Additional Praise for *Modeling Risk*

"Dr. Johnathan Mun has previously published a number of very popular books dealing with different aspects of risk analysis, associated techniques and tools. This last publication puts all the pieces together. The book is really essential for any professional who wants to address risk evaluation following a logical, concrete, and conclusive approach."

—Jean Louis Vaysse
Vice President Marketing,
Airbus (France)

"Once again, Dr. Mun has created a must-have, must-read book for anyone interested in the practical application of risk analysis. Other books speak in academic generalities, or focus on one area of risk application. This book gets to the heart of the matter with applications for every area of risk analysis. You have a real option to buy almost any book—you should exercise your option and get this one!"

—Glenn Kautt
President and Chairman,
Monitor Group

"Dr. Mun breaks through the hyperbole and presents a clear step-by-step approach revealing to readers how quantitative methods and tools can truly make a difference. In short, he teaches you what is relevant and a must know. I highly recommend this book, especially if you want to effectively incorporate the latest technologies into your decision-making process for your real-world business problems."

—Dr. Paul Finnegan
Vice President, Operations & Development,
Alexion Pharmaceuticals

"A must read for product portfolio managers, *Modeling Risk* captures the risk exposure of strategic investments and provides management with estimates of potential outcomes and options for risk mitigation."

—Rafael E. Gutierrez
Executive Director of Strategic
Marketing and Planning,
Seagate Technology

"Having spent years reading through a barrage of integrated risk management and real options analysis books and being lost in the sea of mathematical-statistical methods with virtually no real-life applications or cases to follow, I stumbled on Dr. Mun's books. The current volume is absolutely the best book in risk, with an excellent balance of practice with theory. The step-by-step instructions, supported by the software, allow even us mere mortals to learn and apply the methodology via reference to his excellent real-life case examples without the need for advanced degrees in mathematics. The analytics are applicable for any industry or company, and especially for me, in the U.S. military acquisition arena."

—Dr. Thomas Housel
Professor, U.S. Naval Postgraduate School

"I refer to books of this high caliber as 'pracademic' education. Dr. Mun combines the practical application of financial tools with intellectual and academic rigor to produce one of the most useful tools risk professionals can use. *Modeling Risk* is required reading for all serious professionals."

—Paul Siegel
Chief Executive Officer, The Globecon Group

"Dr. Mun lays out an approach and toolset that is a must for every program manager to learn and use. Management is all about choices, and Dr. Mun has provided a resource that helps make those choices in an informed, disciplined, replicable, and defensible manner. I heartily recommend *Modeling Risk* as a resource for every organization and individual."

—CAPT Mark D. Wessman (U.S. Navy, Ret.)
President, Wessman Consultancy Group

"Uncertainty is a major concern in life and it is unwise to make a decision without taking risk into consideration. Consequently, *Modeling Risk* has this complex risk topic explained in an exceptional way, by covering all the dimensions of risk elements and taking the reader directly to understanding and applying the knowledge with practical examples built in a spreadsheet and a great Risk Simulator software platform."

—Agustín Velázquez Afonso
Senior Economist, Central Bank of Venezuela

"Some risk concepts imply complicated mathematical formulations. In *Modeling Risk*, Dr. Mun provides intuitive and understandable interpretations of these concepts. In addition, they are very well complemented with practical cases."

—Luis Melo
Senior Econometrician,
Central Bank of Colombia

"*Modeling Risk* provides powerful and practical analytics and advanced methodologies with an elegant balance of theory and practice, making it useful in a variety of industries and applications."

—Kim Kovacs
Chief Executive Officer,
OptionEase, Inc.

"Dr. Mun's flexible methodologies, models, and applications are suitable for applying dynamic statistical analysis to quantify and mitigate risk for the effective management of the enterprise. His comprehensive Risk Analysis and Modeling suite provides a full range of capabilities to implement portfolio risk management techniques consistent with best practices that have proven successful in the marketplace. In today's world, change and uncertainty are constants. Such an environment requires a stronger focus on integrated risk management practices within organizations that are quantifiable to strategically deal with uncertainty, to capitalize on opportunities, and to increase involvement of the stakeholders to ensure that optimal solutions are considered in the decision-making process."

—Raymond Heika
Director of Strategic Planning,
Northrop Grumman Corporation

"Dr. Johnathan Mun's book is a sparkling jewel in my finance library. He demonstrates a deep understanding of the underlying mathematical theory and an ability to reduce complex concepts to lucid explanations and examples. For this reason, he's my favorite writer in this field. Experienced professionals will appreciate Dr. Mun's competence in boiling down complex math to a clear presentation of the essential solutions to financial risk, corporate finance, and forecasting."

—Janet Tavakoli
President, Tavakoli Structured Finance

Modeling Risk

Founded in 1807, John Wiley & Sons is the oldest independent publishing company in the United States. With offices in North America, Europe, Australia and Asia, Wiley is globally committed to developing and marketing print and electronic products and services for our customers' professional and personal knowledge and understanding.

The Wiley Finance series contains books written specifically for finance and investment professionals as well as sophisticated individual investors and their financial advisors. Book topics range from portfolio management to e-commerce, risk management, financial engineering, valuation and financial instrument analysis, as well as much more.

For a list of available titles, visit our Web site at www.WileyFinance.com.

Modeling Risk

Applying Monte Carlo Risk Simulation, Strategic Real Options, Stochastic Forecasting, and Portfolio Optimization

Second Edition

JOHNATHAN MUN

WILEY

John Wiley & Sons, Inc.

Published by John Wiley & Sons, Inc., Hoboken, New Jersey.
Published simultaneously in Canada.

For general information on our other products and services or for technical support, please contact our Customer Care Department within the United States at (800) 762-2974, outside the United States at (317) 572-3993 or fax (317) 572-4002.

Designations used by companies to distinguish their products are often claimed as trademarks. In all instances where John Wiley & Sons, Inc. is aware of a claim, the product names appear in initial capital or all capital letters. Readers, however, should contact the appropriate companies for more complete information regarding trademarks and registration.

Wiley also publishes its books in a variety of electronic formats. Some content that appears in print may not be available in electronic books. For more information about Wiley products, visit our web site at www.wiley.com.

ISBN 978-0-470-59221-2

Printed in the United States of America

10 9 8 7 6 5 4 3 2 1

For Penny and Jayden.
In a world where risk and uncertainty abound,
you are the only constants in my life.

Delight yourself in the Lord and he will give
you the desires of your heart.

Psalms 37:4

Contents

PART FOUR

Industry Applications

CHAPTER 7

PART NINE

Risk Management

CHAPTER 15

CHAPTER 16

Preface

We live in an environment fraught with risk and operate our businesses in a risky world, as higher rewards only come with risks. Ignoring the element of risk when corporate strategy is being framed and when tactical projects are being implemented would be unimaginable. In addressing the issue of risk, *Modeling Risk* provides a novel view of evaluating business decisions, projects, and strategies by taking into consideration a unified strategic portfolio analytical process. This book provides a qualitative and quantitative description of risk, as well as introductions to the Integrated Risk Management methods used in identifying, quantifying, applying, predicting, valuing, hedging, diversifying, and managing risk through rigorous examples of the methods' applicability in the decision-making process.

Pragmatic applications are emphasized in order to demystify the many elements inherent in risk analysis. A black box will remain a black box if no one can understand the concepts despite its power and applicability. It is only when the black box becomes transparent so that analysts can understand, apply, and convince others of its results, value-add, and applicability, that the approach will receive widespread influence. The demystification of risk analysis is achieved by presenting step-by-step applications and multiple business cases, as well as discussing real-life applications.

This book is targeted at both the uninitiated professional and those well versed in risk analysis—there is something for everyone. It is also appropriate for use at the second-year M.B.A. level or as an introductory Ph.D. textbook. A DVD comes with the book, including a trial version of the Risk Simulator and Real Options Super Lattice Solver software and associated Excel models.

JOHNATHAN MUN

San Francisco, California
jcmun@realoptionsvaluation.com
June 2010

What's New in the Second Edition

The second edition of *Modeling Risk* includes many updated and new discussions, examples, exercises, and case studies. Because there are numerous hands-on exercises suitable for in-class and homework assignments, this new edition is more user-friendly as a textbook at the university level.

Specifically, Chapter 1 includes a new discussion of the Markowitz efficient frontier on why risk is important in making decisions and the elements of risk to return ratios. Chapter 2 has additional discussions on the mathematical equations of the first four moments of a distribution and on using coefficient of variation and Value at Risk as alternative risk measures. In Chapter 3, the modeling techniques in Excel have been updated to include Excel 2007 and Excel 2010. Chapter 5 is completely updated with the latest version of Risk Simulator when used in Excel 2007 and Excel 2010, including two detailed step-by-step exercises on running simulations and correlated simulations. Next, in Chapter 6, there is an updated discussion on tornado and sensitivity analysis; data diagnostic and statistical analysis routines for testing heteroskedasticity, multicollinearity, and others; and five hands-on detailed exercises on running sensitivity analysis, distributional fitting and hypothesis tests, probability distributions, bootstrap simulations, and data diagnostics.

Chapter 7 includes a new case study on risk-based project management for schedule planning by running simulations. Chapter 8 adds more details on advanced forecasting techniques such as AUTO ARIMA, Cubic Spline, Maximum Likelihood (Logit, Tobit, Probit), Econometrics and Auto Econometrics, Markov Chains, Stochastic Processes, and a variety of GARCH models including GJR/A/I/T/EGARCH models, to complement the existing approaches such as time series decomposition, multiple regression, and extrapolation. A section on the pitfalls of forecasting, discussing items such as structural shifts, causality loops, nonstationarity, stochastic processes, nonlinearity, outliers, and so forth has been added to Chapter 9.

Added to Chapter 11 are four detailed example cases on using stochastic optimization, efficient frontier, and superspeed simulation-optimization techniques for project selection, portfolio optimization, investment allocation, and optimal pricing, as well as a detailed hands-on set of exercises in optimization. Chapter 12 includes updated real options stories and getting started examples, while Chapter 13 is completely revamped to showcase the latest version of Real Options SLS where real options, financial options, and exotic options can be quickly valued. Chapter 14 has a few new case studies on market and credit risk as it applies to Basel II banking requirements and an oil and gas royalty negotiation case study applying risk analytics for the State of California. Chapter 16 concludes with a new section of recommendations on how to take risk analysis into a company and obtain a higher level of adoption. The book also has a new accompanying DVD with free getting started modeling videos, examples, and models.

Acknowledgments

T he author is greatly indebted to David Mercier, David Bittlingmeier, Robert Fourt, Professor Morton Glantz, Dr. Charles Hardy, Steve Hoye, Professor Bill Rodney, Larry Pixley, Dr. Tom Housel, Lt. Commander Cesar Rios, Ken Cobleigh, Pat Haggerty, Larry Blair, Andy Roff, Tony Jurado, and Commander Mark Rhoades for their business case contributions.

J.M.

About the Author

Dr. Johnathan C. Mun is the founder, chairman, and CEO of Real Options Valuation, Inc. (ROV), a consulting, training, and software development firm specializing in strategic real options, financial valuation, Monte Carlo simulation, stochastic forecasting, optimization, and risk analysis located in northern Silicon Valley, California. ROV has partners around the world including Beijing, Chicago, Colombia, Hong Kong, India, Italy, Japan, Korea, Mexico City, New York, Nigeria, Shanghai, Singapore, Spain, Zurich, and other countries globally. ROV also has a local office in Shanghai.

Dr. Mun is also the chairman of the International Institute of Professional Education and Research (IIPER), an accredited global organization staffed by professors from named universities from around the world that provides the Certified in Risk Management (CRM) designation, among others. He is the creator of many different powerful software tools including Risk Simulator, Real Options SLS Super Lattice Solver, Modeling Toolkit, Employee Stock Options Valuation, ROV BizStats, ROV Modeler Suite (ROV Basel II Modeler, ROV Risk Modeler, ROV Optimizer, and ROV Valuator), ROV Compiler, ROV Extractor and Evaluator, ROV Dashboard, ROV Quantitative Data Miner, and other software applications, as well as the risk-analysis training DVD. He holds public seminars on risk analysis and CRM programs. He has authored 11 books published by John Wiley & Sons and Elsevier Science, including *Modeling Risk: Applying Monte Carlo Risk Simulation, Strategic Real Options, Stochastic Forecasting, and Portfolio Optimization*, First Edition (2006) and Second Edition (2010); *The Banker's Handbook on Credit Risk* (2008); *Advanced Analytical Models: 800 Models and 300 Applications from Basel II Accord to Wall Street and Beyond* (2008); *Real Options Analysis: Tools and Techniques*, First Edition (2003) and Second Edition (2005); *Real Options Analysis Course: Business Cases* (2003); *Applied Risk Analysis: Moving Beyond Uncertainty* (2003); and *Valuing Employee Stock Options* (2004). His books and software are being used at top universities around the world, including the Bern Institute in Germany, Chung-Ang University in South Korea, Georgetown University, ITESM in Mexico, Massachusetts Institute of Technology, U.S. Naval Postgraduate School, New York University, Stockholm University in Sweden,

University of the Andes in Chile, University of Chile, University of Pennsylvania Wharton School, University of York in the United Kingdom, and Edinburgh University in Scotland, among others.

Currently a finance and economics professor, Dr. Mun has taught courses in financial management, investments, real options, economics, and statistics at the undergraduate and the graduate M.B.A. levels. He teaches and has taught at universities all over the world, from the U.S. Naval Postgraduate School (Monterey, California) and University of Applied Sciences (Switzerland and Germany) as full professor, to Golden Gate University, San Francisco State University, St. Mary's College, and University of San Francisco (California), and has chaired many graduate research M.B.A. thesis and Ph.D. dissertation committees. He also teaches weeklong risk analysis, real options analysis, and risk analysis for managers' public courses where participants can obtain the CRM designation on completion. He is a senior fellow at the Magellan Center and sits on the board of standards at the American Academy of Financial Management. He was formerly Vice President of Analytics at Decisioneering, Inc., where he headed the development of options and financial analytics software products, analytical consulting, training, and technical support, and where he was the creator of the Real Options Analysis Toolkit software, the older and much less powerful predecessor of the Real Options Super Lattice software. Prior to joining Decisioneering, he was a Consulting Manager and Financial Economist in the Valuation Services and Global Financial Services practice of KPMG Consulting and a Manager with the Economic Consulting Services practice at KPMG LLP. He has extensive experience in econometric modeling, financial analysis, real options, economic analysis, and statistics. During his tenure at Real Options Valuation, Inc., Decisioneering, and KPMG Consulting, he taught and consulted on a variety of real options, risk analysis, financial forecasting, project management, and financial valuation issues for more than 300 multinational firms (current and former clients include 3M, Airbus, Boeing, BP, Chevron Texaco, Financial Accounting Standards Board, Fujitsu, GE, Goodyear, Microsoft, Motorola, Pfizer, Timken, U.S. Department of Defense, U.S. Navy, Veritas, and many others). His experience prior to joining KPMG included being department head of financial planning and analysis at Viking Inc. of FedEx, performing financial forecasting, economic analysis, and market research. Prior to that, he did financial planning and freelance financial consulting work.

Dr. Mun received a Ph.D. in finance and economics from Lehigh University, where his research and academic interests were in the areas of investment finance, econometric modeling, financial options, corporate finance, and microeconomic theory. He also has an M.B.A. in business administration, an MS in management science, and a BS in biology and physics. He is

Certified in Financial Risk Management, Certified in Financial Consulting, and Certified in Risk Management. He is a member of the American Mensa, Phi Beta Kappa Honor Society, and Golden Key Honor Society as well as several other professional organizations, including the Eastern and Southern Finance Associations, American Economic Association, and Global Association of Risk Professionals. In addition, he has written many academic articles published in the *Journal of the Advances in Quantitative Accounting and Finance*, the *Global Finance Journal*, the *International Financial Review*, the *Journal of Financial Analysis*, the *Journal of Applied Financial Economics*, the *Journal of International Financial Markets, Institutions and Money*, the *Financial Engineering News*, and the *Journal of the Society of Petroleum Engineers*.

Modeling
Risk

Introduction

This book is divided into nine parts starting from a discussion of what risk is and how it is quantified, to how risk can be predicted, diversified, taken advantage of, hedged, and, finally, managed. The first part deals with *risk identification* where the different aspects of business risks are identified, including a brief historical view of how risk was evaluated in the past. The second part deals with *risk evaluation* explaining why disastrous ramifications may result if risk is not considered in business decisions. Part Three pertains to *risk quantification* and details how risk can be captured quantitatively through step-by-step applications of Monte Carlo simulation. Part Four deals with *industry applications* and examples of how risk analysis is applied in practical day-to-day issues in oil and gas, pharmaceutical, financial planning, hospital risk management, and executive compensation problems. Part Five pertains to *risk prediction* where the uncertain and risky future is predicted using analytical time-series methods. Part Six deals with how *risk diversification* works when multiple projects exist in a portfolio. Part Seven's *risk mitigation* discussion deals with how a firm or management can take advantage of risk and uncertainty by implementing and maintaining flexibility in projects. Part Eight provides a second installment of *business cases* where risk analysis is applied in banking, real estate, military strategy, automotive parts aftermarket, and global earth observation systems. Part Nine provides a capstone discussion of applying *risk management* in companies, including how to obtain senior management's buy-in and implementing a change of perspective in corporate culture as it applies to risk analysis. This book is an update of *Applied Risk Analysis* (John Wiley & Sons, 2004) to include coverage of the author's own Risk Simulator software and Real Options Super Lattice Solver software. Following is a synopsis of the material covered in each chapter of the book.

PART ONE—RISK IDENTIFICATION

Chapter 1—Moving Beyond Uncertainty

To the people who lived centuries ago, risk was simply the inevitability of chance occurrence beyond the realm of human control. We have been

1

struggling with risk our entire existence, but, through trial and error and through the evolution of human knowledge and thought, have devised ways to describe and quantify risk. Risk assessment should be an important part of the decision-making process; otherwise bad decisions may be made. Chapter 1 explores the different facets of risk within the realms of applied business risk analysis, providing an intuitive feel of what risk is.

PART TWO—RISK EVALUATION

Chapter 2—From Risk to Riches

The concepts of risk and return are detailed in Chapter 2, illustrating their relationships in the financial world, where a higher-risk project necessitates a higher expected return. How are uncertainties estimated and risk calculated? How do you convert a measure of uncertainty into a measure of risk? These are the topics covered in this chapter, starting from the basics of statistics to applying them in risk analysis, and including a discussion of the different measures of risk.

Chapter 3—A Guide to Model-Building Etiquette

Chapter 3 addresses some of the more common errors and pitfalls analysts make when creating a new model by explaining some of the proper modeling etiquettes. The issues discussed range from file naming conventions and proper model aesthetics to complex data validation and Visual Basic for Applications (VBA) scripting. An appendix is provided on some VBA modeling basics and techniques of macros and forms creation.

PART THREE—RISK QUANTIFICATION

Chapter 4—On the Shores of Monaco

Monte Carlo simulation in its simplest form is just a random number generator useful for forecasting, estimation, and risk analysis. A simulation calculates numerous scenarios of a model by repeatedly picking values from the probability distribution for the uncertain variables and using those values for the event—events such as totals, net profit, or gross expenses. Simplistically, think of the Monte Carlo simulation approach as repeatedly picking golf balls out of a large basket. Chapter 4 illustrates why simulation is important through the flaw of averages example. Excel is used to perform rudimentary simulations, and simulation is shown as a logical next step extension to traditional approaches used in risk analysis.

Chapter 5—Test Driving Risk Simulator

Chapter 5 guides the user through applying the world's premier risk analysis and simulation software: *Risk Simulator*. With a few simple mouse clicks, the reader will be on his or her way to running sophisticated Monte Carlo simulation analysis to capture both uncertainty and risks using the enclosed DVD's Risk Simulator trial software. In addition, the interpretation of said analysis is also very important. The best analysis in the world is only as good as the analyst's ability to understand, utilize, present, report, and convince management or clients of the results.

Chapter 6—Pandora's Toolbox

Powerful simulation-related tools such as bootstrapping, distributional fitting, hypothesis test, correlated simulation, multidimensional simulation, tornado charts, and sensitivity charts are discussed in detail in Chapter 6, complete with step-by-step illustrations. These tools are extremely valuable to analysts working in the realm of risk analysis. The applicability of each tool is discussed in detail. For example, the use of nonparametric bootstrapping simulation as opposed to parametric Monte Carlo simulation approaches is discussed. An appendix to this chapter deals with the technical specifics of goodness-of-fit tests.

PART FOUR—INDUSTRY APPLICATIONS

Chapter 7—Extended Business Cases I: Pharmaceutical and Biotech Negotiations, Oil and Gas Exploration, Financial Planning with Simulation, Hospital Risk Management, Risk-Based Executive Compensation Valuation, and Risk-Based Schedule Planning

Chapter 7 contains the first installment of actual business cases from industry applying risk analytics. Business cases were contributed by a variety of industry experts on applying risk analysis in the areas of oil and gas exploration, pharmaceutical biotech deal making, financial planning, hospital risk management, executive compensation valuation, and risk-based project management.

PART FIVE—RISK PREDICTION

Chapter 8—Tomorrow's Forecast Today

Chapter 8 focuses on applying Risk Simulator to run time-series forecasting methods, multivariate regressions, nonlinear extrapolation, stochastic process forecasts, and Box-Jenkins ARIMA. In addition, the issues of seasonality and trend are discussed, together with the eight time-series decomposition models most commonly used by analysts to forecast future events given historical data. The software applications of each method are discussed in detail, complete with their associated measures of forecast errors and potential pitfalls.

Chapter 9—Using the Past to Predict the Future

The main thrust of Chapter 9 is time-series and regression analysis made easy. Starting with some basic time-series models, including exponential smoothing and moving averages, and moving on to more complex models, such as the Holt–Winters' additive and multiplicative models, the reader will manage to navigate through the maze of time-series analysis. The basics of regression analysis are also discussed, complete with pragmatic discussions of statistical validity tests as well as the pitfalls of regression analysis, including how to identify and fix heteroskedasticity, multicollinearity, and autocorrelation. The five appendixes that accompany this chapter deal with the technical specifics of interval estimations in regression analysis, ordinary least squares, and some pitfalls in running regressions, including detecting and fixing heteroskedasticity, multicollinearity, and autocorrelation.

PART SIX—RISK DIVERSIFICATION

Chapter 10—The Search for the Optimal Decision

In most business or analytical models, there are variables over which you have control, such as how much to charge for a product or how much to invest in a project. These controlled variables are called *decision variables*. Finding the optimal values for decision variables can make the difference between reaching an important goal and missing that goal. Chapter 10 details the optimization process at a high level, with illustrations on solving deterministic optimization problems manually, using graphs, and applying Excel's Solver add-in. (Chapter 11 illustrates the solution to optimization problems under uncertainty, mirroring more closely real-life business conditions.)

Chapter 11—Optimization Under Uncertainty

Chapter 11 illustrates two optimization models with step-by-step details. The first model is a discrete portfolio optimization of projects under uncertainty. Given a set of potential projects, the model evaluates all possible discrete combinations of projects on a "go" or "no-go" basis such that a budget constraint is satisfied, while simultaneously providing the best level of returns subject to uncertainty. The best projects will then be chosen based on these criteria. The second model evaluates a financial portfolio's continuous allocation of different asset classes with different levels of risks and returns. The objective of this model is to find the optimal allocation of assets subject to a 100 percent allocation constraint that still maximizes the Sharpe ratio, or the portfolio's return-to-risk ratio. This ratio will maximize the portfolio's return subject to the minimum risks possible while accounting for the cross-correlation diversification effects of the asset classes in a portfolio.

PART SEVEN—RISK MITIGATION

Chapter 12—What Is So Real About Real Options, and Why Are They Optional?

Chapter 12 describes what real option analysis is, who has used the approach, how companies are using it, and what some of the characteristics of real options are. The chapter describes real options in a nutshell, providing the reader with a solid introduction to its concepts without the need for its theoretical underpinnings. Real options are applicable if the following requirements are met: traditional financial analysis can be performed and models can be built; uncertainty exists; the same uncertainty drives value; management or the project has strategic options or flexibility to either take advantage of these uncertainties or to hedge them; and management must be credible to execute the relevant strategic options when they become optimal to do so.

Chapter 13—The Black Box Made Transparent: Real Options Super Lattice Solver Software

Chapter 13 introduces the readers to the world's first true real options software applicable across all industries. The chapter illustrates how a user can get started with the software in a few short moments after it has been installed. The reader is provided with hands-on experience with the Real

Options Super Lattice Solver to obtain immediate results—a true test when the rubber meets the road.

PART EIGHT—MORE INDUSTRY APPLICATIONS

Chapter 14—Extended Business Cases II: Real Estate, Banking, Military Strategy, Automotive Aftermarkets, Global Earth Observation Systems, Employee Stock Options, Oil and Gas Royalty Lease Negotiations, Real Options and IT Enterprise Risk Security, and Basel II Credit and Market Risk Analysis

Chapter 14 contains the second installment of actual business cases from industry applying risk analytics. Business cases were contributed by a variety of industry experts applying simulation, optimization, and real options analysis in the areas of real estate, banking, military strategy, automotive parts aftermarket, global earth observing systems, employee stock options, oil field lease negotiations for the state of California, IT enterprise risk analysis, and Basel II banking credit and market risk modeling.

PART NINE—RISK MANAGEMENT

Chapter 15—The Warning Signs

The risk analysis software applications illustrated in this book are extremely powerful tools and could prove detrimental in the hands of untrained and unlearned novices. Management, the end user of the results from said tools, must be able to discern if quality analysis has been performed. Chapter 15 delves into the 30-some problematic issues most commonly encountered by analysts applying risk analysis techniques, and how management can spot these mistakes. While it might be the job of the analyst to create the models and use the fancy analytics, it is senior management's job to challenge the assumptions and results obtained from the analysis. Model errors, assumption and input errors, analytical errors, user errors, and interpretation errors are some of the issues discussed in this chapter. Some of the issues and concerns raised for management's consideration in performing due diligence include challenging distributional assumptions, critical success factors, impact drivers, truncation, forecast validity, endpoints, extreme values, structural breaks, values at risk, *a priori* expectations, back-casting, statistical validity, specification errors, out of range forecasts, heteroskedasticity, multicollinearity, omitted variables, spurious relationships, causality and correlation, autoregressive processes, seasonality, random walks, and stochastic processes.

Chapter 16—Changing a Corporate Culture

Advanced analytics is hard to explain to management. So, how do you get risk analysis accepted as the norm into a corporation, especially if your industry is highly conservative? It is a guarantee in companies like these that an analyst showing senior management a series of fancy and mathematically sophisticated models will be thrown out of the office together with his or her results, and have the door slammed shut. Change management is the topic of discussion in Chapter 16. Explaining the results and convincing management appropriately go hand in hand with the characteristics of the analytical tools, which, if they satisfy certain change management requisites, can make acceptance easier. The approach that guarantees acceptance has to be three pronged: Top, middle, and junior levels must all get in on the action. Change management specialists underscore that change comes more easily if the methodologies to be accepted are applicable to the problems at hand, are accurate and consistent, provide value-added propositions, are easy to explain, have comparative advantage over traditional approaches, are compatible with the old, have modeling flexibility, are backed by executive sponsorship, and are influenced and championed by external parties including competitors, customers, counterparties, and vendors.

ADDITIONAL MATERIAL

The book concludes with the 10 mathematical tables used in the analyses throughout the book and the answers to the questions at the end of each chapter. The DVD included with the book holds 30-day trial versions of Risk Simulator and Real Options Super Lattice Solver software, as well as sample models and getting started videos to help the reader get a jump start on modeling risk.

Risk Identification

Moving Beyond Uncertainty

CHAPTER 1

A BRIEF HISTORY OF RISK:
WHAT EXACTLY IS RISK?

Since the beginning of recorded history, games of chance have been a popular pastime. Even in Biblical accounts, Roman soldiers cast lots for Christ's robes. In earlier times, chance was something that occurred in nature, and humans were simply subjected to it as a ship is to the capricious tosses of the waves in an ocean. Even up to the time of the Renaissance, the future was thought to be simply a chance occurrence of completely random events and beyond the control of humans. However, with the advent of games of chance, human greed has propelled the study of risk and chance to ever more closely mirror real-life events. Although these games initially were played with great enthusiasm, no one actually sat down and figured out the odds. Of course, the individual who understood and mastered the concept of chance was bound to be in a better position to profit from such games of chance. It was not until the mid-1600s that the concept of chance was properly studied, and the first such serious endeavor can be credited to Blaise Pascal, one of the fathers of modern choice, chance, and probability.[1] Fortunately for us, after many centuries of mathematical and statistical innovations from pioneers such as Pascal, Bernoulli, Bayes, Gauss, LaPlace, and Fermat, our modern world of uncertainty can be explained with much more elegance through methodological applications of risk and uncertainty.

To the people who lived centuries ago, risk was simply the inevitability of chance occurrence beyond the realm of human control. Nonetheless, many phony soothsayers profited from their ability to convincingly profess their clairvoyance by simply stating the obvious or reading the victims' body language and telling them what they wanted to hear. We modern-day humans, ignoring for the moment the occasional seers among us, with our fancy technological achievements, are still susceptible to risk and uncertainty. We may be able to predict the orbital paths of planets in our solar system with astounding accuracy or the escape velocity required to shoot a man from the Earth to the Moon, but when it comes to predicting a firm's revenues the following year, we are at a loss. Humans have been struggling with risk our entire existence but, through trial and error, and through the evolution of human knowledge and thought, have devised ways to describe, quantify, hedge, and take advantage of risk.

Clearly the entire realm of risk analysis is great and would most probably be intractable within the few chapters of a book. Therefore, this book is concerned with only a small niche of risk, namely, *applied business risk modeling and analysis*. Even in the areas of applied business risk analysis, the diversity is great. For instance, business risk can be roughly divided into the areas of operational risk management and financial risk management. In financial risk, one can look at market risk, private risk, credit risk, default risk, maturity risk, liquidity risk, inflationary risk, interest rate risk, country risk, and so forth. This book focuses on the application of risk analysis in the sense of how to adequately apply the tools to identify, understand, quantify, and diversify risk such that it can be hedged and managed more effectively. These tools are generic enough that they can be applied across a whole spectrum of business conditions, industries, and needs.

Finally, understanding this text in its entirety together with *Real Options Analysis*, Second Edition (John Wiley & Sons, 2005) and the associated Risk Simulator and Real Options SLS software are required prerequisites for the Certified Risk Management or CRM certification (see www.realoptionsvaluation.com for more details).

UNCERTAINTY VERSUS RISK

Risk and uncertainty are very different-looking animals, but they are of the same species; however, the lines of demarcation are often blurred. A distinction is critical at this juncture before proceeding and worthy of segue. Suppose I am senseless enough to take a skydiving trip with a good friend and we board a plane headed for the Palm Springs desert. While airborne at 10,000 feet and watching our lives flash before our eyes, we realize that in our haste we forgot to pack our parachutes on board. However, there is an old, dusty, and dilapidated emergency parachute on the plane. At that point, both my friend and I have the same level of uncertainty—the uncertainty of whether the old parachute will open, and if it does not, whether we will fall to our deaths. However, being the risk-adverse, nice guy I am, I decide to let my buddy take the plunge. Clearly, he is the one taking the plunge and the same person taking the risk. I bear no risk at this time while my friend bears all the risk.[2] However, we both have the same level of uncertainty as to whether the parachute will actually fail. In fact, we both have the same level of uncertainty as to the outcome of the day's trading on the New York Stock Exchange—which has absolutely no impact on whether we live or die that day. Only when he jumps and the parachute opens will the uncertainty become resolved through the passage of time, events, and action. However, even when the uncertainty is resolved with the opening of the parachute, the risk still exists as to whether he will land safely on the ground below.

Therefore, risk is something one bears and is the outcome of uncertainty. Just because there is uncertainty, there could very well be no risk. If the only thing that bothers a U.S.-based firm's CEO is the fluctuation in the foreign exchange market of the Zambian kwacha, then I might suggest shorting some kwachas and shifting his portfolio to U.S.-based debt. This uncertainty, if it does not affect the firm's bottom line in any way, is only uncertainty and not risk. This book is concerned with risk by performing uncertainty analysis—the same uncertainty that brings about risk by its mere existence as it impacts the value of a particular project. It is further assumed that the end user of this uncertainty analysis uses the results appropriately, whether the analysis is for identifying, adjusting, or selecting projects with respect to their risks, and so forth. Otherwise, running millions of fancy simulation trials and letting the results "marinate" will be useless. By running simulations on the foreign exchange market of the kwacha, an analyst sitting in a cubicle somewhere in downtown San Francisco will in no way reduce the risk of the kwacha in the market or the firm's exposure to the same. Only by using the results from an uncertainty simulation analysis and finding ways to hedge or mitigate the quantified fluctuation and downside risks of the firm's foreign exchange exposure through the derivatives market could the analyst be construed as having performed risk analysis and risk management.

To further illustrate the differences between risk and uncertainty, suppose we are attempting to forecast the stock price of Microsoft (MSFT). Suppose MSFT is currently priced at $25 per share, and historical prices place the stock at 21.89% volatility. Now suppose that for the next 5 years, MSFT does not engage in any risky ventures and stays exactly the way it is, and further suppose that the entire economic and financial world remains constant. This means that *risk* is fixed and unchanging; that is, volatility is unchanging for the next 5 years. However, the price uncertainty still increases over time; that is, the width of the forecast intervals will still increase over time. For instance, Year 0's forecast is known and is $25. However, as we progress one day, MSFT will most probably vary between $24 and $26. One year later, the uncertainty bounds may be between $20 and $30. Five years into the future, the boundaries might be between $10 and $50.

So, in this example, *uncertainties increase while risks remain the same.* Therefore, risk is not equal to uncertainty. This idea is, of course, applicable to any forecasting approach whereby it becomes more and more difficult to forecast the future even though the risk remains the same. Now, if risk changes over time, the bounds of uncertainty get more complicated (e.g., uncertainty bounds of sinusoidal waves with discrete event jumps).

In other instances, risk and uncertainty are used interchangeably. For instance, suppose you play a coin-toss game—bet $0.50 and if heads come up you win $1, but you lose everything if tails appear. The risk here is you lose everything because the risk is that tails may appear. The uncertainty here is that tails may appear. Given that tails appear, you lose everything; hence, uncertainty brings with it risk. Uncertainty is the possibility of an event occurring, and risk is the ramification of such an event occurring. People tend to use these two terms interchangeably.

In discussing uncertainty, there are three levels of uncertainties in the world: the *known*, the *unknown*, and the *unknowable*. The known is, of course, what we know will occur and are certain of its occurrence (contractual obligations or a guaranteed event); the unknown is what we do not know and can be simulated. These events will become known through the passage of time, events, and action (the uncertainty of whether a new drug or technology can be developed successfully will become known after spending years and millions on research programs—it will either work or not, and we will know this in the future), and these events carry with them risks, but these risks will be reduced or eliminated over time. However, unknowable events carry both uncertainty and risk such that the totality of the risk and uncertainty may not change through the passage of time, events, or actions. These are events such as when the next tsunami or earthquake will hit, or when another act of terrorism will occur around the world. When an event occurs, uncertainty becomes resolved, but risk still remains (another one may or may not hit tomorrow). In traditional analysis, we care about the known factors. In risk analysis, we care about the unknown and unknowable factors. The unknowable factors are easy to hedge—get the appropriate insurance! That is, do not do business in a war-torn country, get away from politically unstable economies, buy hazard and business interruption insurance, and so forth. It is for the unknown factors that risk analysis will provide the most significant amount of value.

WHY IS RISK IMPORTANT IN MAKING DECISIONS?

Risk should be an important part of the decision-making process; otherwise bad decisions may be made without an assessment of risk. For instance,

Name of Project	Cost	Returns	Risk
Project X	**$50**	**$50**	**$25**
Project Y	**$250**	**$200**	**$200**
Project Z	**$100**	**$100**	**$10**

Project X for the cost- and budget-constrained manager
Project Y for the returns-driven and nonresource-constrained manager
Project Z for the risk-averse manager
Project Z for the smart manager

FIGURE 1.1 Why is risk important?

suppose projects are chosen based simply on an evaluation of returns; clearly the highest-return project will be chosen over lower-return projects. In financial theory, projects with higher returns will in most cases bear higher risks.[3] Therefore, instead of relying purely on bottom-line profits, a project should be evaluated based on its returns as well as its risks. Figures 1.1 and 1.2 illustrate the errors in judgment when risks are ignored.

Looking at Bang-for-the-Buck, X (2), Y (1), Z (10), Project Z should be chosen...with a $1,000 budget, the following can be obtained:

Project X:	20 Project Xs returning $1,000, with $500 risk
Project Y:	4 Project Ys returning $800, with $800 risk
Project Z:	10 Project Zs returning $1,000, with $100 risk
Project X:	For each $1 return, $0.5 risk is taken
Project Y:	For each $1 return, $1.0 risk is taken
Project Z:	For each $1 return, $0.1 risk is taken
Project X:	For each $1 of risk taken, $2 return is obtained
Project Y:	For each $1 of risk taken, $1 return is obtained
Project Z:	For each $1 of risk taken, $10 return is obtained

Conclusion: Risk is important. Forgoing risks results in making the wrong decision

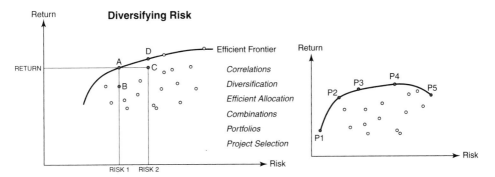

FIGURE 1.2 Adding an element of risk.

> The concepts of risk and uncertainty are related but different. Uncertainty involves variables that are unknown and changing, but uncertainty will become known and resolved through the passage of time, events, and action. Risk is something one bears and is the outcome of uncertainty. Sometimes, risk may remain constant while uncertainty increases over time.

Figure 1.1 lists three *mutually exclusive* projects with their respective costs to implement, expected net returns (net of the costs to implement), and risk levels (all in present values).[4] Clearly, for the budget-constrained manager, the cheaper the project the better, resulting in the selection of Project X.[5] The returns-driven manager will choose Project Y with the highest returns, assuming that budget is not an issue. Project Z will be chosen by the risk-averse manager as it provides the least amount of risk while providing a positive net return. The upshot is that with three different projects and three different managers, three different decisions will be made. Which manager is correct and why?

Figure 1.2 shows that Project Z should be chosen. For illustration purposes, suppose all three projects are independent and mutually exclusive,[6] and that an unlimited number of projects from each category can be chosen but the budget is constrained at $1,000. Therefore, with this $1,000 budget, 20 Project Xs can be chosen, yielding $1,000 in net returns and $500 risks, and so forth. It is clear from Figure 1.2 that Project Z is the best project as for the same level of net returns ($1,000), the least amount of risk is undertaken ($100). Another way of viewing this selection is that for each $1 of returns obtained, only $0.1 amount of risk is involved on average, or that for each $1 of risk, $10 in returns are obtained on average. This example illustrates the concept of *bang for the buck* or getting the best value with the least amount of risk. An even more blatant example is if there are several different projects with identical single-point average net returns of $10 million each. Without risk analysis, a manager should in theory be indifferent in choosing any of the projects.[7] However, with risk analysis, a better decision can be made. For instance, suppose the first project has a 10 percent chance of exceeding $10 million, the second a 15 percent chance, and the third a 55 percent chance. The third project, therefore, is the best bet.

This approach of bang for the buck, or returns to risk ratio, is the cornerstone of the Markowitz efficient frontier in modern portfolio theory. That is, if we constrained the total portfolio risk level and successively allowed it to increase over time, we would obtain several efficient portfolio allocations for different risk characteristics. Thus, different efficient portfolio allocations can be obtained for different individuals with different risk preferences. At the bottom of Figure 1.2, we see a sample Markowitz efficient frontier. In Chapter 11, we revisit this topic in more detail through the use of an example of portfolio optimization of various investment decisions as well as a military portfolio example, to determine the optimal or best allocation of assets and investments or project selection within the context of a portfolio (maximizing a certain objective such as profits or bang-for-the-buck Sharpe ratio subject to certain constraints such as time, budget, cost, risk, and so forth). But briefly, in the chart in Figure 1.2, each dot represents a *portfolio* of multiple projects, projected in a two-dimensional plot of returns (*y*-axis) and risk (*x*-axis). If you compare portfolios A and B, a rational decision maker will choose portfolio A because it has a higher return with the same amount of risk as B. In addition, the same decision maker will choose portfolio A over portfolio C because, for the same returns, A has a lower risk. For similar reasons, D will be chosen over C.

In other words, there are multiple combinations of portfolios that can be developed, but there is an extreme set of portfolios that will yield the highest returns subject to the least amount of risk or the best bang for the buck, and these portfolios lie on the upper end of the curve, named the efficient frontier. We can obtain these portfolio points by running an optimization. *Each point on this graph is an optimization run, and the efficient frontier is simply multiple optimization runs across different and changing constraints.* This approach allows the decision maker flexibility or to have a portfolio of options, an important topic discussed in more detail later (Chapters 12 and 13), rather than be fixed with only a single decision point. In fact, if going from one portfolio to another lies in a steep upward sloping curve (going from P1 to P2 in Figure 1.2), then it is a good idea to move up to the next portfolio, assuming the new portfolio's constraints are acceptable. In other words, a steep positive slope means that for the same amount of risk, the amount of returns you obtain is significantly higher to compensate for the additional resources and risk. In contrast, if the slope is relatively flat (going from P3 to P4), going to the next portfolio on the curve is, perhaps, not such a good idea as only a little marginal return is obtained for a significantly higher risk. However, if additional resources are available and there are no better alternatives, and if the decision maker is willing to take the higher risk for a slight gain, then the next portfolio might still be advisable. At the point where the frontier curves downward (going from P4 to P5), it is no longer efficient and definitely not advisable because for the additional resource constraints required, the risk increases but returns actually decrease, indicating not only diminishing marginal returns, but complete negative marginal returns.

So, when presented with such an analysis, the decision maker can decide which portfolio to undertake, what the resources required will be, and what the projected returns and risks will be.

DEALING WITH RISK THE OLD-FASHIONED WAY

Businesses have been dealing with risk since the beginning of the history of commerce. In most cases, managers have looked at the risks of a particular project, acknowledged their existence, and moved on. Little quantification was performed in the past. In fact, most decision makers look only to single-point estimates of a project's profitability. Figure 1.3 shows an example of a single-point estimate. The estimated net revenue of $30 is simply that, a single point whose probability of occurrence is close to zero.[8] Even in the simple model shown in Figure 1.3, the effects of interdependencies are ignored, and in traditional modeling jargon, we have the problem of *garbage in, garbage out* (GIGO). As an example of interdependencies, the units sold are probably negatively correlated to the price of the product,[9] and positively correlated to the average variable cost;[10] ignoring these effects in a single-point estimate will yield grossly incorrect results. For instance, if the unit sales variable becomes 11 instead of 10, the resulting revenue may not simply be $35. The net revenue may actually decrease due to an increase in variable cost per unit while the sale price may actually be slightly lower to accommodate this increase in unit sales. Ignoring these interdependencies will reduce the accuracy of the model.

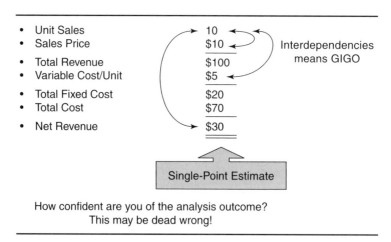

How confident are you of the analysis outcome?
This may be dead wrong!

FIGURE 1.3 Single-point estimate.

A rational manager would choose projects based not only on returns but also on risks. The best projects tend to be those with the best bang for the buck, or the best returns subject to some specified risks.

One approach used to deal with risk and uncertainty is the application of scenario analysis, as seen in Figure 1.4. Suppose the worst-case, nominal-case, and best-case scenarios are applied to the unit sales; the resulting three scenarios' net revenues are obtained. As earlier, the problems of interdependencies are not addressed. The net revenues obtained are simply too variable, ranging from $5 to $55. Not much can be determined from this analysis.

A related approach is to perform *what-if* or *sensitivity* analysis as seen in Figure 1.5. Each variable is perturbed and varied a prespecified amount and the resulting change in net revenues is captured. This approach is great for understanding which variables drive or impact the bottom line the most. A related approach is the use of tornado and sensitivity charts as detailed in Chapter 6, Pandora's Toolbox, which looks at a series of simulation tools. These approaches were usually the extent to which risk and uncertainty analysis were traditionally performed. Clearly, a better and more robust approach is required.

This is the point where simulation comes in. Figure 1.6 shows how simulation can be viewed as simply an extension of the traditional approaches of sensitivity and scenario testing. The critical success drivers or the

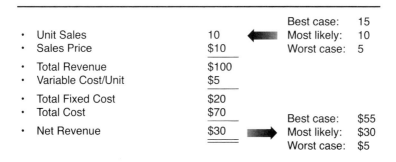

Outcomes are too variable—which will occur?

The best, most likely, and worst-case scenarios are usually simply wild guesses!

FIGURE 1.4 Scenario analysis.

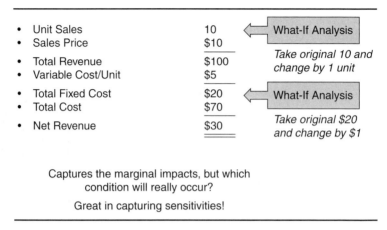

FIGURE 1.5 What-if or sensitivity analysis.

variables that affect the bottom-line net-revenue variable the most, which at the same time are uncertain, are simulated. In simulation, the interdependencies are accounted for by using correlations. The uncertain variables are then simulated thousands of times to emulate all potential permutations and combinations of outcomes. The resulting net revenues from these simulated potential outcomes are tabulated and analyzed. In essence, in its most basic form, simulation is simply an enhanced version of traditional approaches such as sensitivity and scenario analysis but automatically performed for thousands of times while accounting for all the dynamic interactions between the simulated variables. The resulting net revenues from simulation,

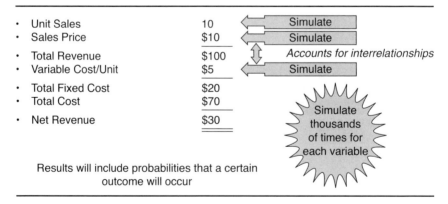

FIGURE 1.6 Simulation approach.

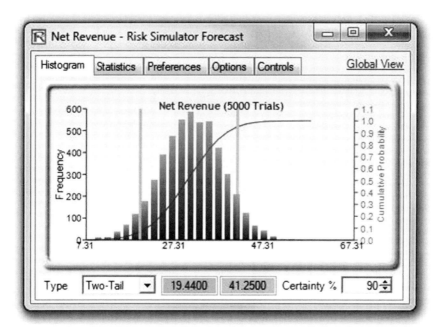

FIGURE 1.7   Simulation results.

as seen in Figure 1.7, show that there is a 90 percent probability that the net revenues will fall between $19.44 and $41.25, with a 5 percent worst-case scenario of net revenues falling below $19.44. Rather than having only three scenarios, simulation created 5,000 scenarios, or trials, where multiple variables are simulated and changing simultaneously (unit sales, sale price, and variable cost per unit), while their respective relationships or correlations are maintained.

THE LOOK AND FEEL OF RISK AND UNCERTAINTY

In most financial risk analyses, the first step is to create a series of free cash flows (FCF), which can take the shape of an income statement or discounted cash-flow (DCF) model. The resulting deterministic free cash flows are depicted on a time line, akin to that shown in Figure 1.8. These cash-flow figures are in most cases forecasts of the unknown future. In this simple example, the cash flows are assumed to follow a straight-line growth curve (of course, other shaped curves also can be constructed). Similar forecasts can be constructed using historical data and fitting these data to a time-series

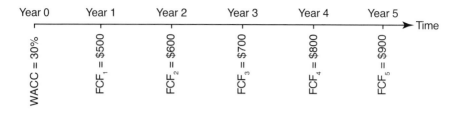

This straight-line cash-flow projection is the basis of DCF analysis. This assumes a static and known set of future cash flows.

FIGURE 1.8   The intuition of risk—deterministic analysis.

model or a regression analysis.[11] Whatever the method of obtaining said forecasts or the shape of the growth curve, these are point estimates of the unknown future. Performing a financial analysis on these static cash flows provides an accurate value of the project if and only if all the future cash flows are known with certainty—that is, no uncertainty exists.

However, in reality, business conditions are hard to forecast. Uncertainty exists, and the actual levels of future cash flows may look more like those in Figure 1.9; that is, at certain time periods, actual cash flows may be above, below, or at the forecast levels. For instance, at any time period, the actual cash flow may fall within a range of figures with a certain percent probability. As an example, the first year's cash flow may fall anywhere between $480 and $520. The actual values are shown to fluctuate around the forecast values at an average volatility of 20 percent.[12] (We use volatility here as a measure of uncertainty; that is, the higher the volatility, the higher the level of uncertainty, where at zero uncertainty, the outcomes are 100 percent certain.)[13] Certainly this example provides a much more accurate view of the true nature of business conditions, which are fairly difficult to predict with any amount of certainty.

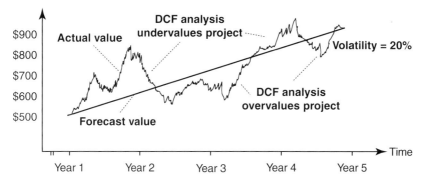

This graph shows that in reality, at different times, actual cash flows may be above, below, or at the forecast value line due to uncertainty and risk.

FIGURE 1.9 The intuition of risk—Monte Carlo simulation.

Figure 1.10 shows two sample actual cash flows around the straight-line forecast value. The higher the uncertainty around the actual cash-flow levels, the higher the volatility. The darker line with 20 percent volatility fluctuates more wildly around the forecast values. These values can be quantified using Monte Carlo simulation fairly easily but cannot be properly accounted for using more simplistic traditional methods such as sensitivity or scenario analyses.

INTEGRATED RISK MANAGEMENT (IRM)®

Before diving into the different risk analysis methods in the remaining chapters of the book, it is important to first understand the *Integrated Risk Management framework* and how these different techniques are related in a risk analysis and risk management context. This framework comprises eight distinct phases of a successful and comprehensive risk analysis implementation, going from a qualitative management screening process to creating clear and

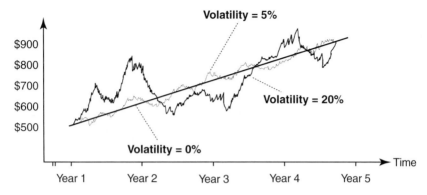

The higher the risk, the higher the volatility and the higher the fluctuation of actual cash flows around the forecast value. When volatility is zero, the values collapse to the forecast straight-line static value.

FIGURE 1.10 The intuition of risk—the face of risk.

concise reports for management. The process was developed by the author based on previous successful implementations of risk analysis, forecasting, real options, valuation, and optimization projects both in the consulting arena and in industry-specific problems. These phases can be performed either in isolation or together in sequence for a more robust integrated analysis.

Figure 1.11 shows the integrated risk analysis process up close. We can segregate the process into the following eight simple steps:

1. Qualitative management screening.
2. Time-series, regression, econometric, and stochastic forecasting.
3. Base case net present value analysis.
4. Monte Carlo simulation.
5. Real options problem framing.
6. Real options modeling and analysis.
7. Portfolio and resource optimization.
8. Reporting and update analysis.

1. Qualitative Management Screening

Qualitative management screening is the first step in any integrated risk analysis process. Management has to decide which projects, assets, initiatives, or strategies are viable for further analysis, in accordance with the firm's mission, vision, goal, or overall business strategy. The firm's mission, vision,

Integrated Risk Management

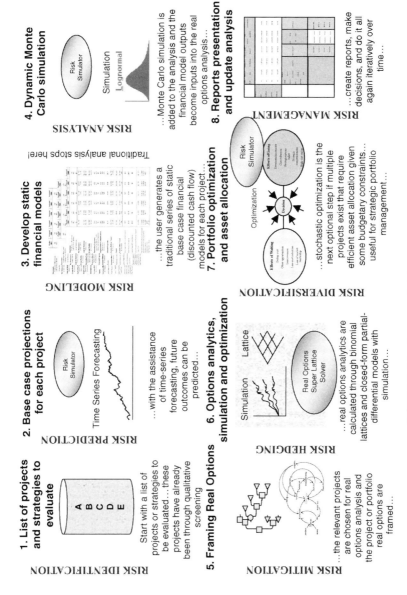

1. List of projects and strategies to evaluate

RISK IDENTIFICATION

Start with a list of projects or strategies to be evaluated...these projects have already been through qualitative screening

2. Base case projections for each project

RISK PREDICTION

Time Series Forecasting

...with the assistance of time-series forecasting, future outcomes can be predicted...

3. Develop static financial models

RISK MODELING

Traditional analysis stops here!

...the user generates a traditional series of static base case financial (discounted cash flow) models for each project...

4. Dynamic Monte Carlo simulation

RISK ANALYSIS

Simulation Lognormal

...Monte Carlo simulation is added to the analysis and the financial model outputs become inputs into the real options analysis...

5. Framing Real Options

RISK MITIGATION

...the relevant projects are chosen for real options analysis and the project or portfolio real options are framed...

6. Options analytics, simulation and optimization

RISK HEDGING

Simulation   Lattice

Real Options Super Lattice Solver

...real options analytics are calculated through binomial lattices and closed-form partial-differential models with simulation...

7. Portfolio optimization and asset allocation

RISK DIVERSIFICATION

Risk Simulator

Optimization   Decision

Effects of Waiting

Effects of Easing

...stochastic optimization is the next optional step if multiple projects exist that require efficient asset allocation given some budgetary constraints... useful for strategic portfolio management...

8. Reports presentation and update analysis

RISK MANAGEMENT

...create reports, make decisions, and do it all again iteratively over time...

FIGURE 1.11 Integrated risk management process.

25

goal, or overall business strategy may include market penetration strategies, competitive advantage, technical, acquisition, growth, synergistic, or globalization issues. That is, the initial list of projects should be qualified in terms of meeting management's agenda. Often at this point the most valuable insight is created as management frames the complete problem to be resolved and the various risks to the firm are identified and flushed out.

2. Time-Series, Regression, Econometric, and Stochastic Forecasting

The future is then forecasted using time-series analysis or multivariate regression analysis if historical or comparable data exist. Otherwise, other qualitative forecasting methods may be used (subjective guesses, growth rate assumptions, expert opinions, Delphi method, and so forth). In a financial context, this is the step where future revenues, sale price, quantity sold, volume, production, and other key revenue and cost drivers are forecasted. See Chapters 8 and 9 for details on forecasting and using the author's Risk Simulator software to run time-series, extrapolation, stochastic process, ARIMA, and regression forecasts.

3. Base Case Net Present Value Analysis

For each project that passes the initial qualitative screens, a discounted cash flow model is created. This model serves as the base case analysis where a net present value (NPV) is calculated for each project, using the forecasted values from the previous step. This step also applies if only a single project is under evaluation. This net present value is calculated using the traditional approach of using the forecast revenues and costs, and discounting the net of these revenues and costs at an appropriate risk-adjusted rate. The return on investment and other profitability, cost-benefit, and productivity metrics are generated here.

4. Monte Carlo Simulation

Because the static discounted cash flow produces only a single-point estimate result, there is oftentimes little confidence in its accuracy given that future events that affect forecast cash flows are highly uncertain. To better estimate the actual value of a particular project, Monte Carlo simulation should be employed next. See Chapters 4 and 5 for details on running Monte Carlo simulations using the author's Risk Simulator software.

Usually, a sensitivity analysis is first performed on the discounted cash flow model; that is, setting the net present value as the resulting variable, we can change each of its precedent variables and note the change in the resulting variable. Precedent variables include revenues, costs, tax rates, discount rates, capital expenditures, depreciation, and so forth, which ultimately flow through the model to affect the net present value figure. By tracing back all these precedent variables, we can change each one by a preset amount and see the effect on the resulting net present value. A graphical representation can then be created, which is often called a tornado chart (see Chapter 6 on using Risk Simulator's simulation analysis tools such as tornado charts, spider charts, and sensitivity charts), because of its shape, where the most sensitive precedent variables are listed first, in descending order of magnitude. Armed with this information, the analyst can then decide which key variables are highly uncertain in the future and which are deterministic. The uncertain key variables that drive the net present value and, hence, the decision are called critical success drivers. These critical success drivers are prime candidates for Monte Carlo simulation. Because some of these critical success drivers may be correlated—for example, operating costs may increase in proportion to quantity sold of a particular product, or prices may be inversely correlated to quantity sold—a correlated Monte Carlo simulation may be required. Typically, these correlations can be obtained through historical data. Running correlated simulations provides a much closer approximation to the variables' real-life behaviors.

5. Real Options Problem Framing

The question now is that after quantifying risks in the previous step, what next? The risk information obtained somehow needs to be converted into *actionable intelligence*. Just because risk has been quantified to be such and such using Monte Carlo simulation, so what, and what do we do about it? The answer is to use real options analysis to hedge these risks, to value these risks, and to position yourself to take advantage of the risks. The first step in real options is to generate a strategic map through the process of framing the problem. Based on the overall problem identification occurring during the initial qualitative management screening process, certain strategic optionalities would have become apparent for each particular project. The strategic optionalities may include, among other things, the option to expand, contract, abandon, switch, choose, and so forth. Based on the identification of strategic optionalities that exist for each project or at each stage of the project, the analyst can then choose from a list of options to analyze in more detail. Real options are added to the projects to hedge downside risks and to take advantage of upside swings.

6. Real Options Modeling and Analysis

Through the use of Monte Carlo simulation, the resulting stochastic discounted cash flow model will have a distribution of values. Thus, simulation models, analyzes, and quantifies the various risks and uncertainties of each project. The result is a distribution of the NPVs and the project's volatility. In real options, we assume that the underlying variable is the future profitability of the project, which is the future cash flow series. An implied volatility of the future free cash flow or underlying variable can be calculated through the results of a Monte Carlo simulation previously performed. Usually, the volatility is measured as the standard deviation of the logarithmic returns on the free cash flow stream. In addition, the present value of future cash flows for the base case discounted cash flow model is used as the initial underlying asset value in real options modeling. Using these inputs, real options analysis is performed to obtain the projects' strategic option values—see Chapters 12 and 13 for details on understanding the basics of real options and on using the Real Options Super Lattice Solver software.

7. Portfolio and Resource Optimization

Portfolio optimization is an optional step in the analysis. If the analysis is done on multiple projects, management should view the results as a portfolio of rolled-up projects because the projects are in most cases correlated with one another, and viewing them individually will not present the true picture. As firms do not only have single projects, portfolio optimization is crucial. Given that certain projects are related to others, there are opportunities for hedging and diversifying risks through a portfolio. Because firms have limited budgets, have time and resource constraints, while at the same time have requirements for certain overall levels of returns, risk tolerances, and so forth, portfolio optimization takes into account all these to create an optimal portfolio mix. The analysis will provide the optimal allocation of investments across multiple projects. See Chapters 10 and 11 for details on using Risk Simulator to perform portfolio optimization.

8. Reporting and Update Analysis

The analysis is not complete until reports can be generated. Not only are results presented, but the process should also be shown. Clear, concise, and precise explanations transform a difficult black-box set of analytics into transparent steps. Management will never accept results coming from black boxes if they do not understand where the assumptions or data originate and what types of mathematical or financial massaging takes place.

Risk analysis assumes that the future is uncertain and that management has the right to make midcourse corrections when these uncertainties become resolved or risks become known; the analysis is usually done ahead of time and, thus, ahead of such uncertainty and risks. Therefore, when these risks become known, the analysis should be revisited to incorporate the decisions made or revising any input assumptions. Sometimes, for long-horizon projects, several iterations of the real options analysis should be performed, where future iterations are updated with the latest data and assumptions.

Understanding the steps required to undertake integrated risk management is important because it provides insight not only into the methodology itself, but also into how it evolves from traditional analyses, showing where the traditional approach ends and where the new analytics start.

QUESTIONS

1. Why is risk important in making decisions?
2. Describe the concept of bang for the buck.
3. Compare and contrast risk and uncertainty.

Risk Evaluation

CHAPTER **2**

From Risk to Riches

TAMING THE BEAST

Risky ventures are the norm in the daily business world. The mere mention of names such as George Soros, John Meriwether, Paul Reichmann, and Nicholas Leeson, or firms such as Long Term Capital Management, Metallgesellschaft, Barings Bank, Bankers Trust, Daiwa Bank, Sumimoto Corporation, Merrill Lynch, and Citibank brings a shrug of disbelief and fear. These names are some of the biggest in the world of business and finance. Their claim to fame is not simply for being the best and brightest individuals or being the largest and most respected firms, but for bearing the stigma of being involved in highly risky ventures that turned sour almost overnight.[1]

George Soros was and still is one of the most respected names in high finance; he is known globally for his brilliance and exploits. Paul Reichmann was a reputable and brilliant real estate and property tycoon. Between the two of them, nothing was impossible, but when they ventured into investments in Mexican real estate, the wild fluctuations of the peso in the foreign exchange market was nothing short of a disaster. During late 1994 and early 1995, the peso hit an all-time low and their ventures went from bad to worse, but the one thing that they did not expect was that the situation would become a lot worse before it was all over and billions would be lost as a consequence.

Long Term Capital Management was headed by Meriwether, one of the rising stars in Wall Street, with a slew of superstars on its management team, including several Nobel laureates in finance and economics (Robert Merton and Myron Scholes). The firm was also backed by giant investment banks. A firm that seemed indestructible literally blew up with billions of dollars in the red, shaking the international investment community with repercussions throughout Wall Street as individual investors started to lose faith in large hedge funds and wealth-management firms, forcing the eventual massive Federal Reserve bailout.

33

Barings was one of the oldest banks in England. It was so respected that even Queen Elizabeth II herself held a private account with it. This multibillion dollar institution was brought down single-handedly by Nicholas Leeson, an employee halfway around the world. Leeson was a young and brilliant investment banker who headed up Barings' Singapore branch. His illegally doctored track record showed significant investment profits, which gave him more leeway and trust from the home office over time. He was able to cover his losses through fancy accounting and by taking significant amounts of risk. His speculations in the Japanese yen went south and he took Barings down with him, and the top echelon in London never knew what hit them.

Had any of the managers in the boardrooms at their respective headquarters bothered to look at the risk profile of their investments, they would surely have made a very different decision much earlier on, preventing what became major embarrassments in the global investment community. If the projected returns are adjusted for risks, that is, finding what levels of risks are required to attain such seemingly extravagant returns, it would be sensible not to proceed.

Risks occur in everyday life that do not require investments in the multimillions. For instance, when would one purchase a house in a fluctuating housing market? When would it be more profitable to lock in a fixed-rate mortgage rather than keep a floating variable rate? What are the chances that there will be insufficient funds at retirement? What about the potential personal property losses when a hurricane hits? How much accident insurance is considered sufficient? How much is a lottery ticket actually worth?

Risk permeates all aspects of life and one can never avoid taking or facing risks. What we can do is understand risks better through a systematic assessment of their impacts and repercussions. This assessment framework must also be capable of measuring, monitoring, and managing risks; otherwise, simply noting that risks exist and moving on is not optimal. This book provides the tools and framework necessary to tackle risks head-on. Only with the added insights gained through a rigorous assessment of risk can one actively manage and monitor risk.

Risks permeate every aspect of business, but we do not have to be passive participants. What we can do is develop a framework to better understand risks through a systematic assessment of their impacts and repercussions. This framework also must be capable of measuring, monitoring, and managing risks.

THE BASICS OF RISK

Risk can be defined simply as any uncertainty that affects a system in an unknown fashion whereby the ramifications are also unknown but bear with them great fluctuation in value and outcome. In every instance, for risk to be evident, the following generalities must exist:

- Uncertainties and risks have a time horizon.
- Uncertainties exist in the future and will evolve over time.
- Uncertainties become risks if they affect the outcomes and scenarios of the system.
- These changing scenarios' effects on the system can be measured.
- The measurement has to be set against a benchmark.

Risk is never instantaneous. It has a time horizon. For instance, a firm engaged in a risky research and development venture will face significant amounts of risk but only until the product is fully developed or has proven itself in the market. These risks are caused by uncertainties in the technology of the product under research, uncertainties about the potential market, uncertainties about the level of competitive threats and substitutes, and so forth. These uncertainties will change over the course of the company's research and marketing activities—some uncertainties will increase while others will most likely decrease through the passage of time, actions, and events. However, only the uncertainties that affect the product directly will have any bearing on the risks of the product being successful. That is, only uncertainties that change the possible scenario outcomes will make the product risky (e.g., market and economic conditions). Finally, risk exists if it can be measured and compared against a benchmark. If no benchmark exists, then perhaps the conditions just described are the norm for research and development activities, and thus the negative results are to be expected. These benchmarks have to be measurable and tangible, for example, gross profits, success rates, market share, time to implementation, and so forth.

> Risk is any uncertainty that affects a system in an unknown fashion and its ramifications are unknown, but it brings great fluctuation in value and outcome. Risk has a time horizon, meaning that uncertainty evolves over time, which affects measurable future outcomes and scenarios with respect to a benchmark.

THE NATURE OF RISK AND RETURN

Nobel Laureate Harry Markowitz's groundbreaking research into the nature of risk and return has revolutionized the world of finance. His seminal work, which is now known all over the world as the *Markowitz Efficient Frontier*, looks at the nature of risk and return. Markowitz did not look at risk as the enemy but as a condition that should be embraced and balanced out through its expected returns. The concept of risk and return was then refined through later works by William Sharpe and others, who stated that a heightened risk necessitates a higher return, as elegantly expressed through the *capital asset pricing model* (CAPM), where the required rate of return on a marketable risky equity is equivalent to the return on an equivalent riskless asset plus a beta systematic and undiversifiable risk measure multiplied by the market risk's return premium. In essence, a higher risk asset requires a higher return. In Markowitz's model, one could strike a balance between risk and return. Depending on the risk appetite of an investor, the optimal or best-case returns can be obtained through the efficient frontier. Should the investor require a higher level of returns, he or she would have to face a higher level of risk. Markowitz's work carried over to finding combinations of individual projects or assets in a portfolio that would provide the best *bang for the buck*, striking an elegant balance between risk and return. In order to better understand this balance, also known as *risk adjustment* in modern risk analysis language, risks must first be measured and understood. The following section illustrates how risk can be measured.

THE STATISTICS OF RISK

The study of statistics refers to the collection, presentation, analysis, and utilization of numerical data to infer and make decisions in the face of uncertainty, where the actual population data is unknown. There are two branches in the study of statistics: descriptive statistics, where data is summarized and described, and inferential statistics, where the *population* is generalized through a small random sample, such that the *sample* becomes useful for making predictions or decisions when the population characteristics are unknown.

A sample can be defined as a subset of the population being measured, whereas the population can be defined as all possible observations of interest of a variable. For instance, if one is interested in the voting practices of all U.S. registered voters, the entire pool of a hundred million registered voters is considered the population, whereas a small survey of one thousand registered voters taken from several small towns across the nation is the sample. The calculated characteristics of the sample (e.g., mean, median, standard deviation) are termed *statistics*, while *parameters* imply that the entire population has been surveyed and the results tabulated. Thus, in decision making, the statistic is of vital importance, seeing that sometimes the entire population is yet unknown (e.g., who are all your customers, what is the total market share) or it is very difficult to obtain all relevant information on the population seeing that it would be too time- or resource-consuming.

In inferential statistics, the usual steps undertaken include:

- Designing the experiment—this phase includes designing the ways to collect all possible and relevant data.
- Collection of sample data—data is gathered and tabulated.
- Analysis of data—statistical analysis is performed.
- Estimation or prediction—inferences are made based on the statistics obtained.
- Hypothesis testing—decisions are tested against the data to see the outcomes.
- Goodness-of-fit—actual data is compared to historical data to see how accurate, valid, and reliable the inference is.
- Decision making—decisions are made based on the outcome of the inference.

Measuring the Center of the Distribution—The First Moment

The first moment of a distribution measures the *expected rate of return* on a particular project. It measures the location of the project's scenarios and possible outcomes on average. The common statistics for the first moment include the mean (average), median (center of a distribution), and mode (most commonly occurring value). Figure 2.1 illustrates the first moment—where,

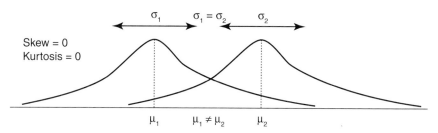

FIGURE 2.1 First moment.

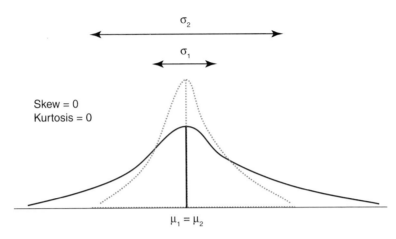

FIGURE 2.2   Second moment.

in this case, the first moment of this distribution is measured by the mean (μ) or average value.

Measuring the Spread of the Distribution—The Second Moment

The second moment measures the spread of a distribution, which is a *measure of risk*. The spread or width of a distribution measures the variability of a variable, that is, the potential that the variable can fall into different regions of the distribution—in other words, the potential scenarios of outcomes. Figure 2.2 illustrates two distributions with identical first moments (identical means) but very different second moments or risks. The visualization becomes clearer in Figure 2.3. As an example, suppose there are two stocks and the first stock's movements (illustrated by the dotted line) with the smaller fluctuation is compared against the second stock's movements (illustrated by the darker line) with a much higher price fluctuation. Clearly an investor would view the stock with the wilder fluctuation as riskier because the outcomes of the more risky stock are relatively more unknown than the less risky stock. The vertical axis in Figure 2.3 measures the stock prices; thus, the more risky stock has a wider range of potential outcomes. This range is translated into a distribution's width (the horizontal axis) in Figure 2.2, where the wider distribution represents the riskier asset. Hence, width or spread of a distribution measures a variable's risks.

Notice that in Figure 2.2, both distributions have identical first moments or central tendencies, but clearly the distributions are very different.

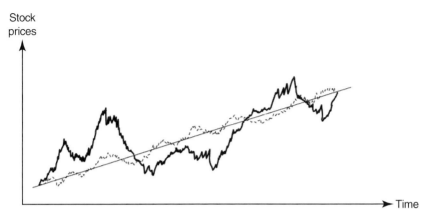

FIGURE 2.3 Stock price fluctuations.

This difference in the distributional width is measurable. Mathematically and statistically, the width or risk of a variable can be measured through several different statistics, including the range, standard deviation (σ), variance, coefficient of variation, volatility, and percentiles.

Measuring the Skew of the Distribution—The Third Moment

The third moment measures a distribution's skewness, that is, how the distribution is pulled to one side or the other. Figure 2.4 illustrates a negative or left skew (the tail of the distribution points to the left), and Figure 2.5 illustrates a positive or right skew (the tail of the distribution points to the right). The mean is always skewed toward the tail of the distribution while the median remains constant. Another way of seeing this is that the mean moves, but the standard deviation, variance, or width may still remain constant.

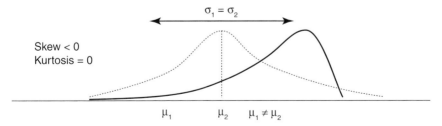

FIGURE 2.4 Third moment (left skew).

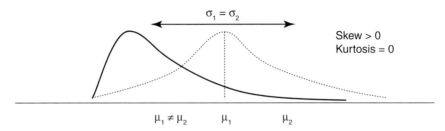

FIGURE 2.5   Third moment (right skew).

If the third moment is not considered, then looking only at the expected returns (e.g., mean or median) and risk (standard deviation), a positively skewed project might be incorrectly chosen! For example, if the horizontal axis represents the net revenues of a project, then clearly a left or negatively skewed distribution might be preferred as there is a higher probability of greater returns (Figure 2.4) as compared to a higher probability for lower level of returns (Figure 2.5). Thus, in a skewed distribution, the median is a better measure of returns, as the medians for both Figures 2.4 and 2.5 are identical, risks are identical, and, hence, a project with a negatively skewed distribution of net profits is a better choice. Failure to account for a project's distributional skewness may mean that the incorrect project may be chosen (e.g., two projects may have identical first and second moments, that is, they both have identical returns and risk profiles, but their distributional skews may be very different).

Measuring the Catastrophic Tail Events of the Distribution—The Fourth Moment

The fourth moment, or kurtosis, measures the peakedness of a distribution. Figure 2.6 illustrates this effect. The background (denoted by the dotted line) is a normal distribution with an excess kurtosis of 0. The new distribution has a higher kurtosis; thus the area under the curve is thicker at the tails with less area in the central body. This condition has major impacts on risk analysis such as for the two distributions in Figure 2.6; the first three moments (mean, standard deviation, and skewness) can be identical, but the fourth moment (kurtosis) is different. This condition means that, although the returns and risks are identical, the probabilities of extreme and catastrophic events (potential large losses or large gains) occurring are higher for a high kurtosis distribution (e.g., stock market returns are leptokurtic or have high kurtosis). Ignoring a project's return's kurtosis may be detrimental. Note that sometimes a normal kurtosis is denoted as 3.0, but in this book we use the measure of excess kurtosis, henceforth simply known as kurtosis. In

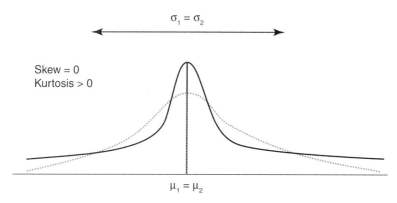

FIGURE 2.6 Fourth moment.

other words, a kurtosis of 3.5 is also known as an excess kurtosis of 0.5, indicating that the distribution has 0.5 additional kurtosis above the normal distribution. The use of excess kurtosis is more prevalent in academic literature and is, hence, used here. Finally, the normalization of kurtosis to a base of 0 makes for easier interpretation of the statistic (e.g., a positive kurtosis indicates fatter-tailed distributions while negative kurtosis indicates thinner-tailed distributions).

Most distributions can be defined up to four moments. The first moment describes the distribution's location or central tendency (expected returns); the second moment describes its width or spread (risks); the third moment, its directional skew (most probable events); and the fourth moment, its peakedness or thickness in the tails (catastrophic losses or gains). All four moments should be calculated and interpreted to provide a more comprehensive view of the project under analysis.

The Functions of Moments

Ever wonder why these risk statistics are called "moments"? In mathematical vernacular, "moment" means *raised to the power of some value*. In other words, the third moment implies that in an equation, three is most probably the highest power. In fact, the equations that follow illustrate the mathematical functions and applications of some moments for a sample statistic. For example, notice that the highest power for the first moment (average) is one; for the second moment (standard deviation), it is two; for the third moment (skew), it is three, and the highest power for the fourth moment (kurtosis) is four.

First Moment: Arithmetic Average or Simple Mean (Sample)

$$\overline{x} = \frac{\sum\limits_{i=1}^{n} x_i}{n}$$

The Excel equivalent function is AVERAGE.

Second Moment: Standard Deviation (Sample)

$$s = \sqrt{\frac{\sum\limits_{i=1}^{n} (x_i - \overline{x})^2}{n-1}}$$

The Excel equivalent function is STDEV for a sample standard deviation.

The Excel equivalent function is STDEVP for a population standard deviation.

Third Moment: Skew

$$skew = \frac{n}{(n-1)(n-2)} \sum\limits_{i=1}^{n} \left(\frac{x_i - \overline{x}}{s}\right)^3$$

The Excel equivalent function is SKEW.

Fourth Moment: Kurtosis

$$kurtosis = \frac{n(n+1)}{(n-1)(n-2)(n-3)} \sum\limits_{i=1}^{n} \left(\frac{x_i - \overline{x}}{s}\right)^4 - \frac{3(n-1)^2}{(n-2)(n-3)}$$

The Excel equivalent function is KURT.

THE MEASUREMENTS OF RISK

There are multiple ways to measure risk in projects. This section summarizes some of the more common measures of risk and lists their potential benefits and pitfalls. The chapter appendix illustrates step-by-step example calculations of some of the more common measurements of risk, which are also briefly defined next:

- *Probability of Occurrence.* This approach is simplistic and yet effective. As an example, there is a 10 percent probability that a project will not break even (it will return a negative net present value indicating losses) within the next 5 years. Further, suppose two similar projects have identical implementation costs and expected returns. Based on a single-point estimate, management should be indifferent between them. However, if risk analysis such as Monte Carlo simulation is performed, the first project might reveal a 70 percent probability of losses compared to only a 5 percent probability of losses on the second project. Clearly, the second project is better when risks are analyzed.

- *Standard Deviation and Variance.* Standard deviation is a measure of the average of each data point's deviation from the mean.[2] This is the most popular measure of risk, where a higher standard deviation implies a wider distributional width and, thus, carries a higher risk. The drawback of this measure is that both the upside and downside variations are included in the computation of the standard deviation. Some analysts define risks as the potential losses or downside; thus, standard deviation and variance will penalize upswings as well as downsides.
- *Semi-Standard Deviation.* The semi-standard deviation only measures the standard deviation of the downside risks and ignores the upside fluctuations. Modifications of the semi-standard deviation include calculating only the values below the mean, or values below a threshold (e.g., negative profits or negative cash flows). This provides a better picture of downside risk but is more difficult to estimate.
- *Volatility.* The concept of volatility is widely used in the applications of real options and can be defined briefly as a measure of uncertainty and risks.[3] Volatility can be estimated using multiple methods, including simulation of the uncertain variables impacting a particular project and estimating the standard deviation of the resulting asset's logarithmic returns over time. This concept is more difficult to define and estimate but is more powerful than most other risk measures in that this single value incorporates all sources of uncertainty rolled into one value.
- *Beta.* Beta is another common measure of risk in the investment finance arena. Beta can be defined simply as the undiversifiable, systematic risk of a financial asset. This concept is made famous through the CAPM, where a higher beta means a higher risk, which in turn requires a higher expected return on the asset.
- *Coefficient of Variation.* The coefficient of variation is simply defined as the ratio of standard deviation to the mean, where risks are common-sized. For example, the distribution of a group of students' heights (measured in meters) can be compared to the distribution of the students' weights (measured in kilograms).[4] This measure of risk or dispersion is applicable when the variables' estimates, measures, magnitudes, or units differ.

- *Value at Risk.* Value at Risk (VaR) was made famous by J. P. Morgan in the mid-1990s through the introduction of its *RiskMetrics* approach, and has thus far been sanctioned by several bank governing bodies around the world. Briefly, it measures the amount of capital reserves at risk given a particular holding period at a particular probability of loss. This measurement can be modified to risk applications by stating, for example, the amount of potential losses a certain percentage of the time during the period of the economic life of the project—clearly, a project with a smaller VaR is better.

- *Worst-Case Scenario and Regret.* Another simple measure is the value of the worst-case scenario given catastrophic losses. Another definition is regret. That is, if a decision is made to pursue a particular project, but if the project becomes unprofitable and suffers a loss, the level of regret is simply the difference between the actual losses compared to doing nothing at all.

- *Risk-Adjusted Return on Capital.* Risk-adjusted return on capital (RAROC) takes the ratio of the difference between the fiftieth percentile (median) return and the fifth percentile return on a project to its standard deviation. This approach is used mostly by banks to estimate returns subject to their risks by measuring only the potential downside effects and ignoring the positive upswings.

The following appendix details the computations of some of these risk measures and is worthy of review before proceeding through the book.

APPENDIX—COMPUTING RISK

This appendix illustrates how some of the more common measures of risk are computed. Each risk measurement has its own computations and uses. For example, certain risk measures are applicable only on time-series data (e.g., volatility) while others are applicable in both cross-sectional and time-series data (e.g., variance, standard deviation, and covariance), while yet others require a consistent holding period (e.g., Value at Risk) or a market comparable or benchmark (e.g., beta coefficient).

Probability of Occurrence

This approach is simplistic yet effective. The probability of success or failure can be determined several ways. The first is through management expectations and assumptions, also known as expert opinion, based on historical occurrences or experience of the expert. Another approach is simply to gather available historical or comparable data, industry averages, academic research, or other third-party sources, indicating the historical probabilities of success or failure (e.g., pharmaceutical R&D's probability of technical success based on various drug indications can be obtained from external research consulting groups). Finally, Monte Carlo simulation can be run on a model with multiple interacting input assumptions and the output of interest (e.g., net present value, gross margin, tolerance ratios, and development success rates) can be captured as a simulation forecast and the relevant probabilities can be obtained, such as the probability of breaking even, probability of failure, probability of making a profit, and so forth. See Chapter 5 for step-by-step instructions on running and interpreting simulations and probabilities.

Standard Deviation and Variance

Standard deviation is a measure of the average of each data point's deviation from the mean. A higher standard deviation or variance implies a wider distributional width and, thus, a higher risk.

The standard deviation can be measured in terms of the population or sample, and for illustration purposes, is shown in the following list, where we define x_i as the individual data points, μ as the population mean, N as the population size, $\bar{x}$ as the sample mean, and n as the sample size:

Population standard deviation:

$$\sigma = \sqrt{\frac{\sum\limits_{i=1}^{n}(x_i - \mu)^2}{N}}$$

and population variance is simply the square of the standard deviation or σ^2. Alternatively, use Excel's *STDEVP* and *VARP* functions for the population standard deviation and variance respectively.

Sample standard deviation:

$$s = \sqrt{\frac{\sum\limits_{i=1}^{n}(x_i - \bar{x})^2}{n-1}}$$

and sample variance is similarly the square of the standard deviation or s^2. Alternatively, use Excel's *STDEV* and *VAR* functions for the sample standard deviation and variance respectively. Figure 2.7 shows the step-by-step computations.

The drawbacks of this measure are that both the upside and downside variations are included in the computation of the standard deviation, and its dependence on the units (e.g., values of x in thousands of dollars versus

	X	X − Mean	Square of (X − Mean)
	−10.50	−9.07	82.2908
	12.25	13.68	187.1033
	−11.50	−10.07	101.4337
	13.25	14.68	215.4605
	−14.65	−13.22	174.8062
	15.65	17.08	291.6776
	−14.50	−13.07	170.8622
Sum	−10.00		
Mean	−1.43		

Population Standard Deviation and Variance

Sum of Square (X − Mean)	1223.6343
Variance = Sum of Square (X − Mean)/N	174.8049
Using Excel's VARP function:	174.8049
Standard Deviation = Square Root of (Sum of Square (X − Mean)/N)	13.2214
Using Excel's STDEVP function:	13.2214

Sample Standard Deviation and Variance

Sum of Square (X − Mean)	1223.6343
Variance = Sum of Square (X − Mean)/(N − 1)	203.9390
Using Excel's VAR function:	203.9390
Standard Deviation = Square Root of (Sum of Square (X − Mean)/(N−1))	14.2807
Using Excel's STDEV function:	14.2807

FIGURE 2.7 Standard deviation and variance computation.

millions of dollars are not comparable). Some analysts define risks as the potential losses or downside; thus, standard deviation and variance penalize upswings as well as downsides. An alternative is the semi-standard deviation.

Semi-Standard Deviation

The semi-standard deviation only measures the standard deviation of the downside risks and ignores the upside fluctuations. Modifications of the semi-standard deviation include calculating only the values below the mean, or values below a threshold (e.g., negative profits or negative cash flows). This approach provides a better picture of downside risk but is more difficult to estimate. Figure 2.8 shows how a sample semi-standard deviation and semi-variance are computed. Note that the computation must be performed manually.

X	X − Mean	Square of (X − Mean)	
−10.50	2.29	5.2327	
12.25	Ignore		(Ignore the positive values)
−11.50	1.29	1.6577	
13.25	Ignore		(Ignore the positive values)
−14.65	−1.86	3.4689	
15.65	Ignore		(Ignore the positive values)
−14.50	−1.71	2.9327	
Sum		−51.1500	
Mean		−12.7875	

Population Standard Deviation and Variance

Sum of Square (X − Mean)	13.2919
Variance = Sum of Square (X − Mean)/N	3.3230
Using Excel's VARP function:	3.3230
Standard Deviation = Square Root of (Sum of Square (X − Mean)/N)	1.8229
Using Excel's STDEVP function:	1.8229

Sample Standard Deviation and Variance

Sum of Square (X − Mean)	13.2919
Variance = Sum of Square (X − Mean)/(N − 1)	4.4306
Using Excel's VAR function:	4.4306
Standard Deviation = Square Root of (Sum of Square (X − Mean)/(N−1))	2.1049
Using Excel's STDEV function:	2.1049

FIGURE 2.8 Semi-standard deviation and semi-variance computation.

Volatility

The concept of volatility is widely used in the applications of real options and can be defined briefly as a measure of uncertainty and risks. Volatility can be estimated using multiple methods, including simulation of the uncertain variables impacting a particular project and estimating the standard deviation of the resulting asset's logarithmic returns over time. This concept is more difficult to define and estimate but is more powerful than most other risk measures in that this single value incorporates all sources of uncertainty rolled into one value. Figure 2.9 illustrates the computation of an annualized volatility. Volatility is typically computed for time-series data only (i.e., data that follows a time series such as stock price, price of oil, interest rates, and so forth). The first step is to determine the relative returns from period

Months	X	Relative Returns	LN (Relative Returns)	Square of (LN Relative Returns − Average)
0	10.50			
1	12.25	1.17	0.1542	0.0101
2	11.50	0.94	−0.0632	0.0137
3	13.25	1.15	0.1417	0.0077
4	14.65	1.11	0.1004	0.0022
5	15.65	1.07	0.0660	0.0001
6	14.50	0.93	−0.0763	0.0169
Sum			0.3228	
Average			0.0538	

Sample Standard Deviation and Variance

Sum of Square (LN Relative Returns − Average)	0.0507
Volatility = Square Root of (Sum of Square (LN Relative Returns − Average)/(N − 1))	10.07%
Using Excel's STDEV function on LN(Relative Returns):	10.07%
Annualized Volatility (Periodic Volatility × Square Root (Periods in a Year))	34.89%

FIGURE 2.9 Volatility computation.

to period, take their natural logarithms (*ln*), and then compute the sample standard deviation of these logged values. The result is the periodic volatility. Then, annualize the volatility by multiplying this periodic volatility by the square root of the number of periods in a year (e.g., 1 if annual data, 4 if quarterly data, and 12 if monthly data are used).

For a more detailed discussion of volatility computation as well as other methods for computing volatility such as using the logarithmic present value approach, management assumptions, and GARCH, or generalized autoregressive conditional heteroskedasticity models, and how a discount rate can be determined from volatility, see *Real Options Analysis*, Second Edition, by Johnathan Mun (John Wiley & Sons, 2005).

Beta

Beta is another common measure of risk in the investment finance arena. Beta can be defined simply as the undiversifiable, systematic risk of a financial asset. This concept is made famous through the CAPM, where a higher beta means a higher risk, which in turn requires a higher expected return on the asset. The beta coefficient measures the relative movements of one asset value to a comparable benchmark or market portfolio; that is, we define the beta coefficient as:

$$\beta = \frac{Cov(x, m)}{Var(m)} = \frac{\rho_{x,m}\sigma_x\sigma_m}{\sigma_m^2}$$

where $Cov(x,m)$ is the population covariance between the asset x and the market or comparable benchmark m, $Var(m)$ is the population variance of m, where both can be computed in Excel using the $COVAR$ and $VARP$ functions. The computed beta will be for the population. In contrast, the sample beta coefficient is computed using the correlation coefficient between x and m or $\rho_{x,m}$ and the sample standard deviations of x and m or using s_x and s_m instead of σ_x and σ_m.

A beta of 1.0 implies that the relative movements or risk of x are identical to the relative movements of the benchmark (see Example 1 in Figure 2.10 where the asset x is simply one unit less than the market asset m, but they both fluctuate at the same levels). Similarly, a beta of 0.5 implies that the relative movements or risk of x is half of the relative movements of the benchmark (see Example 2 in Figure 2.10 where the asset x is simply half the market's fluctuations m). Therefore, beta is a powerful measure but requires a comparable to benchmark its fluctuations.

Coefficient of Variation

The coefficient of variation (CV) is simply defined as the ratio of standard deviation to the mean, where the risks are *common-sized* and *relativized*. For example, a distribution of a group of students' heights (measured in meters) can be compared to the distribution of the students' weights (measured in kilograms). This measure of risk or dispersion is applicable when the variables' estimates, measures, magnitudes, or units differ.

In risk analysis, CV is used in a variety of ways, including risk comparisons and optimization. For instance, suppose you have a portfolio of projects as follows:

	Analyst 1 ($M)	Analyst 2 ($K)	Analyst 3 ($)
Project A	$10.25	$10,250	$10,250,000
Project B	$11.55	$11,550	$11,550,000
Project C	$12.79	$12,790	$12,790,000
Project D	$ 9.57	$ 9,570	$ 9,570,000
Project E	$16.25	$16,250	$16,250,000
Average	$12.08	$12,082	$12,082,000
Standard Deviation	$ 2.64	$ 2,637	$ 2,637,370
Coefficient of Variation	21.83%	21.83%	21.83%

Example 1: Similar fluctuations with the market

Months	X	Market Comparable M
0	10.50	11.50
1	12.25	13.25
2	11.50	12.50
3	13.25	14.25
4	14.65	15.65
5	15.65	16.65
6	14.50	15.50

Sample Beta

Correlation between X and M using Excel's CORREL:	1.0000
Standard deviation of X using Excel's STDEV:	1.8654
Standard deviation of M using Excel's STDEV:	1.8654
Beta Coefficient (Correlation X and M * Stdev X * Stdev M)/(Stdev M * Stdev M)	1.0000

Population Beta

Covariance population using Excel's COVAR:	2.9827
Variance of M using Excel's VARP:	2.9827
Population Beta (Covariance population (X, M)/Variance (M))	1.0000

Example 2: Half the fluctuations of the market

Months	X	Market Comparable M
0	10.50	21.00
1	12.25	24.50
2	11.50	23.00
3	13.25	26.50
4	14.65	29.30
5	15.65	31.30
6	14.50	29.00

Sample Beta

Correlation between X and M using Excel's CORREL:	1.0000
Standard deviation of X using Excel's STDEV:	1.8654
Standard deviation of M using Excel's STDEV:	3.7308
Beta Coefficient (Correlation X and M * Stdev X * Stdev M)/(Stdev M * Stdev M)	0.5000

Population Beta

Covariance population using Excel's COVAR:	5.9653
Variance of M using Excel's VARP:	11.9306
Population Beta (Covariance population (X, M)/Variance (M))	0.5000

FIGURE 2.10 Beta coefficient computation.

The same portfolio of projects was computed by three different analysts: one uses millions of dollars; another denominates the values as thousands of dollars; and the third simply uses dollars. It is the same portfolio of projects, but if we relied solely on standard deviation as the measure of risk, then Analyst 3 would say that the portfolio has a much higher risk than Analyst 2 or 1 would. So, standard deviation is a good measure of *absolute risk levels*, denominated in its own units. However, notice that the CV yields exactly the same value for all three analysts.

Coefficient of variation is a good measure of *relative risk*. In fact, you can now use CV to compare the relative risk across multiple projects of different types and magnitude (e.g., compare a multibillion-dollar's relative risk to a multithousand dollar project). Also, standard deviations and averages are denominated in the original units in which the values were measured (if the original project was measured in dollars, then average and standard deviation are denominated in dollars), whereas CV is a relative measure and is unitless (standard deviation divided by average where we have dollar unit divided by dollar unit making the new variable unitless). That is, CV can be written as a decimal or percentage, allowing it to be comparable across multiple types of projects (e.g., comparing a U.S. dollar denominated project in billions of dollars to a Euro denominated multimillion dollar project).

Finally, CV is the second moment divided by the first moment, or standard deviation divided by the mean, which can be loosely described as buck for the bang. Take the inverse of CV and you have bang for the buck. In fact, the Sharpe ratio that is often used in portfolio optimization is the inverse of CV. The Sharpe ratio is $S = \frac{E[R] - R_{rf}}{\sigma}$, which is nothing but the expected return $E[R]$, or sometimes written as average return μ, less some benchmark returns such as the risk-free rate R_{rf}, divided by the standard deviation or risk σ. Sometimes, the benchmark is set to zero for simplicity, we have $S = \frac{\mu}{\sigma}$, which is nothing but the inverse of the CV. Due to its relative characteristic, the Sharpe ratio or return to risk ratio, and, by extension, the CV or risk to return ratio are used in portfolio optimization to determine the best bang for the buck to reconstruct the efficient frontier as described in Chapter 1, which, again, was simply the optimal portfolio allocation given the risk-return levels of all possible combinations in a portfolio.

Value at Risk (Value at Stake)

Value at Risk (VaR) was made famous by J. P. Morgan in the mid-1990s through the introduction of its *RiskMetrics* approach, and has thus far been sanctioned by several bank-governing bodies around the world. Briefly, it measures the amount of capital reserves at risk given a particular holding period at a particular probability of loss. This measurement can be modified to risk applications by stating, for example, the amount of potential losses a certain percentage of the time during the period of the economic life of the project.

Economic capital is critical to a bank as it links a bank's earnings and returns to risks that are specific to a business line or business opportunity. In addition, these economic capital measurements can be aggregated into a portfolio of holdings. In such situations, VaR is used in trying to understand how the entire organization is affected by the various risks of each holding as aggregated into a portfolio, after accounting for cross-correlations among various holdings. VaR measures the maximum possible loss given some predefined probability level (e.g., 99.90 percent) over some holding period or time horizon (e.g., 10 days). Senior management at the bank usually selects the probability or confidence interval, which is typically a decision made by senior management that reflects the board's risk appetite. Stated another way, we can define the probability level as the bank's desired probability of surviving per year. In addition, the holding period is usually chosen such that it coincides with the time period it takes to liquidate a loss position.

VaR can be computed several ways. Two main families of approaches exist: structural closed-form models and Monte Carlo risk simulation. The latter is a much more powerful approach. Instead of simply correlating individual business lines or assets, Monte Carlo risk simulation can correlate entire probability distributions using mathematical copulas and simulation algorithms, by using Risk Simulator. In addition, tens to hundreds of thousands of scenarios can be generated using simulation, providing a powerful stress testing mechanism for valuing VaR. Distributional fitting methods are applied to reduce the thousands of data points into their appropriate probability distributions, allowing their modeling to be handled with greater ease.

For our purposes, we can loosely define VaR as the left-tail or the right-tail values given some probability. Figure 2.11 illustrates the right-tail VaR and left-tail VaR as used in risk analysis for projects and portfolios. For instance, if we say there is a *right-tail VaR$_{10\%}$ of $X*, we simply mean that there is a 90 percent probability that you will get less than or equal to $X, and a 10 percent chance you will get more than $X. The inverse is true for the left-tail VaR. And it really depends what variable you are looking at before you can determine if a high or low VaR is desirable. For instance, if you are modeling returns or profits, a *higher* right-tail $X VaR value is more desirable than a lower VaR, and a *higher* $X left-tail VaR is better than a low left-tail VaR (e.g., I have a 90 percent chance of making at least $10M as compared to $1M). So, this analysis means that the value at "risk" should be higher. The opposite is true if you are modeling cost or risk of a project, where you would and should prefer a *lower* VaR (e.g., would you prefer to have a project with a 90 percent chance of exceeding $10M in cost or $1M

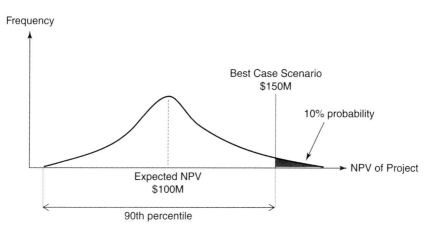

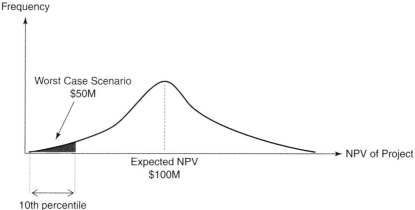

FIGURE 2.11 Value at risk.

in cost?), and in this case, the value at "risk" should be lower. Think about it carefully and draw the pictures to convince yourself.

Finally, if you are using VaR as a measure of the width of the distribution and, by extension, the second moment and the uncertainty of the project, a lower left-tail VaR or higher right-tail VaR implies a wider distribution and, hence, a higher level of *uncertainty* (but the risks may not be equally distributed, so we use the term *uncertainty* in this context).

For more technical details on modeling VaR in a banking environment, see my other books, including *Advanced Analytical Models: 800 Functions and 300 Models from Basel II to Wall Street and Beyond* (John Wiley & Sons, 2008). In Chapters 95 and 160 through 164 of that book, you find detailed VaR analysis including applications of static covariance, simulation, and optimization models to minimize VaR for a bank's economic capital requirements.

Worst-Case Scenario and Regret

Another simple measure is the value of the worst-case scenario given catastrophic losses. An additional definition is regret; that is, if a decision is made to pursue a particular project, but if the project becomes unprofitable and suffers a loss, the level of regret is simply the difference between the actual losses compared to doing nothing at all. This analysis is very similar to the VaR but is not time dependent. For instance, a financial return on investment model can be created and a simulation is run. The 5 percent worst-case scenario can be read directly from the forecast chart in Risk Simulator.

Risk-Adjusted Return on Capital

Risk-adjusted return on capital (RAROC) takes the ratio of the difference between the fiftieth percentile P_{50} or its median return and the fifth percentile P_5 return on a project to its standard deviation σ, written as:

$$RAROC = \frac{P_{50} - P_5}{\sigma}$$

This approach is used mostly by banks to estimate returns subject to their risks by measuring only the potential downside effects and truncating the distribution to the worst-case 5 percent of the time, ignoring the positive upswings, while at the same time common sizing to the risk measure of standard deviation. Thus, RAROC can be seen as a measure that combines standard deviation, CV, semi-standard deviation, and worst-case scenario analysis. This measure is useful when applied with Monte Carlo simulation, where the percentiles and standard deviation measurements required can be obtained through the forecast chart's statistics view in Risk Simulator.

QUESTIONS

1. What is the efficient frontier and when is it used?
2. What are inferential statistics and what steps are required in making inferences?
3. When is using standard deviation less desirable than using semi-standard deviation as a measure of risk?

4. If comparing three projects with similar first, second, and fourth moments, would you prefer a project that has no skew, a positive skew, or a negative skew?

5. If comparing three projects with similar first to third moments, would you prefer a project that is leptokurtic (high kurtosis), mesokurtic (average kurtosis), or platykurtic (low kurtosis)? Explain your reasoning with respect to a distribution's tail area. Under what conditions would your answer change?

6. What are the differences and similarities between Value at Risk and worst-case scenario as a measure of risk?

CHAPTER 3

A Guide to
Model-Building Etiquette

The first step in risk analysis is the creation of a model. A model can range from a simple three-line calculation in an Excel spreadsheet (e.g., $A + B = C$) to a highly complicated and oftentimes convoluted series of interconnected spreadsheets. Creating a proper model takes time, patience, strategy, and practice. Evaluating or learning a complicated model passed down to you that was previously created by another analyst may be rather cumbersome. Even the person who built the model revisits it weeks or months later and tries to remember what was created can sometimes find it challenging. It is indeed difficult to understand what the model originator was thinking of when the model was first built. As most readers of this book are Excel users, this chapter lists some model building blocks that every professional model builder should at least consider implementing in his or her Excel spreadsheets.

> As a rule of thumb, always remember to document the model; separate the inputs from the calculations and the results; protect the models against tampering; make the model user-friendly; track changes made in the model; automate the model whenever possible; and consider model aesthetics.

DOCUMENT THE MODEL

One of the major considerations in model building is its documentation. Although this step is often overlooked, it is crucial in order to allow continuity, survivorship, and knowledge transfer from one generation of model builders to the next. Inheriting a model that is not documented from a predecessor will only frustrate the new user. Some items to consider in model documentation include the following:

- *Strategize the Look and Feel of the Model.* Before the model is built, the overall structure of the model should be considered. This conceptualization includes how many sections the model will contain (e.g., each workbook file applies to a division; while each workbook has 10 worksheets representing each department in the division; and each worksheet has three sections, representing the revenues, costs, and miscellaneous items) as well as how each of these sections are related, linked, or replicated from one another.
- *Naming Conventions.* Each of these workbooks and worksheets should have a proper name. The recommended approach is simply to provide each workbook and worksheet a descriptive name. However, one should always consider brevity in the naming convention but yet provide sufficient description of the model. If multiple iterations of the model are required, especially when the model is created by several individuals over time, the date and version numbers should be part of the model's file name for proper archiving, backup, and identification purposes.
- *Executive Summary.* In the first section of the model, there should always be a welcome page with an executive summary of the model. The summary may include the file name, location on a shared drive, version of the model, developers of the model, and any other pertinent information, including instructions, assumptions, caveats, warnings, or suggestions on using the model.
- *File Properties.* Make full use of Excel's file properties (*File | Properties*) [Excel 2007/2010: *Office Button, Prepare, Properties.*]. This simple action may make the difference between an orphaned model and a model that users will have more faith in as to how current or updated it is (Figure 3.1).
- *Document Changes and Tweaks.* If multiple developers work on the model, when the model is saved, the changes, tweaks, edits, and modifications should always be documented such that any past actions can be undone should it become necessary. This simple practice also provides a method to track the changes that have been made versus a list of bugs or development requirements.
- *Illustrate Formulas.* Consider illustrating and documenting the formulas used in the model, especially when complicated equations and calculations are required. Use Excel's Equation Editor to do this (*Insert | Object | Create New | Microsoft Equation*) [Excel 2007/2010: *Insert* TAB,

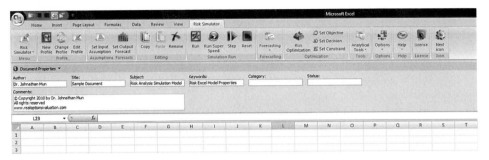

FIGURE 3.1 Excel's file properties dialog box.

Object, Create New, Microsoft Equation.], but also remember to provide a reference for more advanced models.

- *Results Interpretation.* In the executive summary, on the reports or results summary page, include instructions on how the final analytical results should be interpreted, including what assumptions are used when building the model, any theory the results pertain to, any reference material detailing the technical aspects of the model, data sources, and any conjectures made to obtain certain input parameters.

- *Reporting Structure.* A good model should have a final report after the inputs have been entered and the analysis is performed. This report may be as simple as a printable results worksheet or as a more sophisticated macro that creates a new document (e.g., Risk Simulator has a reporting function that provides detailed analysis on the input parameters and output results).

- *Model Navigation.* Consider how a novice user will navigate between modules, worksheets, or input cells. One consideration is to include navigational capabilities in the model. These navigational capabilities range from a simple set of naming conventions (e.g., sheets in a workbook can be named "1. Input Data," "2. Analysis," and "3. Results") where the user can quickly and easily identify the relevant worksheets by their TAB names (Figure 3.2), to more sophisticated methods. More sophisticated navigational methods include using hyperlinks and Visual Basic for Applications (VBA) code.

For instance, in order to create hyperlinks to other sheets from a main navigational sheet, click on *Insert | Hyperlink | Place in This Document*

⏮ ◀ ▶ ⏭ \\ **1. Input Data** ∕ 2. Analysis ∕ 3. Results ∕

FIGURE 3.2 Worksheet TAB names.

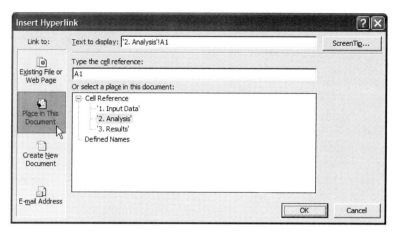

FIGURE 3.3 Insert hyperlink dialog box.

in Excel. Choose the relevant worksheet to link to within the workbook (Figure 3.3). Place all these links in the main navigational sheet and place only the relevant links in each sheet (e.g., only the main menu and Step 2 in the analysis are available in the Step 1 worksheet). These links can also be named as "next" or "previous," to further assist the user in navigating a large model. The second and more protracted approach is to use VBA codes to navigate the model. Refer to the appendix at the end of this chapter—A Primer on VBA Modeling and Writing Macros—for sample VBA codes used in said navigation and automation.

> Document the model by strategizing the look and feel of the model, have an adequate naming convention, have an executive summary, include model property descriptions, indicate the changes and tweaks made, illustrate difficult formulas, document how to interpret results, provide a reporting structure, and make sure the model is easy to navigate.

SEPARATE INPUTS, CALCULATIONS, AND RESULTS

- *Different Worksheets for Different Functions.* Consider using a different worksheet within a workbook for the model's input assumption (these assumptions should all be accumulated into a single sheet), a set of calculation worksheets, and a final set of worksheets summarizing the results. These sheets should then be appropriately named and grouped for easy identification. Sometimes, the input worksheet also has some key model results—this arrangement is very useful as a *management dashboard*, where slight tweaks and changes to the inputs can be made by management and the fluctuations in key results can be quickly viewed and captured.

- *Describe Input Variables.* In the input parameter worksheet, consider providing a summary of each input parameter, including where it is used in the model. Sometimes, this can be done through cell comments instead (*Insert | Comment*) [Excel 2007/2010: *Right-click*, *Insert Comment*; or on the *Review* TAB, *New Comment*.].
- *Name Input Parameter Cells.* Consider naming individual cells by selecting an input cell, typing the relevant name in the *Name Box* on the upper left corner of the spreadsheet, and hitting Enter (the arrow in Figure 3.4 shows the location of the name box). Also, consider naming ranges by selecting a range of cells and typing the relevant name in the *Name Box*. For more complicated models where multiple input parameters with similar functions exist, consider grouping these names. For instance, if the inputs "cost" and "revenues" exist in two different divisions, consider using the following hierarchical naming conventions (separated by periods in the names) for the Excel cells:

Cost.Division.A
Cost.Division.B
Revenues.Division.A
Revenues.Division.B

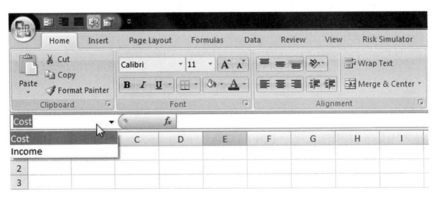

FIGURE 3.4   Name box in Excel.

- *Color Coding Inputs and Results.* Another form of identification is simply to color code the input cells one consistent color, while the results, which are usually mathematical functions based on the input assumptions and other intermediate calculations, should be color coded differently.
- *Model Growth and Modification.* A good model should always provide room for growth, enhancement, and update analysis over time. When additional divisions are added to the model, or other constraints and input assumptions are added at a later date, there should be room to maneuver. Another situation involves data updating, where, in the future, previous sales forecasts have now become reality and the actual sales now replace the forecasts. The model should be able to accommodate this situation. Providing the ability for data updating and model growth is where modeling strategy and experience count.
- *Report and Model Printing.* Always consider checking the overall model, results, summary, and report pages for their print layouts. Use Excel's *File | Print Preview* [Excel 2007/2010: *Office Button, Print, Print Preview.*] capability to set up the page appropriately for printing. Set up the headers and footers to reflect the dates of the analysis as well as the model version for easy comparison later. Use links, automatic fields, and formulas whenever appropriate (e.g., the Excel formula "$=Today()$" is a volatile field that updates automatically to the latest date when the spreadsheet model was last saved).

Separate inputs, calculations, and results by creating different worksheets for different functions, describing input variables, naming input parameters, color coding inputs and results, providing room for model growth and subsequent modifications, and considering report and model printing layouts.

PROTECT THE MODELS

- *Protect Workbook and Worksheets.* Consider using spreadsheet protection (*Tools | Protection*) [Excel 2007/2010: *Review* TAB, *Protect Sheet*, and *Protect Workbook.*] in your intermediate and final results summary sheet to prevent user tampering or accidental manipulation. Passwords are also recommended here for more sensitive models.[1]

- *Hiding and Protecting Formulas.* Consider setting cell properties to hide, lock, or both hide and lock cells (*Format | Cells | Protection*) [Excel 2007/2010: *Home* TAB, *Format* (Cells section), *Format Cells, Protection*; or use *Ctrl + 1* and select *Protection.*], then protect the worksheet (*Tools | Protection*) [Excel 2007/2010: *Review* TAB, *Protect Sheet.*] to prevent the user from accidentally overriding a formula (by locking a cell and protecting the sheet), or still allow the user to see the formula without the ability to irreparably break the model by deleting the contents of a cell (by locking but not hiding the cell and protecting the sheet), or to prevent tampering with and viewing the formulas in the cell (by both locking and hiding the cell and then protecting the sheet).

Protect the models from user tampering at the workbook and worksheet levels through password protecting workbooks, or through hiding and protecting formulas in the individual worksheet cells.

MAKE THE MODEL USER-FRIENDLY: DATA VALIDATION AND ALERTS

- *Data Validation.* Consider preventing the user from entering bad inputs through spreadsheet validation. Prevent erroneous inputs through data validation (*Data | Validation | Settings*) [Excel 2007/2010: *Data* TAB, *Data Validation, Data Validation.*] where only specific inputs are allowed. Figure 3.5 illustrates data validation for a cell accepting only positive inputs. The *Edit | Copy* and *Edit | Paste Special* [Excel 2007/2010: *Home* TAB, *Paste, Paste Special.*] functions can be used to replicate the data validation if validation is chosen in the *Paste Special* command.
- *Error Alerts.* Provide error alerts to let the user know when an incorrect value is entered through data validation (*Data | Validation | Error Alert*) [Excel 2007/2010: *Data* TAB, *Data Validation, Data Validation, Error Alerts.*] shown in Figure 3.6. If the validation is violated, an error message box will be executed (Figure 3.7).
- *Cell Warnings and Input Messages.* Provide warnings and input messages when a cell is selected where the inputs required are ambiguous (*Data | Validation | Input Message*) [Excel 2007/2010: *Data* TAB, *Data Validation, Data Validation, Input Message.*]. The message box can be set up to appear whenever the cell is selected, regardless of the data validation. This message box can be used to provide additional

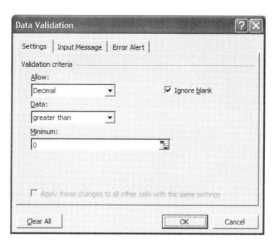

FIGURE 3.5   Data validation dialog box.

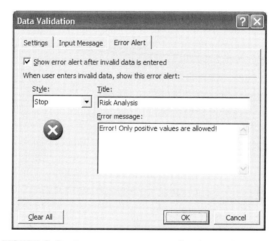

FIGURE 3.6   Error message setup for data validation.

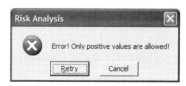

FIGURE 3.7   Error message for data validation.

information to the user about the specific input parameter or to provide suggested input values.

- *Define All Inputs.* Consider including a worksheet with named cells and ranges, complete with their respective definitions and where each variable is used in the model.

Make the model user-friendly through data validation, error alerts, cell warnings, and input messages, as well as defining all the inputs required in the model.

TRACK THE MODEL

- *Insert Comments.* Consider inserting comments for key variables (*Insert | Comment*) [Excel 2007/2010: *Review* TAB, *New Comment*; or *right-click* on a cell and *Insert Comment.*] for easy recognition and for quick reference. Comments can be easily copied into different cells through the *Edit | Paste Special | Comments* procedure.

- *Track Changes.* Consider tracking changes if collaborating with other modelers (*Tools | Track Changes | Highlight Changes*) [Excel 2007/2010: *Review* TAB, *Track Changes, Highlight Changes.*]. Tracking all changes is not only important, but it is also a courtesy to other model developers to note the changes and tweaks that were made.

- *Avoid Hard-Coding Values.* Consider using formulas whenever possible and avoid hard-coding numbers into cells other than assumptions and inputs. In complex models, it would be extremely difficult to track down where a model breaks because a few values are hard-coded instead of linked through equations. If a value needs to be hard-coded, it is by definition an input parameter and should be listed as such.

- *Use Linking and Embedding.* Consider object linking and embedding of files and objects (*Edit | Paste Special*) [Excel 2007/2010: *Home* TAB, *Paste, Paste Special.*] rather than using a simple paste function. This way, any changes in the source files can be reflected in the linked file. If linking between spreadsheets, Excel automatically updates these linked sheets every time the target sheet is opened. However, to avoid the irritating dialog pop-ups to update links every time the model is executed, simply turn off the warnings through *Edit | Links | Startup Prompt.*

Track the model by inserting comments, using the track changes functionality, avoiding hard-coded values, and using the linking and embedding functionality.

AUTOMATE THE MODEL WITH VBA

Visual Basic for Applications (VBA) is a powerful Excel tool that can assist in automating a significant amount of work. Although detailed VBA coding is beyond the scope of this book, an introduction to some VBA applications is provided in the appendix to this chapter—A Primer on VBA Modeling and Writing Macros—specifically addressing the following six automation issues:

1. Consider creating VBA modules for repetitive tasks (*Alt-F11* or *Tools | Macro | Visual Basic Editor*). For Excel 2007/2010, you need to add these tools icons before you can access them. Click on the *Office Button*, choose *Excel Options*, *Customize*, change the *Choose Commands From* drop list to *Developer Tab*, then select and double-click on each of the following: *Insert Controls*, *Record Macros*, *Control Properties*, *Visual Basic*. You can now access these functionalities on the Excel quick links icons on top of the Excel menu.
2. Add custom equations in place of complex and extended Excel equations.
3. Consider recording macros (*Tools | Macro | Record New Macro*) [Excel 2007/2010: *Record Macro* icon on quick links menu after customizing it—see instructions in the first point above.] for repetitive tasks or calculations.
4. Consider placing automation forms in your model (*View | Toolbar | Forms*) [Excel 2007/2010: *Record Macro* icon on quick links menu after customizing it—see instructions in the first point above.] and the relevant codes to support the desired actions.
5. Consider constraining users to only choosing specific inputs (*View | Toolbar | Forms*) [Excel 2007/2010: *Record Macro* icon on quick links menu after customizing it—see instructions in the first point above.] and insert drop-list boxes and the relevant codes to support the desired actions.
6. Consider adding custom buttons and menu items on the user's model within Excel to locate and execute macros easily.

Use VBA to automate the model, including adding custom equations, macros, automation forms, and predefined buttons.

MODEL AESTHETICS AND CONDITIONAL FORMATTING

- *Units.* Consider the input assumption's units and preset them accordingly in the cell to avoid any confusion. For instance, if a discount-rate input cell is required, the inputs can either be typed in as 20 or 0.2 to represent 20%. By avoiding a simple input ambiguity through preformatting the cells with the relevant units, user and model errors can be easily avoided.
- *Magnitude.* Consider the input's potential magnitude, where a large input value may obfuscate the cell's view by using the cell's default width. Change the format of the cell either to automatically reduce the font size to accommodate the higher magnitude input (*Format | Cells | Alignment | Shrink to Fit*) [Excel 2007/2010: *Home* TAB, *Format, Format Cells*; or use *Ctrl+1*.] or have the cell width sufficiently large to accommodate all possible magnitudes of the input.
- *Text Wrapping and Zooming.* Consider wrapping long text in a cell (*Format | Cells | Alignment | Wrap Text*) [Excel 2007/2010: *Home* TAB, *Format, Format Cells*; or use *Ctrl+1*.] for better aesthetics and view. This suggestion also applies to the zoom size of the spreadsheet. Remember that zoom size is worksheet specific and not workbook specific.
- *Merging Cells.* Consider merging cells in titles (*Format | Cells | Alignment | Merge Cells*) [Excel 2007/2010: *Home* TAB, *Format, Format Cells*; or use *Ctrl+1*.] for a better look and feel.
- *Colors and Graphics.* Colors and graphics are integral parts of a model's aesthetics as well as functional elements to determine if a cell is an input, a calculation, or a result. A careful blend of background colors and foreground graphics goes a long way in terms of model aesthetics.
- *Grouping.* Consider grouping repetitive columns or insignificant intermediate calculations (*Data | Group and Outline | Group*).
- *Hiding Rows and Columns.* Consider hiding extra rows and columns (select the relevant rows and columns to hide by selecting their row or column headers, and then choose *Format | Rows or Columns | Hide*) [Excel 2007/2010: *Home* TAB, *Format* (Cells section), *Hide and Unhide Rows and Columns.*] that are deemed as irrelevant intermediate calculations.

- *Conditional Formatting.* Consider conditional formatting such that if a cell's calculated result is a particular value (e.g., positive versus negative profits), the cell or font changes to a different color (*Format | Conditional Formatting*) [Excel 2007/2010: *Home* TAB, *Conditional Formatting* (Styles section), *New Rule*.].
- *Auto Formatting.* Consider using Excel's auto formatting for tables (*Format | Auto Format*) [Excel 2007/2010: *Home* TAB, *Format as Table*, select a style.]. Auto formatting will maintain the same look and feel throughout the entire Excel model for consistency.
- *Custom Styles.* The default Excel formatting can be easily altered, or alternatively, new styles can be added (*Format | Styles | New*) [Excel 2007/2010: *Home* TAB, *Cell Styles*, *New Cell Style*.]. Styles can facilitate the model-building process in that consistent formatting is applied throughout the entire model by default and the modeler does not have to worry about specific cell formatting (e.g., shrink to fit and font size can be applied consistently throughout the model).
- *Custom Views.* In larger models where data inputs and output results are all over the place, consider using custom views (*View | Custom Views | Add*) [Excel 2007/2010: *Views* TAB, *Custom View*.]. This custom view feature allows the user to navigate through a large model spreadsheet with ease, especially when navigational macros are added to these views (see the appendix to this chapter—A Primer on VBA Modeling and Writing Macros—for navigating custom views using macros). In addition, different size zooms on areas of interest can be created within the same spreadsheet through custom views.

Model aesthetics are preserved by considering the input units and magnitude, text wrapping and zooming views, cell merges, colors and graphics, grouping items, hiding excess rows and columns, conditional formatting, auto formatting, custom styles, and custom views.

APPENDIX—A PRIMER ON VBA MODELING AND WRITING MACROS

The Visual Basic Environment (VBE)

In Excel, access the VBE by hitting *Alt-F11* or *Tools | Macro | Visual Basic Environment* [Excel 2007/2010: *Office Button, Excel Options, Customize, Developer Tab* (from the Choose Commands drop list) select *Visual Basic* and double-click to add to quick icons list, then you can access this icon at the top of Excel's menu; or use *Alt+F11*.]. The VBE looks like Figure 3.8.

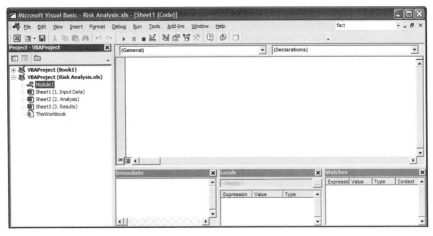

FIGURE 3.8   Visual Basic environment.

Select the VBA project pertaining to the opened Excel file (in this case, it is the *Risk Analysis.xls* file). Click on *Insert | Module* and double-click on the Module icon on the left window to open the module. You are now ready to start coding in VBA.

Custom Equations and Macros

Two Basic Equations   The following example illustrates two basic equations. They are simple combination and permutation functions. Suppose that there are three variables, A, B, and C. Further suppose that two of these variables are chosen randomly. How many pairs of outcomes are possible? In a combination, order is not important and the following three pairs of outcomes are possible: AB, AC, and BC. In a permutation, order is important and matters; thus, the following six pairs of outcomes are possible: AB, AC, BA, BC, CA, and CB. The equations are:

$$Combination = \frac{(\text{Variable})!}{(\text{Choose})!(\text{Variable} - \text{Choose})!} = \frac{3!}{2!(3-2)!} = 3$$

$$Permutation = \frac{(\text{Variable})!}{(\text{Variable} - \text{Choose})!} = \frac{3!}{(3-2)!} = 6$$

If these two equations are widely used, then creating a VBA function will be more efficient and will avoid any unnecessary errors in larger models when Excel equations have to be created repeatedly. For instance, the manually inputted equation will have to be: *=fact(A1)/(fact(A2)*fact(A1–A2))* as compared to a custom function created in VBA where the function in Excel will now be *=combine(A1,A2)*. The mathematical expression is exaggerated

	A	B	C	D	E	F	G
1							
2							
3		Variable		3			
4		Choose		2			
5		Combinations		3	<< "=Combine(3,2)"		
6		Permutations		6	<< "=Permute(3,2)"		

FIGURE 3.9   Excel spreadsheet with custom functions.

if the function is more complex, as will be seen later. The VBA code to be entered into the previous module (Figure 3.8) for the two simple equations is:

*Public Function Combine(Variable As Double, Choose As Double) _
As Double
Combine = Application.Fact(Variable) / (Application.Fact(Choose) * _
Application.Fact(Variable – Choose))
End Function*

*Public Function Permute(Variable As Double, Choose As Double) _
As Double
Permute = Application.Fact(Variable) / Application.Fact(Variable – _
Choose)
End Function*

Once the code is entered, the functions can be executed in the spreadsheet.

Figure 3.9 shows the spreadsheet environment with the custom function. If multiple functions were entered, the user can also get access to those functions through the *Insert | Function* [Excel 2007/2010: *Formulas* TAB, *Insert Function.*] dialog wizard by choosing the user-defined category and scrolling down to the relevant functions (Figure 3.10). The functions arguments box

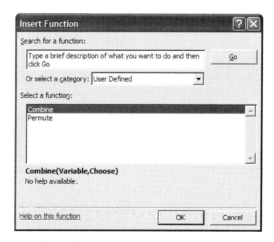

FIGURE 3.10   Insert function dialog box.

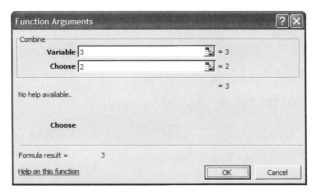

FIGURE 3.11 Function arguments box.

comes up for the custom function chosen (Figure 3.11), and entering the relevant inputs or linking to input cells can be accomplished here.

Following are the VBA codes for the Black–Scholes models for estimating call and put options. The equations for the Black–Scholes are shown below and are simplified to functions in Excel named "BlackScholesCall" and "BlackScholesPut."

$$Call = S\Phi\left[\frac{\ln(S/X) + (rf + \sigma^2/2)T}{\sigma\sqrt{T}}\right]$$

$$-Xe^{-rf(T)}\Phi\left[\frac{\ln(S/X) + (rf - \sigma^2/2)T}{\sigma\sqrt{T}}\right]$$

$$Put = Xe^{-rf(T)}\Phi\left[-\frac{\ln(S/X) + (rf - \sigma^2/2)T}{\sigma\sqrt{T}}\right]$$

$$-S\Phi\left[-\frac{\ln(S/X) + (rf + \sigma^2/2)T}{\sigma\sqrt{T}}\right]$$

Public Function BlackScholesCall(Stock As Double, Strike As _
Double, Time As Double, Riskfree _
As Double, Volatility As Double) As Double
Dim D1 As Double, D2 As Double
*D1 = (Log(Stock / Strike) + (Riskfree + 0.5 * Volatility ^ 2) * _*
*Time) / (Volatility * Sqr(Time))*
*D2 = D1 – Volatility * Sqr(Time)*
*BlackScholesCall = Stock * Application.NormSDist(D1) – Strike * _*
*Exp(–Time * Riskfree) ***
Application.NormSDist(D2)
End Function

```
Public Function BlackScholesPut(Stock As Double, Strike As _
   Double, Time As Double, Riskfree _
   As Double Volatility As Double) As Double
Dim D1 As Double, D2 As Double
D1 = (Log(Stock / Strike) + (Riskfree – 0.5 * Volatility ^ 2) * _
   Time) / (Volatility * Sqr(Time))
D2 = D1 – Volatility * Sqr(Time)
BlackScholesPut = Strike * Exp(–Time * Riskfree) * _
   Application.NormSDist(–D2) – Stock *
   Application.NormSDist(–D1)
End Function
```

As an example, the function BlackScholesCall(100,100,1,5%,25%) results in 12.32 and BlackScholesPut(100,100,1,5%,25%) results in 7.44. Note that *Log* is a natural logarithm function in VBA and that *Sqr* is square root, and make sure there is a space before the underscore in the code. The underscore at the end of a line of code indicates the continuation of the line of code on the next line.

Form Macros   Another type of automation is form macros. In Excel, select *View | Toolbars | Forms* [Excel 2007/2010: *Office Button, Excel Options, Customize*, choose *Developer Tab* from *Choose Commands From*, double-click on *Insert Controls* and on *Control Properties*.] and the forms toolbar will appear. Click on the insert drop-list icon as shown in Figure 3.12 and drag it into an area in the spreadsheet to insert the drop list. Then create a drop-list table as seen in Figure 3.13 (cells B10 to D17). Point at the drop list and use the right mouse click to select *Format Control | Control*. Enter the input range as cells C11 to C15, cell link at C16, and five drop-down lines (Figure 3.14).

In Figure 3.13, the index column simply lists numbers 1 to *n*, where *n* is the total number of items in the drop-down list (in this example, *n* is 5). Here, the index simply converts the items (annually, semiannually, quarterly, monthly, and weekly) into corresponding indexes. The choices column in the input range is the named elements in the drop list. The value column lists the variables associated with the choice (semiannually means

FIGURE 3.12   Forms icon bar.

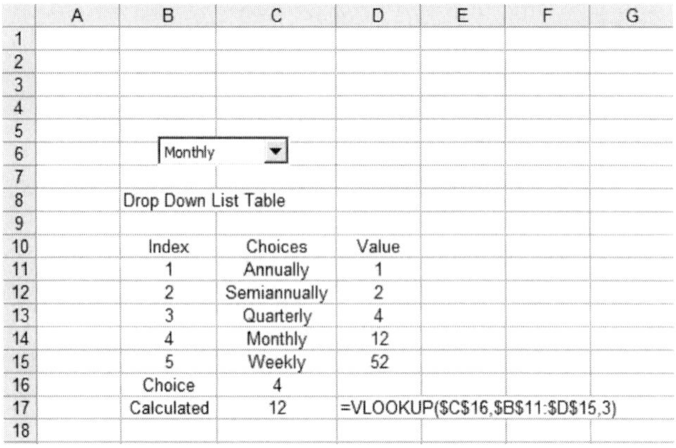

	A	B	C	D	E	F	G
1							
2							
3							
4							
5							
6		Monthly ▼					
7							
8		Drop Down List Table					
9							
10		Index	Choices	Value			
11		1	Annually	1			
12		2	Semiannually	2			
13		3	Quarterly	4			
14		4	Monthly	12			
15		5	Weekly	52			
16		Choice	4				
17		Calculated	12	=VLOOKUP($C$16,$B$11:$D$15,3)			
18							

FIGURE 3.13   Creating a drop-down box.

there are 2 periods in a year, or monthly means there are 12 periods in a year). Cell C16 is the choice of the user selection; that is, if the user chooses monthly on the drop list, cell C16 will become 4, and so forth, as it is linked to the drop list in Figure 3.14. Cell C17 in Figure 3.13 is the equation

$$=VLookup(\$C\$16,\$B\$11:\$D\$15,3)$$

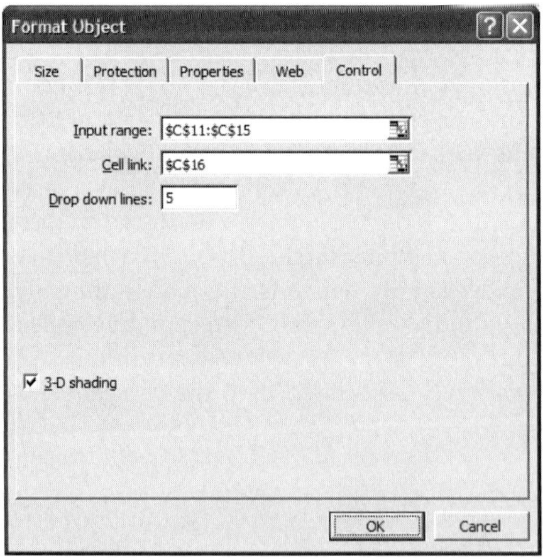

FIGURE 3.14   Format object dialog box.

where the *VLookup* function will look up the value in cell C16 (the cell that changes in value depending on the drop-list item chosen) with respect to the first column in the area B11:D15, matches the corresponding row with the same value as in cell C16, and returns the value in the third column (3). In Figure 3.13, the value is 12. In other words, if the user chooses quarterly, then cell C16 will be 3, and cell C17 will be 4. Clearly, in proper model building, this entire table will be hidden somewhere out of the user's sight (placed in the extreme corners of the spreadsheet or in a distant corner and its font color changed to match the background, making it disappear or placed in a hidden worksheet). Only the drop list will be shown and the models will link to cell C17 as an input parameter. This situation forces the user to choose only from a list of predefined inputs and prevents any accidental insertion of invalid inputs.

Navigational VBA Codes   A simple macro to navigate to sheet "2. Analysis" is shown here. This macro can be written in the VBA environment or recorded in the *Tools | Macros | Record New Macro* [Excel 2007/2010: Use the *Record Macros* icon after you add it using the *Office Button*, *Excel Options, Customize, Developer Tab* is chosen from the drop list, and double-clicking on *Record Macros*.], then perform the relevant navigational actions (i.e., clicking on the "2. Analysis" sheet and hitting the stop recording button), return to the VBA environment, and open up the newly recorded macro.

Sub MoveToSheet2()
Sheets("2. Analysis").Select
End Sub

However, if custom views (*View | Custom Views | Add*) [Excel 2007/2010: *View* TAB, *Custom Views*.] are created in Excel worksheets (to facilitate finding or viewing certain parts of the model such as inputs, outputs, etc.), navigations can also be created through the following, where a custom view named "results" had been previously created:

Sub CustomView()
ActiveWorkbook.CustomViews("Results").Show
End Sub

Form buttons can then be created and these navigational codes can be attached to the buttons. For instance, click on the fourth icon in the forms icon bar (Figure 3.12) and insert a form button in the spreadsheet and assign

	A	B
1	**User:**	John
2	**Date:**	15 July, 2004
3		
4	**Sales Data**	
5	January	$ 10,000.00
6	February	$ 11,000.00
7	March	$ 12,000.00
8	April	$ 13,000.00
9	May	$ 14,000.00
10	June	$ 15,000.00
11	Sum	$ 75,000.00
12		
13	Commissions %	15.00%
14	Commissions Paid	**$ 11,250.00**
15		
16		Calculate
17		

FIGURE 3.15   Simple automated model.

the relevant macros created previously. (If the select macro dialog does not appear, right-click the form button and select *Assign Macro*.)

Input Boxes   Input boxes are also recommended for their ease of use. The following illustrates some sample input boxes created in VBA, where the user is prompted to enter certain restrictive inputs in different steps or wizards. For instance, Figure 3.15 illustrates a simple sales commission calculation model, where the user inputs are the colored and boxed cells. The resulting commissions (cell B11 times cell B13) will be calculated in cell B14. The user would start using the model by clicking on the *Calculate* form button. A series of input prompts will then walk the user through inputting the relevant assumptions (Figure 3.16).

The code can also be set up to check for relevant inputs, that is, sales commissions have to be between 0.01 and 0.99. The full VBA code is shown next. The code is first written in VBA, and then the form button is placed in the worksheet that calls the VBA code.

FIGURE 3.16   Sample input box.

```
Sub UserInputs()
Dim User As Variant, Today As String, Sales As Double, _
   Commissions As Double
Range("B1").Select
User = InputBox("Enter your name:")
ActiveCell.FormulaR1C1 = User
Range("B2").Select
Today = InputBox("Enter today's date:")
ActiveCell.FormulaR1C1 = Today

Range("B5").Select
Sales = InputBox("Enter the sales revenue:")
ActiveCell.FormulaR1C1 = Sales
Dim N As Double

For N = 1 To 5
   ActiveCell.Offset(1, 0).Select
   Sales = InputBox("Enter the sales revenue for the following _
      period:")
ActiveCell.FormulaR1C1 = Sales
Next N

Range("B13").Select
Commissions = 0
Do While Commissions < 0.01 Or Commissions > 0.99
   Commissions = InputBox("Enter recommended commission rate _
      between 1% and 99%:")
Loop
ActiveCell.FormulaR1C1 = Commissions
Range("B1").Select
End Sub
```

Forms and Icons   Sometimes, for globally used macros and VBA scripts, a menu item or an icon can be added to the user's spreadsheet. These new icons and menus are applicable in Excel XP and 2003 only. For Excel 2007/2010, you will need *VSTO* tools and *.NET* ribbons add-in tools to create your own menu tabs and icon sets. Insert a new menu item by clicking on *Tools | Customize | Commands | New Menu* and dragging the *New Menu* item list to the Excel menu bar to a location right before the *Help* menu. Click on *Modify Selection* and rename the menu item accordingly (e.g., Risk Analysis). Also, an ampersand ("&") can be placed before a letter in the menu item name to underline the next letter such that the menu can be accessed through

FIGURE 3.17   Custom menu and icon.

the keyboard by hitting the *Alternate* key and then the corresponding letter key. Next, click on *Modify Selection | Begin a Group* and then drag the *New Menu* item list again to the menu bar, but this time, right under the Risk Analysis group. Now, select this submenu item and click on *Modify Selection | Name* and rename it *Run Commissions*. Then, *Modify Selection | Assign Macro* and assign it to the User Input macro created previously.

Another method to access macros (other than using menu items or *Tools | Macro | Macros*, or *Alt-F8*) is to create an icon on the icon toolbar. To do this, click on *Tools | Customize | Toolbars | New*. Name the new toolbar accordingly and drag it to its new location anywhere on the icon bar. Then, select the *Commands | Macros | Custom Button*. Drag the custom button icon to the new toolbar location. Select the new icon on the toolbar and click on *Modify Selection | Assign Macro*. Assign the User Input macro created previously. The default button image can also be changed by clicking on *Modify Selection | Change Button Image* and selecting the relevant icon accordingly, or from an external image file. Figure 3.17 illustrates the new menu item (Risk Analysis) and the new icon in the shape of a calculator, where selecting either the menu item or the icon will evoke the User Input macro, which walks the user through the simple input wizard.

EXERCISES

1. Create an Excel worksheet with each of the following components activated:
   a. Cells in an Excel spreadsheet with the following data validations: no negative numbers are allowed, only positive integers are allowed, only numerical values are allowed.
   b. Create a form macro drop list (see the appendix to this chapter) with the following 12 items in the drop list: January, February, March, . . . December. Make sure the selection of any item in the drop list will change a corresponding cell's value.
2. Go through the VBA examples in the appendix to this chapter and re-create the following macros and functions for use in an Excel spreadsheet:
   a. Create a column of future sales with the following equation for future sales (Years 2 to 11): *Future sales = (1+RAND())*(Past Year Sales)*

for 11 future periods starting with the current year's sales of $100 (Year 1). Then, in VBA, create a macro using the *For . . . Next* loop to simulate this calculation 1,000 times and insert a form button to activate the macro in the Excel worksheet.

b. Create the following income function in VBA for use in the Excel spreadsheet: *Income = Benefits − Cost*. Try out different benefits and cost inputs to make sure the function works properly.

Risk Quantification

CHAPTER 4

On the Shores of Monaco

Monte Carlo simulation, named for the famous gambling capital of Monaco, is a very potent methodology. For the practitioner, simulation opens the door for solving difficult and complex but practical problems with great ease. Perhaps the most famous early use of Monte Carlo simulation was by the Nobel physicist Enrico Fermi (sometimes referred to as the father of the atomic bomb) in 1930, when he used a random method to calculate the properties of the newly discovered neutron. Monte Carlo methods were central to the simulations required for the Manhattan Project, where in the 1950s Monte Carlo simulation was used at Los Alamos for early work relating to the development of the hydrogen bomb, and became popularized in the fields of physics and operations research. The Rand Corporation and the U.S. Air Force were two of the major organizations responsible for funding and disseminating information on Monte Carlo methods during this time, and today there is a wide application of Monte Carlo simulation in many different fields including engineering, physics, research and development, business, and finance.

Simplistically, Monte Carlo simulation creates artificial futures by generating thousands and even hundreds of thousands of sample paths of outcomes and analyzes their prevalent characteristics. In practice, Monte Carlo simulation methods are used for risk analysis, risk quantification, sensitivity analysis, and prediction. An alternative to simulation is the use of highly complex stochastic closed-form mathematical models. For analysts in a company, taking graduate-level advanced math and statistics courses is just not logical or practical. A brilliant analyst would use all available tools at his or her disposal to obtain the same answer the easiest and most practical way possible. And in all cases, when modeled correctly, Monte Carlo simulation provides similar answers to the more mathematically elegant methods. In addition, there are many real-life applications where closed-form models do not exist and the only recourse is to apply simulation methods. So, what exactly is Monte Carlo simulation and how does it work?

WHAT IS MONTE CARLO SIMULATION?

Today, fast computers have made possible many complex computations that were seemingly intractable in past years. For scientists, engineers, statisticians, managers, business analysts, and others, computers have made it possible to create models that simulate reality and aid in making predictions, one of which is used in simulating real systems by accounting for randomness and future uncertainties through investigating hundreds and even thousands of different scenarios. The results are then compiled and used to make decisions. This is what Monte Carlo simulation is all about.

Monte Carlo simulation in its simplest form is a random number generator that is useful for forecasting, estimation, and risk analysis. A simulation calculates numerous scenarios of a model by repeatedly picking values from a user-predefined *probability distribution* for the uncertain variables and using those values for the model. As all those scenarios produce associated results in a model, each scenario can have a forecast. Forecasts are events (usually with formulas or functions) that you define as important outputs of the model.

Think of the Monte Carlo simulation approach as picking golf balls out of a large basket repeatedly with replacement. The size and shape of the basket depend on the distributional *input assumption* (e.g., a normal distribution with a mean of 100 and a standard deviation of 10, versus a uniform distribution or a triangular distribution) where some baskets are deeper or more symmetrical than others, allowing certain balls to be pulled out more frequently than others. The number of balls pulled repeatedly depends on the number of *trials* simulated. For a large model with multiple related assumptions, imagine the large model as a very large basket, where many baby baskets reside. Each baby basket has its own set of colored golf balls that are bouncing around. Sometimes these baby baskets are linked with each other (if there is a *correlation* between the variables), forcing the golf balls to bounce in tandem, whereas in other uncorrelated cases, the balls are bouncing independently of one another. The balls that are picked each time from these interactions within the model (the large basket) are tabulated and recorded, providing a *forecast output* result of the simulation.

WHY ARE SIMULATIONS IMPORTANT?

An example of why simulation is important can be seen in the case illustration in Figures 4.1 and 4.2, termed the Flaw of Averages.[1] The example is most certainly worthy of more detailed study. It shows how an analyst may be misled into making the wrong decisions without the use of simulation. Suppose you are the owner of a shop that sells perishable goods and you

Actual		Average	5.00
Inventory Held	5		
	6	Historical Data	(5 Yr)
Perishable Cost	$100	Month	Actual
Fed Ex Cost	$175	1	12
		2	11
Total Cost	$100	3	7
		4	0

Your company is a retailer in perishable goods and you were tasked with finding the optimal level of inventory to have on hand. If your inventory exceeds actual demand, there is a $100 perishable cost while a $175 Fed Ex cost is incurred if your inventory is insufficient to cover the actual level of demand. These costs are on a per unit basis. Your first inclination is to collect historical demand data as seen on the right, for the past 60 months. You then take a simple average, which was found to be 5 units. Hence, you select 5 units as the optimal inventory level. You have just committed a major mistake called the Flaw of Averages!

The actual demand data are shown here on the right. Rows 19 through 57 are hidden to conserve space. Being the analyst, what must you then do?

Month	Actual
5	0
6	2
7	7
8	0
9	11
10	12
11	0
12	9
13	3
14	5
15	0
16	2
17	1
18	10
58	3
59	2
60	17

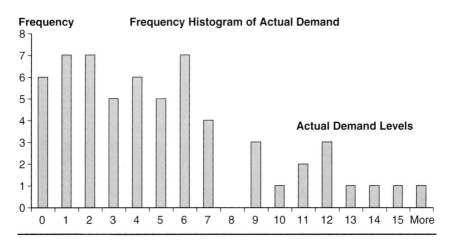

FIGURE 4.1 The flaw of averages example.

Simulated Average
Actual Demand   8.53
Inventory Held   9.00

Simulated Demand Range	From 7.21 to 9.85
Simulated Cost Range	From 178.91 to 149

Perishable Cost $100
Fed Ex Cost $175
Total Cost $46.88

The best method is to perform a nonparametric simulation where we use the actual historical demand levels as inputs to simulate the most probable level of demand going forward, which we found as 8.53 units. Given this demand, the lowest cost is obtained through a trial inventory of 9 units, a far cry from the original Flaw of Averages estimate of 5 units.

Trial Inventory	Total Cost
1.00	$1,318
2.00	$1,143
3.00	$968
4.00	$793
5.00	$618
6.00	$443
7.00	$268
8.00	$93
9.00	$47
10.00	$147
11.00	$247
12.00	$347
13.00	$447
14.00	$547
15.00	$647
16.00	$747

FIGURE 4.2 Fixing the flaw of averages with simulation.

need to make a decision on the optimal inventory to have on hand. Your new-hire analyst was successful in downloading five years worth of monthly historical sales levels and she estimates the average to be five units. You then make the decision that the optimal inventory to have on hand is five units. You have just committed the flaw of averages. As the example shows, the obvious reason why this error occurs is that the distribution of historical demand is highly skewed while the cost structure is asymmetrical. For example, suppose you are in a meeting, and your boss asks what everyone made last year. You take a quick poll and realize that the salaries range from $60,000 to $150,000. You perform a quick calculation and find the average to be $100,000. Then, your boss tells you that he made $20 million last year! Suddenly, the average for the group becomes $1.5 million. This value of $1.5 million clearly in no way represents how much each of your peers made last year. In this case, the median may be more appropriate. Here you see that simply using the average will provide highly misleading results.[2]

Continuing with the example, Figure 4.2 shows how the right inventory level is calculated using simulation. The approach used here is called *nonparametric* bootstrap simulation. It is nonparametric because in this simulation approach, no distributional parameters are assigned. Instead of assuming some preset distribution (normal, triangular, lognormal, or the like) and its required parameters (mean, standard deviation, and so forth) as required in a Monte Carlo *parametric* simulation, nonparametric simulation uses the data themselves to tell the story.

Imagine that you collect five years worth of historical demand levels and write down the demand quantity on a golf ball for each month. Throw all 60 golf balls into a large basket and mix the basket randomly. Pick a golf ball out at random and write down its value on a piece of paper, then replace the ball in the basket and mix the basket again. Do this 60 times and calculate the average. This process is a single grouped trial. Perform this entire process several thousand times, with replacement. The distribution of these thousands of averages represents the outcome of the simulation forecast. The expected value of the simulation is simply the average value of these thousands of averages. Figure 4.2 shows an example of the distribution stemming from a nonparametric simulation. As you can see, the optimal inventory rate that minimizes carrying costs is nine units, far from the average value of five units previously calculated in Figure 4.1.

Clearly, each approach has its merits and disadvantages. Nonparametric simulation, which can be easily applied using Risk Simulator's custom distribution,[3] uses historical data to tell the story and to predict the future. Parametric simulation, however, forces the simulated outcomes to follow well-behaving distributions, which is desirable in most cases. Instead of having to worry about cleaning up any messy data (e.g., outliers and nonsensical values) as is required for nonparametric simulation, parametric simulation starts fresh every time.

Monte Carlo simulation is a type of parametric simulation, where specific distributional parameters are required before a simulation can begin. The alternative approach is nonparametric simulation where the raw historical data is used to tell the story and no distributional parameters are required for the simulation to run.

COMPARING SIMULATION WITH TRADITIONAL ANALYSES

Figure 4.3 illustrates some traditional approaches used to deal with uncertainty and risk. The methods include performing sensitivity analysis,

(*Text continues on p. 88.*)

Point Estimates

This is a simple example of a Point Estimate approach. The issues that arise may include the risk of how confident you are in the unit sales projections, the sales price, and the variable unit cost.

Since the bottom line Net Income is the key financial performance indicator here, an uncertainty in future sales volume will be impounded into the Net Income calculation. How much faith do you have in your calculation based on a simple point estimate?

Recall the Flaw of Average example where a simple point estimate could yield disastrous conclusions.

Unit Sales	10	[10 units × $10 per unit]
Unit Price	$10	
Total Revenue	$100	
Unit Variable Cost	$5	[$20 Fixed + ($5 × 10) Variable]
Fixed Cost	$20	
Total Cost	$70	
Net Income	$30	[$100 − $70]

Sensitivity Analysis

Here, we can make unit changes to the variables in our simple model to see the final effects of such a change. Looking at the simple example, we know that only Unit Sales, Unit Price, and Unit Variable Cost can change. This is since Total Revenues, Total Costs, and Net Income are calculated values while Fixed Cost is assumed to be fixed and unchanging, regardless of the amount of sales units or sales price. Changing these three variables by one unit shows that from the original $40, Net Income has now increased $5 for Unit Sales, increased $10 for Unit Price, and decreased $10 for Unit Variable Cost.

Unit Sales	11	[Change 1 unit]
Unit Price	$10	
Total Revenue	$110	[Up $10]
Unit Variable Cost	$5	
Fixed Cost	$20	
Total Cost	$75	[Up $5]
Net Income	$35	

Unit Sales	10	
Unit Price	$11	[Change 1 unit]
Total Revenue	$110	
Unit Variable Cost	$5	
Fixed Cost	$20	[Change 1 unit]
Total Cost	$70	
Net Income	$40	

Unit Sales	10	
Unit Price	$10	
Total Revenue	$100	
Unit Variable Cost	$6	[Change 1 unit]
Fixed Cost	$20	
Total Cost	$80	
Net Income	$20	[Down $10]

Hence, we know that Unit Price has the most positive impact on the Net Income bottom line and Unit Variable Cost the most negative impact. In terms of making assumptions, we know that additional care must be taken when forecasting and estimating these variables. However, we still are in the dark concerning which sensitivity set of results we should be looking at or using.

Scenario Analysis

In order to provide an added element of variability, using the simple example above, you can perform a Scenario Analysis, where you would change values of key variables by certain units given certain assumed scenarios. For instance, you may assume three economic scenarios where unit sales and unit sale prices will vary. Under a good economic condition, unit sales go up to 14 at $11 per unit. Under a nominal economic scenario, units sales will be 10 units at $10 per unit. Under a bleak economic scenario, unit sales decrease to 8 units but prices per unit stays at $10.

		[Good Economy]
Unit Sales	14	
Unit Price	$11	
Total Revenue	$154	
Unit Variable Cost	$5	
Fixed Cost	$20	
Total Cost	$90	
Net Income	$64	

		[Average Economy]
Unit Sales	10	
Unit Price	$10	
Total Revenue	$100	
Unit Variable Cost	$5	
Fixed Cost	$20	
Total Cost	$70	
Net Income	$30	

		[Bad Economy]
Unit Sales	8	
Unit Price	$10	
Total Revenue	$80	
Unit Variable Cost	$5	
Fixed Cost	$20	
Total Cost	$60	
Net Income	$20	

Looking at the Net Income results, we have $64, $30 and $20. The problem here is, the variation is too large. Which condition do I think will most likely occur and which result do I use in my budget forecast for the firm? Although Scenario Analysis is useful in ascertaining the impact of different conditions, both advantageous and adverse, the analysis provides little insight to which result to use.

FIGURE 4.3 Point estimates, sensitivity analysis, scenario analysis, probabilistic scenarios, and simulation.

	Probability	Net Income
Good Economy	35%	$64.00
Average Economy	40%	$30.00
Bad Economy	25%	$20.00
EMV		$39.40

Unit Sales	10
Unit Price	$10
Total Revenue	$100

Unit Variable Cost	$5
Fixed Cost	$20
Total Cost	$70

Net Income	$30

By performing the simulation thousands of times, we essentially perform thousands of sensitivity analyses and scenario analyses given different sets of probabilities. These are all set in the original simulation assumptions (types of probability distributions, the parameters of the distributions and which variables to simulate).

The results calculated from the simulation output can then be interpreted as follows:

Discussions about types of distributional assumptions to use and the actual simulation approach will be discussed later.

Probabilistic Scenario Analysis

We can always assign probabilities that each scenario will occur, creating a Probabilistic Scenario Analysis and simply calculate the Expected Monetary Value (EMV) of the forecasts. The results here are more robust and reliable than a simple scenario analysis since we have collapsed the entire range of potential outcomes of $64, $30, and $20 into a single expected value. This value is what you would expect to get on average.

Simulation Analysis

Looking at the original model, we know that through Sensitivity Analysis, Unit Sales, Unit Price and Unit Variable Cost are three highly uncertain variables. We can then very easily simulate these three unknowns thousands of times (based on certain distributional assumptions) to see what the final Net Income value looks like.

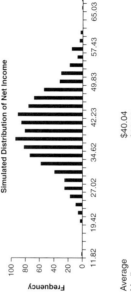

Simulated Distribution of Net Income

Average	$40.04
Median	$39.98
Mode	$46.63
Standard Deviation	$8.20
95% Confidence Interval	Between $56.16 and $24.09

FIGURE 4.3 (*Continued*)

scenario analysis, and probabilistic scenarios. The next step is the application of Monte Carlo simulation, which can be seen as an extension to the next step in uncertainty and risk analysis. Figure 4.4 shows a more advanced use of Monte Carlo simulation for forecasting.[4] The examples in Figure 4.4 show how Monte Carlo simulation can be really complicated, depending on its use. The enclosed DVD's Risk Simulator software has a stochastic process module that applies some of these more complex stochastic forecasting models, including Brownian Motion, mean-reversion, and random-walk models.

USING RISK SIMULATOR AND EXCEL
TO PERFORM SIMULATIONS

Simulations can be performed using Excel. However, more advanced simulation packages such as Risk Simulator perform the task more efficiently and have additional features preset in each simulation. We now present both Monte Carlo parametric simulation and nonparametric bootstrap simulation using Excel and Risk Simulator.

The examples in Figures 4.5 and 4.6 are created using Excel to perform a limited number of simulations on a set of probabilistic assumptions. We assume that having performed a series of scenario analyses, we obtain a set of nine resulting values, complete with their respective probabilities of occurrence. The first step in setting up a simulation in Excel for such a scenario analysis is to understand the function "*RAND()*" within Excel. This function is simply a random number generator Excel uses to create random numbers from a uniform distribution between 0 and 1. Then translate this 0 to 1 range using the assigned probabilities in our assumption into ranges or bins. For instance, if the value $362,995 occurs with a 55% probability, we can create a bin with a range of 0.00 to 0.55. Similarly, we can create a bin range of 0.56 to 0.65 for the next value of $363,522, which occurs 10% of the time, and so forth. Based on these ranges and bins, the nonparametric simulation can now be set up.

Figure 4.5 illustrates an example with 5,000 sets of trials. Each set of trials is simulated 100 times; that is, in each simulation trial set, the original numbers are picked randomly with replacement by using the Excel formula *VLOOKUP(RAND(),$D$16:$F$24,3)*, which picks up the third column of data from the D16 to F24 area by matching the results from the *RAND()* function and data from the first column.

The average of the data sampled is then calculated for each trial set. The distribution of these 5,000 trial sets' averages is obtained and the probability distribution is shown at the bottom of Figure 4.5. According to the Central Limit Theorem, the average of these sample averages will approach the real

A Simple Simulation Example

We need to perform many simulations to obtain a valid distribution.

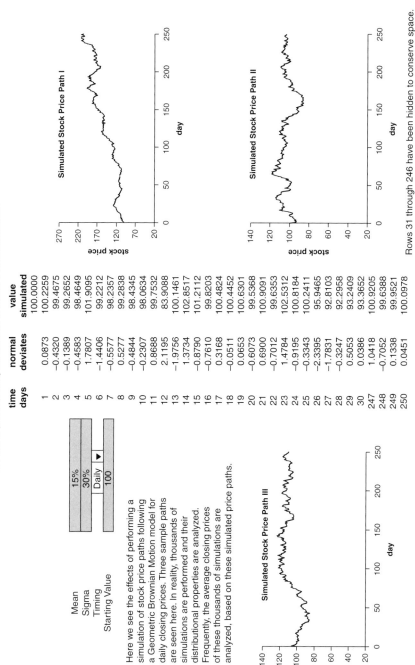

Mean	15%
Sigma	30%
Timing	Daily ▶
Starting Value	100

Here we see the effects of performing a simulation of stock price paths following a Geometric Brownian Motion model for daily closing prices. Three sample paths are seen here. In reality, thousands of simulations are performed and their distributional properties are analyzed. Frequently, the average closing prices of these thousands of simulations are analyzed, based on these simulated price paths.

time days	normal deviates	value simulated
		100.0000
1	0.0873	100.2259
2	−0.4320	99.4675
3	−0.1389	99.2652
4	−0.4583	98.4649
5	1.7807	101.9095
6	−1.4406	99.2212
7	−0.5577	98.2357
8	0.5277	99.2838
9	−0.4844	98.4345
10	−0.2307	98.0634
11	0.8688	99.7532
12	2.1195	83.9088
13	−1.9756	100.1461
14	1.3734	102.8517
15	−0.8790	101.2112
16	−0.7610	99.8203
17	0.3168	100.4824
18	−0.0511	100.4452
19	0.0653	100.6301
20	−0.6073	100.9091
21	0.6900	100.9091
22	−0.7012	99.6353
23	1.4784	102.5312
24	−0.9195	100.8184
25	−0.3343	100.2411
26	−2.3395	95.9465
27	−1.7831	92.8103
28	−0.3247	92.2958
29	0.5053	93.2409
30	0.0386	93.3652
247	1.0418	100.9205
248	−0.7052	99.6388
249	0.1338	99.9521
250	0.0451	100.0978

Rows 31 through 246 have been hidden to conserve space.

FIGURE 4.4 Conceptualizing the lognormal distribution. (*Continues*)

89

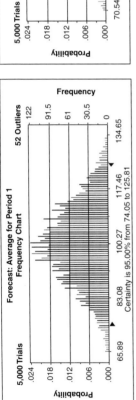

Forecast: Average for Period 1
Frequency Chart

5,000 Trials   52 Outliers

83.08   100.27   117.46
Certainty is 95.00% from 74.05 to 125.81

Forecast: Average for Period 20
Frequency Chart

5,000 Trials   40 Outliers

88.38   106.23   124.08
Certainty is 90.00% from 83.53 to 127.51

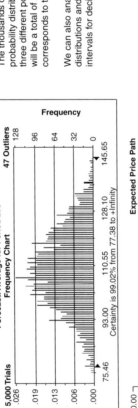

Forecast: Average for Period 250
Frequency Chart

5,000 Trials   47 Outliers

93.00   110.55   128.10
Certainty is 99.02% from 77.38 to +Infinity

The thousands of simulated price paths are then tabulated into probability distributions. Here are three sample price paths at three different points in time, for periods 1, 20, and 250. There will be a total of 250 distributions for each time period, which corresponds to the number of trading days a year.

We can also analyze each of these time-specific probability distributions and calculate relevant statistically valid confidence intervals for decision-making purposes.

We can then graph out the confidence intervals together with the expected values of each forecasted time period.

Notice that as time increases, the confidence interval widens since there will be more risk and uncertainty as more time passes.

Expected Price Path

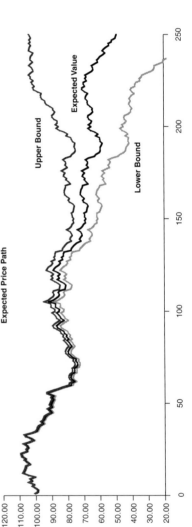

FIGURE 4.4 (*Continued*)

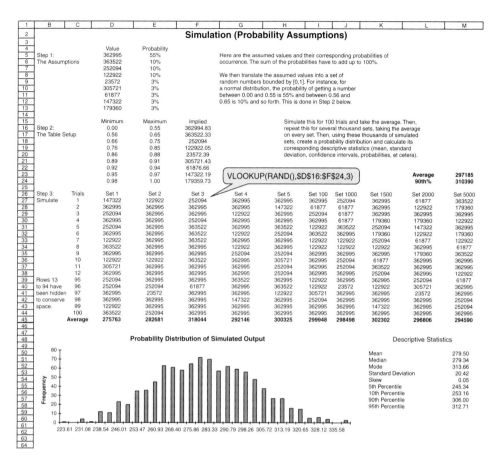

FIGURE 4.5 Simulation using Excel I.

true mean of the population at the limit. In addition, the distribution will most likely approach normality when a sufficient set of trials is performed. Clearly, running this nonparametric simulation manually in Excel is fairly tedious. An alternative is to use Risk Simulator's custom distribution, which does the same thing but in an infinitely faster and more efficient fashion. Chapter 6, Pandora's Toolbox, illustrates some of these simulation tools in more detail.

Nonparametric simulation is a very powerful tool but it is only applicable if data are available. Clearly, the more data there are, the higher the level of precision and confidence in the simulation results. However, when no data exist or when a valid systematic process underlies the data set (e.g., physics, engineering, economic relationship), parametric

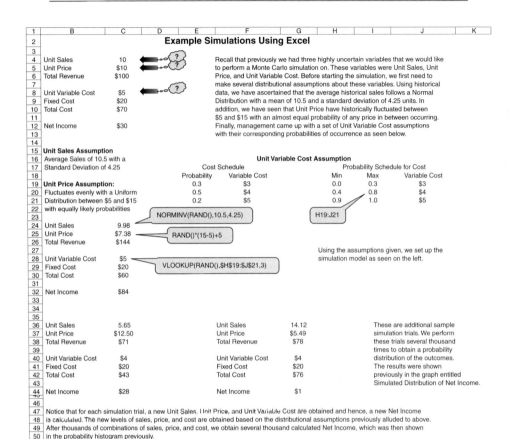

FIGURE 4.6   Simulation using Excel II.

simulation may be more appropriate, where exact probabilistic distributions are used.

> The *RAND()* function in Excel is used to generate random numbers for a uniform distribution between 0 and 1. *RAND()∗(B−A)+A* is used to generate random numbers for a uniform distribution between A and B. *NORMSINV(RAND())* generates random numbers from a standard normal distribution with mean of zero and variance of one.

Monte Carlo Simulation on Financial Analysis

Project A

	2001	2002	2003	2004	2005		
Revenues	$1,010	$1,111	$1,233	$1,384	$1,573	NPV	$126
Opex/Revenue Multiple	0.09	0.10	0.11	0.12	0.13	IRR	15.68%
Operating Expenses	$91	$109	$133	$165	$210	Risk Adjusted Discount Rate	12.00%
EBITDA	$919	$1,002	$1,100	$1,219	$1,363	Growth Rate	3.00%
FCF/EBITDA Multiple	0.20	0.25	0.31	0.40	0.56	Terminal Value	$8,692
Free Cash Flows	($1,200)	$187	$246	$336	$486	$760	Terminal Risk Adjustment	30.00%
Initial Investment	($1,200)					Discounted Terminal Value	$2,341
						Terminal to NPV Ratio	18.52
Revenue Growth Rates	10.00%	11.00%	12.21%	13.70%	15.58%	Payback Period	3.89
						Simulated Risk Value	$390

Project B

	2001	2002	2003	2004	2005		
Revenues	$1,200	$1,404	$1,683	$2,085	$2,700	NPV	$149
Opex/Revenue Multiple	0.09	0.10	0.11	0.12	0.13	IRR	33.74%
Operating Expenses	$108	$138	$181	$249	$361	Risk Adjusted Discount Rate	19.00%
EBITDA	$1,092	$1,266	$1,502	$1,836	$2,340	Growth Rate	3.75%
FCF/EBITDA Multiple	0.10	0.11	0.12	0.14	0.16	Terminal Value	$2,480
Free Cash Flows	($400)	$109	$139	$183	$252	$364	Terminal Risk Adjustment	30.00%
Initial Investment	($400)					Discounted Terminal Value	$668
						Terminal to NPV Ratio	4.49
Revenue Growth Rates	17.00%	19.89%	23.85%	29.53%	38.25%	Payback Period	2.83
						Simulated Risk Value	$122

Project C

	2001	2002	2003	2004	2005		
Revenues	$950	$1,069	$1,219	$1,415	$1,678	NPV	$29
Opex/Revenue Multiple	0.13	0.15	0.17	0.20	0.24	IRR	15.99%
Operating Expenses	$124	$157	$205	$278	$395	Risk Adjusted Discount Rate	15.00%
EBITDA	$827	$912	$1,014	$1,136	$1,283	Growth Rate	5.50%
FCF/EBITDA Multiple	0.20	0.25	0.31	0.40	0.56	Terminal Value	$7,935
Free Cash Flows	($1,100)	$168	$224	$309	$453	$715	Terminal Risk Adjustment	30.00%
Initial Investment	($1,100)					Discounted Terminal Value	$2,137
						Terminal to NPV Ratio	74.73
Revenue Growth Rates	12.50%	14.06%	16.04%	18.61%	22.08%	Payback Period	3.88
						Simulated Risk Value	$53

Project D

	2001	2002	2003	2004	2005		
Revenues	$1,200	$1,328	$1,485	$1,681	$1,932	NPV	$26
Opex/Revenue Multiple	0.08	0.08	0.09	0.09	0.10	IRR	21.57%
Operating Expenses	$90	$107	$129	$159	$200	Risk Adjusted Discount Rate	20.00%
EBITDA	$1,110	$1,221	$1,355	$1,522	$1,732	Growth Rate	1.50%
FCF/EBITDA Multiple	0.14	0.16	0.19	0.23	0.28	Terminal Value	$2,648
Free Cash Flows	($750)	$159	$200	$259	$346	$483	Terminal Risk Adjustment	30.00%
Initial Investment	($750)					Discounted Terminal Value	$713
						Terminal to NPV Ratio	26.98
Revenue Growth Rates	10.67%	11.80%	13.20%	14.94%	17.17%	Payback Period	3.38
						Simulated Risk Value	$56

	Implementation Cost	Sharpe Ratio	Weight	Project Cost	Project NPV	Risk Parameter	Payback Period	Technology Level	Tech Mix
Project A	$1,200	0.02	5.14%	$62	$6	29%	3.89	5	0.26
Project B	$400	0.31	25.27%	$101	$38	15%	2.83	3	0.76
Project C	$1,100	0.19	34.59%	$380	$10	21%	3.88	2	0.69
Project D	$750	0.17	35.00%	$263	$9	17%	3.38	4	1.40
Total	$3,450	0.17	100.00%	$806	$63	28%	3.49	3.5	3.11

Constraints:

	Lower Barrier	Upper Barrier	
Budget	$0	$900	(10 percentile at top 900)
Payback Mix	0.10	1.00	
Technology Mix	0.40	4.00	
Per Project Mix	5%	35%	

FIGURE 4.7 Simulation using Risk Simulator.

Using Excel to perform simulations is easy and effective for simple problems. However, when more complicated problems arise, such as the one presented next, the use of more specialized simulation packages is warranted. Risk Simulator is such a package. In the example shown in Figure 4.7, the cells for "Revenues," "Opex," "FCF/EBITDA Multiple," and "Revenue Growth Rates" (dark gray) are the assumption cells, where we enter our distributional input assumptions, such as the type of distribution the variable follows and what the parameters are. For instance, we can say that revenues follow a normal distribution with a mean of $1,010 and a standard deviation of $100, based on analyzing historical revenue data for the firm. The net present value (NPV) cells are the forecast output cells, that is, the results of these cells are the results we ultimately wish to analyze. Refer to Chapter 5, Test Driving Risk Simulator, for details on setting up and getting started with using the Risk Simulator software.

QUESTIONS

1. Compare and contrast parametric and nonparametric simulation.
2. What is a stochastic process (e.g., Brownian Motion)?
3. What does the *RAND()* function do in Excel?
4. What does the *NORMSINV()* function do in Excel?
5. What happens when both functions are used together, that is, *NORMSINV(RAND())*?

CHAPTER 5

Test Driving Risk Simulator

This chapter provides the novice risk analyst an introduction to the *Risk Simulator* software for performing Monte Carlo simulation, a trial version of which is included in the book's DVD. The chapter starts off by illustrating what Risk Simulator does and what steps are taken in a Monte Carlo simulation, as well as some of the more basic elements in a simulation analysis. The chapter then continues with how to interpret the results from a simulation and ends with a discussion of correlating variables in a simulation as well as applying precision and error control. As software versions with new enhancements are continually released, be sure to review the software's user manual for more up-to-date details on using the latest version of the software.

GETTING STARTED WITH RISK SIMULATOR

The Risk Simulator is a Monte Carlo simulation, forecasting, optimization, and risk analytics software. It is written in Microsoft .NET C# and functions together with Excel as an add-in. When you have the software installed, simply start Excel and you will see a new menu item called Risk Simulator. If you are using Excel 2007 or Excel 2010, you will see a new tab called Risk Simulator as well as some large icons that you can access. The examples referenced throughout this book use Risk Simulator version 2010 or later, with the following languages: English, Chinese (Simplified), Chinese (Traditional), French, German, Italian, Japanese, Korean, Portuguese, Spanish.

This software is also compatible and often used with the *Real Options SLS (Super Lattice Solver)* software (see Chapters 12 and 13), both developed by the author. The different functions or modules in both software applications are briefly described in the list that follows. Note that there are other software applications such as the ROV Basel II Modeling Toolkit, ROV Employee Stock Options Valuation Toolkit, ROV Compiler, ROV

Risk Extractor and Evaluator, ROV BizStats, ROV Modeler, ROV Valuator, ROV Dashboard, and others, also created by the same company that developed Risk Simulator, but introduced in this book. You can get more information on these tools by visiting www.realoptionsvaluation.com, where you can also view some free modeling videos and obtain white papers, case studies, and other free models.

In fact, it is *highly recommended* that you first watch the getting started videos on the DVD or attempt the step-by-step exercises at the end of this chapter *before* reading the text in this chapter. The videos and exercises will get you started immediately, whereas the text in this chapter focuses more on the theory and detailed explanations of the properties of simulation. You can also view the videos online at www.realoptionsvaluation.com/risksimulator.html.

- The *Simulation Module* allows you to run simulations in your existing Excel-based models, generate and extract simulation forecasts (distributions of results), perform distributional fitting (automatically finding the best-fitting statistical distribution), compute correlations (maintain relationships among simulated random variables), identify sensitivities (creating tornado and sensitivity charts), test statistical hypotheses (finding statistical differences between pairs of forecasts), run bootstrap simulation (testing the robustness of result statistics), and run custom and nonparametric simulations (simulations using historical data without specifying any distributions or their parameters for forecasting without data or applying expert opinion forecasts).
- The *Forecasting Module* can be used to generate automatic time-series forecasts (with and without seasonality and trend), multivariate regressions (modeling relationships among variables), nonlinear extrapolations (curve fitting), stochastic processes (random walk, mean-reversion, jump-diffusion, and mixed processes), Box-Jenkins ARIMA (econometric forecasts), Auto ARIMA, basic econometrics and auto-econometrics (modeling relationships and generating forecasts), exponential J curves, logistic S curves, GARCH models and its multiple variations (modeling and forecasting volatility), maximum likelihood models for limited dependent variables (logit, tobit, and probit models), Markov chains, trendlines, spine curves, and others.
- The *Optimization Module* is used for optimizing multiple decision variables subject to constraints to maximize or minimize an objective, and can be run either as a static optimization, as dynamic and stochastic optimization under uncertainty together with Monte Carlo simulation, or as a stochastic optimization with super speed simulations. The software can handle linear and nonlinear optimizations with binary,

integer, and continuous variables, as well as generate Markowitz efficient frontiers.

- The *Analytical Tools Module* allows you to run segmentation clustering, hypothesis testing, statistical tests of raw data, data diagnostics of technical forecasting assumptions (e.g., heteroskedasticity, multicollinearity, and so forth), sensitivity and scenario analyses, overlay chart analysis, spider charts, tornado charts, and many other powerful tools.
- The Real Options Super Lattice Solver is another stand-alone software that complements Risk Simulator, used for solving simple to complex real options problems. See Chapters 12 and 13 for more details on the concept, software, and applications of real options analysis.

The following sections walk you through the basics of the *Simulation Module* in Risk Simulator, while future chapters provide more details on the applications of other modules. To follow along, make sure you have Risk Simulator installed on your computer to proceed. Be sure to see About the DVD at the end of this book for directions on installing your 30-day trial software. Also note that there are additional hands-on exercises available at the end of certain chapters in which you can get step-by-step instructions on running sample models using Risk Simulator.

RUNNING A MONTE CARLO SIMULATION

Typically, to run a simulation in your existing Excel model, the following five steps have to be performed:

1. Start a new simulation profile or open an existing profile.
2. Define input assumptions in the relevant cells.
3. Define output forecasts in the relevant cells.
4. Run simulation.
5. Interpret the results.

If desired, and for practice, open the example file called *Basic Simulation Model* and follow along with the examples provided here on creating a simulation. The example file can be found by first starting Excel, and then clicking on *Risk Simulator | Example Models | 02 Basic Simulation Model.*

Start a New Simulation Profile

To start a new simulation, you must first create a simulation profile. A simulation profile contains a complete set of instructions on how you would like

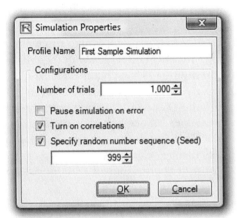

FIGURE 5.1 New simulation profile.

to run a simulation; that is, all the assumptions, forecasts, and run preferences. Having profiles facilitates creating multiple scenarios of simulations. That is, using the same exact model, several profiles can be created, each with its own specific simulation properties and requirements. The same person can create different test scenarios using different distributional assumptions and inputs, or multiple persons can test their own assumptions and inputs on the same model.

- Start Excel and create a new model or open an existing one (you can use the Basic Simulation Model example to follow along).
- Click on *Risk Simulator | New Simulation Profile.*
- Specify a title for your simulation as well as all other pertinent information (Figure 5.1) as described in the following items.
- *Title.* Specifying a simulation title allows you to create multiple simulation profiles in a single Excel model. Using a title means that you can now save different simulation scenario profiles within the same model without having to delete existing assumptions and changing them each time a new simulation scenario is required. You can always change the profile's name later (*Risk Simulator | Edit Profile*).
- *Number of trials.* This is where the number of simulation trials required is entered. That is, running 1,000 trials means that 1,000 different iterations of outcomes based on the input assumptions will be generated. You can change this as desired, but the input has to be positive integers. The default number of runs is 1,000 trials. You can use precision and error control to automatically help determine how many simulation

trials to run (see the section on precision and error control later in this chapter for details).

■ *Pause simulation on error.* If checked, the simulation stops every time an error is encountered in the Excel model. That is, if your model encounters a computation error (e.g., some input values generated in a simulation trial may yield a divide by zero error in one of your spreadsheet cells), the simulation stops. This feature is important to help audit your model to make sure there are no computational errors in your Excel model. However, if you are sure the model works, then there is no need for this preference to be checked.

■ *Turn on correlations.* If checked, correlations between paired input assumptions will be computed. Otherwise, correlations will all be set to zero and a simulation is run assuming no cross correlations between input assumptions. As an example, applying correlations will yield more accurate results if indeed correlations exist and will tend to yield a lower forecast confidence if negative correlations exist. After turning on correlations here, you can later set the relevant correlation coefficients on each assumption generated (see the section on correlations and precision control later in this chapter for more details).

■ *Specify random number sequence.* Simulation, by definition, will yield slightly different results every time a simulation is run. Different results occur by virtue of the random number generation routine in Monte Carlo simulation; this characteristic is a theoretical fact in all random number generators. However, when making presentations, if you require the same results (such as especially when the report being presented shows one set of results and during a live presentation you would like to show the same results being generated, or when you are sharing models with others and would like the same results to be obtained every time), then check this preference and enter in an initial seed number. The seed number can be any positive integer. Using the same initial seed value, the same number of trials, and the same input assumptions, the simulation will always yield the same sequence of random numbers, guaranteeing the same final set of results.

Note that once a new simulation profile has been created, you can come back later and modify these selections. In order to do this, make sure that the current active profile is the profile you wish to modify, otherwise, click on *Risk Simulator | Change Simulation Profile*, select the profile you wish to change and click *OK* (Figure 5.2 shows an example where there are multiple profiles and how to activate a selected profile). Then, click on *Risk Simulator | Edit Simulation Profile* and make the required changes. You can also duplicate or rename an existing profile. When creating multiple profiles

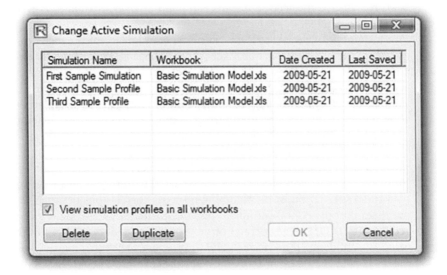

FIGURE 5.2 Change active simulation.

in the same Excel model, make sure to provide each profile a unique name so you can tell them apart later on. Also, these profiles are stored inside hidden sectors of the Excel *.xls or *.xlsx file and you do not have to save any additional files. The profiles and their contents (assumptions, forecasts, etc.) are automatically saved when you save the Excel file. Finally, the last profile that is active when you exit and save the Excel file will be the one that is opened the next time the Excel file is accessed.

Define Input Assumptions

The next step is to set input assumptions in your model. Note that assumptions can only be assigned to cells without any equations or functions (i.e., typed-in numerical values that are inputs in a model), whereas output forecasts can only be assigned to cells with equations and functions (i.e., outputs of a model). Recall that assumptions and forecasts cannot be set unless a simulation profile already exists. Do the following four steps to set new input assumptions in your model:

1. Make sure a Simulation Profile exists, open an existing profile, or start a new profile (*Risk Simulator | New Simulation Profile*).
2. Select the cell you wish to set an assumption on (e.g., cell G8 in the Basic Simulation Model example).
3. Click on *Risk Simulator | Set Input Assumption* or click on the set input assumption icon in the Risk Simulator icon toolbar.

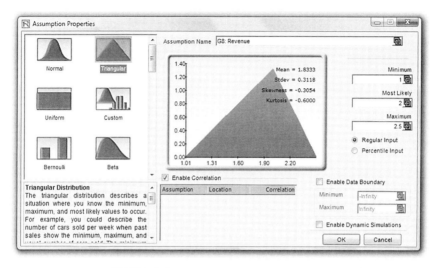

FIGURE 5.3   Setting an input assumption.

4. Select the relevant distribution you want, enter the relevant distribution parameters (e.g., select *Triangular* distribution and use *1*, *2*, and *2.5* as the minimum, most likely, and maximum values), and hit *OK* to insert the input assumption into your model (Figure 5.3).

Note that you can also set assumptions by selecting the cell you wish to set the assumption on and, using the mouse right-click, access the shortcut Risk Simulator menu to set an input assumption. In addition, for expert users, you can set input assumptions using the Risk Simulator *RS Functions*: select the cell of choice, click on Excel's *Insert*, *Function*, and select the *All Category*, and scroll down to the *RS* functions list (we do not recommend using RS functions unless you are an expert user). If using RS functions for the first time, you would need to install this add-in by going to *Start*, *Programs*, *Real Options Valuation*, *Risk Simulator*, *Tools*, and right-click on *Install Functions*, and choose *Run As Administrator*. For the examples going forward, we suggest following the basic instructions in accessing menus and icons.

Notice that in the Assumption Properties, there are several key areas worthy of mention. Figure 5.4 shows the different areas:

- *Assumption Name.* This is an optional area that allows you to enter in unique names for the assumptions to help track what each of the assumptions represents. Good modeling practice is to use short but precise assumption names.

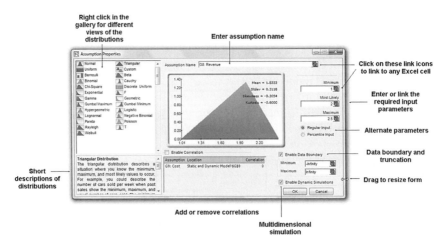

FIGURE 5.4   Assumption properties.

- *Distribution Gallery.* This area to the left shows all of the different distributions available in the software. To change the views, right click anywhere in the gallery and select large icons, small icons, or list. More than two dozen distributions are available.
- *Input Parameters.* Depending on the distribution selected, the required relevant parameters are shown. You may either enter the parameters directly or link them to specific cells in your worksheet. Hard-coding or typing the parameters is useful when the assumption parameters are assumed not to change. Linking to worksheet cells is useful when the input parameters need to be visible or are allowed to be changed (click on the link icon to link an input parameter to a worksheet cell).
- *Enable Data Boundary.* This feature is typically not used by the average analyst but exists for truncating the distributional assumptions. For instance, if a normal distribution is selected, the theoretical boundaries are between negative infinity and positive infinity. However, in practice, the simulated variable exists only within some smaller range, and this range can then be entered to truncate the distribution appropriately.
- *Correlations.* Pairwise correlations can be assigned to input assumptions here. If assumptions are required, remember to check the *Turn on Correlations* preference by clicking on *Risk Simulator | Edit Simulation Profile*. See the discussion on correlations later in this chapter for more details about assigning correlations and the effects correlations will have on a model. Notice that you can either truncate a distribution or correlate it to another assumption but not both.

- *Short Descriptions*. These exist for each of the distributions in the gallery. The short descriptions explain when a certain distribution is used as well as the input parameter requirements. See Understanding Probability Distributions at the end of this chapter for details on each distribution type available in the software.
- *Regular Input and Percentile Input*. This option allows the user to perform a quick due diligence test of the input assumption. For instance, if setting a normal distribution with some mean and standard deviation inputs, you can click on the percentile input to see what the corresponding 10th and 90th percentiles are.
- *Enable Dynamic Simulation*. This option is unchecked by default, but if you wish to run a multidimensional simulation (i.e., if you link the input parameters of the assumption to another cell that is itself an assumption, you are simulating the inputs, or simulating the simulation), then remember to check this option. Dynamic simulation will not work unless the inputs are linked to other changing input assumptions.

Note: If you are following along with the example, continue by setting another assumption on cell G9. This time use the *Uniform* distribution with a minimum value of 0.9 and a maximum value of 1.1. Then, proceed to defining the output forecasts in the next step.

Define Output Forecasts

The next step is to define output forecasts in the model. Forecasts can only be defined on output cells with equations or functions. The following three steps describe the set forecast process:

1. Select the cell you wish to set a forecast on (e.g., cell G10 in the Basic Simulation Model example).
2. Click on *Risk Simulator* and select *Set Output Forecast* or click on the set output forecast icon on the Risk Simulator icon toolbar.
3. Enter the relevant information and click *OK*.

Note that you can also set output forecasts by selecting the cell you wish to set the assumption on and, using the mouse right-click, access the shortcut Risk Simulator menu to set an output forecast.

Figure 5.5 illustrates the set output forecast properties:

- *Forecast Name*. Specify the name of the forecast cell. This is important because when you have a large model with multiple forecast cells,

FIGURE 5.5 Set output forecast.

naming the forecast cells individually allows you to access the right results quickly. Do not underestimate the importance of this simple step. Good modeling practice is to use short but precise assumption names.

- *Forecast Precision.* Instead of relying on a guesstimate of how many trials to run in your simulation, you can set up precision and error controls. When an error-precision combination has been achieved in the simulation, the simulation will pause and inform you of the precision achieved, making the number of simulation trials an automated process and eliminating guesses on the required number of trials to simulate. Review the section on precision and error control later in this chapter for more specific details.
- *Show Forecast Window.* This property allows the user to show or not show a particular forecast window. The default is to always show a forecast chart.

Run Simulation

If everything looks right, simply click on *Risk Simulator | Run Simulation* or click on the *Run* icon on the Risk Simulator toolbar and the simulation will proceed. You may also reset a simulation after it has run to rerun it (*Risk Simulator | Reset Simulation* or the reset simulation icon on the toolbar) or to pause it during a run. Also, the *step* function (*Risk Simulator | Step Simulation* or the step simulation icon on the toolbar) allows you to simulate a single trial, one at a time, useful for educating others on simulation (i.e., you can show that at each trial, all the values in the assumption cells are being replaced and the entire model is recalculated each time). You can also access the run simulation menu by right-clicking anywhere in the model and selecting *Run Simulation.*

Risk Simulator also allows you to run the simulation at extremely fast speed, called Super Speed. To do this, click on *Risk Simulator | Run Super Speed Simulation* or use the run super speed icon. Notice how much faster the super speed simulation runs. In fact, for practice, click on *Reset Simulation* and then *Edit Simulation Profile,* change the *Number of Trials* to *100,000,* and click on *Run Super Speed.* It should only take a few seconds to run. However, be aware that super speed simulation will not run if the model has errors, VBA (Visual Basic for Applications), or links to external data sources or applications. In such situations, you will be notified and the regular speed simulation will be run instead. Regular speed simulations are always able to run even with errors, VBA, or external links.

Interpret the Forecast Results

The final step in Monte Carlo simulation is to interpret the resulting forecast charts. Figures 5.6 to 5.13 show the forecast chart and the corresponding statistics generated after running the simulation. Typically, the following features are important in interpreting the results of a simulation:

- *Forecast Chart.* The forecast chart shown in Figure 5.6 is a probability histogram that shows the frequency counts of values occurring in the

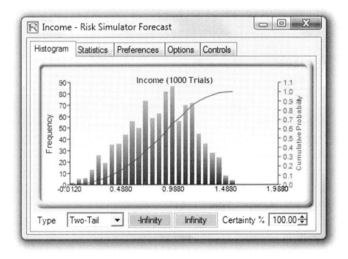

FIGURE 5.6 Forecast chart.

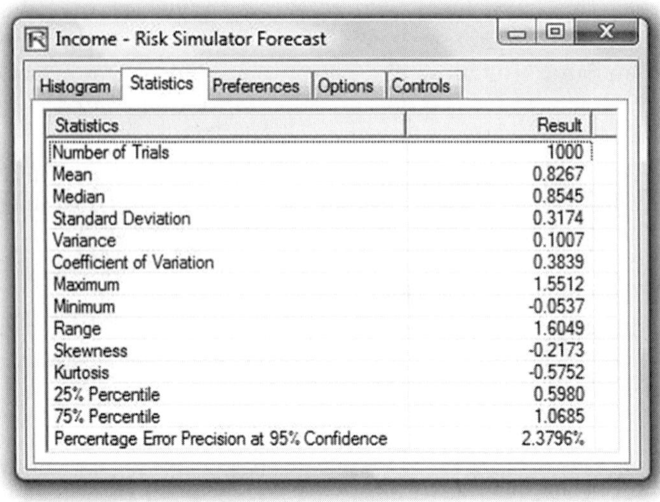

Statistics	Result
Number of Trials	1000
Mean	0.8267
Median	0.8545
Standard Deviation	0.3174
Variance	0.1007
Coefficient of Variation	0.3839
Maximum	1.5512
Minimum	-0.0537
Range	1.6049
Skewness	-0.2173
Kurtosis	-0.5752
25% Percentile	0.5980
75% Percentile	1.0685
Percentage Error Precision at 95% Confidence	2.3796%

FIGURE 5.7 Forecast statistics.

total number of trials simulated. The vertical bars show the frequency of a particular x value occurring out of the total number of trials, while the cumulative frequency (smooth line) shows the total probabilities of all values at and below x occurring in the forecast.

- *Forecast Statistics*. The forecast statistics shown in Figure 5.7 summarize the distribution of the forecast values in terms of the four moments of a distribution. See the section on understanding the forecast statistics in Chapter 2 for more details on what some of these statistics mean. You can rotate between the histogram and statistics tab by depressing the space bar.
- *Preferences*. The preferences tab in the forecast chart (Figure 5.8) allows you to change the look and feel of the charts. For instance, if *Always Show Window On Top* is selected, the forecast charts will always be visible regardless of what other software are running on your computer. *Histogram Resolution* allows you to change the number of bins of the histogram, anywhere from 5 bins to 100 bins. Also, the *Data Update Interval* section allows you to control how fast the simulation runs versus how often the forecast chart is updated. That is, if you wish to see the forecast chart updated at almost every trial, this feature will slow down the simulation as more memory is being allocated to updating the chart versus running the simulation. This option is merely a user preference

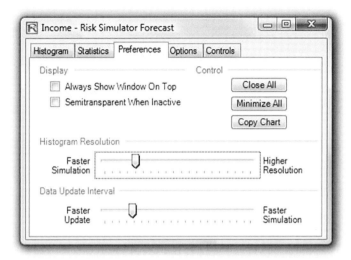

FIGURE 5.8   Forecast chart preferences.

and in no way changes the results of the simulation, just the speed of completing the simulation. To further increase the speed of the simulation, you can minimize Excel while the simulation is running, thereby reducing the memory required to visibly update the Excel spreadsheet and freeing up the memory to run the simulation. The *Close All* and *Minimize All* controls all the open forecast charts, and *Copy Chart* allows you to copy the histogram into clipboard where you can paste it into other applications.

- *Options.* This forecast chart option (Figure 5.9, top) allows you to show all the forecast data or to filter in/out values that fall within some specified interval you choose, or within some standard deviation you choose. Also, the precision level can be set here for this specific forecast to show the error levels in the statistics view. See the section on precision and error control later in this chapter for more details. *Show the Following Statistics on Histogram* is a user preference if the mean, median, first quartile, and third quartile lines (25th and 75th percentiles) should be displayed on the forecast chart.

- *Controls.* This tab (Figure 5.9, bottom) has all the functionalities in allowing you to change the type, color, size, zoom, tilt, 3D, and other things in the forecast chart, as well as providing overlay charts (PDF, CDF) and running distributional fitting on your forecast data (see the Data Fitting sections for more details on this methodology).

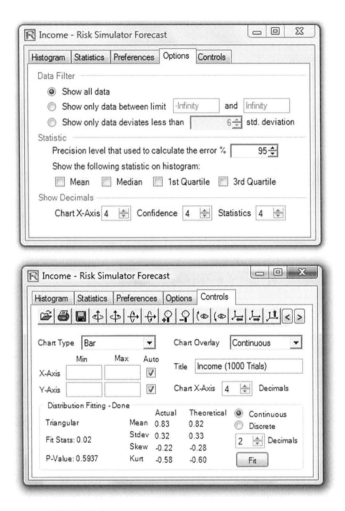

FIGURE 5.9 Forecast chart options and controls.

USING FORECAST CHARTS AND CONFIDENCE INTERVALS

In forecast charts, you can determine the probability of occurrence called *confidence intervals*. That is, given two values, what are the chances that the outcome will fall between these two values? Figure 5.10 illustrates that there is a 90% probability that the final outcome (in this case, the level of

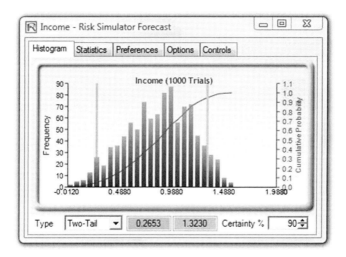

FIGURE 5.10 Forecast chart two-tail confidence interval.

income) will be between $0.2653 and $1.3230. The two-tailed confidence interval can be obtained by first selecting *Two-Tail* as the type, entering the desired certainty value (e.g., 90), and hitting *TAB* on the keyboard. The two computed values corresponding to the certainty value will then be displayed. In this example, there is a 5% probability that income will be below $0.2653 and another 5% probability that income will be above $1.3230. That is, the two-tailed confidence interval is a symmetrical interval centered on the median or 50th percentile value. Thus, both tails will have the same probability.

Alternatively, a one-tail probability can be computed. Figure 5.11 shows a *Left-Tail* selection at 95% confidence (i.e., choose *Left-Tail* ≤ as the type, enter 95 as the certainty level, and hit *TAB* on the keyboard). This means that there is a 95% probability that the income will be at or below $1.3230 or a 5% probability that income will be above $1.3230, corresponding perfectly with the results seen in Figure 5.10.

In addition to evaluating what the confidence interval is (i.e., given a probability level and finding the relevant income values), you can determine the probability of a given income value (Figure 5.12). For instance, what is the probability that income will be less than or equal to $1? To do this, select the *Left-Tail* ≤ probability type, enter 1 into the value input box, and hit *TAB*. The corresponding certainty will then be computed (in this case, there is a 67.70% probability income will be at or below $1).

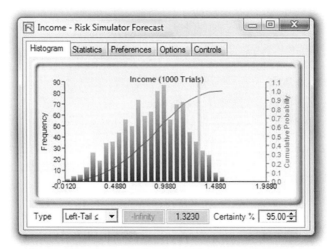

FIGURE 5.11   Forecast chart one-tail confidence interval.

For the sake of completeness, you can select the *Right-Tail* > probability type and enter the value 1 in the value input box, and hit *TAB* (Figure 5.13). The resulting probability indicates the right-tail probability past the value 1, that is, the probability of income exceeding $1 (in this case, we see that there is a 32.30% probability of income exceeding $1). The sum of 32.30% and 67.70% is, of course 100%, the total probability under the curve.

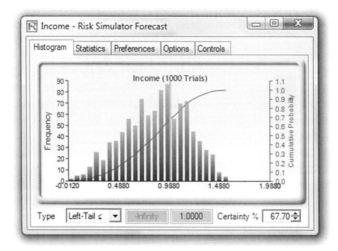

FIGURE 5.12   Forecast chart probability evaluation.

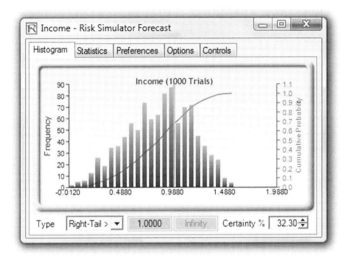

FIGURE 5.13   Forecast chart probability evaluation.

TIPS

- The forecast window is resizable by clicking on and dragging its bottom right corner. It is always advisable that before rerunning a simulation, the current simulation should be reset (*Risk Simulator | Reset Simulation*).
- Remember that you will need to hit *TAB* on the keyboard to update the chart and results when you type in the certainty values or right- and left-tail values.
- You can also hit the *Spacebar* on the keyboard repeatedly to cycle among the histogram, statistics, preferences, options, and control tabs.
- In addition, if you click on *Risk Simulator | Options,* you can access several different options for Risk Simulator, including allowing Risk Simulator to start each time Excel starts or to only start when you want it to (by going to *Start | Programs | Real Options Valuation | Risk Simulator | Risk Simulator*), change the *cell colors* of assumptions and forecasts, as well as turn *cell comments* on and off (cell comments will allow you to see which cells are input assumptions and which are output forecasts as well as their respective input parameters and names). Do spend some time experimenting with the forecast chart outputs and various bells and whistles, especially the *Controls* tab.
- You can also click on the *Global View* (top right corner of the forecast charts) to view all the tabs in a single comprehensive interface, and return to the regular view by clicking on the *Normal View* link.

CORRELATIONS AND PRECISION CONTROL

The Basics of Correlations

The correlation coefficient is a measure of the strength and direction of the relationship between two variables, and it can take on any values between -1.0 and $+1.0$. That is, the correlation coefficient can be decomposed into its sign (positive or negative relationship between two variables) and the magnitude or strength of the relationship (the higher the absolute value of the correlation coefficient, the stronger the relationship).

The correlation coefficient can be computed in several ways. The first approach is to manually compute the correlation r of two variables x and y using:

$$r_{x,y} = \frac{n \sum x_i y_i - \sum x_i \sum y_i}{\sqrt{n \sum x_i^2 - \left(\sum x_i\right)^2} \sqrt{n \sum y_i^2 - \left(\sum y_i\right)^2}}$$

The second approach is to use Excel's *CORREL* function. For instance, if the 10 data points for x and y are listed in cells A1:B10, then the Excel function to use is *CORREL (A1:A10, B1:B10)*.

The third approach is to run Risk Simulator's *Multi-Fit Tool*, and the resulting correlation matrix will be computed and displayed.

It is important to note that correlation does not imply causation. Two completely unrelated random variables might display some correlation, but this does not imply any causation between the two (e.g., sunspot activity and events in the stock market are correlated, but there is no causation between the two).

There are two general types of correlations: parametric and nonparametric correlations. Pearson's correlation coefficient is the most common correlation measure and is usually referred to simply as the correlation coefficient. However, Pearson's correlation is a parametric measure, which means that it requires both correlated variables to have an underlying normal distribution and that the relationship between the variables is linear. When these conditions are violated, which is often the case in Monte Carlo simulation, the nonparametric counterparts become more important. Spearman's rank correlation and Kendall's tau are the two nonparametric alternatives. The Spearman correlation is most commonly used and is most appropriate when applied in the context of Monte Carlo simulation—there is no dependence on normal distributions or linearity, meaning that correlations between different variables with different distribution can be applied. In order to compute the Spearman correlation, first rank all the x and y variable values and then apply the Pearson's correlation computation.

In the case of Risk Simulator, the correlation used is the more robust nonparametric Spearman's rank correlation. However, to simplify the simulation process, and to be consistent with Excel's correlation function, the correlation inputs required are those of the Pearson's correlation coefficient. Risk Simulator will then apply its own algorithms to convert them into Spearman's rank correlation, thereby simplifying the process. However, to simplify the user interface, we allow users to enter the more common Pearson's product-moment correlation (e.g., computed using Excel's *CORREL* function), while in the mathematical codes, we convert these simple correlations into Spearman's rank-based correlations for distributional simulations.

Applying Correlations in Risk Simulator

Correlations can be applied in Risk Simulator in several ways:

- When defining assumptions (*Risk Simulator | Set Input Assumption*), simply enter the correlations into the correlation matrix grid in the Distribution Gallery.
- With existing data, run the Multi-Fit tool (*Risk Simulator | Tools | Distributional Fitting – Multiple Variable*) to perform distributional fitting and to obtain the correlation matrix between pairwise variables. If a simulation profile exists, the assumptions fitted will automatically contain the relevant correlation values.
- With existing assumptions, you can click on *Risk Simulator | Tools | Edit Correlations* to enter the pairwise correlations of all the assumptions directly in one user interface.

Note that the correlation matrix must be positive definite. That is, the correlation must be mathematically valid. For instance, suppose you are trying to correlate three variables: grades of graduate students in a particular year, the number of beers they consume a week, and the number of hours they study a week. One would assume that the following correlation relationships exist:

Grades and Beer: −	The more they drink, the lower the grades (no show on exams)
Grades and Study: +	The more they study, the higher the grades
Beer and Study: −	The more they drink, the less they study (drunk and partying all the time)

However, if you input a negative correlation between Grades and Study, and assuming that the correlation coefficients have high magnitudes, the correlation matrix will be nonpositive definite. It would defy logic, correlation requirements, and matrix mathematics. However, smaller coefficients can sometimes still work even with the bad logic. When a nonpositive or bad correlation matrix is entered, Risk Simulator will automatically inform you and offer to adjust these correlations to something that is semi-positive definite while still maintaining the overall structure of the correlation relationship (the same signs as well as the same relative strengths).

The Effects of Correlations in Monte Carlo Simulation

Although the computations required to correlate variables in a simulation are complex, the resulting effects are fairly clear. Figure 5.14 shows a simple correlation model (Correlation Effects Model in the example folder). The calculation for revenue is simply price multiplied by quantity. The same model is replicated for no correlations, positive correlation (+0.8), and negative correlation (−0.8) between price and quantity.

The resulting statistics are shown in Figure 5.15. Notice that the standard deviation of the model without correlations is 0.1450, compared to 0.1886 for the positive correlation and 0.0717 for the negative correlation. That is, for simple models, negative correlations tend to reduce the average spread of the distribution and create a tight and more concentrated forecast distribution as compared to positive correlations with larger average spreads. However, the mean remains relatively stable. This result implies that correlations do little to change the expected value of projects but can reduce or increase a project's risk.

Figure 5.16 illustrates the results after running a simulation, extracting the raw data of the assumptions, and computing the correlations between

Correlation Model

	Without Correlation	Positive Correlation	Negative Correlation
Price	$2.00	$2.00	$2.00
Quantity	1.00	1.00	1.00
Revenue	$2.00	$2.00	$2.00

To replicate this model, use the following assumptions:
Prices are set as Triangular Distributions (1.8, 2.0, 2.2) while
Quantity is set as Uniform Distributions (0.9, 1.1) with correlations
set at 0.0, +0.8, −0.8 at 1,000 trials with seed value 123456.

FIGURE 5.14 Simple correlation model.

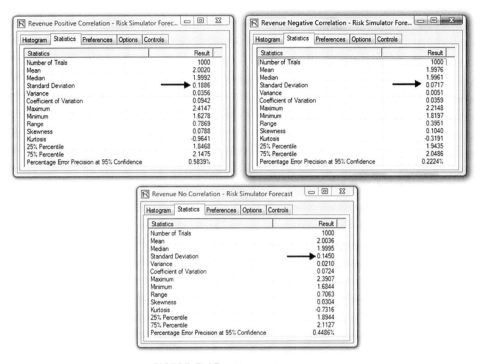

FIGURE 5.15   Correlation results.

the variables. The figure shows that the input assumptions are recovered in the simulation. That is, you enter +0.8 and –0.8 correlations, and the resulting simulated values have the same correlations.

Precision and Error Control

One powerful tool in Monte Carlo simulation is that of precision control. For instance, how many trials are considered sufficient to run in a complex model? Precision control takes the guesswork out of estimating the relevant number of trials by allowing the simulation to stop if the level of prespecified precision is reached.

The precision control functionality lets you set how precise you want your forecast to be. Generally speaking, as more trials are calculated, the confidence interval narrows and the statistics become more accurate. The precision control feature in Risk Simulator uses the characteristic of confidence intervals to determine when a specified accuracy of a statistic has been

These are the extracted raw values from the simulation. They are then correlated to verify that indeed the correlations that were entered in the assumptions would be the correlations that actually were modeled. The Pearson's Correlation Coefficient is a linear parametric correlation, and the results indicate that the correlations entered (+0.80 and −0.80) are indeed the correlations between the variables.

Price Positive Correlation	Quantity Positive Correlation		Price Negative Correlation	Quantity Negative Correlation	
1.95	0.91		1.89	1.06	
1.92	0.95		1.98	1.05	
2.02	1.04	Pearson's	1.89	1.09	Pearson's
2.04	1.03	Correlation:	1.88	1.04	Correlation:
1.69	0.91	*0.80*	1.96	0.93	*−0.80*
1.98	1.05		2.02	0.93	
2.05	1.03		2.00	1.02	
1.87	0.91		1.86	1.04	
1.84	0.91		1.96	1.02	
2.06	1.03		1.90	1.02	
1.98	1.01		1.92	1.10	
1.99	0.96		2.00	1.02	

FIGURE 5.16 Correlations recovered.

reached. For each forecast, you can specify the confidence interval for the precision level.

Make sure that you do not confuse three different terms: error, precision, and confidence. Although they sound similar, the concepts are significantly different from one another. A simple illustration is in order. Suppose you are a taco shell manufacturer and are interested in finding out how many broken taco shells there are on average in a box of 100 shells. One way to do this is to collect a sample of prepackaged boxes of 100 taco shells, open them, and count how many of them are actually broken. You manufacture 1 million boxes a day (this is your *population*), but you randomly open only 10 boxes (this is your *sample* size, also known as your number of *trials* in a simulation). The number of broken shells in each box is as follows: 24, 22, 4, 15, 33, 32, 4, 1, 45, and 2. The calculated average number of broken shells is 18.2. Based on these 10 samples or trials, the average is 18.2 units, while based on the sample, the 80% confidence interval is between 2 and 33 units (that is, 80% of the time, the number of broken shells is between 2 and 33 *based on this sample size or number of trials run*). However, how

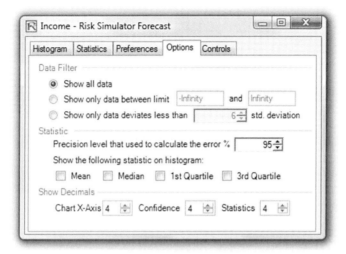

FIGURE 5.17 Setting the forecast's precision level.

sure are you that 18.2 is the correct average? Are 10 trials sufficient to establish this?

The confidence interval between 2 and 33 is too wide and too variable. Suppose you require a more accurate average value where the error is ±2 taco shells 90% of the time—this means that if you open *all* 1 million boxes manufactured in a day, 900,000 of these boxes will have broken taco shells on average at some mean unit ±2 tacos. How many more taco shell boxes would you then need to sample (or trials run) to obtain this level of precision? Here, the 2 tacos is the error level while the 90% is the level of precision. If sufficient numbers of trials are run, then the 90% confidence interval will be identical to the 90% precision level, where a more precise measure of the average is obtained such that 90% of the time, the error, and, hence, the confidence will be ±2 tacos. As an example, say the average is 20 units, then the 90% confidence interval will be between 18 and 22 units, where this interval is precise 90% of the time, where in opening all 1 million boxes, 900,000 of them will have between 18 and 22 broken tacos. The number of trials required to hit this precision is based on the sampling error equation of

$$\overline{x} \pm Z\frac{s}{\sqrt{n}}$$

where

$$Z\frac{s}{\sqrt{n}}$$

is the error of 2 tacos, $\bar{x}$ is the sample average, Z is the standard-normal Z-score obtained from the 90% precision level, s is the sample standard deviation, and n is the number of trials required to hit this level of error with the specified precision.

Figures 5.17 and 5.18 illustrate how precision control can be performed on multiple simulated forecasts in Risk Simulator. This feature prevents the user from having to decide how many trials to run in a simulation and eliminates all possibilities of guesswork. Figure 5.17 illustrates the forecast chart with a 95% precision level set. This value can be changed and will be reflected in the *Statistics* tab as shown in Figure 5.18.

APPENDIX—UNDERSTANDING PROBABILITY DISTRIBUTIONS

This chapter demonstrates the power of Monte Carlo simulation, but in order to get started with simulation, one first needs to understand the concept of probability distributions. This appendix continues with the use of the

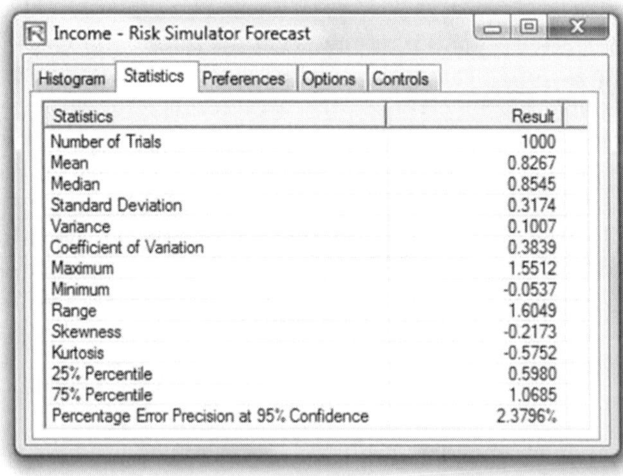

Statistics	Result
Number of Trials	1000
Mean	0.8267
Median	0.8545
Standard Deviation	0.3174
Variance	0.1007
Coefficient of Variation	0.3839
Maximum	1.5512
Minimum	-0.0537
Range	1.6049
Skewness	-0.2173
Kurtosis	-0.5752
25% Percentile	0.5980
75% Percentile	1.0685
Percentage Error Precision at 95% Confidence	2.3796%

FIGURE 5.18   Computing the error.

author's Risk Simulator software and shows how simulation can be very easily and effortlessly implemented in an existing Excel model. A limited trial version of the Risk Simulator software is available on the enclosed DVD-ROM (to obtain a permanent version, please visit the author's web site at www.realoptionsvaluation.com). Professors can obtain free semester-long computer lab licenses for their students and themselves if this book and the simulation/options valuation software are used and taught in an entire class.

To begin to understand probability, consider this example: You want to look at the distribution of nonexempt wages within one department of a large company. First, you gather raw data—in this case, the wages of each nonexempt employee in the department. Second, you organize the data into a meaningful format and plot the data as a frequency distribution on a chart. To create a frequency distribution, you divide the wages into group intervals and list these intervals on the chart's horizontal axis. Then you list the number or frequency of employees in each interval on the chart's vertical axis. Now you can easily see the distribution of nonexempt wages within the department.

A glance at the chart illustrated in Figure 5.19 reveals that the employees earn from $7 to $9 per hour. You can chart this data as a probability distribution. A probability distribution shows the number of employees in each interval as a fraction of the total number of employees. To create a probability distribution, you divide the number of employees in each interval by the total number of employees and list the results on the chart's vertical axis.

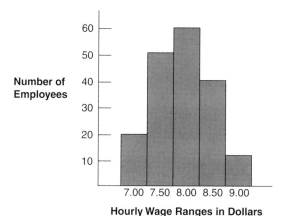

FIGURE 5.19 Frequency histogram I.

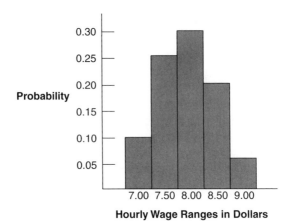

FIGURE 5.20 Frequency histogram II.

The chart in Figure 5.20 shows the number of employees in each wage group as a fraction of all employees; you can estimate the likelihood or probability that an employee drawn at random from the whole group earns a wage within a given interval. For example, assuming the same conditions exist at the time the sample was taken, the probability is 0.20 (a one in five chance) that an employee drawn at random from the whole group earns $8.50 an hour.

Probability distributions are either discrete or continuous. *Discrete probability distributions* describe distinct values, usually integers, with no intermediate values and are shown as a series of vertical bars. A discrete distribution, for example, might describe the number of heads in four flips of a coin as 0, 1, 2, 3, or 4. *Continuous probability distributions* are actually mathematical abstractions because they assume the existence of every possible intermediate value between two numbers; that is, a continuous distribution assumes there is an infinite number of values between any two points in the distribution. However, in many situations, you can effectively use a continuous distribution to approximate a discrete distribution even though the continuous model does not necessarily describe the situation exactly.

Selecting a Probability Distribution

Plotting data is one method for selecting a probability distribution. The following steps provide another process for selecting probability distributions that best describe the uncertain variables in your spreadsheets.

To select the correct probability distribution, use the following three steps:

1. Look at the variable in question. List everything you know about the conditions surrounding this variable. You might be able to gather valuable information about the uncertain variable from historical data. If historical data are not available, use your own judgment, based on experience, listing everything you know about the uncertain variable.
2. Review the descriptions of the probability distributions.
3. Select the distribution that characterizes this variable. A distribution characterizes a variable when the conditions of the distribution match those of the variable.

Alternatively, if you have historical, comparable, contemporaneous, or forecast data, you can use Risk Simulator's distributional fitting modules to find the best statistical fit for your existing data. This fitting process will apply some advanced statistical techniques to find the best distribution and its relevant parameters that describe the data.

Probability Density Functions, Cumulative Distribution Functions, and Probability Mass Functions

In mathematics and Monte Carlo simulation, a probability density function (PDF) represents a *continuous* probability distribution in terms of integrals. If a probability distribution has a density of $f(x)$, then intuitively the infinitesimal interval of $[x, x + dx]$ has a probability of $f(x)\ dx$. The PDF therefore can be seen as a smoothed version of a probability histogram; that is, by providing an empirically large sample of a continuous random variable repeatedly, the histogram using very narrow ranges will resemble the random variable's PDF. The probability of the interval between $[a, b]$ is given by

$$\int_a^b f(x)dx$$

which means that the total integral of the function f must be 1.0. *It is a common mistake to think of f(a) as the probability of a. This is incorrect. In fact, f(a) can sometimes be larger than 1—consider a uniform distribution* between 0.0 and 0.5. The random variable x within this distribution will have $f(x)$ greater than 1. The probability, in reality, is the function $f(x)dx$ discussed previously, where dx is an infinitesimal amount.

The cumulative distribution function (CDF) is denoted as $F(x) = P(X \leq x)$, indicating the probability of X taking on a less than or equal value to x. Every CDF is monotonically increasing, is continuous from the right, and at the limits, has the following properties:

$$\lim_{x \to \infty} F(x) = 0 \quad \text{and} \quad \lim_{x \to \infty} F(x) = 1$$

Further, the CDF is related to the PDF by

$$F(b) - F(a) = P(a \leq X \leq b) = \int_a^b f(x)dx$$

where the PDF function f is the derivative of the CDF function F.

In probability theory, a probability mass function, or PMF, gives the probability that a *discrete* random variable is exactly equal to some value. The PMF differs from the PDF in that the values of the latter, defined only for continuous random variables, are not probabilities; rather, its integral over a set of possible values of the random variable is a probability. A random variable is discrete if its probability distribution is discrete and can be characterized by a PMF. Therefore, X is a discrete random variable if

$$\sum_u P(X = u) = 1$$

as u runs through all possible values of the random variable X.

Discrete Distributions

Following is a detailed listing of the different types of probability distributions that can be used in Monte Carlo simulation. This listing is included in the current appendix for the reader's reference.

Bernoulli or Yes/No Distribution   The Bernoulli distribution is a discrete distribution with two outcomes (e.g., head or tails, success or failure, 0 or 1). The Bernoulli distribution is the binomial distribution with one trial and can be used to simulate Yes/No or Success/Failure conditions. This distribution is the fundamental building block of other more complex distributions. For instance:

- *Binomial distribution.* Bernoulli distribution with higher number of n total trials and computes the probability of x successes within this total number of trials.
- *Geometric distribution.* Bernoulli distribution with higher number of trials and computes the number of failures required before the first success occurs.
- *Negative binomial distribution.* Bernoulli distribution with higher number of trials and computes the number of failures before the xth success occurs.

The mathematical constructs for the Bernoulli distribution are as follows:

$$P(x) = \begin{cases} 1 - p & \text{for } x = 0 \\ p & \text{for } x = 1 \end{cases}$$

or

$$P(x) = p^x(1 - p)^{1-x}$$

$$Mean = p$$

$$Standard\ Deviation = \sqrt{p(1 - p)}$$

$$Skewness = \frac{1 - 2p}{\sqrt{p(1 - p)}}$$

$$Excess\ Kurtosis = \frac{6p^2 - 6p + 1}{p(1 - p)}$$

The probability of success (p) is the only distributional parameter. Also, it is important to note that there is only one trial in the Bernoulli distribution, and the resulting simulated value is either 0 or 1.

Input requirements:

Probability of success >0 and <1 (that is, $0.0001 \le p \le 0.9999$).

Binomial Distribution   The binomial distribution describes the number of times a particular event occurs in a fixed number of trials, such as the number of heads in 10 flips of a coin or the number of defective items out of 50 items chosen.

The three conditions underlying the binomial distribution are:

1. For each trial, only two outcomes are possible that are mutually exclusive.
2. The trials are independent—what happens in the first trial does not affect the next trial.
3. The probability of an event occurring remains the same from trial to trial.

$$P(x) = \frac{n!}{x!(n-x)!} p^x (1-p)^{(n-x)} \text{ for } n > 0; x = 0, 1, 2, \ldots n;$$

$$\text{and } 0 < p < 1$$

$$Mean = np$$

$$Standard\ Deviation = \sqrt{np(1-p)}$$

$$Skewness = \frac{1-2p}{\sqrt{np(1-p)}}$$

$$Excess\ Kurtosis = \frac{6p^2 - 6p + 1}{np(1-p)}$$

The probability of success (p) and the integer number of total trials (n) are the distributional parameters. The number of successful trials is denoted x. It is important to note that probability of success (p) of 0 or 1 are trivial conditions and do not require any simulations, and, hence, are not allowed in the software.

Input requirements:

Probability of success > 0 and < 1 (that is, $0.0001 \le p \le 0.9999$).

Number of trials ≥ 1 or positive integers and $\le 1,000$ (for larger trials, use the normal distribution with the relevant computed binomial mean and standard deviation as the normal distribution's parameters).

Discrete Uniform   The discrete uniform distribution is also known as the *equally likely outcomes* distribution, where the distribution has a set of N elements, and each element has the same probability. This distribution is related to the uniform distribution, but its elements are discrete and not continuous.

The mathematical constructs for the discrete uniform distribution are as follows:

$$P(x) = \frac{1}{N} \text{ ranked value}$$

$$Mean = \frac{N+1}{2} \text{ ranked value}$$

$$Standard\ Deviation = \sqrt{\frac{(N-1)(N+1)}{12}} \text{ ranked value}$$

$$Skewness = 0 \text{ (that is, the distribution is perfectly symmetrical)}$$

$$Excess\ Kurtosis = \frac{-6(N^2+1)}{5(N-1)(N+1)} \text{ ranked value}$$

Input requirements:

Minimum < Maximum and both must be integers (negative integers and zero are allowed)

Geometric Distribution   The geometric distribution describes the number of trials until the first successful occurrence, such as the number of times you need to spin a roulette wheel before you win.

The three conditions underlying the geometric distribution are:

1. The number of trials is not fixed.
2. The trials continue until the first success.
3. The probability of success is the same from trial to trial.

The mathematical constructs for the geometric distribution are as follows:

$$P(x) = p(1-p)^{(x-1)} \quad \text{for} \quad 0 < p < 1 \quad \text{and} \quad x = 1, 2, \ldots, n$$

$$Mean = \frac{1}{p} - 1$$

$$Standard\ Deviation = \sqrt{\frac{1-p}{p^2}}$$

$$Skewness = \frac{2-p}{\sqrt{1-p}}$$

$$Excess\ Kurtosis = \frac{p^2 - 6p + 6}{1-p}$$

The probability of success (*p*) is the only distributional parameter. The number of successful trials simulated is denoted *x*, which can only take on positive integers.

Input requirements:

Probability of success > 0 and < 1 (that is, $0.0001 \le p \le 0.9999$). It is important to note that probability of success (*p*) of 0 or 1 are trivial conditions and do not require any simulations, and, hence, are not allowed in the software.

Hypergeometric Distribution The hypergeometric distribution is similar to the binomial distribution in that both describe the number of times a particular event occurs in a fixed number of trials. The difference is that binomial distribution trials are independent, whereas hypergeometric distribution trials change the probability for each subsequent trial and are called *trials without replacement*. For example, suppose a box of manufactured parts is known to contain some defective parts. You choose a part from the box, find it is defective, and remove the part from the box. If you choose another part from the box, the probability that it is defective is somewhat lower than for the first part because you have removed a defective part. If you had replaced the defective part, the probabilities would have remained the same, and the process would have satisfied the conditions for a binomial distribution.

The three conditions underlying the hypergeometric distribution are:

1. The total number of items or elements (the population size) is a fixed number, a finite population. The population size must be less than or equal to 1,750.
2. The sample size (the number of trials) represents a portion of the population.
3. The known initial probability of success in the population changes after each trial.

The mathematical constructs for the hypergeometric distribution are as follows:

$$P(x) = \frac{\frac{(N_x)!}{x!(N_x - x)!} \frac{(N - N_x)!}{(n - x)!(N - N_x - n + x)!}}{\frac{N!}{n!(N - n)!}}$$

$$\text{for} \quad x = Max(n - (N - N_x), 0), \ldots, Min(n, N_x)$$

$$Mean = \frac{N_x n}{N}$$

$$Standard\ Deviation = \sqrt{\frac{(N - N_x)N_x n(N - n)}{N^2(N - 1)}}$$

$$Skewness = \frac{(N - 2N_x)(N - 2n)}{N - 2}\sqrt{\frac{N - 1}{(N - N_x)N_x n(N - n)}}$$

$$Excess\ Kurtosis = \frac{V(N, N_x, n)}{(N - N_x)N_x n(-3 + N)(-2 + N)(-N + n)}\ where$$

$$V(N, Nx, n) = (N - N_x)^3 - (N - N_x)^5 + 3(N - N_x)^2 N_x - 6(N - N_x)^3 N_x$$
$$+ (N - N_x)^4 Nx + 3(N - N_x)N_x^2 - 12(N - N_x)^2 N_x^2 + 8(N - N_x)^3 N_x^2 + N_x^3$$
$$- 6(N - N_x)N_x^3 + 8(N - N_x)^2 N_x^3 + (N - N_x)N_x^4 - N_x^5 - 6(N - N_x)^3 N_x$$
$$+ 6(N - N_x)^4 N_x + 18(N - N_x)^2 N_x n - 6(N - N_x)^3 N_x n + 18(N - N_x)N_x^2 n$$
$$- 24(N - N_x)^2 N_x^2 n - 6(N - N_x)^3 n - 6(N - N_x)N_x^3 n + 6N_x^4 n$$
$$+ 6(N - N_x)^2 n^2 - 6(N - N_x)^3 n^2 - 24(N - N_x)N_x n^2 + 12(N - N_x)^2 N_x n^2$$
$$+ 6N_x^2 n^2 + 12(N - N_x)N_x^2 n^2 - 6N_x^3 n^2$$

The number of items in the population (N), trials sampled (n), and number of items in the population that have the successful trait (N_x) are the distributional parameters. The number of successful trials is denoted x.
Input requirements:

Population $\geq$ 2 and integer
Trials $>$ 0 and integer
Successes $>$ 0 and integer
Population $>$ Successes
Trials $<$ Population
Population $<$ 1,750

Negative Binomial Distribution   The negative binomial distribution is useful for modeling the distribution of the number of trials until the rth successful occurrence, such as the number of sales calls you need to make to close a total of 10 orders. It is essentially a *superdistribution* of the geometric distribution. This distribution shows the probabilities of each number of trials in excess of r to produce the required success r.

The three conditions underlying the negative binomial distribution are:

1. The number of trials is not fixed.
2. The trials continue until the rth success.
3. The probability of success is the same from trial to trial.

The mathematical constructs for the negative binomial distribution are as follows:

$$P(x) = \frac{(x + r - 1)!}{(r - 1)!x!} p^r (1 - p)^x \text{ for } x = r, r + 1, \ldots; \text{ and } 0 < p < 1$$

$$Mean = \frac{r(1 - p)}{p}$$

$$Standard\ Deviation = \sqrt{\frac{r(1 - p)}{p^2}}$$

$$Skewness = \frac{2 - p}{\sqrt{r(1 - p)}}$$

$$Excess\ Kurtosis = \frac{p^2 - 6p + 6}{r(1 - p)}$$

The probability of success (p) and required successes (r) are the distributional parameters.

Input requirements:

Successes required must be positive integers > 0 and $< 8,000$.

Probability of success > 0 and < 1 (that is, $0.0001 \leq p \leq 0.9999$). It is important to note that probability of success (p) of 0 or 1 are trivial conditions and do not require any simulations, and, hence, are not allowed in the software.

Poisson Distribution   The Poisson distribution describes the number of times an event occurs in a given interval, such as the number of telephone calls per minute or the number of errors per page in a document.

The three conditions underlying the Poisson distribution are:

1. The number of possible occurrences in any interval is unlimited.
2. The occurrences are independent. The number of occurrences in one interval does not affect the number of occurrences in other intervals.

3. The average number of occurrences must remain the same from interval to interval.

The mathematical constructs for the Poisson are as follows:

$$P(x) = \frac{e^{-\lambda}\lambda^x}{x!} \text{ for } x \text{ and } \lambda > 0$$

$$Mean = \lambda$$

$$Standard\ Deviation = \sqrt{\lambda}$$

$$Skewness = \frac{1}{\sqrt{\lambda}}$$

$$Excess\ Kurtosis = \frac{1}{\lambda}$$

Rate (λ) is the only distributional parameter.
Input requirements:

Rate > 0 and $\leq 1{,}000$ (that is, $0.0001 \leq$ rate $\leq 1{,}000$)

Continuous Distributions

Beta Distribution   The beta distribution is very flexible and is commonly used to represent variability over a fixed range. One of the more important applications of the beta distribution is its use as a conjugate distribution for the parameter of a Bernoulli distribution. In this application, the beta distribution is used to represent the uncertainty in the probability of occurrence of an event. It is also used to describe empirical data and predict the random behavior of percentages and fractions, as the range of outcomes is typically between 0 and 1.

The value of the beta distribution lies in the wide variety of shapes it can assume when you vary the two parameters, alpha and beta. If the parameters are equal, the distribution is symmetrical. If either parameter is 1 and the other parameter is greater than 1, the distribution is J-shaped. If alpha is less than beta, the distribution is said to be positively skewed (most of the values are near the minimum value). If alpha is greater than beta, the distribution is negatively skewed (most of the values are near the maximum value).

The mathematical constructs for the beta distribution are as follows:

$$f(x) = \frac{(x)^{(\alpha-1)}(1-x)^{(\beta-1)}}{\left[\dfrac{\Gamma(\alpha)\Gamma(\beta)}{\Gamma(\alpha+\beta)}\right]} \quad \text{for } \alpha > 0; \ \beta > 0; \ x > 0$$

$$Mean = \frac{\alpha}{\alpha + \beta}$$

$$Standard\ Deviation = \sqrt{\frac{\alpha\beta}{(\alpha+\beta)^2(1+\alpha+\beta)}}$$

$$Skewness = \frac{2(\beta-\alpha)\sqrt{1+\alpha+\beta}}{(2+\alpha+\beta)\sqrt{\alpha\beta}}$$

$$Excess\ Kurtosis = \frac{3(\alpha+\beta+1)[\alpha\beta(\alpha+\beta-6)+2(\alpha+\beta)^2]}{\alpha\beta(\alpha+\beta+2)(\alpha+\beta+3)} - 3$$

Alpha (α) and beta (β) are the two distributional shape parameters, and Γ is the gamma function.

The two conditions underlying the beta distribution are:

1. The uncertain variable is a random value between 0 and a positive value.
2. The shape of the distribution can be specified using two positive values.

Input requirements:

Alpha and beta > 0 and can be any positive value

Cauchy Distribution or Lorentzian Distribution or Breit–Wigner Distribution   The Cauchy distribution, also called the Lorentzian distribution or Breit–Wigner distribution, is a continuous distribution describing resonance behavior. It also describes the distribution of horizontal distances at which a line segment tilted at a random angle cuts the x-axis.

The mathematical constructs for the Cauchy or Lorentzian distribution are as follows:

$$f(x) = \frac{1}{\pi}\frac{\gamma/2}{(x-m)^2 + \gamma^2/4}$$

The Cauchy distribution is a special case where it does not have any theoretical moments (mean, standard deviation, skewness, and kurtosis) as they are all undefined.

Mode location (m) and scale (γ) are the only two parameters in this distribution. The location parameter specifies the peak or mode of the distribution, while the scale parameter specifies the half-width at half-maximum of the distribution. In addition, the mean and variance of a Cauchy or Lorentzian distribution are undefined.

In addition, the Cauchy distribution is the Student's t distribution with only 1 degree of freedom. This distribution is also constructed by taking the ratio of two standard normal distributions (normal distributions with a mean of zero and a variance of one) that are independent of one another.

Input requirements:

Location can be any value

Scale > 0 and can be any positive value

Chi-Square Distribution   The chi-square distribution is a probability distribution used predominantly in hypothesis testing, and it is related to the gamma distribution and the standard normal distribution. For instance, the sums of independent normal distributions are distributed as a chi-square (χ^2) with k degrees of freedom:

$$Z_1^2 + Z_2^2 + \cdots + Z_k^2 \overset{d}{\sim} \chi_k^2$$

The mathematical constructs for the chi-square distribution are as follows:

$$f(x) = \frac{2^{(-k/2)}}{\Gamma(k/2)} x^{k/2-1} e^{-x/2} \text{ for all } x > 0$$

$$Mean = k$$

$$Standard\ Deviation = \sqrt{2k}$$

$$Skewness = 2\sqrt{\frac{2}{k}}$$

$$Excess\ Kurtosis = \frac{12}{k}$$

The gamma function is written as Γ. Degrees of freedom k is the only distributional parameter.

The chi-square distribution can also be modeled using a gamma distribution by setting the shape parameter as $k/2$ and scale as $2S^2$, where S is the scale.

Input requirements:

Degrees of freedom > 1 and must be an integer < 1,000

Exponential Distribution The exponential distribution is widely used to describe events recurring at random points in time, such as the time between failures of electronic equipment or the time between arrivals at a service booth. It is related to the Poisson distribution, which describes the number of occurrences of an event in a given interval of time. An important characteristic of the exponential distribution is the "memoryless" property, which means that the future lifetime of a given object has the same distribution, regardless of the time it existed. In other words, time has no effect on future outcomes.

The mathematical constructs for the exponential distribution are as follows:

$$f(x) = \lambda e^{-\lambda x} \text{ for } x \geq 0; \ \lambda > 0$$

$$Mean = \frac{1}{\lambda}$$

$$Standard\ Deviation = \frac{1}{\lambda}$$

$Skewness = 2$ (this value applies to all sucess rate λ inputs)

$Excess\ Kurtosis = 6$ (this value applies to all sucess rate λ inputs)

Success rate (λ) is the only distributional parameter. The number of successful trials is denoted x.

The condition underlying the exponential distribution is:

The exponential distribution describes the amount of time between occurrences.

Input requirements:

Rate > 0 and ≤ 300

Extreme Value Distribution or Gumbel Distribution The extreme value distribution (Type 1) is commonly used to describe the largest value of a response over a period of time, for example, in flood flows, rainfall, and earthquakes. Other applications include the breaking strengths of materials, construction design, and aircraft loads and tolerances. The extreme value distribution is also known as the Gumbel distribution.

The mathematical constructs for the extreme value distribution are as follows:

$$f(x) = \frac{1}{\beta} z e^{-Z} \text{ where } z = e^{\frac{x-m}{\beta}} \text{ for } \beta > 0; \text{ and any value of } x \text{ and } m$$

$$Mean = m + 0.577215\beta$$

$$Standard\ Deviation = \sqrt{\frac{1}{6}\pi^2\beta^2}$$

$$Skewness = \frac{12\sqrt{6}(1.2020569)}{\pi^3} = 1.13955 \text{ (this applies for all values of mode and scale)}$$

$$Excess\ Kurtosis = 5.4 \text{ (this applies for all values of mode and scale)}$$

Mode (m) and scale (β) are the distributional parameters.

There are two standard parameters for the extreme value distribution: mode and scale. The mode parameter is the most likely value for the variable (the highest point on the probability distribution). The scale parameter is a number greater than 0. The larger the scale parameter, the greater the variance.

Input requirements:

Mode can be any value

Scale > 0

F Distribution or Fisher–Snedecor Distribution   The F distribution, also known as the Fisher–Snedecor distribution, is another continuous distribution used most frequently for hypothesis testing. Specifically, it is used to test the statistical difference between two variances in analysis of variance tests and likelihood ratio tests. The F distribution with the numerator degree of freedom n and denominator degree of freedom m is related to the chi-square distribution in that:

$$\frac{\chi_n^2/n}{\chi_m^2/m} \overset{d}{=} F_{n,m} \text{ or } f(x) = \frac{\Gamma\left(\frac{n+m}{2}\right)\left(\frac{n}{m}\right)^{n/2} x^{n/2-1}}{\Gamma\left(\frac{n}{2}\right)\Gamma\left(\frac{m}{2}\right)\left[x\left(\frac{n}{m}\right)+1\right]^{(n+m)/2}}$$

$$Mean = \frac{m}{m-2}$$

$$Standard\ Deviation = \frac{2m^2(m+n-2)}{n(m-2)^2(m-4)} \text{ for all } m > 4$$

$$Skewness = \frac{2(m + 2n - 2)}{m - 6} \sqrt{\frac{2(m - 4)}{n(m + n - 2)}}$$

$$Excess\ Kurtosis = \frac{12(-16 + 20m - 8m^2 + m^3 + 44n - 32mn + 5m^2n - 22n^2 + 5mn^2)}{n(m - 6)(m - 8)(n + m - 2)}$$

The numerator degree of freedom n and denominator degree of freedom m are the only distributional parameters.

Input requirements:

Degrees of freedom numerator and degrees of freedom denominator both > 0 integers

Gamma Distribution (Erlang Distribution) The gamma distribution applies to a wide range of physical quantities and is related to other distributions: lognormal, exponential, Pascal, Erlang, Poisson, and chi-square. It is used in meteorological processes to represent pollutant concentrations and precipitation quantities. The gamma distribution is also used to measure the time between the occurrence of events when the event process is not completely random. Other applications of the gamma distribution include inventory control, economic theory, and insurance risk theory.

The gamma distribution is most often used as the distribution of the amount of time until the rth occurrence of an event in a Poisson process. When used in this fashion, the three conditions underlying the gamma distribution are:

1. The number of possible occurrences in any unit of measurement is not limited to a fixed number.
2. The occurrences are independent. The number of occurrences in one unit of measurement does not affect the number of occurrences in other units.
3. The average number of occurrences must remain the same from unit to unit.

The mathematical constructs for the gamma distribution are as follows:

$$f(x) = \frac{\left(\dfrac{x}{\beta}\right)^{\alpha - 1} e^{-\frac{x}{\beta}}}{\Gamma(\alpha)\beta} \quad \text{with any value of } \alpha > 0 \text{ and } \beta > 0$$

$$Mean = \alpha\beta$$

$$Standard\ Deviation = \sqrt{\alpha\beta^2}$$

$$Skewness = \frac{2}{\sqrt{\alpha}}$$

$$Excess\ Kurtosis = \frac{6}{\alpha}$$

Shape parameter alpha (α) and scale parameter beta (β) are the distributional parameters, and Γ is the gamma function.

When the alpha parameter is a positive integer, the gamma distribution is called the Erlang distribution, used to predict waiting times in queuing systems, where the Erlang distribution is the sum of independent and identically distributed random variables each having a memoryless exponential distribution. Setting n as the number of these random variables, the mathematical construct of the Erlang distribution is:

$$f(x) = \frac{x^{n-1}e^{-x}}{(n-1)!}\ \text{for all } x > 0 \text{ and all positive integers of } n$$

Input requirements:

Scale beta > 0 and can be any positive value

Shape alpha ≥ 0.05 and any positive value

Location can be any value

Logistic Distribution   The logistic distribution is commonly used to describe growth, that is, the size of a population expressed as a function of a time variable. It also can be used to describe chemical reactions and the course of growth for a population or individual.

The mathematical constructs for the logistic distribution are as follows:

$$f(x) = \frac{e^{\frac{\mu-x}{\alpha}}}{\alpha\left[1 + e^{\frac{\mu-x}{\alpha}}\right]^2}\ \text{for any value of } \alpha \text{ and } \mu$$

$$Mean = \mu$$

$$Standard\ Deviation = \sqrt{\frac{1}{3}\pi^2\alpha^2}$$

Skewness $= 0$ (this applies to all mean scale inputs)

Excess Kurtosis $= 1.2$ (this applies to all mean scale inputs)

Mean (μ) and scale (α) are the distributional parameters.

There are two standard parameters for the logistic distribution: mean and scale. The mean parameter is the average value, which for this distribution is the same as the mode, because this distribution is symmetrical. The scale parameter is a number greater than 0. The larger the scale parameter, the greater the variance.

Input requirements:

Scale > 0 and can be any positive value

Mean can be any value

Lognormal Distribution   The lognormal distribution is widely used in situations where values are positively skewed, for example, in financial analysis for security valuation or in real estate for property valuation, and where values cannot fall below zero.

Stock prices are usually positively skewed rather than normally (symmetrically) distributed. Stock prices exhibit this trend because they cannot fall below the lower limit of zero but might increase to any price without limit. Similarly, real estate prices illustrate positive skewness and are lognormally distributed as property values cannot become negative.

The three conditions underlying the lognormal distribution are:

1. The uncertain variable can increase without limits but cannot fall below zero.
2. The uncertain variable is positively skewed, with most of the values near the lower limit.
3. The natural logarithm of the uncertain variable yields a normal distribution.

Generally, if the coefficient of variability is greater than 30 percent, use a lognormal distribution. Otherwise, use the normal distribution.

The mathematical constructs for the lognormal distribution are as follows:

$$f(x) = \frac{1}{x\sqrt{2\pi}\ln(\sigma)}e^{-\frac{[\ln(x)-\ln(\mu)]^2}{2[\ln(\sigma)]^2}} \text{ for } x > 0; \ \mu > 0 \text{ and } \sigma > 0$$

$$Mean = \exp\left(\mu + \frac{\sigma^2}{2}\right)$$

$$Standard\ Deviation = \sqrt{\exp(\sigma^2 + 2\mu)[\exp(\sigma^2) - 1]}$$

$$Skewness = \left[\sqrt{\exp(\sigma^2) - 1}\right](2 + \exp(\sigma^2))$$

$$Excess\ Kurtosis = \exp\left(4\sigma^2\right) + 2\exp(3\sigma^2) + 3\exp(2\sigma^2) - 6$$

Mean (μ) and standard deviation (σ) are the distributional parameters. Input requirements:

Mean and standard deviation both > 0 and can be any positive value

Lognormal Parameter Sets   By default, the lognormal distribution uses the arithmetic mean and standard deviation. For applications for which historical data are available, it is more appropriate to use either the logarithmic mean and standard deviation, or the geometric mean and standard deviation.

Normal Distribution   The normal distribution is the most important distribution in probability theory because it describes many natural phenomena, such as people's IQs or heights. Decision makers can use the normal distribution to describe uncertain variables such as the inflation rate or the future price of gasoline.

The three conditions underlying the normal distribution are:

1. Some value of the uncertain variable is the most likely (the mean of the distribution).
2. The uncertain variable could as likely be above the mean as it could be below the mean (symmetrical about the mean).
3. The uncertain variable is more likely to be in the vicinity of the mean than further away.

The mathematical constructs for the normal distribution are as follows:

$$f(x)\frac{1}{\sqrt{2\pi}\sigma}e^{-\frac{(x-\mu)^2}{2\sigma^2}} \text{ for all values of } x \text{ and } \mu; \text{ while } \sigma > 0$$

Mean $= \mu$

Standard Deviation $= \sigma$

Skewness $= 0$ (this applies to all inputs of mean and standard deviation)

Excess Kurtosis $= 0$ (this applies to all inputs of mean and standard deviation)

Mean (μ) and standard deviation (σ) are the distributional parameters.

Input requirements:

Standard deviation > 0 and can be any positive value
Mean can be any value

Pareto Distribution The Pareto distribution is widely used for the investigation of distributions associated with such empirical phenomena as city population sizes, the occurrence of natural resources, the size of companies, personal incomes, stock price fluctuations, and error clustering in communication circuits.

The mathematical constructs for the pareto are as follows:

$$f(x) = \frac{\beta L^\beta}{x^{(1+\beta)}} \text{ for } x > L$$

$$Mean = \frac{\beta L}{\beta - 1}$$

$$Standard\ Deviation = \sqrt{\frac{\beta L^2}{(\beta - 1)^2 (\beta - 2)}}$$

$$Skewness = \sqrt{\frac{\beta - 2}{\beta}} \left[\frac{2(\beta + 1)}{\beta - 3} \right]$$

$$Excess\ Kurtosis = \frac{6(\beta^3 + \beta^2 - 6\beta - 2)}{\beta(\beta - 3)(\beta - 4)}$$

Location (L) and shape (β) are the distributional parameters.

There are two standard parameters for the pareto distribution: location and shape. The location parameter is the lower bound for the variable. After you select the location parameter, you can estimate the shape parameter. The shape parameter is a number greater than 0, usually greater than 1. The larger the shape parameter, the smaller the variance and the thicker the right tail of the distribution.

Input requirements:

Location > 0 and can be any positive value
Shape ≥ 0.05

Student's t Distribution The Student's t distribution is the most widely used distribution in hypothesis testing. This distribution is used to estimate the mean of a normally distributed population when the sample size is small, and is used to test the statistical significance of the difference between two sample means or confidence intervals for small sample sizes.

The mathematical constructs for the t distribution are as follows:

$$f(t) = \frac{\Gamma[(r+1)/2]}{\sqrt{r\pi}\,\Gamma[r/2]}(1 + t^2/r)^{-(r+1)/2}$$

where $t = \dfrac{x - \overline{x}}{s}$ and Γ is the gamma function

Mean $= 0$ (this applies to all degrees of freedom r except if the distribution is shifted to another nonzero central location)

$$\text{Standard Deviation} = \sqrt{\frac{r}{r-2}}$$

Skewness $= 0$ (this applies to all degrees of freedom r)

$$\text{Excess Kurtosis} = \frac{6}{r-4} \text{ for all } r > 4$$

Degree of freedom r is the only distributional parameter.

The t distribution is related to the F-distribution as follows: The square of a value of t with r degrees of freedom is distributed as F with 1 and r degrees of freedom. The overall shape of the probability density function of the t distribution also resembles the bell shape of a normally distributed variable with mean 0 and variance 1, except that it is a bit lower and wider or is leptokurtic (fat tails at the ends and peaked center). As the number of degrees of freedom grows (say, above 30), the t distribution approaches the normal distribution with mean 0 and variance 1.

Input requirements:

Degrees of freedom ≥ 1 and must be an integer

Triangular Distribution   The triangular distribution describes a situation where you know the minimum, maximum, and most likely values to occur. For example, you could describe the number of cars sold per week when past sales show the minimum, maximum, and usual number of cars sold.

The three conditions underlying the triangular distribution are:

1. The minimum number of items is fixed.
2. The maximum number of items is fixed.

3. The most likely number of items falls between the minimum and maximum values, forming a triangular-shaped distribution, which shows that values near the minimum and maximum are less likely to occur than those near the most likely value.

The mathematical constructs for the triangular distribution are as follows:

$$f(x) \begin{cases} \dfrac{2(x - Min)}{(Max - Min)(Likely - Min)} & \text{for } Min < x < Likely \\[2ex] \dfrac{2(Max - x)}{(Max - Min)(Max - Likely)} & \text{for } Likely < x < Max \end{cases}$$

$$Mean = \frac{1}{3}(Min + Likely + Max)$$

$$Standard\ Deviation = \sqrt{\frac{1}{18}(Min^2 + Likely^2 + Max^2 - MinMax - MinLikely - MaxLikely)}$$

$$Skewness = \frac{\sqrt{2}(Min + Max - 2Likely)(2Min - Max - Likely)(Min - 2Max + Likely)}{5(Min^2 + Max^2 + Likely^2 - MinMax - MinLikely - MaxLikely)^{3/2}}$$

$Excess\ Kurtosis = -0.6$ (this applies to all inputs of Min, Max, and $Likely$)

Minimum value (*Min*), most likely value (*Likely*), and maximum value (*Max*) are the distributional parameters.
Input requirements:

$Min \leq Most\ Likely \leq Max$ and can also take any value

However, $Min < Max$ and can also take any value

Uniform Distribution   With the uniform distribution, all values fall between the minimum and maximum and occur with equal likelihood.
The three conditions underlying the uniform distribution are:

1. The minimum value is fixed.
2. The maximum value is fixed.
3. All values between the minimum and maximum occur with equal likelihood.

The mathematical constructs for the uniform distribution are as follows:

$$f(x) = \frac{1}{Max - Min} \text{ for all values such that } Min < Max$$

$$Mean = \frac{Min + Max}{2}$$

$$Standard\ Deviation = \sqrt{\frac{(Max - Min)^2}{12}}$$

Skewness $= 0$ (this applies to all inputs of *Min* and *Max*)

Excess Kurtosis $= -1.2$ (this applies to all inputs of *Min* and *Max*)

Maximum value (*Max*) and minimum value (*Min*) are the distributional parameters.

Input requirements:

Min < *Max* and can take any value

Weibull Distribution (Rayleigh Distribution) The Weibull distribution describes data resulting from life and fatigue tests. It is commonly used to describe failure time in reliability studies as well as the breaking strengths of materials in reliability and quality control tests. Weibull distributions are also used to represent various physical quantities, such as wind speed.

The Weibull distribution is a family of distributions that can assume the properties of several other distributions. For example, depending on the shape parameter you define, the Weibull distribution can be used to model the exponential and Rayleigh distributions, among others. The Weibull distribution is flexible. When the Weibull shape parameter is equal to 1.0, the Weibull distribution is identical to the exponential distribution. The Weibull location parameter lets you set up an exponential distribution to start at a location other than 0.0. When the shape parameter is less than 1.0, the Weibull distribution becomes a steeply declining curve. A manufacturer might find this effect useful in describing part failures during a burn-in period.

The mathematical constructs for the Weibull distribution are as follows:

$$f(x) = \frac{\alpha}{\beta}\left[\frac{x}{\beta}\right]^{\alpha-1} e^{-\left(\frac{x}{\beta}\right)^{\alpha}}$$

Mean $= \beta\Gamma(1 + \alpha^{-1})$

Standard Deviation $= \beta^2\left[\Gamma(1 + 2\alpha^{-1}) - \Gamma^2(1 + \alpha^{-1})\right]$

Skewness $= \dfrac{2\Gamma^3(1 + \beta^{-1}) - 3\Gamma(1 + \beta^{-1})\Gamma(1 + 2\beta^{-1}) + \Gamma(1 + 3\beta^{-1})}{\left[\Gamma(1 + 2\beta^{-1}) - \Gamma^2(1 + \beta^{-1})\right]^{3/2}}$

Excess Kurtosis $=$

$$\frac{-6\Gamma^4(1+\beta^{-1}) + 12\Gamma^2(1+\beta^{-1})\Gamma(1+2\beta^{-1}) - 3\Gamma^2(1+2\beta^{-1}) - 4\Gamma(1+\beta^{-1})\Gamma(1+3\beta^{-1}) + \Gamma(1+4\beta^{-1})}{\left[\Gamma(1+2\beta^{-1}) - \Gamma^2(1+\beta^{-1})\right]^2}$$

Location (L), shape (α), and scale (β) are the distributional parameters, and Γ is the gamma function.

Input requirements:

Scale > 0 and can be any positive value

Shape ≥ 0.05

Location can take on any value

APPENDIX—ROV COMPILER: PROTECTS AND CONVERTS EXCEL FILES INTO EXECUTABLE EXE

For the sake of completeness, this appendix illustrates the ROV Compiler software, which is extremely handy for Excel modelers. This software is meant to be used to convert Microsoft Excel XP, 2003, 2007, and 2010 files to *extract an existing model into pure mathematical relationships and code such that the same model can be used as usual but the intellectual property of the model is protected.* You can now use Excel as a software development tool instead of as only a modeling tool. That is, suppose you are an expert in a certain industry such as pharmaceuticals, biotechnology, manufacturing, banking, insurance, aeronautics, and so forth, and further suppose that you have developed Excel models and worksheets that are appropriate for use by others in the same field. You can now use ROV Compiler to create executable EXE files from your existing Excel models, lock up the mathematical and computational logic into binary code and create extremely secure hardware-locked license protection of your file, and distribute the file like a software program. When run, the compiled file will have the exact look and feel of Excel, minus the ability of accessing critical calculation logic, plus the ability to be secured and licensed like a regular software program. There exists public domain software that will crack Excel passwords quickly and effortlessly, but such software will not work on compiled files.

By running the extracted model, several items are accomplished, namely:

- Any existing Excel 2002, 2003, 2007, 2010 files and beyond can be compiled–extracted from Excel .xls or .xlsx files and turned into binary mathematical code, and the file will become a self-executable EXE file that, when run, will open in Excel. The file will function exactly like an Excel file, with all of the Excel functionalities, but the end user will not have access to the calculations, functions, or logic. It will look and feel like Excel but the computations are all embedded in binary format that is encrypted and not accessible to the end user.
- All of the business intelligence and relationships are maintained but will no longer be visible to the end user, allowing the model creator to

safely and securely distribute the model without losing control of any intellectual property or company secrets.

- The compiled model can be locked using an AES encryption (military-strength protection) and can only be accessible using the correct password or license key codes (with computer hardware locking algorithms).
- The compiled model cannot be changed by the end user. This feature maintains a strict quality control and prevents malicious tampering or accidental breakage of the model (e.g., equations and functions with broken links, wrong functions, and calculations).

The compiled file can also be used by third-party software applications in a Component Based Modeling environment. For instance, the end user might have his or her own software or database with predefined calculations. The compiled file is linked into and is a part of this existing proprietary system. This proprietary system simply obtains the inputs to link into the compiled file, and the compiled model will perform the computations and return the required outputs.

Figure 5.21 shows a sample screen shot of the security settings for the compiled file where you can convert your Excel file (Figure 5.22) and

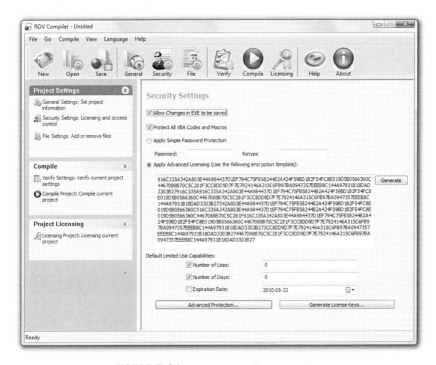

FIGURE 5.21 ROV compiler protection.

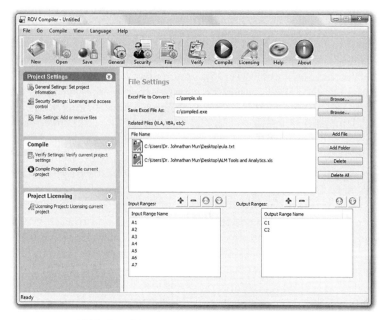

FIGURE 5.22 ROV compiler file conversion.

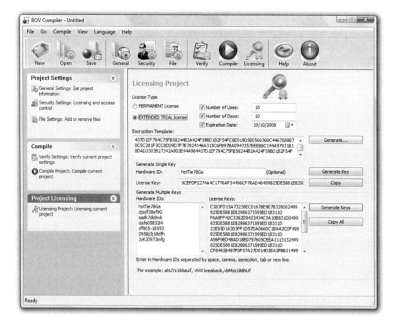

FIGURE 5.23 ROV compiler licensing.

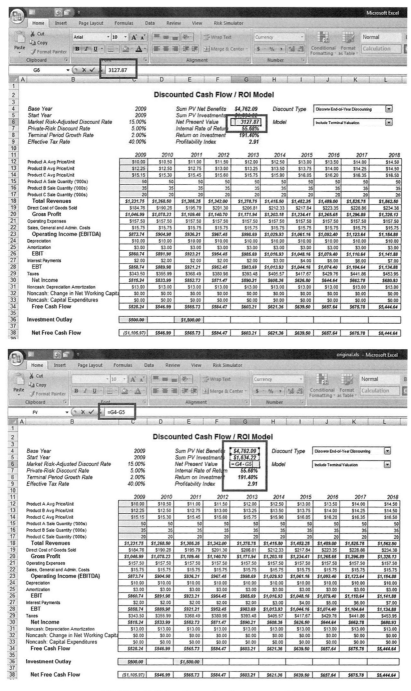

FIGURE 5.24 Completely protected file.

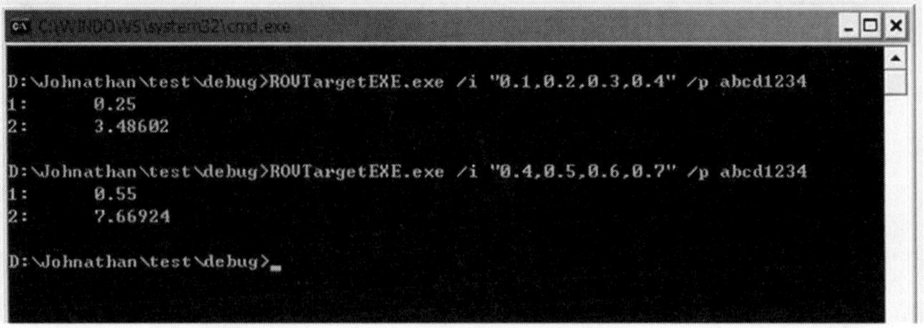

```
D:\Johnathan\test\debug>ROVTargetEXE.exe /i "0.1,0.2,0.3,0.4" /p abcd1234
1:      0.25
2:      3.48602

D:\Johnathan\test\debug>ROVTargetEXE.exe /i "0.4,0.5,0.6,0.7" /p abcd1234
1:      0.55
2:      7.66924

D:\Johnathan\test\debug>_
```

FIGURE 5.25   Console model.

enable advanced license protection that is hardware locked to the end user's computer and contains some advanced encryption templates to which only you would have access. The license generated (Figure 5.23) can only be used by the computer with the unique Hardware ID. The top of Figure 5.24 shows the protected and compiled file while the bottom picture shows the original file. Notice that the protected file looks and feels exactly the same as the original file, but all of the calculations, equations, computations, VBA codes, and so forth are completely protected and embedded inside compiled binary codes that cannot be cracked. Finally, if required, the executable file can be embedded into other proprietary software products and can be run in code (Figure 5.25), without the need of ever opening up the Excel file. For more detailed information, you can watch the getting started videos on the DVD as well as visit www.realoptionsvaluation.com/rovcompiler.html.

APPENDIX—ROV EXTRACTOR AND EVALUATOR: RUNS EXTREME SUPER SPEED SIMULATIONS AND CONVERTS EXCEL MODELS INTO A CALCULATOR ENVIRONMENT

Yet another powerful tool is the ROV Risk Extractor and Evaluator software, which is meant to be used inside of Microsoft Excel 2007 and 2010 to extract an existing model into pure mathematical relationships and code such that the same model can be run completely outside and independent of Excel. By running the extracted model, several items are accomplished:

- All of the business intelligence and relationships are maintained but will no longer be visible to the end user, allowing the model creator to safely and securely distribute the model without losing control of any intellectual property or company secrets.

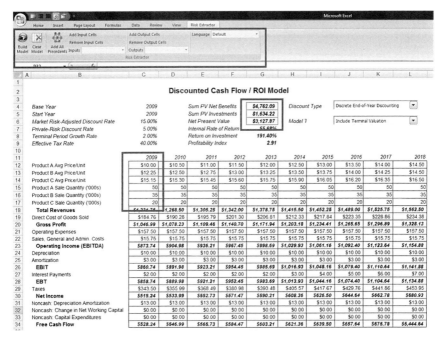

FIGURE 5.26   ROV risk extractor.

- A large model that can take a long time to run in Excel can now be run at extremely fast speeds in the lifted model. You can open ROV Extractor directly in Excel and select the specific cells to set as inputs and outputs before lifting the model (Figure 5.26).
- The large Excel model can now be turned into a calculator-like environment (Figure 5.27), where all the end user has to do is enter the inputs and obtain the outputs. Imagine it as akin to creating a large Visual Basic function in Excel, but instead of a simple function with several lines of computations, this function is an entire Excel workbook with many interconnected worksheets.
- Large-scale Monte Carlo risk simulations with a large number of trials can be performed at very high speeds. Figure 5.28 illustrates a model that was subjected to a 100,000-trial simulation and it took less than a few quick seconds to complete! If you are a large entity such as a bank or investment firm, or some large manufacturer requiring large-scale simulations to be run, this is the best platform to do so. You can develop the model in Excel, then lift the model using ROV Extractor, and run the simulations in ROV Evaluator.

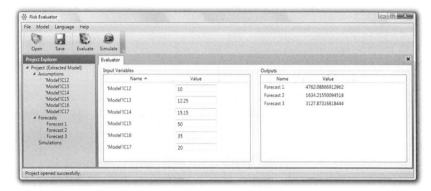

FIGURE 5.27 ROV risk evaluator.

- The extracted model can be locked using an AES encryption (military-strength protection) and can only be accessible using the correct password.
- Large models with many irrelevant parts are identified and, additionally, you can identify the main key inputs and outputs you wish to have modeled. For instance, in a model such as A + B + C = D, B + E = F,

FIGURE 5.28 Extreme super speed simulation.

and if F is chosen as the key output, only B and E are relevant. Computational time for the model is decreased by identifying critical inputs, and the model can then be optimized to run even faster once the model thread is identified.

■ The extracted model cannot be changed by the end user. Thus a strict quality control is maintained and malicious tampering or accidental breakage of the model (e.g., equations and functions with broken links, wrong functions and calculations) are prevented.

■ The extracted file can also be used by third-party software applications in a Component Based Modeling environment. For instance, the end user might have his or her own software or database with predefined calculations. The extracted file is linked into and is a part of this existing proprietary system. This proprietary system simply obtains the inputs to link into the extracted file and the extracted model will perform the computations at high speed and return the required outputs.

For more detailed information, you can watch the getting started videos on the DVD as well as visit www.realoptionsvaluation.com/rovextractor.html.

QUESTIONS

1. Why do you need to have profiles in a simulation?
2. Explain the differences between Pearson's product moment correlation coefficient and Spearman's rank-based correlation.
3. Will more or fewer trials be required to obtain: higher error levels, higher precision levels, and a wider confidence interval?
4. Explain the differences between error and precision and how these two concepts are linked.
5. If you know that two simulated variables are correlated but do not have the relevant correlation value, should you still go ahead and correlate them in a simulation?

Following are some hands-on exercises using Risk Simulator. The example files are located on *Start, Programs, Real Options Valuation, Risk Simulator, Examples*.

EXERCISES

Exercise 1: Basic Simulation Model

This sample model illustrates how to use Risk Simulator for:

1. Running a Monte Carlo Risk Simulation
2. Using Forecast Charts
3. Interpreting the Risk Statistics
4. Setting Seed Values
5. Running Super Speed Simulation
6. Setting Run Preferences (Simulation Properties)
7. Extracting Simulation Data
8. Creating a Simulation Report and Forecast Statistics Table
9. Creating Forecast Statistics Using the RS Functions
10. Saving a Simulation Run's Forecast Charts
11. Creating New and Switching Among Simulation Profiles
12. Distributional Truncation and Multidimensional Simulation

Model Background

File Name: Basic Simulation Model.xls

Access: **Risk Simulator | Example Models | 02 Basic Simulation Model**

Prerequisites: Risk Simulator 2010 or later, Chapters 1 and 2 of *Modeling Risk*

The *Static and Dynamic Model* worksheet illustrates a simple model with two input assumptions (revenue and cost) and an output forecast (income) as seen in Figure 5.29. The model on the left is a static model with single-point estimates while the model on the right is a dynamic model on which we will set Monte Carlo input assumptions and output forecasts. After running the simulation, the results can be extracted and further analyzed. In this model we can also learn to set different simulation preferences,

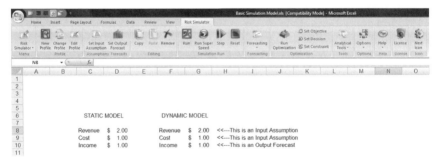

FIGURE 5.29 Basic simulation model.

to run a simulation, how to set seed values, and much more. To perform these exercises, you will need to have Risk Simulator version 2010 or later installed and working.

Running a Monte Carlo Risk Simulation To set up and run a simulation model using Risk Simulator is as simple as 1-2-3; that is, create a new profile, set inputs and outputs, and then run. To follow along, open the example Basic Simulation Model and do the following:

1. Select *Risk Simulator | New Simulation Profile* (or click on the New Profile icon), provide it with a name (e.g., "Practice Simulation") and leave everything else as is (we come back later and revisit some of these settings).

2. Select cell *G8* and click on *Risk Simulator | Set Input Assumption* (or click on the Set Input Assumption icon), then select *Triangular Distribution* and set the *Min = 1.50, Most Likely = 2.00, Max = 2.25*, and then hit *OK* (Figure 5.30).

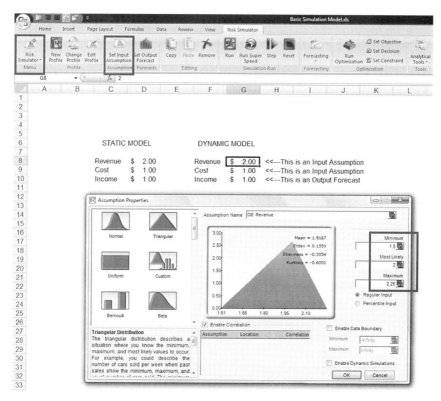

FIGURE 5.30 Setting an input assumption.

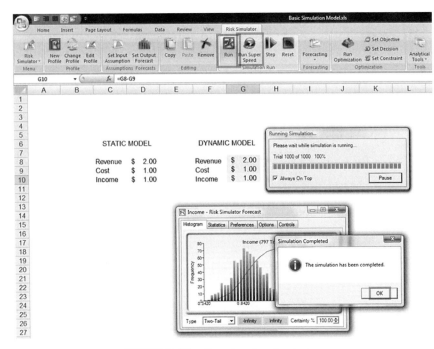

FIGURE 5.31   Running the simulation.

3. Select cell *G9* and set another input assumption. This time use *Uniform Distribution* with *Min = 0.85* and *Max = 1.25*.
4. Select cell *G10* and set that cell as the output forecast by clicking on *Risk Simulator | Set Output Forecast*. You can use the default name "Income" that it picked up from the model.
5. Select *Risk Simulator | Run Simulation* (or click on the Run icon) to start the simulation.

Figure 5.31 shows the simulation run. At the end of the simulation, click *OK*. There are a few things to notice here. The first is that the resulting model at the end of the simulation run returns the same results as the static model. That is, two dollars minus one dollar is equal to one dollar. However, what simulation does is create thousands of possible outcomes of "around two dollars" in revenue minus thousands of possible outcomes of "around one dollar" cost, resulting in the income of "around one dollar." The results are shown as a histogram, complete with the risk statistics, which we review later in this exercise.

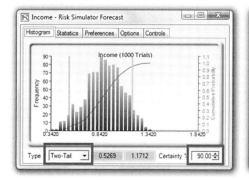 

FIGURE 5.32 Simulation results and forecast charts.

Using Forecast Charts The forecast chart (Figure 5.32) is shown when the simulation is running. Once simulation is completed, the forecast chart can be used. The forecast chart has several tabs: *Histogram, Statistics, Preferences, Options,* and *Controls.* Of particular interest are the first two, the histogram and statistics tabs. For instance, the first tab shows the output forecast's probability distribution in the form of a histogram, where the specific values can be determined using the certainty boxes.

In the *Histogram* tab, select *Two-Tail*, enter *90* in the *Certainty* box, and hit *TAB* on your keyboard. The 90% confidence interval is shown (0.5269 and 1.1712). This result means that there is a 5% chance that the income will fall below \$0.5269, and another 5% chance that it will be above \$1.1712. Alternatively, you can select *Left-Tail* ≤ and enter *1.0* on the input box, hit *TAB*, and see that the left-tail certainty is 76.30%, indicating that there is a 76.30% chance that the income will fall at or below \$1.0 (or that there is a 23.70% chance that income will exceed \$1.0). Note that your results will *not* be exactly the same as what we illustrate here due to the theoretical fact that we are running a simulation of random numbers. Please do not be concerned at this point, and continue on to the seed value exercise next for more details on how to get the same simulation results going forward.

Interpreting the Risk Statistics The *Statistics* tab illustrates the statistical results of the forecast variable. Refer to Chapter 2 for more details on how to interpret and use these risk profile statistics in risk analysis and risk management. Note that your results will not be exactly the same as those illustrated here because a simulation (random number generation) was run, and by definition, the results will not be exactly the same every time. However, if a seed value is set (see next section), the results will be identical in every single run.

Optional Exercises   For additional exercise, view the *Preferences, Options,* and *Controls* tabs and play with some of the settings. Specifically, try the following:

- Preferences:
  a. Try selecting and deselecting the *Always Show Windows on Top* option. Navigate around different applications that might be open and notice the behavior of the forecast chart.
  b. Run a simulation with at least three forecasts and select *Semitransparent When Inactive* on all three forecast charts (e.g., use your own model or in cell G11, set it to be =G10, in G12, set it also to be =G10, set these two cells G11 and G12 as output forecasts, and then run a simulation). Then, minimize all other software applications, leaving these three forecast charts visible, overlay one chart on top of another, then click anywhere on the desktop to deactivate the forecast charts. Notice how you can now compare different forecast charts.
  c. Change the *Histogram Resolution* to different levels and view the *Histogram* to see how the shape changes.
  d. Also, if you have multiple forecast charts up and running and you forget to reset the previous simulation (resetting the simulation will clear all the forecast charts and simulated data from temporary memory, allowing you to rerun another simulation), you can *Minimize All Charts, Close All Charts,* or *Copy* a specific chart (you can set up the chart any way you like and then copy the chart to clipboard and paste it into another software such as Microsoft Word or Microsoft PowerPoint) from this tab.
- Options:
  a. Play with the *Data Filter* by showing only limited data such as only 2 standard deviations from the mean, or a specific range of values. Go back to the *Histogram* and notice the change in the chart; go back to the *Statistics* tab and notice that the computed risk statistics are now based on the truncated data and not the entire data set.
  b. You can also select the *Statistic* to show, or the number of *Decimals* to show in the *Histogram* chart and *Statistics* tabs. This option may come in handy if you wish to obtain higher precision of the results (more decimals) or show fewer decimals for large value results.
- Controls:
  a. From this tab, you can control and change how the histogram looks by changing the orientation, color, 2D and 3D aspects of the chart, background, type of overlay curve to show (CDF versus

PDF), chart types, and many other chart controls. Try out several of these items and see what happens to the histogram chart each time.

b. You can also perform a distributional fitting of the forecast results and obtain the theoretical versus empirical moments of the distribution (see the *Distributional Data Fitting* exercise for more details on how distribution fitting routines work), or show the fitted distribution's theoretical curve on top of the empirical histogram (first click on *Fit*, then select either *Continuous* or *Discrete* from the *Chart Overlay* drop list, and then go back to the *Histogram* tab to view the resulting charts).

c. Finally, you can change the *Chart Type* (Bar, Cylinder, Pyramid, and so forth), *Chart Title*, *Min* and *Max* values of the chart axes, and the *Decimals* to show on the chart. Try out several of these items and see what happens to the histogram chart each time.

If you are using Risk Simulator 2010 or later, you can click on the *Global View* link on the right corner of the forecast chart to view all the aforementioned tabs and functionalities in a single view, or click on the *Normal View* link to return to the tabbed view described above.

Setting Seed Values

1. Reset the simulation by selecting *Risk Simulator | Reset Simulation*.
2. Select *Risk Simulator | Edit Simulation Profile* (Figure 5.33).

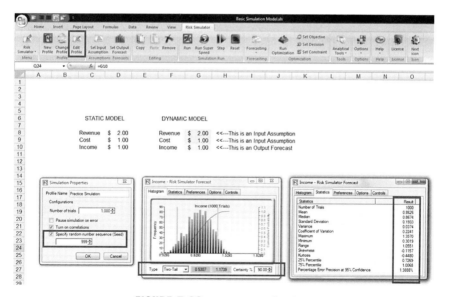

FIGURE 5.33 Using a seed value.

3. Select the *check* box for random number sequence and enter in a seed value (e.g., *999*) and click *OK* (Figure 5.33).

4. *Run* the simulation and verify that the results are the same as the results obtained in Figure 5.33. In fact, run the simulation a few more times, and each time verify that the results are identical.

Note that the random number sequence or seed number has to be a positive integer value. Running the same model with the same assumptions and forecasts with an identical seed value and same number of trials will always yield the same results. The number of simulation trials to run can be set in the same run properties box (Figure 5.33). Setting a seed value is important especially when you wish to obtain the same values in each simulation run. Say, for example, that you need the live model to return the same results as a printed report during a presentation. If the results in your live demonstration are slightly off compared to the printed results, questions may arise as to their validity. By having a seed value, the results are guaranteed to always be the same.

Let us now revisit the confidence interval analysis after you have run another simulation with the seed value. Figure 5.34 illustrates the results of these manipulations:

1. Select *Two-Tail*, enter a *Certainty* of *90*, and hit *TAB* on the keyboard. You will obtain the two-tailed 90% confidence interval of 0.5307 and 1.1739, which means that 90% of the time, the income level will be between these two values, with a 5% chance it will be below 0.5307 and 5% it will be above 1.1739.

2. To verify the 5% result above, select *Left-Tail* <, enter a *Certainty* of *5*, and hit *TAB*. You will obtain the value of 0.5307, indicating that there is a 5% chance you will receive an income less than 0.5307.

3. Next, select *Left-Tail* ≤, enter in the value *1*, and hit *TAB*. This time, *instead of providing a probability to receive a value, you provide a value to receive the probability*. In this case, it states that you have a 74.30% chance that your income will be less than or equal to the 1.000 value that your static single-point model had predicted. In fact, in Figure 5.33, you see that the mean or average income value is 0.8626. In other words, *the expected value (mean) is not the same as the value expected (in your original single-point estimate static model)*.

4. Select *Right-Tail* >, enter in *1*, and hit *TAB*. Here you can see the complement of the Left-Tail ≤ value. In other words, the value you receive, 25.70%, indicates the probability you will make more than your target of 1.000, and if you take 100% minus 25.70%, you obtain 74.30%, the Left-Tail ≤ value. When doing this exercise, make sure you select the correct inequality signs (less than, less than or equal to, greater than, greater than or equal to).

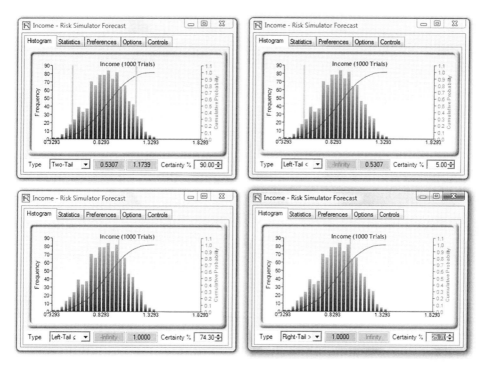

FIGURE 5.34 Left-, right-, and two-tail probabilities (simulation results with seed values).

Running Super Speed Simulation

1. Reset the simulation by selecting *Risk Simulator | Reset Simulation*.
2. Select *Risk Simulator | Run Super Speed Simulation* (Figure 5.31).

Notice how much faster the super speed simulation runs. In fact, for practice, *Reset the Simulation*, *Edit Simulation Profile*, and change the *Number of Trials* to 100,000, and *Run Super Speed*. It should only take a few seconds to run. However, be aware that super speed simulation will not run if the model has errors, VBA (visual basic for applications), or links to external data sources or applications. In such situations, you will be notified and the regular speed simulation will be run instead. Regular speed simulations are always able to run even with errors, VBA, or external links.

Setting Run Preferences (Simulation Properties)   The run preferences or *Simulation Properties* dialog box that came up when you first created a new profile or edited the current profile (Figure 5.33), allows you to specify the *Number of Trials* to run in a particular simulation (by default it will be 1,000 trials). In theory, the higher the number of trials, the more precise the results (try rerunning the simulation again and this time, keep an eye on the *Percentage Error Precision at 95% Confidence* value in the *Statistics* tab, which should decrease as you increase the number of trials). Refer to Chapter 5 for more details on interpreting these risk statistics, and on error precision confidence, and for how to use them in making decisions. In addition, *Pause Simulation on Error* can be set up so that the simulation will stop running if a computational error in Excel is encountered (e.g., #NUM or #ERROR), which is a good tool for ascertaining if your model is set up correctly. If this option is not checked, any errors will be ignored and only the valid results will be used in the forecast charts. Correlations can also be specified between pairs of input assumptions, and if *Turn on Correlations* is selected, these specified correlations will be imputed in the simulation. See the *Correlation Risk Effects* exercise for how to set up correlations and to understand how correlations affect the outcome of your results, the theory of risk diversification, portfolio effects on distributional moments, and others.

Extracting Simulation Data The simulation's assumptions and forecast data are stored in memory until the simulation is reset or when Excel is closed. If required, these raw data can be extracted into a separate Excel sheet. To extract the data, simply:

1. Edit Simulation Profile, reset the Number of Trials to 1,000 and then Run the simulation.
2. After the simulation is completed, select *Risk Simulator | Tools | Extract Data* (you can also access this function by clicking on the *Next* icon repeatedly until you get to the tools icon ribbon, and then click on the *Data Extraction* icon as shown in Figure 5.35).
3. *Choose the relevant assumptions or forecasts* to extract, select New Excel Worksheet as the extraction format, and click *OK*.

Optional Exercise The 1,000 simulated revenue and cost values will be extracted, as well as the computed forecast income variable (Figure 5.35). Note that if you had not first run a simulation, the extracted data report would be empty, as there are no values to extract. Try clicking on the *Select . . .* button a few times to see what happens.

Optional Exercise Using the extracted data, apply Excel's functions to compute all of the risk statistics, for example, the mean, median, standard

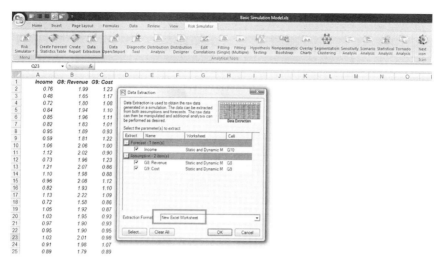

FIGURE 5.35 Extracting simulation data.

deviation, and so forth, and compare to make sure the results are identical to those obtained in Risk Simulator's forecast statistics tab. Hint: Use the following Excel functions for this exercise: AVERAGE(), STDEV(), VAR(), SKEW(), KURT(), MIN(), MAX().

Creating a Simulation Report and Forecast Statistics Table

The simulation's input assumptions and output forecasts, as well as the detailed risk statistics, can also be extracted after a simulation has been run. *Assuming the simulation has already been run*, simply:

1. Select *Risk Simulator | Tools | Create Report* (you can also access this function by clicking on the *Next* icon repeatedly until you get to the tools icon ribbon, and then click on the *Create Report* icon as shown in Figure 5.35). Spend some time reviewing the report that is generated.

2. Select *Risk Simulator | Tools | Create Forecast Statistics Table* (you can also access this function by clicking on the *Next* icon repeatedly until you get to the tools icon ribbon, and then click on the *Create Forecast Statistics Table* icon as shown in Figure 5.35). Here you can select the forecasts you wish to show. In this simple example, we only have one forecast, but in larger models, you can select multiple forecasts at once. We suggest you try creating this statistics table with the other exercises.

Creating Forecast Statistics Using the RS Functions   You can also obtain the forecast statistics not in a report format, but in a specific cell by using the Risk Simulator function call. For example, do the following:

1. Save the example file and then exit Excel and click on *Start | Programs | Real Options Valuation | Risk Simulator | Tools | Install Functions*. When the installation is complete in a few short seconds, hit the spacebar to close the black console pad and start Excel. Note: If you are running Windows Vista or Windows 7, right-click on *Install Functions* in the *Start* menu and choose *Run As Administrator*.
2. Reopen the example at *Risk Simulator | Example Models | 02 Basic Simulation Model* and run a simulation in super speed *Risk Simulator | Run Super Speed Simulation*.
3. Select cell *G12* and click on the *FX* (insert function) icon in Excel or click on and select the *ALL* category and scroll down to the RS functions list. Here you see several set input assumption functions for various distributions. The last item on the RS list is *RSForecastStatistic*. Select this function or you can type this function directly in the cell. For instance, type in =*RSForecastStatistic(G10, "Average")*, where G10 is the forecast output cell and "Average" is the statistic you wish to obtain. Remember to keep the quotes ("") and you can replace the Average parameter with any of the following: *Average, CoefficientofVariation, Median, Maximum, StandardDeviation, Minimum, Variance, Range, Skewness, Percentile75, Kurtosis, Certainty1.0, Percentile99.9*. In fact, you can use *"PercentileXX.XX"* and *"CertaintyXX.XX"* and just replace the X with your own number for a left-tail < value. The Percentile parameter means you enter the percentage and receive the value X, whereas for the Certainty parameter, you enter the value X and get the left-tail percentage.
4. Just for practice, reset the simulation, run a regular speed simulation, and notice that the statistics will keep changing as you run the simulation, and that it stops at the final result when the simulation completes. You can now use this function call as part of your model. One quick note: If you run a super speed simulation, the function call will not be updated automatically. You will have to select the cell with the function after the simulation is run, hit *F2* on the keyboard, and then hit *Enter* to update the function calculation.

Saving a Simulation Run's Forecast Charts   Suppose you run a large model and want to save the forecast charts. You can do so in Risk Simulator by saving the results as a *RiskSim* file format. Saving the forecast charts allows

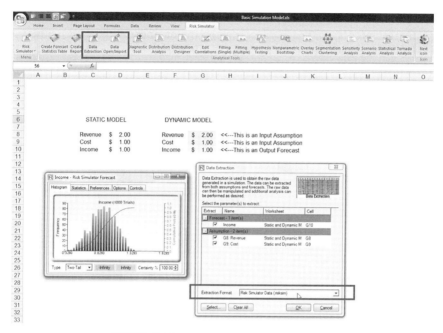

FIGURE 5.36 Extracting to a RiskSim file.

you to reopen the results without having to rerun the simulation, thereby saving you some time.

1. Run a simulation as usual.
2. Select *Risk Simulator | Tools | Data Extraction/Export* (you can also access this function by clicking on the *Next* icon repeatedly until you get to the tools icon ribbon, and then click on the *Data Extraction* icon). Here you select the Extraction Format as *Risk Simulator Data (RiskSim)* file (Figure 5.36). Save the file to the desired location. You can now save and exit Excel.
3. Open Excel and select *Risk Simulator | Tools | Data Open/Import* (you can also access this function by clicking on the *Next* icon repeatedly until you get to the tools icon ribbon, and click on the *Data Open/Import* icon). Select the RiskSim file you saved previously and the forecast charts will now reappear.

Creating New and Switching Among Simulation Profiles The same model can have multiple Risk Simulator profiles. That is, different users of the same model can, in fact, create their own simulation input assumptions, forecasts, run preferences, and so forth. All these preferences are stored in separate simulation profiles and each profile can be run independently. This is a powerful feature that allows multiple users to run the same model their own way, or for the same user to run the model under different simulation conditions, thereby allowing for scenario analysis on Monte Carlo simulation. To create different profiles and switch among different profiles, simply:

1. Create several new profiles by clicking on *Risk Simulator | New Simulation Profile* and provide each new profile with a unique name.
2. Add the relevant assumptions and forecasts, or change the run preferences as desired in each simulation profile.
3. Switch among different profiles by clicking on *Risk Simulator | Change Active Simulation*.

Note that you can create as many profiles as you wish but each profile needs to have its own unique name. Also, you can select an existing profile and click on *Duplicate* (Figure 5.37) to duplicate all the input assumptions and output forecasts that are in this profile, which means you do not have to replicate all these manually. You can then change to this new profile and make any modifications as required. From this user interface, you can also *Delete* any unwanted profiles (but note that you need to have at least one profile active in the model, which means that you can delete any profile you choose but you cannot delete all of them as one profile must be left in

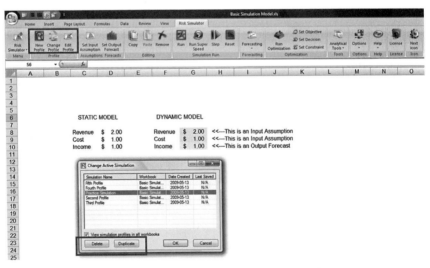

FIGURE 5.37   Multiple profiles in Risk Simulator.

the model). You can also click on a profile, click again on the name of the profile, and *rename* the profile as required.

Finally, as you save the Excel file, you will also save these profiles in the same Excel file. Profiles are stored in a special hidden segment of the Excel file and will be available to you as you open the Excel file in the future. For further practice, try saving the Excel file and then reopening the file again; notice that all your profiles and settings are still available. Just bear in mind that if you have multiple profiles, the last profile used will be the profile that is activated by default when the Excel file is opened the next time. Depending on what you are trying to do, you may need to remember to *Change the Profile* to the one you wish to use before you start running any simulations.

Distributional Truncation and Multidimensional Simulation *Distributional truncation* or *data boundaries* are typically not used by the average analyst but exist for truncating the distributional assumptions. For instance, if a normal distribution is selected, the theoretical boundaries are between negative infinity and positive infinity. However, in practice, the simulated variable exists only within some smaller range, and this range can then be entered to truncate the distribution appropriately. Not considering truncation is a major error users commit, especially when using the triangular distribution. The triangular distribution is simple and intuitive. As a matter of fact, it is probably the most widely used distribution in Risk Simulator, apart from the normal and uniform distributions. Simplistically, the triangular distribution looks at the minimum value, the most probable value, and the maximum value. These three inputs are often confused with the worst-case, nominal-case, and best-case scenarios. This assumption is indeed incorrect.

In fact, a worst-case scenario can be translated as a highly unlikely condition that will still occur given a percentage of the time. For instance, one can model the economy as high, average, and low, analogous to the worst-case, nominal-case, and best-case scenarios. Thus, logic would dictate that the worst-case scenario might have, say, a 15 percent chance of occurrence, the nominal-case, a 50 percent chance of occurrence, and a 35 percent chance that a best-case scenario will occur. This approach is what is meant by using a best-, nominal-, and worst-case scenario analysis. However, compare that to the triangular distribution, where the minimum and maximum cases will almost never occur, with a probability of occurrence set at zero!

For instance, see Figure 5.38, where the worst-, nominal-, and best-case scenarios are set as 5, 10, and 15, respectively. Note that at the extreme values, the probability of 5 or 15 occurring is virtually zero, as the areas under the curve (the measure of probability) of these extreme points are zero. In other words, 5 and 15 will almost never occur. Compare that to the economic scenario where these extreme values have either a 15 percent or

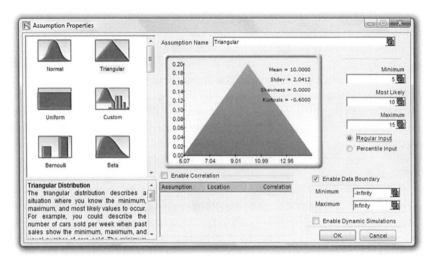

FIGURE 5.38   Sample triangular distribution.

35 percent chance of occurrence. Instead, distributional truncation should be considered here. The same applies to any other distribution. Figure 5.39 illustrates a truncated normal distribution where the extreme values do not extend to both positive and negative infinities, but are truncated at 7 and 13.

Another critical activity is looking at *Alternate Parameters*, that is, to look at the same distribution but through a different set of parameters.

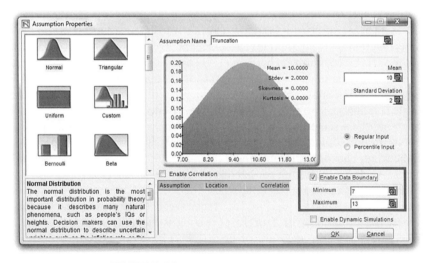

FIGURE 5.39   Truncating a distribution.

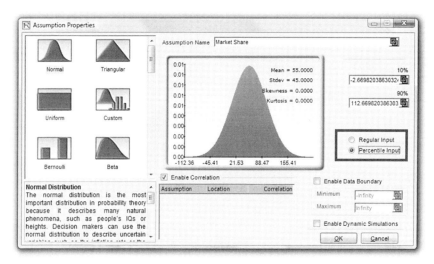

FIGURE 5.40 Alternate parameters.

For instance, if a *normal distribution* is used in simulating market share, and the mean is set at 55% with a standard deviation of 45%, one should be extremely worried. Using Risk Simulator's *Percentile Input* selection in the *Set Input Assumption* user interface, the 10th and 90th percentiles indicate a value of –2.67 percent and 112.67 percent (Figure 5.40). Clearly these values cannot exist under actual conditions. How can a product have –2.67 or 112.67 percent of the market share? The alternate-parameters function is a powerful tool to use in conditions such as these. Almost always, the first thing that should be done is to use alternate parameters to ascertain the logical upper and lower values of an input parameter. So, even if you obtained the 55% and 45% through distributional fitting (which, by the way, is correct, because the fit was probably very strong in the center of the normal distribution), by virtue of a theoretical fitting routine, the entire normal distribution will be fitted, and the normal distribution's tails extend from negative infinity to positive infinity, which is clearly outside the range of the norm for market share. So, using the alternate parameters will quickly allow you to visualize the 10th and 90th percentiles, and then you can decide to change the distribution or still use the distribution but apply distributional truncation as discussed previously. See the exercise on distributional analysis tools for obtaining other percentiles for any distribution, other than the default 10% and 90% as described here.

Finally, on the issue of *multidimensional simulation* or *dynamic simulation*, Figures 5.41 and 5.42 illustrate how this works. Suppose you have

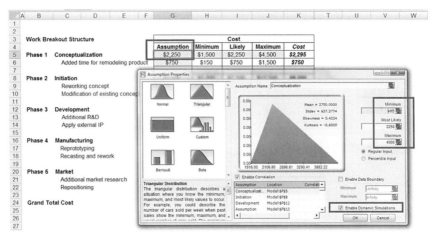

FIGURE 5.41   Dynamic or multidimensional simulation.

a model like the one shown, and further suppose that you have an input Triangular distribution assumption in cell G5, and you used the link icon to link its input parameters to other cells (H5, I5, and J5 for the minimum, most likely, and maximum values) as shown in Figure 5.41. Typically, this is a basic assumption and you are all done. However, what if the minimum, most likely, and maximum inputs are themselves uncertain? If that is the case then you can set an input assumption for these inputs (cells H5, I5, J5). In other words, if you have an assumption that is linked to other cells, and these other cells themselves are assumptions, you have just created a two-layer simulation (of course, you can add additional layers where these input cells are again linked to other cells that are simulated and so forth, creating a multidimensional simulation model). If you do this, remember to select the *Enable Dynamic Simulation* checkbox (Figure 5.41) on the assumption that links to other assumptions (Figure 5.42). So, if you ran a 1,000-trial simulation, instead of having a single Triangular distribution and picking random numbers from this single distribution, there are actually 1,000 triangular distributions, where at each trial, there will be new parameters for this Triangular distribution, and a random number is selected from this distribution, and then on the next trial, you repeat the entire process. This multidimensional simulation approach allows you to simulate uncertain input parameters into the simulation.

There is one little word of caution: Do not overdo the multidimensional layers, because suppose you are using a Triangular distribution with Min = A, Most Likely = B, and Max = C. And suppose A is a uniform distribution with Min = D and Max = E. If C is also another uniform distribution with

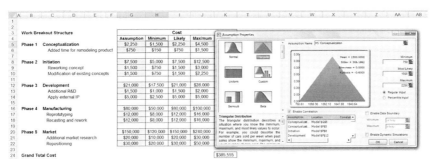

FIGURE 5.42　Input parameter as an assumption.

Min = F and Max = G, all is well as long as E and F do not cross each other. Put another way, if you accidentally set E > F, then there will be times in a random simulation where the random value E is higher than F. This result means that A > C in the original distribution, which violates the input requirements, causing the simulation stop and creating an error (i.e., the maximum value is less than the minimum value in the Triangular distribution; this cannot work and the simulation stops). So, if you are confused by distributional truncation, it might be best to avoid using it.

Exercise 2: Correlation Effects Model

This sample model illustrates how to use Risk Simulator for:

1. Setting Up a Simulation's Input Assumptions and Output Forecasts
2. Copying, Pasting, and Deleting Simulation Assumptions and Forecasts
3. Running Correlated Simulations, Comparing Results between Correlated and Uncorrelated Models
4. Extracting and Manually Computing and Verifying the Assumptions' Correlations
5. Pearson's Product Moment Linear Correlation and Spearman's Nonlinear Rank Correlation

Model Background

File Name: Correlation Risk Effects Model.xls

Access: **Risk Simulator | Example Models | 04 Correlation Risk Effects Model**

Prerequisites: Risk Simulator 2010 or later, Completed Basic Simulation Model Exercise, Chapter 5 of Modeling Risk (Section: Correlations and Precision Control)

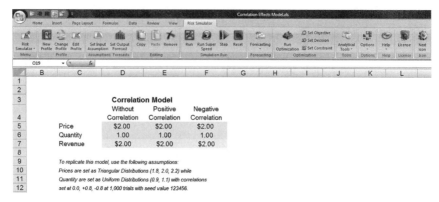

FIGURE 5.43 Correlation model.

This model illustrates the effects of correlated simulation versus uncorrelated simulation. That is, whether a pair of simulated assumptions is not correlated, positively correlated, or negatively correlated, the results can sometimes be very different. In addition, the simulated assumptions' raw data are extracted after the simulation and manual computations of their pairwise correlations are performed. The results indicate that the input correlations hold after the simulation.

Setting Up a Simulation's Input Assumptions and Output Forecasts Open the model *Risk Simulator | Example Models | 04 Correlation Risk Effects Model*. Go to the Correlation Model worksheet (Figure 5.43). Follow the instructions shown on the following pages to set up and run this model.

Copying, Pasting, and Deleting Simulation Assumptions and Forecasts We will replicate the assumptions and forecasts per the instructions on the worksheet by setting the input assumptions for price and quantity, and forecast outputs for revenue. When setting up the input assumptions, you can practice by setting up one assumption at a time, or set up a single assumption and then use the Risk Simulator copy and paste technique to replicate the assumptions across multiple cells at once. Follow these eight steps:

Procedures

1. Create a new profile: *Risk Simulator | New Profile* (or use the *New Profile* icon) and give it a name.
2. Select cell *D5* for the price without correlation. Click on *Risk Simulator | Set Input Assumption* (or use the *Set Input Assumption* icon), select the *Triangular* distribution, and set the parameters as *1.8, 2.0,* and *2.2* as instructed on the worksheet (Figure 5.44). Click *OK* when done.

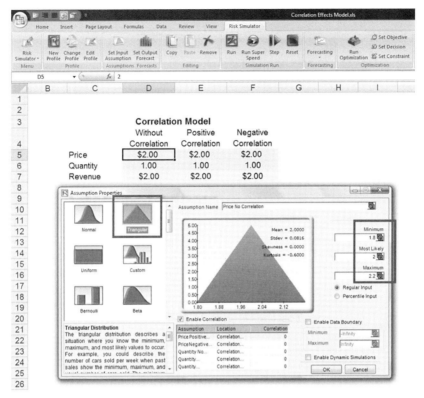

FIGURE 5.44 Setting an input assumption.

3. Select cell *D5* again, after the assumption has been set, and click on *Risk Simulator | Copy Parameter* (or use the *Copy* icon in the Risk Simulator toolbar). Make sure you *do not* use Excel's copy or Ctrl+C or right-click Copy, because using Excel copy will only copy the cell contents, color, equations, and font. Only by using Risk Simulator's copy can you copy the input assumption and its parameters.

4. Select cells *E5* and *F5* and click on *Risk Simulator | Paste Parameter* (or use the *Paste* icon in the Risk Simulator toolbar). Again, make sure you do not hit Enter and do not use Excel's paste function or Ctrl+V, as this will only paste the Excel cell contents and not the input assumptions (Figure 5.45).

5. Select cell *D6* and repeat the process above, this time using a *Uniform* distribution with *0.9* and *1.1* as the input parameters. Copy/paste the parameters for cells *E6* and *F6*.

6. Select cell *D7* and set it as an output forecast by clicking on *Risk Simulator | Set Output Forecast* (or use the *Set Output Forecast* icon), and

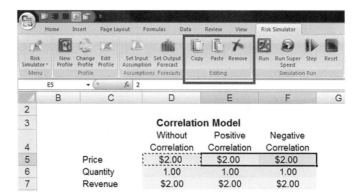

FIGURE 5.45 Simulation parameter copy and paste.

link the forecast name to cell *D4*. Then, select cell *D7* again, copy the parameter, and select cells *E7* and *F7* to paste the parameters using Risk Simulator copy and paste. Later, remember to review the tip presented in the next section for an important reminder on copy and pasting.

7. Next, set the correlations among the variables. There are two ways to set correlations: You can set correlations one pair of assumptions at a time or set them in a correlation matrix all at once. We will explore both approaches as follows:

a. As cell E5 is supposed to be correlated to cell E6, select cell *E5* and click on *Risk Simulator | Set Input Assumption* (or use the *Set Input Assumption* icon) once again. This time, look at the *pair-wise correlation section* (Figure 5.46). You may click and drag to enlarge the user interface form as well as to increase the width of the three columns for assumptions, location, and correlation. Find the input assumption for E6, enter the correlation of *0.8* and hit *ENTER* on the keyboard (Figure 5.46). Remember to hit Enter on the keyboard when you are done entering the correlation, otherwise the software will think that you are still typing in the input box. Click *OK* when done. For the sake of completeness, select cell E6 and again set an input assumption, and notice that by setting the assumption in cell E5 previously and correlating it to E6, cell E6 automatically correlates back to E5. Repeat the correlation process for cell F5 and F6.

b. Click on *Risk Simulator | Tools | Edit Correlations* and you will be provided with a correlation tool (Figure 5.47). Select the *Show Cell Name* checkbox and you can select the variables you wish to correlate or click on *Select All* to show all of them. In the correlation matrix section, enter the correlation value (correlations have to be between −1 and 1, and zeroes are allowed, of course). Notice that the correlation matrix shown is a full square matrix and the upper triangle mirrors

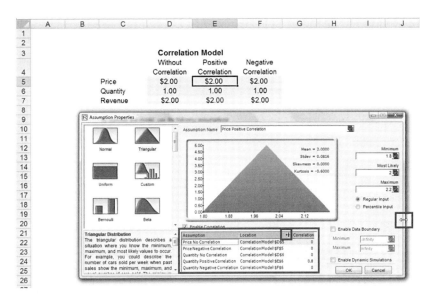

FIGURE 5.46 Pairwise correlations (manual).

the lower triangle. So, all you need to do is enter the correlation on either the upper or lower triangle and hit *Enter* on the keyboard. The value will be updated in both upper and lower triangles. Click *OK* when done. Also, note that the user interface allows you to *Paste* in a correlation matrix. This tool comes in handy if you wish the correlation matrix to be visible in Excel. When you have an existing matrix in Excel, you can copy the matrix and then paste it here (making sure the matrix you copied is square and the upper and lower triangles have identical pairwise correlation values). You are now done with setting correlations. For the sake of completeness, you can select any one of the input assumptions and set assumption again to make sure that the correlations are set up correctly (Figure 5.46).

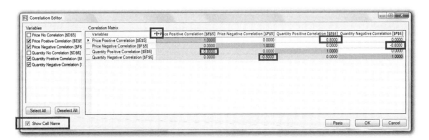

FIGURE 5.47 Pairwise correlations (matrix).

8. Run the simulation by clicking on *Risk Simulator | Run Simulation* (or use the *Run Simulation* icon) and interpret the results. Proceed to the next section for an interpretation of the results. You can also try running *Super Speed Simulation* for faster results.

TIP: For the copy and paste in Risk Simulator, this quick tip will come in handy when you are setting inputs and outputs on larger models. When you select a cell and use the Risk Simulator Copy function, it copies everything into Windows clipboard, including the cell's value, equation, function, color, font, and size, as well as Risk Simulator assumptions, forecasts, or decision variables. Then, as you apply the Risk Simulator Paste function, you have two options. The first option is to apply the Risk Simulator Paste directly, and all cell values, color, font, equation, functions *and* parameters will be pasted, akin to the example above. However, the second option is to first click *Escape* on the keyboard, and then apply the Risk Simulator Paste. *Escape* tells Risk Simulator that you only wish to paste the Risk Simulator assumption, forecast or decision variable, and *not* the cell's values, color, equation, function, font, and so forth. Hitting *Escape* before pasting allows you to maintain the target cell's values and computations, and pastes only the Risk Simulator parameters.

TIP: In Risk Simulator version 2010, you can also click on the *View Correlation Charts* tool to view sample representations of how different correlation levels look when variables are plotted on a scatter chart, and you can also use this tool to compute correlations of your raw data.

TIP: In Risk Simulator version 2010, you can select multiple cells with assumptions and forecasts, and use Risk Simulator copy and paste functionalities.

Running Correlated Simulations, Comparing Results between Correlated and Uncorrelated Models
The resulting simulation statistics indicate that the negatively correlated variables provide a tighter or smaller standard deviation or overall risk level on the model. This relationship exists because negative correlations provide a diversification effect on the variables and, hence, tend to make the standard deviation slightly smaller. Thus, we need to make sure to input correlations when there indeed are correlations between variables. Otherwise this interacting effect will not be accounted for in the simulation.

The positive correlation model has a larger standard deviation because a positive correlation tends to make both variables travel in the same direction, making the extreme ends wider and, hence, increases the overall risk. Therefore, the model without any correlations will have a standard deviation between the positive and negative correlation models.

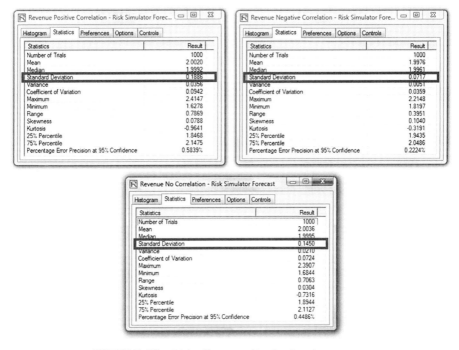

FIGURE 5.48 Risk effects on distributional moments.

Notice that the expected value or mean does not change much. In fact, if sufficient simulation trials are run, the theoretical and empirical values of the mean remain the same. The first moment (central tendency or expected value) does not change with correlations. Only the second moment (spread or risk and uncertainty) will change with correlations (Figure 5.48).

Note that this characteristic exists only in simple models with a positive relationship. That is, a Price × Quantity model is considered a "positive" relationship model (as are Price + Quantity), where a negative correlation decreases the range and a positive correlation increases the range. The opposite is true for negative relationship models. For instance, Price / Quantity or Price − Quantity would be a negative relationship model, where a positive correlation will reduce the range of the forecast variable, and a negative correlation will increase the range. Finally, for more complex models (e.g., larger models with multiple variables interacting with positive and negative relationships and sometimes with positive and negative correlations), the results are hard to predict and cannot be determined theoretically. Only by running a simulation can the true results of the range and outcomes be determined. In such a scenario, Tornado Analysis and Sensitivity Analysis would be more appropriate.

**Extracting and Manually Computing and Verifying the Assumptions'
Correlations** For additional exercise, run the simulation and then extract
the simulated data. Then run a correlation computation and see if the correlations are similar to what you have entered into Risk Simulator.

Procedures

1. Run the simulation: *Risk Simulator | Run Simulation* (or use the *Run
   Simulation* icon). Click *OK* when simulation is done.
2. Extract the data: *Risk Simulator | Tools | Data Extraction and Export*
   (or use the *Data Extraction* icon under the *Analytical Tools* ribbon).
   Select *New Excel Worksheet* and you can click the *Select All...* button
   repeatedly to select only the forecasts, only the assumptions, or all forecasts and assumptions at once (Figure 5.49). Let's just select *all* forecasts
   and assumptions and click *OK* to extract the data.
3. Go to the extracted data worksheet and use Excel's CORREL function
   to compute the pairwise correlations of the simulated data. For example,
   Figure 5.50 illustrates that the computed correlations are +0.8 and −0.8
   for the positive and negative correlation pairs, plus the uncorrelated pair

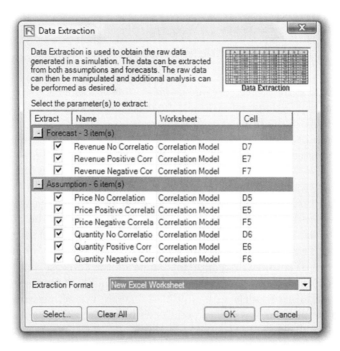

FIGURE 5.49 Data extraction.

	Revenue No Correlation	Revenue Positive Correlation	Revenue Negative Correlation	Price No Correlation	Price Positive Correlation	Price Negative Correlation	Quantity No Correlation	Quantity Positive Correlation	Quantity Negative Correlation			
2	2.08	1.77	2.00	2.08	1.95	1.89	1.00	0.91	1.06			
3	1.83	1.83	2.08	1.89	1.92	1.98	0.97	0.95	1.05	0.03	Equation: =CORREL(D2:D1001,G2:G1001)
4	2.10	2.10	2.06	2.05	2.02	1.89	1.03	1.04	1.09	0.80	Equation: =CORREL(E2:E1001,H2:H1001)
5	2.19	2.09	1.95	2.04	2.04	1.88	1.08	1.03	1.04	-0.80	Equation: =CORREL(F2:F1001,I2:I1001)
6	2.07	1.71	1.82	2.04	1.89	1.96	1.01	0.91	0.93			
7	1.92	2.07	1.89	2.09	1.98	2.02	0.92	1.05	0.93			
8	2.01	2.11	2.04	1.92	2.05	2.00	1.05	1.03	1.02			
9	2.05	1.71	1.93	2.05	1.87	1.86	1.00	0.91	1.04			
10	2.04	1.67	1.99	1.93	1.84	1.96	1.06	1.03	1.02			
11	1.95	2.13	1.94	1.95	2.06	1.90	1.00	1.03	1.02			
12	1.98	2.00	2.11	1.98	1.98	1.92	1.00	1.01	1.10			
13	1.80	1.91	2.03	1.91	1.99	2.00	0.94	0.96	1.02			
14	1.92	1.95	2.02	1.88	1.93	1.84	1.03	1.01	1.10			
15	2.11	2.04	2.01	2.17	2.01	1.83	0.98	1.02	1.09			
16	2.05	1.75	1.98	1.97	1.89	1.81	1.04	0.93	1.10			
17	2.13	2.02	2.12	1.94	2.04	2.01	1.10	0.99	1.05			
18	1.92	1.72	2.05	2.03	1.86	1.87	0.94	0.92	1.09			
19	1.79	1.79	1.94	1.92	1.94	1.90	0.93	0.92	0.98			
20	1.93	2.11	1.99	2.03	2.11	1.81	0.95	1.00	1.10			
21	2.07	2.17	1.94	2.10	2.10	2.09	0.98	1.03	0.93			
22	2.17	1.71	2.03	2.13	1.88	1.96	1.02	0.91	1.04			

FIGURE 5.50 Correlation of simulated values.

is close to zero (the correlation is never exactly equal to zero because of the randomness effect, and 0.03 is statistically significantly identical to zero in this case). In other words, the correlations we inputted originally are maintained in the simulation model.

Pearson's Product Moment Linear Correlation and Spearman's Nonlinear Rank Correlation Typically, when we use the term *correlation*, we usually mean a linear correlation. And, of course, correlations can take on any value between −1 and +1, inclusive, which means that the correlation coefficient has a sign (direction) and magnitude (strength). The problem arises when there is nonlinearity and we use linear correlations.

Figure 5.51 illustrates a few scatter charts with a pairwise X and Y variables (e.g., hours of study and school grades). If we draw an imaginary best-fitting line in the scatter diagram, we can see the approximate correlation (we will show a computation of correlation in a moment, but for now, let's just visualize). Part A shows a relatively high positive correlation coefficient (R) of about 0.7 as an increase in X means an increase in Y, so there is a positive slope and therefore a positive correlation. Part B shows an even stronger negative correlation (negatively sloped, an increase of X means a decrease of Y and vice versa). It has slightly higher magnitude because the dots are closer to the line. In fact, when the dots are exactly on the line, as in Part D, the correlation is +1 (if positively sloped) or −1 (if negatively sloped), indicating a perfect correlation. Part C shows a situation where the curve is perfectly flat, or has zero correlation, where, regardless of the X value, Y remains unchanged, indicating that there is no relationship. These are all basic and good.

The problem arises when there are nonlinear relationships (typically the case in a many real-life situations) as shown in Figure 5.52. Part E shows an exponential relationship between X and Y. If we use a nonlinear

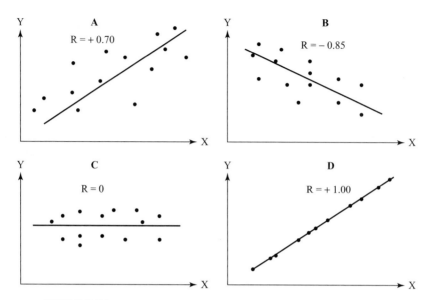

FIGURE 5.51   Correlation of simulated values (linear relationships).

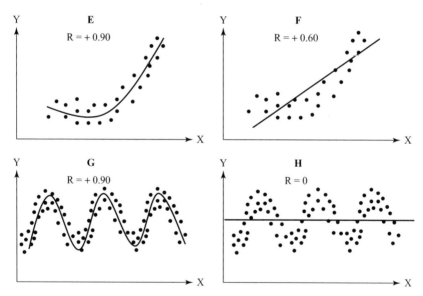

FIGURE 5.52   Correlation of simulated values (nonlinear relationships).

correlation, we get +0.9, but if we use a linear correlation, it is much lower at 0.6 (Part F), which means that there is information that is not picked up by the linear correlation. The situation gets a lot worse when we have a sinusoidal relationship, as in Parts G and H. The nonlinear correlation picks up the relationship nicely with a 0.9 correlation coefficient; using a linear correlation, the best-fitting line is literally a flat horizontal line, indicating zero correlation. However, just looking at the picture would tell you that there is a relationship. *So, we must therefore distinguish between linear and nonlinear correlations, because as we have seen in this exercise, correlation affects risk, and we are dealing with risk analysis!*

The linear correlation coefficient is also known as the Pearson's product moment correlation coefficient. It is computed by

$$R = \frac{\sum_{i=1}^{n} (X_i - \overline{X})(Y_i - \overline{Y})}{\sqrt{\sum_{i=1}^{n} (X_i - \overline{X})^2 (Y_i - \overline{Y})^2}}$$

and assumes that the underlying distribution is normal or near-normal such as the T-distribution. Therefore, this is a parametric correlation. You can use Excel's *CORREL* function to compute this effortlessly. The nonlinear correlation is the Spearman's nonparametric rank-based correlation, which does not assume any underlying distribution, making it a nonparametric measure. The approach to Spearman's nonlinear correlation is simple. Using the original data we first "linearize" the data and then apply the Pearson's correlation computation to get the Spearman's correlation. Typically, whenever there is nonlinear data, we can linearize it by either using a *LOG* function (or equivalently, an *LN* or natural log function) or a *RANK* function. The table below illustrates this effect. The original value is clearly nonlinear (it is 10^x where x is from 0 to 5). However, if you apply a log function, the data becomes linear (1, 2, 3, 4, 5), or when you apply ranks, the rank (either high to low or low to high) is also linear. Once we have linearized the data, we can apply the linear Pearson's correlation. To summarize, Spearman's nonparametric nonlinear correlation coefficient is obtained by first ranking the data and then applying Pearson's parametric linear correlation coefficient.

Value	LOG(Value)	RANK(Value)
1	0	1
10	1	2
100	2	3
1000	3	4
10000	4	5
100000	5	6

Pandora's Toolbox

This chapter deals with the Risk Simulator software's analytical tools. These analytical tools are discussed through example applications of the Risk Simulator software, complete with step-by-step illustrations. These tools are very valuable to analysts working in the realm of risk analysis. The applicability of each tool is discussed in detail in this chapter. All of the example files used in this chapter are found by starting Excel and going to the *Risk Simulator* menu and selecting *Example Models*. There are also multiple highly recommended step-by-step exercises at the end of this chapter that will provide detailed hands-on practice in the tools and techniques presented in this chapter, with more detailed interpretation of the results, as well as special tips and tricks.

TORNADO AND SENSITIVITY TOOLS IN SIMULATION

Theory

One of the powerful simulation tools is tornado analysis—it captures the static impacts of each variable on the outcome of the model; that is, the tool automatically perturbs each variable in the model a preset amount, captures the fluctuation on the model's forecast or final result, and lists the resulting perturbations ranked from the most significant to the least. Figures 6.1 through 6.6 illustrate the application of a tornado analysis. For instance, Figure 6.1 is a sample discounted cash-flow model where the input assumptions in the model are shown. The question is, what are the critical success drivers that affect the model's output the most? That is, what really drives the net present value of $96.63 or which input variable impacts this value the most?

The tornado chart tool can be obtained through *Simulation | Tools | Tornado Analysis*. To follow along the first example, open the *Tornado and Sensitivity Charts (Linear)* file in the examples folder. Figure 6.2 shows this sample model where cell G6, containing the net present value, is chosen as the

Discounted Cash Flow Model

Base Year	2005	Sum PV Net Benefits	$1,896.63	
Market Risk-Adjusted Discount Rate	15.00%	Sum PV Investments	$1,800.00	
Private-Risk Discount Rate	5.00%	Net Present Value	$96.63	
Annualized Sales Growth Rate	2.00%	Internal Rate of Return	18.80%	
Price Erosion Rate	5.00%	Return on Investment	5.37%	
Effective Tax Rate	40.00%			

	2005	2006	2007	2008	2009
Product A Avg Price/Unit	$10.00	$9.50	$9.03	$8.57	$8.15
Product B Avg Price/Unit	$12.25	$11.64	$11.06	$10.50	$9.98
Product C Avg Price/Unit	$15.15	$14.39	$13.67	$12.99	$12.34
Product A Sale Quantity ('000s)	50.00	51.00	52.02	53.06	54.12
Product B Sale Quantity ('000s)	35.00	35.70	36.41	37.14	37.89
Product C Sale Quantity ('000s)	20.00	20.40	20.81	21.22	21.65
Total Revenues	$1,231.75	$1,193.57	$1,156.57	$1,120.71	$1,085.97
Direct Cost of Goods Sold	$184.76	$179.03	$173.48	$168.11	$162.90
Gross Profit	$1,046.99	$1,014.53	$983.08	$952.60	$923.07
Operating Expenses	$157.50	$160.65	$163.86	$167.14	$170.48
Sales, General and Admin. Costs	$15.75	$16.07	$16.39	$16.71	$17.05
Operating Income (EBITDA)	$873.74	$837.82	$802.83	$768.75	$735.54
Depreciation	$10.00	$10.00	$10.00	$10.00	$10.00
Amortization	$3.00	$3.00	$3.00	$3.00	$3.00
EBIT	$860.74	$824.82	$789.83	$755.75	$722.54
Interest Payments	$2.00	$2.00	$2.00	$2.00	$2.00
EBT	$858.74	$822.82	$787.83	$753.75	$720.54
Taxes	$343.50	$329.13	$315.13	$301.50	$288.22
Net Income	$515.24	$493.69	$472.70	$452.25	$432.33
Noncash Depreciation Amortization	$13.00	$13.00	$13.00	$13.00	$13.00
Noncash: Change in Net Working Capital	$0.00	$0.00	$0.00	$0.00	$0.00
Noncash: Capital Expenditures	$0.00	$0.00	$0.00	$0.00	$0.00
Free Cash Flow	$528.24	$506.69	$485.70	$465.25	$445.33

Investment Outlay	$1,800.00				

Financial Analysis

Present Value of Free Cash Flow	$528.24	$440.60	$367.26	$305.91	$254.62
Present Value of Investment Outlay	$1,800.00	$0.00	$0.00	$0.00	$0.00
Net Cash Flows	($1,271.76)	$506.69	$485.70	$465.25	$445.33

FIGURE 6.1 Sample discounted cash flow model.

target result to be analyzed. The target cell's precedents in the model are used in creating the tornado chart. Precedents are all the input and intermediate variables that affect the outcome of the model. For instance, if the model consists of $A = B + C$, and where $C = D + E$, then B, D, and E are the precedents for A (C is not a precedent as it is only an intermediate calculated value). Figure 6.2 also shows the testing range of each precedent variable used to estimate the target result. If the precedent variables are simple inputs, then the testing range will be a simple perturbation based on the range chosen (e.g., the default is ±10 percent). Each precedent variable can be

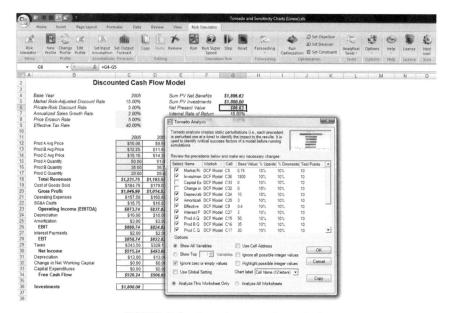

FIGURE 6.2   Running tornado analysis.

perturbed at different percentages if required. A wider range is important as it is better able to test extreme values rather than smaller perturbations around the expected values. In certain circumstances, extreme values may have a larger, smaller, or unbalanced impact (e.g., nonlinearities may occur where increasing or decreasing economies of scale and scope creep in for larger or smaller values of a variable) and only a wider range will capture this nonlinear impact.

Procedure

Use the following steps to create a tornado analysis:

1. Select the single output cell (i.e., a cell with a function or equation) in an Excel model (e.g., cell G6 is selected in our example).
2. Select *Risk Simulator | Tools | Tornado Analysis*.
3. Review the precedents and rename them as appropriate (renaming the precedents to shorter names allows a more visually pleasing tornado and spider chart) and click *OK*. Alternatively, click on *Use Cell Address* to apply cell locations as the variable names.

Tips and Additional Notes on Running a Tornado Analysis

Here are some tips on running tornado analysis and further details on the options available in the tornado analysis user interface (Figure 6.2):

- Tornado analysis should never be run just once. It is meant as a model diagnostic tool, which means that it should ideally be run several times on the same model. For instance, in a large model, Tornado can be run the first time using all of the default settings and all precedents should be shown (select *Show All Variables*). The result may be a large report and long (and potentially unsightly) tornado charts. Nonetheless, this analysis provides a great starting point to determine how many of the precedents are considered critical success factors. For example, the tornado chart may show that the first 5 variables have high impact on the output, while the remaining 200 variables have little to no impact, in which case, a second Tornado analysis is run showing fewer variables (e.g., select the *Show Top 10 Variables* if the first 5 are critical, thereby creating a satisfactory report and tornado chart that shows a contrast between the key factors and less critical factors. You should never show a tornado chart with only the key variables without showing some less critical variables as a contrast to their effects on the output). Finally, the default testing points can be increased from ±10% of the parameter to some larger value to test for nonlinearities (the spider chart will show nonlinear lines and tornado charts will be skewed to one side if the precedent effects are nonlinear).
- *Use Cell Address* is always a good idea if your model is large, allowing you to identify the location (worksheet name and cell address) of a precedent cell. If this option is not selected, the software will apply its own fuzzy logic in an attempt to determine the name of each precedent variable (sometimes the names might end up being confusing in a large model with repeated variables or the names might be too long, possibly making the tornado chart unsightly).
- The *Analyze This Worksheet* and *Analyze All Worksheets* options allow you to control whether the precedents should only be part of the current worksheet or include all worksheets in the same workbook. This option comes in handy when you are only attempting to analyze an output based on values in the current sheet versus performing a global search of all linked precedents across multiple worksheets in the same workbook.
- *Use Global Setting* is useful when you have a large model and you wish to test all the precedents at say, ±50% instead of the default 10%. Instead of having to change each precedent's test values one at a time,

you can select this option, change one setting, and *click somewhere else* in the user interface to change the entire list of the precedents. Deselecting this option will allow you to control the changing of test points one precedent at a time.

- *Ignore Zero or Empty Values* is an option turned on by default where precedent cells with zero or empty values will not be run in the tornado. This is the typical setting.
- *Highlight Possible Integer Values* is an option that quickly identifies all possible precedent cells that currently have integer inputs. This function is sometimes important if your model uses switches (e.g., functions such as *if* a cell is 1, then something happens, and *if* a cell has a 0 value, something else happens, or integers such as 1, 2, 3, and so forth, which you do not wish to test). For instance, ±10% of a flag switch value of 1 will return a test value of 0.9 and 1.1, both of which are irrelevant and incorrect input values in the model, and Excel may interpret the function as an error. This option, when selected, will quickly highlight potential problem areas for tornado analysis. You can determine which precedents to turn on or off manually, or you can use the *Ignore Possible Integer Values* to turn all of them off simultaneously.

Results Interpretation

Figure 6.3 shows the resulting tornado analysis report, which indicates that capital investment has the largest impact on net present value (NPV), followed by tax rate, average sale price and quantity demanded of the product lines, and so forth. The report contains four distinct elements:

1. Statistical summary listing the procedure performed.
2. A sensitivity table (Table 6.1) shows the starting NPV base value of $96.63 and how each input is changed (e.g., investment is changed from $1,800 to $1,980 on the upside with a +10 percent swing, and from $1,800 to $1,620 on the downside with a −10 percent swing). The resulting upside and downside values on NPV are −$83.37 and $276.63, with a total change of $360, making it the variable with the highest impact on NPV. The precedent variables are ranked from the highest impact to the lowest impact.
3. The spider chart (Figure 6.4) illustrates these effects graphically. The y-axis is the NPV target value whereas the x-axis depicts the percentage change on each of the precedent values (the central point is the base case value at $96.63 at 0 percent change from the base value of each precedent). Positively sloped lines indicate a positive relationship or effect while negatively sloped lines indicate a negative relationship

Statistical Summary

One of the powerful simulation tools is the tornado chart—it captures the static impacts of each variable on the outcome of the model. That is, the tool automatically perturbs each precedent variable in the model a user-specified preset amount, captures the fluctuation on the model's forecast or final result, and lists the resulting perturbations ranked from the most significant to the least. Precedents are all the input and intermediate variables that affect the outcome of the model. For instance, if the model consists of $A = B + C$, where $C = D + E$, then B, D, and E are the precedents for A (C is not a precedent as it is only an intermediate calculated value). The range and number of values perturbed is user-specified and can be set to test extreme values rather than smaller perturbations around the expected values. In certain circumstances, extreme values may have a larger, smaller, or unbalanced impact (e.g., nonlinearities may occur where increasing or decreasing economies of scale and scope creep occurs for larger or smaller values of a variable) and only a wider range will capture this nonlinear impact.

A tornado chart lists all the inputs that drive the model, starting from the input variable that has the most effect on the results. The chart is obtained by perturbing each precedent input at some consistent range (e.g., ± 10% from the base case) one at a time, and comparing their results to the base case. A spider chart looks like a spider with a central body and its many legs protruding. The positively sloped lines indicate a positive relationship, while a negatively sloped line indicates a negative relationship. Further, spider charts can be used to visualize linear and nonlinear relationships. The tornado and spider charts help identify the critical success factors of an output cell in order to identify the inputs to simulate. The identified critical variables that are uncertain are the ones that should be simulated. Do not waste time simulating variables that are neither uncertain nor have little impact on the results.

Result

	Base Value: 96.6261638553219			Input Changes		
Precedent Cell	Output Downside	Output Upside	Effective Range	Input Downside	Input Upside	Base Case Value
Investment	$276.63	($83.37)	360.00	$1,620.00	$1,980.00	$1,800.00
Tax Rate	$219.73	($26.47)	246.20	36.00%	44.00%	40.00%
A Price	$3.43	$189.83	186.40	$9.00	$11.00	$10.00
B Price	$16.71	$176.55	159.84	$11.03	$13.48	$12.25
A Quantity	$23.18	$170.07	146.90	45.00	55.00	50.00
B Quantity	$30.53	$162.72	132.19	31.50	38.50	35.00
C Price	$40.15	$153.11	112.96	$13.64	$16.67	$15.15
C Quantity	$48.05	$145.20	97.16	18.00	22.00	20.00
Discount Rate	$138.24	$57.03	81.21	13.50%	16.50%	15.00%
Price Erosion	$116.80	$76.64	40.16	4.50%	5.50%	5.00%
Sales Growth	$90.59	$102.69	12.10	1.80%	2.20%	2.00%
Depreciation	$95.08	$98.17	3.08	$9.00	$11.00	$10.00
Interest	$97.09	$96.16	0.93	$1.80	$2.20	$2.00
Amortization	$96.16	$97.09	0.93	$2.70	$3.30	$3.00
Capex	$96.63	$96.63	0.00	$0.00	$0.00	$0.00
Net Capital	$96.63	$96.63	0.00	$0.00	$0.00	$0.00

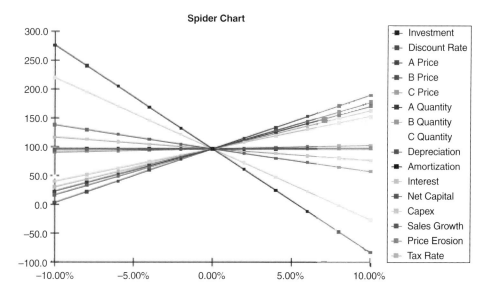

FIGURE 6.3 Tornado analysis report.

TABLE 6.1 Sensitivity Table

	Base Value: 96.62616385532...19			Input Changes		
Precedent Cell	Output Downside	Output Upside	Effective Range	Input Downside	Input Upside	Base Case Value
Investment	$276.63	($83.37)	360.00	$1,620.00	$1,980.00	$1,800.00
Tax Rate	$219.73	($26.47)	246.20	36.00%	44.00%	40.00%
A Price	$3.43	$189.83	186.40	$9.00	$11.00	$10.00
B Price	$16.71	$176.55	159.84	$11.03	$13.48	$12.25
A Quantity	$23.18	$170.07	146.90	45.00	55.00	50.00
B Quantity	$30.53	$162.72	132.19	31.50	38.50	35.00
C Price	$40.15	$153.11	112.96	$13.64	$16.67	$15.15
C Quantity	$48.05	$145.20	97.16	18.00	22.00	20.00
Discount Rate	$138.24	$57.03	81.21	13.50%	16.50%	15.00%
Price Erosion	$116.80	$76.64	40.16	4.50%	5.50%	5.00%
Sales Growth	$90.59	$102.69	12.10	1.80%	2.20%	2.00%
Depreciation	$95.08	$98.17	3.08	$9.00	$11.00	$10.00
Interest	$97.09	$96.16	0.93	$1.80	$2.20	$2.00
Amortization	$96.16	$97.09	0.93	$2.70	$3.30	$3.00
Capex	$96.63	$96.63	0.00	$0.00	$0.00	$0.00
Net Capital	$96.63	$96.63	0.00	$0.00	$0.00	$0.00

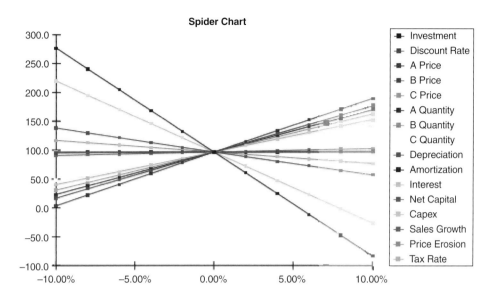

Spider Chart

FIGURE 6.4 Spider chart.

(e.g., investment is negatively sloped, which means that the higher the investment level, the lower the NPV). The absolute value of the slope indicates the magnitude of the effect computed as the percentage change in the result given a percentage change in the precedent (a steep line indicates a higher impact on the NPV y-axis given a change in the precedent x-axis).

4. The tornado chart (Figure 6.5) illustrates the results in another graphical manner, where the highest impacting precedent is listed first. The x-axis is the NPV value with the center of the chart being the base case condition. Green (lighter) bars in the chart indicate a positive effect while red (darker) bars indicate a negative effect. Therefore, for investments, the red (darker) bar on the right side indicates a negative effect of investment on higher NPV—in other words, capital investment and NPV are negatively correlated. The opposite is true for price and quantity of products A to C (their green or lighter bars are on the right side of the chart).

Notes

Remember that tornado analysis is a *static* sensitivity analysis applied on each input variable in the model; that is, each variable is perturbed individually and the resulting effects are tabulated. This makes tornado analysis a key component to execute before running a simulation. One of the very

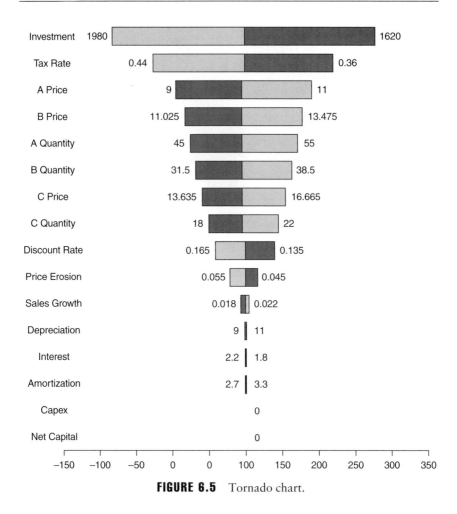

FIGURE 6.5   Tornado chart.

first steps in risk analysis is where the most important impact drivers in the model are captured and identified. The next step is to identify which of these important impact drivers are uncertain. These uncertain impact drivers are the critical success drivers of a project, where the results of the model depend on these critical success drivers. These variables are the ones that should be simulated. Do not waste time simulating variables that are neither uncertain nor have little impact on the results. Tornado charts assist in identifying these critical success drivers quickly and easily. Following this example, it might be that price and quantity should be simulated, assuming that the required investment and effective tax rate are both known in advance and unchanging.

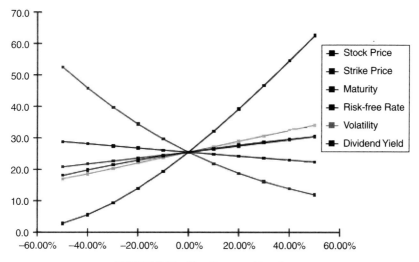

FIGURE 6.6 Nonlinear spider chart.

Although the tornado chart is easier to read, the spider chart is important to determine if there are any nonlinearities in the model. For instance, Figure 6.6 shows another spider chart where nonlinearities are fairly evident (the lines on the graph are not straight but curved). The example model used is *Tornado and Sensitivity Charts (Nonlinear)*, which applies the Black–Scholes option pricing model. Such nonlinearities cannot be ascertained from a tornado chart as readily, and may be important information in the model or provide decision makers important insight into the model's dynamics. For instance, in this Black–Scholes model, the fact that stock price and strike price are nonlinearly related to the option value is important to know. This characteristic implies that option value will not increase or decrease proportionally to the changes in stock or strike price, and that there might be some interactions between these two prices as well as other variables. As another example, an engineering model depicting nonlinearities might indicate that a particular part or component, when subjected to a high enough force or tension, will break. Clearly, it is important to understand such nonlinearities.

SENSITIVITY ANALYSIS

Theory

A related feature is sensitivity analysis. While tornado analysis (tornado charts and spider charts) applies static perturbations *before* a simulation

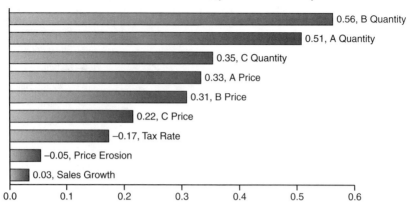

FIGURE 6.7   Sensitivity chart without correlations.

run, sensitivity analysis applies dynamic perturbations created *after* the simulation run. Tornado and spider charts are the results of static perturbations, meaning that each precedent or assumption variable is perturbed a preset amount one at a time, and the fluctuations in the results are tabulated. In contrast, sensitivity charts are the results of dynamic perturbations in the sense that multiple assumptions are perturbed simultaneously and their interactions in the model and correlations among variables are captured in the fluctuations of the results. Tornado charts, therefore, identify which variables drive the results the most and, hence, are suitable for simulation, whereas sensitivity charts identify the impact to the results when multiple interacting variables are simulated together in the model. This effect is clearly illustrated in Figure 6.7. Notice that the ranking of critical success drivers is similar to the tornado chart in the previous examples. However, if correlations are added between the assumptions, Figure 6.8 shows a very different picture. Notice, for instance, price erosion had little impact on NPV, but when some of the input assumptions are correlated, the interaction that exists between these correlated variables makes price erosion have more impact. Note that tornado analysis cannot capture these correlated dynamic relationships. Only after a simulation is run will such relationships become evident in a sensitivity analysis. A tornado chart's presimulation critical success factors will therefore sometimes be different from a sensitivity chart's postsimulation critical success factor. The postsimulation critical success factors should be the ones that are of interest as these more readily capture the model precedents' interactions.

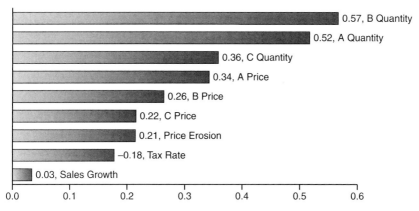

Nonlinear Rank Correlation (Net Present Value)

0.57, B Quantity

0.52, A Quantity

0.36, C Quantity

0.34, A Price

0.26, B Price

0.22, C Price

0.21, Price Erosion

−0.18, Tax Rate

0.03, Sales Growth

0.0 0.1 0.2 0.3 0.4 0.5 0.6

FIGURE 6.8   Sensitivity chart with correlations.

Procedure

Use the following steps to create a sensitivity analysis:

1. Open or create a model, define assumptions and forecasts, and run the simulation—the example here uses the Tornado and Sensitivity Charts (Linear) file.
2. Select *Risk Simulator | Tools | Sensitivity Analysis*.
3. Select the forecast of choice to analyze and click *OK* (Figure 6.9).

Note that sensitivity analysis cannot be run unless assumptions and forecasts have been defined, and a simulation has been run.

Results Interpretation

The results of the sensitivity analysis comprise a report and two key charts. The first is a nonlinear rank correlation chart (Figure 6.10) that ranks from highest to lowest the assumption–forecast correlation pairs. These correlations are nonlinear and nonparametric, making them free of any distributional requirements (i.e., an assumption with a Weibull distribution can be compared to another with a Beta distribution). The results from this chart are fairly similar to that of the tornado analysis seen previously (of course, without the capital investment value, which we decided was a known value and hence was not simulated), with one special exception. Tax rate was relegated to a much lower position in the sensitivity analysis chart

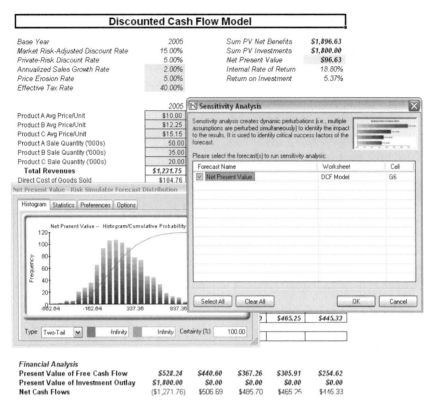

FIGURE 6.9   Running sensitivity analysis.

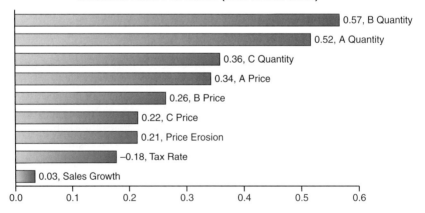

FIGURE 6.10   Rank correlation chart.

(Figure 6.10) as compared to the tornado chart (Figure 6.5). This is because by itself, tax rate will have a significant impact, but once the other variables are interacting in the model, it appears that tax rate has less of a dominant effect (because tax rate has a smaller distribution as historical tax rates tend not to fluctuate too much, and also because tax rate is a straight percentage value of the income before taxes, where other precedent variables have a larger effect on NPV). This example proves that performing sensitivity analysis after a simulation run is important to ascertain if there are any interactions in the model and if the effects of certain variables still hold. The second chart (Figure 6.11) illustrates the percent variation explained; that is, of the fluctuations in the forecast, how much of the variation can be explained by each of the assumptions after accounting for all the interactions among variables? Notice that the sum of all variations explained is usually close to 100 percent (sometimes other elements impact the model, but they cannot be captured here directly), and if correlations exist, the sum may sometimes exceed 100 percent (due to the interaction effects that are cumulative).

Notes

Tornado analysis is performed before a simulation run while sensitivity analysis is performed after a simulation run. Spider charts in tornado analysis can consider nonlinearities while rank correlation charts in sensitivity analysis can account for nonlinear and distributional-free conditions.

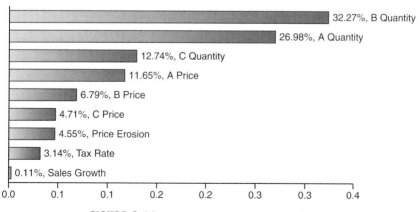

Percent Variation Explained (Net Present Value)

FIGURE 6.11 Contribution to variance chart.

DISTRIBUTIONAL FITTING: SINGLE VARIABLE AND MULTIPLE VARIABLES

Theory

Another powerful simulation tool is distributional fitting; that is, which distribution does an analyst or engineer use for a particular input variable in a model? What are the relevant distributional parameters? If no historical data exist, then the analyst must make assumptions about the variables in question. One approach is to use the Delphi method, where a group of experts are tasked with estimating the behavior of each variable. For instance, a group of mechanical engineers can be tasked with evaluating the extreme possibilities of a spring coil's diameter through rigorous experimentation or guesstimates. These values can be used as the variable's input parameters (e.g., uniform distribution with extreme values between 0.5 and 1.2). When testing is not possible (e.g., market share and revenue growth rate), management can still make estimates of potential outcomes and provide the best-case, most-likely case, and worst-case scenarios, whereupon a triangular or custom distribution can be created.

However, if reliable historical data are available, distributional fitting can be accomplished. Assuming that historical patterns hold and that history tends to repeat itself, then historical data can be used to find the best-fitting distribution with their relevant parameters to better define the variables to be simulated. Figure 6.12, Figure 6.13, and Figure 6.14 illustrate a distributional-fitting example. The following illustration uses the *Data Fitting* file in the examples folder.

Procedure

Use the following steps to perform a distribution fitting model:

1. Open a spreadsheet with existing data for fitting (e.g., use the Data Fitting example file).
2. Select the data you wish to fit not including the variable name (data should be in a single column with multiple rows).
3. Select *Risk Simulator | Tools | Distributional Fitting (Single-Variable)*.
4. Select the specific distributions you wish to fit to or keep the default where all distributions are selected and click *OK* (Figure 6.12).
5. Review the results of the fit, choose the relevant distribution you want, and click *OK* (Figure 6.13).

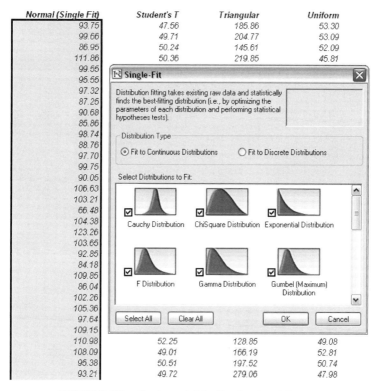

Normal (Single Fit)	Student's T	Triangular	Uniform
93.75	47.56	185.86	53.30
99.66	49.71	204.77	53.09
86.95	50.24	145.61	52.09
111.86	50.36	219.85	45.81
99.55			
95.55			
97.32			
87.25			
90.68			
85.86			
98.74			
88.76			
97.70			
99.75			
90.05			
106.63			
103.21			
66.48			
104.38			
123.26			
103.65			
92.85			
84.18			
109.85			
86.04			
102.26			
105.36			
97.64			
109.15			
110.98	52.25	128.85	49.08
108.09	49.01	166.19	52.81
95.38	50.51	197.52	50.74
93.21	49.72	279.06	47.98

FIGURE 6.12   Single-variable distributional fitting.

Results Interpretation

The null hypothesis (H_o) being tested is such that the fitted distribution is the same distribution as the population from which the sample data to be fitted come. Thus, if the computed p-value is lower than a critical alpha level (typically 0.10 or 0.05), then the distribution is the wrong distribution. Conversely, the *higher the p-value, the better the distribution fits the data*. Roughly, you can think of p-value as a *percentage explained*; that is, if the p-value is 0.9727 (Figure 6.13), then setting a normal distribution with a mean of 99.28 and a standard deviation of 10.17 explains about 97.27 percent of the variation in the data, indicating an especially good fit. The data was from a 1,000-trial simulation in Risk Simulator based on a normal distribution with a mean of 100 and a standard deviation of 10. Because only 1,000 trials were simulated, the resulting distribution is fairly close to the specified distributional parameters, and in this case, about a 97.27 percent precision.

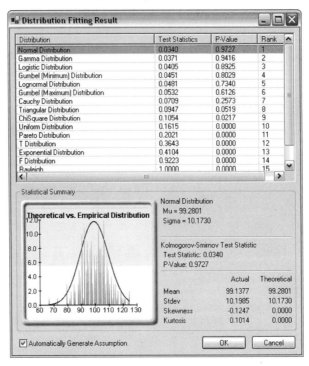

FIGURE 6.13   Distributional fitting result.

Both the results (Figure 6.13) and the report (Figure 6.14) show the test statistic, p-value, theoretical statistics (based on the selected distribution), empirical statistics (based on the raw data), the original data (to maintain a record of the data used), and the assumption complete with the relevant distributional parameters (i.e., if you selected the option to automatically generate assumption and if a simulation profile already exists). The results also rank all the selected distributions and how well they fit the data.

Fitting Multiple Variables

For fitting multiple variables, the process is fairly similar to fitting individual variables. However, the data should be arranged in columns (i.e., each variable is arranged as a column) and all the variables are fitted. The same analysis is performed when fitting multiple variables as when single variables are fitted. The difference here is that only the final report will be generated and you do not get to review each variable's distributional rankings. If the rankings are important, run the single-variable fitting procedure instead, on one variable at a time.

Statistical Summary

Fitted Assumption   99.14

Fitted Distribution   Normal Distribution
    Mu   99.28
    Sigma   10.17

Kolmogorov-Smirnov Statistic   0.03
P-Value for Test Statistic   0.9727

	Actual	Theoretical
Mean	99.28	99.28
Standard Deviation	10.17	10.17
Skewness	0.00	0.00
Excess Kurtosis	0.00	0.00

Theoretical vs. Empirical Distribution

Original Fitted Data

93.75	99.66	86.95	11.86	99.55	95.55	97.32	87.25	90.68	85.86	98.74	88.76	97.70
99.75	90.05	106.63	103.21	66.48	104.38	123.26	103.65	92.85	84.18	109.85	86.04	102.26
105.36	97.64	109.15	110.98	108.09	95.38	93.21	83.86	100.17	110.17	103.72	120.52	95.09
115.18	83.64	90.23	92.44	92.37	92.70	110.81	72.67	104.23	96.47	121.15	94.92	77.26
103.45	96.75	93.91	101.91	134.14	90.95	107.13	92.02	96.43	96.35	88.30	108.48	113.50
101.40	104.72	102.43	113.59	124.15	109.24	105.34	104.57	97.83	94.39	116.19	84.66	101.17
106.13	107.17	95.83	106.67	92.42	79.64	94.15	106.00	113.45	92.63	94.51	93.05	96.19
100.85	83.34	111.82	118.12	87.17	103.66	106.93	82.45	102.74	86.82	106.68	89.61	94.56
101.34	91.32	102.02	82.51	104.46	84.72	105.05	108.40	106.59	109.43	92.49	94.52	94.00
105.92	88.13	96.41	101.45	79.93	89.68	102.91	114.95	92.58	94.05	107.90	111.05	90.58
97.09	105.44	94.95	102.55	77.41	108.53	90.54	100.41	106.83	99.63	79.71	89.32	116.30
98.27	101.73	90.84	74.45	102.24	103.34	96.51	114.55	93.94	106.29	102.95	112.73	98.09
108.20	105.80	106.48	102.88	104.93	103.00	99.10	108.52	101.31	88.17	90.62	96.53	106.03
109.12	104.23	90.34	95.12	102.03	100.00	118.17	99.06	81.89	104.29	92.68	114.69	102.49
119.21	106.20	88.26	92.45	105.15	103.79	100.84	95.19	85.10	97.25	87.65	97.58	111.44
99.52	89.83	97.86	90.96	97.14								

FIGURE 6.14 Distributional fitting report.

Procedure

The procedure for fitting multiple variables is as follows:

1. Open a spreadsheet with existing data for fitting.
2. Select the data you wish to fit (data should be in multiple columns with multiple rows).
3. Select *Risk Simulator | Tools | Distributional Fitting (Multi-Variable)*.
4. Review the data, choose the types of distributions you want to fit to, and click *OK*.

Notes

Notice that the statistical ranking methods used in the distributional fitting routines are the chi-square test and Kolmogorov–Smirnov test. The former is used to test discrete distributions and the latter, continuous distributions. Briefly, a hypothesis test coupled with the maximum likelihood procedure with an internal optimization routine is used to find the best-fitting parameters on each distribution tested and the results are ranked from the best fit to the worst fit. There are other distributional fitting tests such as the Anderson–Darling and Shapiro–Wilks; however, these tests are very sensitive parametric tests and are highly inappropriate in Monte Carlo simulation distribution-fitting routines when different distributions are being tested. Due to their parametric requirements, these tests are most suited for testing normal distributions and distributions with normal-like behaviors (e.g., binomial distribution with a high number of trials and symmetrical probabilities) and will provide less accurate results when performed on non-normal distributions. Take great care when using such parametric tests. The Kolmogorov–Smirnov and chi-square tests employed in Risk Simulator are nonparametric and semiparametric in nature and are better suited for fitting normal and nonnormal distributions.

BOOTSTRAP SIMULATION

Theory

Bootstrap simulation is a simple technique that estimates the reliability or accuracy of forecast statistics or other sample raw data. Bootstrap simulation can be used to answer a lot of confidence- and precision-based questions in simulation. For instance, suppose an identical model (with identical assumptions and forecasts but without any random seeds) is run by 100 different people. The results will clearly be slightly different. The question is, if we collected all the statistics from these 100 people, how will the mean be distributed, or the median, or the skewness, or excess kurtosis? Suppose one person has a mean value of, say, 1.50, while another 1.52. Are these two values statistically significantly different from one another or are they statistically similar and the slight difference is due entirely to random chance? What about 1.53? So, how far is far enough to say that the values are statistically different? In addition, if a model's resulting skewness is –0.19, is this forecast distribution negatively skewed or is it statistically close enough to zero to state that this distribution is symmetrical and not skewed? Thus, if we bootstrapped this forecast 100 times, that is, run a 1,000-trial simulation for 100 times and collect the 100 skewness coefficients, the skewness distribution would indicate how far zero is away from –0.19. If the 90 percent confidence on the bootstrapped skewness distribution contains the value zero, then we can state that on a 90 percent confidence level, this distribution is symmetrical and not skewed, and the value –0.19 is statistically close enough to zero. Otherwise, if zero falls outside of this 90 percent confidence area, then this distribution is negatively skewed. The same analysis can be applied to excess kurtosis and other statistics.

Essentially, bootstrap simulation is a hypothesis testing tool. Classical methods used in the past relied on mathematical formulas to describe the accuracy of sample statistics. These methods assume that the distribution of a sample statistic approaches a normal distribution, making the calculation of the statistic's standard error or confidence interval relatively easy. However, when a statistic's sampling distribution is not normally distributed or easily found, these classical methods are difficult to use. In contrast, bootstrapping analyzes sample statistics empirically by repeatedly sampling the data and creating distributions of the different statistics from each sampling. The classical methods of hypothesis testing are available in Risk Simulator and are explained in the next section. Classical methods provide higher power in their tests but rely on normality assumptions and can only be used to test the mean and variance of a distribution, as compared to bootstrap simulation, which provides lower power but is nonparametric and distribution-free, and can be used to test any distributional statistic.

Procedure

Use the following steps to run a bootstrap simulation:

1. Run a simulation with assumptions and forecasts.
2. Select *Risk Simulator | Tools | Nonparametric Bootstrap*.
3. Select only *one* forecast to bootstrap, select the statistic(s) to bootstrap, and enter the number of bootstrap trials and click *OK* (Figure 6.15).

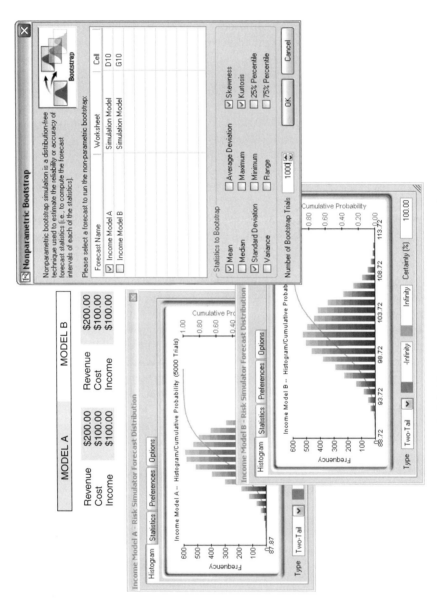

FIGURE 6.15 Nonparametric bootstrap simulation.

Results Interpretation

Figure 6.16 illustrates some sample bootstrap results. For instance, the 90 percent confidence for the skewness statistic is between –0.0189 and 0.0952, such that the value 0 falls within this confidence, indicating that on a 90 percent confidence, the skewness of this forecast is not statistically significantly different from zero, or that this distribution can be considered as symmetrical and not skewed. Conversely, if the value 0 falls outside of this confidence, then the opposite is true: The distribution is skewed (positively skewed if the forecast statistic is positive, and negatively skewed if the forecast statistic is negative). The example file used was *Hypothesis Testing and Bootstrap Simulation*.

Notes

The term *bootstrap* comes from the saying, "to pull oneself up by one's own bootstraps," and is applicable because this method uses the distribution of statistics themselves to analyze the statistics' accuracy. Nonparametric simulation is simply randomly picking golf balls from a large basket with replacement where each golf ball is based on a historical data point. Suppose there are 365 golf balls in the basket (representing 365 historical data points). Imagine if you will that the value of each golf ball picked at random is written on a large whiteboard. The results of the 365 balls picked with replacement are written in the first column of the board with 365 rows of numbers. Relevant statistics (mean, median, mode, standard deviation, and so forth) are calculated on these 365 rows. The process is then repeated, say, five thousand times. The whiteboard will now be filled with 365 rows and 5,000 columns. Hence, 5,000 sets of statistics (that is, there will be 5,000 means, 5,000 medians, 5,000 modes, 5,000 standard deviations, and so forth) are tabulated and their distributions shown. The relevant *statistics of the statistics* are then tabulated, where from these results one can ascertain how confident the simulated statistics are. Finally, bootstrap results are important because according to the *Law of Large Numbers* and *Central Limit Theorem* in statistics, the mean of the sample means is an unbiased estimator and approaches the true population mean when the sample size increases.

HYPOTHESIS TESTING

Theory

A hypothesis test is performed when testing the means and variances of two distributions to determine if they are statistically identical or statistically

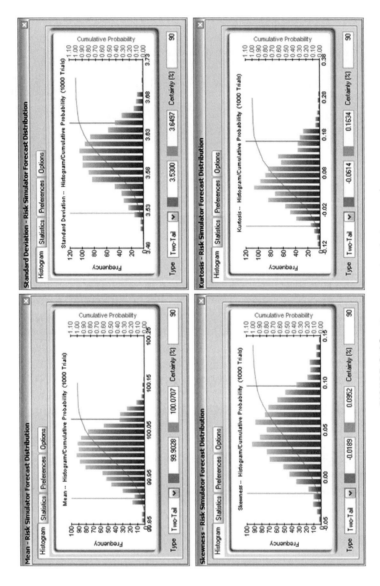

FIGURE 6.16 Bootstrap simulation results.

different from one another; that is, to see if the differences between the means and variances of two different forecasts that occur are based on random chance or if they are, in fact, statistically significantly different from one another.

This analysis is related to bootstrap simulation with several differences. Classical hypothesis testing uses mathematical models and is based on theoretical distributions. This means that the precision and power of the test is higher than bootstrap simulation's empirically based method of simulating a simulation and letting the data tell the story. However, the classical hypothesis tests are only applicable for testing two distributions' means and variances (and by extension, standard deviations) to see if they are statistically identical or different. In contrast, nonparametric bootstrap simulation can be used to test for any distributional statistics, making it more useful, but the drawback is its lower testing power. Risk Simulator provides both techniques from which to choose.

Procedure

Use the following steps to run a hypothesis test:

1. Run a simulation with at least two forecasts.
2. Select *Risk Simulator | Tools | Hypothesis Testing*.
3. Select the two forecasts to test, select the type of hypothesis test you wish to run, and click *OK* (Figure 6.17).

Results Interpretation

A two-tailed hypothesis test is performed on the null hypothesis (H_o) such that the two variables' population means are statistically identical to one another. The alternative hypothesis (H_a) is such that the population means are statistically different from one another. If the calculated p-values are less than or equal to 0.01, 0.05, or 0.10 alpha test levels, it means that the null hypothesis is rejected, which implies that the forecast means are statistically significantly different at the 1 percent, 5 percent, and 10 percent significance levels. If the null hypothesis is not rejected when the p-values are high, the means of the two forecast distributions are statistically similar to one another. The same analysis is performed on variances of two forecasts at a time using the pairwise F-test. If the p-values are small, then the variances (and standard deviations) are statistically different from one another. Otherwise, for large p-values, the variances are statistically identical to one another. See Figure 6.18. The example file used was *Hypothesis Testing and Bootstrap Simulation*.

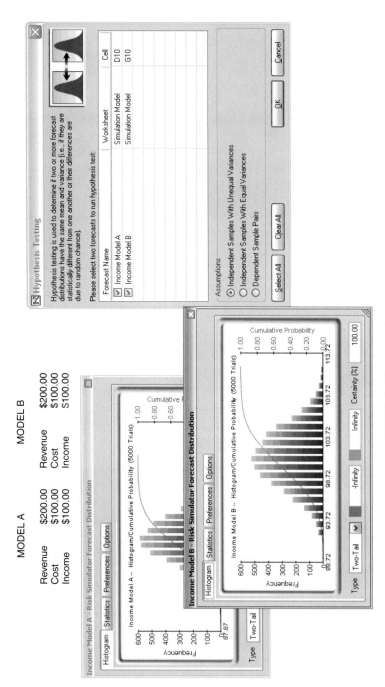

FIGURE 6.17 Hypothesis testing.

Hypothesis Test on the Means and Variances of Two Forecasts

Statistical Summary

A hypothesis test is performed when testing the means and variances of two distributions to determine if they are statistically identical or statistically different from one another; that is, to see if the differences between two means and two variances that occur are based on random chance or they are, in fact, different from one another. The two-variable t-test with unequal variances (the population variance of forecast 1 is expected to be different from the population variance of forecast 2) is appropriate when the forecast distributions are from different populations (e.g., data collected from two different geographical locations, two different operating business units, and so forth). The two variable t-test with equal variances (the population variance of forecast 1 is expected to be equal to the population variance of forecast 2) is appropriate when the forecast distributions are from similar populations (e.g., data collected from two different engine designs with similar specifications, and so forth). The paired dependent two-variable t-test is appropriate when the forecast distributions are from similar populations (e.g., data collected from the same group of customers but on different occasions, and so forth).

A two-tailed hypothesis test is performed on the null hypothesis H_o such that the two variables' population means are statistically identical to one another. The alternative hypothesis is that the population means are statistically different from one another. If the calculated p-values are less than or equal to 0.01, 0.05, or 0.10, the hypothesis is rejected, which implies that the forecast means are statistically significantly different at the 1%, 5%, and 10% significance levels. If the null hypothesis is not rejected when the p-values are high, the means of the two forecast distributions are statistically similar to one another. The same analysis is performed on variances of two forecasts at a time using the pairwise F-Test. If the p-values are small, then the variances (and standard deviations) are statistically different from one another, otherwise, for large p-values, the variances are statistically identical to one another.

Result

Hypothesis Test Assumption	Unequal Variances
Computed t-statistic:	−0.32947
P-value for t-statistic:	0.74181
Computed F-statistic:	1.026723
P-value for F-statistic:	0.351212

FIGURE 6.18   Hypothesis testing results.

Notes

The two-variable t-test with unequal variances (the population variance of forecast 1 is expected to be different from the population variance of forecast 2) is appropriate when the forecast distributions are from different populations (e.g., data collected from two different geographical locations or two different operating business units). The two-variable t-test with equal variances (the population variance of forecast 1 is expected to be equal to the population variance of forecast 2) is appropriate when the forecast distributions are from similar populations (e.g., data collected from two different engine designs with similar specifications). The paired dependent two-variable t-test is appropriate when the forecast distributions are from exactly the same population and subjects (e.g., data collected from the same group of patients before an experimental drug was used and after the drug was applied).

DATA EXTRACTION, SAVING SIMULATION RESULTS, AND GENERATING REPORTS

A simulation's raw data can be very easily extracted using Risk Simulator's *Data Extraction* routine. Both assumptions and forecasts can be extracted, but a simulation must first be run. The extracted data can then be used for a variety of other analyses and the data can be extracted to different formats—for use in spreadsheets, databases, and other software products.

Procedure

To extract a simulation's raw data, use the following steps:

1. Open or create a model, define assumptions and forecasts, and run the simulation.
2. Select *Risk Simulator | Tools | Data Extraction*.
3. Select the assumptions and/or forecasts you wish to extract the data from and click *OK*.

The simulated data can be extracted and saved to an Excel worksheet, a text file (for easy import into other software applications), or as a *RiskSim* file, which can be reopened as Risk Simulator forecast charts at a later date. Finally, you can create a simulation report of all the assumptions and forecasts in your model by going to *Risk Simulator | Tools | Create Report*. This is an efficient way to gather all the simulation inputs in one concise report.

CUSTOM MACROS

Simulation can also be run while harnessing the power of Visual Basic for Applications (VBA) in Excel. For instance, the examples in Chapter 3 on running models with VBA codes can be used in tandem with Risk Simulator. For an illustration of how to set the macros or customized functions to run with simulation, see the VBA Macro hands-on exercise (Retirement Funding with Inflation) at the end of this chapter.

DISTRIBUTIONAL ANALYSIS TOOL

The distributional analysis tool is a statistical probability tool in Risk Simulator that is rather useful in a variety of settings. It can be used to compute the probability density function (PDF), which is also called the probability mass function (PMF) for discrete distributions (these terms are used interchangeably), where given some distribution and its parameters, we can determine the probability of occurrence given some outcome x. In addition, the cumulative distribution function (CDF) can be computed, which is the

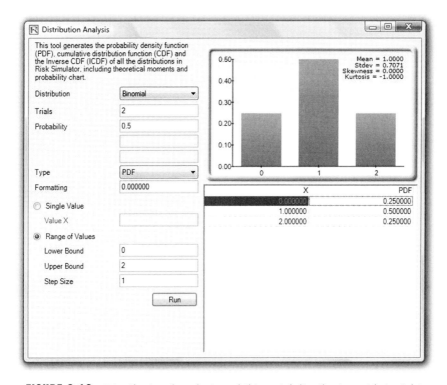

FIGURE 6.19   Distributional analysis tool (binomial distribution with 2 trials).

sum of the PDF values up to this x value. Finally, the inverse cumulative distribution function (ICDF) is used to compute the value x given the cumulative probability of occurrence. The following pages provide example uses of PDF, CDF, and ICDF. Also remember to try some of the exercises at the end of this chapter for more hands-on applications of probability distribution analysis using this tool.

This tool is accessible via *Risk Simulator | Tools | Distributional Analysis*. As an example of its use, Figure 6.19 shows the computation of a binomial distribution (i.e., a distribution with two outcomes, such as the tossing of a coin, where the outcome is either Head or Tail, with some prescribed probability of heads and tails). Suppose we toss a coin two times and set the outcome Head as a success. We use the binomial distribution with Trials = 2 (tossing the coin twice) and Probability = 0.50 (the probability of success, of getting Heads). Selecting the PDF and setting the range of values x as from 0 to 2 with a step size of 1 (this means we are requesting the values 0, 1, 2 for x), the resulting probabilities are provided in the table and in a

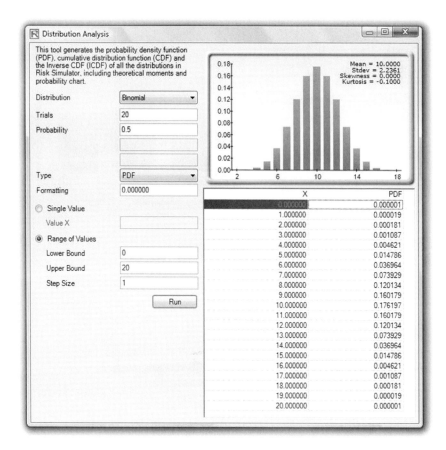

FIGURE 6.20　Distributional analysis tool (binomial distribution with 20 trials).

graphic format, as well as the theoretical four moments of the distribution. As the outcomes of the coin toss are Heads-Heads, Tails-Tails, Heads-Tails, and Tails-Heads, the probability of getting exactly no Heads is 25%, of getting one Head is 50%, and of getting two Heads is 25%. Similarly, we can obtain the exact probabilities of tossing the coin, say 20 times, as seen in Figure 6.20. The results are again presented both in tabular and in graphic formats.

Figure 6.21 shows the same binomial distribution but now the CDF is computed. The CDF is simply the sum of the PDF values up to the point x. For instance, in Figure 6.20, we see that the probabilities of 0, 1, and 2 are 0.000001, 0.000019, and 0.000181, whose sum is 0.000201, which is

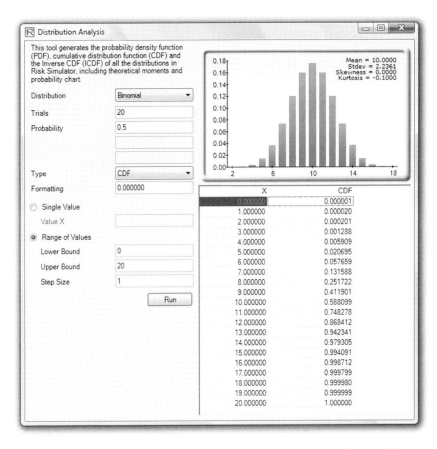

FIGURE 6.21 Distributional analysis tool (binomial CDF with 20 trials).

the value of the CDF at $x = 2$ in Figure 6.21. Whereas the PDF computes the probabilities of getting exactly 2 heads, the CDF computes the probability of getting no more than 2 heads or up to 2 heads (or probabilities of 0, 1, and 2 heads). Taking the complement (i.e., $1 - 0.00021$) obtains 0.999799, or 99.9799%, which is the probability of getting at least 3 heads or more.

Using this distributional analysis tool, distributions even more advanced can be analyzed, such as the gamma, beta, negative binomial, and many others in Risk Simulator. As further example of the tool's use in a continuous distribution and the ICDF functionality, Figure 6.22 shows the standard normal distribution (normal distribution with a mean or *mu* of zero and standard deviation or *sigma* of one), where we apply the ICDF

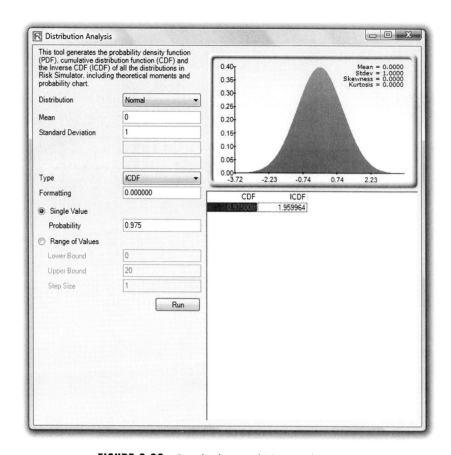

FIGURE 6.22 Standard normal ICDF and Z-score.

to find the value of x that corresponds to the cumulative probability of 97.50% (CDF). That is, a one-tail CDF of 97.50% is equivalent to a two-tail 95% confidence interval (there is a 2.50% probability in the right tail and 2.50% in the left tail, leaving 95% in the center or confidence interval area, which is equivalent to a 97.50% area for one tail). The result is the familiar Z-Score of 1.96. Therefore, using this distributional analysis tool, the standardized scores for other distributions, and the exact and cumulative probabilities of other distributions can all be obtained quickly and easily. See the exercises at the end of this chapter for more hands-on applications using the binomial, negative binomial, and other distributions.

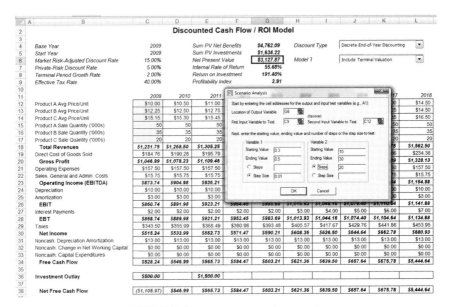

FIGURE 6.23 Scenario analysis tool.

SCENARIO ANALYSIS TOOL

The scenario analysis tool in Risk Simulator allows you to run multiple scenarios quickly and effortlessly by changing one or two input parameters to determine the output of a variable. Figure 6.23 illustrates how this tool works on the discounted cash flow sample model (Model 7 in Risk Simulator's Example Models folder). In this example, cell G6 (net present value) is selected as the output of interest, whereas cells C9 (effective tax rate) and C12 (product price) are selected as inputs to perturb. You can set the starting and ending values to test as well as the step size or the number of steps to run between these starting and ending values. The result is a scenario analysis table (Figure 6.24), where the row and column headers are the two input variables and the body of the table shows the net present values. This scenario analysis tool is available via *Risk Simulator | Tools | Scenario Analysis*.

SEGMENTATION CLUSTERING TOOL

A final analytical technique of interest is that of segmentation clustering. Figure 6.25 illustrates a sample data set. You can select the data and run the

SCENARIO ANALYSIS TABLE

Output Variable:	$G$6	Initial Base Case Value:		$3,127.37					
Column Variable:	$C$12	Min: 10 Max:		30 Steps:			20 Stepsize: —		
Row Variable:	$C$9	Min: 0.3 Max:		0.5 Steps:		—	Stepsize:		0.01

	$10.00	$11.00	$12.00	$13.00	$14.00	$15.00	$16.00	$17.00	$18.00	$19.00
30.00%	$3,904.83	$4,134.43	$4,364.04	$4,593.64	$4,823.24	$5,052.84	$5,282.44	$5,512.04	$5,741.64	$5,971.24
31.00%	$3,827.14	$4,053.46	$4,279.78	$4,506.10	$4,732.42	$4,958.74	$5,185.06	$5,411.39	$5,637.71	$5,864.03
32.00%	$3,749.44	$3,972.48	$4,195.52	$4,418.56	$4,641.61	$4,864.65	$5,087.69	$5,310.73	$5,533.77	$5,756.81
33.00%	$3,671.75	$3,891.51	$4,111.27	$4,331.03	$4,550.79	$4,770.55	$4,990.31	$5,210.07	$5,429.83	$5,649.60
34.00%	$3,594.05	$3,810.53	$4,027.01	$4,243.49	$4,459.97	$4,676.45	$4,892.94	$5,109.42	$5,325.90	$5,542.38
35.00%	$3,516.35	$3,729.55	$3,942.76	$4,155.96	$4,369.16	$4,582.36	$4,795.56	$5,008.76	$5,221.96	$5,435.16
36.00%	$3,438.66	$3,648.58	$3,858.50	$4,068.42	$4,278.34	$4,488.26	$4,698.18	$4,908.10	$5,118.03	$5,327.95
37.00%	$3,360.96	$3,567.60	$3,774.24	$3,980.88	$4,187.53	$4,394.17	$4,600.81	$4,807.45	$5,014.09	$5,220.73
38.00%	$3,283.27	$3,486.63	$3,689.99	$3,893.35	$4,096.71	$4,300.07	$4,503.43	$4,706.79	$4,910.15	$5,113.51
39.00%	$3,205.57	$3,405.65	$3,605.73	$3,805.81	$4,005.89	$4,205.97	$4,406.06	$4,606.14	$4,806.22	$5,006.30
40.00%	$3,127.87	$3,324.67	$3,521.48	$3,718.28	$3,915.08	$4,111.88	$4,308.68	$4,505.48	$4,702.28	$4,899.08
41.00%	$3,050.18	$3,243.70	$3,437.22	$3,630.74	$3,824.26	$4,017.78	$4,211.30	$4,404.82	$4,598.35	$4,791.87
42.00%	$2,972.48	$3,162.72	$3,352.96	$3,543.20	$3,733.45	$3,923.69	$4,113.93	$4,304.17	$4,494.41	$4,684.65
43.00%	$2,894.79	$3,081.75	$3,268.71	$3,455.67	$3,642.63	$3,829.59	$4,016.55	$4,203.51	$4,390.47	$4,577.43
44.00%	$2,817.09	$3,000.77	$3,184.45	$3,368.13	$3,551.81	$3,735.49	$3,919.18	$4,102.86	$4,286.54	$4,470.22
45.00%	$2,739.39	$2,919.79	$3,100.20	$3,280.60	$3,461.00	$3,641.40	$3,821.80	$4,002.20	$4,182.60	$4,363.00
46.00%	$2,661.70	$2,838.82	$3,015.94	$3,193.06	$3,370.18	$3,547.30	$3,724.42	$3,901.54	$4,078.66	$4,255.79
47.00%	$2,584.00	$2,757.84	$2,931.68	$3,105.52	$3,279.37	$3,453.21	$3,627.05	$3,800.89	$3,974.73	$4,148.57
48.00%	$2,506.31	$2,676.87	$2,847.43	$3,017.99	$3,188.55	$3,359.11	$3,529.67	$3,700.23	$3,870.79	$4,041.35
49.00%	$2,428.61	$2,595.89	$2,763.17	$2,930.45	$3,097.73	$3,265.01	$3,432.29	$3,599.52	$3,766.86	$3,934.14
50.00%	$2,350.91	$2,514.91	$2,678.92	$2,842.92	$3,006.92	$3,170.92	$3,334.92	$3,498.92	$3,662.92	$3,826.92

FIGURE 6.24   Scenario analysis table.

tool through *Risk Simulator | Tools | Segmentation Clustering*. Figure 6.25 shows a sample segmentation of two groups. That is, taking the original data set, we run some internal algorithms (a combination or k-means hierarchical clustering and other method of moments in order to find the best-fitting groups or natural statistical clusters) to statistically divide or segment the original data set into two groups. You can see the two-group memberships in Figure 6.25. Clearly, you can segment this data set into as many groups as you wish. This technique is valuable in a variety of settings including marketing (market segmentation of customers into various customer relationship management groups, etc.), physical sciences, engineering, and others.

STRUCTURAL BREAK ANALYSIS

A structural break tests whether the coefficients in different datasets are equal, and this test is most commonly used in time-series analysis to test for the presence of a structural break. A time-series dataset can be divided into two subsets, and each subset is tested on the other and on the entire dataset to statistically determine if indeed there is a break starting at a particular

| Initial Base Case Value: | $10.00 |
| Initial Base Case Value: | 40.00% |

$20.00	$21.00	$22.00	$23.00	$24.00	$25.00	$26.00	$27.00	$28.00	$29.00	$30.00
$6,200.85	$6,430.45	$6,660.05	$6,889.65	$7,119.25	$7,348.85	$7,578.45	$7,808.05	$8,037.65	$8,267.26	$8,496.86
$6,090.35	$6,316.67	$6,542.99	$6,769.31	$6,995.63	$7,221.96	$7,448.28	$7,674.60	$7,900.92	$8,127.24	$8,353.56
$5,979.85	$6,202.89	$6,425.94	$6,648.98	$6,872.02	$7,095.06	$7,318.10	$7,541.14	$7,764.18	$7,987.22	$8,210.26
$5,869.36	$6,089.12	$6,308.88	$6,528.64	$6,748.40	$6,968.16	$7,187.92	$7,407.68	$7,627.45	$7,847.21	$8,066.97
$5,758.86	$5,975.34	$6,191.82	$6,408.30	$6,624.79	$6,841.27	$7,057.75	$7,274.23	$7,490.71	$7,707.19	$7,923.67
$5,648.36	$5,861.57	$6,074.77	$6,287.97	$6,501.17	$6,714.37	$6,927.57	$7,140.77	$7,353.97	$7,567.17	$7,780.38
$5,537.87	$5,747.79	$5,957.71	$6,167.63	$6.377.55	$6,587.47	$6,797.39	$7,007.32	$7,217.24	$7,427.16	$7,637.08
$5,427.37	$5,634.01	$5,840.65	$6,047.30	$6,253.94	$6,460.58	$6,667.22	$6,873.86	$7,080.50	$7,287.14	$7,493.78
$5,316.88	$5,520.24	$5,723.60	$5,926.96	$6,130.32	$6,333.68	$6,537.04	$6,740.40	$6.943.76	$7,147.13	$7,350.49
$5,206.38	$5,406.46	$5,606.54	$5,806.62	$6,006.70	$6,206.79	$6,406.87	$6,606.95	$6.807.03	$7,007.11	$7,207.19
$5,095.88	$5,292.68	$5,489.49	$5,686.29	$5,883.09	$6,079.89	$6,276.69	$6,473.49	$6,670.29	$6,867.09	$7,063.89
$4,985.39	$5,178.91	$5,372.43	$5,565.95	$5,759.47	$5,952.99	$6,146.51	$6,340.03	$6,533.56	$6,727.08	$6,920.60
$4,874.89	$5,065.13	$5,255.37	$5,445.61	$5,635.86	$5,826.10	$6,016.34	$6,206.58	$6,396.82	$6,587.06	$6,777.30
$4,764.40	$4,951.36	$5,138.32	$5,325.28	$5,512.24	$5,699.20	$5,886.16	$6,073.12	$6,260.08	$6,447.04	$6,634.01
$4,653.90	$4,837.58	$5,021.26	$5,204.94	$5,388.62	$5,572.30	$5,755.98	$5,939.67	$6,123.35	$6,307.03	$6,490.71
$4,543.40	$4,723.80	$4,904.20	$5,084.61	$5,265.01	$5,445.41	$5,625.81	$5,806.21	$5,986.61	$6,167.01	$6,347.41
$4,432.91	$4,610.03	$4,787.15	$4,964.27	$5,141.39	$5,318.51	$5,495.63	$5,672.75	$5,849.87	$6,027.00	$6,204.12
$4,322.41	$4,496.25	$4,670.09	$4,843.93	$5,017.77	$5,191.62	$5,365.46	$5,539.30	$5,713.14	$5,886.98	$6,060.82
$4,211.91	$4,382.48	$4,553.04	$4,723.60	$4,894.16	$5,064.72	$5,235.28	$5,405.84	$5,576.40	$5,746.96	$5,917.52
$4,101.42	$4,268.70	$4,435.98	$4,603.26	$4,770.54	$4,937.82	$5,105.10	$5,272.38	$5,439.67	$5,606.95	$5,774.23
$3,990.92	$4,154.92	$4,318.92	$4,482.92	$4,646.93	$4,810.93	$4,974.93	$5,138.93	$5,302.93	$5,466.93	$5,630.93

time period. The structural break test is often used to determine whether the independent variables have different impacts on different subgroups of the population, such as to test if a new marketing campaign, activity, major event, acquisition, divestiture, or other variable has an impact on the time-series data. Suppose the dataset has 100 time-series data points; you can set various breakpoints to test, for instance, data points 10, 30, and 51 (this

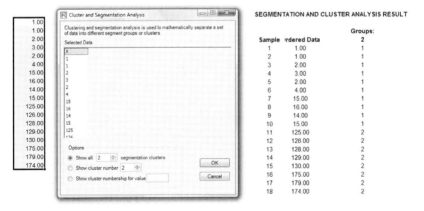

FIGURE 6.25 Segmentation clustering tool and results.

means that three structural break tests will be performed on the following dataset: data points 1–9 compared with 10–100; data points 1–29 compared with 30–100; and 1–50 compared with 51–100, to see whether indeed at the start of data points 10, 30, and 51 there is a break in the underlying structure). A one-tailed hypothesis test is performed on the null hypothesis (H_o) such that the two data subsets are statistically similar to one another; that is, there is no statistically significant structural break. The alternative hypothesis (H_a) is that the two data subsets are statistically different from one another, indicating a possible structural break. If the calculated p-values are less than or equal to 0.01, 0.05, or 0.10, this means that the hypothesis is rejected, which implies that the two data subsets are statistically significantly different at the 1%, 5%, and 10% significance levels. High p-values indicate there is no statistically significant structural break.

DETRENDING AND DESEASONALIZING

This tool in Risk Simulator deseasonalizes and detrends your original data to take out any seasonal and trending components. In forecasting models, this is the process of removing the effects of accumulating datasets from seasonality and trend to show only the absolute changes in values and to allow potential cyclical patterns to be identified after removing the general drift, tendency, twists, bends, and effects of seasonal cycles of a set of time-series data. For example, a detrended dataset may be necessary to see a more accurate account of a company's sales in a given year more clearly by shifting the entire dataset from a slope to a flat surface to better see the underlying cycles and fluctuations.

Many time-series data exhibit seasonality where certain events repeat themselves after some time period or seasonality period (e.g., ski resorts' revenues are higher in winter than in summer, and this predictable cycle will repeat itself every winter). Seasonality periods represent how many periods would have to pass before the cycle repeats itself (e.g., 24 hours in a day, 12 months in a year, 4 quarters in a year, 60 minutes in an hour, and so forth). This tool deseasonalizes and detrends your original data to take out any seasonal components. A seasonal index greater than 1 indicates a high period or peak within the seasonal cycle, and a value below 1 indicates a dip in the cycle.

PRINCIPAL COMPONENT ANALYSIS

Principal component analysis is a way of identifying patterns in data, and recasting the data in such as way as to highlight their similarities and differences. Patterns of data are very difficult to find in high dimensions when multiple variables exist, and higher-dimensional graphs are very difficult to represent and interpret. Once the patterns in the data are found, they can be compressed and the number of dimensions is now reduced. This reduction of data dimensions does not mean much reduction in loss of information. Instead, similar levels of information can now be obtained by a smaller number of variables.

APPENDIX—GOODNESS-OF-FIT TESTS

Several statistical tests exist for deciding if a sample set of data comes from a specific distribution. The most commonly used are the Kolmogorov–Smirnov test and the chi-square test. Each test has its advantages and disadvantages. The following sections detail the specifics of these tests as applied in distributional fitting in Monte Carlo simulation analysis. These two tests are used in Risk Simulator's distributional fitting routines.

Other goodness-of-fit tests such as the Anderson–Darling, Lilliefors, Jacque–Bera, and Wilkes–Shapiro are not used as these are parametric tests and their accuracy depends on the data set being normal or near-normal. Therefore, the results of these tests are oftentimes suspect or yield inconsistent results.

Kolmogorov–Smirnov Test

The Kolmogorov–Smirnov (KS) test is based on the empirical distribution function of a sample data set and belongs to a class of *nonparametric tests*. This nonparametric characteristic is the key to understanding the KS test, which simply means that the distribution of the KS test statistic does not depend on the underlying cumulative distribution function being tested. Nonparametric simply means no predefined distributional parameters are required. In other words, the KS test is applicable across a multitude of underlying distributions. Another advantage is that it is an exact test as compared to the chi-square test, which depends on an adequate sample size for the approximations to be valid. Despite these advantages, the KS test has several important limitations. It only applies to continuous distributions, and it tends to be more sensitive near the center of the distribution than at the distribution's tails. Also, the distribution must be fully specified.

Given N ordered data points $Y_1, Y_2, \ldots Y_N$, the empirical distribution function is defined as $E_n = n_i/N$ where n_i is the number of points less than Y_i where Y_i values are ordered from the smallest to the largest value. This is a step function that increases by $1/N$ at the value of each ordered data point.

The null hypothesis is such that the data set follows a specified distribution while the alternate hypothesis is that the data set does not follow the specified distribution. The hypothesis is tested using the KS statistic defined as

$$KS = \max_{1 \leq i \leq N} \left| F(Y_i) - \frac{i}{N} \right|$$

where F is the theoretical cumulative distribution of the continuous distribution being tested that must be fully specified (i.e., the location, scale, and shape parameters cannot be estimated from the data).

As the null hypothesis is that the data follows some specified distribution, when applied to distributional fitting in Risk Simulator, a low p-value (e.g., less than 0.10, 0.05, or 0.01) indicates a bad fit (the null hypothesis is rejected) while a high p-value indicates a statistically good fit.

Chi-Square Test

The chi-square (CS) goodness-of-fit test is applied to binned data (i.e., data put into classes), and an attractive feature of the CS test is that it can be applied to any univariate distribution for which you can calculate the cumulative distribution function. However, the values of the CS test statistic are dependent on how the data is binned and the test requires a sufficient sample size in order for the CS approximation to be valid. This test is sensitive to the choice of bins. The test can be applied to discrete distributions such as the binomial and the Poisson, while the KS test is restricted to continuous distributions.

The null hypothesis is such that the data set follows a specified distribution while the alternate hypothesis is that the data set does not follow the specified distribution. The hypothesis is tested using the CS statistic defined as

$$\chi^2 = \sum_{i=1}^{k} (O_i - E_i)^2 / E_i$$

where O_i is the observed frequency for bin i and E_i is the expected frequency for bin i. The expected frequency is calculated by

$$E_i = N(F(Y_U) - F(Y_L))$$

TABLE 6.2 Chi-Square Test

Alpha Level (%)	Cutoff
10	32.00690
5	35.17246
1	41.63840

Note: Chi-square goodness-of-fit test sample critical values. Degrees of freedom: 23.

where F is the cumulative distribution function for the distribution being tested, Y_U is the upper limit for class i, Y_L is the lower limit for class i, and N is the sample size.

The test statistic follows a CS distribution with $(k - c)$ degrees of freedom where k is the number of nonempty cells and c is the number of estimated parameters (including location and scale parameters and shape parameters) for the distribution + 1. For example, for a three-parameter Weibull distribution, $c = 4$. Therefore, the hypothesis that the data are from a population with the specified distribution is rejected if $\chi^2 > \chi^2(\alpha, k - c)$ where $\chi^2(\alpha, k - c)$ is the CS percent point function with $k - c$ degrees of freedom and a significance level of α (see Table 6.2).

Again, as the null hypothesis is such that the data follow some specified distribution, when applied to distributional fitting in Risk Simulator, a low p-value (e.g., less than 0.10, 0.05, or 0.01) indicates a bad fit (the null hypothesis is rejected) while a high p-value indicates a statistically good fit.

QUESTIONS

1. Name the key similarities and differences between a tornado chart and a spider chart. Then, compare tornado and spider charts with sensitivity analysis.
2. In distributional fitting, sometimes you may not get the distribution you thought is the right fit as the best choice. Why is this so? Also, why does the beta distribution usually come up as one of the top few candidates as the best-fitting distribution?
3. Briefly explain what a hypothesis test is.
4. How is bootstrap simulation related to precision and error control in simulation?
5. In sensitivity analysis, how is percent variation explained linked to rank correlation?

Additional hands-on exercises are presented in the following pages. These exercises require Risk Simulator to be installed and application of the techniques presented in this chapter.

EXERCISES

Exercise 1: Tornado, Spider, Sensitivity, and Scenario Analyses

This exercise illustrates how to use Risk Simulator for running:

1. Static Sensitivity, Dynamic Sensitivity, and Scenario Analysis
2. Tornado and Spider Analysis: Presimulation Sensitivity Analysis (Linear)
3. Tornado and Spider Analysis: Presimulation Sensitivity Analysis (Nonlinear)
4. Sensitivity Analysis: Postsimulation Sensitivity Analysis
5. Scenario Analysis
6. Optimization Basics

Model Background

File Name: Tornado and Sensitivity Charts (Linear).xls and Tornado and Sensitivity Charts (Nonlinear).xls

Access: **Risk Simulator | Example Models | 22 Tornado and Sensitivity Charts (Linear)**

Access: **Risk Simulator | Example Models | 23 Tornado and Sensitivity Charts (Nonlinear)**

Prerequisites: Risk Simulator 5.2 or later, Chapter 6 of *Modeling Risk* (Section: Tornado and Sensitivity)

The example model we use illustrates a simple discounted cash flow model and shows how sensitivity analysis can be performed both prior to running a simulation and after a simulation is run (Figure 6.26). Tornado and Spider charts are static sensitivity analysis tools useful for determining which variables impact the key results the most. That is, each precedent variable is perturbed a set amount and the key result is analyzed to determine which input variables are the critical success factors with the most impact. In contrast, Sensitivity charts are dynamic, in that all precedent variables are perturbed together in a simultaneous fashion (the effects of autocorrelations,

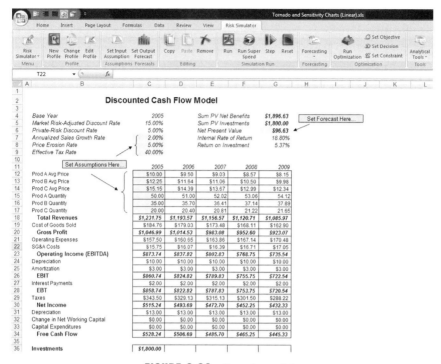

FIGURE 6.26 Sample model.

cross-correlations, and interactions are all captured in the resulting Sensitivity chart). Therefore, a Tornado static analysis is run *before* a simulation while a Sensitivity analysis is run *after* a simulation.

Static Sensitivity, Dynamic Sensitivity, and Scenario Analysis Before we get started, there are a few terminology issues we need to get out of the way. There are similarities and differences among these terms and it is best to cover them up front as these terms are used throughout this exercise and the reports.

- **Static Sensitivity.** Just as the name indicates, this analysis is static, which means that if you have a model A + B = C and C is selected as the output to analyze, it will identify A and B as the inputs that precede C, or as its *precedents*. Then, because of the static nature of this analysis, we start off with A and B at their original values, and then we tweak A to see the effects on C, while holding B constant. Then, we revert A to its original value and tweak B to see the effects on C. Therefore, each precedent is tweaked one at a time, creating a static sensitivity table and chart. In Risk Simulator, we call this the Tornado analysis, where we show the precedent with the largest effect first, followed by the second largest effect and so forth, creating a tornado funnel shape chart. Alternatively, if you take the tornado chart and put it on its side and let all the bars fall onto the x-axis as a baseline, we have a Pareto chart.

- **Dynamic Sensitivity.** In dynamic sensitivity, suppose we have another model, $A + B + C = D$. In this case, A, B, and C are, of course, the precedents to D. However, if only A and C are set as simulation assumptions, only A and C are considered inputs to be tested in a dynamic sensitivity model. This is because, to run a dynamic analysis, we need to dynamically change things, and the only way to do so is through the use of simulation. Therefore, *dynamic sensitivity can only be run after a simulation is run.* And because B is not an assumption, B is only a single point estimate and cannot be tested. Only A and C can be tested in a dynamic sensitivity (B can only be tested if we run a static sensitivity such as a Tornado analysis). In addition, if you set correlations between A and C, the resulting sensitivity analysis will change. Suppose you have another model, $A + B + C + \ldots + X + Y + Z$, and suppose that the values are not correlated and are ranked from having the most effect to the least in the same order. Now further suppose we apply a correlation between A and Z, and let's just say we set the correlation to be $+0.95$. What happens is that the data generated for both A and Z will move together in the same direction, and the dynamic sensitivity analysis will pick up this relationship and will relegate A to a lower rank and increase Z to a higher rank in terms of effect on the model. We will see this result later in the exercise.

- **Scenario Analysis.** Scenario analysis is literally selecting one or more variables on purpose, changing these values within a range, and capturing the results in a table. Again, assume we have a model such as $A + B + C = D$. We can run a scenario analysis by changing B from the value 2 to 100 with a step size of 2 each time. This means that A and C will be left unchanged, whereas B will be set to 2, then 4, 6, 8, ..., 100 and each time, we keep an eye on the resulting value D. The final result is a scenario analysis table showing 50 scenarios of B and the resulting 50 scenarios of D.

Simulation and optimization analysis requires and implements these techniques in one way or another. For instance, simulation is nothing but scenario analysis run in a dynamic way for thousands of times in a statistical and mathematical algorithm with each scenario input variable having its own characteristics, like a normal distribution with a mean and standard deviation, and thus creating a specific distributional shape and probabilities of occurrence, rather than testing a straight range of values as done in scenario analysis. In other words, simulation is scenario analysis on super steroids! On the one hand, scenario analysis can also be seen as tornado static sensitivity analysis but performed on specific variables. On the other hand, static sensitivity runs scenario analysis with a specified range such as ±10% on all precedent variables, not just selected ones. Finally, dynamic sensitivity runs a simulation and then tests its sensitivity to the output, and this process combines both sensitivity analysis and simulation.

Tornado and Spider Charts: Presimulation Sensitivity Analysis (Linear)

To run this model, simply:

1. Start Excel and open the example model *Risk Simulator | Example Models | 22 Tornado and Sensitivity Charts* (Linear).
2. Go to the *DCF Model* worksheet and select the NPV result cell *G6*.
3. Go to *Risk Simulator | Tools | Tornado Analysis* (or click on the *Tornado* icon) and click *OK* (Figure 6.27).

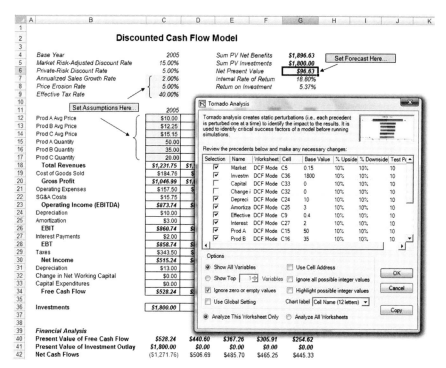

FIGURE 6.27 Running a tornado analysis (linear).

4. Go to the generated tornado analysis report worksheet and review the report (Figure 6.28). The report generated illustrates the sensitivity table (starting base value of the key variable as well as the perturbed values and the precedents). The precedent with the highest impact (range of output) is listed first. The Tornado chart illustrates this analysis graphically. The Spider chart performs the same analysis but also accounts for nonlinear effects. That is, if the input variables have a nonlinear effect on the output variable, the lines on the Spider chart will be curved.

5. Go back to the *DCF Model* and rerun the tornado analysis. This time, spend a little more time on the user interface. You can test out various settings such as the ones listed below. In each setting, see the effects on the report.

   a. Show All Variables versus Show Top N Variables allows you to decide how long the Tornado chart and table should be. Sometimes in a large model there might be a significant number of precedents, and, in most cases, you do not need to see all of them, just the top few that have the largest impact on the model.

   b. Use Cell Address is always a good idea if your model is large, allowing you to identify the location (worksheet name and cell address) of a precedent cell. If this option is not selected, the software will apply its own fuzzy logic in an to attempt to determine the name of each precedent variable (sometimes the names might end up being confusing in a large model with repeated variables or the names might be too long, possibly making the Tornado chart unsightly).

   c. Analyze This Worksheet and Analyze All Worksheets options allow you to control if the precedents should only be part of the current worksheet or include all worksheets in the same workbook. This option comes in handy when you are only attempting to analyze an output based on values in the current sheet versus performing a global search of all linked precedents across multiple worksheets in the same workbook.

   d. Use Global Setting is useful when you have a large model and you wish to test all the precedents at say, ±50% instead of the default 10%. Instead of having to change each precedent's test values one at a time, you can select this option, change one setting, and click somewhere else in the user interface and the entire list of the precedents will change. Deselecting this option will allow you control of changing test points one precedent at a time.

   e. Ignore Zero or Empty Values is an option turned on by default where precedent cells with zero or empty values will not be run in the Tornado. This is the typical setting.

Tornado and Spider Charts

Statistical Summary

One of the powerful simulation tools is the tornado chart—it captures the static impacts of each variable on the outcome of the model. That is, the tool automatically perturbs each precedent variable in the model a user-specified preset amount, captures the fluctuation on the model's forecast or final result, and lists the resulting perturbations ranked from the most significant to the least. Precedents are all the input and intermediate variables that affect the outcome of the model. For instance, if the model consists of A = B + C, where C = D + E, then B, D, and E are the precedents for A (C is not a precedent as it is only an intermediate calculated value). The range and number of values perturbed is user-specified and can be set to test extreme values rather than smaller perturbations around the expected values. In certain circumstances, extreme values may have a larger, smaller, or unbalanced impact (e.g., nonlinearities may occur where increasing or decreasing economies of scale and scope occurs for larger or smaller values of a variable) and only a wider range will capture this nonlinear impact.

A tornado chart lists all the inputs that drive the model, starting from the input variable that has the most effect on the results. The chart is obtained by perturbing each precedent input at some consistent range (e.g., ±10% from the base case) one at a time, and comparing their results to the base case. A spider chart looks like a spider with a central body and its many legs protruding. The positively sloped line indicates a positive relationship, while a negatively sloped line indicates a negative relationship. Further, spider charts can be used to visualize linear and nonlinear relationships. The tornado and spider charts help identify the critical success factors of an output cell in order to identify which inputs to simulate. The identified critical variables that are uncertain are the ones that should be simulated. Do not waste time simulating variables that are neither uncertain nor have little impact on the results.

Result

	Base Value 96.62616385532190			Input Changes		
Precedent Cell	Output Downside	Output Upside	Effective Range	Input Downside	Input Upside	Base Case Value
C36: Investments	276.62616	-83.373836	360.00	$1,620.00	$1,980.00	$1,800.00
C9: Effective Tax Rate	219.72693	-26.474599	246.20	36.00%	44.00%	40.00%
C12: Prod A Avg Price	3.4255424	189.82679	186.40	$9.00	$11.00	$10.00
C13: Prod B Avg Price	16.706631	176.5457	159.84	$11.03	$13.48	$12.25
C15: Prod A Quantity	23.177498	170.07483	146.90	45.00	55.00	50.00
C16: Prod B Quantity	30.533	162.71933	132.19	31.50	38.50	35.00
C14: Prod C Avg Price	40.146587	153.10574	112.96	$13.64	$16.67	$15.15
C17: Prod C Quantity	48.047369	145.20496	97.16	18.00	22.00	20.00
C5: Market Risk-Adjusted Discount Rate	138.23913	57.029841	81.21	13.50%	16.50%	15.00%
C8: Price Erosion Rate	116.80381	76.640952	40.16	4.50%	5.50%	5.00%
C7: Annualized Sales Growth Rate	90.588354	102.68541	12.10	1.80%	2.20%	2.00%
C24: Depreciation	95.084173	98.168155	3.08	$9.00	$11.00	$10.00
C25: Amortization	96.163566	97.088761	0.93	$2.70	$3.30	$3.00
C27: Interest Payments	97.088761	96.163566	0.93	$1.80	$2.20	$2.00

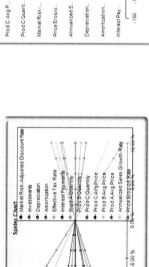

FIGURE 6.28 Linear tornado analysis report.

    f. Highlight Possible Integer Values is an option that quickly identifies all possible precedent cells that currently have integer inputs. This is sometimes important if your model uses switches (e.g., functions such as *if* a cell is 1, then something happens, and *if* a cell has a 0 value, something else happens, or integers such as 1, 2, 3, and so forth, which you do not wish to test). For instance, ±10% of a flag switch value of 1 will return a test value of 0.9 and 1.1, both of which are irrelevant and incorrect input values in the model, and Excel may interpret the function as an error. This option, when selected, will quickly highlight potential problem areas for Tornado analysis and you can determine which precedents to turn on or off manually, or you can use the Ignore Possible Integer Values to turn all of them off simultaneously.

    g. Chart Label is also handy in that sometimes certain cell names are too long and they cut into the chart and table. If that is the case, select *Use Cell Address* for shorter and more precise chart labels.

Note: Tornado analysis should never be run just once. It is meant as a model diagnostic tool, which means that it should ideally be run several times on the same model. For instance, in a large model, Tornado can be run the first time using all of the default settings and all precedents should be shown (select *Show All Variables*). This single analysis may result in a large report and long (and potentially unsightly) Tornado charts. Nonetheless, it provides a great starting point to determine how many of the precedents are considered critical success factors (e.g., the Tornado chart may show that the first 5 variables have high impact on the output, while the remaining 200 variables have little to no impact), in which case, a second Tornado analysis is run showing fewer variables (e.g., select the *Show Top 10 Variables* if the first 5 are critical, thereby creating a nice report and a Tornado chart that shows a contrast between the key factors and less critical factors; that is, you should never show a Tornado chart with only the key variables without showing some less critical variables as a contrast to their effects on the output). Finally, the default testing points can be increased from the ±10% to some larger value to test for nonlinearities (the Spider chart will show nonlinear lines and Tornado charts will be skewed to one side if the precedent effects are nonlinear).

Tornado and Spider Charts: Presimulation Sensitivity Analysis (Nonlinear)

    1. Open the example model *Risk Simulator | Example Models | 23 Tornado and Sensitivity Charts* (Nonlinear).

2. Go to the *Black-Scholes Model* worksheet and select the Black-Scholes result cell *E13*.

3. Go to *Risk Simulator | Tools | Tornado Analysis* (or click on the *Tornado* icon) and this time, select *Use Global Settings* and change the percentage upside to 80%. Then click somewhere else on the grid and the entire column of upside percentages will change to match your new input. Repeat to set the percentage downside to 80%. Click *OK* when done (Figure 6.29).

4. Go to the generated report worksheet and examine the results. Notice the nonlinear effects in this model (Figure 6.30).

   - Exercise Question: What do the green and red colors mean on the tornado chart?
   - Exercise Question: What do the linear versus nonlinear spider chart lines mean and the symmetrical versus asymmetrical bars in the tornado chart mean?
   - Exercise Question: What do the values beside the tornado chart's horizontal bars mean and what does the x-axis of the tornado chart represent?
   - Exercise Question: What do the x-axis and y-axis values represent in the spider chart?
   - Exercise Question: What significance does the slope of the spider chart's lines have? For instance, what is the difference between a variable with a positive slope versus a negative slope, and how about comparing two lines where one is steeper and another is less steep? What about if you have a strictly vertical line or a strictly horizontal line?
   - Exercise Question: How do you compute the effective range on the tornado analysis report table?

Sensitivity Analysis: Postsimulation Sensitivity Analysis   To run this exercise, simply:

1. Go back to the linear model or reopen it from *Risk Simulator | Example Models | 22 Tornado and Sensitivity Charts* (Linear).

2. Some sample input assumptions and forecasts have already been set for this model, so just run the simulation using *Risk Simulator | Run Simulation* (or click on the *Run* icon).

3. After the simulation is complete, click *OK* and then select *Risk Simulator | Tools | Sensitivity Analysis* (Figure 6.31). Select *Cell Name* for the *Chart Label* and click *OK* to run the analysis.

4. Go to the newly generated sensitivity report and review the results (Figure 6.32).

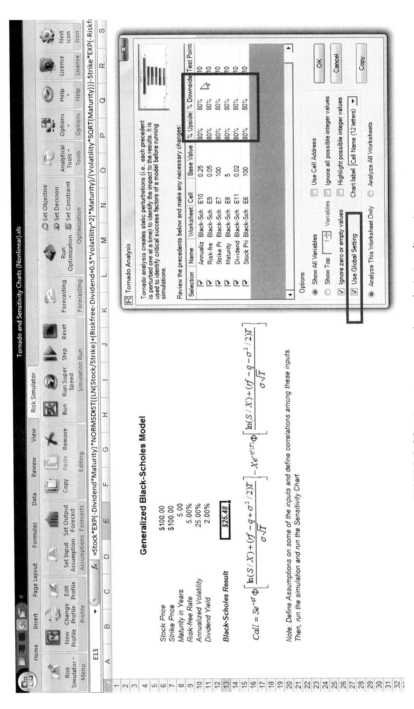

FIGURE 6.29 Running a tornado analysis (nonlinear).

Tornado and Spider Charts

Statistical Summary

One of the powerful simulation tools is the tornado chart—it captures the static impacts of each variable on the outcome of the model. That is, the tool automatically perturbs each precedent variable in the model a user-specified preset amount, captures the fluctuation on the model's forecast or final result, and lists the resulting perturbations ranked from the most significant to the least. Precedents are all the input and intermediate variables that affect the outcome of the model. For instance, if the model consists of $A = B + C$, where $C = D + E$, then B, D, and E are the precedents for A (C is not a precedent as it is only an intermediate calculated value). The range and number of values perturbed is user-specified and can be set to test extreme values rather than smaller perturbations around the expected values. In certain circumstances, extreme values may have a larger, smaller, or unbalanced impact (e.g., nonlinearities may occur where increasing or decreasing economies of scale and scope creep occurs for larger or smaller values of a variable) and only a wider range will capture this nonlinear impact.

A tornado chart lists all the inputs that drive the model, starting from the input variable that has the most effect on the results. The chart is obtained by perturbing each precedent input at some consistent range (e.g., ±10% from the base case) one at a time, and comparing their results to the base case. A spider chart looks like a spider with a central body and its many legs protruding. The positively sloped line indicates a positive relationship, while a negatively sloped line indicates a negative relationship. Further, spider charts can be used to visualize linear and nonlinear relationships. The tornado and spider charts help identify the critical success factors of an output cell in order to identify the inputs to simulate. The identified critical variables that are uncertain are the ones that should be simulated. Do not waste time simulating variables that are neither uncertain nor have little impact on the results.

Result

Precedent Cell	Base Value 25.4786764688884			Input Changes			
	Output Downside	Output Upside	Effective Range	Input Downside	Input Upside	Base Case Value	
E6: Stock Price	0.0287306	87.665051	87.64	$20.00	$180.00	$100.00	
E7: Strike Price	74.912288	7.6196425	67.29	$20.00	$180.00	$100.00	
E10: Annualized Volatility	12.994074	39.051155	26.06	5.00%	45.00%	25.00%	
E8: Maturity in Years	11.123762	32.718244	21.59	1.00	9.00	5.00	
E9: Risk-free Rate	18.190168	33.439471	15.25	1.00%	9.00%	5.00%	
E11: Dividend Yield	30.997461	20.725439	10.27	0.40%	3.60%	2.00%	

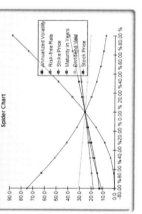

FIGURE 6.30 Nonlinear tornado analysis report.

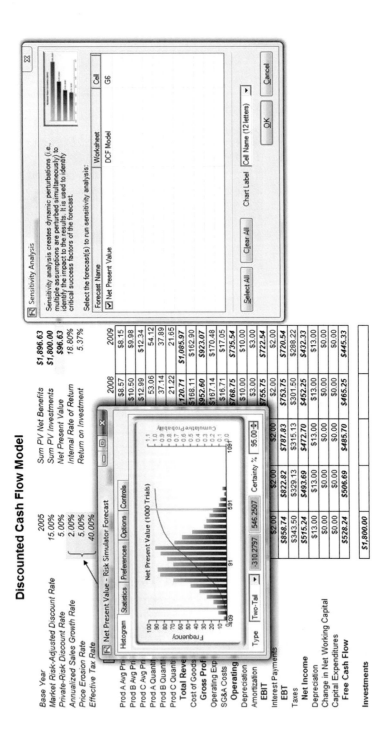

FIGURE 6.31 Dynamic sensitivity analysis.

- Exercise Question: Is this sensitivity analysis a static or dynamic sensitivity?
- Exercise Question: What do the red and green bars mean in the sensitivity charts?
- Exercise Question: What is the nonlinear rank correlation (Spearman nonparametric rank correlation) and what does it measure? Why do we use it rather than a regular linear correlation (Pearson's product moment correlation coefficient)?
- Exercise Question: What is the percent variation explained and what does it measure? How does it compare with the coefficient of determination (R-square) obtained from a regression analysis?

5. Reset the simulation *Risk Simulator | Reset Simulation* (or click on the *Reset* icon) and go back to the model worksheet. Select cell *C7* annualized growth rate and set a correlation of *0.85* with the effective tax rate cell *C9* (Figure 6.33). *Run the simulation* and *run the sensitivity analysis* one more time and compare this new correlated simulation report (Figure 6.34) with the report without correlations (Figure 6.32).
   - Exercise Question: What happens to the sensitivity results when you have a correlated simulation?
   - Exercise Question: What happens to the ranking of C7 before a correlation and after a correlation?

Scenario Analysis   To run this exercise, simply:

1. Go back to the linear model or reopen it from *Risk Simulator | Example Models | 22 Tornado and Sensitivity Charts* (Linear).
2. Click on *Risk Simulator | Tools | Scenario Analysis* (or use the *Scenario Analysis* icon in the *Analytical Tools* ribbon set) and input the values as seen in Figure 6.35. You can click on the *link* icons to link to a cell or type in the cell address directly. *Location of output variable* is the location of the cell you wish to test, and you can enter either one or two input variables to test and their *starting* and *ending* values as well as the *number of steps* to take between these starting and ending values or the *step size* to take. Review the scenario report results (Figure 6.36).

Optimization Basics   Just a quick note before we leave this exercise. The scenario analysis you ran a few moments ago looks at either a one- or two-dimensional table, and from this table you can identify the results, including the highest or lowest NPV values. In a later exercise, we will look at optimization, where you can have multidimensional scenario analysis that can take on billions and trillions of sets of combinations quickly and automatically, to find the optimal results.

Sensitivity Analysis

Statistical Summary

Sensitivity charts are dynamic perturbations created after the simulation run. Sensitivity charts are dynamic perturbations in the sense that multiple assumptions are perturbed simultaneously and their interactions are captured in the fluctuations of the results. In contrast, Tornado charts are static perturbations, meaning that each precedent or assumption variable is perturbed a preset amount and the fluctuations in the results are tabulated. Tornado charts therefore identify which variables drive the results the most and hence are suitable for determining which variables to simulate (that is, they are used before a simulation), whereas Sensitivity charts identify the impact to the results when multiple interacting variables are simulated together in the model (that is, they are used after a simulation).

The Nonlinear Rank Correlation charts indicate the rank correlations between each assumption and the target forecast, and are depicted from the highest absolute value to the lowest absolute value. Positive correlations are shown in green while negative correlations are shown in red. Rank correlation is used instead of a regular correlation coefficient as it captures nonlinear effects between variables. In contrast, the Percent Variation Explained computes how much of the variation in the forecast variable can be explained by the variations in each of the assumptions by itself in a dynamic simulated environment. These charts show the sensitivity of the target forecast to the simulated assumptions.

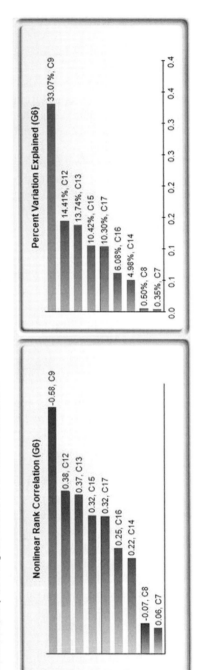

FIGURE 6.32 Dynamic sensitivity analysis report.

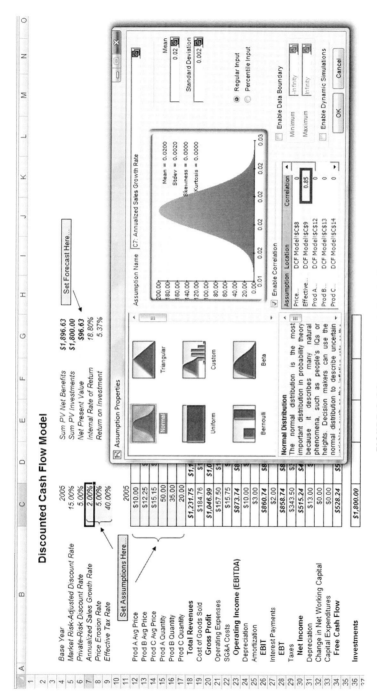

FIGURE 6.33 Correlated simulation.

Sensitivity Analysis

Statistical Summary

Sensitivity charts are dynamic perturbations created after the simulation run. Sensitivity charts are dynamic perturbations in the sense that multiple assumptions are perturbed simultaneously and their interactions are captured in the fluctuations of the results. In contrast, Tornado charts are static perturbations, meaning that each precedent or assumption variable is perturbed a preset amount and the fluctuations in the results are tabulated. Tornado charts therefore identify which variables drive the results the most and hence are suitable for determining which variables to simulate (that is, they are used before a simulation), whereas Sensitivity charts identify the impact to the results when multiple interacting variables are simulated together in the model (that is, they are used after a simulation).

The Nonlinear Rank Correlation charts indicate the rank correlations between each assumption and the target forecast, and are depicted from the highest absolute value to the lowest absolute value. Positive correlations are shown in green while negative correlations are shown in red. Rank correlation is used instead of a regular correlation coefficient as it captures nonlinear effects between variables. In contrast, the Percent Variation Explained computes how much of the variation in the forecast variable can be explained by the variations in each of the assumptions by itself in a dynamic simulated environment. These charts show the sensitivity of the target forecast to the simulated assumptions.

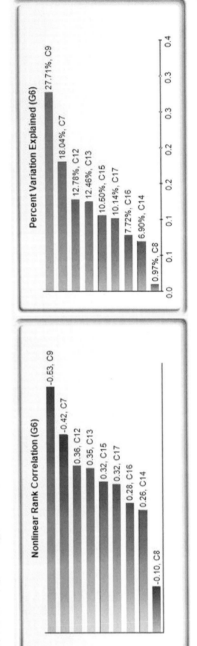

FIGURE 6.34 Dynamic sensitivity report of correlated simulation.

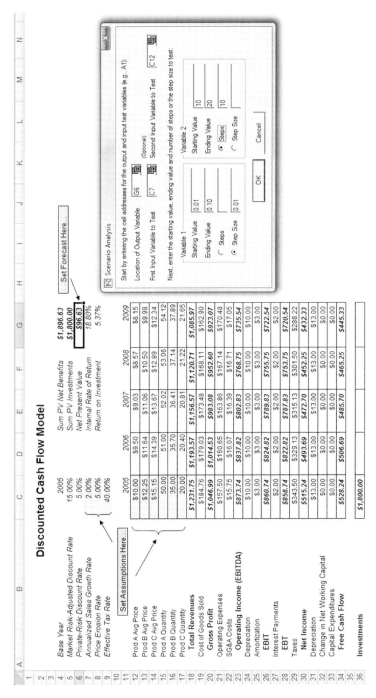

FIGURE 6.35 Scenario analysis.

Scenario Analysis Table

Output Variable: $G$6	Initial Base Case Value:			$96.63		10.00 Stepsize:		Initial Base Case Value:		$10.00
Column Variable: $C$12	Min: $12.00	10.00 Max:		20.00 Steps:		— Stepsize:		0.01 Initial Base Case Value:		2.00%
Row Variable: $G$7	Min:	0.01 Max:		0.10 Steps:		Stepsize:				

	$ 10.00	$ 11.00	$ 12.00	$ 13.00	$ 14.00	$ 15.00	$ 16.00	$ 17.00	$ 18.00	$ 19.00	$ 20.00
1.00%	$ 66.65	$158.35	$250.04	$341.74	$433.43	$525.13	$616.82	$ 708.52	$ 800.22	$ 891.91	$ 983.61
2.00%	$ 96.63	$189.83	$283.03	$376.23	$469.43	$562.63	$655.83	$ 749.03	$ 842.23	$ 935.43	$1,028.63
3.00%	$127.14	$221.87	$316.60	$411.34	$506.07	$600.80	$695.53	$ 790.27	$ 885.00	$ 979.73	$1,074.46
4.00%	$158.19	$254.49	$350.78	$447.07	$543.36	$639.65	$735.95	$ 832.24	$ 928.53	$1,024.82	$1,121.11
5.00%	$189.80	$287.68	$385.56	$483.44	$581.32	$679.20	$777.08	$ 874.96	$ 972.84	$1,070.72	$1,168.59
6.00%	$221.96	$321.46	$420.95	$520.45	$619.94	$719.44	$818.93	$ 918.43	$1,017.93	$1,117.42	$1,216.92
7.00%	$254.69	$355.83	$456.97	$558.11	$659.25	$760.39	$861.53	$ 962.67	$1,063.81	$1,164.95	$1,266.09
8.00%	$288.00	$390.81	$493.62	$596.44	$699.25	$802.06	$904.88	$1,007.69	$1,110.50	$1,213.31	$1,316.13
9.00%	$321.89	$426.40	$530.92	$635.43	$739.95	$844.46	$948.98	$1,053.49	$1,158.01	$1,262.52	$1,367.04
10.00%	$356.36	$462.61	$568.86	$675.10	$781.35	$887.60	$993.85	$1,100.10	$1,206.34	$1,312.59	$1,418.84

FIGURE 6.36 Scenario analysis report.

Exercise 2: Data Fitting

This sample model illustrates how to use Risk Simulator for:

1. Fitting a Single Variable to Existing Data
2. Fitting Multiple Variables to Existing Data
3. Simulating, Extracting Data, and Refitting to Distributions
4. Hypothesis Tests and Fitting Statistics
5. Delphi Method and Custom Distributions

Model Background

File Name: Data Fitting.xls

Access: **Risk Simulator | Example Models | 06 Data Fitting**

Prerequisites: Risk Simulator 5.2 or later, Completed Basic Simulation Model Exercise, Chapter 6 of *Modeling Risk* (Section: Distributional Fitting)

This example illustrates how existing sample data can be used to find the statistically best-fitting distribution. By doing so, we also confirm the simulation results through the distributional fitting routine, that is, we simulate a particular distribution, extract its raw data, and refit it back to all distributions.

Fitting a Single Variable to Existing Data   To run this model, simply:

1. Start Excel and open the example model at *Risk Simulator | Example Models | 06 Data Fitting*. Go to the *Raw Data* worksheet and select cells *C2:C201* (Figure 6.37).
2. Start a new profile by clicking *Risk Simulator | New Profile* (or click the *New Profile* icon).
3. Click on *Risk Simulator | Tools | Distributional Fitting* (Single Variable).
4. Make sure *Fit Continuous Distributions* is selected and all distributions are checked then click *OK*. The resulting fit of all distributions is shown. Select the best fit that is ranked first, view the statistics, and click *OK*.
5. A report will be generated (Figure 6.38) indicating all the relevant statistics as well as the data used for fitting (for future reference). Note that if a *simulation profile* exists and if the *Automatically Generate Assumption* choice is selected, then the report will contain an assumption that is the best fit. Otherwise, only the type of distribution and its relevant input assumptions are provided. You can repeat this exercise on the remaining data points provided.

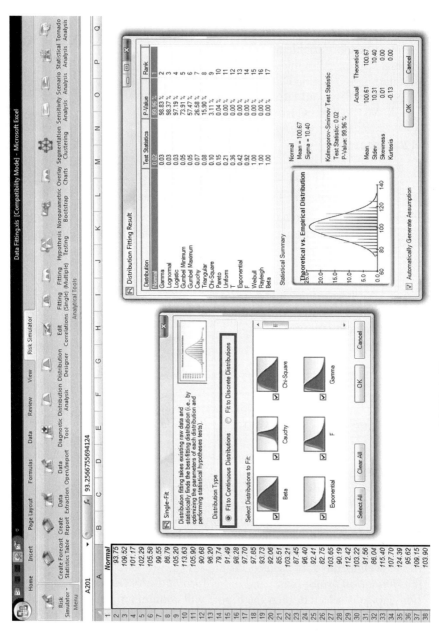

FIGURE 6.37 Single variable data fitting.

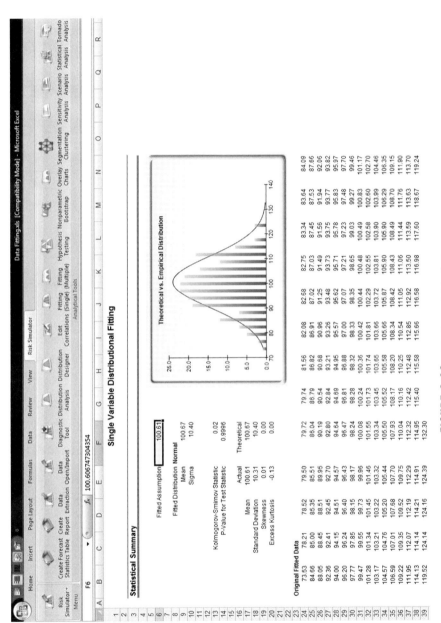

FIGURE 6.38 Single variable fitting report.

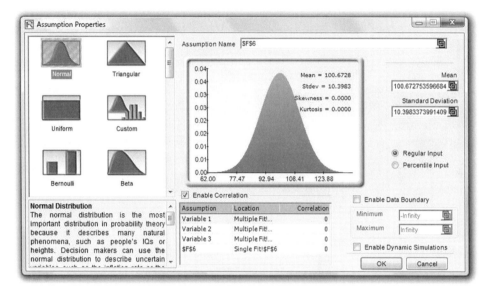

FIGURE 6.39 Auto fitted assumption.

6. Go the report and select the cell with the assumption and then go to *Risk Simulator | Set Input Assumption* and you will be able to see the assumption and the parameters automatically set up for you (Figure 6.39). Compare the input parameters and distribution with those listed in the report.

7. Go back to the Raw Data worksheet and re-run the distributional fitting. This time make sure *Fit Discrete Distributions* is selected and all distributions are checked then click *OK*.

   - Exercise Question: What are the two tests used in distributional fitting?
   - Exercise Question: Do you want a low p-value or a high p-value when doing a distributional fitting, that is, are distributions with high p-values ranked better or worse than low p-values?
   - Exercise Question: What is a p-value anyway?
   - Exercise Question: What is the null hypothesis that is being tested?
   - Exercise Question: Are higher or lower values of the test statistics better?

Note: There are several key points to remember. First, more data implies a better statistical fit. Do not fit to very few data points and expect a good fit. Second, only positive discrete data (integers) can be fitted to discrete distributions. When negative values or continuous data exist, you should always fit to continuous distributions. Third, certain distributions are related to other distributions through their statistical properties. For example, a T-distribution becomes a normal distribution when degrees of freedom is high, a Poisson distribution can be used to approximate a binomial, or a normal can be used to approximate a Poisson, hypergeometric, and binomial. There are many other such relationships, and just because the fit is not exactly to the distribution expected does not mean the data are bad or the routine is incorrect. It simply means that another distribution is better suited for the data. Finally, distributions like beta and gamma are extremely flexible and can take on many shapes (we have another exercise that illustrates this), and so do not be surprised if these distributions sometimes show up at a high ranking fit.

Fitting Multiple Variables to Existing Data   To run this model, simply:

1. Go to the *Raw Data* worksheet, create a new profile (*Risk Simulator | New Profile*) and select the area *C1:E201* and run the multiple variable fitting routine by selecting *Risk Simulator | Tools | Distributional Fitting* (Multi-Variable) (Figure 6.40).
2. Click on the *Distribution Type* list box on the top of the user interface. Then select the binomial distribution type and change it to *Discrete* distribution. Keep the *Include Correlations Above Absolute Value* at its automatically computed value and the selection checked, and click *OK* to run the fitting routines.
3. Go to the newly generated report (Figure 6.41) and spend a minute reviewing the results. Then review the correlation matrix by going to *Risk Simulator | Tools | Edit Correlations* and clicking on *Select All* (Figure 6.42) to review the pairwise cross-correlations.
   - Exercise Question: Why are all the correlations zero?
   - Exercise Question: In layman's terms, what does statistically significant correlation mean?
   - Exercise Question: What do the actual empirical versus theoretical distribution moments mean?
4. Rerun the multiple fitting routine by repeating steps 1 and 2 above, making sure you create a new profile with a new unique name so you can differentiate which fitted values are in which profile. When you repeat these steps, keep the *Include Correlations Above Absolute Value* and change the value to *0*. That is, all correlations, whether positive or negative, as long as it is not zero, will be used. Run the report and view the correlation matrix just like in Step 3 above to review the correlations.

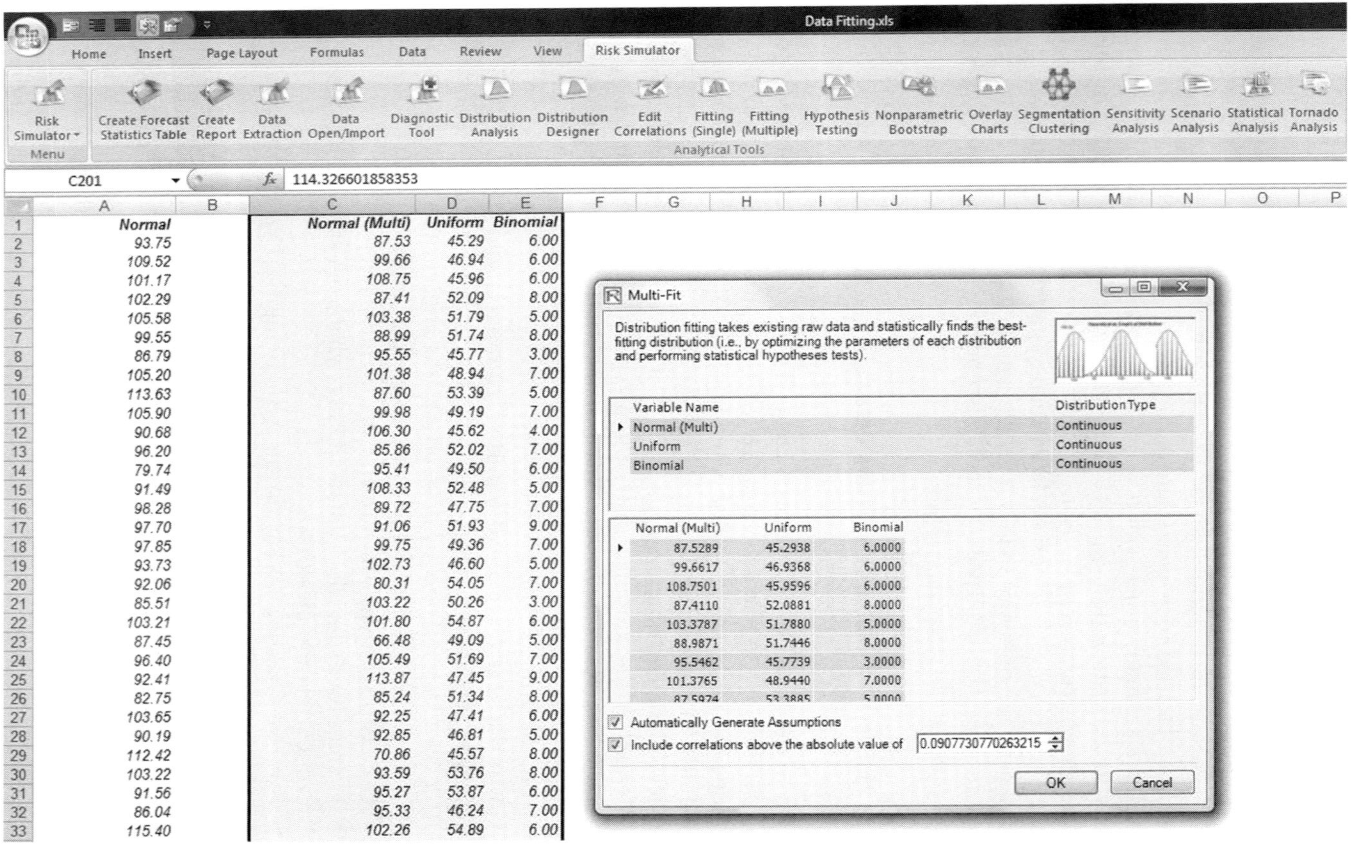

FIGURE 6.40 Multiple variables fitting.

Multiple Variables Distributional Fitting

Statistical Summary

	Variable Name Normal (Multi) 99.18		Variable Name Uniform 49.83		Variable Name Binomial 6.73	
Best-Fit Assumption						
Fitted Distribution	Normal		Uniform		Gumbel(Maximum)	
	Mu	99.34	Minimum	44.84	Alpha	6.38
	Sigma	10.48	Maximum	54.89	Beta	1.26
Kolmogorov-Smirnov Statistic		0.03		0.04		0.14
P-Value for Test Statistic		0.9845		0.8110		0.0005
	Actual	Theoretical	Actual	Theoretical	Actual	Theoretical
Mean	99.18	99.34	49.83	49.87	6.73	7.11
Standard Deviation	10.33	10.48	2.96	2.90	1.49	1.61
Skewness	−0.12	0.00	0.02	0.00	−0.51	1.14
Excess Kurtosis	0.19	0.00	−1.32	−1.20	−0.06	2.40

Correlation Matrix

	Normal	Uniform	Binomial
Normal	1		
Uniform	0.0007	1	
Binomial	−0.0693	−0.0044	1

FIGURE 6.41 Multiple variables fitting report with correlations.

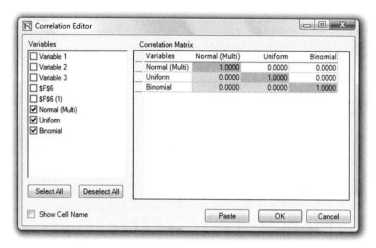

FIGURE 6.42 Not statistically significant correlations.

Note: You can replicate the fitting routine on multiple variables simultaneously (variables must be arranged in columns) instead of one at a time.
When performing a Multiple Variable Fitting, make sure to select the right
distribution types for the variables. For example, select *continuous* for the
first two and *discrete* for the third distribution in our model. Further, you
can either select the data with the names or without the names, and if you
do not select the variable name when fitting, you can enter the variable
names in the fitting dialog box. Also, if you have an existing profile, you can
select the *Automatically Generate Assumptions* option such that the report
will have assumptions set up for you. Further, these assumptions will also
include correlations. The question is then what correlation coefficient is significant for this data set (i.e., is a correlation of 0.0151 significant or merely a
residual effect of randomness and should not be incorporated? What about
0.016 or 0.15, and so forth)? Risk Simulator will automatically compute
the statistical significance cutoff level (in this case, any correlation above
the absolute value of 0.0907 is statistically significant) and if you select this
option, the software will ignore all correlations below the absolute value of
this significance level (we use absolute values because correlations can be
either positive or negative).

Simulating, Extracting Data, and Refitting to Distributions   For additional
practice you can run a simulation on an assumption and run a fitting back
to find the best distribution.

To run this example, simply:

1. Start a new workbook in Excel. Create a new profile by clicking *Risk Simulator | New Profile*. Then select cell *A1* and create an assumption *Risk Simulator | Set Input Assumption* (or use the *Set Input Assumption* icon). Select something simple such as *Normal* distribution and make the *Mean 100* and *Standard Deviation 10*.
2. Go to cell *A2*, set the equation = *A1*, and set this cell as a forecast *Risk Simulator | Set Output Forecast* (or use the *Set Output Forecast* icon).
3. *Risk Simulator | Run Simulation*. At the end of simulation, you can refit the simulated data two ways, first using the forecast chart and, second, by extracting the data and refitting the distribution. We will work on both methods in this exercise.
   a. In the forecast chart, go to the *Controls* tab. Click on the *Fit* button and you can see that the 1,000 raw data captured in the forecast chart are all fitted to the best distribution, which in this case is normal, as expected. Here you can see the theoretical and empirical moments of the distribution (Figure 6.43) as well as the p-value of the fit.
   b. Extract the data *Risk Simulator | Tools | Data Extract and Export* to obtain the raw simulated data. Then, select the data, perform the single distributional fitting, and compare the results in the generated report with the forecast chart's controls tab fitting routine.
      - Exercise Question: What are the differences between raw data fitting and using the forecast chart's controls tab fitting?

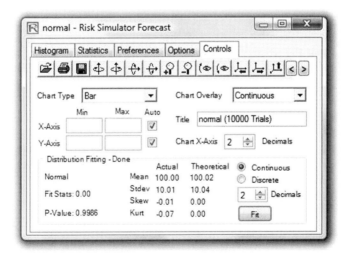

FIGURE 6.43 Forecast chart distributional fit.

4. For practice, reset the simulation, edit the active profile to run 10,000 simulation trials, run the simulation at super speed, and perform a fitting using the forecast chart's controls section.

Hypothesis Tests and Fitting Statistics   There is another exercise on Bootstrapping and Hypothesis Testing that will provide additional information and practice in running a hypothesis test. Nonetheless, briefly, the *null hypothesis* that is being tested in distribution fitting is that "The distribution being tested is the correct distribution." In other words, the algorithm or procedure in distribution fitting is fairly straightforward:

- Using the data, go through each distribution one at a time.
- For each distribution, perform an inverted optimization approach to find the best-fitting input parameters to the distribution that minimizes the fitting errors.
- Perform the Kolmogorov–Smirnov or chi-square test to determine the fit.
- Obtain the p-values of the fit.
- Rank the distributions from best fit to the worst fit.

Delphi Method and Custom Distributions   In a distributional fitting environment, higher p-values are better. The question is how high a p-value do you need to be comfortable with the fit? Clearly a fit of 0.95 is great versus 0.10, which is not that good at all. But what about values in between these two? In most cases, it is really up to the user to make this determination. Nonetheless, in situations where you do not have data, or not enough data points exist or the p-value fit is really low, there is an alternative: the use of the Custom Distribution to make your own distribution. This customized distribution is powerful and applicable because it has multiple advantageous characteristics, including the fact that you will always get a 100% fit or a p-value of 1 because it is nonparametric in nature and the approach uses the data to tell the story. That is, every data point will be used in the distribution. This custom distribution is perfect for use in the Delphi subject matter expert approach as well as for historical simulation, where all historical data are used and simulated.

To run this example, simply:

1. Start a new workbook in Excel. Create a new profile by clicking *Risk Simulator | New Profile* and then enter some data like those shown in Figure 6.44. *Select the data* and click *Edit | Copy* in

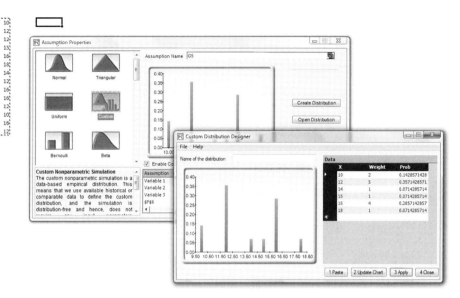

FIGURE 6.44   Custom distribution.

Excel or use Ctrl+C or right-click and copy the cells into the Windows clipboard.

2. Select any empty cell and set an assumption *Risk Simulator | Set Input Assumption*. Select the *Custom* distribution and click on *Create Distribution*. Then, in the custom distribution designer interface, just follow the numbers for the four steps: *1 Paste, 2 Update Chart, 3 Apply,* and *4 Close*. Then back in the set assumptions properties, click *OK* to set the assumption.

3. Click on the *Step Simulation* icon a few times to see the value in the cell changing. You will see that it is randomly selecting the numbers from the original dataset, where numbers that have the highest probability of occurrence or are repeated more often in the original dataset are selected more often, of course.

Exercise 3: Distributional Analysis and Overlay Charts

This sample model illustrates how to use Risk Simulator for:

1. Basics of PDF, CDF, ICDF, and Types of Probability Distributions
2. Distributional Analysis (Empirical Simulation and Theoretical PDF)

3. Simple Getting Started Applications of PDF and CDF
4. Computing Theoretical Probabilities of Events for Six Sigma Quality Control
5. Overlay Charts and Distributional Comparisons

Model Background

File Name: Overlay Charts.xls

Access: **Risk Simulator | Example Models | 14 Overlay Charts**

Prerequisites: Risk Simulator 5.2 or later, Completed Basic Simulation Model Exercise, Chapter 5 of *Modeling Risk* (Appendix: Understanding Probability Distributions)

Basics of PDF, CDF, ICDF, and Types of Probability Distributions In this exercise, you learn how to use the statistical probability *Distributional Analysis* tool in Risk Simulator that is very useful in a variety of settings. This tool can be used to compute the *probability density function* (PDF), which is also called the *probability mass function* (PMF) for discrete distributions (we will use these terms interchangeably), where given some distribution and its parameters, we can determine the probability of occurrence given some outcome x. In addition, the *cumulative distribution function* (CDF) can also be computed, which is the sum of the PDF values up to this x value. Finally, the *inverse cumulative distribution function* (ICDF) is used to compute the value x given the cumulative probability of occurrence.

Distributional Analysis (Empirical Simulation and Theoretical PDF) Before we begin, let's briefly discuss the difference between using a simulation's resulting probabilities and using the statistical probability *Distributional Analysis* tool (Figure 6.45). If both the probability of an event happening and its probability distribution type are known for certain and the scenario is a basic situation (e.g., tossing a coin 10 times where no complex modeling is required), then the statistical probability analysis is sufficient, and the result will be a single probability value or a table of probability of outcomes. Conversely, in more complex situations where there are multiple variables and they are interacting with one another, and where a model needs to be built (e.g., cash flow return on investment model), we have no choice but to revert to risk simulation by setting multiple input assumptions and correlations, and running the simulation thousands of times to obtain the resulting probabilities.

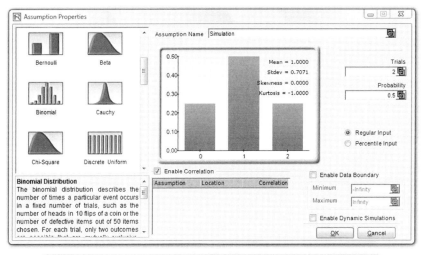

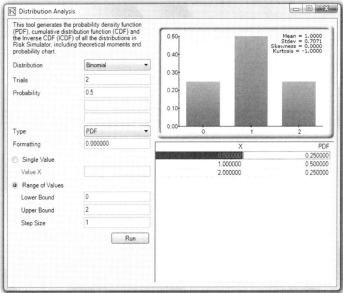

FIGURE 6.45 Distributional analysis tool.

Simple Getting Started Applications of PDF and CDF This distributional analysis tool is accessible via *Risk Simulator | Tools | Distributional Analysis*. As an example, Figure 6.45 shows the computation of a binomial distribution (i.e., a distribution with two outcomes, such as the tossing of a coin, where the outcome is either Head or Tail, with some prescribed probability of heads and tails). Suppose we toss a coin two times, and set the outcome

Head as a success. We use the binomial distribution with Trials = 2 (tossing the coin twice) and Probability = 0.50 (the probability of success, of getting Heads). Selecting the PDF and setting the range of values x as from 0 to 2 with a step size of 1 (this means we are requesting the values 0, 1, 2 for x), the resulting probabilities are provided in the table and in a graphical format, as well as the theoretical four moments of the distribution. As the outcomes of the coin toss is Heads-Heads, Tails-Tails, Heads-Tails, and Tails-Heads, the probability of getting exactly no Heads is 25%, one Head is 50%, and two Heads is 25%.

Similarly, we can obtain the exact probabilities of tossing the coin, say, 20 times, as seen in Figure 6.46. The results are presented both in table and graphical formats. Figure 6.46 shows the same binomial distribution but now the CDF is computed. The CDF is simply the sum of the PDF values up to the point x. For instance, in Figure 6.45 (left panel), we see that the probabilities of 0, 1, and 2 are 0.000001, 0.000019, and 0.000181, whose sum is 0.000201, which is the value of the CDF at $x = 2$ in Figure 6.46. Whereas the PDF computes the probabilities of getting exactly 2 heads, the CDF computes the probability of getting no more than 2 heads or up to 2 heads (or probabilities of 0, 1, and 2 heads). Taking the complement (i.e., 1 − 0.00021) obtains 0.999799 or 99.9799%, which is the probability of getting at least 3 heads or more.

Using this *Distributional Analysis* tool, even more advanced distributions can be analyzed, such as the gamma, beta, negative binomial, and many others in Risk Simulator. As a further example of the tool's use in a continuous distribution and the ICDF functionality, Figure 6.47 shows the standard normal distribution (normal distribution with a mean of zero and standard deviation of one), where we apply the ICDF to find the value of x that corresponds to the cumulative probability of 97.50% (CDF). That is, a one-tail CDF of 97.50% is equivalent to a two-tail 95% confidence interval (there is a 2.50% probability in the right-tail and 2.50% in the left-tail, leaving 95% in the center or confidence interval area, which is equivalent to a 97.50% area for one-tail). The result is the familiar Z-Score of 1.96. Therefore, using this *Distributional Analysis* tool, the standardized scores for other distributions and the exact and cumulative probabilities of other distributions can all be obtained quickly and easily.

Figure 6.48 illustrates another discrete distribution example by applying the Poisson distribution, a distribution that is used when trying to measure events occurring in a specific area and time (for instance, the average number of people standing in line at a McDonald's or waiting in line for a teller at a bank branch, the number of customers showing up at a restaurant, people missing their flights in a specific hour). Let us assume that the average number of people calling up a customer service center per hour is 2.5 individuals (we

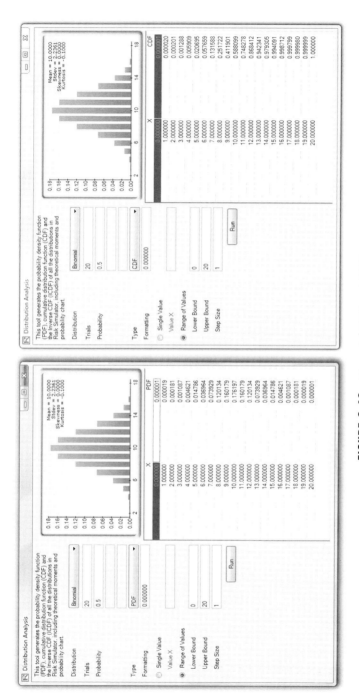

FIGURE 6.46 Binomial PDF and CDF.

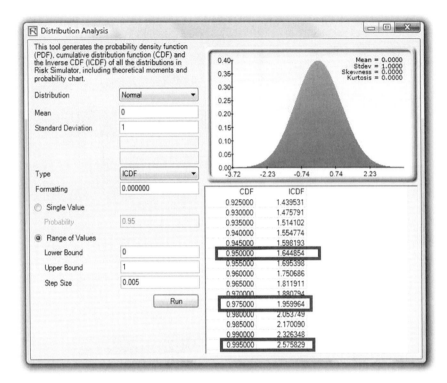

FIGURE 6.47   Standard normal CDF and ICDF.

set Lambda or average value to 2.5 in Figure 6.48), we can determine that the probability of having 0 phone calls per hour is 8.20%, the probability of exactly 1 call per hour is 20.52%, 2 calls per hour is 25.65%, and so forth, by using the PDF function. Conversely, using the CDF function, we know that there is a 54.38% chance that you will get 0 or 1 or 2 calls per hour, or less than or equal to 2 calls per hour, or no more than 2 calls per hour. Of course, the probability of getting more than 2 calls is 100% − 54.38%, or 45.62% (the total probabilities for all numbers of calls will add to 100%). If you wish to be 99% sure that you will have enough customer sales representatives available to handle these incoming calls, you will need to have sufficient staff to handle up to 7 calls per hour.

- Exercise Question: How do you know what to set in terms of the upper bound and lower bound for the range of values to show in the table?
- Exercise Question: What is the probability you will have *no more than* 5 calls per hour?

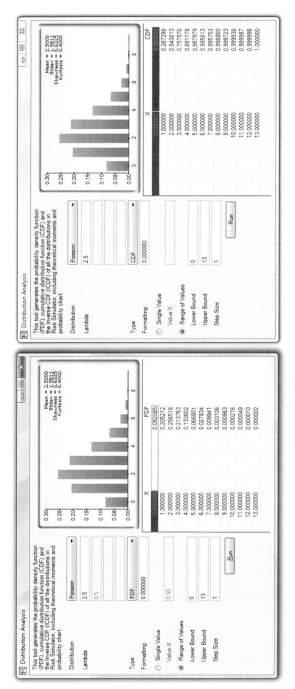

FIGURE 6.48 Poisson PDF and CDF.

- Exercise Question: What is the probability you will have *at least 3* calls per hour?
- Exercise Question: What is the probability you will have *exactly either 2 or 3* calls per hour?

The negative binomial distribution is useful for modeling the distribution of the number of additional trials required on top of the number of successful occurrences required (R). For instance, in order to close a total of 10 sales opportunities, how many extra sales calls would you need to make above 10 calls given some probability of success in each call? The x-axis shows the number of additional calls required or the number of failed calls. The number of trials is not fixed, the trials continue until the Rth success, and the probability of success is the same from trial to trial. Probability of success (P) and number of successes required (R) are the distributional parameters. Such a model can be applied in a multitude of situations, such as the cost of sales cold calls, the budget required to train military recruits, and so forth. The simple example shown below illustrates how a negative binomial distribution works. Suppose that a salesperson is tasked with making cold calls and a resulting sale is considered a success while no sale means a failure. Suppose that, historically, the proportion of sales to all calls is 30%. We can model this scenario using the negative binomial distribution by setting the *Successes Required* (R) to equal 2 and the *Probability of Success* (P) as 0.3. For instance, say the salesperson makes 2 calls and the success rate is 30% per call and they are statistically independent of one another. There can be four possible outcomes (SS, SF, FS, FF, where S stands for success, and F for failure). The probability of SS is 0.3 × 0.3, or 9%; SF and FS is 0.3 × 0.7, or 21%; and FF is 0.7 × 0.7, or 49%. Therefore, there is a 9% chance that 2 calls are sufficient and no additional calls are required to get the 2 successes required. In other words, $X = 0$ has a probability of 9% if we define X as the additional calls required beyond the 2 calls.

Extending to 3 calls, we have many possible outcomes, but the key outcomes we care about are 2 successful calls, which we can define as the following combinations: SSS, SSF, SFS, and FSS. Their respective probabilities are computed below (e.g., FSS is computed by 0.7 × 0.3 × 0.3 = 6.30%). Now, the combinatorial sequence SSS and SSF do not require a third call because the first two calls have already been successful. Further, SFF, FSF, FFS, and FFF all fail the required 2 call success as they only have either zero or one successful call. So, the sum total probability of the situations requiring a third call to make exactly 2 calls successful out of 3 is 12.60%. All other values are listed in the tool.

Clearly, doing the above exercise for a large combinatorial problem with many required successes would be difficult and intractable. However, we can

	2 Call Example			3 Call Example	
	Success	Failure		Success	Failure
Call 1	30%	70%	Call 1	30%	70%
Call 2	30%	70%	Call 2	30%	70%
			Call 3	30%	70%

Success + Success	9%			
Success + Failure	21%	Success + Success + Success	2.70%	*Not require 3rd call*
Failure + Success	21%	Success + Success + Failure	6.30 %	*Not require 3rd call*
Failure + Failure	49%	**Success + Failure + Success**	6.30 %	***Requires 3rd call***
Sum	*100%*	**Failure + Success + Success**	6.30 %	***Requires 3rd call***
Both Successful (R = 2)	9%	Success + Failure + Failure	14.70%	*Fails 2-call required*
		Failure + Success + Failure	14.70%	*Fails 2-call required*
		Failure + Failure + Success	14.70%	*Fails 2-call required*
		Failure + Failure + Failure	34.30%	*Fails 2-call required*
		Sum	*100.00%*	
		Sum (Requires 3rd call)	**12.60%**	

obtain the same results using Risk Simulator's *Distributional Analysis* tool running a negative binomial distribution with $R = 2$ and $P = 0.3$ (Figure 6.49). Notice that the probability of $X = 0$ is exactly what we had computed, 9%, and $X = 1$ yields 12.60%.

Computing Theoretical Probabilities of Events for Six Sigma Quality Control
In this section, we continue using the *Distributional Analysis* tool and illustrate the manual computations used to obtain the exact probabilities of the occurrence of events for quality control purposes. These tools are illustrated through some simple discrete distributions. The section continues with some continuous distributions for the purposes of theoretical hypotheses tests. Then hypothesis testing on empirically simulated data is presented, where we use theoretical distributions to simulate empirical data and run hypotheses tests.

Binomial Distribution   The binomial distribution describes the number of times a particular event occurs in a fixed number of trials, such as the number of heads in 10 flips of a coin or the number of defective items out of 50 items chosen. For each trial, only two outcomes are possible that are mutually exclusive. The trials are independent, where what happens in the first trial does not affect the next trial. The probability of an event occurring remains the same from trial to trial. Probability of success (p) and the number of total trials (n) are the distributional parameters. The

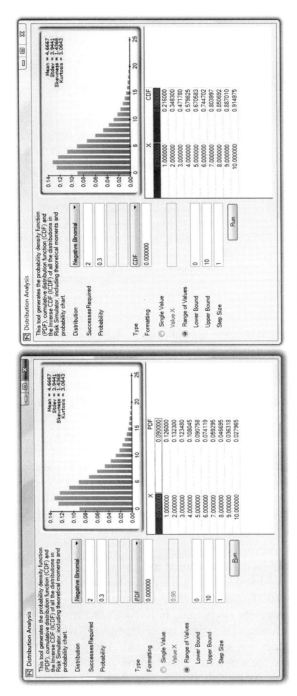

FIGURE 6.49 Negative Binomial PDF and CDF.

number of successful trials is denoted x (the x-axis of the probability distribution graph). The input requirements in the distribution include: Probability of success > 0 and < 1 (e.g., $p \geq 0.0001$ and $p \leq 0.9999$), Number of Trials ≥ 1, and integers ≤ 1000.

Example: If the probability of obtaining a part that is defective is 50%, what is the probability that in selecting 4 parts at random, there will be no defective part, or 1 defective part, or 2 defective parts, and so forth? Recreate the probability mass function or probability density function (PDF):

Probability of no defects $P(x = 0)$: 6.25%:

$$C_0^4(.5)^0(.5)^{4-0} = \frac{4!}{0!(4-0)!}(.5)^0(.5)^{4-0} = \frac{1}{16} = 6.25\%$$

Probability of one defect $P(x = 1)$: 25.00%:

$$C_1^4(.5)^1(.5)^{4-1} = \frac{4!}{1!(4-1)!}(.5)^1(.5)^3 = \frac{4}{16} = 25\%$$

Probability of two defects $P(x = 2)$: 37.50%:

$$C_2^4(.5)^2(.5)^{4-2} = \frac{4!}{2!(4-2)!}(.5)^2(.5)^2 = \frac{6}{16} = 37.50\%$$

Probability of three defects $P(x = 3)$: 25.00%:

$$C_3^4(.5)^3(.5)^{4-3} = \frac{4!}{3!(4-3)!}(.5)^3(.5)^1 = \frac{4}{16} = 25\%$$

Probability of four defects $P(x = 4)$: 6.25%:

$$C_4^4(.5)^4(.5)^{4-4} = \frac{4!}{4!(4-4)!}(.5)^4(.5)^0 = \frac{1}{16} = 6.25\%$$

Total probabilities: 100.00%

where we define $P(x = 0)$ as the probability (P) of the number of successes of an event (x), and the mathematical combination (C).

In addition, you can sum up the probabilities to obtain the cumulative distribution function (CDF):

Probability of no defects $P(x = 0)$:

$$6.25\% \text{ computed as } P(x = 0)$$

Probability of up to 1 defect $P(x< = 1)$:

$$31.25\% \text{ computed as } P(x = 0) + P(x = 1)$$

Probability of up to 2 defects $P(x< = 2)$:

$$68.75\% \text{ computed as } P(x = 0) + P(x = 1) + P(x = 2)$$

Probability of up to 3 defects $P(x< = 3)$:

$$93.75\% \text{ computed as } P(x = 0) + P(x = 1) + P(x = 2) + P(x = 3)$$

Probability of up to 4 defects $P(x< = 4)$:

$$100.00\% \text{ computed as } P(x=0) + P(x=1) + P(x=2) + P(x=3) + P(x=4)$$

The same analysis can be performed using the Distribution Analysis tool in Risk Simulator. For instance, you can start the tool by clicking on *Risk Simulator | Tools | Distributional Analysis*, selecting *Binomial*, entering *4* for Trials and *0.5* for *Probability*, then selecting PDF as the type of analysis, and a range of between *0* and *4* with a step of *1*. The resulting table and PDF distribution is exactly as computed as seen in Figure 6.50. For practice, confirm the computed CDF values above using the *Distributional Analysis* tool.

In addition, the four distributional moments can be determined using the tool:

Mean or Average	2.00
Standard Deviation	1.00
Skewness Coefficient	0.00
Kurtosis (Excess)	−0.50

Poisson Distribution   The Poisson distribution describes the number of times an event occurs in a given space or time interval, such as the number of telephone calls per minute or the number of errors per page in a document (Figure 6.51). The number of possible occurrences in any interval is unlimited; the occurrences are independent. The number of occurrences in

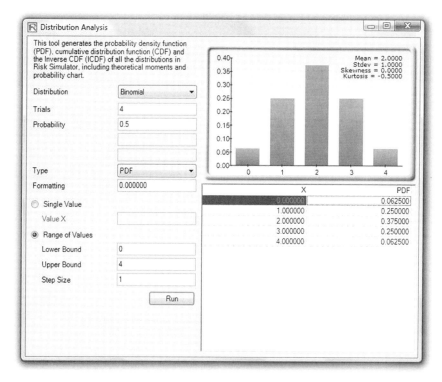

FIGURE 6.50 Distributional analysis for a binomial PDF.

one interval does not affect the number of occurrences in other intervals, and the average number of occurrences must remain the same from interval to interval. Rate or Lambda is the only distributional parameter. The input requirement for the distribution is Rate > 0 and ≤ 1000.

Exercise Question: A tire service center has the capacity of servicing 6 customers in an hour. From prior experience, on average 3 show up an hour. The owner is afraid that there might insufficient manpower to handle an overcrowding of more than 6 customers. What is the probability that there will be exactly 6 customers? What about 6 or more customers? (See Figure 6.52.)

Normal Distribution   The normal distribution is the most important distribution in probability theory because it describes many natural phenomena, such as people's IQs or heights. Decision makers can use the normal distribution to describe uncertain variables such as the inflation rate or the future price of gasoline. Some value of the uncertain variable is the most likely (the

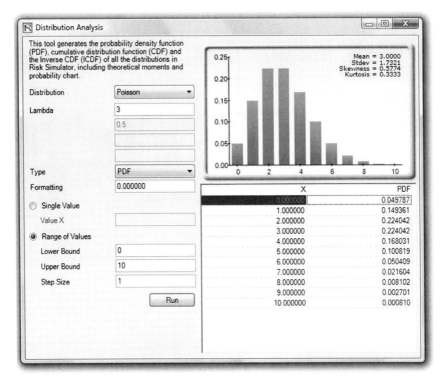

FIGURE 6.51   PDF on a Poisson.

mean of the distribution), the uncertain variable could as likely be above the mean as it could be below the mean (symmetrical about the mean), and the uncertain variable is more likely to be in the vicinity of the mean than farther away. Mean (μ) and standard deviation (σ) are the distributional parameters. The input requirements include: Mean can take on any value and Standard Deviation > 0 and can be any positive value.

Exercise Question: You observe that in the past, on average, your manufactured batteries last for 15 months with a standard deviation of 1.5 months. Assume that the battery life is normally distributed. If a battery is randomly selected, find the probability that it has a life of less than 16.5 months or over 16.5 months. Using the tool, we obtain CDF of X = 16.5 months as 84.13%, which means that there is 84.13% chance that the manufactured batteries last up to 16.5 months, and $1 - 0.8413$ or 15.87% chance the batteries will last over 16.5 months (Figure 6.53).

Exercise Question: Alternatively, suppose you wish to provide a 12-month warranty on your batteries, that is, if the battery dies before

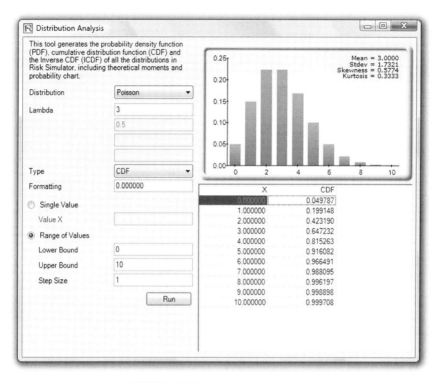

FIGURE 6.52 CDF on a Poisson.

12 months, you will give a full refund. What are the chances that you may have to provide this refund?

Using the tool, we find that the CDF for X = 12 is a 2.28% chance that a refund will have to be issued (Figure 6.54).

So far, we have been computing the probabilities of events occurring using the PDF and CDF functions and tools. We can also reverse the analysis and obtain the X values given some probability, using the inverse cumulative distribution function (ICDF), as seen next.

Exercise Question: If the probability calculated in the above problem is too high and, hence, too costly for you and you wish to minimize the cost and probability of having to refund your customers down to a 1% probability, what would be a suitable warranty date (in months)?

The answer is that to provide anything less than an 11.51 month guarantee will most likely result in less than or equal to a 1% chance of a return. To obtain the results here, we use the ICDF analysis in the Distributional Analysis tool (Figure 6.55).

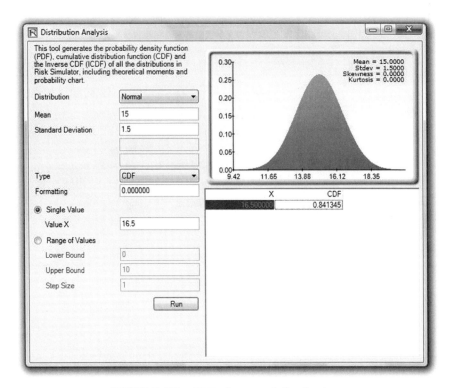

FIGURE 6.53   CDF of a normal distribution.

Hypothesis Tests in a Theoretical Situation   This section illustrates how to continue using the *Distributional Analysis* tool to simplify theoretical hypothesis tests.

Exercise Question: Sometimes, we need to obtain certain X values given a certainty and probability level for the purposes of hypothesis testing. This is where the ICDF comes in handy. For instance, suppose a light bulb manufacturer needs to test if its bulbs can last, on average, 1,000 burning hours. If the plant manager randomly samples 100 light bulbs and finds that the sample average is 980 hours with a standard deviation of 80 hours, at a 5% significance level (two-tails), do the light bulbs last an average of 1,000 hours?

There are several methods for solving this problem, including the use of confidence intervals, Z-scores, and p-values. For example, we are testing the null hypothesis H_o: Population Mean $= 1,000$ and the alternate hypothesis H_a: Population Mean is *not* 1,000. Using the Z-score approach, we first obtain the Z-score equivalent to a two-tail alpha of 5% (which means one-tail

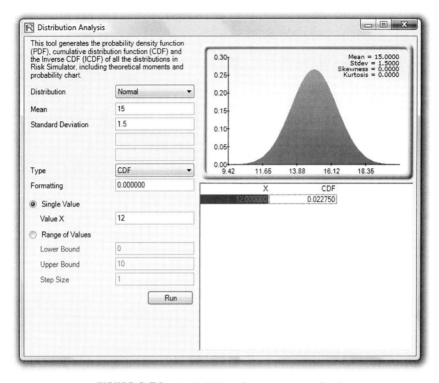

FIGURE 6.54 Probability of a guarantee refund.

is 2.5%, and using the Distributional Analysis tool we get the $Z = 1.96$ at a CDF of 97.50%, equivalent to a one-tail p-value of 2.5%). Using the *Distributional Analysis* tool, set the distribution to Normal with a mean of zero and standard deviation of one (this is the standard normal Z distribution). Then, compute the ICDF for 0.975 or 97.5% CDF, which provides an X value of 1.9599 or 1.96 (Figure 6.56).

Using the confidence interval formula, we get:

$$\mu \pm Z \left(\frac{s}{\sqrt{n}} \right)$$

$$1000 \pm 1.96 \left(\frac{80}{\sqrt{100}} \right)$$

$$1000 \pm 15.68$$

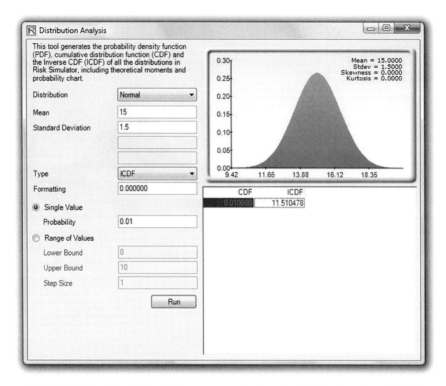

FIGURE 6.55　Obtaining the inverse cumulative distribution function (ICDF).

This result means that the statistical confidence interval is between 984.32 and 1015.68. As the sample mean of 980 falls outside this confidence interval, we reject the null hypothesis and conclude that the true population mean is different from 1,000 hours.

A much quicker and simpler approach is to use the *Distributional Analysis* tool directly. Seeing that we are performing a statistical sample, we first need to correct for small sampling size bias by correcting the standard deviation to get:

$$\frac{s}{\sqrt{n}} = \frac{80}{\sqrt{100}} = 8$$

Then we can find the CDF relating to the sample mean of 980. We see that the CDF p-value is 0.0062, less than the alpha of 0.025 one-tail (or 0.50 two-tail), which means we reject the null hypothesis and conclude that the

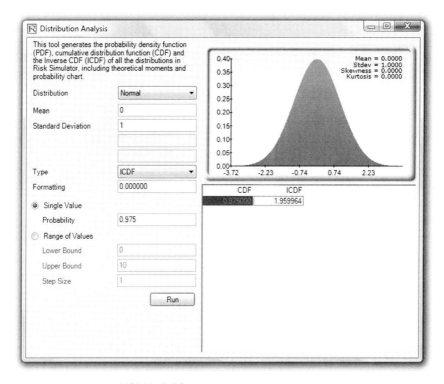

FIGURE 6.56 Standard normal Z-score.

population mean is statistically significantly different from the 1,000 hours tested (Figure 6.57).

Yet another alternative is to use the ICDF method for the mean and sampling adjusted standard deviation and compute the X values corresponding to the 2.5% and 97.5% levels. The results indicate that the 95% two-tail confidence interval is between 984.32 and 1,015.68 as computed previously. Hence, 980 falls outside this range, meaning that the sample value of 980 is statistically far away from the hypothesized population of 1,000 (i.e., the unknown true population based on a statistical sampling test can be determined to be not equal to 1,000). See Figure 6.58.

Note that we adjust the sampling standard deviation only because the population is large and we sample a small size. However, if the population standard deviation is known, we do not divide it by the square root of N (sample size).

Exercise Question: In another example, suppose it takes, on average, 20 minutes with a standard deviation of 12 minutes to complete a certain

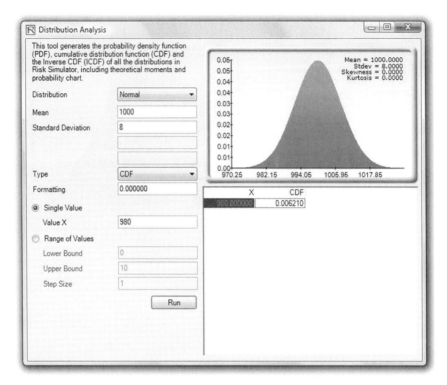

FIGURE 6.57   Obtaining p-values using distributional analysis tool.

manufacturing task. Based on a sample of 36 workers, what is the probability that you will find someone completing the task taking between 18 and 24 minutes?

Again, we adjust the sampling standard deviation to be 12 divided by the square root of 36, or equivalent to 2. The CDFs for 18 and 24 are 15.86% and 97.72%, respectively, yielding the difference of 81.86%, which is the probability of finding someone taking between 18 and 24 minutes to complete the task. See Figure 6.59.

Exercise Question: Sometimes, when the sample size is small, we need to revert to using the Student's T-distribution. For instance, suppose a plant manager studies the life of a particular battery and samples 10 units. The sample mean is 5 hours with a sample standard deviation of 1 hour. What is the 95% confidence interval for the battery life?

Using the T distribution, we set the degrees of freedom as $n - 1$ or 9, with a mean location of 0 for a standard T distribution. The ICDF for 0.975 or 97.5% (5% two-tail means 2.5% on one-tail, creating a

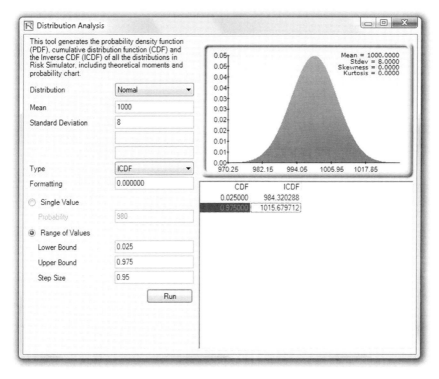

FIGURE 6.58 Computing statistical confidence intervals.

complement of 97.5%) is equivalent to 2.262 (Figure 6.60). So, the 95% statistical confidence interval is:

$$\bar{x} \pm t \frac{s}{\sqrt{n}}$$
$$5 \pm 2.262 \frac{1}{\sqrt{10}}$$
$$5 \pm 0.71$$

Therefore, the confidence interval is between 4.29 and 5.71.

Overlay Charts and Distributional Comparisons In this section, we look at Overlay Charts in Risk Simulator. As you can already tell, sometimes it might be advantageous to overlay several probability distributions on top of one another to compare how they look, as well as to learn the characteristics of specific distributions. For instance, the binomial distribution we have been

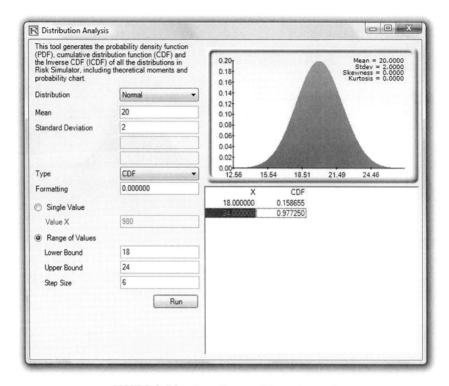

FIGURE 6.59   Sampling confidence interval.

so fond of earlier in this exercise can take on a variety of shapes (Figure 6.61) when different probabilities of success (*P*) and number of trials (*N*) are used. When *N* is a high value, the distribution becomes more symmetrical and approaches the normal distribution (due to the central limit theorem and the law of large numbers), and, in fact, the normal distribution is a good approximation when *N* is fairly large.

As another example, the Beta distribution is a fairly flexible distribution where depending on the input parameters you use, you can get a variety of different shapes and sizes (Figure 6.62). Specifically, if *Alpha* = *Beta* = 1, the distribution is exactly that of a Uniform distribution. When both *Alpha* = *Beta*, the distribution is fairly symmetrical. The larger the *Alpha* and *Beta* parameters, while at the same time being equal, makes the distribution more symmetrical and normal (notice that the skewness is zero and the excess kurtosis is close to zero, indicative of a normal distribution). Further, when *Alpha* < *Beta*, we have a positive skew, and if *Alpha* > *Beta*, we have a negative skew. Further, if either *Alpha* or *Beta* is 1 and the other is 2, we

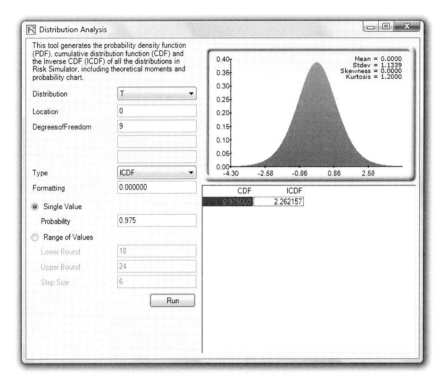

FIGURE 6.60   Standard T-distribution.

have a Triangular distribution, when *Alpha = Beta = 2*, we have a mound distribution, and if *Alpha = 2* and *Beta > Alpha*, we have a lognormal distribution.

We will now work on an exercise to run the *Overlay Chart* tool by comparing and overlaying input assumptions with forecast outputs (Figure 6.63), as well as looking at comparing input assumptions with various distributions or the same distribution using different input parameters (Figure 6.64).

To get started with this exercise, follow the instructions below:

1. Start Excel, open the example model *Risk Simulator | Example Models | 14 Overlay Charts*, and run a simulation by selecting *Risk Simulator | Run Simulation* (or clicking on the *Run Simulation* icon). You can also run super speed simulation if you wish. Click *OK* when the simulation is done.

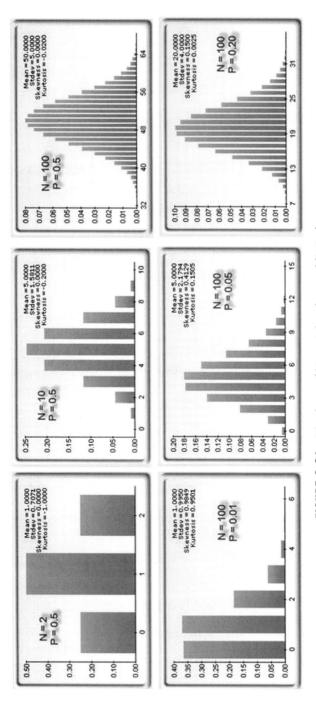

FIGURE 6.61 The faces of binomial and central limit theorem.

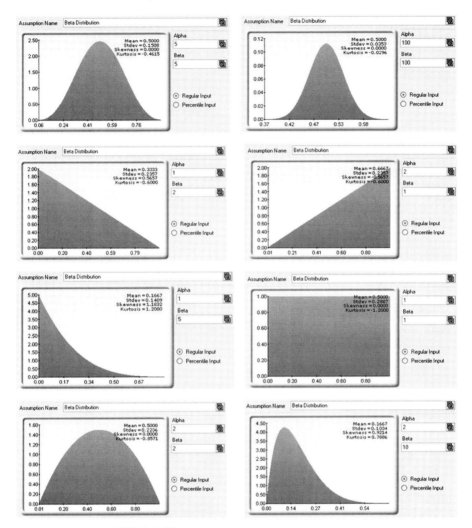

FIGURE 6.62   The faces of Beta on overlay chart.

2. Click on *Risk Simulator | Tools | Overlay Charts* and replicate some of the overlay charts in Figure 6.63, specifically:
   a. Overlay PDF Bar chart with Revenue A, Revenue E, Income A, Income E
   b. Overlay PDF Line chart with Revenue A, Revenue B, Income A, Income B

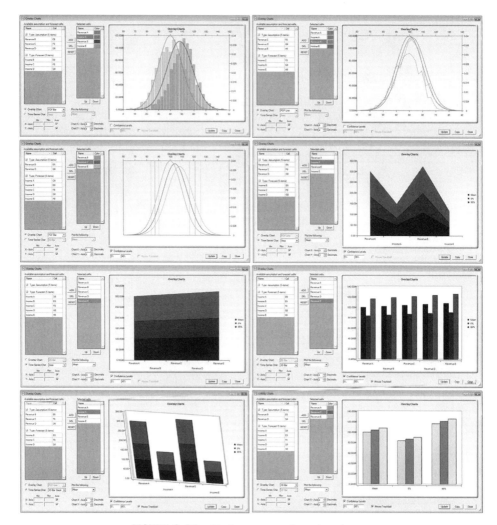

FIGURE 6.63 Various types of overlay charts.

c. Overlay PDF Bar chart with Revenue A, Revenue B, Revenue C (turn confidence on and off)
d. Overlay 3D Bar chart with Revenue A, Revenue C, Revenue E
e. Time Series Area chart with Revenue A, Revenue E, Income A, Income E
f. Time Series Area chart with Revenues A to E

g. Time Series 3D Bar chart with Revenues A to E
h. Time Series 3D Bar Stack chart with Revenue A, Revenue E, Income A, Income E

3. Open a new workbook in Excel and create a new profile. Go to an empty cell and set an input assumption. Use the Beta distribution, set the parameters to be *Alpha* = *2*, *Beta* = *3*, and give it a name (e.g., "Beta 2,3"). Then, go down to the next cell and set another assumption with a *Beta* (*2,4*) distribution, and then another cell with *Beta* (*2,5*), while naming them appropriately each time. Run a simulation, and run the overlay chart. Select these three assumptions for the overlay chart and run the PDF line chart (Figure 6.64).

Note: With a similar approach, you can now keep trying and comparing other theoretical distributions using the input assumptions method. Remember, if only assumptions are used in the overlay chart, the theoretical distributions will be shown. If only output forecasts are chosen, the empirical distributions will be shown, and if both assumptions and forecasts are chosen, the theoretical distributions will be overlaid against the empirical distribution results. In all cases, the theoretical distributions look like nice smooth curves, whereas empirical distributions are shown as bars or irregular curves. Of course, you can change the colors of each variable by clicking on the color tags beside each selected distribution.

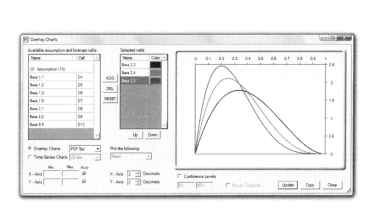

FIGURE 6.64 The faces of Beta on overlay chart.

Exercise 4: Bootstrap Simulation, Hypothesis Testing, and Segmentation Clustering

This sample model illustrates how to use Risk Simulator for:

1. Nonparametric Bootstrap Simulation
2. Theoretical Hypothesis Tests
3. Segmentation Clustering

Model Background

File Name: Hypothesis Testing and Bootstrap Simulation.xls

Access: **Risk Simulator | Example Models | 08 Hypothesis Testing and Bootstrap Simulation**

Prerequisites: Risk Simulator 5.2 or later, Completed the Basic Simulation Exercise

Nonparametric Bootstrap Simulation Bootstrap simulation is a simple technique that estimates the reliability or accuracy of forecast statistics or other sample raw data. Essentially, bootstrap simulation is used in hypothesis testing where we use the empirical resampling approach; that is, using the actual simulated data and resampling the simulation multiple times. In contrast, classical or traditional methods rely on mathematical formulas to describe the accuracy of sample statistics where these methods assume that the distribution of a sample statistic approaches a normal distribution, making the calculation of the statistic's standard error or confidence interval relatively easy. We used these methods in the previous exercise, "Distributional Analysis and Overlay Charts," and will use them in the next segment of this exercise, where additional theoretical hypothesis tests are run. However, when a statistic's sampling distribution is not normally distributed or easily found, these classical methods are difficult to use or are invalid. In contrast, bootstrapping analyzes sample statistics empirically by repeatedly sampling the data and creating distributions of the different statistics from each sampling.

In essence, nonparametric bootstrap simulation can be thought of as simulation based on a simulation. Thus, after running a simulation, the resulting statistics are displayed, but the accuracy of such statistics and their statistical significance are sometimes in question. For instance, if a simulation run's skewness statistic is –0.10, is this distribution truly negatively skewed or is the slight negative value attributable to random chance? What about –0.15, –0.20, and so forth? That is, how far is far enough such

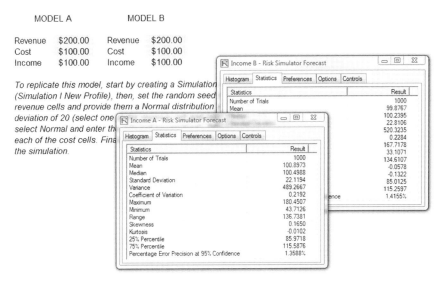

MODEL A

Revenue	$200.00
Cost	$100.00
Income	$100.00

MODEL B

Revenue	$200.00
Cost	$100.00
Income	$100.00

To replicate this model, start by creating a Simulation (Simulation I New Profile), then, set the random seed revenue cells and provide them a Normal distribution deviation of 20 (select one select Normal and enter th each of the cost cells. Fina the simulation.

Income B - Risk Simulator Forecast

Histogram | Statistics | Preferences | Options | Controls

Statistics	Result
Number of Trials	1000
Mean	99.8767
	100.2395
	22.8106
	520.3235
	0.2284
	167.7178
	33.1071
	134.6107
	-0.0578
	-0.1322
	85.0125
	115.2597
	1.4155%

Income A - Risk Simulator Forecast

Histogram | Statistics | Preferences | Options | Controls

Statistics	Result
Number of Trials	1000
Mean	100.8973
Median	100.4988
Standard Deviation	22.1194
Variance	489.2667
Coefficient of Variation	0.2192
Maximum	180.4507
Minimum	43.7126
Range	136.7381
Skewness	0.1650
Kurtosis	-0.0102
25% Percentile	85.9718
75% Percentile	115.5876
Percentage Error Precision at 95% Confidence	1.3588%

FIGURE 6.65   Simulation modeling results.

that this distribution is considered to be negatively skewed? The same question can be applied to all the other statistics. Is one distribution statistically identical to another distribution with regard to some computed statistics or are they significantly different? Figure 6.65 illustrates some sample bootstrap results. For instance, the 90% confidence for the skewness statistic is between 0.0500 and 0.2585, such that the value 0 falls outside of this confidence interval, indicating that on a 90% confidence, the skewness of this forecast is statistically significantly different from zero, or that this distribution can be considered as positively skewed and not symmetrical. Conversely, if the value 0 falls inside of this confidence, then the opposite is true, the distribution is symmetrical.

Think of it another way: If I have a simple or complicated model (Figure 6.65) and if there is no seed value set in the simulation, each time I run the simulation, I get slightly different values. So, suppose the resulting distribution's skew is 0.1650. How do I test to see if this is just random white noise such that this value is close enough to zero to say it is statistically significantly no different from zero? Or perhaps it is statistically significantly positive. Well, I call up 100 of my best buddies and send them each the same model and ask all of them to do me a big favor and run the simulation 1,000 trials (Figure 6.66). This means each person will have his or her own forecast chart and forecast statistics. So, there will be 100 averages, 100 standard deviations, 100 skew, 100 kurtosis, and so forth. I

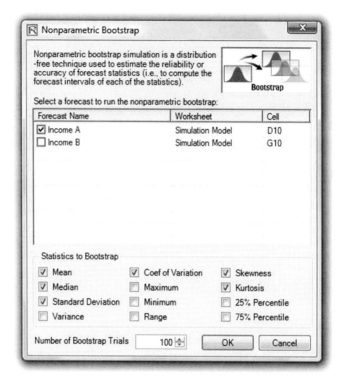

FIGURE 6.66 Running a bootstrap simulation.

call each of them back up and gather all the data and plot the 100 skews in a histogram, and the result is the bootstrapped simulation as shown in Figure 6.67. So, if 90 out of 100 of my buddies (90% confidence interval in Figure 6.67), call me back and provide me a positive skew value, chances are that the real skew is positive! In fact, in Figure 6.67, we actually see that almost 100% of the values are positive, indicating a statistically significant positive skew. In contrast, if the 90% confidence interval straddles zero (the range is positive and negative), such as for the kurtosis measure in Figure 6.67, or in the analogy, 90 out of a 100 friends who call me up provide me both positive and negative values close to zero, I cannot tell if the kurtosis is statistically different than zero and I would correctly infer that there is zero kurtosis.

In other words, bootstrap simulation can be thought of as running a statistical analysis on the statistics, or getting the precision and confidence interval of the statistics, or determining if the simulated forecast statistic is statistically significant. It works well because according to the Law of Large

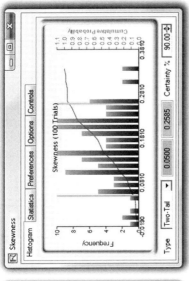
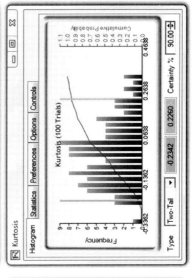
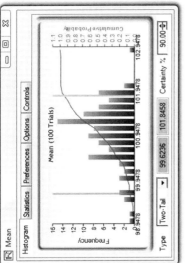
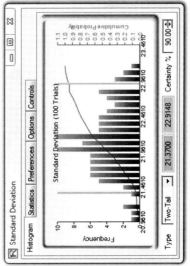

FIGURE 6.67 Bootstrap results and interpretation.

273

Numbers and Central Limit Theorem in statistics, the mean of the sample means is an unbiased estimator and approaches the true population mean when the sample size increases.

To run the exercise, follow the steps below:

1. Start Excel and open the example model *Risk Simulator | Example Models | 08 Hypothesis Testing and Bootstrap Simulation*. Run a simulation as usual by going to *Risk Simulator | Run Simulation* (or click on the *Run* icon), and click *OK* when the simulation is done (Figure 6.65).

2. Click on *Risk Simulator | Tools | Nonparametric Bootstrap* (or click on the *Next* icon repeatedly until you see the *Analytical Tools* ribbon set, and from here you can click on the *Nonparametric Bootstrap* icon). In our example, select *Income A* and then check some of the statistics you wish to test, including *mean, skew,* and *kurtosis* (Figure 6.66) and click *OK*.

3. Review the bootstrap simulation results and create two-tailed confidence intervals for 90%, 95%, and 99%.

   ▪ Exercise Question: Why do we use these 90%, 95%, and 99% confidence levels?

   ▪ Exercise Question: Why do we use two-tails? When can and should we use one-tail, and if so, should it be a left-tail or right-tail confidence?

Theoretical Hypothesis Tests   To run the hypothesis test, use the following procedures:

1. Rerun the same simulation and click on *Risk Simulator | Tools | Hypothesis Test*, and choose two forecasts at a time (in our example model, there are only two forecasts, so make sure both of them are chosen). Select the type of statistical tests you wish to run (for this example, keep the default selection) and click *OK* (Figure 6.68).

2. Review the created statistical analysis report and try to understand the results of the hypothesis test (Figure 6.69).

A hypothesis test is performed when testing the means and variances of two distributions to determine if they are statistically identical or statistically different from one another. It is performed to see if the differences between two means and two variances that occur are based on random chance or are, in fact, different from one another. The two-variable t-test with unequal variances (the population variance of forecast 1 is expected to be different from the population variance of forecast 2) is appropriate when the forecast distributions are from different populations (e.g., data collected from two different geographical locations, two different operating business units,

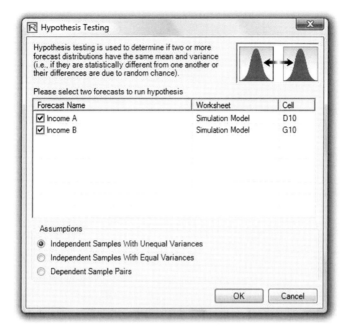

FIGURE 6.68   Hypothesis test types.

and so forth). The two-variable t-test with equal variances (the population variance of forecast 1 is expected to be equal to the population variance of forecast 2) is appropriate when the forecast distributions are from similar populations (e.g., data collected from two different engine designs with similar specifications and so forth). The paired dependent two-variable t-test is appropriate when the forecast distributions are from similar populations (e.g., data collected from the same group of customers but on different occasions, and so forth). A two-tailed hypothesis test is performed on the null hypothesis H_o such that the two variables' population means are statistically identical to one another.

The alternative hypothesis is that the population means are statistically different from one another. If the calculated p-values are less than or equal to 0.01, 0.05, or 0.10, this means that the hypothesis is rejected, which implies that the forecast means are statistically significantly different at the 1%, 5%, and 10% significance levels. If the null hypothesis is not rejected when the p-values are high, the means of the two forecast distributions are statistically similar to one another. The same analysis is performed on variances of two forecasts at a time using the pairwise F-test. If the p-values are small, then

Hypothesis Test on the Means and Variances of Two Forecasts

Statistical Summary

A hypothesis test is performed when testing the means and variances of two distributions to determine if they are statistically identical or statistically different from one another. That is, to see if the differences between two means and two variances that occur are based on random chance or they are in fact different from one another. The two-variable t-test with unequal variances (the population variance of forecast 1 is expected to be different from the population variance of forecast 2) is appropriate when the forecast distributions are from different populations (e.g., data collected from two different geographical locations, two different operating business units, and so forth). The two-variable t-test with equal variances (the population variance of forecast 1 is expected to be equal to the population variance of forecast 2) is appropriate when the forecast distributions are from similar populations (e.g., data collected from two different engine designs with similar specifications, and so forth). The paired dependent two-variable t-test is appropriate when the forecast distributions are from similar populations (e.g., data collected from the same group of customers but on different occasions, and so forth).

A two-tailed hypothesis test is performed on the null hypothesis H_0 such that the two variables' population means are statistically identical to one another. The alternative hypothesis is that the population means are statistically different from one another. If the calculated p-values are less than or equal to 0.01, 0.05, or 0.10, this means that the hypothesis is rejected, which implies that the forecast means are statistically significantly different at the 1%, 5%, and 10% significance levels. If the null hypothesis is not rejected when the p-values are high, the means of the two forecast distributions are statistically similar to one another. The same analysis is performed on variances of two forecasts at a time using the pairwise F-test. If the p-values are small, then the variances (and standard deviations) are statistically different from one another, otherwise, for large p-values, the variances are statistically identical to one another.

Result

Hypothesis Test Assumption:	Unequal Variances:
Computed t-statistic:	1.015722
P-value for t-statistic:	0.309885
Computed F-statistic:	1.063476
P-value for F-statistic:	0.330914

FIGURE 6.69 Hypothesis test results.

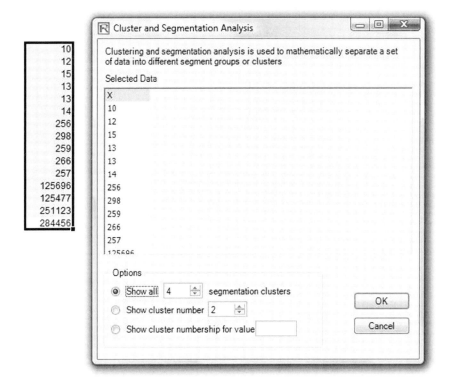

FIGURE 6.70 Segmentation clustering.

the variances (and standard deviations) are statistically different from one another; otherwise, for large p-values, the variances are statistically identical to one another. See Figures 6.68 and 6.69 for details.

Segmentation Clustering Segmentation clustering is the technique of taking a large dataset and running some algorithms that combine k-means hierarchical analysis, data clustering with centroids and Euclidean mean distance measures, and other method of moments to find the best-fitting groups or natural statistical clusters to statistically divide or segment the original dataset into multiple naturally occurring groups. You can see the two-group memberships in Figure 6.70, which illustrates how this is done, and Table 6.2 shows the results of segmenting into two, three, and four groups. Clearly you can segment this dataset into as many groups as you wish. This technique is valuable in a variety of settings including marketing (market segmentation of customers into various customer relationship

TABLE 6.2 Clustering Results

Sample	Ordered Data	Groups		
		2	3	4
1	10	1	1	1
2	12	1	1	1
3	15	1	1	1
4	13	1	1	1
5	13	1	1	1
6	14	1	1	1
7	256	1	1	1
8	298	1	1	1
9	259	1	1	1
10	266	1	1	1
11	257	1	1	1
12	125696	1	2	2
13	125477	1	2	2
14	251123	2	3	3
15	284456	2	3	4

management groups, and so forth), physical sciences, engineering, and others.

To run the exercise on segmentation clustering, follow the steps below:

1. Start a new worksheet and enter in some sample data in a column. You can reuse the sample dataset shown in Figure 6.70. Then select the data (Figure 6.70).
2. Click on *Risk Simulator | Tools | Segmentation Clustering*, and choose any one of the three options. To get started, simply select the first option to *Show All Segmentation Clusters,* select 2 clusters to show, and click *OK*. Review the results that are generated.
3. Repeat the segmentation example but this time use more clusters; for example, set *4* clusters and then run and review the results.
   - Exercise Question: The values 251123 and 284456 look similar but why, when you segment the data into 4 groups, are these two values assigned to different group memberships?
   - Exercise Question: What other applications can you think of that might benefit from using segmentation clustering techniques?

Exercise 5: Data Diagnostics and Statistical Analysis

This sample model illustrates how to use Risk Simulator for:

1. Running Data Diagnostics
2. Running Statistical Analysis

Model Background

> File Name: Regression Diagnostics.xls
>
> Access: **Risk Simulator | Example Models | 16 Regression Diagnostics**
>
> Prerequisites: Risk Simulator 5.2 or later, Chapter 9 (Pitfalls of Forecasting)

Sometimes when you have a lot of data, what do you do with it? In this exercise, we will look at two powerful tools in Risk Simulator, for running data diagnostics and statistical analysis.

Running Data Diagnostics   To run this exercise, use the following procedures:

1. Start Excel and open the example model *Risk Simulator | Example Models | 16 Regression Diagnostics*.
2. Go to the Time Series Data worksheet and select the data you want to analyze, including the data headers (Figure 6.71).
3. Click on *Risk Simulator | Tools | Diagnostic Tool*, select the dependent variable and click *OK*.
   - Exercise Question: What are some of the basic requirements and assumptions in a multiple regression analysis? In other words, if these assumptions are violated, your regression analysis and other related forecast methods will be biased and sometimes invalid.
4. Review the generated report and try to understand what each test is for and how to interpret the results. You can review the *Pitfalls of Forecasting* section for more high-level explanations of these tests and what they do:
   - Heteroskedasticity
   - Micronumerosity
   - Outliers
   - Nonlinearity

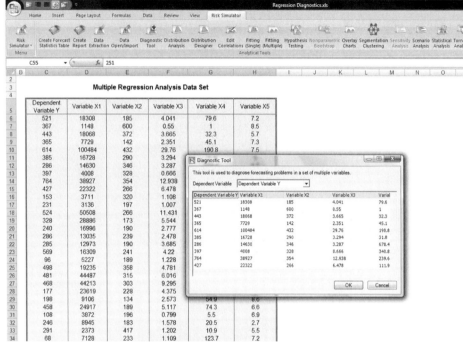

FIGURE 6.71   Data diagnostics.

- Autocorrelation of the Dependent Variable
  - Autocorrelation
  - Partial Autocorrelation
- Distributive Lags of the Independent Variables
- Test for Normality and Sphericity of Errors
- Nonstationarity Analysis of Dependent Variable
  - Brownian motion stochastic process parameter estimation
  - Mean-reversion stochastic process parameter estimation
  - Jump-diffusion stochastic process parameter estimation
- Multicollinearity Analysis of Independent Variables
  - Correlation Matrix
  - Variance Inflation Factor
- Correlation Analysis of All Variables
  - Linear Correlation
  - Nonlinear Correlation
  - Statistical Significance Tests of Correlations
- Charts

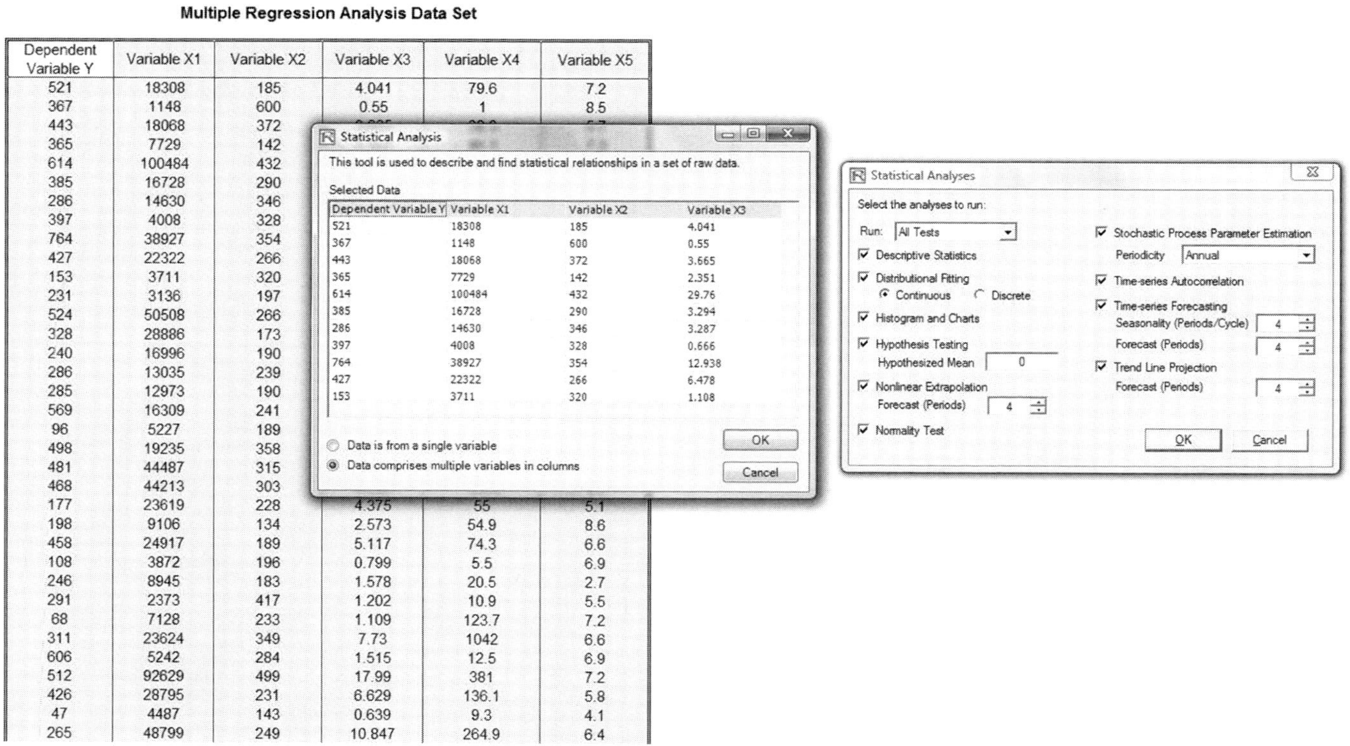

Multiple Regression Analysis Data Set

Dependent Variable Y	Variable X1	Variable X2	Variable X3	Variable X4	Variable X5
521	18308	185	4.041	79.6	7.2
367	1148	600	0.55	1	8.5
443	18068	372			
365	7729	142			
614	100484	432			
385	16728	290			
286	14630	346			
397	4008	328			
764	38927	354			
427	22322	266			
153	3711	320			
231	3136	197			
524	50508	266			
328	28886	173			
240	16996	190			
286	13035	239			
285	12973	190			
569	16309	241			
96	5227	189			
498	19235	358			
481	44487	315			
468	44213	303			
177	23619	228	4.375	55	5.1
198	9106	134	2.573	54.9	8.6
458	24917	189	5.117	74.3	6.6
108	3872	196	0.799	5.5	6.9
246	8945	183	1.578	20.5	2.7
291	2373	417	1.202	10.9	5.5
68	7128	233	1.109	123.7	7.2
311	23624	349	7.73	1042	6.6
606	5242	284	1.515	12.5	6.9
512	92629	499	17.99	381	7.2
426	28795	231	6.629	136.1	5.8
47	4487	143	0.639	9.3	4.1
265	48799	249	10.847	264.9	6.4

Statistical Analysis

This tool is used to describe and find statistical relationships in a set of raw data.

Selected Data

Dependent Variable Y	Variable X1	Variable X2	Variable X3
521	18308	185	4.041
367	1148	600	0.55
443	18068	372	3.665
365	7729	142	2.351
614	100484	432	29.76
385	16728	290	3.294
286	14630	346	3.287
397	4008	328	0.666
764	38927	354	12.938
427	22322	266	6.478
153	3711	320	1.108

○ Data is from a single variable
● Data comprises multiple variables in columns

OK   Cancel

Statistical Analyses

Select the analyses to run:

Run: All Tests

☑ Descriptive Statistics
☑ Distributional Fitting (● Continuous ○ Discrete)
☑ Histogram and Charts
☑ Hypothesis Testing   Hypothesized Mean [0]
☑ Nonlinear Extrapolation
   Forecast (Periods) [4]
☑ Normality Test

☑ Stochastic Process Parameter Estimation   Periodicity [Annual]
☑ Time-series Autocorrelation
☑ Time-series Forecasting   Seasonality (Periods/Cycle) [4]
   Forecast (Periods) [4]
☑ Trend Line Projection   Forecast (Periods) [4]

OK   Cancel

FIGURE 6.72 Statistical analysis.

281

Running Statistical Analysis   To run this exercise, use the following procedures:

1. Select the data you wish to analyze (Figure 6.72). You can use the same model (Regression Diagnostics) or you can open another example in *Risk Simulator | Example Models | 18 Statistical Analysis*. Then go to the *Data* worksheet, making sure the data to analyze are selected.
2. Click on *Risk Simulator | Tools | Statistical Analysis*, and choose whether the dataset selected is a single variable or multiple variables arranged in columns, and click *OK*.
3. You can now select the tests to run or keep and run all tests by default, and click *OK*.
   - Exercise Question: When you are done reviewing the forecast charts, how do you close them all at once without having to exit each one individually?
4. Review the generated report and try to understand what each test is for and how to interpret the results. This tool runs and tests the following items:
   - Descriptive Statistics
   - Single Variable Distributional Fitting
   - Hypothesis Test (t-Test on the Population Mean of One Variable)
   - Nonlinear Extrapolation
   - Test for Normality
   - Stochastic Process Parameter Estimations
   - Autocorrelation
   - Time-Series Forecasting
   - Linear Trend Line Projection

PART Four

Industry Applications

Extended Business Cases I: Pharmaceutical and Biotech Negotiations, Oil and Gas Exploration, Financial Planning with Simulation, Hospital Risk Management, Risk-Based Executive Compensation Valuation, and Risk-Based Schedule Planning

This chapter provides the first installment of six extended business cases. The first case pertains to the application of Monte Carlo simulation and risk analysis in the biotech and pharmaceutical industries. The case details the use of risk analysis for deal making and structuring, and is contributed by Dr. Charles Hardy. The second case in this chapter is contributed by Steve Hoye, a veteran of the oil and gas industry. Steve details the risks involved in oil exploration and production by illustrating a comprehensive oil exploration case from cradle to grave. Then, a financial planning case is presented by Tony Jurado, in considering the risks involved in retirement planning. The next case illustrates how Monte Carlo simulation coupled with queuing theory can be applied to hospital planning, and is contributed by Larry Pixley, an expert consultant in the health-care sector. Finally, Patrick Haggerty illustrates how simulation can be used to engineer a risk-based executive compensation plan, and Mark Rhoades shows us how to perform risk-based schedule planning and project management with simulations.

CASE STUDY: PHARMACEUTICAL AND BIOTECH DEAL STRUCTURING

This business case is contributed by Dr. Charles Hardy, principal of BioAxia Incorporated of Foster City, California, a consulting firm specializing in valuation and quantitative deal structuring for bioscience firms. He is also chief financial officer and director of business development at Panorama Research, a biotechnology incubator in the San Francisco Bay Area. Dr. Hardy has a Ph.D. in pathobiology from the University of Washington in Seattle, Washington, and an M.B.A. in finance and entrepreneurship from the University of Iowa in Iowa City, Iowa. He has functioned in a variety of roles for several start-up companies, including being CEO of Pulmogen, an early-stage medical device company. Dr. Hardy lives and works in the San Francisco Bay Area.

Smaller companies in the biotechnology industry rely heavily on alliances with pharmaceutical and larger companies to finance their R&D expenditures. Pharmaceutical and larger organizations in turn depend on these alliances to supplement their internal R&D programs. In order for smaller organizations to realize the cash flows associated with these alliances, they must have a competent and experienced business development component to negotiate and structure these crucial deals. In fact, the importance of these business collaborations to the survival of most young companies is so great that deal-making experience, polished business-development skills, and a substantial network of contacts are all frequent assets of the most successful executives of start-up and early-stage biotechnology companies.

Although deal-making opportunities for biotech companies are abundant because of the pharmaceutical industry's need to keep a healthy pipeline of new products in development, in recent years deal-making opportunities have lessened. Intuitively, then, firms have to be much more careful in the way they structure and value the deals in which they do get the opportunity to participate. However, despite this importance, a large number of executives prefer to go with comparable business deal structures for these collaborations in the hope of maximizing shareholder value for their firms, or by developing deal terms using their own intuition rather than developing a quantitative methodology for deal valuation and optimization to supplement their negotiation skills and strategies. For companies doing only one deal or less a year, perhaps the risk might be lower by structuring a collaboration based on comparable deal structures; at least they will get as much as the average company, or will they?

As described in this case study, *Monte Carlo simulation, stochastic optimization,* and *real options* are ideal tools for valuing and optimizing the financial terms of collaborative biomedical business deals focused on the development of human therapeutics. A large amount of data associated with clinical trial stage lengths and completion probabilities are publicly available. By quantitatively valuing and structuring deals, companies of all sizes can gain maximum shareholder value at all stages of development, and, most importantly, future cash flows can be defined based on expected cash-flow needs and risk preference.

Deal Types

Most deals between two biotechnology companies or a biotechnology company and pharmaceutical company are strategic alliances where a cooperative agreement is made between two organizations to work together in defined ways with the goal of successfully developing or commercializing products. As the following list describes, there are several different types of strategic alliances:

- *Product Licensing.* A highly flexible and widely applicable arrangement where one party wishes to access the technology of another organization with no other close cooperation. This type of alliance carries very low risk and these types of agreements are made at nearly every stage of pharmaceutical development.
- *Product Acquisition.* A company purchases an existing product license from another company and thus obtains the right to market a fully or partially developed product.
- *Product Fostering.* A short-term exclusive license for a technology or product in a specific market that will typically include hand-back provisions.
- *Comarketing.* Two companies market the same product under different trade names.
- *Copromotion.* Two parties promote the same product under the same brand name.
- *Minority Investment Alliance.* One company buys stock in another as part of a mutually desired strategic relationship.

The historical agreement valued and optimized in this case study is an example of a product-licensing deal.

Financial Terms

Each business deal is decidedly unique, which explains why no "generic" financial model is sufficient to value and optimize every opportunity and collaboration. A biomedical collaborative agreement is the culmination of the combined goals, desires, requirements, and pressures from both sides of the bargaining table, possibly biased in favor of one party by exceptional negotiating skills, good preparation, more thorough due diligence, and accurate assumptions, and less of a need for immediate cash.

The financial terms agreed on for licensing or acquiring a new product or technology depend on a variety of factors, most of which impact the value of the deal. These include but are not limited to:

- Strength of the intellectual property position.
- Exclusivity of the rights agreed on.
- Territorial exclusivity granted.
- Uniqueness of the technology transferred.
- Competitive position of the company.
- Stage of technology developed.
- Risk of the project being licensed or sold.

Although every deal is different, most include: (1) licensing and R&D fees; (2) milestone payments; (3) product royalty payments; and (4) equity investments.

Primary Financial Models

All calculations described in this case study are based on discounted cash-flow (DCF) principals using risk-adjusted discount rates. Here, assets under uncertainty are valued using the following basic financial equation:

$$NPV = \sum_{i=0}^{n} \frac{E(CF_t)}{(1 + r_t + \pi_t)^t}$$

where NPV is the net present value, $E(CF_t)$ is the expected value of the cash flow at time t, r_t is the risk-free rate, and π_t is the risk premium appropriate for the risk of CF_t.

All subcomponents of models described here use different discount rates if they are subject to different risks. In the case of biomedical collaborative agreements, all major subcomponents (licensing fees, R&D costs and funding, clinical costs, milestone payments, and royalties) are frequently subject to many different distinct risks, and thus are all assigned their own discount rates based on a combination of factors, with the subject company's weighted average cost of capital (WACC) used as the base value. To incorporate the uncertain and dynamic nature of these risk assumptions into the model, all of these discount rates are themselves Monte Carlo variables. This discounting supplementation is critical to valuing the deal accurately, and most important for later stochastic optimization.

Historical Deal Background and Negotiated Deal Structure

The deal valued and optimized in this case study was a preclinical, exclusive product-licensing agreement between a small biotechnology company and a larger organization. The biopharmaceutical being valued had one major therapeutic indication, with an estimated market size of $1 billion at the date the deal was signed. The licensee negotiated the right to sublicense. The deal had a variety of funding provisions, with a summary of the financial terms presented in Table 7.1. The licensor estimated it was approximately two years away from filing an investigational new drug (IND) application that would initiate clinical trials in humans. For the purposes of the deal valuation and optimization described here, it is assumed that no information asymmetries exist between the companies forming the collaboration (i.e., both groups feel there is an equally strong likelihood their candidate biopharmaceutical will be a commercial success).

Licensing fees for the historical deal consisted of an up-front fee followed by licensing maintenance fees including multipliers (Table 7.1). Licensing maintenance fees will terminate on any one of the following events: (1) first IND filing by licensor; (2) 10th anniversary of the effective date; and (3) termination of the agreement. Milestone values for the historical deal numbered only three, with a $500,000 payment awarded on IND filing, a $1,500,000 payment on new drug application (NDA) filing, and a $4,000,000 payment on NDA approval (Table 7.1). The negotiated royalties for the historical deal were a flat 2.0 percent of net sales.

As described later in this case, two additional deal scenarios were constructed and stochastically optimized from the historical structure: a higher-value, lower-risk (HVLR) scenario and a higher-value, higher-risk (HVHR) scenario (Table 7.1).

Major Assumptions   Figure 7.1 shows a timeline for all three deal scenarios evaluated. Also shown are the milestone schedules for all three scenarios, along with major assumption data. The total time frame for all deal calculations was 307.9 months, where the candidate pharmaceutical gains a 20 percent maximum market share of a $1 billion market, with a 20 percent standard deviation during the projected 15-year sales period of the pharmaceutical. The market is assumed to grow 1.0 percent annually starting at the effective date of the agreement and throughout the valuation period.

TABLE 7.1 Historical Financial Terms Granted to the Licensor of the Signed Biomedical Collaborative Deal Valued and Optimized in This Case Study

Component	Deal Scenario			Timing
	Historical	Higher-Value, Lower-Risk	Higher-Value, Higher-Risk	
Licensing Fees	$100,000	$125,000	$ 85,000	30 days from effective date
Licensing	$100,000	$125,000	$ 75,000	First anniversary
Maintenance	200,000	250,000	150,000	Second anniversary
Fees	300,000	375,000	225,000	Third anniversary
	400,000	500,000	300,000	Fourth anniversary
	500,000	500,000	300,000	Fifth anniversary
R&D Funding	$250,000	$275,000	$165,000	Per year
Milestone Payments	$500,000	$660,000	$910,000	First IND filing in United States or European equivalent
		895,000		Successful conclusion of Phase I clinical trials in the United States or European equivalent
		1,095,000	1,400,000	Successful conclusion of Phase II clinical trials in the United States or European equivalent
	1,500,000	1,375,000	1,650,000	First PLA[a] (or NDA[b]) filing or European equivalent
	4,000,000	1,675,000	1,890,000	NDA approval in the United States or European equivalent
Royalties	2.0% Net Sales	0.5% Net Sales	5.5%. Net Sales	

[a]Product license application.
[b]New drug application.

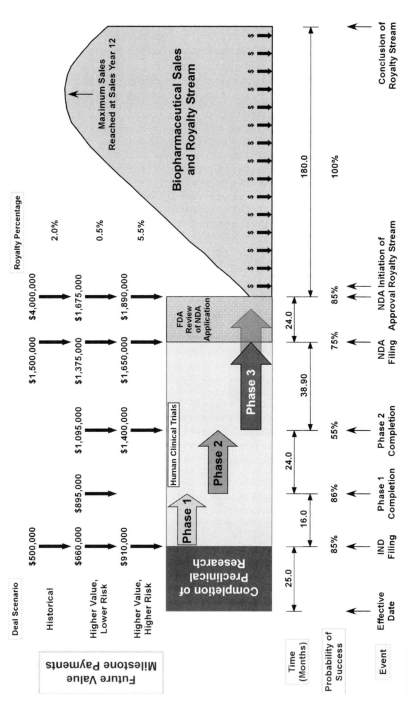

FIGURE 7.1 Timeline for the biomedical licensing deal. Milestone and royalty values for all deal scenarios evaluated are shown. R&D, licensing, and licensing maintenance fees are not shown.

The manufacturing and marketing costs of the potential pharmaceutical were estimated to be 58 percent, an important assumption considering that royalties are paid on net sales, not gross sales. The total market size, market growth rate, maximum market share, and manufacturing and marketing offset are all Monte Carlo variables following lognormal distributions where extreme values are unlikely. Assumptions regarding clinical trial length, completion probabilities, and major variables in the valuation model are also shown in Figure 7.1. All of these values are Monte Carlo assumptions. Throughout this case study, deal values were based on royalties from 15 years of net sales. Royalties were paid on a quarterly basis, not at the end of each sales year. Total R&D costs for the licensor were $200,000 annually, again estimated with a Monte Carlo assumption.

Inflation during the period was assumed to be 1.95 percent annually and average annual pharmaceutical price increases (APPIs) were assumed to be 5.8 percent. Thus, milestones were deflated in value, and royalties inflated by APPI less inflation. For the deal valuation described here, the licensor was assumed to be unprofitable preceding and during the clinical trial process and milestone payments were not subject to taxes. However, royalties from the licensee paid to the licensor were taxed at a 33.0 percent rate.

Deal Valuations

Historical Deal Valuation   Figure 7.2 illustrates the Monte Carlo summary of the historical deal, while Figure 7.3 shows a comparative illustration of each major component of the historical scenario. Mean deal present value was $1,432,128 with a standard deviation of $134,449 (Figure 7.2). The distribution describing the mean was relatively symmetric with a skewness of 0.46. The kurtosis of the distribution, the "peakedness," was 3.47 (excess kurtosis of 0.47), limiting the deal range from $994,954 to $2,037,413. The coefficient of variation (CV), the primary measure of risk for the deal, was low at 9.38 percent. R&D/licensing contributed the most to total deal value with a mean present value of $722,108, while royalties contributed the least with a mean value of $131,092 (Figure 7.3). Milestones in the historical scenario also contributed greatly to the historical deal value with a mean present value of $578,927.

The riskiness of the cash flows varied greatly among individual historical deal components. R&D/licensing cash flows varied the least and had by far the lowest risk with a CV of only 7.48 percent and, proportional to the distribution's mean, had the smallest range among any deal component (data not shown). The present value of milestone cash flows was much more volatile, with a CV of 14.58 percent. Here the range was greater ($315,103 to $1,004,563) with a symmetric distribution having a skewness of only 0.40 (data not shown).

Certainty is 50.00% from $1,338,078 to $1,515,976.

Summary
Certainty level is 50.00%.
Certainty range is from $1,338,115 to $1,516,020.
Display range is from $1,091,067 to $1,772,886.
Entire range is from $994,954 to $2,037,413.
After 10,000 trials, the standard error of the mean is $1,344.

Statistics

Trials	10,000
Mean	$1,432,128
Median	$1,422,229
Standard Deviation	$134,449
Variance	$18,076,644,871
Skewness	0.46
Kurtosis	3.47
Coefficient of Variability	9.38%
Range Minimum	$994,954
Range Maximum	$2,037,413
Range Width	$1,042,459
Mean Standard Error	$1,344

FIGURE 7.2 Historical deal scenario Monte Carlo summary.

Royalty present value was by far the most volatile with a CV of 45.71 percent (data not shown). The kurtosis of royalty present value was large (5.98; data not shown), illustrating the proportionally wide distribution to the small royalty mean ($131,092; Figure 7.3). These data should not be surprising as the royalty cash flows are subject to variability of nearly all Monte Carlo assumptions in the model and are thus highly volatile.

Monte Carlo Assumption and Decision Variable Sensitivities Figure 7.4 shows a tornado chart of historical deal assumptions and decision variables. The probability of IND filing had the largest influence on variation of total deal present value, as all milestones and royalties are dependent on this variable. Interestingly, next came the annual research cost for each full-time equivalent (FTE) for the licensor performing the remaining preclinical work in preparation for an IND filing, followed by the negotiated funding amount of each FTE (Figure 7.4). Thus, an area for the licensor to create shareholder value is to overestimate R&D costs in negotiating the financial terms for the deal, considering R&D/licensing funding contributed 50.42 percent of total deal present value (Figure 7.3). Variables impacting royalty cash flows, such as the royalty discount rate and manufacturing and marketing offset

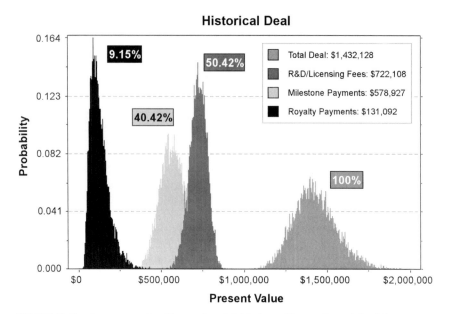

FIGURE 7.3   A comparative illustration I. This is an illustration of the Monte Carlo distributions of the cash-flow present value of the historical deal scenario, along with the distributions of the deal's individual components. Each component has a clearly definable distribution that differs considerably from other deal components, both in value and risk characteristics. The percentage of each component to total deal present value is also shown.

percentages, were more important than the negotiated milestone amounts, although the milestone discount rate was 10th in contribution to variance to the historical deal (Figure 7.4).

Higher-Value, Lower-Risk Deal Valuation

Changes in Key Assumptions and Parameters Differing from the Historical, Signed Deal   The financial structure for the HVLR deal scenario was considerably different from the historical deal (Table 7.1). Indeed, R&D and licensing funding were significantly increased and the milestone schedule was reorganized with five payments instead of the three in the historical deal. In the HVLR scenario, the value of each individual milestone was stochastically optimized using individual restrictions for each payment. While the future value of the milestone payments was actually $300,000 less than the historical deal (Table 7.1), the present value as determined by Monte Carlo analysis was 93.6 percent higher. In devising this scenario, to compensate

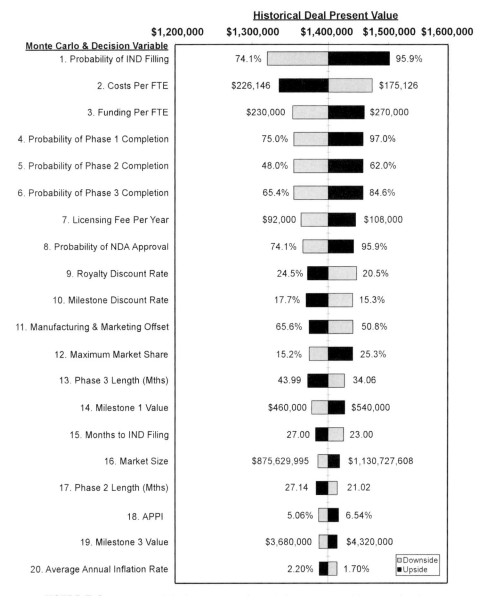

FIGURE 7.4 Historical deal Monte Carlo and decision variable tornado chart.

the licensee for increased R&D/licensing fees and milestone restructuring, the royalty value in the HVLR scenario was reduced to only a 0.5 percent flat rate (Table 7.1).

Deal Valuation, Statistics, and Sensitivities   Figure 7.5 shows the Monte Carlo summary of the HVLR scenario, and Figure 7.6 shows an illustration of present value of the HVLR deal and its three components. The Monte Carlo mean deal value for this scenario was $2,092,617, an increase of 46.1 percent over the historical deal, while total risk was reduced by 16.3 percent as measured by changes in the CV of cash-flow present value (Figures 7.2 and 7.5). This gain in total deal value was achieved by a 93.6 percent increase in the present value of milestone payments (Figures 7.3 and 7.6) along with a 9.6 percent reduction in milestone risk (data not shown). The present value of R&D/licensing funding also increased (30.1 percent) while there is a 22.5 percent reduction in risk. These gains came at the cost of royalty income being reduced by 75.1 percent (Figures 7.3 and 7.6).

The royalty component was so small and the mean so tightly concentrated that the other distributions were comparatively distorted (Panel A,

Certainty is 50.00% from $1,980,294 to $2,200,228.

Summary
Certainty level is 50.00%.
Certainty range is from $1,980,218 to $2,199,958.
Display range is from $1,663,093 to $2,523,897.
Entire range is from $1,475,621 to $2,777,048.
After 10,000 trials, the standard error of the mean is $1,643.

Statistics

Trials	10,000
Mean	$2,092,617
Median	$2,087,697
Standard Deviation	$164,274
Variance	$26,986,218,809
Skewness	0.18
Kurtosis	3.06
Coefficient of Variability	7.85%
Range Minimum	$1,475,620
Range Maximum	$2,777,047
Range Width	$1,301,427
Mean Standard Error	$1,642

FIGURE 7.5   Higher-value, lower-risk deal scenario Monte Carlo.

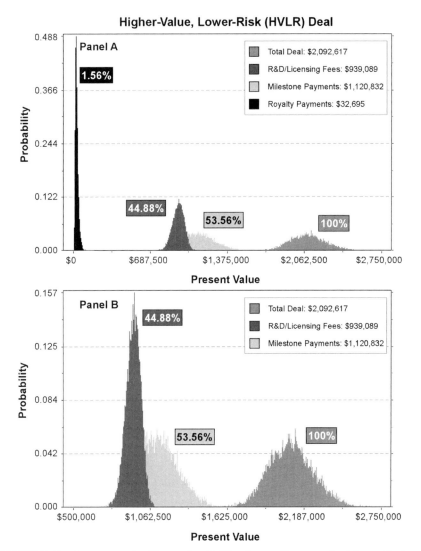

FIGURE 7.6 A comparative illustration II. The figures illustrate the Monte Carlo distributions for cash-flow present value of the HVLR deal scenario along with the distributions of the deal's individual components. Because the royalty cash flows greatly distort the other distributions (Panel A), removing the royalties from the overlay chart allows the other distributions to be more clearly presented (Panel B). The data in Panel B are comparable to a similar representation of the historical deal (Figure 7.3). Here, proportionally, milestones contributed the most to deal value (53.56 percent), followed by R&D/licensing (44.88 percent), while royalties contributed very little (1.56 percent; Panel A).

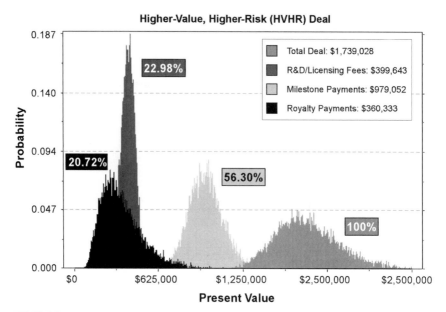

FIGURE 7.7   A comparative illustration III. Illustrations of the Monte Carlo distributions for cash-flow present value of the HVLR deal scenario along with the distributions of the deal's individual components. Here, proportionally, milestones contributed the most to deal value (56.30 percent), followed by R&D/licensing (22.98 percent), while royalties contributed 20.72 percent to total deal value.

Figure 7.6). If the royalty component is removed, the total deal, milestone, and R&D/licensing distributions are more clearly presented (Panel B, Figure 7.6). The milestone percentage of the total HVLR scenario was much higher than the milestone component of the historical deal, while the R&D/licensing fees of the HVLR structure were less than the historical structure (Figures 7.3 and 7.7).

   Cumulatively, the HVLR scenario had a 16.9 percent reduction in risk in comparison to the historical deal (Figures 7.2 and 7.5), where the R&D/licensing and milestone cash flows of HVLR structure were considerably less risky than the historical scenario (data not shown). However, not surprisingly, the risk for the royalty cash flows of the HVLR structure remained nearly identical to that of the historical deal's royalties (data not shown).

Monte Carlo Assumption and Decision Variable Sensitivities   The tornado chart for the HVLR deal is presented in Figure 7.8. As with the historical deal, the probability of IND filing produced the largest variation in the HVLR deal. The annual research cost for each FTE for the licensor

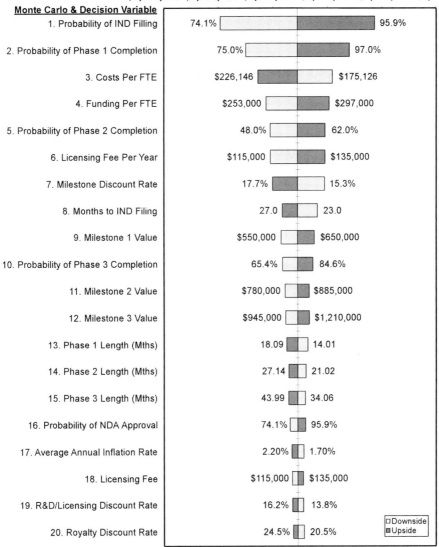

FIGURE 7.8   Higher-value, lower-risk deal scenario Monte Carlo tornado.

performing the remaining preclinical work in preparation for IND filing was third, while the negotiated annual funding amount for each FTE was fourth. The value of each milestone was listed earlier in importance in comparison to the historical deal (Figures 7.4 and 7.8). This result should not be surprising as the present value of total milestones increased 93.6 percent over the historical structure.

The probabilities of completing various clinical trial stages were not clustered as with the historical deal (Figures 7.4 and 7.8). Indeed, the probability of completing Phase 1 was 2nd, the probability of Phase 2 completion 5th, and the probability of Phase 3 completion 10th in predicting variation in total HVLR deal value (Figure 7.8), whereas in the historical deal, these three variables were clustered and ranked 4th through 6th (Figure 7.4). This reorganization is probably because of milestone restructuring where, in the HVLR deal structure, early milestone payments are worth much more (Table 7.1 and Figure 7.1). Among the top 20 most important variables inducing variation in the HVLR deal are the lengths of Phase 1, Phase 2, and Phase 3 clinical trials (13th–15th; Figure 7.8), although their importance was considerably less than the historical deal (Figure 7.4). This is probably because of the reduced royalty component of the HVLR scenario (Table 7.1).

Higher-Value, Higher-Risk Deal Valuation

Changes in Key Assumptions and Parameters Differing from the Historical and HVLR Deal Structures
A variety of financial terms were changed for the HVHR deal structure. First, licensing and licensing maintenance fees were reduced, sometimes substantially (Table 7.1). R&D fees were reduced across the board from the historical deal and the milestone schedule was completely restructured. The historical structure had three payments and the HVLR structure five, with the HVHR deal having only four (Figure 7.1). As shown, the milestone future value for the HVHR deal was reduced to $5,850,000 from $6,000,000 in the historical deal. Like the HVLR deal, the milestone values for the HVHR scenario were stochastically optimized based on specific ranges. The sacrifices gained by lower licensing fees, R&D funding, and milestone restructuring were compensated for by a higher flat royalty rate of 5.5 percent of net sales (Table 7.1).

Deal Valuation, Statistics, and Sensitivities
Figure 7.7 shows an illustration of the total HVHR deal along with its three components. Total deal value for the HVHR scenario was $1,739,028, a 21.4 percent increase from the historical deal and 16.9 percent decrease from the HVLR structure.

TABLE 7.2 Deal Scenario Summary Table as Calculated by Monte Carlo Analysis

Deal Structure	Expected Value	CV	Range Minimum	Range Maximum	Range Width
Historical	$1,432,128	9.38%	$ 994,954	$2,037,413	$1,042,459
Higher-Value, Lower-Risk	2,092,617	7.85	1,475,620	2,777,047	1,301,427
Higher-Value, Higher-Risk	1,739,028	14.33	1,060,603	3,462,679	2,402,076

R&D/licensing present value decreased by 44.7 percent and 57.4 percent from the historical and HVLR deals, respectively (Figures 7.3 through 7.7).

The royalty distribution is much more pronounced and noticeably positively skewed, and illustrates the large downside potential of this deal component. Changes in the royalty percentage also significantly expanded the range maximum for the total deal ($3,462,679) with a range width of $2,402,076, a 130.4 percent increase from the historical and 84.6 percent increase over the HVLR deal widths, respectively (Table 7.2).

Milestone present value increased by 69.1 percent from the historical deal and decreased 12.6 percent from the HVLR scenario, while royalty present value increased 175 percent and 1,002 percent, respectively (Figures 7.3 through 7.7). Both the skewness and kurtosis of total deal value under the HVHR scenario were greater than the other deal structures evaluated (Figures 7.3 through 7.7). This result has to do with the greater royalty component in the HVHR scenario and its associated large cash-flow volatility.

The overall deal risk under the HVHR scenario was the greatest (14.33 percent) in comparison to the historical deal's 9.38 percent and the HVLR scenario's 7.85 percent cash-flow CV, again illustrating the strong royalty component of this deal structure with its greater volatility. With the HVHR deal, R&D/licensing cash flows had much higher risk than either the historical or HVLR deals (data not shown). This increased risk is surely because negotiated R&D funding per FTE and licensing fees were considerably less than the estimated cost per FTE, resulting in more R&D/licensing cash-flow volatility in the HVHR structure. This result again shows the importance of accurate accounting and finance in estimating R&D costs for maximizing this type of licensing deal value.

Monte Carlo Assumption and Decision Variable Sensitivities   The tornado chart for the HVHR deal scenario emphasized the importance of variables directly impacting royalty cash flows (Figure 7.9). Here, the royalty discount

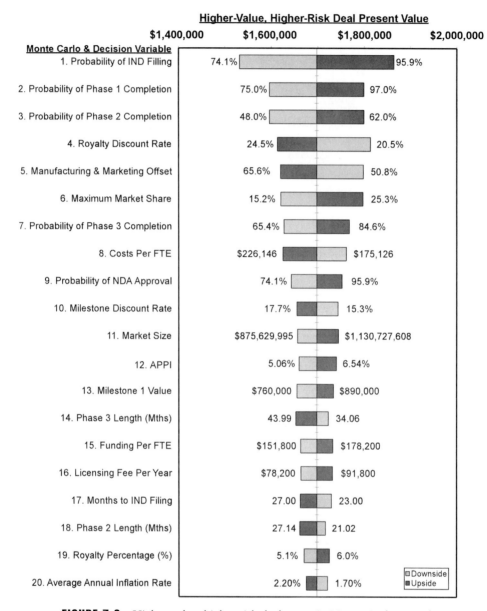

FIGURE 7.9   Higher-value, higher-risk deal scenario Monte Carlo tornado.

Certainty is 50.00% from $1,563,891 to $1,882,975.

Summary
Certainty level is 50.00%.
Certainty range is from $1,563,891 to $1,882,975.
Display range is from $1,132,837 to $2,396,924.
Entire range is from $1,060,603 to $3,462,679.
After 10,000 trials, the standard error of the mean is $2,493.

Statistics

Trials	10,000
Mean	$1,739,028
Median	$1,712,532
Standard Deviation	$249,257
Variance	$62,129,317,618
Skewness	0.77
Kurtosis	4.39
Coefficient of Variability	14.33%
Range Minimum	$1,060,603
Range Maximum	$3,462,679
Range Width	$2,402,076
Mean Standard Error	$2,492

FIGURE 7.10 Higher-value, higher-risk deal scenario Monte Carlo summary.

rate was 4th, manufacturing and marketing offset 5th, and maximum market share capture 6th in impacting total deal present value variation. Total market size and the average APPI were 11th and 12th, respectively. Interestingly, the negotiated royalty percentage was only 19th in contribution to deal variance. Cost per FTE ranked 8th, showing this assumption is important in all deal scenarios (Figures 7.4, 7.8, and 7.9). Figure 7.10 shows the Monte Carlo simulation results for HVHR.

The negotiated first milestone value was the only milestone listed on the sensitivity chart (13th, Figure 7.9), illustrating the importance of milestone structuring (Table 7.1 and Figure 7.1). The first milestone is impacted the least by the time value of money and the probability of completion of each clinical trial stage.

A Structural Comparison of Deal Scenario Returns and Risks

Total deal expected value and risk as measured by the CV of cash-flow present value are shown in Table 7.2. As illustrated here, higher expected value is not necessarily correlated with higher risk, which is contrary to a basic principal in finance where investments of higher risk should always yield higher returns. Thus, these data show why quantitative deal valuation and optimization is critical for *all* companies as higher deal values can be constructed with significantly less risk.

Also shown in Table 7.2 are the range minimums, maximums, and widths of the total deal value distributions as calculated by Monte Carlo analysis for each scenario evaluated. The range minimum is the smallest number and the range maximum is the largest number in a distribution, while the range width is the difference between the range minimum and maximum.

Collaborative business deals in the biotechnology and pharmaceutical industries formed during strategic alliances, such as the one described here, are in fact risky asset portfolios. As such, the standard deviation of a portfolio of assets is less than the weighted average of the component asset standard deviations. To view the impact of diversification of cash-flow streams with the various deal scenarios evaluated in this case study, the weight of each deal component was determined and the weighted average CV of cash-flow present value calculated for each deal scenario (Table 7.3). The CV is used as the primary risk measure because of differences in the scale of the cash flows from individual deal components.

As expected with a portfolio of risky assets, the weighted average of the CV of individual deal components (R&D/licensing funding, milestone payments, and royalties) was always greater than the CV of the total deal present value, illustrating the impact of diversification (Table 7.3). Thus, portfolios of less than perfectly correlated assets always offer better risk–return opportunities than the individual component assets on their own. As such, companies would probably not want to completely forgo receiving milestone payments and royalties for only R&D funding and licensing fees, *if* these deal components can be valued and optimized with reasonable accuracy as described here. By combining assets whose returns are uncorrelated or partially correlated, such as cash flows from milestone payments, royalties, licensing, and R&D funding, risk is reduced (Table 7.3). Risk can be eliminated most rapidly while keeping expected returns as high as possible if a company's cumulative deal repertoire is valued, structured, and balanced from the beginning of a company's evolution and development.

Discussion and Conclusion

The historical deal evaluated in this case study was a preclinical, product-licensing deal for a biopharmaceutical with one major therapeutic indication. For collaborative deal structures containing licensing fees, R&D

TABLE 7.3 Deal Component Weights, Component CVs, Weighted Average Deal CVs, and Calculated Deal CVs

Deal Structure	Weights			Coefficient of Variation (CV)				
	$W_{R\&D}$[a]	W_{Mi}[b]	W_{Ry}[c]	R&D[d]	Milestones	Royalties	W. Avg.[e]	Calculated[f]
Historical	50.42%	40.42%	9.17%	7.47%	14.57%	45.70%	13.84%	9.38%
Higher-Value, Lower-Risk	44.88	53.56	1.56	5.79	13.18	45.95	10.38	7.85
Higher-Value, Higher-Risk	22.98	56.30	20.72	13.40	12.69	46.21	19.80	14.33

[a]Proportion of total deal present value attributable to R&D and licensing fees.
[b]Proportion of total deal present value attributable to milestone payments.
[c]Proportion of total deal present value attributable to royalty payments.
[d]CV in the present value of cash flows from R&D and licensing fees.
[e]Weighted average of the CV of total deal value.
[f]Calculated deal CV by Monte Carlo simulation.

funding, milestone payments, and royalties, each deal component has definable expected values, variances, and widely varying risk characteristics. Alternative deal structures were developed and optimized, all of which had different expected returns and risk levels with the primary risk measure being the CV of cash-flow present values. Thus, nearly any biomedical collaborative deal with the types of financial terms described here can be quantitatively valued, structured, and optimized using financial models, Monte Carlo analysis, stochastic optimization, real options, and portfolio theory.

During this study, the author was at a considerable disadvantage because the historical deal valued and optimized here had already been signed, and he was not present during the negotiation process. Therefore, the author had to make a large number of assumptions when restructuring the financial terms of the agreement. Considering these limitations, this case is not about what is appropriate in the comparative financial terms for a biomedical licensing deal and what is not; rather, the data described here are valuable in showing the quantitative influence of different deal structures on the overall valuation of a biomedical collaborative agreement, and most importantly on the level of overall deal risk, as well as the risk of the individual deal components. The most effective approach using this technique is to work with a negotiator during the development and due diligence, and through the closing process of a collaborative agreement. During this time, data should be continually gathered and the financial models refined as negotiations and due diligence proceed.

CASE STUDY: OIL AND GAS EXPLORATION AND PRODUCTION

This case study is contributed by Steve Hoye. Steve is an independent business consultant with more than 23 years of oil and gas industry experience, specializing in Monte Carlo simulation for the oil and gas industry. Starting with a bachelor of science degree from Purdue University in 1980, he served as a geophysicist with Texaco in Houston, Denver, and Midland, Texas, before earning the M.B.A. degree from the University of Denver in 1997. Since then, Steve has held leadership roles with Texaco as the midcontinent BU technology team leader, and as asset team manager in Texaco's Permian Basin business unit, before starting his consultancy in 2002.

The oil and gas industry is an excellent place to examine and discuss techniques for analyzing risk. The basic business model discussed involves making investments in land rights, geologic data, drilling (services and hardware), and human expertise in return for a stream of oil or gas production that can be sold at a profit. This model is beset with multiple, significant risk factors that determine the resulting project's profitability, including:

- *Dry-Hole Risk.* Investing drilling dollars with no resulting revenue from oil or gas because none is found in the penetrated geologic formation.
- *Drilling Risk.* High drilling costs can often ruin a project's profitability. Although companies do their best to estimate them accurately, unforeseeable geological or mechanical difficulties can cause significant variability in actual costs.
- *Production Risk.* Even when oil or gas reservoirs are discovered by drilling, there is a high probability that point estimates of the size and recoverability of the hydrocarbon reserves over time are wrong.
- *Price Risk.* Along with the cyclical nature of the oil and gas industry, product prices can also vary unexpectedly during significant political events such as war in the Middle East, overproduction and cheating by the OPEC cartel, interruptions in supply such as large refinery fires, labor strikes, or political uprisings in large producing nations (e.g., Venezuela in 2002), and changes in world demand.
- *Political Risk.* Significant amounts of the world's hydrocarbon reserves are controlled by nations with unstable governments. Companies that invest in projects in these countries take significant risks that the governments and leaders with whom they have signed contracts will no longer be in power when earned revenue streams should be shared contractually. In many well-documented cases, corporate investments in property, plants, and equipment (PPE) are simply nationalized by local governments, leaving companies without revenue or the equipment and facilities that they built to earn that revenue.

Oil and gas investments generally are very capital-intensive, often making these risks more than just of passing interest. Business units and entire companies stake their survival on their ability to properly account for these risks as they apportion their capital budgets in a manner that ensures value to their stakeholders. To underline the importance of risk management in the industry, many large oil companies commission high-level corporate panels of experts to review and endorse risk assessments done across all of their business units for large capital projects. These reviews attempt to ensure consistency of risk assessment across departments and divisions that are often under pressure to make their investment portfolios look attractive to corporate leadership as they compete for capital.

Monte Carlo simulation is a preferred approach to the evaluation of the multiple, complex risk factors in the model we discuss. Because of the inherent complexity of these risk factors and their interactions, deterministic solutions are not practical, and point forecasts are of limited use and, at worst, are misleading. In contrast, Monte Carlo simulation is ideal for economic evaluations under these circumstances. Domain experts can individually quantify and describe the project risks associated with their areas of expertise without having to define their overall effect on project economics.[1] Cash-flow models that integrate the diverse risk assumptions for each of the prospect team's experts are relatively straightforward to construct and analyze. Most importantly, the resulting predictions of performance do not result in a simple single-point estimate of the profitability of a given oil and gas prospect. Instead, they provide management with a spectrum of possible outcomes and their related probabilities. Best of all, Monte Carlo simulation provides estimates of the sensitivities of their investment outcomes to the critical assumptions in their models, allowing them to focus money and people on the critical factors that will determine whether they meet the financial goals defined in their business plans. Ultimately, Monte Carlo simulation becomes a project management tool that decreases risk while increasing profits.

In this case study, we explore a practical model of an oil-drilling prospect, taking into account many of the risk factors described earlier. While the model is hypothetical, the general parameters we use are consistent with those encountered drilling in a mature, oil-rich basin in the United States (e.g., Permian Basin of West Texas) in terms of the risk factors and related revenues and expenses. This model is of greater interest as a framework and approach than it is as an evaluation of any particular drilling prospect. Its value is in demonstrating the approach to quantifying important risk assumptions in an oil prospect using Monte Carlo simulation, and analyzing their effects on the profitability forecasts of the project. The techniques described herein are extensible to many other styles and types of oil and gas prospects.

Cash-Flow Model

The model was constructed using Risk Simulator, which provides all of the necessary Monte Carlo simulation tools as an easy-to-use, comprehensive add-in to Microsoft Excel. The model simulates the drilling outcome as being a dry-hole or an oil discovery using dry-hole risk factors for the particular geologic formation and basin. Drilling, seismic, and land-lease costs are incurred whether the well is dry or a discovery. If the well is a discovery, a revenue stream is computed for the produced oil over time using assumptions for product price, and for the oil production rate as it declines over time from its initial value. Expenses are deducted for royalty payments to landowners, operating costs associated with producing the oil, and severance taxes levied by states on the produced oil. Finally, the resulting net cash flows are discounted at the weighted average cost of capital (WACC) for the firm and summed to a net present value (NPV) for the project. Each of these sections of the model is now discussed in more detail.

Dry-Hole Risk

Companies often have proprietary schemes for quantifying the risk associated with not finding any oil or gas in their drilled well. In general, though, there are four primary and independent conditions that must all be encountered in order for hydrocarbons to be found by the drill bit:

1. *Hydrocarbons* must be present.
2. A *reservoir* must be developed in the rock formation to hold the hydrocarbons.
3. An impermeable *seal* must be available to trap the hydrocarbons in the reservoir and prevent them from migrating somewhere else.
4. A *structure* or *closure* must be present that will cause the hydrocarbons (sealed in the reservoir) to pool in a field where the drill bit will penetrate.

Because these four factors are independent and must each be true in order for hydrocarbons to be encountered by the drill bit (and a dry hole to be avoided), the probability of a producing well is defined as:

$$P_{\text{Producing Well}} = P_{\text{Hydrocarbons}} \times P_{\text{Reservoir}} \times P_{\text{Seal}} \times P_{\text{Structure}}$$

Figure 7.11 shows the model section labeled "Dry-Hole Risk," along with the probability distributions for each factor's Monte Carlo assumption. While a project team most often describes each of these factors as a single-point estimate, other methods are sometimes used to quantify these

Dry-Hole Risk Risk Factor	Prob. of Success	Mean	Stdev	Min	Max
Hydrocarbons	89.7%	99.0%	5.0%	0	100%
Structure	89.7%	100.0%	0.0%	0	100%
Reservoir	89.7%	75.0%	10.0%	0	100%
Seal	89.7%	100.0%	0.0%	0	100%
Net Producing Well Prob.:	**64.8%**				
Producing Well [0=no,1=yes]	1				

FIGURE 7.11 Dry-hole risk.

risks. The most effective process the author has witnessed involved the presentation of the geological, geophysical, and engineering factors by the prospect team to a group of expert peers with wide experience in the proposed area. These peer experts then rated each of the risk factors. The resulting distribution of risk factors often appeared near-normally distributed, with strong central tendencies and symmetrical tails. This approach was very amenable to Monte Carlo simulation. It highlighted those factors where there was general agreement about risk and brought the riskiest factors to the foreground where they were examined and specifically addressed.

Accordingly, the assumptions regarding dry-hole risk in this model reflect a relatively low risk profile.[2] Each of the four risk factor assumptions in Figure 7.11 (dark shaded area) are described as normally distributed variables, with the mean and standard deviations for each distribution to the right of the assumption fields. The ranges of these normal distributions are confined and truncated between the *min* and *max* fields, and random samples for any simulation trial outside this range are ignored as unrealistic.

As described earlier, the *Net Producing Well Probability* field in the model corresponds to the product of the four previously described risk factors. These four risk factors are drawn as random samples from their respective normal distributions for each trial or iteration of the simulation. Finally, as each iteration of the Monte Carlo simulation is conducted, the field labeled *Producing Well* generates a random number between zero and one to determine if that simulation resulted in a discovery of oil or a dry hole. If the random number is less than the *Net Producing Well Probability*, it is a producing well and shows the number one. Conversely, if the random number is greater than the *Net Producing Well Probability*, the simulated well is a dry hole and shows zero.

Production Risk

A multiyear stream of oil can be characterized as an initial oil production rate (measured in barrels of oil per day, BOPD), followed by a decline in production rates as the natural reservoir energy and volumes are depleted over time. Reservoir engineers can characterize production declines using a wide array of mathematical models, choosing those that most closely match the geology and producing characteristics of the reservoir. Our hypothetical production stream is described with two parameters:

1. *IP.* The initial production rate tested from the drilled well.
2. *Decline Rate.* An exponentially declining production rate that describes the annual decrease in production from the beginning of the year to

the end of the same year. Production rates in BOPD for our model are calculated by:

$$Rate_{Year\ End} = (1 - Decline\ Rate) \times Rate_{Year\ Begin}$$

Yearly production volumes in barrels of oil are approximated as:

$$Oil\ Volume_{Year} = 365 \times (Rate_{Year\ Begin} + Rate_{Year\ End})/2$$

For Monte Carlo simulation, our model represents the IPs with a log-normal distribution with a mean of 441 BOPD and a standard deviation of 165 BOPD. The decline rate was modeled with a uniform probability of occurrence between 15 percent and 28 percent. To add interest and realism to our hypothetical model, we incorporated an additional constraint in the production model that simulates a situation that might occur for a particular reservoir where higher IPs imply that the production decline rate will be higher. This constraint is implemented by imposing a correlation coefficient of 0.60 between the IP and decline rate assumptions that are drawn from their respective distributions during each trial of the simulation.

The production and operating expense sections of the model are shown in Figure 7.12. Although only the first 3 years are shown, the model accounts for up to 25 years of production. However, when production declines below the economic limit,[3] it will be zeroed for that year and every subsequent year, ending the producing life of the well. As shown, the IP is assumed to occur at the end of Year 0, with the first full year of production accounted for at the end of Year 1.

	Decline Rate	End of Year: 0	1	2	3
BOPD	21.5%	442	347	272	214
Net BBLS / Yr			143,866	112,924	88,636
Price / BBl			$ 20.14	$ 20.14	$ 20.14
Net Revenue Interest	77.4%		77.4%	77.4%	77.4%
Revenue			**$ 2,242,311**	**$ 1,760,035**	**$ 1,381,487**
Operating Costs [$/Barrel]	$ 4.80		$ (690,558)	$ (542,033)	$ (425,453)
Severance Taxes [$]	6.0%	rate	$ (134,539)	$ (105,602)	$ (82,889)
Net Sales			$ 1,417,214	$ 1,112,400	$ 873,145

FIGURE 7.12 Decline rate.

Revenue Section

Revenues from the model flow literally from the sale of the oil production computed earlier. Again there are two assumptions in our model that represent risks in our prospect:

1. *Price.* Over the past two decades, oil prices have varied from $13.63/barrel in 1998 to nearly $30/barrel in 2000.[4] Consistent with the data, our model assumes a normal price distribution with a mean of $20.14 and a standard deviation of $4.43/barrel.
2. *Net Revenue Interest.* Oil companies must purchase leases from mineral interest holders. Along with paying cash to retain the drilling and production rights to a property for a specified time period, the lessee also generally retains some percentage of the oil revenue produced in the form of a royalty. The percentage that the producing company retains after paying all royalties is the net revenue interest (NRI). Our model represents a typical West Texas scenario with an assumed NRI distributed normally with a mean of 75 percent and a standard deviation of 2 percent.

The revenue portion of the model is also shown in Figure 7.12 immediately below the production stream.

The yearly production volumes are multiplied by sampled price per barrel, and then multiplied by the assumed NRI to reflect dilution of revenues from royalty payments to lessees.

Operating Expense Section

Below the revenue portion are operating expenses, which include two assumptions:

1. *Operating Costs.* Companies must pay for manpower and hardware involved in the production process. These expenses are generally described as a dollar amount per barrel. A reasonable West Texas cost would be $4.80 per barrel with a standard deviation of $0.60 per barrel.
2. *Severance Taxes.* State taxes levied on produced oil and gas are assumed to be a constant value of 6 percent of revenue.

Operating expenses are subtracted from the gross sales to arrive at net sales, as shown in Figure 7.12.

Drilling Costs	$ 1,209,632
Completion Cost	$ 287,000
Professional Overhead	$ 160,000
Lease Costs / Well	$ 469,408
Seismic Costs / Well	$ 81,195

FIGURE 7.13 Year 0 expenses.

Year 0 Expenses Figure 7.13 shows the Year 0 expenses assumed to be incurred before oil production from the well (and revenue) is realized. These expenses are:

1. *Drilling Costs.* These costs can vary significantly as previously discussed, due to geologic, engineering, and mechanical uncertainty. It is reasonable to skew the distribution of drilling costs to account for a high-end tail consisting of a small number of wells with very large drilling costs due to mechanical failure and unforeseen geologic or serendipitous occurrences. Accordingly, our distribution is assumed to be lognormal, with a mean of $1.2 million and a standard deviation of $200,000.

2. *Completion Costs.* If it is determined that there is oil present in the reservoir (and we have not drilled a dry hole), engineers must prepare the well (mechanically/chemically) to produce oil at the optimum sustainable rates.[5] For this particular well, we hypothesize our engineers believe this cost is normally distributed with a mean of $287,000 and a standard deviation of $30,000.

3. *Professional Overhead.* This project team costs about $320,000 per year in salary and benefits, and we believe the time they have spent is best represented by a triangular distribution, with a most likely percentage of time spent as 50 percent, with a minimum of 40 percent, and a maximum of 65 percent.

4. *Seismic and Lease Costs.* To develop the proposal, our team needed to purchase seismic data to choose the optimum well location, and to purchase the right to drill on much of the land in the vicinity of the well. Because this well is not the only well to be drilled on this seismic data and land, the cost of these items is distributed over the planned number of wells in the project. Uncertain assumptions are shown in Figure 7.14, and include leased acres, which were assumed to be normally distributed with a mean of 12,000 and a standard deviation of 1,000 acres. The total number of planned wells over which to distribute the costs was assumed to be uniform between 10 and 30. The number of seismic sections acquired was also assumed to be normally distributed with a mean of 50 sections and a standard deviation of 7. These costs are represented as the final two lines of Year 0 expenses in Figure 7.13.

Lease Expense		Comments
Project Lease Acres	12,800	20 sections
Planned Wells	20.0	
Acres / Well	640	
Acreage Price	$ 733.45	$ / acre
Acreage Cost / Well	$ 469,408	

Seismic Expense		
Seismic Sections Acquired	50.0	
Seismic Sections / Well	2.50	
Seismic Cost	$ 32,478.18	$ / section
Seismic Cost / Well	$ 81,195	

FIGURE 7.14   Uncertain assumptions.

Net Present Value Section

The final section of the model sums all revenues and expenses for each year starting at Year 0, discounted at the weighted average cost of capital (WACC—which we assume for this model is 9 percent per year), and summed across years to compute the forecast of NPV for the project. In addition, NPV/I is computed,[6] as it can be used as a threshold and ranking mechanism for portfolio decisions as the company determines how this project fits with its other investment opportunities given a limited capital budget.

Monte Carlo Simulation Results

As we assess the results of running the simulation with the assumptions defined previously, it is useful to define and contrast the point estimate of project value computed from our model using the mean or most likely values of the earlier assumptions. The expected value of the project is defined as:

$$
\begin{aligned}
E_{\text{Project}} &= E_{\text{Dry Hole}} + E_{\text{Producing Well}} \\
&= P_{\text{Dry Hole}} NPV_{\text{Dry Hole}} + P_{\text{Producing Well}} NPV_{\text{Producing Well}}
\end{aligned}
$$

where $P_{\text{Producing Well}}$ = probability of a producing well and $P_{\text{Dry Hole}}$ = probability of a dry hole = $(1 - P_{\text{Producing Well}})$. Using the mean or most likely point estimate values from our model, the expected NPV of the project is $1,250,000, which might be a very attractive prospect in the firm's portfolio.

In contrast, we can now examine the spectrum of outcomes and their probability of occurrence. Our simulation was run with 8,450 trials (trial size selected by precision control) to forecast NPV, which provided a mean NPV plus or minus $50,000 with 95 percent confidence. Figure 7.15 is

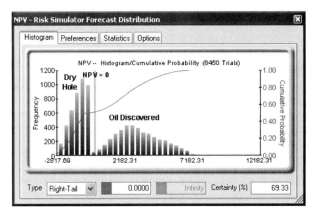

FIGURE 7.15 Frequency distribution of NPV outcomes.

the frequency distribution of NPV outcomes. The distribution is obviously bimodal, with the large, sharp negative NPV peak to the left representing the outcome of a dry hole. The smaller, broader peak toward the higher NPV ranges represents the wider range of more positive NPVs associated with a producing well.

All negative NPV outcomes are to the left of the $NPV = 0$ line (with a lighter shade) in Figure 7.15, while positive outcome NPVs are represented by the area to the right of the $NPV = 0$ line with the probability of a positive outcome (breakeven or better) shown as 69.33 percent. Of interest, the negative outcome possibilities include not only the dry-hole population of outcomes as shown, but also a small but significant portion of producing-well outcomes that could still lose money for the firm. From this information, we can conclude that there is a 30.67 percent chance that this project will have a negative NPV.

It is obviously not good enough for a project of this sort to avoid a negative NPV. The project must return to shareholders something higher than its cost of capital, and, further, must be competitive with other investment opportunities that the firm has. If our hypothetical firm had a hurdle rate of NPV/I greater than 25 percent for its yearly budget, we would want to test our simulated project outcomes against the probability that the project could clear that hurdle rate.

Figure 7.16 shows the forecast distribution of outcomes for NPV/I. The large peak at negative 100 percent again represents the dry-hole case, where in fact the NPV of the outcome is negative in the amount of Year 0 costs incurred, making NPV/I equal to -1. All outcomes for NPV greater than the hurdle rate of 25 percent show that there is a 64 percent probability that the project will exceed that rate. To a risk-sensitive organization, this outcome

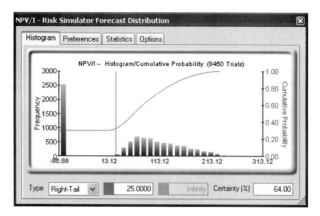

FIGURE 7.16   Forecast distribution of NPV to I ratio.

implies a probability of greater than one in three that the project will fail to clear the firm's hurdle rate—significant risk indeed.

Finally, our simulation gives us the power to explore the sensitivity of our project outcomes to the risks and assumptions that have been made by our experts in building the model. Figure 7.17 shows a sensitivity analysis of the NPV of our project to the assumptions made in our model. This chart shows the correlation coefficient of the top 10 model assumptions to the NPV forecast in order of decreasing correlation.

At this point, the project manager is empowered to focus resources on the issues that will have an impact on the profitability of this project. Given the information from Figure 7.17, we could hypothesize the following actions to address the top risks in this project in order of importance:

- *IP.* The initial production rate of the well has a driving influence on value of this project, and our uncertainty in predicting this rate is causing the

Net Cash Flows	.40	
Reservoir	.17	
Price / BBl 1	.14	
Drilling Costs	−.13	
Decline Rate	.10	
Price / BBl 2	.10	
Planned Wells	.09	
Acreage Price [$/acre]	−.08	
Price / BBl 3	.07	
Operating Costs [$/Barrel]	−.07	

FIGURE 7.17   NPV sensitivity analysis.

largest swing in predicted project outcomes. Accordingly, we could have our team of reservoir and production engineers further examine known production IPs from analogous reservoirs in this area, and perhaps attempt to stratify the data to further refine predictions of IPs based on drilling or completion techniques, geological factors, or geophysical data.

- *Reservoir Risk.* This assumption is the driver of whether the well is a dry hole or producer, and as such it is not surprising that it is a major driving factor. Among many approaches, the project team could investigate the possibility that inadequate analysis of subsurface data is causing many companies to declare dry holes in reservoirs that have hidden producing potential.

- *Oil Price (Year 1) and Drilling Costs.* Both of these items are closely related in their power to affect NPV. Price uncertainty could best be addressed by having a standard price prediction for the firm against which all projects would be compared.[7] Drilling costs could be minimized by process improvements in the drilling team that would tighten the variation of predicted costs from actual costs. The firm could seek out companies with strong track records in their project area for reliable, low-cost drilling.

- *Decline Rate.* The observant reader will note a positive-signed correlation between decline rate and project NPV. At first glance this is unexpected, because we would normally expect that a higher decline rate would reduce the volumes of oil to be sold and hurt the revenue realized by our project. Recall, however, that we correlated higher IPs with higher decline rates in our model assumptions, which is an indirect indication of the power of the IP on the NPV of our project: Despite higher decline rates, the positive impact of higher IPs on our project value is overriding the lost production that occurs because of the rapid reservoir decline. We should redouble our efforts to better predict IPs in our model.

Conclusion

Monte Carlo simulation can be an ideal tool for evaluating oil and gas prospects under conditions of significant and complex uncertainty in the assumptions that would render any single-point estimate of the project outcome nearly useless. The technique provides each member of multidisciplinary work teams a straightforward and effective framework for quantifying and accounting for each of the risk factors that will influence the outcome of his or her drilling project. In addition, Monte Carlo simulation provides management and team leadership something much more valuable than a single forecast of the project's NPV: It provides a probability distribution of the entire spectrum of project outcomes, allowing decision makers to explore any pertinent scenarios associated with the project value. These scenarios could include break-even probabilities as well as scenarios associated with extremely poor project results that could damage the project team's credibility and future access to capital, or outcomes that resulted in highly successful outcomes. Finally, Monte Carlo simulation of oil and gas prospects provides managers and team leaders critical information on which risk factors and assumptions are driving the projected probability of project outcomes, giving them the all-important feedback they need to focus their people and financial resources on addressing those risk assumptions that will have the greatest positive impact on their business, improving their efficiency and adding profits to their bottom line.

CASE STUDY: FINANCIAL PLANNING WITH SIMULATION

Tony Jurado is a financial planner in northern California. He has a BA from Dartmouth College and is a candidate for the Certified Financial Planner designation. Tony specializes in the design and implementation of comprehensive financial plans for high-net-worth individuals. He can be contacted at tony.jurado@alum.dartmouth.org.

Corporate America has increasingly altered the retirement landscape by shifting from defined benefit to defined contribution plans. As the baby boomers retire, they will have different financial planning needs than those of previous generations because they must manage their own retirement funds. A thoughtful financial planner has the ability to positively impact the lives of these retirees.

A Deterministic Plan

Today was the last day of work for Henry Tirement, and, until just now, he and his financial planner, Mr. Determinist, had never seriously discussed what to do with his 401(k) rollover. After a moment of fact gathering with Henry, Mr. D obtains the following information:

- Current assets are $1,000,000 in various mutual funds.
- Current age is 65.
- Desired retirement salary is $60,000 before-tax.

- Expected return on investments is 10 percent.
- Expected inflation is 3 percent.
- Life expectancy is age 95.
- No inheritance considerations.

With his financial calculator, Mr. D concludes that Henry can meet his retirement goals and, in fact, if he died at age 95, he'd have over $3.2 million in his portfolio. Mr. D knows that past performance does not guarantee future results, but past performance is all that we have to go by. With the stock market averaging over 10 percent for the past 75 years, Mr. D feels certain that this return is reasonable. As inflation has averaged 3 percent over the same time period, he feels that this assumption is also realistic. Mr. D delivers the good news to Henry and the plan is put into motion (Table 7.4).

Fast forward to 10 years later. Henry is not so thrilled anymore. He visits the office of Mr. D with his statements in hand and they sit down to discuss the portfolio performance. Writing down the return of each of the past 10 years, Mr. D calculates the average performance of Henry's portfolio (Table 7.5).

"You've averaged 10 percent per year!" Mr. D tells Henry. Befuddled, Henry scratches his head. He shows his last statement to Mr. D that shows a portfolio balance is $501,490.82.

Once again, Mr. D uses his spreadsheet program and obtains the results in Table 7.6.

Mr. D is not certain what has happened. Henry took out $60,000 at the beginning of each year and increased this amount by 3 percent annually. The portfolio return averaged 10 percent. Henry should have over $1.4 million by now.

Sequence of Returns   Sitting in his office later that night, Mr. D thinks hard about what went wrong in the planning. He wonders what would have happened if the annual returns had occurred in reverse order (Table 7.7). The average return is still 10 percent and the withdrawal rate has not changed, but the portfolio ending balance is now $1.4 million. The only difference between the two situations is the sequence of returns. Enlightenment overcomes Mr. D, and he realizes that he has been employing a deterministic planning paradigm during a period of withdrawals.

Withdrawals Versus No Withdrawals   Most financial planners understand the story of Henry. The important point of Henry's situation is that he took withdrawals from his portfolio during an unfortunate sequence of returns. During a period of regular withdrawals, it doesn't matter that his portfolio

TABLE 7.4 The Deterministic Plan

Year	Returns ($)	Beginning Balance ($)	Withdrawal ($)	Ending Balance ($)
1	10.00	1,000,000.00	60,000.00	1,034,000.00
2	10.00	1,034,000.00	61,800.00	1,069,420.00
3	10.00	1,069,420.00	63,654.00	1,106,342.60
4	10.00	1,106,342.60	65,563.62	1,144,856.88
5	10.00	1,144,856.88	67,530.53	1,185,058.98
6	10.00	1,185,058.98	69,556.44	1,227,052.79
7	10.00	1,227,052.79	71,643.14	1,270,950.62
8	10.00	1,270,950.62	73,792.43	1,316,874.01
9	10.00	1,316,874.01	76,006.20	1,364,954.58
10	10.00	1,364,954.58	78,286.39	1,415,335.01
11	10.00	1,415,335.01	80,634.98	1,468,170.03
12	10.00	1,468,170.03	83,054.03	1,523,627.60
13	10.00	1,523,627.60	85,545.65	1,581,890.14
14	10.00	1,581,890.14	88,112.02	1,643,155.93
15	10.00	1,643,155.93	90,755.38	1,707,640.60
16	10.00	1,707,640.60	93,478.04	1,775,578.81
17	10.00	1,775,578.81	96,282.39	1,847,226.07
18	10.00	1,847,226.07	99,170.86	1,922,860.73
19	10.00	1,922,860.73	102,145.98	2,002,786.22
20	10.00	2,002,786.22	105,210.36	2,087,333.45
21	10.00	2,087,333.45	108,366.67	2,176,863.45
22	10.00	2,176,863.45	111,617.67	2,271,770.35
23	10.00	2,271,770.35	114,966.20	2,372,484.56
24	10.00	2,372,484.56	118,415.19	2,479,476.31
25	10.00	2,479,476.31	121,967.65	2,593,259.53
26	10.00	2,593,259.53	125,626.68	2,714,396.14
27	10.00	2,714,396.14	129,395.48	2,843,500.73
28	10.00	2,843,500.73	133,277.34	2,981,245.73
29	10.00	2,981,245.73	137,275.66	3,128,367.08
30	10.00	3,128,367.08	141,393.93	3,285,670.46

returns averaged 10 percent over the long run. It is the sequence of returns combined with regular withdrawals that was devastating to his portfolio. To illustrate this point, imagine that Henry never took withdrawals from his portfolio (Table 7.8).

The time value of money comes into play when withdrawals are taken. When Henry experienced negative returns early in retirement while taking withdrawals, he had less money in his portfolio to grow over time.

TABLE 7.5 The Actual Results

Year	Return %
1	−20.00
2	−10.00
3	9.00
4	8.00
5	12.00
6	−10.00
7	−2.00
8	25.00
9	27.00
10	61.00
Average Return	**10.00**

TABLE 7.6 Portfolio Balance Analysis

Year	Returns (%)	Withdrawal ($)	Ending Balance ($)
1	−20.00	60,000.00	752,000.00
2	−10.00	61,800.00	621,180.00
3	9.00	63,654.00	607,703.34
4	8.00	65,563.62	585,510.90
5	12.00	67,530.53	580,138.01
6	−10.00	69,556.44	459,523.41
7	−2.00	71,643.14	380,122.67
8	25.00	73,792.43	382,912.80
9	27.00	76,006.20	389,771.37
10	61.00	78,286.39	501,490.82

TABLE 7.7 Reversed Returns

Year	Return (%)	Withdrawal ($)	Ending Balance ($)
1	61.00	60,000.00	1,513,400.00
2	27.00	61,800.00	1,843,532.00
3	25.00	63,654.00	2,224,847.50
4	−2.00	65,563.62	2,116,098.20
5	−10.00	67,530.53	1,843,710.91
6	12.00	69,556.44	1,987,053.00
7	8.00	71,643.14	2,068,642.65
8	9.00	73,792.43	2,174,386.74
9	−10.00	76,006.20	1,888,542.48
10	−20.00	78,286.39	1,448,204.87

TABLE 7.8 Returns Analysis Without Withdrawals

Actual Return Sequence with No Withdrawals

Year	Return (%)	Ending Balance ($)
1	−20.00	800,000.00
2	−10.00	720,000.00
3	9.00	784,800.00
4	8.00	847,584.00
5	12.00	949,294.08
6	−10.00	854,364.67
7	−2.00	837,277.38
8	25.00	1,046,596.72
9	27.00	1,329,177.84
10	61.00	2,139,976.32
Average Return	10.00%	

Reverse Return Sequence with No Withdrawals

Year	Return (%)	Ending Balance ($)
1	61.00	1,610,000.00
2	27.00	2,044,700.00
3	25.00	2,555,875.00
4	−2.00	2,504,757.50
5	−10.00	2,254,281.75
6	12.00	2,524,795.56
7	8.00	2,726,779.20
8	9.00	2,972,189.33
9	−10.00	2,674,970.40
10	−20.00	2,139,976.32
Average Return	10.00%	

To maintain his inflation-adjusted withdrawal rate, Henry needed a bull market at the beginning of retirement.

Henry's retirement plan is deterministic because it assumes that returns will be the same each and every year. What Henry and Mr. D didn't understand was that averaging 10 percent over time is very different than getting 10 percent each and every year. As Henry left the office, Mr. D wished he had a more dynamic retirement planning process—one that allowed for varying variables.

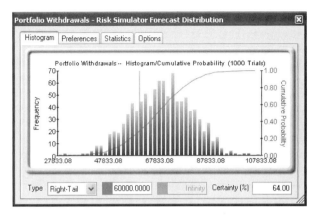

FIGURE 7.18   A 64 percent chance of portfolio survival at $60,000 withdrawals.

Stochastic Planning Using Monte Carlo Simulation

Monte Carlo is a stochastic tool that helps people think in terms of probability and not certainty. As opposed to using a deterministic process, financial planners can use Monte Carlo to simulate risk in investment returns. A financial plan's probability of success can be tested by simulating the variability of investment returns. Typically, to measure this variability, the expected mean and standard deviation of the portfolio's investment returns are used in a Monte Carlo model. What would Mr. D have told Henry had this approach been used?

Using Henry's same information but an expected return of 10 percent with a standard deviation of 17.5 percent, Mr. D can assign success probabilities for how long Henry's money will last. Henry has a 64 percent chance that his portfolio will last 30 years (Figure 7.18). If Henry is not comfortable with that success rate, then Mr. D can increase both expected return and standard deviation, or decrease withdrawals. Mr. D could change the return to 20 percent, but this is obviously not realistic. In Henry's case, it makes more sense to decrease the withdrawal rate. Assuming that Henry will be comfortable with a 70 percent chance of success, then Mr. D needs to lower the annual withdrawal to $55,000 (Figure 7.19).

Expenses Lower Returns

It is truly a misuse of Monte Carlo and unfair to the client to illustrate a plan without fees if an advisory fee is to be charged. If Mr. Determinist charges Henry a 1 percent advisory fee, then this figure must be deducted from

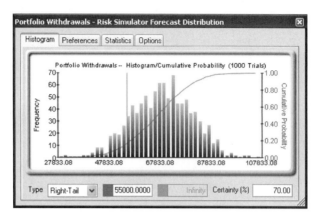

FIGURE 7.19   A 70 percent chance of portfolio survival at $55,000 withdrawals.

the annual return assumption, which will lower the plan's 30-year success probability to 54 percent. In Henry's case, the standard deviation will still be 17.5 percent, which is higher than a standard deviation of a portfolio that averages 9 percent. One can simply modify the Monte Carlo simulation to allow an advisory fee to be included by maintaining the return and standard deviation assumptions and deducting the advisory fee. For Henry's plan to still have a 70 percent success ratio after a 1 percent fee, he can withdraw an inflation-adjusted $47,000 annually, which is notably different from the $55,000 withdrawal rate before fees.

Success Probability

Monte Carlo educates the client about the trade-off between risk and return with respect to withdrawals. The risk is the success probability with which the client is comfortable. The return is the withdrawal rate. The financial planner should understand that a higher success rate amounts to lower withdrawals. A by-product of this understanding is that a higher success rate also increases the chance of leaving money in the portfolio at the client's death. In other words, Henry may be sacrificing lifestyle for an excessive probability of success. For Henry to have a 90 percent chance that his portfolio will last 30 years, he needs to lower his withdrawals to $32,000 (Figure 7.20). An equally important interpretation of this result is that Henry has a 90 percent chance of dying with money in his portfolio. This is money he could have used for vacation, fancy dinners, gifts for his family, or circus tickets.

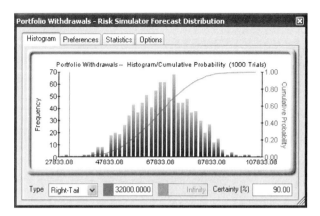

FIGURE 7.20 A 90 percent chance of portfolio survival at $32,000 withdrawals.

Success Tolerance

Going back to Henry's example of withdrawing $47,000 each year, if 5,000 simulation trials are run, a 70 percent success rate means that 3,500 times the plan worked. The 1,500 times the plan failed resulted in Henry being unable to take out $47,000 each and every year for 30 years. What is unclear about the 1,500 failures is how many of these resulted in a withdrawal amount marginally less than $47,000. If Henry takes out $47,000 for 29 years and then only withdraws $46,000 in the last year, is this a failure? Monte Carlo says yes. Most people are more flexible.

Establishing a success tolerance alleviates this problem. If Henry's goal is to take out $47,000 but he would be quite happy with $42,000, then he has a success tolerance of $5,000. This is the same as running a simulation using $42,000 with a zero success tolerance; however, the purpose of the success tolerance is to clearly illustrate to Henry the likelihood that a range of withdrawals will be achieved. By accounting for both the complexities of the market and the flexibility of human response to those complexities, Monte Carlo helps Henry understand, prepare for, and properly choose his risk tolerance.

Bear Markets and Monte Carlo

No matter what financial planning method is used, the reality is that a bear market early in retirement will drastically affect the plan. If Mr. D had used Monte Carlo when Henry first came to him and Henry took out $47,000 in Year 1 and $48,410 in Year 2, the portfolio balance at the end of the second year would have been $642,591. For the portfolio to last another

TABLE 7.9 Simulation-Based Withdrawal Rates

Year	Return (%)	Beginning ($)	End Balance ($)	Monte Carlo Withdrawal ($)	Withdrawal Change (%)	Remaining Years
1	−20.00	1,000,000	762,400	47,000	0	29
2	−10.00	762,400	653,310	36,500	−22	28
3	9.00	653,310	676,683	32,500	−11	27
4	8.00	676,683	693,558	34,500	6	26
5	12.00	693,558	735,904	36,500	6	25
6	−10.00	735,904	627,214	39,000	7	24
7	−2.00	627,214	580,860	34,500	−12	23
8	25.00	580,860	685,137	32,750	−5	22
9	27.00	685,137	819,324	40,000	22	21
10	61.00	819,324	1,239,014	49,750	24	20

28 years and to preserve a 70 percent success rate, Henry must reduce his withdrawal amount to $31,500! The difficulty of this situation is obvious; however, Mr. D is in a position to help Henry make a decision about maintaining his standard of living versus increasing the chances of running out of money.

Table 7.9 illustrates running a Monte Carlo simulation at the end of each year to determine the withdrawal amount that preserves a 70 percent success rate for Henry's plan.

Like most people, Henry will not be enthusiastic about lowering his retirement salary by as much as 22 percent in any year. Without changing the return assumption, Henry's alternative is to accept a lower success rate. If Henry never adjusted his withdrawal rate from the initial $47,000, after 10 years his portfolio value would be $856,496 and his withdrawal would be $61,324 ($47,000 × 1.03^9). The success probability is 60 percent for a portfolio life of 20 years.

Other Monte Carlo Variables

Monte Carlo can simulate more than just investment returns. Other variables that are frequently simulated by financial planners using Monte Carlo include inflation and life expectancy.

Inflation Since 1926, inflation has averaged approximately 3 percent annually with a standard deviation of 4.3 percent. In a plan with inflation-adjusted withdrawals, the change in inflation is significant. According to Ibbotson and Associates, inflation averaged 8.7 percent from the beginning of 1973 until the end of 1982. If such a period of inflation occurred at the beginning of retirement, the effect on a financial plan would be terrible.

Life Expectancy   Using mortality tables, a financial planner can randomize the life expectancy of any client to provide a more realistic plan. According to the National Center for Health Statistics, the average American born in 2002 has a life expectancy of 77.3 years with a standard deviation of 10. However, financial planners should be more concerned with the specific probability that their clients will survive the duration of the plan.

Monte Carlo Suggestions

Financial plans created using Monte Carlo should not be placed on autopilot. As with most forecasting methods, Monte Carlo is not capable of simulating real-life adjustments that individuals make. As previously discussed, if a portfolio experienced severe negative returns early in retirement, the retiree can change the withdrawal amount. It is also important to realize that Monte Carlo plans are only as good as the input assumptions.

Distributions   If Henry is invested in various asset classes, it is important for Mr. D to determine the distinct distribution characteristics of each asset class. The most effective approach to modeling these differences is by utilizing a distribution-fitting analysis in Risk Simulator.

Taxes   Henry Tirement's situation involved a tax-deferred account and a pretax salary. For individuals with nontaxable accounts, rebalancing may cause taxes. In this case, a financial planner using Monte Carlo might employ a tax-adjusted return and a posttax salary might be used. The after-tax account balance should be used in the assumptions for clients with highly concentrated positions and a low tax basis who plan to diversify their investments.

Correlations   It is important to consider any correlations between variables being modeled within Monte Carlo. Cross-correlations, serial correlations, or cross-serial correlations must be simulated for realistic results. For example, it may be shown that a correlation exists between investment returns and inflation. If this is true, then these variables should not be treated as independent of each other.

CASE STUDY: HOSPITAL RISK MANAGEMENT

This case is contributed by Lawrence Pixley, a founding partner of Stroud-water Associates, a management consulting firm for the health-care industry. Larry specializes in analyzing risk and uncertainty for hospitals and physician practices in the context of strategic planning and operational performance analyses. His expertise includes hospital facility planning, hospital/ physician joint ventures, medical staff development, physician compensation packages utilizing a balanced scorecard approach, practice operations assessment, and practice valuations. Larry spent 15 years in health-care management, and has been a consultant for the past three decades, specializing in demand forecasting using scientific management tools including real options analysis, Monte Carlo simulation, simulation-optimization, data envelopment analysis (DEA), queuing theory, and optimization theory. He can be reached at lpixley@stroudwaterassociates.com.

Hospitals today face a wide range of risk factors that can determine success or failure, including:

- Competitive responses both from other hospitals and physician groups.
- Changes in government rules and regulations.
- Razor-thin profit margins.
- Community relations as expressed through zoning and permitting resistance.
- State of the bond market and the cost of borrowing.
- Oligopsony (market with a few buyers) of a few large payers, for example, the state and federal governments.
- Success at fund-raising and generating community support.
- Dependence on key physicians, admitting preferences, and age of medical staff.
- High fixed cost structure.
- Advances in medical technology and their subsequent influence on admissions and lengths of stay.

In addition, hundreds of hospitals across the country are faced with aging facilities. Their dilemma is whether to renovate or relocate to a new site and build an entirely new facility. Many of these hospitals were first constructed in the early 1900s. Residential neighborhoods have grown up around them, locking them into a relatively small footprint, which severely hampers their options for expansion.

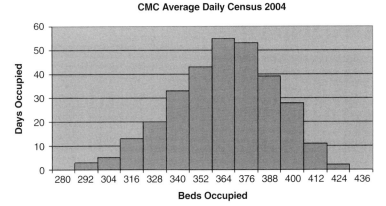

FIGURE 7.21 Histogram of CMC bed occupancy by number of days beds were occupied.

The Problem

Located in a large metropolitan area, CMC is a 425-bed community hospital. The region is highly competitive, with 12 other hospitals located within a 20-mile radius. Like most hospitals of similar size, CMC consists of a series of buildings constructed over a 50-year time span, with three major buildings 50, 30, and 15 years old. All three facilities house patients in double occupancy (or two-bed) rooms.

The hospital has been rapidly outgrowing its current facilities. In the last year alone, CMC had to divert 450 admissions to other hospitals, which meant a loss of $1.6M in incremental revenue. Figure 7.21 shows CMC's average daily census and demonstrates why the hospital is running out of bed space.

Because of this growing capacity issue, the hospital CEO asked his planning team to project discharges for the next 10 years. The planning department performed a trend line analysis using the linear regression function in Excel and developed the chart shown in Figure 7.22. Applying a Poisson distribution to the projected 35,000 discharges, the planners projected a total bed need of 514. They made no adjustment for a change in the average length of stay over that 10-year period, assuming that it would remain constant. See Figure 7.23.

Confronted with the potential need to add 95 beds, the board of directors asked the CEO to prepare an initial feasibility study. To estimate the cost of adding 95 beds to the existing campus, the administrative staff first consulted with a local architect who had designed several small projects for

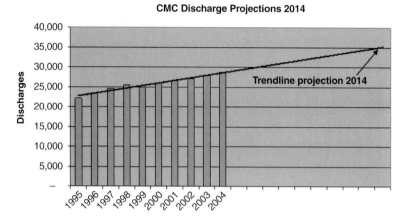

FIGURE 7.22 Trendline projections of CMC discharges for next 10 years (provided by CMC planning department).

the hospital. The architect estimated a cost of $260M to renovate the existing structure and build a new addition, both of which were required to fit 95 more beds within the hospital's current footprint. To accommodate the additional beds on the current site, however, all beds would have to be double occupancy. Single occupancy rooms—the most marketable today—simply could not be accommodated on the present campus.

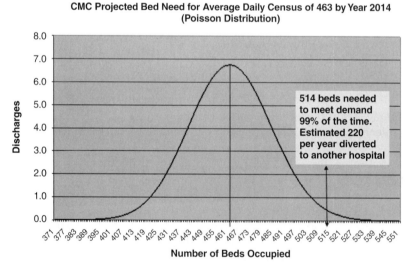

FIGURE 7.23 Projected CMC bed needs based on estimated average daily census of 463 patients for year 2014 (provided by CMC planning department).

In 1990, the hospital board faced a similar decision, whether to build a needed addition on the present campus or to relocate. The board opted to invest $90 million in a major expansion on the current site. Faced with the current dilemma, many of those same board members wished that in 1990 they had been able to better analyze their future options. A number of them expressed regrets that they did not relocate to another campus then. They clearly understood that their current decision—to renovate and add to the existing campus or to relocate—would be a decision the hospital would live with for the next 30 to 50 years.

There was no available site in the town (25 acres minimum), but there was space available in the adjacent town near a new $110 million ambulatory care center the hospital built five years ago. Yet, given the amount invested in the current campus and the uncertainty of how a new location would affect market share, there was real hesitancy to relocate.

The board had other considerations as well. Historically there had been litigation involved every time the hospital tried to expand. The neighboring property owners unsuccessfully opposed the Emergency Department expansion in 1999, but had managed through various legal actions to delay the construction three years. This delay added significantly to the cost of construction, in addition to the revenue lost from not having the modernized facility available as projected.

Two members of the board had attended a conference on the future of hospitals and noted that building more double occupancy rooms was not a good decision for the following reasons:

- By the time the facility was ready for construction, code requirements for new hospital construction would likely dictate single occupancy rooms.
- Patients prefer single rooms and CMC would be at a competitive disadvantage with other hospitals in the area that were already converting to single occupancy.
- Single occupancy rooms require fewer patient transfers and therefore fewer staff.
- Rates of infection were found to be considerably lower.

After receiving a preliminary cost estimate from the architect on a replacement hospital, the CFO presented the analysis shown in Figure 7.24 to the Finance Committee as an initial test of the project's viability. The initial projections for a new hospital estimated construction costs at $670 million. The study estimated a $50 million savings by not funding further capital improvements in the existing buildings. The CFO projected that the hospital would have a debt service capacity of an additional $95 million,

Initial Capital Analysis for New Hospital ($ in M)		
Cost of Project	$	670
Less: Unrestricted Cash	$	(150)
: Deferred Maintenance	$	(50)
: Existing Debt Capacity	$	(100)
: Future Debt Capacity Based on New Volume	$	(95)
: Sale of Assets	$	(56)
: Capital Campaign	$	(150)
Capital Shortfall	$	69

FIGURE 7.24 Capital position analysis for new hospital as prepared by CMC chief financial officer.

assuming that the planning department's volume projections were accurate and that revenue and expense per admission remained static. The balance would have to come from the sale of various properties owned by the hospital and a major capital campaign. Over the years, the hospital had acquired a number of outlying buildings for administrative functions and various clinics that could be consolidated into a new facility. In addition, there was a demand for additional residential property within the town limits, making the hospital's current site worth an estimated $17 million. Although skeptical, the CFO felt that with additional analysis, it could be possible to overcome the projected $69 million shortfall.

The board authorized the administration to seek proposals from architectural firms outside their area. The Selection Committee felt that given the risks of potentially building the wrong-sized facility in the wrong location, they needed firms that could better assess both risks and options. At the same time, as a hedge pending the completion of the analysis, the committee took a one-year option on the 25-acre property in the adjacent town. After a nationwide review, CMC awarded the project analysis to a nationally recognized architectural firm and Stroudwater Associates, with the strategic planning and analytics in Stroudwater's hands.

The Analysis

Stroudwater first needed to test the trend line projections completed by CMC's planning department. Rather than taking simple trend line projections based on past admissions, Stroudwater used a combination of both qualitative and quantitative forecasting methodologies. Before financial projections could be completed, a better estimate of actual bed need was required. Stroudwater segmented the bed need calculation into five key decision areas: population trends, utilization changes, market share, length of stay, and queuing decisions. Given the rapid changes in health-care

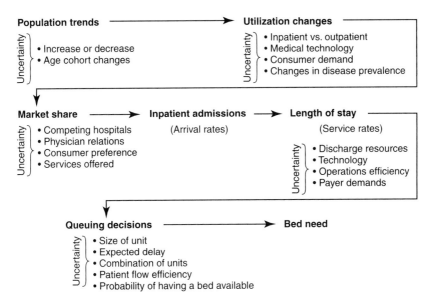

FIGURE 7.25 Stroudwater Associates' methodology for forecasting hospital bed requirements.

technology in particular, it was determined that forecasting beyond 10 years was too speculative, and the board agreed that 10 years was an appropriate period for the analysis. In addition, the hospital wanted to project a minimum of 3 years beyond completion of hospital construction. Because projections were required for a minimum of 10 years, and because of the large number of variables involved, Stroudwater employed Monte Carlo simulation techniques in each of these five decision areas. See Figure 7.25.

For qualitative input to this process, the hospital formed a 15-person steering committee composed of medical staff, board directors, and key administrative staff. The committee met every three weeks during the four-month study and was regularly polled by Stroudwater on key decision areas through the entire process.

In addition, Stroudwater conducted 60 interviews with physicians, board members, and key administrative staff. During the interviews with key physicians in each major service line, Stroudwater consultants were struck by the number of aging physicians that were in solo practice and not planning to replace themselves, a significant risk factor for CMC. The CFO identified another issue: A majority of physicians in key specialties had recently stopped accepting insurance assignments, further putting the hospital

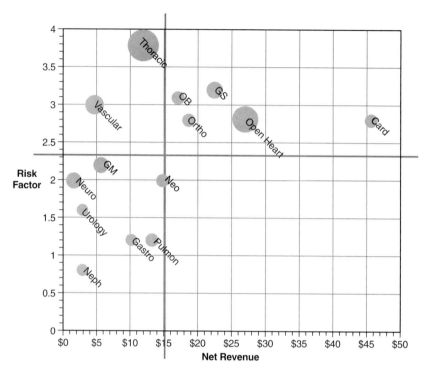

FIGURE 7.26 Bubble chart highlighting service lines considered most at risk (upper right quadrant). Operating margin is represented by the size of the bubble.

at risk vis-à-vis its major competitor whose employed physicians accepted assignment from all payers.

To understand better what service lines were at risk, Stroudwater developed a bubble diagram (Figure 7.26) to highlight areas that needed further business planning before making market share estimates. The three variables were net revenue, operating margin, and a subjective risk factor rating system.

The following risk factors were identified, assigned a weight, rated on a scale of one to five, and plotted on the y-axis:

- Size of practice—percentage of solo and two-physician practices in specialty.
- Average age of physicians in specialty.
- Potential competitive threat from other hospitals.

■ Percentage of admissions coming from outside of service area.

■ Percentage of physicians in the specialty accepting assignment from major insurance carriers.

The analysis revealed five key specialties—orthopedics, obstetrics, general surgery, open-heart surgery, and cardiology—in which CMC's bottom line was at risk, but which also afforded the greatest opportunity for future profitability. To better inform market share estimates, Stroudwater then developed mini-business plans for each of the areas identified in the upper right-hand quadrant of Figure 7.26.

Population Trends   To determine future population numbers in the CMC service area, Stroudwater depended on nationally recognized firms that specialize in population trending. Because hospital utilization is three times higher for over-65 populations, it was important to factor in the ongoing effect of the baby boomers. Stroudwater also asked members of the Steering Committee to review the 2014 population projections and determine what local issues not factored into the professional projections should be considered.

The committee members raised several concerns. There was a distinct possibility of a major furniture manufacturer moving its operations to China, taking some 3,000 jobs out of the primary service area. However, there was also the possibility of a new computer chip factory coming to the area. Stroudwater developed custom distributions to account for these population/employment contingencies.

Utilization Projections   On completion of its population forecasting, Stroudwater turned its attention to calculating discharges per 1,000 people, an area of considerable uncertainty. To establish a baseline for future projections, 2004 discharge data from the state hospital association were used to calculate the hospitalization use rates (discharges per 1,000) for CMC's market. Stroudwater calculated use rates for 34 distinct service lines. See Table 7.10.

Stroudwater factored a number of market forces affecting hospital bed utilization into the utilization trend analyses. The consultants considered the following key factors that might decrease facility utilization:

■ Better understanding of the risk factors for disease, and increased prevention initiatives (e.g., smoking prevention programs, cholesterol-lowering drugs).

■ Discovery/implementation of treatments that cure or eliminate diseases.

TABLE 7.10 Utilization Trends for 2014 by Service Line

Product Line	2004 Discharges	Length of Stay	Population	Discharges 1000	Days 1000	Average Length of Stay	Population	2014 Change in Utilization (%)	Estimated Total Market Discharges
Abortion	137	213	1,193,436	0.12	0.18	1.6	1,247,832	0	1
Adverse Effects	878	2,836	1,193,436	0.74	2.40	3.2	1,247,832	0	9
AIDS and Related	358	3,549	1,193,436	0.30	3.00	9.9	1,247,832	0	3
Burns	66	859	1,193,436	0.07	0.73	10.0	1,247,832	0	
Cardiology	19,113	75,857	1,193,436	16.17	64.19	4.0	1,247,832	18	20,1
Dermatology	435	3,446	1,193,436	0.37	2.92	7.9	1,247,832	0	4
Endocrinology	3,515	18,246	1,193,436	2.97	15.44	5.2	1,247,832	5	3,7
Gastroenterology	9,564	46,103	1,193,436	8.09	39.01	4.8	1,247,832	5	10,0
General Surgery	7,488	51,153	1,193,436	6.34	43.28	6.8	1,247,832	9	7,9
Gynecology	3,056	6,633	1,193,436	2.59	7.31	2.6	1,247,832		3,2
Hematology	1,362	10,325	1,193,436	1.15	8.74	7.6	1,247,832	8	1,4
Infectious Disease	2,043	15,250	1,193,436	1.73	12.90	7.5	1,247,832	0	2,1
Neonatology	1,721	20,239	1,193,436	1.46	17.13	11.8	1,247,832	4	1,8
Neurology	5,338	34,873	1,193,436	4.52	29.51	6.5	1,247,832	12	5,8
Neurosurgery	3,042	13,526	1,193,436	2.57	11.45	4.4	1,247,832	12	3,2
Newborn	11,197	25,007	1,193,436	9.47	21.16	2.2	1,247,832	-5	11,6
Obstetrics	13,720	36,962	1,193,436	11.61	31.28	2.7	1,247,832	-5	14,4
Oncology	1,767	11,563	1,193,436	1.50	9.76	6.5	1,247,832	15	1,5

Source: State Hospital Discharge Survey.

- Consensus documents or guidelines that recommend decreases in utilization.
- Shifts to other sites causing declines in utilization in the original sites
  - As technology allows shifts (e.g., ambulatory surgery).
  - As alternative sites of care become available (e.g., assisted living).
- Changes in practice patterns (e.g., encouraging self-care and healthy lifestyles, reduced length of hospital stay).
- Changes in technology.

Stroudwater also considered the following factors that may increase hospital bed utilization:

- Growing elderly population.
- New procedures and technologies (e.g., hip replacement, stent insertion, MRI).
- Consensus documents or guidelines that recommend increases in utilization.
- New disease entities (e.g., HIV/AIDS, bioterrorism).
- Increased health insurance coverage.
- Changes in consumer preferences and demand (e.g., bariatric surgery, hip and knee replacements).

In all key high-volume services, Stroudwater consultants made adjustments for utilization changes and inserted them into the spreadsheet model, using a combination of uniform, triangular, and normal distributions.

Market Share The Steering Committee asked Stroudwater to model two separate scenarios, one for renovations and an addition to the current campus, and the second for an entirely new campus in the adjacent town. To project the number of discharges that CMC was likely to experience in the year 2014, market share assumptions for both scenarios were made for each major service line.

A standard market share analysis aggregates zip codes into primary and secondary service markets depending on market share percentage. Instead, Stroudwater divided the service area into six separate market clusters using market share, geographic features, and historic travel patterns.

Stroudwater selected eight major service areas that represented 80 percent of the admissions for further analysis and asked committee members and key physicians in each specialty area to project market share. The committee members and participating physicians attended one large meeting where CMC planning department members and Stroudwater consultants jointly presented results from the mini-business plans. Local market trends and results of past patient preference surveys were considered in a discussion that followed. As an outcome from the meeting, participants agreed to focus on specific factors to assist them in estimating market share, including:

- Change in patient preference.
- Proximity of competing hospitals.
- New hospital "halo" effect.
- Change in "hospital of choice" preferences by local physicians.
- Ability to recruit and retain physicians.

Using a customized survey instrument, Stroudwater provided those participating in the exercise with four years of trended market share data; challenging them to create a worst-case, most-likely, and best-case estimate for (1) each of the six market clusters in (2) each of the eight service lines for (3) each campus scenario.

After compiling the results of the survey instrument, Stroudwater assigned triangular distributions to each variable. An exception to the process occurred in the area of cardiac surgery. There was considerable discussion over the impact of a competing hospital potentially opening a cardiothoracic surgery unit in CMC's secondary service market. For the "current campus" scenario, the Steering Committee agreed that if a competing unit were opened it would decrease their market share to the 15 to 19 percent range, and they assigned a 20 percent probability that their competitor would open the unit. Should the competitor not build the unit, a minority of the group felt that CMC's market share would increase significantly to the 27 to 30 percent range; a 30 percent probability was assigned. The remaining members were more conservative and estimated a 23 to 25 percent market share. Similarly, estimates were made for the new campus in which participants felt there were better market opportunities and where losses would be better mitigated should the competing hospital open a new cardiothoracic unit.

Stroudwater used the custom distributions shown in Figure 7.27.

Average Length of Stay   Stroudwater performed length of stay estimates for 400 diagnostic groupings (DRG) using a combination of historic statistics from the National Hospital Discharge Survey of the National Center for Health Statistics and actual CMC data.

Key CMC physicians participated in estimating length of stay based on the benchmark data, their knowledge of their respective fields, and historic CMC data. Stroudwater consultants separately trended historic lengths of stay and developed an algorithm for weighting benchmark data and CMC physician estimates. Length of stay estimates were rolled up into one distribution for each of the major service lines.

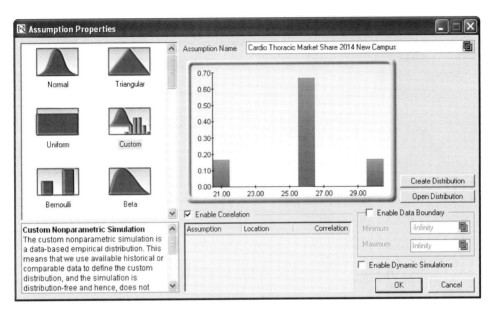

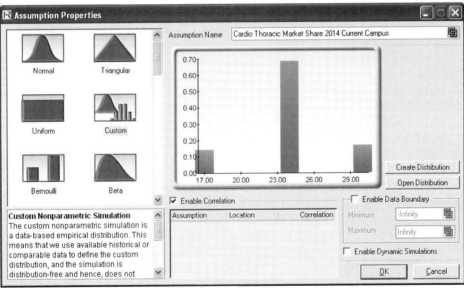

FIGURE 7.27 Cardiothoracic market share using custom distributions comparing market share assumptions for both current and new campus.

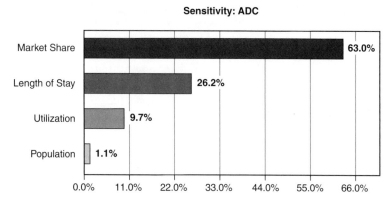

FIGURE 7.28 Sensitivity analysis of key variables in Monte Carlo simulation.

At this point, Stroudwater performed a sensitivity analysis (Figure 7.28) to determine which assumptions were driving the forecasts. Based on the relative unimportance population had on outcome, the population distribution assumptions were dropped in favor of single point estimates.

Queuing Decisions   A typical approach to determining bed need, and the one used by the CMC Planning Department, is to multiply projections for single point admissions by those for single point lengths of stay to determine the total number of patient days. Patient days are divided by 365 to determine the average daily census (ADC). A Poisson distribution is then applied to the ADC to determine the total number of beds required. In addition to the problems of single point estimates, Poisson distributions assume that all arrivals are unscheduled and thus overstate the bed need if any of the services have elective or urgent admissions.

Because CMC had categorized all of its admissions by urgency of the need for a bed, Stroudwater was able to conduct an analysis for each unit and found wide differences in the timing needs for beds ranging from OB with 100 percent emergency factor to Orthopedics with 57 percent of its admissions classified as elective. See Table 7.11.

To deepen the analysis, the physician members of the committee met separately to determine which units could be combined because of natural affinities and similar nursing requirements. The Steering Committee then met to discuss service targets for each category of admission. They agreed that "Emergencies" had to have a bed available immediately, "Urgent" within 48 hours, and "Elective" within 72 hours. Using a multiple channel queuing

TABLE 7.11 Orthopedic/Neurosurgery Admissions Classified by Admission Priority

	Emergency	Urgent	Elective	Total
Total Days	5,540	415	7,894	13,849
Total Admissions	1,497	112	2,133	3,743
Percentage (Admits)	40%	3%	57%	100%

model jointly developed by Dr. Johnathan Mun and Lawrence Pixley, bed needs were determined for each of the major unit groupings. See Table 7.12 and Table 7.13.

Distributions had been set for utilization and market share by service line to determine the arrival rates needed for the queuing model. Length of stay distributions by service line had been determined for the service rate input to the model. Forecast cells for Monte Carlo simulation were set for "Probability of Being Served" for <1, 1–2, and 2–3 days for each of the units respectively.

As its planning criteria, the committee decided on a target rate of 95 percent confidence in having a bed available with a greater than 50 percent certainty. Stroudwater employed an iterative process to the model, rerunning the Monte Carlo simulation until the performance criteria were met. For example, the first run for Orthopedics at 75 beds had a certainty of 47.8 percent at 95 percent confidence level compared to a later run of 78 beds with a certainty of 60.57 percent. The 78-bed figure was adopted. See Figure 7.29.

TABLE 7.12 MGK Blocking Model Showing Bed Need Service Targets

				Bed Needs Service Target		
Unit	Discharges Arrival Rates	Service Rate 1/ALOS	CV	Emergency < 1 day	Urgent 1–2 days	Elective 2–3 days
Medical Cardiology	8.6301	0.0606	142.3973	71%	25%	4%
General Surgery	10.9315	0.0741	147.5753	49%	2%	49%
Orthopedics	17.9795	0.0901	199.5719	40%	3%	57%

TABLE 7.13 MGK Blocking Model with Determination of Beds and Probability of Availability

Unit	Period/ Day 3 No. Beds Per Day	No. Beds Per Period	Beds Busy	Prob. Busy	Prob. Served < 1 Day	Prob. Served 1–2 Days	Prob. Served 2–3 Days
Medical Cardiology	102	34	34	76.3%	99.4%	100.0%	100.0%
General Surgery	66	22	22	84.7%	89.6%	100.0%	100.0%
Orthopedics/ Neuro	78	26	26	81.9%	96.0%	100.0%	100.0%
Total		82					

The Results of the Analysis

The committee's perception was that a new hospital located in a neighboring community closer to its target markets would improve market share in key specialties. That perception was reinforced by Stroudwater's findings in the projected differences in bed need between the two sites. See Table 7.14.

The project architects utilized the bed demand information and completed construction cost projections for each of the two scenarios. With a need for only 39 additional beds on the current campus compared to the

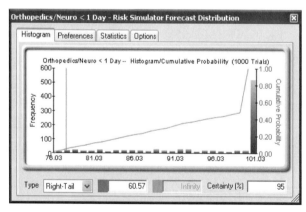

FIGURE 7.29 Frequency distribution for 78 orthopedic beds at new campus site.

TABLE 7.14 Results of Bed Need Projections for Both Current and New Campus Solutions

| | 2004 | 2014 Projections | |
| | Current | Current | New |
Service Line	Campus	Campus	Campus
Obstetrics	47	48	49
Cardiology	41	43	47
Pulmonary	50	55	56
Infectious Disease	18	20	19
Ortho/Neurosurgery	49	69	73
Rehabilitation	16	18	18
Hematology/Oncology	14	15	16
General Surgery	38	41	42
Vascular/Cardiac Surg.	64	60	68
Urology	14	14	16
Gastroenterology	18	21	21
Neurology	18	20	21
Other Medical	12	14	15
Other Surgical	25	26	28
Total Beds	425	464	489

original projection of the need for 95 additional beds, the architects were able to design space that afforded 92 private rooms.

The architects estimated the project cost for the new replacement facility at $587 million compared to $285 million for the renovation/addition option for the current campus. The new campus solution afforded an estimated increase in capital campaign contributions of $125 million and income from sale of assets of $56 million, bringing the borrowing required to an estimated $231 million. Borrowing for the current campus option was estimated to be $110 million.

The pro formas reflected the following advantages to the new campus solution:

- Revenue per admission and per bed was higher with the new campus scenario because of the expected increase in higher margin specialty admissions. Cardiothoracic surgery, for example, contributed $11,600 per case in margin compared to $2,200 for Urology.
- CMC was averaging 6.1 full-time equivalent (FTE) employees per bed in the current facility, much of it due to facility inefficiencies. Stroudwater projected that a renovated campus could bring down

the FTE to occupied bed ratio to 6.0 but projected the new facility at 5.8.

- Utility costs were projected to drop from the current $4.51 to $4.08 per square foot and maintenance costs were expected to drop from $2.46 to $1.40 per square foot.
- Loss of revenue from disruption of operations would be minimized with the new campus solution.
- The adjacent community provided assurances to CMC that it would not experience zoning difficulties should the hospital choose to relocate, whereas because of ongoing community opposition to further construction on the existing campus, a three-year delay in construction was expected.

In addition to the foregoing pro forma presentations (see Tables 7.15 and 7.16), Stroudwater provided the board with the Monte Carlo simulation results for projected profit margin in the year 2014 as shown in Figure 7.30. Interestingly, the profit margins projected for the two scenarios were remarkably similar, with the new hospital scenario having a slightly higher probability of exceeding a 4 percent profit margin. Given the similar outcomes of the pro formas, the board elected to proceed with the new campus solution. They felt that even though moving to the adjacent community was a risk, the risk of remaining on the current site was even greater. They realized that their future expansion options were limited should the projections prove to underrepresent future demand for services, whereas the new campus afforded them a great deal of flexibility for unanticipated events.

A bond rating agency rewarded CMC's approach to risk assessment with a favorable rating. Its opinion letter reflected the following observations:

- CMC received high marks for the decision-making process. The agency appreciated the alternative analysis of building on the present campus compared to a new campus and the unique approach of incorporating uncertainty into the calculation of bed need. It noted that the original projections for a 515-bed facility were scaled back to 489 beds as a result of the analysis.
- CMC received points for involving the physicians in the Steering Committee, and for the fact that CMC administration continually met with the medical staff to provide updates on the analysis.
- The agency felt that the relocation to the new campus was a risk by moving away from existing physician offices, but the risk was not only mitigated but enhanced by a privately owned and developed 300,000 square foot medical office building as part of the new campus. (It noted

TABLE 7.15 Pro Forma for New Hospital Scenario

	FY2007	FY2008	FY2009	FY2010	FY2011	FY2012
Total Operating Revenue	$338,250,000	$350,550,000	$358,360,000	$364,000,000	$361,088,000	$382,720,000
Total Expenses	$314,215,000	$325,641,000	$332,003,200	$336,336,000	$320,762,624	$328,852,160
EBIDA	$ 31,613,900	$ 32,487,900	$ 33,935,700	$ 35,242,900	$ 44,325,376	$ 57,867,840
EBIDA Margin	9.2%	9.1%	9.3%	9.5%	12.2%	15.1%
Total Capital and Other Costs	$ 10,602,167	$ 10,774,367	$ 10,883,707	$ 10,962,667	$ 34,891,167	$ 36,583,630
Operating Income /(Loss)	$ 13,432,833	$ 14,134,633	$ 15,473,093	$ 16,701,333	$ 5,434,209	$ 17,284,210
Operating Margin	4.0%	4.0%	4.3%	4.6%	1.5%	4.5%
Contributions and Investment Income	$ 7,578,900	$ 7,578,900	$ 7,578,900	$ 7,578,900	$ 4,000,000	$ 4,000,000
Net Income/(Loss)	$ 21,011,733	$ 21,713,533	$ 23,051,993	$ 24,280,233	$ 9,434,209	$ 21,284,210
Profit Margin	6.1%	6.1%	6.3%	6.5%	2.6%	5.5%
Income Available for Capital	$ 31,613,900	$ 32,487,900	$ 33,935,700	$ 35,242,900	$ 44,325,376	$ 57,867,840
Debt Service Coverage Ratio	6.1	6.1	6.2	3.3	1.3	3.5

TABLE 7.16 Pro Forma for Current Campus Scenario

	FY2007	FY2008	FY2009	FY2010	FY2011	FY2012
Total Operating Revenue	$338,250,000	$350,550,000	$358,360,000	$364,000,000	$361,088,000	$370,760,000
Total Expenses	$314,215,000	$325,641,000	$332,003,200	$336,336,000	$321,845,888	$326,759,160
EBIDA	$ 31,613,900	$ 32,487,900	$ 33,935,700	$ 35,242,900	$ 43,242,112	$ 48,000,840
EBIDA Margin	9.2%	9.1%	9.3%	9.5%	11.9%	12.9%
Total Capital and Other Costs	$ 10,602,167	$ 10,774,367	$ 10,883,707	$ 10,962,667	$ 23,318,486	$ 23,370,578
Operating Income/(Loss)	$ 13,432,833	$ 14,134,633	$ 15,473,093	$ 16,701,333	$ 15,923,626	$ 20,630,262
Operating Margin	4.0%	4.0%	4.3%	4.6%	4.4%	5.6%
Contributions and Investment Income	$ 7,578,900	$ 7,578,900	$ 7,578,900	$ 7,578,900	$ 4,000,000	$ 4,000,000
Net Income/(Loss)	$ 21,011,733	$ 21,713,533	$ 23,051,993	$ 24,280,233	$ 19,923,626	$ 24,630,262
Profit Margin	6.1%	6.1%	6.3%	6.5%	5.5%	6.6%
Income Available for Capital	$ 31,613,900	$ 32,487,900	$ 33,935,700	$ 35,242,900	$ 43,242,112	$ 48,000,840
Debt Service Coverage Ratio	6.1	6.1	6.2	3.3	2.7	6.1

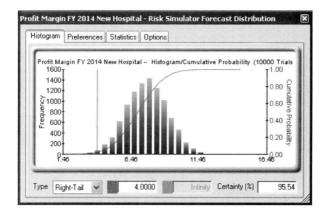

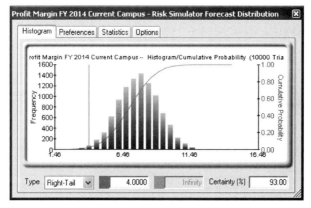

FIGURE 7.30 Frequency distribution of profit margin comparing alternative scenarios.

the lack of room for medical office facilities on the existing campus.) It also accepted the argument that CMC's long-term financial viability was improved by the future ability to recruit and retain physicians, particularly in large group practices.

- The fact that the new hospital would be located adjacent to CMC's ambulatory care center that had already been in full operation for six years was also viewed positively as patients were accustomed to traveling to this site.

- The agency found that management had compellingly examined all reasonable scenarios for patient volume and third-party reimbursement and their impact on earnings and liquidity.

The following were the principal advantages of using applied risk analysis in this case:

- Board members, many of whom were familiar with applied risk analysis in their own industries, were more comfortable making a major relocation decision based on a range of probable outcomes rather than on previously employed single point estimates.
- The bond-rating agency awarded the hospital a favorable bond rating because "what if" scenarios were employed and because of the methods utilized in both identifying and mitigating risk factors.
- The hospital was able to reduce the number of projected beds and hence its overall construction cost because of the more sophisticated queuing methodology employed.

CASE STUDY: RISK-BASED EXECUTIVE COMPENSATION VALUATION

This case was written by Patrick Haggerty, a principal at the executive compensation consulting firm James F. Reda & Associates, LLC. As independent advisors to management and boards, the firm assists companies with designing and implementing executive compensation programs. The firm has significant expertise in valuing long-term incentive awards using guidance provided by FASB Statement No. 123 (Revised 2004), Share-Based Payment (FAS 123(R)), and related interpretations. Through partnering with Dr. Mun and using his option valuation software packages, James F. Reda & Associates, LLC, helps clients determine and understand the compensation expense impact of selecting alternative long-term incentive designs.

This case is based on actual projects performed, but for the purposes of maintaining proprietary information, we use a fictitious entity named Boris Manufacturing, Inc. (Boris). This case study is about the process that Boris used to evaluate alternative long-term incentive (LTI) plan designs and determine the fair value for expensing purposes, as required by the new financial accounting standards. Through the following steps, the management team and the compensation committee worked together to evaluate the advantages and disadvantages of the various LTI vehicles available. The steps undertaken included:

- Reviewing the historical LTI awards made to employees.
- Reviewing the company's LTI plan.
- Conducting a market study.
- Evaluating advantages and disadvantages of each LTI vehicle available.

Ultimately, Boris decided to award restricted stocks that vest on achieving a total shareholder return target. Because the performance condition is total shareholder return, an option-pricing model can be used to determine fair value based on a barrier option, where the stock vests only after breaching a predetermined upper performance barrier. A simple Black–Scholes is not designed to value these types of awards. Instead, Monte Carlo and binomial lattice models like Dr. Mun's Real Options Super Lattice Solver and Risk Simulator software are most appropriate because they include the necessary input factors. FAS 123(R) considers the vesting criteria on Boris's restricted stock award a "market condition," meaning it is stock-price related. This distinction is important because if Boris designed a plan that vests on achieving a nonstock price-related measure (i.e., earnings per share, or EPS, and earnings before interest, taxes, depreciation, and amortization, or EBITDA), the company could not factor the performance condition into the fair value of the award (FAS 123(R) calls this type of performance measure a "performance condition"). For more technical details on valuing regular employee stock options based on the 2004 revised FAS 123, see Dr. Johnathan Mun's case study in Chapter 14 on valuing employee stock options.

Background

Boris Manufacturing Inc. is a publicly traded billion-dollar manufacturer of chemical products. The company has 2,000 employees with approximately 200 management- and executive-level employees. The compensation committee at Boris is responsible for determining executive pay levels and awarding LTIs to all employees. The compensation committee evaluated pay practices among its peer group companies and determined that LTIs should be a significant and important part of total compensation. Accordingly, the company has awarded its management- and executive-level employees LTIs. Historically, Boris awarded stock options to employees because prior to FAS 123(R) the expense was zero—under previous accounting rules, compensation expense was zero for at-the-money stock options if the number of shares awarded are known on the grant date.

Boris's stock option awards have not provided the incentive or link to shareholders that the compensation committee expected. Over the past 4 years, Boris's stock price has been relatively volatile and has generally decreased. Roughly half of the stock options Boris awarded to employees have an exercise price higher than the current stock price or are *underwater*. Further, the company kept awarding more stock options because the stock price continued to fall. As a result, the company has unproductive stock overhang, employees with minimal linkage to shareholders, and few shares remaining in their stock pool. As described next, the compensation committee decided to undertake a study to evaluate these issues.

Compensation Committee Process

To review alternative LTI designs, the compensation committee conducted the following steps:

1. Reviewed historical LTI awards made to employees.
   Purpose: To understand what employees had received in the past such as type of award, current fair value of award, and any gains received.
   Result: Over the past 3 years, Boris awarded approximately 900,000 stock options to employees each year (2.7 million in total). Unfortunately, roughly half are underwater, and very few employees were able to exercise and sell with any gain.
2. Reviewed company's long-term incentive plan.
   Purpose: To understand types of LTI vehicles that Boris shareholders approved in its LTI plan and how many shares are available for awards.
   Result: Boris's LTI plan is very flexible and allows for all types of LTI vehicles, including:
   - Nonqualified stock options (NQSO).
   - Incentive stock options (ISO).
   - Stock-settled stock appreciations rights (Stock SAR).
   - Restricted stock and restricted stock units (RSU).
   - Performance shares and performance units.
     Due to higher than expected stock option grants made over the past 3 years, the company has only 500,000 shares available for future grants. It is likely that Boris will need to go back to shareholders next year, so they want to use the remaining shares wisely.
3. Conducted a market study.
   Purpose: To determine competitive practices for LTI awards, costs, and LTI designs (vesting, performance measures, termination provisions, and holding periods).
   Result: Based on an analysis of industry competitors, the company determined that historical stock option awards were above market levels—on an individual position level, overhang basis, and cost basis. Also, it was determined that many peer group companies are awarding full value shares (i.e., restricted stock and performance shares) rather than stock options. Among the peer group companies that are awarding full value shares with performance conditions, the most common

performance conditions were total shareholder return, earnings per share, and EBITDA.

4. Evaluated advantages and disadvantages of each LTI vehicle available. Table 7.17 summarizes the compensation committee's findings.

Compensation Committee Decision

The compensation committee decided to award restricted stock that vests on achieving a predefined total shareholder return (TSR) target. Key factors that influenced the committee to select this LTI plan included:

- Reduction in overhang and run rate.
- Better link to shareholders.
- Requires minimum acceptable level of performance before payout.
- Promotes stock ownership because executives do not have to sell shares to exercise.

Details of the design include:

Type	Restricted stock
Vesting criteria	Vests on achieving 6 percent annual TSR
Performance period	3 years (average cumulative TSR must exceed 6 percent)
Dividend rights	Participants do not receive dividends until stock has vested
Number of shares	All-or-nothing award, no adjustment in number of shares if TSR is below or above 6 percent

Before selecting the 6 percent TSR target, the compensation committee reviewed Boris's historical TSR. Based on this review, it was determined that Boris's 3-year historical average annualized return is 5.2 percent, and using this and the volatility estimates, we were able to compute the expected distribution of future returns (see Figure 7.31). The committee considered this and set the TSR target and expected range TSR performance at:

TSR Target:	6%
Minimum Expected:	0%
Most Likely:	5%
Max Expected:	9%

TABLE 7.17 Advantages and Disadvantages of LTI Vehicles

LTI Vehicle	FAS 123R Measurement Approach	Key Employee Tax Issue	Key Advantage	Key Disadvantage
NQSOs	Fixed: grant date fair value[a]	Ordinary income tax at exercise	Determine taxable event, upside potential	Potential underwater, highly dilutive
ISOs	Fixed: grant date fair value	Capital gains tax at sale[b]	Capital gains, upside potential	No company tax deduction, ISO rules
Stock SARs	Fixed: grant date fair value	Ordinary income tax at exercise	Limits dilution, upside potential	Potential underwater
Restricted Stock	Fixed: grant date face value[c]	Ordinary income when vested	Retention, no cost to employee	Pay tax when vested, not 162(m) qualified
Restricted Stock Units (paid in stock)	Fixed: grant date face value	Ordinary income when delivered	Flexibility, can include performance	Flexibility subject to 409A rules
Performance Shares	Fixed/variable: stock price fixed, shares adjusted[d]	Ordinary income when vested	Additional shares and higher stock price	Setting performance measures
Performance Units (paid in cash)	Variable:[e] adjusted until paid	Ordinary income when vested	Receive cash, diversify	Cash flow, variable accounting

[a] Fair value based on an option-pricing model, such as Black–Scholes.
[b] If requisite holding periods are met, otherwise same as NQSOs.
[c] Face value equals stock price on grant date.
[d] Stock price fixed on grant date; shares are variable until measurement period is complete.
[e] Mark-to-market accounting until award is paid.

Distribution of Returns at Horizon

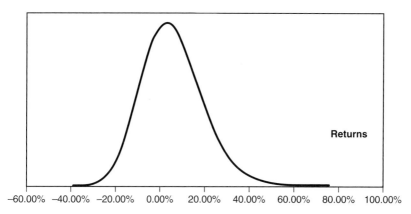

FIGURE 7.31   Boris's projected returns based on historical performance.

The compensation committee considered and analyzed but ultimately decided against the following alternative plan designs. Each one of these alternatives would result in a different fair value calculation.

- Increasing duration of performance period from 3 years to 5 years.
- Vesting award based on company TSR performance against a peer group rather than a predetermined target.
- Awarding performance shares rather than restricted stock (Note: this change does not impact the fair value but impacts the number of shares that will vest).

Compensation Cost Determination

Using FAS 123(R) guidance, Boris determined the fair value of the restricted stock award for expense recognition. Compensation cost for the award will equal the fair value multiplied by the number of restricted shares granted. Determining the fair value for its restricted stock awards is similar to the process Boris had used to determine fair value of its stock option awards under the pro forma disclosure rules of FAS 123. However, a simple Black–Scholes model cannot be used to determine the fair value of an award with a TSR target. Instead, a Monte Carlo simulation model coupled with a binomial lattice model must be used with inputs as detailed next (see Chapters 12 and 13 for details on option valuation techniques). A Monte Carlo simulation model coupled with a binomial model is more appropriate than other closed-form option-pricing models because this analysis has a barrier associated with the payoff structure (i.e., TSR targets), which means only a binomial lattice can be used to model such barrier options. In addition, the potential that Boris's TSR will exceed these targets is highly uncertain and thus we need to run a Monte Carlo simulation to capture its expected value. Therefore, we couple Risk Simulator's Monte Carlo simulation capabilities with the Employee Stock Options Valuation and Real Options SLS software to perform the computations. See the chapters on real options analysis for more details on running the SLS software, or refer to the author's *Real Options Analysis*, Second Edition (John Wiley & Sons, 2005). The following are the assumptions used in the model:

- *Grant date.* This assumption determines the grant date stock price and interest rate assumption.
- *Grant date stock price.* Equals the closing stock price on the grant date, or $20 for this example.
- *Purchase price.* Typically $0 for restricted stock awards.
- *Volatility.* Calculated based on historical stock prices, 30 percent for this example. Significant guidance for determining this assumption is provided in FAS 123(R) and SEC's Staff Accounting Bulletin No. 107.
- *Contractual period.* Equals duration of performance period, 3 years for this example.
- *Dividend yield.* Calculated based on Boris's historical dividend yield, 1 percent for this example.

Dividend Payment Date	Dividend Amount	Stock Price ($)	Quarterly Dividend Yield (%)
3/15/2005	$0.04	15.00	0.27
6/15/2005	$0.04	15.50	0.26
9/15/2005	$0.04	15.75	0.25
12/15/2005	$0.04	16.00	0.25
Sum of quarterly dividend yields			1.03

- *Interest rate.* Based on the U.S. Treasury rates available on the grant date with a maturity equaling the contractual term. For this example, we used a 4 percent interest rate.
- *TSR target.* Boris's compensation committee set the target at 6 percent based on the company's 3-year historical average annualized return of 5.2 percent.

- *Expected range TSR performance.* Sets the parameters for determining the likelihood of achieving the TSR target. The committee thought it would be reasonable to assume a minimum expected TSR of 0 percent and a stretch TSR of 9 percent.
- *Suboptimal exercise multiple.* Set the price at which the participant is expected to exercise. This assumption is set at 10,000, which theoretically renders it unattainable. If this award were a stock option, this assumption could be used if employee exercise behavior indicated a lower level.

The results generated using Risk Simulator's Monte Carlo simulation coupled with the Real Options SLS provides a fair value of $10.27 (Figure 7.32). Real Options SLS software was used to obtain the restricted stock's fair-market valuation, while Risk Simulator was used to simulate the potential TSR values. Thus, if Boris awards 400,000 restricted shares to employees, the compensation cost equals 400,000 × $10.27 = $4,108,000, which is accrued over the performance period of 3 years. If the Monte Carlo simulation model were not used, Boris would be required to use the grant date stock price, $20, resulting in an expense of 400,000 × $20 = $8,000,000. Therefore, by applying the right methodologies as well as the right engineered LTI grants, Boris was able to reduce its expenses by almost 50 percent.

Conclusion

Monte Carlo Simulation models can be used to help design the LTI award by understanding the impact that certain changes have on fair value, and to determine the fair value of the LTI award for expense purposes under FAS 123R. Without the use of such sophisticated methodologies, the fair value would never have been computed correctly and the decision to undertake the right LTI would have been flawed. In addition, such methodologies outlined here can also be used for multiple other applications such as engineering LTIs and stock-based compensations that are tied to, say, a market index such as the S&P 500, or a company's performance (i.e., we can use financial metrics such as net profit margin, gross profits, EBITDA), or perhaps to some commodity price (e.g., price of gold or oil). For technical and application details on FAS 123R and running the Employee Stock Options Valuation software, please refer to the author's book, *Valuing Employee Stock Options (Under 2004 FAS 123)* (John Wiley & Sons, 2004).

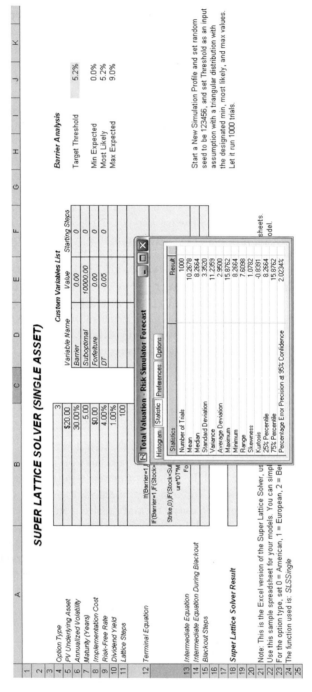

FIGURE 7.32 Total valuation results (sample only) for Boris's LTI.

CASE STUDY: RISK-BASED SCHEDULE PLANNING WITH SIMULATION

Mark Rhoades is a lecturer at the Naval Postgraduate School at Monterey, California. He is a former U.S. Navy Commander and has served as the Deputy Program Manager at the NAVSTAR Global Positioning System Joint Program Office, a systems engineer at the Naval Air Systems Command, and the Program Manager of the Naval Aviation Depot Field Service Repair Teams. Mark has had years of experience in program management, program planning, reliability, and logistics. In addition to teaching graduate-level classes in risk management, he currently runs his own consulting business, Risk and Opportunity Management.

All organizations depend heavily on project planning tools to forecast when various projects will complete. Completing projects within specified times and budgets is critical to facilitate smooth business operations. In our high-technology environment, many things can impact schedule. Technical capabilities can often fall short of expectations. Requirements are insufficient in many cases and need further definition. Tests can bring surprising results—good or bad. A whole host of other reasons can lead to schedule slips. On rare occasions, we may run into good fortune and the schedule can be accelerated. Project schedules are inherently uncertain and change is normal. Therefore, we should expect changes and find the best way to deal with them. So why do projects always take longer than anticipated? The following discussion presents a description on shortcomings in the traditional methods of schedule estimation and how Risk Simulator can be applied to address these shortcomings.

Traditional Schedule Management

Traditional schedule management typically starts with a list of tasks. Next these tasks are put in order and linked from the predecessor to successor for each task. They are typically displayed in either a Gantt chart form or a network. For our discussion, we concentrate on the network. The duration for each task within the network is then developed. The estimated duration for each task is given a single point estimate, even though we know from experience that this estimate should be a range of values. The first error is using a single point estimate. In addition, many people who provide duration estimates try to put their best foot forward and give an optimistic or best-case estimate. If we assume that the probability of achieving this best-case estimate for one task is 20 percent, then the likelihood of achieving the

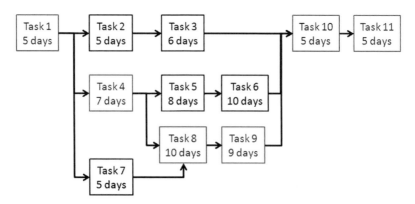

FIGURE 7.33 Schedule network.

best case for two tasks is merely 4 percent (20 percent of 20 percent), and three tasks yields only 0.8 percent. Within a real project with many more tasks, there is only an infinitesimal chance of making the best-case schedule.

Once the task duration estimates have been developed, the network is constructed and the various paths through the network are traced. The task durations are summed along each of these paths, and the one that takes the longest is identified as the critical path. Figure 7.33 illustrates an example network and critical path. The sum of task durations along the critical path is listed as the project completion date. In Figure 7.33, there are four paths through the network from beginning to end. The shortest/quickest path is tasks 1-2-3-10-11 with a total duration of 22 days. The next shortest path is tasks 1-7-8-9-10-11 at 34 days, and then path 1-4-5-6-10-11 at 36 days. Finally, the path 1-4-8-9-10-11 takes the longest at 37 days and is the critical path for this network.

So let us assume that this network of tasks is our part of a larger effort and some other effort upstream of ours has overrun by a day. Our boss has asked us to shorten our schedule by one or two days to get the overall effort back on track. Traditional schedule management has one target: shorten the longest duration item in the critical path. Another approach is to shorten every task on the entire critical path. Because the first technique is more focused, more prone to success, and creates fewer conflicts on our team, let us assume that we will use that one. Hence, we will want to reduce Task 8 from 10 days to 9 days to shorten our schedule and we will satisfy our boss or our customer. Let us leave the traditional methodology at this stage feeling satisfied with our efforts.

Probabilistic Schedule Management

If we agree that task durations can vary, then that uncertainty should be accounted for in our schedule models. A schedule model can be developed by creating a probability distribution for each task, representing the likelihood of completing the particular task at a specific duration. Monte Carlo simulation techniques can then be applied to forecast the entire range of possible project durations.

A simple triangular distribution is a reasonable probability distribution to use to describe the uncertainty for a task's duration. It is a natural fit because if we ask someone to give a range of duration values for a specific task, he or she usually supplies two of the elements: the minimum duration and the maximum duration. We need only ask or determine the most likely duration to complete the triangular distribution. The parameters are simple, intuitively easy to understand, and readily accepted by customers and bosses alike. Other more complex distributions could be used such as the Beta or Weibull but little, if anything, is gained because the determination of the estimated parameters for these distributions is prone to error and the method of determination is not easily explainable to the customer or boss.

To get the best estimates, we should use multiple sources to get the estimates of the minimum, most likely, and maximum values for the task durations. We can talk to the contractor, the project manager, and the people doing the hands-on work and then compile a list of duration estimates. Historical data can also be used, but with caution. While the current project may be similar to past projects, the previous projects usually contain several unique elements or combinations. We can use Figure 7.34 as a guide. Minimum values should reflect optimal utilization of resources. Maximum

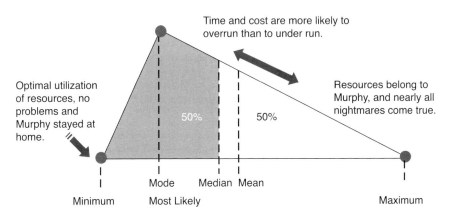

FIGURE 7.34 Triangular distribution.

TABLE 7.18 Range of Task Durations

Task #	Task Name	Dynamic Duration	Minimum	Most Likely	Maximum	Point Estimate
1	Stakeholder Analysis	5.78	4.5	5	6	5
2	Objectives Hierarchy	4.79	4.5	5	6	5
3	Decision Metrics Development	6.16	5.5	6	7	6
4	Functional Analysis	7.78	6	7	9	7
5	Primary Module Rqmts	9.22	7	8	10	8
6	Primary Module Development	10.12	9	10	13	10
7	Secondary Module Functional Analysis	5.42	4.5	5	6	5
8	Secondary Requirements Allocation	10.05	9	10	12	10
9	Secondary Module Development	9.40	8	9	10	9
10	Trade Studies	3.33	2.5	3	4	3
11	Final Development Specification	3.76	2.5	3	4	3

values should take into account substantial problems, but it is not necessary to account for the absolute worst case where everything goes wrong and the problems compound each other. Note that the most likely value will be the value experienced most often, but it is typically less than the median or mean in most cases.

For our example problem, shown in Figure 7.33, the minimum, most likely, and maximum values given in Table 7.18 will be used. We can use Risk Simulator's input assumptions to create triangular distributions based on these minimum, most likely, and maximum parameters. The column of dynamic duration values shown in the table was created by taking one random sample from each of the associated triangular distributions.

After the triangular distributions are created, the next step is to use the schedule network to determine the paths. For the example problem shown Figure 7.33, there are four paths through the network from beginning to end. These paths are shown in Table 7.19 with their associated durations.

TABLE 7.19 Paths and Durations for Example Problem

Path1	Duration1	Path2	Duration2	Path3	Duration3	Path4	Duration4
1	5.78	1	5.78	1	5.78	1	5.78
2	4.79	4	7.78	4	7.78	7	5.42
3	6.16	5	9.22	8	10.05	8	10.05
10	3.33	6	10.12	9	9.40	9	9.40
11	3.76	10	3.33	10	3.33	10	3.33
		11	3.76	11	3.76	11	3.76
Total1	23.81	Total2	39.99	Total3	40.10	Total4	37.73

Overall Schedule Total >>>>>>   **40.0968125** =MAX(Total1,Total2,Total3,Total4)

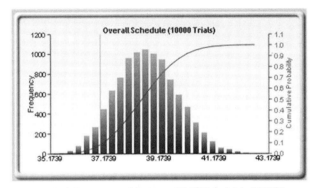

Type: Left-Tail ≤, Lower: -Infinity, Upper: 37.0000, Certainty: 8.2700%

FIGURE 7.35   Results of Monte Carlo analysis.

(Note: When setting up the spreadsheet for the various paths, it is absolutely essential to use the input assumptions for the task durations and then reference these task duration cells when calculating the duration for each path. This method ensures that duration of individual tasks is the same regardless of which path is used.) The overall schedule duration is the maximum of the four paths. In Risk Simulator, we would designate that cell as an Output Forecast. In probabilistic schedule analysis, we are not concerned with the critical path/near-critical path situations because the analysis automatically accounts for all path durations through the calculations.

We can now use Risk Simulator and run a Monte Carlo simulation to produce a forecast for schedule duration. Figure 7.35 shows the results for the example problem. Let us return to the numbers given by the traditional method. The original estimate stated the project would be complete in 37 days. If we use the left-tail function on the forecast chart, we can determine the likelihood of completing the task in 37 days based on the Monte Carlo simulation. In this case, there is a mere 8.27 percent chance of completion within the 37 days. This result illustrates the second shortcoming in the traditional method: Not only is the point estimate incorrect, but it puts us in a high-risk overrun situation before the work even has started! As shown in Figure 7.35, the median value is 38.5 days. Some industry standards recommend using the 80 percent certainty value for most cases, which equates to 39.5 days in the example problem.

Now let us revisit the boss's request to reduce the overall schedule by one day. Where do we put the effort to reduce the overall duration? If we are using probabilistic schedule management, we do not use the critical path; so where do we start? Using Risk Simulator's Tornado and Sensitivity Analysis tools, we can identify the most effective targets for reduction

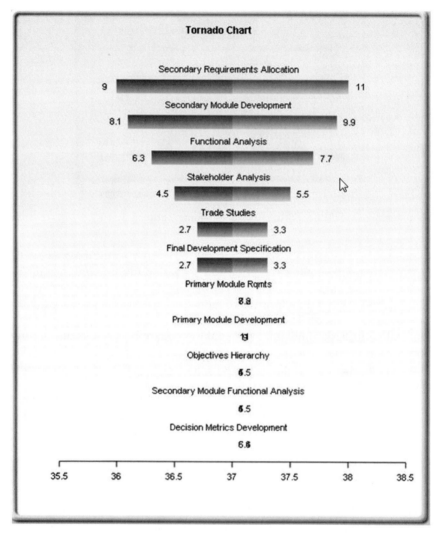

FIGURE 7.36 Tornado chart.

efforts. The tornado chart (Figure 7.36) identifies the most influential variables (tasks) to the overall schedule. This chart provides the best targets to reduce the mean/median values. We cannot address the mean/median without addressing the variation, however. The Sensitivity Analysis tool shows what variables (tasks) contribute the most to the variation in the overall schedule output (see Figure 7.37). In this case, we can see that the variation in Task 4

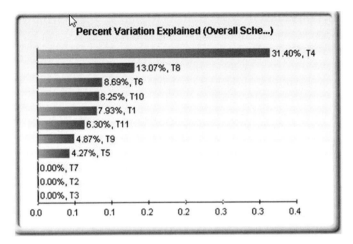

FIGURE 7.37   Sensitivity analysis chart.

is the major contributor to the variation in the overall schedule. Another interesting observation is the variation in Task 6, a task not on the critical path, is also contributing nearly 9 percent of the overall variation.

In this example, reducing the schedule duration for Task 4, Task 8, and Task 9 would pay the most dividends as far as reducing the overall schedule length. Determining the underlying reasons for the substantial variation in Tasks 4, 6, and 8 would likely give better insight into these processes. For example, the variation in Task 4 may be caused by the lack of available personnel. Management actions could be taken to dedicate personnel to the effort and reduce the variation substantially, which would reduce the overall variation and enhance the predictability of the schedule. Digging into the reasons for variation will lead to targets where management actions will be most effective, much more so than simply telling the troops to reduce their task completion time.

Using the network schedule model, we can also experiment to see how different reduction strategies may pay off. For example, taking one day out of Tasks 4, 8, and 9 under the traditional method would lead us to believe that a three-day reduction has taken place, but if we reduce the Most Likely value for Tasks 4, 8, and 9 by one day and run the Monte Carlo risk simulation, we find that the median value is still 37.84, or only a 0.7 day reduction. This small reduction proves that the variation must be addressed. If we reduce the variation by 50 percent, keeping the original minimum and the most likely values, but reducing the maximum value for each distribution, then we reduce the median from 38.5 to 37.84—about the same as reducing the Most Likely values. Taking both actions (reducing the Most Likely and

Maximum values) reduces the median to 36.83, giving us a 55 percent chance of completing within 37 days. This analysis proves that reducing the most likely value and the overall variation is the most effective action.

To get to 36 days, we need to continue to work down the list of tasks shown in the sensitivity and tornado charts addressing each task. If we give Task 1 the same treatment, reducing its most likely and maximum values, then completion within 36 days can be accomplished with a 51 percent certainty, and a 79.25 percent certainty of completing within 37 days. The maximum value for the overall schedule is reduced from more than 42 days to less than 40 days. Substantial management efforts would be needed, however, to reach 36 days at the 80 percent certainty level.

Rules for Schedule Risk Management

When managing the production schedule, use the best-case numbers. If we use the most likely values or, worse yet, the maximum values, production personnel will not strive to hit the best-case numbers thus implementing a self-fulfilling prophecy of delayed completion. When budgeting, we should create the budget for the median outcome but recognize that there is un-certainty in the real world as well as risk. When advertising the schedule to the customer, provide the values that equate to the 75 percent to 80 percent certainty level. In most cases, customers prefer predictability (on-time completion) over potential speedy completion that includes significant risk. Lastly, acknowledge that the "worst case" can conceivably occur and create contingency plans to protect your organization in case it does occur. If the "worst case"/maximum value is unacceptable, then make the appropriate changes in the process to reduce the maximum value of the outcome to an acceptable level.

How to Apply This Method to Larger Networks

Some could argue that this methodology is only good for small networks because it appears that you have to trace all of the paths from beginning to end. We can, however, break up the schedule network to make the problem easier for larger cases. In our example problem, all of the paths came together at Task 10. We can call Task 10 a Merge Event. We can break a large network up into smaller pieces utilizing the merge points to define the boundaries. To further illustrate this technique, we will use the schedule network shown in Figure 7.38.

In Figure 7.38, there are two merge points—Task 12 and Task 18. After we have created Input Assumptions for each task, we can set up our calculations. For this example, we should create the sum of the durations

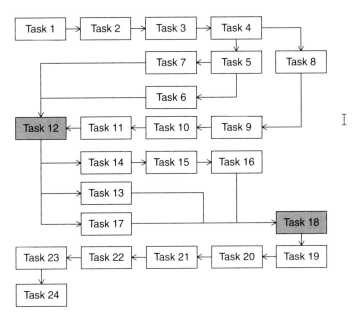

FIGURE 7.38 Example schedule network with multiple merge points.

for Tasks 1-2-3-4 as our first subtotal since these tasks are in series. The second subtotal would be equal to the maximum duration among Tasks 5-6, Task 5-7, and Tasks 8-9-10-11. We would then add the duration of Task 12 as the third subtotal. The fourth subtotal would be the maximum duration among Task 13, Tasks 14-15-16, and Task 17. Lastly we sum the durations of Tasks 18 through 24 as the fifth subtotal. We can then sum all of the five subtotals to determine the overall schedule duration. The spreadsheet cell that sums all five subtotals is set as the Output Forecast for our entire schedule network. The calculations are demonstrated in the spreadsheet shown in Figure 7.39.

Risk Simulator can also be used to take into account correlations between tasks. After we create the Input Assumptions, we can go back and use the *Tools | Edit Correlations* to account for correlations among tasks. For example, if previous experience or data indicates that as Task 8 takes longer the duration for Task 9 will also increase, then there is likely a correlation between those two tasks. If we have paired data, then we can use Risk Simulator's Distribution Fitting (Multi-Variable) tool to determine the correlation values between the two items. This tool also works with more than two items. If we have data from several previous cases, we can use this tool to determine the correlation matrix for all of the tasks. To build

	Task	MIN	ML	MAX	Input Assumption		Summations	Value	Formulas	Description
1	Task	MIN	ML	MAX	Input Assumption					
2	1	2	5	10	5.33		Subtotal1 =	76.03	=SUM(E3:E6)	Tasks 1-2-3-4
3	2	5	10	15	10.48		Subtotal2 =	108.13	=MAX(SUM(E7:E8),SUM(E7,E9),SUM(E10:E13))	Max of (Task 5-6, Tasks 5-7, Tasks 8-9-10-11)
4	3	30	45	90	47.12		Subtotal3 =	18.98	=E14	Task 12
5	4	5	10	15	13.11		Subtotal4 =	88.21	=MAX(E15,SUM(E16:E18),E19)	Max of (Task 13, Task 14-15-16, Task 17)
6	5	30	45	90	74.60		Subtotal5 =	165.52	=SUM(E20:E26)	Tasks 18-19-20-21-22-23-24
7	6	5	10	15	14.04					
8	7	15	25	60	33.53		Total	456.87	=SUM(H3:H7)	Output Forecast
9	8	10	20	60	16.05					
10	9	5	15	30	16.31					
11	10	5	10	15	9.88					
12	11	15	25	45	39.91					
13	12	15	20	30	18.98					
14	13	20	30	45	37.55					
15	14	30	45	60	50.76					
16	15	15	30	45	29.34					
17	16	5	10	20	8.11					
18	17	10	15	25	11.13					
19	18	15	30	60	33.60					
20	19	10	15	30	11.40					
21	20	15	30	60	40.63					
22	21	5	10	15	12.09					
23	22	30	60	90	44.41					
24	23	5	10	15	11.70					
25	24	5	8	12	11.70					

Forecasts

Name	Total
Enabled	Yes
Cell	$H$9

Forecast Precision	
Precision Level	—
Error Level	—

Number of Datapoints	5000
Mean	460.5237
Median	459.7741
Standard Deviation	27.7741
Variance	771.3997
Coefficient of Variation	0.0603
Maximum	557.3585
Minimum	366.8121
Range	190.5464
Skewness	0.1385
Kurtosis	-0.0754
25% Percentile	441.0357
75% Percentile	478.8738
Error Precision at 95%	0.0017

Total (5000 Trials)

Type: Two-Tail; Lower: -Infinity; Upper: Infinity; Certainty: 100.0000%

FIGURE 7.39 Example schedule spreadsheet with multiple merge points.

the most accurate forecast, we should account for correlations whenever we know they exist.

Conclusion

With traditional schedule management, there is only one answer for the scheduled completion date. Each task gets one duration estimate and that estimate is accurate only if everything goes according to plan, not a likely occurrence. With probabilistic schedule management, thousands of trials are run exploring the range of possible outcomes for schedule duration. Each task in the network receives a time estimate distribution, accurately reflecting each task's uncertainty. Correlations can be entered to more accurately model real-world behavior. Critical paths and near critical paths are automatically taken into account, and the output forecast distribution will accurately reflect the entire range of possible outcomes. Using tornado and sensitivity analyses, we can maximize the effectiveness of our management actions to control schedule variations and reduce the overall schedule at high certainty levels.

Risk Prediction

CHAPTER 8

Tomorrow's Forecast Today

Forecasting is the act of predicting the future, whether it is based on historical data or speculation about the future when no history exists. When historical data exist, a quantitative or statistical approach is best, but if no historical data exist, then a qualitative or judgmental approach is usually the only recourse. Figure 8.1 lists the most common methodologies for forecasting.

DIFFERENT TYPES OF FORECASTING TECHNIQUES

Generally, forecasting can be divided into quantitative and qualitative approaches. Qualitative forecasting is used when little to no reliable historical, contemporaneous, or comparable data exist. Several qualitative methods exist such as the Delphi or expert opinion approach (a consensus-building forecast by field experts, marketing experts, or internal staff members), management assumptions (target growth rates set by senior management), as well as market research or external data or polling and surveys (data obtained through third-party sources, industry and sector indexes, or from active market research). These estimates can be either single-point estimates (an average consensus) or a set of prediction values (a distribution of predictions). The latter can be entered into Risk Simulator as a custom distribution and the resulting predictions can be simulated; that is, running a nonparametric simulation using the prediction data points as the custom distribution.

For quantitative forecasting, the available data or data that need to be forecasted can be divided into time-series (values that have a time element to them, such as revenues at different years, inflation rates, interest rates, market share, failure rates, and so forth), cross-sectional (values that are time-independent, such as the grade point average of sophomore students across the nation in a particular year, given each student's levels of SAT scores, IQ, and number of alcoholic beverages consumed per week), or

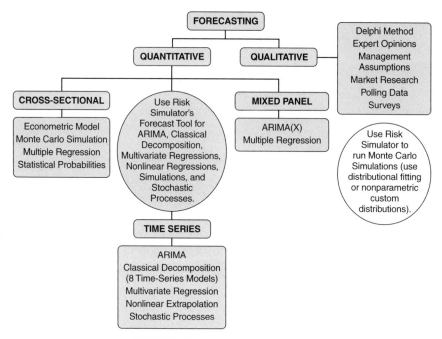

FIGURE 8.1 Forecasting methods.

mixed panel (mixture between time-series and panel data, for example, predicting sales over the next 10 years given budgeted marketing expenses and market share projections, which means that the sales data is time-series but exogenous variables such as marketing expenses and market share exist to help to model the forecast predictions).

Here is a quick review of each methodology and several quick getting started examples in using the software. More detailed descriptions and example models of each of these techniques are found throughout this chapter and in Chapter 9.

1. *ARIMA.* Autoregressive integrated moving average (ARIMA, also known as Box–Jenkins ARIMA) is an advanced econometric modeling technique. ARIMA looks at historical time-series data and performs back-fitting optimization routines to account for historical autocorrelation (the relationship of one value versus another in time), accounts for the stability of the data to correct for the nonstationary characteristics of the data, and this predictive model learns over time by correcting its forecasting errors. Advanced knowledge in econometrics is typically required to build good predictive models using this approach.

2. *Auto ARIMA*. The Auto-ARIMA module automates some of the traditional ARIMA modeling by automatically testing multiple permutations of model specifications and returns the best-fitting model. Running the Auto-ARIMA module is similar to running regular ARIMA forecasts. The differences being that the P, D, Q inputs are no longer required and that different combinations of these inputs are automatically run and compared.

3. *Basic Econometrics*. Econometrics refers to a branch of business analytics, modeling, and forecasting techniques for modeling the behavior or forecasting certain business, economic, finance, physics, manufacturing, operations, and any other variables. Running the Basic Econometrics models is similar to regular regression analysis except that the dependent and independent variables are allowed to be modified before a regression is run.

4. *Basic Auto Econometrics*. This methodology is similar to basic econometrics, but thousands of linear, nonlinear, interacting, lagged, and mixed variables are automatically run on your data to determine the best-fitting econometric model that describes the behavior of the dependent variable. It is useful for modeling the effects of the variables and for forecasting future outcomes, while not requiring the analyst to be an expert econometrician.

5. *Custom Distributions*. Using Risk Simulator, expert opinions can be collected and a customized distribution can be generated. This forecasting technique comes in handy when the data set is small or the goodness-of-fit is bad when applied to a distributional fitting routine.

6. *GARCH*. The generalized autoregressive conditional heteroskedasticity (GARCH) model is used to model historical and forecast future volatility levels of a marketable security (e.g., stock prices, commodity prices, oil prices). The data set has to be a time series of raw price levels. GARCH will first convert the prices into relative returns and then run an internal optimization to fit the historical data to a mean-reverting volatility term structure, while assuming that the volatility is heteroskedastic in nature (changes over time according to some econometric characteristics). Several variations of this methodology are available in Risk Simulator, including EGARCH, EGARCH-T, GARCH-M, GJR-GARCH, GJR-GARCH-T, IGARCH, and T-GARCH.

7. *J-Curve*. The J-curve, or exponential growth curve, is one where the growth of the next period depends on the current period's level and the increase is exponential. This phenomenon means that over time, the values will increase significantly, from one period to another. This model is typically used in forecasting biological growth and chemical reactions over time.

8. *Markov Chains.* A Markov chain exists when the probability of a future state depends on a previous state and when linked together forms a chain that reverts to a long-run steady state level. This approach is typically used to forecast the market share of two competitors. The required inputs are the starting probability of a customer in the first store (the first state) returning to the same store in the next period, versus the probability of switching to a competitor's store in the next state.

9. *Maximum Likelihood on Logit, Probit, and Tobit.* Maximum likelihood estimation (MLE) is used to forecast the probability of something occurring given some independent variables. For instance, MLE is used to predict if a credit line or debt will default given the obligor's characteristics (30 years old, single, salary of $100,000 per year, and total credit card debt of $10,000), or the probability a patient will have lung cancer if the person is a male between the ages of 50 and 60, smokes five packs of cigarettes per month or year, and so forth. In these circumstances, the dependent variable is limited (i.e., limited to being binary 1 and 0 for default/die and no default/live, or limited to integer values such as 1, 2, 3) and the desired outcome of the model is to predict the probability of an event occurring. Traditional regression analysis will not work in these situations (the predicted probability is usually less than zero or greater than one, and many of the required regression assumptions are violated, such as independence and normality of the errors, and the errors will be fairly large).

10. *Multivariate Regression.* Multivariate regression is used to model the relationship structure and characteristics of a certain dependent variable as it depends on other independent exogenous variables. Using the modeled relationship, we can forecast the future values of the dependent variable. The accuracy and goodness-of-fit for this model can also be determined. Linear and nonlinear models can be fitted in the multiple regression analysis.

11. *Nonlinear Extrapolation.* In this methodology, the underlying structure of the data to be forecasted is assumed to be nonlinear over time. For instance, a data set such as 1, 4, 9, 16, 25 is considered to be nonlinear (these data points are from a squared function).

12. *S-Curves.* The S-curve, or logistic growth curve, starts off like a J-curve, with exponential growth rates. Over time, the environment becomes saturated (e.g., market saturation, competition, overcrowding), the growth slows, and the forecast value eventually ends up at a saturation or maximum level. The S-curve model is typically used in forecasting market share or sales growth of a new product from market introduction until maturity and decline, population dynamics, and other naturally occurring phenomenon.

13. *Spline Curves*. Sometimes there are missing values in a time-series data set. For instance, interest rates for years 1 to 3 may exist, followed by years 5 to 8, and then year 10. Spline curves can be used to interpolate the missing years' interest rate values based on the data that exist. Spline curves can also be used to forecast or extrapolate values of future time periods beyond the time period of available data. The data can be linear or nonlinear.

14. *Stochastic Process Forecasting*. Sometimes variables are stochastic and cannot be readily predicted using traditional means. These variables are said to be stochastic. Nonetheless, most financial, economic, and naturally occurring phenomena (e.g., motion of molecules through the air) follow a known mathematical law or relationship. Although the resulting values are uncertain, the underlying mathematical structure is known and can be simulated using Monte Carlo risk simulation. The processes supported in Risk Simulator include Brownian motion random walk, mean-reversion, jump-diffusion, and mixed processes, useful for forecasting nonstationary time-series variables.

15. *Time-Series Analysis and Decomposition*. In well-behaved time-series data (typical examples include sales revenues and cost structures of large corporations), the values tend to have up to three elements: a base value, trend, and seasonality. Time-series analysis uses these historical data and decomposes them into these three elements, and recomposes them into future forecasts. In other words, this forecasting method, like some of the others described, first performs a back-fitting (backcast) of historical data before it provides estimates of future values (forecasts).

RUNNING THE FORECASTING TOOL IN RISK SIMULATOR

In general, to create forecasts, several quick steps are required:

1. Start Excel and enter in or open existing historical data.
2. Select the data and click on *Risk Simulator | Forecasting*.
3. Select the relevant sections (Box–Jenkins ARIMA, Time-Series Analysis, Multivariate Regression, Stochastic Processes, Nonlinear Extrapolation, GARCH, Markov, Econometrics, JS Curves, Trendlines, and others) and enter the relevant inputs.

Figure 8.2 illustrates the *Forecasting* tool and the various methodologies available in Risk Simulator.

The following provides a quick review of each methodology and several quick getting started examples in using the software. The example data

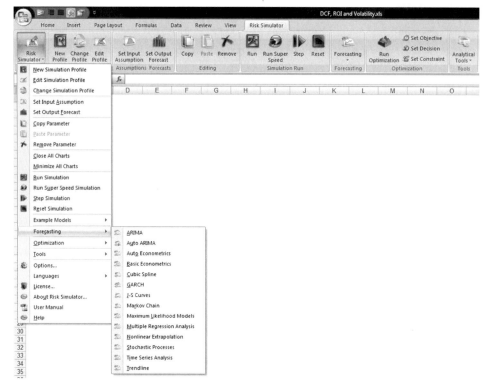

FIGURE 8.2   Risk Simulator's forecasting methods.

files used to create these examples are included in the Risk Simulator software and can be accessed through Excel's Menu: *Risk Simulator | Example Models.*

TIME-SERIES ANALYSIS

Theory

Figure 8.3 lists the eight most common time-series models, segregated by seasonality and trend. For instance, if the data variable has no trend or seasonality, then a single moving-average model or a single exponential-smoothing model would suffice. However, if seasonality exists but no discernible trend is present, either a seasonal additive or seasonal multiplicative model would be better, and so forth.

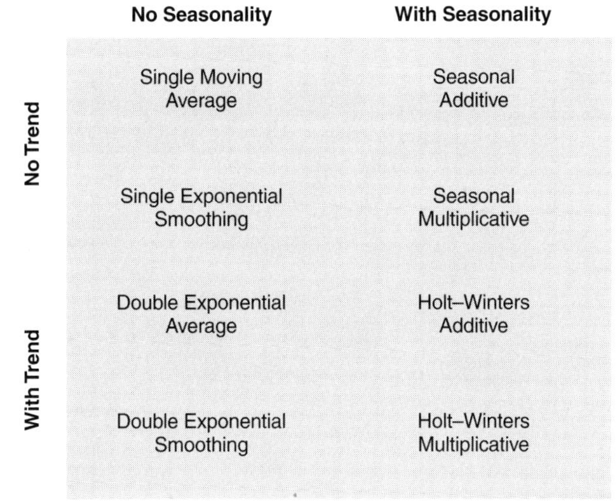

	No Seasonality	With Seasonality
No Trend	Single Moving Average	Seasonal Additive
	Single Exponential Smoothing	Seasonal Multiplicative
With Trend	Double Exponential Average	Holt–Winters Additive
	Double Exponential Smoothing	Holt–Winters Multiplicative

FIGURE 8.3   The eight most common time-series methods.

Procedure

Follow the steps listed to run a time-series analysis:

1. Start Excel and type in or open an existing spreadsheet with the relevant historical data (the following example uses the *Time-Series Forecasting* file in the examples folder).
2. Select the historical data, not including the variable name (data should be listed in a single column).
3. Select *Risk Simulator | Forecasting | Time-Series Analysis*.
4. Choose the model to apply, enter the relevant assumptions, and click *OK*.

Make sure you start a new simulation profile or that there is an existing profile in the model if you want the forecast results to automatically generate simulation assumptions.

To follow along in this example, choose Auto Model Selection, enter 4 for seasonality periods per cycle (select Quarterly seasonality from the drop list or select Custom and enter in the value 4), and forecast for 4 periods. See Figure 8.4.

Results Interpretation

Figure 8.5 illustrates the sample results generated by using the *Forecasting* tool. The model used was a Holt–Winters multiplicative model. Notice that in Figure 8.5, the model-fitting and forecast chart indicate that the trend and

Historical Sales Revenues

Year	Quarter	Period	Sales
2000	1	1	$684.20
2000	2	2	$584.10
2000	3	3	$765.40
2000	4	4	$892.30
2001	1	5	$885.40
2001	2	6	$677.00
2001	3	7	$1,006.60
2001	4	8	$1,122.10
2002	1	9	$1,163.40
2002	2	10	$993.20
2002	3	11	$1,312.50
2002	4	12	$1,545.30
2003	1	13	$1,596.20
2003	2	14	$1,260.40
2003	3	15	$1,735.20
2003	4	16	$2,029.70
2004	1	17	$2,107.80
2004	2	18	$1,650.30
2004	3	19	$2,304.40
2004	4	20	$2,639.40

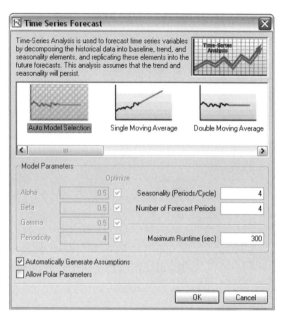

FIGURE 8.4   Time-series analysis.

seasonality are picked up nicely by the Holt–Winters multiplicative model. The time-series analysis report provides the relevant optimized alpha, beta, and gamma parameters, the error measurements, fitted data, forecast values, and forecast-fitted graph. The parameters are simply for reference. Alpha captures the memory effect of the base level changes over time, beta is the trend parameter that measures the strength of the trend, while gamma measures the seasonality strength of the historical data. The analysis decomposes the historical data into these three elements and then recomposes them to forecast the future. The fitted data illustrate the historical data as well as the fitted data using the recomposed model and show how close the forecasts are in the past (a technique called *backcasting*). The forecast values are either single-point estimates or assumptions (if the automatically generated assumptions option is chosen and if a simulation profile exists). The graph illustrates the historical, fitted, and forecast values. The chart is a powerful communication and visual tool to see how good the forecast model is.

Notes

This time-series analysis module contains the eight time-series models seen in Figure 8.3. You can choose the specific model to run based on the trend

Holt-Winters' Multiplicative

Summary Statistics

Alpha, Beta, Gamma	RMSE	Alpha, Beta, Gamma	RMSE
0.00, 0.00, 0.00	914.824	0.00, 0.00, 0.00	914.824
0.10, 0.10, 0.10	415.322	0.10, 0.10, 0.10	415.322
0.20, 0.20, 0.20	187.202	0.20, 0.20, 0.20	187.202
0.30, 0.30, 0.30	118.795	0.30, 0.30, 0.30	118.795
0.40, 0.40, 0.40	101.794	0.40, 0.40, 0.40	101.794
0.50, 0.50, 0.50	102.143		

The analysis was run with alpha = 0.2429, beta = 1.0000, gamma = 0.7797, and seasonality = 4

Time-Series Analysis Summary

When both seasonality and trend exist, more advanced models are required to decompose the data into their base elements: a base-case level (L) weighted by the alpha parameter, a trend component (b) weighted by the beta parameter, and a seasonality component (S) weighted by the gamma parameter. Several methods exist but the two most common are the Holt-Winters' additive seasonality and Holt-Winters' multiplicative seasonality methods. In the Holt-Winters' additive model, the base case level, seasonality, and trend are added together to obtain the forecast fit.

The best-fitting test for the moving average forecast uses the root mean squared errors (RMSE). The RMSE calculates the square root of the average squared deviations of the fitted values versus the actual data points.

Mean Squared Error (MSE) is an absolute error measure that squares the errors (the difference between the actual historical data and the forecast-fitted data predicted by the model) to keep the positive and negative errors from cancelling each other out. This measure also tends to exaggerate large errors by weighting the large errors more heavily than smaller errors by squaring them, which can help when comparing different time-series models. Root Mean Square Error (RMSE) is the square root of MSE and is the most popular error measure, also know as the quadratic loss function. RMSE can be defined as the average of the absolute values of the forecast errors and is highly appropriate when the cost of the forecast errors is proportional to the absolute size of the forecast error. The RMSE is used as the selection criteria for the best-fitting time-series model.

Mean Absolute Percentage Error (MAPE) is a relative error statistic measured as an average percent error of the historical data points and is most appropriate when the cost of the forecast error is more closely related to the percentage error than the numerical size of the error. Finally, an associated measure is the Theil's U statistic, which measures the naivety of the model's forecast. That is, if the Theil's U statistic is less than 1.0, then the forecast method used provides an estimate that is statistically better than guessing.

Period	Actual	Forecast Fit
1	684.20	
2	584.10	
3	765.40	
4	892.30	
5	885.40	684.20
6	677.00	667.55
7	1006.60	935.45
8	1122.10	1198.09
9	1163.40	1112.48
10	993.20	887.95
11	1312.50	1348.38
12	1545.30	1546.53
13	1596.20	1572.44
14	1260.40	1299.20
15	1735.20	1704.77
16	2029.70	1976.23
17	2107.80	2026.01
18	1650.30	1637.26
19	2304.40	2245.93
20	2639.40	2643.09
Forecast 21		2713.69
Forecast 22		2114.79
Forecast 23		2900.42
Forecast 24		3293.81

Error Measurements

RMSE	71.8132
MSE	5157.1348
MAD	53.4071
MAPE	4.50%
Theil's U	0.3054

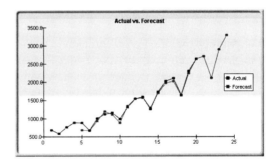

FIGURE 8.5 Example Holt–Winters forecast report.

and seasonality criteria or choose the Auto Model Selection, which will automatically iterate through all eight methods, optimize the parameters, and find the best-fitting model for your data. Alternatively, if you choose one of the eight models, you can also deselect the *optimize* checkboxes and enter your own alpha, beta, and gamma parameters (Figure 8.4). In addition, you would need to enter the relevant seasonality periods if you choose the automatic model selection or any of the seasonal models. The seasonality input has to be a positive integer (e.g., if the data is quarterly, enter *4* as the number of seasons or cycles a year, or enter *12* if monthly data, or any other positive integer representing the data periods of a full cycle—a drop list preset with these inputs is available or apply the Custom selection to enter in your own positive integer value). Next, enter the number of periods to forecast. This value also must be a positive integer. The maximum runtime is set at 300 seconds. Typically, no changes are required. However, when forecasting with a significant amount of historical data, the analysis might take slightly longer, and if the processing time exceeds this runtime, the process will be terminated. You can also elect to have the forecast automatically generate assumptions; that is, instead of single-point estimates, the forecasts will be assumptions. However, to automatically generate assumptions, a simulation profile must first exist. Finally, the polar parameters option allows you to optimize the alpha, beta, and gamma parameters to include zero and one. Certain forecasting software allows these polar parameters while others do not. Risk Simulator allows you to choose which to use. Typically, there is no need to use polar parameters. See Chapter 9 for the technical details on time-series forecasting using the eight decomposition methods.

MULTIVARIATE REGRESSION

Theory

It is assumed that the user is sufficiently knowledgeable about the fundamentals of regression analysis. The general bivariate linear regression equation takes the form of $Y = \beta_0 + \beta_1 X + \varepsilon$, where β_0 is the intercept, β_1 is the slope, and ε is the error term. It is bivariate as there are only two variables, a Y or dependent variable, and an X or independent variable, where X is also known as the regressor (sometimes a bivariate regression is also known as a univariate regression as there is only a single independent variable X). The dependent variable is named as such as it *depends* on the independent variable, for example, sales revenue depends on the amount of marketing costs expended on a product's advertising and promotion, making the dependent variable sales and the independent variable marketing costs. An example of

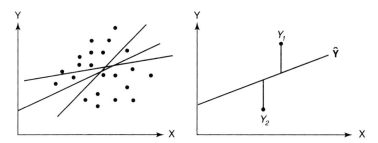

FIGURE 8.6 Bivariate regression.

a bivariate regression is seen as simply inserting the best-fitting line through a set of data points in a two-dimensional plane, as seen on the left panel in Figure 8.6. In other cases, a multivariate regression can be performed, where there are multiple or k number of independent X variables or regressors, where the general regression equation will now take the form of $Y = \beta_0 + \beta_1 X_1 + \beta_2 X_2 + \beta_3 X_3 + \ldots + \beta_k X_k + \varepsilon$. In this case, the best-fitting line will be within a $k + 1$ dimensional plane.

However, fitting a line through a set of data points in a scatter plot as in Figure 8.6 may result in numerous possible lines. The best-fitting line is defined as the single unique line that minimizes the total vertical errors, that is, the sum of the absolute distances between the actual data points (Y_i) and the estimated line ($\hat{Y}$), as shown on the right panel of Figure 8.6. To find the best-fitting unique line that minimizes the errors, a more sophisticated approach is applied, using regression analysis. Regression analysis therefore finds the unique best-fitting line by requiring that the total errors be minimized, or by calculating

$$Min \sum_{i=1}^{n} \left(Y_i - \hat{Y}_i \right)^2$$

where only one unique line minimizes this sum of squared errors. The errors (vertical distances between the actual data and the predicted line) are squared to avoid the negative errors from canceling out the positive errors. Solving this minimization problem with respect to the slope and intercept requires calculating first derivatives and setting them equal to zero:

$$\frac{d}{d\beta_0} \sum_{i=1}^{n} \left(Y_i - \hat{Y}_i \right)^2 = 0 \text{ and } \frac{d}{d\beta_1} \sum_{i=1}^{n} \left(Y_i - \hat{Y}_i \right)^2 = 0$$

which yields the bivariate regression's least squares equations:

$$\beta_1 = \frac{\sum_{i=1}^{n}(X_i - \overline{X})(Y_i - \overline{Y})}{\sum_{i=1}^{n}(X_i - \overline{X})^2} = \frac{\sum_{i=1}^{n} X_i Y_i - \frac{\sum_{i=1}^{n} X_i \sum_{i=1}^{n} Y_i}{n}}{\sum_{i=1}^{n} X_i^2 - \frac{\left(\sum_{i=1}^{n} X_i\right)^2}{n}}$$

$$\beta_0 = \overline{Y} - \beta_1 \overline{X}$$

For multivariate regression, the analogy is expanded to account for multiple independent variables, where $Y_i = \beta_1 + \beta_2 X_{2,i} + \beta_3 X_{3,i} + \varepsilon_i$ and the estimated slopes can be calculated by:

$$\hat{\beta}_2 = \frac{\sum Y_i X_{2,i} \sum X_{3,i}^2 - \sum Y_i X_{3,i} \sum X_{2,i} X_{3,i}}{\sum X_{2,i}^2 \sum X_{3,i}^2 - \left(\sum X_{2,i} X_{3,i}\right)^2}$$

$$\hat{\beta}_3 = \frac{\sum Y_i X_{3,i} \sum X_{2,i}^2 - \sum Y_i X_{2,i} \sum X_{2,i} X_{3,i}}{\sum X_{2,i}^2 \sum X_{3,i}^2 - \left(\sum X_{2,i} X_{3,i}\right)^2}$$

In running multivariate regressions, great care must be taken to set up and interpret the results. For instance, a good understanding of econometric modeling is required (e.g., identifying regression pitfalls such as structural breaks, multicollinearity, heteroskedasticity, autocorrelation, specification tests, nonlinearities, and so forth) before a proper model can be constructed (see Chapter 9 for details).

Procedure

Use the following steps to run a multivariate regression:

1. Start Excel and type in or open your existing data set (the illustration below uses the file *Multiple Regression* in the examples folder).
2. Check to make sure that the data is arranged in columns, select the data including the variable names, and click on *Risk Simulator | Forecasting | Multiple Regression*.
3. Select the dependent variable and check the relevant options (lags, stepwise regression, nonlinear regression, and so forth), and click *OK* (Figure 8.7).

Results Interpretation

Figure 8.8 illustrates a sample multivariate regression result report generated. The report comes complete with all the regression results, analysis

Multiple Regression Analysis Data Set

Aggravated Assault	Bachelor's Degree	Police Expenditure Per Capita	Population in Millions	Population Density (Persons/Sq Mile)	Unemployment Rate
521	18308	185	4.041	79.6	7.2
367	1148	600	0.55	1	8.5
443	18068	372	3.665	32.3	5.7
365	7729	142	2.351	45.1	7.3
614	100484	432			
385	16728	290			
286	14630	346			
397	4008	328			
764	38927	354			
427	22322	266			
153	3711	320			
231	3136	197			
524	50508	266			
328	28886	173			
240	16996	190			
286	13035	239			
285	12973	190			
569	16309	241			
96	5227	189			
498	19235	358			
481	44487	315			
468	44213	303			
177	23619	228			
198	9106	134			
458	24917	189			
108	3872	196			
246	8945	183			
291	2373	417			
68	7128	233			
311	23624	349			
606	5242	284			
512	92629	499			
426	28795	231			
47	4487	143			
265	48799	249	10.847	264.9	6.4
370	14067	195	3.146	45.8	6.7
312	12693	288	2.842	29.6	6
222	62184	229	11.882	265.1	6.9
280	9153	287	1.003	960.3	8.5
759	14250	224	3.487	115.8	6.2
114	3680	161	0.696	9.2	3.4
419	18063	221	4.877	118.3	6.6
435	65112	237	16.987	64.9	6.6
186	11340	220	1.723	21	4.9
87	4553	185	0.563	60.8	6.4
188	28960	260	6.187	156.3	5.8
303	19201	261	4.867	73.1	6.3
102	7533	118	1.793	74.5	10.5
127	26343	268	4.892	90.1	5.4
251	1641	300	0.454	4.7	5.1

Multiple Regression Analysis

Multiple Regression Analysis can be used to run linear regressions with multiple independent variables. These variables can be applied through a series of lags, nonlinear transformations or regressed in a stepwise fashion starting with the most correlated variable.

Dependent Variable   Aggravated Assault

Aggravated Assault	Bachelor's Degree	Police Expenditure Per
521	18308	185
367	1148	600
443	18068	372
365	7729	142
614	100484	432
385	16728	290
286	14630	346
397	4008	328
764	38927	354

Options

☐ Lag Regressors [1] Period(s)   ☐ Stepwise Regression

☐ Non-linear Regression   ☐ Show All Steps

OK   Cancel

FIGURE 8.7   Running a multivariate regression.

of variance results, fitted chart, and hypothesis test results. See Chapter 9 for the technical details on interpreting the results from a regression analysis.

STEPWISE REGRESSION

One powerful automated approach to regression analysis is stepwise regression, and based on its namesake, the regression process proceeds in multiple steps. There are several ways to set up these stepwise algorithms,

Regression Analysis Report

Regression Statistics

R-Squared (Coefficient of Determination)	0.3272
Adjusted R-Squared	0.2508
Multiple R (Multiple Correlation Coefficient)	0.5720
Standard Error of the Estimates (SEy)	149.6720
Number of Observations	50

The R-Squared or Coefficient of Determination indicates that 0.33 of the variation in the dependent variable can be explained and accounted for by the independent variables in this regression analysis. However, in a multiple regression, the Adjusted R-Squared takes into account the existence of additional independent variables or regressors and adjusts this R-Squared value to a more accurate view of the regression's explanatory power. Hence, only 0.25 of the variation in the dependent variable can be explained by the regressors.

The Multiple Correlation Coefficient (Multiple R) measures the correlation between the actual dependent variable (Y) and the estimated or fitted variable (Y) based on the regression equation. This is also the square root of the Coefficient of Determination (R-Squared).

The Standard Error of the Estimates (SEy) describes the dispersion of data points above and below the regression line or plane. This value is used as part of the calculation to obtain the confidence interval of the estimates later.

Regression Results

	Intercept	Bachelor's Degree	Police Expenditure Per Capita	Population in Millions	Population Density (Persons/Sq Mile)	Unemployment Rate
Coefficients	57.9555	−0.0035	0.4644	25.2377	−0.0086	16.5579
Standard Error	108.7901	0.0035	0.2535	14.1172	0.1016	14.7996
t-Statistic	0.5327	−1.0066	1.8316	1.7877	−0.0843	1.1188
p-Value	0.5969	0.3197	0.0738	0.0807	0.9332	0.2693
Lower 5%	−161.2966	−0.0106	−0.0466	−3.2137	−0.2132	−13.2687
Upper 95%	277.2076	0.0036	0.9753	53.6891	0.1961	46.3845

Degrees of Freedom		**Hypothesis Test**	
Degrees of Freedom for Regression	5	Critical t-Statistic (99% confidence with df of 44)	2.6923
Degrees of Freedom for Residual	44	Critical t-Statistic (95% confidence with df of 44)	2.0154
Total Degrees of Freedom	49	Critical t-Statistic (90% confidence with df of 44)	1.6802

The Coefficients provide the estimated regression intercept and slopes. For instance, the Coefficients are estimates of the true; population b values in the following regression equation $Y = b_0 + b1 \times 1 + b2 \times 2 + ... + bn \times n$. The Standard Error measures how accurate the predicted Coefficients are, and the t-Statistics are the ratios of each predicted Coefficient to its Standard Error.

The t-Statistic is used in hypothesis testing, where we set the null hypothesis (H_0) such that the real mean of the Coefficient = 0, and the alternate hypothesis (H_a) such that the real mean of the Coefficient is not equal to 0. A t-test is is performed and the calculated t-Statistic is compared to the critical values at the relevant Degrees of Freedom for Residual. The t-test is very important as it calculates if each of the Coefficients is statistically significant in the presence of the other regressors. This means that the t-test statistically verifies whether a regressor or independent variable should remain in the regression or it should be dropped.

The Coefficient is statistically significant if its calculated t-Statistic exceeds the Critical t-Statistic at the relevant degrees of freedom (df). The three main confidence levels used to test for significance are 90%, 95%, and 99%. If a Coefficient's t-Statistic exceeds the Critical level, it is considered statistically significant. Alternatively, the p-Value calculates each t-Statistic's probability of occurrence, which means that the smaller the p-Value, the more significant the Coefficient. The usual significant levels for the p-Value are 0.01, 0.05, and 0.10, corresponding to the 99%, 95%, and 90% confidence levels.

The Coefficients with their p-Values highlighted in blue indicate that they are statistically significant at the 90% confidence or 0.10 alpha level, while those highlighted in red indicate that they are not statistically significant at any other alpha levels.

FIGURE 8.8 Multivariate regression results.

including the correlation approach, forward method, backward method, and the forward and backward method (these methods are all available in Risk Simulator).

In the correlation method, the dependent variable (Y) is correlated to all the independent variables (X), and a regression is run starting with the X variable with the highest absolute correlation value; then subsequent X variables are added until the p-values indicate that the new X variable is no longer statistically significant. This approach is quick and simple but does not account for interactions among variables, where a new X variable, when added, will statistically overshadow other variables.

Analysis of Variance

	Sums of Squares	Mean of Squares	F-Statistic	p-Value	Hypothesis Test	
Regression	479388.49	95877.70	4.28	0.0029	Critical F-statistic (99% confidence with df of 5 and 44)	3.4651
Residual	985675.19	22401.71			Critical F-statistic (95% confidence with df of 5 and 44)	2.4270
Total	1465063.68				Critical F-statistic (90% confidence with df of 5 and 44)	1.9828

The Analysis of Variance (ANOVA) table provides an F-test of the regression model's overall statistical significance. Instead of looking at individual regressors as in the t-test, the F-test looks at all the estimated Coefficients' statistical properties. The F-Statistic is calculated as the ratio of the Regression's Mean of Squares to the Residual's Mean of Squares. The numerator measures how much of the regression is explained, while the denominator measures how much is unexplained. Hence, the larger the F-Statistic, the more significant the model. The corresponding p-Value is calculated to test the null hypothesis (H_0) where all the Coefficients are simultaneously equal to zero, versus the alternate hypothesis (H_a) in which they are all simultaneously different from zero, indicating a significant overall regression model. If the p-Value is smaller than the 0.01, 0.05, or 0.10 alpha significance, then the regression is significant. The same approach can be applied to the F-Statistic by comparing the calculated F-Statistic with the critical F values at various significance levels.

Forecasting

Period	Actual (Y)	Forecast (F)	Error (E)
1	521.0000	299.5124	221.4876
2	367.0000	487.1243	(120.1243)
3	443.0000	353.2789	89.7211
4	365.0000	276.3296	88.6704
5	614.0000	776.1336	(162.1336)
6	385.0000	298.9993	86.0007
7	286.0000	354.8718	(68.8718)
8	397.0000	312.6155	84.3845
9	764.0000	529.7550	234.2450
10	427.0000	347.7034	79.2966
11	153.0000	266.2526	(113.2526)
12	231.0000	264.6375	(33.6375)
13	524.0000	406.8009	117.1991
14	328.0000	272.2226	55.7774
15	240.0000	231.7882	8.2118
16	286.0000	257.8862	28.1138
17	285.0000	314.9521	(29.9521)
18	569.0000	335.3140	233.6860
19	96.0000	282.0356	(186.0356)
20	498.0000	370.2062	127.7938
21	481.0000	340.8742	140.1258
22	468.0000	427.5118	40.4882
23	177.0000	274.5298	(97.5298)
24	198.0000	294.7795	(96.7795)
25	458.0000	295.2180	162.7820
26	108.0000	269.6195	(161.6195)
27	246.0000	195.5955	50.4045
28	291.0000	364.5004	(73.5004)
29	68.0000	287.0426	(219.0426)
30	311.0000	431.7568	(120.7568)
31	606.0000	323.6399	282.3601
32	512.0000	531.4356	(19.4356)
33	426.0000	325.3641	100.6359
34	47.0000	192.3960	(145.3960)
35	265.0000	378.1250	(113.1250)
36	370.0000	288.6064	81.3936

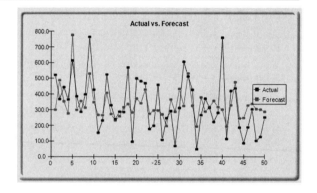

FIGURE 8.8 *(Continued)*

In the forward method, we first correlate Y with all X variables, run a regression for Y on the highest absolute value correlation of X, and obtain the fitting errors. Then, correlate these errors with the remaining X variables, choose the highest absolute value correlation among this remaining set, and run another regression. Repeat the process until the p-value for the latest X variable coefficient is no longer statistically significant; then stop the process.

In the backward method, run a regression with Y on all X variables. Reviewing each variable's p-value, systematically eliminate the variable with the largest p-value; then run a regression again, repeating each time until all p-values are statistically significant.

In the forward and backward method, apply the forward method to obtain three X variables; then apply the backward approach to see if one of them needs to be eliminated because it is statistically insignificant. Repeat the forward method and then the backward method until all remaining X variables have been considered.

STOCHASTIC FORECASTING

Theory

A stochastic process is nothing but a mathematically defined equation that can create a series of outcomes over time, outcomes that are not deterministic in nature; that is, an equation or process that does not follow any simple discernible rule such as price will increase X percent every year or revenues will increase by this factor of X plus Y percent. A stochastic process is by definition nondeterministic, and one can plug numbers into a stochastic process equation and obtain different results every time. For instance, the path of a stock price is stochastic in nature, and one cannot reliably predict the exact stock price path with any certainty. However, the price evolution over time is enveloped in a process that generates these prices. *The process is fixed and predetermined, but the outcomes are not.* Hence, by stochastic simulation, we create multiple pathways of prices, obtain a statistical sampling of these simulations, and make inferences on the potential pathways that the actual price may undertake given the nature and parameters of the stochastic process used to generate the time series. Four stochastic processes are included in Risk Simulator's Forecasting tool, including geometric and exponential Brownian motion or random walk, which is the most common and prevalently used process due to its simplicity and wide-ranging applications. The other three stochastic processes are the mean-reversion process, jump-diffusion process, and a mixed process.

The interesting thing about stochastic process simulation is that historical data are not necessarily required; that is, the model does not have to fit any sets of historical data. Simply compute the expected returns and the volatility of the historical data or estimate them using comparable external data or make assumptions about these values.

Procedure

Run the stochastic forecast by using these two steps:

1. Start the module by selecting *Risk Simulator | Forecasting | Stochastic Processes*.

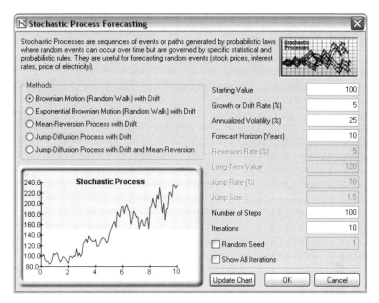

FIGURE 8.9 Stochastic process forecasting.

2. Select the desired process, enter the required inputs, click on update chart a few times to make sure the process is behaving the way you expect it to, and click *OK* (Figure 8.9).

Results Interpretation

Figure 8.10 shows the results of a sample stochastic process. The chart shows a sample set of the iterations while the report explains the basics of stochastic processes. In addition, the forecast values (mean and standard deviation) for each time period are provided. Using these values, you can decide which time period is relevant to your analysis, and set assumptions based on these mean and standard deviation values using the normal distribution. These assumptions can then be simulated in your own custom model.

Notes

Brownian Motion Random Walk Process The Brownian motion random walk process takes the form of

$$\frac{\delta S}{S} = \mu(\delta t) + \sigma \varepsilon \sqrt{\delta t}$$

Stochastic Process Forecasting

Statistical Summary

A stochastic process is a sequence of events or paths generated by probabilistic laws. That is, random events can occur over time but are governed by specific statistical and probabilistic rules. The main stochastic processes include Random Walk or Brownian Motion, Mean-Reversion, and Jump-Diffusion. These processes can be used to forecast a multitude of variables that seemingly follow random trends but yet are restricted by probabilistic laws.

The Random Walk Brownian Motion process can be used to forecast stock prices, prices of commodities, and other stochastic time-series data given a drift or growth rate and a volatility around the drift path. The Mean-Reversion process can be used to reduce the fluctuations of the Random Walk process by allowing the path to target a long-term value, making it useful for forecasting time-series variables that have a long-term rate such as interest rates and inflation rates (these are long-term target rates by regulatory authorities or the market). The Jump-Diffusion process is useful for forecasting time-series data when the variable can occasionally exhibit random jumps, such as oil prices or price of electricity (discrete exogenous event shocks can make prices jump up or down). Finally, these three stochastic processes can be mixed and matched as required.

The results on the right indicate the mean and standard deviation of all the iterations generated at each time step. If the Show All Iterations option is selected, each iteration pathway will be shown in a separate worksheet. The graph generated below shows a sample set of iteration pathways.

Time	Mean	Stdev
0.0000	100.00	0.00
0.1000	106.32	4.05
0.2000	105.92	4.70
0.3000	105.23	8.23
0.4000	109.84	11.18
0.5000	107.57	14.67
0.6000	108.63	19.79
0.7000	107.85	24.18
0.8000	109.61	24.46
0.9000	109.57	27.99
1.0000	110.74	30.81
1.1000	111.53	35.05
1.2000	111.07	34.10
1.3000	107.52	32.85
1.4000	108.26	37.38
1.5000	106.36	32.19
1.6000	112.42	32.16
1.7000	110.08	31.24
1.8000	109.64	31.87
1.9000	110.18	36.43
2.0000	112.23	37.63
2.1000	114.32	33.10
2.2000	111.14	38.42
2.3000	111.03	37.69
2.4000	112.04	37.23
2.5000	112.98	40.84
2.6000	115.74	43.69
2.7000	115.11	43.64
2.8000	114.87	43.70
2.9000	113.28	42.25
3.0000	115.72	43.43
3.1000	120.05	50.48
3.2000	116.69	42.61
3.3000	118.31	45.57
3.4000	116.35	40.82
3.5000	115.71	40.33
3.6000	118.69	41.45
3.7000	121.66	45.34
3.8000	121.40	45.03
3.9000	125.19	48.19
4.0000	129.65	55.44
4.1000	129.61	53.82
4.2000	125.86	49.68
4.3000	125.70	53.79
4.4000	126.72	49.70
4.5000	129.52	50.28
4.6000	132.28	49.70
4.7000	138.47	56.77
4.8000	139.69	66.32
4.9000	140.85	65.95
5.0000	143.61	68.65

Stochastic Process: Brownian Motion (Random Walk) with Drift

Start Value	100	Steps	50.00	Jump Rate	N/A
Drift Rate	5.00%	Iterations	10.00	Jump Size	N/A
Volatility	25.00%	Reversion Rate	N/A	Random Seed	1720050445
Horizon	5	Long-Term Value	N/A		

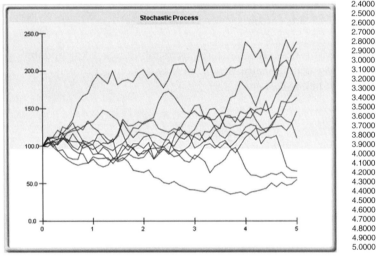

FIGURE 8.10 Stochastic forecast result.

for regular options simulation, or a more generic version takes the form of

$$\frac{\delta S}{S} = (\mu - \sigma^2/2)\delta t + \sigma \varepsilon \sqrt{\delta t}$$

for a geometric process. For an exponential version, we simply take the exponentials, and, as an example, we have

$$\frac{\delta S}{S} = \exp[\mu(\delta t) + \sigma \varepsilon \sqrt{\delta t}]$$

where S = the variable's previous value
   δS = the change in the variable's value from one step to the next
   μ = the annualized growth or drift rate
   σ = the annualized volatility

To estimate the parameters from a set of time-series data, the drift rate and volatility can be found by setting μ to be the average of the natural logarithm of the relative returns $\ln\left[\frac{S_t}{S_{t-1}}\right]$ while σ is the standard deviation of all $\ln\left[\frac{S_t}{S_{t-1}}\right]$ values.

Mean-Reversion Process   The following describes the mathematical structure of a mean-reverting process with drift:

$$\frac{\delta S}{S} = \eta(\overline{S}e^{\mu(\delta t)} - S)\delta t + \mu(\delta t) + \sigma\varepsilon\sqrt{\delta t}$$

In order to obtain the rate of reversion and long-term rate, using the historical data points, run a regression such that $Y_t - Y_{t-1} = \beta_0 + \beta_1 Y_{t-1} + \varepsilon$ and we find $\eta = -\ln[1 + \beta_1]$ and $\overline{S} = -\beta_0/\beta_1$,

where η = the rate of reversion to the mean
   $\overline{S}$ = the long-term value the process reverts to
   Y = the historical data series
   β_0 = the intercept coefficient in a regression analysis
   β_1 = the slope coefficient in a regression analysis

Jump Diffusion Process   A jump diffusion process is similar to a random walk process, but there is a probability of a jump at any point in time. The occurrences of such jumps are completely random, but the probability and magnitude are governed by the process itself.

$$\frac{\delta S}{S} = \eta(\overline{S}e^{\mu(\delta t)} - S)\delta t + \mu(\delta t) + \sigma\varepsilon\sqrt{\delta t} + \theta F(\lambda)(\delta t)$$

for a jump diffusion process,

where θ = the jump size of S
   $F(\lambda)$ = the inverse of the Poisson cumulative probability distribution
   λ = the jump rate of S

The jump size can be found by computing the ratio of the postjump to the prejump levels, and the jump rate can be imputed from past historical data.

The other parameters are found the same way as shown previously. You can also run Risk Simulator's Statistical Analysis tool to calibrate the inputs into these stochastic processes by automatically running econometric models on your raw data to determine their statistical properties.

NONLINEAR EXTRAPOLATION

Theory

Extrapolation involves making statistical forecasts by using historical trends that are projected for a specified period of time into the future. It is only used for time-series forecasts. For cross-sectional or mixed panel data (time series with cross-sectional data), multivariate regression is more appropriate. This methodology is useful when major changes are not expected; that is, causal factors are expected to remain constant or when the causal factors of a situation are not clearly understood. It also helps discourage the introduction of personal biases into the process. Extrapolation is fairly reliable, relatively simple, and inexpensive. However, extrapolation, which assumes that recent and historical trends will continue, produces large forecast errors if discontinuities occur within the projected time period; that is, pure extrapolation of time series assumes that all we need to know is contained in the historical values of the series being forecasted. If we assume that past behavior is a good predictor of future behavior, extrapolation is appealing. This makes it a useful approach when all that is needed are many short-term forecasts.

This methodology estimates the $f(x)$ function for any arbitrary x value, by interpolating a smooth nonlinear curve through all the x values, and using this smooth curve, extrapolates future x values beyond the historical data set. The methodology employs either the polynomial functional form or the rational functional form (a ratio of two polynomials). Typically, a polynomial functional form is sufficient for well-behaved data; however, rational functional forms are sometimes more accurate (especially with polar functions, i.e., functions with denominators approaching zero).

Procedure

Use the following steps to run a nonlinear extrapolation:

1. Start Excel and enter your data or open an existing worksheet with historical data to forecast (the illustration shown next uses the file *Nonlinear Extrapolation* from the examples folder).
2. Select the time-series data and select *Risk Simulator | Forecasting | Nonlinear Extrapolation*.

Year	Month	Period	Sales
2004	1	1	$1.00
2004	2	2	$6.73
2004	3	3	$20.52
2004	4	4	$45.25
2004	5	5	$83.59
2004	6	6	$138.01
2004	7	7	$210.87
2004	8	8	$304.44
2004	9	9	$420.89
2004	10	10	$562.34
2004	11	11	$730.85
2004	12	12	$928.43

Historical Sales Revenues
Polynomial Growth Rates

Historical Net Income
Sinusoidal Growth Rates

Year	Month	Period	Income
2004	1	1	$84.15
2004	2	2	$90.93
2004	3	3	$14.11
2004	4	4	($75.68)
2004	5	5	($95.89)
2004	6	6	($27.94)
2004	7	7	$65.70
2004	8	8	$98.94
2004	9	9	$41.21
2004	10	10	($54.40)
2004	11	11	($100.00)
2004	12	12	($53.66)
2005	1	13	$42.02
2005	2	14	$99.06
2005	3	15	$65.03
2005	4	16	($28.79)
2005	5	17	($96.14)
2005	6	18	($75.10)

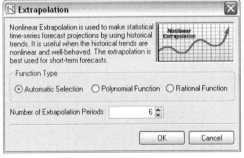

FIGURE 8.11 Running a nonlinear extrapolation.

3. Select the extrapolation type (automatic selection, polynomial function, or rational function are available, but in this example, use automatic selection) and enter the number of forecast period desired (Figure 8.11), and click *OK*.

Results Interpretation

The results report in Figure 8.12 shows the extrapolated forecast values, the error measurements, and the graphical representation of the extrapolation results. The error measurements should be used to check the validity of the forecast and are especially important when used to compare the forecast quality and accuracy of extrapolation versus time-series analysis.

Notes

When the historical data is smooth and follows some nonlinear patterns and curves, extrapolation is better than time-series analysis. However, when the

Nonlinear Extrapolation

Statistical Summary

Extrapolation involves making statistical projections by using historical trends that are projected for a specified period of time into the future. It is only used for time-series forecasts. For cross-sectional or mixed panel data (time-series with cross-sectional data), multivariate regression is more appropriate. This methodology is useful when major changes are not expected, that is, causal factors are expected to remain constant or when the causal factors of a situation are not clearly understood. It also helps discourage the introduction of personal biases into the process. Extrapolation is fairly reliable, relatively simple, and inexpensive. However, extrapolation, which assumes that recent and historical trends will continue, produces large forecast errors if discontinuities occur within the projected time period. That is, pure extrapolation of time series assumes that all we need to know is contained in the historical values of the series that is being forecasted. If we assume that past behavior is a good predictor of future behavior, extrapolation is appealing. This makes it a useful approach when all that is needed are many short-term forecasts.

This methodology estimates the $f(x)$ function for any arbitrary x value, by interpolating a smooth nonlinear curve through all the x values, and using this smooth curve, extrapolates future x values beyond the historical data set. The methodology employs either the polynomial functional form or the rational functional form (a ratio of two polynomials). Typically, a polynomial functional form is sufficient for well-behaved data, however, rational functional forms are sometimes more accurate (especially with polar functions, i.e., functions with denominators approaching zero).

Period	Actual	Forecast Fit
1	1.00	
2	6.73	1.00
3	20.52	−1.42
4	45.25	99.82
5	83.59	55.92
6	138.01	136.71
7	210.87	211.96
8	304.44	304.43
9	420.89	420.89
10	562.34	562.34
11	730.85	730.85
12	928.43	928.43
Forecast 13		1157.03
Forecast 14		1418.57
Forecast 15		1714.95
Forecast 16		2048.00
Forecast 17		2419.55
Forecast 18		2831.39

Error Measurements

RMSE	19.6799
MSE	387.2974
MAD	10.2095
MAPE	31.56%
Theil's U	1.1210

Function Type: Rational

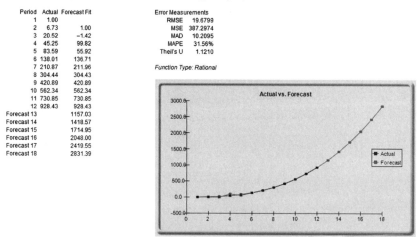

FIGURE 8.12   Nonlinear extrapolation results.

data patterns follow seasonal cycles and a trend, time-series analysis will provide better results. It is always advisable to run both time-series analysis and extrapolation and compare the results to see which has a lower error measure and a better fit.

BOX–JENKINS ARIMA ADVANCED TIME-SERIES

Theory

One very powerful advanced times-series forecasting tool is the ARIMA or autoregressive integrated moving average approach, which assembles three separate tools into a comprehensive model. The first tool segment is the autoregressive or "AR" term, which corresponds to the number of lagged value of the residual in the unconditional forecast model. In essence, the model captures the historical variation of actual data to a forecasting model and uses this variation or residual to create a better predicting model. The second tool segment is the integration order or the "I" term. This integration term corresponds to the number of differencing the time-series to be forecasted goes through to make the time-series data stationary. This element accounts for any nonlinear growth rates existing in the data. The third tool segment is the moving average or "MA" term, which is essentially the moving average of lagged forecast errors. By incorporating these lagged forecast errors, the model in essence learns from its forecast errors or mistakes and corrects for them through a moving average calculation. The ARIMA model follows the Box–Jenkins methodology with each term representing steps taken in the model construction until only random noise remains. Also, ARIMA modeling uses correlation techniques in generating forecasts. ARIMA can be used to model patterns that may not be visible in plotted data. In addition, ARIMA models can be mixed with exogenous variables, but make sure that the exogenous variables have enough data points to cover the additional number of periods to forecast.

There are many reasons why an ARIMA model is superior to common time-series analysis and multivariate regressions. The common finding in time-series analysis and multivariate regression is that the error residuals are correlated with their own lagged values. This serial correlation violates the standard assumption of regression theory that disturbances are not correlated with other disturbances. The primary problems associated with serial correlation are:

- Regression analysis and basic time-series analysis are no longer efficient among the different linear estimators. However, as the error residuals can help to predict current error residuals, we can take advantage of this information to form a better prediction of the dependent variable using ARIMA.
- Standard errors computed using the regression and time-series formula are not correct and are generally understated. If there are lagged dependent variables set as the regressors, regression estimates are biased and inconsistent but can be fixed using ARIMA.

Autoregressive integrated moving average or ARIMA(p,d,q) models are the extension of the AR model that uses three components for modeling the serial correlation in the time-series data. The first component is the autoregressive (AR) term. The AR(p) model uses the p lags of the time series in the equation. An AR(p) model has the form: $y_t = a_1 y_{t-1} + \ldots + a_p y_{t-p} + e_t$. The second component is the integration (d) order term. Each integration order corresponds to differencing the time series. I(1) means differencing the data once. I(d) means differencing the data d times. The third component is the moving average (MA) term. The MA(q) model uses the q lags of the forecast errors to improve the forecast. An MA(q) model has the form: $y_t = e_t + b_1 e_{t-1} + \ldots + b_q e_{t-q}$. Finally, an ARMA(p,q) model has the combined form: $y_t = a_1 y_{t-1} + \ldots + a_p y_{t-p} + e_t + b_1 e_{t-1} + \ldots + b_q e_{t-q}$.

Procedure

To run a Box–Jenkins ARIMA model, follow these steps:

- Start Excel and enter your data or open an existing worksheet with historical data to forecast (the illustration shown next uses the example file *Time-Series Forecasting*).
- Select *Risk Simulator | Forecasting | ARIMA* and select the time-series data.
- Enter the relevant *p*, *d*, and *q* parameters (positive integers only), enter the number of forecast periods desired, and click *OK*.

Results Interpretation

In interpreting the results of an ARIMA model, most of the specifications are identical to the multivariate regression analysis (see Chapter 9, Using the Past to Predict the Future, for more technical details about interpreting the multivariate regression analysis and ARIMA models). However, several additional sets of results are specific to the ARIMA analysis as seen in Figure 8.13. The first is the addition of Akaike Information Criterion (AIC) and Schwarz Criterion (SC), which are often used in ARIMA model selection and identification. That is, AIC and SC are used to determine if a particular model with a specific set of *p*, *d*, and *q* parameters is a good statistical fit. SC imposes a greater penalty for additional coefficients than the AIC, but generally, the model with the lowest AIC and SC values should be chosen. Finally, an additional set of results called the autocorrelation (AC) and partial autocorrelation (PAC) statistics are provided in the ARIMA report.

For instance, if autocorrelation AC(1) is nonzero, it means that the series is first-order serially correlated. If AC dies off more or less geometrically with increasing lags, it implies that the series follows a low-order autoregressive process. If AC drops to zero after a small number of lags, it implies that

ARIMA (Autoregressive Integrated Moving Average)

Regression Statistics

R-Squared (Coefficient of Determination)	0.9999	Akaike Information Criterion (AIC)	4.6213
Adjusted R-Squared	0.9999	Schwarz Criterion (SC)	4.6632
Multiple R (Multiple Correlation Coefficient)	1.0000	Log Likelihood	−1005.13
Standard Error of the Estimates (SEy)	297.52	Durbin-Watson (DW) Statistic	1.8588
Number of Observations	435	Number of Iterations	5

Autoregressive Integrated Moving Average or ARIMA(p,d,q) models are the extension of the AR model that use three components for modeling the serial correlation in the time-series data. The first component is the autoregressive (AR) term. The AR(p) model uses the p lags of the time series in the equation. An AR(p) model has the form: $y(t)=a(1)*y(t-1)+...+a(p)*y(t-p)+e(t)$. The second component is the integration (d) order term. Each integration order corresponds to differencing the time-series. I(1) means differencing the data once. I(d) means differencing the data d times. The third component is the moving average (MA) term. The MA(q) model uses the q lags of the forecast errors to improve the forecast. An MA(q) model has the form: $y(t)=e(t)+b(1)*e(t-1)+...+b(q)*e(t-q)$. Finally, an ARMA(p,q) model has the combined form: $y(t)=a(1)*y(t-1)+...+a(p)*y(t-p)+e(t)+b(1)*e(t-1)+...+b(q)*e(t-q)$.

The R-Squared, or Coefficient of Determination, indicates the percent variation in the dependent variable that can be explained and accounted for by the independent variables in this regression analysis. However, in a multiple regression, the Adjusted R-Squared takes into account the existence of additional independent variables or regressors and adjusts this R-Squared value to a more accurate view the regression's explanatory power. However, under some ARIMA modeling circumstances (e.g., with nonconvergence models), the R-Squared tends to be unreliable.

The Multiple Correlation Coefficient (Multiple R) measures the correlation between the actual dependent variable (Y) and the estimated or fitted variable (Y) based on the regression equation. This correlation is also the square root of the Coefficient of Determination (R-Squared).

The Standard Error of the Estimates (SEy) describes the dispersion of data points above and below the regression line or plane. This value is used as part of the calculation to obtain the confidence interval of the estimates later.

The AIC and SC are often used in model selection. SC imposes a greater penalty for additional coefficients. Generally, the user should select a model with the lowest value of the AIC and SC.

The Durbin-Watson statistic measures the serial correlation in the residuals. Generally, DW less than 2 implies positive serial correlation.

Regression Results

	Intercept	AR(1)	MA(1)
Coefficients	−0.0626	1.0055	0.4936
Standard Error	0.3108	0.0006	0.0420
t-Statistic	−0.2013	1691.1373	11.7633
p-Value	0.8406	0.0000	0.0000
Lower 5%	0.4498	1.0065	0.5628
Upper 95%	−0.5749	1.0046	0.4244

Degrees of Freedom		Hypothesis Test	
Degrees of Freedom for Regression	2	Critical t-Statistic (99% confidence with df of 432)	2.5873
Degrees of Freedom for Residual	432	Critical t-Statistic (95% confidence with df of 432)	1.9655
Total Degrees of Freedom	434	Critical t-Statistic (90% confidence with df of 432)	1.6484

The Coefficients provide the estimated regression intercept and slopes. For instance, the Coefficients are estimates of the true; population b values in the following regression equation $Y = b_0 + b1 \times 1 + b2 \times 2 + ... + bnXn$. The Standard Error measures how accurate the predicted Coefficients are, and the t-Statistics are the ratios of each predicted Coefficient to its Standard Error.

The t-Statistic is used in hypothesis testing, where we set the null hypothesis (H₀) such that the real mean of the Coefficient = 0, and the alternate hypothesis (Hₐ) such that the real mean of the Coefficient is not equal to 0. A t-test is is performed and the calculated t-Statistic is compared to the critical values at the relevant Degrees of Freedom for Residual. The t-test is very important as it calculates if each of the Coefficients is statistically significant in the presence of the other regressors. This means that the t-test statistically verifies whether a regressor or independent variable should remain in the regression or it should be dropped.

The Coefficient is statistically significant if its calculated t-Statistic exceeds the Critical t-Statistic at the relevant degrees of freedom (df). The three main confidence levels used to test for significance are 90%, 95% and 99%. If a Coefficient's t-Statistic exceeds the Critical level, it is considered statistically significant. Alternatively, the p-Value calculates each t-Statistic's probability of occurrence, which means that the smaller the p-Value, the more significant the Coefficient. The usual significant levels for the p-Value are 0.01, 0.05, and 0.10, corresponding to the 99%, 95%, and 90% confidence levels.

The Coefficients with their p-Values highlighted in blue indicate that they are statistically significant at the 90% confidence or 0.10 alpha level, while those highlighted in red indicate that they are not statistically significant at any other alpha levels.

FIGURE 8.13 Box–Jenkins ARIMA forecast report. *(Continues)*

the series follows a low-order moving-average process. In contrast, PAC measures the correlation of values that are k periods apart after removing the correlation from the intervening lags. If the pattern of autocorrelation can be captured by an autoregression of order less than k, then the partial autocorrelation at lag k will be close to zero. The Ljung–Box Q-statistics and their p-values at lag k are also provided, where the null hypothesis

Analysis of Variance

	Sums of Squares	Mean of Squares	F-Statistic	p-Value	Hypothesis Test	
Regression	38415447.53	19207723.76	3171851.1	0.0000	Critical F-statistic (99% confidence with df of 2 and 432)	4.6546
Residual	2616.05	6.06			Critical F-statistic (95% confidence with df of 2 and 432)	3.0166
Total	38418063.58				Critical F-statistic (90% confidence with df of 2 and 432)	2.3149

The Analysis of Variance (ANOVA) table provides an F-test of the regression model's overall statistical significance. Instead of looking at individual regressors as in the t-test, the F-test looks at all the estimated Coefficients' statistical properties. The F-Statistic is calculated as the ratio of the Regression's Mean of Squares to the Residual's Mean of Squares. The numerator measures how much of the regression is explained, while the denominator measures how much is unexplained. Hence, the larger the F-Statistic, the more significant the model. The corresponding p-Value is calculated to test the null hypothesis (Ho) where all the Coefficients are simultaneously equal to zero, versus the alternate hypothesis (Ha) in which they are all simultaneously different from zero, indicating a significant overall regression model. If the p-Value is smaller than the 0.01, 0.05, or 0.10 alpha significance, then the regression is significant. The same approach can be applied to the F-Statistic by comparing the calculated F-Statistic with the critical F values at various significance levels.

Autocorrelation

Time Lag	AC	PAC	Lower Bound	Upper Bound	Q-Stat	Prob
1	0.9921	0.9921	(0.0958)	0.0958	431.1216	-
2	0.9841	(0.0105)	(0.0958)	0.0958	856.3037	-
3	0.9760	(0.0109)	(0.0958)	0.0958	1,275.4818	-
4	0.9678	(0.0142)	(0.0958)	0.0958	1,688.5499	-
5	0.9594	(0.0096)	(0.0958)	0.0958	2,095.4625	-
6	0.9509	(0.0113)	(0.0958)	0.0958	2,496.1572	-
7	0.9423	(0.0124)	(0.0958)	0.0958	2,890.5594	-
8	0.9336	(0.0147)	(0.0958)	0.0958	3,278.5669	-
9	0.9247	(0.0121)	(0.0958)	0.0958	3,660.1152	-
10	0.9156	(0.0139)	(0.0958)	0.0958	4,035.1192	-
11	0.9066	(0.0049)	(0.0958)	0.0958	4,403.6117	-
12	0.8975	(0.0068)	(0.0958)	0.0958	4,765.6032	-
13	0.8883	(0.0097)	(0.0958)	0.0958	5,121.0697	-
14	0.8791	(0.0087)	(0.0958)	0.0958	5,470.0032	-
15	0.8698	(0.0064)	(0.0958)	0.0958	5,812.4256	-
16	0.8605	(0.0056)	(0.0958)	0.0958	6,148.3694	-
17	0.8512	(0.0062)	(0.0958)	0.0958	6,477.8620	-
18	0.8419	(0.0038)	(0.0958)	0.0958	6,800.9622	-
19	0.8326	(0.0003)	(0.0958)	0.0958	7,117.7709	-
20	0.8235	0.0002	(0.0958)	0.0958	7,428.3952	-

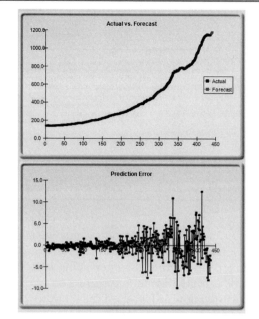

If autocorrelation AC(1) is nonzero, it means that the series is first order serially correlated. If AC(k) dies off more or less geometrically with increasing lag, it implies that the series follows a low-order autoregressive process. If AC(k) drops to zero after a small number of lags, it implies that the series follows a low-order moving-average process. Partial correlation PAC(k) measures the correlation of values that are k periods apart after removing the correlation from the intervening lags. If the pattern of autocorrelation can be captured by an autoregression of order less than k, then the partial autocorrelation at lag k will be close to zero. Ljung-Box Q-statistics and their p-values at lag k has the null hypothesis that there is no autocorrelation up to order k. The dotted lines in the plots of the autocorrelations are the approximate two standard error bounds. If the autocorrelation is within these bounds, it is not significantly different from zero at (approximately) the 5% significance level.

Forecasting

Period	Actual (Y)	Forecast (F)	Error (E)
2	139.4000	139.6056	(0.2056)
3	139.7000	140.0069	(0.3069)
4	139.7000	140.2586	(0.5586)
5	140.7000	140.1343	0.5657
6	141.2000	141.6948	(0.4948)
7	141.7000	141.6741	0.0259
8	141.9000	142.4339	(0.5339)
9	141.0000	142.3587	(1.3587)
10	140.5000	141.0466	(0.5466)
11	140.4000	140.9447	(0.5447)
12	140.0000	140.8451	(0.8451)
13	140.0000	140.2946	(0.2946)
14	139.9000	140.5663	(0.6663)
15	139.8000	140.2823	(0.4823)
16	139.6000	140.2726	(0.6726)
17	139.6000	139.9775	(0.3775)
18	139.6000	140.1232	(0.5231)
19	140.2000	140.0513	0.1487
20	141.3000	140.9862	0.3138
21	141.2000	142.1738	(0.9738)
22	140.9000	141.4377	(0.5377)
23	140.9000	141.3513	(0.4513)
24	140.7000	141.3939	(0.6939)
25	141.1000	141.0731	0.0270
26	141.6000	141.8311	(0.2311)
27	141.9000	142.2065	(0.3065)
28	142.1000	142.4709	(0.3709)
29	142.7000	142.6402	0.0598
30	142.9000	143.4561	(0.5561)
31	142.9000	143.3532	(0.4532)
32	143.5000	143.4040	0.0960
33	143.8000	144.2784	(0.4784)
34	144.1000	144.2966	(0.1966)
35	144.8000	144.7374	0.0626
36	145.2000	145.5692	(0.3692)
37	145.2000	145.7582	(0.5582)
38	145.7000	145.6649	0.0351
39	146.0000	146.4605	(0.4605)
40	146.4000	146.5176	(0.1176)
41	146.8000	147.0891	(0.2891)

FIGURE 8.13 *(Continued)*

being tested is such that there is no autocorrelation up to order k. The dotted lines in the plots of the autocorrelations are the approximate two standard error bounds. If the autocorrelation is within these bounds, it is not significantly different from zero at approximately the 5 percent significance level. Finding the right ARIMA model takes practice and experience. These AC, PAC, SC, and AIC are highly useful diagnostic tools to help identify the correct model specification. Finally, the ARIMA parameter results are obtained using sophisticated optimization and iterative algorithms, which means that although the functional forms look like those of a multivariate regression, they are not the same. ARIMA is a much more computationally intensive and advanced econometric approach.

AUTO ARIMA (BOX–JENKINS ARIMA ADVANCED TIME-SERIES)

Theory

This tool provides analyses identical to the ARIMA module except that the Auto-ARIMA module automates some of the traditional ARIMA modeling by automatically testing multiple permutations of model specifications and returns the best-fitting model. Running the Auto-ARIMA module is similar to running regular ARIMA forecasts. The differences being that the p, d, q inputs are no longer required and that different combinations of these inputs are automatically run and compared.

Procedure

1. Start Excel and enter your data or open an existing worksheet with historical data to forecast (the illustration shown in Figure 8.14 uses the example file *Advanced Forecasting Models* in the *Examples* menu of Risk Simulator).
2. In the *Auto ARIMA* worksheet, select *Risk Simulator | Forecasting | AUTO-ARIMA*. You can also access the method through the *Forecasting* icons ribbon or right-clicking anywhere in the model and selecting the forecasting shortcut menu.
3. Click on the link icon and link to the existing time-series data, enter the number of forecast periods desired, and click *OK*.

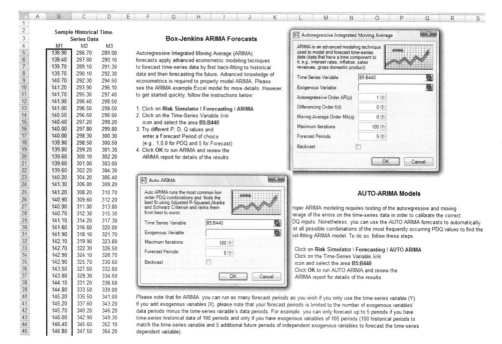

FIGURE 8.14   Auto-ARIMA module.

ARIMA and AUTO-ARIMA Note

For ARIMA and Auto ARIMA, you can model and forecast future periods either by using only the dependent variable (Y), that is, the *Time Series Variable* by itself, or you can insert additional exogenous variables $(X_1, X_2, \ldots, X_n)$ just as in a regression analysis where you have multiple independent variables. You can run as many forecast periods as you wish if you only use the time-series variable (Y). However, if you add exogenous variables (X), be sure to note that your forecast periods are limited to the number of exogenous variables' data periods minus the time-series variable's data periods. For example, you can only forecast up to 5 periods if you have time-series historical data of 100 periods and only if you have exogenous variables of 105 periods (100 historical periods to match the time-series variable and 5 additional future periods of independent exogenous variables to forecast the time-series dependent variable).

BASIC ECONOMETRICS

Theory

Econometrics refers to a branch of business analytics, modeling, and fore-casting techniques for modeling the behavior or forecasting certain business, financial, economic, physical science, and other variables. Running the Basic Econometrics models is similar to regular regression analysis except that the dependent and independent variables are allowed to be modified before a regression is run. The report generated is the same as shown in the Multiple Regression section previously and the interpretations are identical to those described previously.

Procedure

1. Start Excel and enter your data or open an existing worksheet with historical data to forecast (the illustration shown in Figure 8.15 uses the file example file *Advanced Forecasting Models* in the *Examples* menu of Risk Simulator).
2. Select the data in the *Basic Econometrics* worksheet and select *Risk Simulator | Forecasting | Basic Econometrics*.
3. Enter the desired dependent and independent variables (see Figure 8.15 for examples) and click *OK* to run the model and report, or click on *Show Results* to view the results before generating the report in case you need to make any changes to the model.

Notes

- See Chapter 9 for details on interpreting the regression outputs and, by extension, the outputs from a basic econometrics analysis.
- To run an econometric model, simply select the data (B5:G55) including headers and click on *Risk Simulator | Forecasting | Basic Econometrics*. You can then type in the variables and their modifications for the dependent and independent variables (Figure 8.15). Note that only one variable is allowed as the Dependent Variable (Y), whereas multiple variables are allowed in the Independent Variables (X) section, separated by a semicolon (;) and that basic mathematical functions can be used (e.g., LN, LOG, LAG, +, −, /, *, TIME, RESIDUAL, DIFF). Click on *Show Results* to preview the computed model and click *OK* to generate the econometric model report.

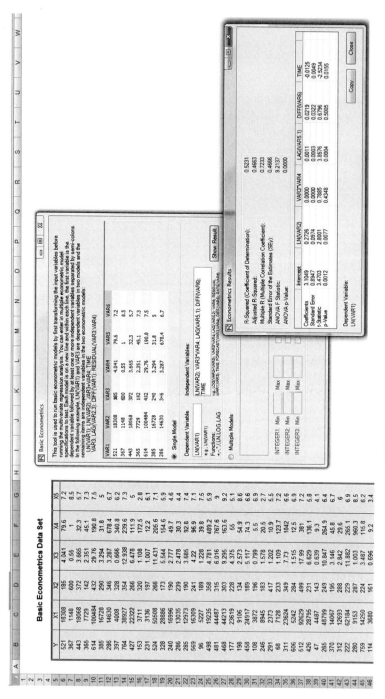

FIGURE 8.15 Basic econometrics module.

- You can also automatically generate Multiple Models by entering a sample model and using the predefined *INTEGER(N)* variable as well as *Shifting Data* up or down specific rows repeatedly. For instance, if you use the variable *LAG(VAR1, INTEGER1)* and you set *INTEGER1* to be between *MIN* = 1 and *MAX* = 3, then the following three models will be run: first *LAG(VAR1,1)*, then *LAG(VAR1,2)*, and, finally, *LAG(VAR1,3)*. Also, sometimes you might want to test if the time-series data has structural shifts or if the behavior of the model is consistent over time by shifting the data and then running the same model. For example, if you have 100 months of data listed chronologically, you can shift down 3 months at a time for 10 times (i.e., the model will be run on months 1–100, 4–100, 7–100, and so forth). Using this *Multiple Models* section in Basic Econometrics, you can run hundreds of models by simply entering a single model equation if you use these predefined integer variables and shifting methods.

J-CURVE AND S-CURVE FORECASTS

Theory

The J-curve, or exponential growth curve, is one where the growth of the next period depends on the current period's level and the increase is exponential. This phenomenon means that over time, the values will increase significantly, from one period to another. This model is typically used in forecasting biological growth and chemical reactions over time.

Procedure

1. Start Excel and select *Risk Simulator | Forecasting | JS Curves*.
2. Select the J- or S-curve type, enter the required input assumptions (see Figures 8.16 and 8.17 for examples), and click *OK* to run the model and report.

The S-curve, or logistic growth curve, starts off like a J-curve, with exponential growth rates. Over time, the environment becomes saturated (e.g., market saturation, competition, overcrowding), the growth slows, and the forecast value eventually ends up at a saturation or maximum level. The S-curve model is typically used in forecasting market share or sales growth of a new product from market introduction until maturity and decline, population dynamics, growth of bacterial cultures, and other naturally occurring variables. Figure 8.17 illustrates a sample S-curve.

J-Curve Exponential Growth Curves

In mathematics, a quantity that grows exponentially is one whose growth rate is always proportional to its current size. Such growth is said to follow an exponential law. This implies that for any exponentially growing quantity, the larger the quantity gets, the faster it grows. But it also implies that the relationship between the size of the dependent variable and its rate of growth is governed by a strict law: direct proportion. The general principle behind exponential growth is that the larger a number gets, the faster it grows. Any exponentially growing number will eventually grow larger than any other number which grows at only a constant rate for the same amount of time. This forecast method is also called a J curve due to its shape resembling the letter J. There is no maximum level of this growth curve. Other growth curves include S-curves and Markov Chains.

To generate a J curve forecast, follow the instructions below:

1. Click on **Risk Simulator I Forecasting I JS Curves**
2. Select **Exponential J Curve** and enter in the desired inputs
   (e.g., Starting Value of **100**, Growth Rate of 5 percent, End Period of 100)
3. Click **OK** to run the forecast and spend some time reviewing the forecast report

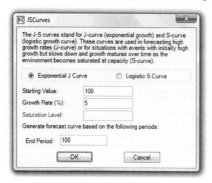

FIGURE 8.16 J-curve forecast.

Logistic S Curve

A logistic function or logistic curve models the S-curve of growth of some variable X. The initial stage of growth is approximately exponential; then, as competition arises, the growth slows, and at maturity, growth stops. These functions find applications in a range of fields, from biology to economics. For example, in the development of an embryo, a fertilized ovum splits, and the cell count grows: 1, 2, 4, 8, 16, 32, 64, etc. This is exponential growth. But the fetus can grow only as large as the uterus can hold; thus other factors start slowing down the increase in the cell count, and the rate of growth slows (but the baby is still growing, of course). After a suitable time, the child is born and keeps growing. Ultimately, the cell count is stable; the person's height is constant; the growth has stopped, at maturity. The same principles can be applied to population growth of animals or humans, and the market penetration and revenues of a product, with an initial growth spurt in market penetration, but over time, the growth slows due to competition and eventually the market declines and matures.

1. Click on **Risk Simulator I Forecasting I JS Curves**
2. Enter in the required inputs (see below for an example)
3. Click **OK** and review the forecast report

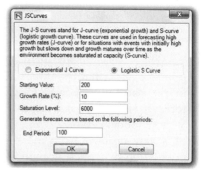

FIGURE 8.17 S-curve forecast.

GARCH VOLATILITY FORECASTS

Theory

The generalized autoregressive conditional heteroskedasticity (GARCH) model is used to compute historical and forecast future volatility levels of a marketable security (e.g., stock prices, commodity prices, oil prices, and so forth). The data set has to be a time series of raw price levels. GARCH will first convert the prices into relative returns and then run an internal optimization to fit the historical data to a mean-reverting volatility term structure, while assuming that the volatility is heteroskedastic in nature (changes over time according to some econometric characteristics). The theoretical specifics of a GARCH model are outside the purview of this book.

Procedure

1. Start Excel, open the example file *Advanced Forecasting Model*, go to the *GARCH* worksheet, and select *Risk Simulator | Forecasting | GARCH*.
2. Click on the link icon, select the *Data Location* and enter the required input assumptions (see Figure 8.18), and click *OK* to run the model and report.

Notes

The typical volatility forecast situation requires $P = 1$, $Q = 1$; Periodicity = number of periods per year (12 for monthly data, 52 for weekly data, 252 or 365 for daily data); Base = minimum of 1 and up to the periodicity value; and Forecast Periods = number of annualized volatility forecasts you wish to obtain. There are several GARCH models available in Risk Simulator, including EGARCH, EGARCH-T, GARCH-M, GJR-GARCH, GJR-GARCH-T, IGARCH, and T-GARCH.

GARCH models are used mainly in analyzing financial time-series data to ascertain their conditional variances and volatilities. These volatilities are then used to value the options as usual, but the amount of historical data necessary for a good volatility estimate remains significant. Usually, several dozen—and even up to hundreds—of data points are required to obtain good GARCH estimates. GARCH is a term that incorporates a family of models that can take on a variety of forms, known as GARCH(p,q), where p and q are positive integers that define the resulting GARCH model and its forecasts. In most cases for financial instruments, a GARCH(1,1) is sufficient

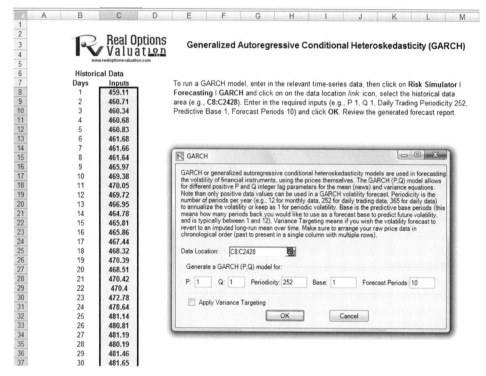

FIGURE 8.18 GARCH volatility forecast.

and is most generally used. For instance, a GARCH(1,1) model takes the form of:

$$y_t = x_t \gamma + \varepsilon_t$$

$$\sigma_t^2 = \omega + \alpha \varepsilon_{t-1}^2 + \beta \sigma_{t-1}^2$$

where the first equation's dependent variable (y_t) is a function of exogenous variables (x_t) with an error term (ε_t). The second equation estimates the variance (squared volatility σ_t^2) at time t, which depends on a historical mean (ω), news about volatility from the previous period, measured as a lag of the squared residual from the mean equation (ε_{t-1}^2), and volatility from the previous period (σ_{t-1}^2).

The exact modeling specification of a GARCH model is beyond the scope of this book. Suffice it to say that detailed knowledge of econometric modeling (model specification tests, structural breaks, and error estimation) is required to run a GARCH model, making it less accessible to the general analyst. Another problem with GARCH models is that the model usually does not provide a good statistical fit. That is, it is impossible to predict the stock market and, of course, equally if not harder to predict a stock's volatility over time. Note that the GARCH function has several inputs as follow:

- *Time-Series Data.* The time series of data in chronological order (e.g., stock prices). Typically, dozens of data points are required for a decent volatility forecast.
- *Periodicity.* A positive integer indicating the number of periods per year (e.g., 12 for monthly data, 252 for daily trading data, and so forth), assuming you wish to annualize the volatility. For getting periodic volatility, enter 1.
- *Predictive Base.* The number of periods back (of the time-series data) to use as a base to forecast volatility. The higher this number, the longer the historical base is used to forecast future volatility.
- *Forecast Period.* A positive integer indicating how many future periods beyond the historical stock prices you wish to forecast.
- *Variance Targeting.* This variable is set as False by default (even if you do not enter anything here) but can be set as True. False means the omega variable is automatically optimized and computed. The suggestion is to leave this variable empty. If you wish to create mean-reverting volatility with variance targeting, set this variable as True.
- *P.* The number of previous lags on the mean equation.
- *Q.* The number of previous lags on the variance equation.

Table 8.1 lists some of the GARCH specifications used in Risk Simulator with two underlying distributional assumptions: one for normal distribution and the other for the t distribution.

For the GARCH-M models, the conditional variance equations are the same in the six variations but the mean questions are different and assumption on z_t can be either normal distribution or t distribution. The estimated parameters for GARCH-M with normal distribution are those five parameters in the mean and conditional variance equations. The estimated parameters for GARCH-M with the t distribution are those five parameters in the mean and conditional variance equations plus another parameter, the degrees of freedom for the t distribution. In contrast, for the GJR models, the mean equations are the same in the six variations and the differences are that the conditional variance equations and the assumption on z_t can be either a normal distribution or t distribution. The estimated parameters for EGARCH and GJR-GARCH with normal distribution are those four parameters in the conditional variance equation. The estimated parameters for GARCH, EARCH, and GJR-GARCH with t distribution are those parameters in the conditional variance equation plus the degrees of freedom for the t distribution. More technical details of GARCH methodologies fall outside of the scope of this book.

MARKOV CHAINS

Theory

A Markov chain exists when the probability of a future state depends on a previous state and when linked together forms a chain that reverts to a long-run steady state level. This Markov approach is typically used to forecast the market share of two competitors. The required inputs are the starting probability of a customer in the first store (the first state) returning

TABLE 8.1 GARCH Specifications Used in Risk Simulator

	$z_t \sim$ Normal Distribution	$z_t \sim$ T-Distribution
GARCH-M Variance in Mean Equation	$y_t = c + \lambda \sigma_t^2 + \varepsilon_t$ $\varepsilon_t = \sigma_t z_t$ $\sigma_t^2 = \omega + \alpha \varepsilon_{t-1}^2 + \beta \sigma_{t-1}^2$	$y_t = c + \lambda \sigma_t^2 + \varepsilon_t$ $\varepsilon_t = \sigma_t z_t$ $\sigma_t^2 = \omega + \alpha \varepsilon_{t-1}^2 + \beta \sigma_{t-1}^2$
GARCH-M Standard Deviation in Mean Equation	$y_t = c + \lambda \sigma_t + \varepsilon_t$ $\varepsilon_t = \sigma_t z_t$ $\sigma_t^2 = \omega + \alpha \varepsilon_{t-1}^2 + \beta \sigma_{t-1}^2$	$y_t = c + \lambda \sigma_t + \varepsilon_t$ $\varepsilon_t = \sigma_t z_t$ $\sigma_t^2 = \omega + \alpha \varepsilon_{t-1}^2 + \beta \sigma_{t-1}^2$
GARCH-M Log Variance in Mean Equation	$y_t = c + \lambda \ln(\sigma_t^2) + \varepsilon_t$ $\varepsilon_t = \sigma_t z_t$ $\sigma_t^2 = \omega + \alpha \varepsilon_{t-1}^2 + \beta \sigma_{t-1}^2$	$y_t = c + \lambda \ln(\sigma_t^2) + \varepsilon_t$ $\varepsilon_t = \sigma_t z_t$ $\sigma_t^2 = \omega + \alpha \varepsilon_{t-1}^2 + \beta \sigma_{t-1}^2$
GARCH	$y_t = x_t \gamma + \varepsilon_t$ $\sigma_t^2 = \omega + \alpha \varepsilon_{t-1}^2 + \beta \sigma_{t-1}^2$	$y_t = \varepsilon_t$ $\varepsilon_t = \sigma_t z_t$ $\sigma_t^2 = \omega + \alpha \varepsilon_{t-1}^2 + \beta \sigma_{t-1}^2$
EGARCH	$y_t = \varepsilon_t$ $\varepsilon_t = \sigma_t z_t$ $\ln\left(\sigma_t^2\right) = \omega + \beta \cdot \ln\left(\sigma_{t-1}^2\right) +$ $\alpha \left[\left\| \dfrac{\varepsilon_{t-1}}{\sigma_{t-1}} \right\| - E(\|\varepsilon_t\|) \right] + r \dfrac{\varepsilon_{t-1}}{\sigma_{t-1}}$ $E(\|\varepsilon_t\|) = \sqrt{\dfrac{2}{\pi}}$	$y_t = \varepsilon_t$ $\varepsilon_t = \sigma_t z_t$ $\ln\left(\sigma_t^2\right) = \omega + \beta \cdot \ln\left(\sigma_{t-1}^2\right) +$ $\alpha \left[\left\| \dfrac{\varepsilon_{t-1}}{\sigma_{t-1}} \right\| - E(\|\varepsilon_t\|) \right] + r \dfrac{\varepsilon_{t-1}}{\sigma_{t-1}}$ $E(\|\varepsilon_t\|) = \dfrac{2\sqrt{v-2}\Gamma((v+1)/2)}{(v-1)\Gamma(v/2)\sqrt{\pi}}$
GJR-GARCH	$y_t = \varepsilon_t$ $\varepsilon_t = \sigma_t z_t$ $\sigma_t^2 = \omega + \alpha \varepsilon_{t-1}^2 +$ $r \varepsilon_{t-1}^2 d_{t-1} + \beta \sigma_{t-1}^2$ $d_{t-1} = \begin{cases} 1 & \text{if } \varepsilon_{t-1} < 0 \\ 0 & \text{otherwise} \end{cases}$	$y_t = \varepsilon_t$ $\varepsilon_t = \sigma_t z_t$ $\sigma_t^2 = \omega + \alpha \varepsilon_{t-1}^2 +$ $r \varepsilon_{t-1}^2 d_{t-1} + \beta \sigma_{t-1}^2$ $d_{t-1} = \begin{cases} 1 & \text{if } \varepsilon_{t-1} < 0 \\ 0 & \text{otherwise} \end{cases}$

Markov Chain Forecast or Markov Process

The Markov Process is useful for studying the evolution of systems over multiple and repeated trials in successive time periods. The system's state at a particular time is unknown, and we are interested in knowing the probability that a particular state exists. For instance, Markov Chains are used to compute the probability that a particular machine or equipment will continue to function in the next time period or whether a consumer purchasing Product A will continue to purchase Product A in the next period or switch to a competitive Product B.

To generate a Markov process, follow the instructions below:

1. Click on **Risk Simulator | Forecasting | Markov Chain**
2. Enter in the relevant state probabilities (e.g., **90** and **80** percents) and click OK
3. Review the forecast report generated

Tip: For an interesting State model, try 10 percent for both probability inputs and see the generated chart.

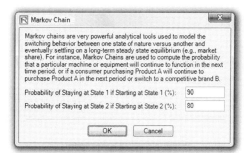

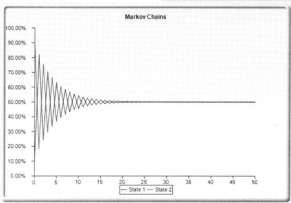

FIGURE 8.19   Markov chains (switching regimes).

to the same store in the next period versus the probability of switching to a competitor's store in the next state.

Procedure

1. Start Excel and select *Risk Simulator | Forecasting | Markov Chain*.
2. Enter the required input assumptions (see Figure 8.19 for an example) and click *OK* to run the model and report.

Note

Set both probabilities to 10 percent and rerun the Markov chain, and you will see the effects of switching behaviors very clearly in the resulting chart as shown at the bottom of Figure 8.19.

MAXIMUM LIKELIHOOD MODELS ON LOGIT, PROBIT, AND TOBIT

Theory

Limited Dependent Variables describe the situation where the dependent variable contains data that are limited in scope and range, such as binary responses (*0* or *1*), truncated, ordered, or censored data. For instance, given a set of independent variables (e.g., age, income, education level of credit card or mortgage loan holders), we can model the probability of default using maximum likelihood estimation (MLE). The response or dependent variable Y is binary; that is, it can have only two possible outcomes that we denote as *1* and *0* (e.g., Y may represent presence/absence of a certain condition, defaulted/not defaulted on previous loans, success/failure of some device, answer yes/no on a survey, and so forth), and we also have a vector of independent variable regressors X, which are assumed to influence the outcome Y. A typical ordinary least squares regression approach is invalid because the regression errors are heteroskedastic and non-normal, and the resulting estimated probability estimates will return nonsensical values of above *1* or below *0*. MLE analysis handles these problems using an iterative optimization routine to maximize a log likelihood function when the dependent variables are limited.

A Logit or Logistic regression is used for predicting the probability of occurrence of an event by fitting data to a logistic curve. It is a generalized linear model used for binomial regression, and like many forms of regression analysis, it makes use of several predictor variables that may be either numerical or categorical. MLE applied in a binary multivariate logistic analysis is used to model dependent variables to determine the expected probability of success of belonging to a certain group. The estimated coefficients for the Logit model are the logarithmic odds ratios and cannot be interpreted directly as probabilities. A quick computation is first required and the approach is simple.

Specifically, the Logit model is specified as *Estimated Y = LN[P_i/ (1 − P_i)]* or conversely, $P_i = EXP(Estimated\ Y)/(1 + EXP(Estimated\ Y))$, and the coefficients β_i are the log odds ratios. So, taking the antilog or *EXP(β_i)* we obtain the odds ratio of $P_i/(1 - P_i)$. This means that with an increase in a unit of β_i the log odds ratio increases by this amount. Finally, the rate of change in the probability $dP/dX = \beta_i P_i(1 - P_i)$. The Standard Error measures how accurate the predicted Coefficients are, and the t-Statistics are the ratios of each predicted Coefficient to its Standard Error and are used in the typical regression hypothesis test of the significance of each estimated parameter. To estimate the probability of success of belonging to a certain group (e.g., predicting if a smoker will develop chest complications given the amount smoked per year), simply compute the *Estimated Y* value using the MLE coefficients. For example, if the model is $Y = 1.1 + 0.005$ *(Cigarettes)* then someone smoking 100 packs per year has an *Estimated Y* of $1.1 + 0.005(100) = 1.6$. Next, compute the inverse antilog of the odds ratio by doing: $EXP(Estimated Y)/[1 + EXP(Estimated Y)] = EXP(1.6)/(1 + EXP(1.6)) = 0.8320$. So, such a person has an *83.20%* chance of developing some chest complications in his lifetime.

A Probit model (sometimes also known as a Normit model) is a popular alternative specification for a binary response model, which employs a probit function estimated using maximum likelihood estimation and the approach is called probit regression. The Probit and Logistic regression models tend to produce very similar predictions where the parameter estimates in a logistic regression tend to be 1.6 to 1.8 times higher than they are in a corresponding Probit model. The choice of using a Probit or Logit is entirely up to convenience, and the main distinction is that the logistic distribution has a higher kurtosis (fatter tails) to account for extreme values. For example, suppose that house ownership is the decision to be modeled, and this response variable is binary (home purchase or no home purchase) and depends on a series of independent variables X_i such as income, age, and so forth, such that $I_i = \beta_0 + \beta_1 X_1 + \ldots + \beta_n X_n$, where the larger the value of I_i, the higher the probability of home ownership. For each family, a critical I^* threshold exists, where if exceeded, the house is purchased, otherwise, no home is purchased, and the outcome probability (P) is assumed to be normally distributed, such that $P_i = CDF(I)$ using a standard normal cumulative distribution function *(CDF)*. Therefore, use the estimated coefficients exactly like those of a regression model and using the *Estimated Y* value, apply a standard normal distribution (you can use Excel's *NORMSDIST* function or Risk Simulator's Distributional Analysis tool by selecting Normal distribution and setting the mean to be *0* and standard deviation to be *1*). Finally, to obtain a Probit or probability unit measure, set $I_i + 5$ (this is because whenever the probability $P_i < 0.5$, the estimated I_i is negative, due to the fact that the normal distribution is symmetrical around a mean of zero).

The Tobit Model (Censored Tobit) is an econometric and biometric modeling method used to describe the relationship between a non-negative dependent variable Y_i and one or more independent variables X_i. A Tobit model is an econometric model in which the dependent variable is censored; that is, the dependent variable is censored because values below zero are not observed. The Tobit model assumes that there is a latent unobservable variable Y^*. This variable is linearly dependent on the X_i variables via a vector of β_i coefficients that determine their interrelationships. In addition, there is a normally distributed error term U_i to capture random influences on this relationship. The observable variable Y_i is defined to be equal to the latent variables whenever the latent variables are above zero and Y_i is assumed to be zero otherwise. That is, $Y_i = Y^*$ if $Y^* > 0$ and $Y_i = 0$ if $Y^* = 0$. If the relationship parameter β_i is estimated by using ordinary least squares regression of the observed Y_i on X_i, the resulting regression estimators are inconsistent and yield downward biased slope coefficients and an upward biased intercept. Only MLE would be consistent for a Tobit model. In the Tobit model, there is an ancillary statistic called sigma, which is equivalent to the standard error of estimate in a standard ordinary least squares regression, and the estimated coefficients are used the same way as a regression analysis.

Procedure

1. Start Excel and open the example file *Advanced Forecasting Model,* go to the *MLE* worksheet, select the data set including the headers, and click on *Risk Simulator | Forecasting | Maximum Likelihood.*
2. Select the dependent variable from the drop-down list (see Figure 8.20) and click *OK* to run the model and report.

Binary Logistic Maximum Likelihood Forecast

Defaulted	Age	Education Level	Years with Current Employer	Years at Current Address	Household Income (Thousands $)	Debt to Income Ratio (%)	Credit Card Debt (Thousands $)	Other Debt (Thousands $)
1	41	3	17	12	176	9.3	11.36	5.01
0	27	1	10	6	31	17.3	1.36	4
0	40	1	15	14				
0	41	1	15	14				
1	24	2	2	0				
0	41	2	5	5				
0	39	1	20	9				
0	43	1	12	11				
1	24	1	3	4				
0	36	1	0	13				
0	27	1	0	1				
0	25	1	4	0				
0	52	1	24	14				
0	37	1	6	9				
0	48	1	22	15				
1	36	2	9	6				
1	36	2	13	6				
0	43	1	23	19				
0	39	1	6	9				
0	41	3	0	21				
0	39	1	22	3				
0	47	1	17	21				
0	28	1	3	6	26	10	0.43	2.17
0	29	1	8	6	27	9.8	0.4	2.24
1	21	2	1	2	16	18	0.24	2.64
0	25	4	0	2	32	17.6	2.14	3.49
0	45	2	9	26	69	6.7	0.71	3.92
0	43	1	25	21	64	16.7	0.95	9.74
0	33	2	12	8	58	18.4	3.08	7.59
0	26	3	2	1	37	14.2	0.2	5.05

(Dialog box overlay)

Logistic Tool

The Maximum Likelihood and Weighted Least Squares models are used when the dependent variable is binary (0, 1) or grouped as successes and failures. It is used to model the expected probability of certain characteristics that belong to a group (e.g., modeling credit default probabilities or probabilities of an event occuring).

Dependent Variable: Defaulted

Defaulted	Age	Education Level
1	41	3
0	27	1
0	40	1
0	41	1
1	24	2
0	41	2
0	39	1
0	43	1

OK   Cancel

FIGURE 8.20 Maximum likelihood module.

SPLINE (CUBIC SPLINE INTERPOLATION AND EXTRAPOLATION)

Theory

Sometimes there are missing values in a time-series data set. For instance, interest rates for years 1 to 3 may exist, followed by years 5 to 8, and then year 10. Spline curves can be used to interpolate the missing years' interest rate values based on the data that exist. Spline curves can also be used to forecast or extrapolate values of future time periods beyond the time period of available data. The data can be linear or nonlinear. Figure 8.21 illustrates how a cubic spline is run and Figure 8.22 shows the resulting forecast report from this module. The Known *X* values represent the values on the x-axis of a chart (in our example, this is Years of the known interest rates, and, usually, the x-axis are the values that are known in advance such as time or years) and the Known *Y* values represent the values on the y-axis (in our case, the known Interest Rates). The y-axis variable is typically the variable you wish to interpolate missing values from or extrapolate the values into the future.

Procedure

1. Start Excel and open the example file *Advanced Forecasting Model,* go to the *Cubic Spline* worksheet, select the data set excluding the headers, and click on *Risk Simulator | Forecasting | Cubic Spline.*
2. The data location is automatically inserted into the user interface if you first select the data, or you can also manually click on the link icon and link the *Known X* values and *Known Y* values (see Figure 8.21 for an example), then enter the required *Starting* and *Ending* values to extrapolate and interpolate, as well as the required *Step Size* between these starting and ending values. Click *OK* to run the model and report (see Figure 8.22).

QUESTIONS

1. What are the differences between time-series forecasting techniques and nonlinear extrapolation?
2. Which forecasting method requires existing data and which method does not?
3. How do you use the software to perform qualitative forecasts?
4. Replicate all the examples in this chapter.
5. Time-series data that exhibit seasonality are easier to forecast than data that exhibit cyclicality. Is this statement true and why or why not?

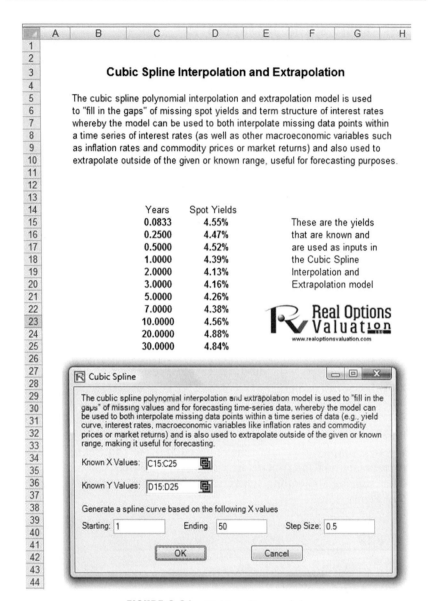

FIGURE 8.21   Cubic spline module.

Cubic Spline Forecasts

The cubic spline polynomial interpolation and extrapolation model is used to "fill in the gaps" of missing values and for forecasting time-series data, whereby the model can be used to both interpolate missing data points within a time series of data (e.g., yield curve, interest rates, macroeconomic variables like inflation rates and commodity prices or market returns) and also used to extrapolate outside of the given or known range, making it useful for forecasting.

Spline Interpolation and Extrapolation Results

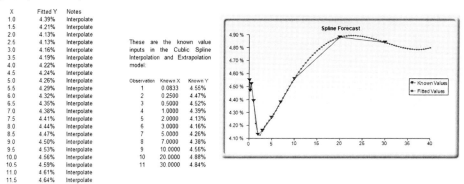

X	Fitted Y	Notes
1.0	4.39%	Interpolate
1.5	4.21%	Interpolate
2.0	4.13%	Interpolate
2.5	4.13%	Interpolate
3.0	4.16%	Interpolate
3.5	4.19%	Interpolate
4.0	4.22%	Interpolate
4.5	4.24%	Interpolate
5.0	4.26%	Interpolate
5.5	4.29%	Interpolate
6.0	4.32%	Interpolate
6.5	4.35%	Interpolate
7.0	4.38%	Interpolate
7.5	4.41%	Interpolate
8.0	4.44%	Interpolate
8.5	4.47%	Interpolate
9.0	4.50%	Interpolate
9.5	4.53%	Interpolate
10.0	4.56%	Interpolate
10.5	4.59%	Interpolate
11.0	4.61%	Interpolate
11.5	4.64%	Interpolate
12.0	4.66%	Interpolate
12.5	4.68%	Interpolate

These are the known value inputs in the Cubic Spline Interpolation and Extrapolation model:

Observation	Known X	Known Y
1	0.0833	4.55%
2	0.2500	4.47%
3	0.5000	4.52%
4	1.0000	4.39%
5	2.0000	4.13%
6	3.0000	4.16%
7	5.0000	4.26%
8	7.0000	4.38%
9	10.0000	4.56%
10	20.0000	4.88%
11	30.0000	4.84%

FIGURE 8.22 Spline forecast results.

The following pages present additional hands-on exercises on forecasting and review all the techniques covered in this chapter.

EXERCISE: FORECASTING

This sample exercise illustrates how to use Risk Simulator for running:

1. Autoregressive Integrated Moving Average (ARIMA)
2. AUTO ARIMA
3. Basic Econometrics and Auto Econometrics
4. Cubic Spline
5. Custom Distribution
6. GARCH
7. J-Curve (Exponential Curve)
8. Markov Chain Process
9. Maximum Likelihood (Logit, Probit, Tobit)
10. Nonlinear Extrapolation
11. Multiple Regression
12. S-Curve (Logistic Curve)

13. Stochastic Processes (Random Walk, Brownian Motion, Mean-Reversion, Jump-Diffusion)
14. Time-Series Decomposition
15. Trendlines

It is assumed that you have reviewed Chapter 8 for all the technical and usability details of these forecasting methods and are somewhat familiar with what each of them are used for.

ARIMA

Autoregressive Integrated Moving Average (ARIMA) forecasts apply advanced econometric modeling techniques to forecast time-series data by first *back-fitting* to historical data and then *forecasting* the future. Advanced knowledge of econometrics is required to properly model ARIMA. Please see the ARIMA example Excel model for more details. However, to get started quickly, follow the instructions below:

1. Start Excel and open the example model *Risk Simulator | Example Models | 01 Advanced Forecast Models.*
2. Go to the *ARIMA* and *AUTO ARIMA* worksheet.
3. Select the data area *B5:B440* and click on *Risk Simulator | Forecasting | ARIMA* and click *OK* (you can keep the default settings for now). Spend some time reviewing the generated ARIMA report.
4. Next, go back to the worksheet and rerun ARIMA. This time you can try different P, D, Q values and enter a different *Forecast Period* of choice (e.g., 1,0,0 for P, D, Q, and 5 for Forecast ... remember that these inputs have to be 0 or positive integers).
5. Run ARIMA again, but this time, click on the link icon to select the data set *B5:B440* on the worksheet for the *time-series variable* and *C5:D445* for the *exogenous variables.*
   - Exercise Question: What does exogenous variable mean?
   - Exercise Question: What types of variables might be well-suited for ARIMA forecasting?
   - Exercise Question: What types of data are appropriate for ARIMA? Time-series, cross-sectional or mixed-panel data?
   - Exercise Question: What are the P, D, Q values used for?
   - Exercise Question: How does ARIMA compare with multiple regression analysis?

Note: For ARIMA and AUTO ARIMA, you can run as many forecast periods as you wish if you only use the time-series variable (*Y*). If you add exogenous variables (*X*), note that your forecast period is limited to the number of exogenous variables' data periods minus the time-series variable's data periods. For example, you can only forecast up to 5 periods if you have time-series historical data of 100 periods and only if you have exogenous variables of 105 periods (100 historical periods to match the time-series variable and 5 additional future periods of independent exogenous variables to forecast the time-series dependent variable).

AUTO ARIMA

Proper ARIMA modeling requires testing of the autoregressive and moving average of the errors on the time-series data in order to calibrate the correct *p, d, q* inputs. Nonetheless, you can use the AUTO ARIMA forecasts to automatically test all possible combinations of the most frequently occurring *p, d, q* values to find the best-fitting ARIMA model. To do so, follow these steps:

1. Start Excel and open the example model *Risk Simulator | Example Models | 01 Advanced Forecast Models*.
2. Go to the *ARIMA* and *AUTO ARIMA* worksheet.
3. Select the data area *B5:B440* and click on *Risk Simulator | Forecasting | AUTO ARIMA* and click *OK*. Review the ARIMA report for details of the results.
4. Run ARIMA again, but this time, click on the link icon to select the data set *B5:B440* on the worksheet for the *time-series variable* and *C5:D445* for the exogenous variables.
   - Exercise Question: What is the difference between ARIMA and AUTO ARIMA?
   - Exercise Question: What additional information is provided in the report and what input parameters are no longer required?

Basic Econometrics and Auto Econometrics

To run an econometric model, follow the instructions below:

1. Start Excel and open the example model *Risk Simulator | Example Models | 01 Advanced Forecast Models*.
2. Go to the *Basic Econometrics* worksheet.
3. Select the data area *B5:G55* and click on *Risk Simulator | Forecasting | Basic Econometrics* and then type in the variables and their modifications for the dependent and independent variables.
   - Dependent Variable: *VAR1*
   - Independent Variables: *VAR2; VAR3; VAR4; VAR5; VAR6*

4. Click on *Show Results* to preview the computed model and click *OK* to generate the econometric model report.
5. Go back to the data and rerun Basic Econometrics. This time, set up the model:
   - Dependent Variable: *LN(VAR1)*
   - Independent Variable: *LN(VAR2); VAR3* VAR4; LAG(VAR5,1); DIFF(VAR6); TIME*
6. Go back to the data one more time and rerun Basic Econometrics. This time, select the *Multiple Models* option. Run the initial model with *VAR1* as the dependent variable and *LAG(VAR5,INTEGER1); VAR3* VAR4* as the independent variable, set *INTEGER1* to be between *1 and 3, Sort by Adjusted R-Square*, and *Shift Data 1 Row Down 5 Times* and click *OK*.
   - Exercise Question: What happens when you perform a shift to multiple econometric models?
   - Exercise Question: How do you model linear, nonlinear, interacting, lag, lead, log, natural log, time-series, difference, and ratios?
7. Go back to the data, select *Risk Simulator | Forecasting | Auto Econometrics*, and this time select *Linear and Nonlinear Interacting*, and then click *OK*. Review the generated report.

Note: Only one variable is allowed as the Dependent Variable (*Y*), whereas multiple variables are allowed in the Independent Variables (*X*) section, separated by a semicolon (;) and basic mathematical functions can be used (e.g., *LN, LOG, LAG, +, −, /, *, TIME, RESIDUAL, DIFF*). You can also automatically generate *Multiple Models* by entering a sample model and using the predefined '*INTEGER(N)*' variable as well as *Shifting Data* up or down specific rows repeatedly. For instance, if you use the variable *LAG(VAR1, INTEGER1)* and you set *INTEGER1* to be between *MIN* = 1 and *MAX* = 3, then the following three models will be run: *LAG(VAR1,1)*, then *LAG(VAR1,2)*, and, finally, *LAG(VAR1,3)*. Using this *Multiple Models* section in Basic Econometrics, you can run hundreds of models by simply entering a single model equation if you use these predefined integer variables and shifting methods.

Cubic Spline

The cubic spline polynomial interpolation and extrapolation model is used to "fill in the gaps" of missing values in that it can be used to both interpolate missing data points within a time series (e.g., interest rates as well as other macroeconomic variables such as inflation rates and commodity prices or market returns) and to extrapolate outside of the given or known range, useful for forecasting purposes.

To run the Cubic Spline forecast, follow the instructions below:

1. Start Excel and open the example model *Risk Simulator | Example Models | 01 Advanced Forecast Models*.
2. Go to the *Cubic Spline* worksheet.
3. Select the data area *C15:D25* and click on *Risk Simulator | Forecasting | Cubic Spline* (check to make sure *C15:C25* is set as the *Known X* values and D15:D25 is set as the *Known Y values*). Enter the desired forecast periods *Starting = 1, Ending = 50, Step Size = 0.5* and click *OK*. Review the generated forecasts and chart.
   - Exercise Question: How do you know which variable should be set as the known Y versus the known X?
   - Exercise Question: What is a spline curve supposed to do?
   - Exercise Question: Is this methodology more appropriate for time-series data and can it be used for cross-sectional data sets with missing intermediate values?

Custom Distribution

To create a custom distribution assumption, follow the instructions below:

1. Start Excel and open the example model *Risk Simulator | Example Models | 01 Advanced Forecast Models*.
2. Go to the *Custom Distribution and Delphi* worksheet.
3. Create a new profile by clicking on *Risk Simulator | New Simulation Profile*.
4. Select the data area *B14:C24* and click on *Edit | Copy in Excel* or use *CTRL+C* to copy the data into temporary clipboard memory and then select any empty cell in the worksheet.
5. Click on *Risk Simulator | Set Input Assumption* and select *Custom* distribution, then click on *Create Distribution*. Then, in the custom distribution designer interface, just click on and follow each of the four steps: *1 Paste, 2 Update Chart, 3 Apply*, and *4 Close*. Finally, back in the set assumptions properties, click *OK* to set the assumption.
6. Click on the *Step Simulation* icon a few times to see the value in the cell changing and you will see that it is randomly selecting the numbers from the original dataset, where numbers that have the highest probability of occurrence or that are repeated more often in the original dataset are selected more often, of course.

- Exercise Question: Why is the custom distribution considered a non-parametric simulation?
- Exercise Question: Is it better to use data fitting to find the best-fitting distribution to run a simulation or to use a custom distribution?
- Exercise Question: What is the p-value for the distributional fitting if we were to apply a hypothesis test to see what the goodness of fit is for a custom distribution?

GARCH

To run a GARCH model, follow the instructions below:

1. Start Excel and open the example model *Risk Simulator | Example Models | 01 Advanced Forecast Models*.
2. Go to the *GARCH* worksheet.
3. Select the data area *C8:C2428* and click on *Risk Simulator | Forecasting | GARCH* (you can also click on the data location link icon to select the historical data area or preselect the data area before starting the GARCH routine). Enter in the required inputs: *P = 1, Q = 1, Daily Trading Periodicity = 252, Predictive Base = 1, Forecast Periods = 10* and click *OK*. Review the generated forecast report and chart.
   - Exercise Question: What variables are most appropriate for running a GARCH model?
   - Exercise Question: Can cross-sectional data be used to run GARCH or is it only restricted to time-series data?
   - Exercise Question: What does GARCH forecast?
   - Exercise Question: Briefly describe what GARCH is used for.
   - Exercise Question: Why is number of days set to 252? Why is it not 365?

J-Curve (Exponential Curve)

In mathematics, a quantity that grows exponentially is one whose growth rate is always proportional to its current size. Such growth is said to follow an exponential law. This law implies that for any exponentially growing quantity, the larger the quantity gets, the faster it grows. But it also implies that the relationship between the size of the dependent variable and its rate of growth is governed by a strict law: direct proportion. This forecast method is also called a J-curve due to its shape resembling the letter J. There is no maximum level of this growth curve.

To generate a J-curve forecast, follow the instructions below:

1. Start Excel and open the example model *Risk Simulator | Example Models | 01 Advanced Forecast Models*.
2. Go to the *J-Curve* worksheet.
3. Click on *Risk Simulator | Forecasting | JS Curves* and click on *J-Curve*, and use *Starting Value = 100, Growth Rate = 5 percent, End Period = 100* and click *OK* to run the forecast and spend some time reviewing the forecast report.
   - Exercise Question: Can J-Curves be used to forecast cross-sectional data or are they only appropriate for time-series data?

Markov Chain Process

The Markov process is useful for studying the evolution of systems over multiple and repeated trials in successive time periods. The system's state at a particular time is unknown, and we are interested in knowing the probability that a particular state exists. For instance, Markov chains are used to compute the probability that a particular machine or equipment will continue to function in the next time period, or whether a consumer purchasing Product A will continue to purchase Product A in the next period or switch to a competitive Product B.

To generate a Markov process, follow the instructions below:

1. Start Excel and open the example model *Risk Simulator | Example Models | 01 Advanced Forecast Models*.
2. Go to the *Markov* worksheet.
3. Click on *Risk Simulator | Forecasting | Markov Chain* and enter in the value of *10* (for 10%) for both state probabilities and click *OK* to create the report and chart. Review the chart and see what happens when the probability is low.
4. Rerun the Markov Chain and this time, set the probabilities to both be at *90%*.
   - Exercise Question: What is the difference between a stochastic process forecast and a Markov chain forecast?
   - Exercise Question: What happens when the state probabilities are small? Why are there such high levels of switching back and forth on the chart as compared to a much lower fluctuation level with high probabilities?

Maximum Likelihood (Logit, Probit, Tobit)

Maximum Likelihood Estimates, or MLE, is a binary multivariate logistic analysis used to model dependent variables to determine the expected probability of success of belonging to a certain group. For instance, given a set of independent variables (e.g., age, income, and education level of credit card or mortgage loan holders), we can model the probability of credit loan default using MLE, or we can determine the probability a person will contract a specific illness or survive this disease given the person's age, social status, blood pressure, medications taken, and so forth. A typical regression model is invalid because the errors are heteroskedastic and non-normal, and the resulting estimated probability estimates will sometimes be above 1 or below 0. MLE analysis handles these problems using an iterative optimization routine. The data here represent a sample of several hundred previous loans, credit, or debt issues. The data show whether each loan had defaulted or not, as well as the specifics of each loan applicant's age, education level (1–3 indicating high school, university, or graduate professional education), years with current employer, and so forth. The idea is to model these empirical data to see which variables affect the default behavior of individuals, using Risk Simulator's Maximum Likelihood Models. The resulting model will help the bank or credit issuer compute the expected probability of default of an individual credit holder having specific characteristics.

To run the analysis, follow the instructions below:

1. Start Excel and open the example model *Risk Simulator | Example Models | 01 Advanced Forecast Models*.
2. Go to the *MLE* worksheet.
3. Select the data area including the headers or cells *B4:J504* and click on *Risk Simulator | Forecasting | Maximum Likelihood*. Select the *Dependent Variable* as *Defaulted* and click *OK*.
   - Exercise Question: What does *limited dependent variable* mean?
   - Exercise Question: What types of dependent variable data can be used in this logit, probit, and tobit model?
   - Exercise Question: Follow the instructions above to compute the expected probability of default of an individual with the following information:

Age	35
Education Level	2
Years with Current Employer	10
Years at Current Address	10
Household Income (Thousands $)	50
Debt to Income Ratio (%)	0
Credit Card Debt (Thousands $)	0
Other Debt (Thousands $)	0

Nonlinear Extrapolation

Nonlinear Extrapolation involves making statistical projections by using historical trends that are projected for a specified period of time into the future. It is only used for time-series forecasts. Extrapolation is fairly reliable, relatively simple, and inexpensive. However, extrapolation, which assumes that recent and historical trends will continue, produces large forecast errors if discontinuities occur within the projected time period.

To run the nonlinear extrapolation model, follow these steps:

1. Start Excel and open the example model *Risk Simulator | Example Models | 01 Advanced Forecast Models*.
2. Go to the *Nonlinear Extrapolation* worksheet.
3. Select the data area excluding the headers or cells *E13:E24* and click on *Risk Simulator | Forecasting | Nonlinear Extrapolation*. Input the number of periods to forecast as *3*, use the *Automatic Selection* option, and click *OK*. Review the report and chart that are created.
   - Exercise Question: What is a polynomial function versus a rational function?
   - Exercise Question: How many periods into the future may be considered a reasonable forecast assuming that there are 12 periods of historical data?
   - Exercise Question: Would this model be appropriate for cross-sectional data?

Multiple Regression

To run the multiple regression analysis, follow these steps:

1. Start Excel and open the example model *Risk Simulator | Example Models | 01 Advanced Forecast Models*.
2. Go to the *Regression* worksheet.
3. Select the data area including the headers or cells *B5:G55* and click on *Risk Simulator | Forecasting | Regression Analysis*. Select the *Dependent Variable* as the variable *Y*, leave everything else alone, and click *OK*. Review the generated report.
   - Exercise Question: Which of the independent variables are statistically insignificant and how can you tell? That is, which statistic did you use?
   - Exercise Question: How good is the initial model's fit?
   - Exercise Question: Delete the entire variable columns of data that are insignificant and re-run the regression (i.e., select the column headers

in Excel's grid, right-click and delete). Compare the R-Square and Adjusted R-Square values for both regressions. What can you determine?

- Exercise Question: Will R-Square always increase when you have more independent variables, regardless of their being statistically significant? How about Adjusted R-Square? Which is a more conservative and appropriate goodness of fit measure?
- Exercise Question: What can you do to increase the Adjusted R-Square of this model? Hint: Consider nonlinearity and some other econometric modeling techniques.
- Exercise Question: Run an Auto Econometric model on this dataset and select the nonlinear and interacting option and see what happens. Does the generated model better fit the data?

S-Curve (Logistic Curve)

A logistic function or logistic curve models the S-curve of growth of some variable X. The initial stage of growth is approximately exponential; then, as competition arises, the growth slows, and at maturity, growth stops. These functions find applications in a range of fields, from biology to economics. For example, in the development of an embryo, a fertilized ovum splits, and the cell count grows: 1, 2, 4, 8, 16, 32, 64, and so forth. This is exponential growth. But the fetus can grow only as large as the uterus can hold; thus other factors start slowing down the increase in the cell count, and the rate of growth slows (but the baby is still growing, of course). After a suitable time, the child is born and keeps growing. Ultimately, the cell count is stable; the person's height is constant; the growth has stopped, at maturity. The same principles can be applied to population growth of animals or humans, and the market penetration and revenues of a product, with an initial growth spurt in market penetration, but over time, the growth slows due to competition and eventually the market declines and matures.

To generate an S-curve forecast, follow the instructions below:

1. Start Excel and open the example model *Risk Simulator | Example Models | 01 Advanced Forecast Models*.
2. Go to the *S-Curve* worksheet.
3. Click on *Risk Simulator | Forecasting | JS Curves* and click on *S-Curve*. Use *Starting Value = 200, Growth Rate = 10 percent, Saturation Level = 6000, End Period = 100* and click *OK* to run the forecast. Spend some time reviewing the forecast report.
   - Exercise Question: Can S-Curves be used to forecast cross-sectional data or are they only appropriate for time-series data?

- Exercise Question: How would one obtain the value of the saturation level? What does saturation level mean?

Stochastic Processes (Random Walk, Brownian Motion, Mean-Reversion, Jump-Diffusion)

A stochastic process is a sequence of events or paths generated by probabilistic laws. That is, random events can occur over time but are governed by specific statistical and probabilistic rules. The main stochastic processes include Random Walk or Brownian motion, Mean-Reversion, and Jump-Diffusion. These processes can be used to forecast a multitude of variables that seemingly follow random trends but yet are restricted by probabilistic laws. We can use Risk Simulator's Stochastic Process module to simulate and create such processes. These processes can be used to forecast a multitude of time-series data including stock prices, interest rates, inflation rates, oil prices, electricity prices, commodity prices, and so forth.

To run this forecast method, follow the instructions below:

1. Start Excel and open the example model *Risk Simulator | Example Models | 01 Advanced Forecast Models.*
2. Click on *Risk Simulator | Forecasting | Stochastic Processes.*
3. Enter a set of relevant inputs or use the existing inputs as a test case. Then, you can select the relevant process to simulate. Click *Update Chart* several times to view the updated computation of a single path each time. When ready, click *OK* to generate the process.
4. Re-run the stochastic process module and try out other processes. Using the default sample inputs, modify some of them and see what happens to the sample generated path as you click *Update Chart* repeatedly. For instance, select the mean-reversion process and change the reversion rate from 5% to 1%, and then to 10% to see what happens to the chart when you click on *Update Chart* a few times. Be very careful with your choice of inputs because sometimes large values will invalidate the process and it will not run.
   - Exercise Question: How does a mean-reversion process compare to a Brownian motion random walk process?
   - Exercise Question: What types of variables might be best suited for a random walk process versus a mean-reversion process versus a jump-diffusion process?

Time-Series Decomposition

Time-series forecasting decomposes the historical data into the baseline, trend, and seasonality, if any. The models then apply an optimization procedure to find the alpha, beta, and gamma parameters for the baseline, trend, and seasonality coefficients and then recompose them into a forecast. In other words, this methodology first applies a "backcast" to find the best-fitting model and best-fitting parameters of the model that minimizes forecast errors, and then proceeds to "forecast" the future based on the historical data that exist. This process assumes that the same baseline growth, trend, and seasonality hold going forward. Even if they do not, say, when there exists a structural shift (e.g., company goes global, has a merger, spin-off, or other significant business activity), the baseline forecasts can be computed and then the required adjustments can be made to the forecasts.

To run these forecast models, follow the steps below:

1. Start Excel and open the example model *Risk Simulator | Example Models | 01 Advanced Forecast Models*.
2. Go to the *Time Series Decomposition* worksheet.
3. Create a new profile at *Risk Simulator | New Simulation Profile* if you wish the software to automatically generate assumptions for the forecast. Otherwise, if you do not need the assumption, a new profile is not required.
4. Select the data excluding the headers or cells *E25:E44*.
5. Click on *Risk Simulator | Forecasting | Time Series Analysis* and choose *Auto Model Selection*, set *Forecast = 4, Periods and Seasonality = 4 Periods*. Note that you can only select *Create Simulation Assumptions* if an existing Simulation Profile exists. Click *OK* to run the analysis. Review the generated report and chart.
   - Exercise Question: What do the alpha, beta, and gamma mean or represent?
   - Exercise Question: What are the three elements that a time-series analysis decomposes into?
   - Exercise Question: Can time-series analysis be used to forecast cross-sectional data? How about for panel data?
   - Exercise Question: How accurate are the forecast results? How can you tell? What does each of the error measures represent in the report?
   - Exercise Question: How is heteroskedasticity modeled in this forecast method? Hint: Look at each of the input assumptions automatically set up in the report.

Trendlines

To run trendlines analysis, follow the steps below:

1. Start Excel and open the example model *Risk Simulator | Example Models | 01 Advanced Forecast Models*.

2. Go to the *Time Series Decomposition* worksheet.

3. Select the data excluding the headers or cells *E25:E44*.

4. Click on *Risk Simulator | Forecasting | Trendlines*, select the trendlines you wish to run or leave everything checked by default, and click *OK* to run. Review the generated report.

   - Exercise Question: Is a low p-value or a high p-value a better fit?
   - Exercise Question: Would you rather have a low or high R-Squared value, and what does R-Square here represent?

CHAPTER 9

Using the Past to Predict the Future

One of the more difficult tasks in risk analysis is forecasting, which includes the forecasting of any variable's future outcomes, for example, sales, revenues, machine failure rates, demand, costs, market share, competitive threats, and so forth. Recall from Chapter 8, Tomorrow's Forecast Today, that the most common quantitative or statistical approaches to forecasting include econometric modeling, multivariate regression, time-series analysis, nonlinear extrapolation, stochastic processes, autoregressive integrated moving average (ARIMA), generalized autoregressive conditional heteroskedasticity (GARCH), and others. Data can be time-dependent, cross-sectional, or panel-based (both pooled time-dependent and cross-sectional data), and specific methods are applicable for specific types of data. Chapter 8 explores the basics of these methods and how to use Risk Simulator to forecast using these approaches, as well as some fundamental theories of these approaches. This chapter explores in more depth time-series and regression analysis through example computations. We start with time-series analysis by exploring the eight most common time-series methods or models as seen in Table 9.1. Regression analysis is then discussed, including the many pitfalls and dangers of applying regression analysis as a novice.

TIME-SERIES FORECASTING METHODOLOGY

Table 9.1 lists the eight most common time-series models, segregated by seasonality and trend. For instance, if the data variable has no trend or seasonality, then a single moving-average model or a single exponential-smoothing model would suffice. However, if seasonality exists but no discernible trend is present, either a seasonal additive or seasonal multiplicative model would be better, and so forth. The following sections explore these models in more detail through computational examples.

TABLE 9.1 The Eight Most Common Time-Series Methods

	No Seasonality	With Seasonality
No	Single Moving Average	Seasonal Additive
Trend	Single Exponential Smoothing	Seasonal Multiplicative
With	Double Moving Average	Holt–Winters Additive
Trend	Double Exponential Smoothing	Holt–Winters Multiplicative

NO TREND AND NO SEASONALITY

Single Moving Average

The single moving average is applicable when time-series data with no trend and seasonality exist. The approach simply uses an average of the actual historical data to project future outcomes. This average is applied consistently moving forward, hence the term *moving average*.

The value of the moving average (MA) for a specific length (n) is simply the summation of actual historical data (Y) arranged and indexed in time sequence (i):

$$MA_n = \frac{\sum\limits_{i=1}^{n} Y_i}{n}$$

An example computation of a 3-month single moving average is seen in Figure 9.1. Here we see that there are 39 months of actual historical data and a 3-month moving average is computed.[1] Additional columns of calculations also exist in the example—calculations that are required to estimate the error of measurements in using this moving-average approach. These errors are important as they can be compared across multiple moving averages (3-month, 4-month, 5-month, and so forth) as well as other time-series models (single moving average, seasonal additive model, and so forth) to find the best fit that minimizes these errors. Figures 9.2 to 9.4 show the calculations used in the moving-average model. Notice that the forecast-fit value in period 4 of 198.12 is a 3-month average of the prior three periods (months 1 through 3). The forecast-fit value for period 5 would then be the 3-month average of months 2 through 4. This process is repeated moving forward until month 40 (Figure 9.3), where every month after that, the forecast is fixed at 664.97. Clearly, this approach is not suitable if there is a trend (upward or downward over time) or if there is seasonality. Thus, error estimation is important when choosing the optimal time-series forecast model. Figure 9.2

Month	Actual	Forecast Fit	$\lvert Error \rvert$	$Error^2$	$\dfrac{\lvert Y_t - \hat{Y}_t \rvert}{Y_t}$	$\left[\dfrac{\hat{Y}_t - Y_t}{Y_{t-1}}\right]^2$	$\left[\dfrac{Y_t - Y_{t-1}}{Y_{t-1}}\right]$	Error	$\left[E_t - E_{t-1}\right]^2$
1	265.22	-	-	-	-	-	-	-	-
2	146.64	-	-	-	-	-	-	-	-
3	182.50	-	-	-	-	-	-	-	-
4	118.54	198.12	79.57	6332.12	67.13%	0.19	0.12	79.57	-
5	180.04	149.23	30.81	949.43	17.11%	0.07	0.27	-30.81	12185.39
6	167.45	160.36	7.09	50.20	4.23%	0.00	0.00	-7.09	562.99
7	231.75	155.34	76.41	5838.18	32.97%	0.21	0.15	-76.41	4805.61
8	223.71	193.08	30.63	938.22	13.69%	0.02	0.00	-30.63	2095.60
9	192.98	207.64	14.66	214.91	7.60%	0.00	0.02	14.66	2051.18
10	122.29	216.15	93.86	8808.84	76.75%	0.24	0.13	93.86	6271.97
11	336.65	179.66	157.00	24647.46	46.63%	1.65	3.07	-157.00	62925.98
12	186.50	217.31	30.81	949.17	16.52%	0.01	0.20	30.81	35270.22
13	194.27	215.15	20.88	435.92	10.75%	0.01	0.00	20.88	98.60
14	149.19	239.14	89.95	8091.27	60.29%	0.21	0.05	89.95	4771.05
15	210.06	176.65	33.41	1115.94	15.90%	0.05	0.17	-33.41	15216.99
16	272.91	184.50	88.40	7815.04	32.39%	0.18	0.09	-88.40	3024.67
17	191.93	210.72	18.79	352.98	9.79%	0.00	0.09	18.79	11489.77
18	286.94	224.96	61.97	3840.48	21.60%	0.10	0.25	-61.97	6522.06
19	226.76	250.59	23.83	567.99	10.51%	0.01	0.04	23.83	7362.34
20	303.38	235.21	68.17	4647.58	22.47%	0.09	0.11	-68.17	8465.03
21	289.72	272.36	17.36	301.32	5.99%	0.00	0.00	-17.36	2582.12
22	421.59	273.29	148.30	21993.55	35.18%	0.26	0.21	-148.30	17146.25
23	264.47	338.23	73.76	5440.32	27.89%	0.03	0.14	73.76	49310.98
24	342.30	325.26	17.04	290.41	4.98%	0.00	0.09	-17.04	8244.63
25	339.86	342.79	2.93	8.56	0.86%	0.00	0.00	2.93	398.71
26	439.90	315.54	124.35	15463.53	28.27%	0.13	0.09	-124.35	16199.87
27	315.54	374.02	58.48	3420.05	18.53%	0.02	0.08	58.48	33428.15
28	438.62	365.10	73.52	5404.80	16.76%	0.05	0.15	-73.52	17423.61
29	400.94	398.02	2.92	8.54	0.73%	0.00	0.01	-2.92	4983.77
30	437.37	385.02	52.34	2739.41	11.97%	0.02	0.01	-52.34	2442.13
31	575.77	425.64	150.13	22539.03	26.07%	0.12	0.10	-150.13	9563.01
32	407.33	471.36	64.03	4099.56	15.72%	0.01	0.09	64.03	45863.59
33	681.92	473.49	208.43	43442.59	30.57%	0.26	0.45	-208.43	74232.65
34	475.78	555.01	79.23	6277.13	16.65%	0.01	0.09	79.23	82746.68
35	581.17	521.68	59.49	3539.49	10.24%	0.02	0.05	-59.49	19243.79
36	647.82	579.62	68.20	4651.17	10.53%	0.01	0.01	-68.20	75.79
37	650.81	568.26	82.55	6814.39	12.68%	0.02	0.00	-82.55	205.92
38	677.54	626.60	50.94	2594.71	7.52%	0.01	0.00	-50.94	999.26
39	666.56	658.72	7.84	61.47	1.18%	0.00	0.00	-7.84	1857.46
Forecast 40	-	664.97	-	-	-	-	-	-	-
Forecast 41	-	664.97	-	-	-	-	-	-	-
Forecast 42	-	664.97	-	-	-	-	-	-	-

RMSE	79.00
MSE	6241.27
MAD	63.00
MAPE	20.80%
Thiel's U	0.80

$$MA_n = \frac{\sum_{i=1}^{n} Y_i}{n} \quad \forall\, i = 1, \ldots, N$$

FIGURE 9.1 Single moving average (3 months).

illustrates a few additional columns of calculations required for estimating the forecast errors. The values from these columns are used in Figure 9.4's error estimation.

Error Estimation (RMSE, MSE, MAD, MAPE, Thiel's U)

Several different types of errors can be calculated for time-series forecast methods, including the mean-squared error (MSE), root mean-squared error

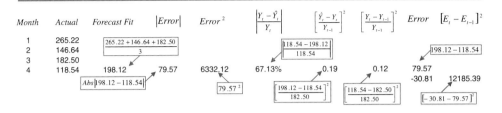

FIGURE 9.2 Calculating single moving average.

(RMSE), mean absolute deviation (MAD), and mean absolute percent error (MAPE).

The MSE is an absolute error measure that squares the errors (the difference between the actual historical data and the forecast-fitted data predicted by the model) to keep the positive and negative errors from canceling each other out. This measure also tends to exaggerate large errors by weighting the large errors more heavily than smaller errors by squaring them, which can help when comparing different time-series models. The MSE is calculated by simply taking the average of the *Error²* column in Figure 9.1. RMSE is the square root of MSE and is the most popular error measure, also known as the *quadratic loss function*. RMSE can be defined as the average of the absolute values of the forecast errors and is highly appropriate when the cost of the forecast errors is proportional to the absolute size of the forecast error.

The MAD is an error statistic that averages the distance (absolute value of the difference between the actual historical data and the forecast-fitted data predicted by the model) between each pair of actual and fitted forecast data points. MAD is calculated by taking the average of the | *Error* | column in Figure 9.1 and is most appropriate when the cost of forecast errors is proportional to the absolute size of the forecast errors.

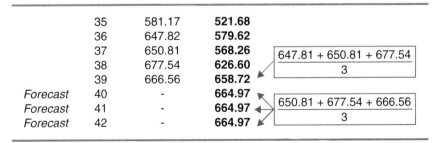

FIGURE 9.3 Forecasting with a single moving average.

RMSE	79.00
MSE	6241.27
MAD	63.00
MAPE	20.80%
Thiel's U	0.80

$$RMSE = \sqrt{\sum_{i=1}^{n} \frac{\left(Error^2\right)}{n}} = \sqrt{MSE}$$

$$MSE = \sum_{i=1}^{n} \frac{\left(Error^2\right)}{n} = RMSE^2$$

$$MAD = \sum_{i=1}^{n} \frac{|Error|_i}{n}$$

$$MAPE = \sum_{i=1}^{n} \frac{\left|\dfrac{Y_t - \hat{Y}_t}{Y_t}\right|_i}{n}$$

$$Theil's\,U = \sqrt{\frac{\sum_{i=1}^{n}\left[\dfrac{\hat{Y}_t - Y_t}{Y_{t-1}}\right]_i^2}{\sum_{i=1}^{n}\left[\dfrac{Y_t - Y_{t-1}}{Y_{t-1}}\right]_i^2}}$$

FIGURE 9.4   Error estimation.

The MAPE is a relative error statistic measured as an average percent error of the historical data points and is most appropriate when the cost of the forecast error is more closely related to the percentage error than the numerical size of the error. This error estimate is calculated by taking the average of the

$$\left|\frac{Y_t - \hat{Y}_t}{Y_t}\right|$$

column in Figure 9.1, where Y_t is the historical data at time t, while $\hat{Y}_t$ is the fitted or predicted data point at time t using this time-series method. Finally, an associated measure is the Theil's U statistic, which measures the naivety of the model's forecast. That is, if the Theil's U statistic is less than 1.0, then the forecast method used provides an estimate that is statistically better than guessing. Figure 9.4 provides the mathematical details of each error estimate.

Single Exponential Smoothing

The second approach to use when no discernible trend or seasonality exists is the single exponential-smoothing method. This method weights past data with exponentially decreasing weights going into the past; that is, the more recent the data value, the greater its weight. This weighting largely overcomes the limitations of moving averages or percentage-change models. The weight used is termed the *alpha* measure. The method is illustrated in Figures 9.5 and 9.6 and uses the following model:

$$ESF_t = \alpha Y_{t-1} + (1 - \alpha)ESF_{t-1}$$

where the exponential smoothing forecast (ESF_t) at time t is a weighted average between the actual value one period in the past (Y_{t-1}) and last

	Alpha 0.10	RMSE 126.26
Month	*Actual*	*Forecast Fit*
1	265.22	
2	146.64	265.22
3	182.50	253.36
4	118.54	246.28
5	180.04	233.50
6	167.45	228.16
7	231.75	222.09
8	223.71	223.05
9	192.98	223.12
10	122.29	220.10
11	336.65	210.32
12	186.50	222.96
13	194.27	219.31
14	149.19	216.81
15	210.06	210.04
16	272.91	210.05
17	191.93	216.33
18	286.94	213.89
19	226.76	221.20
20	303.38	221.75
21	289.72	229.92
22	421.59	235.90
23	264.47	254.46
24	342.30	255.47
25	339.86	264.15
26	439.90	271.72
27	315.54	288.54
28	438.62	291.24
29	400.94	305.98
30	437.37	315.47
31	575.77	327.66
32	407.33	352.47
33	681.92	357.96
34	475.78	390.35
35	581.17	398.90
36	647.82	417.12
37	650.81	440.19
38	677.54	461.26
39	666.56	482.88
Forecast 40	-	501.25

$$ESF_t = \alpha\, Y_{t-1} + (1-\alpha)\, ESF_{t-1}$$

FIGURE 9.5 Single exponential smoothing.

Alpha
0.10

Month	Actual	Forecast Fit
1	265.22	
2	146.64	265.22
3	182.50	253.36
4	118.54	246.28
5	180.04	233.50
6	167.45	228.16
7	231.75	222.09
8	223.71	223.05

$\hat{Y}_2 = Y_1 = 265.22$

$0.1(146.64) + (1 - 0.1)265.22$

$$ESF_t = \alpha\, Y_{t-1} + (1 - \alpha)\, ESF_{t-1}$$

FIGURE 9.6   Calculating single exponential smoothing.

period's forecast (ESF_{t-1}), weighted by the alpha parameter (α). Figure 9.6 shows an example of the computation. Notice that the first forecast-fitted value in month 2 ($\hat{Y}_2$) is always the previous month's actual value (Y_1). The mathematical equation gets used only at month 3 or starting from the second forecast-fitted period.

Optimizing Forecasting Parameters

Clearly, in the single exponential-smoothing method, the alpha parameter was arbitrarily chosen as 0.10. In fact, the optimal alpha has to be obtained for the model to provide a good forecast. Using the model in Figure 9.5, Excel's Solver add-in package is applied to find the optimal alpha parameter that minimizes the forecast errors. Figure 9.7 illustrates Excel's Solver add-in dialog box, where the target cell is set to the RMSE as the objective to be minimized by methodically changing the alpha parameter. As alpha should only be allowed to vary between 0.00 and 1.00 (because alpha is a weight given to the historical data and past period forecasts, and weights can never be less than zero or greater than one), additional constraints are also set up. The resulting optimal alpha value that minimizes forecast errors calculated by Solver is 0.4476. Therefore, entering this alpha value into the model will yield the best forecast values that minimize the errors. Risk Simulator's time-series forecast module takes care of finding the optimal alpha level automatically as well as allowing the integration of risk simulation

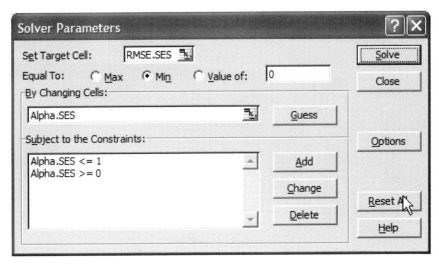

FIGURE 9.7 Optimizing parameters in single exponential smoothing.

parameters (see Chapter 8 for details), but we show the manual approach here using Solver as an illustrative example.

WITH TREND BUT NO SEASONALITY

For data that exhibit a trend but no seasonality, the double moving-average and double exponential smoothing methods work rather well.

Double Moving Average

The double moving-average method smoothes out past data by performing a moving average on a subset of data that represents a moving average of an original set of data. That is, a second moving average is performed on the first moving average. The second moving average application captures the trending effect of the data. Figures 9.8 and 9.9 illustrate the computation involved. The example shown is a 3-month double moving average and the forecast value obtained in period 40 is calculated using the following:

$$Forecast = 2MA_{1,t} - MA_{2,t} + \frac{2}{m-1}[MA_{1,t} - MA_{2,t}]$$

where the forecast value is twice the amount of the first moving average (MA_1) at time t, less the second moving average estimate (MA_2) plus the

Period	Actual	3-month MA $_1$	3-month MA $_2$	Forecast Fit
1	265.22	-	-	-
2	146.64	-	-	-
3	182.50	-	-	-
4	118.54	198.12	-	-
5	180.04	149.23	-	-
6	167.45	160.36	169.24	-
7	231.75	155.34	154.98	142.61
8	223.71	193.08	169.59	156.08
9	192.98	207.64	185.35	240.05
10	122.29	216.15	205.62	252.20
11	336.65	179.66	201.15	237.20
12	186.50	217.31	204.37	136.68
13	194.27	215.15	204.04	243.18
14	149.19	239.14	223.86	237.37
15	210.06	176.65	210.31	269.69
16	272.91	184.50	200.10	109.33
17	191.93	210.72	190.62	153.32
18	286.94	224.96	206.73	250.90
19	226.76	250.59	228.76	261.44
20	303.38	235.21	236.92	294.26
21	289.72	272.36	252.72	231.78
22	421.59	273.29	260.28	311.64
23	264.47	338.23	294.62	299.29
24	342.30	325.26	312.26	425.44
25	339.86	342.79	335.42	351.26
26	439.90	315.54	327.86	357.51
27	315.54	374.02	344.12	290.91
28	438.62	365.10	351.55	433.82
29	400.94	398.02	379.04	392.19
30	437.37	385.03	382.71	435.96
31	575.77	425.64	402.90	389.66
32	407.33	471.36	427.34	471.13
33	681.92	473.49	456.83	559.39
34	475.78	555.01	499.95	506.81
35	581.17	521.68	516.72	665.12
36	647.82	579.62	552.10	531.58
37	650.81	568.26	556.52	634.66
38	677.54	626.60	591.49	591.73
39	666.56	658.72	617.86	696.81
Forecast 40	-	664.97	650.10	740.45

$$Forecast_{t+1} = 2MA_{1,t} - MA_{2,t} + \frac{2}{m-1}\left[MA_{1,t} - MA_{2,t}\right]$$

FIGURE 9.8 Double moving average (3 months).

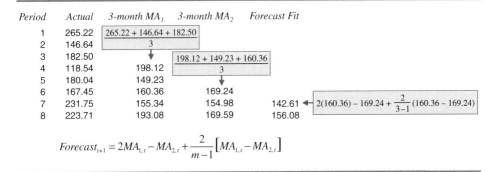

Period	Actual	3-month MA_1	3-month MA_2	Forecast Fit
1	265.22	$\dfrac{265.22 + 146.64 + 182.50}{3}$		
2	146.64			
3	182.50	$\downarrow$	$\dfrac{198.12 + 149.23 + 160.36}{3}$	
4	118.54	198.12		
5	180.04	149.23	$\downarrow$	
6	167.45	160.36	169.24	
7	231.75	155.34	154.98	142.61 ← $2(160.36) - 169.24 + \dfrac{2}{3-1}(160.36 - 169.24)$
8	223.71	193.08	169.59	156.08

$$Forecast_{t+1} = 2MA_{1,t} - MA_{2,t} + \frac{2}{m-1}\left[MA_{1,t} - MA_{2,t}\right]$$

FIGURE 9.9 Calculating double moving average.

difference between the two moving averages multiplied by a correction factor (two divided into the number of months in the moving average, *m*, less one).

Double Exponential Smoothing

The second approach to use when the data exhibit a trend but no seasonality is the double exponential-smoothing method. Double exponential smoothing applies single exponential smoothing twice, once to the original data and then to the resulting single exponential-smoothing data. An alpha (α) weighting parameter is used on the first or single exponential smoothing (*SES*) while a beta (β) weighting parameter is used on the second or double exponential smoothing (*DES*). This approach is useful when the historical data series is not stationary. Figure 9.10 illustrates the double exponential smoothing model, while Figure 9.11 shows Excel's Solver add-in dialog box used to find the optimal alpha and beta parameters that minimize the forecast errors. Risk Simulator's time-series forecast module takes care of finding the optimal alpha level automatically as well as allowing the integration of risk simulation parameters (see Chapter 8 for details), but we show the manual approach here using Solver as an illustrative example. Figure 9.12 shows the computational details. The forecast is calculated using the following:

$$DES_t = \beta(SES_t - SES_{t-1}) + (1 - \beta)DES_{t-1}$$
$$SES_t = \alpha Y_t + (1 - \alpha)(SES_{t-1} + DES_{t-1})$$

Note that the starting value (period 1 for DES in Figure 9.10) can take on different values other than the one shown. In some instances, zero is used when no prior information is available.

Period	Actual	SES	DES	Forecast Fit
		Alpha 0.1593	**Beta** 0.3919	**RMSE** 70.81
1	265.22	265.22	0.00	-
2	146.64	246.33	−7.40	-
3	182.50	229.94	−10.93	238.93
4	118.54	203.01	−17.20	219.01
5	180.04	184.89	−17.56	185.81
6	167.45	167.35	−17.55	167.33
7	231.75	162.85	−12.44	149.80
8	223.71	162.09	−12.44	150.42
9	192.98	160.41	−5.44	154.23
10	122.29	149.76	−7.48	154.96
11	336.65	173.24	4.65	142.28
12	186.50	179.27	5.19	177.90
13	194.27	186.02	5.80	184.46
14	149.19	185.03	3.14	191.82
15	210.06	191.66	4.51	188.17
16	272.91	208.39	9.30	196.17
17	191.93	213.59	7.69	217.69
18	286.94	231.74	11.79	221.28
19	226.76	240.86	10.74	243.53
20	303.38	259.85	13.98	251.60
21	289.72	276.35	14.97	273.82
22	421.59	312.07	23.10	291.32
23	264.47	323.91	18.69	335.17
24	342.30	342.55	18.67	342.60
25	339.86	357.82	17.33	361.22
26	439.90	385.46	21.38	375.15
27	315.54	392.30	15.68	406.84
28	438.62	412.85	17.59	407.97
29	400.94	425.74	15.75	430.44
30	437.37	440.83	15.49	441.49
31	575.77	475.35	22.95	456.32
32	407.33	483.81	17.27	498.30
33	681.92	529.88	28.56	501.08
34	475.78	545.27	23.40	558.44
35	581.17	570.66	24.18	568.67
36	647.82	603.28	27.49	594.84
37	650.81	633.96	28.74	630.77
38	677.54	665.06	29.66	662.69
39	666.56	690.24	27.91	694.72
Forecast 40	-	-	-	718.14
Forecast 41	-	-	-	746.05
Forecast 42	-	-	-	773.95
Forecast 43	-	-	-	801.86

$$DES_t = \beta \, (SES_t - SES_{t-1}) + (1 - \beta)\,DES_{t-1}$$
$$SES_t = \alpha \, Y_t + (1 - \alpha)\,(SES_{t-1} + DES_{t-1})$$

FIGURE 9.10 Double exponential smoothing.

Solver Parameters   [?][X]

Set Target Cell: [RMSE.DES]   [Solve]

Equal To: ○ Max   ● Min   ○ Value of: [0]   [Close]

By Changing Cells:

[AlphaBeta.DES]   [Guess]

Subject to the Constraints: [Options]

OptimalAlpha.DES <= 1   [Add]
OptimalAlpha.DES >= 0
OptimalBeta.DES <= 1   [Change]
OptimalBeta.DES >= 0
          [Reset All]
          [Delete]
          [Help]

FIGURE 9.11   Optimizing parameters in double exponential smoothing.

NO TREND BUT WITH SEASONALITY

Additive Seasonality

If the time-series data have no appreciable trend but exhibit seasonality, then the additive seasonality and multiplicative seasonality methods apply. The additive seasonality method is illustrated in Figures 9.13 and 9.14. The additive seasonality model breaks the historical data into a level (L) or base case component as measured by the alpha parameter (α), and a

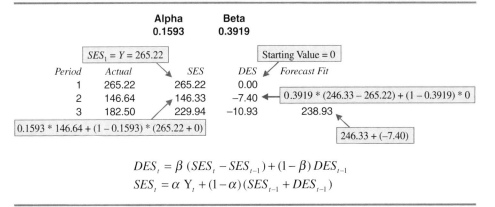

| | Alpha | Beta |
| | 0.1593 | 0.3919 |

$SES_1 = Y = 265.22$ Starting Value = 0

Period	Actual	SES	DES	Forecast Fit
1	265.22	265.22	0.00	
2	146.64	146.33	−7.40	0.3919 * (246.33 − 265.22) + (1 − 0.3919) * 0
3	182.50	229.94	−10.93	238.93

0.1593 * 146.64 + (1 − 0.1593) * (265.22 + 0)

246.33 + (−7.40)

$$DES_t = \beta \, (SES_t - SES_{t-1}) + (1 - \beta) \, DES_{t-1}$$
$$SES_t = \alpha \, Y_t + (1 - \alpha)(SES_{t-1} + DES_{t-1})$$

FIGURE 9.12   Calculating double exponential smoothing.

	Level Alpha 0.33	Seasonal Gamma 0.40		RMSE 93.54
Period	*Actual*	*Level*	*Seasonality*	*Forecast Fit*
1	265.22	-	87.00	-
2	146.64	-	−31.59	-
3	182.50	-	4.27	-
4	118.54	178.23	−59.68	-
5	180.04	150.44	63.85	265.22
6	167.45	166.29	−18.38	118.86
7	231.75	186.25	20.90	170.56
8	223.71	217.93	−33.28	126.57
9	192.98	188.97	39.72	281.78
10	122.29	173.22	−31.51	170.58
11	336.65	219.70	59.63	194.12
12	186.50	219.73	−33.26	186.42
13	194.27	198.47	22.01	259.45
14	149.19	192.67	−36.34	166.96
15	210.06	178.90	48.15	252.31
16	272.91	220.40	1.32	145.63
17	191.93	203.94	8.29	242.41
18	286.94	242.86	−3.91	167.60
19	226.76	221.90	30.69	291.01
20	303.38	248.05	23.10	223.23
21	289.72	258.93	17.36	256.34
22	421.59	313.26	41.35	255.02
23	264.47	287.34	9.09	343.95
24	342.30	297.73	31.76	310.44
25	339.86	305.81	24.09	315.09
26	439.90	336.05	66.55	347.16
27	315.54	326.40	1.05	345.15
28	438.62	352.64	53.62	358.16
29	400.94	360.53	30.67	376.73
30	437.37	363.89	69.35	427.08
31	575.77	432.65	58.34	364.94
32	407.33	406.90	32.17	486.27
33	681.92	486.59	97.07	437.57
34	475.78	460.45	47.56	555.94
35	581.17	480.80	75.29	518.79
36	647.82	524.78	68.82	512.97
37	650.81	534.22	104.94	621.84
38	677.54	565.45	73.58	581.79
39	666.56	573.87	82.31	640.74

$Level\ L_t = \alpha(Y_t - S_{t-s}) + (1-\alpha)(L_{t-1})$

$Seasonality\ S_t = \gamma(Y_t - L_t) + (1-\gamma)(S_{t-s})$

$Forecast\ F_{t+m} = L_t + S_{t+m-s}$

FIGURE 9.13 Additive seasonality with no trend.

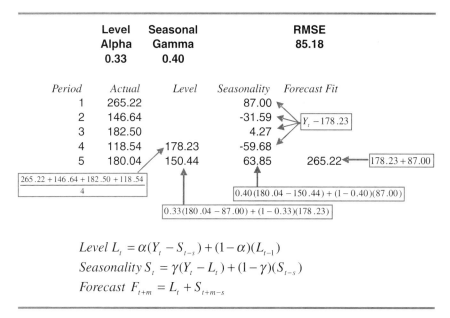

	Level Alpha 0.33	Seasonal Gamma 0.40		RMSE 85.18
Period	*Actual*	*Level*	*Seasonality*	*Forecast Fit*
1	265.22		87.00	
2	146.64		-31.59	
3	182.50		4.27	
4	118.54	178.23	-59.68	
5	180.04	150.44	63.85	265.22

$$Y_t - 178.23$$

$$\frac{265.22 + 146.64 + 182.50 + 118.54}{4}$$

$$178.23 + 87.00$$

$$0.40(180.04 - 150.44) + (1 - 0.40)(87.00)$$

$$0.33(180.04 - 87.00) + (1 - 0.33)(178.23)$$

$$\text{Level } L_t = \alpha(Y_t - S_{t-s}) + (1 - \alpha)(L_{t-1})$$
$$\text{Seasonality } S_t = \gamma(Y_t - L_t) + (1 - \gamma)(S_{t-s})$$
$$\text{Forecast } F_{t+m} = L_t + S_{t+m-s}$$

FIGURE 9.14 Calculating seasonal additive.

seasonality (S) component measured by the gamma parameter (γ). The resulting forecast value is simply the addition of this base case level to the seasonality value. Quarterly seasonality is assumed in the example. (Note that calculations are rounded.)

Multiplicative Seasonality

Similarly, the multiplicative seasonality model requires the alpha and gamma parameters. The difference from additive seasonality is that the model is multiplicative, for example, the forecast value is the multiplication between the base case level and seasonality factor. Figures 9.15 and 9.16 illustrate the computations required. Quarterly seasonality is assumed in the example. (Calculations are rounded.)

WITH SEASONALITY AND WITH TREND

When both seasonality and trend exist, more advanced models are required to decompose the data into their base elements: a base case level (L) weighted by the alpha parameter (α); a trend component (b) weighted by the beta parameter (β); and a seasonality component (S) weighted by the gamma parameter (γ). Several methods exist, but the two most common are the

		Level Alpha 0.22	Seasonal Gamma 0.64	RMSE 95.65
Period	*Actual*	*Level*	*Seasonality*	*Forecast Fit*
1	265.22	-	1.49	-
2	146.64	-	0.82	-
3	182.50	-	1.02	-
4	118.54	178.23	0.67	-
5	180.04	165.35	1.23	265.22
6	167.45	173.93	0.91	136.04
7	231.75	185.72	1.17	178.11
8	223.71	219.61	0.89	123.53
9	192.98	205.42	1.04	270.67
10	122.29	189.36	0.74	187.42
11	336.65	211.65	1.44	221.04
12	186.50	211.10	0.89	188.67
13	194.27	205.43	0.98	220.57
14	149.19	204.47	0.73	152.37
15	210.06	191.32	1.22	294.08
16	272.91	217.55	1.12	169.58
17	191.93	212.61	0.93	213.50
18	286.94	252.73	0.99	156.05
19	226.76	237.67	1.05	308.43
20	303.38	245.03	1.20	266.66
21	289.72	259.92	1.05	228.13
22	421.59	297.16	1.26	257.56
23	264.17	286.97	0.97	311.99
24	342.30	286.78	1.19	343.32
25	339.86	295.18	1.11	300.72
26	439.90	307.02	1.37	373.34
27	315.54	311.30	1.00	297.12
28	438.62	323.87	1.30	371.87
29	400.94	331.95	1.17	360.91
30	437.37	328.97	1.34	455.55
31	575.77	384.87	1.32	328.02
32	407.33	368.95	1.17	499.11
33	681.92	416.60	1.47	433.22
34	475.78	402.47	1.24	560.30
35	581.17	411.24	1.38	529.84
36	647.82	442.93	1.36	482.55
37	650.81	442.86	1.47	651.26
38	677.54	466.08	1.38	549.47
39	666.56	470.02	1.40	642.45

$$\text{Level } L_t = \alpha(Y_t / S_{t-s}) + (1-\alpha)(L_{t-1})$$
$$\text{Seasonality } S_t = \gamma(Y_t / L_t) + (1-\gamma)(S_{t-s})$$
$$\text{Forecast } F_{t+m} = L_t S_{t+m-s}$$

FIGURE 9.15 Multiplicative seasonality with no trend.

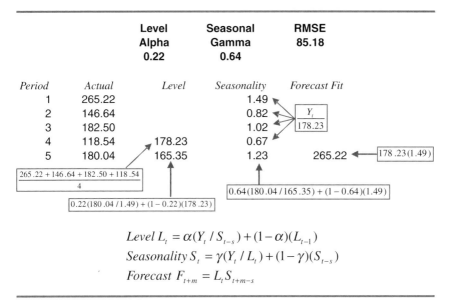

FIGURE 9.16 Calculating seasonal multiplicative.

Holt–Winters additive seasonality and Holt–Winters multiplicative seasonality methods.

Holt–Winters Additive Seasonality

Figures 9.17 and 9.18 illustrate the required computations for determining a Holt–Winters additive forecast model. (Calculations are rounded.)

Holt–Winters Multiplicative Seasonality

Figures 9.19 and 9.20 show the required computation for determining a Holt–Winters multiplicative forecast model when both trend and seasonality exist. (Calculations are rounded.)

REGRESSION ANALYSIS

This section deals with using regression analysis for forecasting purposes. It is assumed that the reader is sufficiently knowledgeable about the fundamentals of regression analysis. Instead of focusing on the detailed theoretical mechanics of the regression equation, we look at the basics of applying regression analysis and work through the various relationships that a regression analysis can capture, as well as the common pitfalls in regression,

	Level Alpha 0.05	Trend Beta 1.00	Seasonal Gamma 0.24		RMSE 77.03
Period	Actual	Level	Trend	Seasonality	Forecast Fit
1	265.22	-	-	87.00	-
2	146.64	-	-	−31.59	-
3	182.50	-	-	4.27	-
4	118.54	178.23	0.00	−59.68	-
5	180.04	174.03	−4.20	67.96	265.22
6	167.45	171.27	−2.76	−25.06	138.25
7	231.75	171.42	0.15	17.45	172.79
8	223.71	177.07	5.65	−34.69	111.89
9	192.98	179.89	2.81	55.06	250.69
10	122.29	180.96	1.07	−32.96	157.64
11	336.65	188.78	7.83	48.11	199.48
12	186.50	197.82	9.04	−29.20	161.92
13	194.27	203.53	5.71	39.94	261.92
14	149.19	207.90	4.37	−39.01	176.27
15	210.06	209.79	1.89	36.86	260.38
16	272.91	216.14	6.35	−8.99	182.49
17	191.93	219.01	2.87	24.19	262.43
18	286.94	227.01	8.00	−15.76	182.87
19	226.76	232.79	5.78	26.78	271.87
20	303.38	242.20	9.41	7.50	229.58
21	289.72	252.30	10.10	27.30	275.80
22	421.59	271.02	18.71	23.34	246.64
23	264.47	287.17	16.15	15.15	316.51
24	342.30	304.87	17.70	14.54	310.82
25	339.86	322.08	17.21	25.06	349.87
26	439.90	343.09	21.01	40.61	362.63
27	315.54	360.97	17.88	0.91	379.26
28	438.62	381.07	20.10	24.65	393.38
29	400.94	399.93	18.86	19.41	426.24
30	437.37	417.70	17.77	35.69	459.40
31	575.77	442.34	24.64	32.06	436.38
32	407.33	462.83	20.49	5.81	491.63
33	681.92	492.14	29.31	59.45	502.72
34	475.78	517.45	25.31	17.50	557.14
35	581.17	543.06	25.62	33.48	574.81
36	647.82	572.29	29.23	22.20	574.49
37	650.81	601.02	28.73	57.18	660.98
38	677.54	631.24	30.22	24.27	647.26
39	666.56	660.07	28.82	27.14	694.95

$$\text{Level } L_t = \alpha(Y_t - S_{t-s}) + (1 - \alpha)(L_{t-1} + b_{t-1})$$
$$\text{Trend } b_t = \beta(L_t - L_{t-1}) + (1 - \beta)(b_{t-1})$$
$$\text{Seasonality } S_t = \gamma(Y_t - L_t) + (1 - \gamma)(S_{t-s})$$
$$\text{Forecast } F_{t+m} = L_t + mb_t + S_{t+m-s}$$

FIGURE 9.17 Holt–Winters additive seasonality with trend.

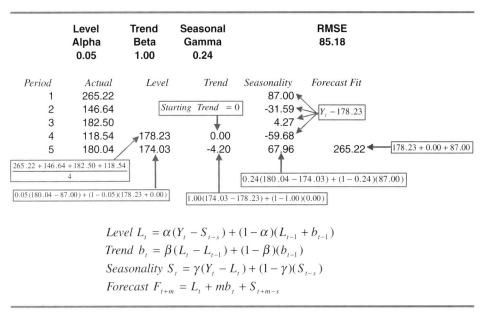

FIGURE 9.18 Calculating Holt–Winters additive.

including the problems of outliers, nonlinearities, heteroskedasticity, auto-correlation, and structural breaks.

The general bivariate linear regression equation takes the form of

$$Y = \beta_0 + \beta_1 X + \varepsilon$$

where β_0 is the intercept, β_1 is the slope, and ε is the error term. It is bivariate as there are only two variables, a Y or dependent variable, and an X or independent variable, where X is also known as the regressor (sometimes a bivariate regression is also known as a univariate regression as there is only a single independent variable X). The dependent variable is named as such as it *depends* on the independent variable, for example, sales revenue depends on the amount of marketing costs expended on a product's advertising and promotion, making the dependent variable sales and the independent variable marketing costs. An example of a bivariate regression is seen as simply inserting the best-fitting line through a set of data points in a two-dimensional plane as seen on the left panel in Figure 9.21. In other cases, a multivariate regression can be performed, where there are multiple or n number of independent X variables, where the general regression equation will now take the form of $Y = \beta_0 + \beta_1 X_1 + \beta_2 X_2 + \beta_3 X_3 + \ldots + \beta_n X_n + \varepsilon$. In this case, the best-fitting line will be within an $n + 1$ dimensional plane.

	Level Alpha 0.04	Trend Beta 1.00	Seasonal Gamma 0.27		RMSE 79.15
Period	Actual	Level	Trend	Seasonality	Forecast Fit
1	265.22	-	-	1.49	-
2	146.64	-	-	0.82	-
3	182.50	-	-	1.02	-
4	118.54	178.23	0.00	0.67	-
5	180.04	176.12	−2.10	1.36	265.22
6	167.45	175.11	−1.02	0.86	143.18
7	231.75	176.01	0.90	1.10	178.26
8	223.71	182.75	6.75	0.82	117.67
9	192.98	187.75	5.00	1.27	257.93
10	122.29	190.90	3.15	0.80	165.60
11	336.65	198.12	7.22	1.27	214.19
12	186.50	206.17	8.06	0.84	167.87
13	194.27	211.98	5.81	1.17	272.12
14	149.19	216.64	4.66	0.77	174.13
15	210.06	219.27	2.63	1.18	280.20
16	272.91	225.66	6.39	0.94	186.67
17	191.93	229.53	3.88	1.08	272.38
18	286.94	238.53	9.00	0.89	179.57
19	226.76	245.48	6.95	1.11	292.61
20	303.38	254.99	9.51	1.01	237.70
21	289.72	264.63	9.63	1.09	286.13
22	421.59	281.63	17.00	1.05	243.42
23	264.47	296.40	14.77	1.05	331.98
24	342.30	312.20	15.80	1.03	314.05
25	339.86	327.45	15.25	1.07	355.98
26	439.90	345.45	18.00	1.11	361.10
27	315.54	361.12	15.67	1.00	382.29
28	438.62	378.54	17.42	1.07	389.23
29	400.94	395.15	16.61	1.06	424.62
30	437.37	411.07	15.91	1.10	458.54
31	575.77	432.37	21.30	1.09	428.40
32	407.33	451.03	18.66	1.02	484.20
33	681.92	476.14	25.11	1.16	496.30
34	475.78	498.73	22.59	1.06	551.41
35	581.17	521.70	22.97	1.10	569.70
36	647.82	547.93	26.23	1.07	556.94
37	650.81	573.70	25.77	1.15	665.46
38	677.54	600.92	27.22	1.08	635.58
39	666.56	627.35	26.43	1.09	690.07

$$Level\ L_t = \alpha(Y_t / S_{t-s}) + (1-\alpha)(L_{t-1} + b_{t-1})$$
$$Trend\ b_t = \beta(L_t - L_{t-1}) + (1-\beta)(b_{t-1})$$
$$Seasonality\ S_t = \gamma(Y_t / L_t) + (1-\gamma)(S_{t-s})$$
$$Forecast\ F_{t+m} = (L_t + mb_t)S_{t+m-s}$$

FIGURE 9.19   Holt–Winters multiplicative seasonality with trend.

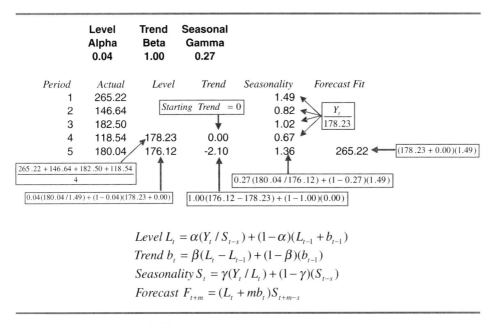

FIGURE 9.20 Calculating Holt–Winters multiplicative.

However, fitting a line through a set of data points in a scatter plot as in Figure 9.21 may result in numerous possible lines. The best-fitting line is defined as the single unique line that minimizes the total vertical errors, that is, the sum of the absolute distances between the actual data points (Y_i) and the estimated line $(\hat{Y})$ as shown on the right panel of Figure 9.21. In order to find the best-fitting line that minimizes the errors, a more sophisticated approach is required, that is, regression analysis.

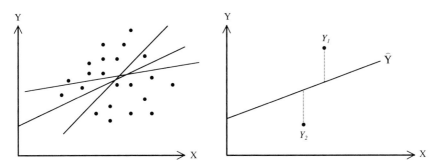

FIGURE 9.21 Bivariate regression.

$$\beta_1 = \frac{\sum\limits_{i=1}^{n}(X_i - \bar{X})(Y_i - \bar{Y})}{\sum\limits_{i=1}^{n}(X_i - \bar{X})^2} = \frac{\sum\limits_{i=1}^{n}X_i Y_i - \frac{\sum\limits_{i=1}^{n}X_i \sum\limits_{i=1}^{n}Y_i}{n}}{\sum\limits_{i=1}^{n}X_i^2 - \frac{\left(\sum\limits_{i=1}^{n}X_i\right)^2}{n}}$$

$$\text{and } \beta_0 = \bar{Y} - \beta_1 \bar{X}$$

FIGURE 9.22 Least squares regression equations.

Regression analysis therefore finds the unique best-fitting line by requiring that the total errors be minimized, or by calculating

$$\text{Min} \sum_{i=1}^{n}(Y_i - \hat{Y}_i)^2$$

where only one unique line minimizes this sum of squared errors. The errors (vertical distance between the actual data and the predicted line) are squared to avoid the negative errors from canceling out the positive errors. Solving this minimization problem with respect to the slope and intercept requires calculating a first derivative and setting them equal to zero:

$$\frac{d}{d\beta_0}\sum_{i=1}^{n}(Y_i - \hat{Y}_i)^2 = 0 \quad \text{and} \quad \frac{d}{d\beta_1}\sum_{i=1}^{n}(Y_i - \hat{Y}_i)^2 = 0$$

which yields the *least squares regression equations* seen in Figure 9.22.

See Appendix—Ordinary Least Squares at the end of this chapter for more details on optimizing this line to find the best-fitting line.

Example Given the following sales amounts ($ millions) and advertising sizes (measured as linear inches by summing up all the sides of an ad) for a local newspaper, answer the accompanying questions.

Advertising size (inch)	12	18	24	30	36	42	48
Sales ($ millions)		5.9	5.6	5.5	7.2	8.0	7.7	8.4

1. Which is the dependent variable and which is the independent variable?
   The independent variable is advertising size, whereas the dependent variable is sales.
2. Manually calculate the slope (β_1) and the intercept (β_0) terms.

X	Y	XY	X²	Y²
12	5.9	70.8	144	34.81
18	5.6	100.8	324	31.36
24	5.5	132.0	576	30.25
30	7.2	216.0	900	51.84
36	8.0	288.0	1296	64.00
42	7.7	323.4	1764	59.29
48	8.4	403.2	2304	70.56
$\Sigma(X) = 210$	$\Sigma(Y) = 48.3$	$\Sigma(XY) = 1534.2$	$\Sigma(X^2) = 7308$	$\Sigma(Y^2) = 342.11$

$$\beta_1 = \frac{1534.2 - \dfrac{210(48.3)}{7}}{7308 - \dfrac{210^2}{7}} = 0.0845 \; and \; \beta_0 = \frac{48.3}{7} - 0.0845 \left[\frac{210}{7}\right] = 4.3643$$

3. What is the estimated regression equation?

$$Y = 4.3643 + 0.0845\,X \quad or \quad Sales = 4.3643 + 0.0845(Size)$$

4. What would the level of sales be if we purchase a 28-inch ad?

$$Y = 4.3643 + 0.0845\,(28) = \$6.73 \; million \; in \; sales$$

(Note that we only predict or forecast and cannot say for certain. This is only an expected value or on average.)

Regression Output

Using the data in the previous example, a regression analysis can be performed using either Excel's Data Analysis add-in or Risk Simulator software.[2] Figure 9.23 shows Excel's regression analysis output. Notice that the coefficients on the intercept and X variable confirm the results we obtained in the manual calculation.

The same regression analysis can be performed using Risk Simulator.[3] The results obtained through Risk Simulator are seen in Figure 9.24. Notice again the identical answers to the slope and intercept calculations. Clearly, there are significant amounts of additional information obtained through

SUMMARY OUTPUT

Regression Statistics	
Multiple R	0.9026
R Square	0.8146
Adjusted R Square	0.7776
Standard Error	0.5725
Observations	7

ANOVA

	df	SS	MS	F	Significance F
Regression	1	7.2014	7.2014	21.9747	0.0054
Residual	5	1.6386	0.3277		
Total	6	8.8400			

	Coefficients	Standard Error	t Stat	P-value	Lower 95%	Upper 95%	Lower 95.0%	Upper 95.0%
Intercept	4.3643	0.5826	7.4911	0.0007	2.8667	5.8619	2.8667	5.8619
X Variable 1	0.0845	0.0180	4.6877	0.0054	0.0382	0.1309	0.0382	0.1309

FIGURE 9.23 Regression output from Excel's Data Analysis add-in.

the Excel and Risk Simulator analyses. Most of these additional statistical outputs pertain to goodness-of-fit measures, that is, a measure of how accurate and statistically reliable the model is.

Goodness-of-Fit

Goodness-of-fit statistics provide a glimpse into the accuracy and reliability of the estimated regression model. They usually take the form of a t-statistic, F-statistic, R-squared statistic, adjusted R-squared statistic, Durbin–Watson statistic, and their respective probabilities. (See the t-statistic, F-statistic, and critical Durbin–Watson tables at the end of this book for the corresponding critical values used later in this chapter.) The following sections discuss some of the more common regression statistics and their interpretation.

The R-squared (R^2), or coefficient of determination, is an error measurement that looks at the percent variation of the dependent variable that can be explained by the variation in the independent variable for a regression analysis. The coefficient of determination can be calculated by:

$$R^2 = 1 - \frac{\sum_{i=1}^{n} (Y_i - \hat{Y}_i)^2}{\sum_{i=1}^{n} (Y_i - \overline{Y})^2} = 1 - \frac{SSE}{TSS}$$

where the coefficient of determination is one less the ratio of the sums of squares of the errors (SSE) to the total sums of squares (TSS). In other words, the ratio of SSE to TSS is the unexplained portion of the analysis; thus, one less the ratio of SSE to TSS is the explained portion of the regression analysis.

Regression Analysis Report

Regression Statistics

R-Squared (Coefficient of Determination)	0.8146
Adjusted R-Squared	0.7776
Multiple R (Multiple Correlation Coefficient)	0.9026
Standard Error of the Estimates (SEy)	0.5725
nObservations	7

The R-squared or coefficient of determination indicates that 0.81 of the variation in the dependent variable can be explained and accounted for by the independent variables in this regression analysis. However, in a multiple regression, the adjusted R-squared takes into account the existence of additional independent variables or regressors and adjusts this R-squared value to a more accurate view of the regression's explanatory power. Hence, only 0.78 of the variation in the dependent variable can be explained by the regressors.

The multiple correlation coefficient (Multiple R) measures the correlation between the actual dependent variable (Y) and the estimated or fitted (Y) based on the regression equation. This is also the square root of the coefficient of determination (R-Squared.)

The standard error of the estimates (SE_y) describes the dispersion of data points above and below the regression line or plane. This value is used as part of the calculation to obtain the confidence interval of the estimates later.

Regression Results

	Intercept	Ad Size
Coefficients	4.3643	0.0845
Standard Error	0.5826	0.0180
t-Statistic	7.4911	4.6877
p-Value	0.0007	0.0054
Lower 5%	2.8667	0.0382
Upper 95%	5.8619	0.1309

Degrees of Freedom		Hypothesis Test	
Degrees of Freedom for Regression	1	Critical t-Statistic (99% confidence with df of 5)	4.0321
Degrees of Freedom for Residual	5	Critical t-Statistic (95% confidence with df of 5)	2.5706
Total Degrees of Freedom	6	Critical t-Statistic (90% confidence with df of 5)	2.0150

The coefficients provide the estimated regression intercept and slopes. For instance, the coefficients are estimates of the true population b values in the following regression equation: $Y = \beta_0 + \beta_1 X_1 + \beta_2 X_2 + ... + \beta_2 X_2$. The standard error measures how accurate the predicted Coefficients are, and the t-Statistics are the ratios of each predicted coefficient to its standard error.

The t-statistic is used in hypothesis testing, where we set the null hypothesis (H_0) such that the real mean of the coefficient = 0, and the alternate hypothesis (H_a) such that the real mean of the Coefficient is not equal to 0. A t-test is performed and the calculated t-statistic is compared to the critical values at the relevant degrees of freedom for residual. The t-test is very important as it calculates if each of the coefficients is statistically significant in the presence of the other regressors. This means that the t-test statistically verifies whether a regressor or independent variable should remain in the regression or it should be dropped.

The coefficient is statistically significant if its calculated t-statistic exceeds the critical t-statistic at the relevant degrees of freedom (df). The three main confidence levels used to test for significance are 90%, 95%, and 99%. If a coefficient's t-statistic exceeds the critical level, it is considered statistically significant. Alternatively, the p-value calculates each t-statistic's probability of occurrence, which means that the smaller the p-value, the more significant the coefficient. The usual significant levels for the p-value are 0.01, 0.05, and 0.10, corresponding to the 99%, 95%, and 99% confidence levels.

The coefficients with their p-values highlighted in blue indicate that they are statistically significant at the 95% confidence or 0.05 alpha level, while those highlighted in red indicate that they are not statistically significant at any of the alpha levels.

Analysis of Variance

	Sums of Squares	Mean of Squares	F-Statistic	P-Value	Hypothesis Test	
Regression	7.2014	7.2014	21.9747	0.0054	Critical t-Statistic (99% confidence with df of 4 and 3)	16.2582
Residual	1.6386	0.3277			Critical t-Statistic (95% confidence with df of 4 and 3)	6.6079
Total	8.8400				Critical t-Statistic (90% confidence with df of 4 and 3)	4.0604

The analysis of variance (ANOVA) table provides an F-test of the regression model's overall statistical significance. Instead of looking at individual regressors as in the t-test, the F-test looks at all the estimated Coefficients statistical properties. The F-statistic is calculated as the ratio of the regression's mean of squares to the residual's mean of squares. The numerator measures how much of the regression is explained, while the denominator measures how much is unexplained. Hence, the larger the F-statistic, the more significant the model. The corresponding p-value is calculated to test the null hypothesis (H_0) where all the coefficients are simultaneously equal to zero, versus the alternate hypothesis (H_a) that they are all simultaneously different from zero, indicating a significant overall regression model. If the p-value is smaller than the 0.01, 0.05, or 0.10 alpha significance, then the regression is significant. The same approach can be applied to the F-statistic by comparing the calculated F-statistic with the critical F-values at various significance levels.

FIGURE 9.24 Regression output from Risk Simulator software.

Forecasting

Period	Actual (Y)	Forecast (F)	Error (E)
1	5.9	5.3786	0.5214
2	5.6	5.8857	(0.2857)
3	5.5	6.3929	(0.8929)
4	7.2	6.9000	0.3000
5	8	7.4071	0.5929
6	7.7	7.9143	(0.2143)
7	8.4	8.4214	(0.0214)

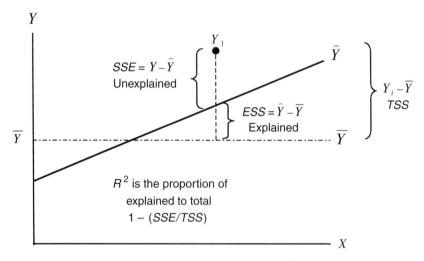

FIGURE 9.24   (*Continued*)

Figure 9.25 provides a graphical explanation of the coefficient of determination. The estimated regression line is characterized by a series of predicted values ($\hat{Y}$); the average value of the dependent variable's data points is denoted $\overline{Y}$; and the individual data points are characterized by Y_i. Therefore, the total sum of squares, that is, the total variation in the data or the total variation about the average dependent value, is the total of the difference between the individual dependent values and its average (seen as the total squared distance of $Y_i - \overline{Y}$ in Figure 9.25). The explained sum of squares, the portion that is captured by the regression analysis, is the total of the difference between the regression's predicted value and the average

FIGURE 9.25   Explaining the coefficient of determination.

dependent variable's data set (seen as the total squared distance of $\hat{Y} - \overline{Y}$ in Figure 9.25). The difference between the total variation (*TSS*) and the explained variation (*ESS*) is the unexplained sums of squares, also known as the sums of squares of the errors (*SSE*).

Another related statistic, the adjusted coefficient of determination, or the adjusted R-squared ($\overline{R}^2$), corrects for the number of independent variables (k) in a multivariate regression through a degrees-of-freedom correction to provide a more conservative estimate:

$$\overline{R}^2 = 1 - \frac{\sum\limits_{i=1}^{n}(Y_i - \hat{Y}_i)^2/(k-2)}{\sum\limits_{i=1}^{n}(Y_i - \overline{Y})^2/(k-1)} = 1 - \frac{SSE/(k-2)}{TSS/(k-1)}$$

The adjusted R-squared should be used instead of the regular R-squared in multivariate regressions because every time an independent variable is added into the regression analysis, the R-squared will increase, indicating that the percent variation explained has increased. This increase occurs even when nonsensical regressors are added. The adjusted R-squared takes the added regressors into account and penalizes the regression equation accordingly, providing a much better estimate of a regression model's goodness-of-fit.

Other goodness-of-fit statistics include the t-statistic and the F-statistic. The former is used to test if *each* of the estimated slope and intercept(s) is statistically significant, that is, if it is statistically significantly different from zero (therefore making sure that the intercept and slope estimates are statistically valid). The latter applies the same concepts but simultaneously for the entire regression equation including the intercept and slope(s). Using the previous example, the following illustrates how the t-statistic and F-statistic can be used in a regression analysis. (See the t-statistic and F-statistic tables at the end of the book for their corresponding critical values.) It is assumed that the reader is somewhat familiar with hypothesis testing and tests of significance in basic statistics.

Example Given the information from Excel's regression output in Figure 9.26, interpret the following:

1. Perform a hypothesis test on the slope and the intercept to see if they are *each* significant at a two-tailed alpha (α) of 0.05.
   The null hypothesis H_o is such that the slope $\beta_1 = 0$ and the alternate hypothesis H_a is such that $\beta_1 \neq 0$. The t-statistic calculated is 4.6877,

ANOVA

	df	SS	MS	F	Significance F
Regression	1	7.2014	7.2014	21.9747	0.0054
Residual	5	1.6386	0.3277		
Total	6	8.8400			

	Coefficients	Standard Error	t Stat	P-value	Lower 95%	Upper 95%	Lower 95.0%	Upper 95.0%
Intercept	4.3643	0.5826	7.4911	0.0007	2.8667	5.8619	2.8667	5.8619
X Variable 1	0.0845	0.0180	4.6877	0.0054	0.0382	0.1309	0.0382	0.1309

FIGURE 9.26   ANOVA and goodness-of-fit table.

which exceeds the t-critical (2.9687 obtained from the t-statistic table at the end of this book) for a two-tailed alpha of 0.05 and degrees of freedom $n - k = 7 - 1 = 6$.[4] Therefore, the null hypothesis is rejected and one can state that the slope is statistically significantly different from 0, indicating that the regression's estimate of the slope is statistically significant. This hypothesis test can also be performed by looking at the t-statistic's corresponding p-value (0.0054), which is less than the alpha of 0.05, which means the null hypothesis is rejected.[5] The hypothesis test is then applied to the intercept, where the null hypothesis H_o is such that the intercept $\beta_0 = 0$ and the alternate hypothesis H_a is such that $\beta_0 \neq 0$. The t-statistic calculated is 7.4911, which exceeds the critical t value of 2.9687 for $n - k$ ($7 - 1 = 6$) degrees of freedom, so, the null hypothesis is rejected, indicating that the intercept is statistically significantly different from 0, meaning that the regression's estimate of the intercept is statistically significant. The calculated p-value (0.0007) is also less than the alpha level, which means the null hypothesis is also rejected.

2. Perform a hypothesis test to see if both the slope and intercept are significant as a whole, in other words, if the estimated model is statistically significant at an alpha (α) of 0.05.

   The simultaneous null hypothesis H_o is such that $\beta_0 = \beta_1 = 0$ and the alternate hypothesis H_a is $\beta_0 \neq \beta_1 \neq 0$. The calculated F-value is 21.9747, which exceeds the critical F-value (5.99 obtained from the table at the end of this book) for k (1) degrees of freedom in the numerator and $n - k$ ($7 - 1 = 6$) degrees of freedom for the denominator, so the null hypothesis is rejected, indicating that both the slope and intercept are simultaneously significantly different from 0 and that the model as a whole is statistically significant. This result is confirmed by the p-value of 0.0054 (significance of F), which is less than the alpha value, thereby rejecting the null hypothesis and confirming that the regression as a whole is statistically significant.

Regression Statistics

R-Squared (coefficient of determination)	0.8146
Adjusted R-Squared	0.7776
Multiple R (multiple correlation coefficient)	0.9026
Standard Error of the Estimates (SE_y)	0.5725
n Observations	7

Regression Results

	Intercept	Ad Size
Coefficients	4.3643	0.0845
Standard Error	0.5826	0.0180
t-Statistic	7.4911	4.6877
p-Value	0.0007	*0.0054*
Lower 5%	2.8667	0.0382
Upper 95%	5.8619	0.1309

FIGURE 9.27 Additional regression output from Risk Simulator.

3. Using Risk Simulator's regression output in Figure 9.27, interpret the R^2 value. How is it related to the correlation coefficient?

The calculated R^2 is 0.8146, meaning that 81.46 percent of the variation in the dependent variable can be explained by the variation in the independent variable. The R^2 is simply the square of the correlation coefficient, that is, the correlation coefficient between the independent and dependent variable is 0.9026.

Regression Assumptions

The following six assumptions are the requirements for a regression analysis to work:

1. The relationship between the dependent and independent variables is *linear*.
2. The expected value of the errors or *residuals is zero*.
3. The errors are *independently and normally distributed*.
4. The variance of the errors is constant or *homoskedastic* and not varying over time.
5. The errors are independent and *uncorrelated* with the explanatory variables.
6. The independent variables are uncorrelated to each other, meaning that no *multicollinearity* exists.

One very simple method to verify some of these assumptions is to use a scatter plot. This approach is simple to use in a bivariate regression scenario. If the assumption of the linear model is valid, the plot of the observed dependent variable values against the independent variable values should suggest a linear band across the graph with no obvious departures from linearity. Outliers may appear as anomalous points in the graph, often in the upper right-hand or lower left-hand corner of the graph. However, a point may be an outlier in either an independent or dependent variable without necessarily being far from the general trend of the data.

If the linear model is not correct, the shape of the general trend of the X–Y plot may suggest the appropriate function to fit (e.g., a polynomial, exponential, or logistic function). Alternatively, the plot may suggest a reasonable transformation to apply. For example, if the X–Y plot arcs from lower left to upper right so that data points either very low or very high in the independent variable lie below the straight line suggested by the data, while the middle data points of the independent variable lie on or above that straight line, taking square roots or logarithms of the independent variable values may promote linearity.

If the assumption of equal variances or homoskedasticity for the dependent variable is correct, the plot of the observed dependent variable values against the independent variable should suggest a band across the graph with roughly equal vertical width for all values of the independent variable. That is, the shape of the graph should suggest a tilted cigar and not a wedge or a megaphone.

A fan pattern like the profile of a megaphone, with a noticeable flare either to the right or to the left in the scatter plot, suggests that the variance in the values increases in the direction where the fan pattern widens (usually as the sample mean increases), and this in turn suggests that a transformation of the dependent variable values may be needed.

As an example, Figure 9.28 shows a scatter plot of two variables: sales revenue (dependent variable) and marketing costs (independent variable). Clearly, there is a positive relationship between the two variables, as is evident from the regression results in Figure 9.29, where the slope of the regression equation is a positive value (0.7447). The relationship is also statistically significant at 0.05 alpha and the coefficient of determination is 0.43, indicating a somewhat weak but statistically significant relationship.

Compare that to a multiple linear regression in Figure 9.30, where another independent variable, pricing structure of the product, is added. The regression's adjusted coefficient of determination (adjusted R-squared) is now 0.62, indicating a much stronger regression model.[6] The pricing variable shows a negative relationship to the sales revenue, a very much expected result, as according to the law of demand in economics, a higher price point necessitates a lower quantity demanded, hence, lower sales revenues (this, of course, assumes an elastic demand curve). The t-statistics and corresponding probabilities (p-values) also indicate a statistically significant relationship.

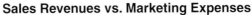

Sales Revenues vs. Marketing Expenses

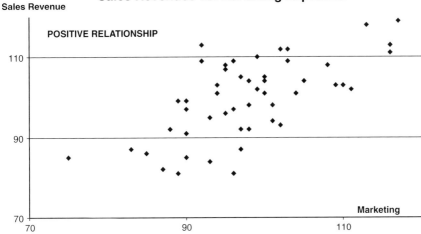

FIGURE 9.28 Scatter plot showing a positive relationship.

Summary:
    Number of series: 2
    Periods to forecast: 12
    Seasonality: none
    Error Measure: RMSE

Series: Sales Revenues

    Method: Multiple Linear Regression

    Statistics:
        R-squared: 0.430
        Adjusted R-squared: 0.4185
        SSE: 2732.9
        F Statistic: 36.263
        F Probability: 2. 32E-7
        Durbin-Watson: 2.370
        No. of Values: 50
        Independent variables: 1 included out of 1 selected

Regression Variables:

Variable	Coefficient	t Statistic	Probability
Constant	26.897	2.215	0.03154
Marketing Expenses	0.7447	6.0219	2.32E-07

FIGURE 9.29 Bivariate regression results for positive relationship.

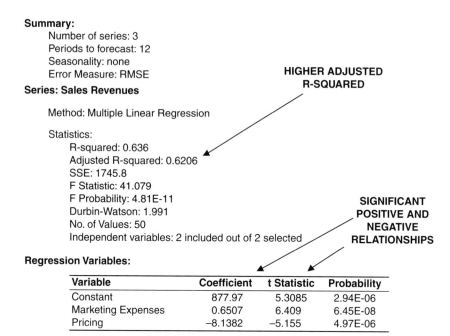

Summary:

  Number of series: 3
  Periods to forecast: 12
  Seasonality: none
  Error Measure: RMSE

HIGHER ADJUSTED R-SQUARED

Series: Sales Revenues

  Method: Multiple Linear Regression

  Statistics:
    R-squared: 0.636
    Adjusted R-squared: 0.6206
    SSE: 1745.8
    F Statistic: 41.079
    F Probability: 4.81E-11
    Durbin-Watson: 1.991
    No. of Values: 50
    Independent variables: 2 included out of 2 selected

SIGNIFICANT POSITIVE AND NEGATIVE RELATIONSHIPS

Regression Variables:

Variable	Coefficient	t Statistic	Probability
Constant	877.97	5.3085	2.94E-06
Marketing Expenses	0.6507	6.409	6.45E-08
Pricing	−8.1382	−5.155	4.97E-06

FIGURE 9.30 Multiple linear regression results for positive and negative relationships.

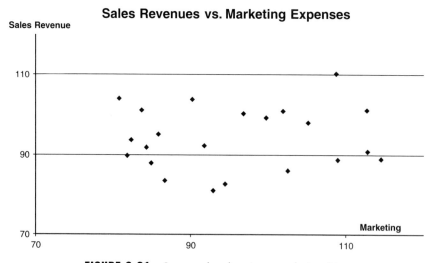

Sales Revenues vs. Marketing Expenses

FIGURE 9.31 Scatter plot showing no relationship.

Summary:

Number of series: 2
Periods to forecast: 12
Seasonality: 12 months
Error Measure: RMSE

Series: Sales Revenues

Method: Multiple Linear Regression

Statistics:
R-squared: 0.066
Adjusted R-squared: 0.04622
SSE: 13661
F Statistic: 3.3743
F Probability: 0.07242
Durbin-Watson: 2.173
No. of Values: 50
Independent variables: 1 included out of 1 selected

LOW R-SQUARED IS AN INDICATION OF LITTLE TO NO RELATIONSHIP

Regression Variables:

Variable	Coefficient	t Statistic	Probability
Constant	82.966	6.0363	2.20E-07
Marketing Expenses	0.2265	1.8369	0.07242

FIGURE 9.32 Multiple regression results showing no relationship.

In contrast, Figure 9.31 shows a scatter plot of two variables with little to no relationship, which is confirmed by the regression result in Figure 9.32, where the coefficient of determination is 0.066, close to being negligible. In addition, the calculated t-statistic and corresponding probability indicate that the marketing-expenses variable is statistically insignificant at the 0.05 alpha level, meaning that the regression equation is not significant (a fact that is also confirmed by the low F-statistic).

THE PITFALLS OF FORECASTING: OUTLIERS, NONLINEARITY, MULTICOLLINEARITY, HETEROSKEDASTICITY, AUTOCORRELATION, AND STRUCTURAL BREAKS

Forecasting is a balance between art and science. Using Risk Simulator can take care of the science, but it is almost impossible to take the art out of forecasting. In forecasting, experience and subject-matter expertise counts. One effective way to support this point is to look at some of the more common problems and violations of the required underlying assumptions of the data and forecast interpretation. Clearly there are many other technical issues, but the following list is sufficient to illustrate the pitfalls of forecasting and why sometimes the art (i.e., experience and expertise) is important:

- Out-of-Range Forecasts
- Nonlinearities
- Interactions
- Self-Selection Bias
- Survivorship Bias
- Control Variables
- Omitted Variables
- Redundant Variables
- Multicollinearity
- Bad-Fitting Model or Bad Goodness-of-Fit
- Error Measurements
- Structural Breaks
- Structural Shifts
- Model Errors (Granger Causality and Causality Loops)
- Autocorrelation, Serial Correlation, Leads and Lags
- Seasonality and Cyclicality
- Specification Errors and Incorrect Econometric Methods
- Micronumerosity
- Bad Data and Data Collection Errors
- Nonstationary Data, Random Walks, Nonpredictability, and Stochastic Processes (Brownian Motion, Mean-Reversion, Jump-Diffusion, Mixed Processes)
- Nonspherical and Dependent Errors
- Heteroskedasticity and Homoskedasticity
- Many other technical issues!

Analysts sometimes use historical data to make *out-of-range forecasts* that, depending on the forecast variable, could be disastrous. Take a simple yet extreme case of a cricket. Did you know that if you caught some crickets, put them in a controlled lab environment, raised the ambient temperature, and counted the average number of chirps per minute, these chirps are relatively predictable? You might get a pretty good fit and a high R-squared value. So, the next time you go out on a date with your spouse or significant other and hear some crickets chirping on the side of the road, stop and count the number of chirps per minute. Then, using your regression forecast equation, you can approximate the temperature, and the chances are that you would be fairly close to the actual temperature. But here are some problems: Suppose you take the poor cricket and toss it into an oven at

450 degrees Fahrenheit, what happens? Well, you are going to hear a large "pop" instead of the predicted 150 chirps per minute! Conversely, toss it into the freezer at −32 degrees Fahrenheit and you will not hear the negative chirps that were predicted in your model. That is the problem of out-of-sample or out-of-range forecasts.

Suppose that in the past, your company spent different amounts in marketing each year and saw improvements in sales and profits as a result of these marketing campaigns. Further assume that, historically, the firm spends between $10M and $20M in marketing each year, and for every dollar spent in marketing, you get $5 back in net profits. Does that mean the CEO should come up with a plan to spend $500M in marketing the next year? After all, the prediction model says there is a 5× return, meaning the firm will get $2.5B in net profit increase. Clearly this is not going to be the case. If it were, why not keep spending infinitely? The issue here is, again, an out-of-range forecast as well as *nonlinearity*. Revenues will not increase linearly at a multiple of five for each dollar spent in marketing expense, going on infinitely. Perhaps there might be some initial linear relationship, but this will most probably become nonlinear, perhaps taking the shape of a logistic S-curve, with a high-growth early phase followed by some diminishing marginal returns and eventual saturation and decline. After all, how many iPhones can a person own? At some point you have reached your total market potential and any additional marketing you spend will further flood the media airwaves and eventually cut into and reduce your profits. This is the issue of *interactions* among variables.

Think of this another way. Suppose you are a psychologist and are interested in student aptitude in writing essays under pressure. So you round up 100 volunteers, give them a pretest to determine their IQ levels, and divide the students into two groups: the brilliant Group A and the not-so-brilliant Group B, without telling the students, of course. Then you administer a written essay test twice to both groups; the first test has a 30-minute deadline and the second test, with a different but comparably difficult question, a 60-minute window. You then determine if time and intelligence has an effect on exam scores. A well-thought-out experiment, or so you think. The results might differ depending on whether you gave the students the 30-minute test first and then the 60-minute test or vice versa. As the not-so-brilliant students will tend to be anxious during an exam, taking the 30-minute test first may increase their stress level, possibly causing them to give up easily. Conversely, taking the longer test first might make them ambivalent and not really care about doing it well. Of course, we can come up with many other issues with this experiment. The point is, there might be some interaction among the sequence of exams taken, intelligence, and how students fare under pressure, and so forth.

The student volunteers are just that, volunteers, and so there might be a *self-selection bias*. Another example of self-selection is a clinical research program on sports-enhancement techniques that might only attract die-hard sports enthusiasts, whereas the couch potatoes among us will not even bother participating, let alone be in the mediagraphics readership of the sports magazines in which the advertisements were placed. Therefore, the sample might be biased even before the experiment ever started. Getting back to the student test-taking volunteers, there is also an issue of *survivorship bias*, where the really not-so-brilliant students just never show up for the essay test, possibly because of their negative affinity towards exams. This fickle-mindedness and many other variables that are not *controlled* for in the experiment may actually be reflected in the exam grade. What about the students' facility with English or whatever language the exam was administered in? How about the number of beers they had the night before (being hung over while taking an exam does not help your grades at all)? These are all *omitted variables*, which means that the predictability of the model is reduced should these variables not be accounted for. It is like trying to predict the company's revenues the next few years without accounting for the price increase you expect, the recession the country is heading into, or the introduction of a new, revolutionary product line.

However, sometimes too much data can actually be bad. Now, let us go back to the students again. Suppose you undertake another research project and sample another 100 students, obtain their grade point average at the university, and ask them how many parties they go to on average per week, the number of hours they study on average per week, the number of beers they have per week (the drink of choice for college students), and the number of dates they go on per week. The idea is to see which variable, if any, affects a student's grade on average. A reasonable experiment, or so you think. The issue in this case is *redundant variables* and, perhaps worse, severe *multicollinearity*. In other words, chances are, the more parties they attend, the more people they meet, the more dates they go on per week, and the more drinks they would have on the dates and at the parties, and being drunk half the time, the less time they have to study! All variables in this case are highly correlated to each other. In fact, you probably only need one variable, such as hours of study per week, to determine the average student's grade point. Adding in all these exogenous variables confounds the forecast equation, making the forecast less reliable.

In fact, as you see later in this chapter, when you have severe multicollinearity, which just means there are multiple variables ("multi") that are changing together ("co-") in a linear fashion ("linearity"), the regression equation cannot be run. In less severe multicollinearity such as with redundant variables, the adjusted R-square might be high but the p-values will be high as well, indicating that you have a *bad-fitting* model. The prediction errors will be large. And while it might be counterintuitive, the problem of multicollinearity, of having too much data, is worse than having less data or having omitted variables. And speaking of bad-fitting models, what is a good R-square *goodness-of-fit* value? This, too, is subjective. How good is your prediction model, and how accurate is it? Unless you measure accuracy using some statistical procedures for your *error measurements* such as those provided by Risk Simulator (e.g., mean absolute deviation, root mean square, p-values, Akaike, and Schwartz criterion, and many others) and perhaps input a distributional assumption around these errors to run a simulation on the model, your forecasts may be highly inaccurate.

Another issue is *structural breaks*. For example, remember the poor cricket? What happens when you take a hammer and smash it? Well, there goes your prediction model! You just had a structural break. A company filing for bankruptcy will see its stock price plummet and delisted on the stock exchange, a major natural catastrophe or terrorist attack on a city can cause such a break, and so forth. *Structural shifts* are less severe changes, such as a recessionary period, or a company going into new international markets, engaged in a merger and acquisition, and so forth, where the fundamentals are still there but values might be shifted upward or downward.

Sometimes you run into a *causality loop* problem. We know that correlation does not imply causation. Nonetheless, sometimes there is a *Granger causation*, which means that one event causes another but in a specified direction, or sometimes there is a *causality loop*, where you have different variables that loop around and perhaps back into themselves. Examples of loops include systems engineering where changing an event in the system causes some ramifications across other events, which feeds back into itself causing a feedback loop. Here is an example of a causality loop going the wrong way: Suppose you collect information on crime rate statistics for the 50 states in the United States for a specific year, and you run a regression model to predict the crime rate using police expenditures per capita, gross state product, unemployment rate, number of university graduates per year, and so forth. And further suppose you see that police expenditures per capita is highly predictive of crime rate, which makes sense, and say the relationship is positive, and if you use these criteria as your prediction model (i.e., the dependent variable is crime rate and independent variable is police expenditure), you have just run into a causality loop issue. That is, you are saying that the higher the police expenditure per capita, the higher the crime rate! Well, then, either the cops are corrupt or they are not really good at their jobs. A better approach might be to use the previous year's police expenditure to predict this year's crime rate; that is, using a *lead* or *lag* on the data. So, more crime necessitates a larger police force, which will, in turn, reduce the crime rate, but going from one step to the next takes time and the lags and leads take the time element into account. Back to the marketing problem, if you spend more on marketing now, you may not see a rise in net income for a few months or even years. Effects are not immediate and the time lag is required to better predict the outcomes.

Many time-series data, especially financial and economic data, are *autocorrelated*; that is, the data is correlated to itself in the past. For instance, January's sales revenue for the company is probably related to the previous month's performance, which itself may be related to the month before. If there is *seasonality* in the variable, then perhaps last January's sales are related to the last 12 months, or January of the year before, and so forth. These seasonal cycles are repeatable and somewhat predictable. You sell more ski tickets in winter than in summer, and, guess what, next winter you will again sell more tickets than next summer, and so forth. In contrast, *cyclicality* such as the business cycle, the economic cycle, the housing cycle, and so forth, is a lot less predictable. You can use autocorrelations (relationship to your own past) and lags (one variable correlated to another variable lagged a certain number of periods) for predictions involving seasonality, but, at the same time, you would require additional data. Usually, you need historical data of at least two seasonal cycles in length to even start running a seasonal model with any level of confidence, otherwise you run into a problem of *micronumerosity*, or lack of data. Regardless of the predictive approach used, the issue of *bad data* is always a concern. Either badly coded data or just data from a bad source, incomplete data points, and *data collection errors* are always a problem in any forecast model.

Next, there is the potential for a *specification error* or using the *incorrect econometric model* error. You can run a seasonal model where there are no seasonalities, thus creating a specification problem, or use an ARIMA when you should be using a GARCH model, creating an econometric model error. Sometimes there are variables that are considered *nonstationary*; that is, the data are not well behaved. These types of variables are really not predictable. An example is stock prices. Try predicting stock prices and you quickly find out that you cannot do a reasonable job at all. Stock prices usually follow something called a random walk, where values are randomly changing all over the place. The mathematical relationship of this random walk is known and is called a *stochastic process*, but the exact outcome is not known for certain. Typically, simulations are required to run random walks, and these stochastic processes come in a variety of forms, including the Brownian motion (e.g., ideal for stock prices), mean-reversion (e.g., ideal for interest rates and inflation), jump-diffusion (e.g., ideal for price of oil and price of electricity), and mixed processes of several forms combined into one. In this case, picking the wrong process is also a specification error.

In most forecasting methods, we assume that the forecast errors are *spherical* or *normally distributed*. That is, the forecast model is the best-fitting model one can develop that minimizes all the forecast errors, which means whatever errors that are left over are random white noise that is normally distributed (a normal distribution is symmetrical, which means you are equally likely to be underestimating as you are overestimating the forecast). If the errors are not normal and skewed, you are either overestimating or underestimating things, and adjustments need to be made. Further, these errors, because they are random, should be random over time, which means that they should be *identically and independently distributed as normal,* or *i.i.d. normal.* If they are not, then you have some autocorrelations in the data and should be building an autocorrelation model instead.

Finally, if the errors are i.i.d. normal, then the data are *homoskedastic*; that is, the forecast errors are identical over time. Think of it as a tube that contains all your data, and you put a skinny stick in that tube. The amount of wiggle room for that stick is the error of your forecast (and, by extension, if your data are spread out, the tube's diameter is large and the wiggle room is large, which means that the error is large; conversely, if the diameter of the tube is small, the error is small, such that if the diameter of the tube is exactly the size of the stick, the prediction error is zero and your R-squared goodness-of-fit is 100 percent). The amount of wiggle room is constant going into the future. This condition is ideal and what you want. The problem is, especially in nonstationary data or data with some *outliers*, that there is *heteroskedasticity*, which means that instead of a constant diameter tube, you now have a cone, with a small diameter initially that increases over time. This fanning out (Figure 9.40) means that there is an increase in wiggle room or errors the further out you go in time. An example of this fanning out is stock prices, where if the stock price today is $50, you can forecast and say that there is a 90 percent probability the stock price will be between $48 and $52 tomorrow, or between $45 and $55 in a week, and perhaps between $20 and $100 in six months, holding everything else constant. In other words, the prediction errors increase over time.

So you see, there are many potential issues in forecasting. Knowing your variables and the theory behind the behavior of these variables is an art that depends a lot on experience, comparables with other similar variables, historical data, and expertise in modeling. There is no such thing as a single model that will solve all these issues automatically. See the sections on Data Diagnostics and Statistical Analysis later in the chapter for the two tools in Risk Simulator that help in identifying some of these problems.

Other than being good modeling practice to create scatter plots prior to performing regression analysis, the scatter plot can also sometimes, on a fundamental basis, provide significant amounts of information regarding the

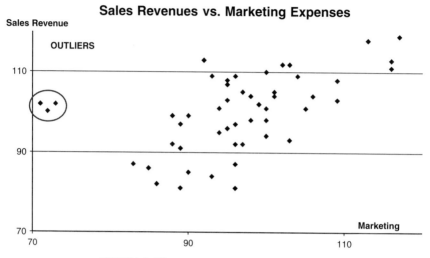

FIGURE 9.33   Scatter plot showing outliers.

behavior of the data series. Blatant violations of the regression assumptions can be spotted easily and effortlessly, without the need for more detailed and fancy econometric specification tests. For instance, Figure 9.33 shows the existence of outliers. Figure 9.34's regression results, which include the outliers, indicate that the coefficient of determination is only 0.252 as compared to 0.447 in Figure 9.35 when the outliers are removed.

Values may not be identically distributed because of the presence of outliers. Outliers are anomalous values in the data. Outliers may have a strong influence over the fitted slope and intercept, giving a poor fit to the bulk of the data points. Outliers tend to increase the estimate of residual variance, lowering the chance of rejecting the null hypothesis. They may be due to recording errors, which may be correctable, or they may be due to the dependent-variable values not all being sampled from the same population. Apparent outliers may also be due to the dependent-variable values being from the same, but nonnormal, population. Outliers may show up clearly in an X–Y scatter plot of the data, as points that do not lie near the general linear trend of the data. A point may be an unusual value in either an independent or dependent variable without necessarily being an outlier in the scatter plot.

The method of least squares involves minimizing the sum of the squared vertical distances between each data point and the fitted line. Because of this, the fitted line can be highly sensitive to outliers. In other words, least squares regression is not resistant to outliers; thus, neither is the fitted-slope estimate.

Summary:
>Number of series: 2
>Periods to forecast: 12
>Seasonality: 12 months
>Error Measure: RMSE

Series: Sales Revenues

>Method: Multiple Linear Regression

>Statistics:
>>R-squared: 0.252
>>Adjusted R-squared: 0.2367
>>SSE: 3417.6
>>F Statistic: 16.198
>>F Probability: 2.01E-4
>>Durbin-Watson: 1.945
>>No. of Values: 50
>>Independent variables: 1 included out of 1 selected

Regression Variables:

Variable	Coefficient	t Statistic	Probability
Constant	53.269	4.5619	3.51E-05
Marketing Expenses	0.4857	4.0247	2.01E-04

FIGURE 9.34   Regression results with outliers.

A point vertically removed from the other points can cause the fitted line to pass close to it, instead of following the general linear trend of the rest of the data, especially if the point is relatively far horizontally from the center of the data (the point represented by the mean of the independent variable and the mean of the dependent variable). Such points are said to have high leverage: the center acts as a fulcrum, and the fitted line pivots toward high-leverage points, perhaps fitting the main body of the data poorly. A data point that is extreme in dependent variables but lies near the center of the data horizontally will not have much effect on the fitted slope, but by changing the estimate of the mean of the dependent variable, it may affect the fitted estimate of the intercept.

However, great care should be taken when deciding if the outliers should be removed. Although in most cases when outliers are removed, the regression results look better, a priori justification must first exist. For instance, if one is regressing the performance of a particular firm's stock returns, outliers caused by downturns in the stock market should be included; these are not truly outliers as they are inevitabilities in the business cycle. Forgoing these outliers and using the regression equation to forecast one's retirement fund

Summary:
>   Number of series: 2
>   Periods to forecast: 12
>   Seasonality: 12 months
>   Error Measure: RMSE

Series: Sales Revenues

>   Method: Multiple Linear Regression

>   Statistics:
>   R-squared: 0.447
>   Adjusted R-squared: 0.4343
>   SSE: 2524.9
>   F Statistic: 36.321
>   F Probability: 2.84E-7
>   Durbin-Watson: 2.242
>   No. of Values: 47
>   Independent variables: 1 included out of 1 selected

COMPARE R-SQUARED BETWEEN REGRESSION WITH OUTLIERS AND WITHOUT OUTLIERS!

Regression Variables:

Variable	Coefficient	t Statistic	Probability
Constant	19.447	1.4512	0.1537
Marketing Expenses	0.8229	6.0267	2.84E-07

FIGURE 9.35   Regression results with outliers deleted.

based on the firm's stocks will yield incorrect results at best. In contrast, suppose the outliers are caused by a single nonrecurring business condition (e.g., merger and acquisition) and such business structural changes are not forecast to recur, then these outliers should be removed and the data cleansed prior to running a regression analysis.

Figure 9.36 shows a scatter plot with a nonlinear relationship between the dependent and independent variables. In a situation such as the one in Figure 9.36, a linear regression will not be optimal. A nonlinear transformation should first be applied to the data before running a regression. One simple approach is to take the natural logarithm of the independent variable (other approaches include taking the square root or raising the independent variable to the second or third power) and regress the sales revenue on this transformed marketing-cost data series. Figure 9.37 shows the regression results with a coefficient of determination at 0.938, as compared to 0.707 in Figure 9.38 when a simple linear regression is applied to the original data series without the nonlinear transformation.

If the linear model is not the correct one for the data, then the slope and intercept estimates and the fitted values from the linear regression will

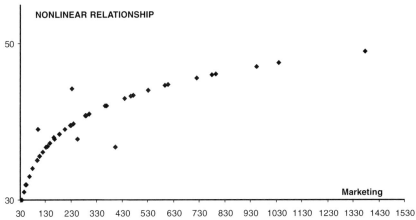

FIGURE 9.36 Scatter plot showing a nonlinear relationship.

Summary:
    Number of series: 2
    Periods to forecast: 12
    Seasonality: none
    Error Measure: RMSE

Series: Sales Revenues

    Method: Multiple Linear Regression

    Statistics:
        R-squared: 0.938
        Adjusted R-squared: 0.9364
        SSE: 101.74
        F Statistic: 722.25
        F Probability: 1.39E-30
        Durbin-Watson: 1.825
        No. of Values: 50
        Independent variables: 1 included out of 1 selected

Regression Variables:

Variable	Coefficient	t Statistic	Probability
Constant	10.208	9.6141	9.03E-13
Nonlinear Marketing Expenses	5.3783	26.875	1.39E-30

FIGURE 9.37 Regression results using a nonlinear transformation.

Summary:
Number of series: 3
Periods to forecast: 12
Seasonality: none
Error Measure: RMSE

Series: Sales Revenues

Method: Multiple Linear Regression

Statistics:
R-squared: 0.707
Adjusted R-squared: 0.7013
SSE: 477.72
F Statistic: 116.04
F Probability: 2.09E-14
Durbin-Watson: 0.992
No. of Values: 50
Independent variables: 1 included out of 1 selected

Regression Variables:

Variable	Coefficient	t Statistic	Probability
Constant	33.358	52.658	4.00E-44
Linear Marketing Expenses	0.01639	10.772	2.09E-14

FIGURE 9.38 Regression results using linear data.

be biased, and the fitted slope and intercept estimates will not be meaningful. Over a restricted range of independent or dependent variables, nonlinear models may be well approximated by linear models (this is in fact the basis of linear interpolation), but for accurate prediction, a model appropriate to the data should be selected. An examination of the X–Y scatter plot may reveal whether the linear model is appropriate. If there is a great deal of variation in the dependent variable, it may be difficult to decide what the appropriate model is. In this case, the linear model may do as well as any other, and has the virtue of simplicity. Refer to Appendix—Detecting and Fixing Heteroskedasticity for specification tests of nonlinearity and heteroskedasticity as well as ways to fix them.

However, great care should be taken here as both the original linear data series of marketing costs should not be added with the nonlinearly transformed marketing costs in the regression analysis. Otherwise, multicollinearity occurs; that is, marketing costs are highly correlated to the natural logarithm of marketing costs, and if both are used as independent variables in a multivariate regression analysis, the assumption of no

Summary:

Number of series: 3
Periods to forecast: 12
Seasonality: none
Error Measure: RMSE

WATCH OUT FOR MULTICOLLINEARITY!

Series: Sales Revenues

Method: Multiple Linear Regression

Statistics:

R-squared: 0.938
Adjusted R-squared: 0.9358
SSE: 100.59
F Statistic: 357.93
F Probability: 3.60E-29
Durbin-Watson: 1.807
No. of Values: 50
Independent variables: 2 included out of 2 selected

USE ADJUSTED R-SQUARED FOR MULTIPLE REGRESSION

NONLINEAR TAKES OVER LINEAR

Regression Variables:

Variable	Coefficient	t Statistic	Probability
Constant	9.0966	4.9143	1.12E-05
Linear Marketing Expenses	−0.001098	−0.7349	0.4661
Nonlinear Marketing Expenses	5.6542	13.275	1.62E-17

FIGURE 9.39   Regression results using both linear and nonlinear transformations.

multicollinearity is violated and the regression analysis breaks down. Figure 9.39 illustrates what happens when multicollinearity strikes. Notice that the coefficient of determination (0.938) is the same as the nonlinear transformed regression (Figure 9.37). However, the adjusted coefficient of determination went down from 0.9364 (Figure 9.37) to 0.9358 (Figure 9.39). In addition, the previously statistically significant marketing-costs variable in Figure 9.38 now becomes insignificant (Figure 9.39) with a probability value increasing from close to zero to 0.4661. A basic symptom of multicollinearity is low t-statistics coupled with a high R-squared (Figure 9.39). See Appendix—Detecting and Fixing Multicollinearity—for further details on detecting multicollinearity in a regression.

Another common violation is heteroskedasticity, that is, the variance of the errors increases over time. Figure 9.40 illustrates this case, where the width of the vertical data fluctuations increases or fans out over time. In this example, the data points have been changed to exaggerate the effect. However, in most time-series analysis, checking for heteroskedasticity is a much more difficult task. See Appendix—Detecting and Fixing Heteroskedasticity for further details. And correcting for heteroskedasticity is an even greater

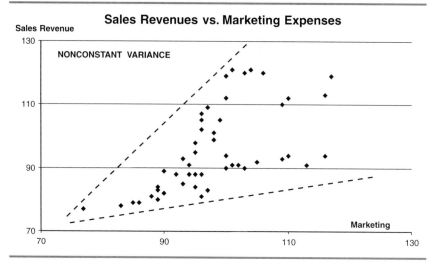

FIGURE 9.40   Scatter plot showing heteroskedasticity with nonconstant variance.

Summary:
Number of series: 2
Periods to forecast: 12
Seasonality: 12 months
Error Measure: RMSE

WATCH OUT FOR HETEROSKEDASTICITY!

Series: Sales Revenues

Method: Multiple Linear Regression

Statistics:
R-squared: 0.398
Adjusted R-squared: 0.3858
SSE: 5190.1
F Statistic: 31.777
F Probability: 8.94E-7
Durbin-Watson: 2.755
No. of Values: 50
Independent variables: 1 included out of 1 selected

Regression Variables:

Variable	Coefficient	t Statistic	Probability
Constant	1.5742	0.09421	0.9253
Marketing Expenses	0.9586	5.6371	8.94E-07

FIGURE 9.41   Regression results with heteroskedasticity.

challenge.[7] Notice in Figure 9.41 that the coefficient of determination drops significantly when heteroskedasticity exists. As is, the current regression model is insufficient and incomplete.

If the variance of the dependent variable is not constant, then the error's variance will not be constant. The most common form of such heteroskedasticity in the dependent variable is that the variance of the dependent variable may increase as the mean of the dependent variable increases for data with positive independent and dependent variables.

Unless the heteroskedasticity of the dependent variable is pronounced, its effect will not be severe: The least-squares estimates will still be unbiased, and the estimates of the slope and intercept will either be normally distributed if the errors are normally distributed, or at least normally distributed asymptotically (as the number of data points becomes large) if the errors are not normally distributed. The estimate for the variance of the slope and overall variance will be inaccurate, but the inaccuracy is not likely to be substantial if the independent-variable values are symmetric about their mean.

Heteroskedasticity of the dependent variable is usually detected informally by examining the X–Y scatter plot of the data before performing the regression. If both nonlinearity and unequal variances are present, employing a transformation of the dependent variable may have the effect of simultaneously improving the linearity and promoting equality of the variances. Otherwise, a weighted least-squares linear regression may be the preferred method of dealing with nonconstant variance of the dependent variable.

OTHER TECHNICAL ISSUES IN
REGRESSION ANALYSIS

If the data to be analyzed by linear regression violate one or more of the linear regression assumptions, the results of the analysis may be incorrect or misleading. For example, if the assumption of independence is violated, then linear regression is not appropriate. If the assumption of normality is violated or outliers are present, then the linear regression goodness-of-fit test may not be the most powerful or informative test available, and this could mean the difference between detecting a linear fit or not. A nonparametric, robust, or resistant regression method, a transformation, a weighted least-squares linear regression, or a nonlinear model may result in a better fit. If the population variance for the dependent variable is not constant, a weighted least-squares linear regression or a transformation of the dependent variable may provide a means of fitting a regression adjusted for the inequality of the variances. Often, the impact of an assumption violation on the linear regression result depends on the extent of the violation (such as how nonconstant the variance of the dependent variable is, or how skewed the dependent variable population distribution is). Some small violations may have little practical effect on the analysis, while other violations may render the linear regression result useless and incorrect. Other potential assumption violations include:

- Lack of independence in the dependent variable.
- Independent variable is random, not fixed.
- Special problems with few data points.
- Special problems with regression through the origin.

Lack of Independence in the Dependent Variable

Whether the independent-variable values are independent of each other is generally determined by the structure of the experiment from which they arise. The dependent-variable values collected over time may be autocorrelated. For serially correlated dependent-variable values, the estimates of the slope and intercept will be unbiased, but the estimates of their variances will not be reliable and hence the validity of certain statistical goodness-of-fit tests will be flawed. An ARIMA model may be better in such circumstances.

The Independent Variable Is Random, Not Fixed

The usual linear regression model assumes that the observed independent variables are fixed, not random. If the independent values are not under the control of the experimenter (i.e., are observed but not set), and if there is in fact underlying variance in the independent variable, but they have the same variance, the linear model is called an errors-in-variables model or structural model. The least-squares fit will still give the best linear predictor of the dependent variable, but the estimates of the slope and intercept will be biased (will not have expected values equal to the true slope and variance). A stochastic forecast model may be a better alternative here.

Special Problems with Few Data Points (Micronumerosity)

If the number of data points is small (also termed *micronumerosity*), it may be difficult to detect assumption violations. With small samples, assumption violations such as nonnormality or heteroskedasticity of variances are difficult to detect even when they are present. With a small number of data points, linear regression offers less protection against violation of assumptions. With few data points, it may be hard to determine how well the fitted line matches the data, or whether a nonlinear function would be more appropriate.

Even if none of the test assumptions are violated, a linear regression on a small number of data points may not have sufficient power to detect a significant difference between the slope and zero, even if the slope is nonzero. The power depends on the residual error, the observed variation in the independent variable, the selected significance alpha level of the test, and the number of data points. Power decreases as the residual variance increases, decreases as the significance level is decreased (i.e., as the test is made more stringent), increases as the variation in the observed independent variable increases, and increases as the number of data points increases. If a statistical significance test with a small number of data points produces a surprisingly nonsignificant probability value, then lack of power may be the reason. The best time to avoid such problems is in the design stage of an experiment, when appropriate minimum sample sizes can be determined, perhaps in consultation with an econometrician, before data collection begins.

Special Problems with Regression Through the Origin

The effects of nonconstant variance of the dependent variable can be particularly severe for a linear regression when the line is forced through the origin: The estimate of variance for the fitted slope may be much smaller than the actual variance, making the test for the slope nonconservative (more likely to reject the null hypothesis that the slope is zero than what the stated significance level indicates). In general, unless there is a structural or theoretical reason to assume that the intercept is zero, it is preferable to fit both the slope and intercept.

REGRESSION AND FORECASTING DIAGNOSTIC TOOL

The regression and forecasting diagnostic tool is the advanced analytical tool in Risk Simulator used to determine the econometric properties of your data. The diagnostics include checking the data for heteroskedasticity, nonlinearity, outliers, specification errors, micronumerosity, stationarity and stochastic properties, normality and sphericity of the errors, and multicollinearity. Each test is described in more detail in their respective reports in the model.

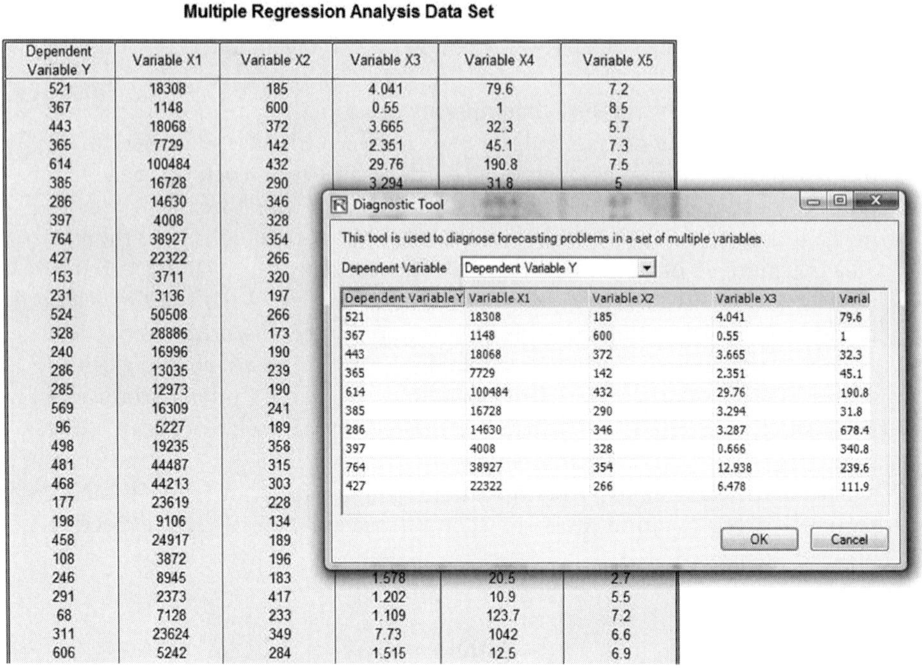

Multiple Regression Analysis Data Set

Dependent Variable Y	Variable X1	Variable X2	Variable X3	Variable X4	Variable X5
521	18308	185	4.041	79.6	7.2
367	1148	600	0.55	1	8.5
443	18068	372	3.665	32.3	5.7
365	7729	142	2.351	45.1	7.3
614	100484	432	29.76	190.8	7.5
385	16728	290	3.294	31.8	5
286	14630	346			
397	4008	328			
764	38927	354			
427	22322	266			
153	3711	320			
231	3136	197			
524	50508	266			
328	28886	173			
240	16996	190			
286	13035	239			
285	12973	190			
569	16309	241			
96	5227	189			
498	19235	358			
481	44487	315			
468	44213	303			
177	23619	228			
198	9106	134			
458	24917	189			
108	3872	196			
246	8945	183	1.578	20.5	2.7
291	2373	417	1.202	10.9	5.5
68	7128	233	1.109	123.7	7.2
311	23624	349	7.73	1042	6.6
606	5242	284	1.515	12.5	6.9

Diagnostic Tool dialog:

This tool is used to diagnose forecasting problems in a set of multiple variables.

Dependent Variable: Dependent Variable Y

Dependent Variable Y	Variable X1	Variable X2	Variable X3	Varial
521	18308	185	4.041	79.6
367	1148	600	0.55	1
443	18068	372	3.665	32.3
365	7729	142	2.351	45.1
614	100484	432	29.76	190.8
385	16728	290	3.294	31.8
286	14630	346	3.287	678.4
397	4008	328	0.666	340.8
764	38927	354	12.938	239.6
427	22322	266	6.478	111.9

OK   Cancel

FIGURE 9.42 Running the data diagnostic tool.

Procedure

1. Open the example model (*Risk Simulator | Examples | Regression Diagnostics*), and go to the *Time-Series Data* worksheet, and select the data including the variable names (cells C5:H55).
2. Click on *Risk Simulator | Tools | Diagnostic Tool*.
3. Check the data and select the *Dependent Variable Y* from the dropdown menu. Click *OK* when finished (Figure 9.42).

A common violation in forecasting and regression analysis is heteroskedasticity; that is, the variance of the errors increases over time (see Figure 9.43 for test results using the diagnostic tool). Visually, the width of the vertical data fluctuations increases or fans out over time, and, typically, the coefficient of determination (R-squared coefficient) drops significantly when heteroskedasticity exists. If the variance of the dependent variable is not constant, then the error's variance will not be constant. Unless the heteroskedasticity of the dependent variable is pronounced, its effect will not be severe: The least-squares estimates will still be unbiased, and the estimates

Diagnostic Results

	Heteroskedasticity		Micronumerosity	Outliers			Nonlinearity	
Variable	W-Test p-value	Hypothesis Test result	Approximation result	Natural Lower Bound	Natural Upper Bound	Number of Potential Outliers	Nonlinear Test p-value	Hypothesis Test result
Y			no problems					
Variable X1	0.2543	Homoskedastic	no problems	−7.86	671.70	2	0.2458	linear
Variable X2	0.3371	Homoskedastic	no problems	−21377.95	64713.03	3	0.0335	nonlinear
Variable X3	0.3649	Homoskedastic	no problems	77.47	445.93	2	0.0305	nonlinear
Variable X4	0.3066	Homoskedastic	no problems	−5.77	15.69	3	0.9298	linear
Variable X5	0.2495	Homoskedastic	no problems	−295.96	628.21	4	0.2727	linear
				3.35	9.38	3		

FIGURE 9.43 Results from tests of outliers, heteroskedasticity, micronumerosity, and nonlinearity.

of the slope and intercept will either be normally distributed if the errors are normally distributed or at least normally distributed asymptotically (as the number of data points becomes large) if the errors are not normally distributed. The estimate for the variance of the slope and overall variance will be inaccurate, but the inaccuracy is not likely to be substantial if the independent-variable values are symmetric about their mean.

If the number of data points is small (micronumerosity), it may be difficult to detect assumption violations. With small sample sizes, assumption violations such as nonnormality or heteroskedasticity of variances are difficult to detect even when they are present. With a small number of data points, linear regression offers less protection against violation of assumptions. With few data points, it may be hard to determine how well the fitted line matches the data, or whether a nonlinear function would be more appropriate. Even if none of the test assumptions are violated, a linear regression on a small number of data points may not have sufficient power to detect a significant difference between the slope and zero, even if the slope is nonzero. The power depends on the residual error, the observed variation in the independent variable, the selected significance alpha level of the test, and the number of data points. Power decreases as the residual variance increases, decreases as the significance level is decreased (i.e., as the test is made more stringent), increases as the variation in observed independent variable increases, and increases as the number of data points increases.

Values may not be identically distributed because of the presence of outliers. Outliers are anomalous values in the data. Outliers may have a strong influence over the fitted slope and intercept, giving a poor fit to the bulk of the data points. Outliers tend to increase the estimate of residual variance, lowering the chance of rejecting the null hypothesis; that is, creating higher prediction errors. They may be due to recording errors, which may be correctable, or they may be due to the dependent-variable values not all being sampled from the same population. Apparent outliers may also be due to the dependent-variable values being from the same, but non-normal, population. However, a point may be an unusual value in either an independent or dependent variable without necessarily being an outlier in the scatter plot. In regression analysis, the fitted line can be highly sensitive to outliers. In other words, least squares regression is not resistant to outliers, thus, neither is the fitted-slope estimate. A point vertically removed from the other points can cause the fitted line to pass close to it, instead of following the general linear trend of the rest of the data, especially if the point is relatively far horizontally from the center of the data. However, great care should be taken when deciding if the outliers should be removed. Although in most cases when outliers are removed, the regression results look better, *a priori* justification must first exist. For instance, if one is regressing the performance of a particular firm's stock returns, outliers caused by downturns in the stock market should be included; these are not truly outliers as they are inevitabilities in the business cycle. Forgoing these outliers and using the regression equation to forecast one's retirement fund based on the firm's stocks will yield incorrect results at best. In contrast, suppose the outliers are caused by a single nonrecurring business condition (e.g., merger and acquisition) and such business structural changes are not forecast to recur, then these outliers should be removed and the data cleansed prior to running a regression analysis. The analysis here only identifies outliers and it is up to the user to determine if they should remain or be excluded.

Sometimes, a nonlinear relationship between the dependent and independent variables is more appropriate than a linear relationship. In such cases, running a linear regression will not be optimal. If the linear model is not the correct form, then the slope and intercept estimates and the fitted values from the linear regression will be biased, and the fitted slope and intercept estimates will not be meaningful. Over a restricted range of independent or dependent variables, nonlinear models may be well approximated by linear models (this is, in fact, the basis of linear interpolation), but for accurate prediction, a model appropriate to the data should be selected. A nonlinear transformation should first be applied to the data before running a regression. One simple approach is to take the natural logarithm of the independent variable (other approaches include taking the square root or raising the independent variable to the second or third power) and run a regression or forecast using the nonlinearly transformed data.

Another typical issue when forecasting time-series data is whether the independent-variable values are truly independent of each other or are actually dependent. Dependent-variable values collected over a time series may be autocorrelated. For serially correlated dependent-variable values, the estimates of the slope and intercept will be unbiased, but the estimates of their forecast and variances will not be reliable and, hence, the validity of certain statistical goodness-of-fit tests will be flawed. For instance, interest rates, inflation rates, sales, revenues, and many other time-series data are typically autocorrelated, where the value in the current period is related to the value in a previous period, and so forth (clearly, the inflation rate in March is related to February's level, which, in turn, is related to January's level, etc.). Ignoring such blatant relationships will yield biased and less accurate forecasts. In such events, an autocorrelated regression model or an ARIMA model may be better suited (*Risk Simulator | Forecasting | ARIMA*). Finally, the autocorrelation functions of a series that is nonstationary tend to decay slowly (see nonstationary report in the model).

If autocorrelation $AC(1)$ is nonzero, it means that the series is first-order serially correlated. If $AC(k)$ dies off more or less geometrically with increasing lag, it implies that the series follows a low-order autoregressive process. If AC(k) drops to zero after a small number of lags, it implies that the series follows a low-order moving-average process. Partial correlation PAC(k) measures the correlation of values that are k periods apart after removing the correlation from the intervening lags. If the pattern of autocorrelation can be captured by an autoregression of order less than k, then the partial autocorrelation at lag k will be close to zero. Ljung–Box Q-statistics and their p-values at lag k have the null hypothesis that there is no autocorrelation up to order k. The dotted lines in the plots of the autocorrelations are the approximate two standard error bounds. If the autocorrelation is within these bounds, it is not significantly different from zero at the 5 percent significance level.

Autocorrelation measures the relationship to the past of the dependent Y variable to itself. Distributive lags, in contrast, are time-lag relationships between the dependent Y variable and different independent X variables. For instance, the movement and direction of mortgage rates tend to follow the Federal Funds Rate but at a time lag (typically 1 to 3 months). Sometimes, time lags follow cycles and seasonality (e.g., ice-cream sales tend to peak during the summer months and are therefore related to last summer's sales, 12 months in the past). The distributive lag analysis (Figure 9.44) shows how the dependent variable is related to each of the independent variables at

Autocorrelation

Time Lag	AC	PAC	Lower Bound	Upper Bound	Q-Stat	Prob
1	0.0580	0.0580	-0.2828	0.2828	0.1786	0.6726
2	-0.1213	-0.1251	-0.2828	0.2828	0.9754	0.6140
3	0.0590	0.0756	-0.2828	0.2828	1.1679	0.7607
4	0.2423	0.2232	-0.2828	0.2828	4.4865	0.3442
5	0.0067	-0.0078	-0.2828	0.2828	4.4890	0.4814
6	-0.2654	-0.2345	-0.2828	0.2828	8.6516	0.1941
7	0.0814	0.0939	-0.2828	0.2828	9.0524	0.2489
8	0.0634	-0.0442	-0.2828	0.2828	9.3012	0.3175
9	0.0204	0.0673	-0.2828	0.2828	9.3276	0.4076
10	-0.0190	0.0865	-0.2828	0.2828	9.3512	0.4991
11	0.1035	0.0790	-0.2828	0.2828	10.0648	0.5246
12	0.1658	0.0978	-0.2828	0.2828	11.9466	0.4500
13	-0.0524	-0.0430	-0.2828	0.2828	12.1394	0.5162
14	-0.2050	-0.2523	-0.2828	0.2828	15.1738	0.3664
15	0.1782	0.2089	-0.2828	0.2828	17.5315	0.2881
16	-0.1022	-0.2591	-0.2828	0.2828	18.3296	0.3050
17	-0.0861	0.0808	-0.2828	0.2828	18.9141	0.3335
18	0.0418	0.1987	-0.2828	0.2828	19.0559	0.3884
19	0.0869	-0.0821	-0.2828	0.2828	19.6894	0.4135
20	-0.0091	-0.0269	-0.2828	0.2828	19.6966	0.4770

Distributive Lags

P-Values of Distributive Lag Periods of Each Independent Variable

Variable	1	2	3	4	5	6	7	8	9	10	11	12
X1	0.8467	0.2045	0.3336	0.9105	0.9757	0.1020	0.9205	0.1267	0.5431	0.9110	0.7495	0.4016
X2	0.6077	0.9900	0.8422	0.2851	0.0638	0.0032	0.8007	0.1551	0.4823	0.1126	0.0519	0.4383
X3	0.7394	0.2396	0.2741	0.8372	0.9808	0.0464	0.8355	0.0545	0.6828	0.7354	0.5093	0.3500
X4	0.0061	0.6739	0.7932	0.7719	0.6748	0.8627	0.5586	0.9046	0.5726	0.6304	0.4812	0.5707
X5	0.1591	0.2032	0.4123	0.5599	0.6416	0.3447	0.9190	0.9740	0.5185	0.2856	0.1489	0.7794

FIGURE 9.44 Autocorrelation and distributive lag results.

various time lags, when all lags are considered simultaneously, to determine which time lags are statistically significant and should be considered.

Another requirement in running a regression model is the assumption of normality and sphericity of the error term. If the assumption of normality is violated or outliers are present, then the linear regression goodness-of-fit test may not be the most powerful or informative test available. Choosing the most appropriate test could mean the difference between detecting a linear fit or not. If the errors are not independent and not normally distributed, it may indicate that the data might be autocorrelated or suffer from nonlinearities or other more destructive errors. Independence of the errors can also be detected in the heteroskedasticity tests (Figure 9.45).

The normality test on the errors performed is a nonparametric test, which makes no assumptions about the specific shape of the population from where the sample is drawn, allowing for smaller sample data sets to be analyzed. This test evaluates the null hypothesis of whether the sample errors were drawn from a normally distributed population versus an alternate hypothesis that the data sample is not normally distributed. If the calculated D-statistic is greater than or equal to the D-critical values at various significance values, then reject the null hypothesis and accept the alternate hypothesis (the errors are not normally distributed). Otherwise, if the D-statistic is less than the D-critical value, do not reject the null hypothesis (the errors are normally distributed). This test relies on two cumulative frequencies: one derived from the sample data set and the second from a theoretical distribution based on the mean and standard deviation of the sample data.

Sometimes, certain types of time-series data cannot be modeled using any other methods except for a stochastic process, because the underlying events are stochastic in nature. For instance, you cannot adequately model and forecast stock prices, interest rates, price of oil, and other commodity prices using a simple regression model because these variables are highly uncertain and volatile, and do not follow a predefined static rule of behavior; in other words, the process is not stationary. Stationarity is checked here using the Runs Test, while another visual clue is found in the Autocorrelation report (the ACF tends to decay slowly). A stochastic process is a sequence of events or paths generated by probabilistic laws. That is, random events can occur over time but are governed by specific statistical and probabilistic rules. The main stochastic processes include random walk or Brownian motion, mean reversion, and jump diffusion. These processes can be used to forecast a multitude of variables that seemingly follow random trends but are restricted by probabilistic laws. The process-generating equation is known in advance, but the actual results generated is unknown (Figure 9.46).

The random walk Brownian motion process can be used to forecast stock prices, prices of commodities, and other stochastic time-series data given a drift or growth rate and volatility around the drift path. The

Test Result

Regression Error Average	0.00
Standard Deviation of Errors	141.83
D Statistic	0.1036
D Critical at 1%	0.1138
D Critical at 5%	0.1225
D Critical at 10%	0.1458

Null Hypothesis: The errors are normally distributed.

Conclusion: The errors are normally distributed at the 1% alpha level.

Errors	*Relative Frequency*	*Observed*	*Expected*	*O-E*
−219.04	0.02	0.02	0.0612	−0.0412
−202.53	0.02	0.04	0.0766	−0.0366
−186.04	0.02	0.06	0.0948	−0.0348
−174.17	0.02	0.08	0.1097	−0.0297
−162.13	0.02	0.10	0.1265	−0.0265
−161.62	0.02	0.12	0.1272	−0.0072
−160.39	0.02	0.14	0.1291	0.0109
−145.40	0.02	0.16	0.1526	0.0074
−138.92	0.02	0.18	0.1637	0.0163
−133.81	0.02	0.20	0.1727	0.0273
−120.76	0.02	0.22	0.1973	0.0227
−120.12	0.02	0.24	0.1985	0.0415
−113.25	0.02	0.26	0.2123	0.0477
−113.12	0.02	0.28	0.2125	0.0675

FIGURE 9.45 Test for normality of errors.

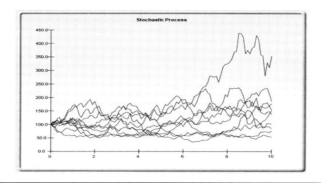

Statistical Summary

The following are the estimated parameters for a stochastic process given the data provided. It is up to you to determine if the probability of fit (similar to a goodness-of-fit computation) is sufficient to warrant the use of a stochastic process forecast, and if so, whether it is a random walk, mean-reversion, or a jump-diffusion model, or combinations thereof. In choosing the right stochastic process model, you will have to rely on past experiences and *a priori* economic and financial expectations of what the underlying data set is best represented by. These parameters can be entered into a stochastic process forecast (**Risk Simulator I Forecasting I Stochastic Processes**).

Periodic					
Drift Rate	-1.48%	Reversion Rate	283.89%	Jump Rate	20.41%
Volatility	88.84%	Long-Term Value	327.72	Jump Size	237.89

Probability of stochastic model fit: 46.48%
A high fit means a stochastic model is better than conventional models.

Runs	20	Standard Normal	-1.7321
Positive	25	P-Value (1-tail)	0.0416
Negative	25	P-Value (2-tail)	0.0833
Expected Run	26		

A low p-value (below 0.10, 0.05, 0.01) means that the sequence is not random and hence suffers from stationarity problems, and an ARIMA model might be more appropriate. Conversely, higher p-values indicate randomness and stochastic process models might be appropriate.

FIGURE 9.46 Stochastic process parameter estimation.

mean-reversion process can be used to reduce the fluctuations of the random walk process by allowing the path to target a long-term value, making it useful for forecasting time-series variables that have a long-term rate such as interest rates and inflation rates (these are long-term target rates by regulatory authorities or the market). The jump-diffusion process is useful for forecasting time-series data when the variable can occasionally exhibit random jumps, such as oil prices or price of electricity (discrete exogenous event shocks can make prices jump up or down). These processes can also be mixed and matched as required.

A note of caution is required here. The stochastic parameters calibration shows all the parameters for all processes and does not distinguish which process is better and which is worse or which process is more appropriate to use. It is up to the user to make this determination. For instance, if we see a 283 percent reversion rate, chances are a mean-reversion process is inappropriate, or a high jump rate of, say, 100 percent most probably means that a jump-diffusion process is probably not appropriate, and so forth. Further, the analysis cannot determine what the variable is and what the data source is. For instance, is the raw data from historical stock prices or is it the historical prices of electricity or inflation rates or the molecular motion of subatomic particles, and so forth. Only the user would know such information, and, hence, using *a priori* knowledge and theory, be able to pick the correct process to use (e.g., stock prices tend to follow a Brownian motion random walk whereas inflation rates follow a mean-reversion process, or a jump-diffusion process is more appropriate should you be forecasting price of electricity).

Multicollinearity exists when there is a linear relationship between the independent variables. When this occurs, the regression equation cannot be estimated at all. In near collinearity situations, the estimated regression equation will be biased and provide inaccurate results. This situation is especially true when a step-wise regression approach is used, where the statistically significant independent variables will be thrown out of the regression mix earlier than expected, resulting in a regression equation that is neither efficient nor accurate. One quick test of the presence of multicollinearity in a multiple regression equation is that the R-squared value is relatively high while the t statistics are relatively low.

Another quick test is to create a correlation matrix between the independent variables. A high cross correlation indicates a potential for autocorrelation. The rule of thumb is that a correlation with an absolute value greater than 0.75 is indicative of severe multicollinearity. Another test for multicollinearity is the use of the Variance Inflation Factor (VIF), obtained by regressing each independent variable to all the other independent variables, obtaining the R-squared value, and calculating the VIF. A VIF exceeding 2.0 can be considered as severe multicollinearity. A VIF exceeding 10.0 indicates destructive multicollinearity (Figure 9.47).

The correlation matrix lists the Pearson's product moment correlations (commonly referred to as the Pearson's R) between variable pairs. The correlation coefficient ranges between −1.0 and +1.0, inclusive. The sign indicates the direction of association between the variables, while the coefficient indicates the magnitude or strength of association. The Pearson's R only measures a linear relationship and is less effective in measuring nonlinear relationships.

To test whether the correlations are significant, a two-tailed hypothesis test is performed and the resulting p-values are computed. P-values less than 0.10, 0.05, and 0.01 are highlighted in blue to indicate statistical significance. In other words, a p-value for a correlation pair that is less than a given significance value is statistically significantly different from zero, indicating that there is a significant linear relationship between the two variables.

Correlation Matrix				
CORRELATION	X2	X3	X4	X5
X1	0.333	0.959	0.242	0.237
X2	1.000	0.349	0.319	0.120
X3		1.000	0.196	0.227
X4			1.000	0.290
				1.000
Variance Inflation Factor				
VIF	X2	X3	X4	X5
X1	1.12	12.46	1.06	1.06
X2		1.14	1.11	1.01
X3			1.04	1.05
X4				1.09

FIGURE 9.47 Multicollinearity errors.

The Pearson's product moment correlation coefficient (R) between two variables $(x$ and $y)$ is related to the covariance (cov) measure where

$$R_{x,y} = \frac{cov_{x,y}}{s_x s_y}$$

The benefit of dividing the covariance by the product of the two variables' standard deviations (s) is that the resulting correlation coefficient is bounded between -1.0 and $+1.0$, inclusive. This parameter makes the correlation a good relative measure to compare among different variables (particularly with different units and magnitude). The Spearman rank-based nonparametric correlation is also included in the analysis. The Spearman's R is related to the Pearson's R in that the data is first ranked and then correlated. The rank correlations provide a better estimate of the relationship between two variables when one or both of them is nonlinear.

It must be stressed that a significant correlation does not imply causation. Associations between variables in no way imply that the change of one variable causes another variable to change. Two variables that are moving independently of each other but in a related path may be correlated but their relationship might be spurious (e.g., a correlation between sunspots and the stock market might be strong, but one can surmise that there is no causality and that this relationship is purely spurious).

STATISTICAL ANALYSIS TOOL

Another very powerful tool in Risk Simulator is the *Statistical Analysis* tool, which determines the statistical properties of the data. The diagnostics run include checking the data for various statistical properties, from basic descriptive statistics to testing for and calibrating the stochastic properties of the data.

Procedure

1. Open the example model (*Risk Simulator | Example Models | Statistical Analysis*), go to the *Data* worksheet, and select the data including the variable names (cells C5:E55).
2. Click on *Risk Simulator | Tools | Statistical Analysis* (Figure 9.48).
3. Check the data type; that is, whether the data selected are from a single variable or multiple variables arranged in rows. In our example, we assume that the data areas selected are from multiple variables. Click *OK* when finished.
4. Choose the statistical tests you wish to perform. The suggestion (and by default) is to choose all the tests. Click *OK* when finished (Figure 9.49).

Spend some time going through the reports generated to get a better understanding of the statistical tests performed (sample reports are shown in Figures 9.50 through 9.53).

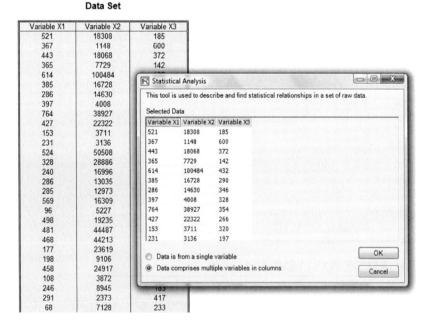

FIGURE 9.48   Running the statistical analysis tool.

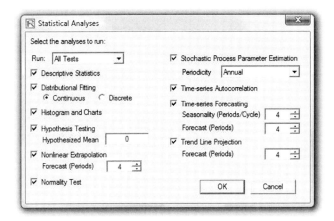

FIGURE 9.49   Statistical tests.

Descriptive Statistics

Analysis of Statistics

Almost all distributions can be described within 4 moments (some distributions require one moment, while others require two moments, and so forth). Descriptive statistics quantitatively capture these moments. The first moment describes the location of a distribution (i.e., mean, median, and mode) and is interpreted as the expected value, expected returns, or the average value of occurrences.

The Arithmetic Mean calculates the average of all occurrences by summing up all of the data points and dividing them by the number of points. The Geometric Mean is calculated by taking the power root of the products of all the data points and requires them to all be positive. The Geometric Mean is more accurate for percentages or rates that fluctuate significantly. For example, you can use Geometric Mean to calculate average growth rate given compound interest with variable rates. The Trimmed Mean calculates the arithmetic average of the data set after the extreme outliers have been trimmed. As averages are prone to significant bias when outliers exist, the Trimmed Mean reduces such bias in skewed distributions.

The Standard Error of the Mean calculates the error surrounding the sample mean. The larger the sample size, the smaller the error such that for an infinitely large sample size, the error approaches zero, indicating that the population parameter has been estimated. Due to sampling errors, the 95% Confidence Interval for the Mean is provided. Based on an analysis of the sample data points, the actual population mean should fall between these Lower and Upper Intervals for the Mean.

Median is the data point where 50% of all data points fall above this value and 50% below this value. Among the three first moment statistics, the median is least susceptible to outliers. A symmetrical distribution has the Median equal to the Arithmetic Mean. A skewed distribution exists when the Median is far away from the Mean. The Mode measures the most frequently occurring data point.

Minimum is the smallest value in the data set while Maximum is the largest value. Range is the difference between the Maximum and Minimum values.

FIGURE 9.50   Sample statistical analysis tool report. (*Continues*)

Descriptive Statistics

The second moment measures a distribution's spread or width, and is frequently described using measures such as Standard Deviations, Variances, Quartiles, and Inter-Quartile Ranges. Standard Deviation indicates the average deviation of all data points from their mean. It is a popular measure as is associated with risk (higher standard deviations mean a wider distribution, higher risk, or wider dispersion of data points around the mean) and its units are identical to original data set's. The Sample Standard Deviation differs from the Population Standard Deviation in that the former uses a degree of freedom correction to account for small sample sizes. Also, Lower and Upper Confidence Intervals are provided for the Standard Deviation and the true population standard deviation falls within this interval. If your data set covers every element of the population, use the Population Standard Deviation instead. The two Variance measures are simply the squared values of the standard deviations.

The Coefficient of Variability is the standard deviation of the sample divided by the sample mean, proving a unit-free measure of dispersion that can be compared across different distributions (you can now compare distributions of values denominated in millions of dollars with one in billions of dollars, or meters and kilograms, etc.). The First Quartile measures the 25th percentile of the data points when arranged from its smallest to largest value. The Third Quartile is the value of the 75th percentile data point. Sometimes quartiles are used as the upper and lower ranges of a distribution as it truncates the data set to ignore outliers. The Inter-Quartile Range is the difference between the third and first quartiles, and is often used to measure the width of the center of a distribution.

Skewness is the third moment in a distribution. Skewness characterizes the degree of asymmetry of a distribution around its mean. Positive skewness indicates a distribution with an asymmetric tail extending toward more positive values. Negative skewness indicates a distribution with an asymmetric tail extending toward more negative values. Kurtosis characterizes the relative peakedness or flatness of a distribution compared to the normal distribution. It is the fourth moment in a distribution. A positive Kurtosis value indicates a relatively peaked distribution. A negative kurtosis indicates a relatively flat distribution. The Kurtosis measured here has been centered to zero (certain other kurtosis measures are centered around 3.0). While both are equally valid, centering across zero makes the interpretation simpler. A high positive Kurtosis indicates a peaked distribution around its center and leptokurtic or fat tails. This indicates a higher probability of extreme events (e.g., catastrophic events, terrorist attacks, stock market crashes) than is predicted in a normal distribution.

Summary Statistics

Statistics	*Variable X1*		
Observations	50.0000	*Standard Deviation (Sample)*	172.9140
Arithmetic Mean	331.9200	*Standard Deviation (Population)*	171.1761
Geometric Mean	281.3247	*Lower Confidence Interval for Standard Deviation*	148.6090
Trimmed Mean	325.1739	*Upper Confidence Interval for Standard Deviation*	207.7947
Standard Error of Arithmetic Mean	24.4537	*Variance (Sample)*	29899.2588
Lower Confidence Interval for Mean	283.0125	*Variance (Population)*	29301.2736
Upper Confidence Interval for Mean	380.8275	*Coefficient of Variability*	0.5210
Median	307.0000	*First Quartile (Q1)*	188.0000
Minimum	47.0000	*Third Quartile (Q3)*	435.0000
Maximum	764.0000	*Inter-Quartile Range*	247.0000
Range	717.0000	*Skewness*	0.4838
		Kurtosis	−0.0952

FIGURE 9.50   *(Continued)*

Hypothesis Test (t-Test on the Population Mean of One Variable)

Statistical Summary

Statistics from Dataset:		*Calculated Statistics:*	
Observations	*50*	*t-Statistic*	*13.5734*
Sample Mean	*331.92*	*P-Value (right-tail)*	*0.0000*
Sample Standard Deviation	*172.91*	*P-Value (left-tailed)*	*1.0000*
		P-Value (two-tailed)	*0.0000*
User Provided Statistics:			
		Null Hypothesis (Ho):	μ *= Hypothesized Mean*
Hypothesized Mean	*0.00*	*Alternate Hypothesis (Ha):*	μ *< > Hypothesized Mean*

Notes: "< >" denotes "greater than" for right-tail, "less than" for left-tail, or "not equal to" for two-tail hypothesis tests.

Hypothesis Testing Summary

The one-variable t-test is appropriate when the population standard deviation is not known but the sampling distribution is assumed to be approximately normal (the t-test is used when the sample size is less than 30 but is also appropriate and in fact, provides more conservative results with larger data sets). This t-test can be applied to three types of hypothesis tests: a two-tailed test, a right-tailed test, and a left-tailed test. All three tests and their respective results are listed below for your reference.

Two-Tailed Hypothesis Test
A two-tailed hypothesis tests the null hypothesis Ho such that the population mean is statistically identical to the hypothesized mean. The alternative hypothesis is that the real population mean is statistically different from the hypothesized mean when tested using the sample dataset. Using a t-test, if the computed p-value is less than a specified significance amount (typically 0.10, 0.05, or 0.01), this means that the population mean is statistically significantly different than the hypothesized mean at 10%, 5%, and 1% significance value (or at the 90%, 95%, and 99% statistical confidence). Conversely, if the p-value is higher than 0.10, 0.05, or 0.01, the population mean is statistically identical to the hypothesized mean and any differences are due to random chance.

Right-Tailed Hypothesis Test
A right-tailed hypothesis tests the null hypothesis Ho such that the population mean is statistically less than or equal to the hypothesized mean. The alternative hypothesis is that the real population mean is statistically greater than the hypothesized mean when tested using the sample dataset. Using a t-test, if the p-value is less than a specified significance amount (typically 0.10, 0.05, or 0.01), this means that the population mean is statistically significantly greater than the hypothesized mean at 10%, 5%, and 1% significance value (or 90%, 95%, and 99% statistical confidence). Conversely, if the p-value is higher than 0.10, 0.05, or 0.01, the population mean is statistically similar or less than the hypothesized mean.

Left-Tailed Hypothesis Test
A left-tailed hypothesis tests the null hypothesis Ho such that the population mean is statistically greater than or equal to the hypothesized mean. The alternative hypothesis is that the real population mean is statistically less than the hypothesized mean when tested using the sample dataset. Using a t-test, if the p-value is less than a specified significance amount (typically 0.10, 0.05, or 0.01), this means that the population mean is statistically significantly less than the hypothesized mean at 10%, 5%, and 1% significance value (or 90%, 95%, and 99% statistical confidence). Conversely, if the p-value is higher than 0.10, 0.05, or 0.01, the population mean is statistically similar or greater than the hypothesized mean and any differences are due to random chance.

Because the t-test is more conservative and does not require a known population standard deviation as in the Z-test, we only use this t-test.

FIGURE 9.51 Sample statistical analysis tool report (hypothesis testing of one variable).

Test for Normality

The Normality test is a form of nonparametric test, which makes no assumptions about the specific shape of the population from which the sample is drawn, allowing for smaller sample data sets to be analyzed. This test evaluates the null hypothesis of whether the data sample was drawn from a normally distributed population, versus an alternate hypothesis that the data sample is not normally distributed. If the calculated p-value is less than or equal to the alpha significance value, then reject the null hypothesis and accept the alternate hypothesis. Otherwise, if the p-value is higher than the alpha significance value, do not reject the null hypothesis. This test relies on two cumulative frequencies: one derived from the sample data set, the second from a theoretical distribution based on the mean and standard deviation of the sample data. An alternative to this test is the Chi-Square test for normality. The Chi-Square test requires more data points to run compared to the Normality test used here.

Test Result

		Data	Relative Frequency	Observed	Expected	O-E
Data Average	331.92	47.00	0.02	0.02.	0.0497	−0.0297
Standard Deviation	172.91	68.00	0.02	0.04	0.0635	−0.0235
D Statistic	0.0859	87.00	0.02	0.06	0.0783	−0.0183
D Critical at 1%	0.1150	96.00	0.02	0.08	0.0862	−0.0062
D Critical at 5%	0.1237	102.00	0.02	0.10	0.0916	0.0082
D Critical at 10%	0.1473	108.00	0.02	0.12	0.0977	0.0223
		114.00	0.02	0.14	0.1038	0.0362
		127.00	0.02	0.16	0.1180	0.0420
Null Hypothesis: The data is normally distributed.		153.00	0.02	0.18	0.1504	0.0296
		177.00	0.02	0.20	0.1851	0.0149
		186.00	0.02	0.22	0.1994	0.0206
		188.00	0.02	0.24	0.2026	0.0374
		198.00	0.02	0.26	0.2193	0.0407
Conclusion: The sample data is normally distributed at the 1% alpha level.		222.00	0.02	0.28	0.2625	0.0175
		231.00	0.02	0.30	0.2797	0.0203
		240.00	0.02	0.32	0.2975	0.0225
		246.00	0.02	0.34	0.3096	0.0304

FIGURE 9.52 Sample statistical analysis tool report (normality test).

Time-Series Forecasting

Time-Series Analysis Summary

Time-series forecasting is used to forecast the future based on historical data, through the decompositon of the historical data into the baseline (alpha). The best-fitting test for the moving average forecast uses the root mean squared errors (RMSE). The RMSE calculates the square root of the average squared deviations of the fitted values versus the actual data points.

Mean Squared Error (MSE) is an absolute error measure that squares the errors (the difference between the actual historical data and the forecast-fitted data predicted by the model) to keep the positive and negative errors from canceling each other out. This measure also tends to exaggerate large errors by weighting the large errors more heavily than smaller errors by squaring them, which can help when comparing different time-series models. Root Mean Square Error (RMSE) is the square root of MSE and is the most popular error measure, also known as the quadratic loss function. RMSE can be defined as the average of the absolute values of the forecast errors and is highly appropriate when the cost of the forecast errors is proportional to the absolute size of the forecast error. The RMSE is used as the selection criteria for the best-fitting time-series model.

Mean Absolute Percentage Error (MAPE) is a relative error statistic measured as an average percent error of the historical data points and is most appropriate when the cost of the forecast error is more closely related to the percentage error than the numerical size of the error. Finally, an associated measure is the Theil's U statistic, which measures the naivety of the model's forecast. That is, if the Theil's U statistic is less than 1.0, then the forecast method used provides an estimate that is statistically better than guessing.

The analysis was run with periodicity = 12

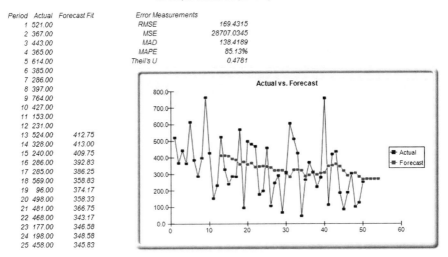

Period	Actual	Forecast Fit		Error Measurements	
1	521.00			RMSE	169.4315
2	367.00			MSE	28707.0345
3	443.00			MAD	138.4189
4	365.00			MAPE	85.13%
5	614.00			Theil's U	0.4781
6	385.00				
7	286.00				
8	397.00				
9	764.00				
10	427.00				
11	153.00				
12	231.00				
13	524.00	412.75			
14	328.00	413.00			
15	240.00	409.75			
16	286.00	392.83			
17	285.00	386.25			
18	569.00	358.83			
19	96.00	374.17			
20	498.00	358.33			
21	481.00	366.75			
22	468.00	343.17			
23	177.00	346.58			
24	198.00	348.58			
25	458.00	345.83			

FIGURE 9.53 Sample statistical analysis tool report (forecasting).

APPENDIX—FORECAST INTERVALS

The forecast interval estimated in a forecast (an approach also used by Risk Simulator) is illustrated in Figure 9.54. The confidence interval (*CI*) is estimated by

$$\hat{Y}_i \pm Z\left[\frac{RMSE}{N-T}\right]N$$

where $\hat{Y}_i$ is the *i*th forecast estimate; Z is the standard-normal statistic (see the standard-normal tables at the end of this book); *RMSE* is the root

Period	Raw Data	**Forecast Values**								
		Forecast	5%	95%						
1	265.22	710.07	586.91	833.23						
2	146.64	701.52	575.03	828.01						
3	182.50	756.04	626.04	886.04						
4	118.54	818.99	685.27	952.71						
5	180.04	794.37	656.71	932.02						
6	167.45	Estimated RMSE		72.951						
7	231.75									
8	223.71									
9	192.98									
10	122.29									
11	336.65									
12	186.50									
13	194.27									
14	149.19									
15	210.06									
36	647.82									
37	650.81									
38	677.54									
39	666.56									

$$CI = \hat{Y} \pm Z \left[\frac{RMSE}{(N-T)} N \right]$$

Period	Forecast (T)	Stdev	Z-statistic	Lower	Upper		
40	1	74.87	1.645	586.91	833.23	**RMSE**	72.951
41	2	76.89	1.645	575.03	828.01	**Data Points (N)**	39
42	3	79.03	1.645	626.03	886.04		
43	4	81.29	1.645	685.27	952.71		
44	5	83.68	1.645	656.71	932.02		

FIGURE 9.54   Forecast interval estimation.

mean-squared error previously calculated; N is the number of historical data points; and T is the forecast period. When N is a relatively small number (usually less than 30), then the same analysis can be performed using the t-statistic in place of the Z-value (see the t-statistic table at the end of this book).

Clearly, this approach is a modification of the more common confidence interval estimate of

$$\hat{Y}_i \pm Z \frac{\sigma}{\sqrt{n}}$$

applicable within a data set. Here, it is assumed that

$$\left[\frac{RMSE}{N-T} \right] N = \frac{\sigma}{\sqrt{n}}$$

and the inclusion of the T variable is simply to adjust for the added degrees of freedom when forecasting outside of the original data set.

APPENDIX—ORDINARY LEAST SQUARES

The following illustrates the concept of the ordinary least-squares regression line. Figure 9.55 shows the data on the dependent variable (Y) and

	A	B	C	D	E	F	G	H
1	Y	X	Slope	Intercept	Predicted	Residual	Squared Resid	
2	1000	3	91.98	2489.16	2765.09	1765.09	3115530.48	
3	3333	3	91.98	2489.16	2765.09	-567.91	322525.70	
4	2222	3	91.98	2489.16	2765.09	543.09	294942.99	
5	1111	2	91.98	2489.16	2673.11	1562.11	2440188.73	
6	5555	3	91.98	2489.16	2765.09	-2789.91	7783617.14	
7	2222	2	91.98	2489.16	2673.11	451.11	203500.54	
8	2222	3	91.98	2489.16	2765.09	543.09	294942.99	
9	5555	3	91.98	2489.16	2765.09	-2789.91	7783617.14	
10	4444	7	91.98	2489.16	3132.99	-1311.01	1718743.79	
11	3333	6	91.98	2489.16	3041.02	-291.98	85255.17	
12	2222	7	91.98	2489.16	3132.99	910.99	829905.16	
13	1111	8	91.98	2489.16	3224.97	2113.97	4468858.59	
14	5555	7	91.98	2489.16	3132.99	-2422.01	5866126.11	
15	2222	6	91.98	2489.16	3041.02	819.02	670785.76	
16	2222	7	91.98	2489.16	3132.99	910.99	829905.16	
17	5555	6	91.98	2489.16	3041.02	-2513.98	6320120.01	
18	4444	5	91.98	2489.16	2949.04	-1494.96	2234908.63	
19	1111	6	91.98	2489.16	3041.02	1930.02	3724958.34	
20	2222	4	91.98	2489.16	2857.06	635.06	403304.67	
21	3333	5	91.98	2489.16	2949.04	-383.96	147426.11	
22	2222	4	91.98	2489.16	2857.06	635.06	403304.67	
23	1111	4	91.98	2489.16	2857.06	1746.06	3048735.05	
24								
25		Optimization Parameter					Excel Estimated Parameter	
26		Intercept			2489.16		Intercept	2489.16
27		Slope			91.98		Slope	91.98
28		Sum of Squared Residuals			52991202.91			
29								

FIGURE 9.55 Using optimization to estimate regression intercept and slope.

independent variable (X) as well as the results estimated using Excel's solver add-in. Arbitrary starting points of the slope and intercept values are fitted back into the data points and the squared residuals are calculated. Then, the optimal slope and intercept values are calculated through minimizing the sum of the squared residuals.

To get started, make sure Excel's Solver is added in by clicking on *Tools | Add-Ins*. Verify that the check-box beside *Solver Add-In* is selected (Figure 9.56). Then, back in the Excel model, click on *Tools | Solver* and make sure the *sum of squared residuals* (cell E28) is set as the target cell to minimize through systematically changing the intercept and slope values (cells E26 and E27) as seen in Figure 9.57.

Solving yields an intercept value of 2489.16 and a slope of 91.98. These results can be verified using Excel's built-in *slope* and *intercept* functions (Figure 9.58). In other words, the ordinary least-squares regression equation approach is the unique line (as described by an intercept and slope) that minimizes all possible vertical errors (total sum of squared residuals), making it the best-fitting line through a data set.

FIGURE 9.56   Excel Solver add-in.

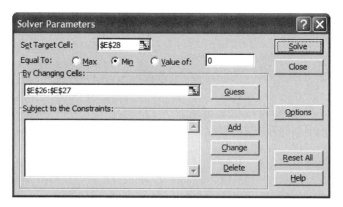

FIGURE 9.57   Excel Solver parameters.

Optimization Parameters			Excel Estimated Parameter	
Intercept	2489.16		Slope	2489.16
Slope	91.98		Intercept	91.98
Sum of Squared Residuals	52991202.91			

FIGURE 9.58   Optimized ordinary least squares results.

APPENDIX—DETECTING AND FIXING HETEROSKEDASTICITY

Several tests exist to test for the presence of heteroskedasticity. These tests also are applicable for testing misspecifications and nonlinearities. The simplest approach is to graphically represent each independent variable against the dependent variable as illustrated earlier in the chapter. Another approach is to apply one of the most widely used models, the White's test, where the test is based on the null hypothesis of no heteroskedasticity against an alternate hypothesis of heteroskedasticity of some unknown general form. The test statistic is computed by an auxiliary or secondary regression, where the squared residuals or errors from the first regression are regressed on all possible (and nonredundant) cross products of the regressors. For example, suppose the following regression is estimated:

$$Y = \beta_0 + \beta_1 X + \beta_2 Z + \varepsilon_t$$

The test statistic is then based on the auxiliary regression of the errors (ε):

$$\varepsilon_t^2 = \alpha_0 + \alpha_1 X + \alpha_2 Z + \alpha_3 X^2 + \alpha_4 Z^2 + \alpha_5 XZ + v_t$$

The nR^2 statistic is the White's test statistic, computed as the number of observations (n) times the centered R-squared from the test regression. White's test statistic is asymptotically distributed as a χ^2 with degrees of freedom equal to the number of independent variables (excluding the constant) in the test regression.

The White's test is also a general test for model misspecification, because the null hypothesis underlying the test assumes that the errors are both homoskedastic and independent of the regressors, and that the linear specification of the model is correct. Failure of any one of these conditions could lead to a significant test statistic. Conversely, a nonsignificant test statistic implies that none of the three conditions is violated. For instance, the resulting F-statistic is an omitted variable test for the joint significance of all cross products, excluding the constant.

One method to fix heteroskedasticity is to make it homoskedastic by using a weighted least-squares (WLS) approach. For instance, suppose the following is the original regression equation:

$$Y = \beta_0 + \beta_1 X_1 + \beta_2 X_2 + \beta_3 X_3 + \varepsilon$$

Further suppose that X_2 is heteroskedastic. Then transform the data used in the regression into:

$$Y = \frac{\beta_0}{X_2} + \beta_1 \frac{X_1}{X_2} + \beta_2 + \beta_3 \frac{X_3}{X_2} + \frac{\varepsilon}{X_2}$$

The model can be redefined as the following WLS regression:

$$Y_{WLS} = \beta_0^{WLS} + \beta_1^{WLS} X_1 + \beta_2^{WLS} X_2 + \beta_3^{WLS} X_3 + v$$

Alternatively, the Park's test can be applied to test for heteroskedasticity and to fix it. The Park's test model is based on the original regression equation, uses its errors, and creates an auxiliary regression that takes the form of:

$$\ln e_i^2 = \beta_1 + \beta_2 \ln X_{k,i}$$

Suppose β_2 is found to be statistically significant based on a t-test, then heteroskedasticity is found to be present in the variable $X_{k,i}$. The remedy therefore is to use the following regression specification:

$$\frac{Y}{\sqrt{X_k^{\beta_2}}} = \frac{\beta_1}{\sqrt{X_k^{\beta_2}}} + \frac{\beta_2 X_2}{\sqrt{X_k^{\beta_2}}} + \frac{\beta_3 X_3}{\sqrt{X_k^{\beta_2}}} + \varepsilon$$

APPENDIX—DETECTING AND FIXING MULTICOLLINEARITY

Multicollinearity exists when there is a linear relationship between the independent variables. When this occurs, the regression equation cannot be estimated at all. In near collinearity situations, the estimated regression equation will be biased and provide inaccurate results. This situation is especially true when a step-wise regression approach is used, where the statistically significant independent variables will be thrown out of the regression mix earlier than expected, resulting in a regression equation that is neither efficient nor accurate.

As an example, suppose the following multiple regression analysis exists, where

$$Y_i = \beta_1 + \beta_2 X_{2,i} + \beta_3 X_{3,i} + \varepsilon_i$$

then the estimated slopes can be calculated through

$$\hat{\beta}_2 = \frac{\sum Y_i X_{2,i} \sum X_{3,i}^2 - \sum Y_i X_{3,i} \sum X_{2,i} X_{3,i}}{\sum X_{2,i}^2 \sum X_{3,i}^2 - \left(\sum X_{2,i} X_{3,i}\right)^2}$$

$$\hat{\beta}_3 = \frac{\sum Y_i X_{3,i} \sum X_{2,i}^2 - \sum Y_i X_{2,i} \sum X_{2,i} X_{3,i}}{\sum X_{2,i}^2 \sum X_{3,i}^2 - \left(\sum X_{2,i} X_{3,i}\right)^2}$$

Now suppose that there is perfect multicollinearity, that is, there exists a perfect linear relationship between X_2 and X_3, such that $X_{3,i} = \lambda X_{2,i}$ for all positive values of λ. Substituting this linear relationship into the slope calculations for β_2, the result is indeterminate. In other words, we have

$$\hat{\beta}_2 = \frac{\sum Y_i X_{2,i} \sum \lambda^2 X_{2,i}^2 - \sum Y_i \lambda X_{2,i} \sum \lambda X_{2,i}^2}{\sum X_{2,i}^2 \sum \lambda^2 X_{2,i}^2 - \left(\sum \lambda X_{2,i}^2\right)^2} = \frac{0}{0}$$

The same calculation and results apply to β_3, which means that the multiple regression analysis breaks down and cannot be estimated given a perfect collinearity condition.

One quick test of the presence of multicollinearity in a multiple regression equation is that the R-squared value is relatively high while the t-statistics are relatively low. (See Figure 9.39 for an illustration of this effect.) Another quick test is to create a correlation matrix between the independent variables. A high cross correlation indicates a potential for multicollinearity. The rule of thumb is that a correlation with an absolute value greater than 0.75 is indicative of severe multicollinearity.

Another test for multicollinearity is the use of the variance inflation factor (VIF), obtained by regressing each independent variable to all the other independent variables, obtaining the R-squared value and calculating the VIF of that variable by estimating:

$$VIF_i = \frac{1}{(1 - R_i^2)}$$

A high VIF value indicates a high R-squared near unity. As a rule of thumb, a VIF value greater than 10 is usually indicative of destructive multicollinearity.

APPENDIX—DETECTING AND FIXING AUTOCORRELATION

One very simple approach to test for autocorrelation is to graph the time series of a regression equation's residuals. If these residuals exhibit some cyclicality, then autocorrelation exists. Another more robust approach to detect autocorrelation is the use of the Durbin–Watson statistic, which estimates the potential for a first-order autocorrelation. The Durbin–Watson test also identifies model misspecification, that is, if a particular time-series variable is correlated to itself one period prior. Many time-series data tend to be autocorrelated to their historical occurrences. This relationship can be due to multiple reasons, including the variables' spatial relationships (similar time and space), prolonged economic shocks and events, psychological inertia, smoothing, seasonal adjustments of the data, and so forth.

The Durbin–Watson statistic is estimated by the sum of the squares of the regression errors for one period prior to the sum of the current period's errors:

$$DW = \frac{\sum (\varepsilon_t - \varepsilon_{t-1})^2}{\sum \varepsilon_t^2}$$

There is a Durbin–Watson critical statistic table at the end of the book that provides a guide as to whether a statistic implies any autocorrelation.

Another test for autocorrelation is the Breusch–Godfrey test, where for a regression function in the form of:

$$Y = f(X_1, X_2, \ldots, X_k)$$

estimate this regression equation and obtain its errors ε_t. Then, run the secondary regression function in the form of:

$$Y = f(X_1, X_2, \ldots, X_k \varepsilon_{t-1}, \varepsilon_{t-2}, \varepsilon_{t-p})$$

Obtain the R-squared value and test it against a null hypothesis of no autocorrelation versus an alternate hypothesis of autocorrelation, where the test statistic follows a chi-square distribution of p degrees of freedom:

$$R^2(n - p) \sim \chi^2_{df=p}$$

Fixing autocorrelation requires more advanced econometric models including the applications of ARIMA (Autoregressive Integrated Moving

Average) or ECM (Error Correction Models). However, one simple fix is to take the lags of the dependent variable for the appropriate periods, add them into the regression function, and test for their significance, for instance:

$$Y_t = f(Y_{t-1}, Y_{t-2}, \ldots, Y_{t-p}, X_1, X_2, \ldots, X_k)$$

QUESTIONS

1. Explain what each of the following terms means:
   a. Time-series analysis
   b. Ordinary least squares
   c. Regression analysis
   d. Heteroskedasticity
   e. Autocorrelation
   f. Multicollinearity
   g. ARIMA
2. What is the difference between the R-squared versus the adjusted R-squared measure in a regression analysis? When is each applicable and why?
3. Explain why if each of the following is not detected properly or corrected for in the model, the estimated regression model will be flawed:
   a. Heteroskedasticity
   b. Autocorrelation
   c. Multicollinearity
4. Explain briefly how to fix the problem of nonlinearity in the data set.

EXERCISE

1. Based on the data in the chapter examples, re-create the following using Excel:
   a. Double-moving average model
   b. Single exponential-smoothing model
   c. Additive seasonality model
   d. Holt–Winters multiplicative model

Risk Diversification

CHAPTER 10

The Search for the Optimal Decision

In most simulation models, there are variables over which you have control, such as how much to charge for a product or how much to invest in a project. These controlled variables are called decision variables. Finding the optimal values for decision variables can make the difference between reaching an important goal and missing that goal. This chapter details the optimization process at a high-level, while Chapter 11, Optimization Under Uncertainty, provides two step-by-step examples of resource optimization and portfolio optimization solved using the Risk Simulator software.

WHAT IS AN OPTIMIZATION MODEL?

In today's highly competitive global economy, companies are faced with many difficult decisions. These decisions include allocating financial resources, building or expanding facilities, managing inventories, and determining product-mix strategies (see Figure 10.1). Such decisions might involve thousands or millions of potential alternatives. Considering and evaluating each of them would be impractical or even impossible. A model can provide valuable assistance in incorporating relevant variables when analyzing decisions and finding the best solutions for making decisions. Models capture the most important features of a problem and present them in a form that is easy to interpret. Models often provide insights that intuition alone cannot. An optimization model has three major elements: decision variables, constraints, and an objective. In short, the optimization methodology finds the best combination or permutation of decision variables (e.g., which products to sell and which projects to execute) in every conceivable way such that the objective is maximized (e.g., revenues and net income) or minimized

An approach used to find the combination of inputs to achieve the best possible output subject to satisfying certain prespecified conditions
- What stocks to pick in a portfolio, as well as the weights of each stock as a percentage of total budget
- Optimal staffing needs for a production line
- Project and strategy selection and prioritization
- Inventory optimization
- Optimal pricing and royalty rates
- Utilization of employees for workforce planning
- Configuration of machines for production scheduling
- Location of facilities for distribution
- Tolerances in manufacturing design
- Treatment policies in waste management

FIGURE 10.1　　What is optimization?

(e.g., risk and costs) while still satisfying the constraints (e.g., budget and resources).

Obtaining optimal values generally requires that you search in an iterative or ad hoc fashion. This search involves running one iteration for an initial set of values, analyzing the results, changing one or more values, rerunning the model, and repeating the process until you find a satisfactory solution. This process can be very tedious and time consuming even for small models, and often it is not clear how to adjust the values from one iteration to the next.

A more rigorous method systematically enumerates all possible alternatives. This approach guarantees optimal solutions if the model is correctly specified. Suppose that an optimization model depends on only two decision variables. If each variable has 10 possible values, trying each combination requires 100 iterations (10^2 alternatives). If each iteration is very short (e.g., 2 seconds), then the entire process could be done in approximately three minutes of computer time.

However, instead of two decision variables, consider six, then consider that trying all combinations requires 1,000,000 iterations (10^6 alternatives). It is easily possible for complete enumeration to take weeks, months, or even years to carry out.

THE TRAVELING FINANCIAL PLANNER

A very simple example is in order. Figure 10.2 illustrates the traveling financial planner problem. Suppose the traveling financial planner has to make three sales trips to New York, Chicago, and Seattle. Further suppose that the order of arrival at each city is irrelevant. All that is important in this

- You have to travel and visit clients in New York, Chicago, and Seattle
- You may start from any city and you will stay at your final city, that is, you will need to purchase three airline tickets
- Your goal is to travel as cheaply as possible given these rates:

Route	Airfare
Seattle – Chicago	$325
Chicago – Seattle	$225
New York – Seattle	$350
Seattle – New York	$375
Chicago – New York	$325
New York – Chicago	$325

- How do you solve the problem?
  - Ad Hoc approach—start trying different combinations
  - Enumeration—look at all possible alternatives

FIGURE 10.2 Traveling financial planner problem.

simple example is to find the lowest total cost possible to cover all three cities. Figure 10.2 also lists the flight costs from these different cities.

The problem here is cost minimization, suitable for optimization. One basic approach to solving this problem is through an ad hoc or brute force method, that is, manually list all six possible permutations as seen in Figure 10.3. Clearly the cheapest itinerary is going from the East Coast to the West Coast, going from New York to Chicago and finally on to Seattle.[1] Here, the problem is simple and can be calculated manually, as there are three cities and hence six possible itineraries.[2] However, add two more cities and the total number of possible itineraries jumps to 120.[3] Performing an ad hoc calculation will be fairly intimidating and time consuming. On a larger scale, suppose there are 100 cities on the salesman's list, the possible itineraries will be as many as 9.3×10^{157}. The problem will take many years to calculate manually, which is where optimization software steps in, automating the search for the optimal itinerary.

The example illustrated up to now is a deterministic optimization problem, that is, the airline ticket prices are known ahead of time and are assumed to be constant. Now suppose the ticket prices are not constant but are uncertain, following some distribution (e.g., a ticket from Chicago to Seattle averages $325, but is never cheaper than $300 and usually never exceeds $500).[4] The same uncertainty applies to tickets for the other cities. The problem now becomes an *optimization under uncertainty*. Ad hoc and brute force approaches simply do not work. Software such as Risk Simulator

Seattle-Chicago-New York $325 + $325 = **$650**

Seattle-New York-Chicago $375 + $325 = **$700**

Chicago-Seattle-New York $225 + $375 = **$600**

Chicago-New York-Seattle $325 + $350 = **$675**

New York-Seattle-Chicago $350 + $325 = **$675**

New York-Chicago-Seattle $325 + $225 = **$550**

Additionally, say you want to visit San Antonio and Denver

For the five cities to visit (Seattle, Chicago, New York, San Antonio, and Denver) you now have:

$5! = 5 \times 4 \times 3 \times 2 \times 1 = 120$ possible combinations

What about 100 different cities?

$100! = 100 \times 99 \times 98 \dots \times 1 =$
93,326,215,443,944,200,000,000,000,000,000,000,000,000,000,
000,000,000,000,000,000,000,000,000,000,000,000,000,000,
000,000,000,000,000,000,000,000,000,000,000,000,000,000,
000,000,000,000,000,000,000,000,000,000,000,000,000,000

or 9.3×10^{157} different combinations

FIGURE 10.3 Multiple combinations of the traveling financial planner problem.

can take over this optimization problem and automate the entire process seamlessly. The next section discusses the terms required in an optimization under uncertainty. Chapter 11 illustrates several additional business cases and models with step-by-step instructions.

> Optimization problems can be solved using different approaches, including the use of simplex or graphical methods, brute force, mathematically taking calculus derivatives, or using software that applies smart algorithms and search heuristics to efficiently identify the optimal solutions.

THE LINGO OF OPTIMIZATION

Before embarking on solving an optimization problem, it is vital to understand the terminology of optimization—the terms used to describe certain attributes of the optimization process. These words include decision variables, constraints, and objectives.

Decision variables are quantities over which you have control; for example, the amount of a product to make, the number of dollars to allocate among different investments, or which projects to select from among a limited set. As an example, portfolio optimization analysis includes a go or no-go decision on particular projects. In addition, the dollar or percentage budget allocation across multiple projects also can be structured as decision variables.

Constraints describe relationships among decision variables that restrict the values of the decision variables. For example, a constraint might ensure that the total amount of money allocated among various investments cannot exceed a specified amount or at most one project from a certain group can be selected based on budget constraints, timing restrictions, minimum returns, or risk tolerance levels.

Objectives give a mathematical representation of the model's desired outcome, such as maximizing profit or minimizing cost, in terms of the decision variables. In financial analysis, for example, the objective may be to maximize returns while minimizing risks (maximizing the Sharpe ratio, or the returns-to-risk ratio).

Conceptually, an optimization model might look like Figure 10.4. The solution to an optimization model provides a set of values for the decision variables that optimizes (maximizes or minimizes) the associated objective. If the real business conditions were simple and the future were predictable, all data in an optimization model would be constant, making the model deterministic. In many cases, however, a deterministic optimization model

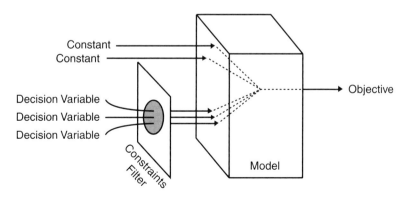

Deterministic Optimization Model

FIGURE 10.4 Visualizing a deterministic optimization.

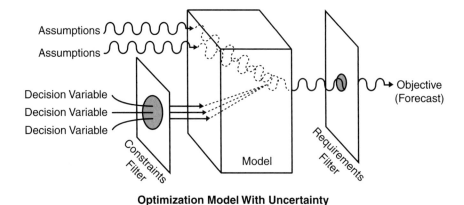

Optimization Model With Uncertainty

FIGURE 10.5 Visualizing a stochastic optimization.

cannot capture all the relevant intricacies of a practical decision-making environment. When a model's data are uncertain and can only be described probabilistically, the objective will have some probability distribution for any chosen set of decision variables. You can find this probability distribution by simulating the model using Risk Simulator. An optimization model under uncertainty has several additional elements, including assumptions and forecasts.

Assumptions capture the uncertainty of model data using probability distributions, whereas forecasts are the frequency distributions of possible results for the model. Forecast statistics are summary values of a forecast distribution, such as the mean, standard deviation, and variance. The optimization process controls the optimization by maximizing or minimizing the objective (see Figure 10.5).

Each optimization model has one objective, a variable that mathematically represents the model's objective in terms of the assumption and decision variables. Optimization's job is to find the optimal (minimum or maximum) value of the objective by selecting and improving different values for the decision variables. When model data are uncertain and can only be described using probability distributions, the objective itself will have some probability distribution for any set of decision variables.

Before embarking on solving an optimization problem, the analyst first has to understand the lingo of optimization: objectives, constraints, decision variables, assumptions, and forecasts.

SOLVING OPTIMIZATION GRAPHICALLY AND USING EXCEL'S SOLVER

Figure 10.6 illustrates a simple multiple constraint optimization problem solved using the graphical method. In this simple example of deterministic linear optimization with linear constraints, the graphical approach is easy to implement. However, great care should be taken when nonlinear constraints exist.[5] Sometimes, optimization models are specified incorrectly. For instance, Figure 10.7 shows problems arising with unbounded solutions (with a solution set at infinity), no feasible solution (where the constraints are too restrictive and impossible to satisfy), and multiple solutions (this is good news for management as it can choose from among several equally optimal solutions).

Figure 10.8 illustrates the same problem but solved using Excel's Solver add-in.[6] Solver is clearly a more powerful approach than the manual graphical method. This situation is especially true when multiple decision variables exist as a multidimensional graph would be required.[7] Figures 10.9 and 10.10 show the use of Solver to optimize a portfolio of projects—the former assumes an integer optimization, where projects are either a go or no-go decision, whereas the latter assumes a continuous optimization, where projects can be funded anywhere from 0 percent to 100 percent.[8]

There is one major limitation of Solver. Specifically, it assumes static and deterministic optimization models and cannot account for risk and uncertainty. In the next chapter, we see how Risk Simulator can be used to run static optimization as well as dynamic optimization and stochastic optimization to account for risks and uncertainty, as well as run investment efficient frontiers.

(*Text continues on page 513.*)

Say there are two products X and Y being manufactured. Product X provides a $20 profit and product Y a $15 profit. Product X takes 3 hours to manufacture and product Y takes 2 hours tc produce. In any given week, the manufacturing equipment can make both products but has a maximum capacity of 300 hours. In addition, based on market demand, management has determined that it cannot sell more than 80 units of X and 100 units of Y in a given week and prefers not to have any inventory on hand. Therefore, management has set these demand levels as the maximum output for products X and Y respectively. The issue now becomes what is the optimal production levels of both X and Y such that profits would be maximized in any given week?

Based on the situation above, we can formulate a linear optimization routine where we have:

The Objective Function: $\quad$ Max $20X + 15Y$

Subject to Constraints: $\quad 3X + 2Y \leq 300$
$\qquad\qquad\qquad\qquad\quad X \leq 80$
$\qquad\qquad\qquad\qquad\quad Y \leq 100$

We can more easily visualize the constraints by plotting them out one at a time as follows:

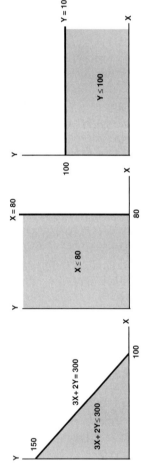

The graph below shows the combination of all three constraints. The shaded region shows the feasible area, where all constraints are simultaneously satisfied. Hence, the optimal decision should fall within this shaded region.

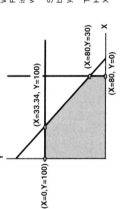

We can easily calculate the intersection points of the constraints. For example, the intersection between Y = 100 and 3X + 2Y = 300 is obtained by solving the equations simultaneously. Substituting, we get 3X + 2(100) = 300. Solving yields X = 33.34 and Y = 100.

Similarly, the intersection between X = 80 and 3X + 2Y = 300 can be obtained by solving the equations simultaneously. Substituting yields 3(80) + 2Y = 300. Solving yields Y = 30 and X = 80.

The other two edges are simply intersections between the axes. Hence, when X = 80, Y = 0 for the X = 80 line and Y = 100 and X = 0 for the Y = 100 line.

From linear programming theory, one of these four intersection edges or extreme values is the optimal solution. One method is simply to substitute each of the end points into the objective function and see which solution set provides the highest profit level.

Using the objective function where Profit = 20X + 15Y and substituting each of the extreme value sets:

When X = 0 and Y = 100:   Profit = $20 (0) + $15 (100) = $1,500
When X = 33.34 and Y = 100:   Profit = $20 (33.34) + $15 (100) = $2,167
When X = 80 and Y = 30:   Profit = $20 (80) + $15 (30) = $2,050
When X = 80 and Y = 0:   Profit = $20 (80) + $15 (0) = $1,600

Here, we see that when X = 33.34 and Y = 100, the profit function is maximized. We can also further verify this by using any combinations of X and Y within the feasible (shaded) area above. For instance, X = 10 and Y = 10 is a combination that is feasible but their profit outcome is only $20 (10) + $15 (10) = $350. We can calculate infinite combinations of X and Y sets but the optimal combination is always going to be at extreme value edges.

We can easily verify which extreme value will be the optimal solution set by drawing the objective function line. If we set the objective function to be:

20X + 15Y = 0   we get X = 20, Y = 15
20X + 15Y = 1200   we get X = 60, Y = 80

If we keep shifting the profit function upwards to the right, we will keep intersecting with the extreme value edges. The edge that provides the highest profit function is the optimal solution set.

In our example, point B is the optimal solution, which was verified by our calculations above, where X = 33.34 and Y = 100.

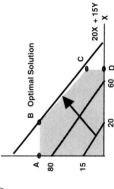

FIGURE 10.6   Solving optimization using linear programming.

There could be potential problems when dealing with linear programming. The three most frequently occurring problems include: Unbounded Solutions, No Feasible Solutions, and Multiple Optimal Solutions.

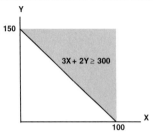

Unbounded Solutions

For instance, if the only constraint was such that $3X + 2Y \geq 300$, we have an unbounded problem. This means the machine can keep working greater than 300 hours without stop. Hence, optimally, in order to generate the most amount of profit, we would keep making products X and Y up to an infinite level. This is essentially management heaven, to produce as much as possible without any budgetary or resource constraints. Obviously, if this is the case, we should assume that the problem has not been defined correctly and perhaps an error has occurred in our mathematical models.

No Feasible Solution

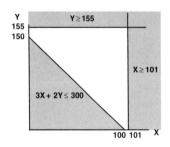

Now suppose we have the following constraints:

$$3X + 2Y \leq 300$$
$$X \geq 101$$
$$Y \geq 155$$

There exists no area where all constraints are binding simultaneously. In essence, any solution generated will by definition not be feasible since there will always be a constraint that is violated. Given a situation like this, it may be that the problem has been framed incorrectly or that we may have to request that management loosen some of its tight constraints since based on its expectations, the project is just not doable. Additional resources are required (greater than 300 hours by purchasing additional machines or hiring more workers) or that the minimum required production levels (155 and 101) be reduced.

Multiple Solutions

Here, we have two extreme values (B and C) that intersect the profit objective function. Both these solution sets are optimal. This is good news for management since it has the option of choosing either combination of X and Y production levels. Other qualitative factors may be utilized on top of quantitative analytical results.

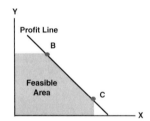

FIGURE 10.7   Potential problems of linear programming.

Using the same previous problem, where we have the following:

The Objective Function: Max 20X + 15Y

Subject to Constraints: 3X + 2Y ≤ 300

$$X \le 80$$
$$Y \le 100$$

We can utilize Excel's Solver add-in to provide a quick analytical solution.

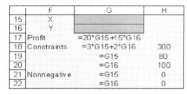

First, we need to set up the spreadsheet model. We have an X and Y variable which is to be solved. Next, we have the profit objective function in cell G17 and the constraints in cells G18 through H22. In order for Solver to perform the calculation, we needed to include two additional requirements, the nonnegative constraints, where we are setting both X and Y to be positive values only. Negative values of production are impossible. Cells H18 to H22 are the target values for the constraints. We then start Solver by clicking on Tools and Solver. (If Solver is not available, you may have to first add it in by clicking on Tools/Add-Ins and selecting Solver. Then, go back to Tools/Solver to run the program).

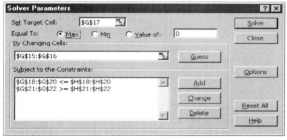

Set the profit calculation as the target cell ($G$17) and select maximization. Set the X and Y unknowns as the cells to change ($G$15:$G$16). Next, click on Add to add the constraints. The constraints could be added one at a time or in a batch group. Add $G$18:$G$20 to be less than or equal to $H$18:$H$20. Then, add in the nonnegative constraints where $G$21:$G$22 is greater than or equal to zero ($H$21:$H$22).

If we let Solver calculate the results, we would obtain the following, where the optimal solution set is when:

X	33.33	
Y	100	
Profit	$2,167	
Constraints	300	300
	33.33	80
	100	100
Nonnegative	33.33	0
	100	0

FIGURE 10.8 Using Excel's Solver in linear programming.

Integer Portfolio Optimization and Integer Linear Programming

	Cost	Return	Risk	Return-Risk Ratio	Allocation	Weighted Cost	Risk Return	Weighted Risk
Project A	$500,000	19%	32%	0.594	0%	$0	0.000	0%
Project B	$625,000	23%	39%	0.590	0%	$0	0.000	0%
Project C	$345,000	15%	22%	0.682	100%	$345,000	0.682	22%
Project D	$290,000	16%	29%	0.552	0%	$0	0.000	0%
Project E	$450,000	17%	25%	0.680	100%	$450,000	0.680	25%
					Sum	$795,000	1.362	47%

Budget Constraint $1,000,000
Each project must be between 10% and 50% allocated in funds

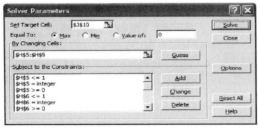

Suppose you have 5 projects you wish to allocate a fixed budget of $500,000 (this is your constraint) among, such that you will maximize the return to risk ratio (this is the objective function) subject to the requirements that each of these projects can be allocated anywhere between 10% and 50% of its total cost. You cannot allocate more than 50% of the cost of a project since you are only in the beginning stages of development while at least 10% of the project should be funded since all five projects have been previously found to be financially feasible. Using Excel's Solver add-in (use Tools/Add-Ins/Solver and then Tools/Solver) we calculate the optimal weights that will maximize the return to risk ratio.

Target cell is the objective function, which in this case is the total return to risk ratio weighted by each project, which is to be maximized.
Next, add additional constraints including the budget constraint where the total cost allocated in the portfolio is ≤ the budget constraint.
In addition, for each project weight, set them to be ≥ 0 and ≤ 1 as well as weight as integers. This is essentially the difference between the prior linear programming and optimization routine which allows fractional projects to be executed while in integer linear programming, projects are either chosen (1.0) or not (0.0) and nothing in between is allowed (integer constraint).

FIGURE 10.9   Excel Solver on integer linear programming.

Portfolio Optimization and Linear Programming

	Cost	Return	Risk	Return-Risk Ratio	Allocation	Weighted Cost	Total Risk-Return	Weighted Risk
Project A	$500,000	19%	32%	0.594	10%	$50,000	0.059	3%
Project B	$625,000	23%	39%	0.590	10%	$62,500	0.059	4%
Project C	$345,000	15%	22%	0.682	50%	$172,500	0.341	11%
Project D	$290,000	16%	29%	0.552	50%	$145,000	0.276	15%
Project E	$450,000	17%	25%	0.680	16%	$70,000	0.106	4%
					Sum	$500,000	0.841	36%

Budget Constraint $500,000
Each project must be between 10% and 50% allocated in funds

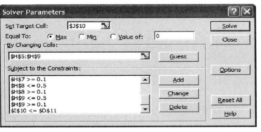

Suppose you have 5 projects you wish to allocate a fixed budget of $500,000 (this is your constraint) among, such that you will maximize the return to risk ratio (this is the objective function) subject to the requirements that each of these projects can be allocated anywhere between 10% and 50% of its total cost. You cannot allocate more than 50% of the cost of a project since you are only in the beginning stages of development while at least 10% of the project should be funded since all five projects have been previously found to be financially feasible. Using Excel's Solver add-in (use Tools/Add-Ins/Solver and then Tools/Solver) we calculate the optimal weights that will maximize the return to risk ratio.

Target cell is the objective function, which in this case is the total return to risk ratio weighted by each project, which is to be maximized.
Next, add additional constraints including the budget constraint where the total cost allocated in the portfolio is ≤ the budget constraint.
In addition, for each project weight, set them to be ≥ 0.1 and ≤ 0.5.

FIGURE 10.10   Excel Solver on continuous linear programming.

QUESTIONS

1. What is the difference between deterministic optimization and optimization under uncertainty?
2. Define then compare and contrast each of the following:
   a. Objective
   b. Constraint
   c. Decision variable
3. Explain what some of the problems are in a graphical linear programming approach and if they can be easily solved.
4. What are some of the approaches to solve an optimization problem? List each approach as well as its corresponding pros and cons.

CHAPTER 11

Optimization Under Uncertainty

T his chapter looks at the optimization process and methodologies in more detail as it pertains to using Risk Simulator. These methodologies include the use of continuous versus discrete integer optimization, as well as static versus dynamic and stochastic optimizations. The chapter then proceeds with several example optimization models to illustrate how the optimization process works. The first is the application of *continuous* optimization under uncertainty for a simple project selection model, where the idea is to allocate 100 percent of an individual's investment among several different asset classes (different types of mutual funds or investment styles: growth, value, aggressive growth, income, global, index, contrarian, momentum, and so forth). The second project deals with *discrete integer* optimization, where the idea is to look at several competing and nonmutually exclusive project choices, each with a different return, risk, and cost profile. The job of the analyst here is to find the best combination of projects that will satisfy the firm's budget constraints while maximizing the portfolio's total value.

The chapter continues by running a portfolio investment efficient frontier by applying some of the advanced settings in Risk Simulator, continued by a stochastic optimization model where simulation is iteratively combined with optimization methods. Next, small case applications in the military on using portfolio optimization and efficient frontier are shown, together with a case on applying the optimal pricing structure on various goods and services by examining the price elasticity of demand. The chapter concludes with several appendixes on running optimization outside of Excel (using ROV Optimizer for linking to large databases and for running large portfolios at super speed) and computing portfolio risk and return levels, as well as a detailed step-by-step set of hands-on exercises on setting up and running your own optimization routines.

OPTIMIZATION PROCEDURES

Many algorithms exist to run optimization and many different procedures exist when optimization is coupled with Monte Carlo simulation. In Risk Simulator, there are three distinct optimization procedures and optimization types as well as different decision variable types. For instance, Risk Simulator can handle *continuous decision variables* (1.2535, 0.2215, and so forth), *integer decision variables* (1, 2, 3, 4), *binary decision variables* (1 and 0 for go and no-go decisions), and *mixed decision variables* (both integers and continuous variables). On top of that, Risk Simulator can handle *linear optimization* (i.e., when both the objective and constraints are all linear equations and functions) and *nonlinear optimizations* (i.e., when the objective and constraints are a mixture of linear and nonlinear functions and equations).

As far as the optimization process is concerned, Risk Simulator can be used to run a *discrete optimization*, that is, an optimization that is run on a discrete or static model, where no simulations are run. In other words, all the inputs in the model are static and unchanging. This optimization type is applicable when the model is assumed to be known and no uncertainties exist. Also, a discrete optimization can first be run to determine the optimal portfolio and its corresponding optimal allocation of decision variables before more advanced optimization procedures are applied. For instance, before running a stochastic optimization problem, a discrete optimization is first run to determine if solutions to the optimization problem exist before a more protracted analysis is performed.

Next, *dynamic optimization* is applied when Monte Carlo simulation is used together with optimization. Another name for such a procedure is *simulation-optimization*; that is, a simulation is first run, then the results of the simulation are applied in the Excel model, and then an optimization is applied to the simulated values. In other words, a simulation is run for N trials, and then an optimization process is run for M iterations until the optimal results are obtained or an infeasible set is found. Using Risk Simulator's optimization module, you can choose which forecast and assumption statistics to use and replace in the model after the simulation is run. Then, these forecast statistics can be applied in the optimization process. This approach is useful when you have a large model with many interacting assumptions and forecasts, and when some of the forecast statistics are required in the optimization. For example, if the standard deviation of an assumption or forecast is required in the optimization model (e.g., computing the Sharpe ratio in asset allocation and optimization problems where we have mean divided by standard deviation of the portfolio), then this approach should be used.

The *stochastic optimization* process, in contrast, is similar to the dynamic optimization procedure with the exception that the entire dynamic optimization process is repeated T times; that is, a simulation with

N trials is run, and then an optimization is run with M iterations to obtain the optimal results. Then the process is replicated T times. The results will be a forecast chart of each decision variable with T values. In other words, a simulation is run and the forecast or assumption statistics are used in the optimization model to find the optimal allocation of decision variables. Then, another simulation is run, generating different forecast statistics, and these new updated values are then optimized, and so forth. Hence, the final decision variables will each have their own forecast chart, indicating the range of the optimal decision variables. For instance, instead of obtaining single-point estimates in the dynamic optimization procedure, you can now obtain a distribution of the decision variables, hence, a range of optimal values for each decision variable, also known as a stochastic optimization.

Finally, an efficient frontier optimization procedure applies the concepts of marginal increments and shadow pricing in optimization; that is, what would happen to the results of the optimization if one of the constraints were relaxed slightly? Say for instance, if the budget constraint is set at $1 million. What would happen to the portfolio's outcome and optimal decisions if the constraint were now $1.5 million, or $2 million, and so forth? This is the concept of the Markowitz efficient frontier in investment finance, where if the portfolio standard deviation is allowed to increase slightly, what additional returns will the portfolio generate? This process is similar to the dynamic optimization process with the exception that *one* of the constraints is allowed to change, and with each change, the simulation and optimization process is run. This process can be run either manually (rerunning optimization several times) or automatically (using Risk Simulator's changing constraint and efficient frontier functionality). As an example, the manual process is: Run a dynamic or stochastic optimization, then rerun another optimization with a new constraint, and repeat that procedure several times. This manual process is important, as by changing the constraint, the analyst can determine if the results are similar or different, and hence whether it is worthy of any additional analysis, or to determine how far a marginal increase in the constraint should be to obtain a significant change in the objective and decision variables. This is done by comparing the forecast distribution of each decision variable after running a stochastic optimization. Alternatively, the automated efficient frontier approach is shown later in the chapter.

One item is worthy of consideration. Other software products exist that supposedly perform stochastic optimization, but, in fact, they do not. For instance, after a simulation is run, then *one* iteration of the optimization process is generated, and then another simulation is run, then the *second* optimization iteration is generated, and so forth. This process is simply a waste of time and resources; that is, in optimization, the model is put through a rigorous set of algorithms, where multiple iterations (ranging from several to thousands of iterations) are required to obtain the optimal results. Hence, generating *one* iteration at a time is a waste of time and resources. The same portfolio can be solved using Risk Simulator in under a minute as compared to multiple hours using such a backward approach. Also, such a simulation-optimization approach will typically yield bad results and is not a stochastic optimization approach. Be extremely careful of such methodologies when applying optimization to your models.

The following are two example optimization problems. One uses continuous decision variables while the other uses discrete integer decision variables. In either model, you can apply discrete optimization, dynamic optimization, stochastic optimization, or even manually generate efficient frontiers with shadow pricing. Any of these approaches can be used for these two examples. Therefore, for simplicity, only the model setup is illustrated and it is up to the user to decide which optimization process to run. Also, the continuous decision variable example uses the nonlinear optimization approach (because the portfolio risk computed is a nonlinear function, and the objective is a nonlinear function of portfolio returns divided by portfolio risks) while the second example of an integer optimization is an example of a linear optimization model (its objective and all of its constraints are linear). Therefore, these two examples encapsulate all of the procedures aforementioned.

CONTINUOUS OPTIMIZATION

Figure 11.1 illustrates the sample continuous optimization model. The example here uses the *11 Optimization Continuous* file found on *Risk Simulator | Example Models*. In this example, there are 10 distinct asset classes (e.g., different types of mutual funds, stocks, or assets) where the idea is to most efficiently and effectively allocate the portfolio holdings such that the best *bang for the buck* is obtained; that is, to generate the best portfolio returns possible given the risks inherent in each asset class. In order to truly understand the concept of optimization, we must delve more deeply into this sample model to see how the optimization process can best be applied.

The model shows the 10 asset classes and each asset class has its own set of annualized returns and annualized volatilities. These return and risk measures are annualized values such that they can be consistently compared across different asset classes. Returns are computed using the geometric average of the relative returns while the risks are computed using the logarithmic relative stock returns approach. See the appendix to this chapter for details on computing the annualized volatility and annualized returns on a stock or asset class.

The Allocation Weights in column E hold the decision variables, which are the variables that need to be tweaked and tested such that the total

ASSET ALLOCATION OPTIMIZATION MODEL

Asset Class Description	Annualized Returns	Volatility Risk	Allocation Weights	Required Minimum Allocation	Required Maximum Allocation	Return to Risk Ratio	Returns Ranking (Hi-Lo)	Risk Ranking (Lo-Hi)	Return to Risk Ranking (Hi-Lo)	Allocation Ranking (Hi-Lo)
Asset Class 1	10.54%	12.36%	10.00%	5.00%	35.00%	0.8524	9	2	7	1
Asset Class 2	11.25%	16.23%	10.00%	5.00%	35.00%	0.6929	7	8	10	1
Asset Class 3	11.84%	15.64%	10.00%	5.00%	35.00%	0.7570	6	7	9	1
Asset Class 4	10.64%	12.35%	10.00%	5.00%	35.00%	0.8615	8	1	5	1
Asset Class 5	13.25%	13.28%	10.00%	5.00%	35.00%	0.9977	5	4	2	1
Asset Class 6	14.21%	14.39%	10.00%	5.00%	35.00%	0.9875	3	6	3	1
Asset Class 7	15.53%	14.25%	10.00%	5.00%	35.00%	1.0898	1	5	1	1
Asset Class 8	14.95%	16.44%	10.00%	5.00%	35.00%	0.9094	2	9	4	1
Asset Class 9	14.16%	16.50%	10.00%	5.00%	35.00%	0.8584	4	10	6	1
Asset Class 10	10.06%	12.50%	10.00%	5.00%	35.00%	0.8045	10	3	8	1

Portfolio Total | 12.6419% | 4.58% | 100.00%

Return to Risk Ratio | 2.7596

Specifications of the optimization model:

Objective: *Maximize Return to Risk Ratio (C18)*
Decision Variables: *Allocation Weights (E6:E15)*
Restrictions on Decision Variables: *Minimum and Maximum Required (F6:G15)*
Constraints: *Portfolio Total Allocation Weights 100% (E17 is set to 100%)*

Additional specifications:

1. One can always maximize portfolio total returns or minimize the portfolio total risk.
2. Incorporate Monte Carlo simulation in the model by simulating the returns and volatility of each asset class and apply Simulation-Optimization techniques.
3. The portfolio can be optimized as is without simulation using Static Optimization techniques.

FIGURE 11.1 Continuous optimization model.

518

weight is constrained at 100% (cell E17). Typically, to start the optimization, we will set these cells to a uniform value, where in this case, cells E6 to E15 are set at 10% each. In addition, each decision variable may have specific restrictions in its allowed range. In this example, the lower and upper allocations allowed are 5% and 35%, as seen in columns F and G. This means that each asset class may have its own allocation boundaries. Next, column H shows the return to risk ratio, which is simply the return percentage divided by the risk percentage, where the higher this value, the higher the *bang for the buck*. The remaining model shows the individual asset class rankings by returns, risk, return to risk ratio, and allocation. In other words, these rankings show at a glance which asset class has the lowest risk, or the highest return, and so forth.

The portfolio's total returns in cell C17 are *SUMPRODUCT(C6:C15, E6:E15)*, that is, the sum of the allocation weights multiplied by the annualized returns for each asset class. In other words, we have $R_P = \omega_1 R_1 + \omega_2 R_2 + \omega_3 R_3 + \ldots + \omega_{10} R_{10}$, where R_P is the return on the portfolio, R_i are the individual returns on the projects, and ω_i are the respective weights or capital allocation across each project.

In addition, the portfolio's diversified risk in cell D17 is computed by taking

$$\sigma_p = \sqrt{\sum_{i=1}^{n} \omega_i^2 \sigma_i^2 + \sum_{i=1}^{n}\sum_{j=1}^{m} 2\omega_i \omega_j \rho_{i,j} \sigma_i \sigma_j}$$

Here, ρ_{ij} are the respective cross correlations between the asset classes. Hence, if the cross correlations are negative, there are risk diversification effects, and the portfolio risk decreases. However, to simplify the computations here, we assume zero correlations among the asset classes through this portfolio risk computation, but assume the correlations when applying simulation on the returns as will be seen later. Therefore, instead of applying static correlations among these different asset returns, we apply the correlations in the simulation assumptions themselves, creating a more dynamic relationship among the simulated return values.

Finally, the return to risk ratio or Sharpe ratio is computed for the portfolio. This value is seen in cell C18 and represents the objective to be maximized in this optimization exercise. To summarize, we have the following specifications in this example model:

Objective:	*Maximize Return to Risk Ratio (C18)*
Decision Variables:	*Allocation Weights (E6:E15)*
Restrictions on Decision Variables:	*Minimum and Maximum Required (F6:G15)*
Constraints:	*Total Allocation Weights Sum to 100% (E17)*

Procedure

Use the following procedure to run an optimization analysis:

1. Open the example file (*Continuous Optimization*) and start a new profile by clicking on *Risk Simulator | New Profile* and provide it a name.
2. The first step in optimization is to set the decision variables. Select cell E6 and set the first decision variable (*Risk Simulator | Optimization | Set Decision*) and click on the link icon to select the name cell (B6), as well as the lower bound and upper bound values at cells F6 and G6. Then, using Risk Simulator copy, copy this cell E6 decision variable and paste the decision variable to the remaining cells in E7 to E15.
3. The second step in optimization is to set the constraint. There is only one constraint here, that is, the total allocation in the portfolio must sum to 100%. So, click on *Risk Simulator | Optimization | Constraints* ... and select *ADD* to add a new constraint. Then, select the cell E17 and make it equal (=) to 100%. Click *OK* when done.
4. The final step in optimization is to set the objective function and start the optimization by selecting the objective cell C18 and *Risk Simulator | Optimization | Set Objective* and then run the optimization by selecting *Risk Simulator | Optimization | Run Optimization* and selecting the optimization of choice (Static Optimization, Dynamic Optimization, or Stochastic Optimization). To get started, select *Static Optimization*. Check to make sure the objective cell is set for C18 and select *Maximize*. You can now review the decision variables and constraints if required, or click *OK* to run the static optimization.
5. Once the optimization is complete, you may select *Revert* to revert back to the original values of the decision variables as well as the objective, or select *Replace* to apply the optimized decision variables. Typically, Replace is chosen after the optimization is done.

Figure 11.2 shows the screen shots of the preceding procedural steps. You can add simulation assumptions on the model's returns and risk (columns C and D) and apply the dynamic optimization and stochastic optimization for additional practice.

Results Interpretation

The optimization's final results are shown in Figure 11.3, where the optimal allocation of assets for the portfolio is seen in cells E6:E15. Given the restrictions of each asset fluctuating between 5 percent and 35 percent, and where the sum of the allocation must equal 100 percent, the allocation that maximizes the return to risk ratio is seen in Figure 11.3.

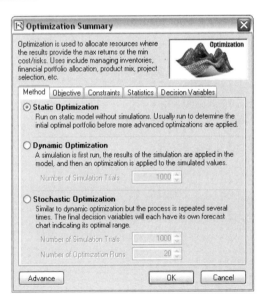

FIGURE 11.2 Running continuous optimization in Risk Simulator.

ASSET ALLOCATION OPTIMIZATION MODEL

Asset Class Description	Annualized Returns	Volatility Risk	Allocation Weights	Required Minimum Allocation	Required Maximum Allocation	Return to Risk Ratio	Returns Ranking (Hi-Lo)	Risk Ranking (Lo-Hi)	Return to Risk Ranking (Hi-Lo)	Allocation Ranking (Hi-Lo)
Asset Class 1	10.54%	12.36%	11.09%	5.00%	35.00%	0.8524	9	2	7	4
Asset Class 2	11.25%	16.23%	6.87%	5.00%	35.00%	0.6929	7	8	10	10
Asset Class 3	11.84%	15.64%	7.78%	5.00%	35.00%	0.7570	6	7	9	9
Asset Class 4	10.64%	12.35%	11.22%	5.00%	35.00%	0.8615	8	1	5	3
Asset Class 5	13.25%	13.28%	12.08%	5.00%	35.00%	0.9977	5	4	2	2
Asset Class 6	14.21%	14.39%	11.04%	5.00%	35.00%	0.9875	3	6	3	5
Asset Class 7	15.53%	14.25%	12.30%	5.00%	35.00%	1.0898	1	5	1	1
Asset Class 8	14.95%	16.44%	8.90%	5.00%	35.00%	0.9094	2	9	4	7
Asset Class 9	14.16%	16.50%	8.37%	5.00%	35.00%	0.8584	4	10	6	8
Asset Class 10	10.06%	12.50%	10.35%	5.00%	35.00%	0.8045	10	3	8	6

Portfolio Total 12.6920%   4.52%   **100.00%**

Return to Risk Ratio 2.8091

Specifications of the optimization model:

Objective: *Maximize Return to Risk Ratio (C18)*
Decision Variables: *Allocation Weights (E6:E15)*
Restrictions on Decision Variables: *Minimum and Maximum Required (F6:G15)*
Constraints: *Portfolio Total Allocation Weights 100% (E17 is set to 100%)*

Additional specifications:

1. One can always maximize portfolio total returns or minimize the portfolio total risk.
2. Incorporate Monte Carlo simulation in the model by simulating the returns and volatility of each asset class and apply Simulation-Optimization techniques.
3. The portfolio can be optimized as is without simulation using Static Optimization techniques.

FIGURE 11.3 Continuous optimization results.

A few important things must be noted when reviewing the results and optimization procedures performed thus far:

- The correct way to run the optimization is to maximize the bang for the buck or returns to risk Sharpe ratio as we have done.
- If instead we maximized the total portfolio returns, the optimal allocation result is trivial and does not require optimization to obtain; that is, simply allocate 5 percent (the minimum allowed) to the lowest eight assets, 35 percent (the maximum allowed) to the highest returning asset, and the remaining (25 percent) to the second-best returns asset. Optimization is not required. However, when allocating the portfolio this way, the risk is a lot higher as compared to when maximizing the returns to risk ratio, although the portfolio returns by themselves are higher.
- In contrast, one can minimize the total portfolio risk, but the returns will now be less.

Table 11.1 illustrates the results from the three different objectives being optimized. From the table, the best approach is to maximize the returns to risk ratio, that is, for the same amount of risk, this allocation provides the highest amount of return. Conversely, for the same amount of return, this allocation provides the lowest amount of risk possible. This approach of *bang for the buck* or returns to risk ratio is the cornerstone of the Markowitz efficient frontier in modern portfolio theory. That is, if we constrain the total portfolio risk levels and successively increase them over time, we will obtain several efficient portfolio allocations for different risk characteristics. Thus, different efficient portfolio allocations can be obtained for different individuals with different risk preferences.

DISCRETE INTEGER OPTIMIZATION

Sometimes, the decision variables are not continuous but discrete integers (e.g., 1, 2, 3) or binary (e.g., 0 and 1). We can use such binary decision

TABLE 11.1 Optimization Results

Objective	Portfolio Returns (%)	Portfolio Risk (%)	Portfolio Returns to Risk Ratio
Maximize Returns to Risk Ratio	12.69	4.52	2.8091
Maximize Returns	13.97	6.77	2.0636
Minimize Risk	12.38	4.46	2.7754

Projects	ENPV	Cost	Risk $	Risk %	Return to Risk Ratio	Profitability Index	Selection
Project 1	$458.00	$1,732.44	$54.96	12.00%	8.33	1.26	1.0000
Project 2	$1,954.00	$859.00	$1,914.92	98.00%	1.02	3.27	1.0000
Project 3	$1,599.00	$1,845.00	$1,551.03	97.00%	1.03	1.87	1.0000
Project 4	$2,251.00	$1,645.00	$1,012.95	45.00%	2.22	2.37	1.0000
Project 5	$849.00	$458.00	$925.41	109.00%	0.92	2.85	1.0000
Project 6	$758.00	$52.00	$560.92	74.00%	1.35	15.58	1.0000
Project 7	$2,845.00	$758.00	$5,633.10	198.00%	0.51	4.75	1.0000
Project 8	$1,235.00	$115.00	$926.25	75.00%	1.33	11.74	1.0000
Project 9	$1,945.00	$125.00	$2,100.60	108.00%	0.93	16.56	1.0000
Project 10	$2,250.00	$458.00	$1,912.50	85.00%	1.18	5.91	1.0000
Project 11	$549.00	$45.00	$263.52	48.00%	2.08	13.20	1.0000
Project 12	$525.00	$105.00	$309.75	59.00%	1.69	6.00	1.0000
Total	$17,218.00	$8,197.44	$7,007	40.70%			12.00
Goal:	MAX	< =$5000					<=6
Sharpe Ratio	2.4573						

ENPV is the expected NPV of each investment or project, while Cost can be the total cost of investment, and Risk is the Coefficient of Variation of the project's ENPV.

FIGURE 11.4 Discrete integer optimization model.

variables as on-off switches or go/no-go decisions. Figure 11.4 illustrates a project selection model where there are 12 projects listed. The example here uses the *Optimization Discrete* file found on *Risk Simulator | Example Models*. Each project, like before, has its own returns (ENPV and NPV for expanded net present value and net present value—the ENPV is simply the NPV plus any strategic real options values), costs of implementation, risks, and so forth. If required, this model can be modified to include required full-time equivalences (FTE) and other resources of various functions, and additional constraints can be set on these additional resources. The inputs into this model are typically linked from other spreadsheet models. For instance, each project will have its own discounted cash flow or returns on investment model. The application here is to maximize the portfolio's Sharpe ratio subject to some budget allocation. Many other versions of this model can be created, for instance, maximizing the portfolio returns, or minimizing the risks, or add additional constraints where the total number of projects chosen cannot exceed 6, and so forth and so on. All of these items can be run using this existing model.

Procedure

Use the following procedure to set up and run the optimization:

1. Open the example file (*Discrete Optimization*) and start a new profile by clicking on *Risk Simulator | New Profile* and provide it a name.
2. The first step in optimization is to set up the decision variables. Set the first decision variable by selecting cell J4, and select *Risk Simulator | Optimization | Set Decision*, click on the link icon to select the name cell (B4), and select the *Binary* variable. Then, using Risk Simulator copy, copy this J4 decision variable cell and paste the decision variable to the remaining cells in J5 to J15.
3. The second step in optimization is to set the constraint. There are two constraints here, that is, the total budget allocation in the portfolio must be less than $5,000 and the total number of projects must not exceed 6. So, click on *Risk Simulator | Optimization | Constraints...* and select *ADD* to add a new constraint. Then, select the cell D17 and make it less than or equal ($\leq$) to 5,000. Repeat by setting cell J17 $\leq$ 6.
4. The final step in optimization is to set the objective function and start the optimization by selecting cell C19 and selecting *Risk Simulator | Optimization | Set Objective* and then run the optimization (*Risk Simulator | Optimization | Run Optimization*) and selecting the optimization of choice (Static Optimization, Dynamic Optimization, or Stochastic Optimization). To get started, select *Static Optimization*. Check to make sure that the objective cell is C19 and select *Maximize*. You can now review the decision variables and constraints if required, or click *OK* to run the static optimization.

Figure 11.5 shows the screen shots of the foregoing procedural steps. You can add simulation assumptions on the model's ENPV and Risk (columns C and F) and apply the dynamic optimization and stochastic optimization for additional practice.

Results Interpretation

Figure 11.6 shows a sample optimal selection of projects that maximizes the Sharpe ratio. In contrast, one can always maximize total revenues, but, as before, this is a trivial process and simply involves choosing the highest returning project and going down the list until you run out of money or exceed the budget constraint. Doing so will yield theoretically undesirable projects as the highest yielding projects typically hold higher risks. Now, if desired,

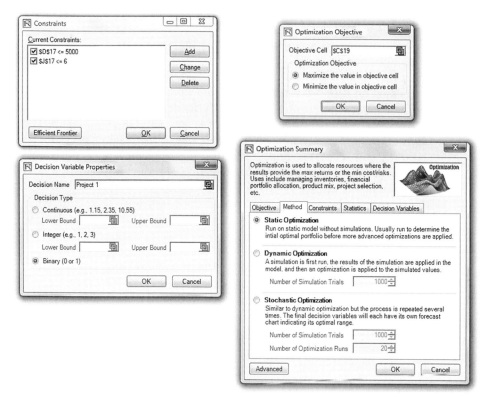

FIGURE 11.5   Running discrete integer optimization in Risk Simulator.

you can replicate the optimization using a stochastic or dynamic optimization by adding in assumptions in the ENPV and/or cost and/or risk values.

EFFICIENT FRONTIER AND ADVANCED OPTIMIZATION SETTINGS

Figure 11.7 shows the efficient frontier constraints for optimization. You can get to this interface by clicking on the *Efficient Frontier* button *after* you have set some constraints. You can now make these constraints changing. That is, each of the constraints can be created to step through between some minimum and maximum value. As an example, the constraint in cell J17 <= 6 can be set to run between 4 and 8 (Figure 11.7). That is, five optimizations will be run, each with the following constraints: J17 <= 4, J17 <= 5, J17 <= 6, J17 <= 7, and J17 <= 8. The optimal results will then be plotted as an efficient frontier and the report will be generated (Figure 11.8).

Projects	ENPV	Cost	Risk $	Risk %	Return to Risk Ratio	Profitability Index	Selection
Project 1	$458.00	$1,732.44	$54.96	12.00%	8.33	1.26	1.0000
Project 2	$1,954.00	$859.00	$1,914.92	98.00%	1.02	3.27	0.0000
Project 3	$1,599.00	$1,845.00	$1,551.03	97.00%	1.03	1.87	1.0000
Project 4	$2,251.00	$1,645.00	$1,012.95	45.00%	2.22	2.37	0.0000
Project 5	$849.00	$458.00	$925.41	109.00%	0.92	2.85	0.0000
Project 6	$758.00	$52.00	$560.92	74.00%	1.35	15.58	1.0000
Project 7	$2,845.00	$758.00	$5,633.10	198.00%	0.51	4.75	0.0000
Project 8	$1,235.00	$115.00	$926.25	75.00%	1.33	11.74	0.0000
Project 9	$1,945.00	$125.00	$2,100.60	108.00%	0.93	16.56	0.0000
Project 10	$2,250.00	$458.00	$1,912.50	85.00%	1.18	5.91	0.0000
Project 11	$549.00	$45.00	$263.52	48.00%	2.08	13.20	1.0000
Project 12	$525.00	$105.00	$309.75	59.00%	1.69	6.00	1.0000
Total	$5,776.00	$3,694.44	$1,539	26.64%			6.00
Goal	MAX	<=$5000					<=6
Sharpe Ratio	3.7543						

ENPV is the expected NPV of each investment or project, while Cost can be the total cost of investment, and Risk is the Coefficient of Variation of the project's ENPV.

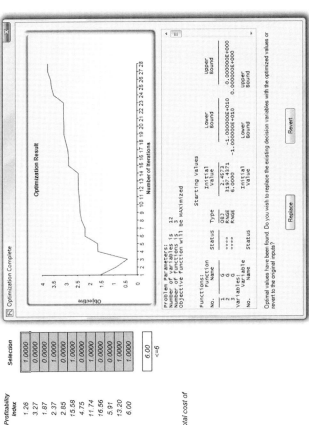

FIGURE 11.6 Optimal selection of projects that maximize the Sharpe ratio.

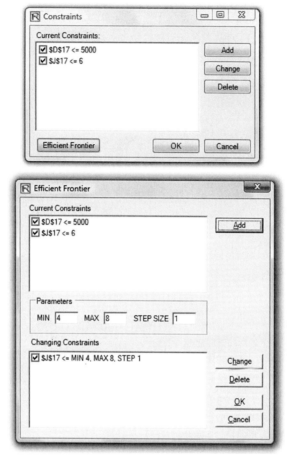

FIGURE 11.7   Generating changing constraints in an efficient frontier.

Specifically, following are the steps required to create a changing constraint:

1. In an optimization model (i.e., a model with Objective, Decision Variables, and Constraints already set up), click on *Risk Simulator | Optimization | Constraints* and then click on *Efficient Frontier.*
2. Select the constraint you want to change or step (e.g., J17), enter the parameters for Min, Max, and Step Size (Figure 11.7), and click *ADD,* then *OK,* and *OK* again. You should deselect the D17 <= 5000 constraint before running.

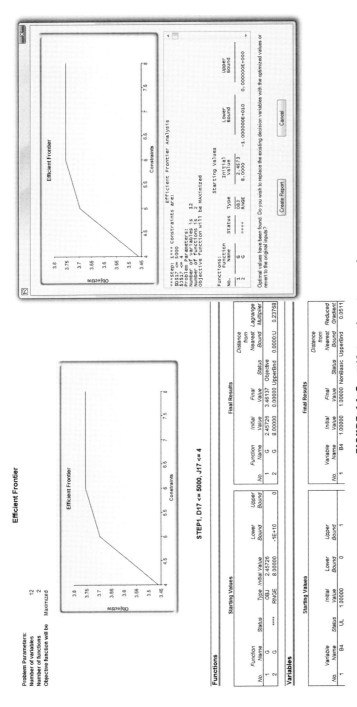

FIGURE 11.8 Efficient frontier results.

3. Run Optimization as usual (*Risk Simulator | Optimization | Run Optimization*). You can choose static, dynamic, or stochastic. To get started, select the *Static Optimization* to run.
4. The results will be shown as a user interface (Figure 11.8). Click on *Create Report* to generate a report worksheet with all the details of the optimization runs.

STOCHASTIC OPTIMIZATION

This example illustrates the application of stochastic optimization using a sample model with four asset classes each with different risk and return characteristics. The idea here is to find the best portfolio allocation such that the portfolio's bang for the buck, or returns to risk ratio, is maximized. That is, the goal is to allocate 100 percent of an individual's investment among several different asset classes (e.g., different types of mutual funds or investment styles: growth, value, aggressive growth, income, global, index, contrarian, momentum, and so forth). This model is different from others because there exists several simulation assumptions (risk and return values for each asset in columns C and D), as seen in Figure 11.9.

A simulation is run, then optimization is executed, and the entire process is repeated multiple times to obtain distributions of each decision variable. The entire analysis can be automated using Stochastic Optimization.

ASSET ALLOCATION OPTIMIZATION MODEL

Asset Class Description	Annualized Returns	Volatility Risk	Allocation Weights	Required Minimum Allocation	Required Maximum Allocation	Return to Risk Ratio	Returns Ranking (Hi-Lo)	Risk Ranking (Lo-Hi)	Return to Risk Ranking (Hi-Lo)	Allocation Ranking (Hi-Lo)
Asset 1	10.60%	12.41%	25.00%	10.00%	40.00%	0.8544	3	2	1	1
Asset 2	11.21%	16.16%	25.00%	10.00%	40.00%	0.6937	1	4	3	1
Asset 3	10.61%	15.93%	25.00%	10.00%	40.00%	0.6660	2	3	4	1
Asset 4	10.52%	12.40%	25.00%	10.00%	40.00%	0.8480	4	1	2	1
Portfolio Total	10.7356%	7.17%	100.00%							
Return to Risk Ratio	1.4970									

Specifications of the optimization model:

Objective: Maximize Return to Risk Ratio (C12)
Decision Variables: Allocation Weights (E6:E9)
Restrictions on Decision Variables: Minimum and Maximum Required (F6:G9)
Constraints: Portfolio Total Allocation Weights 100% (E11 is set to 100%)

Additional specifications:

1. One can always maximize portfolio total returns or minimize the portfolio total risk.
2. Incorporate Monte Carlo simulation in the model by simulating the returns and volatility of each asset class and apply Simulation-Optimization techniques.
3. The portfolio can be optimized as is without simulation using Static Optimization techniques.

FIGURE 11.9 Asset allocation model ready for stochastic optimization.

In order to run an optimization, several key specifications on the model have to be identified first:

Objective: Maximize Return to Risk Ratio (C12)

Decision Variables: Allocation Weights (E6:E9)

Restrictions on Decision Variables: Minimum and Maximum Required (F6:G9)

Constraints: Portfolio Total Allocation Weights 100% (E11 is set to 100%)

Simulation Assumptions: Return and Risk Values (C6:D9)

The model shows the various asset classes. Each asset class has its own set of annualized returns and annualized volatilities. These return and risk measures are annualized values such that they can be consistently compared across different asset classes. Returns are computed using the geometric average of the relative returns, while the risks are computed using the logarithmic relative stock returns approach. See the appendix in this chapter on volatility models for computational details.

Column E, the Allocation Weights, holds the decision variables, which are the variables that need to be tweaked and tested such that the total weight is constrained at 100% (cell E11). Typically, to start the optimization, we will set these cells to a uniform value. In this case, cells E6 to E9 are set at 25% each. In addition, each decision variable may have specific restrictions in its allowed range. In this example, the lower and upper allocations allowed are 10% and 40%, as seen in columns F and G. This setting means that each asset class may have its own allocation boundaries.

Next, column H shows the return to risk ratio, which is simply the return percentage divided by the risk percentage for each asset, where the higher this value, the higher the bang for the buck. The remaining parts of the model show the individual asset class rankings by returns, risk, return to risk ratio, and allocation. In other words, these rankings show at a glance which asset class has the lowest risk, or the highest return, and so forth.

Running an Optimization

To run this model, simply click on *Risk Simulator | Optimization | Run Optimization*. Alternatively, and for practice, you can set up the model using the following steps:

1. Start a new profile (*Risk Simulator | New Profile*).
2. For stochastic optimization, set distributional assumptions on the risk and returns for each asset class. That is, select cell C6, set an assumption

(*Risk Simulator* | *Set Input Assumption*), and make your own assumption as required. Repeat for cells C7 to D9.

3. Select cell E6, define the decision variable (*Risk Simulator* | *Optimization* | *Set Decision* or click on the *Set Decision D* icon), and make it a *Continuous Variable*. Then link the decision variable's name and minimum/maximum required to the relevant cells (B6, F6, G6).

4. Then use the *Risk Simulator Copy* on cell E6, select cells E7 to E9, and use *Risk Simulator Paste* (*Risk Simulator* | *Copy Parameter* and *Risk Simulator* | *Paste Parameter*, or use the copy and paste icons). Remember not to use Excel's regular copy and paste functions.

5. Next, set up the optimization's constraints by selecting *Risk Simulator* | *Optimization* | *Constraints*, selecting *ADD*, and selecting the cell E11 and making it equal 100% (total allocation, and do not forget the % sign).

6. Select cell C12, the objective to be maximized, and make it the objective: *Risk Simulator* | *Optimization* | *Set Objective* or click on the *O* icon.

7. Run the optimization by going to *Risk Simulator* | *Optimization* | *Run Optimization*. Review the different tabs to make sure that all the required inputs in steps 2 and 3 are correct. Select *Stochastic Optimization* and let it run for 500 trials repeated 20 times (Figure 11.10 illustrates these setup steps).

Click *OK* when the simulation completes and a detailed stochastic optimization report will be generated along with forecast charts of the decision variables.

Viewing and Interpreting Forecast Results

Stochastic optimization is performed when a simulation is first run and then the optimization is run. Then the whole analysis is repeated multiple times. The result is a distribution of each decision variable rather than a single-point estimate (Figure 11.11). So instead of saying you should invest 30.53% in Asset 1, the optimal decision is to invest between 30.19% and 30.88% as long as the total portfolio sums to 100%. This way, the results provide management or decision makers a range of flexibility in the optimal decisions, and all the while accounting for the risks and uncertainties in the inputs.

Notes

■ *Super Speed Simulation with Optimization.* You can also run stochastic optimization with super speed simulation. To do this, first reset the

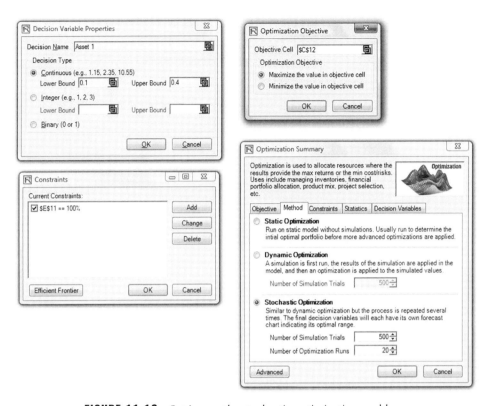

FIGURE 11.10 Setting up the stochastic optimization problem.

optimization by resetting all four decision variables back to 25%. Next select *Run Optimization,* click on the *Advanced* button (Figure 11.10), and select the checkbox for *Run Super Speed Simulation.* Then, in the run optimization user interface, select *Stochastic Optimization* on the *Method* tab and set it to run 500 trials and 20 optimization runs, and click *OK.* This approach will integrate the super speed simulation with optimization. Notice how much faster the stochastic optimization runs. You can now quickly rerun the optimization with a higher number of simulation trials.

- *Simulation Statistics for Stochastic and Dynamic Optimization.* Notice that if there are input simulation assumptions in the optimization model (i.e., these input assumptions are required to run the dynamic or stochastic optimization routines), the *Statistics* tab is now populated in the *Run Optimization* user interface. You can select from the droplist the statistics you want, such as average, standard deviation, coefficient of

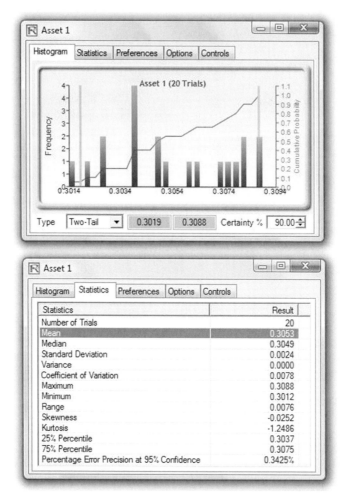

FIGURE 11.11 Simulated results from the stochastic optimization approach.

variation, conditional mean, conditional variance, a specific percentile, and so forth. Thus, if you run a stochastic optimization, a simulation of thousands of trials will first run; then the selected statistic will be computed and this value will be temporarily placed in the simulation assumption cell; then an optimization will be run based on this statistic; then the entire process is repeated multiple times. This method is important and useful for banking applications in computing Conditional Value at Risk or Conditional VaR.

OPTIMIZATION APPLICATION EXAMPLE: MILITARY PORTFOLIO AND EFFICIENT FRONTIER

This section illustrates a sample model from the ROV Modeling Toolkit—another software tool developed by Real Options Valuation, Inc., that contains more than 300 models and 800 functions (there are no trial versions for this software but a sample version of the model is located on the accompanying DVD). Figure 11.12 shows a model with 20 projects with different risk–return characteristics as well as several qualitative measures such as strategic score, military readiness score, tactical score, comprehensive score, and so forth. These scores are obtained through subject-matter experts, for instance, decision makers, leaders, and managers of organizations, where their expert opinions are gathered through the double-blind Delphi method. After being scrubbed (e.g., extreme values are eliminated, large data variations are analyzed, multiple iterations of the Delphi method are performed), their respective scores can be entered into a Distributional Fitting routine to find the best-fitting distribution, or used to develop a Custom Distribution for each project.

The central idea of this model is to find the best portfolio allocation such that the portfolio's total comprehensive strategic score and profits are maximized. That is, it is used to find the best project mix in the portfolio that maximizes the total *Profit* * *Score* measure, where *Profit* points to the portfolio level net returns after considering the risks and costs of each project and the *Score* measures the total comprehensive score of the portfolio, all the while being subject to the constraints on number of projects, budget constraint, full-time equivalent (FTE) resource restrictions, and strategic ranking constraints.

Objective: Maximize total portfolio returns times the portfolio comprehensive score (C28)

Decision Variables: Allocation or go/no-go decision (J5:J24)

Restrictions on Decision Variables: Binary decision variables (0 or 1)

Constraints: Total cost (E26) is less than or equal to $3,800 (in thousands or millions of dollars), less than or equal to 10 projects selected (J26) in the entire portfolio, FTE resources have to be less than or equal to 80 (M26), total strategic ranking for the entire portfolio must be less than or equal to 100 (F26)

Running an Optimization

1. To run this preset model, simply open the profile (*Risk Simulator | Change Profile*) and select *Military Portfolio and Efficient Frontier*.

Military Portfolio Optimization

Project Name	ENPV	NPV	Cost	Strategy Ranking	Return to Rank Ratio	Profitability Index	Selection	Military Score	Tactical Score	FTE Resources	Comprehensive Score
Project 1	$458.00	$150.76	$1,732.44	1.20	381.67	1.09	1	8.10	2.31	1.20	1.98
Project 2	$1,954.00	$245.00	$859.00	9.80	199.39	1.29	1	1.27	4.83	2.50	1.76
Project 3	$1,599.00	$458.00	$1,845.00	9.70	164.85	1.25	1	9.88	4.75	3.60	2.77
Project 4	$2,251.00	$529.00	$1,645.00	4.50	500.22	1.32	1	8.83	1.61	4.50	2.07
Project 5	$849.00	$564.00	$458.00	10.90	77.89	2.23	1	5.02	6.25	5.50	2.94
Project 6	$758.00	$135.00	$52.00	7.40	102.43	3.60	1	3.64	5.79	9.20	3.26
Project 7	$2,845.00	$311.00	$758.00	19.80	143.69	1.41	1	5.27	6.47	12.50	4.04
Project 8	$1,235.00	$754.00	$115.00	7.50	164.67	7.56	1	9.80	7.16	5.30	3.63
Project 9	$1,945.00	$198.00	$125.00	10.80	180.09	2.58	1	5.68	2.39	6.30	2.16
Project 10	$2,250.00	$785.00	$458.00	8.50	264.71	2.71	1	8.29	4.41	4.50	2.67
Project 11	$549.00	$35.00	$45.00	4.80	114.38	1.78	1	7.52	4.65	4.90	2.75
Project 12	$525.00	$75.00	$105.00	5.90	88.98	1.71	1	5.54	5.09	5.20	2.69
Project 13	$516.00	$451.00	$48.00	2.80	184.29	10.40	1	2.51	2.17	4.60	1.66
Project 14	$499.00	$458.00	$351.00	9.40	53.09	2.30	1	9.41	9.49	9.90	4.85
Project 15	$859.00	$125.00	$421.00	6.50	132.15	1.30	1	6.91	9.62	7.20	4.25
Project 16	$684.00	$458.00	$124.00	3.90	226.67	4.69	1	7.06	9.98	7.50	4.46
Project 17	$956.00	$124.00	$521.00	15.40	62.08	1.24	1	1.25	2.50	8.60	2.07
Project 18	$654.00	$164.00	$512.00	21.00	40.67	1.32	1	3.09	2.90	4.30	1.70
Project 19	$195.00	$45.00	$5.00	1.20	162.50	10.00	1	5.25	1.22	4.10	1.86
Project 20	$210.00	$65.00	$21.00	1.00	210.00	5.05	1	2.01	4.06	5.20	2.50
Total	$22,191.00		$10,200.44	162.00			20	116.32	97.65	116.60	56.08
Profit/Rank	$136.98						x <=10				
Profit*Score	$1,244,365.33	Maximize	<=$3800	<=100					<=80		

FIGURE 11.12 The project selection optimization model.

Then run the optimization (*Risk Simulator | Optimization | Run Optimization*) or, for practice, set up the model yourself by following these steps:

2. Start a new profile (*Risk Simulator | New Profile*) and give it a name.
3. In this example, all the allocations are required to be binary (0 or 1) values, so, first select cell J5 and make this a decision variable in the *Integer Optimization* worksheet. Select cell J5 and define it as a decision variable (*Risk Simulator | Optimization | Set Decision,* or click on the *Set Decision* icon) and make it a *Binary Variable.* This setting automatically sets the minimum to 0 and maximum to 1 and can only take on a value of 0 or 1. Then use the *Risk Simulator Copy* on cell J5, select cells J6 to J24, and use *Risk Simulator Paste* (*Risk Simulator | Copy Parameter* and *Risk Simulator | Paste Parameter,* or use the *Risk Simulator* copy and paste icons, not the Excel copy/paste).
4. Next, set up the optimization's constraints by selecting *Risk Simulator | Optimization | Constraints* and selecting *ADD.* Then link to cell E26, and make it <= 3800, select *ADD* one more time, click on the link icon, and point to cell J26 and set it to <=10. Continue with adding the other constraints (cell M26 <= 80 and F26 <= 100).
5. Select cell C28, the objective to be maximized, select *Risk Simulator | Optimization | Set Objective,* choose *Maximize* and *OK.*
6. Then select *Risk Simulator | Optimization | Run Optimization.* Review the different tabs to make sure that all the required inputs in steps 2 and 3 are correct. You may now select the optimization method of choice (e.g., *Static Optimization*) and click *OK* to run the optimization. The model setup is illustrated in Figure 11.13.

Note: Remember that if you want to run either a dynamic or stochastic optimization routine, make sure that first you have assumptions defined in the model. That is, make sure that some of the cells in C5:C24 and E5:F24 are assumptions. The suggestion for this model is to run a *Static Optimization*.

Portfolio Efficient Frontier

Clearly, running the optimization procedure will yield an optimal portfolio of projects where the constraints are satisfied. This result represents a single optimal portfolio point on the efficient frontier, for example, Portfolio B on the chart in Figure 11.14. Then, by subsequently changing some of the constraints, for instance, by increasing the budget and allowed projects, we can rerun the optimization to produce another optimal portfolio given these new constraints. Therefore, a series of optimal portfolio allocations can be determined and graphed. This graphical representation of all optimal

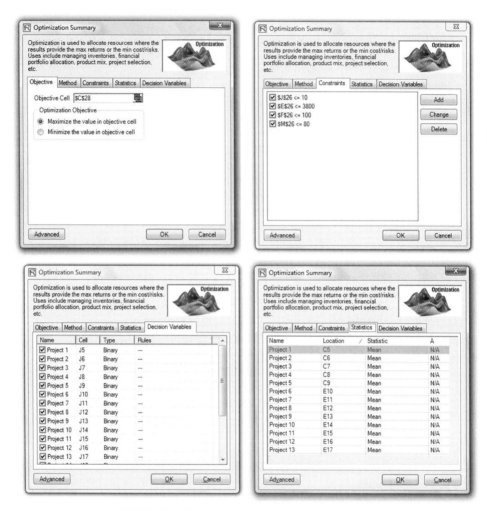

FIGURE 11.13   Setting up an optimization model.

portfolios is called the *Portfolio Efficient Frontier*. At this juncture, each point represents a portfolio allocation, for instance, Portfolio B might represent projects 1, 2, 5, 6, 7, 8, 10, 15, and so forth, while Portfolio C might represent projects 2, 6, 7, 9, 12, 15, and so forth, each resulting in different tactical, military, or comprehensive scores, and portfolio returns. It is up to the decision maker to decide which portfolio represents the best decision and if sufficient resources exist to execute these projects.

Typically, in an efficient frontier analysis, you would select projects where the marginal increase in benefits is positive and the slope is steep.

Budget	Comprehensive Score	Tactical Score	Military Score	Allowed Projects	ROI-RANK Objective
$3,800	33.15	62.64	58.58	10	$470,236
$4,800	36.33	68.85	66.86	11	$521,646
$5,800	38.40	70.46	75.69	12	$623,558
$6,800	39.94	72.14	82.31	13	$659,948
$7,800	39.76	70.05	86.54	14	$676,280

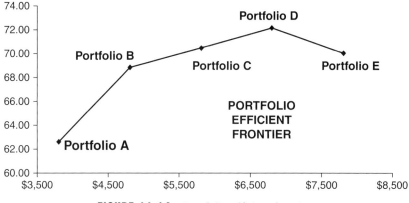

FIGURE 11.14 Portfolio efficient frontier.

In the next example, you would select Portfolio D rather than Portfolio E because the marginal increase is negative on the y-axis (e.g., Tactical Score). That is, spending too much money may actually reduce the overall tactical score, and, hence, this portfolio should not be selected. Also, in comparing portfolios A and B, you would be more inclined to choose B as the slope is steep and the same increase in budget requirements (x-axis) would return a much higher percentage Tactical Score (y-axis). The decision to choose between portfolios C and D would depend on available resources and the decision maker deciding if the added benefits warrant and justify the added budget and costs.

To further enhance the analysis, you can obtain the optimal portfolio allocations for C and D and then run a simulation on each optimal portfolio to decide what the probability that D will exceed C in value is, and whether this probability of occurrence justifies the added costs.

OPTIMIZATION APPLICATION EXAMPLE: OPTIMAL PRICING WITH ELASTICITY

This section illustrates another sample model from the ROV Modeling Toolkit (but a sample version of the model is available on the accompanying

DVD). This model is used to find the optimal pricing levels that will maximize revenues through the use of historical elasticity levels. The price elasticity of demand is a basic concept in microeconomics, which can be briefly described as the percentage change of quantity divided by the percentage change in prices. For example, if, in response to a 10% fall in the price of a good, the quantity demanded increases by 20%, the price elasticity of demand would be $20\%/(-10\%) = -2$. In general, a fall in the price of a good is expected to increase the quantity demanded, so the price elasticity of demand is negative but in some literature, the negative sign is omitted for simplicity (denoting only the absolute value of the elasticity). We can use this concept in several ways, including the point elasticity by taking the first derivative of the inverse of the demand function and multiplying it by the ratio of price to quantity at a particular point on the demand curve:

$$\varepsilon_d = \frac{\delta Q}{\delta P} \cdot \frac{P}{Q}$$

where ε is the price elasticity of demand, P is price, and Q is quantity demanded.

Instead of using instantaneous point elasticities, this example uses the discrete version, where we define elasticity as:

$$\varepsilon_d = \frac{\%\Delta Q}{\%\Delta P} = \frac{Q_2 - Q_1}{\frac{Q_2 + Q_1}{2}} \div \frac{P_2 - P_1}{\frac{P_2 + P_1}{2}} = \frac{Q_2 - Q_1}{Q_2 + Q_1} \cdot \frac{P_2 + P_1}{P_2 - P_1}$$

To further simplify things, we assume that in a category of hotel rooms, cruise ship tickets, airline tickets, or any other products with various categories (e.g., standard room, executive room, suite, and so forth), there is an average price and average quantity of units sold per period. Therefore, we can further simplify the equation to:

$$\varepsilon_d = \frac{Q_2 - Q_1}{\overline{Q}} \div \frac{P_2 - P_1}{\overline{P}} = \frac{\overline{P}}{\overline{Q}} \cdot \frac{Q_2 - Q_1}{P_2 - P_1}$$

where we now use the average price and average quantity demanded values $\overline{P}, \overline{Q}$.

If we have in each category the average price and average quantity sold, as in the model, we can compute the expected quantity sold given a new price provided we have the historical elasticity of demand values. See Figure 11.15.

Historical Analysis

Type	Average Price Sold	Average Quantity Sold	Average Total Revenue
Single	$ 750	200	$150,000.00
Double	$ 812	180	$146,160.00
Deluxe	$ 865	150	$129,750.00
Executive	$1,085	100	$108,500.00
Premium Suite	$1,195	75	$ 89,625.00
Presidential	$1,458	50	$ 72,900.00

FIGURE 11.15 Sample historical pricing.

In other words, if we take:

$$Q_1 - \varepsilon_d(P_2 - P_1)\frac{\overline{Q}}{\overline{P}} = Q_2$$

we would get:

$$Q_1 - \left[\frac{\overline{P}}{\overline{Q}} \cdot \frac{Q_2 - Q_1}{P_2 - P_1}\right](P_2 - P_1)\frac{\overline{Q}}{\overline{P}} = Q_2$$

To illustrate, suppose the price elasticity of demand for a single room during high season at a specific hotel property is 3.15 (we use the absolute value), where the average price last season was $750 and the average quantity of rooms sold was 200 units. What would happen if prices were to change from $750 ($P_1$) to $800 ($P_2$)? That is, what would happen to the quantity sold from 200 units (Q_1)? See Figure 11.16. Note that ε is a

Type	Historical Analysis Average Price Sold	Average Quantity Sold	Average Total Revenue	Price Elasticity of Demand	Allocated New Price	Projected Quantity Sold
Single	$750	200	$150,000.00	3.15	$800.00	158
Double	$812	180	$146,160.00	2.85	$800.00	188
Deluxe	$865	150	$129,750.00	2.55	$1,000.00	90
Executive	$1,085	100	$108,500.00	2.35	$1,000.00	118
Premium Suite	$1,195	75	$89,625.00	1.65	$1,000.00	95
Presidential	$1,458	50	$72,900.00	1.45	$1,000.00	73

FIGURE 11.16 Elasticity simulation.

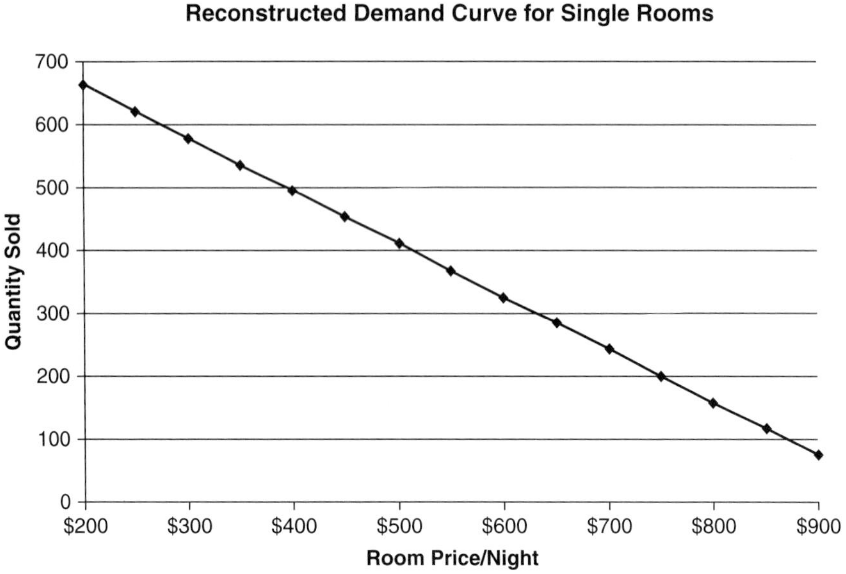

Reconstructed Demand Curve for Single Rooms

FIGURE 11.17   Reconstructed demand curve for a single room.

negative value but we simplify as a positive value here to be consistent with economic literature.

Using the preceding equation, we compute the newly predicted quantity demanded at $800 per night to be:

$$Q_2 = Q_1 - \varepsilon_d(P_2 - P_1)\frac{\overline{Q}}{\overline{P}} = 200 - 3.15(800 - 750)\frac{200}{750} = 158$$

The higher the price, the lower the quantity demanded, and vice versa. Indeed, the entire demand curve can be reconstructed by applying different price levels. For instance, the demand curve for the single room is reconstructed in Figure 11.17.

Optimization Procedures

Using the principles of price elasticity of demand, we can now figure out the optimal pricing structure of these hotel rooms by setting:

Objective: Maximize total revenues

Constraints: Number of rooms available per type

Decision Variables: Price to charge for each type of room

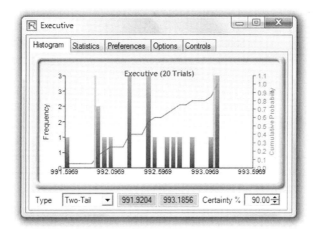

FIGURE 11.18 Distribution of stochastic optimization decision variable.

This model already has the optimization set up. To run it directly, do the following:

1. Go to the *Model* worksheet and click on *Risk Simulator | Change Profile* and choose the *Optimal Pricing with Elasticity* profile.
2. Click on the *Run Optimization* icon or click on *Risk Simulator | Optimization | Run Optimization*.
3. Select the *Method* tab and select either *Static Optimization* if you wish to view the resulting optimal prices or *Stochastic Optimization* to run simulation with optimization multiple times, to obtain a range of optimal prices.

The results from a stochastic optimization routine are seen in the *Report* worksheet. In addition, several forecast charts will be visible once the stochastic optimization routine completes. For instance, looking at the Executive suites, select *Two-Tail*, type 90 in the Certainty box, and hit *TAB* on the keyboard to obtain the 90% confidence level (e.g., the optimal price to charge for the season is between $991 and $993 per night). See Figure 11.18.

To reset the model manually, do the following:

1. Go to the *Model* worksheet, click on *Risk Simulator | New Profile*, and give the new profile a name.
2. *Reset* the values on prices. That is, enter 800 for cells H7, H8 and 1000 for cells H9 to H12. We choose these values so that we determine the

initial starting prices that are easy to remember, versus the optimized price levels later on.

3. Set the objective. Select cell J15 and click on the O (set objective) icon or click *Risk Simulator | Optimization | Set Objective*.

4. Set the decision variables. Select cell H7 and click on the D (set decision variable) icon or click *Risk Simulator | Optimization | Set Decision*. Select *Continuous* and give it the relevant lower and upper bounds (see columns M and N) or click on the link icons and link the lower and upper bounds (cells M7 and N7).

5. Set the constraints. Click on the C icon or *Risk Simulator | Optimization | Constraints* and add the capacity constraints on the maximum number of available rooms (e.g., click *ADD* and link cell I7 and make it "<= 250").

6. Click on the *Run Optimization* icon or click on *Risk Simulator | Optimization | Run Optimization*.

7. Select the *Method* tab and select either *Static Optimization* if you wish to view the resulting optimal prices, or *Stochastic Optimization* to run simulation with optimization multiple times, to obtain a range of optimal prices. But remember that to run a stochastic optimization procedure, you need to have assumptions set up. Select cell G7 and click on *Risk Simulator | Set Input Assumption* and set an assumption of your choice or choose *Normal distribution* and use the default values. Repeat for cells G8 to G12, one at a time, and then you can run a stochastic optimization.

APPENDIX—ROV MODELER SUITE: SERVER-BASED APPLICATIONS FOR RUNNING DATA-INTENSIVE MODELS AT EXTREMELY HIGH SPEEDS

Throughout the book, we look at individual Excel-based models to simplify the discussions and explanations. Nonetheless, these Excel models are limited in that they can only run on a limited set of data (e.g., Excel has a maximum number of rows and columns per worksheet) and might be much slower than, say, a bank would consider optimal (because of Excel's computational overhead of including graphics, equations, and cell-by-cell platform). Banks typically have thousands, if not millions, of transactions per day across all their branches, and some of these credit and market risk analyses have to be done frequently and quickly. In this appendix, we introduce the server-based applications, where millions of data points and computations can be run within seconds or minutes on a server. The same analytics and models in the two software programs described throughout this book are now run in pure mathematical software codes, making the computations blazing fast and capable of handling large data sets.

This server-based software is called ROV Modeler Suite and it is divided into a few application modules:

- *ROV Risk Modeler.* Risk Modeler is a simulation and analytical module that focuses on general analytics and modeling, forecasting, and simulation, as well as credit risk and market risk for Basel II based on a bank's existing data tables. It provides many models to simulate, fit, forecast, and value, and reports the results to the user. Existing data tables are based on the user's requirements such as linking to an existing database (e.g., Oracle OFDM, SQL, CSV, DSN, ODBC, Excel, flat text files, and other proprietary database systems), manually inputting data, or setting simulation assumptions, and so forth. This module can be used for computing, forecasting, and simulating risk analytics including historical back-fitting, time-series forecasts (ARIMA), volatility computations (GARCH), credit and market risk (PD, LGD, VAR, EAD), and other applications.

- *ROV Risk Optimizer.* Risk Optimizer is an advanced optimization module that can be used to optimize large portfolios and to find optimal decision variables. The decision variables can be discrete, continuous, integer, or binary, and the objective function can be linear or nonlinear. In addition, Risk Optimizer allows the user to link to existing data tables to run simulations, find the best-fitting models, and couple these techniques with optimization. It works exactly like Risk Simulator's optimization module described throughout this chapter, but it runs completely independently of Excel at super high speeds.

- *ROV Risk Valuator.* Risk Valuator is the application of more than 600 functions and models. Users can input the required data for the selected model and this application will return the computed results very quickly. This module is useful for valuing derivative instruments, debt instruments, exotic options, and options-embedded instruments, as well as multiple types of financial models.

  The 600-plus advanced models are categorized into the following groups of applications:

  - Advanced Math Functions
  - Basic Finance Models
  - Basic Options Models
  - Bond Math, Options, Pricing, and Yields
  - Credit Risk Analysis
  - Delta Gamma Hedging
  - Exotic Options and Derivatives

- Financial Ratios
- Forecasting, Extrapolation, and Interpolation
- Probability Distributions
- Put-Call Parity and Option Sensitivities
- Real Options Analysis
- Value at Risk, Volatility, Portfolio Risk and Return

System Architecture

The entire system architecture of this server-based application can be divided into three parts: the first level is the product's main application, which is the user interface; the second level is the data map, which is used to input the data to compute from various methods such as linking to existing databases or manually inputting the data, and so forth; the last level is the lowest level, which links the database to a *query*, *insert*, and *get* value function to and from data tables. Figure 11.19 illustrates the system architecture.

Figure 11.20 illustrates the first level of the system architecture, the user interface. A user can create new profiles for saving the data that will be used

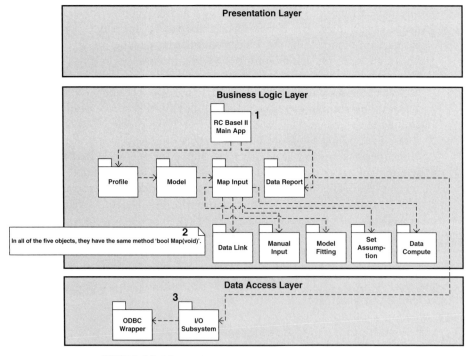

FIGURE 11.19 System architecture of Risk Modeler.

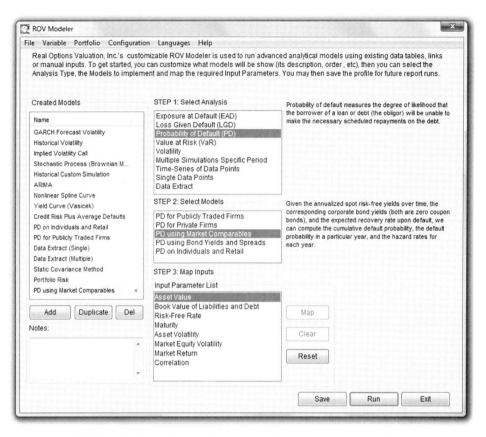

FIGURE 11.20 Risk Modeler main application interface (Level 1).

in the procedure (*File | New Profile*). In *Step 1*, the user selects the Analysis type, and, based on the type chosen, a list of models will be shown in *Step 2*. The user can then select models and *ADD* as many as required, which will then appear in the *Created Models* list box for updating and editing. In *Step 3*, the list of required input assumptions and parameters will be shown for each model. The user can then map, clear, or reset the parameter values by clicking the *MAP*, *CLEAR*, or *RESET* buttons (short descriptions for each step are provided). Clicking on the *SAVE* button will save all the data to the Profile that the user had previously created. When all the required inputs have been populated, clicking *RUN* will compute the models selected.

When selecting a parameter in the *Step 3* list box in the main application and clicking the *MAP* button, the *Input Parameter Mapping* dialog will display. There are five methods afforded to the user, as seen in

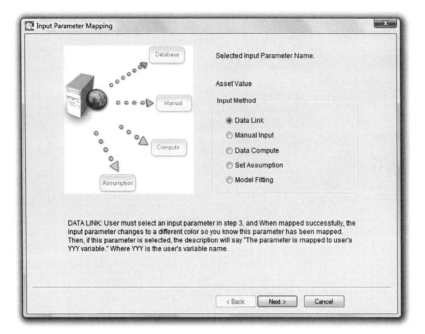

FIGURE 11.21 Input Parameter Mapping user interface (Level 2).

Figure 11.21. Selecting *Data Link* will allow the user to link to an existing database or Excel to access existing data. Selecting *Manual Input* will show a dialog requiring manual input of a specific variable. Selecting *Data Compute* shows a variable and data calculator to compute the parameter's value by incorporating other parameters or constants. Selecting *Set Assumption* will provide the user the ability to choose the simulation distribution and input the risk simulation assumption values. Selecting *Model Fitting* will fit some existing data to 24 potential relevant distributions for that parameter.

There are seven types of ODBC data connect for accessing existing data (Figure 11.22). For instance, in the Oracle data connect, the user needs to set up the required login inputs such as User and Password to access the database. When clicking on the *OK* button, the software will call the database connect method to connect the specified database. For different types of ODBC applications, the software codes are wrapped with popular calling methods such as *CONNECT*, *QUERY*, and so forth.

Other types of database and software connections are also possible, for example, through Excel worksheets and plain text files such as comma-delimited settings files (CSV), as well as other proprietary software databases.

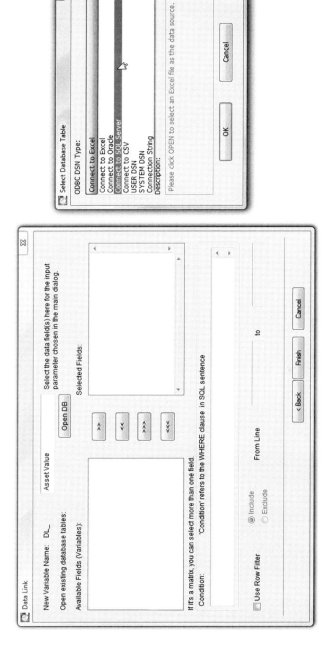

FIGURE 11.22 Link database user interface (Level 3).

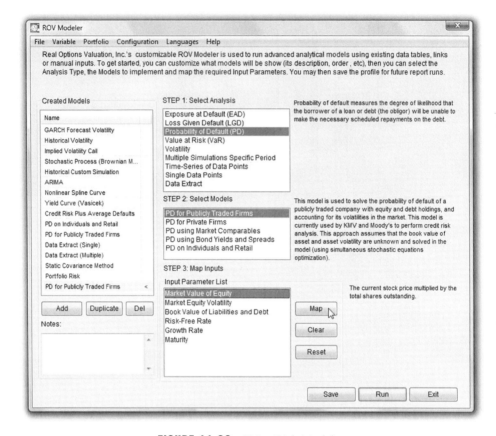

FIGURE 11.23   Using Risk Modeler.

For the *Risk Optimizer* module, users can input values directly or use the same three-level approach previously described to link input variables and output results with existing databases. The user only needs to select the required model, input the required parameters' values, and run the analysis.

Risk Modeler

This section includes a simple example showcasing how to use Risk Modeler. After Risk Modeler has been successfully installed, start the application to show the main user dialog. Click on *File | New Profile* to create a new profile. Then select *Probability of Default (PD)* in the *Step 1* list box and *PD for Publicly Traded Firms* in *Step 2*. Next, click on *Market Value Equity* in *Step 3* (Figure 11.23). Then, click on *MAP* and the program will open another

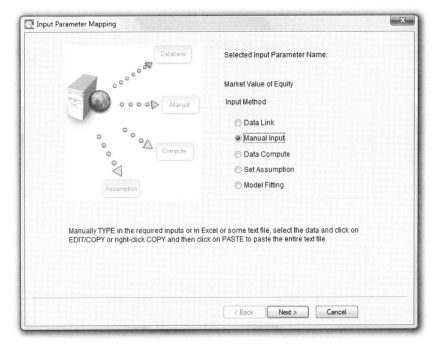

FIGURE 11.24   Parameter mapping.

dialog named *Input Parameter Mapping*. Click on the *Manual Input* radio button and hit *Next* (Figure 11.24).

When the *Manual Input* dialog opens (Figure 11.25), enter a variable name such as *Var1* and click the third radio button to manually input 3000. Then click on *Finish* to close this dialog. The program will return to the main application dialog. Using the same method, enter the following values for the required input parameters (enter any variable name as required):

Market Equity Volatility	0.45
Book Value Liabilities and Debt	10000
Risk-Free	0.05
Growth Rate	0.07
Maturity	1.00

Alternatively, the user can copy multiple data points from an existing spreadsheet, a text file, or some other software application and paste these values directly into the data area. A flat text file can also be uploaded to

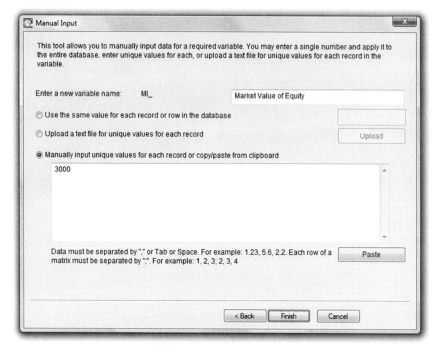

FIGURE 11.25 Manual inputs.

populate this variable. Finally, for some special models, the input parameter to the selected variable might be constant for all cases, and the software allows the ability to populate an entire data table with the same value (e.g., risk-free rate for a specific time period is the same regardless of the transaction type or credit listing).

When all the parameters have populated values, click on the *RUN* button in the main application dialog. There are several options the user can select (Figure 11.26). For this example, select the first choice and click *OK*.

The Result dialog (Figure 11.27) shows the computed values using the input parameters specified. Click the *OK* button to close the Result dialog. The focus will return to the Main application dialog.

Risk Optimizer

Here is another simple example showcasing how to use the *Risk Optimizer* module. After the Risk Modeler Suite has been successfully installed, start the Risk Optimizer application. The user interface has several tabs, *Method,*

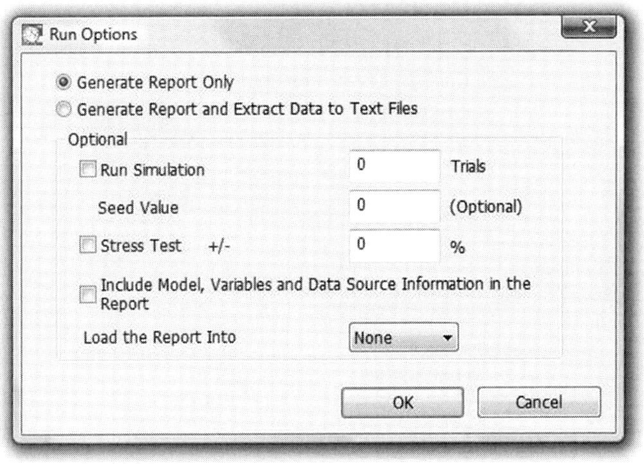

FIGURE 11.26 Running the report.

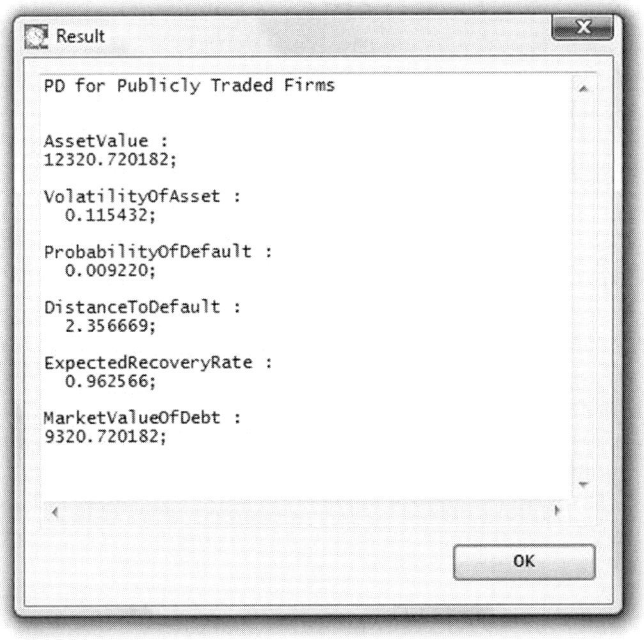

FIGURE 11.27 Results.

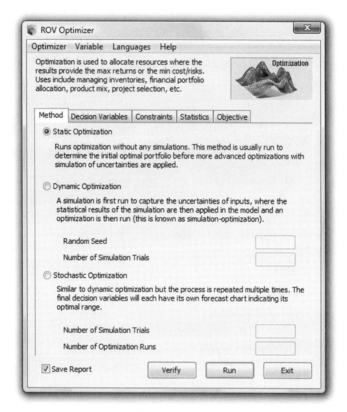

FIGURE 11.28   Risk optimizer.

Decision Variables, Constraints, Statistics, and *Objective* (Figure 11.28). To get started, select the *Method* tab and click on *Static Optimization.*

Next, click on the *Decision Variables* tab and *ADD* to add some variables. For instance, we have four different variables (*Asset 1* to *Asset 4*), and each asset can be set to take continuous, integer, binary, or discrete values. For our simple illustration, set the variables to all be *Continuous* between 0.10 and 0.40 (i.e., only asset allocations between 10% and 40% are allowed). Keep adding 4 different asset classes as decision variables as shown in Figure 11.29.

Next, click on the *Constraints* tab and *ADD* (Figure 11.30). Then, in the Expression input box, enter the constraints (you can double-click on the list of variables and the variable string will be transferred up to the Expression box). In our simple example, the sum of the decision variables

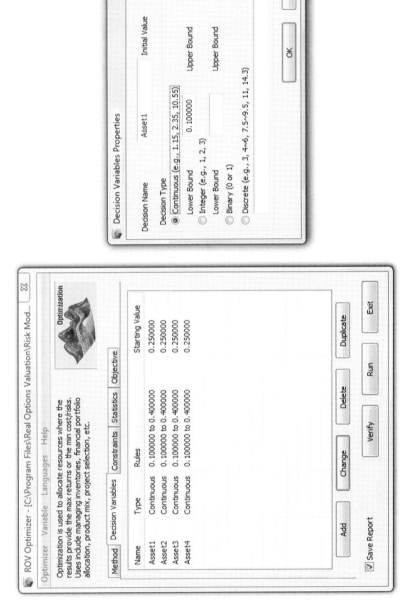

FIGURE 11.29 Setting decision variables.

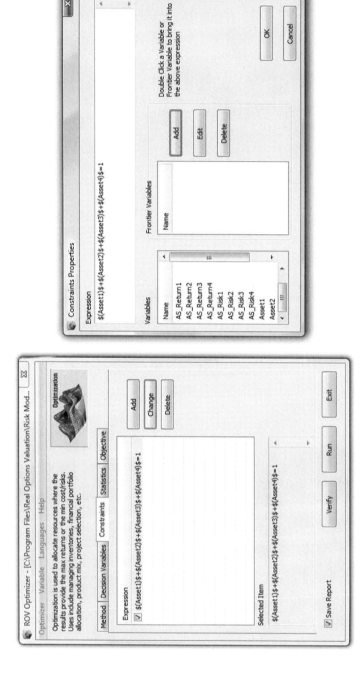

FIGURE 11.30 Setting constraints.

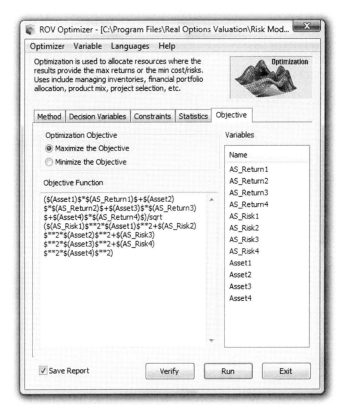

FIGURE 11.31 Setting the optimization objective.

must equal 1.0 (i.e., the total allocation of asset classes must total 100% in an investment portfolio).

Next, select the *Objective* tab and decide if you wish to run *Maximization* or *Minimization* on your objective. In addition, enter the relevant Objective Expression as outlined in Figure 11.31. You can double-click on the list of Variables to bring the variable name string to the Objective Expression input box.

When completed, click on *RUN* to obtain the results of your optimization (Figure 11.32).

You may also use Risk Optimizer to link to an existing database such as Oracle or generate your own data tables to optimize. For instance, clicking on the *Variable | Variable Management* menu (Figure 11.33) accesses the Variable Management tool, which will, in turn, allow you to *Add*, *Edit*, or *Delete* variables. For instance, by clicking on *ADD*, the familiar *Input*

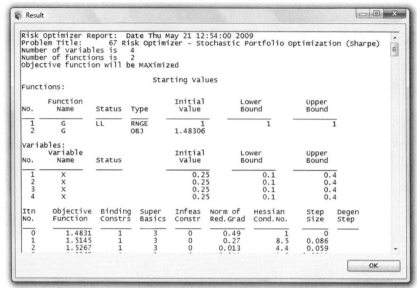

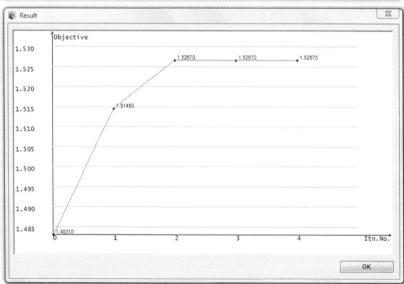

FIGURE 11.32 Optimization results.

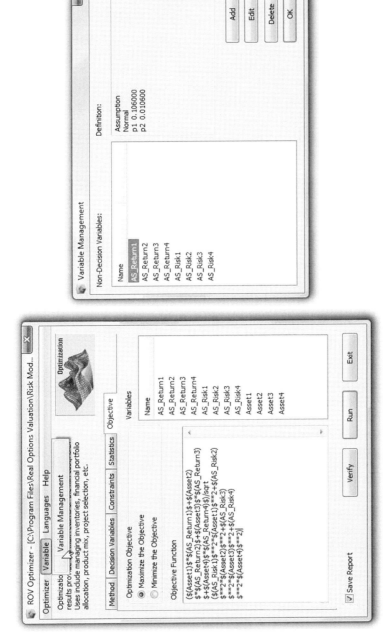

FIGURE 11.33 Variable management.

Parameter Mapping tool appears (Figure 11.24), allowing you to link, compute, paste, simulate, or fit existing data for use in the optimization process.

Finally, if *Dynamic* or *Stochastic Optimization* is selected (Figure 11.28), and if the variables have risk simulation assumptions associated with them, you can then access the *Statistics* tab, whereby you can make use of the simulated statistical properties to run stochastic optimization on. It is highly suggested that you try some of the example profiles such as the Markowitz efficient frontier and stochastic optimization.

Risk Valuator

Risk Valuator is used to perform quick computations from simple and basic models to advanced analytical models, and can handle single point values or a series of values. After installing the software, start Risk Valuator. Simply select the model type in the *Model Category* box and select the model of interest in the *Model Selection* box (Figure 11.34). The required input parameters will then be listed. Single point inputs (e.g., 10 or 10.4532) will be in the *single input parameters* area, whereas multiple data requirements will be shown in the *multiple series input parameters* area. When entering a single series of multiple data points, use commas or spaces to separate the values (e.g., a time series of 6 months of interest rates can be entered either as 0.12, 0.124, 0.112, 0.1, 0.09, 0.16 or simply as 0.12 0.124 0.112 0.1 0.09 0.16).

Sometimes, certain models, such as the Value at Risk (VaR) model using the standard correlation method, require different columns of data and a correlation matrix. For instance, the goal is to compute the portfolio VaR using this model, where there are three asset classes, each with its own amounts, specific daily volatility for each asset class, and a square correlation matrix among these asset classes. In such a situation, the amounts and volatility inputs will have to be entered as a single column (hit *ENTER* at the end of entering a value, to create a new line, designating a new asset class), and the correlation matrix will be separated by commas for the same row with different columns, and semicolons for different rows. This Risk Valuator module does not allow the user to link to various databases or simulate. To do so, use the Risk Modeler module instead. Many of the same models exist in both places. The Risk Valuator module is used to quickly obtain results without having to link to databases and so forth. Risk Valuator can also be used to compute more advanced models such as the Box–Jenkins ARIMA forecast (Figure 11.35). In summary, Risk Modeler can be used to

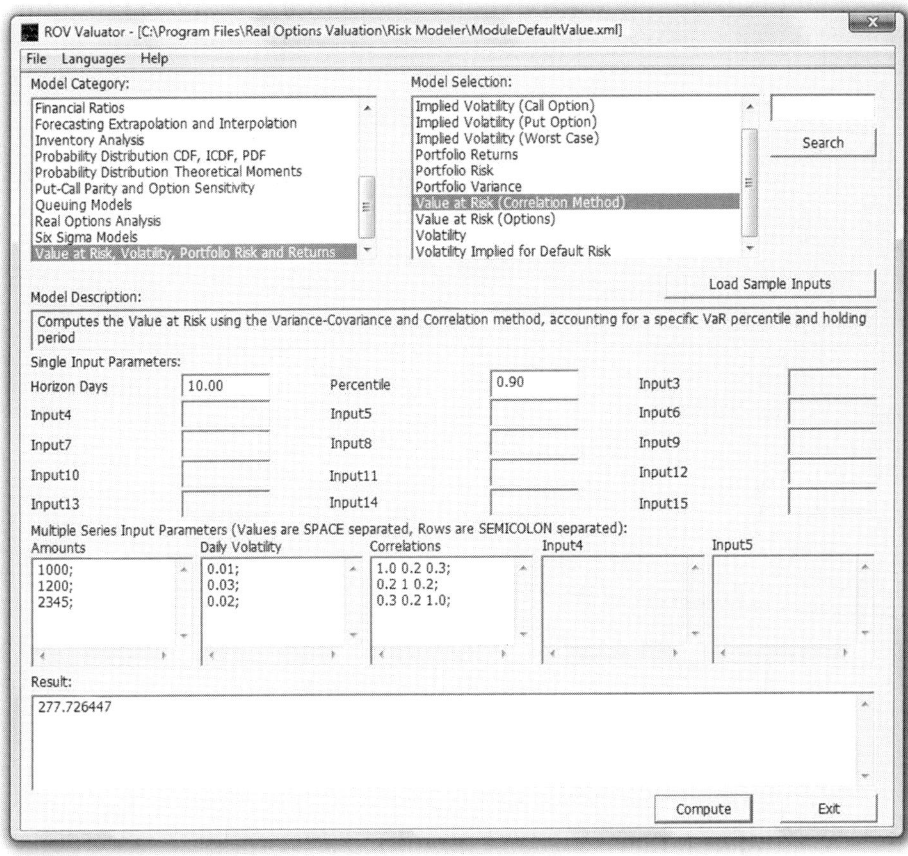

FIGURE 11.34 Portfolio Value at Risk model solved using Risk Valuator.

run highly data-intensive models, and it allows the user to link to existing databases and yet run forecasting, simulation, and optimization algorithms, coupled with the advanced analytical models for credit and market risks as specified by Basel II.

This appendix only illustrates the basics of this tool, whereas the user manual and getting started videos available at *www.realoptionsvaluation .com/rovmodeler.html* provide much more detail on how to use the ROV Modeler Suite with Oracle and other databases, linking to and from other data sources, embedding ROV Compiler files, performing computations and data validation, executing SQL commands for data cleansing, running simulations, and many other approaches.

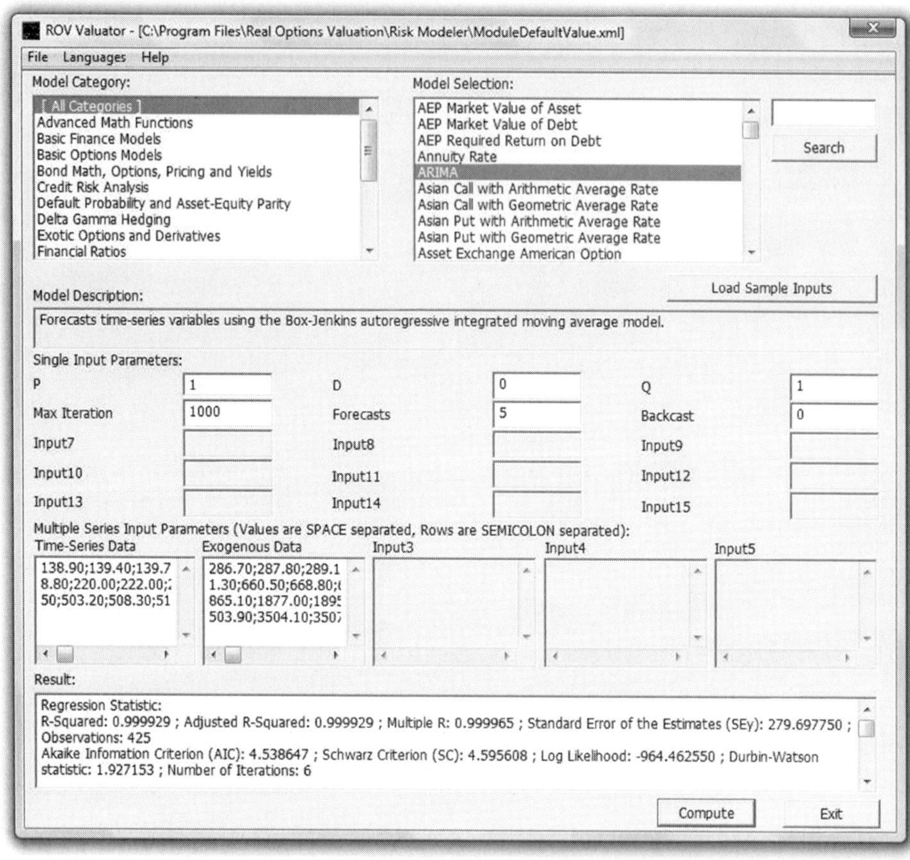

FIGURE 11.35   Complex ARIMA model solution.

APPENDIX—COMPUTING ANNUALIZED RETURNS AND RISK FOR PORTFOLIO OPTIMIZATION

Figure 11.36 illustrates a quick example using Microsoft's historical stock prices for computing the annualized return and annualized volatility risk. It shows the stock prices for Microsoft downloaded from Yahoo! Finance, a publicly available free resource (visit http://finance.yahoo.com and enter a stock symbol, e.g., MSFT for Microsoft, click on *Quotes: Historical Prices*, select *Weekly*, and select the period of interest to download the data to a spreadsheet for analysis). The data in columns A and B are downloaded from Yahoo.

Historical Data			Volatility Computations		Returns Computations								
Week	Closing Price		LN Relative Returns	Moving Average Volatilities	Relative Returns	Absolute Returns	Moving Average Absolute Returns	Moving Average Geometric Returns					
27-Dec-04	26.64		-0.0108	17.87%	0.9892	-1.08%	10.04%	7.69%					
20-Dec-04	26.93		0.0019	17.84%	1.0019	0.19%	11.98%	9.55%					
13-Dec-04	26.88		-0.0045	17.85%	0.9956	-0.44%	11.27%	10.22%					
6-Dec-04	27.00		-0.0055	18.00%	0.9945	-0.55%	14.36%	10.14%					
29-Nov-04	27.15		0.0235	18.13%	1.0238	2.38%	17.50%	13.31%			One-Year Annualized Volatility Analysis		
22-Nov-04	26.52		-0.0098	18.03%	0.9903	-0.97%	16.17%	13.52%					
15-Nov-04	26.78		-0.0011	18.10%	0.9989	-0.11%	19.56%	15.54%			Average Annualized Volatility		21.89%
8-Nov-04	26.81		0.0223	18.20%	1.0225	2.25%	18.13%	18.05%			Median Annualized Volatility		22.30%
1-Nov-04	26.22		0.0468	18.28%	1.0480	4.80%	13.56%	14.26%					
25-Oct-04	25.02		0.0084	17.71%	1.0085	0.85%	8.63%	7.21%					
18-Oct-04	24.81		-0.0092	17.80%	0.9908	-0.92%	6.02%	6.24%			One-Year Annualized Returns Analysis		
11-Oct-04	25.04		0.0000	19.68%	1.0000	0.00%	-1.09%	5.38%					
4-Oct-04	25.04		-0.0091	19.69%	0.9909	-0.91%	-0.46%	-2.99%			Arithmetic Average Return		8.54%
27-Sep-04	25.27		0.0346	19.68%	1.0352	3.52%	-0.13%	-1.45%			Geometric Average Return		6.16%
20-Sep-04	24.41		-0.0082	19.62%	0.9919	-0.81%	-0.50%	-5.50%					
13-Sep-04	24.61		0.0008	20.52%	1.0008	0.08%	-5.59%	-1.57%					
7-Sep-04	24.59		0.0139	21.30%	1.0140	1.40%	0.05%	-7.74%					
30-Aug-04	24.25		-0.0127	21.25%	0.9874	-1.26%	-1.51%	-3.56%					
23-Aug-04	24.56		0.0123	22.29%	1.0124	1.24%	6.77%	-2.45%					
16-Aug-04	24.26		0.0066	22.29%	1.0066	0.66%	6.70%	3.10%					
9-Aug-04	24.10		-0.0041	22.42%	0.9959	-0.41%	8.68%	3.59%					
2-Aug-04	24.20		-0.0488	22.42%	0.9524	-4.76%	8.92%	6.62%					
26-Jul-04	25.41		0.0163	21.97%	1.0164	1.64%	11.44%	11.33%					
19-Jul-04	25.00		0.0198	22.11%	1.0200	2.00%	7.12%	7.43%					
12-Jul-04	24.51		-0.0138	22.02%	0.9863	-1.37%	5.12%	2.73%					
6-Jul-04	24.85		-0.0250	22.04%	0.9753	-2.47%	4.96%	4.11%					
28-Jun-04	25.48		0.0000	22.07%	1.0000	0.00%	10.49%	5.07%					
21-Jun-04	25.48		0.0079	22.30%	1.0079	0.79%	13.88%	8.10%					

FIGURE 11.36 Computing annualized return and risk. (*Continues*)

31	14-Jun-04	25.28	0.0574	22.48%	1.0591	5.91%	10.44%	10.64%
32	7-Jun-04	23.87	0.0311	22.71%	1.0315	3.15%	11.34%	2.20%
33	1-Jun-04	23.14	-0.0107	22.86%	0.9893	-1.07%	12.33%	5.69%
34	24-May-04	23.39	0.0129	23.19%	1.0130	1.30%	9.56%	10.84%
35	17-May-04	23.09	0.0013	23.21%	1.0013	0.13%	9.89%	5.61%
36	10-May-04	23.06	0.0030	23.87%	1.0030	0.30%	4.46%	7.10%
37	3-May-04	22.99	-0.0134	24.07%	0.9867	-1.33%	1.17%	1.36%
38	26-Apr-04	23.30	-0.0527	24.05%	0.9487	-5.13%	3.49%	-0.34%
39	19-Apr-04	24.56	0.0903	23.67%	1.0945	9.45%	12.11%	5.92%
40	12-Apr-04	22.44	-0.0124	21.92%	0.9877	-1.23%	1.55%	0.31%
41	5-Apr-04	22.72	-0.0144	22.50%	0.9857	-1.43%	8.19%	0.44%
42	29-Mar-04	23.05	0.0322	22.76%	1.0327	3.27%	6.07%	7.15%
43	22-Mar-04	22.32	0.0158	22.59%	1.0159	1.59%	4.49%	0.31%
44	15-Mar-04	21.97	-0.0296	23.72%	0.9708	-2.92%	-4.23%	0.41%

FIGURE 11.36 (Continued)

The formula in cell D3 is simply *LN(B3/B4)* to compute the natural logarithmic value of the relative returns week after week, and is copied down the entire column. The formula in cell E3 is *STDEV(D3:D54)*SQRT(52)* which computes the annualized (by multiplying the square root of the number of weeks in a year) volatility (by taking the standard deviation of the entire 52 weeks of the year 2004 data). The formula in cell E3 is then copied down the entire column to compute a moving window of annualized volatilities. The volatility used is this example is the average of a 52-week moving window, which covers two years of data; that is, cell M8's formula is *AVERAGE(E3:E54)*, where cell E54 has the following formula: *STDEV(D54:D105)*SQRT(52)*, and, of course, row 105 is January 2003. This means that the 52-week moving window captures the average volatility over a two-year period and smoothes the volatility such that infrequent but extreme spikes will not dominate the volatility computation. Of course, a median volatility should also be computed. If the median is far off from the average, the distribution of volatilities is skewed and the median should be used; otherwise, the average should be used. Finally, these 52 volatilities can be fed into Monte Carlo simulation, using the Risk Simulator software's custom distribution to run a nonparametric simulation or to perform a data fitting procedure to find the best-fitting distribution to simulate.

In contrast, we can compute the annualized returns either using the arithmetic average method or the geometric average method. Cell G3 computes the absolute percentage return for the week where the formula for the cell is *(B3–B4)/B4*, and the formula is copied down the entire column. Then, the moving average window is computed in cell H3 as *AVERAGE(G3:G54)*52*, where the average weekly returns are obtained and annualized by multiplying them with 52, the number of weeks in a year. Note that averages are additive and can be multiplied directly by the number of weeks in a year versus volatility, which is not additive. Only volatility squared is additive, which means that the periodic volatility computed previously needs to be multiplied by the square root of 52. The arithmetic average return in cell M14 is, hence, the average of a 52-week period of the moving average or *AVERAGE(H3:H54)*. Similarly, the geometric average return is the average of the 52-week moving window of the geometric returns, that is, cell M15 is simply *AVERAGE(I3:I54)*, where in cell I3, we have *(POWER(B3/B54,1/52)–1)*52*, the geometric average computation. The arithmetic growth rate is typically higher than the geometric growth rate when the returns period to period are volatile. Typically, the geometric growth rate (with a moving average window) should be used.

EXERCISE: OPTIMIZATION

This sample model illustrates how to use Risk Simulator for:

1. Running Static, Dynamic, and Stochastic Optimization with Continuous Decision Variables
2. Optimization with Discrete Integer Decision Variables
3. Efficient Frontier and Advanced Optimization Settings

Model Background

File Name: Basic Simulation Model.xls

Access: **Risk Simulator | Example Models | 11 Optimization Continuous**

Access: **Risk Simulator | Example Models | 12 Optimization Discrete**

Access: **Risk Simulator | Example Models | 13 Optimization Stochastic**

Prerequisites: Risk Simulator 5.2 or later, Chapters 10 and 11 of *Modeling Risk*

Running Static, Dynamic, and Stochastic Optimization with Continuous Decision Variables

Figure 11.37 illustrates the sample continuous optimization model. In this example, there are 10 distinct asset classes (e.g., different types of mutual funds, stocks, or assets) where the idea is to most efficiently and effectively allocate the portfolio holdings such that the best bang-for-the-buck is obtained. In other words, we want to generate the best portfolio returns possible given the risks inherent in each asset class. In order to truly understand the concept of optimization, we have to delve more deeply into this sample model to see how the optimization process can best be applied. The model shows the 10 asset classes and each asset class has its own set of annualized returns and annualized volatilities. These return and risk measures are annualized values such that they can be consistently compared across different asset classes. Returns are computed using the geometric average of the relative returns, while the risks are computed using the logarithmic relative stock returns approach.

The Allocation Weights in column E holds the decision variables, which are the variables that need to be tweaked and tested such that the total weight is constrained at 100% (cell E17). Typically, to start the optimization, we will set these cells to a uniform value, where in this case, cells E6 to E15 are set at 10% each. In addition, each decision variable may

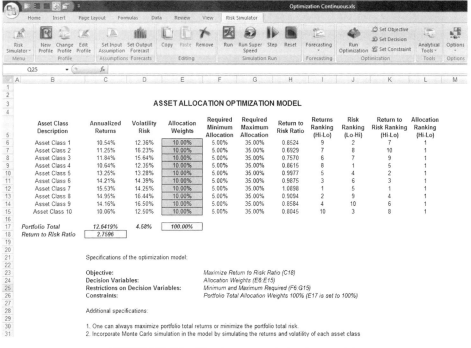

FIGURE 11.37 Continuous optimization model.

have specific restrictions in its allowed range. In this example, the lower and upper allocations allowed are 5% and 35%, as seen in columns F and G. This means that each asset class may have its own allocation boundaries. Next, column H shows the return to risk ratio, which is simply the return percentage divided by the risk percentage; the higher this value, the higher the bang-for-the-buck. The remaining columns show the individual asset class rankings by returns, risk, return to risk ratio, and allocation. In other words, these rankings show at a glance which asset class has the lowest risk, or the highest return, and so forth. The portfolio's total returns in cell C17 is $SUMPRODUCT(C6:C15, E6:E15)$; that is, the sum of the allocation weights multiplied by the annualized returns for each asset class. In other words, we have $R_P = \omega_A R_A + \omega_B R_B + \omega_C R_C + \omega_D R_D$, where R_P is the return on the portfolio, $R_{A,B,C,D}$ are the individual returns on the projects, and $\omega_{A,B,C,D}$ are the respective weights or capital allocation across each project. In addition, the portfolio's diversified risk in cell D17 is computed by taking $\sigma_P = \sqrt{\sum_{i=1}^{i} \omega_i^2 \sigma_i^2 + \sum_{i=1}^{n} \sum_{j=1}^{m} 2\omega_i \omega_j \rho_{i,j} \sigma_i \sigma_j}$. Here, $\rho_{i,j}$

are the respective cross-correlations between the asset classes—hence, if the cross-correlations are negative, there are risk diversification effects, and the portfolio risk decreases. However, to simplify the computations here, we assume zero correlations among the asset classes through this portfolio risk computation, but assume the correlations when applying simulation on the returns as will be seen later. Therefore, instead of applying static correlations among these different asset returns, we apply the correlations in the simulation assumptions themselves, creating a more dynamic relationship among the simulated return values. Finally, the return to risk ratio or Sharpe Ratio is computed for the portfolio. This value is seen in cell C18, and represents the objective to be maximized in this optimization exercise.

The following are the specifications in this example optimization model:

Objective:	Maximize Return to Risk Ratio (C18)
Decision Variables:	Allocation Weights (E6:E15)
Restrictions on Decision Variables:	Minimum and Maximum Required (F6:G15)
Constraints:	Total Allocation Weights Sum to 100% (E17)

Procedure

1. Start Excel and open the example file *Risk Simulator | Example Models | 11 Optimization Continuous*.
2. Start a new profile with *Risk Simulator | New Profile* (or click on the *New Profile* icon) and give it a name.
3. The first step in optimization is to set the decision variables. Select cell E6 and set the first decision variable (*Risk Simulator | Optimization | Set Decision*) or click on the *D* icon. Then click on the link icon to select the name cell (B6), as well as the lower bound and upper bound values at cells F6 and G6. Then, using Risk Simulator Copy, copy this cell E6 decision variable and paste the decision variable to the remaining cells in E7 to E15.
4. The second step in optimization is to set the constraint. There is only one constraint here, that is, the total allocation in the portfolio must sum to 100%. So, click on *Risk Simulator | Optimization | Constraints . . .* or click on the *C* icon, and select *ADD* to add a new constraint. Then, select the cell *E17* and make it equal (=) to 100%. Click *OK* when done.
   - Exercise Question: Would you get the same results if you set E7 = 1 instead of 100%?
   - Exercise Question: In the constraints user interface, what does the Efficient Frontier button mean and how does it work?

5. The final step in optimization is to set the objective function. Select cell *C18* and click on *Risk Simulator | Optimization | Set Objective* or click on the *O* icon. Check to make sure the objective cell is set for C18 and select *Maximize*.

6. Start the optimization by going to *Risk Simulator | Optimization | Run Optimization* or click on the *Run Optimization* icon and select the optimization of choice (Static Optimization, Dynamic Optimization, or Stochastic Optimization). To get started, select *Static Optimization*. You can now review the objective, decision variables, and constraints in each tab if required, or click *OK* to run the static optimization.
   - Exercise Question: In the Run Optimization user interface, click on the *Statistics* tab and you see that there is nothing there. Why?

7. Once the optimization is complete, you may select *Revert* to revert back to the original values of the decision variables as well as the objective, or select *Replace* to apply the optimized decision variables. Typically, Replace is chosen after the optimization is done. Then review the *Results Interpretation* section below before proceeding to the next step in the exercise.

8. Now reset the decision variables by typing *10%* back into all cells from *E6* to *E15*. Then, select cell *C6* and *Risk Simulator | Set Input Assumption* and use the default *Normal* distribution and the default parameters. This is only an example run and we really do not need to spend time to set proper distributions. Repeat setting the normal assumptions for cells *C7* to *C15*.
   - Exercise Question: Should you or should you not copy the first assumption in cell C6 and then copy and paste the parameters to cells C7:C15? And if we copy and paste the assumptions, what is the difference between using *Risk Simulator Copy and Paste* functions as opposed to using Excel's copy and paste function? What happens when you first hit *Escape* before applying *Risk Simulator Paste*?
   - Exercise Question: Why do we need to enter *10%* back into the cells?

9. Now run the optimization *Risk Simulator | Optimization | Run Optimization* and this time select *Dynamic Optimization* in the *Method* tab. When completed, click on *Revert* to go back to the original 10% decision variables.
   - Exercise Question: What was the difference between the static optimization run in Step 6 above and dynamic optimization?

10. Now run the optimization *Risk Simulator | Optimization | Run Optimization* a third time, but this time, select *Stochastic Optimization* in the *Method* tab. Then notice several things.
    - First, click on the *Statistics* tab and see that this tab is now populated. Why is this the case and how do you use this statistics tab?

- Second, click on the *Advanced* button and select the checkbox *Run Super Speed Simulation*. Then click *OK* to run the optimization. What do you see? How is super speed integrated into stochastic optimization?
11. Access the advanced options by going to *Risk Simulator | Optimization | Run Optimization* and clicking the *Advanced* button. Spend some time trying to understand what each element means and how it is pertinent to optimization.
12. After running the stochastic optimization, a report is created. Spend some time reviewing the report and try to understand what it means, as well as review the forecast charts generated for each decision variable.

Figure 11.38 shows the screen shots of the procedural steps given above. You can add simulation assumptions on the model's returns and risk (columns C and D) and apply the dynamic optimization and stochastic optimization for additional practice.

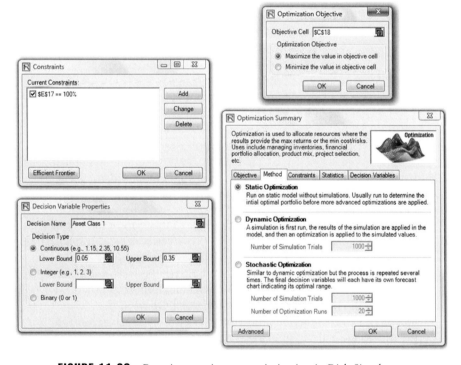

FIGURE 11.38 Running continuous optimization in Risk Simulator.

Results Interpretation   The optimization's final results are shown in Figure 11.39, where the optimal allocation of assets for the portfolio is seen in cells E6:E15. That is, given the restrictions of each asset fluctuating between 5% and 35%, and where the sum of the allocation must equal 100%, the allocation that maximizes the return to risk ratio is seen in Figure 11.39. A few important things have to be noted when reviewing the results and optimization procedures performed thus far:

- The correct way to run the optimization is to maximize the bang-for-the-buck or returns to risk Sharpe Ratio as we have done.
- If instead we maximized the total portfolio returns, the optimal allocation result is trivial and does not require optimization to obtain. That is, simply allocate 5% (the minimum allowed) to the lowest 8 assets, 35% (the maximum allowed) to the highest returning asset, and the remaining (25%) to the second-best returns asset. Optimization is not required. However, when allocating the portfolio this way, the risk is a lot higher as compared to when maximizing the returns to risk ratio, although the portfolio returns by themselves are higher.
- In contrast, one can minimize the total portfolio risk, but the returns will now be less.

The following table illustrates the results from the three different objectives being optimized:

Objective:	Portfolio Returns	Portfolio Risk	Portfolio Returns to Risk Ratio
Maximize Returns to Risk Ratio	12.69%	4.52%	2.8091
Maximize Returns	13.97%	6.77%	2.0636
Minimize Risk	12.38%	4.46%	2.7754

From the table it can be seen that the best approach is to maximize the returns to risk ratio. That is, for the same amount of risk, this allocation provides the highest amount of return. Conversely, for the same amount of return, this allocation provides the lowest amount of risk possible. This approach of bang-for-the-buck or returns to risk ratio is the cornerstone of the Markowitz efficient frontier in modern portfolio theory. That is, if we constrained the total portfolio risk level and successively increased it over time we will obtain several efficient portfolio allocations for different risk characteristics. Thus, different efficient portfolio allocations can be obtained for different individuals with different risk preferences.

ASSET ALLOCATION OPTIMIZATION MODEL

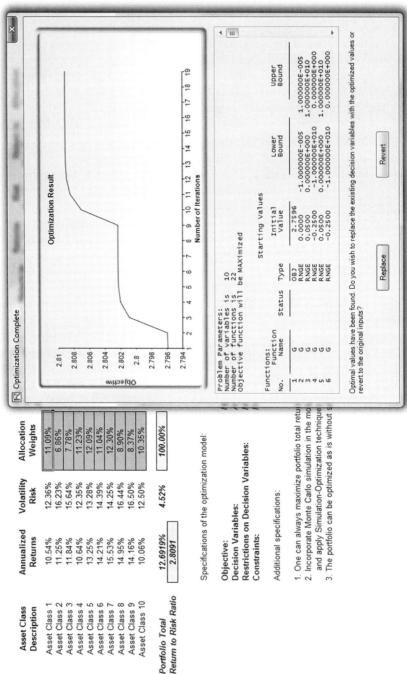

Asset Class Description	Annualized Returns	Volatility Risk	Allocation Weights
Asset Class 1	10.54%	12.36%	11.09%
Asset Class 2	11.25%	16.23%	6.86%
Asset Class 3	11.84%	15.64%	7.78%
Asset Class 4	10.64%	12.35%	11.23%
Asset Class 5	13.25%	13.28%	12.09%
Asset Class 6	14.21%	14.39%	11.04%
Asset Class 7	15.53%	14.25%	12.30%
Asset Class 8	14.95%	16.44%	8.90%
Asset Class 9	14.16%	16.50%	8.37%
Asset Class 10	10.06%	12.50%	10.35%
Portfolio Total	12.6919%	4.52%	100.00%
Return to Risk Ratio	2.8091		

Specifications of the optimization model:

Objective:
Decision Variables:
Restrictions on Decision Variables:
Constraints:

Additional specifications:

1. One can always maximize portfolio total retur
2. Incorporate Monte Carlo simulation in the mo
   and apply Simulation-Optimization technique
3. The portfolio can be optimized as is without s

FIGURE 11.39 Continuous optimization results.

572

Optimization with Discrete Integer Decision Variables

Sometimes, the decision variables are not continuous but discrete integers (e.g., 1, 2, 3) or binary (e.g., 0 and 1). In the binary situation, we can use such optimization as on-off switches or go/no-go decisions. Figure 11.40 illustrates a project selection model where there are 12 projects listed. The example here uses the *Risk Simulator | Example Models | 12 Optimization Discrete* model. As before, each project has its own returns (ENPV and NPV for expanded net present value and net present value—the ENPV is simply the NPV plus any strategic real options values), costs of implementation, risks, and so forth. If required, this model can be modified to include required full-time equivalences (FTE) and other resources of various functions, and additional constraints can be set on these additional resources. The inputs into this model are typically linked from other spreadsheet models. For instance, each project will have its own discounted cash flow or returns on investment model. The application here is to maximize the portfolio's Sharpe Ratio subject to some budget allocation. Many other versions of this model can be created, for instance, maximizing the portfolio returns, or minimizing the risks, or adding additional constraints where the total number of projects chosen cannot exceed 6, and so forth and so on. All of these items can be run using this existing model.

Procedure

1. Open the example file and start a new profile by clicking on *Risk Simulator | New Profile* and give it a name (Figure 11.40 shows the screen shots of these procedures).
2. The first step in optimization is to set up the decision variables. Set the first decision variable by selecting cell *J4*, and select *Risk Simulator | Optimization | Set Decision* or click on the *D* icon. Then, click on the *link* icon to select the name cell (*B4*), and select the *Binary* variable. Then, using Risk Simulator copy, copy this cell J4 decision variable and paste the decision variable to the remaining cells in *J5* to *J15*. This is the best method if you have only several decision variables and you can name each decision variable with a unique name for identification later (see Figure 11.41).
   - Exercise Question: What is the main purpose of linking the name to cell B4 before doing the copy and paste parameters?
   - Exercise Question: Does it matter if you hit or not hit *Escape* before pasting the parameters?

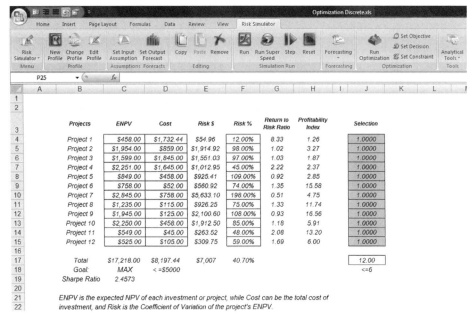

FIGURE 11.40 Discrete integer optimization model.

3. The second step in optimization is to set the constraint. There are two constraints here: The total budget allocation in the portfolio must be less than $5,000 and the total number of projects must not exceed 6. So, click on *Risk Simulator | Optimization | Constraints . . .* or click on the *C* icon and select *ADD* to add a new constraint. Then, select the cell *D17* and make it *D17 <= 5000.* Repeat by setting cell *J17 <= 6.*
   - Exercise Question: Why do we use <= instead of =?
   - Exercise Question: Sometimes when there are no feasible results or the optimization does not run, changing the equal sign to the inequality helps. Why?
   - Exercise Question: What would you do if you wanted D17 < 5000 instead of <= 5000?
   - Exercise Question: Explain what would happen to the binding constraints if you set only one constraint and it is D17 <= 8200 or only J17 <= 12?
4. The final step in optimization is to set the objective function and start the optimization by selecting cell *C19* and selecting *Risk Simulator | Optimization | Set Objective,* then run the optimization using *Risk Simulator | Optimization | Run Optimization* and selecting the optimization of

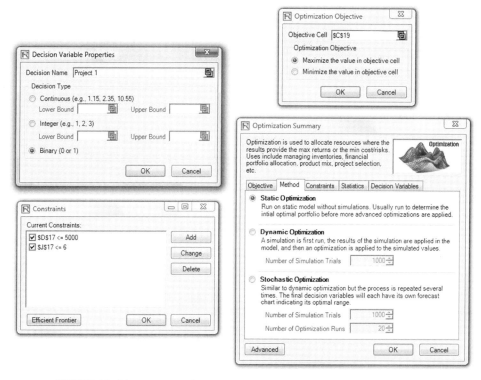

FIGURE 11.41 Running discrete integer optimization in Risk Simulator.

choice (Static Optimization, Dynamic Optimization, or Stochastic Optimization). To get started, select *Static Optimization*. Check to make sure that the objective cell is either the Sharpe Ratio or portfolio returns to risk ratio and select *Maximize*. You can now review the decision variables and constraints if required, or click *OK* to run the static optimization. Figure 11.42 shows a sample optimal selection of projects that maximizes the Sharpe Ratio.

- Exercise Question: If instead you maximized total revenues by changing the existing objective, this becomes a trivial model and simply involves choosing the highest returning project and going down the list until you run out of money or exceed the budget constraint. Doing so will yield theoretically undesirable projects as the highest yielding projects typically hold higher risks. Do you agree? What other variables can be used as objective in this model, if any?

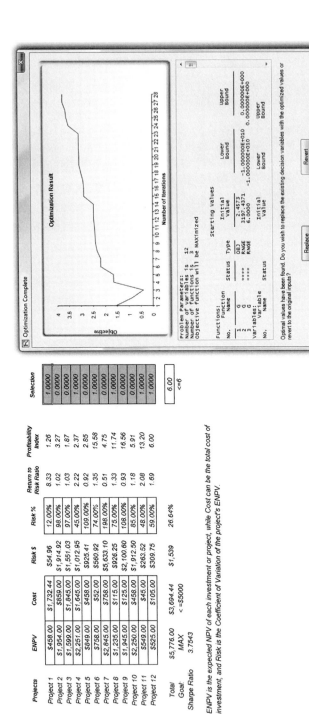

Projects	ENPV	Cost	Risk $	Risk %	Return to Risk Ratio	Profitability Index		Selection
Project 1	$458.00	$1,732.44	$54.96	12.00%	8.33	1.26		1.0000
Project 2	$1,954.00	$859.00	$1,914.92	98.00%	1.02	3.27		0.0000
Project 3	$1,599.00	$1,845.00	$1,551.03	97.00%	1.03	1.87		0.0000
Project 4	$2,251.00	$1,645.00	$1,012.95	45.00%	2.22	2.37		1.0000
Project 5	$849.00	$458.00	$925.41	109.00%	0.92	2.85		0.0000
Project 6	$758.00	$52.00	$560.92	74.00%	1.35	15.58		1.0000
Project 7	$2,845.00	$758.00	$5,633.10	198.00%	0.51	4.75		0.0000
Project 8	$1,235.00	$115.00	$926.25	75.00%	1.33	11.74		1.0000
Project 9	$1,945.00	$125.00	$2,100.60	108.00%	0.93	16.56		0.0000
Project 10	$2,250.00	$458.00	$1,912.50	85.00%	1.18	5.91		0.0000
Project 11	$549.00	$45.00	$263.52	48.00%	2.08	13.20		1.0000
Project 12	$525.00	$105.00	$309.75	59.00%	1.69	6.00		1.0000
Total	$5,776.00	$3,694.44	$1,539	26.64%				6.00
Goal:	MAX	<=$5000						<=6
Sharpe Ratio	3.7543							

ENPV is the expected NPV of each investment or project, while Cost can be the total cost of investment, and Risk is the Coefficient of Variation of the project's ENPV.

FIGURE 11.42 Optimal selection of projects that maximizes the Sharpe Ratio.

- Exercise Question: If we use coefficient of variation instead of return to risk ratio, would we maximize or minimize this variable?
- Exercise Question: How would you model a situation where, say, one project is the prerequisite for another or if two or more projects are mutually exclusive? How do you model the following?
  - You cannot do Project 2 by itself without Project 1, but you can do Project 1 on its own without Project 2.
  - Either Project 3 or Project 4 can be chosen but not both.
  - Each project has some full time equivalence (FTE) employees required to be involved, and the company has a limited number of FTEs.

5. Now add simulation assumptions on the model's ENPV and cost variables (columns C and D) and apply dynamic optimization for additional practice.

Efficient Frontier and Advanced Optimization Settings

Figure 11.43 shows the *Constraints* for optimization. Here, if you clicked on the *Efficient Frontier* button *after* you have set some constraints, you can now make these constraints changing. That is, each of the constraints can be created to step through between some maximum and minimum value. As an example, the constraint in cell *J17* $<= 6$ can be set to run between

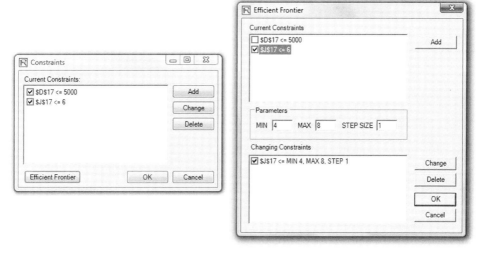

FIGURE 11.43 Generating changing constraints in an efficient frontier.

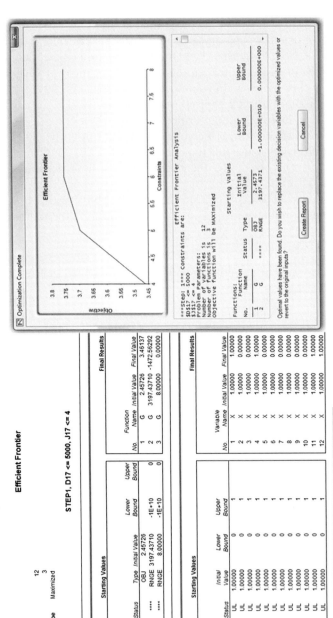

FIGURE 11.44 Efficient frontier results.

4 and *8* (Figure 11.43). That is, five optimizations will be run, each with the following constraints: *J17* <= *4, J17* <= *5, J17* <= *6, J17* <= *7* and *J17* <= *8.* The optimal results will then be plotted as an efficient frontier and the report will be generated (Figure 11.44). Specifically, the following illustrates the steps required to create a changing constraint:

1. In an optimization model (i.e., a model with Objective, Decision Variables and Constraints already set up), click on *Risk Simulator | Optimization | Constraints* and click on *Efficient Frontier.*
2. Select the constraint you want to change or step, *J17,* and enter the parameters for *Min, Max,* and *Step Size* (Figure 11.43). Then click *ADD* and then *OK* and *OK* again. Also, *uncheck* the first constraint of *D17* <= *5000.*
3. Run Optimization as usual, *Risk Simulator | Optimization | Run Optimization* or click on the *Run Optimization* icon. You can choose static, dynamic, or stochastic when running an efficient frontier, but to get started, choose the static optimization routine.
   ▪ Exercise Question: What happens if you run a stochastic optimization with efficient frontier? What is the step-by-step process that it goes through?
   ▪ Exercise Question: What happens if you do not uncheck the first constraint?
4. The results will be shown as a user interface (Figure 11.43). Click on *Create Report* to generate a report worksheet with all the details of the optimization runs.
   ▪ Exercise Question: How do you interpret the efficient frontier? Is a steeper curve better or a flatter curve? Can the curve slope downwards and if so, what does that mean?

QUESTIONS

1. Compare and contrast between a discrete versus continuous decision variable when used in an optimization under uncertainty.
2. Create an Excel model for a continuous optimization problem with the following parameters:
   a. A stock portfolio consisting of four individual stocks, each with its own return and risk profile—each return and risk value has its own distributional assumption that is correlated to one another.

   b. The optimization problem is to efficiently allocate your resources to those individual stocks such that the best bang for the buck is achieved—use a Sharpe ratio (portfolio returns to risk ratio).

   c. Optimize this portfolio of stocks through the Sharpe ratio and progressively create and show the Markowitz efficient frontier of stock allocations.

Seven

Risk Mitigation

CHAPTER 12

What Is So Real About Real Options, and Why Are They Optional?

T his chapter provides the reader a cursory look at and quick introduction to real options analysis. It explains why only running simulations, forecasting, and optimization are not sufficient in a comprehensive risk management paradigm; that is, time-series forecasting and Monte Carlo simulation are used for *identifying*, *predicting*, and *quantifying* risks. The question that should be asked is, so what and what next? Quantifying and understanding risk is one thing, but turning this information into *actionable intelligence* is another. Real options analysis, when applied appropriately, allows you to *value* risk, creating strategies to *mitigate* risk, and how to position yourself to *take advantage* of risk. It is highly recommended that you refer to *Real Options Analysis: Tools and Techniques*, Second Edition (John Wiley & Sons, 2005) also by the author, in order to learn more about the theoretical as well as pragmatic step-by-step computational details of real options analysis.

WHAT ARE REAL OPTIONS?

In the past, corporate investment decisions were cut and dried. Buy a new machine that is more efficient, make more products costing a certain amount, and if the benefits outweigh the costs, execute the investment. Hire a larger pool of sales associates, expand the current geographical area, and if the marginal increase in forecast sales revenues exceeds the additional salary and implementation costs, start hiring. Need a new manufacturing plant? Show that the construction costs can be recouped quickly and easily by the increase in revenues the plant will generate through new and improved products, and the initiative is approved.

However, real-life business conditions are a lot more complicated. Your firm decides to go with an e-commerce strategy, but multiple strategic paths exist. Which path do you choose? What are the options you have? If you choose the wrong path, how do you get back on the right track? How do you value and prioritize the paths that exist? You are a venture capitalist firm with multiple business plans to consider. How do you value a start-up firm with no proven track record? How do you structure a mutually beneficial investment deal? What is the optimal timing to a second or third round of financing?

> Business conditions are fraught with uncertainty and risks. These uncertainties hold with them valuable information. When uncertainty becomes resolved through the passage of time, actions, and events, managers can make the appropriate midcourse corrections through a change in business decisions and strategies. Real options incorporate this learning model, akin to having a strategic road map, whereas traditional analyses that neglect this managerial flexibility will grossly undervalue certain projects and strategies.

Real options are useful not only in valuing a firm through its strategic business options, but also as a strategic business tool in capital investment decisions. For instance, should a firm invest millions in a new e-commerce initiative? How does a firm choose among several seemingly cashless, costly, and unprofitable information-technology infrastructure projects? Should a firm indulge its billions in a risky research and development initiative? The consequences of a wrong decision can be disastrous or even terminal for certain firms. In a traditional discounted cash-flow model, these questions cannot be answered with any certainty. In fact, some of the answers generated through the use of the traditional discounted cash-flow model are flawed because the model assumes a static, one-time decision-making process whereas the real options approach takes into consideration the strategic managerial options certain projects create under uncertainty and management's flexibility in exercising or abandoning these options at different points in time, when the level of uncertainty has decreased or has become known over time.

The real options approach incorporates a learning model, such that management makes better and more informed strategic decisions when some levels of uncertainty are resolved through the passage of time, actions, and events. The discounted cash-flow analysis assumes a static investment decision and assumes that strategic decisions are made initially with no recourse to choose other pathways or options in the future. To create a good analogy of real options, visualize it as a strategic road map of long and winding roads with multiple perilous turns and branches along the way. Imagine the intrinsic and extrinsic value of having such a road map or global positioning system when navigating through unfamiliar territory, as well as having road signs at every turn to guide you in making the best and most informed driving decisions. Such a strategic map is the essence of real options.

The answer to evaluating such projects lies in real options analysis, which can be used in a variety of settings, including pharmaceutical drug development, oil and gas exploration and production, manufacturing, start-up valuation, venture capital investment, information technology infrastructure, research and development, mergers and acquisitions, e-commerce and e-business, intellectual capital development, technology development, facility expansion, business project prioritization, enterprise-wide risk management, business unit capital budgeting, licenses, contracts, intangible asset valuation, and the like. The following section illustrates some business cases and how real options can assist in identifying and capturing additional strategic value for a firm.

THE REAL OPTIONS SOLUTION IN A NUTSHELL

Simply defined, real options methodology is a systematic approach and integrated solution using financial theory, economic analysis, management science, decision sciences, statistics, and econometric modeling in applying options theory in valuing real physical assets, as opposed to financial assets, in a dynamic and uncertain business environment where business decisions are flexible in the context of strategic capital investment decision making, valuing investment opportunities, and project capital expenditures.

Real options are crucial in:

- Identifying different corporate investment decision pathways or projects that management can navigate given highly uncertain business conditions.
- Valuing each of the strategic decision pathways and what it represents in terms of financial viability and feasibility.
- Prioritizing these pathways or projects based on a series of qualitative and quantitative metrics.
- Optimizing the value of strategic investment decisions by evaluating different decision paths under certain conditions or using a different sequence of pathways that can lead to the optimal strategy.

- Timing the effective execution of investments and finding the optimal trigger values and cost or revenue drivers.
- Managing existing or developing new optionalities and strategic decision pathways for future opportunities.

ISSUES TO CONSIDER

Strategic options do have significant intrinsic value, but this value is only realized when management decides to execute the strategies. Real options theory assumes that management is logical and competent and that management acts in the best interests of the company and its shareholders through the maximization of wealth and minimization of risk of losses. For example, suppose a firm owns the rights to a piece of land that fluctuates dramatically in price. An analyst calculates the volatility of prices and recommends that management retain ownership for a specified time period, where within this period there is a good chance that the price of real estate will triple. Therefore, management owns a call option, an *option to wait* and defer sale for a particular time period. The value of the real estate is therefore higher than the value that is based on today's sale price. The difference is simply this option to wait. However, the value of the real estate will not command the higher value if prices do triple but management decides not to execute the option to sell. In that case, the price of real estate goes back to its original levels after the specified period, and then management finally relinquishes its rights.

> Strategic optionality value can only be obtained if the option is executed; otherwise, all the options in the world are worthless.

Was the analyst right or wrong? What was the true value of the piece of land? Should it have been valued at its explicit value on a deterministic case where you know what the price of land is right now, and therefore this is its value; or should it include some types of optionality where there is a good probability that the price of land could triple in value, hence, the piece of land is truly worth more than it is now and should therefore be valued accordingly? The latter is the real options view. The additional strategic optionality value can only be obtained if the option is executed; otherwise, all the options in the world are worthless. This idea of *explicit* versus *implicit* value becomes highly significant when management's compensation is tied directly to the actual performance of particular projects or strategies.

To further illustrate this point, suppose the price of the land in the market is currently $10 million. Further, suppose that the market is highly liquid and volatile and that the firm can easily sell off the land at a moment's notice within the next 5 years, the same amount of time the firm owns the rights to the land. If there is a 50 percent chance the price will increase to $15 million and a 50 percent chance it will decrease to $5 million within this time period, is the property worth an expected value of $10 million? If the price rises to $15 million, management should be competent and rational enough to execute the option and sell that piece of land immediately to capture the additional $5 million premium. However, if management acts inappropriately or decides to hold off selling in the hopes that prices will rise even further, the property value may eventually drop back down to $5 million. Now, how much is this property really worth? What if there happens to be an *abandonment option*? Suppose there is a perfect counterparty to this transaction who decides to enter into a contractual agreement whereby, for a contractual fee, the counterparty agrees to purchase the property for $10 million within the next 5 years, regardless of the market price and executable at the whim of the firm that owns the property. Effectively, a safety net has been created whereby the minimum floor value of the property has been set at $10 million (less the fee paid); that is, there is a limited downside but an unlimited upside, as the firm can always sell the property at market price if it exceeds the floor value. Hence, this strategic *abandonment option* has increased the value of the property significantly. Logically, with this abandonment option in place, the value of the land with the option is definitely worth more than $10 million. The land price is stochastic and uncertain with some volatility (risk) and has some inherent probability distribution. The distribution's left tail is the downside risk and the right tail is upside value, and having an abandonment option (in this example, a price protection of $10 million) means that you take a really sharp knife and you slice off the distribution's left tail at $10 million because the firm will never have to deal with the situation of selling the land at anything lower than $10 million. What happens is that the distribution's left-tail risk has been truncated and reduced, making the distribution now positively skewed; and the expected return or average value moves to the right. In other words, strategic real options in this case provided a *risk reduction and value enhancement strategy* to the firm. Therefore, this option has value (e.g., insurance policies require a premium or price to obtain, and you can think of this abandonment option as a price protection insurance against any downside movements), and the idea is to determine what the fair market value is, whether the option is indeed worth it, the optimal timing to execute the option, and so forth. The real options approach seeks to value this additional inherent flexibility. Real options analysis allows the firm to determine how much this safety downside insurance or abandonment option is worth (i.e., what is the fair-market value of the contractual fee to obtain the option?), the optimal trigger price (i.e., at what price will it be optimal to sell the land?), and the optimal timing (i.e., what is the optimal amount of time to hold on to the land?).

IMPLEMENTING REAL OPTIONS ANALYSIS

First, it is vital to understand that real options analysis is *not* a simple set of equations or models. It is an *entire decision-making process* that enhances the traditional decision analysis approaches. It takes what has been tried-and-true financial analytics and evolves it to the next step by pushing the envelope of analytical techniques. In addition, it is vital to understand that 50 percent of the value in real options analysis is simply thinking about it. Another 25 percent of the value comes from the number crunching activities, while the final 25 percent comes from the results interpretation and explanation to management. Several issues should be considered when attempting to implement real options analysis:

- *Tools.* The correct tools are important. These tools must be more comprehensive than initially required because analysts will grow into them over time. Do not be restrictive in choosing the relevant tools. Always provide room for expansion. Advanced tools will relieve the analyst of detailed model building and let him or her focus instead on 75 percent of the value—thinking about the problem and interpreting the results. Chapter 13 illustrates the use of Real Options Super Lattice Solver (SLS) software and how even complex and customized real options problems can be solved with great ease.
- *Resources.* The best tools in the world are useless without the relevant human resources to back them up. Tools do not eliminate the analyst, but enhance the analyst's ability to effectively and efficiently execute the analysis. The right people with the right tools will go a long way. Because there are only a few true real options experts in the world who truly understand the theoretical underpinnings of the models as well as the practical applications, care should be taken in choosing the correct team. A team of real options experts is vital in the success of the initiative. A company should consider building a team of in-house experts to implement real options analysis and to maintain the ability for continuity, training, and knowledge transfer over time. Knowledge and experience in the theories, implementation, training, and consulting are the core requirements of this team of individuals. This is why training is vital. For instance, the Certified in Risk Management (CRM) certification program provides analysts and managers

the opportunity to immerse themselves in the theoretical and real-life applications of simulation, forecasting, optimization, and real options (see www.realoptionsvaluation.com for more details).

- *Senior Management Buy-In.* The analysis buy-in has to be top-down where senior management drives the real options analysis initiative. A bottom-up approach where a few inexperienced junior analysts try to impress the powers that be will fail miserably.

TYPES OF REAL OPTIONS STRATEGIES

- **Abandonment Option:** An abandonment option provides the holder the right but not the obligation to sell off and abandon some project, asset, or property at a prespecified price and term.
- **Barrier Option:** A barrier option means that the option becomes live and available for execution and consequently the value of the strategic option depends on either breaching or not breaching an artificial barrier.
- **Expansion Option:** An expansion option provides management the right and ability to expand into different markets, products, and strategies or to expand its current operations under the right conditions.
- **Chooser Option:** A chooser option implies that management has the flexibility to choose among several strategies, including the option to expand, abandon, switch, contract, and combinations of other exotic options.
- **Contraction Option:** A contraction option provides management the right and ability to contract its operations under the right conditions, thereby saving on expenses.
- **Deferment Option (Timing Option, Option to Wait):** This type of option is also a purchase option or an option to wait.
- **Sequential Compound Option:** A sequential compound option means that the execution and value of future strategic options depend on previous options in sequence of execution.
- **Switching Option:** A switching option provides the right and ability but not the obligation to switch among different sets of business operating conditions, including different technologies, markets, or products.

Execution Option Types

And for all of these options, you can have different allowed execution times, including American, European, Bermudan, and Asian options. American options allow you to execute at any time before and up to and including the expiration date. European options allow you to execute only on a specific

date, typically the expiration date itself. Bermudan options are a mix between European and American in that there is a blackout or vesting period
when you cannot execute the option, but you can do so at any time after
this blackout period and up to and including expiration (e.g., an employee
stock option usually has a 10-year maturity and a 4-year vesting period,
where you cannot exercise the option within this first four years and you
lose the option if you leave your job during this vesting period, but once
this requisite service period has passed, the option is yours and you can
exercise it at any time between year 4 and year 10). Finally, Asian options
are look-back options, where specific conditions in the option are dependent
on some factor in the future (e.g., United Airlines buys some Airbus A380
planes where they sign the purchase order today for delivery of the planes
in two years, and the price of the plane is dependent on the average market
price between now and two years, a period that is in the future when the
purchase order was placed, but will be the past once the planes and final
payment changes hands two years from now, and both parties can look back
to this pricing period to obtain the final sale price of the planes). So, you
can have an American Abandonment option or a European Abandonment
option, and so forth.

INDUSTRY LEADERS EMBRACING REAL OPTIONS

Automobile and Manufacturing Industry

In automobile and manufacturing, General Motors (GM) applies real options to create *switching option*s in producing its new series of autos. This
option is essentially to use a cheaper resource over a given period of time.
GM holds excess raw materials and has multiple global vendors for similar
materials with excess contractual obligations above what it projects as necessary. The excess contractual cost is outweighed by the significant savings
of switching vendors when a certain raw material becomes too expensive in
a particular region of the world. By spending the additional money in contracting with vendors and meeting their minimum purchase requirements,
GM has essentially paid the premium on purchasing a *switching option,*
which is important especially when the price of raw materials fluctuates
significantly in different regions around the world. Having an option here
provides the holder a hedging vehicle against pricing risks.

Computer Industry

In the computer industry, HP-Compaq used to forecast sales in foreign
countries months in advance. It then configured, assembled, and shipped
the highly specific configuration printers to these countries. However, given

that demand changes rapidly and forecast figures are seldom correct, the preconfigured printers usually suffer the higher inventory holding cost or the cost of technological obsolescence. HP-Compaq can create an *option to wait* and defer making any decisions too early through building assembly plants in these foreign countries. Parts can then be shipped and assembled in specific configurations when demand is known, possibly weeks in advance rather than months in advance. These parts can be shipped anywhere in the world and assembled in any configuration necessary, while excess parts are interchangeable across different countries. The premium paid on this option is building the assembly plants, and the upside potential is the savings in making wrong demand forecasts.

Airline Industry

In the airline industry, Boeing spends billions of dollars and takes several years to decide if a certain aircraft model should even be built. Should the wrong model be tested in this elaborate strategy, Boeing's competitors may gain a competitive advantage relatively quickly. Because so many technical, engineering, market, and financial uncertainties are involved in the decision-making process, Boeing can conceivably create an *option to choose* through parallel development of multiple plane designs simultaneously, knowing well the increasing cost of developing multiple designs simultaneously with the sole purpose of eliminating all but one in the near future. The added cost is the premium paid on the option. However, Boeing will be able to decide which model to abandon or continue when these uncertainties and risks become known over time. Eventually, all the models will be eliminated save one. This way, the company can hedge itself against making the wrong initial decision and benefit from the knowledge gained through parallel development initiatives.

Oil and Gas Industry

In the oil and gas industry, companies spend millions of dollars to refurbish their refineries and add new technology to create an *option to switch* their mix of outputs among heating oil, diesel, and other petrochemicals as a final product, using real options as a means of making capital and investment decisions. This option allows the refinery to switch its final output to one that is more profitable based on prevailing market prices, to capture the demand and price cyclicality in the market.

Telecommunications Industry

In the telecommunications industry, in the past, companies like Sprint and AT&T installed more fiber-optic cable and other telecommunications infrastructure than any other company in order to create a *growth option* in the future by providing a secure and extensive network and to create a high barrier to entry, providing a first-to-market advantage. Imagine having to justify to the board of directors the need to spend billions of dollars on infrastructure that will not be used for years to come. Without the use of real options, this decision would have been impossible to justify.

Utilities Industry

In the utilities industry, firms have created an *option to execute* and an *option to switch* by installing cheap-to-build inefficient energy generator *peaker* plants to be used only when electricity prices are high and to shut down when prices are low. The price of electricity tends to remain constant until it hits a certain capacity utilization trigger level, when prices shoot up significantly. Although this occurs infrequently, the possibility still exists, and by having a cheap standby plant, the firm has created the option to turn on the switch whenever it becomes necessary, to capture this upside price fluctuation.

Real Estate Industry

In the real estate arena, leaving land undeveloped creates an option to develop at a later date at a more lucrative profit level. However, what is the optimal wait time or the optimal trigger price to maximize returns? In theory, one can wait for an infinite amount of time, and real options provide the solution for the optimal timing and optimal price trigger value.

Pharmaceutical Research and Development Industry

In pharmaceutical or research and development initiatives, real options can be used to justify the large investments in what seems to be cashless and unprofitable under the discounted cash flow method but actually creates *compound expansion options* in the future. Under the myopic lenses of a traditional discounted cash flow analysis, the high initial investment of, say, a billion dollars in research and development may return a highly uncertain projected few million dollars over the next few years. Management will conclude under a net present value analysis that the project is not financially feasible. However, a cursory look at the industry indicates that research and development is performed everywhere. Hence, management must see an intrinsic strategic value in research and development. How is this intrinsic strategic value quantified? A real options approach would optimally time and spread the billion dollar initial investment into a multiple-stage investment structure. At each stage, management has an *option to wait* and see what happens as well as the *option to abandon* or the *option to expand* into the subsequent stages. The ability to defer cost and proceed only if situations are permissible creates value for the investment.

High-Tech and e-Business Industry

In e-business strategies, real options can be used to prioritize different e-commerce initiatives and to justify those large initial investments that have an uncertain future. Real options can be used in e-commerce to create incremental investment stages compared to a large one-time investment (invest a little now, wait and see before investing more) as well as create *options to abandon* and other future growth options.

Mergers and Acquisitions

In valuing a firm for acquisition, you should not only consider the revenues and cash flows generated from the firm's operations but also the strategic options that come with the firm. For instance, if the acquired firm does not operate up to expectations, an *abandonment option* can be executed where it can be sold for its intellectual property and other tangible assets. If the firm is highly successful, it can be spun off into other industries and verticals or new products and services can be eventually developed through the execution of an *expansion option*. In fact, in mergers and acquisition, several strategic options exist. For instance, a firm acquires other entities to enlarge its existing portfolio of products or geographic location or to obtain new technology (*expansion option*); or to divide the acquisition into many smaller pieces and sell them off as in the case of a corporate raider (*abandonment option*); or it merges to form a larger organization due to certain synergies and immediately lays off many of its employees (*contraction option*). If the seller does not value its real options, it may be leaving money on the negotiation table. If the buyer does not value these strategic options, it is undervaluing a potentially highly lucrative acquisition target.

All these cases where the high cost of implementation with no apparent payback in the near future seems foolish and incomprehensible in the traditional discounted cash flow sense are fully justified in the real options sense when taking into account the strategic options the practice creates for the future, the uncertainty of the future operating environment, and management's flexibility in making the right choices at the appropriate time.

MORE SAMPLE APPLICATIONS AND SHORT CASES

Expansion and Compound Options: The Case of the Operating System

You are the Chief Technology Officer of a large multinational corporation, and you know that your firm's operating systems are antiquated and require an upgrade, say, to the new Microsoft Windows 7 and Server 2008 series from the antiquated Windows XP platform. You arrange a meeting with the CEO, letting him in on the situation. The CEO quips back immediately, saying that he will support your initiative if you can prove to him that the monetary benefits outweigh the costs of implementation—a simple and logical request. You immediately arrange for a demonstration of the new operating system, and the highly technical experts from Microsoft provide you and your boss a marvelous presentation of the system's capabilities and value-added enhancements that took in excess of a few million dollars and several years to develop. The system even fixes itself in times of dire circumstances and is overall more reliable and stable than its predecessors. You get more excited by the minute and have made up your mind to get the much-needed product upgrade. There is still one hurdle, the financial hurdle, to prove not only that the new system provides a better operating environment, but also that the plan of action is financially sound. Granted, the more efficient and sophisticated system will make your boss's secretary a much happier person and hence more productive. Then again, so will an extra week's worth of vacation and a bigger bonus check, both of which are a lot cheaper and easier to implement. The new system will not help your sales force sell more products and generate higher revenues because the firm looks state-of-the-art only if a customer questions what version of Windows operating system you are using—hardly an issue that will arise during a sales call. Then again, when has using the latest software ever assisted in closing a deal, especially when you are a contract global-freight and logistics solutions provider?

You lose sleep over the next few days pondering the issue, and you finally decide to assemble a task force made up of some of your top IT personnel. The six of you sit in a room considering the same issues and trying to brainstorm a few really good arguments. You link up the value-added propositions provided in the Microsoft technician's presentation and come up with a series of potential cost-reduction drivers. Principally, the self-preservation and self-fixing functionality will mean less technical assistance and help-desk calls, freeing up resources and perhaps leading to the need for fewer IT people on staff. Your mind races through some quick figures, you feel your heart pounding faster, and you see a light at the end of the tunnel. Finally you will have your long-awaited operating system, and all your headaches will go away. Wait, not only does it reduce the help-desk time, but also it increases efficiency because employees will no longer have to call or hold for technical assistance.

Your team spends the next few days scouring through mountains of data on help-desk calls and issues—thank God for good record-keeping and relational databases. Looking for issues that could potentially become obsolete with the new system, you find that at least 20 percent of your help-desk calls could be eliminated by having the new system in place because it is more stable, is capable of self-fixing these critical issues, can troubleshoot internal hardware conflicts, and so forth. Besides, doesn't employee morale count? Satisfied with your analysis, you approach the CEO and show him your findings.

Impressed with your charts and analytical rigor in such a short time frame, he asks several quick questions and points out several key issues. The cost reduction in technical assistance is irrelevant because you need these people to install and configure the new system. The start-up cost and learning curve might be steep, and employees may initially have a tough time adjusting to the new operating environment—help-desk calls may actually increase in the near future, albeit slowing down in time. But the firm's mission has always been to cultivate its employees and not to fire them needlessly. Besides, there are five people on staff at the help desk and a 20 percent reduction means one less full-time employee out of 5,000 in the entire firm—hardly a cost-reduction strategy! As for the boss's secretary's productivity, you noticed two first-class air tickets to Maui on his desk, and you are pretty sure one of them is for her. Your mind races with alternate possibilities—including taking a trip to Hawaii with a high-powered digital-zoom camera but deciding against it on your way out. He notices your wandering eyes and tries to change the subject. You still have not sufficiently persuaded your boss on getting the new operating system, and you are up a tree and out on a limb. Thoughts of going shopping for a camera haunt you for the rest of the day.

Sound familiar? Firms wrestle with similar decisions daily, and vendors wrestling with how to make their products more marketable have to first address this financial and strategic issue. Imagine you are the sales director for Microsoft, or any software and hardware vendor for that matter. How do you close a sale like this?

Performing a series of simple traditional analyses using a discounted cash-flow methodology or economic justification based on traditional analyses will fail miserably, as we have seen above. The quantifiable financial benefits do not exceed the high implementation costs. How do you justify and correctly value such seemingly cashless and cash-flow draining projects? The answer lies in real options. Instead of being myopic and focusing on current savings, the implementation of large-scale servers or operating systems will generate future strategic options for the firm. That is, having the servers and system in place provides you a springboard to a second-, third-, or fourth-phase IT implementation. That is, having a powerful connected system gives you the technical feasibility to pursue online collaboration, global data access, videoconferencing, digital signatures, encryption security, remote installations, document recovery, and the like, which would be impossible to do without it. Hence, the value of upgrading to a new system provides the firm an *expansion option,* which is the right and ability, but not the obligation, to invest and pursue some of these value-added technologies. Some of these technologies such as security enhancements and global data access can be highly valuable to your global freight company's supply chain management. You may further delineate certain features into groups of options to execute at the same time—that is, create a series of *sequential compound options* where the success of one group of initiatives depends on the success of another in sequence, similar to a stage-gate investment process. Notice that using an extrapolation of the traditional analytic approaches would be inappropriate here because all these implementation possibilities are simply options that a senior manager has, and not guaranteed execution by any means. When you view the whole strategic picture, value is created and identified where there was not any before, thereby making you able to clearly justify financially your plans for the upgrade. You would be well on your way to getting your new operating system installed.

Expansion Options: The Case of the e-Business Initiative

The e-business boom has been upon us for a few years now, and finally the investment bank you work for has decided to join the Internet age. You get a decree from the powers that be to come up with a solid e-commerce initiative. The CEO calls you into his office and spends an hour expounding on the wisdom of bringing the firm closer to the electronic Web. After hours of meetings, you are tasked with performing a feasibility analysis, choosing the right strategy, and valuing the wisdom of going e-commerce. Well, it sounds simple enough, or so you think.

The next two weeks are spent with boardroom meetings, conference calls with e-commerce consulting firms, and bottles of Alka-Seltzer. Being a newly endowed expert on the e-business strategies after spending two weeks in Tahiti on a supposedly world-renowned e-commerce crash course, you realize you really still know nothing. One thing is for certain: the Internet has revolutionized the way businesses are run. The traditional *Sun Tzu* business environment of "know thy enemy and know thyself and in a hundred battles you will be victorious" had not met the Internet. The competitive playing field has been leveled, and your immediate competitors are no longer the biggest threat. The biggest threat is globalization, when new competitors halfway around the world crawl out of the woodwork and take half of your market-share just because they have a fancy web site capable of attracting, diverting, and retaining Web traffic, and capable of taking orders around the world, and you do not. Perhaps the CEO is right; it is a do-or-die scenario. When a 12-year-old girl can transform her parent's fledgling trinket store into an overnight success by going to the Internet, technology seems to be the biggest foe of all. You either ride the technological wave or are swept under.

Convinced of the necessity of e-commerce and the strong desire to keep your job, you come up with a strategic game plan. You look at the e-commerce options you have and try to ascertain the correct path to traverse, knowing well that if you pick the wrong one, it can be ultimately disastrous, for you and your firm, in that particular order. In between updating your curriculum vitae, you decide to spend some time pondering the issues. You realize that there are a large number of options in going e-commerce, and you have decided on several potential pathways to consider as they are most appropriate to the firm's core business.

Do we simply create a static web site with nice graphics, text explaining what we do, and perhaps a nice little map showing where we are located and the hours of availability, and get fired? Do we perhaps go a little further and provide traditional banking services on the Web? Perhaps a way for our customers to access their accounts, pay bills, trade stocks, apply for loans, and perhaps get some free stock advice or free giveaways and pop-up ads to divert traffic on the Web? Perhaps we can take it to the extreme and use state-of-the-art technology to enable items like digital television access, live continuous streaming technology, equity trading on personal digital assistants and cellular phones, interaction with and direct access to floor specialists and traders on the New York Stock Exchange for the larger clients, and all the while using servers in Enron-like offshore tax havens (all the while assuming you don't get caught and implode like Enron did). The potentials are endless.

You suddenly feel queasy, and the inkling of impending doom. What about competition? Ameritrade and a dozen other online trading firms currently exist. Most major banks are already on the Web, and they provide the same services. What makes us so special? Then again, if we do not follow the other players, we may be left out in the cold. Perhaps there are some ways to differentiate our services. Perhaps some sort of geographical expansion; after all, the Internet is global, so why shouldn't we be? What about market penetration effects and strategies, country risk analysis, legislative and regulatory risks? What if the strategy is unsuccessful? What will happen then? Competitive effects are unpredictable. The threats of new entrants and low barriers to entry may elicit even more competitors than you currently have. Is the firm ready to play in the big leagues and fight with the virtual offshore banking services? Globalization—what an ugly word it is right about now. What about new technology: Do we keep spending every time something new comes out? What about market share, market penetration, positioning, and being first to market with a new and exciting product? What about future growth opportunities, e-traffic management, and portal security? The lists go on and on. Perhaps you should take a middle ground, striking an alliance with established investment banking firms with the applicable IT infrastructure already in place. Why build when you can buy? You reach for your Alka-Seltzer and realize you need something much stronger.

How do you prioritize these potential strategies, perform a financial and strategic feasibility analysis, and make the right decision? Will the firm survive if we go down the wrong path? If we find out we are on the wrong path, can we navigate our way back to the right one? What options can we create to enable this? Which of these strategies is optimal? Upon identifying what these strategies are, including all their downstream *expansion options,* you can then value each of these strategic pathways. The identification, valuation, prioritization, and selection of strategic projects are where real options analysis can provide great insights and value. Each project initiative should not be viewed in its current state. Instead, all downstream opportunities should be viewed and considered as well. Otherwise, wrong decisions can be made because only projects with immediate value will be chosen, while projects that carry with them great future potential are abandoned simply because management is setting its sights on the short term.

Expansion and Sequential Options: The Case of the Pharmaceutical R&D

Being the chief chemist of a small pharmaceutical firm that is thinking of developing a certain drug useful in gene therapy, you have the responsibility to determine the right biochemical compounds to create. Understanding well that the future of the firm rests on pursuing and developing the right portfolio of drugs, you take your evaluation task seriously. Currently, the firm's management is uncertain whether to proceed with developing a group of compounds and is also uncertain regarding the drug development's financial feasibility. From historical data and personal experience, you understand that development "home runs" are few and far between. As a matter of fact, you realize that less than 5 percent of all compounds developed are superstars. However, if the right compounds are chosen, the firm will own several valuable patents and bolster its chances of receiving future rounds of funding. Armed with that future expectation, you evaluate each potential compound with care and patience.

For example, one of the compounds you are currently evaluating is called Creatosine. Management knows that Creatosine, when fully developed, can be taken orally, but has the potential to be directly injected into the bloodstream, which increases its effectiveness. Because there is great uncertainty in the development of Creatosine, management decides to develop the oral version for now and wait for a period of several years before deciding on investing additional funds to develop the injectable version. Thus, management has created an *expansion option*—that is, the option but not the obligation to expand Creatosine into an injectable version at any time between now and several years. By incorporating real options strategy, your firm has mitigated its risks in developing the drug into both an oral and injectable form at initiation. By waiting, scientific and market risks become resolved through the passage of time, and your firm can then decide whether to pursue the second injectable phase. This risk-hedging phenomenon is common in financial options and is applicable here for real options.

However, there are other drug compounds to analyze as well. You go through the list with a fine-tooth comb and realize that you must evaluate each drug by not only its biochemical efficacies, but also by its financial feasibility. Given the firm's current capital structure, you would need to not only value, prioritize, and select the right compounds, but also find the optimal portfolio mix of compounds, subject to budget, timing, and risk constraints. On top of that, you would have to value your firm as a whole in terms of a portfolio of strategic options. The firm's value lies not only in its forecast revenues less its costs subject to time valuation of money but also in all the current research and development initiatives under way, where a single home run will double or triple the firm's valuation. These so-called future *growth options*, which are essentially growth opportunities that the firm has, are highly valuable. These *growth options* are simply *expansion options* because your firm owns the right infrastructure, resources, and technology to pursue these future opportunities but not the obligation to do so unless both internal research and external market conditions are amenable.

Another approach you decide to use is to create a strategic development road map, knowing that every drug under development has to go through multiple phases. At each phase, depending on the research results, management can decide to continue its development to the next phase or abandon it assuming it does not meet certain prespecified criteria. That is, management has the *option to choose* whether a certain compound will continue to the next stage. Certain drugs in the initial phases go through a *sequential compound option*, where the success of the third phase, for example, depends on the success of the second phase, which in turn depends on the success of the first phase in the stage-gate drug development cycle. Valuing such sequences of options using a traditional approach of taking expected values with respect to the probabilities of success is highly dubious and incorrect. The valuation will be incorrect at best and highly misleading at worst, driving management to select the wrong mix of compounds at the wrong time.

Expansion and Switching Options: The Case of the Oil and Gas Exploration and Production

The oil and gas industry is fraught with strategic options problems because oil and gas exploration and production involves significant amounts of risk and uncertainty. For example, when drilling for oil, the reservoir properties, fluidic properties, trap size and geometry, porosity, seal containment, oil and gas in place, expulsion force, losses due to migration, development costs, and so forth are all unknowns. How then is a reservoir engineer going to recommend to management the value of a particular drill site? Let us explore some of the more frequent real options problems encountered in this industry.

Being a fresh M.B.A. graduate from a top finance program, you are hired by a second-tier independent oil and gas firm, and your first task is to value several primary and secondary reservoir recovery wells. You are called into your boss's office, and she requested that you do an independent financial analysis on a few production wells. You were given a stack of technical engineering documents to review. After spending a fortnight scouring through several books on the fundamentals of the oil and gas industry, you finally have some basic understanding of the intricacies of what a secondary recovery well is. Needing desperately to impress your superiors, you decide to investigate a little further into some new analytics for solving these types of recovery-well problems.

Based on your incomplete understanding of the problem, you begin to explore all the possibilities and come to the conclusion that the best analytics to use may be the application of a Monte Carlo simulation and real options analysis. Instead of simply coming up with the value of the project, you decide to also identify where value can be added to the projects by incorporating strategic real optionality.

Suppose that the problem you are analyzing is a primary drilling site that has its own natural energy source, complete with its gas cap on one side and a water drive on the other. These energy sources maintain a high upward pressure on the oil reservoir to increase the ease of drilling and, therefore, the site's productivity. However, knowing that the level of energy may not be sustainable for a long time and its efficacy is unknown currently, you recognize that one of the strategies is to create an *expansion option* to drill a secondary recovery well near the primary site. Instead of drilling, you can use this well to inject water or gas into the ground, thereby increasing the upward pressure and keeping the reservoir productive. Building this secondary well is an option and not an obligation for the next few years.

The first recommendation seems to make sense given that the geological structure and reservoir size are difficult to estimate. Yet these are not the only important considerations; the price of oil in the market is also something that fluctuates dramatically and should be considered. Assuming that the price of oil is a major factor in management's decisions, your second recommendation includes separating the project into two stages. The first stage is to drill multiple wells in the primary reservoir, which will eventually maximize on its productivity. At that time a second phase can be implemented through smaller satellite reservoirs in the surrounding areas that are available for drilling but are separated from the primary reservoir by geological faults. This second stage is also an *expansion option* on the first: when the price of oil increases, the firm is then able to set up new rigs over the satellite reservoirs, drill, and complete these wells. Then, using the latest technology in subsurface robotics, the secondary wells can be tied back into the primary platform, thereby increasing and expanding the productivity of the primary well by some expansion factor. Obviously, although this is a strategic option that the firm has, the firm does not have the obligation to drill secondary wells unless the market price of oil is favorable enough. Using some basic intuition, you plug some numbers into your models and create the optimal oil price levels such that secondary drillings are profitable. However, given your brief conversation with your boss and your highly uncertain career future, you decide to dig into the strategy a little more.

Perhaps the company already has several producing wells at the reservoir. If that is so, the analysis should be tweaked such that instead of being an *expansion option* by drilling more wells, the firm can retrofit these existing wells in strategic locations from producers into injectors, creating a *switching option*. Instead of drilling more wells, the company can use the existing wells to inject gas or water into the surrounding geological areas in the hopes that this will increase the energy source, forcing the oil to surface at a higher rate. Obviously, these secondary production wells should be switched into injectors when the recovery rate of the secondary wells is relatively low and the marginal benefits of the added productivity on primary wells far outstrip the retrofit costs. In addition, some of the deep-sea drilling platforms that are to be built in the near future can be made into *expansion options*, where slightly larger platforms are built at some additional cost (premium paid to create this option), such that if oil prices are optimally high, the flexible capacity inherent in this larger platform can be executed to boost production.

Finally, depending on the situation involved, you can also create a *sequential compound option* for the reservoir. That is, the firm can segregate its activities into different phases. Specifically, we can delineate the strategic option into four phases. Phases I to III are exploration wells, and Phase IV is a development well.

Phase I: Start by performing seismic surveys to get information on the structures of subsurface reservoirs (the costs incurred include shooting the survey, processing data, and mapping).

Phase II: If autoclines and large structures are found, drill an exploration well; if not, then abandon now.

Phase III: If the exploration well succeeds industrially or commercially (evaluated on factors such as cost, water depth, oil price, rock, reservoir, and fluid properties), drill more delineation or "step out" wells to define the reservoir.

Phase IV: If the reservoir is productive enough, commit more money for full development (platform building, setting platform, drilling development wells).

Abandonment Options: The Case of the Manufacturer

You work for a midsize hardware manufacturing firm located in the heartland of America. Having recently attended a corporate finance seminar on real options, you set out to determine whether you can put some of your newfound knowledge to good use within the company. Currently, your firm purchases powerful laser-guided robotic fabrication tools that run into tens and even hundreds of millions of dollars each. These tools have to be specially ordered more than a year in advance, due to their unique and advanced specifications. They break down easily, and if any one of the three machines that your firm owns breaks down, it can be disastrous because part of the manufacturing division may have to be shut down temporarily for a period exceeding a year. So, is it always desirable to have at least one fabrication tool under order at all times, just as a precaution? A major problem arises when the newly ordered tool arrives, but the three remaining ones are fully functional and require no replacement. The firm has simply lost millions of dollars. In retrospect, certainly having a backup machine sitting idle that costs millions of dollars is not optimal. However, millions can also be lost if indeed a tool breaks down and a replacement is a year away. The question is, what do you do, and how can real options be used in this case, both as a strategic decision-making tool and valuation model?

Using traditional analysis, you come up to a dead end, as the tool's breakdown has never been consistent and the ordered parts never arrive on schedule. Turning to real options, you decide to create a strategic option with the vendor. Instead of having to wait more than a year before a new machine arrives, while during that time not knowing when your existing machines will break down, you decide to create a mutually agreeable contract. Your firm decides to put up a certain amount of money and to enter into a contractual agreement whereby the vendor will put you on its preferred list. In addition, your firm spends some development funds to retrofit your manufacturing equipment to an open architecture and modular configuration, allowing quickly replaceable and interchangeable parts. This cuts down delivery time from one year to two months. If your firm does not require the equipment, you will have to pay a penalty exit fee equivalent to a certain percentage of the machine's dollar value amount, within a specified period, on a ratcheted scale, with different exit penalties at different exit periods. In essence, you have created an *abandonment option* where your firm has the right not to purchase the equipment should circumstances force your hand, but hedging yourself to obtain the machine at a moment's notice should there be a need. The price of the option's premium is the contractual price paid for such an arrangement. The savings come in the form of not having to close down part of your plant and losing revenues. By incorporating real options insights into the problem, the firm saves millions and ends up with the optimal decision.

Expansion and Barrier Options: The Case of the Lost Venture Capitalist

You work in a venture capital firm and are in charge of the selection of strategic business plans and performing financial analysis on their respective financial feasibility and operational viability. The firm gets more than a thousand business plans a year, and your boss does not have the time to go through each of them in detail and relies on you to sniff out the ones with the maximum potential in the least amount of time. Besides, the winning plans do not wait for money. They often have money chasing after them. Having been in the field of venture capital funding for 10 years and having survived the bursting of the dot-com bubble, your judgment is highly valued in the firm. However, with the changing economic and competitive landscape, even seemingly bad ideas may turn into the next IPO success story. Given the opportunity of significant investment returns, the money lost on bad ideas is a necessary evil in not losing out on the next "eBay" or "Yahoo!" just because the CEO is not a brilliant business plan author.

Your qualitative judgment may still be valid, but the question is, what next? What do you do after you have selected your top 100 candidates? How do you efficiently allocate the firm's capital to minimize risk and maximize return? Picking the right firms the wrong way only gets you so far, especially when banking on start-ups hoping for new technological breakthroughs. A diversified portfolio of firms is always prudent, but a diversified portfolio of the right firms is much better. Prioritizing, ranking, and coming up with a solid financing structure for funding start-ups is tricky business, especially when traditional valuation methodologies do not work.

The new economy provides many challenges for the corporate decision maker. Market equity value of a firm now depends on expectations and anticipation of future opportunities in novel technologies rather than on a traditional bricks-and-mortar environment. This shift in underlying fundamentals from tangible goods to technological innovation has created an issue in valuing the firm. Even the face of the intangibles created by technological innovation has changed. In most cases, a significant portion of a firm's value or its strategic investment options is derived from the firm's intangibles. Intangibles generally refer to elements in a business that augment the revenue-generating process but do not themselves have a physical or monetary appearance while still holding significant value to the firm. Intangibles may range from more traditional items like intellectual property, property rights, patents, branding, and trademarks to a new generation of so-called e-intangibles created in the new economy.

Examples of this new generation of e-intangibles include items like marketing intangible, process and product technologies, trade dress, customer loyalty, branding, proprietary software, speed, search engine efficiency, online data catalogs, server efficiency, traffic control and diversion, streaming technology, content, experience, collaborative filtering, universal-resource-locator naming conventions, hubs, Web page hits, imprints, blogs, and community relationships. New entries in the e-commerce economy over the past few years include the financial sector (bank wires, online bill payments, online investing), health care sector (cross-border medical teaching), retail auctions and others (e-pocket books, Web magazines, Web papers, eBay, Twitter, Facebook, Google). The new trend seems to continue, and new start-ups emerge in scores by the minute to include sophisticated and complex structures like online cross-border banking services, virtual offshore banks, cross-border medical diagnostic imaging, and online-server game playing. However, other less sophisticated e-business strategies have also been booming of late, including service-based web sites, which provide a supposedly value-added service at no charge to the consumers such as online greeting cards and online e-invitations. Lower barriers to entry and significant threat of new entrants and substitution effects characterize these strategies.

Even using fairly well-known models like the discounted cash flow analysis is insufficient to value these types of firms. For instance, as a potential venture capitalist, how do you go about identifying the intangibles and intellectual property created when traditional financial theory is insufficient to justify or warrant such outrageous price-to-earnings multiples? Trying to get on the bandwagon in initial public offerings with large capital gains is always a good investment strategy, but randomly investing in start-ups with little to no fundamental justification of potential future profitability is a whole other issue. Perhaps there is a fundamental shift in the way the economy works today or is expected to work in the future as compared to the last decade. Whether there is indeed an irrational exuberance in the economy, or whether there is perhaps a shift in the fundamentals, we need a newer, more accurate, and sophisticated method of quantifying the value of such intangibles.

How do you identify, value, select, prioritize, justify, optimize, time, and manage large corporate investment decisions with high levels of uncertainty such that when a decision is made, the investment becomes irreversible? How do you value and select among several start-up firms to determine whether they are ideal venture candidates, and how do you create an optional financing structure? These types of cashless return investments provide no immediate increase in revenues, and the cost savings are only marginal compared to their costs. How do you justify such outrageous market equity prices?

There must be a better way to value these investment opportunities. Having read press releases by Motley Fool on Credit Suisse First Boston, and how the firm used real options to value stocks of different companies, you begin looking into the possibilities of applying real options yourself. The start-up firm has significant value even when its cash flow situation is hardly something to be desired because the firm has strategic *growth options*. That is, a particular start-up may have some technology that may seem untested today, but it has the *option to expand* into the marketplace quickly and effortlessly should the technology prove to be highly desirable in the near future. Obviously the firm has the right to also pursue other ancillary technologies but only if the market conditions are conducive enough. The venture firm can capitalize on this *option to expand* by hedging itself with multiple investments within a venture portfolio. The firm can also create strategic value through setting up contractual agreements with a *barrier option* and *option to defer* where for the promise of seed financing, the venture firm has the right of first refusal, but not the obligation, to invest in a second- or third-round should the start-up achieve certain management-set goals or barriers. The cost of this *barrier option* is seed financing, which is akin to the premium paid on a stock option. Should the option be in-the-money, the option will be executed through second- and third-round financing. By obtaining this strategic option, the venture firm has locked itself into a guaranteed favorable position should the start-up be highly successful, similar to the characteristics of a financial call option of unlimited upside potential. At the same time, the venture firm has hedged itself against missing the opportunity with limited downside proportional to the expenditure of a minimal amount of seed financing.

When venture capital firms value a group of companies, they should consider all the potential upsides available to these companies. These strategic options may well prove valuable. A venture firm can also hedge itself through the use of barrier-type or deferment options. The venture firm should then go through a process of portfolio optimization analysis to decide what proportion of its funds should be disseminated to each of the chosen firms. This portfolio optimization analysis will maximize returns and minimize the risks borne by the venture firm on a portfolio level subject to budget or other constraints.

Compound Expansion Options: The Case of the Internet Start-Up

In contrast, one can look at the start-up entrepreneur. How do you obtain venture funding, and how do you position the firm such that it is more attractive to the potential investor? Your core competency is in developing software or Web-enabled vehicles on the Internet, not financial valuation. How do you then structure the financing agreements such that they will be more attractive yet at the same time not detrimental to your operations, strategic plans, or worse, your personal equity stake? What are your projected revenues and costs? How do you project these values when you haven't even started your business yet? Are you undervaluing your firm and its potential such that an unscrupulous venture firm will capitalize on your lack of sophistication and take a larger piece of the pie for itself? What are your strategic alternatives when you are up and running, and how do you know it's optimal for you to proceed with the next phase of your business plan?

All these questions can be answered and valued through a real options framework. Knowing what strategic options your firm has is significant because this value-added insight not only provides the firm an overall strategic road map but also increases its value. The real option that may exist in this case is something akin to a *compound expansion option*. For example, the firm can expand its product and service offerings by branching out into ancillary technologies or different applications, or expanding into different vertical markets. However, these expansions will most certainly occur in stages, and the progression from one stage to another depends heavily on the success of the previous stages.

All these cases where the high cost of implementation with no apparent payback in the near future seems foolish and incomprehensible in the traditional discounted cash-flow sense are fully justified in the real options sense when taking into account the strategic options the practice creates for the future, the uncertainty of the future operating environment, and management's flexibility in making the right choices at the appropriate time.

WHAT THE EXPERTS ARE SAYING

The trend in the market is quickly approaching the acceptance of real options, as can be seen from the following sample publication excerpts below.
According to an article by Credit Suisse (2009):

Real options will become an increasingly important tool in security analysis. Real options provide the analytical flexibility that standard valuation frameworks lack.

According to an article in *Forbes Business Finance* (2007):

An even more accurate method for evaluating risk in space projects is called real options analysis. It has changed valuation from the old static NPV model to a dynamic model based on specific risks.

IBM Institute for Business Value (2002) says that:

Real options recognize that today's investments give investors the choice of pursuing further investments later, if conditions appear favorable, or abandoning the project if the environment has deteriorated. The capital investment made today provides future flexibility that can and must be valued, but is often missed by traditional DCF or ROI measures. Borrowing from both finance and strategy, real options can provide a way to analyze the value of investing in initiatives made under uncertainty.

According to an article by some MIT professors (2001):

The integration of real options analysis will radically change the design of public and private systems. It will change the processes of system design, the way planners deal with uncertainly and risk. It will also change the outcomes, the kinds of elements designers build into the system as they develop it. Real options analysis explains this coming evolution, and presents cases documenting the changes in attitude and the results already occurring.

According to an article by the Center of Economics of Innovation and Technological Change (2007):

Real options show that risk can be influenced through managerial flexibility, which becomes a central instrument for value creation.

According to an article in *Bloomberg Wealth Manager* (November 2001):

Real options provide a powerful way of thinking and I can't think of any analytical framework that has been of more use to me in the past five years that I've been in this business.

According to a *Wall Street Journal* article (February 2000):

Investors who, after its IPO in 1997, valued only Amazon.com's prospects as a book business would have concluded that the stock was significantly overpriced and missed the subsequent extraordinary price appreciation. Though assessing the value of real options is challenging, without doing it an investor has no basis for deciding whether the current stock price incorporates a reasonable premium for real options or whether the shares are simply overvalued.

CFO Europe (July/August 1999) cites the importance of real options in that:

A lot of companies have been brainwashed into doing their valuations on a one-scenario discounted cash-flow basis and sometimes our recommendations are not what intuition would suggest, and that's where the real surprises come from—and with real options, you can tell exactly where they came from.

According to a *BusinessWeek* article (June 1999):

The real options revolution in decision making is the next big thing to sell to clients and has the potential to be the next major business breakthrough. Doing this analysis has provided a lot of intuition you didn't have in the past and that as it takes hold, it's clear that a new generation of business analysts will be schooled in options thinking. Silicon Valley is fast embracing the concepts of real options analytics, in its tradition of fail fast so that other options may be sought after.

In *Products Financiers* (April 1999):

Real options is a new and advanced technique that handles uncertainty much better than traditional evaluation methods. Because many managers feel that uncertainty is the most serious issue they have to face, there is no doubt that this method will have a bright future as any industry faces uncertainty in its investment strategies.

A *Harvard Business Review* article (September/October 1998) hits home:

Unfortunately, the financial tool most widely relied on to estimate the value of a strategy is the discounted cash flow, which assumes that we will follow a predetermined plan regardless of how events unfold. A better approach to valuation would incorporate both the uncertainty inherent in business and the active decision making required for a strategy to succeed. It would help executives to think strategically on their feet by capturing the value of doing just that—of managing actively rather than passively and real options can deliver that extra insight.

This chapter and the next provide a novel approach to applying real options to answering these issues and more. In particular, a real options framework is presented. It takes into account managerial flexibility in adapting to ever-changing strategic, corporate, economic, and financial environments over time as well as the fact that in the real business world, opportunities and uncertainty exist and are dynamic in nature. This book provides a real options process framework to identify, justify, time, prioritize, value, and manage corporate investment strategies under uncertainty in the context of applying real options.

The recommendations, strategies, and methodologies outlined here are not meant to replace traditional discounted cash-flow analysis but to complement it when the situation and the need arise. The entire analysis could be done, or parts of it could be adapted to a more traditional approach. In essence, the process methodology outlined starts with traditional analyses and continues with value- and insight-adding analytics, including Monte Carlo simulation, forecasting, real options analysis, and portfolio optimization. The real options approach outlined is not the only viable alternative nor will it provide a set of infallible results. However, if utilized correctly with the traditional approaches, it may lead to a set of more robust, accurate, insightful, and plausible results. The insights generated through real options analytics provide significant value in understanding a project's true strategic value.

CRITICISMS, CAVEATS, AND MISUNDERSTANDINGS IN REAL OPTIONS

Before embarking on a real options analysis, analysts should be aware of several caveats. The following five requirements need to be satisfied before a real options analysis can be run:

1. *A financial model must exist.* Real options analysis requires the use of an existing discounted cash-flow model, as real options build on the existing tried-and-true approaches of current financial modeling techniques. If a model does not exist, it means that strategic decisions have already been made and no financial justifications are required, and hence, there is no need for financial modeling or real options analysis.

2. *Uncertainties must exist.* Without uncertainty, the option value is worthless. If everything is known for certain in advance, then a discounted cash-flow model is sufficient. In fact, when volatility (a measure of risk and uncertainty) is zero, everything is certain, the real options value is zero, and the total strategic value of the project or asset reverts to the net present value in a discounted cash-flow model.

3. *Uncertainties must affect decisions when the firm is actively managing the project and these uncertainties must affect the results of the financial model.* These uncertainties will then become risks, and real options can be used to hedge the downside risk and take advantage of the upside uncertainties.

4. *Management must have strategic flexibility or options to make mid-course corrections when actively managing the projects.* Otherwise, do not apply real options analysis when there are no options or management flexibility to value.

5. *Management must be smart enough and credible enough to execute the options when it becomes optimal to do so.* Otherwise, all the options in the world are useless unless they are executed appropriately, at the right time, and under the right conditions.

There are also several criticisms against real options analysis. It is vital that the analyst understands what they are and what the appropriate responses are, prior to applying real options.

- *Real options analysis is merely an academic exercise and is not practical in actual business applications.* Nothing is further from the truth. Although it was true in the past that real options analysis was merely academic, many corporations have begun to embrace and apply real options analysis. Also, its concepts are very pragmatic, and with the use of the Real Options Super Lattice Solver software, even difficult problems can be easily solved, as will become evident later in the next chapter. This book and software have helped bring the theoretical a lot closer to practice. Firms are using it and universities are teaching it. It is only a matter of time before real options analysis becomes part of normal financial analysis.

- *Real options analysis is just another way to bump up and incorrectly increase the value of a project to get it justified.* Again, nothing is further from the truth. If a project has significant strategic options but the analyst does not value them appropriately, he or she is leaving money on the table. In fact, the analyst will be incorrectly undervaluing the project or asset. Also, one of the foregoing requirements states that one should never run real options analysis unless strategic options and flexibility exist. If they do not exist, then the option value is zero, but if they do exist, neglecting their valuation will grossly and significantly underestimate the project or asset's value.

- *Real options analysis ends up choosing the highest risk projects, as the higher the volatility, the higher the option value.* This criticism is also incorrect. The option value is zero if no options exist. However, if a project is highly risky and has high volatility, then real options analysis becomes more important; that is, if a project is strategic but is risky, then you better incorporate, create, integrate, or obtain strategic real options to reduce and hedge the downside risk and take advantage of the upside uncertainties. Therefore, this argument is actually heading in the wrong direction. It is not that real options will overinflate a project's value, but for risky projects, you should create or obtain real options to reduce the risk and increase the upside, thereby increasing the total strategic value of the project. Also, although an option value is always greater than or equal to zero, sometimes the cost to obtain certain options may exceed its benefit, making the entire strategic value of the option negative, although the option value itself is always zero or positive.

So, it is incorrect to say that real options will always increase the value of a project or only risky projects are selected. People who make these criticisms do not truly understand how real options work. However, having said that, real options analysis is just another financial analysis tool, and the old axiom of *garbage in, garbage out* still holds. But if care and due diligence are exercised, the analytical process and results can provide highly valuable insights. In fact, this author believes that 50 percent (rounded, of course) of the challenge and value of real options analysis is simply thinking about it. Understanding that you have options, or obtaining options to hedge the risks and take advantage of the upside, and to think in terms of strategic options, is half the battle. Another 25 percent of the value comes from actually running the analysis and obtaining the results. The final 25 percent of the value comes from being able to explain it to management, to your clients, and to yourself, such that the results become actionable, and not merely another set of numbers.

QUESTIONS

1. Create your own definition of real options analysis; that is, define real options analysis in a paragraph.
2. What are some of the possible approaches used to solve a real options analysis problem?
3. In choosing the right methodology to be used in a real options analysis, what are some of the key requirements that should be considered?
4. What are the necessary conditions that must exist before real options analysis can be applied on a project?
5. What is the major limitation of only using Monte Carlo simulation to perform risk analysis?

CHAPTER 13

The Black Box Made Transparent: Real Options Super Lattice Solver Software

The Real Options Super Lattice Solver (SLS) software comprises several modules, including the Single Super Lattice Solver (SLS), Multiple Super Lattice Solver (MSLS), Multinomial Lattice Solver (MNLS), Lattice Maker, SLS Excel Solution, Advanced Exotic Financial Options Valuator, and SLS Functions. These modules are highly powerful and customizable binomial and multinomial lattice solvers, as well as closed-form models (partial differential equations, variance reduction, path-dependent simulation, and other analytical models) that can be used to solve many types of options (including the three main families of options: *real options*, which deals with physical and intangible assets; *financial options*, which deals with financial assets and the investments of such assets; and *employee stock options*, which deals with financial assets provided to employees within a corporation). Note: See "About the DVD-ROM" for installation instructions and prerequisites for this software.

- The Single Asset Model is used primarily for solving options with a *single underlying asset* using binomial lattices. Even highly complex options with a single underlying asset can be solved using the SLS.
- The Multiple Asset Model is used for solving options with *multiple underlying assets* and sequential compound options with *multiple phases* using binomial lattices. Highly complex options with multiple underlying assets and phases can be solved using the MSLS.
- The Multinomial Model uses *multinomial lattices* (trinomial, quadranomial, pentanomial) to solve specific options that cannot be solved using binomial lattices.
- The Lattice Maker is used to create lattices in Excel with visible and live equations, useful for running Monte Carlo simulations with the Risk

Simulator software (an Excel add-in, risk-based simulation, forecasting, and optimization software also developed by Real Options Valuation, Inc.) or for linking to and from other spreadsheet models. The lattices generated also include decision lattices where the strategic decisions to execute certain options and the optimal timing to execute these options are shown.

- The Advanced Exotic Financial Options Valuator is a comprehensive calculator of more than 250 functions and models, from basic options to exotic options (e.g., from Black-Scholes and multinomial lattices to closed-form differential equations and analytical methods for valuing exotic options, as well as other options-related models such as bond options, volatility computations, delta-gamma hedging). This valuator complements the ROV Risk Modeler and ROV Valuator software tools, with more than 800 functions and models between them, also developed by Real Options Valuation, Inc. (ROV), which are capable of running at extremely fast speeds, handling large data sets, and linking into existing ODBC-compliant databases (e.g., Oracle, SAP, Access, Excel, CSV, and others).

- The SLS Excel Solution implements the SLS and MSLS computations within the Excel environment, allowing users to access the SLS and MSLS functions directly in Excel. This feature facilitates model building, formula and value linking and embedding, and running simulations, and provides the user sample templates to create such models.

- The SLS Functions are additional real options and financial options models accessible directly through Excel. This module facilitates model building, linking and embedding, and running simulations.

- The Option Charts are used to visually analyze the payoff structure of the options under analysis, the sensitivity and scenario tables of options to various inputs, convergence of the lattice results, and other valuable analyses.

The SLS software is created by the author. This software also accompanies the materials presented at different training courses on real options, simulation, and employee stock options valuation taught by Dr. Mun. While the software and its models are based on his books, the training courses cover the real options subject matter in more depth, including the solution of sample business cases and the framing of real options of actual cases. It is highly suggested that the user familiarizes him- or herself with the fundamental concepts of real options in *Real Options Analysis: Tools and Techniques,* Second Edition (John Wiley & Sons, 2005) prior to attempting an in-depth real options analysis using this software. This chapter does not cover some of the fundamental topics already discussed in that book.

Note: The first edition of *Real Options Analysis: Tools and Techniques* published in 2002 shows the *Real Options Analysis Toolkit* software, an older precursor to the *Super Lattice Solver,* also created by Dr. Johnathan Mun. The *Real Options Super Lattice Solver* supersedes the *Real Options Analysis Toolkit* by providing the following enhancements, and is introduced in *Real Options Analysis,* Second Edition (2005):

- Runs 100 times faster and is completely customizable and flexible.
- All inconsistencies, computation errors, and bugs have been fixed and verified.
- Allows for changing input parameters over time (customized options).
- Allows for changing volatilities over time.
- Incorporates Bermudan (vesting and blackout periods) and Customized Options.
- Flexible modeling capabilities in creating or engineering your own customized options.
- Includes general enhancements to accuracy, precision, and analytical prowess.
- Includes more than 250 exotic options models (closed-form, exotic, multinomial lattice).

As the creator of both the Super Lattice Solver and Real Options Analysis Toolkit (ROAT) software, the author suggests that the reader focuses on using the Super Lattice Solver because it provides many powerful enhancements and analytical flexibility over its predecessor, ROAT.

The software will work on most foreign operating systems such as foreign language Windows or Excel, and the SLS software has been tested to work on most international Windows operating systems with just a quick change in settings by clicking on *Start | Control Panel | Regional and Language Options.* Select *English (United States).* This change is required because the numbering convention is different in foreign countries (e.g., one thousand dollars and fifty cents is written as 1,000.50 in the United States versus 1.000,50 in certain European countries).

SINGLE ASSET SUPER LATTICE SOLVER

Figure 13.1 illustrates the SLS software's main screen. After installing the software, the user can access the SLS main screen by clicking on *Start | Programs | Real Options Valuation | Real Options SLS | Real Options SLS.* From this main screen, you can run the Single Asset model, Multiple Asset model, Multinomial model, Lattice Maker, and Advanced Exotic Financial

FIGURE 13.1 Single Super Lattice Solver (SLS).

Options Valuator; open example models; or open an existing model. You can move your mouse over any one of the items to obtain a short description of what that module does. Finally, Real Options SLS supports eight languages, including English, Chinese, French, German, Italian, Japanese, Portuguese, and Spanish, and you can change the language using the droplist on the main screen.

You can also purchase or install a newly obtained permanent license from this main screen by clicking on each of the two license links. Refer to "About the DVD-ROM" at the end of this book to obtain and install the 30-day trial license.

To access the SLS Functions, SLS Excel Solutions, or a sample volatility computation file, go to *Start | Programs | Real Options Valuation | Real Options SLS | Real Options SLS* and select the relevant module.

Single Asset SLS Examples

To help you get started, several simple examples are in order. A simple European call option is computed in this example using SLS. To follow along, in the main screen, click on New Single Asset Model and then click on *File | Examples | Plain Vanilla Call Option I*. This example file will be loaded into the SLS software as seen in Figure 13.2. The starting PV Underlying Asset or starting stock price is $100, and the Implementation Cost or strike price is $100 with a 5-year maturity. The annualized risk-free rate of return is 5 percent, and the historical, comparable, or future expected annualized volatility is 10 percent. Click on *RUN* (or Alt-R) and a 100-step

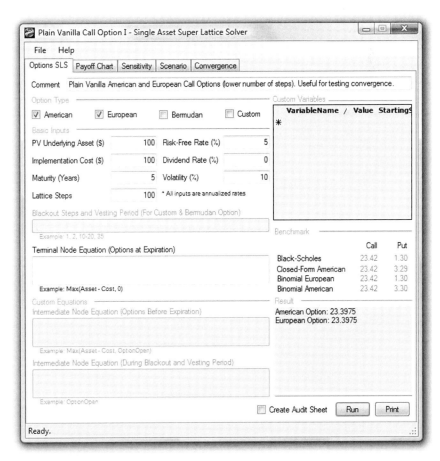

FIGURE 13.2   SLS results of a simple European and American call option.

binomial lattice is computed with the results indicating a value of $23.3975 for both the European and American call options. Benchmark values using Black-Scholes and partial differential Closed-Form American approximation models as well as standard plain-vanilla Binomial American and Binomial European Call and Put Options with 1,000-step binomial lattices are also computed. Notice that only the American and European options are selected and the computed results are for these simple plain-vanilla American and European call options.

The benchmark results use both closed-form models (Black-Scholes and Closed-Form Approximation models) and 1,000-step binomial lattices on plain-vanilla options. You can change the steps to *1000* in the basic inputs section to verify that the answers computed are equivalent to the benchmarks as seen in Figure 13.3. Notice that, of course, the values computed for the American and European options are identical to each other and identical

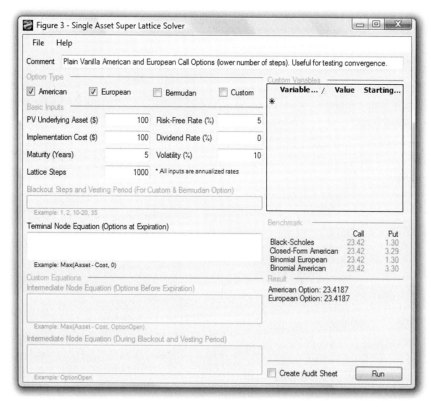

FIGURE 13.3   SLS comparing results with benchmarks.

to the benchmark values of $23.4187, as it is never optimal to exercise a standard plain-vanilla call option early if there are no dividends. Be aware that the higher the lattice step, the longer it takes, of course, to compute the results. It is advisable to start with lower lattice steps to make sure the analysis is robust and then progressively increase lattice steps to check for results convergence.

Alternatively, you can enter Terminal and Intermediate Node Equations for a call option to obtain the same results. Notice that using 100 steps and creating your own Terminal Node Equation of *Max(Asset-Cost,0)* and Intermediate Node Equation of *Max(Asset-Cost,OptionOpen)* will yield the same answer. When entering your own equations, make sure that *Custom* option is first checked.

> When entering your own equations, make sure that Custom option is first checked.

Figure 13.4 illustrates how the analysis is done. Notice that the value $23.3975 in Figure 13.4 agrees with the value in Figure 13.2. The Terminal Node Equation is the computation that occurs at maturity, while the Intermediate Node Equation is the computation that occurs at all periods prior to maturity, and is computed using backward induction. The term "OptionOpen" represents "keeping the option open" and is often used in the Intermediate Node Equation when analytically representing the fact that the option is not executed but kept open for possible future execution. Therefore, in Figure 13.4, the Intermediate Node Equation *Max(Asset-Cost,OptionOpen)* represents the profit maximization decision of either executing the option or leaving it open for possible future execution. In contrast, the Terminal Node Equation of *Max(Asset-Cost,0)* represents the profit maximization decision at maturity of either executing the option if it is in-the-money or allowing it to expire worthless if it is at-the-money or out-of-the-money.

In addition, you can create an Audit Worksheet in Excel to view a sample 10-step binomial lattice by checking the box *Generate Audit Worksheet*. For instance, loading the example file *Plain Vanilla Call Option I* and selecting the box creates a worksheet as seen in Figure 13.5. There are several items that should be noted about this audit worksheet:

- The audit worksheet generated will show the first 10 steps of the lattice, regardless of how many you enter. That is, if you enter 1,000 steps, the

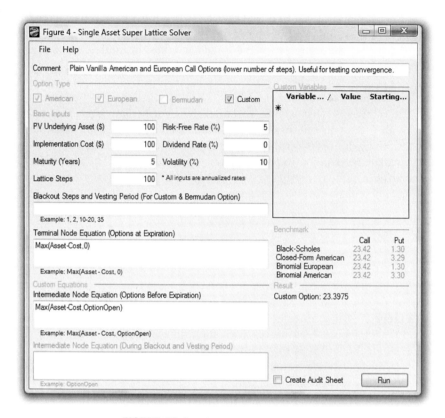

FIGURE 13.4 Custom equation inputs.

first 10 steps will be generated. If a complete lattice is required, simply enter 10 steps in the SLS and the full 10-step lattice will be generated instead. The Intermediate Computations and Results are for the Super Lattice, based on the number of lattice steps entered and not based on the 10-step lattice generated. To obtain the Intermediate Computations for 10-step lattices, simply rerun the analysis inputting *10* as the lattice steps. This way, the Audit Worksheet generated will be for a 10-step lattice, and the results from SLS will now be comparable (Figure 13.6).

- The worksheet only provides values as it is assumed that the user was the one who entered the terminal and intermediate equations, hence there is really no need to re-create these equations in Excel again. The user can always reload the SLS file and view the equations or print out the form if required (by clicking on *File | Print*).

Option Valuation Audit Sheet

Assumptions

PV Asset Value ($)	$100.00
Implementation Cost ($)	$100.00
Maturity (Years)	5.00
Risk-free Rate (%)	5.00%
Dividends (%)	0.00%
Volatility (%)	10.00%
Lattice Steps	100
Option Type	Custom

Terminal Equation	Max(Asset-Cost,0)
Intermediate Equation	Max(Asset-Cost,OptionOpen)
Intermediate Equation (Blackouts)	

Intermediate Computations

Stepping Time (dt)	0.0500
Up Step Size (up)	1.0226
Down Step Size (down)	0.9779
Risk-neutral Probability	0.5504

Results

Auditing Lattice Result (10 steps)	23.19
Super Lattice Results	23.40

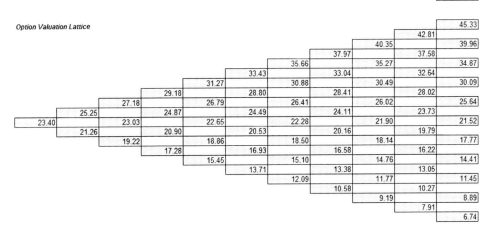

FIGURE 13.5 SLS-generated audit worksheet.

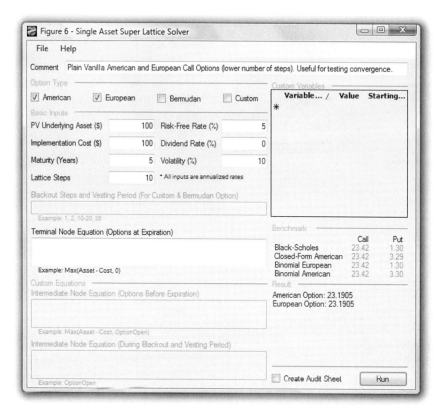

FIGURE 13.6   SLS results with a 10-step lattice.

The software also allows you to save or open analysis files. That is, all the inputs in the software will be saved and can be retrieved for future use. The results will not be saved because you may accidentally delete or change an input and the results will no longer be valid. In addition, rerunning the super lattice computations will only take a few seconds, and it is always advisable for you to rerun the model when opening an old analysis file.

You may also enter Blackout Steps. These are the steps on the super lattice that will have different behaviors than the terminal or intermediate steps. For instance, you can enter *1000* as the lattice steps, *0-400* as the blackout steps, and some Blackout Equation (e.g., *OptionOpen*). This means that for the first 400 steps, the option holder can only keep the option open. Other examples include entering *1, 3, 5, 10* if these are the lattice steps where blackout periods occur. You will have to calculate the relevant steps within the lattice where the blackout exists. For instance, if the blackout exists in years 1 and 3 on a 10-year, 10-step lattice, then steps 1, 3 will be the blackout dates. This blackout step feature comes in handy when analyzing options with holding periods, vesting periods, or periods where the option cannot be executed. Employee stock options have blackout and vesting periods, and certain contractual real options have periods during which the option cannot be executed (e.g., cooling-off periods, or proof of concept periods).

If equations are entered into the Terminal Node Equation box and American, European, or Bermudan Options are chosen, the terminal node equation you entered will be the one used in the super lattice for the terminal nodes. However, for the intermediate nodes, the American option will assume the same terminal node equation plus the ability to keep the option open; the European option will assume that the option can only be kept open and not executed; while the Bermudan option will assume that during the blackout lattice steps, the option will be kept open and cannot be executed. If you also wish to enter the Intermediate Node Equation, the *Custom* option should be first chosen (otherwise you cannot use the Intermediate Node Equation box). The *Custom* option result will use all the equations you have entered in the Terminal, Intermediate, and Intermediate with Blackout sections.

The Custom Variables list is where you can add, modify, or delete custom variables, the variables that are required beyond the basic inputs. For instance, when running an abandonment option, you will require the salvage value. You can add this in the Custom Variables list, provide it a name (a variable's name must be a single word without spaces), the appropriate value, and the starting step when this value becomes effective. For example, if you have multiple salvage values (i.e., if salvage values change over time), you can enter the same variable name (e.g., *salvage*) several times, but each time, its value changes and you can specify when the appropriate salvage value becomes effective. For instance, in a 10-year, 100-step super lattice problem where there are two salvage values—$100 occurring within the first 5 years and increases to $150 at the beginning of Year 6—you can enter two salvage variables with the same name: $100 with a starting step of 0 and $150 with a starting step of 51. Be careful here as Year 6 starts at step 51 and not 61. That is, for a 10-year option with a 100-step lattice, we have Steps 1–10 = Year 1; Steps 11–20 = Year 2; Steps 21–30 = Year 3; Steps 31–40 = Year 4; Steps 41–50 = Year 5; Steps 51–60 = Year 6; Steps 61–70 = Year 7; Steps 71–80 = Year 8; Steps 81–90 = Year 9; and Steps 91–100 = Year 10. Finally, incorporating 0 as a blackout step indicates that the option cannot be executed immediately.

A Custom Variable's name must be a single continuous word.

MULTIPLE ASSET SUPER LATTICE SOLVER

The MSLS is an extension of the SLS in that the MSLS can be used to solve options with multiple underlying assets and multiple phases. The MSLS allows the user to enter multiple underlying assets as well as multiple valuation lattices (Figure 13.7). These valuation lattices can call to user-defined custom variables. Some examples of the types of options that the MSLS can be used to solve include:

- Sequential Compound Options (two-, three-, and multiple-phased sequential options)
- Simultaneous Compound Options (multiple assets with multiple simultaneous options)
- Chooser and Switching Options (choosing among several options and underlying assets)
- Floating Options (choosing between calls and puts)
- Multiple Asset Options (3D binomial option models)

The MSLS software has several areas including a *Maturity* and *Comment* area. The *Maturity* value is a global value for the entire option, regardless of how many underlying or valuation lattices exist. The *Comment* field is for your personal notes describing the model you are building. There is also a *Blackout and Vesting Period Steps* section and a *Custom Variables* list similar to the SLS. The MSLS also allows you to create audit worksheets. Notice, too, that the user interface is resizable (e.g., you can click and drag the right side of the form to make it wider, as shown in Figure 13.8).

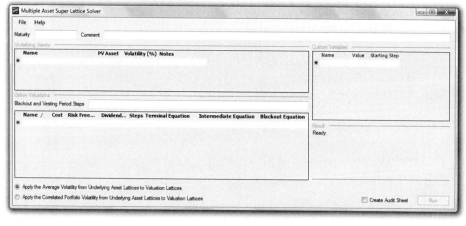

FIGURE 13.7 Multiple Super Lattice Solver.

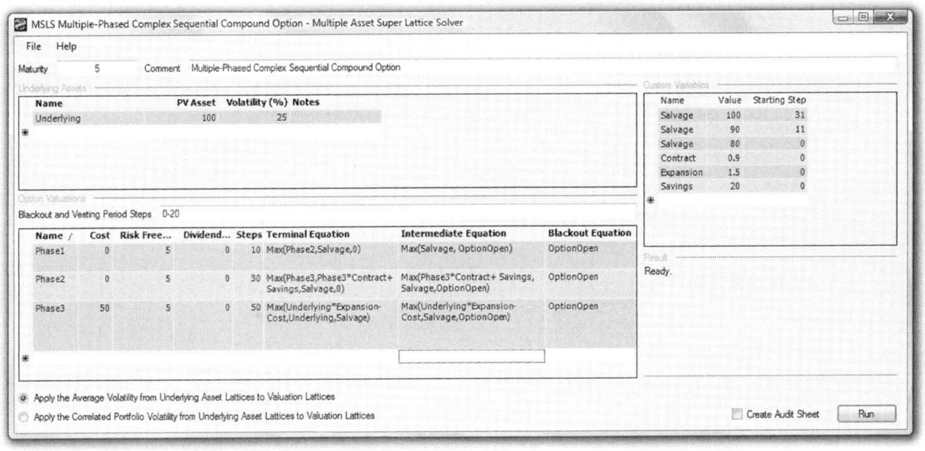

FIGURE 13.8   Resized Multiple Super Lattice Solver.

To illustrate the power of the MSLS, a simple illustration is in order. Click on *Start | Programs | Real Options Valuation | Real Options SLS | Real Options SLS*. In the Main Screen, click on *New Multiple Asset Option Model*, and then select *File | Examples | Simple Two Phased Sequential Compound Option*. Figure 13.9 shows the MSLS example loaded. In this simple example, a single underlying asset is created with two valuation phases.

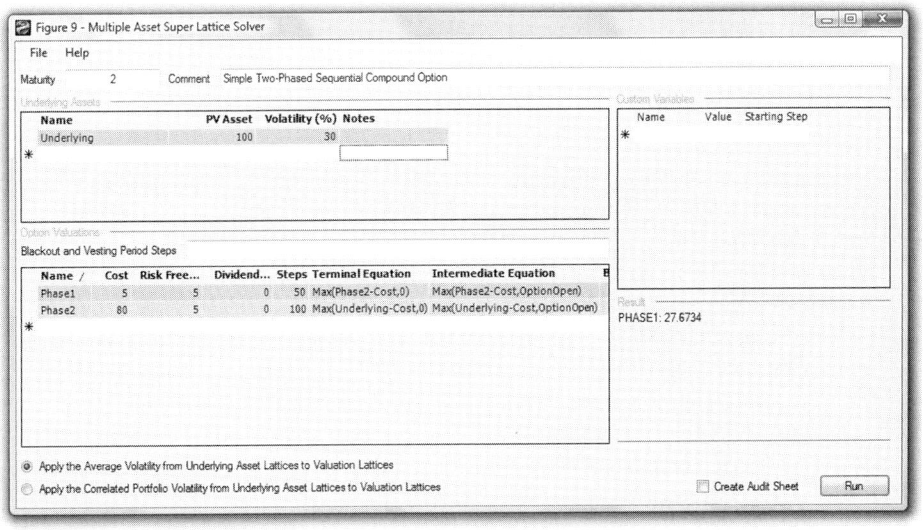

FIGURE 13.9   MSLS solution to a simple two-phased sequential compound option.

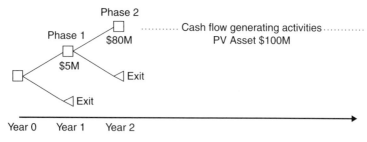

FIGURE 13.10 Strategy tree for two-phased sequential compound option.

The strategy tree for this option is seen in Figure 13.10. The project is executed in two phases—the first phase within the first year costs $5 million, while the second phase occurs within two years but only after the first phase is executed, and costs $80 million, both in present value dollars. The PV Asset of the project is $100 million (NPV is therefore $15 million) and faces 30 percent volatility in its cash flows. The computed strategic value using the MSLS is $27.67 million, indicating that there is a $12.67 million in option value. That is, spreading out and staging the investment into two phases has significant value (an expected value of $12.67 million to be exact). See the sections on compound options for more examples and results interpretation.

MULTINOMIAL SUPER LATTICE SOLVER

The Multinomial Lattice Solver (MNLS) is another module of the Real Options Super Lattice Solver software. The MNLS applies multinomial lattices—where multiple branches stem from each node—such as trinomials (three branches), quadranomials (four branches), and pentanomials (five branches). Figure 13.11 illustrates the MNLS module. The module has a Basic Inputs section, where all of the common inputs for the multinomials are listed. Then, there are four sections with four different multinomial applications complete with the additional required inputs and results for both American and European call and put options. To follow along with this simple example, in the *Main Screen*, click on *New Multinomial Option Model*, select *File | Examples | Trinomial American Call Option*, set dividend to 0 percent, and then hit *Run*.

Figure 13.11 shows a sample call and put option computation using trinomial lattices. Note that the results shown in Figure 13.11 using a 50-step lattice are equivalent to the results shown in Figure 13.2 using a 100-step binomial lattice. In fact, a trinomial lattice or any other multinomial

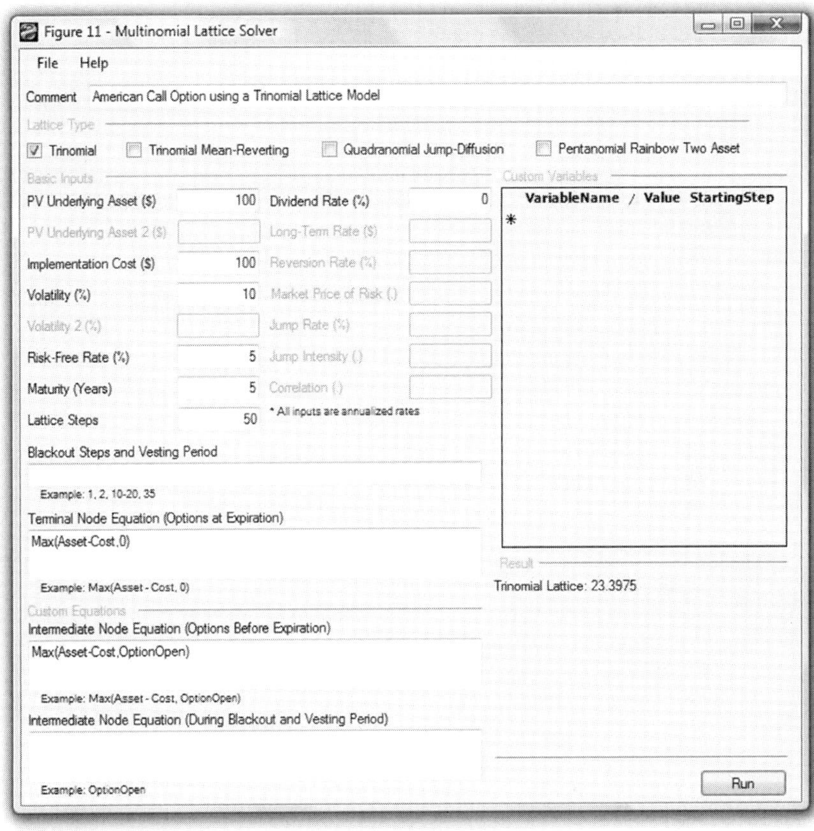

FIGURE 13.11   Multinomial Lattice Solver.

lattice provides identical answers to the binomial lattice at the limit, but convergence is achieved faster at lower steps. Because both yield identical results at the limit but trinomials are much more difficult to calculate and take a longer computation time, in practice, the binomial lattice is usually used instead. Nonetheless, using the SLS software, the computation times are only seconds, making this traditionally difficult to run model computable almost instantly. However, a trinomial is required only under one special circumstance: when the underlying asset follows a mean-reverting process.

With the same logic, quadranomials and pentanomials yield identical results as the binomial lattice with the exception that these multinomial lattices can be used to solve the following different special limiting conditions:

- *Trinomials.* Results are identical to binomials and are most appropriate when used to solve mean-reverting underlying assets.
- *Quadranomials.* Results are identical to binomials and are most appropriate when used to solve options whose underlying assets follow jump-diffusion processes.
- *Pentanomials.* Results are identical to binomials and are most appropriate when used to solve two underlying assets that are combined, called rainbow options (e.g., price and quantity are multiplied to obtain total revenues, but price and quantity each follows a different underlying lattice with its own volatility, but both underlying parameters could be correlated to one another).

SLS LATTICE MAKER

The Lattice Maker module is capable of generating binomial lattices and decision lattices with visible formulas in an Excel spreadsheet (it is compatible with Excel XP, 2003, 2007, and 2010). Figure 13.12 illustrates an example option generated using this module. The illustration shows the module inputs (you can obtain this module by clicking on *Create A Lattice* from the *Main Screen*) and the resulting output lattice. Notice that the visible equations are linked to the existing spreadsheet, which means this module will come in handy when running Monte Carlo simulations or when used to link to and from other spreadsheet models. The results can also be used as a presentation and learning tool to peep inside the analytical black box of binomial lattices. Last but not least, a decision lattice is also available with specific decision nodes indicating expected optimal times of execution of certain options in this module. The results generated from this module are identical to those generated using the SLS and Excel functions, but has the added advantage of a visible lattice (lattices of up to 200 steps can be generated using this module).

SLS EXCEL SOLUTION (SLS, MSLS, AND CHANGING VOLATILITY MODELS IN EXCEL)

The SLS software also allows you to create your own models in Excel using customized functions. This is an important functionality because certain models may require linking from other spreadsheets or

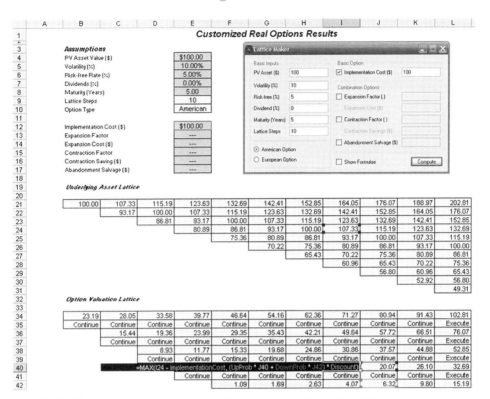

FIGURE 13.12 Lattice Maker module and worksheet results with visible equations.

databases, run certain Excel macros and functions, or certain inputs need to be simulated, or inputs may change over the course of modeling your options. This Excel compatibility allows you the flexibility to innovate within the Excel spreadsheet environment. Specifically, the sample worksheet solves the SLS, MSLS, and Changing Volatility model.

To illustrate, Figure 13.13 shows a Customized Abandonment Option solved using SLS (from the *Single Asset Module*, click on *File | Examples | Abandonment Customized Option*). The same problem can be solved using the *SLS Excel Solution* by clicking on *Start | Programs | Real Options Valuation | Real Options SLS | Excel Solution*. The sample solution is seen in Figure 13.14. Notice that the results are the same using the SLS versus the SLS Excel Solution file. The only difference is that in the Excel Solution, the function (Figure 13.14) has an added input, specifically, the *Option Type*. If the option type value is set to 0, you get an American

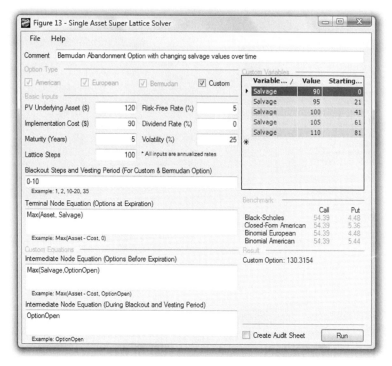

FIGURE 13.13 Customized abandonment option using SLS.

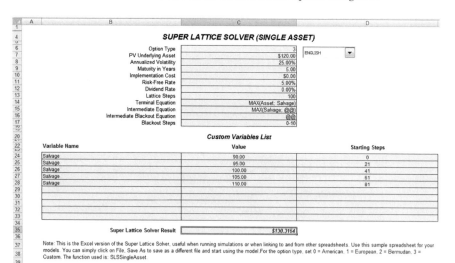

FIGURE 13.14 Customized abandonment option using SLS Excel Solution.

option; 1 for European option; 2 for Bermudan option; and 3 for customized options. You can use the template provided by simply clicking on *File | Save As* in Excel and use the new file for your own modeling needs.

Similarly, the MSLS can also be solved using the SLS Excel Solver. Figure 13.15 shows a complex multiple-phased sequential compound option solved using the SLS Excel Solver. The results shown are identical to the results generated from the MSLS module (example file: *Multiple Phased Complex Sequential Compound Option*). One small note of caution here is that if you add or reduce the number of option valuation lattices, make sure you change the function's link for the *MSLS Result* to incorporate the right number of rows; otherwise the analysis will not compute properly. For example, the default shows three option valuation lattices, and by selecting the *MSLS Results* cell in the spreadsheet and clicking on *Insert | Function*, you will see that the function links to cells A27:I29 for these three rows for the OVLattices input in the function. If you add another option valuation lattice, change the link to A27:I30, and so forth. You can also leave the list of custom variables as is. The results will not be affected if these variables are not used in the custom equations.

Finally, Figure 13.16 shows a Changing Volatility and Changing Risk-free Rate Option. In this model, the volatility and risk-free yields are allowed to change over time and a nonrecombining lattice is required to solve the option. In most cases, it is recommended that you create option models without the changing volatility term structure because getting a single volatility is difficult enough let alone a series of changing volatilities over time. If different volatilities that are uncertain need to be modeled, run a Monte Carlo simulation on volatilities instead. This model should only be used when the volatilities are modeled robustly, are rather certain, and change over time. The same advice applies to a changing risk-free rate term structure.

SLS FUNCTIONS

The software also provides a series of SLS functions that are directly accessible in Excel. To illustrate its use, start the SLS Functions by clicking on *Start | Programs | Real Options Valuation | Real Options SLS | SLS Functions*, and Excel will start. When in Excel, you can click on the function wizard icon or simply select an empty cell and click on *Insert | Function*. While in Excel's equation wizard, select the *ALL* category and scroll down to the functions starting with the SLS prefixes. Here you will see a list of SLS functions that are ready for use in Excel. Figure 13.17 shows the Excel equation wizard.

MULTIPLE SUPER LATTICE SOLVER (MULTIPLE ASSET & MULTIPLE PHASES)

ENGLISH ▼

| Maturity in Years | 5.00 |
| Blackout Steps | 0-20 |

| Result | $134.0802 |

Underlying Asset Lattices

Lattice Name	PV Asset	Volatility %	Riskfree Rate	Dividend Rate
Underlying	100.00	25.00		

Custom Variables

Variable Name	Value	Starting Steps
Salvage	100.00	31
Salvage	90.00	11
Salvage	80.00	0
Contract	0.90	0
Expansion	1.50	0
Savings	20.00	0

Option Valuation Lattices

Lattice Name	Implementation Cost	Riskfree Rate	Dividend Rate	Lattice Steps	Terminal Equation	Intermediate Equation	Intermediate Blackout Equation
Phase3	50.00	5.00	0.00	50	Max(Underlying*Expansion-Cost:Underlying:Salvage)	Max(Underlying*Expansion-Cost:Salvage)	@@
Phase2	0.00	5.00	0.00	30	Max(Phase3:Phase3*Contract+Savings:Salvage:0)	Max(Phase3*Contract+Savings:Salvage:@@)	@@
Phase1	0.00	5.00	0.00	10	Max(Phase2:Salvage:0)	Max(Salvage:@@)	@@

Note: This is the Excel version of the Multiple Super Lattice Solver, useful when running simulations or when linking to and from other spreadsheets. Use this sample spreadsheet for your models. You can simply click on File, Save As to save as a different file and start using the model. The function used is: SLSMultipleAsset. One small note of caution here is that if you add or reduce the number of option valuation lattices make sure you change the function's link for the MSLS Result to incorporate the right number of rows otherwise the analysis will not compute properly. For example, the default shows 3 option valuation lattices and by selecting the MSLS Results cell F5 and clicking on Insert | Function, you will see that the function links to cells A24:H26 for these three rows for the OVLattices input in the function. If you add another option valuation lattice, change the link to A24:H27, and so forth.

FIGURE 13.15 Complex sequential compound option using SLS Excel Solver.

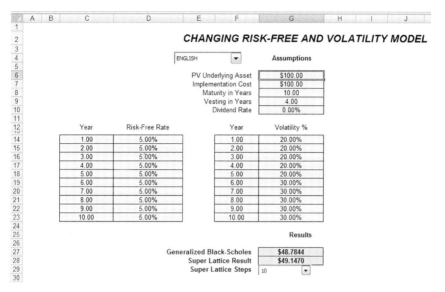

FIGURE 13.16 Changing volatility and risk-free rate option.

Start the Excel Fuctions module and select the *ALL* category when in Excel's function wizard, then scroll down to access the SLS functions.

You may have to check your macro security settings before starting in Excel XP and 2003 (*Tools, Macro, Security,* and make sure *Security* is set to *Medium* or below) as well as in Excel 2007 and 2010 (click on the large *Office* button on the top left corner of Excel, click on *Excel Options, Trust Center, Trust Center Settings, Add-Ins,* uncheck all three options, then click on *Macro Settings,* select *Enable All Macros,* check *Trust Access to the VBA project,* and click *OK*).

Suppose you select the first function, *SLSBinomialAmericanCall* and hit *OK*. Figure 13.17 shows how the function can be linked to an existing Excel model. The values in cells B1 to B7 can be linked from other models or spreadsheets, can be created using VBA macros, or can be dynamic and changing as in when running a simulation.

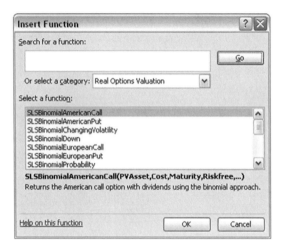

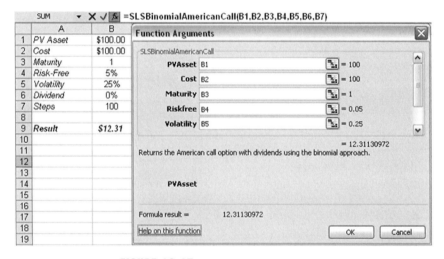

FIGURE 13.17 Excel's equation wizard.

Note: Be aware that certain functions require many input variables, and Excel's equation wizard can only show five variables at a time. Therefore, remember to scroll down the list of variables by clicking on the vertical scroll bar to access the rest of the variables.

This concludes a quick overview and tour of the software. You are now equipped to start using the SLS software in building and solving real options, financial options, and employee stock options problems. However, it is highly recommended that you first review Dr. Johnathan Mun's *Real Options Analysis: Tools and Techniques,* Second Edition (John Wiley & Sons, 2006) for details on the theory and application of real options. And if you are a new user of Real Options SLS or have upgraded from an older version, do spend some time reviewing the Key SLS Notes and Tips starting on the next few pages to familiarize yourself with the modeling intricacies of the software. Also, remember to spend some time watching some of the free getting started videos on the accompanying DVD to help you get a jump-start on using the software.

EXOTIC FINANCIAL OPTIONS VALUATOR

The Exotic Financial Options Valuator is a comprehensive calculator of more than 250 functions and models, from basic options to exotic options (e.g., from Black-Scholes to multinomial lattices to closed-form differential equations and analytical methods for valuing exotic options, as well as other options-related models such as bond options, volatility computations, delta-gamma hedging). Figure 13.18 illustrates the Valuator. You can click on the *Load Sample Values* button to load some samples to get started. Then, select the *Model Category* (left panel) as desired and select the *Model* (right panel) you wish to run. Click *Compute* to obtain the result. Note that this valuator complements the ROV Risk Modeler and ROV Valuator software tools, with more than 800 functions and models, also developed by Real Options Valuation, Inc. (ROV), which are capable of running at extremely fast speeds and handling large data sets and linking into existing ODBC-compliant databases (e.g., Oracle, SAP, Access, Excel, CSV, and others). Finally, if you wish to access these 800 functions (including the ones in this Exotic Financial Options Valuator tool), use the ROV Modeling Toolkit software instead, where, in addition to having access to these functions and more, you can run Monte Carlo simulation on your models using ROV's Risk Simulator software.

PAYOFF CHARTS, TORNADO SENSITIVITY, SCENARIO, AND CONVERGENCE ANALYSIS

The main Single Asset SLS module also comes with payoff charts, sensitivity tables, scenario analysis, and convergence analysis (Figure 13.19). To run

FIGURE 13.18   Exotic Financial Options Valuator.

these analyses, first create a new model or open and run an existing model (e.g., from the first tab, *Options SLS*, click on *File*, *Examples*, and select *Plain Vanilla Call Option I*; then hit *Run* to compute the option value and click on any one of the tabs). To use these tools, you need to first have a model specified in the main *Options SLS* tab. Here are brief explanations of these tabs and how to use their corresponding controls as shown in Figure 13.19:

> *Payoff Chart*. The *Payoff Chart* tab (A) allows you to generate a typical option payoff chart where you have the ability to choose the input variable to chart (B) by entering some minimum and maximum values (C) to chart, as well as its step size (e.g., setting minimum as 20 and maximum as 200 with a step of 10 means to run the analysis for the values 20, 30, 40, ... , 180, 190, 200) and lattice steps (the

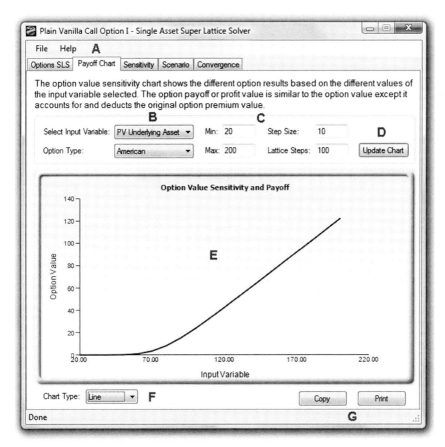

FIGURE 13.19 Payoff charts, sensitivity analysis, scenario tables, and convergence analysis. (*Continues*)

lower the lattice step number, the faster the analysis runs but the less precise the results—see the following discussion of *Lattice Step Convergence Analysis* for more details). Click *Update Chart* (D) to obtain a new payoff chart (E) each time. The default is to show a line chart (F), but you can opt to choose area or bar charts, and the generated chart and table can be copied and pasted into other applications or printed out as is (G). If you do not enter any minimum and maximum values, the software automatically picks some default test values for you, the PV Underlying Asset is chosen by default, and the typical hockey-stick payoff chart will be displayed. Finally, there will be a warning message if any of the original input

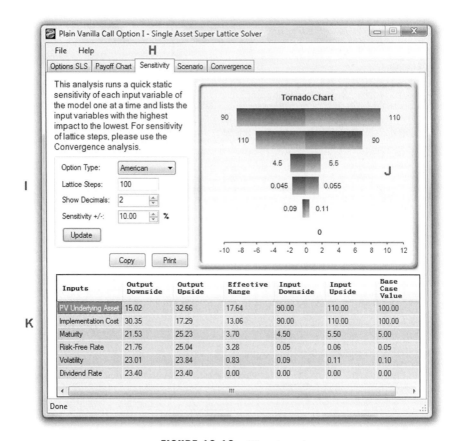

FIGURE 13.19   (*Continues*)

is zero, requiring you to manually insert these minimum, maximum, and step size values in order to generate the payoff chart.

Tornado Sensitivity Analysis. The *Sensitivity* tab (H) runs a quick static sensitivity of each input variable of the model one at a time and lists the input variables with the highest impact to the lowest impact. You can control the option type, lattice steps, and sensitivity percentage to test (I). The results will be returned in the form of a tornado chart (J) and sensitivity analysis table (K). Tornado analysis captures the static impacts of each input variable on the outcome of the option value by automatically perturbing each input some preset ±% amount, captures the fluctuation on the option value's result, and lists the resulting perturbations ranked from the most significant to the least. The results are shown as a sensitivity table with the starting base case value, the perturbed input upside and

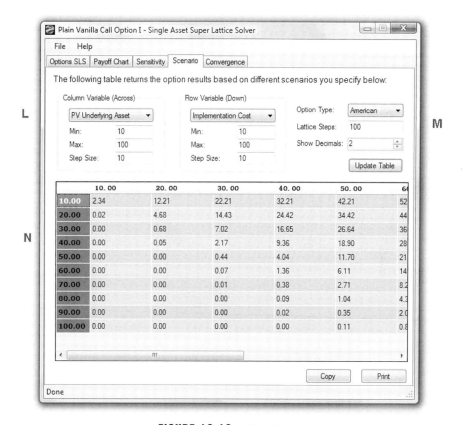

FIGURE 13.19 (*Continues*)

downside, the resulting option value's upside and downside, and the absolute swing or impact. The precedent variables are ranked from the highest impact to the lowest impact. The tornado chart illustrates this data in graphic form. Green bars (lighter shade) in the chart indicate a positive effect, while red bars (darker shade) indicate a negative effect on the option value. For example, Implementation Cost's red bar is on the right side, indicating a negative effect of investment cost—in other words, for a simple call option, implementation cost (option strike price) and option value are negatively correlated. The opposite is true for PV Underlying Asset (stock price) where the green bar is on the right side of the chart, indicating a positive correlation between the input and output.

Scenario Analysis. The *Scenario* tab runs a two-dimensional scenario of two input variables (L) based on the selected option type and lattice

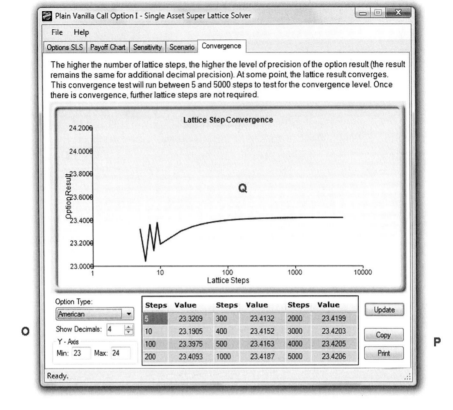

FIGURE 13.19 *(Continued)*

steps (M) and returns a scenario analysis table (N) of the resulting option values based on the various combinations of inputs.

Lattice Step Convergence Analysis. The *Convergence* tab shows the option results from 5 to 5,000 steps—the higher the number of steps, the higher the level of precision (granularity in lattices increases)—where at some point the results of the lattice converge and once convergence is achieved, no additional lattice steps are required. The number of steps is set by default from 5 to 5,000, but you can select the option type and number of decimals to show (O), and the convergence chart is displayed (Q) depending on your selection. You can also copy or print the table with the chart as required (P).

KEY SLS NOTES AND TIPS

Here are some noteworthy changes from the previous version and interesting tips on using Real Options SLS:

- The *User Manual* is accessible within SLS, MSLS, or MNLS. For instance, simply start the Real Options SLS software and create a new model or open an existing SLS, MSLS, or MNLS model. Then click on *Help | User Manual*.
- *Example Files* are accessible directly in the SLS Main Screen; when in the SLS, MSLS, or MNLS models, you can access the example files at *File | Examples*.
- Current *License* information can be obtained in SLS, MSLS, or MNLS at *Help | About*.
- A *Variable List* is available in SLS, MSLS, and MNLS by going to *Help | Variable List*. Specifically, the following are allowed variables and operators in the *custom equations* boxes:

Asset	−value of the underlying asset at the current step (in currency)
Cost	−implementation cost (in currency)
Dividend	−value of dividend (in percent)
Maturity	−years to maturity (in years)
OptionOpen	−value of keeping the option open (formerly @@ in version 1.0)
RiskFree	−annualized risk-free rate (in percent)
Step	−integer representing the current step in the lattice
LatticeSteps	−the total lattice steps in the model
Volatility	−annualized volatility (in percent)
−	−subtract
!	−not
!=, <>	−not equal
&	−and
*	−multiply
/	−divide
^	−power
|	−or
+	−add
<, >, <=, >=	−comparisons
=	−equal

- *OptionOpen at Terminal Nodes* in SLS or MSLS. If *OptionOpen* is specified as the Terminal Node equation, the value will always evaluate to *Not a Number* error (NaN). This is clearly a user error as *OptionOpen* cannot apply at the terminal nodes.

- *Unspecified interval of custom variables.* If a specified interval in which a custom variable has no value, the value is assumed zero. For example, suppose a model exists with 10 steps where a custom variable "*myVar*" of value 5 starts at step 6 exists. This specification means *myVar* will be substituted with the value 5 from step 6 onward. However, the model did not specify the value of *myVar* from steps 0 to 5. In this situation, the value of *myVar* is assumed to be 0 for steps 0 to 5.

- *Compatibility with SLS 1.0.* Super Lattice Solver 6.0 has a user interface similar to the previous version with the exception that SLS, MSLS, MNLS, and Lattice Maker are all integrated into one Main Screen. The data files created in SLS 1.0 can be loaded in SLS 6.0. However, because SLS 6.0 includes advanced features that do not exist in the previous version, the models created in SLS 1.0 may not run in SLS 6.0 without some minor modifications. The following lists the differences between SLS 1.0 and SLS 6.0:

  - The "@@" variable in SLS 1.0 has been replaced by "*OptionOpen*" in SLS 6.0. Therefore, SLS 6.0 still recognizes "@@" as a special variable and will automatically convert it to "*OptionOpen*" before it runs. Consequently, a potential problem exists because a model that defines "OptionOpen" as a custom variable will have errors as *OptionOpen* is now a special variable.

  - A model that uses advanced worksheet functions in the custom equations will not work. Functions supported include ABS, ACOS, ASIN, ATAN2, ATAN, CEILING, COS, COSH, EXP, FLOOR, LOG, MAX, MIN, REMAINDER, ROUND, SIN, SINH, SQRT, TAN, TANH, TRUNCATE, and IF.

  - Variables in SLS 6.0 are case sensitive except for function names. Models that mix and match cases will not work in SLS 6.0. Therefore, it is suggested that when using custom variables in SLS and MSLS, you are consistent with the use of case for the custom variable names.

- *AND() and OR() functions* are missing and are replaced with special characters in SLS 6.0. The "&" and " | " symbols represent the AND and OR operators. For example: "Asset > 0 | Cost < 0" means "OR (Asset > 0, Cost < 0)," while "Asset > 0 & Cost < 0" is "AND (Asset > 0, Cost < 0)."

- *Blackout Step Specifications.* To define the blackout steps, use the following examples as a guide:

3	Step 3 is a blackout step.
3, 5	Steps 3 and 5 are blackout steps.
3, 5–7	Steps 3, 5, 6, 7 are blackout steps.
1, 3, 5–6	Steps 1, 3, 5, 6 are blackout steps.
5–7	Steps 5, 6, 7 are blackout steps.
5–10|2	Steps 5, 7, 9 are blackout steps (the | symbol means skip size).
5–14|3	Steps 5, 8, 11, 14 are blackout steps.
5–6|3	Step 5 is a blackout step.
5–6 | 3	Step 5 is a blackout step (white spaces are ignored).

- *Identifiers.* An identifier is a sequence of characters that begins with a–z, A–Z, _ or \$. After the first character, a–z, A–Z, 0–9, _, \$ are valid characters in the sequence. Note that space is not a valid character. However, it can be used if the variable is enclosed in a pair of curly braces {}. Identifiers are case sensitive, except for function names. The following are some examples of valid identifiers: myVariable, MYVARIABLE, _myVariable, __myVariable, \$myVariable, {This is a single variable}.
- *Numbers.* A number can be an *integer*, defined as one or more characters between 0 and 9. The following are some examples of integers: 0, 1, 00000, 12345. Another type of number is a *real number*. The following are some examples of real numbers: 0., 3., 0.0, 0.1, 3.9, .5, .934, .3E3, 3.5E-5, 0.2E-4, 3.2E+2, 3.5e-5,
- *Operator Precedence.* The operator precedence when evaluating the equations is shown in the following list. However, if there are two terms with two identical precedence operators, the expression is evaluated from left to right.

()	– parenthesized expression has highest precedence
!, –	– not, and unary minus. e.g., −3
^	
*, /	
+, −	
=, <>, !=, <, <=, >, >=	
&, |	

- *Mathematical Expression.* The following shows some examples of valid equations usable in the *custom equations* boxes. Review the rest of the user manual, recommended texts, and example files for more illustrations of actual options equations and functions used in SLS 6.0.

- Max(Asset-Cost,0)
- Max(Asset-Cost,OptionOpen)
- 135
- 12 + 24 ∗ 12 + 24 ∗ 36 / 48
- 3 + ABS(−3)
- 3∗MAX(1,2,3,4) (− MIN(1,2,3,4)
- SQRT(3) + ROUND(3) ∗ LOG(12)
- IF(a > 0, 3, 4): returns 3 if a > 0, else 4
- ABS + 3
- MAX(a + b, c, MIN(d,e), a > b)
- IF(a > 0 | b < 0, 3, 4)
- IF(c <> 0, 3, 4)
- IF(IF(a <= 3, 4, 5) <> 4, a, a − b)
- MAX({My Cost 1} − {My Cost 2}, {Asset 2} + {Asset 3})

EXERCISES

Exercise 1: Basic American, European, and Bermudan Call Options

The following are exercises on solving strategic real options problems using Real Options SLS software (the exercises here require version 6.0 or later). It is assumed that you have already successfully reviewed Chapters 12 and 13, and have the software installed and ready to use. This first exercise illustrates how to use Real Options SLS for solving:

1. American Call Options
2. European Call Options
3. Bermudan Call Options
4. The Value Differential among American, European, and Bermudan Options
5. Custom Equations in Call and Put Options
6. Input Impacts on a Call and Put Option

Figure 13.20 shows the computation of basic American, European, and Bermudan options without dividends (example file used: *File | Examples | Basic American, European, versus Bermudan Call Options*), while Figure 13.21 shows the computation of the same options but with a dividend yield. Of course, European options can only be executed at termination and not

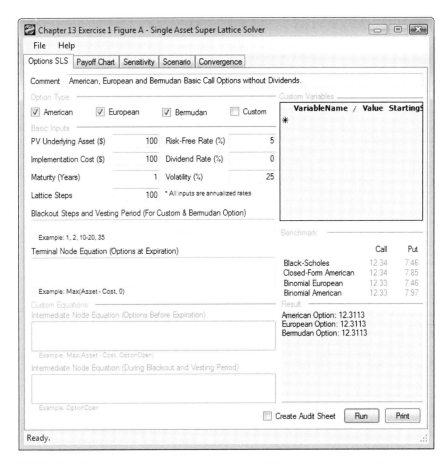

FIGURE 13.20 Simple American, Bermudan, and European options without dividends.

before, while in American options, early exercise is allowed, versus a Bermudan option where early exercise is allowed except during blackout or vesting periods. Notice that the results for the three options without dividends are identical for simple call options, but they differ when dividends exist. When dividends are included, the simple call option values for American $\geq$ Bermudan $\geq$ European in most basic cases, as seen in Figure 13.21 (insert a 5% dividend rate and blackout steps of 0–50). Of course, this generality can be applied only to plain vanilla call options and do not necessarily apply to other exotic options (e.g., Bermudan options with vesting and suboptimal exercise behavior multiples tend to sometimes carry a higher value when

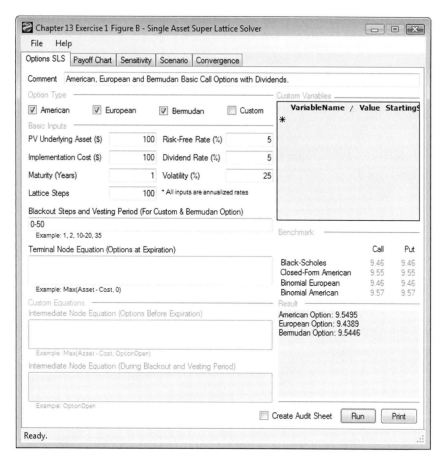

FIGURE 13.21 Simple American, Bermudan, and European Options with dividends and blackout steps.

blackouts and vesting occur than regular American options with the same suboptimal exercise parameters).

Exercises

1. Using Real Options SLS, re-create the first call option without dividends.
   a. Prove that the binomial lattice method, when sufficient steps exist, converge to the closed-form Black-Scholes result in the benchmark section of the software. Use the Convergence analysis to assist you.

b. Look at the Payoff Chart and explain what is on the x-axis and y-axis, and how you would replicate drawing the chart.

c. Use the Sensitivity analysis to determine which input has the highest effect on the option value.

2. Re-create and solve the American, European, and Bermudan call options with a 5% dividend rate using Real Options SLS software as illustrated.

a. Prove that the Bermudan call option value decreases as the blackout steps increase, until the point where the option value equals the European call option. Explain your findings.

b. What happens to the value differential among these three types of options as dividends increase? What does dividend represent in the real options context? (Hint: What are opportunity costs, cost of deferment, and cost outlay?)

c. Select the *Custom Option* checkbox and replicate each of the results above using your own "Max(Asset-Cost)" and "OptionOpen" equations.

d. For each of the inputs below, determine whether an increase in its input value will increase or decrease the value of a plain vanilla call option: asset value (stock), implementation cost (strike), maturity, risk-free rate, dividend, volatility.

3. Create a put option instead of a call option. How would the custom equations differ? For each of the inputs below, determine whether an increase in its input value will increase or decrease the value of a plain vanilla call option: asset value (stock), implementation cost (strike), maturity, risk-free rate, dividend, volatility.

Exercise 2: American, European, Bermudan, and Customized Abandonment Options

This exercise illustrates how to use Real Options SLS for solving:

1. American Abandonment Options
2. European Abandonment Options
3. Bermudan Abandonment Options
4. Customized Abandonment Options
5. The Effects of Vesting and Blackout Periods
6. Optimal Trigger Values
7. The Effects of Opportunity Cost, Leakage, and Cost of Waiting
8. Risk Simulation on Lattice Models using Risk Simulator and Lattice Maker

The *Abandonment Option* looks at the value of a project's or asset's flexibility in being abandoned over the life of the option. As an example, suppose that a firm owns a project or asset and that based on traditional discounted cash flow (DCF) models, it estimates the present value of the asset (*PV Underlying Asset*) to be $120M (for the abandonment option this is the net present value of the project or asset). Monte Carlo simulation indicates that the *Volatility* of this asset value is significant, estimated at 25%. Under these conditions, there is a lot of uncertainty as to the success or failure of this project (the volatility calculated models the different sources of uncertainty and computes the risks in the discounted cash flow [DCF] model including price uncertainty, probability of success, competition, cannibalization, and so forth), and the value of the project might be significantly higher or significantly lower than the expected value of $120M. Suppose an abandonment option is created where a counterparty is found and a contract is signed that lasts 5 years (*Maturity*) such that for some monetary consideration now, the firm has the ability to sell the asset or project to the counterparty at any time within these 5 years (indicative of an American option) for a specified *Salvage* of $90M. The counterparty agrees to this $30M discount and signs the contract.

What has just occurred is that the firm bought itself a $90M insurance policy. That is, if the asset or project value increases above its current value, the firm may decide to continue funding the project, or sell it off in the market at the prevailing fair market value. Alternatively, if the value of the asset or project falls below the $90M threshold, the firm has the right to execute the option and sell off the asset to the counterparty at $90M. In other words, a safety net of sorts has been erected to prevent the value of the asset from falling below this salvage level. Thus, how much is this safety net or insurance policy worth? One can create competitive advantage in negotiation if the counterparty does not have the answer and you do. Further assume that the 5-year Treasury Note *Risk-Free Rate* (zero coupon) is 5% from the U.S. Department of Treasury (www.treas.gov). The *American Abandonment Option* results in Figure 13.22 show a value of $125.48M, indicating that the option value is $5.48M as the present value of the asset is $120M. Hence, the *maximum* value one should be willing to pay for the contract on *average* is $5.48M. This resulting expected value weights the continuous probabilities that the asset value exceeds $90M versus when it does not (where the abandonment option is valuable). Also, it weights when the timing of executing the abandonment is optimal such that the expected value is $5.48M.

In addition, some experimentation can be conducted. Changing the salvage value to $30M (this means a $90M discount from the starting asset value) yields a result of $120M, or $0M for the option. This result means

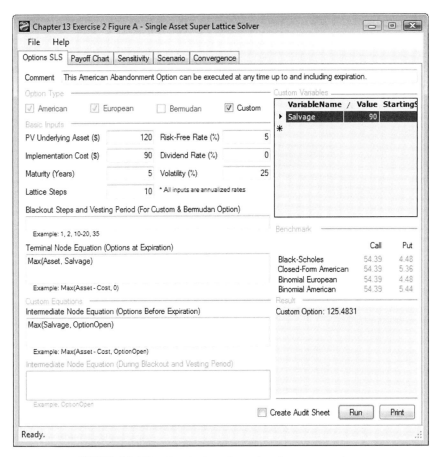

FIGURE 13.22   Simple American abandonment option.

that the option or contract is worthless because the safety net is set so low that it will never be utilized. Conversely, setting the salvage level to thrice the prevailing asset value or $360M would yield a result of $360M, which means that there is no option value, there is no value in waiting and having this option, or simply, execute the option immediately and sell the asset if someone is willing to pay three times the value of the project right now. Thus, you can keep changing the salvage value until the option value disappears, indicating the *optimal trigger value* has been reached. For instance, if you enter $166.80 as the salvage value, the abandonment option analysis yields a result of $166.80, indicating that at this price and above, the optimal decision is to sell the asset immediately. At any lower salvage value, there is option value, and at any higher salvage value, there will be no option value. This breakeven salvage point is the optimal trigger value. Once the market price of this asset exceeds this value, it is optimal to abandon. Finally, adding a *Dividend Rate*, the *cost of waiting before abandoning the asset* (e.g., the annualized taxes and maintenance fees that have to be paid if you keep the asset and not sell it off, measured as a percentage of the present value of the asset) will decrease the option value. Hence, the breakeven trigger point, where the option becomes worthless, can be calculated by successively choosing higher dividend levels. This breakeven point again illustrates the trigger value at which the option should be optimally executed immediately, but this time with respect to a dividend yield. That is, if the *cost of carry* or holding on to the option, or the option's *leakage value* is high, that is, if the *cost of waiting* is too high, do not wait and execute the option immediately.

Figure 13.23 shows the same abandonment option but with a 100-step lattice. To follow along, open the Single Asset SLS example file: *File | Examples | Abandonment American Option*. Notice that the 10-step lattice yields $125.48 while the 100-step lattice yields $125.45, indicating that the lattice results have achieved convergence. The Terminal Node Equation is *Max(Asset,Salvage)* which means the decision at maturity is to decide if the option should be executed, selling the asset and receiving the salvage value, or not to execute, holding on to the asset. The Intermediate Node Equation used is *Max(Salvage,OptionOpen)* indicating that before maturity, the decision is either to execute early in this American option to abandon and receive the salvage value, or to hold on to the asset, and hence hold on to and keeping the option open for potential future execution, denoted simply as *OptionOpen*. To run the European version of the abandonment option, the Intermediate Node Equation is set to *OptionOpen*, as early execution is prohibited before maturity. Of course, being only able to execute the option at maturity is worth less ($124.5054 compared to $125.4582) than being able to exercise earlier. The example files used are: *File | Examples | Abandonment American Option* and *File | Examples | Abandonment European Option*. For example, the airline manufacturer in the previous case example can agree to a buy-back provision that can be exercised at any time by the airline customer versus only at a specific date at the end of five years—the former American option will clearly be worth more than the latter European option.

Sometimes, a Bermudan option is appropriate, where there might be a vesting period or blackout period when the option cannot be executed. For instance, the contract stipulates that for the 5-year abandonment buy-back contract, the airline customer cannot execute the abandonment option within the first 2.5 years. This is run using a Bermudan option with

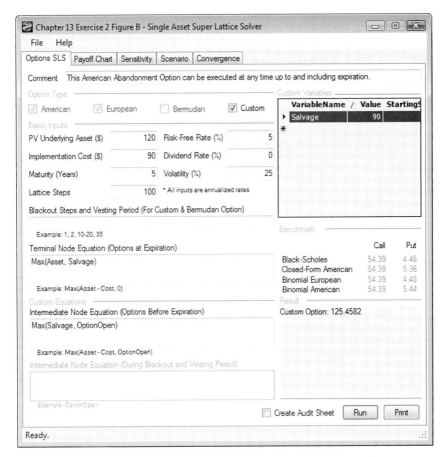

FIGURE 13.23 American abandonment option with 100-step lattice.

a 100-step lattice on 5 years, where the blackout steps are 0–50. This means that during the first 50 steps (as well as right now or step 0), the option cannot be executed. This is modeled by inserting *OptionOpen* into the Intermediate Node Equation During Blackout and Vesting Periods. This forces the option holder to only keep the option open during the vesting period, preventing execution during this blackout period. You can see that the American option is worth more than the Bermudan option, which is worth more than the European option, by virtue of each option type's ability to execute early and the frequency of execution possibilities.

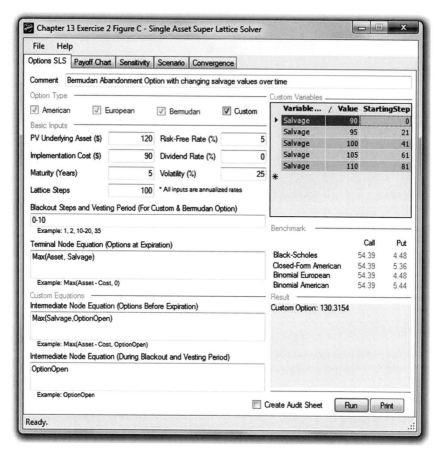

FIGURE 13.24 Customized abandonment option.

Sometimes, the salvage value of the abandonment option may change over time. To illustrate, in the previous example of an acquisition of a start-up firm, the intellectual property will most probably increase over time because of continued research and development activities, thereby changing the salvage values over time. An example is seen in Figure 13.24, where there are five salvage values over the 5-year abandonment option. This can be modeled by using the Custom Variables. Type in the *Variable Name*, *Value*, and *Starting Step* and hit *ENTER* to input the variables one at a time as seen in Figure 13.24's Custom Variables list. Notice that the same variable name (*Salvage*) is used but the values change over time, and the starting steps represent when these different values become effective. For instance, the salvage value $90 applies at step 0 until the next salvage value of $95 takes over at step 21. This means that for a 5-year option with a 100-step lattice, the first year including the current period (steps 0 to 20) will have a salvage value of $90, which then increases to $95 in the second year (steps 21 to 40), and so forth. Notice that as the value of the firm's intellectual property increases over time, the option valuation results also increase, which makes logical sense. You can also model in blackout vesting periods for the first 6 months (steps 0–10 in the blackout area). The blackout period is typical of contractual obligations of abandonment options where during specified periods, the option cannot be executed (a cooling-off period). Note that you may use *TAB* on the keyboard to move from the variable name column to the value column, and on to the starting step column. However, remember to hit *ENTER* on the keyboard to insert the variable and to create a new row so that you may enter a new variable.

Exercises

1. Replicate the abandonment options as illustrated above, solving for the American, European, Bermudan, and Custom types using Real Options SLS.
   a. Generate Audit Sheets in the analysis.
   b. Generate the live lattice using the Lattice Maker module and apply a Monte Carlo simulation on the real options lattice model using Risk Simulator.
2. Other applications of the abandonment option include buy-back lease provisions in a contract (guaranteeing a specified asset value); asset preservation flexibility; insurance policies; walking away from a project and selling off its intellectual property; purchase price of an acquisition. Solve the following abandonment options:
   a. An aircraft manufacturer sells its planes of a particular model in the primary market for, say, $30M each to various airline companies. Airlines are usually risk-averse and may find it hard to justify buying an additional plane with all the uncertainties in the economy, demand, price competition, and fuel costs. When uncertainties become resolved over time, airline carriers may have to reallocate and reroute their existing portfolio of planes globally, and an excess plane on the tarmac is costly. The airline can sell the excess plane in the secondary market where smaller regional carriers buy used planes, but the price uncertainty is very high and is subject to significant volatility, of say, 45%, and may fluctuate wildly between $10M and $25M for this class of aircraft. The aircraft manufacturer can reduce the airline's risk by providing a buy-back provision or abandonment option,

where at anytime within the next five years, the manufacturer agrees to buy back the plane at a guaranteed residual salvage price of $20M, at the request of the airline. The corresponding risk-free rate for the next five years is 5%. This reduces the downside risk of the airline, and hence reduces its risk, chopping off the left tail of the price fluctuation distribution, and shifting the expected value to the right. This abandonment option provides risk reduction and value enhancement to the airline. (Hint: Applying the abandonment option in SLS using a 100-step binomial lattice, this option is worth $3.52M. If the airline is the smarter counterparty and calculates this value and gets this buy-back provision for free as part of the deal, the aircraft manufacturer has just lost over 10% of its aircraft value that it left on the negotiation table. Information and knowledge is highly valuable in this case.)

b. A high-tech disk-drive manufacturer is thinking of acquiring a small start-up firm with a new micro drive technology (a super-fast and high-capacity pocket hard drive) that may revolutionize the industry. The start-up is for sale and its asking price is $50M based on an NPV fair market value analysis some third-party valuation consultants have performed. The manufacturer can either develop the technology themselves or acquire this technology through the purchase of the firm. The question is, how much is this firm worth to the manufacturer, and is $50M a good price? Based on internal analysis by the manufacturer, the NPV of this micro drive is expected to be $45M, with a cash flow volatility of 40%, and it would take another 3 years before the micro drive technology is successful and goes to market. Assume that the three-year risk-free rate is 5%. In addition, it would cost the manufacturer $45M in present value to develop this drive internally. If using an NPV analysis, the manufacturer should build the drive itself. However, if you include an abandonment option analysis where if this specific micro drive does not work, the start-up still has an abundance of intellectual property (patents and proprietary technologies) as well as physical assets (buildings and manufacturing facilities) that can be sold in the market at up to $40M. (Hint: The abandonment option together with the NPV yields $51.83, making buying the start-up worth more than developing the technology internally, and making the purchase price of $50M worth it.) See the section on Expansion Option for more examples on how this start-up's technology can be used as a platform to further develop newer technologies that can be worth much more than just the abandonment option.

Exercise 3: American, European, Bermudan, and Customized Contraction Options

This exercise illustrates how to use Real Options SLS for solving:

1. American Contraction Options
2. European Contraction Options
3. Bermudan Contraction Options
4. Customized Contraction Options

A *Contraction Option* evaluates the flexibility value of being able to reduce production output or to contract the scale and scope of a project when conditions are not as amenable, thereby reducing the value of the asset or project by a *Contraction Factor*, but at the same time creating some cost *Savings*. As an example, suppose you work for a large aeronautical manufacturing firm that is unsure of the technological efficacy and market demand for its new fleet of long-range supersonic jets. The firm decides to hedge itself through the use of strategic options, specifically an option to contract 10% of its manufacturing facilities at any time within the next 5 years (i.e., the *Contraction Factor* is 0.9).

Suppose that the firm has a current operating structure whose static valuation of future profitability using a discounted cash flow model (in other words, the present value of the expected future cash flows discounted at an appropriate market risk-adjusted discount rate) is found to be $1,000M (*PV Asset*). Using Monte Carlo simulation, you calculate the implied volatility of the logarithmic returns of the asset value of the projected future cash flows to be 30%. The risk-free rate on a riskless asset (5-year U.S. Treasury Note with zero coupons) is found to be yielding 5%.

Further, suppose the firm has the option to contract 10% of its current operations at any time over the next 5 years, thereby creating an additional $50 million in savings after this contraction. These terms are arranged through a legal contractual agreement with one of its vendors, who had agreed to take up the excess capacity and space of the firm. At the same time, the firm can scale back and lay off part of its existing workforce to obtain this level of savings (in present values).

The results indicate that the strategic value of the project is $1,001.71M (using a 10-step lattice as seen in Figure 13.25), which means that the NPV currently is $1,000M and the additional $1.71M comes from this contraction option. This result is obtained because contracting now yields 90% of $1,000M + $50M, or $950M, which is less than staying in business and not contracting and obtaining $1,000M. Therefore, the optimal decision is to not contract immediately but keep the ability to do so open for the future.

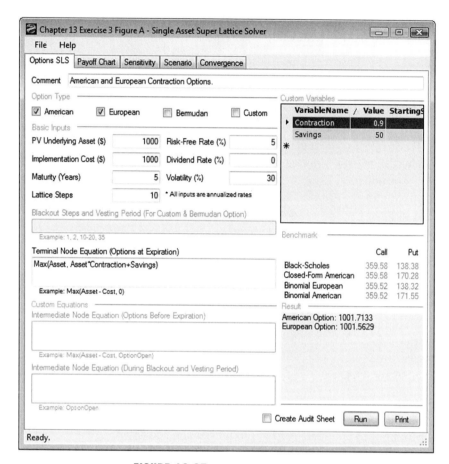

FIGURE 13.25 Contraction option.

Hence, in comparing this optimal decision of $1,000M to $1,001.71M of being able to contract, the option to contract is worth $1.71M. This should be the maximum amount the firm is willing to spend to obtain this option (contractual fees and payments to the vendor counterparty).

In contrast, if *Savings* were $200M instead, then the strategic project value becomes $1,100M, which means that starting at $1,000M and contracting 10% to $900M and keeping the $200M in savings, yields $1,100M in total value. Hence, the additional option value is $0M, which means that it is optimal to execute the contraction option immediately as there is no option value and no value to wait to contract. So, the value of executing now is $1,100M as compared to the strategic project value of $1,100M;

there is no additional option value, and the contraction should be executed immediately. That is, instead of asking the vendor to wait, the firm is better off executing the contraction option now and capturing the savings.

Other applications include shelving an R&D project by spending a little to keep it going but reserving the right to come back to it should conditions improve; the value of synergy in a merger and acquisition where some management personnel are let go to create the additional savings; reducing the scope and size of a production facility; reducing production rates; a joint venture or alliance, and so forth.

Figure 13.26 illustrates a customized option where there is a blackout period and the savings from contracting change over time (example file used

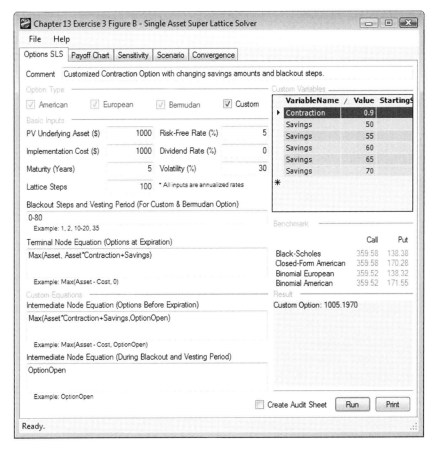

FIGURE 13.26 Customized option to contract with changing savings.

is *File | Examples | Contraction Customized Option*). These results are for the aeronautical manufacturing example.

Exercises

1. Replicate the two illustrations above for the basic contraction option and customized contraction option with changing savings, and answer the following questions:
    a. How would you run a simulation on a contraction option by simulating some of the inputs?
    b. How does simulating the input Savings compare analytically to the approach illustrated above with a changing Savings value at different lattice steps? Explain how each approach is doing something different.
2. Solve the following two cases:
    a. A large oil and gas company is embarking on a deep-sea drilling platform that will cost the company billions to implement. A DCF analysis is run and the NPV is found to be $500M over the next 10 years of economic life of the offshore rig. The 10-year risk-free rate is 5%, and the volatility of the project is found to be at an annualized 45% using historical oil prices as a proxy. If the expedition is highly successful (oil prices are high and production rates are soaring), then the company will continue its operations. However, if things are not looking too good (oil prices are low or moderate and production is only decent), it is difficult for the company to abandon operations (why lose everything when net income is still positive although not as high as anticipated and not to mention the environmental and legal ramifications of simply abandoning an oil rig in the middle of the ocean). Hence, the oil company decides to hedge its downside risk through an American Contraction Option. The oil company was able to find a smaller oil and gas company (a former partner on other explorations) to be interested in a joint venture. The joint venture is structured such that the oil company pays this smaller counterparty a lump sum right now for a 10-year contract whereby at any time and at the oil company's request, the smaller counterparty will have to take over all operations of the offshore oil rig (i.e., taking over all operations and hence all relevant expenses) and keep 30% of the net revenues generated. The counterparty is in agreement because it does not have to partake in the billions of dollars required to implement the rig in the first place, and it actually obtains some cash up front for this contract to assume the downside risk. The oil company is also in agreement because it reduces its own risks if oil prices are low and production is not up to par, and it ends

up saving over $75M in present value of total overhead expenses, which can then be reallocated and invested somewhere else. (Hint: In this example, the contraction option using a 100-step lattice is valued to be $14.24M using SLS. This means that the maximum amount that the counterparty should be paid should not exceed this amount. Of course, the option analysis can be further complicated by analyzing the actual savings on a present value basis. For instance, if the option is exercised within the first 5 years, the savings is $75M but if exercised during the last 5 years, then the savings is only $50M. The revised option value is now $10.57M).

b. A manufacturing firm is interested in outsourcing its manufacturing of children's toys to a small province in China. By doing so, it will produce overhead savings of more than $20M in present value over the economic life of the toys. However, outsourcing this internationally will mean lower quality control, delayed shipping problems, added importing costs, and assuming the added risks of unfamiliarity with the local business practices. In addition, the firm will consider outsourcing only if the quality of the workmanship in this Chinese firm is up to the stringent quality standards it requires. The NPV of this particular line of toys is $100M with 25% volatility. The firm's executives decide to purchase a contraction option by locating a small manufacturing firm in China, spending some resources to try out a small-scale proof of concept (thereby reducing the uncertainties of quality, knowledge, import-export issues, and so forth). If successful, the firm will agree to give this small Chinese manufacturer 20% of its net income as remuneration for their services, plus some start-up fees. The question is, how much is this option to contract worth; that is, how much should the firm be willing to pay, on average, to cover the initial start-up fees plus the costs of this proof of concept stage? (Hint: A contraction option valuation result using SLS shows that the option is worth $1.59M, assuming a 5% risk-free rate for the 1-year test period. So, as long as the total costs for a pilot test costs less than $1.59, it is optimal to obtain this option, especially if it means potentially being able to save more than $20M).

Exercise 4: American, European, Bermudan, and Customized Expansion Options

This exercise illustrates how to use Real Options SLS for solving:

1. American Expansion Options
2. European Expansion Options

3. Bermudan Expansion Options
4. Customized Expansion Options
5. Optimal Trigger Values
6. Opportunity Cost of Waiting

The *Expansion Option* values the flexibility to expand from a current existing state to a larger or expanded state. Therefore, an existing state or condition must first be present in order to use the expansion option. That is, there must be a base case to expand upon. If there is no base case state, then the simple *Execution Option* (calculated using the simple *Call Option*) is more appropriate, where the issue at hand is whether or not to execute a project immediately or to defer execution.

As an example, suppose a growth firm has a static valuation of future profitability using a discounted cash flow model (in other words, the present value of the expected future cash flows discounted at an appropriate market risk-adjusted discount rate) that is found to be $400 million (*PV Asset*). Using Monte Carlo simulation, you calculate the implied *Volatility* of the logarithmic returns on the assets based on the projected future cash flows to be 35%. The *Risk-Free Rate* on a riskless asset (5-year U.S. Treasury Note with zero coupons) for the next 5 years is found to be 7%.

Further, suppose that the firm has the option to expand and double its operations by acquiring its competitor for a sum of $250 million (*Implementation Cost*) at any time over the next 5 years (*Maturity*). What is the total value of this firm, assuming that you account for this expansion option? The results in Figure 13.27 indicate that the strategic project value is $638.73M (using a 100-step lattice), which means that the expansion option value is $88.73M. This result is obtained because the net present value of executing immediately is $400M × 2 − $250M, or $550M. Thus, $638.73M less $550M is $88.73M, the value of the ability to *defer* and to wait and see before executing the expansion option. The example file used is *File | Examples | Expansion American and European Option*.

Exercises

1. Replicate the basic expansion option illustration above. Make sure you are able to obtain the same results.
2. We will now learn about Optimal Trigger Values. Using the same model in the first question, increase the dividend rate to, say, 2% and notice that both the American and European Expansion Options are now worth less, and that the American Expansion Option is worth more than the European Expansion Option by virtue of the American Option's ability for early execution. The dividend rate implies that the cost of waiting

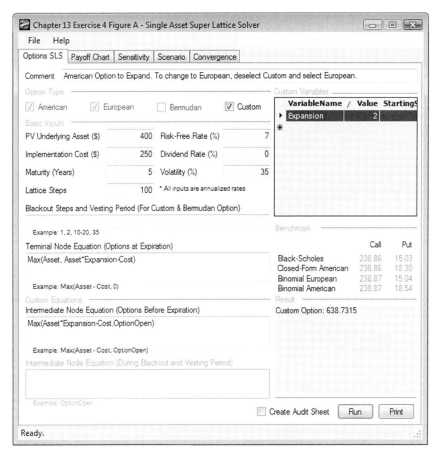

FIGURE 13.27 American and European options to expand with a 100-step lattice.

to expand, to defer and not execute, the *opportunity cost of waiting on executing the option*, and the cost of holding the option is high, then the ability to defer reduces. In addition, increase the Dividend Rate to 4.9% and see that the binomial lattice's Custom Option result reverts to $550 (the static, expand-now scenario), indicating that the option is worthless. This result means if the cost-of-waiting as a proportion of the asset value (as measured by the dividend rate) is too high, then execute now and stop wasting time deferring the expansion decision! Of course, this decision can be reversed if the volatility is significant enough to compensate for the cost of waiting. That is, it might be worth something to wait and see if the uncertainty is too high even if the cost to wait is high.

3. Using Real Options SLS, show how you can create a customized expansion option with changing expansion factors over time and changing execution cost over time, all the while with some vesting or blackout periods where the option cannot be executed.

4. Other applications of this option simply abound! To illustrate, here are some additional quick exercises of the expansion option (as before, providing some additional sample exercises):

   a. Suppose a pharmaceutical firm is thinking of developing a new type of insulin that can be inhaled and the drug will directly be absorbed into the blood stream. A novel and honorable idea. Imagine what this means to diabetics who no longer need painful and frequent injections. The problem is, this new type of insulin requires a brand new development effort but if the uncertainties of the market, competition, drug development, and FDA approval are high, perhaps a base insulin drug that can be ingested is first developed. The ingestible version is a required precursor to the inhaled version. The pharmaceutical firm can decide to either take the risk and fast track development into the inhaled version or buy an option to defer, to first wait and see if the ingestible version works. If this precursor works, then the firm has the option to expand into the inhaled version. How much should the firm be willing to spend on performing additional tests on the precursor and under what circumstances should the inhaled version be implemented directly? Suppose the intermediate precursor development work yields an NPV of $100M, but at any time within the next 2 years, an additional $50M can be further invested into the precursor to develop it into the inhaled version, which will triple the NPV. However, after modeling the risk of technical success and uncertainties in the market (competitive threats, sales, and pricing structure), the annualized volatility of the cash flows using the logarithmic present value returns approach comes to 45%. Suppose the risk-free rate is 5% for the 2-year period. (Hint: Using the SLS, the analysis results yields $254.95M, indicating that the option value to wait and defer is worth more than $4.95M after accounting for the $250M NPV if executing now. In playing with several scenarios, the breakeven point is found when dividend yield is 1.34%. This means that if the cost of waiting [lost net revenues in sales by pursuing the smaller market rather than the larger market, and loss of market share by delaying] exceeds $1.34M per year, then it is not optimal to wait and the pharmaceutical firm should engage in the inhaled version immediately. The loss in returns generated each year does not sufficiently cover the risks incurred.)

b. An oil and gas company is currently deciding on a deep-sea exploration and drilling project. The platform provides an expected NPV of $1,000M. This project is fraught with risks (price of oil and production rate are both uncertain) and the annualized volatility is computed to be 55%. The firm is thinking of purchasing an expansion option by spending an additional $10M to build a slightly larger platform that it does not currently need, but if the price of oil is high, or when production rate is low, the firm can execute this expansion option and execute additional drilling to obtain more oil to sell at the higher price, which will cost another $50M, thereby increasing the NPV by 20%. The economic life of this platform is 10 years and the risk-free rate for the corresponding term is 5%. Is obtaining this slightly larger platform worth it? (Hint: Using the SLS, the option value is worth $27.12M when applying a 100-step lattice. Therefore, the option cost of $10M is worth it. However, this expansion option will not be worth it if annual dividends exceed 0.75% or $7.5M a year—this is the annual net revenues lost by waiting and not drilling as a percentage of the base case NPV.)

Exercise 5: Contraction, Expansion, and Abandonment Options

This exercise illustrates how to use Real Options SLS for solving:

1. American, Bermudan, European, Customized Contraction, Expansion, and Abandonment Options
2. Competing and Mutually Exclusive Options
3. Dominant and Dominated Options

The *Contraction, Expansion, and Abandonment Option* applies when a firm has three *competing and mutually exclusive* options on a single project to choose from at different times up to the time of expiration. Be aware that this is a mutually exclusive set of options. That is, you cannot execute any combinations of expansion, contraction, or abandonment at the same time. Only one option can be executed at any time. That is, for mutually exclusive options, use a single model to compute the option value as seen in Figure 13.28 (example file used: *File | Examples | Expand Contract Abandon American and European Option*). However, if the options are non-mutually exclusive, calculate them individually in different models and add up the values for the total value of the strategy (that is, solve the option to contract,

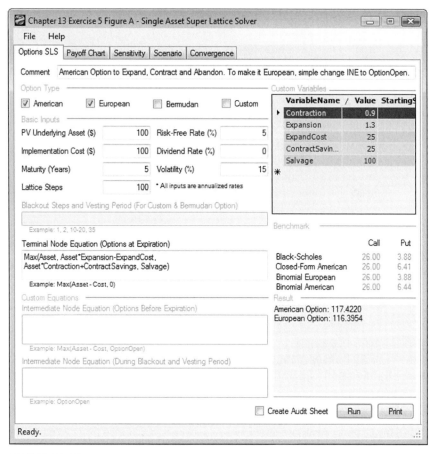

FIGURE 13.28   American, European, and custom options to expand, contract, and abandon.

then solve the option to expand, and then the option to abandon, each in its own model, and sum all of their option values).

Figure 13.29 (example file used: *File | Examples | Expand Contract Abandon Customized Option II*) illustrates a more complex custom option where during some earlier period of vesting, the option to expand does not exist yet (perhaps the technology being developed is not yet mature enough in the early stages to be expanded into some spin-off technology). In addition, during the post-vesting period but prior to maturity, the option to contract or abandon does not exist (perhaps the technology is now being reviewed for spin-off opportunities), and so forth. Finally, the input parameters (salvage

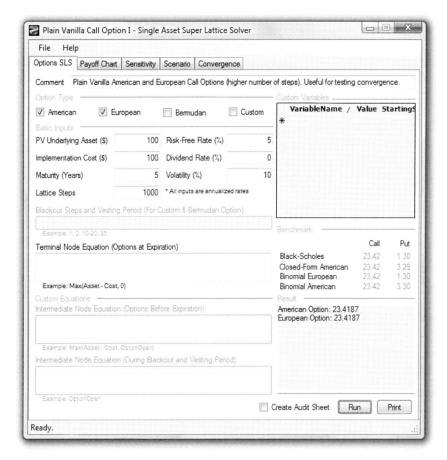

FIGURE 13.29 Custom options with mixed expand, contract, and abandon capabilities with changing input parameters.

value) are allowed to change over time perhaps accounting for the increase in project, asset, or firm value if abandoned at different times.

Exercises

1. Replicate the first example illustrated above using Real Options SLS.
2. Using the results from the first model, compare them with the results of summing three models run independently. Which option value is larger and why? Hint: Explain the analysis and results in terms of mutually

exclusive options and non–mutually exclusive options. Which one is worth more and why?

3. What happens when you have a dominant versus a dominated option? Run the following and explain your results:
   a. Using the first model and the original inputs, change the Contraction Savings from 25 to 100 and explain your results.
   b. Using the first model and the original inputs, change the Salvage value from 100 to 300 and explain your results.
   c. Using the first model and the original inputs, change the Expansion Cost from 25 to 1 and explain your results.
   d. Replicate the three exercises (a–c) above using the Lattice Solver and explain what you see in terms of the decision lattice. What do you observe as dominant and dominated options?

Exercise 6: Complex Sequential Compound Options

This exercise illustrates how to use Real Options SLS for solving:

1. Basic Two-Phased Sequential Compound Options
2. Multiple-Phased Sequential Compound Options (Stage-Gate Development)
3. Customized Complex Mixed Sequential Compound Options (Mixed-Gate Strategies)
4. The Expected Value of Information

Basic Two-Phased Sequential Compound Options *Sequential Compound Options* are applicable for research and development investments or any other investments that have multiple stages. The Real Options SLS (multiple assets/phases module) is required for solving Sequential Compound Options. The easiest way to understand this option is to start with a two-phased example as seen in Figure 13.30. In the two-phased example, management has the ability to decide if Phase II (PII) should be implemented after obtaining the results from Phase I (PI). For example, a pilot project or market research in PI indicates that the market is not yet ready for the product, hence PII is not implemented. All that is lost is the PI sunk cost, not the entire investment cost of both PI and PII. An example below illustrates how the option is analyzed.

The illustration in Figure 13.30 is valuable in explaining and communicating to senior management the aspects of an American Sequential Compound Option and its inner workings. In the illustration, the *Phase I* investment of –\$5M (in present value dollars) in Year 1 is followed by *Phase II* investment of –\$80M (in present value dollars) in Year 2. Hopefully, positive net free cash flows (CF) will follow in Years 3 to 6, yielding

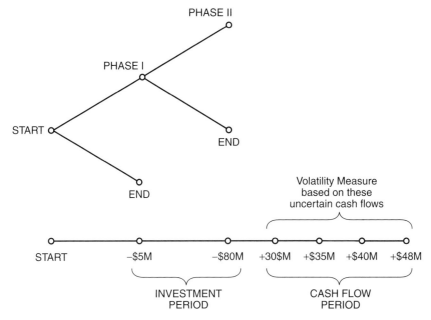

FIGURE 13.30 Graphical representation of a two-phased sequential compound option.

a sum of *PV Asset* of $100M (CF discounted at, say, a 9.7% discount or hurdle rate), and the *Volatility* of these CFs is 30%. At a 5% risk-free rate, the strategic value is calculated at $27.67 as seen in Figure 13.31 using a 100-step lattice, which means that the strategic option value of being able to *defer* investments and to *wait and see* until more information becomes available and uncertainties become resolved is worth $12.67M because the NPV is worth $15M ($100M – $5M – $85M). In other words, the *Expected Value of Perfect Information* is worth $12.67M, which indicates that assuming market research can be used to obtain credible information to decide if this project is a good one, the maximum the firm should be willing to spend in Phase I is *on average no more than* $17.67M (i.e., $12.67M + $5M) if PI is part of the market research initiative, or simply $12.67M otherwise. If the cost to obtain the credible information exceeds this value, then it is optimal to take the risk and execute the entire project immediately at $85M. The Multiple Asset module example file used is: *File | Examples | Simple Two-Phased Sequential Compound Option.*

In contrast, if the volatility decreases (uncertainty and risk are lower), the strategic option value decreases. In addition, when the cost of waiting (as

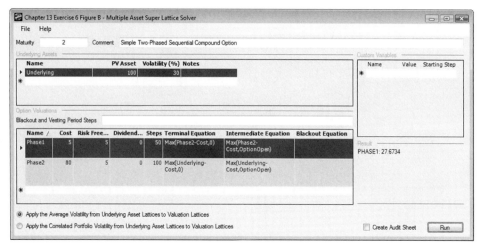

FIGURE 13.31   Solving a two-phased sequential compound option.

described by the *Dividend Rate* as a percentage of the *Asset Value*) increases, it is better not to defer and wait that long. Therefore, the higher the dividend rate, the lower the strategic option value. For instance, at an 8% dividend rate and 15% volatility, the resulting value reverts to the NPV of $15M, which means that the option value is zero, and that it is better to execute immediately as the cost of waiting far outstrips the value of being able to wait given the level of volatility (uncertainty and risk). Finally, if risks and uncertainty increase significantly even with a high cost of waiting (e.g., 7% dividend rate at 30% volatility), it is still valuable to wait.

This model provides the decision maker with a view into the optimal balancing between *waiting for more information* (Expected Value of Perfect Information) and the *cost of waiting*. You can analyze this balance by creating strategic *options to defer* investments through development stages where at every stage the project is reevaluated as to whether it is beneficial to proceed to the next phase. Based on the input assumptions used in this model, the *Sequential Compound Option* results show the strategic value of the project, and the NPV is simply the *PV Asset* less both phases' *Implementation Costs*. In other words, the strategic option value is the difference between the calculated strategic value minus the NPV. It is recommended for your consideration that the volatility and dividend inputs are varied to determine their interactions—specifically, where the breakeven points are for different combinations of volatilities and dividends. Thus, using this information, you can make better *go* or *no-go decisions* (for instance, breakeven volatility points can be traced back into the discounted cash flow model to estimate the probability of crossing over and that this ability to wait becomes valuable).

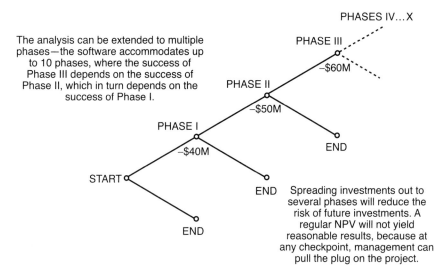

The analysis can be extended to multiple phases—the software accommodates up to 10 phases, where the success of Phase III depends on the success of Phase II, which in turn depends on the success of Phase I.

PHASES IV...X

PHASE III

−$60M

PHASE II

−$50M

PHASE I

−$40M

START

END

END

END

Spreading investments out to several phases will reduce the risk of future investments. A regular NPV will not yield reasonable results, because at any checkpoint, management can pull the plug on the project.

FIGURE 13.32 Graphical representation of a multiphased sequential compound option.

Multiple-Phased Sequential Compound Options (Stage-Gate Development)

The Sequential Compound Option can similarly be extended to multiple phases with the use of MSLS. A graphical representation of a multiphased or stage-gate investment is seen in Figure 13.32. The example illustrates a multiphase project, where at every phase management has the option and flexibility to either continue to the next phase if everything goes well, or to terminate the project otherwise. Based on the input assumptions, the results in the Real Options SLS (multiple assets/phases module) indicate the calculated strategic value of the project, while the NPV of the project is simply the *PV Asset* less all *Implementation Costs* (in present values) if implementing all phases immediately. Therefore, with the strategic option value of being able to defer and wait before implementing future phases because due to the volatility, there is a possibility that the asset value will be significantly higher. Hence, the ability to wait before making the investment decisions in the future is the option value or the strategic value of the project less the NPV.

Figure 13.33 shows the results using Real Options SLS. Notice that due to the backward induction process used, the analytical convention is to start with the last phase and going all the way back to the first phase (the Multiple Asset module's example file used: *File | Examples | Sequential Compound Option for Multiple Phases*). In NPV terms the project is worth −$500. However, the total strategic value of the stage-gate investment option is worth $41.78. This means that although on an NPV basis the investment

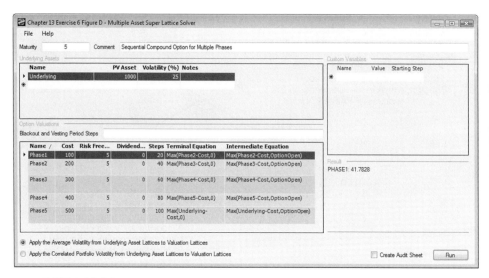

FIGURE 13.33 Solving a multiphased sequential compound option using MSLS.

looks bad, in reality, by hedging the risks and uncertainties through sequential investments, the option holder can pull out at any time and not have to keep investing unless things look promising. If after the first phase things look bad, pull out, and stop investing and the maximum loss will be $100 (Figure 13.33) and not the entire $1,500 investment. If, however, things look promising, the option holder can continue to invest in stages. The expected value of the investments in present values after accounting for the probabilities that things will look bad (and hence stop investing) versus things looking great (and hence continuing to invest), is worth an average of $41.78M.

Notice that the option valuation result will always be greater than or equal to zero (e.g., try reducing the volatility to 5% and increasing the dividend yield to 8% for all phases). When the option value is very low or zero, this means that it is not optimal to defer investments and that this stage-gate investment process is not optimal here. The cost of waiting is too high (high dividend) or that the uncertainties in the cash flows are low (low volatility), hence, invest if the NPV is positive. In such a case, although you obtain a zero value for the option, the analytical interpretation is significant! A zero or very low value is indicative of an optimal decision not to wait.

Customized Complex Mixed Sequential Compound Options (Mixed-Gate Strategies)

The Sequential Compound Option can be further complicated by adding customized options at each phase as illustrated in Figure 13.34, where at every phase, there may be different combinations of mutually exclusive options including the flexibility to stop investing, *abandon* and *salvage*

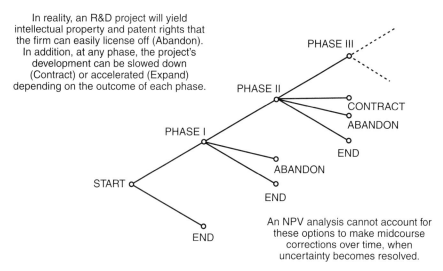

In reality, an R&D project will yield intellectual property and patent rights that the firm can easily license off (Abandon). In addition, at any phase, the project's development can be slowed down (Contract) or accelerated (Expand) depending on the outcome of each phase.

PHASE III

PHASE II

CONTRACT

ABANDON

PHASE I

END

ABANDON

START

END

END

An NPV analysis cannot account for these options to make midcourse corrections over time, when uncertainty becomes resolved.

FIGURE 13.34   Graphical representation of a complex multiphased sequential compound option.

the project in return for some value, *expand* the scope of the project into another project (e.g., spin-off projects and expand into different geographical locations), *contract* the scope of the project resulting in some savings, or continue on to the next phase. The seemingly complicated option can be very easily solved using Real Options SLS as seen in Figure 13.35 (example file used: *File | Examples | Multiple Phased Complex Sequential Compound Option*).

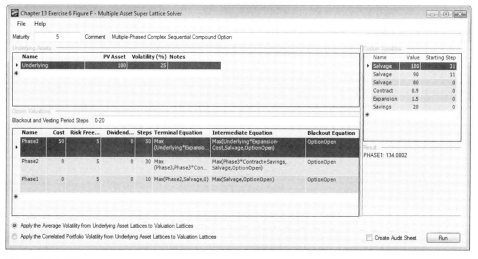

FIGURE 13.35   Solving a complex multiphased sequential compound option using MSLS.

To illustrate, Figure 13.35's MSLS path-dependent sequential option uses the following inputs:

Phase 3	Terminal:	Max(Underlying*Expansion-Cost,Underlying,Salvage)
	Intermediate:	Max(Underlying*Expansion-Cost,Salvage,OptionOpen)
	Steps:	50
Phase 2	Terminal:	Max(Phase3,Phase3*Contract+Savings,Salvage,0)
	Intermediate:	Max(Phase3*Contract+Savings,Salvage,OptionOpen)
	Steps:	30
Phase 1	Terminal:	Max(Phase2,Salvage,0)
	Intermediate:	Max(Salvage,OptionOpen)
	Steps:	10

More Industry Applications

Extended Business Cases II: Real Estate, Banking, Military Strategy, Automotive Aftermarkets, Global Earth Observation Systems, Employee Stock Options, Oil and Gas Royalty Lease Negotiations, Real Options and IT Enterprise Risk Security, Basel II Credit and Market Risk Analysis, and IT Information Security Intrusion Risk Management

This chapter provides ten additional applied case studies. The first case is contributed by Robert Fourt and Professor Bill Rodney on real estate development using real options analysis techniques. For more details on the techniques used in this case—specifically relating to optimal timing, binomial lattices, and state-pricing approaches—refer to *Real Options Analysis*, Second Edition, by Johnathan Mun (John Wiley & Sons, 2005) and *Real Options Analysis Course* also by Johnathan Mun (John Wiley & Sons, 2003). The second case is contributed by Professor Morton Glantz on the application of risk analysis, simulation, and optimization under uncertainty with respect to credit risk modeling in the banking industry. The third case is contributed by Dr. Tom Housel and Lt. Commander Cesar Rios on applying real options analysis and Monte Carlo simulation at the U.S. Navy and Department of Defense. The fourth case is on the billion-dollar automotive aftermarket by Larry Blair and Andy Roff. The fifth case is by Dr. Johnathan Mun and several senior engineers and analysts from Boeing, including Ken Cobleigh, on the Global Earth Observation System of Systems. The sixth case, also by Dr. Mun, looks at how Super Lattice Solver can be used to solve complex employee stock options and executive compensation with suboptimal exercise behaviors and performance barriers. Case number seven deals with a multibillion dollar oil and gas lease negotiation on behalf of the state of California, with analyses conducted by Dave Mercier (chief economist of the California State Lands Commission) and Dr. Mun. The eighth case deals with IT enterprise risk security and operational risk analysis by David Bittlingmeier. The next case shows how the Basel II banking requirements on credit and market risk analysis can be modeled, from computing the probability of default and credit exposure of a bank to hedging against foreign exchange and interest rate risk. The last case by Mark Benyovsky illustrates risk analysis on an IT security attack and how risk analysis can assist in making the optimal investment decision.

CASE STUDY: UNDERSTANDING RISK AND OPTIMAL TIMING IN A REAL ESTATE DEVELOPMENT USING REAL OPTIONS ANALYSIS

This case study is contributed by Robert Fourt (contact: Gerald Eve, 7 Vere Street, London W1G OJB, UK, +44(0)2074933338, rfourt@ geraldeve.com) and Bill Rodney (contact: Cass Business School, 106 Bunhill Row, London, EC1Y8TZ, UK, +44(0)2070408600, whr@dial.pipex.com). Robert is a partner within the planning and development team of UK-based real estate consultants, Gerald Eve. He specializes in development consultancy, providing advice on a wide range of schemes to corporate and public sector clients with a particular emphasis on strategy, finance, and project management. Gerald Eve is a multidisciplinary practice employing more than 300 people operating from a head office in central London and a regional network that spans the United Kingdom. The firm provides specialist advice in all real estate sectors. Bill is a senior lecturer in real estate finance at the Cass Business School, as well as undertaking research and providing advice to a number of institutions on real estate risk analysis, financing strategies, and the risk pricing of PPP/PFI projects. The Cass Business School (part of the City University) is a leading European center for finance research, investment management, and risk assessment and benefits from its location in the heart of London's financial district and involvement of leading practitioners in its teaching and research.

Consideration of risk and its management is key in most real estate investment and development opportunities. Recognition of this, particularly in recent years, has led to various financial techniques being employed, including simulation analysis and Value at Risk (VaR), to assess various proposed transactions. The U.K. Investment Property Forum has sought to establish a real estate sector standard for risk. This standard for risk has provided a greater insight into the risk structure and returns on investments for management to review. Notwithstanding these approaches, they have nevertheless largely relied on traditional deterministic appraisals as a basis for assessing risk and return.

An addition to understanding the risks and returns of a project is to apply a real options analysis (ROA). In commercial real estate, the application of an ROA to date has largely been academically driven. While this has provided a strong theoretical base with complex numerical and analytical techniques employed, there has been limited practical application. This lack in some respects is surprising, given that real estate contains a multiplicity of embedded real options due to its intrinsic nature and that the sector operates under conditions of uncertainty. In particular, real estate development provides flexibility in deferring, commencing, or abandoning a project, which in turn are options that convey value.

This case example, which focuses on a large site in the town center of Croydon, 20 minutes from central London in the United Kingdom, highlights the differences of an investment's risk structure and average return when comparing a static net present value (NPV) to an ROA approach. It also illustrates the apparent irrationality of why land is left undeveloped in downtown locations despite the apparent redevelopment potential, an issue that has been the subject of several seminal real option real estate papers (see Notes at the end of this case).

The ROA approach for this example initially formed the basis for advice to the Council (local authority), which was working closely with an investor developer. For this case study, the analysis is from the perspective of the investor in seeking to understand the optimal timing for development and its associated risk structure. In order to maintain confidentiality and simplify certain steps, prices and issues referred to have been adapted.

The right or flexibility to develop (i.e., construct) land is a real option and this often comes in the form of an American call option. This case study utilizes a binomial lattice approach and methodology. The call option is combined with an American put to sell the site either to the Council at open market value (OMV) or as a result of compulsory purchase order (CPO). Therefore, the strategic decision is whether to defer, sell (i.e., abandon), or develop. This flexibility conveys value, which is not captured by a conventional deterministic or NPV appraisal.

A five-step ROA approach was adopted and comprised:

> Stage I   Mapping or framing the problem.
> Stage II   Base scoping appraisal (deterministic).
> Stage III   Internal and external uncertainty inputs.
> Stage IV   Real options quantitative analysis.
> Stage V   Explanation and strategic decisions.

Three quantitative variations using a lattice approach were considered: a binomial lattice; state pricing; and a binomial lattice with two volatility variables. The reasoning for this approach is explained later. A Monte Carlo analysis was undertaken at both the deterministic analysis (Stage II) and with the ROA (Stage IV), which further illustrates the risk profile comparison between real options and NPV.

The lattice approach allows for decisions to be taken at each node. This features provides an investor with the ability to determine the optimal timing with respect to development, or to defer, or to abandon (disposal of the property).

The basic simplified details of this case study are as follows:

- An undeveloped town center site of approximately 2.43 ha (6 acres) adjacent to a major public transport interchange.
- A comprehensive mixed-use scheme has been granted planning permission comprising: a supermarket (7,756 sq m, 83,455 sq ft); retail units (6,532 sq m, 68,348 sq ft); restaurants and bar (7,724 sq m, 83,110 sq ft); health club and swimming pool (4,494 sq m, 48,355 sq ft); night club (3,718 sq m, 40,006 sq ft); casino (2,404 sq m, 25,867 sq ft); offices (12,620 sq m, 135,791 sq ft); and a car park (500 spaces).
- A Fund acquired part of the site (in a larger portfolio acquisition) at a book (accounting) cost of £8m, reflecting the development potential. It also inherited option agreements with other adjoining landowners in order to assemble the entirety of the site, which would result in a total site acquisition cost of £12.75m, thereby enabling the implementation of a comprehensive scheme.
- The costs of holding the site and keeping the options open with the other landowners are £150,000pa. Income from a car park on the site is £50,000pa. Therefore, net outgoings are £100,000pa (totaling £500k over 5 years, that is, this is assumed to be an intrinsic sunk cost in developing the site).
- The Council wishes to see the site comprehensively developed for the scheme and has granted permission. It also has a long-held objective

of developing a sports and entertainment arena in the center of Croydon. Under an agreement with the investor in conjunction with granting the planning permission, the Council has said it would acquire the land at OMV (i.e., equivalent to the book cost) at any time up to 5 years from grant of planning permission should the investor wish to sell and not implement the scheme. Thereafter, the Council would acquire the site using CPO powers (a statutory procedure) if comprehensive development has not been started. The case for granting a CPO is believed to be given, among other reasons, due to the fragmented ownership and that this high-profile site has lain undeveloped for many years. Compensation from the Council to the Fund in acquiring the site via a CPO based on a *no scheme* world (i.e., ignoring any development potential) has been calculated at £5m.

Stage I: Mapping the Problem

Three basic real options were identified that conveyed *flexibility* in terms of optionality in real estate development. They were the option to abandon (i.e., sell), the option to defer investment, and the option to execute (i.e., implement the development). Any of these should be exercised prior to the expiration of 5 years given that the site would be compulsorily acquired at what the Fund estimated as being at subbook value under a CPO. In addition to these options, the option to alter the planning permission subject to market circumstances could also be added. While this would often occur in practice, it is not examined in this instance. The optionality of achieving an optimal tenant mix could also be considered.

As indicated earlier, these options are American (two calls and one put), although the decision just prior to the expiration of 5 years or the CPO could be considered a European put and therefore should be calculated as such.

The Croydon market was considered uncertain in terms of occupier requirements and rental levels, which were sensitive to general real estate market movements for both offices and retail. The ability to attract a supermarket operator and a major office pre-let were seen as key prerequisites prior to implementation of construction. The scheme would not be developed speculatively.

An ROA strategy matrix was prepared. Table 14.1 provides a simplified summary. It is evident from Table 14.1 that even in applying a qualitative analysis, values may evolve asymmetrically. There could be a considerable upside relative to the downside. It was a characteristic of the Croydon office market, for example, that other competitor office schemes if implemented could encourage office sector activity and upward pricing of space with a high probability of occupier relocations. In this instance the investor did

TABLE 14.1   ROA Development Strategy Matrix

Strategy/ Approach	Type of Development	Market Factors	Planning Issues	Timing	Embedded Option Appraisal
Pessimistic	Comprehensive Development	Poor office market; uncertain retail requirements	Reduce office content; reconfigure retail	3–5 yrs	Defer or sell
Cautious		Occupiers require 50% of offices; anchor retail tenant but at low rent gain	Consider phasing offices and retail (review planning obligations)	2–4 yrs	Defer or develop/ expansion option
Optimistic		Major office pre-let; quality anchor retailers secured; demand is high for all uses in the scheme	Consider increasing office content	1–3 yrs	Develop and expansion option

not have other real estate holdings in the town center. If the investor did, implementation of the scheme may also be considered a strategic (growth) option and could be analyzed as such.

Stage II: Base-Scoping Approach

A cash-flow residual development appraisal was produced, with key value drivers of the scheme being the supermarket and office components accounting for 47.15 percent of the expected capital value of the entire project. An overall blended yield of 7.8 percent was expected, which in market terms was considered cautious. An office rent of £215 per sq m (£20 per sq ft) was applied, although this was considered to have

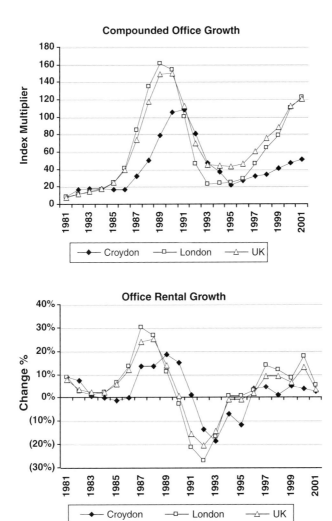

FIGURE 14.1 Croydon office rental and compounded growth.
(*Source:* Data from IPD 2001)

underperformed London's (and United Kingdom) office growth as illustrated in the two graphs in Figure 14.1. Total office returns also underperformed London (and the United Kingdom), which is in line with historic patterns for Croydon.

Costs comprised land acquisition, construction, professional fees, other agents' fees and costs, and finance (rolled up interest on costs). Land and

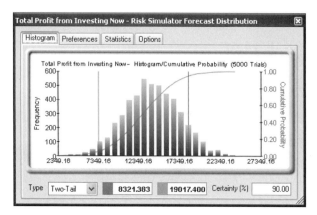

FIGURE 14.2   Base scoping Monte Carlo analysis.

construction costs excluding profit totaled £90.48m. The gross development value (GDV) of the scheme was £105.76m. It was considered by the investor that, for a project of this scale, a developer's profit on cost of 17.5 percent would be required (although profit on land was acceptable at 10 percent). The scheme on this basis outlined previously was marginally producing a total profit of £15.28m, in other words, a deterministic (NPV) measure of development profit. The next stage was to consider the project risks in a state without strategic flexibility.

A Monte Carlo simulation analysis was undertaken based on key input variables of supermarket and office rents and yields and office construction costs (a fuller analysis with other variables was initially undertaken and then narrowed down to key variables together with preliminary sensitivity and scenario analysis). The results are shown in the frequency chart in Figure 14.2.

Figure 14.2 shows a mean total profit return of £13.7m (90 percent certainty range of £8.3m to £19.0m) against a minimum required return of £14.7m (assuming 10 percent and 17.5 percent profit on land and construction cost, respectively). These returns can be compared with the ROA and explanation that incorporate a simulation of the option values in Figure 14.7 and Table 14.3, which appear in a later section. It should be noted that the project risk testing and use of simulation analysis, as illustrated earlier, is in itself a complex area, as highlighted earlier in this book.

Stage III: Internal and External Uncertainty Inputs

The base scoping provided a useful measure of the financial internal uncertainties and their interdependencies. In addition, it was necessary to regard specialist reports concerning construction constraints, cost variables, and programming. These also aided the simulation analysis in Stage II.

An ROA requires an assessment of volatility, a key input into the risk-neutral framework of real options pricing. In this instance, state pricing was also used. An assessment of the magnitude of the upside and downside within an underlying lattice in order to capture the likely asymmetry of the Croydon market was therefore undertaken.

As volatility is key to ROA, research and subsequent analysis are critical in obtaining suitable input data and then reviewing the resultant computations in Stage V. Indexes, as outlined later, are based on professional valuations as opposed to market transactions. Academic papers have highlighted the potential for what is known as valuation "smoothing" within the indexes with the result that volatility of real estate may be understated. Various techniques and data sources have been used for backing out true, historic, implied, and expected volatility in real estate over alternative time frames. However, this remains a significant area of research. The following approach has been simplified for practical reasons in obtaining appropriate volatility rates for this case study.

The U.K. Investment Property Databank (IPD) data on office and retail rental growth and total returns for Croydon, London, and the United Kingdom between 1981 and 2002 were analyzed. As investment performance is judged on total returns, these volatility figures were used with respect to the underlying asset value. Volatility of total returns for office and retail for three periods—1981–2002(1); 1991–2002(2); and 1995–2001(3)—are shown in Figure 14.3. Both graphs show volatility decreasing over the three periods from a range of 8.6 percent to 12.1 percent (offices) and 6.4 percent to 8.7 percent (retail) to 2.4 percent to 3.3 percent (offices) and 1.15 percent to 3.4 percent (retail). These appear to be low volatility rates compared to empirical research.

Another way of considering the volatility over this period for offices and retail is on a 5-year rolling basis as shown in the two charts in Figure 14.4.

From Figure 14.4 we see that the Croydon office market showed an average volatility of 8.95 percent (range 2.2 percent to 14.7 percent), which was below both London (average 11.39 percent, range 4.1 percent to 24.1 percent) and the United Kingdom (average 10.12 percent, range 2.6 percent to 10.9 percent). For retail (except in Croydon) the volatility levels were generally lower than for offices, with the Croydon market showing an average of 10.27 percent (range 3.2 percent to 18.9 percent) compared with a London average of 9.29 percent (range 3.5 percent to 19 percent) and the United Kingdom average of 7.46 percent (range 1.5 percent to 14.3 percent).

It is necessary for the underlying asset to arrive at a single volatility, that is, combining retail and offices. Further research and analysis in practice was

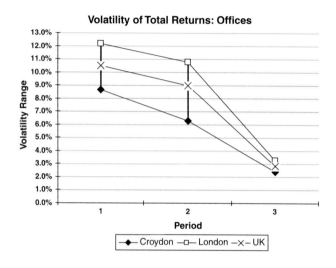

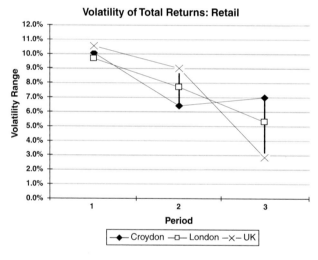

FIGURE 14.3 Croydon retail and office volatility of total returns. (*Source:* Data from IPD 2001)

undertaken, including cross correlations. For the purposes here, a figure of 10 percent with an analysis range of between 5 percent and 35 percent is utilized, taking account of sector empirical studies and desmoothing of base indexes.

So far as the price probability falls under the ROA analytical approach state pricing, this has regard to compounded growth in capturing the

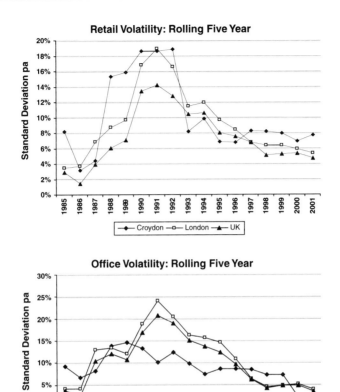

FIGURE 14.4 Croydon retail and office returns—5-year rolling volatility. (*Source:* Data from IPD 2001)

asymmetry of future underlying asset changes. Again, further research in practice was undertaken. Indeed, an alternative approach in option pricing would be via a jump-diffusion whereby an initial jump (i.e., upside) could be followed by a reversion to appropriate volatility levels. Nonrecombining lattices or multiple recombining lattices with changing volatilities could also achieve similar results. For state pricing, the upstate was assumed at 15 percent and downstate, 5 percent. See Johnathan Mun's *Real Options Analysis*, Second Edition (John Wiley & Sons, 2005) for technical details.

So far as costs were concerned, cost inflation was set at 5 percent and cost volatility at 5 percent. The latter was considered low in comparison to empirical examples and therefore was analyzed within a range of 5 percent to 25 percent. U.K.-published construction cost indexes have been criticized as not reflecting the true volatility found in the sector. This criticism has again led to other alternative measures and proxies being sought and analyzed, including traded call options of construction companies.

Stage IV: Real Options (Quantitative) Analysis

The three lattice approaches together with the inputs and assumptions outlined earlier were computed. The cost of implementation input excluded profit on cost and land in order to directly compare the option price to development profit. The value input was that derived from the deterministic appraisal. Under each approach, the lattices were as follows:

- An underlying asset pricing lattice, the price evolution.
- An underlying cost lattice, the cost growth or evolution.
- The value of exercising the development, in simple terms the NPV in each moment of time of making an investment.
- A valuation lattice, where the value would be the maximum of price less cost; the option to defer less the intrinsic sunk costs; or the offer to be acquired by the Council. The termination boundary (year 5) would be the maximum of the underlying price less costs or the offer to be acquired by the Council.
- A decision lattice, which was based on the valuation lattice in determining at each node whether to defer, sell, or develop.

Option values were calculated under each of the three approaches, which were then compared to the development profit of the deterministic approach, as shown in Table 14.2. In each case the value (profit) of the

TABLE 14.2 A Comparison of Real Option Values with NPV

	ROA		
NPV (£m)	Binomial (£m)	State Pricing (£m)	Binomial (Dual Volatility) (£m)
15.28[a]	18.13	18.09	23.77
Additional Value Created by ROA	2.85	2.81	8.49

[a]This amount represents the total profit of investing now of which £14.7m would be the minimum required return.

option to defer (i.e., now or later) is higher than the current or expected profit of investing immediately. The difference in the real option values results from the evolution of the lattice and risk-neutral pricing of each approach.

Stage V: Explanation

The option price takes into account all possible future outcomes under the three ROA approaches that were not captured by the deterministic analysis. It was, however, necessary to consider the sensitivity of the inputs, particularly with respect to volatility (price and cost) and price probabilities under state pricing as well as the impact on the decision lattice at the different nodes. The decision lattices in Figure 14.5 (with time in years in bold) are set out for comparative purposes.

Taking an overview with regard to all of the approaches, development should probably be deferred in years 1 and 2; deferral or selling were the dominant options in year 3; and development should only probably be envisaged in years 4 or 5. This scheme essentially provided an analytical underpinning for a professional judgment and decision framework. The surface graphs in Figure 14.6 illustrated the sensitivity for each approach. Figure 14.6 clearly indicated the effect and interaction of volatility on the option price (OP), which again emphasized the importance attached to establishing base volatility inputs as discussed earlier in Stage II. This analysis in practice was analyzed and reported on further. A Monte Carlo analysis of each option price was undertaken and the frequency charts are set out in Figure 14.7 together with a certainty level of 90 percent. These charts can be compared to the base-scoping frequency chart (Figure 14.2) and illustrate the narrowing (particularly with state pricing) of the risk structure and higher average return.

It was notable that the risk structure range's downside of the three approaches was relatively similar, being between £16.2m and £18.6m (see Table 14.3). In this particular instance, the downsides provided useful benchmarks to the minimum required return of £14.7m under an NPV approach, as an alternative measure to comparing average returns. Notwithstanding this NPV result, the upsides under the three approaches were significant.

The investor, as a result of an ROA, could clearly form a strategy in terms of optimal timing or whether to invest at all. The flexibility of this decision created additional value over and above a conventional valuation of the development. This additional value would perhaps be incorporated within a price, if the investor were to dispose of the opportunity to a third party at the beginning of the period.

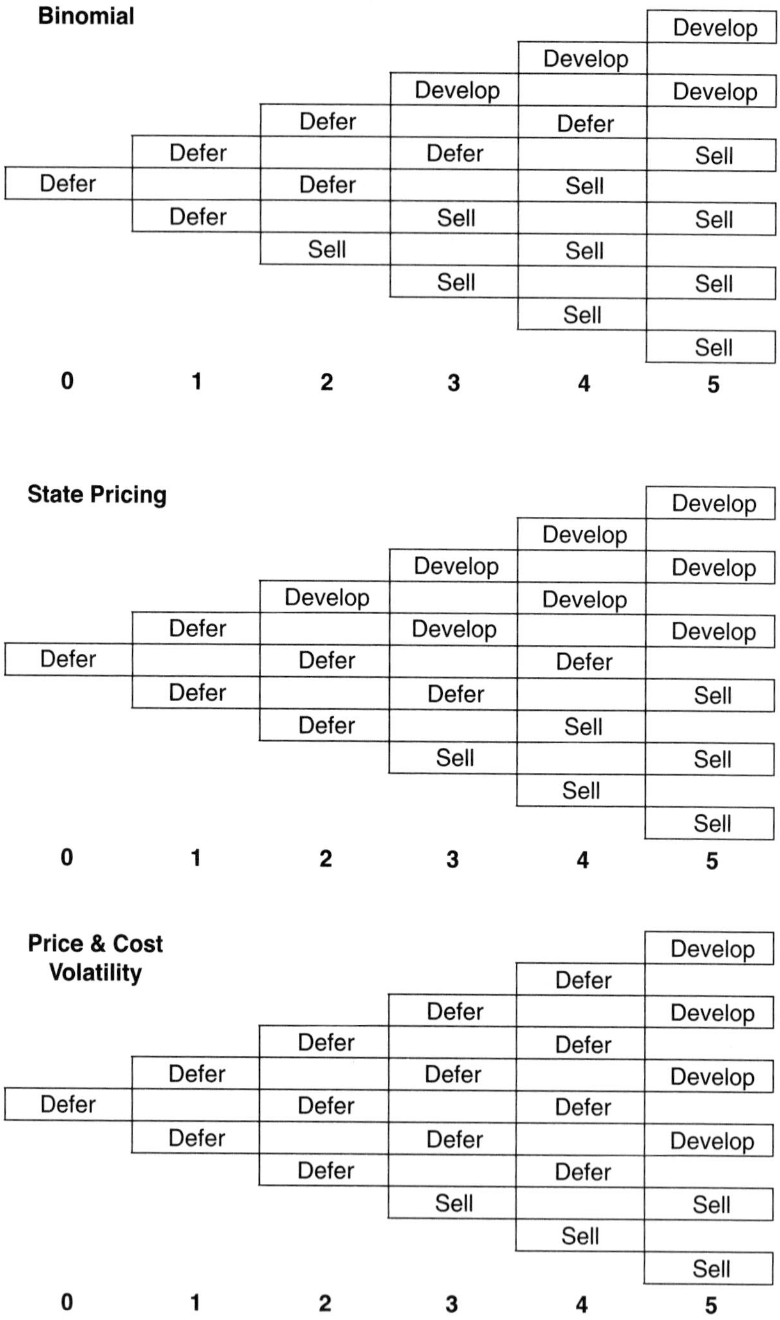

Binomial

0	1	2	3	4	5
					Develop
				Develop	
			Develop		Develop
		Defer		Defer	
	Defer		Defer		Sell
Defer		Defer		Sell	
	Defer		Sell		Sell
		Sell		Sell	
			Sell		Sell
				Sell	
					Sell

State Pricing

0	1	2	3	4	5
					Develop
				Develop	
			Develop		Develop
		Develop		Develop	
	Defer		Develop		Develop
Defer		Defer		Defer	
	Defer		Defer		Sell
		Defer		Sell	
			Sell		Sell
				Sell	
					Sell

Price & Cost Volatility

0	1	2	3	4	5
					Develop
				Defer	
			Defer		Develop
		Defer		Defer	
	Defer		Defer		Develop
Defer		Defer		Defer	
	Defer		Defer		Develop
		Defer		Defer	
			Sell		Sell
				Sell	
					Sell

FIGURE 14.5 Binomial lattices.

(A) Binomial Lattice: Price Volatility & Time Sensitivity

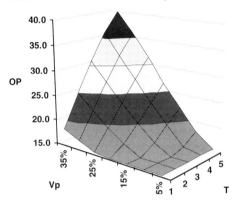

(B) State Pricing: Up & Down Sensitivity

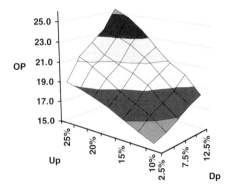

(C) Cost & Value Volatility Sensitivity

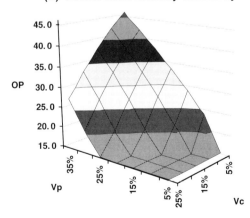

FIGURE 14.6 Croydon ROA sensitivity graphs.

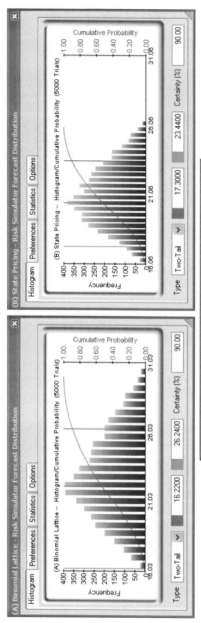

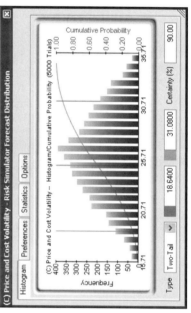

FIGURE 14.7 ROA Monte Carlo application.

TABLE 14.3 Simulated NPV and Option Values Croydon (Average and Range)

	Average Return (£m)	Risk Structure Range 90% (£m)	Percentage Above Required Return (£m)
NPV	14.7	8.3–19.0	(6.8)
Binomial Lattice	21.1	16.2–26.2	43.5
State Pricing	20.6	17.3–23.4	40.0
Binomial (Cost/Price Volatility)	25.1	18.6–31.1	70.7

The real option paradigm when applied to real estate potentially highlights, on one hand, the seemingly intuitive action of investors and, on the other hand, undervalued investment opportunities and suboptimal decisions. As such the ROA, as illustrated previously, therefore provides another approach and valuable layer to the risk analysis and potential returns of real estate investment and development.

Notes

The following papers provide further reading on the subjects of investment risk, volatility measures, and real options in real estate development:

Brown, G., and G. Matysiak. *Real Estate Investment, A Capital Market Approach*. London: Financial Times Prentice Hall, 2000.

Grenadier, S. "The Strategic Exercise of Options: Development Cascades and Overbuilding in Real Estate Markets." *Journal of Finance* 51, no. 5 (1996): 1653–1679.

Quigg, L. "Empirical Testing of Real Option-Pricing Models." *Journal of Finance* 68, no. 2 (1993): 621–639.

Sing, T. "Optimal Timing of Real Estate Development under Uncertainty." *Journal of Property Investment & Finance*, Special Issue: Real Options, 19, no. 1 (2001): 35–52.

Titman, S. "Urban Land Prices under Uncertainty." *The American Economic Review* 75, no. 3 (1985): 505–514.

Ward, C. "Arbitrage and Investment in Commercial Property." *Journal of Business & Accounting* 9, no. 1 (1982): 93–108.

Williams, J. "Real Estate Development as an Option." *Journal of Real Estate Finance and Economics* 4, no. 2 (1991): 191–208.

CASE STUDY: USING STOCHASTIC OPTIMIZATION AND VALUATION MODELS TO EVALUATE THE CREDIT RISK OF CORPORATE RESTRUCTURING

This business case is contributed by Professor Morton Glantz. Professor Glantz is on the finance faculty of Fordham Graduate Business School in New York. He is widely published in financial journals and has authored a number of books, including Optimal Trading Strategies, Managing Bank Risk, Scientific Financial Management, *and* Loan Management Risk.

Companies restructure their product mix to boost sales and profits, to increase shareholder value, or to survive when the corporate structure becomes impaired. In successful restructurings, management not only actualizes lucrative new projects, but abandons existing projects when they no longer yield sufficient returns, thereby channeling resources to more value-creating uses.

At one level, restructuring can be viewed as changes in financing structures and management. At another level, restructuring may be operational—in response to production overhauls, market trends, technology, and industry or macroeconomic disturbances. It is often the essence of strategy formulation—that is, management's response to changes in the environment to creatively deploy internal resources—that improves the firm's competitive position. Indeed, changing operating and financial structures in pursuit of a long-run strategy is a key corporate goal—the most direct path to shareholder value.

For banks called on to finance corporate restructurings, things are a bit different. For example, most loans provide a fixed return over fixed periods that are dependent on interest rates and the borrower's ability to pay. A good loan will be repaid on time and in full. It is hoped that the bank's cost of funds will be low, with the deal providing attractive risk-adjusted returns. If the borrower's business excels, *the bank will not participate in upside corporate values* (except for a vicarious pleasure in the firm's success). However, if a borrower ends up financially distressed, lenders share much, perhaps most, of the pain.

Two disparate goals—controlling default (credit) risk, the bank's objective, and value maximization, a traditional corporate aspiration—are often at odds, particularly if borrowers want term money to finance excessively aggressive projects. In the vast majority of cases of traditional credit analysis, where the spotlight focuses on deterministically drawn projections, hidden risks are often exceedingly difficult to uncover. Devoid of viable projections, bankers will time and again fail to bridge gaps between their agendas and client aspirations.

This case study offers ways for bankers to advance both their analytics and communication skills—senior bank officials and clients like to "get the deal done" and ensure risk/reward agendas are set in equilibrium. Undeniably, the direct way to achieve results is to take a stochastic view of strategic plans rather than relying inappropriately on deterministic base case or conservative scenarios. Let us start with the following fundamentals:

- Stochastically driven optimization models allow bankers to more realistically represent the flow of random variables.
- In negotiating restructuring loans, borrowers (and bankers) can determine under stochastic assumptions optimal amounts to invest in or borrow to finance projects.
- McKinsey & Company, Inc.,[1] suggests that business units should be defined and separated into lines of business. Business units should be broken down into the smallest components and analyzed at the base level first.
- Consolidating financials, rather than consolidated reports, should be used to perform business-unit valuations.
- Knowing the market value and volatility of the borrower's assets is crucial in determining the probability of default.
- A firm's leverage has the effect of magnifying its underlying asset volatility. As a result, industries with low-asset volatility can take on larger amounts of leverage, whereas industries with high-asset volatility tend to take on less.
- After restructuring is optimized at the unit stage, unit level valuations are linked to the borrower's consolidated worksheet to process corporate valuations.

The Business Case

Consider the data in the Excel spreadsheets depicted in Figures 14.8, 14.9, and 14.10. The worksheets depict management's original restructuring plan. ABC Bank is asked to approve a $3,410,000 loan facility for the hypothetical firm RI Furniture Manufacturing LTD. Management wants to restructure four of its operating subsidiaries. In support of the facility, the firm supplied the bank with deterministic base case and conservative consolidating and consolidated projections—income statement, balance sheet, and cash flows.

The deterministic or static forecasts tendered the bank limited the variability of outcomes. From a banker's perspective it is often difficult to single

	Distribution	Operating Profit Margin Range	Operating Profit Margin Most Likely
All Weather Resin Wicker Sets	Triangular	5.5% – 12.6%	11.0%
Commuter Mobile Office Furniture	Triangular	6.5% – 8.7%	7.5%
Specialty Furniture	Triangular	0.5% – 5.3%	4.7%
Custom Built Furniture	Uniform	3.3% – 6.6%	None

FIGURE 14.8 Distributional assumptions.

out which of a series of *strategic options* the borrower should pursue if the bank fails to understand differences in the range and distribution shape of possible outcomes and the most likely result associated with each option. Indeed an overly aggressive restructuring program might reduce the firm's credit grade and increase default probabilities. We will not let this happen. Undeniably, this deal deserves stochastic analytics rather than a breadbasket consisting of passé deterministic tools.

From deterministic consolidating projections, bankers developed a stochastic spreadsheet depicted in Figure 14.10. This spreadsheet included maximum/minimum investment ranges supporting restructuring in each of four product lines. Using optimization along with the deterministic McKinsey DCF Valuation 2000 Model, the firm's bankers came up with a stochastic solution. On a unit level, they developed a probability distribution assigned to each uncertain element in the forecast, established an optimal funding array for the various business combinations, and held cash-flow volatility to acceptable levels, preserving the credit grade (again at the unit level). Finally, the last optimization (worksheet) was linked to the consolidating/consolidated DCF valuation worksheet(s). The firm's bankers then determined postrestructuring equity values, specific confidence levels, and probabilities that asset values fall below debt values.

Product Line	Lower Bound	Upper Bound
All Weather Resin Wicker Sets	1,000,000	1,250,000
Commuter Mobile Office Furniture	600,000	1,000,000
Specialty Furniture	570,000	1,100,000
Custom Built Furniture	400,000	900,000

FIGURE 14.9 Investment boundaries.

	B	C	D	E	F
1	**RI Furniture Co. Limited: Strategic Plan**				
2					
3		*Annual*	*Lower*	*Upper*	
4	*Proposed New Product Lines*	*operating return*	*bound*	*bound*	
5	All Weather Resin Wicker Sets	9.7%	$1,000,000	$1,250,000	
6	Commuter Mobile Office Furniture	7.6%	$600,000	$1,000,000	
7	Specialty Furniture	3.5%	$570,000	$1,100,000	
8	Custom Built Furniture	5.0%	$400,000	$900,000	
9					
10					
11		*Amount*		Constraint	
12	*Decision variables*	*invested*			
13	All Weather Resin Wicker Sets	$1,125,000		Decision Variables	
14	Commuter Mobile Office Furniture	$800,000		prior to optimization	
15	Specialty Furniture	$835,000			Total amount
16	Custom Built Furniture	$650,000			invested
17	*Total expected return*	$231,058		Objective	$3,410,000
18	*(Annual operating return X Amount invested)*				

FIGURE 14.10 Borrower's original strategic restructuring plan (reworked by the bank in a stochastic mode, not yet optimized).

Business History

RI Furniture started operations in 1986. The firm manufactures a full line of indoor and outdoor furniture. Operating subsidiaries targeted for restructuring, depicted later, represent approximately 65 percent of consolidated operations.

- *All Weather Resin Wicker Sets.* This furniture comes with a complete aluminum frame with handwoven polypropylene resin produced to resist weather. *Operating profit margin distributions and investment ranges for each subsidiary are shown in Figures 14.8 through 14.10.*
- *Commuter Mobile Office Furniture.* The commuter rolls from its storage location to any work area and sets up in minutes. It integrates computer peripherals (monitor, CPU tower, keyboard, and printer) in a compact, secure mobile unit.
- *Specialty Furniture.* After restructuring, this business segment will include production of hotel reception furniture, cafe furniture, canteen furniture, restaurant seating, and banqueting furniture.
- *Custom-Built Furniture.* Furniture will be custom built in the firm's own workshop or sourced from a host of reputable manufacturers both at home and abroad.

The analysis was run by placing a constraint on the $3,410,000 investment—that is, the bank's facility cannot exceed $3,410,000. Later we place an additional constraint: the forecast variable's volatility. From the information in Figures 14.8 and 14.9, the bank developed the spreadsheet depicted in Figure 14.10.

Using optimization, a constraint on investment/loan facility was entered:

All Weather Resin Wicker Sets + Commuter Mobile Office Furniture +
Specialty Furniture + Custom Built Furniture <= 3410000.

Note that investment falls to within the constraint boundary, while expected return increased.

Simulation statistics reveal that volatility of the expected return (the forecast variable), as measured by the standard deviation, was $20,000. Again, *volatility of operating results affects the volatility of assets.* This point is important. Suppose we determine the market value of a corporation's assets as well as the volatility of that value. Moody's KMV demonstrates that volatility measures the propensity of asset values to change within a given time period. This information determines the probability of default, given the corporation's obligations. For instance, KMV suggests that if the current asset market value is $150 million and a corporation's debt is $75 million and is due in 1 year, then default will occur if the asset value turns out to be less than $75 million in 1 year. Thus, as a prudent next step, bankers discuss the first optimization run (Figure 14.11) with management

	A	B	C	D	E	F
10						
11			Amount		Constraint	
12		Decision variables	invested			
13		All Weather Resin Wicker Sets	$1,247,100		Decision Variables	
14		Commuter Mobile Office Furniture	$993,671		prior to optimization	
15		Specialty Furniture	$570,000			Total amount
16		Custom Built Furniture	$598,998			invested
17		Total expected return	$245,757		Objective	$3,409,769
18		(Annual operating return X Amount invested)				
19						

Total Expected Return - Risk Simulator Forecast Distribution ⊠

Histogram | Preferences | Statistics | Options

Statistics	Result
Number of Trials	1000
Mean	248378.1019
Median	248845.3630
Standard Deviation	20278.0716
Variance	411200188.4180
Average Deviation	15951.5389
Maximum	314095.8767
Minimum	176695.9212
Range	137399.9555
Skewness	-0.0396
Kurtosis	0.2564
25% Percentile	234474.0950
75% Percentile	261455.6607
Error Precision at 95% confidence	0.5060%

FIGURE 14.11 Run two optimization results.

	B	C	D	E	F
10					
11		*Amount*		Constraint	
12	*Decision variables*	*invested*			
13	All Weather Resin Wicker Sets	$1,000,000			
14	Commuter Mobile Office Furniture	$993,225	Decision Variables		
15	Specialty Furniture	$723,457	prior to optimization		Total amount
16	Custom Built Furniture	$614,420			invested
17	Total expected return	$227,889		Objective	$3,331,102
18	(Annual operating return X Amount invested)				
19			Expected	Total	
20	Summary		Return	Investment	Standard Deviation
21	Borrower's Original Projections		$231,058	$3,410,000	n/a
22	Run One: Original Projections Optimized		$245,757	$3,409,769	$20,373
23	Run Two: Project Volatility Constraint		$227,889	$3,331,102	$17,800
24	Run Two: Project Volatility Actual				$17,701
25	Expected Return and Loan Reduction		$17,868	$78,667	
26	(Bank Requirement: Reduce Project Risk)				
27					
28				Run One	Run Two
29	Investment (Loan Amounts)	Original Strategy	Optimized; No	Optimized; Risk	
30		Not Optimized	Risk Constraint	Constraint	
31	All Weather Resin Wicker Sets	$1,125,000	$1,247,100	$1,000,000	
32	Commuter Mobile Office Furniture	$800,000	$993,671	$993,225	
33	Specialty Furniture	$835,000	$570,000	$723,457	
34	Custom Built Furniture	$650,000	$598,998	$614,420	
35	Total	$3,410,000	$3,409,769	$3,331,102	

FIGURE 14.12   Final optimization results.

on three levels: (1) maximum expected return, (2) optimal investments/loan facility, and (3) volatility of expected return. If volatility is unacceptable, the standard deviation must be reduced to preserve credit grade integrity. We assume the bank requires project standard deviation to be equal to or below $17,800.

The final simulation shown in Figure 14.12 produced an optimization that reconciled both risk/reward agendas discussed earlier. The loan facility effectively reduces to (optimized) $3,331,102, and because the firm requires less money, financial leverage improves. We note that $227,889 is the maximized expected return, lower than the $245,757 produced with no volatility constraint—lower risk reduces rewards.

The story does not end here; our analysis up to now was restricted to the unit level—that is, business segments involved in the restructuring. While the spreadsheet in Figure 14.12 worked its stochastic wonders, it *must now link to consolidating and consolidated discounted cash-flow (DCF) valuation worksheets.* Consolidated DCF valuations provide a *going-concern* value—the value driven by a company's future economic strength. RI Furniture value is determined by the present value of future cash flows for a specific forecast horizon (projection period) plus the present value of cash flow *beyond* the forecast horizon (residual or terminal value).

In other words, the firm's value depends on cash-flow potential and the risks (threats) of those future cash flows. These perceived risks or threats help define the discounting factor used to measure cash flows in present value terms. Cash flow depends on the industry and the economic outlook for RI Furniture's products, current and future competition, sustainable competitive advantage, projected changes in demand, and this borrower's capacity to grow in light of its past financial and operating performance. Risk factors that the firm's bankers will examine carefully include their borrower's financial condition; quality, magnitude, and volatility of cash flows; financial and operating leverage; and management's capacity to sustain operations on a profitable basis. *These primary attributes cannot be ignored when bankers determine distributions associated with assumption variables.*

Simulation and optimization embedded into powerful valuation models provides an intuitive advantage; it is a decidedly efficient and precise way to get deals analyzed, done, and sold.

CASE STUDY: REAL OPTIONS AND KVA IN MILITARY STRATEGY AT THE UNITED STATES NAVY

This case was written by Lieutenant Commander Cesar Rios in collaboration with Dr. Tom Housel and Dr. Johnathan Mun. Lieutenant Commander Rios is an intelligence officer for the U.S. Navy assigned to the Third Expeditionary Strike Group in San Diego, California. Dr. Tom Housel is a professor of Information Sciences at the Naval Postgraduate School in Monterey, California. Please contact Dr. Housel with any questions about the case at tjhousel@nps.edu.

Millions of dollars are spent by the United States military for information technology (IT) investments on Quick Reaction Capability Information Warfare (IW) and intelligence collection systems. To evaluate and select projects yielding maximum benefits to the government, valuation tools are critical to properly define, capture, and measure the total value of those investments. This case study applies Knowledge Value-Added (KVA) and Real Options valuation techniques to the Naval Cryptologic Carry-On Program (CCOP) systems used in the intelligence collection process, with particular focus on human capital and IT processes. The objective is to develop a model and methodology to assist in the budgeting process for IW systems. The methodology had to be capable of producing measurable objectives so existing and future CCOP systems could be evaluated.

The Challenge

The Chief of Naval Operations directed its CCOP Office to focus on three goals for fiscal year 2005: efficiencies, metrics, and return on investment. Given this mandate, CCOP Program Manager Lieutenant Commander (LCDR) Brian Prevo had the difficult choice of how much funding to allocate among the 12 IW CCOP systems currently in his portfolio. Should he merely allocate an equal amount of continuous funding? Should he ask which ones needed the most funding to continue or upgrade? Should he ask the users which ones they preferred? To make appropriate budget decisions, LCDR Prevo had to analyze the operating performance of each CCOP program by developing metrics, measuring efficiencies, and calculating the return on investment. Moreover, he had to identify which investment options supported the United States Navy's Global Intelligence, Surveillance, and Reconnaissance (ISR) mission. LCDR Prevo teamed with researchers at the Naval Postgraduate School (NPS). He enlisted Professor Thomas Housel and Professor Johnathan Mun at NPS's Graduate School of Operations and Information Sciences to identify valuation techniques to help manage his CCOP portfolio. Prevo also sought the aid of NPS student LCDR Cesar Rios, a Naval Cryptologist and Information Warfare Officer. Rios had operated CCOP systems and other IW systems while conducting ISR missions from various Navy platforms, including ships and aircraft. As the team leader and subject matter expert, LCDR Rios worked with Dr. Housel and Dr. Mun to conduct the analysis required to make the optimal portfolio management decision in his CCOP strategies.

Background

Intelligence is a critical component of U.S. security strategy. It is the first line of defense against threats poised by hostile states and terrorists, according to the National Security Strategy (NSS) of the United States.[2] After the tragic events of September 11, a new world emerged where intelligence techniques from the Cold War era were inadequate to meet the new and complex security threats to the United States. Several initiatives were launched to transform the country's intelligence capabilities to keep pace with emerging threats, including:

- Establishing a new framework for intelligence warning providing seamless and integrated warning across the spectrum of threats facing the nation and its allies.
- Developing new methods for collecting information to sustain intelligence advantage.

- Investing in future capabilities while working to protect them through a more vigorous effort to prevent the compromise of intelligence capabilities.
- Collecting intelligence against the terrorist danger across the government with all-source analysis.[3]

Expenditures on U.S. intelligence activities are estimated at $40 billion annually and a significant amount of that total is spent on ISR activities. The ISR are the systems that gather, process, and disseminate intelligence. The ISR systems cover a multitude of systems and programs for acquiring and processing information needed by national security decision makers and military commanders. The ISR systems range in size from small, hand-held cameras to billion dollar satellites. Some ISR programs collect basic information for a wide range of analytical products, whereas others are designed to acquire data for specific weapons systems. Some are "national" systems, collecting information for government agencies, whereas others are "tactical" systems intended to support military commanders on the battlefield. The ISR programs are currently grouped into three major categories: the National Intelligence Program (NIP), the Joint Military Intelligence Program (JMIP), and Tactical Intelligence and Related Activities (TIARA).

Most intelligence used by the military comes from the Defense Intelligence Agency (DIA), which produces some HUMINT, MASINT, and a large portion of the Department of Defense's (DoD) strategic, long-term analysis; the National Security Agency (NSA), which produces most SIGINT; and the National Imagery and Mapping Agency (NIMA), which produces most IMINT.[4] To a lesser extent, the military intelligence community also consists of the Central Intelligence Agency (CIA), State Department, Department of Energy, Department of Justice, and Department of Treasury.

Navy ISR

The Naval Transformation Roadmap of 2003 calls for the reengineering of maritime ISR to align with the DoD's 5000 Series and joint warfighting concepts. Goals are to redefine standards and metrics and ensure interoperability while providing the warfighter-required capabilities in a timely, cost-effective, and efficient manner. Maritime ISR lies at the core of the Naval Operational Doctrine and is an essential element in improving the speed and effectiveness of naval and joint operations. With today's security threats, it is necessary to expand the range of ISR options available to the commander and ensure decision superiority across the range of military operations in accordance with the NSS.

The Intelligence Collection Process (ICP) is the way tactical Navy ISR units of ships, aircraft, and other platforms complete intelligence requests.

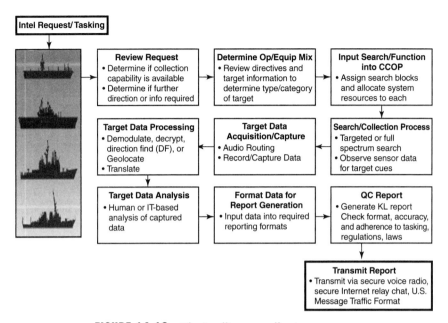

FIGURE 14.13 The intelligence collection process.

Once requests are received, human disciplines and IT technologies are used together to search, acquire, process, and report results back to tactical users (i.e., fleet staffs and strike groups), and national-level consumers (i.e., NSA). The generalized process is shown in Figure 14.13.

Each subprocess is further broken down into individual actions that may be required to perform the subprocess in the ICP. For example, the subprocess Target Data Processing can be broken down into a number of tasks:

1. Human-based (no automation required)
   a. Manual copy directly into report
   b. Human translation and processing
2. IT-based
   a. Direct transfer into report
      (1) Demodulate
         (a) All IT-based
         (b) Human enabled
      (2) Decrypt
         (a) All IT-based
         (b) Human enabled

    b. Direction finding
       (1) Automatic—Local line of bearing (LOB)
       (2) Human-enabled—Local LOB
       (3) Human-enabled—B-rep request
    c. Geolocation
       (1) Special processing

Established in 1994, CCOP developed state-of-the-art ISR capabilities for Combatant Command requirements for a quick-reaction surface, subsurface, and airborne cryptologic carry-on capability. Approximately 100 cryptologic-capable surface ships are currently in the U.S. Navy inventory. Each one is a potential user of carry-on equipment, along with numerous subsurface and air platforms. Although CCOP systems have broad scope and functions, basic capabilities include:

- Tactical surveillance, targeting.
- Passive detection, classification, tracking, enemy intent at extended range.
- Analysis tools allowing interpretation and reporting of the potential or known meaning of intercepted data.
- Correlation and tracking.

As part of the Advanced Cryptologic Systems Engineering program, CCOP utilizes commercial off-the-shelf (COTS) technology, government off-the-shelf (GOTS) technology, and modular, open systems architectures. COTS and GOTS technologies, when applied to ISR system functionalities, typically require various levels of integration to leverage on-board capabilities to provide system and mission management, product reporting, and data analysis support. COTS and GOTS also require some level of adaptation or modification to meet fleet requirements. Before deployment for operational use, systems must be systematically tested to ensure suitable and reliable operation. They must also be tested for network vulnerabilities (if connected to Navy or joint networks), and tested against joint interoperability requirements.

Valuation Techniques

Assessing information technology investments is a daunting challenge. Although several valuation methods are used to measure and justify IT investments, return on investment (ROI) is the most widely used metric to measure past, present, and potential future performance. Other techniques are used to measure the impact of IT on organizations at the corporate and subcorporate levels. Although approaches differ, the objectives are similar and that is to provide managers with metrics to measure tangible IT investments and intangible knowledge assets. Corporate-level approaches determine the contribution of both IT and knowledge assets on the overall performance of the organization. Subcorporate-level approaches look internally at the subprocesses involved in the production of organizational output and attempt to establish a measure for the benefits of knowledge and IT assets within each subprocess.

ROI in the Public Sector

ROI yields insights for managers and investors making high-level strategic business decisions, yet what if an organization does not produce measurable revenues such as the U.S. DoD? Traditional ROI metrics cannot measure the total value of IT investments made by public sector entities. When conducting an ROI analysis for the public sector, there are several considerations:

- Lack of measurable revenues and profits makes it challenging to determine the overall benefit stream produced by the organization.
- Concrete data is often difficult to collect amid an abundance of seemingly intangible soft data.
- ROI depends on costs and benefits; recipients of benefits or stakeholders are not easily identifiable because potential beneficiaries are program participants, managers of participants, program sponsors, or taxpayers.
- Certain government services are essential for the public good and must be provided, regardless of the accountability or cost.

Budgets of public sector organizations are under increased scrutiny, with stakeholders, managers, and taxpayers demanding higher levels of accountability and transparency of public investment. Compounding the problem further are increased regulations such as the Government Performance Results Act of 1993 (GPRA), requiring the establishment of strategic planning and performance measurement in programs for the accountability of their expenditures. These challenges have forced public sector organizations to adopt quantifiable methods to produce the required metrics for measuring the *total value* of services and products.

ROI in DoD Programs

Funding for many intelligence programs comes from the DoD, which requires all IT programs be managed as investments and not acquisitions. To achieve this goal and meet other government regulations and legislation such as the GPRA and the Information Technology Management and Results Act (ITMRA), the DoD has established performance measures in the IT investment process. Although profitability is not the primary goal of the DoD and other nonprofit organizations, there is pressure to ensure efficient use of taxpayers' money and deliver maximum value to citizens and communities.

Many issues are inherent in determining overall value and risks with ISR systems acquisitions. Technological complexities from the use of COT/GOTS systems, open architectures systems, evolving software standards, shortened acquisitions timelines, and funding instability all contribute to risks in Navy ISR systems. Although the DoD has instituted rigorous types of testing and evaluation (T&E) for all of its programs and projects to mitigate risk, metrics for IT systems have lacked the requisite depth for meaningful valuation. Crucial to successful T&E is the development of measurable key performance parameters (KPPs) and measures of effectiveness (MOEs) to provide accurate projections of system performance in a variety of operational environments.

Another issue in the DoD case is the translation of outputs into monetary benefits. Whereas in the commercial case, a price per unit is assigned to the outputs, there is no equivalent pricing mechanism in the DoD or nonprofit case. This presents a problem when conducting empirical financial analysis and in particular when seeking a baseline from which to formulate sound fiscal decisions. Valuation methodologies used by DoD for acquisitions must include a common framework for understanding, evaluating, and justifying the impact of government IT investments on the overall successful completion of the national security mission of the United States. KVA methodology is a viable valuation technique for that purpose.

Knowledge Value-Added Methodology

Knowledge Value-Added (KVA) was developed by Dr. Thomas Housel and Dr. Valery Kanevsky almost two decades ago to estimate the value added by knowledge assets, both human and IT. It is based on the premise that businesses and other organizations produce outputs (e.g., products and services) through a series of processes and subprocesses, which change into raw inputs (i.e., labor into services, information into reports). Changes made on the inputs by organizational processes to produce outputs are the equivalent corresponding changes in entropy. Entropy is defined in the *American Heritage Dictionary* as a "measure of the degree of disorder [or change] in a closed system." In the business context, it can be used as a surrogate for the amount of changes that a process makes to inputs to produce the resulting outputs.[5]

Describing all process outputs in common units allows managers to assign revenues and costs to those units at any given point in time. With the resulting information, traditional accounting and financial performance and profitability metrics can be applied at the suborganizational level. KVA differs from other financial models in two important respects: It provides a method to analyze the metrics at a suborganizational level and allows for the allocation of cost and revenue across subprocesses for accounting purposes.

Knowledge value-added uses knowledge-based metaphor to operationalize the relationship between change in entropy and value added. The units of change induced by a process to produce an output are described in terms of the knowledge required to make the changes. More specifically, the time it takes the average learner "to acquire the procedural knowledge required to produce a process output provides a practical surrogate for the corresponding changes in entropy."[6]

The KVA, Monte Carlo simulation, and real options methodologies are applied to the USS *Readiness* in this case study to demonstrate how program managers can build metrics to conduct a financial analysis of each CCOP system at the process and subprocess levels. Managers and senior decision makers can thereby establish monetary values for traditionally intangible assets such as knowledge.

The USS *Readiness*

The goal of this case study is to assess the effectiveness and efficiency of CCOP systems in the Navy ISR mission. With KVA methodology, metrics are produced and the CCOP portfolio can be compared on existing and future programs. This section reviews how KVA is applied in two of the subprocesses in the CCOP program: Search/Collection Process (P4) and Format Data for Report Generation (P8).

The USS *Readiness* is a fictitious U.S. Navy warship outfitted to conduct ISR missions.[7] Along with the general manning, the ship has a contingent of IW operators performing intelligence collection processes utilizing CCOP systems. The ship is on a typical six-month deployment and receives daily tasking for ISR collection at national and tactical levels. Onboard the USS *Readiness* is an ISR crew of IW Officers: Division Officer, Division Leading Petty Officer, Signals Operators, and Comms Operators. Each IW officer performs certain processes in the ICP. After a request is received, the ISR crew produces a variety of reports that include raw intelligence reports, technical reports, analyst-to-analyst exchanges, and daily collection summaries. USS *Readiness* is outfitted with four CCOP systems (A, B, C, and D).

As shown in Table 14.4, CCOP systems may be used in a single subprocess or across multiple subprocesses along with the existing infrastructure available in each particular platform. Additionally, some systems such as CCOP A are highly complex and comprised multiple subsystems. With the help of KVA, the proxy revenues and costs are obtained and are shown in Table 14.5. Clearly, in the corporate setting, revenues and costs can be

TABLE 14.4 USS *Readiness* CCOP Systems

	Subprocess Name	CCOP A	CCOP B	CCOP C	CCOP D
P1	Review request/tasking	X			
P2	Determine op/equip mix	X			
P3	Input search function/coverage plan	X			
P4	Search/collection process	X	X		
P5	Target data acquisition/capture	X	X		
P6	Target data processing	X	X	X	X
P7	Target data analysis	X		X	X
P8	Format data for report generation	X			
P9	QC report	X			
P10	Transmit report	X			

obtained quickly and easily, but KVA is required when applied to the public sector.

Table 14.6 lists the preliminary results where ROK is the return on knowledge (a productivity ratio), ROKA is the return on knowledge assets, a profitability ratio, and ROKI is the return on knowledge investment, the value equation.

The KVA provides the structured data required to perform various methods of risk analysis and performance projections such as real options analysis. This combination of KVA historical performance metrics, simulation, and real options analysis will enable the CCOP Program Office and the U.S. Navy to estimate and compare the future value added of different mixes of human assets and systems as well as a range of new initiatives for the deployment and employment options of both.

TABLE 14.5 P4 and P8 Cost Allocation for CCOP C, D, and Fixed IT Infrastructure

Proxy Revenue Assigned to CCOP C Process K ($US)	Cost Assigned to CCOP C Process K ($US)	Proxy Revenue Assigned to CCOP D Process K ($US)	Cost Assigned to CCOP D Process K ($US)	Proxy Revenue Assigned to Fixed Infras Process K ($US)	Cost Assigned to Fixed Infras Process K ($US)
$	$			$ 28,156	$ 10,250
$	$			$ 13,868	$ 10,250
$58,253	$12,000	$19,906	$63,462	$241,667	$102,500

TABLE 14.6 P4 and P8 KVA Metrics

| | KVA Metrics for Total K | | | |
	Subprocess Name	ROK as Ratio	ROK (%)	ROKA (%)	ROKI (%)
P4	Search/collection	3.39	339.01	70.50	239.01
P8	Format data for report generation	0.80	79.63	–25.59	–20.37
Metrics for aggregated		14.10	1410.20	157.31	410.20

Analyzing Real Options

A real options analysis was performed to determine the prospective value of three basic options over a 3-year period (Figure 14.14). The eight-step real options analysis process with KVA data was used to estimate the value of the options as seen earlier in this book.

The first option (A—Remote to Shore) was to use the various CCOP systems in a way that would allow all the data they generated to be viewed by a geographically remote center, the idea being that if all the intelligence collection processing could be done remotely in a consolidated center, fewer intelligence personnel would be required on ships. The idea of remoting capabilities to a consolidated center is a popular movement in the military to cut costs and provide more shore-based operations to support warfighting capabilities. This is akin to the consolidation of service operations in businesses—for example, in larger, but fewer, call centers.

The second option (B—Direct Support) focused on how the CCOP's equipment and operators could be moved from ship to ship. When a ship came into port for maintenance, repair, or modernization, the idea was to move the CCOP equipment and operators to ships that were about to be deployed. This way, fewer sets of CCOP equipment and operators would be needed to service the intelligence gathering needs of the fleet.

The third option (C—Permanent SSES) basically kept the CCOP systems and operators assigned to given ships at all times. This approach required more operators and CCOP systems raising the potential costs but providing more control of the intelligence capability by the ships and fleet commanders.

The results of the analysis (Figure 14.15) indicated that the highest value was for option C. The result ran contrary to the expected cost savings of options A and B. However, because KVA provided a monetized numerator in the form of surrogate revenue, it was possible to see the effects of greater outputs-revenue for option C. Option C is the preferred option of the commanders of the fleet and ships because it affords greater

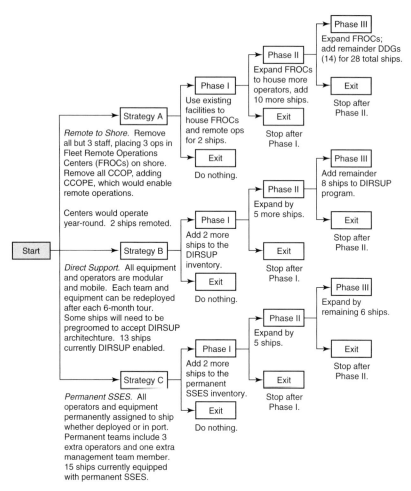

FIGURE 14.14   Staging three path-dependent real options strategies for CCOPs.

control of the intelligence assets for their specific operations. So, intuitively, these commanders favored option C, but prior to the real options with KVA data analysis, they had no relatively objective way to support their intuitions.

It is possible that with time and experience, the remoting option would provide greater benefits-revenue per cost than data collection techniques because remoting provides more robust operations from ship platforms. But, the current bandwidth limitations of the naval operating environment mitigate against remoting systems that have high bandwidth requirements.

Summary Results	Strategy A	Strategy B	Strategy C
PV Option Cost (Year 1)	$348,533	$1,595,697	$1,613,029
PV Option Cost (Year 2)	$4,224,487	$3,043,358	$4,494,950
PV Option Cost (Year 3)	$3,688,994	$10,105,987	$8,806,643
PV Revenues	$24,416,017	$33,909,554	$48,420,096
PV Operating Costs	$16,220,188	$16,765,513	$9,951,833
PV Net Benefit	$8,195,829	$17,144,041	$28,868,264
PV Cost to Purchase Option	$425,000	$169,426	$72,611
Maturity in Years	3.00	3.00	3.00
Average Risk-Free Rate	3.54%	3.54%	3.54%
Dividend Opportunity Cost	0.00%	0.00%	0.00%
Volatility	26.49%	29.44%	15.04%
Total Strategic Value with Options	$1,386,355	$4,466,540	$15,231,813

FIGURE 14.15   Summary of real options analysis results.

The CCOP's program office has asked for further analysis using the KVA and real options methodologies. Software that applies KVA, simulation, and real options analysis are routinely in the process of being deployed with a naval strike group to enable ongoing monitoring of the performance of the data collection process and its supporting CCOP systems. The next step will be to include the use of this software to enable the commanders and program executives to make projections about the best options for deploying the CCOP systems to support the intelligence needs of the naval commanders and other intelligence gathering and analysis agencies in the federal government.

CASE STUDY: MANUFACTURING AND SALES IN THE AUTOMOTIVE AFTERMARKET

This case study was written by Andy Roff and Larry Blair with modeling assistance from the author. Both Andy and Larry are executives from the automotive aftermarket who have owned and managed several businesses. They each have 30-plus years of experience, specifically in the provision of information systems for the shared benefit of both suppliers and distributors. They can be contacted at larblair2@aol.com.

Background and History of the Automotive Aftermarket

The automotive aftermarket (AAM) started soon after the first horseless carriage made its way on to the world's roads more than a century ago.

It happened perhaps within a couple of days when the original dog-clutch gave in to the abuse of its erstwhile horse-driving operator! And thus, the AAM was born the moment the first screw needed replacement. Over time, as makes and models of automobiles multiplied, so did the manufacturers of parts to repair and keep them running—some commissioned by the auto makers—with various manufacturing "pattern" parts of varying quality and durability. As of the time of writing, the world APA is approximately $800 billion per year, with a 3 percent expected growth rate going forward.

With so many different parts and suppliers, there was a need for reference books to identify the correct item, so giving birth to the parts catalog. Nothing much changed until the introduction of the microfiche in the 1960s, and that was used almost exclusively by the car makers' service and parts network. In skilled hands, this quasi-electronic database brought efficiency and speed to the parts sales and automotive repair processes. However, the wealth and complexity of the largely graphic-based content made its adoption by the competitive aftermarket nonviable.

Instead, the ubiquitous personal computer became a natural tool for the advent of electronic cataloguing in the early 1980s. A major hurdle that still had to be overcome was that the various proprietary systems demanded a high level of specific data formatting, which was an extremely costly exercise to undertake and conflicted with the existing print-oriented legacy practices of the catalog authors. Also, there was little point in the major aftermarket suppliers each devising and installing their own e-catalog versions when each one would demand a separate hardware platform to run on. Worse, these platforms could not integrate with the computerized point-of-sale (PoS) tills that were introduced in the late 1970s.

This demand vacuum was just too big, both conceptually and given the constraints of the available technology. The first European attempt concentrated on providing a standalone terminal, bringing together parts from multiple providers in a "bookcase" format. There was a common drill-down of available car makes and models with access to information compiled by each aftermarket supplier and designed for dissemination by trade associations. This system originated in the Netherlands and was also licensed for use in the United Kingdom during the early 1990s.

Although eventually a commercial failure, this system's introduction forced the parts suppliers and manufacturers to focus on e-data provision and begin the shift from a print-centric catalog-building mentality. This shift was reinforced by the ambitions of national parts distribution chains to provide "tied" e-catalogs and the leading PoS providers to add e-cataloguing capabilities to their terminals. Both initiatives increased the demands for e-data from suppliers and manufacturers.

In the United States, a national PoS provider decided on a massive investment in 1984, leading to the introduction of a dedicated, integrated e-catalog in 1985, followed by a European version 5 years later.

So the manufacturers' primary "shop window" took the form of these third-party e-cataloguing systems. They were forced to become less possessive about their data, had less control of timeliness and accuracy in the way it was presented to the marketplace, and had to provide multiple versions of the e-catalogs for the various national chains and third-party providers. In some cases, they were even obliged to pay to have it placed on display.

The Issues Facing the Industry

There is a silver lining to this particular cloud. Given that the formats of the data are now becoming increasingly common and indexed to an industry standard—in the United States, industry-sponsored lists are available—data will become increasingly consistent with a faster time to market. Now that technology is more advanced, graphics and illustrations on the part's characteristics, its location on the car, fitting tips, and other key information can all be linked into such a catalog. All of these improvements will help to increase the quality of the buying experience and enable individual manufacturers the ability to distinguish their offerings.

And there's more. Manufacturers' products can be accurately linked to a list of cars and that list of cars can be linked to state-provided car population statistics. Now production and distribution strategies can be subjected to risk analysis, simulation, forecasting, optimization, and real options analysis. When all the possible components impacting on a decision to manufacture or source the supply of a given replacement part are taken into consideration, it shows just how fragile and error-prone traditional decision-making methods must be.

The Analytical Complexity

An example case study is based on Casky Automotive Electrics, Inc., a theoretical private company specializing in the design and manufacturing of automotive products in support of the original equipment manufacturing (OEM) sector of the automotive industry. Casky's specialty is rotating electrics, commonly known as *alternators* and *starters*. The company has close ties with both Ford and General Motors (GM), and these firms have provided Casky with a basis for growing their business in both North America and Europe. As a development partner to two of the world's largest automotive manufacturers, Casky has supported the development programs of both manufacturers with engineering expertise that has led to manufacturing contracts for starter motors for some of the most recognized car models on the road. Those relationships have also led to contracts for some of the newest hybrid models in which fuel efficiency is maximized. These models place an even greater burden on the starter motor and therefore increase its cost and complexity. Casky has won a contract for the starter motor for the hypothetical new Phalanx hybrid minivan that was introduced by GM in 2005. GM has placed orders for the units that will be fitted to the cars during their assembly. However, Casky has also won the contract for the service support of the dealer network for replacement of starters as required by service demands. The automotive manufacturing industry is one of the largest (considering both economic value and employment) in those countries having a high vehicle registration. Certainly North America and Europe account for most of the vehicle registrations in the world and highest per capita ratios of car registrations in comparison to the general population.

Initial total sales of the Phalanx are predicted at 100,000 per year, rising to 150,000 in year 2 and reducing to 100,000 in year 3. Sales predictions for similar models in the past have been accurate to ±5 percent. The vehicle will be manufactured in mainland Europe and primarily marketed in Europe and North America. The eventual population of the model will vary across the European and North American states but will aggregate 55 percent and 45 percent in the two markets. Vehicle population statistics will be available annually from various external suppliers. A face-lift, as opposed to an all-new, model will be marketed in year 4, and sales are predicted to recover to 150,000 before declining steadily to 75,000 in year 5 prior to an all-new model launch. The total predicted model population will therefore be 575,000 with an annual scrap rate—attrition through either insurance total loss or being uneconomical to repair—of 2 percent compounded annually. There are two gasoline and one diesel versions with a prediction of equal demand for all three engine variations across the model range, with these engines serving both the original and face-lift versions, but not the all-new model.

Caskey is chosen to provide the starting motor for all three engines. It supplies only new, as opposed to reconditioned, units both to GM and the automotive aftermarket (AAM). Each starting motor unit is different, having been specifically designed for a specific model, and has different wear characteristics with a minimum time before failure (MTBF) of 100,000 miles for the smaller gas engine, 85,000 miles for the larger gas engine, and 100,000 miles for the diesel version. The average annual user mileage is predicted at 12,000 for the smaller gas engine and 15,000 for both the larger gas engine and the diesel. There is a 2-year warranty on the units sold in mainland Europe and 3 years in the United Kingdom, Ireland, and North America.

There is a demand from GM of sufficient stock on hand for 1 week's production with a zero failure rate at fitting. The unexpected failure rate (that is, before MTBF and therefore resulting in a warranty claim) is 1:10,000. GM's retail service network has 250 outlets in Europe and 150 in North America, and each must hold at least two of each unit at the model launch. Caskey has three European and two North American distribution warehouses that service both GM's retail network and the AAM through both independent and chain parts retailers. The margin is the least on sales to GM, +20 percent to the national chains, and +25 percent to the independents.

Caskey expects to supply 90 percent of units sold through GM's service network outside of warranty claims, but competes from the 4th year onward with other new unit manufacturers and in the 5th year onward with unit reconditioners. There is a single European new unit manufacturer with a distribution network in North America that introduces a modified starting motor, which also fits another model with an existing and out-of-warranty model with a similar population and engine mix. This new unit manufacturer expects to gain an initial 10 percent of the market for the new model, rising by 2 percent compound and 50 percent of the additional model where it was one of two vehicle parts manufacturers (VPMs) selected for the original equipment. Two unit reconditioners enter the market in North America and three in Europe, each expecting a 5 percent share of the market and each distributing only to the AAM. The reconditioners' ability to service the market is directly related to the return of worn units, which in the first year of their operation (year 5 of production) is 100 percent from GM, reducing in subsequent years as more units from the other new unit VPM wear out. The MTBF for the reconditioned units is only 66 percent of that for the all-new units.

The Analytical Framework Applying Risk Analysis, Simulation, Forecasting, and Optimization

Setting up and solving the problem is not a trivial task, requiring facility with Risk Simulator's Monte Carlo simulation, forecasting, and optimization routines. Figure 14.16 illustrates a forecast model of the automobile demand based on the assumptions listed previously. Minimum, maximum, and most likely value ranges are also listed and each of the period's demand values is simulated (Figure 14.17); that is, the European and U.S. demands for each quarter are simulated such that the expected values of each year are in line with the foregoing assumptions of 100, 150, 100, 150, and 75 thousand vehicles, respectively.

Figure 14.18 illustrates the modeling of the additional requirements and restrictions of the demand forecasts, such as failure rates of the parts, scrap rates of the automobile model, and average miles driven per year.

Period	Europe	USA	Total	Running Total	Annual Totals	Minimum Europe	Most Likely Europe	Maximum Europe	Minimum USA	Most Likely USA	Maximum USA
								Possible Ranges for Actual Auto Demand			
Year 1 Q1	11,001	8,996	20,000	20,000		10,451	11,001	11,551	8,546	8,996	9,445
Year 1 Q2	13,767	11,242	25,000	45,000		13,079	13,767	14,455	10,680	11,242	11,804
Year 1 Q3	19,266	15,763	35,000	80,000		18,303	19,266	20,230	14,974	15,763	16,551
Year 1 Q4	10,998	8,999	20,000	100,000	100,000	10,448	10,998	11,547	8,549	8,999	9,449
Year 2 Q1	16,497	13,504	30,000	130,000		15,672	16,497	17,322	12,828	13,504	14,179
Year 2 Q2	20,615	13,504	37,500	167,500		19,584	20,615	21,646	16,057	16,902	17,747
Year 2 Q3	28,892	23,629	52,500	220,000		27,447	28,892	30,336	22,448	23,629	24,810
Year 2 Q4	16,499	13,503	30,000	250,000	150,000	15,674	16,499	17,324	12,828	13,503	14,178
Year 3 Q1	10,997	8,995	20,000	270,000		10,447	10,997	11,547	8,546	8,995	9,445
Year 3 Q2	13,746	11,246	25,000	295,000		13,059	13,746	14,434	10,684	11,246	11,809
Year 3 Q3	19,253	15,737	35,000	330,000		18,290	19,253	20,216	14,951	15,737	16,524
Year 3 Q4	11,004	9,007	20,000	350,000	100,000	10,453	11,004	11,554	8,557	9,007	9,458
Year 4 Q1	16,500	13,498	30,000	380,000		15,675	16,500	17,325	12,823	13,498	14,173
Year 4 Q2	20,619	16,890	37,500	417,500		19,588	20,619	21,650	16,046	16,890	17,735
Year 4 Q3	28,882	23,637	52,500	470,000		27,438	28,882	30,326	22,455	23,637	24,819
Year 4 Q4	16,487	13,504	30,000	500,000	150,000	15,663	16,487	17,311	12,828	13,504	14,179
Year 5 Q1	8,246	6,757	15,000	515,000		7,834	8,246	8,658	6,419	6,757	7,094
Year 5 Q2	10,307	8,433	18,750	533,750		9,792	10,307	10,823	8,012	8,433	8,855
Year 5 Q3	14,434	11,802	26,250	560,000		13,712	14,434	15,156	11,212	11,802	12,392
Year 5 Q4	8,255	6,746	15,000	575,000	75,000	7,843	8,255	8,668	6,409	6,746	7,083
Grand Total	316,266	258,790	575,000			300,452	316,266	332,079	245,850	258,790	271,729

FIGURE 14.16 Automobile demand forecast.

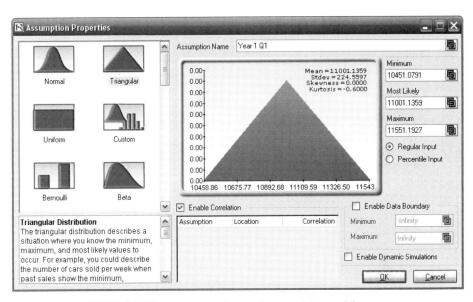

FIGURE 14.17   Monte Carlo simulation of demand forecast.

Note that all the highlighted cells in Figures 14.16 and 14.18 are simulation assumptions and each value is simulated thousands of times in the model. Next, an optimization model is developed based on these uncertainties in demand levels, as shown in Figure 14.19. In this model, we see that the decision variables are the quantity to manufacture; that is, to find the optimal quantity to manufacture given the uncertainty-based forecasted demand levels. Price per unit, failure rates, and average driving distance per year for a vehicle are all accounted for in the model. The analysis provides the optimal quantity to manufacture such that the total net profits are maximized, subject to excess costs of surplus and shortages in quantity on hand.

Initial Projected Scrap Rate	1.99%	(Range is from 1.50% to 2.5% per year)
Postwarranty Scrap Rate	10.82%	(Range is from 8% to 15% per year)
Projected Miles Driven Per Year	12,000	(Range is from 10,000–14,000 for small petrol engines)
	15,000	(Range is from 13,000–17,000 for large petrol engines)
	14,989	(Range is from 13,000–17,000 for diesel engines)
Average Warranty	100,000 (miles)	
Prewarranty Failure Rate	0.01%	(Range is from 0.01% to 0.02% per week)
Postwarranty Failure Rate	0.15%	(Range is from 0.05% to 0.20% per week)

FIGURE 14.18   Additional requirements.

Expected Period	Auto Parts Demand Forecast Europe	Auto Parts Demand Forecast USA	Auto Parts Demand Forecast Total	Miles Driven	Quantity to Manufacture	Required Min	Required Max	Shortage or Surplus	Marginal Cost	Total Sales	Price Unit	Min Price	Max Price	Stochastic Sales
Year 1 Q1	83	68	152	3,747	400	200	500	248	$ (248.21)	$ 11,384.55	$ 74.88	$ 50.00	$100.00	$ 11,291.05
Year 1 Q2	188	154	342	7,495	400	200	500	58	$ (58.46)	$ 25,615.24	$ 74.78	$ 50.00	$100.00	$ 25,539.16
Year 1 Q3	334	273	607	11,242	224	200	500	-383	$ (459.81)	$ 18,800.00	$ 75.06	$ 50.00	$100.00	$ 16,812.41
Year 1 Q4	417	342	759	14,989	225	200	500	-534	$ (640.76)	$ 16,875.00	$ 74.65	$ 50.00	$100.00	$ 16,795.51
Year 2 Q1	543	444	987	18,736	977	300	2,000	-10	$ (11.59)	$109,912.50	$ 112.31	$ 75.00	$150.00	$109,729.00
Year 2 Q2	699	527	1,271	22,484	978	300	2,000	-293	$ (351.93)	$110,025.00	$ 112.00	$ 75.00	$150.00	$109,540.33
Year 2 Q3	918	751	1,670	26,231	978	300	2,000	-692	$ (830.08)	$110,025.00	$ 112.55	$ 75.00	$150.00	$110,078.79
Year 2 Q4	1,044	854	1,897	29,978	978	300	2,000	-919	$ (1,103.31)	$110,025.00	$ 111.30	$ 75.00	$150.00	$108,853.36
Year 3 Q1	1,127	922	2,049	33,725	1,586	500	4,000	-463	$ (555.86)	$237,900.00	$ 148.90	$100.00	$200.00	$236,163.21
Year 3 Q2	1,231	1,008	2,239	37,473	1,586	500	4,000	-653	$ (783.55)	$237,900.00	$ 151.04	$100.00	$200.00	$239,546.39
Year 3 Q3	1,378	1,127	2,505	41,220	1,586	500	4,000	-919	$ (1,102.32)	$237,900.00	$ 147.99	$100.00	$200.00	$234,717.81
Year 3 Q4	1,461	1,195	2,656	44,967	1,586	500	4,000	-1,069	$ (1,283.27)	$238,050.00	$ 148.44	$100.00	$200.00	$235,580.13
Year 4 Q1	1,586	1,298	2,884	48,715	2,251	500	4,000	-633	$ (759.70)	$337,650.00	$ 149.12	$100.00	$200.00	$335,671.99
Year 4 Q2	1,743	1,426	3,169	52,462	2,252	500	4,000	-917	$ (1,100.04)	$337,800.00	$ 152.04	$100.00	$200.00	$342,396.00
Year 4 Q3	1,961	1,605	3,567	56,209	2,252	500	4,000	-1,315	$ (1,578.19)	$337,800.00	$ 150.20	$100.00	$200.00	$338,241.96
Year 4 Q4	2,087	1,708	3,795	59,956	2,252	500	4,000	-1,543	$ (1,851.42)	$337,800.00	$ 150.49	$100.00	$200.00	$338,897.62
Year 5 Q1	2,150	1,759	3,909	63,704	2,782	500	4,000	-1,127	$ (1,352.04)	$417,300.00	$ 151.17	$100.00	$200.00	$420,552.35
Year 5 Q2	2,228	1,824	4,051	67,451	2,782	500	4,000	-1,269	$ (1,522.80)	$417,300.00	$ 150.71	$100.00	$200.00	$419,276.61
Year 5 Q3	2,338	1,913	4,250	71,198	2,782	500	4,000	-1,468	$ (1,761.88)	$417,300.00	$ 150.03	$100.00	$200.00	$417,384.52
Year 5 Q4	2,400	1,964	4,364	74,946	2,782	500	4,000	-1,582	$ (1,898.49)	$417,300.00	$ 148.95	$100.00	$200.00	$414,391.63
Year 6 Q1	2,353	1,925	4,277	78,693	2,786	500	4,000	-1,491	$ (1,789.63)	$417,900.00	$ 151.00	$100.00	$200.00	$420,674.40
Year 6 Q2	2,306	1,887	4,192	82,440	2,786	500	4,000	-1,406	$ (1,687.63)	$417,900.00	$ 149.22	$100.00	$200.00	$415,723.94
Year 6 Q3	2,260	1,849	4,109	86,187	2,787	500	4,000	-1,322	$ (1,546.46)	$418,050.00	$ 148.80	$100.00	$200.00	$414,703.62
Year 6 Q4	2,215	1,812	4,027	89,935	2,787	500	4,000	-1,240	$ (1,488.47)	$418,050.00	$ 148.93	$100.00	$200.00	$415,055.05
Year 7 Q1	2,171	1,776	3,947	93,682	3,947	500	4,000	0	$ (0.43)	$592,050.00	$ 149.16	$100.00	$200.00	$688,741.26
Year 7 Q2	2,128	1,741	3,869	97,429	3,869	500	4,000	0	$ (0.08)	$580,338.17	$ 150.50	$100.00	$200.00	$582,285.22
Year 7 Q3	9,871	8,076	17,948	101,176 *Warranty Expires*	4,000	500	4,000	-13,948	$ (16,737.06)	$600,000.00	$ 248.15	$100.00	$200.00	$593,796.91
Year 7 Q4	8,804	7,203	16,006	104,924	4,000	500	4,000	-12,006	$ (14,407.69)	$600,000.00	$ 150.91	$100.00	$200.00	$603,657.11
Year 8 Q1	7,851	6,424	14,275	108,671	4,000	500	4,000	-10,275	$ (12,330.26)	$600,000.00	$ 151.07	$100.00	$200.00	$604,279.89
Year 8 Q2	7,002	5,729	12,731	112,418	4,000	500	4,000	-8,731	$ (10,477.52)	$600,000.00	$ 150.93	$100.00	$200.00	$603,708.20
Year 8 Q3	6,245	5,109	11,354	116,166	4,000	500	4,000	-7,453	$ (8,825.16)	$600,000.00	$ 149.51	$100.00	$200.00	$598,020.37
Year 8 Q4	5,569	4,557	10,126	119,913	4,000	500	4,000	-6,126	$ (7,351.51)	$600,000.00	$ 151.25	$100.00	$200.00	$604,988.39
Year 9 Q1	4,967	4,064	9,031	123,660	4,000	500	4,000	-5,031	$ (6,037.25)	$600,000.00	$ 150.33	$100.00	$200.00	$601,315.42
Year 9 Q2	4,430	3,624	8,054	127,407	4,000	500	4,000	-4,054	$ (4,865.13)	$600,000.00	$ 150.79	$100.00	$200.00	$603,151.05
Year 9 Q3	3,951	3,232	7,183	131,155	4,000	500	4,000	-3,183	$ (3,819.79)	$600,000.00	$ 150.17	$100.00	$200.00	$600,671.48
Year 9 Q4	3,523	2,883	6,406	134,902	4,000	500	4,000	-2,406	$ (2,887.50)	$600,000.00	$ 149.10	$100.00	$200.00	$596,392.93
Year 10 Q1	3,142	2,571	5,713	138,649	3,858	500	4,000	-1,856	$ (2,226.45)	$578,700.00	$ 150.14	$100.00	$200.00	$579,252.36
Year 10 Q2	2,802	2,293	5,095	142,396	3,858	500	4,000	-1,237	$ (1,484.93)	$578,700.00	$ 149.96	$100.00	$200.00	$578,548.04
Year 10 Q3	2,499	2,045	4,544	146,144	3,859	500	4,000	-685	$ (822.40)	$578,850.00	$ 150.89	$100.00	$200.00	$582,296.17
Year 10 Q4	2,229	1,824	4,053	149,891	3,859	500	4,000	-194	$ (232.61)	$578,850.00	$ 148.00	$100.00	$200.00	$571,137.56
Year 11 Q1	1,988	1,627	3,614	153,638	2,531	500	4,000	-1,083	$ (1,300.20)	$379,650.00	$ 149.92	$100.00	$200.00	$379,435.92
Year 11 Q2	1,773	1,451	3,224	157,496	2,531	500	4,000	-693	$ (831.08)	$379,650.00	$ 150.23	$100.00	$200.00	$380,226.69
Year 11 Q3	1,581	1,294	2,875	161,133	2,532	500	4,000	-343	$ (411.50)	$379,800.00	$ 150.56	$100.00	$200.00	$381,210.00
Year 11 Q4	1,410	1,154	2,564	164,880	2,532	500	4,000	-32	$ (38.37)	$379,800.00	$ 148.24	$100.00	$200.00	$375,336.46
Year 12 Q1	1,258	1,029	2,287	168,627	2,000	300	2,000	-287	$ (344.00)	$300,000.00	$ 150.02	$100.00	$200.00	$300,038.57
Year 12 Q2	1,122	918	2,039	172,375	1,661	300	2,000	-378	$ (454.02)	$249,150.00	$ 150.70	$100.00	$200.00	$250,312.34
Year 12 Q3	1,000	818	1,819	176,122	1,661	300	2,000	-158	$ (189.34)	$249,150.00	$ 149.70	$100.00	$200.00	$248,656.93
Year 12 Q4	892	730	1,622	179,869	1,322	300	2,000	-300	$ (360.08)	$198,300.00	$ 150.56	$100.00	$200.00	$199,034.29
Year 13 Q1	796	651	1,447	183,617	500	200	500	-947	$ (1,135.96)	$ 75,000.00	$ 151.45	$100.00	$200.00	$ 75,726.91
Year 13 Q2	710	581	1,290	187,364	500	200	500	-790	$ (948.20)	$ 75,000.00	$ 150.21	$100.00	$200.00	$ 75,106.59
Year 13 Q3	633	518	1,151	191,111	500	200	500	-651	$ (780.76)	$ 75,000.00	$ 149.66	$100.00	$200.00	$ 74,829.28
Year 13 Q4	564	462	1,026	194,858	500	200	500	-526	$ (631.42)	$ 75,000.00	$ 150.37	$100.00	$200.00	$ 75,186.06

FIGURE 14.19 Optimization model.

For instance, say we have a marginal holding or carrying cost of $1.00 for each surplus unit manufactured versus a cost of $1.20 marginal excess net losses in sales if there is a shortage in manufactured parts with respect to sales demand. In addition, at least 800 units must be available within the first 6 months to cover the two-unit minimum per outlet for the 400 outlets worldwide. Finally, the manufactured output cannot exceed 1.50 times the forecasted values per year, to prevent any glut in the market. Monte Carlo simulation and forecasting methodologies were applied as well as dynamic optimization techniques. The actual part quantities that should be manufactured that maximize net profits, minimize excess losses, and are all the while subject to the relevant minimum and maximum manufactured parts are illustrated in Figure 14.19 and charted in Figure 14.20. As can be seen in the chart, it is optimal to start with a small quantity initially when the Phalanx is introduced, and gradually but with a stepwise progression, increase the number of parts as the car gets older. The quantity peaks between years 7 and 10 when warranties expire and when the parts are most needed, and then gradually decreases over time as the cars are decommissioned, sold, or scrapped.

Using these advanced risk analysis techniques, we are able to predict the optimal manufacturing output and the life cycle of a specific part based on

However, we require two parts per outlet for 250 outlets in Europe and 150 outlets in the United States. So, the first period requires 800 units.

Assumed Cost of a Surplus unit: $1.00   (Additional carrying cost losses per unit)
Assumed Cost of a Shortage unit: $1.20   (Additional sales loss per unit)

Constraints:
1. First 6 months must be at least 800 units: 800
2. Each year we cannot manufacture more than 1.5 times the forecasted demands:

Year	Manufactured	Limit
1	1,249	1,859
2	3,911	5,825
3	6,345	9,449
4	9,007	13,415
5	11,128	16,574
6	11,146	16,606
7	15,816	41,770
8	16,000	48,487
9	16,000	30,675
10	15,434	19,406
11	10,126	12,277
12	6,644	7,767
13	2,000	4,914

FIGURE 14.20 Optimal quantity and manufacturing constraints.

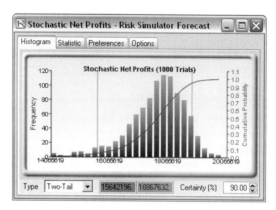

FIGURE 14.21   The 90 percent confidence interval.

historical data and simulating thousands of potential outcomes and scenarios in an optimization model. In fact, we can take this one step further and on completion of the optimization analysis, reapply simulation and obtain the probabilities of the net revenues for this particular part, as seen in Figures 14.21, 14.22, and 14.23.

Figure 14.21 shows that the 90 percent confidence interval of the net profits for this particular part is between $15.64 and $18.87 million over its lifetime. In fact, the expected value or mean net profit is $17.54 million (Figure 14.22). Finally, using the simulated results, we can compare the profitability of one part versus another. For instance, suppose we have an alternative part that the company is deciding on manufacturing and the expected net profit payoff is $15.0 million. We can determine that by manufacturing the current parts, there is a 91.20 percent probability that this current part's net profits will exceed the alternative business line.

Statistics	Result
Number of Trials	1000
Mean	1.754064E+007
Median	1.768675E+007
Standard Deviation	9.702058E+005
Variance	9.412994E+011
Average Deviation	7.463943E+005
Maximum	1.977128E+007
Minimum	1.391331E+007
Range	5.857964E+006
Skewness	-0.8801
Kurtosis	1.1070
25% Percentile	1.701109E+007
75% Percentile	1.821140E+007
Percentage Error Precision at 95% Confidence	0.3428%

FIGURE 14.22   The simulated statistics.

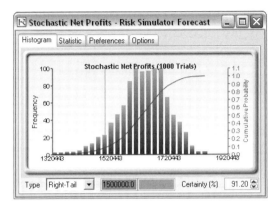

FIGURE 14.23 Sample breakeven points.

In contrast, had optimization and simulation risk analysis not been performed, the results would have been a highly suboptimal set of results. For instance, based on the required minimum and maximum production required in each period, say we manufacture at the average of the forecasted values; the total net profits would have been $13.43 million or manufacturing at the required minimum required values returns $0.71 million in net profits. Therefore, given such huge swings in values, running optimization guarantees the maximum possible net profits of $17.54 million subject to the uncertainties and risks inherent in the demand forecasts.

To conclude, Monte Carlo simulation, forecasting, and optimization are crucial in determining the risk elements and uncertainties of pricing and demand levels. In addition, the analysis provides a set of valid optimal quantities to manufacture given these uncertainty demand levels, all the while considering the risk of the business line. Thus, using risk analysis, decision makers can not only decide which business lines or parts to manufacture, but how much to manufacture, when to manufacture them, and, if required, to decide the optimal price points to sell the parts, maximize profits, and minimize any losses and risks.

CASE STUDY: THE BOEING COMPANY'S STRATEGIC ANALYSIS OF THE GLOBAL EARTH OBSERVATION SYSTEM OF SYSTEMS

This case study was written by Ken Cobleigh, Dan Compton, and Bob Wiebe, from the Boeing Company in Seattle, Washington, with assistance from the author. This is an actual consulting project performed by Ken, Dan, Bob, and the author on the GEOSS system. Although the facts were

correct at the time of writing, the analysis has been significantly simplified
for the purposes of this case study.

A Background on the Global Earth Observation System of Systems

On February 16, 2005, 61 countries agreed to a plan that, over the next 10 years, humanity will revolutionize its understanding of the earth and how it works. Agreement for a 10-year implementation plan for a Global Earth Observation System of Systems, known as GEOSS, was reached by member countries of the Group on Earth Observations at the Third Observation Summit held in Brussels. Nearly 40 international organizations also support the emerging global network. The number of participating countries has nearly doubled, and interest has accelerated since the December 2004 tsunami devastated parts of Asia and Africa. In the coming months, more countries and global organizations are expected to join the historic initiative. The GEOSS project will help all nations involved produce and manage their information in a way that benefits the environment and humanity by taking the pulse of the planet. The beneficiaries are divided into nine major categories, as depicted in Figure 14.24.

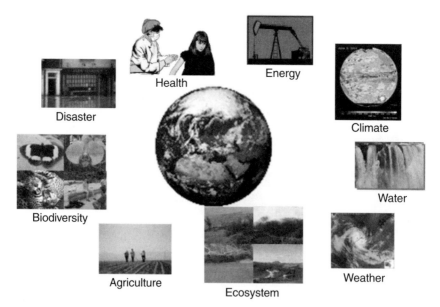

FIGURE 14.24   Societal benefits from earth observations.

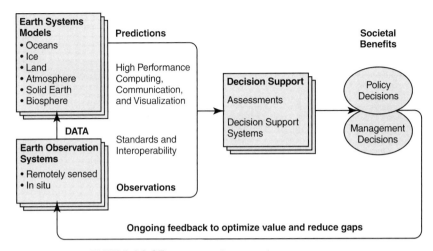

FIGURE 14.25   GEOSS dynamic decision process.

The data can come from satellites, airplanes, balloons, ships, radars, river gauges, ground weather stations, buoys, and field data collected on recorders as well as data collected with pencil and paper. An end-to-end architecture was derived from the basic needs of the system and defined into three groups: the observations systems and other domain data; the GEOSS information architecture; and the user communities. This is shown in Figures 14.25 and 14.26. Some of the applications can be as basic as measuring an ecosystem's biodiversity of animal life to measuring, capturing, analyzing, and better predicting natural disasters like tsunamis, earthquakes, hurricanes, and so forth, providing a global early warning system, saving lives in the process.

Currently, several issues must be overcome in order to allow a long-term high-level vision such as the GEOSS to become a reality. An assessment was made with the technical GEOSS community, which comprised several subcommittees; the one the authors consulted with was the architecture subcommittee. The major issues are summarized in the following list:

- Capability of supporting multiple data formats and exchanging between formats.
- Agree on a new standard format for raw and processed data for new systems.
- Provide information assurance (knowing the data will arrive uncorrupted).
- Provide data, information security, and controlled access (country restrictions, classified data, and so forth).

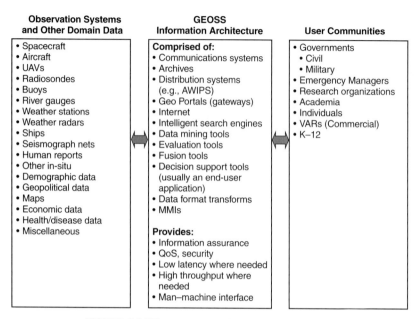

Observation Systems and Other Domain Data	GEOSS Information Architecture	User Communities

• Spacecraft
• Aircraft
• UAVs
• Radiosondes
• Buoys
• River gauges
• Weather stations
• Weather radars
• Ships
• Seismograph nets
• Human reports
• Other in-situ
• Demographic data
• Geopolitical data
• Maps
• Economic data
• Health/disease data
• Miscellaneous
	Comprised of:
	• Communications systems
	• Archives
	• Distribution systems
	   (e.g., AWIPS)
	• Geo Portals (gateways)
	• Internet
	• Intelligent search engines
	• Data mining tools
	• Evaluation tools
	• Fusion tools
	• Decision support tools
	   (usually an end-user
	   application)
	• Data format transforms
	• MMIs
	
	Provides:
	• Information assurance
	• QoS, security
	• Low latency where needed
	• High throughput where
	   needed
	• Man–machine interface
		• Governments
		   • Civil
		   • Military
		• Emergency Managers
		• Research organizations
		• Academia
		• Individuals
		• VARs (Commercial)
		• K–12

FIGURE 14.26   GEOSS end-to-end architecture.

- Assure easy use of data and information including training, data mining, and other usability tools.
- Enable the creation and use of decision support tools.
- Allow data and knowledge products (higher-level processed products through the use of multiple sensor fusing).
- Assure easy global access.
- Allow data and knowledge products (higher level processed products through the use of multiple sensor and nonsensor fusing).
- Provide high throughput end to end.
- Support nonelectronic transfer of data and information.
- Provide low latency.

As can be seen, many of these high level issues are going to be politically and economically charged. For instance, is the economic benefit decided by the country's gross domestic product or wealth, or by the countries that are in the most need of the benefits? Clearly, a lot of discussions and negotiations need to occur before such a system can be realized. And most likely, it will happen in stages.

One current problem is that many systems are built as stand-alone or stovepipe systems. Their data do not easily register, correlate, or fuse with data from other systems, although in a few cases this is not true, as in some of the National Oceanographic and Atmospheric Administration (NOAA) applications. Another key issue is that many countries simply are not open to sharing their data with the world, even though there are obvious advantages to doing so. They may feel their national security or exclusive economic zones (the 200 nautical mile offshore areas from most countries) are at risk. These issues will need to be resolved before a working implementation can occur. Once these issues are resolved, it is obvious how powerful such a system of systems will be.

A Background on Systems Dynamics

In order to perform a strategic analysis of the GEOSS system, we need to apply Monte Carlo simulation and real options analysis, and couple them with a systems dynamics model. Therefore a quick segue is required here to briefly explain the basics of systems dynamics.

Although systems engineering is a disciplined approach to identifying and specifying requirements as well as architecting systems, systems dynamics allows one to observe the behavior of a system under given circumstances. One such model that makes this possible is the Ventana Vensim model, which allows one to conceptualize, document, simulate, analyze, and optimize models of dynamic systems. Systems dynamics models allow models to be built from causal loops or stocks and flow diagrams. By connecting words with arrows, relationships among system variables are entered and recorded as causal connections. This information is used by the mathematical equations in the model to help form a complete simulation model. The model can be analyzed through the building process, looking at the causes and uses of a variable, and the loops involving the variable. When you have built a model that can be simulated, systems dynamics let you thoroughly explore the behavior of the model.

As a simple example, Figure 14.27 shows the rabbit and fox population behavior and the interaction between the two populations within a systems dynamics model. The model has slider bars built into the birth rates, the initial population, and the average life for the rabbit and fox populations, as well as the fox food requirements and the carrying capacity of the rabbit population. As these bars are adjusted, the remaining variables change the number of births (population and deaths of rabbits and foxes, rabbit crowding, fox consumption of rabbits, and fox food availability). Variables can also be expressed as lookup tables. In this way, we can investigate the behavior of the rabbit and fox population and their interrelationships.

Of course, a model is only as good as its builder and the underlying assumptions. However, systems dynamics have built-in tools that help the builder assess if the model makes sense and the units are correct.

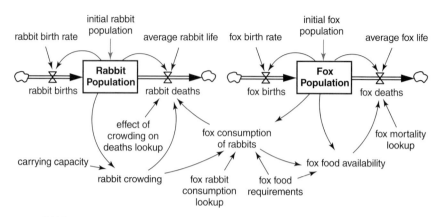

FIGURE 14.27   Sample fox-rabbit population systems dynamics model.

Creation of GEOSS Systems Dynamics Model

Next, the GEOSS model was created using systems dynamics concepts and based on the U.S. military's Office of Force Transformation's model of Network Centric Operations (NCO) as shown in Figure 14.28. The tenets of the NCO model were then modeled. When presented to the GEOSS experts, it was noticed that the tenets of NCO could be slightly modified to fit the GEOSS model, as shown in Figure 14.29.

> • A robustly networked force improves information sharing.
> • Information sharing and collaboration enhance the quality of information and shared situational awareness.
> • Shared situational awareness enables collaboration and self-synchronization, and enhances sustainability and speed of command.
> • These in turn dramatically increase mission effectiveness.

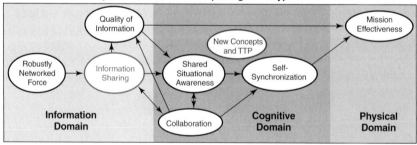

FIGURE 14.28   The Office of Force Transformation NCO model tenets.

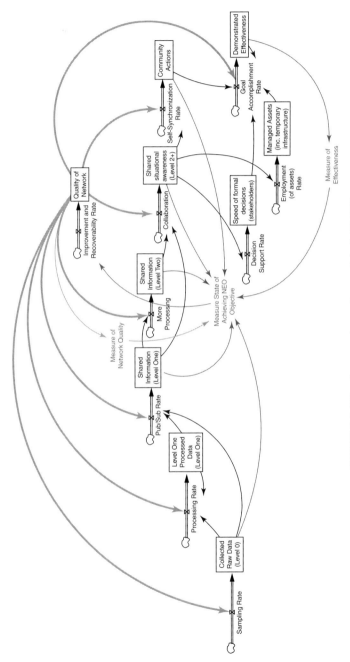

FIGURE 14.29 Systems dynamics model of GEOSS.

Seventy-four technology areas were defined to be required for this large-scale System of Systems (SoS) architecture to operate. An optimization run was then done to determine the most influential technologies in determining system effectiveness, which is largely driven by collaboration. Next, the link to real options analysis was accomplished so the relative value of each technology area could be assessed.

Real Options Valuation Integration and Cost–Benefit Results

The social and economic benefits of a fully developed GEOSS system are very substantial. For instance, according to the U.S. Environmental Protection Agency (EPA), the following is only a small list of the potential benefits:

- We could more accurately know the severity of next winter's weather, with strong implications for emergency managers, transportation, energy and medical personnel, farmers, families, manufacturers, store owners, and others. Weather- and climate-sensitive industries account for one-third of the nation's gross domestic product (GDP), or $3 trillion.
- We could forecast weather one degree Fahrenheit more accurately, saving at least $1 billion annually in U.S. electricity costs.
- With coastal storms reflecting 71 percent, or $7 billion, of U.S. disaster losses every year, improved forecasting would have a major favorable impact on preparedness.
- In the United States, at a cost of $4 billion annually, weather is responsible for about two-thirds of aviation delays—$1.7 billion of which would be avoidable with better observations and forecasts.
- Benefits from more effective air quality monitoring could provide real-time information as well as accurate forecasts that, days in advance, could enable us to mitigate the effects of poor quality through proper transportation and energy use.
- Benefits from ocean instrumentation that, combined with improved satellite earth-observing coverage, could provide revolutionary world-wide and regional climate forecasts, enabling us, for example, to predict years of drought.
- Benefits from real-time monitoring and forecasting of the water quality in every watershed and accompanying coastal areas could provide agricultural interests with immediate feedback and forecasts of the correct amount of fertilizers and pesticides to apply to maximize crop generation at minimum cost, helping to support both healthy ecosystems and greatly increased U.S. fishery output and value from coastal tourism.

- Globally, an estimated 300 million to 500 million people worldwide are infected with malaria each year and about one million die from this largely preventable disease. With a linked international system, we could pinpoint where the next outbreak of SARS, or bird flu, or West Nile virus, or malaria is likely to hit.
- Natural hazards such as earthquakes, volcanoes, landslides, floods, wildfires, extreme weather, coastal hazards, sea ice, and space weather, plus major pollution events, impose a large burden on society. In the United States, the economic cost of disasters averages tens of billions of dollars per year. Disasters are a major cause of loss of life and property. The ability of GEOSS to predict, monitor, and respond to natural and technological hazards is a key consideration in reducing the impact of disasters.

Currently, thousands of individual pieces of technology are gathering earth observations globally. These individual pieces of technologies are demonstrating their value in estimating crop yields, monitoring water and air quality, and improving airline safety. For instance, according to the EPA, U.S. farmers gain about $15 of value for each $1 spent on weather forecasting. Benefits to U.S. agriculture from altering planting decisions are estimated at more than $250 million. The annual economic return to the United States from NOAA's El Niño ocean-observing and forecast system is between 13 and 26 percent. In the meantime, there are thousands of moored and free-floating data buoys in the world's oceans, thousands of land-based environmental stations, and more than 50 environmental satellites orbiting the globe, all providing millions of data sets, but most of these technologies do not yet talk to each other. Until they do, as in a comprehensive GEOSS system, there will always be blind spots and scientific uncertainty. Scientists really cannot know what is happening on our planet without taking the earth's pulse everywhere it beats, all around the globe. Therefore, the challenge is to connect the scientific dots—to build a system of systems that will yield the science on which sound policy must be built.

Strategic Option Pathways

Due to the nature and scope of the project being a global effort, this case study does not expound on all the numerical analyses involved in the quantification of the strategic real options and risk analysis currently being performed. However, a sample strategic tree used for framing real options analysis is provided next to illustrate some of the potential options that GEOSS has. Of course, the entire universe of strategic option pathways and courses of action is a lot more significant than the simple examples

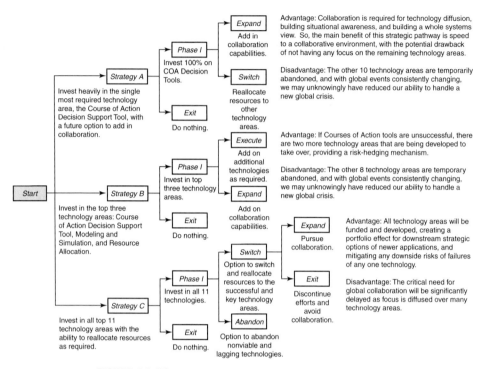

FIGURE 14.30   Sample real options strategies for GEOSS.

illustrated next. See the author's other books on real options for more details on generating strategy trees, as well as modeling and quantifying the real options values using the SLS software (e.g., see *Real Options Analysis: Tools and Techniques*, Second Edition [John Wiley & Sons, 2005] by Dr. Johnathan Mun).

To illustrate the basics of the GEOSS options, Figure 14.30 shows three sample pathways of the technology development required as part of a global earth observation system.

Strategy A is to invest heavily in the single most required technology area, the Courses of Action Decision Support tools. It has been determined that Courses of Action technology development builds future options at a faster rate than other technology development because of their influence on collaboration. Collaboration is required for technology diffusion, building situational awareness, and building a whole systems view. The main benefit of this strategic pathway is the speed to a collaborative environment, with the potential drawback of not having any focus on the remaining technology areas.

Strategy B is to invest in the top three technology areas, namely, the Courses of Action Decision Support tools; Modeling and Simulation Decision Support tools; and Resource Allocation tools. One set of technology combinations enables the development of certain follow-on options and activities. So, if Courses of Action tools are unsuccessful, there are two more technology areas that are being developed to take over, providing a risk-hedging mechanism. However, the disadvantage is that the other eight technology areas are temporarily abandoned, and with global events consistently changing, we may unknowingly have reduced our ability to handle a new global crisis.

Strategy C is to invest in the top 11 technology areas but scale them so that more important technologies get a proportionately higher percentage of the overall investment funding. The advantage is that all technology areas will be funded and developed, creating a portfolio effect for downstream strategic options of newer applications, and mitigating any downside risks of failures of any one technology. However, the disadvantage is that the critical need for global collaboration will be significantly delayed as focus is diffused over many technology areas.

Each of these simple example strategic paths has exit points and each also has an option of whether the technology should be tackled in-house or by some large integrator such as the Boeing Company or by smaller vendors with other expertise in these areas. These are nested options or options within options.

Of course the efforts are ongoing and would pose rather significant analytical and resource challenges. However, with the combinations of simulation, real options, systems dynamics, and optimization tools, the analysis methodology and results can become more valid and robust.

CASE STUDY: VALUING EMPLOYEE STOCK OPTIONS UNDER THE 2004 FAS 123R

This case study is based on Dr. Johnathan Mun's Valuing Employee Stock Options: Under 2004 FAS 123R *(John Wiley & Sons, 2004). This case study and book apply the same software FASB used to create the valuation examples in FAS 123R's section A87. It was this software application and the training seminars provided by the author for the Board of Directors at FASB, and one-on-one small group trainings for the project managers and research fellows at FASB, that convinced FASB of the pragmatic applications of employee stock options (ESO) valuation. The author consulted for and taught FASB about ESO valuation and is also the creator of the ESO Valuation Toolkit software used by FASB as well as many corporations and consultants.*

Executive Summary

In what the *Wall Street Journal* calls "among the most far-reaching steps that the Financial Accounting Standards Board (FASB) has made in its 30 year history,"[8] in December 2004 FASB released a final revised Statement of Financial Accounting Standard 123 (FAS 123R, or simply denoted as FAS 123) on Share-Based Payment amending the old FAS 123 and 95 issued in October 1995.[9] Basically, the proposal states that starting June 15, 2005, all new and portions of existing employee stock option (ESO) awards that have not yet vested will have to be expensed. In anticipation of the Standard, many companies such as GE and Coca-Cola had already voluntarily expensed their ESOs at the time of writing, while hundreds of other firms were scrambling to look into valuing their ESOs.

The goal of this case study is to provide the reader a better understanding of the valuation applications of FAS 123's preferred methodology—the binomial lattice—through a systematic and objective assessment of the methodology and comparing its results with the Black–Scholes model (BSM). This case study shows that, with care, FAS 123 valuation can be implemented accurately. The analysis performed uses a customized binomial lattice that takes into account real-life conditions such as vesting, employee suboptimal exercise behavior, forfeiture rates, and blackouts, as well as changing dividends, risk-free rates, and volatilities over the life of the ESO. This case study introduces the FAS 123 concept, followed by the different ESO valuation methodologies (closed-form BSM, binomial lattices, and Monte Carlo simulation) and their impacts on valuation. It is shown here that by using the right methodology that still conforms to the FAS 123 requirements, firms can potentially reduce their expenses by millions of dollars a year by avoiding the unnecessary overvaluation of the naïve BSM, using instead a modified and customized binomial lattice model that takes into account suboptimal exercise behavior, forfeiture rates, vesting, blackout dates, and changing inputs over time.

Introduction

The binomial lattice is the preferred method of calculating the fair-market valuation of ESOs in the FAS 123 requirements, but critics argue that companies do not necessarily have the resources in-house or the data availability to perform complex valuations that are both consistent with these new requirements and still able to pass an audit. Based on a prior published study by the author that was presented to the FASB Board in 2003, it is concluded that the BSM, albeit theoretically correct and elegant, is insufficient and inappropriately applied when it comes to quantifying the fair-market value of ESOs.[10] This is because the BSM is applicable only to European options without dividends, where the holder of the option can exercise the option only on its maturity date and the underlying stock does not pay any dividends.[11] However, in reality, most ESOs are American-type[12] options with dividends, where the option holder can execute the option at any time up to and including the maturity date while the underlying stock pays dividends. In addition, under real-world conditions, ESOs have a time to *vesting* before the employee can execute the option, which may also be contingent on the firm and/or the individual employee attaining a specific performance level (e.g., profitability, growth rate, or stock price hitting a minimum barrier before the options become live), and subject to *forfeitures* when the employee leaves the firm or is terminated prematurely before reaching the vested period. In addition, certain options follow a *tranching* or graduated scale, where a certain percentage of the stock option grants becomes exercisable every year.[13] Also, employees exhibit erratic exercise behavior where the option will be executed only if it exceeds a particular multiple of the strike price; this is termed the *suboptimal exercise behavior multiple*. Next, the option value may be sensitive to the expected economic environment, as characterized by the term structure of interest rates (i.e., the U.S. Treasuries yield curve) where the risk-free rate changes during the life of the option. Finally, the firm may undergo some corporate restructuring (e.g., divestitures, or mergers and acquisitions that may require a stock swap that changes the volatility of the underlying stock). All these real-life scenarios make the BSM insufficient and inappropriate when used to place a fair-market value on the option grant.[14] In summary, firms can implement a variety of provisions that affect the fair value of the options. The closed-form models such as the BSM or the Generalized Black–Scholes (GBM)—the latter accounts for the inclusion of dividend yields—are inflexible and cannot be modified to accommodate these real-life conditions. Hence, the binomial lattice approach is preferred.

Under very specific conditions (European options without dividends) the binomial lattice and Monte Carlo simulation approaches yield identical values to the BSM, indicating that the two former approaches are robust and exact at the limit. However, when specific real-life business conditions are modeled (i.e., probability of forfeiture, probability the employee leaves or is terminated, time-vesting, suboptimal exercise behavior, and so forth), only the binomial lattice with its highly flexible nature will provide the true fair-market value of the ESO. The BSM takes into account only the following inputs: stock price, strike price, time to maturity, a single risk-free rate, and a single volatility. The GBM accounts for the same inputs as well as a single dividend rate. Hence, in accordance with the FAS 123 requirements, the BSM and GBM fail to account for real-life conditions. In contrast, the binomial lattice can be customized to include the stock price, strike price, time to maturity, a single risk-free rate and/or multiple risk-free rates changing over time, a single volatility and/or multiple volatilities changing over time, a single dividend rate and/or multiple dividend rates changing over time, plus all the other real-life factors including, but not limited to, vesting periods, suboptimal early exercise behavior, blackout periods, forfeiture rates, stock price and performance barriers, and other exotic contingencies. Note that the binomial lattice results revert to the GBM if these real-life conditions are negligible.

The two most important and convincing arguments for using binomial lattices are (1) that FASB requires it and states that the binomial lattice is the preferred method for ESO valuation and (2) that lattices can substantially reduce the cost of the ESO by more appropriately mirroring real-life conditions. Here is a sample of FAS 123's requirements discussing the use of binomial lattices:

> *B64. As discussed in paragraphs A10–A17, closed-form models are one acceptable technique for estimating the fair value of employee share options. However, a lattice model (or other valuation technique, such as a Monte Carlo simulation technique, that is not based on a closed-form equation) can accommodate the term structures of risk-free interest rates and expected volatility, as well as expected changes in dividends over an option's contractual term. A lattice model also can accommodate estimates of employees' option exercise patterns and post-vesting employment termination during the option's contractual term, and thereby can more fully reflect the effect of those factors than can an estimate developed using a closed-form model and a single weighted-average expected life of the options.*
>
> *A15. The Black–Scholes–Merton formula assumes that option exercises occur at the end of an option's contractual term, and that expected volatility, expected dividends, and risk-free interest rates are constant over the option's term. If used to estimate the fair value of instruments in the scope of this Statement, the Black–Scholes–Merton formula must be adjusted to take account of certain characteristics of employee share options and similar instruments that are not consistent with the model's assumptions (for example, the ability to exercise before the end of the option's contractual term). Because of the nature of the formula, those adjustments take the form of weighted average assumptions about*

those characteristics. In contrast, a lattice model can be designed to accommodate dynamic assumptions of expected volatility and dividends over the option's contractual term, and estimates of expected option exercise patterns during the option's contractual term, including the effect of blackout periods. Therefore, the design of a lattice model more fully reflects the substantive characteristics of a particular employee share option or similar instrument. Nevertheless, both a lattice model and the Black–Scholes–Merton formula, as well as other valuation techniques that meet the requirements in paragraph A8, can provide a fair value estimate that is consistent with the measurement objective and fair-value-based method of this Statement. However, if an entity uses a lattice model that has been modified to take into account an option's contractual term and employees' expected exercise and post-vesting employment termination behavior, the expected term is estimated based on the resulting output of the lattice. For example, an entity's experience might indicate that option holders tend to exercise their options when the share price reaches 200 percent of the exercise price. If so, that entity might use a lattice model that assumes exercise of the option at each node along each share price path in a lattice at which the early exercise expectation is met, provided that the option is vested and exercisable at that point. Moreover, such a model would assume exercise at the end of the contractual term on price paths along which the exercise expectation is not met but the options are in-the-money at the end of the contractual term. That method recognizes that employees' exercise behavior is correlated with the price of the underlying share. Employees' expected post-vesting employment termination behavior also would be factored in. Expected term, which is a required disclosure (paragraph A240), then could be estimated based on the output of the resulting lattice.

In fact, some parts of the FAS 123 Final Requirements cannot be modeled with a traditional Black–Scholes model. A lattice is required to model items such as suboptimal exercise behavior multiple, forfeiture rates, vesting, blackout periods, and so forth. This case study and the software used to compute the results use both a binomial (and trinomial) lattice as well as closed-form Black–Scholes models to compare the results. The specific FAS 123 paragraphs describing the use of lattices include:

A27. However, if an entity uses a lattice model that has been modified to take into account an option's contractual term and employees' expected exercise and post-vesting employment termination behavior, the expected term is estimated based on the resulting output of the lattice. For example, an entity's experience might indicate that option holders tend to exercise their options when the share price reaches 200 percent of the exercise price. If so, that entity might use a lattice model that assumes exercise of the option at each node along each share price path in a lattice at which the early exercise expectation is met, provided that the option is vested and exercisable at that point.

A28. Other factors that may affect expectations about employees' exercise and post-vesting employment termination behavior include the following:

a. The vesting period of the award. An option's expected term must at least include the vesting period.

b. Employees' historical exercise and post-vesting employment termination behavior for similar grants.

c. Expected volatility of the price of the underlying share.

d. Blackout periods and other coexisting arrangements such as agreements that allow for exercise to automatically occur during blackout periods if certain conditions are satisfied.

e. Employees' ages, lengths of service, and home jurisdictions (that is, domestic or foreign).

Therefore, based on the preceding justifications, and in accordance with the requirements and recommendations set forth by the revised FAS 123, which prefers the binomial lattice, it is hereby concluded that the customized binomial lattice is the best and preferred methodology to calculate the fair-market value of ESOs.

Application of the Preferred Method

In applying the customized binomial lattice methodology, several inputs have to be determined:

- Stock price at grant date.
- Strike price of the option grant.
- Time to maturity of the option.
- Risk-free rate over the life of the option.
- Dividend yield of the option's underlying stock over the life of the option.
- Volatility over the life of the option.
- Vesting period of the option grant.

- Suboptimal exercise behavior multiples over the life of the option.
- Forfeiture and employee turnover rates over the life of the option.
- Blackout dates postvesting when the options cannot be exercised.

The analysis assumes that the employee cannot exercise the option when it is still in the vesting period. Further, if the employee is terminated or decides to leave voluntarily during this vesting period, the option grant will be forfeited and presumed worthless. In contrast, after the options have been vested, employees tend to exhibit erratic exercise behavior where an option will be exercised only if it breaches the suboptimal exercise behavior multiple.[15] However, the options that have vested must be exercised within a short period if the employee leaves voluntarily or is terminated, regardless of the suboptimal behavior threshold—that is, if forfeiture occurs (measured by the historical option forfeiture rates as well as employee turnover rates). Finally, if the option expiration date has been reached, the option will be exercised if it is in-the-money, and expire worthless if it is at-the-money or out-of-the-money. The next section details the results obtained from such an analysis.

ESO Valuation Toolkit Software

It is theoretically impossible to solve a large binomial lattice ESO valuation without the use of software algorithms.[16] The analyses results in this case study were performed using the author's Employee Stock Options Valuation Toolkit 1.1 software (Figure 14.31), which is the same software used by FASB to convince itself that ESO valuation is pragmatic and manageable. In fact, FASB used this software to calculate the valuation example in the Final FAS 123 release in sections A87–A88 (illustrated later). Figure 14.32 shows a sample module for computing the Customized American Option using binomial lattices with vesting, forfeiture rate, suboptimal exercise behavior multiple, and changing risk-free rates and volatilities over time. The Real Options Super Lattice Solver software also can be used to create any customized ESO model using binomial lattices, FASB's favored method.

The software shows the applications of both closed-form models such as the BSM/GBM and binomial lattice methodologies. By using binomial lattice methodologies, more complex ESOs can be solved. For instance, the Customized Advanced Option (Figure 14.32) shows how multiple variables can be varied over time (risk-free, dividend, volatility, forfeiture rate, suboptimal exercise behavior multiple, and so forth). In addition, for added flexibility, the Super Lattice Solver module allows the expert user to create and solve his or her own customized ESO. This feature allows management to experiment with different flavors of ESO as well as to engineer one that

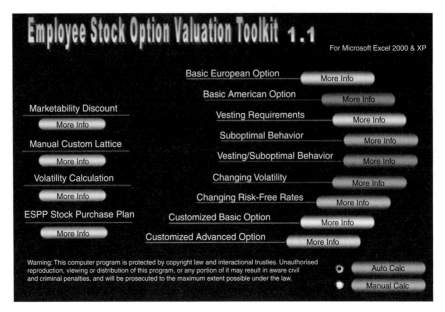

FIGURE 14.31   ESO Valuation Toolkit 1.1 software.

Customized American Option

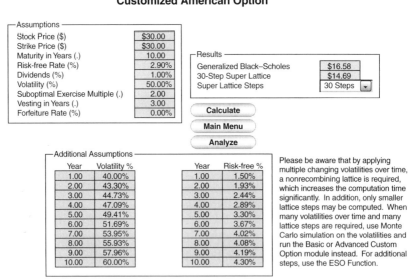

FIGURE 14.32   Customized advanced option model.

would suit its needs, by balancing fair and equitable value to employees, with cost minimization to its shareholders.

Figure 14.32 shows the solution of the case example provided in section A87 of the Final 2004 FAS 123 standards. Specifically, A87–A88 state:

> *A87. The following table shows assumptions and information about the share options granted on January 1, 20X5.*
>
> *Share options granted 900,000*
> *Employees granted options 3,000*
> *Expected forfeitures per year 3.0%*
> *Share price at the grant date $30*
> *Exercise price $30*
> *Contractual term (CT) of options 10 years*
> *Risk-free interest rate over CT 1.5% to 4.3%*
> *Expected volatility over CT 40% to 60%*
> *Expected dividend yield over CT 1.0%*
> *Suboptimal exercise factor 2*
>
> *A88. This example assumes that each employee receives an equal grant of 300 options. Using as inputs the last 7 items from the table above, Entity T's lattice-based valuation model produces a fair value of $14.69 per option. A lattice model uses a suboptimal exercise factor to calculate the expected term (that is, the expected term is an output) rather than the expected term being a separate input. If an entity uses a Black–Scholes–Merton option-pricing formula, the expected term would be used as an input instead of a suboptimal exercise factor.*

Figure 14.32 shows the result as $14.69, the answer that FASB uses in its example. The forfeiture rate of 3 percent used by FASB's example is applied outside of the model to discount for the quantity reduced over time. The software allows the ability to input the forfeiture rates (pre- and postvesting) inside or outside of the model. In this specific example, we set forfeiture rate to zero in Figure 14.32 and adjust the quantity outside, just as FASB does, in A91:

> *The number of share options expected to vest is estimated at the grant date to be 821,406 (900,000 × .97³).*

In fact, using the ESO Valuation Toolkit software and Excel's goal seek function, we can find that the expected life of this option is 6.99 years. We can then justify the use of 6.99 years as the input into a modified GBM to obtain the same result at $14.69, something that cannot be done without the use of the binomial lattice approach.

Technical Justification of Methodology Employed

This section illustrates some of the technical justifications that make up the price differential between the GBM and the customized binomial lattice models. Figure 14.33 shows a tornado chart and how each input variable in a customized binomial lattice drives the value of the option.[17] Based on the chart, it is clear that volatility is not the single key variable that drives option value. In fact, when vesting, forfeiture, and suboptimal behavior elements are added to the model, their effects dominate that of volatility. The chart illustrated is based on a typical case and cannot be generalized across all cases.

In contrast, volatility is a significant variable in a simple BSM as can be seen in Figure 14.34. This is because there is less interaction among input variables due to the fewer input variables, and for most ESOs that are issued at-the-money, volatility plays an important part when there are no other dominant inputs.

In addition, the interactions among these new input variables are non-linear. Figure 14.35 shows a spider chart[18] where it can be seen that vesting,

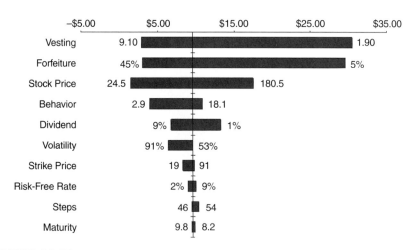

FIGURE 14.33 Tornado chart listing the critical input factors of a customized binomial model.

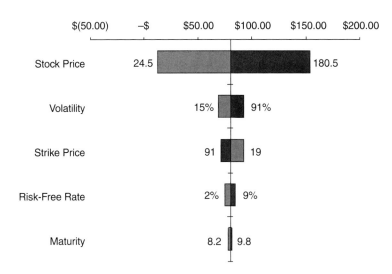

FIGURE 14.34   Tornado chart listing the critical input factors of the BSM.

forfeiture rates, and suboptimal exercise behavior multiples have nonlinear effects on option value. That is, the lines in the spider chart are not straight but curve at certain areas, indicating that there are nonlinear effects in the model. This means that we cannot generalize these three variables' effects on option value (for instance, we cannot generalize that if a 1 percent increase in forfeiture rate will decrease option value by 2.35 percent, it

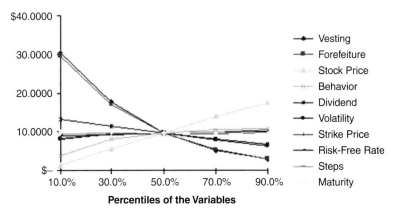

FIGURE 14.35   Spider chart showing the nonlinear effects of input factors in the binomial model.

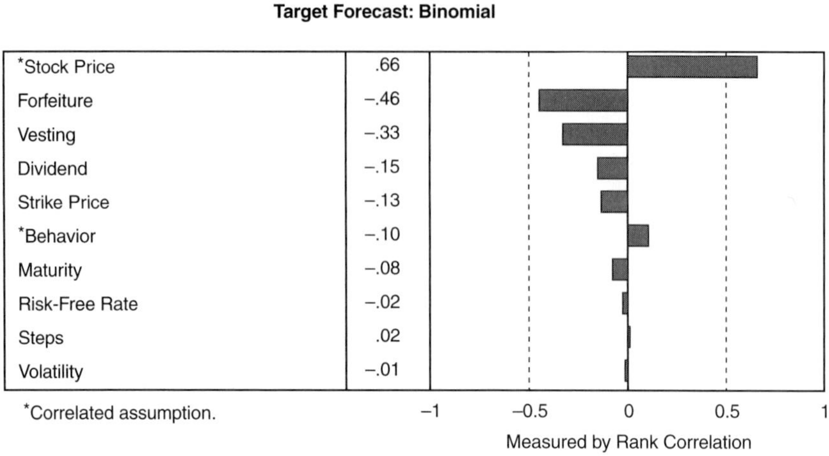

Target Forecast: Binomial

*Stock Price	.66	
Forfeiture	−.46	
Vesting	−.33	
Dividend	−.15	
Strike Price	−.13	
*Behavior	−.10	
Maturity	−.08	
Risk-Free Rate	−.02	
Steps	.02	
Volatility	−.01	

*Correlated assumption.

−1   −0.5   0   0.5   1

Measured by Rank Correlation

FIGURE 14.36 Dynamic sensitivity with simultaneously changing input factors in the binomial model.

means that a 2 percent increase in forfeiture rate drives option value down 4.70 percent, and so forth). This is because the variables interact differently at different input levels. The conclusion is that we really cannot say a priori what the direct effects are of changing one variable on the magnitude of the final option value. More detailed analysis will have to be performed in each case.

Although the tornado and spider charts illustrate the impact of each input variable on the final option value, the effects are static; that is, one variable is tweaked at a time to determine its ramifications on the option value. However, as shown, the effects are sometimes nonlinear, which means we need to change all variables simultaneously to account for their interactions. Figure 14.36 shows a Monte Carlo simulated dynamic sensitivity chart where forfeiture, vesting, and suboptimal exercise behavior multiple are determined to be important variables, while volatility is again relegated to a less important role. The dynamic sensitivity chart perturbs all input variables simultaneously for thousands of trials, and captures the effects on the option value. This approach is valuable in capturing the net interaction effects among variables at different input levels.

From this preliminary sensitivity analysis, we conclude that incorporating forfeiture rates, vesting, and suboptimal exercise behavior multiple is vital to obtaining a fair-market valuation of ESOs due to their significant contributions to option value. In addition, we cannot generalize each input's effects on the final option value. Detailed analysis has to be performed to obtain the option's value every time.

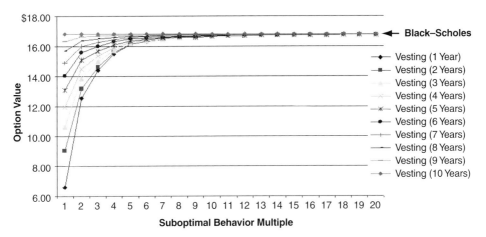

FIGURE 14.37 Impact of suboptimal exercise behavior and vesting on option value in the binomial model. (Assumptions used: stock and strike price of $25, 10-year maturity, 5% risk-free rate, 50% volatility, 0% dividends, suboptimal exercise behavior multiple range of 1–20, vesting period of 1–10 years, and tested with 100–5,000 binomial lattice steps.)

Options with Vesting and Suboptimal Behavior

Further investigation into the elements of suboptimal behavior[19] and vesting yields the chart shown in Figure 14.37. Here we see that at lower suboptimal exercise behavior multiples (within the range of 1 to 6), the stock option value can be significantly lower than that predicted by the BSM. With a 10-year vesting stock option, the results are identical regardless of the suboptimal exercise behavior multiple—its flat line bears the same value as the BSM result. This is because for a 10-year vesting of a 10-year maturity option, the option reverts to a perfect European option, where it can be exercised only at expiration. The BSM provides the correct result in this case.

However, when the suboptimal exercise behavior multiple is low, the option value decreases because employees holding the option will tend to exercise the option suboptimally—that is, the option will be exercised earlier and at a lower stock price than optimal. Hence, the option's upside value is not maximized. As an example, suppose an option's strike price is $10 while the underlying stock is highly volatile. If an employee exercises the option at $11 (this means a 1.10 suboptimal exercise multiple), he or she may not be capturing the entire upside potential of the option as the stock price can go up significantly higher than $11 depending on the underlying volatility. Compare this to another employee who exercises the option when the stock price is $20 (suboptimal exercise multiple of 2.0) versus one who

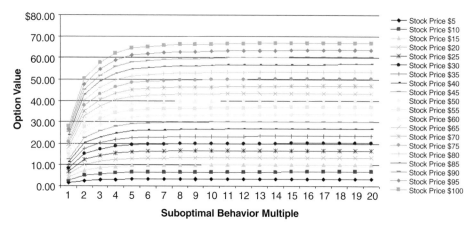

FIGURE 14.38 Impact of suboptimal exercise behavior and stock price on option value in the binomial model. (Assumptions used: stock and strike price range of $5 to $100, 10-year maturity, 5% risk-free rate, 50% volatility, 0% dividends, suboptimal exercise behavior multiple range of 1–20, 4-year vesting, and tested with 100–5,000 binomial lattice steps.)

does so at a much higher stock price. Thus, lower suboptimal exercise behavior means a lower fair-market value of the stock option. This suboptimal exercise behavior has a higher impact when stock prices at grant date are forecast to be high. Figure 14.38 shows that (at the lower end of the suboptimal multiples) a steeper slope occurs the higher the initial stock price at grant date.

Figure 14.39 shows that for higher volatility stocks, the suboptimal region is larger and the impact to option value is greater, but the effect is gradual. For instance, for the 100 percent volatility stock, the suboptimal region extends from a suboptimal exercise behavior multiple of 1.0 to approximately 9.0 versus from 1.0 to 2.0 for the 10 percent volatility stock. In addition, the vertical distance of the 100 percent volatility stock extends from $12 to $22 with a $10 range, as compared to $2 to $10 with an $8 range for the 10 percent volatility stock. Therefore, the higher the stock price at grant date and the higher the volatility, the greater the impact of suboptimal behavior will be on the option value. *In all cases*, the BSM results are the horizontal lines in the charts (Figures 14.38 and 14.39). That is, the BSM will always generate the maximum option value assuming optimal behavior, and overexpense the option significantly. A GBM or BSM cannot be modified to account for this suboptimal exercise behavior; only the binomial lattice can be used.

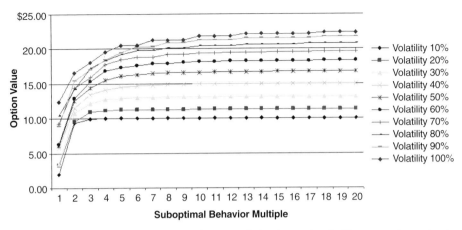

FIGURE 14.39 Impact of suboptimal exercise behavior and volatility on option value in the binomial model. (Assumptions used: stock and strike price of $25, 10-year maturity, 5% risk-free rate, 10–100% volatility range, 0% dividends, suboptimal exercise behavior multiple range of 1–20, 1-year vesting, and tested with 100–5,000 binomial lattice steps.)

Options with Forfeiture Rates

Figure 14.40 illustrates the reduction in option value when the forfeiture rate increases. The rate of reduction changes depending on the vesting period. The longer the vesting period, the more significant the impact of forfeitures will be, illustrating once again the nonlinear interacting relationship between vesting and forfeitures (i.e., the lines in Figure 14.40 are curved and nonlinear). This is intuitive because the longer the vesting period, the lower the compounded probability that an employee will still be employed in the firm and the higher the chances of forfeiture, reducing the expected value of the option.

Again, we see that the BSM result is the highest possible value assuming a 10-year vesting in a 10-year maturity option with zero forfeiture (Figure 14.40). In addition, forfeiture rates can be negatively correlated to stock price—if the firm is doing well, its stock price usually increases, making the option more valuable and making the employees less likely to leave and the firm less likely to lay off its employees. Because the rate of forfeitures is uncertain (forfeiture rate fluctuations typically occur in the past due to business and economic environments, and will most certainly fluctuate again in the future) and is negatively correlated to the stock price, we can also apply a correlated Monte Carlo simulation on forfeiture rates in conjunction with the customized binomial lattices (shown later in this case study). The BSM will always generate the maximum option value assuming all options will

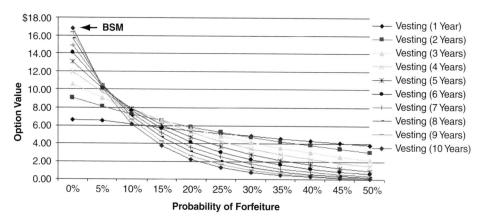

FIGURE 14.40　Impact of forfeiture rates and vesting on option value in the binomial model. (Assumptions used: stock and strike price of $25, 10-year maturity, 5% risk-free rate, 50% volatility, 0% dividends, suboptimal behavior 1.01, vesting period of 1–10 years, forfeiture range 0–50%, and tested with 100–5,000 binomial lattice steps.)

fully vest and will overexpense the option significantly. The ESO Valuation software can account for forfeiture rates, while the accompanying Super Lattice Solver can account for different prevesting and postvesting forfeiture rates in the lattices.

Options Where Risk-Free Rate Changes Over Time

Another input assumption is the risk-free rate. Figure 14.41 illustrates the effects of changing risk-free rates over time on option valuation. When other exotic inputs are added, the changing risk-free lattice model has an overall lower valuation. In addition, due to the time value of money, discounting more heavily in the future will reduce the option's value. In other words, Figure 14.41 compares an upward sloping yield curve, a downward sloping yield curve, risk-free rate smile, and risk-free rate frown. When the term structure of interest rates increases over time, the option value calculated using a customized changing risk-free rate binomial lattice is lower ($24.31) than that calculated using an average of the changing risk-free rates ($25.92) base case. The reverse is true for a downward-sloping yield curve. In addition, Figure 14.41 shows a risk-free yield curve frown (low rates followed by high rates followed by low rates) and a risk-free yield curve smile (high rates followed by low rates followed by high rates). The results indicate that using a single average rate will overestimate an upward-sloping yield curve,

Basic Input Parameters		Year	Static Base Case	Increasing Risk-Free Rates	Decreasing Risk-Free Rates	Risk-Free Rate Smile	Risk-Free Rate Frown
Stock Price	$100.00	1	5.50%	1.00%	10.00%	8.00%	3.50%
Strike Price	$100.00	2	5.50	3.00	9.00	7.00	4.00
Maturity	10.00	3	5.50	3.00	8.00	5.00	5.00
Volatility	45.00	4	5.50	4.00	7.00	4.00	7.00
Dividend Rate	4.00	5	5.50	5.00	6.00	3.50	8.00
Lattice Steps	1000	6	5.50	6.00	5.00	3.50	8.00
Suboptimal Behavior	1.80	7	5.50	7.00	4.00	4.00	7.00
Vesting Period	4.00	8	5.50	8.00	3.00	5.00	5.00
Forfeiture Rate	10.00	9	5.50	9.00	2.00	7.00	4.00
		10	5.50	10.00	1.00	8.00	3.50
		Average	5.50	5.50	5.50	5.50	5.50
BSM using 5.50% Average Rate			$37.45	$37.45	$37.45	$37.45	$37.45
Forfeiture Modified BSM using 5.50% Average Rate			$33.71	$33.71	$33.71	$33.71	$33.71
Changing Risk-Free Binomial Lattice			$25.92	$24.31	$27.59	$26.04	$25.76

FIGURE 14.41 Effects of changing risk-free rates on option value. These results only illustrate a typical case and should not be generalized across all possible case.

underestimate a downward-sloping yield curve, underestimate a yield curve smile, and overestimate a yield curve frown. Therefore, whenever appropriate, use all available information in terms of forward risk-free rates, one rate for each year.

Options Where Volatility Changes Over Time

Figure 14.42 illustrates the effects of changing volatilities on an ESO. If volatility changes over time, the BSM ($71.48) using the average volatility over time will *always* overestimate the true option value when there are other exotic inputs. In addition, compared to the $38.93 base case, slowly increasing volatilities over time from a low level has lower option values, while a decreasing volatility from high values and volatility smiles and frowns have higher values than using the average volatility estimate.

Options Where Dividend Yield Changes Over Time

Dividend yield is a simple input that can be obtained from corporate dividend policies or publicly available historical market data. It is the total dividend payments computed as a percentage of stock price that is paid out over the course of a year. The typical dividend yield is between 0 percent and

Basic Input Parameters		Year	Static Base Case	Increasing Volatilities	Decreasing Volatilities	Volatility Smile	Volatility Frown
Stock Price	$100.00	1	55.00%	10.00%	100.00$	80.00%	35.00%
Strike Price	$100.00	2	55.00	20.00	90.00	70.00	40.00
Maturity	10.00	3	55.00	30.00	80.00	50.00	50.00
Risk-Free Rate	5.50	4	55.00	40.00	70.00	40.00	70.00
Dividend Rate	0.00	5	55.00	50.00	60.00	35.00	80.00
Lattice Steps	10	6	55.00	60.00	50.00	35.00	80.00
Suboptimal Behavior	1.80	7	55.00	70.00	40.00	40.00	70.00
Vesting Period	4.00	8	55.00	80.00	30.00	50.00	50.00
Forfeiture Rate	10.00	9	55.00	90.00	20.00	70.00	40.00
		10	55.00	100.00	10.00	80.00	35.00
		Average	55.00	55.00	55.00	55.00	55.00
BSM using 5.50% Average Rate			$71.48	$71.48	$71.48	$71.48	$71.48
Forfeiture Modified BSM using 5.50% Average Rate			$64.34	$64.34	$64.34	$64.34	$64.34
Changing Risk-Free Binomial Lattice			$38.93	$32.35	$45.96	$39.56	$39.71

FIGURE 14.42   Effects of changing volatilities on option value.

7 percent. In fact, about 45 percent of all publicly traded firms in the United States pay dividends. Of those that pay a dividend, 85 percent have a yield of 7 percent or below, and 95 percent have a yield of 10 percent or below.[20] Dividend yield is an interesting variable with very little interaction with other exotic input variables. It has a close to linear effect on option value, whereas the other exotic input variables do not. For instance, Figure 14.43 illustrates the effects of different maturities on the same option. The higher the maturity, the higher the option value, but the option value increases at a decreasing rate.

Maturity	Option Value	Change
1	$25.16	—
2	32.41	28.84%
3	35.35	9.08
4	36.80	4.08
5	37.87	2.91
6	38.41	1.44
7	38.58	0.43

FIGURE 14.43   Nonlinear effects of maturity. (Assumptions used: stock price and strike price are set at $100, 5% risk-free rate, 75% volatility, and 1,000 steps in the customized lattice, 1.8 behavior multiple, 1-year vesting, 10% forfeiture rate.)

Dividend Rate	1.8 Behavior Multiple, 4-Year Vesting, 10% Forfeiture Rate		1.8 Behavior Multiple, 1-Year Vesting, 10% Forfeiture Rate		3.0 Behavior Multiple, 1-Year Vesting, 10% Forfeiture Rate	
	Option Value	Change	Option Value	Change	Option Value	Change
0%	$42.15		$42.41		$49.07	
1	39.94	−5.24%	41.47	−2.20%	47.67	−2.86%
2	37.84	−5.27	40.55	−2.22	46.29	−2.89
3	35.83	−5.30	39.65	−2.24	44.94	−2.92
4	33.92	−5.33	38.75	−2.26	43.61	−2.95
5	32.10	−5.37	37.87	−2.28	42.31	−2.98

Dividend Rate	$50 Stock Price, 1.8 Behavior Multiple, 1-Year Vesting, 10% Forfeiture Rate		1.8 Behavior Multiple, 1-Year Vesting, 5% Forfeiture Rate	
	Option Value	Change	Option Value	Change
0%	$21.20		$45.46	
1	20.74	−2.20%	44.46	−2.20%
2	20.28	−2.22	43.47	−2.23
3	19.82	−2.24	42.49	−2.25
4	19.37	−2.26	41.53	−2.27
5	18.93	−2.28	40.58	−2.29

FIGURE 14.44   Near-linear effects of dividends.

In contrast, Figure 14.44 illustrates the near-linear effects of dividends even when some of the exotic inputs have been changed. Whatever the change in variable is, the effects of dividends are always very close to linear. While Figure 14.44 illustrates many options with unique dividend rates, Figure 14.45 illustrates the effects of changing dividends over time on a single option. That is, the results shown in Figure 14.44 are based on comparing

Scenario	Option Value	Change	Notes
Static 3% Dividend	$39.65	0.00%	Dividends are kept steady at 3%
Increasing Gradually	$40.94	3.26%	1% to 5% with 1% increments (average of 3%)
Decreasing Gradually	$38.39	−3.17%	5% to 1% with −1% increments (average of 3%)
Increasing Jumps	$41.70	5.19%	0%, 0%, 5%, 5%, 5% (average of 3%)
Decreasing Jumps	$38.16	−3.74%	5%, 5%, 5%, 0%, 0% (average of 3%)

FIGURE 14.45   Effects of changing dividends over time. (Assumptions used: stock price and strike price are set at $100, 5-year maturity, 5% risk-free rate, 75% volatility, 1,000 steps in the customized lattice, 1.8 behavior multiple, 10% forfeiture rate, and 1-year vesting.)

different options with different dividend rates, whereas the results shown in Figure 14.45 are based on a single option whose underlying stock's dividend yields are changing over the life of the option.

Clearly, a changing-dividend option has some value to add in terms of the overall option valuation results. Therefore, if the firm's stock pays a dividend, then the analysis should also consider the possibility of dividend yields changing over the life of the option.

Options Where Blackout Periods Exist

Another item of interest is blackout periods, the dates that ESOs cannot be executed. These dates are usually several weeks before and several weeks after an earnings announcement (usually on a quarterly basis). In addition, only senior executives with fiduciary responsibilities have these blackout dates, and, hence, their proportion is relatively small compared to the rest of the firm. Figure 14.46 illustrates the calculations of a typical ESO with different blackout dates. In the case where there are only a few blackout days a month, there is little difference between options with blackout dates and those without blackout dates. In fact, if the suboptimal exercise behavior multiple is small (a 1.8 ratio is assumed in this case), blackout dates at strategic times will actually prevent the option holder from exercising suboptimally and sometimes even increase the value of the option ever so slightly.

The analysis shown as Figure 14.46 assumes only a small percentage of blackout dates in a year (e.g., during several days in a year, the ESO cannot be executed). This may be the case for certain so-called brick-and-mortar companies, and, as such, blackout dates can be ignored. However, in other firms such as those in the biotechnology and high-tech industries, blackout periods play a more significant role. For instance, in a biotech firm, blackout

Blackout Dates	Option Value
No Blackouts	$43.16
Every 2 years evenly spaced	43.16
First 5 years annual blackouts only	43.26
Last 5 years annual blackouts only	43.16
Every 3 months for 10 years	43.26

FIGURE 14.46 Effects of blackout periods on option value. (Assumptions used: stock and strike price of $100, 75% volatility, 5% risk-free rate, 10-year maturity, no dividends, 1-year vesting, 10% forfeiture rate, and 1,000 lattice steps.)

% Difference between no blackout periods versus significant blackouts	Volatility (25%)	Volatility (30%)	Volatility (35%)	Volatility (40%)	Volatility (45%)	Volatility (50%)
Forfeiture Rate (5%)	−17.33%	−13.18%	−10.26%	−9.21%	−7.11%	−5.95%
Forfeiture Rate (6%)	−19.85%	−15.17%	−11.80%	−10.53%	−8.20%	−6.84%
Forfeiture Rate (7%)	−22.20%	−17.06%	−13.29%	−11.80%	−9.25%	−7.70%
Forfeiture Rate (8%)	−24.40%	−18.84%	−14.71%	−13.03%	−10.27%	−8.55%
Forfeiture Rate (9%)	−26.44%	−20.54%	−16.07%	−14.21%	−11.26%	−9.37%
Forfeiture Rate (10%)	−28.34%	−22.15%	−17.38%	−15.35%	−12.22%	−10.17%
Forfeiture Rate (11%)	−30.12%	−23.67%	−18.64%	−16.45%	−13.15%	−10.94%
Forfeiture Rate (12%)	−31.78%	−25.11%	−19.84%	−17.51%	−14.05%	−11.70%
Forfeiture Rate (13%)	−33.32%	−26.48%	−21.00%	−18.53%	−14.93%	−12.44%
Forfeiture Rate (14%)	−34.77%	−27.78%	−22.11%	−19.51%	−15.78%	−13.15%
Forfeiture Rate (14%)	−34.77%	−27.78%	−22.11%	−19.51%	−15.78%	−13.15%

FIGURE 14.47 Effects of significant blackouts (different forfeiture rates and volatilities). (Assumptions used: stock and strike price range of $30 to $100, 45% volatility, 5% risk-free rate, 10-year maturity, dividend range 0–10%, vesting of 1–4 years, 5–14% forfeiture rate, suboptimal exercise behavior multiple range of 1.8–3.0, and 1,000 lattice steps.)

periods may extend 4–6 weeks every quarter, straddling the release of its quarterly earnings. In addition, blackout periods prior to the release of a new product may exist. Therefore, the proportion of blackout dates with respect to the life of the option may reach upward of 35–65 percent per year. In such cases, blackout periods will significantly affect the value of the option. For instance, Figure 14.47 illustrates the differences between a customized binomial lattice with and without blackout periods. By adding in the real-life elements of blackout periods, the ESO value is further reduced by anywhere between 10 percent and 35 percent depending on the rate of forfeiture and volatility. As expected, the reduction in value is nonlinear, as the effects of blackout periods will vary depending on the other input variables involved in the analysis.

Figure 14.48 shows the effects of blackouts under different dividend yields and vesting periods, while Figure 14.49 illustrates the results stemming from different dividend yields and suboptimal exercise behavior multiples. Clearly, it is almost impossible to predict the exact impact unless a detailed analysis is performed, but the range can be generalized to be typically between 10 percent and 20 percent. Blackout periods can only be modeled in a binomial lattice and not in the BSM/GBM.

% Difference between no blackout periods versus significant blackouts	Vesting (1)	Vesting (2)	Vesting (3)	Vesting (4)
Dividends (0%)	−8.62%	−6.93%	−5.59%	−4.55%
Dividends (1%)	−9.04%	−7.29%	−5.91%	−4.84%
Dividends (2%)	−9.46%	−7.66%	−6.24%	−5.13%
Dividends (3%)	−9.90%	−8.03%	−6.56%	−5.43%
Dividends (4%)	−10.34%	−8.41%	−6.90%	−5.73%
Dividends (5%)	−10.80%	−8.79%	−7.24%	−6.04%
Dividends (6%)	−11.26%	−9.18%	−7.58%	−6.35%
Dividends (7%)	−11.74%	−9.58%	−7.93%	−6.67%
Dividends (8%)	−12.22%	−9.99%	−8.29%	−6.99%
Dividends (9%)	−12.71%	−10.40%	−8.65%	−7.31%
Dividends (10%)	−13.22%	−10.81%	−9.01%	−7.64%

FIGURE 14.48 Effects of significant blackouts (different dividend yields and vesting periods).

Nonmarketability Issues

The 2004 FAS 123 revision does not explicitly discuss the issue of nonmarketability; that is, ESOs are neither directly transferable to someone else nor freely tradable in the open market. Under such circumstances, it can be argued based on sound financial and economic theory that a nontradable and nonmarketable discount can be appropriately applied to the ESO. However, this is not a simple task.

A simple and direct application of a discount should not be based on an arbitrarily chosen percentage *haircut* on the resulting binomial lattice result. Instead, a more rigorous analysis can be performed using a *put option*. A call option is the contractual right, but not the obligation, to *purchase* the underlying stock at some predetermined contractual strike price within a specified time, while a put option is a contractual right, but not the obligation, to *sell* the underlying stock at some predetermined contractual price within a specified time. Therefore, if the holder of the ESO cannot sell or transfer the rights of the option to someone else, then the holder of the option has given up his or her rights to a put option (i.e., the employee has written or sold the firm a put option). Calculating the put option and discounting this value from the call option provides a theoretically correct and justifiable nonmarketability and nontransferability discount to the existing option.

However, care should be taken in analyzing this haircut or discounting feature. The same inputs that go into the customized binomial lattice to

FIGURE 14.49 Effects of significant blackouts (different dividend yields and exercise behaviors).

% Difference between no blackout periods versus significant blackouts	Dividends (0%)	Dividends (1%)	Dividends (2%)	Dividends (3%)	Dividends (4%)	Dividends (5%)	Dividends (6%)	Dividends (7%)	Dividends (8%)	Dividends (9%)	Dividends (10%)
Suboptimal Behavior Multiple (1.8)	-1.01%	-1.29%	-1.58%	-1.87%	-2.16%	-2.45%	-2.75%	-3.06%	-3.36%	-3.67%	-3.98%
Suboptimal Behavior Multiple (1.9)	-1.01%	-1.29%	-1.58%	-1.87%	-2.16%	-2.45%	-2.75%	-3.06%	-3.36%	-3.67%	-3.98%
Suboptimal Behavior Multiple (2.0)	-1.87%	-2.29%	-2.72%	-3.15%	-3.59%	-4.04%	-4.50%	-4.96%	-5.42%	-5.90%	-6.38%
Suboptimal Behavior Multiple (2.1)	-1.87%	-2.29%	-2.72%	-3.15%	-3.59%	-4.04%	-4.50%	-4.96%	-5.42%	-5.90%	-6.38%
Suboptimal Behavior Multiple (2.2)	-4.71%	-5.05%	-5.39%	-5.74%	-6.10%	-6.46%	-6.82%	-7.19%	-7.57%	-7.95%	-8.34%
Suboptimal Behavior Multiple (2.3)	-4.71%	-5.05%	-5.39%	-5.74%	-6.10%	-6.46%	-6.82%	-7.19%	-7.57%	-7.95%	-8.34%
Suboptimal Behavior Multiple (2.4)	-4.71%	-5.05%	-5.39%	-5.74%	-6.10%	-6.46%	-6.82%	-7.19%	-7.57%	-7.95%	-8.23%
Suboptimal Behavior Multiple (2.5)	-6.34%	-6.80%	-7.28%	-7.77%	-8.26%	-8.76%	-9.27%	-9.79%	-10.32%	-10.86%	-11.41%
Suboptimal Behavior Multiple (2.7)	-6.34%	-6.80%	-7.28%	-7.77%	-8.26%	-8.76%	-9.27%	-9.79%	-10.32%	-10.86%	-11.41%
Suboptimal Behavior Multiple (2.8)	-6.34%	-6.80%	-7.28%	-7.77%	-8.26%	-8.76%	-9.27%	-9.79%	-10.32%	10.86%	-11.41%
Suboptimal Behavior Multiple (2.9)	-8.62%	-9.04%	-9.46%	-9.90%	-10.34%	-10.80%	-11.26%	-11.74%	-12.22%	-12.71%	-13.22%
Suboptimal Behavior Multiple (3.0)	-8.62%	-9.04%	-9.46%	-9.90%	-10.34%	-10.80%	-11.26%	-11.74%	-12.22%	-12.71%	-13.22%

Customized Binomial Lattice (Option Valuation)	Behavior (1.20)	Behavior (1.40)	Behavior (1.60)	Behavior (1.80)	Behavior (2.00)	Behavior (2.20)	Behavior (2.40)	Behavior (2.60)	Behavior (2.80)	Behavior (3.00)
Forfeiture (0.00%)	$24.57	$30.53	$36.16	$39.90	$43.15	$45.87	$48.09	$49.33	$50.40	$51.31
Forfeiture (4.00%)	$22.69	$27.65	$32.19	$35.15	$37.67	$39.74	$41.42	$42.34	$43.13	$43.80
Forfeiture (10.00%)	$21.04	$25.22	$28.93	$31.29	$33.27	$34.88	$36.16	$36.86	$37.45	$37.94
Forfeiture (15.00%)	$19.58	$23.13	$26.20	$28.11	$29.69	$30.94	$31.93	$32.46	$32.91	$33.29
Forfeiture (20.00%)	$18.28	$21.32	$23.88	$25.44	$26.71	$27.70	$28.48	$28.89	$29.23	$29.52
Forfeiture (25.00%)	$17.10	$19.73	$21.89	$23.17	$24.20	$25.00	$25.61	$25.93	$26.19	$26.41
Forfeiture (30.00%)	$16.02	$18.31	$20.14	$21.21	$22.06	$22.70	$23.19	$23.44	$23.65	$23.82
Forfeiture (35.00%)	$15.04	$17.04	$18.61	$19.51	$20.20	$20.73	$21.12	$21.32	$21.49	$21.62
Forfeiture (40.00%)	$14.13	$15.89	$17.24	$18.00	$18.58	$19.01	$19.33	$19.49	$19.63	$19.73

FIGURE 14.50 Customized binomial lattice valuation results. (Assumptions used: stock and strike price of $100, 10-year maturity, 1-year vesting, 35% volatility, 0% dividends, 5% risk-free rate, suboptimal exercise behavior multiple range of 1.2–3.0, forfeiture range of 0–40%, and 1,000 step customized lattice.)

calculate a call option should also be used to calculate a customized binomial lattice for a put option. That is, the put option must also be under the same risks (volatility that can change over time), economic environment (risk-free rate structure that can change over time), corporate financial policy (a static or changing dividend yield over the life of the option), contractual obligations (vesting, maturity, strike price, and blackout dates), investor irrationality (suboptimal exercise behavior), firm performance (stock price at grant date), and so forth.

Although nonmarketability discounts or haircuts are not explicitly discussed in FAS 123, the valuation analysis is performed here for the sake of completeness. It is up to each firm's management to decide if haircuts should and can be applied. Figure 14.50 shows the customized binomial lattice valuation results of a typical ESO. Figure 14.51 shows the results from a nonmarketability analysis performed using a down-and-in upper barrier modified put option with the same exotic inputs (vesting, blackouts, forfeitures, suboptimal behavior, and so forth) calculated using the customized binomial lattice model.[21] The discounts range from 22 percent to 53 percent. These calculated discounts look somewhat significant but are actually in line with market expectations.[22] As these discounts are not explicitly sanctioned by FASB, the author cautions their use in determining the fair-market value of the ESOs.

Haircut (Customized Binomial Lattice Modified Put)	Behavior (1.20)	Behavior (1.40)	Behavior (1.60)	Behavior (1.80)	Behavior (2.00)	Behavior (2.20)	Behavior (2.40)	Behavior (2.60)	Behavior (2.80)	Behavior (3.00)
Forfeiture (0.00%)	$11.33	$11.33	$11.33	$11.33	$11.33	$11.33	$11.33	$11.33	$11.33	$11.33
Forfeiture (5.00%)	$10.76	$10.76	$10.76	$10.76	$10.76	$10.76	$10.76	$10.76	$10.76	$10.76
Forfeiture (10.00%)	$10.23	$10.23	$10.23	$10.23	$10.23	$10.23	$10.23	$10.23	$10.23	$10.23
Forfeiture (15.00%)	$9.72	$9.72	$9.72	$9.72	$9.72	$9.72	$9.72	$9.72	$9.72	$9.72
Forfeiture (20.00%)	$9.23	$9.23	$9.23	$9.23	$9.23	$9.23	$9.23	$9.23	$9.23	$9.23
Forfeiture (25.00%)	$8.77	$8.77	$8.77	$8.77	$8.77	$8.77	$8.77	$8.77	$8.77	$8.77
Forfeiture (30.00%)	$8.34	$8.34	$8.34	$8.34	$8.34	$8.34	$8.34	$8.34	$8.34	$8.34
Forfeiture (35.00%)	$7.92	$7.92	$7.92	$7.92	$7.92	$7.92	$7.92	$7.92	$7.92	$7.92
Forfeiture (40.00%)	$7.52	$7.52	$7.52	$7.52	$7.52	$7.52	$7.52	$7.52	$7.52	$7.52

Nonmarketability and Nontransferability Discount (%)	Behavior (1.20)	Behavior (1.40)	Behavior (1.60)	Behavior (1.80)	Behavior (2.00)	Behavior (2.20)	Behavior (2.40)	Behavior (2.60)	Behavior (2.80)	Behavior (3.00)
Forfeiture (0.00%)	46.09%	37.09%	31.32%	28.39%	26.25%	24.69%	23.55%	22.96%	22.47%	22.07%
Forfeiture (5.00%)	47.43%	38.92%	33.43%	30.62%	28.57%	27.08%	25.98%	25.42%	24.95%	24.57%
Forfeiture (10.00%)	48.60%	40.55%	35.35%	32.68%	30.73%	29.32%	28.28%	27.75%	27.31%	26.95%
Forfeiture (15.00%)	49.62%	42.01%	37.08%	34.57%	32.73%	31.40%	30.43%	29.93%	29.53%	29.19%
Forfeiture (20.00%)	50.52%	43.31%	38.66%	36.29%	34.57%	33.33%	32.42%	31.96%	31.59%	31.28%
Forfeiture (25.00%)	51.32%	44.48%	40.09%	37.86%	36.25%	35.10%	34.26%	33.84%	33.49%	33.22%
Forfeiture (30.00%)	52.03%	45.53%	41.38%	39.29%	37.79%	36.72%	35.95%	35.56%	35.25%	35.00%
Forfeiture (35.00%)	52.67%	46.48%	42.56%	40.60%	39.20%	38.21%	37.50%	37.15%	36.86%	36.63%
Forfeiture (40.00%)	53.24%	47.34%	43.64%	41.80%	40.49%	39.57%	38.92%	38.60%	38.34%	38.14%

FIGURE 14.51 Nonmarketability and nontransferability discount.

Expected Life Analysis

As seen previously, the 2004 Final FAS 123 Sections A15 and B64 expressly prohibit the use of a modified BSM with a single expected life. This means that instead of using an expected life as the *input* into the BSM to obtain the similar results as in a customized binomial lattice, the analysis should be done the other way around. That is, using vesting requirements, suboptimal exercise behavior multiples, forfeiture or employee turnover rates, and the other standard option inputs, calculate the valuation results using the customized binomial lattice. This result can then be compared with a modified BSM and the expected life can then be *imputed*. Excel's goal-seek function

Customized Binomial Lattice Results to Impute the Expected Life for BSM
Applying Different Suboptimal Behavior Multiples

Stock Price	$20.00	$20.00	$20.00	$20.00	$20.00	$20.00	$20.00
Strike Price	$20.00	$20.00	$20.00	$20.00	$20.00	$20.00	$20.00
Maturity	10.00	10.00	10.00	10.00	10.00	10.00	10.00
Risk-Free Rate	3.50%	3.50%	3.50%	3.50%	3.50%	3.50%	3.50%
Dividend	0.00%	0.00%	0.00%	0.00%	0.00%	0.00%	0.00%
Volatility	50.00%	50.00%	50.00%	50.00%	50.00%	50.00%	50.00%
Vesting	4.00	4.00	4.00	4.00	4.00	4.00	4.00
Suboptimal Behavior	**1.10**	**1.50**	**2.00**	**2.50**	**3.00**	**3.50**	**4.00**
Forfeiture Rate	0.00%	0.00%	0.00%	0.00%	0.00%	0.00%	0.00%
Lattice Steps	1000	1000	1000	1000	1000	1000	1000
Binomial	$8.94	$10.28	$11.03	$11.62	$11.89	$12.18	$12.29
BSM	$12.87	$12.87	$12.87	$12.87	$12.87	$12.87	$12.87
Expected Life	*4.42*	*5.94*	*6.95*	*7.83*	*8.26*	*8.74*	*8.93*
Modified BSM	$8.94	$10.28	$11.03	$11.62	$11.89	$12.18	$12.29

FIGURE 14.52   Imputing the expected life for the BSM using the binomial lattice results.

can be used to obtain the imputed expected life of the option by setting the BSM result equal to the customized binomial lattice. The resulting expected life can then be compared with historical data as a secondary verification of the results, that is, if the expected life falls within reasonable bounds based on historical performance. This is the correct approach because measuring the expected life of an option is very difficult and inaccurate.

Figure 14.52 illustrates the use of Excel's goal-seek function on the ESO Valuation Toolkit software to impute the expected life into the BSM model by setting the BSM results equal to the customized binomial lattice results.

Figure 14.53 illustrates another case where the expected life can be imputed, but this time the forfeiture rates are not set at zero. In this case, the BSM results will need to be modified. For example, the customized binomial lattice result of $5.41 is obtained with a 15 percent forfeiture rate. This means that the BSM result needs to be BSM(1−15%) = $5.41 using the modified expected life method. The expected life that yields the BSM value of $6.36 ($5.41/85% is $6.36, and $6.36(1−15%) is $5.41) is 2.22 years.

Dilution

In most cases, the effects of dilution can be safely ignored as the proportion of ESO grants is relatively small compared to the total equity issued by the company. In investment finance theory, the market has already anticipated

Customized Binomial Lattice Results to Impute the Expected Life for BSM
Applying Different Forfeiture Rates

Stock Price	$20.00	$20.00	$20.00	$20.00	$20.00	$20.00	$20.00
Strike Price	$20.00	$20.00	$20.00	$20.00	$20.00	$20.00	$20.00
Maturity	10.00	10.00	10.00	10.00	10.00	10.00	10.00
Risk-Free Rate	3.50%	3.50%	3.50%	3.50%	3.50%	3.50%	3.50%
Dividend	0.00%	0.00%	0.00%	0.00%	0.00%	0.00%	0.00%
Volatility	50.00%	50.00%	50.00%	50.00%	50.00%	50.00%	50.00%
Vesting	4.00	4.00	4.00	4.00	4.00	4.00	4.00
Suboptimal Behavior	1.50	1.50	1.50	1.50	1.50	1.50	1.50
Forfeiture Rate	0.00%	.250%	5.00%	7.50%	10.00%	12.50%	15.00%
Lattice Steps	1000	1000	1000	1000	1000	1000	1000
Binomial	$10.28	$9.23	$8.29	$7.44	$6.69	$6.02	$5.41
BSM	$12.87	$12.87	$12.87	$12.87	$12.87	$12.87	$12.87
Expected Life	*5.94*	*4.71*	*3.77*	*3.03*	*2.45*	*1.99*	*1.61*
Modified BSM*	$10.28	$9.23	$8.29	$7.44	$6.69	$6.02	$5.41
Expected Life	*5.94*	*4.97*	*4.19*	*3.55*	*3.02*	*2.59*	*2.22*
Modified BSM**	$10.28	$9.23	$8.29	$7.44	$6.69	$6.02	$5.41

*Note: Uses the binomial lattice result to impute the expected life for a modified BSM.
**Note: Uses the binomial lattice but also accounts for the forfeiture rate to modify the BSM.

FIGURE 14.53 Imputing expected life for the BSM using lattice results under nonzero forfeiture rates.

the exercise of these ESOs and the effects have already been accounted for in the stock price. Once a new grant is announced, the stock price will immediately and fully incorporate this news and account for any dilution that may occur. This means that as long as the valuation is performed after the announcement is made, then the effects of dilution are nonexistent. The 2004 FAS 123 revisions do not explicitly provide guidance in this area. Given that FASB provides little guidance on dilution (Section A39), and because forecasting stock prices (as part of estimating the effects of dilution) is fairly difficult and inaccurate at best, plus the fact that the dilution effects are minimal (small in proportion compared to all the equity issued by the firm), the effects of dilution are assumed to be minimal and can be safely ignored.

Applying Monte Carlo Simulation for Statistical Confidence and Precision Control

Next, Monte Carlo simulation can be applied to obtain a range of calculated stock option fair values. That is, any of the inputs into the stock options valuation model can be chosen for Monte Carlo simulation if they are uncertain and stochastic. Distributional assumptions are assigned to these variables, and the resulting option values using the BSM, GBM, path simulation, or binomial lattices are selected as forecast cells. These modeled uncertainties include the probability of forfeiture and the employees' suboptimal exercise behavior.

The results of the simulation are essentially a distribution of the stock option values. Keep in mind that the simulation application here is used to vary the inputs to an options valuation model to obtain a range of results, not to model and calculate the options themselves. However, simulation can be applied both to simulate the inputs to obtain the range of options results and to solve the options model through path-dependent simulation. For instance, the simulated input assumptions are those inputs that are highly uncertain and can vary in the future, such as stock price at grant date, volatility, forfeiture rates, and suboptimal exercise behavior multiples. Clearly, variables that are objectively obtained, such as risk-free rates (U.S. Treasury yields for the next 1 month to 20 years are published), dividend yield (determined from corporate strategy), vesting period, strike price, and blackout periods (determined contractually in the option grant) should not be simulated. In addition, the simulated input assumptions can be correlated. For instance, forfeiture rates can be negatively correlated to stock price—if the firm is doing well, its stock price usually increases, making the option more valuable, thus making the employees less likely to leave and the firm less likely to lay off its employees. Finally, the output forecasts are the option valuation results. In fact, Monte Carlo simulation is allowed and recommended in FAS 123 (Sections B64, B65, and footnotes 48, 52, 74, and 97).

Figure 14.54 shows the results obtained using the customized binomial lattices based on single-point inputs of all the variables. The model takes exotic inputs such as vesting, forfeiture rates, suboptimal exercise behavior multiples, blackout periods, and changing inputs (dividends, risk-free rates, and volatilities) over time. The resulting option value is $31.42. This analysis can then be extended to include simulation. Figure 14.55 illustrates the use of simulation coupled with customized binomial lattices (Risk Simulator software was used to simulate the input variables).

Rather than randomly deciding on the correct number of trials to run in the simulation, statistical significance and precision control are set up to run the required number of trials automatically. A 99.9 percent statistical confidence on a $0.01 error precision control was selected and 145,510 simulation trials were run.[23] This highly stringent set of parameters means that an adequate number of trials will be run to ensure that the results will fall within a $0.01 error variability 99.9 percent of the time. For instance, the simulated average result was $31.32 (Figure 14.55). This means that 999 out of 1,000 times, the true option value will be accurate to within $0.01 of $31.32. These measures are statistically valid and objective.[24]

Risk-Free Rate		Volatility		Dividend Yield		Suboptimal Behavior	
Year	Rate	Year	Rate	Year	Rate	Year	
1	3.50%	1	35.00%	1	1.00%	1	1.80
2	3.75	2	35.00	2	1.00	2	1.80
3	4.00	3	35.00	3	1.00	3	1.80
4	4.15	4	45.00	4	1.50	4	1.80
5	4.20	5	45.00	5	1.50	5	1.80

		Forfeiture Rate		Blackout Dates	
		Year	Rate	Month	Step
Stock Price	$100	1	5.00%	12	12
Strike Price	$100	2	5.00	24	24
Time to Maturity	5	3	5.00	36	36
Vesting Period	1	4	5.00	48	48
Lattice Steps	60	5	5.00	60	60
Option value	**$31.42**				

FIGURE 14.54 Single-point result using a customized binomial lattice.

Number of Steps

The higher the number of lattice steps, the higher the precision of the results. Figure 14.56 illustrates the convergence of results obtained using a BSM closed-form model on a European call option without dividends, and comparing its results to the basic binomial lattice. Convergence is generally achieved at 1,000 steps. As such, the analysis results will use 1,000 steps whenever possible.[25] Due to the high number of steps required to generate the results, software-based mathematical algorithms are used.[26] For instance, a nonrecombining binomial lattice with 1,000 steps has a total of

Statistic	Value	Precision
Trials	145,510	
Mean	$31.32	$0.01
Median	$31.43	$0.02
Mode	—	
Standard Deviation	$1.57	$0.01
Variance	$2.46	
Skewness	−0.21	
Kurtosis	2.43	
Coeff. of Variability	0.05	
Range Minimum	$26.59	
Range Maximum	$35.62	
Range Width	$9.03	
Mean Std. Error	$0.00	

*Tested for $0.01 precision at 99.90% confidence.

FIGURE 14.55 Options valuation result at $0.01 precision with 99.9 percent confidence.

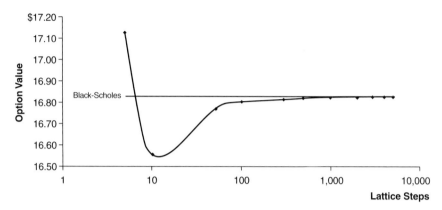

FIGURE 14.56   Convergence of the binomial lattice to closed-form solutions.

2×10^{301} nodal calculations to perform, making manual computation impossible without the use of specialized algorithms.[27] Figure 14.57 illustrates the calculation of convergence by using progressively higher lattice steps. The progression is based on sets of 120 steps (12 months per year multiplied by 10 years). The results are tabulated and the median of the average results is calculated. It shows that 4,200 steps is the best estimate in this customized binomial lattice, and this input is used throughout the analysis.[28]

Conclusion

It has been more than 30 years since Fischer Black, Myron Scholes, and Robert Merton derived their option pricing model, and significant advancements have been made; therefore, do not restrict stock option pricing to one specific model (the BSM/GBM) while a plethora of other models and applications can be explored. The three mainstream approaches to valuing stock options are closed-form models (e.g., BSM, GBM, and American option approximation models), Monte Carlo simulation, and binomial lattices. The BSM and GBM will typically *overstate* the fair value of ESOs where there is suboptimal early exercise behavior coupled with vesting requirements and option forfeitures. In fact, firms using the BSM and GBM to value and expense ESOs may be *significantly* overstating their true expense. The BSM requires many underlying assumptions before it works and, as such, has significant limitations, including being applicable only for European options without dividends. In addition, American option approximation models are very complex and difficult to create in a spreadsheet. The BSM *cannot* account for American options, options based on stocks that pay dividends (the GBM model can, however, account for dividends

Stock Price	$45.17	$45.17	$45.17	$45.17	$45.17	$45.17	$45.17	$45.17	$45.17	$45.17	$45.17	$45.17	$45.17	$45.17
Strike Price	$45.17	$45.17	$45.17	$45.17	$45.17	$45.17	$45.17	$45.17	$45.17	$45.17	$45.17	$45.17	$45.17	$45.17
Maturity	10	10	10	10	10	10	10	10	10	10	10	10	10	10
Risk-Free Rate	1.21%	1.21%	1.21%	1.21%	1.21%	1.21%	1.21%	1.21%	1.21%	1.21%	1.21%	1.21%	1.21%	1.21%
Volatility	49.91%	49.91%	49.91%	49.91%	49.91%	49.91%	49.91%	49.91%	49.941%	49.91%	49.91%	49.91%	49.91%	49.91%
Dividend	0%	0%	0%	0%	0%	0%	0%	0%	0%	0%	0%	0%	0%	0%
Lattice Steps	10	50	100	120	600	1200	1800	2400	3000	3600	4200	4800	5400	6000
Suboptimal Behavior	1.8531	1.8531	1.8531	1.8531	1.8531	1.8531	1.8531	1.8531	1.8531	1.8531	1.8531	1.8531	1.8531	1.8531
Vesting	0.08	0.08	0.08	0.08	0.08	0.08	0.08	0.08	0.08	0.08	0.08	0.08	0.08	0.08
Binomial Option Value	$20.55	$17.82	$17.32	$18.55	$17.55	$13.08	$13.11	$12.93	$12.88	$12.91	$13.00	$13.08	$12.93	$13.06

Segments	Steps	Results	Average
1	120	$18.55	$13.91
5	600	$17.55	$13.48
10	1200	$13.08	$13.00
15	1800	$13.11	$12.99
20	2400	$12.93	$12.97
25	3000	$12.83	$12.99
30	3600	$12.91	$13.00
35	4200	$13.00	$13.02
40	4800	$13.03	$12.99
45	5400	$12.93	$13.06
50	6000	$13.06	
		Median	$13.00

FIGURE 14.57 Convergence of the customized binomial lattice.

in a European option), forfeitures, underperformance, stock price barriers, vesting periods, changing business environments and volatilities, suboptimal early exercise behavior, and a slew of other conditions. Monte Carlo simulation when used alone is another option valuation approach, but is restricted only to European options. Simulation can be used in two different ways: to solve the option's fair-market value through path simulations of stock prices, or used in conjunction with other approaches (e.g., binomial lattices and closed-form models) to capture multiple sources of uncertainty in the model.

Binomial lattices are flexible and easy to implement. They are capable of valuing American-type stock options with dividends but require computational power. Software applications should be used to facilitate this computation. Binomial lattices can be used to calculate American options paying dividends and can be easily adapted to solve ESOs with exotic inputs and used in conjunction with Monte Carlo simulation to account for the uncertain input assumptions (e.g., probabilities of forfeiture, suboptimal exercise behavior, vesting, underperformance) and to obtain a high precision at statistically valid confidence intervals. Based on the analyses throughout the case study, it is recommended that the use of a model that assumes an ESO is European style when, in fact, the option is American style with the other exotic variables should not be permitted, as this substantially overstates compensation expense. Many factors influence the fair-market value of ESOs, and a binomial lattice approach to valuation that considers these factors should be used. With due diligence, real-life ESOs can absolutely be valued using the customized binomial lattice approach as shown in this case study, where the methodology employed is pragmatic, accurate, and theoretically sound.

CASE STUDY: OIL AND GAS ROYALTY LEASE NEGOTIATION

This case was contributed by David Mercier, vice president of corporate development at Bonanza Creek Energy. Mr. Mercier has executive experience in starting, financing, and selling businesses. As the chief of finance, economics, and accounting for the California State Lands Commission Mineral Resources Division, he was responsible for maximizing the value of more than 20,000 barrels of oil per day. His responsibilities included profit-sharing negotiations, crude oil and natural gas marketing, royalty accounting, financial review of lease assignments, financial risk management, and revenue forecasting and budgeting. In short, with more than 20 years of experience, Mr. Mercier has worked in every aspect of the energy business.

He has published and presented numerous technical papers and has written case studies for risk modeling text books. He has presented many papers throughout the United States on maximizing value using a royalty rate that slides with oil price. California was the first state to employ this type of royalty. He is a member of the Society of Petroleum Engineers and was a California Natural Gas Committee member. Prior to joining the State Lands Commission, Mr. Mercier worked as an environmental consultant for TRC, a process engineer for Mobil Oil Company, and a commodity trader. He is an active member of and donor to the Autism Society of America. He holds a B.S. degree in petroleum engineering, University of Southern California (USC), an M.B.A. degree (finance), is Certified in Risk Management (CRM), and completed the SDRM (Strategic Decision and Risk Management) program at Stanford University.

Background

Since 1938, the California State Lands Commission (SLC, or "Commission") has had exclusive jurisdiction over the leasing of oil and gas from offshore state lands. In March 2005, Plains Exploration & Production Company (PXP) applied to the California State Lands Commission and County of Santa Barbara for a new state lease and onshore permits to allow development of the Tranquillon Ridge field, located in state waters offshore from Vandenberg Air Force Base. PXP plans to use an existing platform, Platform Irene, which is currently used to produce oil and gas from the adjacent Pt. Pedernales field, in federal waters (Figure 14.58). Like the oil produced from Pt. Pedernales, oil produced from Tranquillon Ridge would be sent to shore by pipeline and processed at the Lompoc Oil and Gas Plant (LOGP); therefore, no new construction. However, the project requires a new state lease

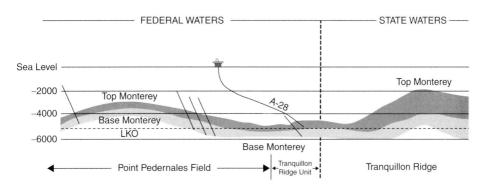

FIGURE 14.58 Picture of the development.

to allow "extended reach drilling" from Platform Irene into the Tranquillon Ridge field.

The lease could be issued under an exception to the California Coastal Sanctuary Act (1984), which allows a new lease if oil or gas from state-owned tide and submerged lands "are being drained by means of producing wells upon adjacent federal lands and the lease is in the best interests of the state" (Pub. Res. Code §6244.). In this case, PXP is draining oil and gas from state tide and submerged lands from wells drilled on Platform Irene. The parties to the Settlement Agreement believe the provisions that have been negotiated are in the best interests of the state, not only because they provide specific environmental benefits, but also because they set a new precedent for full mitigation of the impact of industrial development in the county and the state.

The Agreement

A previous proposal to develop the Tranquillon Ridge Field, by Nuevo Energy Company, was opposed by local environmental groups and denied by the County of Santa Barbara in 2002. When PXP made a similar proposal, the environmental groups again raised objections, based on the fact that the drilling operations would extend the life of the existing facilities. PXP responded by agreeing to include a termination date for the Tranquillon Ridge Project. This commitment goes well beyond any legal requirements, which allow oil companies to continue operations so long as they are producing commercially viable quantities of oil and gas.

The Environmental Defense Center (EDC), Get Oil Out! (GOO!), and Citizens Planning Association of Santa Barbara (CPA) signed an historic and unprecedented agreement in Santa Barbara, California. The agreement allowed for development by PXP of the Tranquillon Ridge Oil and Gas Field offshore Lompoc, while curtailing the life of existing oil and gas operations.

In addition to the royalty schedule, PXP agreed to the following:

- The Tranquillon Ridge Project will include an "end date" that will prohibit any extension of the life of existing oil and gas operations.
- PXP will phase out other oil and gas production operations in the county, both offshore near Pt. Arguello and Pt. Conception and onshore near Lompoc.
- All greenhouse gas emissions from the Tranquillon Ridge Project will be mitigated or offset, resulting in carbon neutrality.
- PXP will donate an additional $1,500,000 to reduce greenhouse gas emissions in the county.

- PXP will convey approximately 3,900 acres of land, including approximately 3,700 acres adjacent to the Burton Mesa Ecological Reserve in the Lompoc Valley and up to 200 acres on the Gaviota Coast, for the benefit of the public.

The Negotiated Royalty Rate Schedule

The California State Lands Commission (CSLC) finance and economics chief, David Mercier, together with Dr. Johnathan Mun ("Consultant"), designed, evaluated, and negotiated the royalty schedule illustrated in Figure 14.59 with PXP.

Why Use a Priced-Based Sliding Scale Royalty?

In the United States, oil and gas property owners typically charge the producer a royalty rate, with the most common being 16.7 percent of the gross revenue. The initial analysis illustrated the benefits of using an oil price-based sliding scale royalty: The royalty rate is low when the price is low and vice versa. This type of royalty schedule can benefit both the royalty owner and operator by encouraging operator investment, mitigating royalty-induced production drops, and lowering the likelihood of abandonment. Increasing

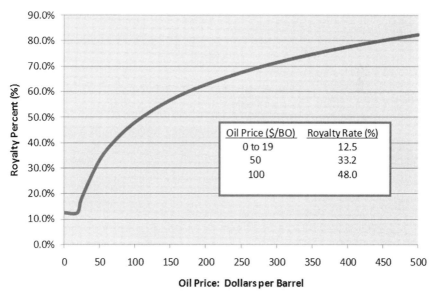

Oil Price ($/BO)	Royalty Rate (%)
0 to 19	12.5
50	33.2
100	48.0

FIGURE 14.59 State royalty rate versus oil price.

the amount of investment in development projects will likely increase the production rate, field value, and royalty revenue:

(*Royalty Revenue = Oil Price * Production Rate * Rate Rate*)

Traditionally, many royalty owners have tried to get the highest fixed royalty rate possible, thinking that a higher rate naturally translates into more royalty revenue. This approach has resulted in royalties that need to be renegotiated when the oil price goes lower than predicted to prevent premature abandonment. Negotiating the highest possible royalty rate the producer will accept should never be the royalty owner's strategy. High royalty rates do not necessarily maximize royalty revenue.

In any profit-sharing agreement the (royalty owner–operator) economic interdependence is large; these negotiations should not be treated as a zero-sum game (like chess) where someone wins and the other loses. When the royalty rate is high and the oil price is low, a royalty owner–operator win-lose relationship usually ends up lose-lose in the long term. The only way the royalty owner can win in the long term is to make sure the royalty rate is low when the price is low and vice versa. This arrangement ensures that the royalty rate is not so high at low oil prices that it triggers premature field abandonment or royalty-induced production drops (lose-lose).

To better understand how the royalty rate affects an operation, it is important to note that an X percent royalty rate has the same effect on an operator's shut-in, drilling, and well-work decisions as an X percent reduction in oil price or an X percent increase in operating costs.

Net profits sharing contracts are progressive systems employed in many places around the world; however, typically, these contracts require the mineral owner to be constantly evaluating the details of the operation. For many operations this additional accounting expense is cost-prohibitive. This continuous auditing of the operation to ensure proper payment can be costly for both the mineral owner and operator. Accounting disputes can often lead to expensive litigation and a serious deterioration of the mineral owner–operator relationship. Huge amounts of value can be lost (for both parties) if the operation's human and financial resources shift focus from optimizing the value of the field to expensive litigation/arbitration. Also, net profit contracts, as compared with royalty contracts, may expose the mineral owner to increased financial liability—the risk of negative cash flow or negative balance. Increased financial risk is not bad when it comes with a proportionate amount of increased benefit. However, because of the strong correlation between operator profits and oil price, a royalty schedule that tracks oil price can provide the same or better (if designed properly) revenue stream without all the administrative costs associated with the typical net-profits types of agreements.

Royalty Design Strategy

The royalty schedule (Figure 14.59) is the result of thousands of scenario combinations and permutations of royalty rates and PXP's IRR as well as other metrics. This royalty schedule was developed to maximize the total NPV of the project, and to the state. At the same time, the constraint is that PXP needs to be profitable given these royalty rates. At royalty rates that are too high, PXP will find the project unprofitable and not proceed with development.

Analysis Steps and Modeling

Building the Decision Model The first step to develop the optimal royalty schedule was building the financial model in Excel. Before building the model, some time was taken to plan the model's structure. A decision diagram provided a high-level blueprint of the model's structure. The decision diagram emphasizes which inputs are used to calculate the results and how the uncertain inputs may be interdependent on each other.

The model flow is sequential, first identifying the input variables (oil price, expense, etc.), then setting up the calculations, and then providing the summary output metrics.

Evaluating the Tornado Diagram After the model was built, a tornado diagram was generated. This is actually a great debugging tool because it varies all of the inputs. The example tornado summary shown in Figure 14.60 details how each input variable affected the state's and PXP's NPV, and which inputs were the most important.

Not surprisingly, the main critical success factors in this project are:

- Oil price
- Royalty rates
- Volume/production risk
- Discount or hurdle rate

Distributional Analysis After identifying which input variables affect the state's and PXP's NPV, the oil price history uncertainty was captured into the model using distributional analysis.

Preliminary Analysis: GARCH Volatility Estimates After understanding the key impact drivers in the model, the focus was on calibrating these variables. Thousands of simulation trials and scenarios were run on these key impact drivers to determine the outcome of the project. In other words,

Tornado Summary

CSLC Precedent Cell	Base Value: 2766.89539618279			Input Changes		
	Output Downside	Output Upside	Effective Range	Input Downside	Input Upside	Base Case Value
Royalty Function (H7)	$ 2,199	$ 3,335	$ 1,137	0.19	0.24	0.21
Oil Price	$ 2,373	$ 3,173	$ 800	90.00	110.00	100.00
Royalty Function (H6)	$ 3,059	$ 2,475	$ 583	0.46	0.56	0.51
Volume Risking	$ 2,490	$ 3,044	$ 553	0.90	1.10	1.00
SLC Discount Rate	$ 2,919	$ 2,625	$ 294	7.2%	8.8%	8.0%
			$ 3,367			

PXP Precedent Cell	Base Value: 1786.5447300599			Input Changes		
	Output Downside	Output Upside	Effective Range	Input Downside	Input Upside	Base Case Value
Royalty Function (H7)	$ 2,262	$ 1,311	$ 952	0.19	0.24	0.21
Royalty Function (H6)	$ 1,542	$ 2,031	$ 488	0.46	0.56	0.51
Volume Risking	$ 1,550	$ 2,023	$ 473	0.90	1.10	1.00
Oil Price	$ 1,648	$ 1,915	$ 267	$ 90	$ 110	$ 100
PXP Discount Rate	$ 1,911	$ 1,673	$ 238	9.7%	11.8%	10.8%
			$ 2,418			

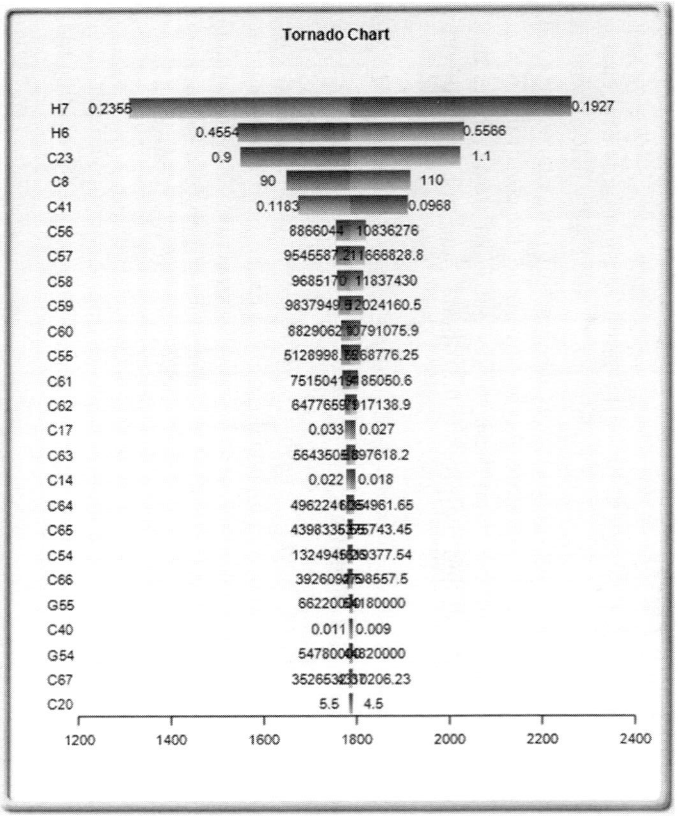

FIGURE 14.60 Tornado summary and chart.

Single Variable Distributional Fitting

Statistical Summary

Fitted Distribution	*Gumbel (Maximum)*
Alpha	67.06
Beta	12.70
Kolmogorov-Smirnov Statistic	0.07
P-Value for Test Statistic	0.1102

	Actual	Theoretical
Mean	74.45	74.39
Standard Deviation	13.00	16.29
Skewness	0.36	1.14
Excess Kurtosis	-1.16	2.40

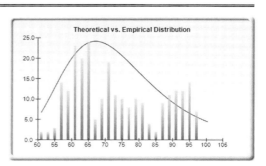

FIGURE 14.61   Historical oil price distribution.

less attention was paid to those variables that have little impact on the outcome of the project. After all, why spend too much time calibrating the inputs to the variables that have negligible effects on the NPV of the project (e.g., the variables at the bottom of the tornado chart)?

As oil price is the major impact driver, our next step was to determine the risk and volatility of this variable by looking at historical oil prices (Figure 14.61). Figure 14.62 shows the results from a GARCH (generalized autoregressive conditional heteroskedasticity) model that was run to forecast the volatility of the price of oil using historical price levels. Figure 14.63 shows some sample oil price data coupled with macroeconomic variables such as gross domestic product and variables such as inflation and interest rates. These were entered into some advanced econometric models in order to forecast the levels of oil prices and its uncertainties (Figure 14.64 shows some sample results from ARIMA, or autoregressive integrated moving average, models). The results from these analyses were then used to recalibrate the cash flow models, where tens of thousands of simulation trials were run to determine the returns and risks of the project both to the state and PXP.

Risk Analysis (Monte Carlo Risk-Based Simulation)   To properly determine the risks and uncertainties involved in the project, we employed Monte Carlo risk simulation and ran 1,000 to 100,000 simulation trials on the financial and economic models to account for all possible outcomes. The variables we simulated were those found to be the most sensitive in driving the NPV and IRR of the project. These critical success factors (e.g., price of oil and oil production) were difficult to forecast with any certainty, hence we employed simulation techniques to handle these uncertainties.

GARCH: Generalized Autoregressive Conditional Heteroskedasticity (Volatility Forecast)

GARCH models are used mainly for computing the volatility on liquid and tradable assets such as stocks in financial options; this model is sometimes used for other traded assets such as price of oil and price of electricity. The drawback is that a lot of data is required, advanced econometric modeling expertise is required, and this approach is highly susceptible to user manipulation. The benefit is that rigorous statistical analysis is performed to find the best-fitting volatility curve, providing different volatility estimates over time. GARCH is a term that incorporates a family of models that can take on a variety of forms, known as GARCH (P,Q), where P and Q are positive integers that define the resulting GARCH model and its forecasts. In most cases for financial instruments, a GARCH

GARCH Model (P, Q)	1,1	Periodicity (Periods/Year)	12
Optimized Alpha	0.3243	Predictive Base	1
Optimized Beta	0.5756	Forecast Periods	3
Optimized Omega	0.0009	Variance Targeting	FALSE

Period	Data	Volatility
0	59.40	
1	58.26	
2	59.45	23.43%
3	60.47	20.83%
4	60.91	19.06%
5	59.44	17.70%
6	57.73	17.47%
7	56.76	17.64%
8	55.36	17.10%
9	55.92	17.17%
10	56.45	16.60%
11	57.59	16.26%
12	57.07	16.43%
13	56.39	16.15%
14	55.34	16.06%
15	53.00	16.26%
16	53.57	18.08%
17	53.40	17.17%
18	52.10	16.50%
19	50.85	16.81%
20	48.77	16.96%
21	46.21	18.32%
22	48.73	20.22%
23	50.39	21.14%
24	51.26	20.08%
25	48.74	18.59%
26	47.83	20.00%
27	47.84	18.60%
28	48.31	17.36%

GARCH or generalized autoregressive conditional heteroskedasticity models are used in forecasting the volatility of financial instruments, using the prices themselves. The GARCH (P,Q) model allows for different positive P and Q integer lag parameters for the mean (news) and variance equations. Note than only positive data values can be used in a GARCH volatility forecast. Periodicity is the number of periods per year (e.g., 12 for monthly data, 252 for daily trading data, 365 for daily data) to annualize the volatility or keep as 1 for periodic volatility. Base is the predictive base periods (this means how many periods back you would like to use as a forecast base to predict future volatility, and is typically between 1 and 12). Variance Targeting means if you wish the volatility forecast to revert to an imputed long-run mean over time. Make sure to arrange your raw price data in chronological order (past to present in a single

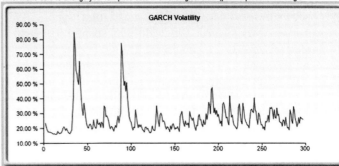

FIGURE 14.62   Generalized autoregressive conditional heteroskedasticity (volatility forecast).

Figures 14.65 through 14.71 illustrate a small sample set of the analysis performed, and the descriptions of our findings are listed here:

- Figure 14.65 shows simulation forecast results that indicate the state's NPV levels and NPV share of the total NPV of the project, assuming that the best-case scenario occurs. The 90 percent confidence interval means that 90 percent of the time, given all that can occur in terms of price of oil and actual production as well as other uncertainties (assuming that production is at full capacity), the state will yield an NPV of between $1.21B and $4.59B, which is equivalent to obtaining between 55.51 percent and 68.70 percent of the total NPV. This result

	A	B	C	D	E	F	G	H	I
1	Date	U.S. Natural Gas Wellhead Price (Dollars per Thousand Cubic Feet)		Date	Cushing, OK Crude Oil Future Contract 1 (Dollars per Barrel)	CPI	Adjusted Contract Crude Oil Price	Adjusted Natural Gas Wellhead Price	PXP Contract Crude Oil Price
392	Jul-2005	6.71		Jul-2005	59.03	201.4		7.31	55.94
393	Aug-2005	6.48		Aug-2005	64.99	203.1		7.00	61.07
394	Sep-2005	8.95		Sep-2005	65.55	205.8		9.54	60.79
395	Oct-2005	10.33		Oct-2005	62.27	206.9		10.95	57.44
396	Nov-2005	9.89		Nov-2005	58.34	205.6		10.55	54.16
397	Dec-2005	9.08		Dec-2005	59.45	203.9		9.77	55.65
398	Jan-2006	8.02		Jan-2006	65.54	206		8.54	60.72
399	Feb-2006	6.86		Feb-2006	61.93	207.5		7.25	56.96
400	Mar-2006	6.44		Mar-2006	62.97	208.5		6.78	57.64
401	Apr-2006	6.38		Apr-2006	70.16	210.5		6.65	63.61
402	May-2006	6.24		May-2006	70.96	212.4		6.44	63.76
403	Jun-2006	5.78		Jun-2006	70.97	211.1		6.01	64.16
404	Jul-2006	5.92		Jul-2006	74.46	211.4		6.14	67.22
405	Aug-2006	6.56		Aug-2006	73.08	211.9		6.79	65.82
406	Sep-2006	6.06		Sep-2006	63.9	212.9		6.24	57.28
407	Oct-2006	5.09		Oct-2006	59.14	211.4		5.28	53.39
408	Nov-2006	6.72		Nov-2006	59.4	211.1		6.98	53.70
409	Dec-2006	6.76		Dec-2006	62.09	210.6		7.04	56.27
410	Jan-2007	5.92		Jan-2007	54.35	212.584		6.11	48.79
411	Feb-2007	6.66		Feb-2007	59.39	214.76		6.80	52.78
412	Mar-2007	6.56		Mar-2007	60.74	216.5		6.65	53.55
413	Apr-2007	6.84		Apr-2007	64.04	217.845		6.89	56.11
414	May-2007	6.98		May-2007	63.53	218.596		7.00	55.47
415	Jun-2007	6.86		Jun-2007	67.53	217.273		6.93	59.32
416	Jul-2007	6.19		Jul-2007	74.15	217.454		6.24	65.08
417	Aug-2007	5.9		Aug-2007	72.36	217.33		5.96	63.54
418	Sep-2007	5.61		Sep-2007	79.63	217.697		5.65	69.81
419	Oct-2007	6.25		Oct-2007	85.66	218.696		6.27	74.75
420				Nov-2007	94.63	219.943			82.11
421				Dec-2007	91.74	219.373			79.81

FIGURE 14.63 Oil price forecasts using macroeconomic factors.

also means that in the 5 percent worst-case scenario, if production is at full capacity, the state will yield at least $1.21B (55.51 percent NPV share). This amount increases the possibility that the state will not get any more than $4.59B (68.70 percent NPV share) 5 percent of the time (that the state will only be able to beat these values at the absolute best-case scenario will occur less than 5 percent of the time).

- Figure 14.66 shows the same analysis as done for Figure 14.65 with the average NPV at $2.80B, or 62.74 percent NPV share if the production is at full capacity.

AUTO-ARIMA (Autoregressive Integrated Moving Average)

Regression Statistics

R-Squared (Coefficient of Determination)	0.9633	Akaike Information Criterion (AIC)	4.7115
Adjusted R-Squared	0.9630	Schwarz Criterion (SC)	4.7695
Multiple R (Multiple Correlation Coefficient)	0.9815	Log Likelihood	-692.59
Standard Error of the Estimates (SEy)	13.33	Durbin-Watson (DW) Statistic	2.0070
Number of Observations	294	Number of Iterations	6

Autoregressive Integrated Moving Average or ARIMA(p,d,q) models are the extension of the AR model that use three components for modeling the serial correlation in the time-series data. The first component is the autoregressive (AR) term. The AR(p) model uses the p lags of the time series in the equation. An AR(p) model has the form: $y(t)=a(1)*y(t-1)+...+a(p)*y(t-p)+e(t)$.The second component is the integration (d) order term. Each integration order corresponds to differencing the time series. I(1) means differencing the data once. I(d) means differencing the data d times. The third component is the moving average (MA) term. The MA(q) model uses the q lags of the forecast errors to improve the forecast. An MA(q) model has the form: $y(t)=e(t)+b(1)*e(t-1)+...+b(q)*e(t-q)$.Finally, an ARMA(p,q) model has the combined form: $y(t)=a(1)*y(t-1)+...+a(p)*y(t-p)+e(t)+b(1)*e(t-1)+...+b(q)*e(t-q)$

The R-Squared, or Coefficient of Determination, indicates the percent variation in the dependent variable that can be explained and accounted for by the independent variables in this regression analysis. However, in a multiple regression, the Adjusted R-Squared takes into account the existence of additional independent variables or regressors and adjusts this R-Squared value to a more accurate view the regression's explanatory power. However, under some ARIMA modeling circumstances (e.g., with nonconvergence models), the R-Squared tends to be unreliable.

The Multiple Correlation Coefficient (Multiple R) measures the correlation between the actual dependent variable (Y) and the estimated or fitted (Y) based on the regression equation. This correlation is also the square root of the Coefficient of Determination (R-Squared).

The Standard Error of the Estimates (SEy) describes the dispersion of data points above and below the regression line or plane. This value is used as part of the calculation to obtain the confidence interval of the estimates later.

The AIC and SC are often used in model selection. SC imposes a greater penalty for additional coefficients. Generally, the user should select a model with the lowest value of the AIC and SC.

The Durbin-Watson statistic measures the serial correlation in the residuals. Generally, DW less than 2 implies positive serial correlation.

Regression Results

	Intercept	AR(1)	MA(1)
Coefficients	0.7421	0.9796	0.2874
Standard Error	0.5320	0.0147	0.0571
t-Statistic	1.3950	66.6201	5.0313
p-Value	0.1641	0.0000	0.0000
Lower 5%	1.6199	1.0038	0.3816
Upper 95%	-0.1357	0.9553	0.1931

Degrees of Freedom		Hypothesis Test	
Degrees of Freedom for Regression	2	Critical t-Statistic (99% confidence with df of 291)	2.5928
Degrees of Freedom for Residual	291	Critical t-Statistic (95% confidence with df of 291)	1.9681
Total Degrees of Freedom	293	Critical t-Statistic (90% confidence with df of 291)	1.6501

Autocorrelation

Time Lag	AC	PAC	Lower Bound	Upper Bound	Q-Stat	Prob
1	0.9583	0.9583	(0.1164)	0.1164	272.7748	-
2	0.9117	(0.0826)	(0.1164)	0.1164	520.4740	-
3	0.8706	0.0489	(0.1164)	0.1164	747.1625	-
4	0.8296	(0.0316)	(0.1164)	0.1164	953.8689	-
5	0.7966	0.0841	(0.1164)	0.1164	1,144.7658	-
6	0.7690	0.0325	(0.1164)	0.1164	1,323.4421	-
7	0.7453	0.0404	(0.1164)	0.1164	1,491.8665	-
8	0.7234	0.0081	(0.1164)	0.1164	1,651.1049	-
9	0.7029	0.0171	(0.1164)	0.1164	1,801.9631	-
10	0.6859	0.0422	(0.1164)	0.1164	1,946.1286	-
11	0.6590	(0.1255)	(0.1164)	0.1164	2,079.6593	-
12	0.6307	0.0003	(0.1164)	0.1164	2,202.4158	-
13	0.6051	0.0067	(0.1164)	0.1164	2,315.7966	-
14	0.5800	0.0049	(0.1164)	0.1164	2,420.3514	-
15	0.5484	(0.1111)	(0.1164)	0.1164	2,514.1731	-
16	0.5187	0.0099	(0.1164)	0.1164	2,598.3934	-
17	0.4962	0.0544	(0.1164)	0.1164	2,675.7356	-
18	0.4737	(0.0197)	(0.1164)	0.1164	2,746.4771	-
19	0.4500	(0.0362)	(0.1164)	0.1164	2,810.5473	-
20	0.4316	0.0379	(0.1164)	0.1164	2,869.6993	-

Forecasting

Period	Actual (Y)	Forecast (F)	Error (E)
2	58.2609	58.9272	(0.6664)
3	59.4452	57.6212	1.8240
4	60.4724	59.4971	0.9753
5	60.9053	60.2593	0.6460
6	59.4446	60.5888	(1.1442)
7	57.7311	58.6435	(0.9124)
8	56.7621	57.0316	(0.2695)
9	55.3630	56.2671	(0.9042)
10	55.9174	54.7142	1.2032
11	56.4486	55.8629	0.5857
12	57.5938	56.2058	1.3880
13	57.0702	57.5582	(0.4880)
14	56.3888	56.5061	(0.1173)
15	55.3367	55.9452	(0.6085)
16	52.9967	54.7735	(1.7768)
17	53.5671	52.1455	1.4216
18	53.4029	53.6234	(0.2205)
19	52.1006	52.9906	(0.8901)
20	50.8523	51.5225	(0.6702)
21	48.7739	50.3629	(1.5890)
22	46.2088	48.0630	(1.8542)

FIGURE 14.64　　Oil price forecasts using advanced econometric ARIMA models.

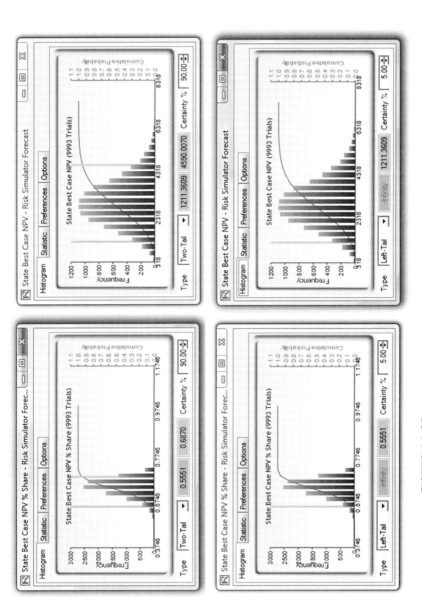

FIGURE 14.65 A sample of state's risk profile I (simulation results).

State Best Case NPV % Share - Risk Simulator Forec...

Histogram | **Statistic** | Preferences | Options

Statistics	Result
Number of Trials	9993
Mean	0.6274
Median	0.6317
Standard Deviation	0.0413
Variance	0.0017
Coefficient of Variation	0.0658
Maximum	1.0000
Minimum	0.3579
Range	0.6421
Skewness	-0.5370
Kurtosis	1.6773
25% Percentile	0.6028
75% Percentile	0.6564
Percentage Error Precision at 95% Confidence	0.1291%

State Best Case NPV - Risk Simulator Forecast

Histogram | **Statistic** | Preferences | Options

Statistics	Result
Number of Trials	9993
Mean	2803.5461
Median	2752.6646
Standard Deviation	1027.9473
Variance	1.056676E+006
Coefficient of Variation	0.3667
Maximum	7403.9008
Minimum	128.4847
Range	7275.4161
Skewness	0.3451
Kurtosis	0.0925
25% Percentile	2075.0334
75% Percentile	3461.4980
Percentage Error Precision at 95% Confidence	0.7189%

FIGURE 14.66   A sample of state's risk profile II (simulation results).

- Figure 14.67 shows the results of the analysis when the level of production is at the most likely middle-case scenario, where the state will be receiving an expected average of $744M and between 68.67 percent and 87.07 percent of the NPV share. The worse the situation, the higher the percentage NPV share the state receives because it carries no risk whereas PXP takes all the risk (although both the state and PXP will have reduced NPV dollar values).
- Figure 14.68 illustrates the results for PXP. In the best-case and most likely mid-case, the NPV on a 90 percent confidence interval shows that PXP will always have a significant NPV. The only way PXP will not obtain positive NPV values is when production is super low and close to a standstill, under the worst-case scenario.
- Figure 14.69 illustrates PXP's probability of success in generating a positive NPV for the entire project, at the sliding royalty rate proposed

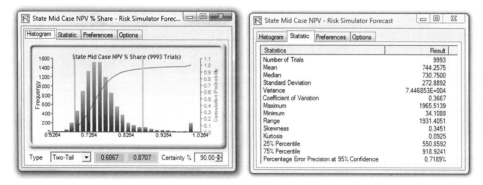

FIGURE 14.67   A sample of state's risk profile III (simulation results).

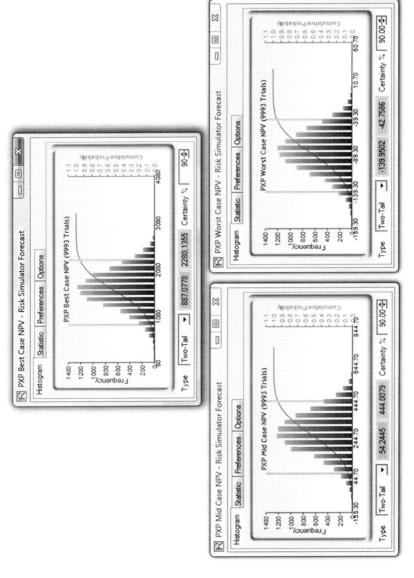

FIGURE 14.68 A sample of PXP's risk profile I (simulation results).

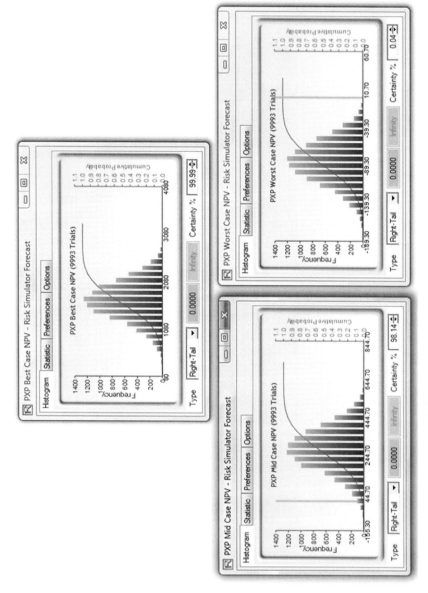

FIGURE 14.69 A sample of PXP's risk profile II (simulation results).

by the state. There is a 99.99 percent and 98.14 percent chance that NPV will be positive in the best- and most likely mid-case scenarios for PXP. This result indicates that there is less than a 2 percent chance that the project will be unprofitable, whereas 98.14 percent of the time, this project is lucrative and profitable for PXP. The only exception, again, is when production is at the worst-case scenario and output is close to a standstill.

- Figure 14.70, in contrast to the preceding figures, illustrates PXP's IRR on a pretax level. In the best-case scenario, PXP's IRR has a 100 percent chance of exceeding 55 percent, the required threshold for most high-risk projects such as undefined oil and gas exploration projects. Even in the most likely case, there is more than a 98 percent probability that the IRR exceeds PXP's hurdle rate of 25 percent, and in the worst-case scenario, a 45.80 percent chance of that occurring.

In summary, PXP's risks were nominal and the upside potential significant. To further decrease PXP's downside risks, David Mercier, chief of finance, economics, and accounting, and the economic consultant, Dr. Johnathan Mun, performed the real options analysis whereby PXP can start with three wells as a proof of concept to delineate the reservoir. If done properly, these three wells (limited total costs to drill, as compared to the total number of wells and injectors required in a full development) will help limit the downside risks and losses to PXP, while providing a significant upside. Therefore, the risks are mitigated, and, depending on the results of the three test wells, PXP can decide if it wants to pursue developing and completing all additional wells. Thus, the risks specified using simulation as previously illustrated would be diminished to a level that is close to zero, with the total loss being the expenses used to drill the three wells. The upside leverage is significant. For instance, say the total cost of drilling the three test wells is $53M. In the best-case scenario where 90 percent of the time at full production yields an NPV of $2.28B, PXP has leveraged its upside by almost 43 times. In the absolute worst-case scenario, the total losses for PXP will be the $53M spent on test drilling the three wells.

Strategic Real Options Analysis (Risk Mitigation) For PXP, if the best-case or most likely mid-case scenario occurs, its NPV value is still highly positive, indicating a profitable project in general. However, if the worst-case scenario occurs, with limited production, the project might end up being unprofitable. This is clearly a risk that PXP has to undertake, even with up to a projected 30 percent geological chance of failure (dry hole). To mitigate this risk, PXP can first drill three exploratory wells (Phase I in Figure 14.71). On the one hand, if these three wells prove to be successful (the reservoir

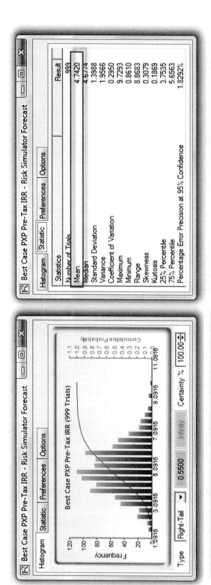

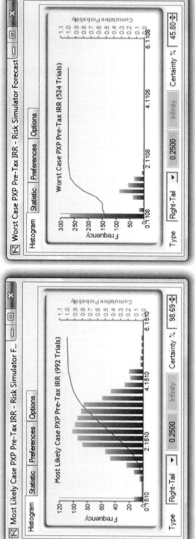

FIGURE 14.70 PXP's risk profile III (simulation results).

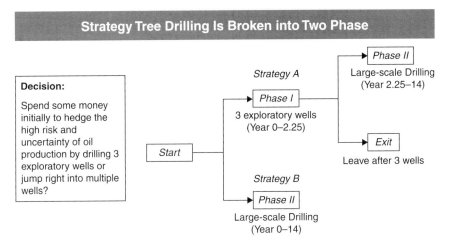

This added value allows the royalty schedule to be shifted up <u>8%</u> to 48% at $100/BO.
The option to exit after three wells reduces risk and increases the project's expected value

FIGURE 14.71 Sequential compound two-phased option.

is clearly delineated and the geological uncertainties of the reservoir are resolved and known), then PXP can pursue additional or large-scale drilling of the other wells in Phase II. On the other hand, if Phase I proves that there are issues with the reservoir, PXP can simply exit and abandon the drilling altogether. By creating a Phase I and Phase II development process, PXP can delineate the wells and reduce its risks. Instead of paying all of the capital expenditures immediately, the maximum that will be lost will be the cost to drill the three exploratory wells.

This risk mitigation technique is known in real options analysis as a sequential compound or phased option. This stage-gate process allows PXP to reduce its total losses should the worst-case scenario become reality, capping the total loss at three wells drilled, as compared to a large-scale development. By using this technique, the uncertainty and risks become resolved over the passage of actions, time, and events. PXP will and should optimally execute Phase II only if Phase I proves to be highly successful. Figure 14.72 illustrates the analysis performed to value the strategic option.

Optimal Royalty Rate Determination (Optimization and Scenario Analysis)

The next part of the analysis is the determination of the optimal royalty rate schema. The approach used was that of an optimization, where thousands of scenario combinations and permutations of royalty rates and PXP's IRR

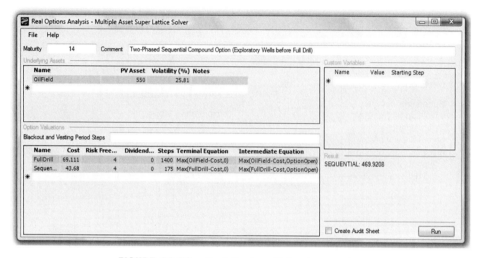

FIGURE 14.72 Real Options Valuation results.

were determined, and the optimal confidence band was determined. This band was developed to maximize the total NPV of the project while maximizing the returns to the state without leaving additional money on the negotiation table. At the same time, the constraint is such that PXP will still be profitable given these royalty rates. At rates higher than those in the optimal band, PXP will find the project unprofitable and the optimal decision is to abandon it. It is important to note that IRR was evaluated along with the many other financial metrics. (Note: A smaller investment and a better rate of return may have a higher IRR, but an investor's total wealth may be increased more with a larger investment and a lower IRR. Therefore, IRR doesn't provide any insight into the magnitude of the investment.) PXP's NPV was also considered in the sample optimization to ensure that it increases with increasing oil price. Figure 14.73 illustrates a small subset of these scenarios.

Analysis Conclusion

Based on the detailed economic and financial modeling performed by Staff and the economic Consultant, we came to the conclusion that the sliding royalty rate is the optimal scheme for the PXP project. The analysis took into consideration the risk and volatility of oil price and production decline rates, running stochastic simulations covering hundreds of thousands of potential outcomes, creating an optimization frontier of

Sample PXP IRR

Scenario Analysis Table

Output Variable:	PXP AVG IRR	Initial Base Case Va	0.47			
Column Variable:	Oil Price	Min: 0.00	Max: 0.00	Steps: 1.00	Steps: —	Steps 0.04 Initial Base Case Value:
Row Variable:	Royalty Rate	Min: 0.00	Max: 500.00	Steps: 500.00	Steps: —	Steps 20.00 Initial Base Case Value:

	12%	16%	20%	24%	28%	32%	36%	40%	44%	48%	52%	56%	60%	64%	68%	72%	76%	80%	Calculated Royalty (%)
0	—	—	—	—	—	—	—	—	—	—	—	—	—	—	—	—	—	—	12.5%
20	-0.65	-0.68	-0.72	-0.75	-0.79	-0.83	-0.97	—	—	—	—	—	—	—	—	—	—	—	13.5%
40	-0.04	-0.10	-0.15	-0.21	-0.26	-0.32	-0.38	-0.43	-0.49	-0.55	-0.61	-0.68	-0.74	-0.82	—	—	—	—	28.4%
60	0.53	0.45	0.37	0.29	0.21	0.13	0.05	-0.03	-0.12	-0.20	-0.28	-0.37	-0.46	-0.54	-0.64	-0.73	-0.86	—	37.1%
80	1.10	0.99	0.89	0.78	0.67	0.57	0.46	0.35	0.25	0.14	0.03	-0.08	-0.19	-0.30	-0.42	-0.54	-0.66	-0.80	43.2%
100	1.66	1.53	1.40	1.26	1.13	1.00	0.87	0.74	0.60	0.47	0.33	0.20	0.06	-0.07	-0.21	-0.35	-0.50	-0.65	48.0%
120	2.21	2.06	1.90	1.74	1.59	1.43	1.27	1.11	0.95	0.80	0.64	0.47	0.31	0.15	-0.01	-0.18	-0.35	-0.52	51.9%
140	2.77	2.58	2.40	2.22	2.04	1.85	1.67	1.49	1.30	1.12	0.93	0.75	0.56	0.37	0.19	-0.01	-0.20	-0.40	55.2%
160	3.32	3.11	2.90	2.69	2.49	2.28	2.07	1.86	1.65	1.44	1.23	1.02	0.81	0.60	0.38	0.17	-0.05	-0.28	58.1%
180	3.87	3.64	3.40	3.17	2.94	2.70	2.47	2.23	2.00	1.76	1.53	1.29	1.05	0.82	0.58	0.33	0.09	-0.16	60.6%
200	4.42	4.16	3.90	3.64	3.38	3.12	2.86	2.60	2.34	2.08	1.82	1.56	1.30	1.03	0.77	0.50	0.23	-0.04	62.8%
220	4.97	4.68	4.40	4.11	3.83	3.54	3.26	2.97	2.69	2.40	2.12	1.83	1.54	1.25	0.96	0.67	0.37	0.08	64.9%
240	5.51	5.21	4.90	4.59	4.28	3.97	3.65	3.34	3.03	2.72	2.41	2.10	1.78	1.47	1.15	0.84	0.52	0.19	66.7%
260	6.06	5.73	5.39	5.06	4.72	4.39	4.05	3.71	3.38	3.04	2.70	2.36	2.02	1.68	1.34	1.00	0.66	0.31	68.5%
280	6.61	6.25	5.89	5.53	5.17	4.81	4.44	4.08	3.72	3.36	2.99	2.63	2.27	1.90	1.53	1.17	0.80	0.42	70.0%
300	7.16	6.77	6.38	6.00	5.61	5.22	4.84	4.45	4.06	3.67	3.29	2.90	2.51	2.12	1.72	1.33	0.93	0.54	71.5%
320	7.70	7.29	6.88	6.47	6.06	5.64	5.23	4.82	4.41	3.99	3.58	3.16	2.75	2.33	1.91	1.49	1.07	0.65	72.9%
340	8.25	7.81	7.38	6.94	6.50	6.06	5.62	5.19	4.75	4.31	3.87	3.43	2.99	2.55	2.10	1.66	1.21	0.76	74.2%
360	8.80	8.33	7.87	7.41	6.94	6.48	6.02	5.55	5.09	4.62	4.16	3.69	3.23	2.76	2.29	1.82	1.35	0.88	75.4%
380	9.34	8.86	8.37	7.88	7.39	6.90	6.41	5.92	5.43	4.94	4.45	3.96	3.47	2.97	2.48	1.99	1.49	0.99	76.6%
400	9.89	9.38	8.86	8.35	7.83	7.32	6.80	6.29	5.77	5.26	4.74	4.22	3.71	3.19	2.67	2.15	1.63	1.10	77.7%
420	10.44	9.90	9.36	8.82	8.28	7.74	7.20	6.66	6.11	5.57	5.03	4.49	3.95	3.40	2.86	2.31	1.76	1.21	78.7%
440	10.98	10.42	9.85	9.29	8.72	8.15	7.59	7.02	6.46	5.89	5.32	4.75	4.19	3.62	3.05	2.47	1.90	1.32	79.7%
460	11.53	10.94	10.35	9.76	9.16	8.57	7.98	7.39	6.80	6.20	5.61	5.02	4.42	3.83	3.23	2.64	2.04	1.44	80.7%
480	12.07	11.46	10.84	10.22	9.61	8.99	8.37	7.76	7.14	6.52	5.90	5.28	4.66	4.04	3.42	2.80	2.18	1.55	81.6%
500	12.62	11.98	11.34	10.69	10.05	9.41	8.77	8.12	7.48	6.84	6.19	5.55	4.90	4.26	3.61	2.96	2.31	1.66	82.5%

FIGURE 14.73 Sample optimal range of royalty rates developed by running thousands of alternate scenarios.

all possible combinations and permutations of oil prices and royalty rates. Other nonfinancial factors as well as factors such as the land donation, potential payment of additional county taxes, tax rebates and incentives, donation to develop certain green technology or environmental offsets (hybrid buses, parks, and the like) were outside the purview of this financial analysis, but are nonetheless important aspects in the negotiations.

Project Update

On January 29, 2009, the State Lands Commission voted down the project two (Lt. Governor Garamendi and State Controller John Chiang) against one (Deputy Finance Director Tom Sheehy). As of writing this case study, PXP has appealed to the State Legislature to get the State Lands Commission's vote overturned.

CASE STUDY: HOW REAL OPTIONS MITIGATES IT ENTERPRISE SECURITY RISKS

This case was written by David M. Bittlingmeier (david@bittlingmeier.com). David has a B.S. from St. Mary's College and an M.S. from Golden Gate University, and has numerous years in strategic enterprise security, designing, developing, and implementing various enterprise policies and procedures, enterprise-wide security awareness training, business continuity, project management, and technical consultation experience, where he has provided professional judgments and advice to all levels of management. As a consultant, he has worked on ensuring compliance with industry best practices, business continuity, disaster recovery planning, ISO 17799, NIST standards, OCC, Basel II, BITS regulation, and has offered enterprise security management perspective for executives seeking an unbiased source of education, insight, and expertise in order to ensure the success of their business. In addition, he has consulted with (ISC)2, where he was both part of the team that developed/modified the training to prepare security professionals for the CISSP exam and then was/is a supervisor during the CISSP exams, wrote the strategic security plan for one of the major departments of the State of California, speaks at International Enterprise Security Conferences, is an ongoing attendee of the U.S. Secret Service San Francisco Electronic Crimes Task Force, was a contributor of Risk Analysis: 1st Step in HIPAA Security publication, as well as being a member of the High Technology Crime Investigation Association, Inc. David has received praise for his ability to explain complexity in lay terms from various sources such as San Francisco Mayor's Criminal Justice Council, California Youth Authority, and others.

This case study provides a quick overview of IT Enterprise Risk Management analysis drawn from numerous local, national, and international security reviews he has completed, including, yet not necessarily limited to, third-party service companies, mail services, various outsourcing functions/ processes, venture capitalist projects, insurance companies, financial companies, and so forth from multimillion to multibillion dollar organizations, and as such the case study is an illustration of those robust review processes. Within the case study is a short composite case with a sample report that outlines both issues and possible solutions, which highlights the need for Bittlingmeier & Associates, LLC and Real Options Valuation, Inc. (BAROV) methodologies. Finally, adding the strategic real options and integrated risk analysis such as applying Monte Carlo risk simulations offer solutions to the effective allocation of major funds on enterprise security projects. While the benefits of IT are clear, managing the risks that can be introduced to the business from IT processes, policies, and technology failures are not easily inferred and yet these risks can have serious impacts in terms of achieving compliance with:

- Regulations
- Protecting brand reputation
- Ensuring overall corporate performance

The process introduced in this case study is the Risk Assessment Process (RAP) process, which helps facilitate excellence in governance by aligning:

- IT policy, risk, and operations management
- Corporate business initiatives
- Strategy
- Operational standards
- Enterprise security

RAP is a comprehensive solution that reduces the cost, complexity, and cumbersome nature of complying with numerous regulatory mandates. RAP facilitates the ongoing review, attestation, and remediation process, while helping to identify similarities between regulations to reduce redundancy and duplication of effort and provides the confidence that compliance is achievable, risks are mitigated, and corporate policies and procedures are enforced. As regulatory pressures continue to mount, businesses that take a more practical, cross-regulatory approach to managing compliance will alleviate increasing cost and complexity while gaining valuable insight into risks to key business processes that could affect the company's performance in the form of legal action, fines, penalties, and damage to a company's reputation.

Enterprise Security Risk Management is a complex and difficult problem that can be made efficient and manageable through RAP's consolidation, identification, and harmonization of overlapping regulatory demands—interdependencies that cannot be seen using spreadsheets—and enables transparency and visibility to stakeholders throughout the organization. The process ensures that risks are properly associated to business strategy and needs while it helps to manage a multitude of technology risks. Such processes have become increasingly more difficult and require a holistic approach wherein the interdependencies between risk and business performance are easily understood and manageable. For example, currently organizations in general have had to rely on a fragmented and disparate approach to managing supplier risks. Reliance on a silo risk management approach is not only costly and inefficient, it lacks the contextual understanding of the real impacts that risk in technology processes and policies have on the business.

In today's highly regulated business environment, companies are required to comply with a multitude of global regulatory mandates, including privacy, industry, and process regulations. Regardless of a company's current compliance environment, similarities across regulations create overlapping management, documentation, and audit demands, which can overwhelm efforts to effectively identify and manage risk. RAP makes governance practicable, enabling a company to sustain compliance across multiple best practice frameworks and regulations while managing IT control and risk according to the business processes they support. With RAP, a company will instill risk management and governance as part of the corporate culture, making procedures more effective and efficient while providing management with peace of mind that the corporate brand is protected, providing management with the visibility, control, and decision support required to manage supplier risk and optimize business performance. RAP is a key building block in implementing an enterprise-wide security risk management approach as it delivers a policy-driven, process-centric way to manage risk through:

- Control assessments
- User surveys
- Logical and repeatable workflow
- Industry standard best practices criteria

We are able to apply Risk Simulator input assumptions to both BAROV and Client Company's subject matter expert risk rankings, and then run simulations on the matrices in order to determine the total grand risk score for the Client Company (see Figure 14.77). Furthermore, we are able to develop optimization models where each element may be subject to a decision variable in terms of the cost required to correct any outstanding issues, compared to possible benefits/losses obtained from having/not having an "in compliance" security level, and run it based on the Client Company's budget constraints. Using probabilistic distributions obtained from the simulation(s), we are now able to identify the chances that a specific category's risk and impact may exceed tolerable limits, as well as identify the critical success factors (sensitivity analysis and Tornado analysis are usually run on these assessment matrices). A strategy is then created of multiple phases (sequential compound option) on when certain elements of the issue(s) identified can/need(s) to be first to be fixed, when it/they then becomes the less/more critical in other phase(s), all the while were so warranted accounting for interrelationships among any/all Enterprise projects. For example, if a certain project requires another as a prerequisite (say some platform technology that first needs to be implemented before any subsequent projects can be implemented) or any mutually exclusive redundant projects (the implementation of one project makes another obsolete or unnecessary). At the end of the day, at what point does not stopping project A become cost effective and/or project B becoming cost-effective or ending project A completely or moving toward project B become the best and optimal overall strategy? As most companies have hundreds of these projects, BAROV could demonstrate both the dependency and the costs between projects, thereby giving a pragmatic real-world risk of project A versus project B, and so forth.

Based on a company's business objectives, the inherent risks associated will determine the tier ranking system using a value of 1 to 5 Likert scale (the scale can also be color-coordinated such as: 1 = Green, 2 = Yellow, 3 = Orange, 4 = Red, 5 = Black), indicating the level of risk involved, from low to high. In general, compliance reviews dictate that formal reviews must be conducted on at least an annual basis, and more frequently if warranted based on risk. Using a pragmatic, real-world-based stance in conducting reviews we understand how policy, procedures, and management controls mitigate risk. Based on a comprehensive and customizable risk-assessment approach, this RAP methodology can be used across multiple industries and functions. It can be used as the basis for performing up-front due-diligence, a one-time controls review, or an annual assessment of controls and/or best practices (Figure 14.74 illustrates this compliance core methodology).

A Sample Implementation

This sample implementation is derived from extensive on-site reviews (companies' names and proprietary information are intentionally kept confidential and we only present a generic example case) in the United States, India, and China, of due-diligence reviews across numerous industries including yet not limited to financial services, insurance companies, onshore/offshore IT service providers, manufacturing, and other functional areas for compliance issues in general, while specifically reviewing Enterprise Security of internal,

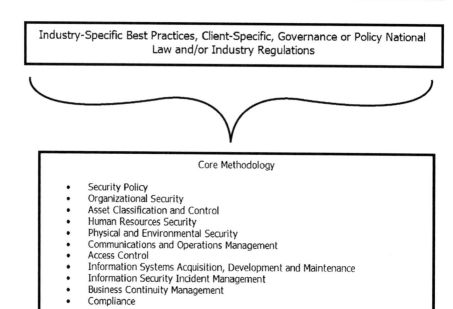

FIGURE 14.74   Assurance of compliance with legal requirements.

external, outsourced, and offshore service security, highlighting the needs for
BAROV methodologies to ensure enterprise security that meets or exceeds
industry-standard security practices that are cost-effective, robust, function-
ally effective, and real time. Information systems are designed and deployed
to support business and legal requirements, leverage cost efficiencies, and
improve internal and external communication. However, organizations,
like the people they are designed to serve, are organic—they grow, evolve,
and change continuously. It is impossible for the infrastructures supporting
such environments to maintain their secure integrity and cost-effectiveness
without persistent vigilance and wisely spent renewed investment, which
BAROV allows and facilitates. Striking the balance between sharing information among all necessary parties and maintaining adequate protection
for the company's proprietary information is crucial in any business environment. In a networked world, information is the central nervous system
for the organization with the risk of proprietary knowledge and confidential information being exposed to potential perpetrators. These perpetrators
prey on the vulnerabilities that are inevitable in an IT system. Opportunities emerging from such vulnerabilities range from defacing corporate web
sites to stealing valuable assets where infrastructure resources are appropri-
ated covertly for seditious activities. Eradicating all threats would make the

infrastructure useless. System security and performance objectives tend to be at odds. However, steps can be taken to optimize and balance these seemingly diametrically opposed poles. BAROV has developed the process and assessment methods to help companies have a way to cost-effectively identify, prioritize, and achieve their security goals without depleting system performance. A summary of the four phases applied and nine processes are shown later in this case study, providing a summary of BAROV's usual recommend tasks, using a prioritized approach that qualitatively considers security benefits and levels of effort. The methodology is developed to help initiate discussions regarding which recommendations to implement immediately, in the future, or not at all, within the context of the company's business requirements, security goals, and budget constraints. Due to the limited scope of this case study, any company-specific requirements would need a unique and detailed analysis prior to the remediation efforts here.

Sample Analysis Report

This section shows a sample BAROV analysis report issued to a company based on answers provided during personal interviews with the company's staff and on independent examination of documents and facilities by the BAROV team. The company analyzed is a multinational billion-dollar organization that is currently outsourcing a relatively small quantity of work items to Outsourced Company and before expanding its activities, hired BAROV to review the risks, if any, related to this business expansion and outsourcing activities, with a detailed report that outlines the risks and steps to either remove or mitigate the said risks that are identified.

Approach   BAROV identified certain risks in its contract operations using agreed on work programs to address the risks. We also reviewed more than four dozen presentations and hundreds of documents in both English and Chinese, covering all the major policies and procedures within the scope of this engagement. Furthermore, we interviewed more than 42 company employees and the results of our review are presented in the form of an assessment report.

Findings   After careful review of our findings and recommendations regarding the activities supporting Outsourced Company combined with their staffs' responses, we present the following overall finding. With minor correction actions, as pointed out by the team and completed while on-site, no instances of substantial nonconformance to the expectations matrix in the methodology were found in our review of Outsourced Company.

This does not mean there is absolutely no risk, but our review did not uncover any significant risks within Outsourced Company's operations or systems of internal control. In our professional judgment, the management controls operated by Outsourced Company mitigate the risks identified by the Client Company.

Recommendations During our review process, we made numerous recommendations to Outsourced Company regarding process improvements that could increase mitigation of risk, reduce the opportunity for error, or generally improve Outsourced Company's policy and procedures. The fact that Outsourced Company agreed to implement all of the recommendations documented in this report showed their interest in being viewed as a world-class service provider; most were done immediately, but due to the effort needed, a few remain to be completed as outlined in the findings section. Although the responsiveness of Outsourced Company to the risks of the existing business relationship is both reasonable and adequate, it should be noted that differences in relevant law, regulations, standards, and audit practices with the United States merit recommendation that Outsourced Company conduct annual external/independent reviews of the ongoing adequacy of operations. These annual reviews should demonstrate that no material risks exist, or have developed, with the business relationship and service. In our professional judgment, Outsourced Company provides the following characteristics essential to the Client Company:

- Management is dedicated to "Best of Breed" Enterprise Security
- Environment is highly secure
- Infrastructure is robust and backed up
- Policy and procedures are adequate, with two caveats:
  - Translation to English would make them more accessible
  - Improvements in organization would make them more cohesive
- Material control processes are effective and followed

Scope of Assessment and Report This report is not an audit report or an internal controls certification. It is an independent assessment of specifically identified performance criteria agreed to by Client Company and for the exclusive use of Client Company. It is the sole responsibility of Client Company to determine the adequacy of the controls, take steps to ameliorate any deficiencies as soon as practicable, and conduct a follow-up review to verify remediation. This report provides a narrative of the review conducted by a team from BAROV on-site in Outsourced Company's factory during the specified contractual period. The report is based on answers provided during personal interviews with Outsourced Company's staff and on independent examination of documents and facilities by the BAROV team. BAROV employed the staff and proprietary methodology of its affiliates to conduct this review.

Background   Outsourced Company began its operations (on some specified date) and currently employs approximately 1,600 personnel in one plant. There are plans to build multiple plants over the next 10 years at the same campus. Current capacity is 1.25 million manufactured units per year, with plans to double capacity by 2015. Client Company is currently outsourcing a relatively small item to Outsourced Company. Client Company is concerned about security and controls in all of its operations, including those contracted to Outsourced Company. Client Company engaged BAROV to review enterprise security at Outsourced Company.

Our relationship with the Outsourced Company was at the highest professional level at all times. From time to time, this excellent working relationship seemed strained. We learned near the end of our visit that Outsourced Company had previously experienced a similar review from a different customer and during the review was told everything was going great; however, the final report to the customer's executives was less than flattering. In hindsight, what we perceived as a misunderstanding about the scope of our review was an understandable tension about our motivation. This underlying caution on the part of Outsourced Company, combined with the language difficulties and the disjointed structure of the documentation, required that we occasionally needed to review the same items more than once. In the end, the misunderstanding about our scope and working style was resolved.

Approach   We reviewed over four dozen presentations and hundreds of documents in both English and Chinese covering all the major policies and procedures within the scope of this engagement. We interviewed more than 42 Outsourced Company employees.

Risk Assessment   Following our methodology, the project scope is determined by performing an independent risk assessment of the services outsourced. For this project, Client Company directed the work toward those areas it deemed most important.

Scope of Review   Based on our understanding of Client Company's situation and underlying risk, we performed the following work programs for this review:

- Security Policies
- IT Security Infrastructure
- Access Control—both physical and logical

- Business Continuation Management
- Malicious Software
- Network Management
- Cryptology and Files
- Materials Management
- Inventory Controls

Prior Audits or Reviews

Internal Audit Report   We viewed a copy of the latest internal audit report. BAROV's translator read the cover page and told us that there were no outstanding issues, but since it was written in Chinese we were unable to validate the contents. After conferring with Client Company it was decided that a full translation was low-priority for our review.

Assessment Reports   Each work program is summarized in a stand-alone Assessment Report (AR) in the following format. Each work program begins with a set of definitions and expectations that are repeated in this section of the AR for clarity in reading the report:

- *Situation*—This section describes the current policy and procedures (P&P) environment, with references to relevant documents in the work papers.
- *Findings*—This section presents the results of our inspection, citing specific incidents of nonconformance or issues that require discussion. We will specifically identify these incidents or issues as Item A, Item B, or Item C.
- *Recommendations*—We recommend the following actions: Item A, Item B, and Item C.
- *Disposition*—With regard to Item A, the Service Provider agrees with our recommendation and has already made changes that mitigate Item A. With regard to Item B, the Service Provider agrees with our recommendation and will make appropriate changes that mitigate Item B. With regard to Item C, the Service Provider believes that this issue is adequately addressed in another manner.
- *Conclusions*—This section provides our overall impression of this area of the assessment.
- *Follow up*—We recommend that Client Company ask the Service Provider to provide documentation of changes that mitigate Item B within a certain period to confirm the agreed upon changes. We recommend that Client Company review the Item C issue with regard to Client Company's policy, procedures, and governance framework.

Client Company should promptly discuss the Service Provider position with regard to Item C and ratify the approach or request that the Service Provider make changes to mitigate Client Company's concern.

Work Papers

The report described above is fully supported by professional documentation or work papers (WP), which are maintained by BAROV. These work papers are contained in four folders with the contents as follows:

- Tab A—Work Program
- Tab B—Additional Pages to Work Program
- Tab C—Service Provider Documentation
- Tab D—Other Documents including Service Provider Policy

The following is a sample of a work paper, specifically on IT security policy.

WP 1: Security Policy

Suppliers should have adhered to a documented Enterprise Security Policy and Procedures (P&P) manual to ensure that only properly approved users are granted access to information systems and assets. Users should be granted access on a need-to-know basis, according to job responsibilities. There exists an information security policy, approved by management that is published and communicated to all personal who are responsible for its maintenance and review according to a defined review process. As part of the report, we will provide a situational awareness document, and list our findings, recommendations for correction, prescribed disposition of the problem, and any follow-up required. As an example of a follow up, we may recommend that the Client Company ask Outsourced Company to provide a copy of the agreed changes to the P&P within six months to confirm the changes required. We recommend that Client Company review the identified issues with regard to Client Company policy, procedures, and governance framework. Client Company should promptly discuss Outsourced Company's position and ratify the P&P approach or request that Outsourced Company make changes to mitigate Client Company's concerns.

Quantitative Risk Simulation, Real Options Analysis, and Portfolio Optimization WP2 to WP11 have been left out in this case study, but the sample seen in Figures 14.75 through 14.77 illustrate a Pre-Assessment Ranking Matrix used to understand the specific risk within a specific industry and rate those risks in order of risks to be reviewed. Using the example matrix

Assumptions:

Manager's information has been received
Rated for an On-site review
After all eleven (11) domains are completed the draft report needs to be completed. If issues need to be resolved do so, otherwise
publish draft. After draft has been approved the Executive Summary needs to be completed, once approved published.

Fill out each of the eleven (11) workpages as required:

1. Security Policy
2. Organizational Security
3. Asset Classification and Control
4. Human Resources Security
5. Physical and Environmental Security
6. Communications and Operations Management
7. Access Control
8. Information Systems Acquisition, Development and Maintenance
9. Information Security Incident Management
10. Business Continuity Management
11. Compliance

with the following information:

(7) Page ___ of ___ (name):	Date: on-site	Prepared by: Your Name
Company ABC		

Page ___ of ___   needs to be filled out by hand as you ask the questions and receive the answers

Yes/No/NA   Comments may be completed by hand or by computer (note this section will broaden as you type) please see samples below:

	Rate	Yes/No/NA Comments
Questions/Control Activities: Does your organization have a formal Information Security Policy, which is published and approved by management?	1	A comprehensive formal Information Security Policy, which is published and approved by management which far exceeds industry standards was reviewed
	Rate	Yes/No/NA Comments
Questions/Control Activities: Does your organization have a formal Information Security Policy, which is published and approved by management?	2	I reviewed their Information Security Policy, which is published and approved by management which meets industry standards

FIGURE 14.75   List of working papers.

in Figure 14.76, we apply Risk Simulator input assumptions to the subject matter expert risk rankings, and we run simulations on the matrix in order to determine the total grand risk score for the Client Company. Using probabilistic distributions obtained from the simulation, we are now able to identify the chances that a specific category's risk and impact may exceed tolerable limits, as well as identify the critical success factors (sensitivity analysis and Tornado analysis were run on this assessment matrix). Furthermore, we developed an optimization model where each element was subject to a decision variable in terms of the cost required to correct any outstanding issues, compared to the benefit obtained from having an in-compliance security level, and ran it based on the Client Company's budget constraints. We were then able to create a strategy of multiple phases (sequential compound option) on when certain elements of the issues identified can first be fixed. Following this is the less critical next phase, all the while accounting for interrelationships among IT projects. For example, if a certain project requires another as a prerequisite (some platform technology that first needs

	2.8 Overall Rating			
	Strategic	Reputation	Compliance	Transactional
Probability Risk Assessment				
1 Security Policy	1	1.25	1.5	1.75
2 Organizational Security	2	2.25	2.5	2.75
3 Asset classification and control	3	3.25	3.5	3.5
4 Human Resources Security	4	4.25	4.5	4.75
5 Physical and Environmental Security	5	3	3	3
6 Communications and Operations Management	3	3	3	3
7 Access Control	3	3	3	3
8 Information Systems Acquisition, Development and Maintenance	3	3	3	3
9 Information Security Incident Management	3	3	3	3
10 Business Continuity Management	3	3	3	3
11 Compliance	3	3	3	3
Impact Risk Assessment				
1 Security Policy	5	2	2	1
2 Organizational Security	5	3	2	3
3 Asset classification and control	5	2	1	2
4 Human Resources Security	5	1	2	2
5 Physical and Environmental Security	5	1	1	3
6 Communications and Operations Management	5	2	2	2
7 Access Control	5	2	3	1
8 Information Systems Acquisition, Development and Maintenance	5	3	2	1
9 Information Security Incident Management	5	1	2	1
10 Business Continuity Management	5	1	1	2
11 Compliance	5	2	2	3

Risk free score is One (1) and the highest risk is Five (5)

1   2   3   4   5

Values that are accepted	1	1.25	1.5	1.75	2
Values that are accepted	2.25	2.5	2.75	3	3.25
Values that are accepted	3.5	3.75	4	4.25	4.5
Values that are accepted	4.75	5			

FIGURE 14.76 Assessment matrix.

to be implemented before any subsequent projects can be implemented) or mutually exclusive redundant projects (the implementation of one project makes another obsolete or unnecessary).

In keeping with the belief that neither "cookie-cutter" nor "boil the ocean" approaches are cost-effective or appropriate, we use the following enterprise security assessment methodology to plan for a customized program. Our security assessment consists of four phases and nine processes. Phase 1 has four processes, Phase 2 has two processes, Phase 3 has two processes and Phase 4 has one process (Table 14.7).

Each phase is designed to produce meaningful results for the organization. Please see the attached sample forms previously used to get a flavor of the details that might be requested. Phase 1 examines the enterprise by eliciting information from people working in multiple levels of the enterprise. Phase 1 also derives the security requirements of the enterprise, based on the need for confidentiality, integrity, and/or availability of the key information assets. This phase is important because it helps in integrating unique perspectives and knowledge from multiple organizational levels and helps to build an enterprise-wide view of assets, threats, protection strategies, and risk indicators. This information can then be used to establish the security requirements of the enterprise, which is the goal of the first phase. Phase 2 is then applied to identify infrastructure issues and builds on the

Probability/Impact/Raw Score -- (5=highest risk, 1=no risk)
Executive Summary Prioritization Criteria Matrix

Overall Rating 2.8

1=lowest   11=highest

	Strategic	Reputation	Compliance	Transactional	Priority
Security Policy	3.0	1.6	1.8	1.4	1
Organizational Security	3.5	2.6	2.3	2.9	4
Asset classification and control	4.0	2.6	2.3	2.8	8
Human Resources Security	4.5	2.6	3.3	3.4	11
Physical and Environmental Security	5.0	2.0	2.0	3.0	9
Communications and Operations Management	4.0	2.5	2.5	2.5	5
Access Control	4.0	3.0	3.0	2.0	5
Information Systems Acquisition, Develop and Maint	4.0	2.0	2.5	2.0	5
Information Security Incident Management	4.0	2.0	2.0	2.5	2
Business Continuity Management	4.0	2.5	2.5	3.0	9
Compliance					

Matrix

Legend:
- Security Policy
- Physical and Environmental Security
- Information Security Incident Management
- Organizational Security
- Communications and Operations Management
- Business Continuity Management
- Asset classification and control
- Access Control
- Compliance
- Human Resources Security
- Information Systems Acquisition, Develop and Maint

Strategic
Reputation
Compliance
Transactional

012345

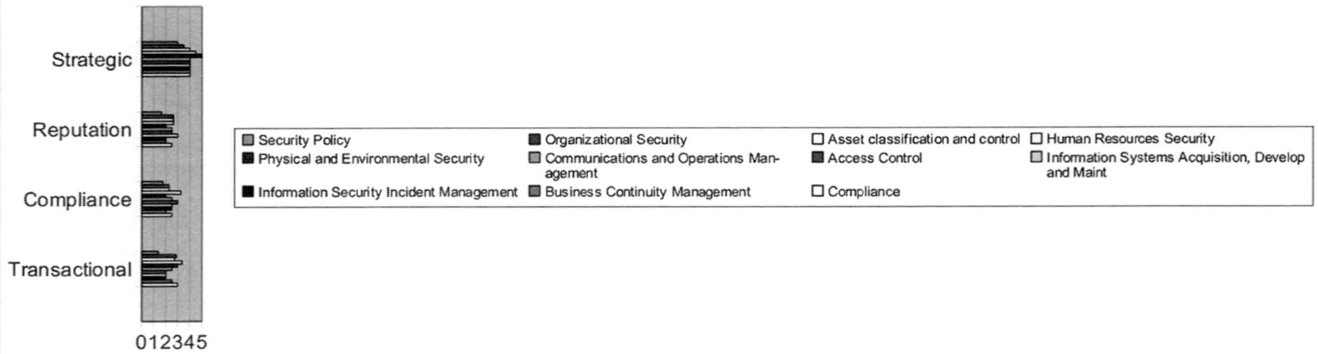

Risk free score is One (1) and the highest risk is Five (5)

1 2 3 4 5

FIGURE 14.77 Ranking matrix.

TABLE 14.7 Summary of Four Phases and Nine Processes

Phase 1	**Enterprise-Wide Security Requirements**
Process 1	Identify Enterprise Knowledge
Process 2	Identify Operational Area Knowledge
Process 3	Identify Staff Knowledge
Process 4	Establish Security Requirements
Phase 2	**Identify Infrastructure Issues**
Process 5	Map Information Assets to Information Infrastructure
Process 6	Perform Infrastructure Vulnerability Evaluation
Phase 3	**Determine Security Management Strategy**
Process 7	Conduct Multi-Dimensional Risk Analysis
Process 8	Develop Protection Strategy
Phase 4	**Develop Customized Training Program**
Process 9	Develop Security Knowledge Gap Strategy

information identified during Phase 1. It uses the asset and threat information from Phase 1 to identify the high-priority components of the information infrastructure. Phase 2 also evaluates the information infrastructure to identify infrastructure vulnerabilities that are exposing the enterprise's assets as well as missing policies and practices. At the conclusion of Phase 2, the high-priority information infrastructure components, missing policies and practices, and vulnerabilities would have been identified. Phase 3 is then applied to determine the security risk management strategy, which involves analysis of assets, threats, and vulnerability information in the context of intrusion scenarios to identify and prioritize the information security risks to the organization. In addition, it develops and implements a protection strategy in the organization to reduce the risk to the enterprise. Therefore, Phase 3 creates a comprehensive risk management plan for implementing the protection strategy and managing risks on a continual basis. The prioritized list of risks generated is used in conjunction with information from the previous phases to develop a protection strategy for the enterprise and to establish a comprehensive plan for managing security risks, which are among the goals of Phase 3. In addition, should the information supplied by staff-level employees indicate that there was some dissatisfaction among some of the employees in the company, specifically, any technical issues, these disgruntled insiders might have both the motive and the means to steal the information and would add to the risks, thereby in all probability adding to the complexity of the project. By performing a comprehensive risk assessment that considers asset, threat, and vulnerability information and puts it into the context of the enterprise, the risks facing the enterprise can be identified. In addition, personnel from all levels can understand risks when they are put into the context of the enterprise, and can make sensible decisions concerning a protection strategy.

- Phase 1:
  - Process 1: Identify Enterprise Knowledge. This process identifies what senior managers perceive to be the key assets and their values, the threats to those assets, indicators of risk, and the current protection strategy employed by the enterprise.
  - Process 2: Identify Operational Area Knowledge. This process identifies what operational area managers perceive to be the key assets and their values, the threats to those assets, indicators of risk, and the current protection strategy employed by the enterprise.
  - Process 3: Identify Staff Knowledge. This process identifies what staff-level personnel perceive to be the key assets and their values, the threats to those assets, indicators of risk, and the current protection strategy employed by the enterprise.
  - Process 4: Establish Security Requirements. This process integrates the individual perspectives identified in the first three processes to produce an enterprise view of the assets.
- Phase 2: Uses the asset and threat information from Phase 1 to identify the high-priority components of the information infrastructure (both the physical infrastructure and the computing infrastructure). It also evaluates the information infrastructure to identify vulnerabilities. Standard catalogs of information about intrusion scenarios and vulnerabilities are used as a basis for evaluating the infrastructure. The ultimate goal of Phase 2 is to identify missing policies and practices as well as infrastructure vulnerabilities. The following two processes comprise Phase 2:
  - Process 5: Map Information Assets to Information Infrastructure. This process combines Phase 1 asset and threat information with staff knowledge about the information infrastructure to establish asset locations, access paths, and data flows. This leads to the identification of the high-priority infrastructure components.
  - Process 6: Perform Infrastructure Vulnerability Evaluation. This process combines the knowledge about assets, threats, risk indicators, and security requirements determined in Phase 1 with staff knowledge about the information infrastructure and standard catalogs of intrusion scenarios and vulnerabilities to identify missing policies and practices as well as infrastructure vulnerabilities.
- Phase 3: This phase is applied to determine the security risk management strategy, and has two subprocesses. They analyze the assets, threats, and vulnerability information in the context of intrusion scenarios to identify and prioritize the risks to the enterprise. In addition, a protection

strategy is developed and implemented in the enterprise. The ultimate goal of Phase 3 is to identify risks to the enterprise and develop a protection strategy to mitigate the highest priority risks. The following two processes comprise Phase 3:

- Process 7: Conduct Multidimensional Risk Analysis. This process analyzes the assets, threats, and vulnerability information identified in Phases 1 and 2 using intrusion scenarios to produce a set of risks to the enterprise. The risk attributes of impact and probability are estimated and then used to prioritize the risks.

- Process 8: Develop Protection Strategy. This process develops the protection strategy by identifying candidate mitigation strategies and then selecting the appropriate ones based on factors such as cost and available resources. This process also develops a comprehensive security risk management plan for implementing the protection strategy and managing risks on a continual basis.

- Phase 4: This phase is used to develop customized training programs by analyzing the assets, threats, and vulnerability information in the context of intrusion scenarios, so that an organization can begin to understand what information is at risk. With this understanding, it can create and implement a protection strategy designed to reduce the overall risk exposure of its information assets. The following process comprises a single subprocess:

- Process 9: Develop Security Knowledge Gap Strategy. This process combines all the above information and industry-specific issues to tailor a training program that "fits" the organization and its current situation to meet current best practices as well as due diligence in its security practices.

CASE STUDY: BASEL II CREDIT RISK AND MARKET RISK

Analytical Techniques for Modeling Probability of Default, Loss Given Default, Economic Capital, Value at Risk, Portfolio Optimized Value at Risk, Interest Rates and Yield Curve, Delta-Gamma Hedging, Floating and Fixed Rates, Foreign Exchange Risk Hedging, Volatility, Commodity Prices, and Over-the-Counter Exotic Options

This case study is written by the author based on consulting projects that he had performed on banks globally, and the case illustrations apply the Risk Simulator, Modeling Toolkit, and Real Options SLS software applications. For more details on some of these applications, please see two of the author's books, Advanced Analytical Models *(John Wiley & Sons, 2008)* and The Banker's Handbook on Credit Risk: Implementing Basel II *(Elsevier Science Academic Press, 2008). This is only meant to be a case study illustrating sample implementations at banks using risk analytic methods and the discussions are not meant to be step-by-step instructions.*

With the new Basel II Accord, internationally active banks are now required to compute their own risk capital requirements using the internal ratings-based (IRB) approach. Not only is adequate risk capital analysis important as a compliance obligation, it provides banks with the ability to optimize their capital through the ability to compute and allocate risks, perform performance measurements, execute strategic decisions, increase competitiveness, and enhance profitability. This case discusses the various *scientific risk management* approaches required to implement an IRB method, as well as the step-by-step models and methodologies in implementing and valuing economic capital, Value at Risk (VaR), probability of default, and loss given default, the key ingredients required in an IRB approach, through the use of advanced analytics such as Monte Carlo and historical risk simulation, portfolio optimization, stochastic forecasting, and options analysis. This case shows the use of Risk Simulator and the Modeling Toolkit (Basel II Toolkit) software in computing and calibrating these critical input parameters. Instead of dwelling on theory or revamping what has already been written many times over, this case focuses solely on the practical modeling applications of the key ingredients to the Basel II Accord.

To follow along with the analyses in this case, we assume that the reader already has Risk Simulator, Real Options SLS, and the Basel II Modeling Toolkit installed, and is somewhat familiar with the basic functions of each software program. If not, please refer to www.realoptionsvaluation.com (click on the *Downloads* link or use the enclosed DVD) and watch the getting started videos, read some of the getting started case studies, or install the latest trial versions of these software programs and their extended licenses. You can download and install the demo version of Modeling Toolkit from the web site and use the password: "heteroskedasticity" when prompted. There is no trial version available; only demo versions or permanent and fully-functional versions are currently available.

Probability of Default

Probability of default measures the degree of likelihood that the borrower of a loan or debt (the obligor) will be unable to make the necessary scheduled repayments on the debt, thereby defaulting on the debt. Should the obligor be unable to pay, the debt is in default, and the lenders of the debt have legal avenues to attempt a recovery of the debt, or at least partial repayment of the entire debt. The higher the default probability a lender estimates a borrower to have, the higher the interest rate the lender will charge the borrower as compensation for bearing the higher default risk.

Probability of default models are categorized as *structural* or *empirical*. Structural models look at a borrower's ability to pay based on market data such as equity prices, market and book values of asset and liabilities, as well as the volatility of these variables, and hence are used predominantly to estimate the probability of default of *companies* and *countries*, most applicable within the areas of commercial and industrial banking. In contrast, empirical models or credit scoring models are used to quantitatively determine the probability that a loan or loan holder will default, where the loan holder is an individual, by looking at historical portfolios of loans held, where individual characteristics are assessed (e.g., age, educational level, debt to income ratio, and other variables), making this second approach more applicable to the retail banking sector.

Structural Models of Probability of Default   Probability of default models is a category of models that assesses the likelihood of default by an obligor. They differ from regular credit scoring models in several ways. First of all, credit scoring models are usually applied to smaller credits—individuals or small businesses whereas default models are applied to larger credits—corporation or countries. Credit scoring models are largely statistical, regressing instances of default against various risk indicators, such as an obligor's income, home renter or owner status, years at a job, educational level, and debt to income ratio, something that will be shown later in this case. Structural default models in contrast directly model the default process, and are typically calibrated to market variables, such as the obligor's stock price, asset value, book value of debt, or the credit spread on its bonds. Default models have many applications within financial institutions. They are used to support credit analysis and for finding the probability that a firm will default, to value counterparty credit risk limits, or to apply financial engineering techniques in developing credit derivatives or other credit instruments.

The example illustrated next uses the Merton probability of default model. This model is used to solve the probability of default of a publicly traded company with equity and debt holdings, and accounting for its volatilities in the market (Figure 14.78). This model is currently used by KMV and Moody's to perform credit risk analysis. This approach assumes that the book value of asset and asset volatility are unknown and solved in the model, and that the company is relatively stable and the growth rate of the company's assets are stable over time (e.g., not in start-up mode).

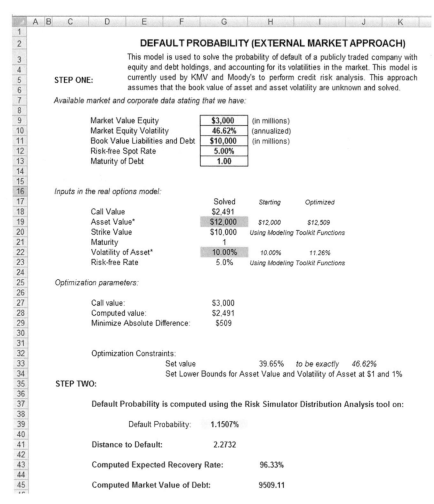

FIGURE 14.78 Probability of default model for external public firms.

The model uses several simultaneous equations in options valuation theory coupled with optimization to obtain the implied underlying asset's market value and volatility of the asset in order to compute the probability of default and distance to default for the firm.

Illustrative Example: Structural Probability of Default Models on Public Firms It is assumed that at this point, the reader is well versed in running simulations and optimizations in Risk Simulator. The example model used is the *Probability of Default – External Options Model* and can be accessed through *Modeling Toolkit | Prob of Default | External Options Model (Public Company)*.

To run this model (Figure 14.78), enter in the required inputs such as the market value of equity (obtained from market data on the firm's capitalization, that is, stock price times number of shares outstanding), equity volatility (computed in the Volatility or LPVA worksheets in the model), book value of debt and liabilities (the firm's book value of all debt and liabilities), the risk-free rate (the prevailing country's risk-free interest rate for the same maturity as the debt), and the debt maturity (the debt maturity to be analyzed, or enter 1 for the annual default probability). The comparable option parameters are shown in cells G18 to G23. All these comparable inputs are computed except for Asset Value (the market value of asset) and the Volatility of Asset. You will need to input some rough estimates as a starting point so that the analysis can be run. The rule of thumb is to set the volatility of the asset in G22 to be one-fifth to half of the volatility of equity computed in G10, and the market value of asset (G19) to be approximately the sum of the market value of equity and book value of liabilities and debt (G9 and G11).

Then, an optimization needs to be run in Risk Simulator in order to obtain the desired outputs. To do this, set Asset Value and Volatility of Asset as the decision variables (make them continuous variables with a lower limit of 1% for volatility and $1 for asset, as both these inputs can only take on positive values). Set cell G29 as the objective to minimize as this is the absolute error value. Finally, the constraint is such that cell H33, the implied volatility in the default model is set to exactly equal the numerical value of the equity volatility in cell G10. Run a static optimization using Risk Simulator.

If the model has a solution, the absolute error value in cell G29 will revert to zero (Figure 14.79). From here, the probability of default (measured in percent) and distance to default (measured in standard deviations) are computed in cells G39 and G41.

Then, using the resulting probability of default, the relevant credit spread required can be determined using the *Credit Analysis – Credit Premium* model or some other credit spread tables (such as using the *Internal Credit Risk Rating* model).

The results indicate that the company has a probability of default at 0.87% with 2.37 standard deviations to default, indicating good creditworthiness (Figure 14.79).

Illustrative Example: Structural Probability of Default Models on Private Firms In addition, several other structural models exist for computing the probability of default of a firm. Specific models are used depending on

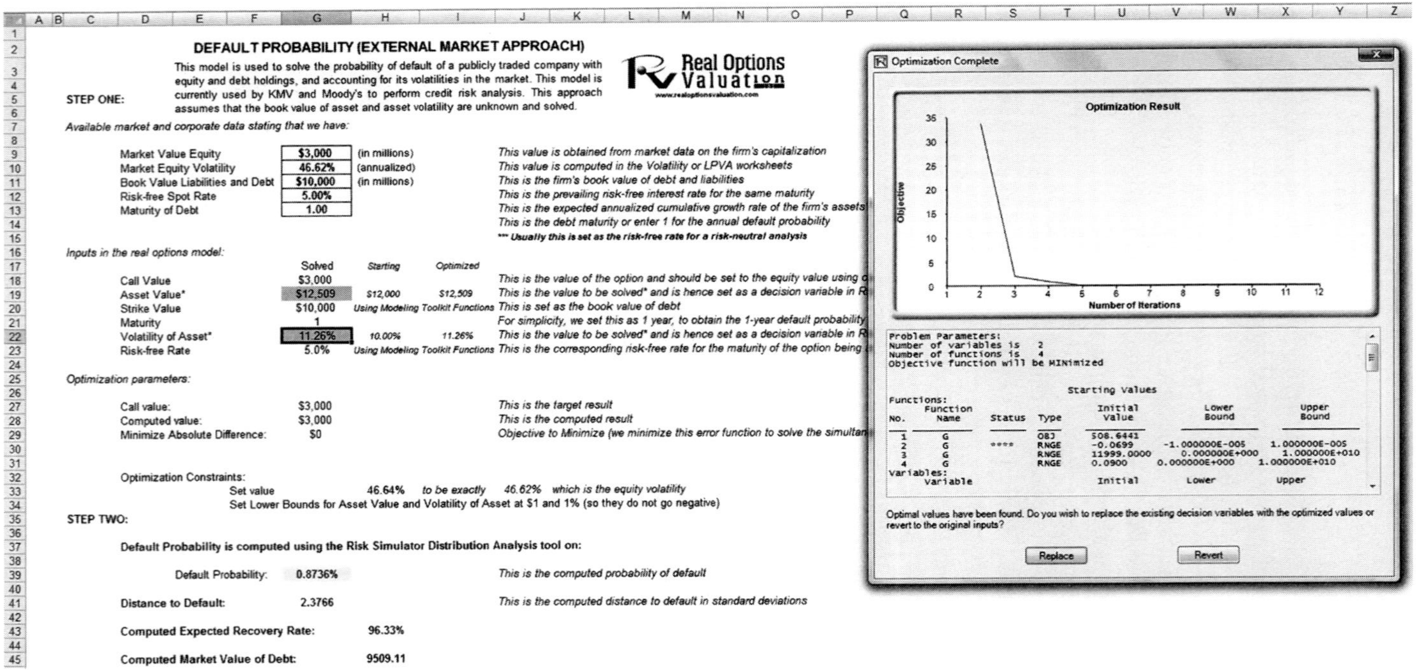
DEFAULT PROBABILITY (EXTERNAL MARKET APPROACH)
This model is used to solve the probability of default of a publicly traded company with equity and debt holdings, and accounting for its volatilities in the market. This model is currently used by KMV and Moody's to perform credit risk analysis. This approach assumes that the book value of asset and asset volatility are unknown and solved.
Real Options Valuation
STEP ONE:
Available market and corporate data stating that we have:
Market Value Equity $3,000 (in millions)
Market Equity Volatility 46.62% (annualized)
Book Value Liabilities and Debt $10,000 (in millions)
Risk-free Spot Rate 5.00%
Maturity of Debt 1.00
This value is obtained from market data on the firm's capitalization
This value is computed in the Volatility or LPVA worksheets
This is the firm's book value of debt and liabilities
This is the prevailing risk-free interest rate for the same maturity
This is the expected annualized cumulative growth rate of the firm's assets
This is the debt maturity or enter 1 for the annual default probability
*** Usually this is set as the risk-free rate for a risk-neutral analysis
Inputs in the real options model:
Solved Starting Optimized
Call Value $3,000
Asset Value* $12,509 $12,000 $12,509
Strike Value $10,000 Using Modeling Toolkit Functions
Maturity 1
Volatility of Asset* 11.26% 10.00% 11.26%
Risk-free Rate 5.0% Using Modeling Toolkit Functions
This is the value of the option and should be set to the equity value using
This is the value to be solved* and is hence set as a decision variable in
This is set as the book value of debt
For simplicity, we set this as 1 year, to obtain the 1-year default probability
This is the value to be solved* and is hence set as a decision variable in
This is the corresponding risk-free rate for the maturity of the option being
Optimization parameters:
Call value: $3,000
Computed value: $3,000
Minimize Absolute Difference: $0
This is the target result
This is the computed result
Objective to Minimize (we minimize this error function to solve the simultan
Optimization Constraints:
Set value 46.64% to be exactly 46.62% which is the equity volatility
Set Lower Bounds for Asset Value and Volatility of Asset at $1 and 1% (so they do not go negative)
STEP TWO:
Default Probability is computed using the Risk Simulator Distribution Analysis tool on:
Default Probability: 0.8736%
This is the computed probability of default
Distance to Default: 2.3766
This is the computed distance to default in standard deviations
Computed Expected Recovery Rate: 96.33%
Computed Market Value of Debt: 9509.11
Optimization Complete
Optimization Result
Objective
Number of Iterations
Problem Parameters:
Number of variables is 2
Number of functions is 4
Objective function will be MINimized
Starting Values
Functions:
No. Function Name Status Type Initial Value Lower Bound Upper Bound
1 G OBJ 508.6441
2 G **** RNGE -0.0699 -1.000000E-005 1.000000E-005
3 G RNGE 11999.0000 0.000000E+000 1.000000E+010
4 G RNGE 0.0900 0.000000E+000 1.000000E+010
Variables:
Variable Initial Lower Upper
Optimal values have been found. Do you wish to replace the existing decision variables with the optimized values or revert to the original inputs?
Replace
Revert

FIGURE 14.79 Optimized model results showing probability of default.

CREDIT RISK DEFAULT PROBABILITY (OPTIONS APPROACH)

VALUING DEFAULT PROBABILITY AND DISTANCE TO DEFAULT BASED ON
OPTIONS MODELING OF INTERNAL DEBT

Input Assumptions	
Asset Book Value	$12.0000
Debt Book Value	$10.0000
Maturity	1.0000
Risk-free Rate	7.00%
Volatility of Asset	10.00%

Probability of Default	0.6695%
Distance to Default	2.4732

This is the options approach to computing the probability of default and distance to default of a company assuming that the book values of asset and debt are known, as are the asset volatilities and anticipated annual growth rates. If the book value of assets or volatility of assets are not known and the company is publicly traded, use the External Markets model instead. This model assumes these inputs are known or the company is privately held and not traded.

Function: B2ProbabilityDefaultMertonII (Asset Value, Strike, Maturity, Riskfree, Asset Volatility)
Function: B2ProbabilityDefaultMertonDefaultDistance(Asset Value, Strike, Maturity, Asset Volatility, Riskfree Rate)

FIGURE 14.80 Probability of default of a privately held company.

the need and availability of data. In the previous example, the firm is a publicly traded firm, with stock prices and equity volatility that can be readily obtained from the market. In this next example, we assume that the firm is privately held, meaning that there would be no market equity data available. It essentially computes the probability of default or the point of default for the company when its liabilities exceed its assets, given the asset's growth rates and volatility over time (Figure 14.80). It is recommended that before using this model, the previous model on external publicly traded company is first reviewed. Similar methodological parallels exist between these two models, whereby this example builds upon the knowledge and expertise of the previous example.

In Figure 14.80, the example firm with an asset value of $12M and a book value of debt at $10M with significant growth rates of its internal assets and low volatility returns a 0.67% probability of default. In addition, instead of relying on the valuation of the firm, external market benchmarks can be used if such data are available. In Figure 14.81, we see that additional input assumptions such as the market fluctuation (market returns and volatility) and relationship (correlation between the market benchmark and the company's assets) are required. The model used is the *Probability of Default – Merton Market Options Model* accessible from *Modeling Toolkit | Prob of Default | Merton Market Options Model (Industry Comparable)*.

Empirical Models of Probability of Default   As mentioned previously, empirical models of probability of default are used to compute an individual's default probability, applicable within the retail banking arena, where

MERTON MODEL OF DEBT DEFAULT PROBABILITY
VALUING THE PROBABILITY OF DEFAULT BASED ON MARKET RELATIONSHIPS

Input Assumptions

Asset Value	$100.0000
Debt Value	$50.0000
Time to Maturity	1.00
Risk-free Rate	5.00%
Volatility of Asset	20.00%
Market Volatility	10.00%
Market Return	8.00%
Correlation	0.00

Probability of Default   0.0150%

This models the probability of default for both public and private companies using an index or set of comparables (the market), assuming that the company's asset and debt book values are known, as well as the asset's annualized volatility. Based on this volatility and the correlation of the company's assets to the market, we can determine the probability of default.

Function: B2ProbabilityDefaultMertonI (Asset, Debt, Maturity, Riskfree, Asset Volatility, Market Volatility, Market Return, Correlation)

FIGURE 14.81 Default probability of a privately held entity calibrated to market fluctuations.

empirical or actual historical or comparable data exist on past credit defaults. The dataset in Figure 14.82 represents a sample of several thousand previous loans, credit or debt issues. The data show whether each loan had defaulted or not (0 for no default, and 1 for default), as well as the specifics of each loan applicant's age, education level (1–3 indicating high school, university, or graduate professional education), years with current employer, and so forth. The idea is to model these empirical data to see which variables

PROBABILITY OF DEFAULT (EMPIRICAL METHOD USING MAXIMUM LIKELIHOOD MODELS ON HISTORICAL DATA)

Defaulted	Age	Education Level	Years with Current Employer	Years at Current Address	Household Income (Thousands $)	Debt to Income Ratio (%)	Credit Card Debt (Thousands $)	Other Debt (Thousands $)
1	41	3	17	12	176	9.3	11.36	5.01
0	27	1	10	6	31	17.3	1.36	4
0	40	1	15	14	55	5.5	0.86	2.17
0	41	1	15	14	120	2.9	2.66	0.82
1	24	2	2	0	28	17.3	1.79	3.06
0	41	2	5	5	25	10.2	0.39	2.16
0	39	1	20	9	67	30.6	3.83	16.67
0	43	1	12	11	38	3.6	0.13	1.24
1	24	1	3	4	19	24.4	1.36	3.28
0	36	1	0	13	25	19.7	2.78	2.15
0	27	1	0	1	16	1.7	0.18	0.09
0	25	1	4	0	23	5.2	0.25	0.94
0	52	1	24	14	64	10	3.93	2.47
0	37	1	6	9	29	16.3	1.72	3.01
0	48	1	22	15	100	9.1	3.7	5.4
1	36	2	9	6	49	8.6	0.82	3.4
1	36	2	13	6	41	16.4	2.92	3.81
0	43	1	23	19	72	7.6	1.18	4.29
0	39	1	6	9	61	5.7	0.56	2.91
0	41	3	0	21	26	1.7	0.1	0.34
0	39	1	22	3	52	3.2	1.15	0.51
0	47	1	17	21	43	5.6	0.59	1.82
0	28	1	3	6	26	10	0.43	2.17
0	29	1	8	6	27	9.8	0.4	2.24
1	21	2	1	2	16	18	0.24	2.64
0	25	4	0	2	32	17.6	2.14	3.49
0	45	2	9	26	69	6.7	0.71	3.92
0	43	1	25	21	64	16.7	0.95	9.74

The data here represents a sample of several hundred previous loans, credit, or debt issues. The data show whether each loan had defaulted or not, as well as the specifics of each loan applicant's age, education level (1-3 indicating high school, university, or graduate professional education), years with current employer and so forth. The idea is to model these empirical data to see which variables affect the default behavior of individuals, using Risk Simulator's Maximum Likelihood Models. The resulting model will help the bank or credit issuer compute the expected probability of default of an individual credit holder of having specific characteristics.

To run the analysis, select the data on the left or any other data set (include the headers) and make sure that the data have the same length for all variables, without any missing or invalid data. Then, click on **Risk Simulator | Forecasting | Maximum Likelihood Models**. A sample set of results are provided in the MLE worksheet, complete with detailed instructions on how to compute the expected probability of default of an individual.

FIGURE 14.82 Empirical analysis of probability of default.

affect the default behavior of individuals, using Risk Simulator's *Maximum Likelihood Estimation* (MLE) tool. The resulting model will help the bank or credit issuer compute the expected probability of default of an individual credit holder having specific characteristics.

Illustrative Example on Applying Empirical Models of Probability of Default
The example file is *Probability of Default – Empirical* and can be accessed through *Modeling Toolkit | Prob of Default | Empirical (Individuals)*. To run the analysis, select the data set (include the headers) and make sure that the data have the same length for all variables, without any missing or invalid data points. Then, using Risk Simulator, click on *Risk Simulator | Forecasting | Maximum Likelihood Models*. A sample set of results is provided in the MLE worksheet, complete with detailed instructions on how to compute the expected probability of default of an individual.

The MLE approach applies a modified binary multivariate logistic analysis to model dependent variables to determine the expected probability of success of belonging to a certain group. For instance, given a set of independent variables (e.g., age, income, education level of credit card or mortgage loan holders), we can model the probability of default using MLE. A typical regression model is invalid because the errors are heteroskedastic and nonnormal, and the resulting estimated probability forecast will sometimes be above 1 or below 0. MLE analysis handles these problems using an iterative optimization routine. The computed results show the coefficients of the estimated MLE intercept and slopes.[29]

The coefficients estimated are actually the logarithmic odds ratios and cannot be interpreted directly as probabilities. A quick but simple computation is first required. The approach is simple. To estimate the probability of success of belonging to a certain group (e.g., predicting if a debt holder will default given the amount of debt he or she holds), simply compute the estimated Y value using the MLE coefficients. Figure 14.83 illustrates an individual with eight years at a current employer and current address, a low 3% debt to income ratio, and $2,000 in credit card debt has a log odds ratio of –3.1549. Then, the inverse antilog of the odds ratio is obtained by computing:

$$\frac{\exp(estimated\ Y)}{1 + \exp(estimated\ Y)} = \frac{\exp(-3.1549)}{1 + \exp(-3.1549)} = 0.0409$$

So, such a person has a 4.09% chance of defaulting on the new debt. Using this probability of default, you can then use the *Credit Analysis – Credit Premium* model to determine the additional credit spread to charge

MLE Results

| Log Likelihood Value | | −200.507 | | | |

Variable	Coefficients	Standard Error	Z- Statistic	p-Value	Sample Inputs
	−1.7003	0.7512	−2.2634	0.0236	
Age	0.0279	0.0205	1.3588	0.1742	
Education Level	0.0728	0.1447	0.5028	0.6151	
Years with Current Employer	−0.2528	0.0391	−6.4644	0.0000	*8.000*
Years at Current Address	−0.0952	0.0271	−3.5064	0.0005	*8.000*
Household Income (Thousands $)	0.0009	0.0125	0.0754	0.9399	
Debt to Income Ratio (%)	0.0750	0.0396	1.8934	0.0583	*3.000*
Credit Card Debt (Thousands $)	0.5521	0.1324	4.1697	0.0000	*2.000*
Other Debt (Thousands $)	0.0461	0.1005	0.4592	0.6461	

| | | | | *Log Odds Ratio* | *−3.1549* |
| | | | | *Default Probability* | *4.09%* |

FIGURE 14.83   MLE results.

this person given this default level and the customized cash flows anticipated from this debt holder.

Loss Given Default and Expected Losses

As shown previously, probability of default is a key parameter for computing credit risk of a portfolio. In fact, the Basel II Accord requires the probability of default, as well as other key parameters such as the loss given default (LGD) and exposure at default (EAD) be reported as well. The reason is that a bank's expected loss is equivalent to:

Expected Losses = (Probability of Default) × (Loss Given Default) × (Exposure at Default)

or simply: $EL = PD \times LGD \times EAD$

PD and LGD are both percentages, whereas EAD is a value. As we have shown how to compute PD in the previous section, we will now revert to some estimations of LGD. There are again several methods used to estimate LGD. The first is through a simple empirical approach where we set $LGD = 1 - Recovery\ Rate$. That is, whatever is not recovered at default is the loss at default, computed as the charge off (net of recovery) divided by the outstanding balance:

$$LGD = 1 - \text{Recovery Rate}$$
$$\text{or}$$
$$LGD = \frac{\text{Charge Offs (Net of Recovery)}}{\text{Outstanding Balance at Default}}$$

Therefore, if market data or historical information is available, LGD can be segmented by various market conditions, types of obligor, and other pertinent segmentations (use Risk Simulator's segmentation tool to perform this). LGD can then be readily read off a chart.

A second approach to estimate LGD is more attractive in that if the bank has available information, it can attempt to run some econometric models to create the best fitting model under an ordinary least squares approach. By using this approach, a single model can be determined and calibrated, and this same model can be applied under various conditions, and no data mining is required. However, in most econometric models, a normal-transformation will have to be performed first. Suppose the bank has some historical LGD data (Figure 14.84), the best-fitting distribution can be found using Risk Simulator by first selecting the historical data, and then clicking on *Risk Simulator | Tools | Distributional Fitting (Single Variable)* to perform the fitting routine. The example's result is a beta distribution for the thousands of LGD values. The p-value can also be evaluated for the goodness of fit of the theoretical distribution (i.e., the higher the p-value, the better the distributional fit, so in this example, the historical LGD fits a beta distribution 81% of the time, indicating a good fit).

Next, using the Distribution Analysis tool in Risk Simulator, obtain the theoretical mean and standard deviation of the fitted distribution (Figure 14.85). Then, transform the LGD variable using the *B2NormalTransform* function in the Modeling Toolkit software. For instance, the value 49.69% will be transformed and normalized to 28.54% (Figure 14.84). Using this newly transformed data set, you can now run some nonlinear econometric models to determine LGD.

The following is a partial list of independent variables that might be significant for a bank, in terms of determining and forecasting the LGD value:

- Debt to capital ratio
- Profit margin
- Revenue

Past LGD	Normalized
49.69%	28.54%
25.76%	18.27%
14.61%	11.84%
26.91%	18.83%
18.47%	14.33%
21.29%	15.95%
26.00%	18.39%
11.84%	9.76%
51.85%	29.41%
19.35%	14.84%
24.74%	17.76%
15.68%	12.57%
14.35%	11.66%
21.36%	15.98%
35.31%	22.65%
50.71%	28.95%
28.58%	19.63%
5.96%	3.77%
3.84%	0.38%
21.70%	16.17%
71.28%	37.64%
23.49%	17.12%
20.25%	15.36%
44.01%	26.26%
31.27%	20.87%
40.86%	24.98%
26.54%	18.65%
25.29%	18.04%
28.51%	19.60%
55.40%	30.84%
31.57%	21.00%
16.30%	12.98%
24.37%	17.57%
8.46%	6.70%
77.08%	40.52%

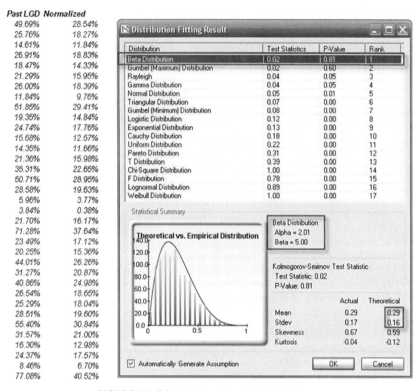

FIGURE 14.84 Fitting historical LGD data.

- Current assets to current liabilities
- Risk rating at default and one year before default
- Industry
- Authorized balance at default
- Collateral value
- Facility type
- Tightness of covenant
- Seniority of debt
- Operating income to sales ratio (and other efficiency ratios)
- Total asset, total net worth, total liabilities

Economic Capital and Value at Risk

Economic capital is critical to a bank as it links a bank's earnings and returns to risks that are specific to a business line or business opportunity. In addition, these economic capital measurements can be aggregated into a

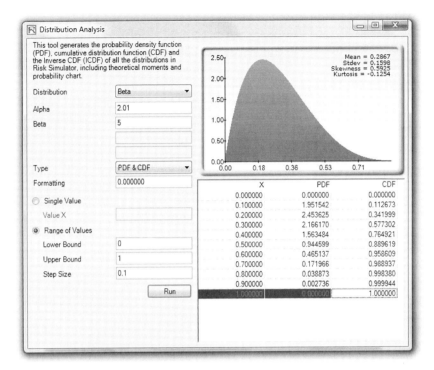

FIGURE 14.85   Distributional analysis tool.

portfolio of holdings. Value at Risk (VaR) is used in trying to understand how the entire organization is affected by the various risks of each holding as aggregated into a portfolio, after accounting for their cross-correlations among various holdings. VaR measures the maximum possible loss given some predefined probability level (e.g., 99.90%) over some holding period or time horizon (e.g., 10 days). The selected probability or confidence interval is typically a decision made by senior management at the bank and reflects the board's risk appetite. Stated another way, we can define the probability level as the bank's desired probability of surviving per year. In addition, the holding period is usually chosen such that it coincides with the time period it takes to liquidate a loss position.

VaR can be computed several ways. Two main families of approaches exist: structural closed-form models and Monte Carlo risk simulation approaches. We will showcase both methods in this case, starting with the structural models.

The second and much more powerful approach is the use of Monte Carlo risk simulation. Instead of simply correlating individual business lines or assets in the structural models, entire probability distributions can be correlated using more advanced mathematical copulas and simulation algorithms in Monte Carlo simulation methods, by using Risk Simulator. In addition, tens to hundreds of thousands of scenarios can be generated using simulation, providing a very powerful stress-testing mechanism for valuing VaR. In addition, distributional fitting methods are applied to reduce the thousands of data points into their appropriate probability distributions, allowing their modeling to be handled with greater ease.

Illustrative Example: Structural VaR Models   The first VaR example model shown is the *Value at Risk – Static Covariance Method,* accessible through *Modeling Toolkit | Value at Risk | Static Covariance Method.* This model is used to compute the portfolio's VaR at a given percentile for a specific holding period, after accounting for the cross-correlation effects between the assets (Figure 14.86). The daily volatility is the annualized volatility divided by the square root of trading days per year. Typically, positive correlations tend to carry a higher VaR compared to zero correlation asset mixes, whereas negative correlations reduce the total risk of the portfolio through the diversification effect (Figures 14.86 and 14.87). The approach used is a portfolio VaR with correlated inputs, where the portfolio has multiple asset holdings with different amounts and volatilities. Each asset is also correlated to each other. The covariance or correlation structural model is used to compute the VaR given a holding period or horizon and percentile value (typically 10 days at 99% confidence). Of course, the example only illustrates a few assets or business lines or credit lines for simplicity's sake. Nonetheless, using the functions in the Modeling Toolkit, many more lines, assets, or businesses can be modeled (the function B2VaRCorrelationMethod is used in this example).

Illustrative Example: VaR Models Using Monte Carlo Risk Simulation   The model used is *Value at Risk – Portfolio Operational and Capital Adequacy* and is accessible through *Modeling Toolkit | Value at Risk | Portfolio Operational and Capital Adequacy.* This model shows how operational risk and credit risk parameters are fitted to statistical distributions and their resulting distributions are modeled in a portfolio of liabilities to determine the Value at Risk (e.g., 99.50th percentile certainty) for the capital requirement under Basel II requirements. It is assumed that the historical data of the operational risk impacts (Historical Data worksheet) are obtained through econometric modeling of the Key Risk Indicators.

The *Distributional Fitting Report* worksheet is a result of running a distributional fitting routine in Risk Simulator to obtain the appropriate

VALUE AT RISK (VARIANCE-COVARIANCE METHOD)

Asset Allocation	Amount	Daily Volatility
Asset A	$1,000,000.00	1.20%
Asset B	$2,000,000.00	2.00%
Asset C	$3,000,000.00	1.89%
Asset D	$4,000,000.00	3.25%
Asset E	$5,000,000.00	4.20%

Correlation Matrix	Asset A	Asset B	Asset C	Asset D	Asset E
Asset A	1.0000	0.1000	0.1000	0.1000	0.1000
Asset B	0.1000	1.0000	0.1000	0.1000	0.1000
Asset C	0.1000	0.1000	1.0000	0.1000	0.1000
Asset D	0.1000	0.1000	0.1000	1.0000	0.1000
Asset E	0.1000	0.1000	0.1000	0.1000	1.0000

Horizon (Days)	10
Percentile	99.00%

Value at Risk (Daily)	$655,915.30
Value at Risk (Horizon)	$2,074,186.30

Daily Value at Risk (Positive Correlations)	$2,074,186.30
Daily Value at Risk (Zero Correlations)	$1,889,345.26
Daily Value at Risk (Negative Correlations)	$1,684,340.28

FIGURE 14.86 Computing Value at Risk using the structural covariance method.

Correlation Matrix	Asset A	Asset B	Asset C	Asset D	Asset E
Asset A	1.0000	0.1000	0.1000	0.1000	0.1000
Asset B	0.1000	1.0000	0.1000	0.1000	0.1000
Asset C	0.1000	0.1000	1.0000	0.1000	0.1000
Asset D	0.1000	0.1000	0.1000	1.0000	0.1000
Asset E	0.1000	0.1000	0.1000	0.1000	1.0000

Correlation Matrix	Asset A	Asset B	Asset C	Asset D	Asset E
Asset A	1.0000	0.0000	0.0000	0.0000	0.0000
Asset B	0.0000	1.0000	0.0000	0.0000	0.0000
Asset C	0.0000	0.0000	1.0000	0.0000	0.0000
Asset D	0.0000	0.0000	0.0000	1.0000	0.0000
Asset E	0.0000	0.0000	0.0000	0.0000	1.0000

Correlation Matrix	Asset A	Asset B	Asset C	Asset D	Asset E
Asset A	1.0000	-0.1000	-0.1000	-0.1000	-0.1000
Asset B	-0.1000	1.0000	-0.1000	-0.1000	-0.1000
Asset C	-0.1000	-0.1000	1.0000	-0.1000	-0.1000
Asset D	-0.1000	-0.1000	-0.1000	1.0000	-0.1000
Asset E	-0.1000	-0.1000	-0.1000	-0.1000	1.0000

FIGURE 14.87 Different correlation levels.

distribution for the operational risk parameter. Using the resulting distributional parameters, we model each liability's capital requirements within an entire portfolio. Correlations can also be inputted if required between pairs of liabilities or business units. The resulting Monte Carlo simulation results show the Value at Risk or VaR capital requirements.

Note that an appropriate empirically based historical VaR cannot be obtained if distributional fitting and risk-based simulations were not first run. Only by running simulations will the VaR be obtained. To perform distributional fitting, follow the steps below:

1. In the *Historical Data* worksheet (Figure 14.88), select the data area (cells C5:L104) and click on *Risk Simulator | Tools | Distributional Fitting (Single Variable)*.
2. Browse through the fitted distributions and select the best-fitting distribution (in this case, the exponential distribution with a particularly high p-value fit, as shown in Figure 14.89) and click *OK*.
3. You may now set the assumptions on the *Operational Risk Factors* with the exponential distribution (fitted results show *Lambda* = 1) in the Credit Risk worksheet. Note that the assumptions have already been set for you in advance. You may set it by going to cell F27 and clicking on *Risk Simulator | Set Input Assumption,* selecting *Exponential* distribution and entering 1 for the *Lambda* value and clicking *OK*. Continue this process for the remaining cells in column F or simply perform a *Risk Simulator Copy* and *Risk Simulator Paste* on the remaining cells:
   a. Note that since the cells in column F have assumptions set, you will first have to clear them if you wish to reset and copy/paste parameters. You can do so by first selecting cells F28:F126 and clicking on the *Remove Parameter* icon or select *Risk Simulator | Remove Parameter*.
   b. Then select cell F27, click on the *Risk Simulator Copy* icon or select *Risk Simulator | Copy Parameter*, and then select cells F28:F126 and click on the *Risk Simulator Paste* icon or select *Risk Simulator | Paste Parameter*.
4. Next, additional assumptions can be set such as the probability of default using the Bernoulli distribution (column H) and *Loss Given Default* (column J). Repeat the procedure in Step 3 if you wish to reset the assumptions.
5. Run the simulation by clicking on the *Run* icon or clicking on *Risk Simulator | Run Simulation*.
6. Obtain the Value at Risk by going to the forecast chart once the simulation is done running and selecting *Left-Tail* and typing in 99.50. Hit *TAB* on the keyboard to enter the confidence value and obtain the VaR of $25,959 (Figure 14.90).

Basel II - Credit Risk and Capital Requirement (Portfolio-Based)

This model applies the Basel II requirements on capital adequacy and modeling the operational risk of probability of default on 100 loans as well as the loss given default. These values are fitted based on the bank's historical loss data (Historical Data and Distributional Fitting Report sheets) using Risk Simulator. Then, the relevant historical simulation assumptions are set in this model (Credit Risk sheet) and a Monte Carlo risk-based simulation was run in Risk Simulator to determine the expected capital required and 99.50% Value at Risk (VaR). A simulation has to be run in order to determine the VaR.

Market Factor	2.000
Weighting:	
Macro	50%
Micro	50%
Correlation	100%

Rating level	P (Default) - Long term
2	0.5%
3	1.0%
4	1.5%
5	2.0%
6	2.5%
7	3.0%
	5.0%

	Static	Stochastic with Risk-Simulation
Expected Value of Total Capital	$11,734.54	$11,112.81
VaR 99.50% of Total Capital	$30,888.34	$25,959.60

Without running historical simulations, the 99.50% VaR cannot be obtained directly. The only recourse is to apply a theoretical distributional analysis using the fitted distributions' empirical parameters and estimating the theoretical cumulative density function value at 99.50%, and computing the relevant theoretical confidence level of the required capital (thereby requiring too much capital) and at worst, wrong.

Bank loan	Size of loan	Rating grade	P (Default) - Long term	Operational Risk Factor	P (Default) - Now	Default?	LGD% Static	LGD% Stochastic	Losses Static	Losses Stochastic
1	$ 13,274.73	5	2.5%	2.000	5.00%	0	30.0%	30.0%	$ 199.12	$ -
2	$ 14,215.77	6	3.0%	2.000	6.00%	0	30.0%	30.0%	$ 255.88	$ -
3	$ 9,003.59	1	0.5%	2.000	1.00%	0	30.0%	30.0%	$ 27.01	$ -
4	$ 1,324.27	3	1.5%	2.000	3.00%	0	30.0%	30.0%	$ 11.92	$ -
5	$ 11,203.14	1	0.5%	2.000	1.00%	0	30.0%	30.0%	$ 33.61	$ -
6	$ 5,480.61	4	2.0%	2.000	4.00%	0	30.0%	30.0%	$ 65.77	$ -
7	$ 9,853.12	5	2.5%	2.000	5.00%	0	30.0%	30.0%	$ 147.80	$ -
8	$ 12,356.22	3	1.5%	2.000	3.00%	0	30.0%	30.0%	$ 111.21	$ -
9	$ 8,255.80	4	2.0%	2.000	4.00%	0	30.0%	30.0%	$ 99.07	$ -
10	$ 1,662.99	2	1.0%	2.000	2.00%	0	30.0%	30.0%	$ 9.98	$ -

	Static	Stochastic
Sum	$11,734.54	$ -
Static 99.50%	$30,888.34	

Portfolio Losses - Risk Simulator Forecast

Portfolio Losses (1000 Trials)

Type: Left-Tail   25955.800   Certainty (%)   99.50

Portfolio Losses - Risk Simulator Forecast

Statistics	Result
Number of Trials	1000
Mean	1.11128E+004
Median	1.06799E+004
Standard Deviation	5597.8726
Variance	3.13361E+007
Average Deviation	4522.4248
Maximum	3.16772E+004
Minimum	0.0000
Range	3.16772E+004
Skewness	0.4724
Kurtosis	-0.1656
25% Percentile	6678.1717
75% Percentile	1.46639E+004
Percentage Error Precision at 95% Confidence	3.1221%

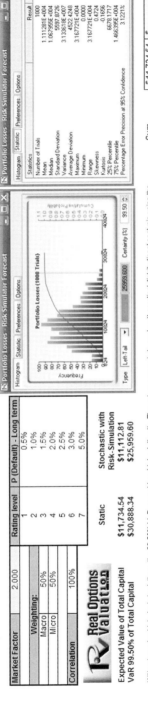

FIGURE 14.88 Sample historical bank loans.

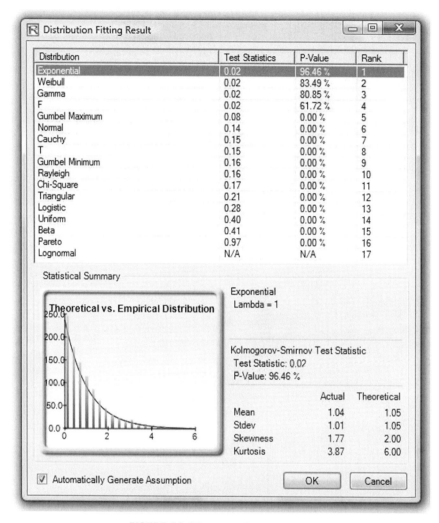

FIGURE 14.89   Data fitting results.

Another example on VaR computation is shown next, where the model *Value at Risk – Right Tail Capital Requirements* is used, and available through *Modeling Toolkit | Value at Risk | Right Tail Capital Requirements*.

This model shows the capital requirements per Basel II requirements (99.95th percentile capital adequacy based on a specific holding period's Value at Risk). Without running risk-based historical and Monte Carlo simulation using Risk Simulator, the required capital is $37.01M

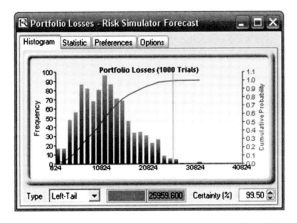

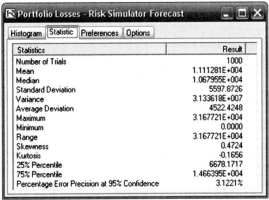

FIGURE 14.90 Simulated forecast results and the 99.50% Value at Risk value.

(Figure 14.91) as compared to only $14.00M required using a correlated simulation (Figure 14.92). This is due to the cross-correlations between assets and business lines, and can only be modeled using Risk Simulator. This lower VaR is preferred as banks can now be required to hold less required capital and can reinvest the remaining capital in various profitable ventures, thereby generating higher profits.

1. To run the model, click on *Risk Simulator | Run Simulation* (if you had other models open, make sure you first click on *Risk Simulator | Change Simulation | Profile*, and select the *Tail VaR* profile before starting).
2. When simulation is complete, select *Left-Tail* in the forecast chart and enter in 99.95 in the *Certainty* box and hit *TAB* on the keyboard to obtain the value of $14.00M Value at Risk for this correlated simulation.

Real Options Valuation
www.realoptionsvaluation.com

TAIL VALUE AT RISK MODEL (BASEL II REQUIREMENT)

Line of Business	Mean Required Capital	99.95th Percentile	Capital Required	Allocation Weights	Minimum Allowed	Maximum Allowed	
Business 1	$10.50	$36.52	$26.01	10.00%	5.00%	15.00%	3.48
Business 2	$11.12	$47.52	$36.39	10.00%	5.00%	15.00%	4.27
Business 3	$11.77	$48.99	$37.22	10.00%	5.00%	15.00%	4.16
Business 4	$10.77	$37.34	$26.56	10.00%	5.00%	15.00%	3.47
Business 5	$13.49	$49.52	$36.03	10.00%	5.00%	15.00%	3.67
Business 6	$14.24	$55.59	$41.35	10.00%	5.00%	15.00%	3.91
Business 7	$15.60	$60.24	$44.64	10.00%	5.00%	15.00%	3.86
Business 8	$14.95	$64.69	$49.74	10.00%	5.00%	15.00%	4.33
Business 9	$14.15	$61.02	$46.87	10.00%	5.00%	15.00%	4.31
Business 10	$10.08	$35.37	$25.29	10.00%	5.00%	15.00%	3.51
Portfolio Total	$12.67	$49.68	$37.01	100.00%			
Total Capital Required			$14.00				

Correlation Matrix

	1	2	3	4	5	6	7	8	9	10
1										
2	-0.20									
3	-0.13	0.35								
4	-0.05	0.01	0.00							
5	0.23	0.50	0.15	0.00						
6	0.00	0.00	-0.15	0.00	0.03					
7	0.25	0.00	-0.26	0.01	0.10	-0.10				
8	0.36	-0.25	-0.60	-0.30	0.00	0.00	-0.15			
9	-0.01	-0.20	0.16	0.04	-0.01	0.01	0.00	0.00		

FIGURE 14.91 Right-tail VaR model.

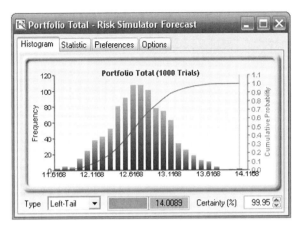

FIGURE 14.92   Simulated results of the portfolio VaR.

3. Note that the assumptions have already been set for you in advance in the model in cells *C6:C15*. However, you may set it again by going to cell C6 and clicking on *Risk Simulator | Set Input Assumption*, selecting your distribution of choice or use the default *Normal Distribution* or perform a distributional fitting on historical data and click *OK*. Continue this process for the remaining cells in column C. You may also decide to first *Remove Parameters* of these cells in column C and set your own distributions. Further, correlations can be set manually when assumptions are set (Figure 14.93) or by going to *Simulation | Edit Correlations* (Figure 14.94) after all the assumptions are set.

If risk simulation was not run, the VaR or economic capital required would have been $37M, as opposed to only $14M. All cross-correlations between business lines have been modeled, as are stress and scenario tests, and thousands and thousands of possible iterations are run. Individual risks are now aggregated into a cumulative portfolio level VaR.

Efficient Portfolio Allocation and Economic Capital VaR   As a side note, by performing portfolio optimization, a portfolio's VaR can actually be reduced. We start by first introducing the concept of stochastic portfolio optimization through an illustrative hands-on example. Then, using this portfolio optimization technique, we apply it to four business lines or assets to compute the VaR or an un-optimized versus an optimized portfolio of assets, and see the difference in computed VaR. You will note that at the end, the optimized portfolio bears less risk and has a lower required economic capital.

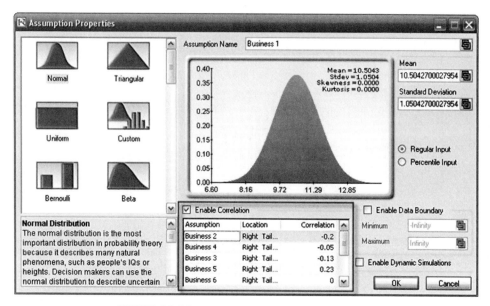

FIGURE 14.93   Setting correlations one at a time.

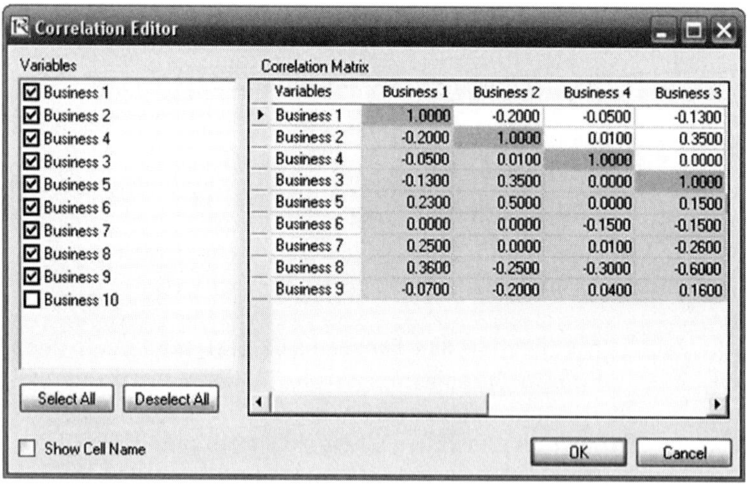

FIGURE 14.94   Setting correlations using the correlation matrix routine.

	A	B	C	D	E	F	G
1							
2							**Real Options**
3		VALUE AT RISK WITH ASSET ALLOCATION OPTIMIZATION MODEL					**Valuation**
4							www.realoptionsvaluation.com
5		Asset Class Description	Annualized Returns	Volatility Risk	Allocation Weights	Required Minimum Allocation	Required Maximum Allocation
6		S&P 500	7.10%	9.80%	10.00%	10.00%	40.00%
7		Small Cap	9.51%	14.35%	27.30%	10.00%	40.00%
8		High Yield	15.90%	22.50%	22.70%	10.00%	40.00%
9		Govt Bonds	4.50%	7.25%	40.00%	10.00%	40.00%
10				*Total Weight:*	*100.00%*		
11							
12		Correlation Matrix	S&P 500	Small Cap	High Yield	Govt Bonds	
13		S&P 500	1.0000	0.7400	0.6500	0.5500	
14		Small Cap	0.7400	1.0000	0.4200	0.3100	
15		High Yield	0.6500	0.4200	1.0000	0.2300	
16		Govt Bonds	0.5500	0.3100	0.2300	1.0000	
17							
18		Covariance Matrix	S&P 500	Small Cap	High Yield	Govt Bonds	
19		S&P 500	0.0096	0.0104	0.0143	0.0039	
20		Small Cap	0.0104	0.0206	0.0136	0.0032	
21		High Yield	0.0143	0.0136	0.0506	0.0038	
22		Govt Bonds	0.0039	0.0032	0.0038	0.0053	
23							
24		Starting Value	$1,000,000.00				
25		Term (Years)	5.00				
26							
27		Annualized Return	8.72%	Profit/Loss	$87,151.94		
28		Portfolio Risk	9.84%	Return to Risk Ratio	88.59%		
29		Ending Value	$1,087,151.94				
30							
31		Specifications of the optimization model:					
32							
33		Objective:		*Maximize Return to Risk Ratio (E28)*			
34		Decision Variables:		*Allocation Weights (E6:E9)*			
35		Restrictions on Decision Variables:		*Minimum and Maximum Required (F6:G9)*			
36		Constraints:		*Portfolio Total Allocation Weights 100% (E10 is set to 100%)*			
37							
38		Notice that the 10% VaR of profit/loss for a simple 25% allocation yields $42,157 as compared to a VaR of $35,815 for an optimized					
39		portfolio allocation of assets. The VaR is reduced by having a better portfolio allocation. Further, the portfolio risk is also reduced as well					
40		the fluctuations of the profit and loss results (coefficient of variability) but at the expense of slightly lower profits (low risk, low returns).					
41		This model is already set up and ready to run an optimization analysis.					

FIGURE 14.95   Computing Value at Risk (VaR) with simulation.

Illustrative Example: Portfolio Optimization and the Effects on Portfolio VaR   Now that we understand the concepts of optimized portfolios, let us now see what the effects are on computed economic capital through the use of a correlated portfolio VaR. This model uses Monte Carlo simulation and optimization routines in Risk Simulator to minimize the VaR of a portfolio of assets (Figure 14.95). The file used is *Value at Risk – Optimized and Simulated Portfolio VaR*, which is accessible via *Modeling Toolkit | Value at Risk | Optimized and Simulated Portfolio VaR*. In this example model, we intentionally used only 4 asset classes to illustrate the effects of an optimized portfolio, whereas in real life, we can extend this to cover a multitude of asset classes and business lines. In addition, we now illustrate the use of a left-tail VaR, as opposed to a right-tail VaR, but the concepts are similar.

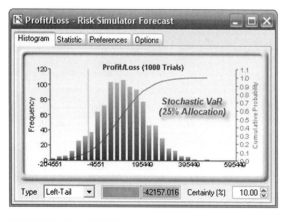

FIGURE 14.96   Nonoptimized Value at Risk.

First, simulation is used to determine the 90% left-tail VaR (this means that there is a 10% chance that losses will exceed this VaR for a specified holding period). With an equal allocation of 25% across the 4 asset classes, the VaR is determined using simulation (Figure 14.96). The annualized returns are uncertain and hence simulated. The VaR is then read off the forecast chart. Then, optimization is run to find the best portfolio subject to the 100% allocation across the 4 projects that will maximize the portfolio's bang-for-the-buck (returns to risk ratio). The resulting optimized portfolio is then simulated once again and the new VaR is obtained (Figure 14.97). The VaR of this optimized portfolio is a lot less than the not optimized portfolio. That is, the expected loss is $35.8M instead of $42.2M, which means that the bank will have a lower required economic capital if the portfolio of holdings is first optimized.

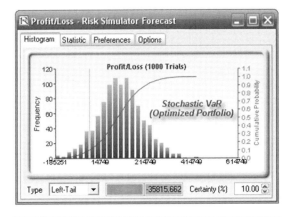

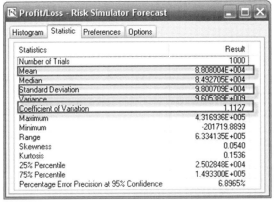

FIGURE 14.97   Optimal portfolio's Value at Risk through optimization and simulation.

Market Risk Analysis

Illustrative Example: Risk Analysis—Interest Rate Risk

File Name: Risk Analysis – Interest Rate Risk

Location: *Modeling Toolkit | Risk Analysis | Interest Rate Risk*

Brief Description: Applies duration and convexity measures to account for a bond's sensitivity and how interest rate shifts can affect the new bond price, and how this new bond price can be approximated using these sensitivity measures

Requirements: Modeling Toolkit, Risk Simulator

Modeling Toolkit Functions Used: B2BondPriceDiscrete, B2ModifiedDuration, B2ConvexityDiscrete

INTEREST RATE RISK

Face Value	$100.00
Coupon Rate	5.50%
Maturity	30.00
Current Interest Rate	5.50%
Interest Rate Shift	0.25%

Original Bond Price	$100.00	
Modified Duration	14.5337	
Convexity	321.0265	
	Duration and Convexity	**Using New Rates**
New Price After Shift	$96.47	$96.46
Price Change After Shift	-3.53%	-3.54%

Cash Flow	Interest Rates	Year	Shifted Interest Rates
$5.50	5.50%	1	5.75%
$5.50	5.50%	2	5.75%
$5.50	5.50%	3	5.75%
$5.50	5.50%	4	5.75%
$5.50	5.50%	5	5.75%
$5.50	5.50%	6	5.75%
$5.50	5.50%	7	5.75%
$5.50	5.50%	8	5.75%
$5.50	5.50%	9	5.75%
$5.50	5.50%	10	5.75%

FIGURE 14.98   Interest rate risk.

Banks selling fixed income products and vehicles need to understand interest rate risks. This model uses duration and convexity to show how fixed income products react under various market conditions. To compare the effects of interest rate and credit risks on fixed income investments, this model uses modified duration and convexity (discrete discounting) to analyze the effects of a change in interest rates on the value of a bond or debt (Figure 14.98).

Duration and convexity are sensitivity measures that describe exposure to parallel shifts in the spot interest rate yield curve, applicable to individual fixed income instruments or entire fixed income portfolios. These sensitivities cannot warn of exposure to more complex movements in the spot curve, including tilts and bends, only parallel shifts. The idea behind duration is simple. Suppose a portfolio has a duration measure of 2.5 years. This means that the portfolio's value will decline about 2.5% for each 1% increase in interest rates—or rise about 2.5% for each 1% decrease in interest rates. Typically, a bond's duration will be positive but exotic instruments such as mortgage-backed securities may have negative durations, or portfolios that short fixed income instruments or pay fixed for floating on an interest rate swap. Inverse floaters tend to have large positive durations. Their values change significantly for small changes in rates. Highly leveraged fixed-income portfolios tend to have large (positive or negative) durations.

In contrast, convexity summarizes the second-most significant piece of information, or the nonlinear curvature of the yield curve, whereas duration measures the linear or first-approximation sensitivity. Duration and convexity have traditionally been used as tools for immunization or asset-liability management. To avoid exposure to parallel spot curve shifts, an organization (such as an insurance company or defined benefit pension plan) with significant fixed income exposures might perform duration matching by structuring its assets so that their duration matches the duration of its liabilities so the two offset each other. Even more effective (but less frequently practical) is duration-convexity matching, in which assets are structured so that durations and convexities match.

Illustrative Example: Risk Hedging—Delta-Gamma Hedging

File Name: Risk Analysis – Delta Gamma Hedge

Location: *Modeling Toolkit | Risk Analysis | Delta Gamma Hedge*

Brief Description: Sets up a delta-gamma riskless and costless hedge in determining the number of call options to sell and buy, number of common stocks to buy, and the borrowing amount required, to set up a perfect arbitrage-free hedge

Requirements: Modeling Toolkit

Modeling Toolkit Functions Used: B2DeltaGammaHedgeCallSold, B2DeltaGammaHedgeSharesBought, B2DeltaGammaHedgeMoneyBorrowed

The Delta-Gamma hedge provides a hedge against larger changes in the asset value (Figure 14.99). This is done by buying some equity shares and a call option, which are funded by borrowing some amount of money and selling a call option at a different strike price. The net amount is a zero sum game, making this hedge completely effective in generating a zero delta and zero gamma for the portfolio. Just like in a delta hedge, where the total portfolio's delta is zero (e.g., to offset a positive delta of some underlying assets, call options are sold to generate sufficient negative delta

DELTA-GAMMA HEDGE

Asset	$100.00
Strike for Call Sold	$95.00
Strike for Call Bought	$100.00
Maturity for Call Sold	0.50
Maturity for Call Bought	0.75
Riskfree	8.00%
Volatility	20.00%
DividendRate	3.00%

Sell Calls	$9.7258
Shares to Buy	($6.9058)
Buy Calls	($9.1991)
Borrow This Amount	$6.3791
Delta-Gamma-Neutral Position Sum	$0.0000

FIGURE 14.99   Delta-gamma hedging.

to completely offset the existing deltas to generate a zero delta portfolio). The problem of delta neutral portfolios is that secondary changes, that is, larger shocks are not hedged. Delta-gamma hedged portfolios, on the contrary, hedge both delta and gamma risk, making it much more expensive to generate. The typical problem with such a hedging vehicle is that in larger quantities, buying and selling additional options or underlying assets may change the market value and prices of the same instruments used to perform the hedge. Therefore, typically, a dynamic hedge or continuously changing hedge portfolios might be required.

Illustrative Example: Risk Hedging—Delta Hedging

> **File Name:** Risk Analysis – Delta Hedge
>
> **Location:** *Modeling Toolkit | Risk Analysis | Delta Hedge*
>
> **Brief Description:** Sets up a delta riskless and costless hedge in determining the number of call options to sell, number of common stocks to buy, and the borrowing amount required to set up a costless hedge
>
> **Requirements:** Modeling Toolkit
>
> **Modeling Toolkit Functions Used:** B2DeltaHedgeCallSold, B2DeltaHedgeSharesBought, B2DeltaHedgeMoneyBorrowed

The Delta hedge provides a hedge against small changes in the asset value by buying some equity shares of the asset and financing it through selling a call option and borrowing some money (Figure 14.100). The net should be

DELTA HEDGE

Asset	$100.00
Strike	$95.00
Maturity	0.50
Riskfree	8.00%
Volatility	20.00%
DividendRate	3.00%

Sell 1 Call	$9.7258
Shares to Buy	($71.8275)
Borrow This Amount	$62.1018
Delta-Neutral Position Sum	$0.0000

FIGURE 14.100   Delta hedging.

a zero sum game to provide a hedge where the portfolio's delta is zero. For instance, an investor computes the portfolio delta of some underlying asset, and offsets this delta through buying or selling some additional instruments such that the new instruments will offset the delta of the existing underlying assets. Typically, say an investor holds some stocks or commodity like gold in the long position, creating a positive delta for the asset. To offset this, he or she sells some calls to generate negative delta, such that the amount of the call options sold on the gold is sufficient to offset the delta in the portfolio.

Illustrative Example: Risk Hedging—Effects of Fixed versus Floating Rates (Swaps)

File Name: Risk Hedging – Effects of Fixed versus Floating Rates

Location: *Modeling Toolkit | Risk Hedging | Effects of Fixed versus Floating Rates*

Brief Description: Sets up various levels of hedging to determine the impact on earnings per share

Requirements: Modeling Toolkit

This model illustrates the impact to financial earnings and earnings before interest and taxes (EBIT) on a hedged versus unhedged position (Figure 14.101). The hedge is done through interest rate swap payments. Various scenarios of swaps (different combinations of fixed rate versus floating rate debt are tested and modeled) can be generated in this model to determine the impact to earnings per share (EPS) and other financial metrics. The foreign

IMPACTS OF FIXED VERSUS FLOATING RATE INTEREST PAYMENTS

Assumptions

EBIT	$3,000,000
Shares Outstanding	$500,000
Tax Rate	40.00%
Total Debt	$8,000,000
Fixed Interest Rate	7.00%
LIBOR	6.00%
10-Year Swap Rate	5.00%

		Scenarios		
Initial Debt Structure (before swap)	Current	1	2	3
% of Total Debt in Fixed-rate Debt	50.00%	50.00%	50.00%	50.00%
% of Total Debt in Floating-rate Debt	50.00%	50.00%	50.00%	50.00%
Desired Debt Structure (after swap)				
% of Total Debt in Fixed-rate Debt	50.00%	30.00%	100.00%	0.00%
% of Total Debt in Floating-rate Debt	50.00%	70.00%	0.00%	100.00%
Change in Interest Rates	0.00%	1.00%	0.50%	0.10%
Financials				
Fixed-rate Debt	7.00%	7.00%	7.00%	7.00%
Floating-rate Debt	8.00%	9.00%	8.50%	8.10%
EBIT	3,000,000	3,000,000	3,000,000	3,000,000
Interest Expense	(600,000)	(672,000)	(560,000)	(648,000)
Net Income before Taxes	2,400,000	2,328,000	2,440,000	2,352,000
Earnings	1,440,000	1,396,800	1,464,000	1,411,200
EPS	2.8800	2.7936	2.9280	2.8224
Change in Interest Expense		72,000	(40,000)	48,000
Change in Earnings		(43,200)	24,000	(28,800)

FIGURE 14.101   Impacts of an unhedged versus hedged position.

exchange cash flow hedge model (shown next) goes into more detail on the hedging aspects of foreign exchange through the use of risk simulation.

Illustrative Example: Risk Hedging—Foreign Exchange Cash Flow Model

File Name: Risk Hedging – Foreign Exchange Cash Flow Model

Location: *Modeling Toolkit | Risk Hedging | Foreign Exchange Cash Flow Model*

Brief Description: This model illustrates how to use Risk Simulator for simulating foreign exchange rates to determine if the value of a hedged fixed exchange rate or floating unhedged rate is worth more

Requirements: Modeling Toolkit, Risk Simulator

This is a cash flow model used to illustrate the effects of hedging foreign exchange rates (Figure 14.102). The tornado sensitivity analysis illustrates that foreign exchange rate, or forex, has the highest effects on the profitability of the project (shown in the Excel model). Suppose for the moment that the project undertaken is in a foreign country (FC) and the values obtained are denominated in FC currency, and the parent company is in the United States (U.S.) and requires that the net revenues be repatriated back to the U.S. The question we try to ask here is what is the appropriate forex rate to hedge at and the appropriate costs for that particular rate? Banks will be able to provide your firm with the appropriate pricing structure for various exchange forward rates but by using the model here, we can determine the added value of the hedge, and hence can decide if the value added exceeds the cost to obtain the hedge. This model is already preset for you to run a simulation on.

The *Forex Data* worksheet shows historical exchange rates between the FC and U.S. Dollar. Using these values, we can create a *custom* distribution (we simply used the rounded values in our illustration), which is already preset in this example model.

However, should you wish to replicate creating the simulation model, you can follow the steps below:

1. Start a new profile (*Risk Simulator | New Profile*) and give it an appropriate name.
2. Go to the *Forex Data* worksheet and select the data in cells K6:K490 and click on *Edit | Copy* or Ctrl + C.
3. Select an empty cell (e.g., cell K4) and click on *Risk Simulator | Set Input Assumption* and select *Custom Distribution*.
4. Click on *Paste* to paste the data into the custom distribution, then *Update Chart* to view the results on the chart. Then, *File | Save* and save the newly created distribution to your hard drive. Close the set assumption dialog.
5. Go to the *Model* worksheet and select the *Forex* cell (J9) and click on *Risk Simulator | Set Input Assumption*, and choose *Custom*, then, click on *Open* a distribution and select the previously saved custom distribution.
6. You may continue to set assumptions across the entire model, and set the NPV cell (G6) as a forecast (*Risk Simulator | Set Output Forecast*).
7. RUN the simulation with the custom distribution to denote an unhedged position. You can then rerun the simulation but this time, delete the custom distribution (use the *Delete Simulation Parameter* icon and not Excel's delete function or the keyboard's delete key) and enter in the

Cash Flow Model

Base Year	2006
Start Year	2006
Discount Rate	15.00%
Private-Risk Discount Rate	5.00%
Terminal Period Growth Rate	2.00%
Tax Rate	40.00%

Sum PV Net Benefits	FC 3,809.62
Sum PV Investments	FC 1,389.08
Net Present Value	FC 2,420.54
Internal Rate of Return	54.64%
Return on Investment	174.25%
Profitability Index	2.74
Forex Rate (USD/FC)	0.85000

	2006	2007	2008	2009	2010	2011	2012	2013	2014	2015
Prod A Price	FC 10.00	FC 10.50	FC 11.00	FC 11.50	FC 12.00	FC 12.00	FC 12.00	FC 12.00	FC 12.00	FC 12.00
Prod B Price	FC 12.25	FC 12.50	FC 12.75	FC 13.00	FC 13.25	FC 13.25	FC 13.25	FC 13.25	FC 13.25	FC 13.25
Prod C Price	FC 15.15	FC 15.30	FC 15.45	FC 15.60	FC 15.75	FC 15.75	FC 15.75	FC 15.75	FC 15.75	FC 15.75
Prod A Quantity	50	50	50	50	50	50	50	50	50	50
Prod B Quantity	35	35	35	35	35	35	35	35	35	35
Prod C Quantity	20	20	20	20	20	20	20	20	20	20
Total Revenues (Local Currency)	FC 1,231.75	FC 1,268.50	FC 1,305.25	FC 1,342.00	FC 1,378.75	FC 1,378.75	FC 1,378.75	FC 1,378.75	FC 1,378.75	FC 1,378.75
Direct Cost of Goods Sold	FC 184.76	FC 190.28	FC 195.79	FC 201.30	FC 206.81	FC 206.81	FC 206.81	FC 206.81	FC 206.81	FC 206.81
Gross Profit	FC 1,046.99	FC 1,078.23	FC 1,109.46	FC 1,140.70	FC 1,171.94	FC 1,171.94	FC 1,171.94	FC 1,171.94	FC 1,171.94	FC 1,171.94
Operating Expenses	FC 157.50	FC 157.50	FC 157.50	FC 157.50	FC 157.50	FC 157.50	FC 157.50	FC 157.50	FC 157.50	FC 157.50
Sales, General and Admin. Costs	FC 15.75	FC 15.75	FC 15.75	FC 15.75	FC 15.75	FC 15.75	FC 15.75	FC 15.75	FC 15.75	FC 15.75
Operating Income (EBITDA)	FC 873.74	FC 904.98	FC 936.21	FC 967.45	FC 998.69	FC 998.69	FC 998.69	FC 998.69	FC 998.69	FC 998.69
Depreciation	FC 10.00	FC 10.00	FC 10.00	FC 10.00	FC 10.00	FC 10.00	FC 10.00	FC 10.00	FC 10.00	FC 10.00
Amortization	FC 3.00	FC 3.00	FC 3.00	FC 3.00	FC 3.00	FC 3.00	FC 3.00	FC 3.00	FC 3.00	FC 3.00
EBIT	FC 860.74	FC 891.98	FC 923.21	FC 954.45	FC 985.69	FC 985.69	FC 985.69	FC 985.69	FC 985.69	FC 985.69
Interest	FC 2.00	FC 2.00	FC 2.00	FC 2.00	FC 2.00	FC 3.00	FC 3.00	FC 4.00	FC 6.00	FC 7.00
EBT	FC 858.74	FC 889.98	FC 921.21	FC 952.45	FC 983.69	FC 982.69	FC 981.69	FC 980.69	FC 979.69	FC 978.69
Taxes	FC 343.50	FC 355.99	FC 368.49	FC 380.98	FC 393.48	FC 393.08	FC 392.68	FC 392.28	FC 391.88	FC 391.48
Net Income	FC 515.24	FC 533.99	FC 552.73	FC 571.47	FC 590.21	FC 589.61	FC 589.01	FC 588.41	FC 587.81	FC 587.21
Depreciation/Amort	FC 13.00	FC 13.00	FC 13.00	FC 13.00	FC 13.00	FC 13.00	FC 13.00	FC 13.00	FC 13.00	FC 13.00
Net Working Capital	FC 0.00	FC 0.00	FC 0.00	FC 0.00	FC 0.00	FC 0.00	FC 0.00	FC 0.00	FC 0.00	FC 0.00
Capital Expenditures	FC 0.00	FC 0.00	FC 0.00	FC 0.00	FC 0.00	FC 0.00	FC 0.00	FC 0.00	FC 0.00	FC 0.00
Free Cash Flow	FC 528.24	FC 546.99	FC 565.73	FC 584.47	FC 603.21	FC 602.61	FC 602.01	FC 601.41	FC 600.81	FC 4,709.36
Investments	FC 500.00		FC 1,500.00							
Net Free Cash Flow	-FC 1,105.97	FC 546.99	FC 565.73	FC 584.47	FC 603.21	FC 602.61	FC 602.01	FC 601.41	FC 600.81	FC 4,709.36

FIGURE 14.102 Hedging foreign exchange risk cash flow model.

relevant hedged exchange rate, indicating a fixed rate. You may create a report after each simulation to compare the results.

From the sample analysis, we see the following:

	Mean ($000)	Stdev ($000)	% Confidence ($000)	CV (%)
Unhedged	2292.82	157.94	2021 to 2550	6.89
Hedged at 0.85	2408.81	132.63	2199 to 2618	5.51
Hedged at 0.83	2352.13	129.51	2147 to 2556	5.51
Hedged at 0.80	2267.12	124.83	2069 to 2463	5.51

From this table, several things are evident:

- The higher the hedged exchange rate is, the more profitable the project (e.g., 0.85 USD/FC is worth more than 0.80 USD/FC).
- The relative risk ratio, computed as the coefficient of variation (CV, or the standard deviation divided by the mean), is the same regardless of the exchange rate, as long as it is hedged.
- The CV is lower for hedged positions than unhedged positions, indicating that the relative risk is reduced by hedging.
- It seems that the exchange rate hedge should be above 0.80, such that the hedged position is more profitable than the unhedged.
- In comparing a hedged versus unhedged position, we can determine the amount of money the hedging is worth, for instance, going with a 0.85 USD/FC means that on average the hedge is worth $115,990 (computed as $2,408.81 – $2,292.82 denominated in thousands). This means that as long as the cost of the hedge is less than this amount, it is a good idea to pursue the hedge.

Illustrative Example: Risk Hedging—Hedging Foreign Exchange Exposure

File Name: Risk Hedging – Hedging Foreign Exchange Exposure

Location: *Modeling Toolkit | Risk Hedging | Hedging Foreign Exchange Exposure*

Brief Description: This model illustrates how to use Risk Simulator for simulating foreign exchange rates to determine the value of a hedged currency option position

Requirements: Modeling Toolkit, Risk Simulator

Hedging Foreign Exchange Exposure with Currency Options

Months	Jan	Feb	Mar	April	May	June	July
FX Spot Rate (HKD/USD)	7.80	7.40	7.60	7.30	7.10	7.20	7.40
FX Strike Rate (HKD/USD)	7.80	7.80	7.80	7.80	7.80	7.80	7.80
Maturity (Years)	0.5833	0.5000	0.4167	0.3333	0.2500	0.1667	0.0833
Risk Free Rate US	6.08%	6.08%	6.08%	6.08%	6.08%	6.08%	6.08%
Risk Free Rate HK	5.06%	5.06%	5.06%	5.06%	5.06%	5.06%	5.06%
Volatility	15.00%	15.00%	15.00%	15.00%	15.00%	15.00%	15.00%
Quantity of Options Hedge Position	10,000,000	10,000,000	10,000,000	10,000,000	10,000,000	10,000,000	10,000,000
Currency Put Option Value (HKD/USD)	0.3229	0.5191	0.3795	0.5533	0.7012	0.6034	0.4102
Market Value of Hedge	3,229,135	5,191,009	3,794,813	5,532,845	7,012,229	6,034,435	4,102,320
Intrinsic Value	0	4,000,000	2,000,000	5,000,000	7,000,000	6,000,000	4,000,000
Time Value	3,229,135	1,191,009	1,794,813	532,845	12,229	34,435	102,320

FINANCIAL STATEMENTS IMPACTS - MARK TO MARKET

Balance Sheet (in 000's)	Jan	Feb	Mar	April	May	June	July
Option Contract	3,229,135	5,191,009	3,794,813	5,532,845	7,012,229	6,034,435	4,102,320
Other Comp Income (SE)		4,000,000	2,000,000	5,000,000	7,000,000	6,000,000	4,000,000

Income Statement (in 000's)							
Hedge Effectiveness gain or loss per period		(2,038,126)	603,805	(1,261,969)	(520,615)	22,206	67,884
Hedge Effectiveness sum of all periods							(3,126,816)
Market Cost of Hedge (Current Period)							3,229,135
Income from Option Exercise							4,000,000
Net Valuation of Hedging							770,865
Income from Hedging							74,770,865
Income from No Hedge							74,000,000
Loss Distribution from Hedging							3,229,135
Loss Distribution from No Hedge							4,000,000

FIGURE 14.103　Hedging currency exposures with currency options.

This model is used to simulate possible foreign exchange spot and future prices and the effects on the cash flow statement of a company under a freely floating exchange rate versus using currency options to hedge the foreign exchange exposure (Figure 14.103).

Figure 14.104 shows the effects of the Value at Risk (VaR) of a hedged versus unhedged position. Clearly the right-tailed VaR of the loss distribution is higher without the currency options hedge. Figure 14.104 shows that there is a lower risk, lower risk to returns ratio, higher returns, and less swing in the outcomes of a currency hedged position than an exposed position, with Figure 14.105 showing the simulated forecast statistics of the loss distribution. Finally, Figure 14.106 shows the hedging effectiveness, that is, how often the hedged is in the money and become usable.

Illustrative Example: Volatility—Implied Volatility

File Name: Volatility – Implied Volatility

Location: *Modeling Toolkit | Volatility | Implied Volatility*

Brief Description: This model computes the implied volatilities using an internal optimization routine, given the values of a call or put option, as well as all their required inputs

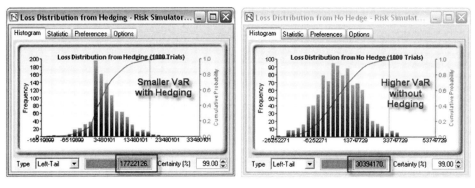

FIGURE 14.104   Values at Risk (VaR) of hedged versus unhedged positions.

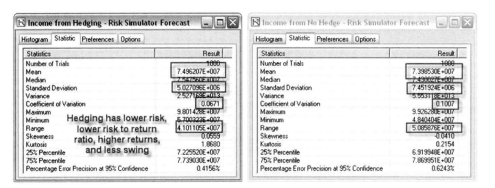

FIGURE 14.105   Forecast statistics of the loss distribution.

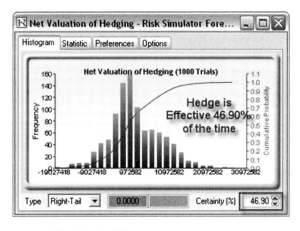

FIGURE 14.106   Hedging effectiveness.

Requirements: Modeling Toolkit, Risk Simulator

Modeling Toolkit Function Used: B2ImpliedVolatilityCall, B2Implied VolatilityPut

This implied volatility computation is based on an internal iterative optimization, which means it will work under typical conditions (without extreme volatility values, i.e., too small or too large). It is always good modeling technique to recheck the imputed volatility using an options model to make sure the answers coincide with each other before adding more sophistication to the model. That is, given all the inputs in an option analysis as well as the option value, the volatility can be imputed (Figure 14.107).

Illustrative Example: Volatility—Volatility Computations

File Name: Volatility – Volatility Computations

Location: *Modeling Toolkit | Volatility | Volatility Computations*

Brief Description: This model uses Risk Simulator to apply Monte Carlo simulation in order to compute a project's volatility measure

Requirements: Modeling Toolkit, Risk Simulator

There are several ways to estimate the volatility used in the option models. The most common and valid approaches are:

- **Logarithmic Cash Flow Returns Approach or Logarithmic Stock Price Returns Approach:** This method is used mainly for computing the volatility on liquid and tradable assets such as stocks in financial

IMPLIED VOLATILITY FUNCTION

Asset	$100.00
Strike	$95.00
Maturity	0.50
Risk-free	8.00%
Volatility	25.00%
DividendRate	3.00%

Call Option	$10.9126
Put Option	$3.6764

Implied Volatility Calculation
Call Option	25.00%
Put Option	25.00%

FIGURE 14.107   Getting the implied volatility from options.

options; however, it is sometimes used for other traded assets such as price of oil and price of electricity. The drawback is that discounted cash flow models with only a few cash flows will generally overstate the volatility and this method cannot be used when negative cash flows occur. This means that this volatility approach is only applicable for financial instruments and not for real options analysis. The benefits include its computational ease, transparency, and modeling flexibility of the method. In addition, no simulation is required to obtain a volatility estimate. The approach is simply to take the annualized standard deviation of the logarithmic relative returns of the time-series data as the proxy for volatility. The Modeling Toolkit function B2Volatility is used to compute this volatility, where the time series of stock prices is arranged in time series (can be chronological or reverse chronological). See the Log Cash Flow Returns example model under the Volatility section of Modeling Toolkit for details.

- **Exponentially Weighted Moving Average (EWMA) Models:** This approach is similar to the previous approach of logarithmic cash flow returns approach, using the B2Volatility function, to compute the annualized standard deviation of the natural logarithms of relative stock returns. The difference here is that the most recent value will have a higher weight than values further in the past. A *lambda* or weight variable is required (typically, industry standards set this at 0.94), where the most recent volatility is weighted at this lambda value, and the period before that is (1 – lambda), and so forth. See the EWMA example model under the Volatility section of Modeling Toolkit for details.

- **Logarithmic Present Value Returns Approach:** This approach is used mainly when computing the volatility on assets with cash flows. A typical application is in real options. The drawback of this method is that simulation is required to obtain a single volatility and is not applicable for highly traded liquid assets such as stock prices. The benefit includes the ability to accommodate certain negative cash flows and applies more rigorous analysis than the logarithmic cash flow returns approach, providing a more accurate and conservative estimate of volatility when assets are analyzed. In addition, within say, a cash flow model, multiple simulation assumptions can be set up (we can insert any types of risks and uncertainties such as related assumptions, correlated distributions and nonrelated inputs, multiple stochastic processes, and so forth), and we allow the model to distill all the interacting risks and uncertainties in these simulated assumptions, and we obtain the single value volatility, which represents the integrated risk of the project. See the Log Asset Returns example model under the Volatility section of Modeling Toolkit for details.

- **Management Assumptions and Guesses:** This approach is used for both financial options and real options. The drawback is that the volatility estimates are very unreliable and are only subjective best guesses. The benefit of this approach is its simplicity—this method is easy to explain to management the concept of volatility, both in execution and interpretation. That is, most people understand what probability is, but have a hard time understanding what volatility is. Using this approach, we can impute one from another. See the Probability to Volatility example model under the Volatility section of Modeling Toolkit for details.
- **Generalized Autoregressive Conditional Heteroskedasticity (GARCH) Models:** These models are used mainly for computing the volatility of liquid and tradable assets such as stocks in financial options, but are sometimes used for other traded assets such as price of oil and price of electricity. The drawback is that a lot of data is required, advanced econometric modeling expertise is required, and this approach is highly susceptible to user manipulation. The benefit is that rigorous statistical analysis is performed to find the best-fitting volatility curve, providing different volatility estimates over time. The EWMA model is a simple weighting model whereas the GARCH model is a more advanced analytical and econometric model that requires advanced algorithms such as generalized method of moments to obtain the volatility forecasts.

See the GARCH model in Chapter 8 for more technical details on running this forecast approach as well as the Appendix in Chapter 2 for details on computing volatility. Risk Simulator also has the data diagnostic tool and statistical analysis tool (see Chapter 6 for details) that can quickly compute the volatility of any time-series dataset. Finally, in the Real Options SLS software folder, there is a Volatility example model that illustrates these computations in more detail.

Illustrative Example: Yield Curve—CIR Model

File Name: Yield Curve – CIR Model

Location: *Modeling Toolkit | Yield Curve | CIR Model*

Brief Description: This is the CIR model for estimating and modeling the term structure of interest rates and yield curve approximation assuming the interest rates are mean-reverting

Requirements: Modeling Toolkit, Risk Simulator

Modeling Toolkit Function Used: B2CIRBondYield

The yield curve is the time-series relationship between interest rates and the time to maturity of the debt. The more formal mathematical description of this relationship is called the term structure of interest rates. The yield curve can take on various shapes. The normal yield curve means that yields rise as maturity lengthens and the yield curve is positively sloped, reflecting investor expectations for the economy to grow in the future (and hence an expectation that inflation rates will rise in the future). An inverted yield curve occurs when the opposite occurs, where the long-term yields fall below short-term yields, and long-term investors will settle for lower yields now if they think the economy will slow or even decline in the future, indicative of a worsening economic situation in the future (and hence, an expectation that inflation will remain low in the future). Another potential situation is a flat yield curve, signaling uncertainty in the economy. The yield curve can also be humped or show a smile or a frown. The yield curve over time can change in shape through a twist or bend, a parallel shift, or a movement on one end versus another.

As the yield curve is related to inflation rates as discussed above, and central banks in most countries have the ability to control monetary policy to target inflation rates, inflation rates are mean-reverting in nature. This also implies that interest rates are mean-reverting, as well as stochastically changing over time.

This section shows the Cox-Ingersoll-Ross (CIR) model that is used to compute the term structure of interest rates and yield curve (Figure 14.108). The CIR model assumes a mean-reverting stochastic interest rate. The rate of reversion and long-run mean rates can be determined using Risk Simulator's statistical analysis tool. If the long-run rate is higher than the current short rate, the yield curve is upward sloping, and vice versa.

Illustrative Example: Yield Curve—Curve Interpolation BIM Model

File Name: Yield Curve – Curve Interpolation BIM

Location: *Modeling Toolkit | Yield Curve | Curve Interpolation BIM*

Brief Description: This is the BIM model for estimating and modeling the term structure of interest rates and yield curve approximation using a curve interpolation method

Requirements: Modeling Toolkit, Risk Simulator

Modeling Toolkit Function Used: B2YieldCurveBIM

A number of alternative methods exist for estimating the term structure of interest rates and the yield curve. Some are fully specified stochastic term structure models while others are simply interpolation models. The former

CIR MODEL
YIELD CURVE CONSTRUCTION

Input Assumptions

Time to Maturity of the Bond or Debt (Years)	1.00
Risk-free Rate (Short Rate)	3.00%
Long-run Mean Rate	8.00%
Annualized Volatility of Interest Rate	6.00%
Market Price of Interest Rate Risk	0.00%
Rate of Mean Reversion	25.00%

Yield of Zero Coupon Bond   3.5744%

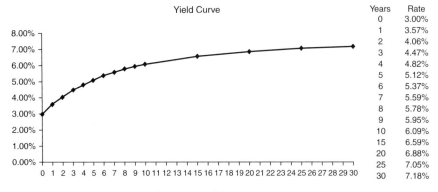

Years	Rate
0	3.00%
1	3.57%
2	4.06%
3	4.47%
4	4.82%
5	5.12%
6	5.37%
7	5.59%
8	5.78%
9	5.95%
10	6.09%
15	6.59%
20	6.88%
25	7.05%
30	7.18%

FIGURE 14.108   CIR model.

are models such as the CIR and Vasicek models (illustrated in other sections in this book), while the latter are interpolation models such as the Bliss or Nelson approach. This section looks at the Bliss interpolation model (Figure 14.109) for generating the term structure of interest rates and yield curve estimation. This model requires several input parameters whereby their estimations require some econometric modeling techniques to calibrate their values. The Bliss approach is a modification of the Nelson-Siegel method by adding an additional generalized parameter. Virtually any yield curve shape can be interpolated using these models, which are widely used at banks around the world.

Illustrative Example: Yield Curve—Curve Spline Interpolation and Extrapolation

> **File Name:** Yield Curve – Spline Interpolation and Extrapolation
>
> **Location:** *Modeling Toolkit | Yield Curve | Spline Interpolation and Extrapolation*

YIELD CURVE - INTERPOLATION MODEL

Beta 0	0.0500
Beta 1	0.1000
Beta 2	0.1000
Lambda 1	0.2000
Lambda 2	0.2000

Time	Rate
0	8.91%
1	7.00%
2	6.33%
3	6.00%
4	5.80%
5	5.67%
6	5.57%
7	5.50%
8	5.44%
9	5.40%
10	5.36%
11	5.33%
12	5.31%
13	5.29%
14	5.27%
15	5.25%
16	5.24%
17	5.22%
18	5.21%
19	5.20%
20	5.19%
21	5.18%
22	5.17%
23	5.17%
24	5.16%
25	5.15%
26	5.15%
27	5.14%
28	5.14%
29	5.13%
30	

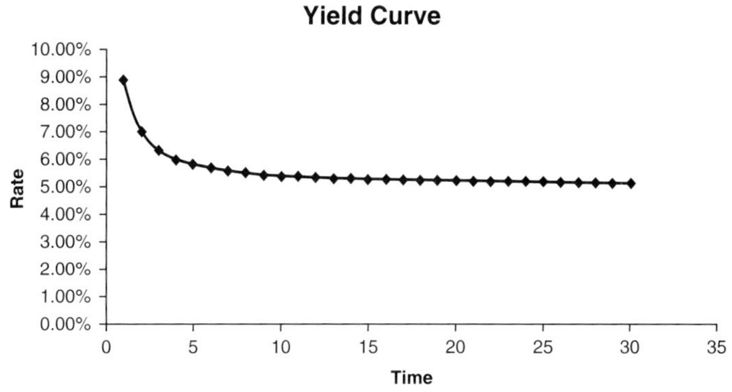

FIGURE 14.109 BIM Model.

Brief Description: This is the multidimensional cubic spline model for estimating and modeling the term structure of interest rates and yield curve approximation using a curve interpolation and extrapolation methods

Requirements: Modeling Toolkit, Risk Simulator

Modeling Toolkit Function Used: B2CubicSpline

The cubic spline polynomial interpolation and extrapolation model is used to "fill in the gaps" of missing spot yields and term structure of interest rates whereby the model can be used to both interpolate missing data points within a time series of interest rates (as well as other macroeconomic variables such as inflation rates and commodity prices or market returns) and also used to extrapolate outside of the given or known range, useful for forecasting purposes. In Figure 14.110, the actual U.S. Treasury risk-free rates are shown, and entered into the model as known values. The timing of these

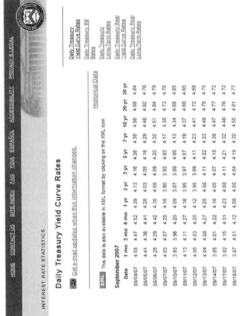

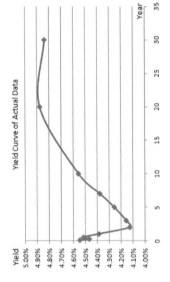

INTEREST RATE STATISTICS

Daily Treasury Yield Curve Rates

Get e-mail updates when this information changes.

This data is also available in XML format by clicking on the XML icon.

Historical Data

September 2007

Date	1 mo	3 mo	6 mo	1 yr	2 yr	3 yr	5 yr	7 yr	10 yr	20 yr	30 yr
09/04/07	4.55	4.47	4.52	4.39	4.13	4.16	4.26	4.38	4.56	4.88	4.84
09/05/07	4.41	4.36	4.41	4.28	4.03	4.05	4.16	4.29	4.48	4.82	4.78
09/06/07	4.28	4.29	4.42	4.30	4.08	4.09	4.20	4.32	4.51	4.84	4.79
09/07/07	4.03	4.07	4.20	4.10	3.90	3.92	4.03	4.17	4.38	4.73	4.70
09/10/07	3.93	3.96	4.20	4.09	3.87	3.89	4.00	4.13	4.34	4.68	4.65
09/11/07	4.13	4.11	4.27	4.16	3.95	3.97	4.07	4.19	4.37	4.68	4.65
09/12/07	4.00	4.03	4.20	4.12	3.95	3.99	4.11	4.23	4.41	4.72	4.66
09/13/07	4.04	4.08	4.27	4.20	4.08	4.11	4.22	4.33	4.49	4.79	4.75
09/14/07	3.85	4.01	4.22	4.16	4.05	4.07	4.18	4.30	4.47	4.77	4.72
09/17/07	3.82	4.15	4.31	4.23	4.08	4.11	4.21	4.32	4.48	4.76	4.72
09/18/07	3.87	4.01	4.12	4.08	4.00	4.04	4.19	4.32	4.50	4.81	4.77

These are the yields that are known and are used as inputs in the Cubic Spline Interpolation and Extrapolation model

Years	Spot Yields
0.0833	4.55%
0.2500	4.47%
0.5000	4.52%
1.0000	4.39%
2.0000	4.13%
3.0000	4.16%
5.0000	4.26%
7.0000	4.38%
10.0000	4.56%
20.0000	4.88%
30.0000	4.84%

Spline Interpolation and Extrapolation Results

Years	Yield	Notes
0.5	4.52%	Interpolate
1.0	4.39%	Interpolate
1.5	4.21%	Interpolate
2.0	4.13%	Interpolate
2.5	4.13%	Interpolate
3.0	4.16%	Interpolate
3.5	4.19%	Interpolate
4.0	4.22%	Interpolate
4.5	4.24%	Interpolate
5.0	4.26%	Interpolate
5.5	4.29%	Interpolate
6.0	4.32%	Interpolate
6.5	4.35%	Interpolate
7.0	4.38%	Interpolate
7.5	4.41%	Interpolate
8.0	4.44%	Interpolate
8.5	4.47%	Interpolate
9.0	4.50%	Interpolate
9.5	4.53%	Interpolate
10.0	4.56%	Interpolate
10.5	4.59%	Interpolate
11.0	4.61%	Interpolate
11.5	4.64%	Interpolate
12.0	4.66%	Interpolate
12.5	4.68%	Interpolate
13.0	4.70%	Interpolate
13.5	4.72%	Interpolate
14.0	4.74%	Interpolate

FIGURE 14.110 Cubic spline model.

spot yields are entered as Years (the known X value inputs), whereas the known risk-free rates are the known Y values. Using the "B2Cubicspline" function, we can now interpolate the in-between risk-free rates that are missing as well as the rates outside of the given input dates. For instance, the risk-free Treasury rates given include 1-month, 3-month, 6-month, 1-year, and so forth, until the 30-year rate. Using these data, we can interpolate the rates for, say, 5 months or 9 months, and so forth, as well as extrapolate beyond the 30-year rate.

Illustrative Example: Yield Curve—Forward Rates from Spot Rates

File Name: Yield Curve – Forward Rates from Spot Rates

Location: *Modeling Toolkit | Yield Curve | Forward Rates from Spot Rates*

Brief Description: This is a bootstrap model used to determine the implied forward rate given two spot rates

Requirements: Modeling Toolkit, Risk Simulator

Modeling Toolkit Function Used: B2ForwardRate

Given two spot rates (from Year 0 to some future time periods), you can determine the implied forward rate between these two time periods. For instance, if the spot rate from Year 0 to Year 1 is 8%, and the spot rate from Year 0 to Year 2 is 7% (both yields are known currently), the implied forward rate from Year 1 to Year 2 (that will occur based on current expectations) is 6%. This is simplified by using the B2ForwardRate function in Modeling Toolkit (Figure 14.111).

FORWARD RATES
COMPUTING FORWARD RATES FROM SPOT RATES

Input Assumptions

Spot Rate 1	8.00%
Spot Rate 2	7.00%
Time of Spot Rate 1	1.00
Time of Spot Rate 2	2.00

Forward Rate   6.00%

FIGURE 14.111   Forward rate extrapolation.

Illustrative Example: Yield Curve—Vasicek Model

File Name: Yield Curve – Vasicek Model

Location: *Modeling Toolkit | Yield Curve | Vasicek Model*

Brief Description: The Vasicek model is used to create the term structure of interest rates and to reconstruct the yield curve assuming the underlying interest rates are mean-reverting and stochastic

Requirements: Modeling Toolkit, Risk Simulator

Modeling Toolkit Function Used: B2VasicekBondYield

This is the Vasicek model used to compute the term structure of interest rates and yield curve. The Vasicek model assumes a mean-reverting stochastic interest rate (Figure 14.112). The rate of reversion and long-run mean rates can be determined using Risk Simulator's statistical analysis tool. If the

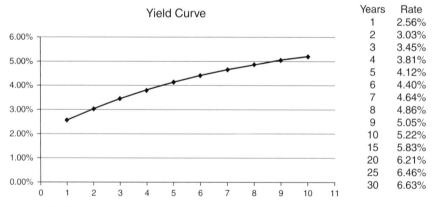

VASICEK MODEL
YIELD CURVE CONSTRUCTION

Input Assumptions

Time to Maturity of the Bond or Debt (Years)	1.00
Risk-free Rate (Short Rate)	2.00%
Long-run Mean Rate	8.00%
Annualized Volatility of Interest Rate	2.00%
Market Price of Interest Rate Risk	0.00%
Rate of Mean Reversion	20.00%

Yield of Zero Coupon Bond   2.5562%

Years	Rate
1	2.56%
2	3.03%
3	3.45%
4	3.81%
5	4.12%
6	4.40%
7	4.64%
8	4.86%
9	5.05%
10	5.22%
15	5.83%
20	6.21%
25	6.46%
30	6.63%

FIGURE 14.112   Using the Vasicek model to generate a yield curve.

long-run rate is higher than the current short rate, the yield curve is upward sloping, and vice versa.

The yield curve is the time-series relationship between interest rates and the time to maturity of the debt. The more formal mathematical description of this relationship is called the term structure of interest rates. As discussed previously, the yield curve can take on various shapes. The normal yield curve means that yields rise as maturity lengthens and the yield curve is positively sloped, reflecting investor expectations for the economy to grow in the future (and hence an expectation that inflation rates will rise in the future). An inverted yield curve occurs when the opposite occurs, where the long-term yields fall below short-term yields, and long-term investors will settle for lower yields now if they think the economy will slow or even decline in the future, indicative of a worsening economic situation in the future (and hence an expectation that inflation will remain low in the future). Another potential situation is a flat yield curve, signaling uncertainty in the economy. The yield curve can also be humped or show a smile or a frown. The yield curve over time can change in shape through a twist or bend, a parallel shift, or a movement on one end versus another.

As the yield curve is related to inflation rates as discussed above, and central banks in most countries have the ability to control monetary policy to target inflation rates, inflation rates are mean-reverting in nature. This also implies that interest rates are mean-reverting, as well as stochastically changing over time.

A Czech mathematician, Oldrich Vasicek, in a 1977 paper proved that bond prices on a yield curve over time and various maturities are driven by the short end of the yield curve, or the short-term interest rates, using a risk-neutral martingale measure. In his work the mean-reverting Ornstein-Uhlenbeck process was assumed, hence the resulting Vasicek model requires that a mean-reverting interest rate process be modeled (rate of mean reversion and long-run mean rates are both inputs in the Vasicek model).

Illustrative Example: Stochastic Forecasting of Interest Rates and Stock Prices

File Name: Forecasting – Stochastic Processes

Location: *Modeling Toolkit | Forecasting | Stochastic Processes*

Brief Description: This sample model illustrates how to simulate Stochastic Processes (Brownian Motion Random Walk, Mean-Reversion, Jump-Diffusion, and Mixed Models)

Requirements: Modeling Toolkit, Risk Simulator

A stochastic process is a sequence of events or paths generated by probabilistic laws. That is, random events can occur over time but are governed by specific statistical and probabilistic rules. The main stochastic processes include Random Walk or Brownian Motion, Mean-Reversion, and Jump-Diffusion. These processes can be used to forecast a multitude of variables that seemingly follow random trends but yet are restricted by probabilistic laws. We can use Risk Simulator's *Stochastic Process* module to simulate and create such processes. These processes can be used to forecast a multitude of time-series data including stock prices, interest rates, inflation rates, oil prices, electricity prices, commodity prices, and so forth.

Stochastic Process Forecasting

To run this model, simply:

1. Select *Simulation | Forecasting | Stochastic Processes*.
2. Enter a set of relevant inputs or use the existing inputs as a test case (Figure 14.113).

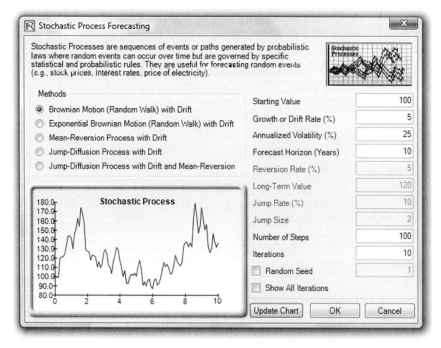

FIGURE 14.113   Running a stochastic process forecast.

3. Select the relevant process to simulate.

4. Click on *Update Chart* to view the updated computation of a single path or click *OK* to create the process.

Model Results Analysis

For your convenience, the analysis report sheet is included in the model. A stochastic time-series chart and forecast values are provided in the report as well as each step's time period, mean, and standard deviation of the forecast (see Chapter 8 for technical details of using this stochastic process forecast technique and Chapter 6 for the data diagnostic and statistical analysis tools for calibrating the input parameters for the stochastic process models). The mean values can be used as the single point estimate or assumptions can be manually generated for the desired time period. That is, finding the appropriate time period, create an assumption with a normal distribution with the appropriate mean and standard deviation computed. A sample chart with 10 iteration paths is included to graphically illustrate the behavior of the forecasted process.

CASE STUDY: IT INFORMATION SECURITY INTRUSION RISK MANAGEMENT

This case study illustrates an information systems security attack profile and provides decision analysis and support on the optimal investment. The model is contributed by Mark A. Benyovszky, Managing Director of Zero Delta Center for Enterprise Alignment. Zero Delta CfEA is a research and development organization that specializes in helping companies to align their strategic and tactical efforts.

There are several models illustrated in this case study and available in the Modeling Toolkit. First, the IT Bandwidth Requirements for Streaming Media model shows how to create forecasts for media streaming environments for off-peak and peak media consumption cycles. The model explains how to use historical time-series data to establish an understanding of the future demand for media consumption. This model also explores how the Delphi Method can be used when historical data do not exist or when there is significant uncertainty surrounding the demand for new media types that require more bandwidth or have chattier communication channels.

The IT Intrusion Management model shows how to create an information systems security attack profile, determine the probabilities of occurrence of different types of attacks, assess the financial and operational impact that an attack has on an organization, and arrive at the level of investment in technology security solutions (e.g., intrusion detection systems, intrusion prevention systems, and network behavior analysis solutions) necessary to mitigate the profiled attacks.

Finally, the IT Storage and CPU Demand model illustrates how to create forecasts for future information system storage and CPU demand. The model explains how to use historical time-series data to establish an understanding of the future demand for media storage and computing cycles. This model also explores how the Delphi Method can be used when historical data do not exist or when there is significant uncertainty surrounding the demand for new media types that require more storage space and where CPU cycles are being consumed by expensive encoding and decoding processes.

Organizations of all sizes rely on technology to support a wide range of business processes that span the spectrum from back-office finance and accounting to mid-office manufacturing, distribution, and other operational support functions to front-office sales, marketing, and customer support functions. As a general rule of thumb, larger organizations have more complex system environments and significantly greater volumes of data along with a wide range of different types of information.

If you were to look across industries, you would see different degrees of sensitivity of both the systems and information that are employed. For example, financial and insurance companies store critical and very sensitive information (financial transactions and personal medical histories) about their customers, or that an energy company engaged in gas transmission and distribution relies on critical technology systems that control the flow of gas through complex pipeline networks.

Regardless of the specific industry an organization is involved with or the size of the company, the underlying technology systems and the data and information they consume and produce are significant business assets. Like any asset, they must be protected. In order to protect these assets, we must understand what their individual and collective risk profiles look like.

Protecting these assets is of paramount concern. Technology systems are interconnected across private, semiprivate, and public networks. Every second (perhaps you prefer nanoseconds, picoseconds, or attoseconds, depending on your geekiness factor) of every day, information moves across these networks; most of the time the information moves about intentionally, whereas on other occasions it does not.

We can think of this information and these systems in the context of an information security asset portfolio. It is important for us to quantify the value of each class of system or set of information, which will help us to understand, according to a scale of sensitivity, which assets require greater protection, as higher-value assets are likely to be greater targets for attack (based on the basic risk/reward equation).

We can then apply various methods against the portfolio to determine the composite (high-level view) risk level of the portfolio, risk profiles of categories of assets, and individual asset risk profiles (detailed view). This approach enables us to gain a better grasp on our information and technology asset portfolio, and provides us with the ability to determine how much to invest to protect each class of assets.

While the specific approaches and processes that are required to perform this initial portfolio structuring are beyond the scope of this case study, determining the probabilities of events occurring against these assets and what the resultant outcomes are likely to be is at the center of our discussion. This case study will assume that this structuring process has already been completed. Specifically, there are five steps to undergo:

Step 1: Create environment details.

Step 2: Create attack models.

Step 3: Create attack scenarios.

Step 4: Determine financial impact.

Step 5: Arrive at investment decision.

Now, let us get on with the heart of our discussion. Monte Carlo simulation provides us with an effective way to estimate losses associated with a given attack. Monte Carlo simulation addresses the "flaw of averages" problem that plagues many single-point estimates or estimates based on standard averages.

For the sake of this discussion, we will explore how we applied this approach to a large gas transmission and distribution company. The company (which we refer to as Acme T&D) is one of the largest natural gas transmission and distribution companies in North America. Acme T&D has an extensive gas pipeline network that supplies natural gas to wholesalers and retailers in some of the largest markets throughout North America.

Energy companies fit in a unique category of organizations that use technology at the core of their business operations. Acme T&D relies on an extensive industrial control system known in the industry as Supervisory Control and Data (SCADA) and Process Control Monitor (PCM) systems. These systems are composed of a number of devices that are distributed throughout the gas pipeline network; these components are used to control the flow of gas through the network. They supply critical information, such as gas flow rate, temperature of gas, and pressure at various points through the network, to a system operator who then makes certain decisions about what to do to keep the pipeline at an operationally efficient level—always supplying gas where and when it is needed in a dynamic environment that changes continually.

These systems are critical not only to the operations of Acme T&D but also to the greater infrastructure of the United States. If the transmission and distribution of natural gas are interrupted for a significant period of time, the interruption can have downstream effects that could be devastating economically (the suspended operations of manufacturing companies that rely on natural gas) or personally (lack of gas to run a furnace in the cold of winter).

Clearly, these SCADA system(s) would be categorized as business-critical assets with the highest priority placed on their protection.

Step 1: Create Environment Details

When we consider the extent to which an attack will cause damage, we must identify the factors that drive the top end of our model. These factors will be different for each company (with similarities for companies within the same industry).

For Acme T&D our greatest concerns, from an operational perspective, are the count and types of networks in the environment, and employee productivity (we will take into account separately how operations are impacted when a threat impacts a SCADA network). The reason for using employee productivity as a factor is that when networks are down or systems are unreachable (for whatever reason), employees are directly impacted (we use this in this example because of its universal relevance across industry domains).

Acme T&D Network Counts	
Enterprise Network Count	16
SCADA Network Count	4
PCM Network Count	1
Total Networks	21

As an aside, and as previously alluded to, the factors that drive the model will change based on industry characteristics. For example, a financial institution may wish to use the economic losses associated with stolen credit card data as a primary factor to drive the model, in addition to employee productivity losses and so forth.

Acme T&D has approximately 10,000 employees. We must determine the payroll expenses (fully burdened) per hour. We are simplifying this model intentionally—it is not likely that 10,000 employees are working all at once (e.g., some percentage of employees may be on a shift rotation schedule). A sample computation is shown next:

$$Total\ Employee\ Cost\ per\ Hour = Employee\ Count\ \times \frac{Salary}{2,000}$$

where 2,000 is the number of hours worked per employee each calendar year (2,080 less 80 hours for holidays); and the salary input is the fully burdened amount at the average of all employees.

The model is based on various types of attack. We determine the probability that each attack will occur and to what extent it will cause damage (economic and operational) to the organization. We then create a separate model (our attack portfolio), which will allow us to simulate multiple attacks occurring against different networks in the environment and the resultant impacts in aggregate. We classify attacks based on two variables—the frequency and impact of the attack.

An attack as profiled in Class I is considered an average attack (see Table 14.8). An average attack could be considered a low-impact worm, a Trojan horse, or a virus that may affect various network systems and employee computers. Acme T&D has a variety of tools deployed in the network to mitigate these types of attacks; however, no tool is 100% effective. This is where the value of Monte Carlo simulation is realized.

Minimum 0.7

Most Likely 0.8

Maximum 1.0

Now we construct the remaining elements of the model. We will use standard (and very conservative) estimates for the probability of occurrence of an attack.

Table 14.8 illustrates how the top end of the model comes together. We place the attack types across the columns of the model and we create the network structure and impact structure components.

Step 2: Create Attack Models

We must first create a common attack model and categorize the different types of attacks that exist. The classes of attacks are based on the severity level of the attack (from average to extreme). We also indicate the extent

TABLE 14.8 Qualitative Assessments of Attack Classes

Attack Class	Severity Level of Attack	Type of Attack	Extent of Damage	Recovery Approach
Class I	Average	Benign worm, Trojan horse, virus, or equivalent	Limited. Most damage occurs at host level.	Mostly automated, but may require some human intervention.
Class II	Slightly above average	Worm, Trojan horse, virus, or equivalent designed to create some damage or consume resources	Limited. Damage can occur at the host and network level.	Human intervention is required. Humans use tools that require interaction and expertise.
Class III	Moderately above average	Worm, Trojan horse, or equivalent designed to create significant damage and consume resources	Noticeable damage at host and network levels. Automated tools have limited effect to combat attacker.	Significant human intervention is required. Personnel require physical access to host machines and network environments.
Class IV	Significantly above average	Concentrated attack by hacker using a variety of tools and techniques to compromise systems	Significant damage to important/ sensitive data. May also include damage to host machines as Trojans and other tools are used to circumvent detection and mitigation techniques.	Extensive human intervention is required. Data and systems recovery is necessary. Multiple techniques and methods are necessary to fully recover.
Class V	Extreme case	Concentrated attack by hacker or groups of hackers who are trying to compromise infor-mation/systems and have malicious intent	Critical damage to important/sensitive information. Irreversible damage to systems/ hardware.	Extensive human intervention is required. External experts are required to assess and recover environment.

of damage that an attack produces and the recovery details associated with each class of attack. This classification structure provides us with a basic framework we can leverage throughout the analysis exercise. We have five classes of attacks structured in our model. The descriptors are qualitative in nature (see Table 14.8).

We create current state and future state models for the classes of attacks. The purpose for creating current and future state models is so that we can compare the models to each other. The current state model is based on the technology and approaches that are currently in use (our preexisting investments) to detect, mitigate, and recover from each respective type of attack. The future state model is based on a set of new technologies (our future investments) that can be deployed in the environment to enhance the security of the environment, mitigate a wider range of attacks, and more rapidly recover from various types of attacks.

These types of attacks will be consistent across our current and future state models. There are a number of variables that are a part of our attack models. They include:

% of network impacted.

% of employees impacted.

Productivity loss (hours/employee).

Costs to recover employees.

Hours to recover employees.

Note that the models are populated with static values that are single-point estimates and averages. For example, a Class I attack in the current state attack model has a 10% Network Impacted value and a 5-hour Productivity Loss value.

How can we be absolutely certain that a Class I attack will always impact 10% of the networks and result in a productivity loss of 5 hours per employee (along with the other variables included in the model)? We cannot be sure with a reliable degree of confidence. Therefore, any analysis based on single-point estimates or averages is flawed.

Monte Carlo simulation allows us to refine our assumptions and provides us with a mechanism to perturb these variables in a dynamic fashion. While we have solved the problem of dealing with averages, we are faced with a new challenge: What are the appropriate ranges to use to perturb the values, and how should these perturbations behave throughout the simulation?

To gather these values, we leveraged the Delphi Method. Following the Delphi Method approach, we interviewed a number of technical experts

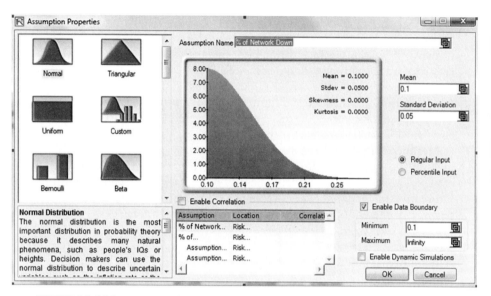

FIGURE 14.114 Truncated percent of Network Impacted simulation assumption.

in the environment who had knowledge of prior attacks and the extent to which tools were used to mitigate them. The expert panel provided the details necessary to determine how the model variables might behave and what their respective upper and lower boundary values may be.

Figure 14.114 illustrates how we have adapted the % of Network Impacted value for a Class I attack. The original value was based on an average of 10%. Upon closer inspection and after some discussion, our panel of experts determined that such an attack is unlikely to impact less than 10% of the network and may in fact impact a greater percentage of the network before it is identified and stopped, preventing further damage. Using Monte Carlo simulation, we create an assumption for this value and select a normal distribution. We truncate the left side (or minimum value) of the distribution to take into account the 10% floor and provide some movement toward the right side (or maximum value) of the distribution. We set the mean to 10% and standard deviation to 5%. The resultant distribution indicates a minimum value of 10%, a mean of 10% (our average), and a maximum value of approximately 25%.

We have introduced into our model a very powerful feature. Our model better reflects reality by taking into account the uncertainty associated with this value. We use this same approach for the other values and select and adjust the distributions accordingly. To further illustrate this point,

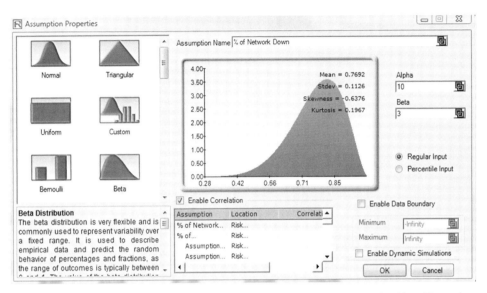

FIGURE 14.115 Percent of Network Impacted simulation assumption of a Class V attack.

Figure 14.115 is taken from the Class V attack column. A Class V attack is considered an extreme event. The probability of occurrence is very low, and the damage caused is expected to be extreme or catastrophic in nature. An analogous event would be a volcano eruption or an earthquake (they may evoke a tsunami wave, for example, especially if located in the South Pacific) that occurs once every 100 years.

The Gumbel Maximum Distribution is ideally suited for this type of catastrophic event. This distribution model is positively skewed and is designed to produce a higher probability of lower numbers and a lower probability of extreme values. We set the alpha value to 70 and the beta to 10. This results in a mean of 75.7722 and a standard deviation of 12.8255. It is important to note the third and fourth moments of this distribution. Skewness coefficient is 1.1395 (indicating the positively skewed nature of the distributions) and kurtosis coefficient is 2.400 (indicating the extent to which extreme events should occur in the distribution).

This distribution model better reflects reality vis-à-vis extreme attacks. We can see in Figure 14.116 that there are higher probabilities to the left of the mean than to the right. However, the model has taken into account the extreme distributions to the far right of the median.

The original analysis based on averages indicated that for this scenario, the total financial losses are $21,741,176. If we follow our "1 in 3"

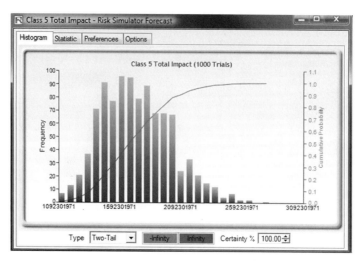

FIGURE 14.116 Forecast distribution of a Class V impact.

approach, we find that the number is adjusted downward to $18,0174,729 or by a little over 12%. As you explore the model in more detail, you will note the use of various distributions for each class of attack.

We adjust these figures for each scenario to take into account the greater variability of more advanced and staged attacks. We know that as attacks gain more sophistication there are more unknowns about how far-reaching or to what extent damage will occur. Hence, the mean and standard deviation parameters can be adjusted to take into account this variability.

Model Results

Impact to Operational Productivity   We have determined that the average fully burdened salary per employee is $80,000. For Scenario I, we estimate that an attack that affects each employee results in 5 hours of lost productivity. It costs Acme T&D $39.22 per employee per hour of lost productivity. For an attack profile we modeled in Scenario I where 10% of the networks and 10% of employees are impacted results in a total productivity loss of $196,078.43 (see Table 14.9).

Recovery Costs   Attacks generally result in some form of damage (more often than not the damage is nonphysical in nature). It is often necessary

TABLE 14.9 Modeling Results from Scenario I

Lost Revenues Impact to Operational Productivity	$196,078.43
Assumption—Average Salary/Employee (Fully Burdened)	$ 80,000
Assumption—Total Time to Fully Recover/Employee (Hours)	5
Productivity Cost/Hour	$ 39.22
Costs to Recover/Employee	$50
Assumption (Hours to Recover)	1
Costs to Recover Networks	$ 4,800
Assumption—Hours to Recover	12
Resources per Network	5
Cost per Hour	$ 50
Total Costs to Recover Employees	$ 50,000
Total Costs to Recover Networks	$ 4,800
Total Impact	$246,078.43

to deploy technical personnel to remediate the impacted environments and systems. There are two dimensions to this remediation. There is network remediation (resetting/reconfiguring network routers, switches, firewalls, etc.) and client remediation (ghosting client machines, patching software, reinstalling/reconfiguring software, etc.).

Our model takes into account the number of resources and the time necessary to recover the networks and the same for recovering employees. For Scenario I the costs are $50,000 and $4,800, respectively.

Total Impact We now sum up all of the separate loss components of the model:

$$Loss(Productivity) + Loss(Network\ Recovery) + Loss(Employee\ Recovery)$$

For Scenario I, we have total losses of $147,647.

In the model, there are four additional scenarios. For each scenario we tweak the assumptions to better fit the attack profiles. The percentages of networks down and employees impacted increase for each scenario.

Exposing the Flaw of Averages

	Class I Attack	Class II Attack	Class III Attack	Class IV Attack	Class V Attack
Total Impact (Original)	$147,647	$616,471	$1,933,235	$5,223,529	$21,741,176
Total Impact (Revised)	$310,616	$714,145	$1,679,616	$7,507,908	$23,817,256
Variance (%)	210.38%	115.84%	86.88%	143.73%	109.55%

The next step of our modeling efforts involves creating a portfolio of attacks. This step will provide us with the answer to the question: How much should Acme T&D invest in security solutions to mitigate the risks associated with the attacks profiled?

Step 3: Create Attack Scenarios

Now that we have determined the estimated costs associated with different types of attacks, we are ready to move on to creating the attack scenarios. The attack scenarios will provide us with the total losses realized during a specified period of time.

We have created six attack scenarios. The attack scenarios consider the occurrence of different types of attacks over a 5-year period. By creating different scenarios, we can consider different foreseeable futures. This approach allows an organization to determine how it wishes to view the world from a risk planning and risk mitigation standpoint.

The degree to which an organization will tolerate risk varies greatly. Some organizations are more tolerant of risk and will invest less in mitigating technologies and approaches, whereas other organizations that are more risk averse will invest substantially more in order to reduce their risk profiles.

One can think of this type of investment as an insurance policy—juggling premium with payout—or from a strategic real options perspective of risk mitigation. The scenarios provide us with a landscape view from lowest to highest possible losses. We explore two different approaches to determining the probability of attacks occurring across a specified time line. The first approach involves the use of the Delphi Method. We interview a number of subject matter and technical experts who are asked to produce five different likely scenarios for various attack profiles. We provide some guidance and suggest to each expert that the scenarios should range from a most likely

| | Scenario I | | | | | |
	Year 1	Year 2	Year 3	Year 4	Year 5	Totals
Class I Attacks	1	0	1	1	0	3
Class II Attacks	0	0	0	0	1	1
Class III Attacks	0	0	0	0	0	0
Class IV Attacks	0	0	0	0	0	0
Class V Attacks	0	0	0	0	0	0
Class I Attack Impact CS	309,579	0	309,579	309,579	0	928,737
Class I Attack Impact FS	44,632	0	44,632	44,632	0	133,896
Class II Attack Impact CS	0	0	0	0	713,288	713,288
Class II Attack Impact FD	0	0	0	0	303,871	303,871
Class III Attack Impact CS	0	0	0	0	0	0
Class III Attack Impact FS	0	0	0	0	0	0
Class IV Attack Impact CS	0	0	0	0	0	0
Class IV Attack Impact FS	0	0	0	0	0	0
Class V Attack Impact CS	0	0	0	0	0	0
Class V Attack Impact FS	0	0	0	0	0	0
Impact Based on Current State	309,579	0	309,579	309,579	713,288	1,642,025
Impact Based on Future State	44,632	0	44,632	44,632	303,871	437,767
Variance	85.58%	#DIV/0!	85.58%	85.58%	57.40%	73.34%
Risk Adjustment	264,947	0	264,947	264,947	409,417	1,204,258

FIGURE 14.117 Scenario I attack profile of a future state.

scenario to a least likely scenario. This team of experts is then brought together to discuss the ranges across the spectrum. After various conversations and some debate, the team collectively determines to reduce the total scenarios (5 experts × 5 scenarios = 25) to the final 5. These scenarios are reflected as Scenarios I through V on the Attack Scenarios spreadsheet.

Figure 14.117 illustrates a Scenario I attack profile. On our defined scale of least likely to most likely, this scenario is most likely to be realized. The experts provided the count of each type of attack that occurs within our 5-year period and further determined the years in which the attacks will occur.

We have carried over our financial impact information from our previous exercise. For each class of attack we have current state and future state impact costs.

The first section of the model includes the classes of attacks. For Scenario I, we have determined that three Class I attacks will occur in years 1, 3, and 4. In addition we have determined that one Class II attack will occur in year 5.

The second section of the model includes the impact values from the attack models. We include in this model both the current state and future state impact values. These values are computed for each year and are summed in the totals column. The variance value indicates the percentage reduction from current to future state loss values. By investing in the proposed technologies, we can reduce by 73.34% the total losses for this scenario. The risk adjustment value is the difference between the current state impact and future state impact values. This value is carried over to the next step of our analysis.

We use this same model to create the other attack scenarios. Figure 14.118 illustrates the Scenario IV attack profile. This scenario represents the

Scenario IV						
	Year 1	Year 2	Year 3	Year 4	Year 5	Totals
Class I Attacks	0	0	0	0	0	0
Class II Attacks	0	0	0	0	0	0
Class III Attacks	0	0	0	0	0	0
Class IV Attacks	0	0	0	0	0	0
Class V Attacks	0	0	0	0	1	1
Class I Attack Impact CS	0	0	0	0	0	0
Class I Attack Impact FS	0	0	0	0	0	0
Class II Attack Impact CS	0	0	0	0	0	0
Class II Attack Impact FD	0	0	0	0	0	0
Class III Attack Impact CS	0	0	0	0	0	0
Class III Attack Impact FS	0	0	0	0	0	0
Class IV Attack Impact CS	0	0	0	0	0	0
Class IV Attack Impact FS	0	0	0	0	0	0
Class V Attack Impact CS	0	0	0	0	23,791,472	23,791,472
Class V Attack Impact FS	0	0	0	0	16,095,255	16,095,255
Impact Based on Current State	0	0	0	0	23,791,472	23,791,472
Impact Based on Future State	0	0	0	0	16,095,255	16,095,255
Variance					32.35%	32.35%
Risk Adjustment	0	0	0	0	7,696,217	7,696,217

FIGURE 14.118 Scenario IV attack profile of a future state.

opposite end of the spectrum. In this scenario the company is successful in preventing all classes of attacks until year 5, where a Class V attack occurs. This is the scenario of the infamous "hacker with malicious intent" who makes a concentrated effort to circumvent intrusion management technologies with the specific desire to cause significant harm to the organization. For Acme T&D this scenario could perhaps reflect the sentiments of a terrorist who has a desire to gain access to the critical gas pipeline systems in order to cause a catastrophic failure to the pipeline network.

One could argue that such an approach to determining these probabilities lacks scientific rigor or can be significantly biased—either intentionally or unintentionally. Consider technical experts who firmly believe that their skills are second to none with respect to effectively deploying and managing an armory of intrusion management technology. They may be biased to create scenarios that are on the conservative end of the spectrum, significantly coloring the reality of the environment or threat landscape. If we pin our decision on this approach, a crafty hacker who has superior skills to these individuals may easily circumvent these technologies and successfully realize his or her attack objectives and goals.

Conversely, consider the doomsday character who is constantly pondering the worst-case scenario and has a strong voice in the room. He or she may be overly aggressive with the attack scenarios, creating unrealistic models that result in doom and gloom.

How can one test for these biases? Is there a way to independently determine the probabilities and likelihoods of events? Indeed there is a way, and it is again found in Monte Carlo simulation.

Scenario VI represents our independent attack scenario. You may consider this the control model. This is our expert who is neutral to all biases. The probabilities of occurrence are factually driven and leverage a distribution model that is focused on the discrete nature of these events—an event either happens or it doesn't.

The Poisson distribution provides us with the ability to address the unique aspects of occurrence probabilities. Figure 14.119 illustrates how we can leverage the Poisson distribution for modeling an attack. These events are discrete in nature—they either occur or don't occur. For a Class I attack we set the lambda value to 1.5984. This creates a distribution model that ranges from 0 to 6. Note on the left side of the model the probability scale. We can see that this lambda value results in a 20% nonoccurrence outcome. Or, in other words, 80% of the time a class I attack will occur at least one time (at a rate of approximately 33%) and may occur up to 6 times within our time interval at a rate of, say, 0.01%.

Compare this to a Poisson distribution model for a Class V extreme attack. We set the lambda value to 0.0012 to reflect this. It results in a

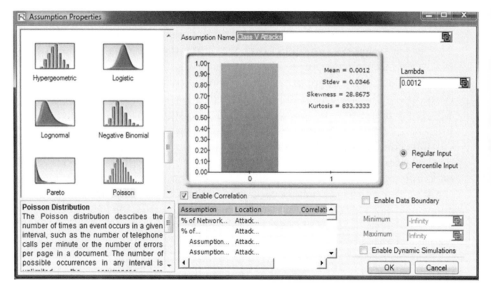

FIGURE 14.119   Poisson distribution assumption.

distribution model where this event will not occur 99.9988% of the time. There is only a 0.0012% chance that the event will occur in any given trial.

You may wonder why, if Monte Carlo simulation can be used reliably to arrive at probabilities of occurrence, we choose to use two different methods for determining probabilities. There are three primary reasons:

1. *To Reduce the "Fear of the Black Box" Phenomenon.* People who are not familiar with analytical techniques or the details associated with statistical methods have a tendency to treat analysis and the resultants outputs as black box–generated values. There is a natural fear to mistrust the unknown. By leveraging both statistical methods and expert opinion interviews, laypersons observing the analysis and output can rationalize in their minds how the results were generated and how they were validated or refuted. It also provides an avenue for the layperson to provide input (vis-à-vis his or her own opinions) into the equation.

2. *To Spur Additional Dialogue and Debate.* The interview process inherently spurs additional dialogue among the expert panel. My experience has been that the more divergence of opinions, the more debate occurs, which results in more robust and more refined models. The process may require more work, but, more often than not, the value of the outcome is greater than the additional effort.

3. *As a Litmus Test of Expert Opinions.* Conversely, if we rely solely on the input of expert opinions without thinking through and modeling out the statistical side of the equation, we may fall victim to tunnel vision.

While it is beyond the scope of this case study, these models could be further enhanced by creating forecasts for different types of attacks and determining the probabilities of becoming a victim for each attack. These enhancements could be realized by using historical data (what is published in the public domain along with an organization's own data).

For the purposes of simplicity, we leveraged the Delphi Method to create the various attack scenarios. The attack scenario total impact values range from $1,547,895 to $23,791,472—quite a significant range. How do we determine how much to invest to mitigate the risks associated with attacks?

Step 4: Determine Financial Impact

We are now ready to explore different investment scenarios to offset the risks of attacks. We now have more reliable estimates for the various classes of attacks and can take this financial information and turn it through a classical net present value (NPV) and discounted cash flow (DCF) analysis.

Our NPV/DCF analysis also has six different scenarios that will follow the same scenario structure as those previously defined. We follow this same approach through the entire analysis. It allows us to see multiple sides of the problem and arrive at a more reliable outcome.

We return to our original investment estimate (as provided by the client) of $2,000,000, which was previously arrived at through a variety of network and systems analyses. This amount reflects the investment necessary to upgrade and enhance the intrusion management systems currently distributed throughout the environment.

At a high level, this investment will result in:

- The replacement of intrusion detection systems (IDSs) with intrusion prevention systems (IPSs).
- An increased deployment of IPS devices at additional points throughout the network—from network perimeter to network core.
- The deployment of Network Behavior Analysis (NBA) solutions at various points throughout the network along with data collection and analysis engines necessary to detect anomalies and suspect network and traffic behavior.

The logical question is: Does a $2,000,000 investment adequately address the risks associated with the attacks and their likelihood of occurrence in this environment? Add to this: Is it too much or too little?

SCENARIO I

	Year 1	Year 2	Year 3	Year 4	Year 5	Totals
Capital Investments	(2,000,000)	(300,000)	(300,000)	(300,000)	(300,000)	
Risk Adjustment	264,947	0	264,947	409,417	409,417	1,348,728
Net Cash Flow	(1,735,053)	(300,000)	(35,053)	109,417	109,417	

NPV	($1,708,918,00)
IRR	−42.36%

FIGURE 14.120 DCF and NPV analysis.

If you recall from the previous steps, we created two different aspects of our models: current state and future state views. The basic premise of our argument is that no technology or set of technologies can provide 100% protection from all classes of attacks. However, we can intelligently place technology throughout the environment that mitigates these attacks. And these technologies will have varying degrees of success with respect to eliminating altogether the attack or significantly reducing the damage produced or the amount of time necessary to recover from an attack. What is important to us, then, is the reduction of losses. The investment decision is how much we should invest to reduce our losses. This is the basis behind our current state and future state views. We now move on to create our DCF and NPV analysis scenarios. Figure 14.120 illustrates Scenario I.

We create our 5-year time horizon and determine the timing and intensity of capital investments (our intrusion management technology solutions). The Risk Adjustment value is the difference between the current state impact less the future state impact for each year in this scenario (as modeled previously during the attack scenario step). We compute our net cash flows for each year, sum up the values, and then apply our NPV and internal rate of return (IRR) calculations (note: we use the MIRR function in Excel to better adapt to negative values). We also have unknowns associated with this model. We don't know precisely a few critical inputs into the model. We must account for these uncertainties. The following lists the additional inputs required to run the NPV analysis:

DCF/NPV Input Parameters	
Discount Rate	10%
Finance Rate	5%
Reinvestment Rate	7%
Equipment Annual Maintenance	15%

where we define the following parameters:

Discount Rate. The standard discount rate on the cash flows.

Finance Rate. The cost of capital or financing rate used to acquire the desired assets.

Reinvestment Rate. The return on the free cash flows that are reinvested.

Equipment Annual Maintenance. The annual maintenance fees and service fees associated with keeping the various technology solutions current (software upgrades, signature updates).

We apply Monte Carlo–based distributions to each value. For example, we may have varying degrees of success negotiating annual maintenance fees on the various equipment we decide to purchase. For this value we use a normal distribution with the mean set to 15% (industry average for a company of Acme T&D's size) and the standard deviation set to 0.015%, which gives us a range of between just less than 12% and slightly more than 18% (both of which are realistic outer limits). Next, Figure 14.121 represents what the expert team believed to be the planning case—in other words, the team members agreed that they should plan their efforts and investments based on this scenario. This is also the scenario we use for our unbiased expert.

Based on this case, we are expecting a total of eight attacks during a 5-year period. Our current state model suggests that we would incur losses of $11,650,567 in this scenario; our future state model suggests losses of $4,600,118. As mentioned earlier, our DCF/NPV analysis is concerned with the net difference, which in this case is $6,990.449. The model takes into account when these losses occur and when the difference is realized. We then compute the NPV and IRR values. Using the $2,000,000 assumption

SCENARIO VI

	Year 1	Year 2	Year 3	Year 4	Year 5	Totals
Capital Investments	(2,000,000)	(300,000)	(300,000)	(300,000)	(300,000)	
Risk Adjustment	264,947	264,947	813,973	5,381,635	264,947	6,990,449
Net Cash Flow	(1,735,053)	(35,053)	513,973	5,081,635	(35,053)	

NPV	$2,228,925.15
IRR	35.32%

FIGURE 14.121 DCF and NPV analysis on Scenario VI.

as our capital investment in intrusion management technologies, we can see that this scenario results in a positive NPV of $2,228,925.15, which results in a 35.32% IRR on our investment. Clearly, this model supports a $2,000,000 investment. This model in isolation would suggest that we could nearly double the initial investment and still have a positive NPV and IRR (the threshold to negative NPV is $3,666,000 year 1 expense following standard computations for all other variables in the model).

Step 5: Arrive at Investment Decision

We are now near the end of our analysis. We have a solid understanding of what our current and future risks are vis-à-vis the losses we are likely to incur across a variety of attack scenarios. We know that a $2,000,000 investment is within the range of reason. However, we also know that we could invest more and as a result further reduce our risk of losses. Alternatively, we could invest less and rely on the relatively low probability of being a target of a severe or catastrophic event.

We are at a crossroad. There is no absolute right or wrong decision for any organization. The decision makers in your organization must choose the best decision based on all of the available facts, on expert opinion, and in light of the organization's culture.

Consider that the analysis is relatively conservative in nature. Consider that the most conservative and least biased model (the model generated by our independent expert) suggests that 80% of the time losses will be greater than $1,857,474 (current state), and if we implement our proposed future state technology plan these losses will reduce to $267,792, resulting in a total loss reduction of $1,589,742. Follow this same mode of thinking and be on

Loss Reduction	$813,973		$7,696,217
Investment IRR	35.32%		−100%
Total Loss	$23,791,472		$813,973
Investment	$0		$3,666,000

More Risk Tolerant   **More Risk Averse**

FIGURE 14.122 Risk tolerance levels.

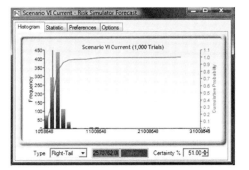 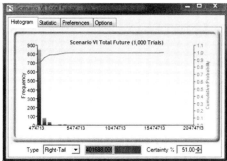

FIGURE 14.123 Simulation forecast risk tolerance levels.

the greater side of a betting man—51% of the time losses will be greater than $2,570,762 (current state) and $401,688 (future state), yielding $2,169,074 in loss reductions. Figure 14.122 illustrates an example set of risk tolerance and required investment levels, and the resulting simulation forecast distributions shown in Figure 14.123 further illustrate the probabilistic levels of these risk tolerances.

Risk Management

CHAPTER 15

The Warning Signs

T he finding of absence is very different from an absence of findings. How does management appropriately evaluate the validity and applicability of analytical results? How should management challenge the assumptions used in the analysis? What are some of the questions that should be asked? This chapter deals with some of the more difficult questions when evaluating the results of Monte Carlo risk simulation, stochastic forecasting, portfolio optimization, and strategic real options analysis.

THE PROBLEM OF NEGLIGENT ENTRUSTMENT

Power tools such as Risk Simulator and Real Options Super Lattice Solver took years to build and many more years to be perfected. It is extremely likely that a new user can simply pick up software products such as these and hit the ground running immediately. However, some knowledge of the theoretical underpinnings is required. In short, to create and perform sophisticated modeling, the analyst first needs to understand some of the underlying assumptions and approaches used in these analytics. Otherwise, it is akin to giving a three-year-old child a loaded machine gun. The correct term for this situation might be "negligent entrustment." In fact, when the rubber meets the road, more often than not, even so-called *power users* are perplexed and have a difficult time using these tools with respect to their models and business cases. These software tools, despite their analytical power, are just tools. They do not replace the analyst in any way. In fact, tools such as these only accouter the analyst with the appropriate analytics at their fingertips and do not by themselves make the relevant decisions. Such tools only relieve the analyst from having facility with fancy mathematics in order to build sophisticated models. As stated previously, 50 percent of the challenge in decision making is simply thinking about the problem, with 25 percent being the actual modeling and analytics, and the remaining 25 percent being able to convince and explain the results to senior management, clients, colleagues, and yourself.

MANAGEMENT'S DUE DILIGENCE

It might be the job of the analyst to create the models and use the fancy analytics, but it is senior management's job to challenge the assumptions and results obtained from said analysis. For instance, Figure 15.1 lists some of the issues that may arise when running a multivariate regression analysis and time-series forecasting. Although it may not be senior management's job to understand the mathematical or theoretical implications of these issues, management must nonetheless have a good grasp of what they mean.

The following sections are written specifically for senior management who are recipients of different types of advanced analyses results. The next section starts off with a general set of warning signs and moves on to the specifics of each analytical methodology used throughout this book.

SINS OF AN ANALYST

In general, warning signs can be grouped into five categories:

1. Model errors
2. Assumption and input errors
3. Analytical errors
4. User errors
5. Interpretation errors

Model errors are the errors an analyst would make while creating models. For instance, a financial model created in Excel may have errors

- Out of Range Forecasts
- Structural Breaks
- Specification Errors
- Omitted and Redundant Variables
- Heteroskedasticity and Homoskedasticity
- Multicollinearity
- Spurious Regression and Time Dependency
- Autocorrelation and Serial Correlation
- Correlation versus Causation
- Random Walks
- Mean Reversions
- Jump Processes
- Stochastic Processes

FIGURE 15.1 Warning signs in regression analysis.

stemming from broken links, incorrect functions and equations, poor modeling practices, or a break in the knowledge transfer between the originator of the model and subsequent users as well as successors of the model. This error can be eliminated through diligence on the part of the model creator. Good model-building practices also can assist in eliminating messy models. These practices include:

- Good documentation of the approaches used in the model as well as the integration and connectivity of the subparts that exist in the model.
- Creating a starting page that is linked through hyperlinks or macros with sufficient descriptions of each subpage or worksheet.
- Differentiating assumption input sheets from the models actually performing the number crunching, and from the results or reports page.
- Allowing changes to be made only on the input assumptions page and not directly in the model to prevent accidentally breaking the model.

For a detailed listing of good model-building practices and modeling etiquette, refer to Chapter 3, A Guide to Model-Building Etiquette.

Assumption and input errors are more difficult to tackle. These errors include the inputs required to make the model compute; for example, items such as levels of competitive threats, levels of technological success, revenue projections, income growth rates, market share determination, and so forth. Many of these determinant factors are almost impossible to determine. In fact, the old adage of *garbage in, garbage out* holds true here. The analyst can only do so much.

Multiple approaches exist to help clean up these so-called garbage assumptions. One way is simply to use expert knowledge and advice. For instance, the Delphi method requires the presence of a group of expert engineers in a room to discuss the levels of technological success rates. These engineers with intimate knowledge of the potential success rates are able to provide valuable insights that would otherwise be unavailable to a financial analyst sitting in front of a computer, far removed from the everyday technological challenges. Senior management, based on their many years of experience and expertise, can often provide valuable insights into what certain market outcomes may be. A double-blind experiment also can be conducted, where experts in a group are asked on anonymous questionnaires what their objective estimates of an outcome are. These quantitative outcomes are then tabulated and, on occasion, more experienced participants' comments will be weighted more heavily. The expected value is then used in the model. Here, Monte Carlo simulation can be applied on the distribution of the outcomes related to these expert testimonies. A custom distribution can be constructed using Risk Simulator, which relates back to the weights given to each outcome, or a simple nonparametric custom distribution simulation can also be applied on all possible outcomes obtained. Obviously, if there are ample historical data, then it is relatively easier to project the future, whether it is using some time-series forecast, regression analysis, or Monte Carlo simulation. *When in doubt, simulate!* Instead of arguing and relying on a particular single-point input value of a particular variable, an analyst can just simulate it around the potential outcomes of that input, whether it is the worst-case scenario, nominal-case scenario, or best-case scenario using a triangular distribution or some other distribution through expert assumptions.

No matter the approach used to obtain the data, management must test and challenge these assumptions. One way is to create tornado and sensitivity charts. The variables that drive the bottom line the most (the variable of interest, e.g., net present value, net income, return on investment) that are unpredictable and subject to uncertain levels of fluctuations are the ones that management should focus on. These critical success factors are the ones that management should care about, not some random variable that has little to no effect on the bottom line no matter how attractive or important the variable may be in other instances.

The upshot being that the more expert knowledge and historical data that exist, the better the assumption estimates will be. A good test of the assumptions used is through the application of back-casting, as opposed to forecasting, which looks forward into the future. Back-casting uses historical data to test the validity of the assumptions. One approach is to take the historical data, fit them to a distribution using Risk Simulator's distributional-fitting routines, and test the assumption input. Observe where the assumption value falls within this historical distribution. If it falls outside of the distribution's normal set of parameters (e.g., 95 percent or 99 percent confidence intervals), then the analyst should be able to better describe why there will be a potential structural shift going forward (e.g., mergers and acquisition, divestiture, reallocation of resources, economic downturn, entry of formidable competition). In forecasting, similar approaches can be used such as historical data-fitting of the forecast model and holdout approaches (i.e., some historical data are left out in the original forecast model but are used in the subsequent forecast-fitting to verify the model's accuracy).

READING THE WARNING SIGNS IN MONTE CARLO SIMULATION

Monte Carlo simulation is a very potent methodology. Statisticians and mathematicians sometimes dislike it because it solves difficult and often intractable problems with too much simplicity and ease. Instead, mathematical purists would prefer the more elegant approach: the old-fashioned way. Solving a fancy stochastic mathematical model provides a sense of accomplishment and completion as opposed to the brute force method. Monte Carlo creates artificial futures by generating thousands and even millions of sample paths of outcomes and looks at their prevalent characteristics. For analysts in a company, taking graduate-level advanced mathematics courses is neither logical nor practical. A brilliant analyst would use all available tools at his or her disposal to obtain the same answer the easiest way possible. One such tool is Monte Carlo simulation using Risk Simulator. The major benefit that Risk Simulator brings is its simplicity of use. The major downfall that Risk Simulator brings is also its simplicity of use!

Here are 14 due-diligence issues management should evaluate when an analyst presents a report with a series of advanced analytics using simulation.

1. How Are the Distributions Obtained? One thing is certain: If an analyst provides a report showing all the fancy analyses undertaken and one of these analyses is the application of Monte Carlo simulation of a few dozen variables, where each variable has the same distribution (e.g., triangular distribution), management should be very worried indeed and with good reason. One might be able to accept the fact that a few variables are triangularly distributed, but to assume that this holds true for several dozen other variables is ludicrous. One way to test the validity of distributional assumptions is to apply historical data to the distribution and see how far off one is.

Another approach is to take the distribution and test its alternate parameters. For instance, if a normal distribution is used on simulating market share, and the mean is set at 55 percent with a standard deviation of 45 percent, one should be extremely worried. Using Risk Simulator's alternate-parameter function, the 10th and 90th percentiles indicate a value of -2.67 percent and 112.67 percent. Clearly these values cannot exist under actual conditions. How can a product have -2.67 or 112.67 percent of the market share? The alternate-parameters function is a very powerful tool to use in conditions such as these. Almost always, the first thing that should be done is the use of alternate parameters to ascertain the logical upper and lower values of an input parameter.

2. How Sensitive Are the Distributional Assumptions? Obviously, not all variables under the sun should be simulated. For instance, a U.S.-based firm doing business within the 48 contiguous states should not have to worry about what happens to the foreign exchange market of the Zairian zaire. Risk is something one bears and is the outcome of uncertainty. Just because there is uncertainty, there could very well be no risk. If the only thing that bothers a U.S.-based firm's CEO is the fluctuation of the Zairian zaire, then I might suggest shorting some zaires and shifting his or her portfolio to U.S.-based bonds.

In short, simulate when in doubt, but simulate the variables that actually have an impact on what you are trying to estimate. Two very powerful tools to decide which variables to analyze are tornado and sensitivity charts. Make sure the simulated variables are the critical success factors—variables that have a significant impact on the bottom line being estimated while at the same time being highly uncertain and beyond the control of management.

3. What Are the Critical Success Factors? Critical success factors are related to how sensitive the resulting bottom line is to the input variables and assumptions. The first step that should be performed before using Monte Carlo simulation is the application of tornado charts. Tornado charts help identify which variables are the most critical to analyze. Coupled with management's and the analyst's expertise, the relevant critical success factors—the variables that drive the bottom line the most while being highly uncertain and beyond the control of management—can be determined and simulated. Obviously the most sensitive variables should receive the most amount of attention.

4. Are the Assumptions Related, and Have Their Relationships Been Considered? Simply defining assumptions on variables that have significant impact without regard to their interrelationships is also a major error most analysts make. For instance, when an analyst simulates revenues, he or she could conceivably break the revenue figures into price and quantity, where the resulting revenue figure is simply the product of price and quantity. The problem is if both price and quantity are considered as independent variables occurring in isolation, a major error arises. Clearly, for most products, the law of demand in economics takes over, where the higher the price of a product, ceteris paribus, or holding everything else constant, the quantity demanded of the same product decreases. Ignoring this simple economic truth, where both price and quantity are assumed to occur independently of one another, means that the possibility of a high price and a high quantity demanded may occur simultaneously, or vice versa. Clearly this condition will never occur in real life; thus, the simulation results will most certainly be flawed. The revenue or price estimates can also be further disaggregated into several product categories, where each category is correlated to the rest of the group (competitive products, product life cycle, product substitutes, complements, and cannibalization). Other examples include the possibility of economies of scale (where a higher production level forces cost to decrease over time), product life cycles (sales tend to decrease over time and plateau at a saturation rate), and average total costs (the average of fully allocated cost decreases initially and increases after it hits some levels of diminishing returns). Therefore, relationships, correlations, and causalities have to be modeled appropriately. If data are available, a simple correlation matrix can be generated through Excel to capture these relationships.

5. Considered Truncation?   Truncation is a major error Risk Simulator users commit, especially when using the infamous triangular distribution. The triangular distribution is very simple and intuitive. As a matter of fact, it is probably the most widely used distribution in Risk Simulator, apart from the normal and uniform distributions. Simplistically, the triangular distribution looks at the minimum value, the most probable value, and the maximum value. These three inputs are often confused with the worst-case, nominal-case, and best-case scenarios. This assumption is indeed incorrect.

In fact, a worst-case scenario can be translated as a highly unlikely condition that *will* still occur given a percentage of the time. For instance, one can model the economy as high, average, and low, analogous to the worst-case, nominal-case, and best-case scenarios. Thus, logic would dictate that the worst-case scenario might have, say, a 15 percent chance of occurrence, the nominal-case, a 50 percent chance of occurrence, and a 35 percent chance that a best-case scenario will occur. This approach is what is meant by using a best-, nominal-, and worst-case scenario analysis. However, compare that to the triangular distribution, where the minimum and maximum cases will almost never occur, with a probability of occurrence set at zero!

For instance, see Figure 15.2, where the worst-, nominal-, and best-case scenarios are set as 5, 10, and 15, respectively. Note that at the extreme values, the probability of 5 or 15 occurring is virtually zero, as the areas under the curve (the measure of probability) of these extreme points are zero. In other words, 5 and 15 will almost *never* occur. Compare that to the economic scenario where these extreme values have either a 15 percent or 35 percent chance of occurrence. Instead, distributional truncation should be considered here. The same applies to any other distribution. Figure 15.3 illustrates a truncated normal distribution where the extreme values do not extend to both positive and negative infinities, but are truncated at 7 and 13.

6. How Wide Are the Forecast Results?   I have seen models that are as large as 300MB with over 1,000 distributional assumptions. When you have a model that big with so many assumptions, there is a huge problem! For one, it takes an unnecessarily long time to run in Excel, and for another, the results generated are totally bogus. One thing is certain: The final forecast distribution of the results will most certainly be too large to use to make

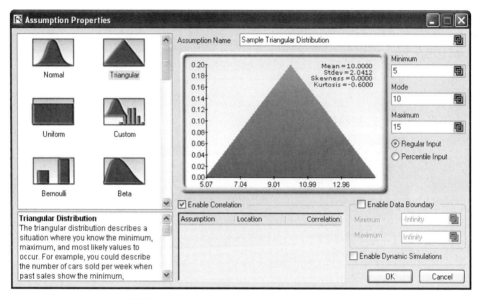

FIGURE 15.2   Sample triangular distribution.

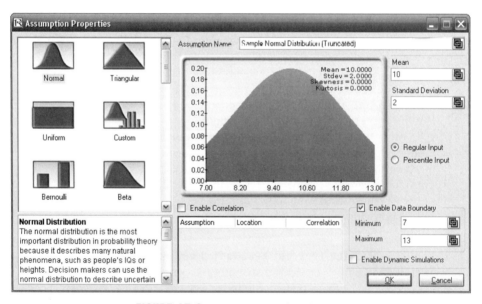

FIGURE 15.3   Truncating a distribution.

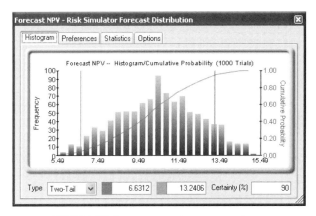

FIGURE 15.4   Truncated extreme values.

any definitive decision. Besides, what is the use of generating results that are close to a range between negative and positive infinity?

The results that you obtain should fall within decent parameters and intervals. One good check is to simply look at the single-point estimates. In theory, the single-point estimate is based on all precedent variables at their respective expected values. Thus, if one perturbs these expected values by instituting distributions about their single-point estimates, then the resulting single-point bottom line estimate should also fall within this forecast interval.

7. What Are the End Points and Extreme Values?   Mistaking end points is both an error of interpretation and a user error. For instance, Figure 15.4 illustrates the results obtained from a financial analysis with extreme values between $5.49 million and $15.49 million. By making the leap that the worst possible outcome is $5.49 million and the best possible outcome is $15.49 million, the analyst has made a major error. Clicking on the *Options* menu and *Data Filter* area, one can choose any display range (Figure 15.5).

Clearly, if the *show data less than 2 standard deviations* option is chosen, the graph looks somewhat different (the endpoints are now 6.34 and 14.34 as compared to 5.49 and 15.49), indicating the actual worst and best cases (Figure 15.6). Of course, the interpretation would be quite different here than with the 2 standard deviations option chosen.

8. Are There Breaks Given Business Logic and Business Conditions?   Assumptions used in the simulation may be based on valid historical data, which means that the distributional outcomes would be valid if the firm indeed existed in the past. However, going forward, historical data may not

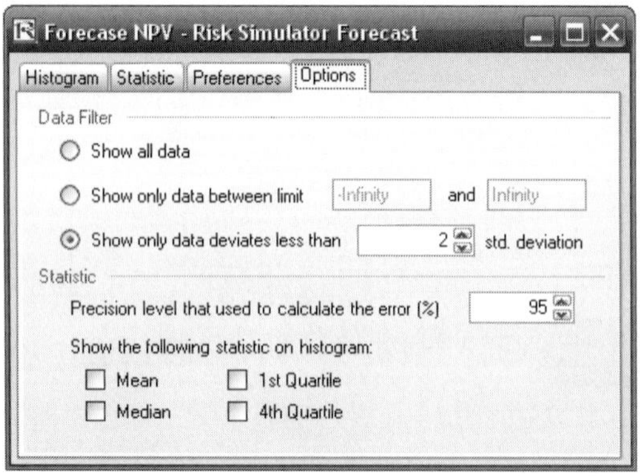

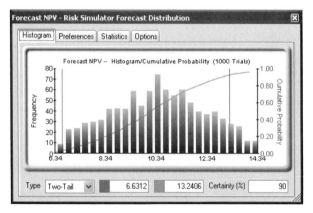

FIGURE 15.5　Display range preferences.

be the best predictor of the future. In fact, past performance is no indicator of future ability to perform, especially when structural breaks in business conditions are predicted to occur. Structural breaks include situations where firms decide to go global, acquire other firms, divest part of their assets, enter into new markets, and so forth. The resulting distributional forecasts need to be revalidated based on these conditions. The results based on past performance could be deemed as the base-case scenario, with additional adjustments and add-ons as required. This situation is especially true in the research and development arena, where by definition of research and development, things that are yet to be developed are new and novel in nature; thus by definition, there exist no historical data on which to base the future forecasts. In situations such as these, it is best to rely on experience and

FIGURE 15.6　Display range using fixed end points.

expert opinions of future outcomes. Other approaches where historical data do not exist include using market proxies and project comparables—where current or historical projects and firms with similar functions, markets, and risks are used as benchmarks.

9. Do the Results Fall Within Expected Economic Conditions? One of the most dangerous traps analysts fall into is the trap of data mining. Rather than relying on solid theoretical frameworks, analysts let the data sort things out by themselves. For instance, analysts who blindly use stepwise regression and distributional fitting fall directly into this data-mining trap. Instead of relying on theory *a priori*, or before the fact, analysts use the results to explain the way things look, *a posteriori*, or after the fact.

A simple example is the prediction of the stock market. Using tons of available historical data on the returns of the Standard & Poor's 500 index, an analyst runs a multivariate stepwise regression using over a hundred different variables ranging from economic growth, gross domestic product, and inflation rates, to the fluctuations of the Zairian zaire, to who won the Super Bowl and the frequency of sunspots on particular days. Because the stock market by itself is unpredictable and random in nature, as are sunspots, there seems to be some relationship over time. Although this relationship is purely spurious and occurred out of happenstance, a stepwise regression and correlation matrix will still pick up this spurious relationship and register the relationship as statistically significant. The resulting analysis will show that sunspots do in fact explain fluctuations in the stock market. Therefore, is the analyst correct in setting up distributional assumptions based on sunspot activity in the hopes of beating the market? When one throws a computer at data, it is almost certain that a spurious connection will emerge.

The lesson learned here is to look at particular models with care when trying to find relationships that may seem on the surface to be valid, but in fact are spurious and accidental in nature, and that holding all else constant, the relationship dissipates over time. Merely correlating two randomly occurring events and seeing a relationship is nonsense and the results should not be accepted. Instead, analysis should be based on economic and financial rationale. In this case, the economic rationale is that the relationship between sunspots and the stock market is completely accidental and should thus be treated as such.

10. What Are the Values at Risk? Remember the story about my friend and me going skydiving in the first chapter? Albeit fictitious, it illustrates the differences between risk and uncertainty. When applying Monte Carlo simulation, an analyst is looking at uncertainty; that is, distributions are applied to different variables that drive a bottom-line forecast. Figure 15.7

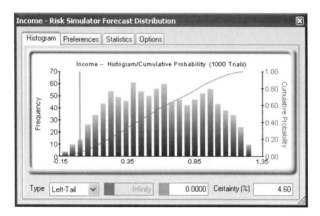

STATIC MODEL

Revenue	$	2.00
Cost	$	1.00
Income	$	1.00

DYNAMIC MODEL

Revenue	$	2.00	<<--- This is an Input Assumption
Cost	$	1.00	<<--- This is an Input Assumption
Income	$	1.00	<<--- This is an Output Forecast

FIGURE 15.7 Illustrating the differences between risk and uncertainty.

shows a very simple calculation, where on a deterministic basis, if revenue is $2 and cost is $1, the resulting net income is simply $1 (i.e., $2 – $1). However, in the dynamic model, where revenue is "around $2" and cost is "around $1," the net income is "around $1." This "around" comment signifies the uncertainty involved in each of these variables. The resulting variable will also be an "around" number. In fact, when Risk Simulator is applied, the resulting single-point estimate also ends up being $1. The only difference being that there is a forecast distribution surrounding this $1 value. By performing Monte Carlo simulation, a level of uncertainty surrounding this single-point estimate is obtained. Risk analysis has *not yet* been done. Only uncertainty analysis has been done thus far. By running simulations, only the levels of uncertainty have been quantified if the reports are shown but the results are not used to adjust for risk.

For instance, one can in theory simulate everything under the sun, including the fluctuations of the Zairian zaire, and if the Zairian zaire has no impact on the project being analyzed, capturing the uncertainty surrounding the currency does not mean one has managed, reduced, or analyzed the project's foreign exchange risks. It is only when the results are analyzed and used appropriately that risk analysis has been done. For instance, if an analyst is evaluating three similar projects where each project has an expected value of $1 in net income but with different distributions, no new information is realized. However, only when the results are used appropriately, where we say the first project has a $0.30 value at the fifth percentile, while the second and third projects have $0.20 and –$0.10 values at the fifth percentile, will risk analysis have been done. Holding everything else constant, the best project is clearly the first project, where in the worst-case scenario 5 percent of the time, the minimum amount to be gained is $0.30, the largest of the three. Obviously, other measures can be used, including the mean divided by the standard deviation (creating the inverse of the coefficient of variability or bang-for-the-buck measure), risk-adjusted return on capital (RAROC or median less the fifth percentile divided by the volatility), and so forth, as detailed in Chapter 2, From Risk to Riches. Suffice it to say, as long as the risk adjustment is applied appropriately across all projects for comparability purposes, the measurement will be valid. The upshot being that simply noting the uncertainty levels around a value is not risk analysis. It is only when this value is adjusted according to its risk levels has risk analysis actually been performed.

11. How Do the Assumptions Compare to Historical Data and Knowledge?
Suspect distributional assumptions should be tested through the use of back-casting, which uses historical data to test the validity of the assumptions. One approach is to take the historical data, fit them to a distribution using Risk Simulator's distributional-fitting routines, and test the assumption inputs. See if the distributional-assumption values fall within this historical distribution. If they fall outside of the distribution's normal set of parameters (e.g., 95 percent or 99 percent confidence intervals), then the analyst should better be able to describe and explain this apparent discontinuity, which can very well be because of changing business conditions and so forth.

12. How Do the Results Compare Against Traditional Analysis? A very simple test of the analysis results is through single-point estimates. For instance, remember the $1 net income example? If the single-point estimate shows $1 as the expected value of net income, then, in theory, the uncertainty surrounding this $1 should have the initial single-point estimate somewhere within its forecast distribution. If $1 is not within the resulting forecast distribution, something is amiss here. Either the model used to calculate the original $1 single-point estimate is flawed or the simulation assumptions are flawed. To recap, how can "around $2" minus "around $1" not be "around $1"?

13. Do the Statistics Confirm the Results? Risk Simulator provides a wealth of statistics after performing a simulation. Figure 15.8 shows a sample listing of these statistics, which can be obtained through the *View | Statistics* menu in Risk Simulator. Some of these statistics when used in combination provide a solid foundation of the validity of the results. When

Standard Normal Distribution - Risk Simulator Forecast Distribution ☒

| Histogram | Preferences | Statistics | Options |

Statistics	Result
Number of Trials	10000
Mean	0.0038
Median	-0.0003
Standard Deviation	1.0063
Variance	1.0126
Average Deviation	0.8034
Maximum	4.1971
Minimum	-4.1760
Range	8.3732
Skewness	-0.0169
Kurtosis	0.0187
25% Percentile	-0.6756
75% Percentile	0.6829
Error Precision at 95% confidence	518.5972%

FIGURE 15.8 Standard-normal distribution statistics.

in doubt as to what the *normal*-looking statistics should be, simply run a simulation in Risk Simulator and set the distribution to normal with a mean of 0.00 and a standard deviation of 1.00. This condition would create a standard-normal distribution, one of the most basic statistical distributions. The resulting set of statistics is shown in Figure 15.8. See Chapter 2, From Risk to Riches, for more details on some basic statistics and interpreting distributional moments.

Clearly, after running 10,000 trials, the resulting mean is 0.00 with a standard deviation of 1.00, as specified in the assumption. Of particular interest are the skewness and kurtosis values. For a normally distributed result, the skewness is close to 0.00, and the excess kurtosis is close to 0.00. If the results from your analysis fall within these parameters, it is clear that the forecast values are symmetrically distributed with no excess areas in the tail. A highly positive or negative skew would indicate that something might be going on in terms of some distributional assumptions that are skewing the results either to the left or to the right. This skew may be intentional or something is amiss in terms of setting up the relevant distributions. Also, a significantly higher kurtosis value would indicate that there is a higher probability of occurrence in the tails of the distribution, which means extreme values or catastrophic events are prone to occur more frequently than predicted in most normal circumstances. This result may be expected or not. If not, then the distributional assumptions in the model should be revisited with greater care, especially the extreme values of the inputs.

14. Are the Correct Methodologies Applied? The problem of whether the correct methodology is applied is where user error comes in. The analyst should be able to clearly justify why a lognormal distribution is used instead of a uniform distribution, and so forth, and why distributional fitting is used instead of bootstrap simulation, or why a tornado chart is used instead of a sensitivity chart. All of these methodologies and approaches require some basic levels of understanding, and questions such as these are most certainly required as part of management's due diligence when evaluating an analyst's results.

> Warning signs to watch out for in Monte Carlo simulation and questions to ask include how the distributions are obtained, how sensitive are the distributional assumptions, how to identify the critical success factors, how the distributional assumptions are related, if the distributions are truncated, how wide are the forecast values, what are the end points and extreme values, are there breaks in business logic and conditions, do the results follow economic rationale, what are the values-at-risk, how do the results compare with historical data and knowledge, how do the results compare with traditional analyses, do the statistics confirm expectations, and are the correct methodologies applied.

READING THE WARNING SIGNS IN TIME-SERIES FORECASTING AND REGRESSION

Another frequently used decision-analysis tool is forecasting. One thing is certain: You can never predict the future with perfect accuracy. The best that you can hope for is to get as close as possible. In addition, it is actually okay to be wrong on occasion. As a matter of fact, it is sometimes good to be wrong, as valuable lessons can be learned along the way. It is better to be wrong consistently than to be wrong on occasion, because if you are wrong consistently in one direction, you can correct or reduce your expectations, or increase your expectations when you are consistently overoptimistic or underoptimistic. The problem arises when you are occasionally right and occasionally wrong, and you have no idea when or why it happens. Some of the issues that should be addressed when evaluating time-series or any other forecasting results include the following:

1. Out of Range Forecasts   Not all variables can be forecast using historical data. For instance, did you know that you can predict, rather reliably, the ambient temperature given the frequency of cricket chirps? Collect a bunch of crickets and change the ambient temperature, collect the data, and run a bivariate regression, and you would get a high level of confidence as seen in the coefficient of determination or R-squared value. Given this model, you could reasonably predict ambient temperature whenever crickets chirp, correct? Well, if you answered yes, you have just fallen into the trap of forecasting out of range.

Suppose your model holds up to statistical scrutiny, which it may very well do, assuming you do a good job with the experiment and data collection. Using the model, one finds that crickets chirp more frequently the higher the ambient temperature, and less frequently the colder it gets. What do you presume would happen if one were to toss a poor cricket in the oven and turn it up to 550 degrees? What happens when the cricket is thrown into the freezer instead? What would occur if a Malaysian cricket were used instead of the Arizona reticulated cricket? The quick answer is you can toss your fancy statistical regression model out the window if any of these things happened. As for the cricket in the oven, you would most probably hear the poor thing give out a very loud chirp and then complete silence. Regression and prediction models out of sample, that is, modeling events that are out of place and out of the range of the data collected in ordinary circumstances, on occasion will fail to work, as is clearly evident from the poor cricket.

2. Structural Breaks   Structural breaks in business conditions occur all the time. Some example instances include going public, going private, merger, acquisition, geographical expansion, adding new distribution channels, existence of new competitive threats, union strikes, change of senior management, change of company vision and long-term strategy, economic downturn, and so forth. Suppose you are an analyst at FedEx performing volume, revenue, and profitability metric forecasting of multiple break-bulk stations. These stations are located all around the United States and each station has its own seasonality factors complete with detailed historical data. Some advanced econometric models are applied, ranging from ARIMA (autoregressive integrated moving average) and ECM (error correction models) to GARCH (generalized autoregressive conditional heteroskedasticity) models; these time-series forecasting models usually provide relatively robust forecasts. However, within a single year, management reorganization, union strikes, pilot strikes, competitive threats (UPS, your main competitor, decided to enter a new submarket), revised accounting rules, and a plethora of other *coincidences* simply made all the forecasts invalid. The analyst must decide if these coincidences are just that, coincidences, or if they point to a fundamental structural change in the way global freight businesses are run. Obviously, certain incidences are planned or expected, whereas others are unplanned and unexpected. The planned incidences should thus be considered when performing forecasting.

3. Specification Errors Sometimes, models are incorrectly specified. A nonlinear relationship can be very easily masked through the estimation of a linear model. In the forecasting chapter, running a linear regression model on a clearly nonlinear data set still resulted in statistically valid models and provided decent estimates. Another specification error that is fairly common has to do with autocorrelated and seasonal data sets. Estimating the demand of flowers in a floral chain without accounting for the holidays (Valentine's Day, Mother's Day, and so forth) is a blatant specification error. Failure to clearly use the correct model specification or first sanitizing the data may result in highly erroneous results.

4. Omitted and Redundant Variables This type of model error in multivariate regression exists when regression is used to forecast the future. Suppose an analyst uses multivariate regression to obtain a statistical relationship between a dependent variable (e.g., sales, prices, revenues) and other regressors or independent variables (e.g., economic conditions, advertising levels, market competition) and he or she hopes to use this relationship to forecast the future. Unfortunately, the analyst may not have all the available information at his or her fingertips. If important information is unavailable, an important variable may be omitted (e.g., market saturation effects, price elasticity of demand, threats of emerging technology), or if too much data is available, redundant variables may be included in the analysis (e.g., inflation rate, interest rate, economic growth). It may be counterintuitive, but the problem of redundant variables is more serious than omitted variables.[1] In a situation where redundant variables exist,[2] and if these redundant variables are perfectly correlated or collinear with each other, the regression equation does not exist and cannot be solved. In the case where slightly less severe collinearity exists, the estimated regression equation will be less accurate than without this collinearity. For instance, suppose both interest rates and inflation rates are used as explanatory variables in the regression analysis, where if there is a significant negative correlation between these variables with a time lag, then using both variables to explain sales revenues in the future is redundant. Only one variable is sufficient to explain the relationship with sales. If the analyst uses both variables, the errors in the regression analysis will increase. The prediction errors of an additional variable will increase the errors of the entire regression.

5. Heteroskedasticity If the variance of the errors in a regression analysis increases over time, the regression equation is said to be flawed and suffers from heteroskedasticity. Although this may seem to be a technical matter, many regression practitioners fall into this heteroskedastic trap without even realizing it. See Chapter 9, Using the Past to Predict the Future, for details on heteroskedasticity, testing for its existence, and methods to fix the error.

6. Multicollinearity   One of the assumptions required for a regression to run is that the independent variables are noncorrelated or noncollinear. These independent variables are exactly collinear when a variable is an exact linear combination of the other variables. This error is most frequently encountered when dummy variables are used.[3] A quick check of multicollinearity is to run a correlation matrix of the independent variables.[4] In most instances, the multicollinearity problem will prevent the regression results from being computed. See Chapter 9's Appendix—Detecting and Fixing Multicollinearity—for more details.

7. Spurious Regression, Data Mining, Time Dependency, and Survivorship Bias   Spurious regression is another danger that analysts often run into. This mistake is made through certain uses of data-mining activities. Data mining refers to using approaches such as a step-wise regression analysis, where analysts do not have some prior knowledge of the economic effects of what independent variables drive the dependent variable, and use all available data at their disposal. The analyst then runs a step-wise regression, where the methodology ranks the highest correlated variable to the least correlated variable.[5] Then the methodology automatically adds each successive independent variable in accordance with its correlation until some specified stopping statistical criteria. The resulting regression equation is then taken as the final and best result. The problem with this approach is that some independent variables may simply be randomly moving about while the dependent variable may also be randomly moving about, and their movements depend on time.[6] Suppose this randomness in motion is somehow related at certain points in time but the actual economic fundamentals or financial relationships do not exist. Data-mining activities will pick up the coincidental randomness and not the actual relationship, and the result is a spurious regression; that is, the relationship estimated is bogus and is purely a chance happenstance. Multicollinearity effects may also unnecessarily eliminate highly significant variables from the step-wise regression.

Finally, survivorship bias and self-selection bias are important, as only the best-performing realization will always show up and have the most amount of visibility. For instance, looking to the market to obtain proxy data can be dangerous for only successful firms will be around and have the data. Firms that have failed will most probably leave no trails of their existence, let alone credible market data for an analyst to collect. Self-selection occurs when the data that exist are biased and selective. For instance, pharmacology research on a new cancer treatment will attract cancer patients of all types, but the researchers will clearly only select those patients in the earlier stages of cancer, making the results look more promising than they actually are.

8. Autoregressive Processes, Lags, Seasonality, and Serial Correlation

In time-series data, certain variables are autoregressive in nature; that is, future values of variables such as price, demand, interest rates, inflation rates, and so forth depend on values that occurred in the past, or are autoregressive.[7] This reversion to the past occurs because of many reasons, including seasonality and cyclicality.[8] Because of these cyclical or seasonal and autoregressive effects, regression analysis using seasonal or cyclical independent variables as is will yield inexact results. In fact, some of these autoregressive, cyclical, or seasonal variables will affect the dependent variable differently over time. There may be a time lag between effects. For example, an increase in interest rates may take 1 to 3 months before the mortgage market feels the effects of this decline. Ignoring this time lag will downplay the relationships of highly significant variables.

9. Correlation and Causality

Regression analysis looks at correlation effects, not causality.[9] To say that there is a cause in X (independent variable) that drives the outcome of Y (dependent variable) through the use of regression analysis is flawed. For instance, there is a high correlation between the number of shark attacks and lunch hour around the world. Clearly, sharks cannot tell that it is time to have lunch. However, because lunchtime is the warmest time of the day, this is also the hour that beaches around the world are most densely populated. With a higher population of swimmers, the chances of heightened shark attacks are almost predictable. Lunchtime does not *cause* sharks to go hungry and prompt them to search for food. Just because there is a correlation does not mean that there is causality. Making this leap will provide analysts and management an incorrect interpretation of the results.

10. Random Walks

Certain financial data (e.g., stock prices, interest rates, inflation rates) follow something called a random walk. Random walks can take on different characteristics, including random walks with certain jumps, random walks with a drift rate, or a random walk that centers or reverts to some long-term average value. Even the models used to estimate random walks are varied, from geometric to exponential, among other things. A simple regression equation will yield no appreciable relationship when random walks exist.[10]

11. Jump Processes

Jump processes are more difficult to grasp but are nonetheless important for management to understand and challenge the assumptions of an analyst's results. For instance, the price of oil in the global market may sometimes follow a jump process. When the United States goes to war with another country, or when OPEC decides to cut the production of oil by several billion barrels a year, oil prices will see a sudden jump. Forecasting revenues based on these oil prices over time using historical data may not be the best approach. These sudden probabilistic jumps should most certainly be accounted for in the analysis. In this case, a jump-diffusion stochastic model is more appropriate than simple time-series or regression analyses.

12. Stochastic Processes   Other stochastic processes are also important when analyzing and forecasting the future. Interest rates and inflation rates may follow a mean-reversion stochastic process; that is, interest rates and inflation rates cannot increase or decrease so violently that they fall beyond all economic rationale. In fact, economic factors and pressures will drive these rates to their long-run averages over time. Failure to account for these effects over the long run may yield statistically incorrect estimates, resulting in erroneous forecasts.

> Warning signs to watch out for in time-series forecasting and regression as well as questions to ask include whether the forecasts are out of range, are there structural and business breaks anticipated in the forecast period, are there any misspecifications in the model, are there any possibilities of omitted and redundant variables, are there heteroskedasticity effects, are there any spurious relationships and biases, are there autoregressive lags, are correlations confused with causality, and are there variables that follow a random walk, jump processes, or other stochastic processes.

READING THE WARNING SIGNS IN REAL OPTIONS ANALYSIS

Risk analysis is never complete without the analysis of real options. What are uncertainty and risk analyses good for if one cannot make use of them? Real options analysis looks at the flexibility of a project or management's ability to make midcourse corrections when uncertainty becomes resolved over time. At the outset, real options analysis looks like a very powerful analytical tool, but care should be taken when real options analysis is applied. For instance, consider the following:

1. Do Not Let Real Options Simply Overinflate the Value of a Project

One of the most significant criticisms of real options approaches is that of overinflating the value of a project. This criticism, of course, is false. Real options are applicable if and only if the following requirements are met: traditional financial analysis can be performed and models can be built; uncertainty exists; the same uncertainty drives value; management or the project has strategic options or flexibility to either take advantage of these uncertainties or to hedge them; and management must be credible in executing the relevant strategic options when they become optimal to do so; otherwise all the options in the world would be useless. Thus, an analyst should not simply apply real options analysis to every project that comes across his or her desk, but only to those that are appropriate and ripe for analysis.

An option will always bear a value greater than or equal to zero. Hence, critics argue that by applying real options analysis, a project's value will be artificially inflated. In reality, real options may sometimes appear without cost, but in most cases firms need to pay to acquire these options (e.g., spending money to retrofit a refinery to obtain a switching option to choose between input fuels), and although the value of an option may be positive, its value can be clouded by the cost to obtain the option, making the entire strategy unprofitable and reducing the value of a project. So, although the value of an option is positive, the entire strategy's value may be negative. The lesson here is well learned—do not apply real options analysis on everything in sight, just to those projects that actually do have strategic options. Without doing so may mean leaving money on the table.

2. How Is Volatility Obtained and How Do You Reconcile Its Value?

Fifty percent of the value of a real options analysis is simply thinking about it and realizing that management has the flexibility to make midcourse corrections when uncertainty becomes resolved over time. Twenty-five percent is crunching the numbers, and the remaining 25 percent of the value in applying real options comes from being able to convince and explain the results to management. One of the toughest things to explain is the concept of where and how volatility is obtained. Volatility should be obtained from a project based on a project's level of uncertainty going forward. One major error is to use external market proxies for volatility. Using a firm's stock price to estimate volatility of a single project in a company with hundreds or even thousands of projects is not only incorrect, it is ludicrous. An analyst should, hence, be able to defend the choice of volatility estimates. See Johnathan Mun's *Real*

Options Analysis, Second Edition (John Wiley & Sons, 2005) for details on converting volatility to probability, and explaining volatility to management in an easy to understand manner.

3. What About Competing Options or Options That Have Not Even Been Considered?

If a project has 10 strategic options, do you analyze all 10 options? What about projects in the distant future, where the options are not yet known for certain, that may be highly valuable? For a project with many options, the analyst has to determine which of these options are independent and which are interacting type options. If the options are interacting, dominant strategies will always dominate over less valuable options and the value of the project's total set of options will revert to these dominant options.[11] Thus, do not evaluate all the options in the world if only a few options capture a significant portion of the value. Focus instead on valuing those important or dominant options.

4. The Error of Interpretation of Option Results

Sometimes options come without a cost, while sometimes they do have a cost. On some occasions, option value is tangible or explicit, and sometimes option value is implicit or intangible. As an example, the land seller illustration used in Chapter 13, The Black Box Made Transparent: Real Options Super Lattice Solver Software, looks at the value of having an abandonment option, where if the counterparty signs the contractual agreement, the maximum expected cost of the contract is the option value.[12] However, in the case of some of the illustrations in Chapter 12, What Is So Real About Real Options, and Why Are They Optional? where a research and development outfit performing stage-gate development has the option to abandon at every stage, valuing these options does not automatically mean the IRS or a counterparty will show up at the door and give the company a check in that amount. In this situation, the option value is an intangible or implicit value, useful as a measure against other projects and alternate strategies with or without such a flexibility option value.[13]

> Warning signs to watch out for in real options analysis and questions to ask include whether the real options analysis is applied inappropriately when there are no options such that the value of a project is inappropriately overinflated, how the volatility measure is obtained, are competing or omitted options appropriately considered, and are the results interpreted correctly.

READING THE WARNING SIGNS IN OPTIMIZATION UNDER UNCERTAINTY

Finally, uncertainty and risk analyses are irrelevant if these quantified risks cannot be diversified away. Optimization looks at the ability to diversify away risks to find the best combination of projects subject to some prespecified constraints.

1. Why Are the Decision Variables the Decision Variables? Decision variables are the variables that management has control over (e.g., which projects to execute, which products to manufacture, which vendor to purchase from, which wells to drill). However, sometimes things that are seemingly decision variables at the outset may not exactly be decision variables. For instance, the CEO's pet project is definitely a "go" decision no matter what the analytical results. The internal politics involved in decision making is something that cannot be taken lightly. Decision variables in an optimization analysis should most certainly be decision variables, not decisions that have already been made with the façade that their existence still has to be justified. Finally, certain decision variables are related to other decision variables and this interaction must be considered. For instance, Project A is a precursor to Projects B, C, and D; however, Project C cannot be executed if project B is executed, and Project C is a precursor to Project D.[14]

2. How Certain Are the Optimization Results? Has the analyst looked at enough combinations to obtain the optimal results? In static optimization without simulation, whether it is using Risk Simulator, Excel's goal seek, or Excel's Solver add-in, the optimal solution will be found, if there is one, rather quickly, as the computer can calculate all possible combinations and permutations of inputs to yield the optimal results. However, in optimization under uncertainty,[15] the process will take much longer and the results may not achieve optimality quickly. Even if the results do seem to be optimal, it is hard to tell; thus, it is safer to run the simulation much longer than required. An impatient analyst may fall into the trap of not running sufficient simulation trials to obtain robust stochastic or dynamic optimization results.

3. What Is the Analyst's Level of Training? Little knowledge of probability will lead to more dangerous conclusions than no knowledge at all. Knowledge and experience together will prove to be an impressive combination, especially when dealing with advanced analytics. Almost always, the first step in getting more advanced analytics accepted and rolled out corporate-wide is to have a group of in-house experts trained in both the art and science of advanced analytics. Without a solid foundation, plans on rolling out these analytics will fail miserably.

> Warning signs to watch out for in an optimization under uncertainty and questions to ask include whether the decision variables are indeed decisions to be made, what are the levels of certainty of the results, and what is the level of training of the analyst.

QUESTIONS

1. Define what is meant by negligent entrustment.
2. What are some of the general types of errors encountered by an analyst when creating a model?
3. Why is truncation in a model's assumption important? What would happen to the results if truncation is not applied when it should be?
4. What is a critical success factor?
5. What are some of the normal-looking statistics?
6. What are structural breaks and specification errors, and why are they important?

CHAPTER 16

Changing a Corporate Culture

HOW TO GET RISK ANALYSIS ACCEPTED IN AN ORGANIZATION

Advanced analytics is hard to explain to management.[1] So, how do you get risk analysis accepted as the norm in a corporation, especially if your industry is highly conservative? It is almost a guarantee in conservative companies that an analyst showing senior management a series of fancy, mathematically complex, and computationally sophisticated models will be thrown out of the office together with his or her results and have the door slammed in his or her face. Changing management's thinking is the topic of discussion in this chapter. Explaining results and convincing management appropriately go hand in hand with the characteristics of the advanced analytical tools, which if they satisfy certain change-management requisites, the level and chances of acceptance become easier.

CHANGE-MANAGEMENT ISSUES AND PARADIGM SHIFTS

Change-management specialists have found that there are several criteria to be met before a paradigm shift in thinking is found to be acceptable in a corporation. For example, in order for senior management to accept a new and novel set of advanced analytical approaches—simulation, forecasting, real options, and portfolio optimization—the models and processes themselves must have applicability to the problem at hand and not merely be an academic exercise.[2] Figure 16.1 lists the criteria required for change.

As we saw previously, it is certainly true that large multinationals have embraced the concept of risk analysis with significant fervor and that risk analysis is here to stay.[3] It is not simply an academic exercise, nor is it

"No change of paradigm comes easily"

Criteria for instituting change:

- Method applicability
  - Not just an academic exercise
- Accurate, consistent, and replicable
  - Creates a standard for decision making
- Value-added propositions
  - Competitive advantage over competitors
  - Provide valuable insights otherwise unavailable
- Exposition
  - Making the black box transparent
  - Explaining the value to senior management
- Comparative advantage
  - Better method than the old
  - It takes a good theory to kill an old one
- Compatibility with the old approach
  - Based on the old with significant improvements
- Flexibility
  - Able to be tweaked
  - Covers a multitude of problems
- External influences
  - From "Main Street" to "Wall Street"
  - Communicating to the investment community the value created internally

FIGURE 16.1   Changing a corporate culture.

the latest financial analysis fad that is here today and gone tomorrow. In addition, the process and methodology have to be consistent, accurate, and replicable, that is, they pass the scientific process. Given similar assumptions, historical data, and assertions, one can replicate the results with ease and predictability. This replicability is especially true with the use of software programs such as the ones included on the DVD.

Next, the new method must provide a compelling value-added proposition. Otherwise, it is nothing but a fruitless and time-consuming exercise. The time, resources, and effort spent must be met and even surpassed by the method's added value. This added value is certainly the case in larger capital investment initiatives, where a firm's future or the future of a business unit may be at stake—incorrect and insufficient results may be obtained, and disastrous decisions made if risk analysis is not undertaken.

Other major criteria include the ability to provide the user a comparative advantage over its competitors, which is certainly the case when the additional valuable insights generated through advanced risk analysis will help management identify options, value, prioritize, and select strategic and less risky alternatives that may otherwise be overlooked.

Finally, in order to accept a change in mind-set, the new methodology, analysis, process, or model must be easy to explain and understand. In addition, there has to be a link to previously accepted methods, whether the new methodology is an extension of the old or a replacement of the old due to some clear superior attributes. These last two points are the most difficult to tackle for an analyst. The sets of criteria prior to this are direct and easy to define.

The new set of risk analytics is nothing but an extension of existing methodologies.[4] For instance, Monte Carlo simulation can be explained simply as scenario analysis applied to the nth degree. Simulation is nothing but scenario analysis done thousands of times only not just on a single variable (e.g., the three common scenarios: good economy, average economy, and bad economy complete with their associated probabilities of occurrence and payoffs at each state), but on multiple variables interacting simultaneously, where multiple variables are changing independently or dependently, in a correlated or uncorrelated fashion (e.g., competition, economy, market share, technological efficacy). In fact, the result stemming from new analytics is simply a logical extension of the traditional approaches. Figure 16.2 illustrates this logical extension.

The static model in the illustration shows a revenue value of $2, cost of $1, and the resulting income value, calculated as the difference between the two, of $1. Compare that to the dynamic model, where the same inputs are used but the revenue and cost variables have been subjected to Monte Carlo simulation. Once simulation has been completed, the dynamic model still shows the same single-point estimate of $1 as in the static model. In other words, adding in the more advanced analytics, namely, Monte Carlo simulation, the model and results have not changed. If management still wants the single-point estimate of $1 reported, then so be it. However, by logical extension, if both revenues and costs are uncertain, then by definition, the resulting income will also be uncertain. The forecast chart for the income variable shows this uncertainty of the resulting income with fluctuations around $1. In fact, additional valuable information is obtained using simulation, where the probability or certainty of breakeven or exceeding $0 in income is shown as 95.40 percent in Figure 16.2. In addition, rather than relying on the single-point estimate of $1, simulation reveals that the business only has an 8.90 percent probability of exceeding the single-point estimate of $1 in income (Figure 16.3).

STATIC MODEL			DYNAMIC MODEL			
Revenue	$	2.00	Revenue	$	2.00	<<--- This is an Input Assumption
Cost	$	1.00	Cost	$	1.00	<<--- This is an Input Assumption
Income	$	1.00	Income	$	1.00	<<--- This is an Output Forecast

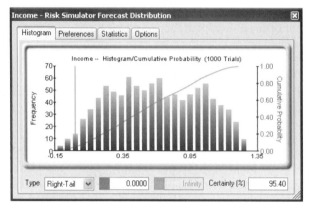

FIGURE 16.2   Monte Carlo simulation as a logical extension of traditional analysis.

If simulation is not applied here, the riskiness of this project will never be clearly elucidated. Imagine if management has multiple but similar types of projects where every project has a single-point estimate of $1. In theory, management should be indifferent in choosing any of these projects. However, if the added element of risk is analyzed, each project may have different probabilities of breakeven and different probabilities of exceeding

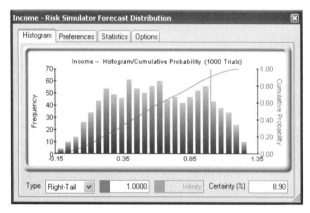

FIGURE 16.3   Probability of exceeding the original $1 income.

the $1 income threshold. Clearly, the project with the least amount of risk should be chosen (i.e., highest probability of breakeven and exceeding the threshold value).

MAKING TOMORROW'S FORECAST TODAY

Firms that are at first skeptical about applying advanced analytics in their decision-making activities should always consider first applying these new rules to smaller projects. Instead of biting off too much immediately, a small-scale project is always preferable. Companies new to advanced risk analytics should first learn to crawl before they start running and head straight for the wall. If management can be eased into the new analytical paradigm slowly, the transition will be more palatable.

Having a vision to change the entire organization's decision-making processes overnight is very admirable but will be very short-lived and bound for disaster. Before an organization can learn to make tomorrow's forecast today, it has to learn from the lessons of yesterday. One approach is to look at high-profile projects in the past. Instead of starting with forecasting, perform some back-casting first. Instead of waiting for years to verify if the results from the analysis were actually correct or valuable, the result from a back-casting analysis is almost immediate. If the analyst is true to himself or herself, using the actual data coupled with the assumptions used in the past (without the advantage of hindsight), the new analytical results can then be compared to the decisions that were made to see if different strategies and decisions would have been undertaken instead. However, care should be taken as corporate politics come into play because the individuals who made the decisions in the past may not take it too kindly when their decisions are negatively scrutinized.

No matter the strategy moving forward, one thing is certain: If senior management buys into the techniques, acceptance will be imminent. Otherwise, a few junior analysts in a cubicle somewhere trying to get management's attention will fail miserably. In retrospect, a midlevel manager trying to impress his or her superiors without the adequate knowledge and support from analysts will not work either.

The approach for successful implementation has to be comprehensive and three pronged. Senior management must keep an open mind to alternatives. Middle management must keep championing the approach and not let minor setbacks be permanent, while attempting to be the conduit of information between the junior analysts and senior management. Finally, analysts should attempt to acquire as much knowledge about the techniques and applications as possible. The worst possible outcome is where extreme expectations are set from high above and the powers that be, while the lower rungs cannot deliver the goods as required.

In order to facilitate adoption of a new set of analytical methods in an organization, several criteria must first be met. To judge the level of potential adoption, the following factors should be considered: whether the method is applicable to the problem at hand, how accurate, consistent, and replicable are the methods, what are the value-added propositions, what is the level of expositional ease, what are the comparative advantages, how compatible is the new method to the old models, how flexible is the new method, and what are some of the external influences in using the methods.

PARTING SHOTS AND A WORD OF CAUTION FROM THE AUTHOR

I sincerely hope that you have enjoyed this book. Modeling risk is clearly a hard and sometimes dry and difficult subject, but I hope that I was successful in making the concepts clearer and simpler to understand. As a professor, my ultimate goal is knowledge transmission, and as a consultant, it is to show and teach you things that are applicable so you can hit the ground running. And as a software developer, it is to create a tool that is super-powerful yet super-simple to use and completely applicable across multiple domains and industries. I hope that I am successful on all counts.

So what now? You spent weeks going through this book, had a few laughs along the way, and learned a new thing or two. How do you take this experience back to your workplace? How do you present this risk analysis approach to someone new to the topic, or worse, to senior management? Here are some suggestions based on some things that the author has been successful with in past consulting engagements and teaching activities, especially if it concerns senior-level management.

- **Practice Makes Perfect.** This adage is true of almost everything in life. Make sure you understand the theory and practice of these risk analysis methods. You really do not want to demonstrate the software, methodology, and applications and be questioned beyond your ability to answer intelligently. Be well-versed and be well-prepared before you broach this topic at work.

- **Low-Hanging Fruits.** The proverbial advice to "not bite off more than you can chew" is apropos here. Do not hit the ground running by analyzing the highest priority, largest, and most cumbersome project in the entire company. Do so only if you are truly well-trained and well-versed in all of the risk concepts. Rather, look for some low-hanging fruits: projects that are simple to tackle, less convoluted, and having clear risks, clear portfolio optimization requirements, sufficient data to run distributional fitting on, well-behaved to run forecast approaches on, clear strategic options, and so forth.
- **Executive Summary.** Using the low-hanging fruits approach, create a two-page executive summary—executives are super busy or get distracted easily, while some are just scared of learning new things, and when reviewing technical stuff they do not really understand, have the attention span of a two-year-old—which just means a single sheet of paper on both sides. Start with the basics such as an introduction to the problem being solved, some basic traditional single-point analysis, and then jump into basic risk analysis methodologies such as a tornado analysis (it is easy enough to run and to describe), a scenario analysis table, perhaps a few three-point high-medium-low triangular distributions (clearly avoid the beta, gamma, or hypergeometric world for now). Then run a simulation and show the forecast chart, with some basic things such as probability of exceeding a certain value, or worst-case scenario Value at Risk, and so forth. You get the idea. By following this approach, you slowly but concretely show the applicability of risk analysis, without all the jargon and at the same time using the company's own projects and terminology. This sort of a summary will go a long way. Do several of these, and preferably across different divisions and departments, showing that these methods are not confined and limited to the finance and strategy department, but are also applicable to the quality control Six Sigma guys down the hall, to marketing strategy and pricing, to research and development, and so forth. And being that it is only two pages (and half of that is occupied by Risk Simulator generated charts and tables anyway), it is simple to do and more likely that senior management will actually review it.
- **Senior Level Buy-In: Elevator Pitch and Keep It Simple, Stupid.** You get the idea. Create your own elevator pitch. What I mean is that you go back to work tomorrow and you run into the chairman of the board, the big cheese himself, walking into the elevator. He says hello and pretends to know your name, but he's a really nice guy, or so you hope. He looks over and asks what you are currently working on. You hastily answer, "modeling risk." There is a moment of silence and you are kicking yourself for saying that. Then the big guy asks you for

more specific details, and, of course, the elevator door closes. You have exactly 30 seconds to explain to him what Integrated Risk Management is and why he should care. Remember, this is the chairman of the board, not a mathematician or financial analyst. The moment you use words such as stochastic, heteroskedasticity, multicollinearity, mean-reversion with jump-diffusion, or kurtosis, he will press the emergency button and toss you out of the elevator! So, what should you say? You should say something like, "Risk is a very important issue that our firm has not really spent too much time on, especially in the current economic situation ... in fact, our competitors X and Y are doing these types of analysis, and it can potentially save us millions of dollars by seeing how to better forecast and allocate our resources to generate a better portfolio of products and services that will reduce our risks, identify optimal pricing points, increase our bottom line," and so forth. He will probably be excited and interested as you have hit enough key points of interest, and you may find yourself riding the elevator to the top floor much more often!

- **Knowledge Is Power.** And just like riding a bicycle, practice makes perfect. Try taking some seminars and training classes on quantitative risk analysis. A highly recommended seminar would be the week-long CRM, or Certified in Risk Management, certification program. See www.realoptionsvaluation.com for more details on this program. Participating in the program allows you to interact with the instructors and other participants as well as forces you to spend an entire week in a classroom and computer lab working on projects, problems, and exercises, and listening to real-life case studies and applications. Having read the book, you would be well prepared, and hedged your risks, for the class and the certification exam if you choose to do so. Also, visit the previously mentioned web site for additional free training videos, case studies, white papers, and applications of risk analysis.

The following are best practices in risk management for organizations from multinational corporations and banks to the U.S. military, and are based on many years of experience consulting for these firms and implementing risk analysis within these organizations:

- **Senior Management Support.** This is vital for success of any integrated risk management implementation within a firm, as without senior management support, this effort will not take root and will fail before it even starts.
- **Senior Management's High-Level Training.** Senior management needs to be trained in at least a half-day session in terms of understanding the key elements of risk management, how it works within organizations,

and what it can do, and to explore multiple business cases at various multinational organizations, both successes and failures. The outcome of this training is the ability to quickly identify what projects might be a best fit for these types of advanced risk management techniques, as well as how to interpret the results and make strategic decisions based on the results.

- **Mandate from Senior Management.** Mandates and standardized rules for certain decision processes in the company are required. For instance, any projects over US$10 million will need a business case justification, and within that business case, certain elements must always exist, such as a tornado sensitivity analysis (which identifies the critical and key success factors within a project, the bottlenecks, and the risks), and each of these identified critical factors will need to be subject to some basic simulation by using ranges as inputs instead of single-point estimates.

- **Middle Management Training.** Typically, when the author performs this training, it is a two-day hands-on computer-based training with business cases illustrating how decisions are made under uncertainty and risk. Middle management needs to understand more than senior management, as their job is to interpret the results for senior management while at the same time be able to take charge and manage the more junior analysts.

- **Analyst Detailed Training.** This is typically a five-day weeklong detailed computer-based hands-on training where analysts are subject to a barrage of hands-on modeling and case study analysis.

- **A Culture of Learning.** The most successful organizations are those interested in change and willing to learn and adapt. The integrated risk management techniques are detailed, vast, and varied, and certainly there are aspects that are useful to all organizations and other aspects that may be less useful to one organization but more useful to another. Without the exposure and culture of embracing learning and change, it would be very difficult to make these risk management techniques successful in a company.

- **A Standardized Language of Risk.** By implementing training sessions for all three levels (senior management, middle management, and junior staff), everyone will have a standardized language or lingo. For example, when the term *simulation* is used, everyone will understand what it means, what it is used for, and why it is required.

- **Standardized Toolset.** To support the decision process, standardized toolsets such as Risk Simulator are a required software application for each person in the organization. This allows interchangeable and group collaboration on strategic decisions, where one staff member can replicate and run another's models and come to the same conclusions.

- **A Centralized Strategic Risk Team.** This team ideally reports indirectly or directly to the chief financial officer or president of the company so that it has exposure and credibility, and the members of the team are hand-picked from the entire organization for their thought leadership and analytical capabilities. These individuals need to be properly trained in Integrated Risk Management, have experience implementing at least several projects, and make up the core of the strategic risk team. The purpose of this team is to provide advice to all analysts in the organization, a gatekeeper or guardian of decision risk analytics, the go-to persons in the organization, and the people who will approve the business cases submitted over a certain threshold based on the mandate from senior management. In other words, they are the gatekeepers in a stage-gate development and investment process, whereby a business case justification or proposal and request for investment will never reach senior management's offices without first passing through this centralized team.
- **Work Cross-Functionally.** Strategic risk management should never be confined to one department or business unit. That is, risk management is not the responsibility of just a financial or sales and marketing department. Instead, most projects within an organization are cross-functional and involve multiple staff members from various departments and divisions. This cross-functional team provides better subject matter experts and creates a diverse and rich view of the decisions and risks.
- **Nothing Beats Hands-On Experience.** Never fully rely on consultants alone. Analysts and staff in an organization need to learn how certain risk management projects are executed, analyzed, and modeled. This provides the organization better control over the decisions and reliability of the inputs, and allows the process to be repeated.
- **Portfolio View.** The entire organization should be viewed as a portfolio and each project or major decision should be viewed in the same way, on how it impacts the organization as a whole. For instance, certain projects that may seem unprofitable may actually be very profitable and strategic if viewed in a portfolio sense (e.g., options to expand, platform technology that can be used to springboard into other more profitable areas later on, sequential stage-gate options of a multiple phased investment or development).

A Word on Closed-Form Partial Differential Equations: They Do Not Work!

It would be a major disservice to the reader if I do not include something about my consulting experience and to point out some potential landmines in the road ahead in terms of actual applications and consulting implementations. At the time of writing, I have successfully trained and consulted in more than 300 corporations around the world these past 15 years in terms of applying advanced analytics and real options analysis, but this was not always the case. The key takeaway and advice I can offer any reader is how you would approach these methods in a company:

- Avoid showing or using advanced equations, models, and functions.
- Avoid any references to advanced terminology.
- Show how simple things are to understand.

Let us face it, C-level executives and senior management of large corporations are usually not mathematical or technical and showing them a series of advanced closed-form partial differential equations will scare them off, piss them off, or turn them off. Regardless of how accurate and well thought out the models might be, or even how correct they are, showing a series of fancy equations and models is not appropriate, and asking the executives to buy-in into the results is a battle not worth fighting for because you will never win. There are several reasons for this:

- First, *you* would have a hard time *explaining* and using these advanced models correctly. Take a look at some sample *basic* closed-form and partial differential equations in the next few pages. How many people actually know what a *Sup* function means or how to solve a recursive model using the Newton-Raphson algorithm? If you write these things out and show them to a senior decision maker, their eyes will glaze over and completely and immediately marginalize all your efforts as purely academic and not applicable to the business at hand.
- Second, speaking of iterative processes, you would have a hard time *solving* these equations. Again, look at some of the sample basic equations in the next few pages. The first set is for a closed-form American call option approximation, and the second is a closed-form equation for a basic European chooser option. Neither of these basic option models can be solved using an Excel spreadsheet. More advanced programming knowledge and mathematics are required. Therefore, how sure are you that you can obtain a solution, and if so, is it correct?
- Third, the models are never always perfect or *appropriate* and always require customization. Okay, that's putting it in a politically correct way. In reality, most of these fancy closed-form partial differential equations are completely useless in any real-life context. For example, take a look at the next few pages and review the part on optimal trigger values. From an initial inspection, this looks like a great idea, and in

fact, it really is, to identify when it might be appropriate to invest in a risky project. But if you start looking at the assumptions and inputs that go into the model, you will see that it is theoretically elegant but practically useless. The creators will get these models published in academic journal articles and get the requisite points for promotion and tenure at a university but the circle of influence is limited to academics, researchers, and professors. Notice that in the entire equation development, deciding on whether to invest in a multimillion-dollar project depends only on two things: profits and cost. What about competition, uncertainty, risks, market reaction, co-opetition strategies, product and market success, geographical location, related product types, contractual structures, negotiated terms, and a million other assumptions? All these have been assumed away, and this generic model is then presented for use in all cases. This is complete garbage. Every company is unique, and every project in a company is unique. Using a single generic model and applying it to every situation will mean that you are taking the company's constraints and decisions and squeezing them into a black box. Any analyst presenting such an analysis and any decision maker accepting such analysis should be terminated immediately. Instead, a model should take on its namesake, to model real life, and not the other way around by changing real life and assuming things away in order to stick the real life into a predetermined or canned model.

- In order to replicate and model a company's real-life situations using closed-form equations, well, you will need a double doctorate in mathematics and finance in order to properly *customize* the model for use. For example, in the simple closed-form American option model illustrated in the following pages, if you wish to change any of the inputs (e.g., making it variable in time by taking a derivative with respect to time, for example, $\delta X/\delta t$) or adding a new variable, and so forth, you will need to re-solve the equation from scratch, and the mathematics is fairly daunting. In fact, regular calculus is insufficient, as these models incorporate a stochastic property (e.g., the phi Φ function is a standard normal cumulative distribution function, and solving it requires facility with stochastic calculus such as using Ito's Lemma). No wonder Myron Scholes and Robert Merton won the Nobel Prize for their work in developing the Black-Scholes-Merton model, and the Black-Scholes-Merton model is pretty much the most basic closed-form European call and put option model there is. Good luck to the general analyst in trying to do this.

Another key takeaway is how you would introduce these advanced analytics at your company or client site. Whenever I broach the subject of advanced analytics contained in this book, I use *simple* terminologies, avoiding big words like real options, differential equations, autoregressive integrated moving average forecasts, generalized autoregressive conditional heteroskedasticity models, and the like. Instead, I use terms like uncertainty and risk, things can go up or down, or basic words like forecasts or seasonality. It really does not matter what method you use when you close your office door and do the number crunching, but the moment you use terminology foreign to the decision maker, you might well get thrown out of the board room and have the door slammed in your face so fast your head will spin! Are you saying that a board room filled with seasoned senior management types with decades of experience, who are quite brilliant and successful at what they do (at least we assume so, otherwise they would not hold the position they do), cannot make a decision and you, a young whippersnapper analyst/consultant, with little exposure in the specific industry, comes in with some black-box advanced analytical models and tell them how they should run their business? You get the picture, and it is not pretty. So, my advice is to keep it simple! Use strategy trees to visualize and draw the solutions, use terms like strategic options or courses of action instead of real options, do not show fancy equations but use things like binomial lattices with up and down branches (now, you might think I am biased toward lattices, and you are indeed correct, because I have found them to work. Analytically, in Risk Simulator, Real Options SLS, ROV Modeling Toolkit, and other software applications I created, there are more than 1,000 models and functions, and most of them are advanced closed-form partial differential equations, and I would not have bothered doing them unless there is value, but for the purposes of consulting and presentations, avoid them like the plague!).

Sample Closed-Form Differential Equations

The following is a sample portion of an American closed-form approximation model using an iterative algorithm:

$$C(S, X, T) = Sup(C + \psi(S/S')^q, S - X)^+$$

$$\psi = (1 - e^{(b-r)T}\Phi\left[\frac{\ln(S/X) + (b + \sigma^2/2)T}{\sigma\sqrt{T}}\right](S'))(S'/q)$$

$$q = \frac{N + 1 + \sqrt{(N^2 + N + 8r)/(1 - e^{-rT})\sigma^2 + 1}}{2}$$

Solving S' with the Newton–Raphson algorithm

The following is a sample closed-form model for a European chooser option. First, solve recursively for the critical I value as below:

$$0 = Ie^{-q(T_C - t)} \Phi \left[\frac{\ln(I/X_C) + (r - q + \sigma^2/2)(T_C - t)}{\sigma\sqrt{T_C - t}} \right]$$

$$- X_C e^{-r(T_C - t)} \Phi \left[\frac{\ln(I/X_C) + (r - q + \sigma^2/2)(T_C - t)}{\sigma\sqrt{T_C - t}} - \sigma\sqrt{T_C - t} \right]$$

$$+ Ie^{-q(T_P - t)} \Phi \left[\frac{-\ln(I/X_P) + (q - r - \sigma^2/2)(T_P - t)}{\sigma\sqrt{T_P - t}} \right]$$

$$- X_P e^{-r(T_P - t)} \Phi \left[\frac{-\ln(I/X_P) + (q - r - \sigma^2/2)(T_P - t)}{\sigma\sqrt{T_P - t}} + \sigma\sqrt{T_P - t} \right]$$

Then using the I value, calculate

$$d_1 = \frac{\ln(S/I) + (r - q + \sigma^2/2)t}{\sigma\sqrt{t}} \quad \text{and} \quad d_2 = d_1 - \sigma\sqrt{t}$$

$$y_1 = \frac{\ln(S/X_C) + (r - q + \sigma^2/2)T_C}{\sigma\sqrt{T_C}} \quad \text{and} \quad y_2 = \frac{\ln(S/X_P) + (r - q + \sigma^2/2)T_P}{\sigma\sqrt{T_P}}$$

$$\rho_1 = \sqrt{t/T_C} \quad \text{and} \quad \rho_2 = \sqrt{t/T_P}$$

$$Option\ Value = Se^{-qT_C} \Omega(d_1; y_1; \rho_1)$$

$$- X_C e^{-rT_C} \Omega(d_2; y_1 - \sigma\sqrt{T_C}; \rho_1) - Se^{-qT_P} \Omega(-d_1; -y_2; \rho_2)$$

$$+ X_P e^{-rT_P} \Omega(-d_2; -y_2 + \sigma\sqrt{T_P}; \rho_2)$$

A related analysis is that of *optimal trigger values*. This analysis is adapted from Chapter 7's appendix in *Real Options Analysis*, Second Edition (John Wiley & Sons, 2006) by Dr. Johnathan Mun. Suppose we create a generic valuation structure for an option value and add a level of complexity, the total implementation cost of an option should be discounted at a risk-free rate (r_f), as we segregate the market risk (Π_G) and private risk (TC), and the structure could be represented as

$$\Pi_{CALL} = \max \left\{ [\Pi_0 - TC], \ \frac{p^G \left(\Pi_1^G\right)}{1+r} - \frac{TC}{1+r_f} \right\}$$

$$= \max \left\{ \left[\pi_0 + \frac{E(\pi_1)}{r} - TC\right]^+, \left[\frac{p^G \pi_1^G \left(\dfrac{r+1}{r}\right)}{1+r} - \frac{TC}{1+r_f} \right]^+ \right\}$$

This simply is to calculate the maximum value of either starting now, which is represented by $[\Pi_0 - TC]$ or starting later, which is represented as $\frac{p^G(\pi_1^G)}{1+r} - \frac{TC}{1+r_f}$. Because the future starting point has been collapsed into a single static state, any starting points in the future can be approximated by the valuation of a single period in the future. Looking at the formulation for the call valuation price structure, if there is a change in total cost, that is, the initial capital outlay, something interesting occurs. The total cost in starting now is not discounted because the outlay occurs immediately. However, if the outlay occurs in the future, the total cost will have to be discounted at the risk-free rate. Therefore, the higher the initial cost outlay, the discounting effect of starting in the future decreases the effective cost in today's dollar, hence making it more efficient to wait and defer the cost until a later time. If the cost is lower and the firm becomes more operationally efficient, it is beneficial to begin now as the value of starting now is greater than waiting. The total cost break-even point can be obtained by solving the call valuation equation above for total cost and can be represented as

$$TC^* = \left[1 - \frac{1}{(1+r_f)^n} \right]^{-1} \left[\pi_0 + \frac{E[\pi_1]}{r} - \frac{p^G \pi_1^G \left(\dfrac{r+1}{r}\right)}{(1+r)^n} \right]$$

If total cost of implementation exceeds TC^* above, it is optimal to wait, and if total cost does not exceed TC^*, it is beneficial to execute the option now. Remember that the optimal trigger value depends on the operational efficiency of the firm as well, because it is a dynamic equation given that the optimal trigger value depends on how much money can be saved with implementation of the Cryogenic modifications. Refer to Chapters 10 and 11 of *Real Options Analysis*, Second Edition (John Wiley & Sons, 2006) by

Dr. Johnathan Mun for details on optimal timing and optimal trigger values computed using binomial lattices.

You probably have no idea what was just said these past few pages, nor should you, and that is precisely the point. The bottom line: In order to get risk analytics to stick in an organization, the right approach is not to intimidate others by showing how smart you are, but to show applicability and how simple it is to apply and understand the analytics, as well as showing the added value and insights obtained in the results. So, good luck and God bless!

Notes

CHAPTER 1   Moving Beyond Uncertainty

1. Peter L. Bernstein, *Against the Gods: The Remarkable Story of Risk* (John Wiley & Sons, 1996).
2. Save the potentiality of a plane crash, at which I would have regretted not taking the parachute.
3. The concepts of high risk and high return are nothing new and are central to the development of the *capital asset pricing model (CAPM)* used to estimate the required rate of return on a project based on its *systematic risk*. In the CAPM model, the higher the risk, the higher the expected rate of return (*ceteris paribus*, or holding everything else constant).
4. Risk can be measured in different ways. In this example, it is measured using the standard deviation of the distribution of returns.
5. This selection is because Project X bears a positive net return (positive net present value) above its implementation cost, making it profitable. Thus, the cheapest project is selected.
6. "Independence" means that the projects themselves are uncorrelated; thus it is assumed that there are no risk-diversification effects. "Mutually exclusive" means that the manager cannot mix and match among the different projects (e.g., 2 Project Xs with 3 Project Ys).
7. This choice, of course, is based purely on financial analysis alone by holding everything else constant (management's taste and preferences, or other strategic values inherent in different projects).
8. On a continuous basis, the probability of hitting exactly $30 ($30.0000000000 and so forth) is close to zero. The probability in a distribution is measured as the area under the curve, which means two values are required; for example, the probability of net revenues being between $29 and $31 is 25 percent. Thus, the area under the curve for a single-point estimate (a single line in a distribution) is close to zero.
9. The *Law of Demand* in economics requires that, in most cases, price and quantity demanded are negatively correlated, in accordance with a downward-sloping demand curve. The exception being Giffen or status goods where a higher price may yield a higher quantity demanded (Porsches are desirable and have a higher status because they are expensive, among other things).
10. A firm's average variable cost curve is U-shaped, with an initial downward slope at lower quantities (economies of scale), hits a global minimum value

where marginal cost equals average variable cost, and then continues to slope upward (diseconomies of scale).

11. See Chapter 9 for details on time-series and regression models.
12. The simulated actual values depicted graphically are based on a geometric Brownian motion with a volatility of 20 percent calculated as the standard deviation of the simulated natural logarithms of historical returns.
13. See Chapters 2 and 3 for details of other measures of risk and uncertainty.

CHAPTER 2   From Risk to Riches

1. Ron Dembo and Andrew Freeman, *Seeing Tomorrow: Rewriting the Rules of Risk* (John Wiley & Sons, 1998). This book provides an interesting nonmathematical review of risk management.
2. That is, the standard deviation of the population (σ) and the standard deviation of a sample (s) are

$$\sigma = \sqrt{\frac{\sum_{i=1}^{N}(x_i - \mu)^2}{N}} \qquad s = \sqrt{\frac{\sum_{i=1}^{n}(x_i - \overline{x})^2}{n-1}}$$

where the standard deviation is the square root of the sum of the deviation of each data point (x_i) from the population mean (μ) or sample mean ($\overline{x}$) squared, and then divided into the population size (N) or sample size (n) less one. For the sample statistic, the division is into n less one to correct for the degrees of freedom in a smaller sample size. The variance is simply the square of the standard deviation.

3. Johnathan Mun, *Real Options Analysis*, Second Edition (John Wiley & Sons, 2005); Johnathan Mun, *Real Options Analysis Course* (John Wiley & Sons, 2003). Refer to these books for details on estimating volatility in a real options context.
4. For instance, the height distribution's mean is 10 m with a standard deviation of 1 m, which yields a coefficient variation of 0.1, versus the weight distribution's mean of 100 kg and a standard deviation of 20 kg, which yields a coefficient of variation of 0.2. Clearly, the weight distribution carries with it more variability.

CHAPTER 3   A Guide to Model-Building Etiquette

1. However, be aware that password busters are abundant and certain spreadsheet models can very easily be hacked by outsiders. A better approach is to convert sensitive functions and macros into ActiveX ".*dll*" files that are encrypted, providing a much higher level of security.

CHAPTER 4   On the Shores of Monaco

1. This example is an adaptation from papers and lectures provided by Professor Sam Savage of Stanford University.
2. In this example, the median is a better measure of central tendency.
3. The same nonparametric simulation can also be applied using Risk Simulator's custom distribution where each occurrence has an equal chance of being selected.
4. The approach used here is the application of a geometric Brownian motion stochastic process for forecasting and simulating potential outcomes.

CHAPTER 5   Test Driving Risk Simulator

1. This approach is valid because in typical simulations, thousands of trials are being simulated and the assumption of normality can be applied.

CHAPTER 7   Extended Business Cases I

1. For example, drilling engineers can review historical drilling cost data and provide a probability distribution of drilling costs in a geographic area in the proposed rock formation. They are not required to know how important this risk is to the project economics versus the risk that an oil and gas reservoir is not present after the well is drilled. This risk is better evaluated by geological/geophysical staff.
2. While "low risk" is a subjective term, the risk in our model reflects a well that might be drilled in or very close to an existing producing oil field in a mature, well-established oil basin such as the Permian Basin of West Texas.
3. The economic limit is the point at which the marginal expense of producing the well exceeds the marginal revenue associated with the oil or gas produced. It is highly dependent on the company's organization and producing infrastructure. For our model we assume 10 BOPD is the economic limit.
4. Calculated from average weekly prices of West Texas Intermediate Crude, then averaged over 52 weeks of each year, from November 1991 to March 2003.
5. Note that if it is determined that the well has not encountered significant oil and gas reserves, the well is not completed and these costs are not incurred. This cost is the only one of the Year 0 costs in our model that is not incurred in the case of a dry hole.
6. NPV/I is simply the net present value of the project divided by the sum of Year 0 investments, and provides a measure of bang for the buck in a capital-rationing corporate environment.
7. In fact, most oil and gas companies do maintain proprietary price forecasts for the purpose of portfolio and investment analysis. Sensitivity of projects to these forecasts suggests that corporations (not just project teams) are well advised

to model the variability in earnings and cash flow that will propagate from unavoidable errors in their proprietary price forecasts.

CHAPTER 9   Using the Past to Predict the Future

1. An arbitrary 3-month moving average is chosen. For modeling purposes, different n-length moving averages should be computed and the one with the least amount of errors should be chosen.
2. To start Excel's Data Analysis, first click on the *Tools* menu in Excel and select *Add-Ins*. Then make sure the check box beside *Analysis Tool Pak* is selected and hit *OK*. Then return to the *Tools* menu and select *Data Analysis*. The *Regression* functionality should now exist.
3. See Chapter 8, Tomorrow's Forecast Today, for specifics on using Risk Simulator.
4. The critical *t-statistic* can be found in the t-distribution table at the end of this book, by looking down the two-tailed alpha 0.025 (alpha 0.05 for two tails means that each tail has an area of 0.025) and cross-referencing it to 6 degrees of freedom. The degrees of freedom is calculated as the number of data points, n (7), used in the regression, less the number of independent regressors, k (1).
5. As this is a two-tailed hypothesis test, the alpha should be halved, which means that as long as the p-value calculated is less than 0.025 (half of 0.05), then the null hypothesis should be rejected.
6. The adjusted R-squared is used here as this is a multivariate regression, and the adjustment in the coefficient of determination accounts for the added independent variable.
7. The two most notable and challenging econometric models include the ARCH (autoregressive conditional heteroskedasticity) and GARCH (generalized autoregressive conditional heteroskedasticity) models.

CHAPTER 10   The Search for the Optimal Decision

1. For a total cost of $550 for the entire trip.
2. The number of possible itineraries is the factorial of the number of cities, that is, $3! = 3 \times 2 \times 1 = 6$.
3. A total of five cities means $5! = 5 \times 4 \times 3 \times 2 \times 1 = 120$.
4. A triangular distribution can be applied here, with the minimum level set at $300, most likely a value of $325, and a maximum level set at $500.
5. The straight lines in Figure 10.6 would now be nonlinear and the problem would be difficult to solve graphically.
6. To access Solver, start Excel, click on *Tools | Add-Ins*. Make sure the check box beside *Solver Add-In* is selected. Solver can then be accessed by clicking on *Tools | Solver*.
7. A two-decision variable optimization problem requires a two-dimensional graph, which means an n-decision variable problem requires the use of an

n-dimensional graph, making the problem mathematically and manually intractable using the graphical method.

8. Chapter 11, Optimization Under Uncertainty, illustrates a similar portfolio-optimization process but under uncertainty using Risk Simulator.

CHAPTER 14 Extended Business Cases II

1. McKinsey & Company, Inc., Tom Copeland, Tim Koller, and Jack Murrin, *Valuation: Measuring and Managing the Value of Companies*, Third Edition (John Wiley & Sons, 2000).

2. United States. President. The National Security Strategy of the United States of America. Washington, White House, 2002. Internet: 1 June, 2005: www.whitehouse.gov/nsc/nss.pdf p. 30.

3. United States. President. The National Security Strategy of the United States of America. Washington, White House, 2002. Internet: 1 June, 2005: www.whitehouse.gov/nsc/nss.pdf p. 30.

4. Judy G. Chizek, "Military Transformation: Intelligence, Surveillance and Reconnaissance," Congressional Research Services, January 17, 2003, p. 2.

5. T. Housel, O. El Sawy, J. Zhong, and W. Rodgers, "Models for Measuring the Return on Information Technology: A Proof of Concept Demonstration," 22nd International Conference on Information Systems, December, 2001, p. 13.

6. Ibid.

7. The ISR Mission is generally conducted at a highly classified level, so specifics of the ICP and CCOP are not available to the public. For the purpose of this academic research, much of the data was estimated or inferred based on realistic sampling of unclassified process information. Information on human capital, such as salaries and operator training, is public information and was gathered from sources such as the Stay Navy web site and the Center for Information Dominance (CID) training documentation. The equipment data was also derived or inferred from documentation provided by the OPNAV N20 staff and the Space and Naval Warfare Command (SPAWAR). Other information such as number of process outputs and executions was extrapolated from samples gathered via interviews with ISR crews currently operating on board deployed U.S. Navy surface ships.

8. *Wall Street Journal*, April 21, 2004.

9. Financial Accounting Standards Board web site: www.fasb.org.

10. See Johnathan Mun's *Real Options Analysis*, Second Edition (John Wiley & Sons, 2005), for details on the case study.

11. The GBM accounts for dividends on European options, but the basic BSM does not.

12. American options are exercisable at any time up to and including the expiration date. European options are exercisable only at termination or maturity expiration date. Most ESOs are a mixture of both—European option during the vesting period (the option cannot be exercised prior to vesting) reverting to an American option after the vesting period.

13. These could be cliff vesting (the options are all void if the employee leaves or is terminated before this cliff vesting period) or graded monthly/quarterly/annually vesting (a certain proportion of the options vest after a specified period of employment service to the firm).

14. The BSM described herein refers to the original model developed by Fisher Black, Myron Scholes, and Robert Merton. Although significant advances have been made such that the BSM can be modified to take into consideration some of the exotic issues discussed in this case study, it is mathematically very complex and is highly impractical for use.

15. This multiple is the ratio of the stock price when the option is exercised to the contractual strike price, and is tabulated based on historical information. Post- and near-termination exercise behaviors are excluded.

16. For instance, a 1,000-step nonrecombining binomial lattice will require 2×10^{301} computations, and even after combining all of the world's fastest supercomputers together, will take longer than the lifetime of the sun to compute!

17. A tornado chart lists all the inputs that drive the model, starting from the input variable that has the most effect on the results. The chart is obtained by perturbing each input at some consistent range (e.g., ±10 percent from the base case) one at a time, and comparing their results to the base case. Different input levels yield different tornado charts, but in most cases, volatility is not the only dominant variable. Forfeiture, vesting, and suboptimal exercise behavior multiples all tend to either dominate over or be as dominant as volatility.

18. A spider chart looks like a spider with a central body and its many legs protruding. The positively sloped lines indicate a positive relationship (e.g., the higher the stock price, the higher the option value), while a negatively sloped line indicates a negative relationship. Further, spider charts can be used to visualize linear and nonlinear relationships.

19. People tend to exhibit suboptimal exercise behavior due to many reasons, for example, the need for liquidity, risk adversity, personal preferences, and expectations.

20. Of the 6,553 stocks analyzed, 2,924 of them pay dividends, with 2,140 of them yielding at or below 5 percent, 2,282 at or below 6 percent, 2,503 at or below 7 percent, and 2,830 at or below 10 percent.

21. An alternative method is to calculate the relevant carrying cost adjustment by artificially inserting an inflated dividend yield to convert the ESO into a "soft option," thereby discounting the value of the ESO. This method is more difficult to apply and is susceptible to more subjectivity than using a put option.

22. Cedric Jolidon finds the mean values of marketability discounts to be between 20 percent and 35 percent in his article, "The Application of the Marketability Discount in the Valuation of Swiss Companies" (Swiss Private Equity Corporate Finance Association). A typical marketability range of 10–40% was found in several discount court cases. In the *CPA Journal* (February 2001), M. Greene and D. Schnapp found that a typical range was somewhere between 30% and 35%. Another article in the *Business Valuation Review* finds that 35 percent

is the typical value (Jay Abrams, "Discount for Lack of Marketability"). In the *Fair Value* newsletter, Michael Paschall finds that 30–50% is the typical marketability discount used in the market.

23. Any level of precision and confidence can be chosen. Here, the 99.9 percent statistical confidence with a $0.01 error precision ($0.01 fluctuation around the average option value) is fairly restrictive. Of course, the level of precision attained is contingent on the inputs and their distributional parameters being accurate.

24. This assumes that the inputs are valid and accurate.

25. A 1,000-step customized binomial lattice is generally used unless otherwise noted. Sometimes increments from 1,000 to 5,000 steps may be used to check for convergence. However, due to the nonrecombining nature of changing volatility options, a lower number of steps may have to be employed.

26. This proprietary algorithm was developed by Dr. Johnathan Mun based on his analytical work with FASB in 2003–2004; his books: *Valuing Employee Stock Options Under the 2004 FAS 123 Requirements* (John Wiley & Sons, 2004), *Real Options Analysis: Tools and Techniques*, Second Edition (John Wiley & Sons, 2005), *Real Options Analysis Course* (John Wiley & Sons, 2003), and *Applied Risk Analysis: Moving Beyond Uncertainty* (John Wiley & Sons, 2003); creation of his software, Real Options Super Lattice Solver; academic research; and previous valuation consulting experience at KPMG Consulting.

27. A nonrecombining binomial lattice bifurcates (splits into two) every step it takes, so starting from one value, it branches out to two values on the first step (2^1), two becomes four in the second step (2^2), and four becomes eight in the third step (2^3), and so forth, until the 1,000th step (2^{1000} or over 10^{301} values to calculate; the world's fastest supercomputer cannot calculate the result within our lifetimes).

28. The Law of Large Numbers stipulates that the central tendency (mean) of a distribution of averages is an unbiased estimator of the true population average. The results from 4,200 steps show a mean value that is comparable to the median of the distribution of averages, and, hence, 4,200 as the number of steps is chosen as the input into the binomial lattice.

29. For instance, the coefficients are estimates of the true population β values in the following equation $Y = \beta_0 + \beta_1 X_1 + \beta_2 X_2 + \ldots + \beta_n X_n$. The standard error measures how accurate the predicted coefficients are, and the Z-statistics are the ratios of each predicted coefficient to its standard error. The Z-statistic is used in hypothesis testing, where we set the null hypothesis (Ho) such that the real mean of the coefficient is equal to zero, and the alternate hypothesis (Ha) such that the real mean of the coefficient is not equal to zero. The Z-test is important as it calculates if each of the coefficients is statistically significant in the presence of the other regressors. This means that the Z-test statistically verifies whether a regressor or independent variable should remain in the model or it should be dropped. That is, the smaller the p-value, the more significant the coefficient. The usual significant levels for the p-value are 0.01, 0.05, and 0.10, corresponding to the 99%, 95%, and 90% confidence levels.

CHAPTER 15   The Warning Signs

1. The problem of omitted variables is less vital as an analyst will simply have to work with all available data. If everything about the future is known, then why bother forecasting? If there is no uncertainty, then the future is known with certainty.

2. The problem of redundant variables is also known as multicollinearity.

3. For instance, if a dummy variable on sex is used (i.e., "0" for male and "1" for female), then a regression equation with *both* dummy variables will be perfectly collinear. In such a situation, simply drop one of the dummy variables as they are mutually exclusive of each other.

4. Make sure there are no independent variables that are perfectly or almost perfectly correlated to each other. In addition, correlation analysis can be performed to test the linear relationships among the independent variables.

5. If Y is the dependent variable and X_i is the independent variable, then the correlation pairs are between all possible combinations of Y and X_i.

6. Interest rates tend to be time dependent (mean-reverting over longer periods of time) and demand for a product that is not related to interest rate movements may also be time dependent (exhibiting cyclicality and seasonality effects).

7. The term "auto" means self and "regressive" means reverting to the past. Hence, the term "autoregressive" means to revert back to one's own past history.

8. Seasonality effects are usually because of periodicities in time (12-month seasonality in a year, 4-quarter seasonality in a year, 7-day seasonality in a week, etc.) while cyclical effects are because of larger influences without regard to periodicities (e.g., business cycle movements and technological innovation cycles).

9. However, there are other approaches used to estimate causality, for example, Granger causality approaches look at statistical causalities.

10. More advanced econometric models are required to estimate random walks, including methods using differences and unit root models.

11. See *Real Options Analysis*, Second Edition (John Wiley & Sons, 2005) and *Real Options Analysis Course* (John Wiley & Sons, 2003) for details on interacting options in evaluating the chooser option.

12. In this case, the option value is explicit, or something that is tangible, and the seller of the option can actually acquire this value.

13. Therefore, management's compensation should not be tied to actualizing this implicit option value.

14. This means the decision strategies are: A–B, A–C, and A–C–D.

15. Optimization under uncertainty means to run a set of simulations for a certain number of trials (e.g., 1,000 trials), pause, estimate the forecast distributions, test a set of combinations of decision variables, and rerun the entire analysis again, for hundreds to thousands of times.

CHAPTER 16   Changing a Corporate Culture

1. Advanced analytics are all the applications discussed in this book, including simulation, time-series forecasting, regression, optimization, and real options analysis.

2. Examples of an academic exercise that has little pragmatic application for general consumption in the areas of advanced analytics include sensitivity simulation, variance reduction, closed-form partial-differential models, and so forth. These are mathematically elegant approaches, but they require analysts with advanced degrees in finance and mathematics to apply, making the methodology and results very difficult to explain to management.

3. The case is made through the many actual business cases and examples throughout this book.

4. This is particularly true for Monte Carlo simulation where simulation cannot be applied unless there already is a spreadsheet model.

Tables You Really Need

Standard Normal Distribution (partial area)

Standard Normal Distribution (full area)

Student's t-Distribution (one tail and two tails)

Durbin–Watson Critical Values (alpha 0.05)

Normal Random Numbers (standard normal distribution's random number generated $\sim (N(0,1))$)

Random Numbers (multiple digits)

Uniform Random Numbers (uniform distribution's random number generated between 0.0000 and 1.0000)

Chi-Square Critical Values

F-Distribution Critical Statistics (alpha one tail 0.10)

F-Distribution Critical Statistics (alpha one tail 0.05)

F-Distribution Critical Statistics (alpha one tail 0.025)

F-Distribution Critical Statistics (alpha one tail 0.01)

Real Options Analysis Values (1-year maturity at 5% risk-free rate)

Real Options Analysis Values (3-year maturity at 5% risk-free rate)

Real Options Analysis Values (5-year maturity at 5% risk-free rate)

Real Options Analysis Values (7-year maturity at 5% risk-free rate)

Real Options Analysis Values (10-year maturity at 5% risk-free rate)

Real Options Analysis Values (15-year maturity at 5% risk-free rate)

Real Options Analysis Values (30-year maturity at 5% risk-free rate)

Standard Normal Distribution (partial area)

Z	0.00	0.01	0.02	0.03	0.04	0.05	0.06	0.07	0.08	0.09
0.0	0.0000	0.0040	0.0080	0.0120	0.0160	0.0199	0.0239	0.0279	0.0319	0.0359
0.1	0.0398	0.0438	0.0478	0.0517	0.0557	0.0596	0.0636	0.0675	0.0714	0.0753
0.2	0.0793	0.0832	0.0871	0.0910	0.0948	0.0987	0.1026	0.1064	0.1103	0.1141
0.3	0.1179	0.1217	0.1255	0.1293	0.1331	0.1368	0.1406	0.1443	0.1480	0.1517
0.4	0.1554	0.1591	0.1628	0.1664	0.1700	0.1736	0.1772	0.1808	0.1844	0.1879
0.5	0.1915	0.1950	0.1985	0.2019	0.2054	0.2088	0.2123	0.2157	0.2190	0.2224
0.6	0.2257	0.2291	0.2324	0.2357	0.2389	0.2422	0.2454	0.2486	0.2517	0.2549
0.7	0.2580	0.2611	0.2642	0.2673	0.2704	0.2734	0.2764	0.2794	0.2823	0.2852
0.8	0.2881	0.2910	0.2939	0.2967	0.2995	0.3023	0.3051	0.3078	0.3106	0.3133
0.9	0.3159	0.3186	0.3212	0.3238	0.3264	0.3289	0.3315	0.3340	0.3365	0.3389
1.0	0.3413	0.3438	0.3461	0.3485	0.3508	0.3531	0.3554	0.3577	0.3599	0.3621
1.1	0.3643	0.3665	0.3686	0.3708	0.3729	0.3749	0.3770	0.3790	0.3810	0.3830
1.2	0.3849	0.3869	0.3888	0.3907	0.3925	0.3944	0.3962	0.3980	0.3997	0.4015
1.3	0.4032	0.4049	0.4066	0.4082	0.4099	0.4115	0.4131	0.4147	0.4162	0.4177
1.4	0.4192	0.4207	0.4222	0.4236	0.4251	0.4265	0.4279	0.4292	0.4306	0.4319
1.5	0.4332	0.4345	0.4357	0.4370	0.4382	0.4394	0.4406	0.4418	0.4429	0.4441
1.6	0.4452	0.4463	0.4474	0.4484	0.4495	0.4505	0.4515	0.4525	0.4535	0.4545
1.7	0.4554	0.4564	0.4573	0.4582	0.4591	0.4599	0.4608	0.4616	0.4625	0.4633
1.8	0.4641	0.4649	0.4656	0.4664	0.4671	0.4678	0.4686	0.4693	0.4699	0.4706
1.9	0.4713	0.4719	0.4726	0.4732	0.4738	0.4744	0.4750	0.4756	0.4761	0.4767
2.0	0.4772	0.4778	0.4783	0.4788	0.4793	0.4798	0.4803	0.4808	0.4812	0.4817
2.1	0.4821	0.4826	0.4830	0.4834	0.4838	0.4842	0.4846	0.4850	0.4854	0.4857
2.2	0.4861	0.4864	0.4868	0.4871	0.4875	0.4878	0.4881	0.4884	0.4887	0.4890
2.3	0.4893	0.4896	0.4898	0.4901	0.4904	0.4906	0.4909	0.4911	0.4913	0.4916
2.4	0.4918	0.4920	0.4922	0.4925	0.4927	0.4929	0.4931	0.4932	0.4934	0.4936
2.5	0.4938	0.4940	0.4941	0.4943	0.4945	0.4946	0.4948	0.4949	0.4951	0.4952
2.6	0.4953	0.4955	0.4956	0.4957	0.4959	0.4960	0.4961	0.4962	0.4963	0.4964
2.7	0.4965	0.4966	0.4967	0.4968	0.4969	0.4970	0.4971	0.4972	0.4973	0.4974
2.8	0.4974	0.4975	0.4976	0.4977	0.4977	0.4978	0.4979	0.4979	0.4980	0.4981
2.9	0.4981	0.4982	0.4982	0.4983	0.4984	0.4984	0.4985	0.4985	0.4986	0.4986
3.0	0.4987	0.4987	0.4987	0.4988	0.4988	0.4989	0.4989	0.4989	0.4990	0.4990

Example: For a Z-value of 1.96, refer to the 1.9 row and 0.06 column for the area of 0.4750. This means there is 47.50% in the shaded region and 2.50% in the single tail. Similarly, there is 95% in the body or 5% in both tails.

Standard Normal Distribution (full area)

Z	0.00	0.01	0.02	0.03	0.04	0.05	0.06	0.07	0.08	0.09
0.0	0.5000	0.5040	0.5080	0.5120	0.5160	0.5199	0.5239	0.5279	0.5319	0.5359
0.1	0.5398	0.5438	0.5478	0.5517	0.5557	0.5596	0.5636	0.5675	0.5714	0.5753
0.2	0.5793	0.5832	0.5871	0.5910	0.5948	0.5987	0.6026	0.6064	0.6103	0.6141
0.3	0.6179	0.6217	0.6255	0.6293	0.6331	0.6368	0.6406	0.6443	0.6480	0.6517
0.4	0.6554	0.6591	0.6628	0.6664	0.6700	0.6736	0.6772	0.6808	0.6844	0.6879
0.5	0.6915	0.6950	0.6985	0.7019	0.7054	0.7088	0.7123	0.7157	0.7190	0.7224
0.6	0.7257	0.7291	0.7324	0.7357	0.7389	0.7422	0.7454	0.7486	0.7517	0.7549
0.7	0.7580	0.7611	0.7642	0.7673	0.7704	0.7734	0.7764	0.7794	0.7823	0.7852
0.8	0.7881	0.7910	0.7939	0.7967	0.7995	0.8023	0.8051	0.8078	0.8106	0.8133
0.9	0.8159	0.8186	0.8212	0.8238	0.8264	0.8289	0.8315	0.8340	0.8365	0.8389
1.0	0.8413	0.8438	0.8461	0.8485	0.8508	0.8531	0.8554	0.8577	0.8599	0.8621
1.1	0.8643	0.8665	0.8686	0.8708	0.8729	0.8749	0.8770	0.8790	0.8810	0.8830
1.2	0.8849	0.8869	0.8888	0.8907	0.8925	0.8944	0.8962	0.8980	0.8997	0.9015
1.3	0.9032	0.9049	0.9066	0.9082	0.9099	0.9115	0.9131	0.9147	0.9162	0.9177
1.4	0.9192	0.9207	0.9222	0.9236	0.9251	0.9265	0.9279	0.9292	0.9306	0.9319
1.5	0.9332	0.9345	0.9357	0.9370	0.9382	0.9394	0.9406	0.9418	0.9429	0.9441
1.6	0.9452	0.9463	0.9474	0.9484	0.9495	0.9505	0.9515	0.9525	0.9535	0.9545
1.7	0.9554	0.9564	0.9573	0.9582	0.9591	0.9599	0.9608	0.9616	0.9625	0.9633
1.8	0.9641	0.9649	0.9656	0.9664	0.9671	0.9678	0.9686	0.9693	0.9699	0.9706
1.9	0.9713	0.9719	0.9726	0.9732	0.9738	0.9744	0.9750	0.9756	0.9761	0.9767
2.0	0.9772	0.9778	0.9783	0.9788	0.9793	0.9798	0.9803	0.9808	0.9812	0.9817
2.1	0.9821	0.9826	0.9830	0.9834	0.9838	0.9842	0.9846	0.9850	0.9854	0.9857
2.2	0.9861	0.9864	0.9868	0.9871	0.9875	0.9878	0.9881	0.9884	0.9887	0.9890
2.3	0.9893	0.9896	0.9898	0.9901	0.9904	0.9906	0.9909	0.9911	0.9913	0.9916
2.4	0.9918	0.9920	0.9922	0.9925	0.9927	0.9929	0.9931	0.9932	0.9934	0.9936
2.5	0.9938	0.9940	0.9941	0.9943	0.9945	0.9946	0.9948	0.9949	0.9951	0.9952
2.6	0.9953	0.9955	0.9956	0.9957	0.9959	0.9960	0.9961	0.9962	0.9963	0.9964
2.7	0.9965	0.9966	0.9967	0.9968	0.9969	0.9970	0.9971	0.9972	0.9973	0.9974
2.8	0.9974	0.9975	0.9976	0.9977	0.9977	0.9978	0.9979	0.9979	0.9980	0.9981
2.9	0.9981	0.9982	0.9982	0.9983	0.9984	0.9984	0.9985	0.9985	0.9986	0.9986
3.0	0.9987	0.9987	0.9987	0.9988	0.9988	0.9989	0.9989	0.9989	0.9990	0.9990

Example: For a Z-value of 2.33, refer to the 2.3 row and 0.03 column for the area of 0.99. This means there is 99% in the shaded region and 1% in the one-sided left or right tail.

Student's t-Distribution
(one and two tails)

one tail | | | | | | two tail

alpha	0.1	0.05	0.025	0.01	0.005	alpha	0.1	0.05	0.025	0.01	0.005
df = 1	3.0777	6.3137	12.7062	31.8210	63.6559	df = 1	6.3137	12.7062	25.4519	63.6559	127.3211
2	1.8856	2.9200	4.3027	6.9645	9.9250	2	2.9200	4.3027	6.2054	9.9250	14.0892
3	1.6377	2.3534	3.1824	4.5407	5.8408	3	2.3534	3.1824	4.1765	5.8408	7.4532
4	1.5332	2.1318	2.7765	3.7469	4.6041	4	2.1318	2.7765	3.4954	4.6041	5.5975
5	1.4759	2.0150	2.5706	3.3649	4.0321	5	2.0150	2.5706	3.1634	4.0321	4.7733
6	1.4398	1.9432	2.4469	3.1427	3.7074	6	1.9432	2.4469	2.9687	3.7074	4.3168
7	1.4149	1.8946	2.3646	2.9979	3.4995	7	1.8946	2.3646	2.8412	3.4995	4.0294
8	1.3968	1.8595	2.3060	2.8965	3.3554	8	1.8595	2.3060	2.7515	3.3554	3.8325
9	1.3830	1.8331	2.2622	2.8214	3.2498	9	1.8331	2.2622	2.6850	3.2498	3.6896
10	1.3722	1.8125	2.2281	2.7638	3.1693	10	1.8125	2.2281	2.6338	3.1693	3.5814
15	1.3406	1.7531	2.1315	2.6025	2.9467	15	1.7531	2.1315	2.4899	2.9467	3.2860
20	1.3253	1.7247	2.0860	2.5280	2.8453	20	1.7247	2.0860	2.4231	2.8453	3.1534
25	1.3163	1.7081	2.0595	2.4851	2.7874	25	1.7081	2.0595	2.3846	2.7874	3.0782
30	1.3104	1.6973	2.0423	2.4573	2.7500	30	1.6973	2.0423	2.3596	2.7500	3.0298
35	1.3062	1.6896	2.0301	2.4377	2.7238	35	1.6896	2.0301	2.3420	2.7238	2.9961
40	1.3031	1.6839	2.0211	2.4233	2.7045	40	1.6839	2.0211	2.3289	2.7045	2.9712
45	1.3007	1.6794	2.0141	2.4121	2.6896	45	1.6794	2.0141	2.3189	2.6896	2.9521
50	1.2987	1.6759	2.0086	2.4033	2.6778	50	1.6759	2.0086	2.3109	2.6778	2.9370
100	1.2901	1.6602	1.9840	2.3642	2.6259	100	1.6602	1.9840	2.2757	2.6259	2.8707
200	1.2858	1.6525	1.9719	2.3451	2.6006	200	1.6525	1.9719	2.2584	2.6006	2.8385
300	1.2844	1.6499	1.9679	2.3388	2.5923	300	1.6499	1.9679	2.2527	2.5923	2.8279
500	1.2832	1.6479	1.9647	2.3338	2.5857	500	1.6479	1.9647	2.2482	2.5857	2.8195
100000	1.2816	1.6449	1.9600	2.3264	2.5759	100000	1.6449	1.9600	2.2414	2.5759	2.8071

Example: For an alpha in the single right tail area of 2.5% with 15 degrees of freedom, the critical t value is 2.1315.

Durbin–Watson Critical Values (alpha 0.05)

	k = 1		k = 2		k = 3		k = 4		k = 5	
n	D_L	D_U	D_L	D_U	D_L	D_U	D_L	D_U	D_L	D_U
15	1.08	1.36	0.95	1.54	0.82	1.75	0.69	1.97	0.56	2.21
16	1.10	1.37	0.98	1.54	0.86	1.73	0.74	1.93	0.62	2.15
17	1.13	1.38	1.02	1.54	0.90	1.71	0.78	1.90	0.67	2.10
18	1.16	1.39	1.05	1.53	0.93	1.69	0.82	1.87	0.71	2.06
19	1.18	1.40	1.08	1.53	0.97	1.68	0.86	1.85	0.75	2.02
20	1.20	1.41	1.10	1.54	1.00	1.67	0.90	1.83	0.79	1.99
21	1.22	1.42	1.13	1.54	1.03	1.66	0.93	1.81	0.83	1.96
22	1.24	1.43	1.15	1.54	1.05	1.66	0.96	1.80	0.86	1.94
23	1.26	1.44	1.17	1.54	1.08	1.66	0.99	1.79	0.90	1.92
24	1.27	1.45	1.19	1.55	1.10	1.66	1.01	1.78	0.93	1.90
25	1.29	1.45	1.21	1.55	1.12	1.65	1.04	1.77	0.95	1.89
26	1.30	1.46	1.22	1.55	1.14	1.65	1.06	1.76	0.98	1.88
27	1.32	1.47	1.24	1.56	1.16	1.65	1.08	1.76	1.01	1.86
28	1.33	1.48	1.26	1.56	1.18	1.65	1.10	1.75	1.03	1.85
29	1.34	1.48	1.27	1.56	1.20	1.65	1.12	1.74	1.05	1.84
30	1.35	1.49	1.28	1.57	1.21	1.65	1.14	1.74	1.07	1.83
31	1.36	1.50	1.30	1.57	1.23	1.65	1.16	1.74	1.09	1.83
32	1.37	1.50	1.31	1.57	1.24	1.65	1.18	1.73	1.11	1.82
33	1.38	1.51	1.32	1.58	1.26	1.65	1.19	1.73	1.13	1.81
34	1.39	1.51	1.33	1.58	1.27	1.65	1.21	1.73	1.15	1.81
35	1.40	1.52	1.34	1.58	1.28	1.65	1.22	1.73	1.16	1.80
36	1.41	1.52	1.35	1.59	1.29	1.65	1.24	1.73	1.18	1.80
37	1.42	1.53	1.36	1.59	1.31	1.66	1.25	1.72	1.19	1.80
38	1.43	1.54	1.37	1.59	1.32	1.66	1.26	1.72	1.21	1.79
39	1.43	1.54	1.38	1.60	1.33	1.66	1.27	1.72	1.22	1.79
40	1.44	1.54	1.39	1.60	1.34	1.66	1.29	1.72	1.23	1.79
45	1.48	1.57	1.43	1.62	1.38	1.67	1.34	1.72	1.29	1.78
50	1.50	1.59	1.46	1.63	1.42	1.67	1.38	1.72	1.34	1.77
55	1.53	1.60	1.49	1.64	1.45	1.68	1.41	1.72	1.38	1.77
60	1.55	1.62	1.51	1.65	1.48	1.69	1.44	1.73	1.41	1.77
65	1.57	1.63	1.54	1.66	1.50	1.70	1.47	1.73	1.44	1.77
70	1.58	1.64	1.55	1.67	1.52	1.70	1.49	1.74	1.46	1.77
75	1.60	1.65	1.57	1.68	1.54	1.71	1.51	1.74	1.49	1.77
80	1.61	1.66	1.59	1.69	1.56	1.72	1.53	1.74	1.51	1.77
85	1.62	1.67	1.60	1.70	1.57	1.72	1.55	1.75	1.52	1.77
90	1.63	1.68	1.61	1.70	1.59	1.73	1.57	1.75	1.54	1.78
95	1.64	1.69	1.62	1.71	1.60	1.73	1.58	1.75	1.56	1.78
100	1.65	1.69	1.63	1.72	1.61	1.74	1.59	1.76	1.57	1.78

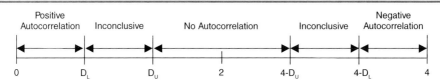

Example: For 30 observations (n) of a multivariate regression with three independent variables, the critical Durbin–Watson statistics are 1.21 (D_L) and 1.65 (D_U). If the calculated Durbin–Watson is 1.05, there is positive autocorrelation.

Normal Random Numbers (standard normal distribution's random number generated $\sim N(0,1)$)

	1	2	3	4	5	6	7	8	9	10
1	-1.0800	-0.5263	-0.7099	-0.3124	0.0216	-0.7768	-0.0752	0.4273	0.7708	0.1887
2	-1.1028	1.0904	-0.9228	-0.8831	-1.7909	0.6459	0.8982	-0.9736	-0.8630	0.1361
3	-0.8336	0.1454	-1.5907	1.0843	0.6271	1.1925	1.4669	0.5701	-2.7364	0.2500
4	0.2296	-0.2436	-0.0639	0.2307	-0.0560	-1.8494	0.6068	-0.2562	0.2168	-0.0261
5	1.2795	-0.6267	0.3133	0.3831	0.8894	0.9869	1.6185	0.7713	0.1421	-0.9623
6	1.2079	-0.8924	0.0491	0.0250	-0.5501	-0.8312	0.5067	-0.4316	0.7880	0.3858
7	-0.9474	-1.1758	-2.0242	-1.1567	-0.3838	0.8031	-0.5129	1.3572	-0.6772	1.0510
8	-0.7296	-0.8073	0.1137	-0.3553	-2.5826	-0.2768	0.0300	0.6233	-2.0171	-1.0818
9	0.0939	-0.1833	0.5550	0.38C9	0.4096	0.0930	0.0257	-0.0603	-2.3620	-0.2656
10	-1.2110	-0.3240	0.8859	0.3776	-1.9103	2.0585	0.5215	-1.3543	-0.6975	-1.5965
11	-0.4614	-0.7827	0.8294	0.4460	-0.6563	0.4167	-0.3699	-0.0852	0.5010	0.3579
12	-0.5282	1.2526	-0.3289	1.5912	0.8460	1.2919	-0.6255	-0.2466	0.6740	1.6007
13	1.1204	0.5921	0.3115	0.1986	-0.6793	0.0694	-0.2777	0.5517	-0.5385	1.2437
14	-0.3726	0.0955	-2.3786	-1.7042	0.6656	0.0641	0.3874	1.1669	-0.6837	-0.0934
15	-0.5656	-0.0949	-0.3845	-0.6864	0.9967	0.0695	1.4614	1.0945	-1.2097	-1.4070
16	-0.2430	-2.4107	-2.5924	0.2724	-0.0967	-0.0315	-0.8218	0.2390	0.5987	-0.6879
17	-0.2820	-0.4370	0.7358	-0.3511	-0.2308	-0.7651	-0.7652	-0.4937	-1.0157	-0.1394
18	-0.3955	0.5096	0.1447	-0.4119	1.3781	-0.7365	0.4475	1.7877	0.3629	1.4260
19	0.1652	-0.4687	0.1058	-0.4183	-0.3782	-2.4017	0.9160	-1.8322	-0.6279	0.0098
20	-0.0504	-1.0931	-1.6450	-0.6165	-0.0279	-0.9539	-1.6489	-0.7252	0.3962	0.8928
21	0.1841	-0.1236	0.7653	-0.9054	0.8158	-0.8576	1.9970	-0.1568	-1.6658	-0.6698
22	-1.1091	0.5140	0.4505	-1.7429	0.0854	0.1573	-2.2687	0.4879	-0.0820	0.4840
23	0.6553	0.4692	0.9139	0.9639	-0.9046	-0.6695	-0.3393	-1.8453	1.0532	0.9795
24	0.5185	0.8624	0.6098	0.7062	0.3533	0.1695	0.1840	-0.5235	0.7202	0.0790
25	-0.6228	-0.0052	0.1012	0.9541	1.4046	-0.2620	-0.2783	0.7601	-0.0375	1.8253
26	0.5867	0.3346	-0.0588	-0.4356	0.0004	0.2037	-1.1411	-0.4674	2.2770	-0.8338

27	0.2450	1.0948	-0.8954	1.0444	-0.2184	-1.1320	1.5127	-0.9275	-0.4799	0.1281
28	-0.0279	-0.1937	-1.2914	-0.9880	1.1571	0.5578	0.4071	1.2601	1.1695	-0.2957
29	-0.4161	-0.5507	-0.4475	0.0689	0.4422	-1.1679	-0.5163	0.3915	-0.7226	0.9784
30	-0.8053	0.3502	-1.4505	-0.5941	-0.7228	-0.7034	-1.0992	0.3020	-0.1026	-1.2502
31	1.0404	0.1097	0.4544	-0.5799	-0.2926	1.2725	-0.5619	-0.0821	-0.5477	1.0231
32	0.2528	0.5059	-1.4190	0.3989	-1.3937	-1.2064	0.0228	-0.6627	1.1379	0.5220
33	-0.2739	-0.9455	-2.2941	0.0276	1.7592	-1.7925	-0.5070	-0.2650	1.5300	-0.3373
34	-0.9423	0.3491	-1.3512	0.4576	1.0860	-0.1653	0.4558	-0.6405	-1.2085	-0.7493
35	0.0883	0.2888	-0.5136	2.1450	-0.0262	2.9286	-1.7310	1.1511	-0.6439	-0.3583
36	-0.4517	0.2437	0.2776	-0.7868	0.1671	1.0155	-0.3549	0.7456	-0.3971	-1.9802
37	-1.1278	-2.3892	-0.2134	0.2925	1.2178	-0.3160	0.9686	-1.2743	-0.0707	1.5162
38	1.3791	-0.4170	-0.1155	-0.1992	-1.1890	1.2458	-1.6882	0.3428	-1.3231	-0.3701
39	0.0819	0.5604	-1.7606	-0.6743	-1.0426	-0.8501	1.1497	0.0442	0.5657	-1.2778
40	-0.4175	0.4203	1.2675	1.2768	-0.4826	-2.3268	0.0747	1.0223	0.2681	-0.3952
41	0.6801	-0.6346	-0.4628	0.1047	1.0032	-1.4099	0.3401	-0.5051	-1.2245	-0.4696
42	0.9200	-0.4411	1.9065	-0.8623	-0.8896	-1.3154	-0.2427	1.4517	0.6037	0.7206
43	-2.0794	-0.0927	1.0023	-0.2296	-0.6263	-0.7918	-0.6372	2.7211	0.3840	-0.5358
44	0.5448	0.6405	0.3647	-1.9654	-1.8430	-0.4946	-0.6691	1.3191	0.9991	1.6156
45	1.0963	1.2051	0.7243	2.3032	-0.4820	2.0831	0.6108	0.8796	0.5527	0.8128
46	-0.9386	1.2509	-2.1745	-0.4204	-0.6400	-1.0716	0.0190	-1.9153	-1.4322	0.0870
47	2.4524	1.5695	-0.6953	-2.4997	-0.0891	-0.5719	-0.9301	-0.3394	-2.6532	-0.0226
48	0.4448	-1.8947	0.7942	0.3552	-0.4288	1.0699	0.7316	-1.1951	1.4356	0.2318
49	0.1323	-0.0470	1.5664	0.1610	0.4068	-1.1848	-1.2338	0.1546	-0.3490	2.4516
50	-0.6323	1.7106	-0.6715	0.2511	0.7708	-0.6902	0.8453	1.1715	1.4897	0.0401

Random Numbers (multiple digits)

	1	2	3	4	5	6	7	8	9	10
1	2721.5177	7927.3605	5509.2000	7755.4229	8910.1600	9583.6638	9063.9590	8043.2820	9974.8278	7685.4216
2	5427.5197	6573.0674	6996.6637	9135.8127	2718.8760	8982.9624	4576.1065	5844.0620	2435.0249	2281.9131
3	1570.2192	5024.3217	6764.9039	1023.2814	6548.8675	3329.6628	4520.5547	9269.9768	6344.4565	2809.3591
4	6617.8598	5903.1769	7002.3606	2085.2144	4792.4796	6844.4960	8697.2448	6543.3337	2982.5475	6500.9816
5	1042.3463	4784.7013	2453.3249	2006.1324	2128.2118	4070.3922	7223.9221	9040.6234	3864.3067	8258.1458
6	5152.2026	2683.5095	3648.9192	7937.8332	9361.6421	6588.8570	9066.6720	7688.1069	4799.6166	4936.4821
7	8092.3323	5697.0313	7446.0071	3138.0076	3274.5303	3064.3907	9283.3996	3169.3531	5119.0202	9799.3380
8	3200.8200	8155.2797	2903.4796	3975.4799	2090.4880	2584.4027	2321.1790	9201.1671	5563.8958	4922.1343
9	2182.8695	9863.5501	3827.3677	5479.6807	5846.3606	7009.6787	1956.4793	9485.3016	6048.6349	4545.7721
10	4929.3461	1009.5500	6692.1558	6563.8505	6478.1138	1457.2554	2607.2569	1772.3479	1130.7805	9296.8716
11	9478.2765	9055.7916	8831.3015	9113.9356	3863.2465	6845.3370	7956.4931	3620.3660	6516.1395	5908.0984
12	1336.6521	6161.7270	8222.4781	5859.3163	8247.4744	8348.0894	6487.8202	6784.5221	4693.3882	5667.7078
13	7460.0083	5643.3684	2422.6688	6932.7146	2091.5401	3917.1395	5129.1433	1218.7031	8785.2712	7050.3969
14	5849.9114	5882.0649	6661.0100	6681.4560	9481.2436	2195.1850	4813.7851	9085.3021	1653.4790	3719.3843
15	6975.6430	9691.5555	6668.4537	7785.4196	6508.2217	9147.5266	9760.7188	1920.8204	1278.8593	5578.9917
16	9178.9897	3759.3978	3947.4711	6015.4509	2645.6605	9933.6472	8250.7021	4046.9983	2472.1532	6918.8681
17	1105.8190	7150.7795	1707.7886	6093.6588	5725.3097	6168.8648	6322.9949	8035.1053	1670.8308	3130.7888
18	4378.4322	8484.7097	7236.2981	4585.2984	6117.0657	1604.2704	6441.3144	9050.4318	1192.4602	3053.1196
19	6589.7603	8938.1669	5639.4775	9210.1063	3355.4245	5526.0291	2033.4076	8997.8637	6921.5642	9584.1109
20	4455.2372	6786.2862	4018.8972	5491.1575	1560.0462	4115.5836	1048.3373	9623.0486	8862.3072	7621.1737
21	4448.7636	6209.5568	9959.7063	3177.2467	1641.8797	6802.2869	8161.5705	1685.3721	1941.6971	8308.9046
22	8654.4590	9343.3206	6653.9854	9692.1930	3929.0176	4784.0031	4596.3431	6587.9375	9035.8024	1517.4567
23	8844.1890	9681.9999	2822.7265	2899.0180	5158.0016	5636.0479	2528.0603	6982.0078	9200.3319	6361.4182
24	7390.3963	5983.7082	5900.1055	3837.7891	8828.4116	7731.9270	3157.1180	1957.9680	6105.4342	4370.7669
25	5203.6897	4338.6493	4776.3189	1129.9635	1273.6261	8183.6248	2281.0786	2374.5525	2381.9855	3381.8613
26	4161.9959	6863.8237	9514.2372	2225.4123	4676.0563	6451.0761	5920.1725	2916.4971	5819.8761	7904.7086

27	8044.9759	8610.4069	8708.4209	8303.2069	6696.6600	5799.8857	9579.7723	6845.5490	1039.0858	8763.7395
28	2587.5116	5853.4249	4388.2114	5526.0319	2061.3728	4644.3832	1388.8595	5890.9486	3907.8750	4141.8542
29	7052.2487	6036.5176	2541.3818	2812.2029	7546.7513	2546.8478	2494.0563	6029.0624	1324.0261	8162.4338
30	1163.9374	1931.4068	6247.8204	7745.6642	3070.3767	5071.9130	6159.3637	3013.1682	1226.8873	8162.4898
31	1714.6545	1523.8375	8509.5616	8306.2575	9657.2873	3120.0271	6688.3472	5159.6344	3671.7474	7133.5930
32	3919.0191	5588.6388	4923.3729	5347.2862	1600.1555	2029.1451	3136.0774	2317.8933	3932.5034	3018.1371
33	5026.6414	2547.0444	4424.7295	4170.3210	7624.0027	5232.2546	5874.4753	4124.2614	5273.4984	5929.6120
34	5621.6736	5358.4125	2870.7415	6454.0855	8476.0039	2736.0572	6719.2599	2753.2847	4911.0976	1791.5700
35	9910.5203	6121.8213	3308.4460	3150.5253	9211.2410	5499.6467	3931.8208	5313.8206	5934.1154	4849.0388
36	4312.4452	8426.2265	8872.6974	1663.1930	9120.5661	5981.5407	2613.1288	5439.7424	9611.6777	5188.4457
37	7626.7677	5387.7439	2935.0787	8309.7795	8246.8356	2074.3136	5736.0131	3286.1149	8836.6044	7193.7667
38	9884.8894	6400.4452	3674.4606	6779.5470	9832.8283	8108.7365	4803.5534	7599.8840	2362.3725	8762.0338
39	3835.9843	9103.7538	2867.9787	6320.5689	2208.7881	3409.7276	7836.5953	5104.6250	3424.2561	6521.1725
40	1337.4881	5372.2827	4089.9067	9875.2185	1422.7835	6058.8479	5847.4650	8856.1609	1258.4403	3044.5864
41	3785.1585	4943.2358	2420.7229	5821.4256	5122.6017	8973.0601	6324.9297	9036.6863	1197.9443	2913.1478
42	8926.2929	6024.7767	4233.9264	2292.9495	1958.8263	5534.9091	8243.9129	9370.1993	9628.7974	2321.1484
43	8900.4838	4553.4951	8777.2026	8809.0081	6170.5223	4601.8483	6653.8133	8002.2370	2871.4168	4085.8857
44	6385.5759	1642.6064	4939.2942	8710.5348	2064.4489	7854.8362	4247.8259	3799.9352	6065.6772	9917.2978
45	9684.0981	5429.2985	6042.3134	5461.5755	8034.5336	5056.7885	1621.9722	9290.8556	4395.0623	9808.8263
46	6385.0021	5007.4273	2845.5347	1898.6996	9031.1549	9874.3671	2061.4315	5221.1304	4624.0654	8847.7553
47	8706.7893	1279.1794	8722.8166	5683.5057	9611.4135	2593.5565	2220.1057	6559.8872	3554.2664	5352.1678
48	4542.1757	5609.2758	9599.0981	7644.5129	8663.3854	7009.6717	1887.5296	7330.2408	9197.2417	3012.4571
49	3242.9899	8305.9299	6439.2860	7130.1905	6503.2924	5736.9502	3489.9470	3671.3190	2925.8024	7207.2956
50	7751.6580	7934.9861	8400.8779	2923.6741	4305.5792	3995.4573	9288.3303	6593.9721	5302.2203	9007.2129

Uniform Random Numbers (uniform distribution's random number generated between 0.0000 and 1.0000)

	1	2	3	4	5	6	7	8	9	10
1	0.8470	0.8006	0.8185	0.5479	0.6664	0.4772	0.8983	0.9434	0.0272	0.1912
2	0.8538	0.1840	0.0235	0.5733	0.5103	0.9165	0.2052	0.6861	0.4069	0.8930
3	0.4816	0.0929	0.0404	0.1688	0.4297	0.1381	0.5717	0.3440	0.3050	0.3347
4	0.1827	0.6090	0.2067	0.0201	0.1809	0.4326	0.5870	0.4826	0.8274	0.4693
5	0.6736	0.7903	0.0910	0.7829	0.9657	0.3531	0.5095	0.4019	0.9799	0.4321
6	0.9953	0.8069	0.5096	0.8088	0.5747	0.5876	0.6151	0.7627	0.3793	0.4698
7	0.7613	0.8829	0.9609	0.6287	0.0849	0.9027	0.2761	0.5469	0.5634	0.0308
8	0.1317	0.7907	0.5440	0.0469	0.7220	0.5695	0.2482	0.3742	0.1409	0.3288
9	0.5269	0.6977	0.4061	0.0950	0.2114	0.4113	0.7619	0.6854	0.1402	0.2956
10	0.9121	0.5435	0.3236	0.6256	0.7646	0.3120	0.8037	0.1198	0.8887	0.5443
11	0.5390	0.4622	0.3459	0.1427	0.7762	0.8186	0.5059	0.1905	0.8696	0.8893
12	0.9055	0.4771	0.6290	0.8068	0.5124	0.9142	0.6397	0.5279	0.2051	0.1220
13	0.6644	0.9212	0.2139	0.3678	0.8107	0.1869	0.5594	0.8278	0.2343	0.9175
14	0.7403	0.1068	0.9122	0.1193	0.5645	0.9703	0.9102	0.3528	0.6891	0.0330
15	0.8611	0.9607	0.1820	0.8349	0.4017	0.2822	0.3624	0.8583	0.1495	0.1532
16	0.4914	0.1137	0.2635	0.6062	0.1728	0.5471	0.1065	0.4250	0.7094	0.3168
17	0.7664	0.6767	0.5264	0.9354	0.9880	0.1942	0.9594	0.2610	0.9933	0.3406
18	0.0126	0.5592	0.3942	0.4020	0.7840	0.8675	0.1734	0.0476	0.3372	0.4067
19	0.5251	0.8027	0.6730	0.9985	0.4706	0.2960	0.3305	0.1006	0.1012	0.4638
20	0.7772	0.4434	0.1596	0.3856	0.0163	0.5783	0.4055	0.1490	0.7172	0.2243
21	0.8973	0.7618	0.4225	0.9524	0.7371	0.3863	0.2146	0.3799	0.8521	0.7857
22	0.1709	0.1966	0.1125	0.1454	0.0325	0.2262	0.3624	0.3600	0.6517	0.4073
23	0.1785	0.6833	0.9500	0.3603	0.8863	0.4362	0.5985	0.2979	0.6837	0.0957
24	0.5644	0.2031	0.9380	0.0418	0.9262	0.6584	0.5958	0.9879	0.4332	0.0198
25	0.3672	0.4599	0.2637	0.9380	0.8343	0.6933	0.4732	0.5802	0.2715	0.1287
26	0.8391	0.1803	0.4345	0.7670	0.5298	0.7905	0.4120	0.9688	0.8540	0.8267

27	0.7135	0.8772	0.5661	0.4345	0.8710	0.6183	0.1704	0.3377	0.1432	0.9205
28	0.9477	0.0880	0.0476	0.2050	0.5699	0.5680	0.3438	0.9242	0.1429	0.0283
29	0.2862	0.0944	0.0698	0.6541	0.5945	0.5464	0.1861	0.8030	0.8177	0.8099
30	0.9237	0.5355	0.9374	0.4701	0.8763	0.3914	0.5917	0.6042	0.0596	0.2829
31	0.5876	0.2458	0.6085	0.6830	0.5682	0.9463	0.5392	0.0854	0.7900	0.3149
32	0.0677	0.4571	0.6932	0.0656	0.3131	0.9006	0.8570	0.7966	0.4101	0.5311
33	0.9369	0.3878	0.8473	0.9510	0.9292	0.1164	0.4611	0.7247	0.7077	0.0106
34	0.1777	0.1686	0.1624	0.9553	0.2083	0.9768	0.2229	0.1562	0.6361	0.0027
35	0.4455	0.5007	0.0395	0.4937	0.9753	0.3447	0.0391	0.6322	0.3977	0.4147
36	0.4002	0.5214	0.1770	0.8398	0.2889	0.5151	0.4960	0.6892	0.4331	0.8813
37	0.4288	0.7095	0.6115	0.1138	0.7932	0.7117	0.6252	0.1275	0.6600	0.0738
38	0.3327	0.3886	0.6723	0.0747	0.7562	0.2142	0.1860	0.9814	0.0407	0.7521
39	0.5113	0.4232	0.2029	0.9034	0.0154	0.6591	0.0515	0.8867	0.5985	0.0338
40	0.2530	0.2622	0.2013	0.0351	0.1554	0.4416	0.0300	0.7017	0.4546	0.6329
41	0.3086	0.7557	0.6003	0.5604	0.6615	0.8889	0.2757	0.8436	0.1147	0.2306
42	0.7732	0.6118	0.3301	0.7272	0.4494	0.4960	0.6787	0.2748	0.4064	0.1111
43	0.6713	0.2170	0.5049	0.7975	0.6739	0.9117	0.0948	0.9233	0.6709	0.6739
44	0.9708	0.0705	0.0987	0.5948	0.1022	0.1206	0.2131	0.3548	0.0826	0.7013
45	0.4756	0.6014	0.8200	0.5208	0.3044	0.4410	0.1012	0.5467	0.7132	0.2751
46	0.6130	0.0888	0.2238	0.1298	0.5416	0.7280	0.9447	0.6551	0.0112	0.5960
47	0.2792	0.7500	0.3124	0.0277	0.3785	0.9622	0.7501	0.6412	0.1556	0.1384
48	0.5724	0.0308	0.7103	0.1949	0.9440	0.9585	0.4508	0.3737	0.7383	0.6845
49	0.2825	0.9384	0.6804	0.3165	0.1243	0.6089	0.2623	0.8008	0.2408	0.9563
50	0.3294	0.4181	0.5703	0.4162	0.8578	0.3346	0.5491	0.1812	0.7001	0.6394

Chi-Square Critical Values

df	0.10	0.09	0.08	0.07	0.06	0.05	0.04	0.03	0.02	0.01
1	2.7055	2.8744	3.0649	3.2830	3.5374	3.8415	4.2179	4.7093	5.4119	6.6349
2	4.6052	4.8159	5.0515	5.3185	5.6268	5.9915	6.4377	7.0131	7.8241	9.2104
3	6.2514	6.4915	6.7587	7.0603	7.4069	7.8147	8.3112	8.9473	9.8374	11.3449
4	7.7794	8.0434	8.3365	8.6664	9.0444	9.4877	10.0255	10.7119	11.6678	13.2767
5	9.2363	9.5211	9.8366	10.1910	10.5962	11.0705	11.6443	12.3746	13.3882	15.0863
6	10.6446	10.9479	11.2835	11.6599	12.0896	12.5916	13.1978	13.9676	15.0332	16.8119
7	12.0170	12.3372	12.6912	13.0877	13.5397	14.0671	14.7030	15.5091	16.6224	18.4753
8	13.3616	13.6975	14.0684	14.4836	14.9563	15.5073	16.1708	17.0105	18.1682	20.0902
9	14.6837	15.0342	15.4211	15.8537	16.3459	16.9190	17.6083	18.4796	19.6790	21.6660
10	15.9872	16.3516	16.7535	17.2026	17.7131	18.3070	19.0208	19.9219	21.1608	23.2093
11	17.2750	17.6526	18.0687	18.5334	19.0614	19.6752	20.4120	21.3416	22.6179	24.7250
12	18.5493	18.9395	19.3692	19.8488	20.3934	21.0261	21.7851	22.7418	24.0539	26.2170
13	19.8119	20.2140	20.6568	21.1507	21.7113	22.3620	23.1423	24.1249	25.4715	27.6882
14	21.0641	21.4778	21.9331	22.4408	23.0166	23.6848	24.4854	25.4931	26.8727	29.1412
15	22.3071	22.7319	23.1992	23.7202	24.3108	24.9958	25.8161	26.8480	28.2595	30.5780
16	23.5418	23.9774	24.4564	24.9901	25.5950	26.2962	27.1356	28.1908	29.6332	31.9999
17	24.7690	25.2150	25.7053	26.2514	26.8701	27.5871	28.4449	29.5227	30.9950	33.4087
18	25.9894	26.4455	26.9467	27.5049	28.1370	28.8693	29.7450	30.8447	32.3462	34.8052
19	27.2036	27.6695	28.1813	28.7512	29.3964	30.1435	31.0367	32.1577	33.6874	36.1908
20	28.4120	28.8874	29.4097	29.9910	30.6488	31.4104	32.3206	33.4623	35.0196	37.5663
21	29.6151	30.0998	30.6322	31.2246	31.8949	32.6706	33.5972	34.7593	36.3434	38.9322
22	30.8133	31.3071	31.8494	32.4526	33.1350	33.9245	34.8672	36.0491	37.6595	40.2894
23	32.0069	32.5096	33.0616	33.6754	34.3696	35.1725	36.1310	37.3323	38.9683	41.6383
24	33.1962	33.7077	34.2690	34.8932	35.5989	36.4150	37.3891	38.6093	40.2703	42.9798
25	34.3816	34.9015	35.4721	36.1065	36.8235	37.6525	38.6417	39.8804	41.5660	44.3140
26	35.5632	36.0914	36.6711	37.3154	38.0435	38.8851	39.8891	41.1461	42.8558	45.6416
27	36.7412	37.2777	37.8662	38.5202	39.2593	40.1133	41.1318	42.4066	44.1399	46.9628
28	37.9159	38.4604	39.0577	39.7213	40.4710	41.3372	42.3699	43.6622	45.4188	48.2782
29	39.0875	39.6398	40.2456	40.9187	41.6789	42.5569	43.6038	44.9132	46.6926	49.5878

31	41.4217	41.9895	42.6120	43.3033	44.0840	44.9853	46.0595	47.4024	49.2263	52.1914
32	42.5847	43.1600	43.7906	44.4909	45.2815	46.1942	47.2817	48.6410	50.4867	53.4857
33	43.7452	44.3278	44.9664	45.6755	46.4759	47.3999	48.5005	49.8759	51.7429	54.7754
34	44.9032	45.4930	46.1395	46.8573	47.6674	48.6024	49.7159	51.1073	52.9953	56.0609
35	46.0588	46.6558	47.3101	48.0364	48.8560	49.8018	50.9281	52.3350	54.2439	57.3420
36	47.2122	47.8163	48.4782	49.2129	50.0420	50.9985	52.1372	53.5596	55.4889	58.6192
37	48.3634	48.9744	49.6440	50.3869	51.2253	52.1923	53.3435	54.7811	56.7304	59.8926
38	49.5126	50.1305	50.8074	51.5586	52.4060	53.3835	54.5470	55.9995	57.9689	61.1620
39	50.6598	51.2845	51.9688	52.7280	53.5845	54.5722	55.7477	57.2151	59.2040	62.4281
40	51.8050	52.4364	53.1280	53.8952	54.7606	55.7585	56.9459	58.4278	60.4361	63.6908
41	52.9485	53.5865	54.2852	55.0603	55.9345	56.9424	58.1415	59.6379	61.6654	64.9500
42	54.0902	54.7347	55.4405	56.2234	57.1062	58.1240	59.3348	60.8455	62.8918	66.2063
43	55.2302	55.8811	56.5940	57.3845	58.2759	59.3035	60.5257	62.0505	64.1156	67.4593
44	56.3685	57.0258	57.7456	58.5437	59.4436	60.4809	61.7144	63.2531	65.3367	68.7096
45	57.5053	58.1689	58.8955	59.7011	60.6094	61.6562	62.9010	64.4535	66.5552	69.9569
46	58.6405	59.3104	60.0437	60.8568	61.7734	62.8296	64.0855	65.6515	67.7714	71.2015
47	59.7743	60.4503	61.1903	62.0107	62.9355	64.0011	65.2679	66.8475	68.9852	72.4432
48	60.9066	61.5887	62.3353	63.1630	64.0959	65.1708	66.4484	68.0413	70.1967	73.6826
49	62.0375	62.7257	63.4788	64.3137	65.2547	66.3387	67.6270	69.2331	71.4060	74.9194
50	63.1671	63.8612	64.6209	65.4629	66.4117	67.5048	68.8039	70.4229	72.6132	76.1538
51	64.2954	64.9954	65.7615	66.6105	67.5673	68.6693	69.9789	71.6109	73.8183	77.3860
52	65.4224	66.1282	66.9006	67.7567	68.7212	69.8322	71.1521	72.7971	75.0215	78.6156
53	66.5482	67.2598	68.0385	68.9015	69.8737	70.9934	72.3238	73.9813	76.2225	79.8434
54	67.6728	68.3902	69.1751	70.0449	71.0248	72.1532	73.4938	75.1639	77.4217	81.0688
55	68.7962	69.5192	70.3104	71.1870	72.1744	73.3115	74.6622	76.3447	78.6191	82.2920
56	69.9185	70.6472	71.4444	72.3278	73.3227	74.4683	75.8291	77.5239	79.8148	83.5136
57	71.0397	71.7740	72.5773	73.4673	74.4697	75.6237	76.9944	78.7015	81.0085	84.7327
58	72.1598	72.8996	73.7090	74.6055	75.6153	76.7778	78.1583	79.8775	82.2007	85.9501
59	73.2789	74.0242	74.8395	75.7426	76.7597	77.9305	79.3208	81.0520	83.3911	87.1658
60	74.3970	75.1477	75.9689	76.8785	77.9029	79.0820	80.4820	82.2251	84.5799	88.3794

Example: For a degree of freedom (k-c) of 23, the critical values are 32.0069 for 10% alpha level (0.10), 35.1725 for 5% alpha level (0.05), and 41.6383 for 1% alpha level (0.01).

F-Distribution Critical Statistics (alpha one tail 0.10)

$\alpha = 0.10$

					Numerator (df)							
Denominator df	1	2	3	4	5	6	7	8	9	10	15	20
1	39.86	49.50	53.59	55.83	57.24	58.20	58.91	59.44	59.86	60.19	61.22	61.74
2	8.53	9.00	9.16	9.24	9.29	9.33	9.35	9.37	9.38	9.39	9.42	9.44
3	5.54	5.46	5.39	5.34	5.31	5.28	5.27	5.25	5.24	5.23	5.20	5.18
4	4.54	4.32	4.19	4.11	4.05	4.01	3.98	3.95	3.94	3.92	3.87	3.84
5	4.06	3.78	3.62	3.52	3.45	3.40	3.37	3.34	3.32	3.30	3.24	3.21
6	3.78	3.46	3.29	3.18	3.11	3.05	3.01	2.98	2.96	2.94	2.87	2.84
7	3.59	3.26	3.07	2.96	2.88	2.83	2.78	2.75	2.72	2.70	2.63	2.59
8	3.46	3.11	2.92	2.81	2.73	2.67	2.62	2.59	2.56	2.54	2.46	2.42
9	3.36	3.01	2.81	2.69	2.61	2.55	2.51	2.47	2.44	2.42	2.34	2.30
10	3.29	2.92	2.73	2.61	2.52	2.46	2.41	2.38	2.35	2.32	2.24	2.20
15	3.07	2.70	2.49	2.36	2.27	2.21	2.16	2.12	2.09	2.06	1.97	1.92
20	2.97	2.59	2.38	2.25	2.16	2.09	2.04	2.00	1.96	1.94	1.84	1.79
25	2.92	2.53	2.32	2.18	2.09	2.02	1.97	1.93	1.89	1.87	1.77	1.72
30	2.88	2.49	2.28	2.14	2.05	1.98	1.93	1.88	1.85	1.82	1.72	1.67
35	2.85	2.46	2.25	2.11	2.02	1.95	1.90	1.85	1.82	1.79	1.69	1.63
40	2.84	2.44	2.23	2.09	2.00	1.93	1.87	1.83	1.79	1.76	1.66	1.61
45	2.82	2.42	2.21	2.07	1.98	1.91	1.85	1.81	1.77	1.74	1.64	1.58
50	2.81	2.41	2.20	2.06	1.97	1.90	1.84	1.80	1.76	1.73	1.63	1.57
100	2.76	2.36	2.14	2.00	1.91	1.83	1.78	1.73	1.69	1.66	1.56	1.49
200	2.73	2.33	2.11	1.97	1.88	1.80	1.75	1.70	1.66	1.63	1.52	1.46
300	2.72	2.32	2.10	1.96	1.87	1.79	1.74	1.69	1.65	1.62	1.51	1.45
500	2.72	2.31	2.09	1.96	1.86	1.79	1.73	1.68	1.64	1.61	1.50	1.44
100000	2.71	2.30	2.08	1.94	1.85	1.77	1.72	1.67	1.63	1.60	1.49	1.42

Example: For an alpha in the single right-tail area of 10% with 10 degrees of freedom in the numerator and 15 degrees of freedom in the denominator, the critical F value is 2.06.

	Numerator (df)										
Denominator df	25	30	35	40	45	50	100	200	300	500	100000
1	62.05	62.26	62.42	62.53	62.62	62.69	63.01	63.17	63.22	63.26	63.33
2	9.45	9.46	9.46	9.47	9.47	9.47	9.48	9.49	9.49	9.49	9.49
3	5.17	5.17	5.16	5.16	5.16	5.15	5.14	5.14	5.14	5.14	5.13
4	3.83	3.82	3.81	3.80	3.80	3.80	3.78	3.77	3.77	3.76	3.76
5	3.19	3.17	3.16	3.16	3.15	3.15	3.13	3.12	3.11	3.11	3.11
6	2.81	2.80	2.79	2.78	2.77	2.77	2.75	2.73	2.73	2.73	2.72
7	2.57	2.56	2.54	2.54	2.53	2.52	2.50	2.48	2.48	2.48	2.47
8	2.40	2.38	2.37	2.36	2.35	2.35	2.32	2.31	2.30	2.30	2.29
9	2.27	2.25	2.24	2.23	2.22	2.22	2.19	2.17	2.17	2.17	2.16
10	2.17	2.16	2.14	2.13	2.12	2.12	2.09	2.07	2.07	2.06	2.06
15	1.89	1.87	1.86	1.85	1.84	1.83	1.79	1.77	1.77	1.76	1.76
20	1.76	1.74	1.72	1.71	1.70	1.69	1.65	1.63	1.62	1.62	1.61
25	1.68	1.66	1.64	1.63	1.62	1.61	1.56	1.54	1.53	1.53	1.52
30	1.63	1.61	1.59	1.57	1.56	1.55	1.51	1.48	1.47	1.47	1.46
35	1.60	1.57	1.55	1.53	1.52	1.51	1.47	1.44	1.43	1.42	1.41
40	1.57	1.54	1.52	1.51	1.49	1.48	1.43	1.41	1.40	1.39	1.38
45	1.55	1.52	1.50	1.48	1.47	1.46	1.41	1.38	1.37	1.36	1.35
50	1.53	1.50	1.48	1.46	1.45	1.44	1.39	1.36	1.35	1.34	1.33
100	1.45	1.42	1.40	1.38	1.37	1.35	1.29	1.26	1.24	1.23	1.21
200	1.41	1.38	1.36	1.34	1.32	1.31	1.24	1.20	1.18	1.17	1.14
300	1.40	1.37	1.34	1.32	1.31	1.29	1.22	1.18	1.16	1.14	1.12
500	1.39	1.36	1.33	1.31	1.30	1.28	1.21	1.16	1.14	1.12	1.09
1000	1.38	1.34	1.32	1.30	1.28	1.26	1.19	1.13	1.11	1.08	1.01

F-Distribution Critical Statistics (alpha one tail 0.05)

$\alpha = 0.05$

Denominator df		Numerator (df)										
	1	2	3	4	5	6	7	8	9	10	15	20
1	161	199	216	225	230	234	237	239	241	242	246	248
2	18.51	19.00	19.16	19.25	19.30	19.33	19.35	19.37	19.38	19.40	19.43	19.45
3	10.13	9.55	9.28	9.12	9.01	8.94	8.89	8.85	8.81	8.79	8.70	8.66
4	7.71	6.94	6.59	6.39	6.26	6.16	6.09	6.04	6.00	5.96	5.86	5.80
5	6.61	5.79	5.41	5.19	5.05	4.95	4.88	4.82	4.77	4.74	4.62	4.56
6	5.99	5.14	4.76	4.53	4.39	4.28	4.21	4.15	4.10	4.06	3.94	3.87
7	5.59	4.74	4.35	4.12	3.97	3.87	3.79	3.73	3.68	3.64	3.51	3.44
8	5.32	4.46	4.07	3.84	3.69	3.58	3.50	3.44	3.39	3.35	3.22	3.15
9	5.12	4.26	3.86	3.63	3.48	3.37	3.29	3.23	3.18	3.14	3.01	2.94
10	4.96	4.10	3.71	3.48	3.33	3.22	3.14	3.07	3.02	2.98	2.85	2.77
15	4.54	3.68	3.29	3.06	2.90	2.79	2.71	2.64	2.59	2.54	2.40	2.33
20	4.35	3.49	3.10	2.87	2.71	2.60	2.51	2.45	2.39	2.35	2.20	2.12
25	4.24	3.39	2.99	2.76	2.60	2.49	2.40	2.34	2.28	2.24	2.09	2.01
30	4.17	3.32	2.92	2.69	2.53	2.42	2.33	2.27	2.21	2.16	2.01	1.93
35	4.12	3.27	2.87	2.64	2.49	2.37	2.29	2.22	2.16	2.11	1.96	1.88
40	4.08	3.23	2.84	2.61	2.45	2.34	2.25	2.18	2.12	2.08	1.92	1.84
45	4.06	3.20	2.81	2.58	2.42	2.31	2.22	2.15	2.10	2.05	1.89	1.81
50	4.03	3.18	2.79	2.56	2.40	2.29	2.20	2.13	2.07	2.03	1.87	1.78
100	3.94	3.09	2.70	2.46	2.31	2.19	2.10	2.03	1.97	1.93	1.77	1.68
200	3.89	3.04	2.65	2.42	2.26	2.14	2.06	1.98	1.93	1.88	1.72	1.62
300	3.87	3.03	2.63	2.40	2.24	2.13	2.04	1.97	1.91	1.86	1.70	1.61
500	3.86	3.01	2.62	2.39	2.23	2.12	2.03	1.96	1.90	1.85	1.69	1.59
100000	3.84	3.00	2.60	2.37	2.21	2.10	2.01	1.94	1.88	1.83	1.67	1.57

Denominator df	Numerator (df)										
	25	30	35	40	45	50	100	200	300	500	100000
1	249	250	251	251	251	252	253	254	254	254	254
2	19.46	19.46	19.47	19.47	19.47	19.48	19.49	19.49	19.49	19.49	19.50
3	8.63	8.62	8.60	8.59	8.59	8.58	8.55	8.54	8.54	8.53	8.53
4	5.77	5.75	5.73	5.72	5.71	5.70	5.66	5.65	5.64	5.64	5.63
5	4.52	4.50	4.48	4.46	4.45	4.44	4.41	4.39	4.38	4.37	4.37
6	3.83	3.81	3.79	3.77	3.76	3.75	3.71	3.69	3.68	3.68	3.67
7	3.40	3.38	3.36	3.34	3.33	3.32	3.27	3.25	3.24	3.24	3.23
8	3.11	3.08	3.06	3.04	3.03	3.02	2.97	2.95	2.94	2.94	2.93
9	2.89	2.86	2.84	2.83	2.81	2.80	2.76	2.73	2.72	2.72	2.71
10	2.73	2.70	2.68	2.66	2.65	2.64	2.59	2.56	2.55	2.55	2.54
15	2.28	2.25	2.22	2.20	2.19	2.18	2.12	2.10	2.09	2.08	2.07
20	2.07	2.04	2.01	1.99	1.98	1.97	1.91	1.88	1.86	1.86	1.84
25	1.96	1.92	1.89	1.87	1.86	1.84	1.78	1.75	1.73	1.73	1.71
30	1.88	1.84	1.81	1.79	1.77	1.76	1.70	1.66	1.65	1.64	1.62
35	1.82	1.79	1.76	1.74	1.72	1.70	1.63	1.60	1.58	1.57	1.56
40	1.78	1.74	1.72	1.69	1.67	1.66	1.59	1.55	1.54	1.53	1.51
45	1.75	1.71	1.68	1.66	1.64	1.63	1.55	1.51	1.50	1.49	1.47
50	1.73	1.69	1.66	1.63	1.61	1.60	1.52	1.48	1.47	1.46	1.44
100	1.62	1.57	1.54	1.52	1.49	1.48	1.39	1.34	1.32	1.31	1.28
200	1.56	1.52	1.48	1.46	1.43	1.41	1.32	1.26	1.24	1.22	1.19
300	1.54	1.50	1.46	1.43	1.41	1.39	1.30	1.23	1.21	1.19	1.15
500	1.53	1.48	1.45	1.42	1.40	1.38	1.28	1.21	1.18	1.16	1.11
100000	1.51	1.46	1.42	1.39	1.37	1.35	1.24	1.17	1.14	1.11	1.01

F-Distribution Critical Statistics (alpha one tail 0.025) α =0.025

Denominator df	1	2	3	4	5	6	7	8	9	10	15	20
					Numerator (df)							
1	648	799	864	900	922	937	948	957	963	969	985	993
2	38.51	39.00	39.17	39.25	39.30	39.33	39.36	39.37	39.39	39.40	39.43	39.45
3	17.44	16.04	15.44	15.10	14.88	14.73	14.62	14.54	14.47	14.42	14.25	14.17
4	12.22	10.65	9.98	9.60	9.36	9.20	9.07	8.98	8.90	8.84	8.66	8.56
5	10.01	8.43	7.76	7.39	7.15	6.98	6.85	6.76	6.68	6.62	6.43	6.33
6	8.81	7.26	6.60	6.23	5.99	5.82	5.70	5.60	5.52	5.46	5.27	5.17
7	8.07	6.54	5.89	5.52	5.29	5.12	4.99	4.90	4.82	4.76	4.57	4.47
8	7.57	6.06	5.42	5.05	4.82	4.65	4.53	4.43	4.36	4.30	4.10	4.00
9	7.21	5.71	5.08	4.72	4.48	4.32	4.20	4.10	4.03	3.96	3.77	3.67
10	6.94	5.46	4.83	4.47	4.24	4.07	3.95	3.85	3.78	3.72	3.52	3.42
15	6.20	4.77	4.15	3.80	3.58	3.41	3.29	3.20	3.12	3.06	2.86	2.76
20	5.87	4.46	3.86	3.51	3.29	3.13	3.01	2.91	2.84	2.77	2.57	2.46
25	5.69	4.29	3.69	3.35	3.13	2.97	2.85	2.75	2.68	2.61	2.41	2.30
30	5.57	4.18	3.59	3.25	3.03	2.87	2.75	2.65	2.57	2.51	2.31	2.20
35	5.48	4.11	3.52	3.18	2.96	2.80	2.68	2.58	2.50	2.44	2.23	2.12
40	5.42	4.05	3.46	3.13	2.90	2.74	2.62	2.53	2.45	2.39	2.18	2.07
45	5.38	4.01	3.42	3.09	2.86	2.70	2.58	2.49	2.41	2.35	2.14	2.03
50	5.34	3.97	3.39	3.05	2.83	2.67	2.55	2.46	2.38	2.32	2.11	1.99
100	5.18	3.83	3.25	2.92	2.70	2.54	2.42	2.32	2.24	2.18	1.97	1.85
200	5.10	3.76	3.18	2.85	2.63	2.47	2.35	2.26	2.18	2.11	1.90	1.78
300	5.07	3.73	3.16	2.83	2.61	2.45	2.33	2.23	2.16	2.09	1.88	1.75
500	5.05	3.72	3.14	2.81	2.59	2.43	2.31	2.22	2.14	2.07	1.86	1.74
100000	5.02	3.69	3.12	2.79	2.57	2.41	2.29	2.19	2.11	2.05	1.83	1.71

Denominator df	Numerator (df)										
	25	30	35	40	45	50	100	200	300	500	100000
1	998	1001	1004	1006	1007	1008	1013	1016	1017	1017	1018
2	39.46	39.46	39.47	39.47	39.48	39.48	39.49	39.49	39.49	39.50	39.50
3	14.12	14.08	14.06	14.04	14.02	14.01	13.96	13.93	13.92	13.91	13.90
4	8.50	8.46	8.43	8.41	8.39	8.38	8.32	8.29	8.28	8.27	8.26
5	6.27	6.23	6.20	6.18	6.16	6.14	6.08	6.05	6.04	6.03	6.02
6	5.11	5.07	5.04	5.01	4.99	4.98	4.92	4.88	4.87	4.86	4.85
7	4.40	4.36	4.33	4.31	4.29	4.28	4.21	4.18	4.17	4.16	4.14
8	3.94	3.89	3.86	3.84	3.82	3.81	3.74	3.70	3.69	3.68	3.67
9	3.60	3.56	3.53	3.51	3.49	3.47	3.40	3.37	3.36	3.35	3.33
10	3.35	3.31	3.28	3.26	3.24	3.22	3.15	3.12	3.10	3.09	3.08
15	2.69	2.64	2.61	2.59	2.56	2.55	2.47	2.44	2.42	2.41	2.40
20	2.40	2.35	2.31	2.29	2.27	2.25	2.17	2.13	2.11	2.10	2.09
25	2.23	2.18	2.15	2.12	2.10	2.08	2.00	1.95	1.94	1.92	1.91
30	2.12	2.07	2.04	2.01	1.99	1.97	1.88	1.84	1.82	1.81	1.79
35	2.05	2.00	1.96	1.93	1.91	1.89	1.80	1.75	1.74	1.72	1.70
40	1.99	1.94	1.90	1.88	1.85	1.83	1.74	1.69	1.67	1.66	1.64
45	1.95	1.90	1.86	1.83	1.81	1.79	1.69	1.64	1.62	1.61	1.59
50	1.92	1.87	1.83	1.80	1.77	1.75	1.66	1.60	1.58	1.57	1.55
100	1.77	1.71	1.67	1.64	1.61	1.59	1.48	1.42	1.40	1.38	1.35
200	1.70	1.64	1.60	1.56	1.53	1.51	1.39	1.32	1.29	1.27	1.23
300	1.67	1.62	1.57	1.54	1.51	1.48	1.36	1.28	1.25	1.23	1.18
500	1.65	1.60	1.55	1.52	1.49	1.46	1.34	1.25	1.22	1.19	1.14
100000	1.63	1.57	1.52	1.48	1.45	1.43	1.30	1.21	1.17	1.13	1.01

F-Distribution Critical Statistics (alpha one tail 0.01) $\alpha = 0.01$

Denominator df	Numerator (df)											
	1	2	3	4	5	6	7	8	9	10	15	20
1	4052	4999	5404	5624	5764	5859	5928	5981	6022	6056	6157	6209
2	98.50	99.00	99.16	99.25	99.30	99.33	99.36	99.38	99.39	99.40	99.43	99.45
3	34.12	30.82	29.46	28.71	28.24	27.91	27.67	27.49	27.34	27.23	26.87	26.69
4	21.20	18.00	16.69	15.98	15.52	15.21	14.98	14.80	14.66	14.55	14.20	14.02
5	16.26	13.27	12.06	11.39	10.97	10.67	10.46	10.29	10.16	10.05	9.72	9.55
6	13.75	10.92	9.78	9.15	8.75	8.47	8.26	8.10	7.98	7.87	7.56	7.40
7	12.25	9.55	8.45	7.85	7.46	7.19	6.99	6.84	6.72	6.62	6.31	6.16
8	11.26	8.65	7.59	7.01	6.63	6.37	6.18	6.03	5.91	5.81	5.52	5.36
9	10.56	8.02	6.99	6.42	6.06	5.80	5.61	5.47	5.35	5.26	4.96	4.81
10	10.04	7.56	6.55	5.99	5.64	5.39	5.20	5.06	4.94	4.85	4.56	4.41
15	8.68	6.36	5.42	4.89	4.56	4.32	4.14	4.00	3.89	3.80	3.52	3.37
20	8.10	5.85	4.94	4.43	4.10	3.87	3.70	3.56	3.46	3.37	3.09	2.94
25	7.77	5.57	4.68	4.18	3.85	3.63	3.46	3.32	3.22	3.13	2.85	2.70
30	7.56	5.39	4.51	4.02	3.70	3.47	3.30	3.17	3.07	2.98	2.70	2.55
35	7.42	5.27	4.40	3.91	3.59	3.37	3.20	3.07	2.96	2.88	2.60	2.44
40	7.31	5.18	4.31	3.83	3.51	3.29	3.12	2.99	2.89	2.80	2.52	2.37
45	7.23	5.11	4.25	3.77	3.45	3.23	3.07	2.94	2.83	2.74	2.46	2.31
50	7.17	5.06	4.20	3.72	3.41	3.19	3.02	2.89	2.78	2.70	2.42	2.27
100	6.90	4.82	3.98	3.51	3.21	2.99	2.82	2.69	2.59	2.50	2.22	2.07
200	6.76	4.71	3.88	3.41	3.11	2.89	2.73	2.60	2.50	2.41	2.13	1.97
300	6.72	4.68	3.85	3.38	3.08	2.86	2.70	2.57	2.47	2.38	2.10	1.94
500	6.69	4.65	3.82	3.36	3.05	2.84	2.68	2.55	2.44	2.36	2.07	1.92
100000	6.64	4.61	3.78	3.32	3.02	2.80	2.64	2.51	2.41	2.32	2.04	1.88

Denominator df	Numerator (df)										
	25	30	35	40	45	50	100	200	300	500	100000
1	6240	6260	6275	6286	6296	6302	6334	6350	6355	6360	6366
2	99.46	99.47	99.47	99.48	99.48	99.48	99.49	99.49	99.50	99.50	99.50
3	26.58	26.50	26.45	26.41	26.38	26.35	26.24	26.18	26.16	26.15	26.13
4	13.91	13.84	13.79	13.75	13.71	13.69	13.58	13.52	13.50	13.49	13.46
5	9.45	9.38	9.33	9.29	9.26	9.24	9.13	9.08	9.06	9.04	9.02
6	7.30	7.23	7.18	7.14	7.11	7.09	6.99	6.93	6.92	6.90	6.88
7	6.06	5.99	5.94	5.91	5.88	5.86	5.75	5.70	5.68	5.67	5.65
8	5.26	5.20	5.15	5.12	5.09	5.07	4.96	4.91	4.89	4.88	4.86
9	4.71	4.65	4.60	4.57	4.54	4.52	4.41	4.36	4.35	4.33	4.31
10	4.31	4.25	4.20	4.17	4.14	4.12	4.01	3.96	3.94	3.93	3.91
15	3.28	3.21	3.17	3.13	3.10	3.08	2.98	2.92	2.91	2.89	2.87
20	2.84	2.78	2.73	2.69	2.67	2.64	2.54	2.48	2.46	2.44	2.42
25	2.60	2.54	2.49	2.45	2.42	2.40	2.29	2.23	2.21	2.19	2.17
30	2.45	2.39	2.34	2.30	2.27	2.25	2.13	2.07	2.05	2.03	2.01
35	2.35	2.28	2.23	2.19	2.16	2.14	2.02	1.96	1.94	1.92	1.89
40	2.27	2.20	2.15	2.11	2.08	2.06	1.94	1.87	1.85	1.83	1.80
45	2.21	2.14	2.09	2.05	2.02	2.00	1.88	1.81	1.79	1.77	1.74
50	2.17	2.10	2.05	2.01	1.97	1.95	1.82	1.76	1.73	1.71	1.68
100	1.97	1.89	1.84	1.80	1.76	1.74	1.60	1.52	1.49	1.47	1.43
200	1.87	1.79	1.74	1.69	1.66	1.63	1.48	1.39	1.36	1.33	1.28
300	1.84	1.76	1.70	1.66	1.62	1.59	1.44	1.35	1.31	1.28	1.22
500	1.81	1.74	1.68	1.63	1.60	1.57	1.41	1.31	1.27	1.23	1.16
100000	1.77	1.70	1.64	1.59	1.55	1.52	1.36	1.25	1.20	1.15	1.01

Real Options Analysis Values (1-year maturity at 5% risk-free rate)

Volatility	Profitability Ratio (% in-the-money)									
	-99%	-90%	-80%	-70%	-60%	-50%	-40%	-30%	-20%	-10%
1%	0.00%	0.00%	0.00%	0.00%	0.00%	0.00%	0.00%	0.00%	0.00%	0.00%
3%	0.00%	0.00%	0.00%	0.00%	0.00%	0.00%	0.00%	0.00%	0.00%	0.04%
5%	0.00%	0.00%	0.00%	0.00%	0.00%	0.00%	0.00%	0.00%	0.00%	0.35%
7%	0.00%	0.00%	0.00%	0.00%	0.00%	0.00%	0.00%	0.00%	0.02%	0.88%
9%	0.00%	0.00%	0.00%	0.00%	0.00%	0.00%	0.00%	0.00%	0.10%	1.52%
11%	0.00%	0.00%	0.00%	0.00%	0.00%	0.00%	0.00%	0.01%	0.30%	2.22%
13%	0.00%	0.00%	0.00%	0.00%	0.00%	0.00%	0.00%	0.05%	0.60%	2.96%
15%	0.00%	0.00%	0.00%	0.00%	0.00%	0.00%	0.01%	0.13%	1.01%	3.72%
17%	0.00%	0.00%	0.00%	0.00%	0.00%	0.00%	0.02%	0.28%	1.49%	4.49%
19%	0.00%	0.00%	0.00%	0.00%	0.00%	0.00%	0.06%	0.50%	2.03%	5.26%
21%	0.00%	0.00%	0.00%	0.00%	0.00%	0.01%	0.13%	0.78%	2.63%	6.05%
23%	0.00%	0.00%	0.00%	0.00%	0.00%	0.02%	0.24%	1.13%	3.26%	6.84%
25%	0.00%	0.00%	0.00%	0.00%	0.00%	0.05%	0.40%	1.54%	3.93%	7.63%
27%	0.00%	0.00%	0.00%	0.00%	0.01%	0.11%	0.61%	2.00%	4.62%	8.43%
29%	0.00%	0.00%	0.00%	0.00%	0.02%	0.18%	0.86%	2.50%	5.33%	9.22%
31%	0.00%	0.00%	0.00%	0.00%	0.04%	0.29%	1.17%	3.05%	6.06%	10.02%
33%	0.00%	0.00%	0.00%	0.00%	0.07%	0.44%	1.52%	3.63%	6.80%	10.82%
35%	0.00%	0.00%	0.00%	0.01%	0.12%	0.62%	1.92%	4.24%	7.55%	11.62%
37%	0.00%	0.00%	0.00%	0.02%	0.18%	0.84%	2.35%	4.88%	8.32%	12.42%
39%	0.00%	0.00%	0.00%	0.03%	0.27%	1.10%	2.82%	5.54%	9.09%	13.21%
41%	0.00%	0.00%	0.00%	0.05%	0.39%	1.39%	3.33%	6.22%	9.86%	14.01%
43%	0.00%	0.00%	0.00%	0.08%	0.53%	1.73%	3.87%	6.91%	10.64%	14.80%
45%	0.00%	0.00%	0.01%	0.13%	0.70%	2.10%	4.44%	7.62%	11.43%	15.60%
47%	0.00%	0.00%	0.01%	0.19%	0.91%	2.50%	5.03%	8.35%	12.22%	16.39%
49%	0.00%	0.00%	0.02%	0.26%	1.14%	2.93%	5.64%	9.09%	13.01%	17.18%
51%	0.00%	0.00%	0.03%	0.36%	1.41%	3.40%	6.28%	9.83%	13.80%	17.97%
53%	0.00%	0.00%	0.05%	0.48%	1.71%	3.90%	6.94%	10.59%	14.60%	18.76%
55%	0.00%	0.00%	0.08%	0.62%	2.03%	4.42%	7.61%	11.35%	15.40%	19.55%
57%	0.00%	0.00%	0.11%	0.78%	2.39%	4.96%	8.30%	12.12%	16.20%	20.33%
59%	0.00%	0.00%	0.16%	0.97%	2.78%	5.54%	9.00%	12.90%	16.99%	21.12%
61%	0.00%	0.00%	0.21%	1.18%	3.19%	6.13%	9.72%	13.68%	17.79%	21.90%
63%	0.00%	0.01%	0.29%	1.42%	3.63%	6.74%	10.44%	14.46%	18.59%	22.68%
65%	0.00%	0.01%	0.37%	1.69%	4.10%	7.37%	11.18%	15.25%	19.39%	23.45%
67%	0.00%	0.02%	0.47%	1.98%	4.59%	8.02%	11.92%	16.04%	20.18%	24.23%
69%	0.00%	0.03%	0.59%	2.30%	5.11%	8.68%	12.68%	16.83%	20.98%	25.00%
71%	0.00%	0.04%	0.73%	2.64%	5.65%	9.36%	13.44%	17.63%	21.77%	25.77%
73%	0.00%	0.06%	0.88%	3.01%	6.21%	10.05%	14.21%	18.42%	22.56%	26.53%
75%	0.00%	0.08%	1.06%	3.40%	6.79%	10.76%	14.98%	19.22%	23.35%	27.30%
77%	0.00%	0.11%	1.26%	3.82%	7.38%	11.47%	15.76%	20.02%	24.14%	28.06%
79%	0.00%	0.15%	1.48%	4.26%	8.00%	12.20%	16.54%	20.82%	24.93%	28.82%
81%	0.00%	0.19%	1.72%	4.72%	8.63%	12.94%	17.32%	21.61%	25.71%	29.57%
83%	0.00%	0.24%	1.98%	5.21%	9.28%	13.68%	18.11%	22.41%	26.49%	30.33%
85%	0.00%	0.30%	2.26%	5.72%	9.94%	14.43%	18.90%	23.21%	27.27%	31.07%
87%	0.00%	0.38%	2.57%	6.24%	10.62%	15.19%	19.70%	24.00%	28.05%	31.82%
89%	0.00%	0.46%	2.90%	6.79%	11.30%	15.95%	20.49%	24.80%	28.83%	32.56%
91%	0.00%	0.56%	3.25%	7.35%	12.00%	16.72%	21.29%	25.59%	29.60%	33.30%
93%	0.00%	0.67%	3.62%	7.93%	12.71%	17.50%	22.09%	26.38%	30.37%	34.04%
95%	0.00%	0.79%	4.01%	8.53%	13.43%	18.28%	22.88%	27.17%	31.13%	34.77%
97%	0.00%	0.93%	4.43%	9.15%	14.16%	19.06%	23.68%	27.96%	31.90%	35.50%
99%	0.00%	1.09%	4.86%	9.78%	14.90%	19.85%	24.48%	28.75%	32.66%	36.23%
101%	0.00%	1.26%	5.32%	10.42%	15.65%	20.64%	25.28%	29.53%	33.41%	36.95%

Example: Suppose a real option exists that has a $110 million present value of free cash flows (S), $100 million in implementation costs (X), 33% volatility, 5% risk-free rate, and a 1-year maturity, estimate the real options value of this simple option. The calculated profitability ratio is $110/$100 or 10% in-the-money. Using the 1-year table, the option value as a percentage of asset is 20.13%, for a 10% profitability ratio and 33% volatility. This means that for the $110 asset value, the option value is 20.13% of $110 or $22.15 million. In addition, if the asset value

Volatility	0%	10%	20%	30%	40%	50%	60%	70%	80%	90%	100%
1%	4.88%	13.52%	20.73%	26.83%	32.06%	36.58%	40.55%	44.05%	47.15%	49.94%	52.44%
3%	4.94%	13.52%	20.73%	26.83%	32.06%	36.58%	40.55%	44.05%	47.15%	49.94%	52.44%
5%	5.28%	13.53%	20.73%	26.83%	32.06%	36.58%	40.55%	44.05%	47.15%	49.94%	52.44%
7%	5.83%	13.57%	20.73%	26.83%	32.06%	36.58%	40.55%	44.05%	47.15%	49.94%	52.44%
9%	6.47%	13.71%	20.74%	26.83%	32.06%	36.58%	40.55%	44.05%	47.15%	49.94%	52.44%
11%	7.15%	13.97%	20.79%	26.83%	32.06%	36.58%	40.55%	44.05%	47.15%	49.94%	52.44%
13%	7.86%	14.32%	20.90%	26.86%	32.06%	36.59%	40.55%	44.05%	47.15%	49.94%	52.44%
15%	8.59%	14.76%	21.08%	26.92%	32.07%	36.59%	40.55%	44.05%	47.15%	49.94%	52.44%
17%	9.33%	15.24%	21.33%	27.02%	32.11%	36.60%	40.55%	44.05%	47.15%	49.94%	52.44%
19%	10.08%	15.78%	21.63%	27.17%	32.18%	36.63%	40.56%	44.05%	47.16%	49.94%	52.44%
21%	10.83%	16.34%	21.99%	27.37%	32.28%	36.67%	40.58%	44.06%	47.16%	49.94%	52.44%
23%	11.58%	16.94%	22.40%	27.62%	32.42%	36.75%	40.62%	44.08%	47.17%	49.94%	52.44%
25%	12.34%	17.55%	22.84%	27.91%	32.60%	36.85%	40.68%	44.11%	47.18%	49.95%	52.45%
27%	13.09%	18.18%	23.31%	28.23%	32.81%	36.99%	40.76%	44.16%	47.21%	49.97%	52.46%
29%	13.85%	18.82%	23.81%	28.60%	33.06%	37.16%	40.87%	44.23%	47.26%	49.99%	52.47%
31%	14.61%	19.47%	24.33%	28.99%	33.35%	37.35%	41.01%	44.32%	47.32%	50.03%	52.50%
33%	15.37%	20.13%	24.87%	29.41%	33.66%	37.58%	41.17%	44.43%	47.39%	50.09%	52.53%
35%	16.13%	20.80%	25.42%	29.85%	34.00%	37.84%	41.36%	44.57%	47.49%	50.16%	52.58%
37%	16.89%	21.47%	25.99%	30.31%	34.36%	38.12%	41.57%	44.73%	47.61%	50.24%	52.65%
39%	17.64%	22.15%	26.57%	30.79%	34.75%	38.42%	41.81%	44.91%	47.75%	50.35%	52.73%
41%	18.40%	22.83%	27.16%	31.28%	35.15%	38.75%	42.07%	45.11%	47.91%	50.47%	52.82%
43%	19.16%	23.52%	27.75%	31.79%	35.57%	39.09%	42.34%	45.34%	48.09%	50.62%	52.94%
45%	19.91%	24.20%	28.36%	32.30%	36.01%	39.46%	42.64%	45.58%	48.29%	50.78%	53.06%
47%	20.67%	24.89%	28.97%	32.83%	36.46%	39.83%	42.96%	45.84%	48.50%	50.95%	53.21%
49%	21.42%	25.58%	29.58%	33.37%	36.92%	40.23%	43.29%	46.12%	48.74%	51.15%	53.37%
51%	22.17%	26.27%	30.20%	33.91%	37.39%	40.63%	43.64%	46.42%	48.99%	51.36%	53.55%
53%	22.92%	26.96%	30.82%	34.46%	37.88%	41.05%	44.00%	46.73%	49.25%	51.58%	53.74%
55%	23.66%	27.65%	31.44%	35.02%	38.37%	41.48%	44.37%	47.05%	49.53%	51.82%	53.95%
57%	24.41%	28.34%	32.07%	35.58%	38.87%	41.92%	44.76%	47.39%	49.82%	52.08%	54.16%
59%	25.15%	29.03%	32.70%	36.15%	39.37%	42.37%	45.15%	47.73%	50.12%	52.34%	54.40%
61%	25.89%	29.72%	33.33%	36.72%	39.88%	42.82%	45.56%	48.09%	50.44%	52.62%	54.64%
63%	26.63%	30.40%	33.96%	37.29%	40.40%	43.29%	45.97%	48.46%	50.76%	52.91%	54.90%
65%	27.37%	31.09%	34.59%	37.87%	40.92%	43.75%	46.39%	48.83%	51.10%	53.21%	55.16%
67%	28.10%	31.78%	35.22%	38.44%	41.44%	44.23%	46.82%	49.22%	51.44%	53.51%	55.44%
69%	28.84%	32.46%	35.86%	39.02%	41.97%	44.71%	47.25%	49.61%	51.80%	53.83%	55.73%
71%	29.57%	33.14%	36.49%	39.61%	42.50%	45.19%	47.69%	50.01%	52.16%	54.16%	56.02%
73%	30.29%	33.83%	37.12%	40.19%	43.04%	45.68%	48.13%	50.41%	52.52%	54.49%	56.32%
75%	31.02%	34.50%	37.75%	40.77%	43.57%	46.17%	48.58%	50.82%	52.90%	54.83%	56.63%
77%	31.74%	35.18%	38.38%	41.35%	44.11%	46.66%	49.03%	51.23%	53.28%	55.18%	56.95%
79%	32.46%	35.86%	39.01%	41.94%	44.65%	47.16%	49.49%	51.65%	53.66%	55.53%	57.27%
81%	33.18%	36.53%	39.64%	42.52%	45.19%	47.66%	49.95%	52.08%	54.05%	55.89%	57.60%
83%	33.89%	37.20%	40.27%	43.11%	45.73%	48.16%	50.41%	52.50%	54.45%	56.25%	57.94%
85%	34.60%	37.87%	40.89%	43.69%	46.27%	48.66%	50.88%	52.93%	54.84%	56.62%	58.28%
87%	35.31%	38.54%	41.52%	44.27%	46.81%	49.17%	51.34%	53.37%	55.25%	56.99%	58.63%
89%	36.02%	39.20%	42.14%	44.85%	47.36%	49.67%	51.81%	53.80%	55.65%	57.37%	58.98%
91%	36.72%	39.87%	42.76%	45.43%	47.90%	50.18%	52.28%	54.24%	56.06%	57.75%	59.33%
93%	37.42%	40.53%	43.38%	46.01%	48.44%	50.68%	52.76%	54.68%	56.47%	58.13%	59.69%
95%	38.11%	41.18%	44.00%	46.59%	48.98%	51.19%	53.23%	55.12%	56.88%	58.52%	60.05%
97%	38.81%	41.84%	44.61%	47.17%	49.52%	51.69%	53.70%	55.57%	57.30%	58.91%	60.41%
99%	39.50%	42.49%	45.23%	47.74%	50.06%	52.20%	54.18%	56.01%	57.71%	59.30%	60.78%
101%	40.18%	43.13%	45.84%	48.32%	50.60%	52.70%	54.65%	56.45%	58.13%	59.69%	61.14%

were $330 million, then the option value is 20.13% of $330 million or $66.44 million as long as the 10% profitability ratio remains the same (implementation cost now becomes $300 million). The option value as a percentage of asset value does not change as long as the maturity, profitability ratio, and volatility remain constant for these tables.

Real Options Analysis Values (3-year maturity at 5% risk-free rate)

Volatility	Profitability Ratio (% in-the-money)									
	-99%	-90%	-80%	-70%	-60%	-50%	-40%	-30%	-20%	-10%
1%	0.00%	0.00%	0.00%	0.00%	0.00%	0.00%	0.00%	0.00%	0.00%	4.37%
3%	0.00%	0.00%	0.00%	0.00%	0.00%	0.00%	0.00%	0.00%	0.19%	4.92%
5%	0.00%	0.00%	0.00%	0.00%	0.00%	0.00%	0.00%	0.03%	1.00%	6.00%
7%	0.00%	0.00%	0.00%	0.00%	0.00%	0.00%	0.01%	0.24%	2.11%	7.23%
9%	0.00%	0.00%	0.00%	0.00%	0.00%	0.00%	0.07%	0.74%	3.35%	8.51%
11%	0.00%	0.00%	0.00%	0.00%	0.00%	0.02%	0.26%	1.49%	4.65%	9.81%
13%	0.00%	0.00%	0.00%	0.00%	0.00%	0.08%	0.62%	2.42%	5.99%	11.12%
15%	0.00%	0.00%	0.00%	0.00%	0.02%	0.22%	1.16%	3.47%	7.35%	12.44%
17%	0.00%	0.00%	0.00%	0.00%	0.06%	0.49%	1.86%	4.62%	8.72%	13.76%
19%	0.00%	0.00%	0.00%	0.01%	0.16%	0.88%	2.70%	5.84%	10.10%	15.08%
21%	0.00%	0.00%	0.00%	0.03%	0.33%	1.40%	3.65%	7.10%	11.48%	16.40%
23%	0.00%	0.00%	0.00%	0.08%	0.60%	2.05%	4.68%	8.40%	12.86%	17.72%
25%	0.00%	0.00%	0.01%	0.18%	0.96%	2.80%	5.80%	9.72%	14.25%	19.04%
27%	0.00%	0.00%	0.02%	0.32%	1.43%	3.66%	6.97%	11.07%	15.63%	20.35%
29%	0.00%	0.00%	0.05%	0.54%	1.99%	4.60%	8.18%	12.43%	17.00%	21.65%
31%	0.00%	0.00%	0.11%	0.83%	2.65%	5.61%	9.44%	13.79%	18.37%	22.96%
33%	0.00%	0.00%	0.19%	1.20%	3.40%	6.69%	10.73%	15.17%	19.74%	24.25%
35%	0.00%	0.01%	0.32%	1.65%	4.23%	7.82%	12.04%	16.55%	21.10%	25.54%
37%	0.00%	0.02%	0.50%	2.18%	5.14%	9.01%	13.38%	17.93%	22.46%	26.83%
39%	0.00%	0.04%	0.73%	2.80%	6.11%	10.23%	14.73%	19.31%	23.81%	28.10%
41%	0.00%	0.07%	1.03%	3.49%	7.15%	11.48%	16.09%	20.69%	25.15%	29.37%
43%	0.00%	0.12%	1.38%	4.26%	8.24%	12.77%	17.46%	22.07%	26.49%	30.64%
45%	0.00%	0.19%	1.81%	5.10%	9.38%	14.08%	18.83%	23.44%	27.81%	31.89%
47%	0.00%	0.28%	2.30%	6.00%	10.56%	15.40%	20.21%	24.81%	29.13%	33.14%
49%	0.00%	0.41%	2.87%	6.96%	11.77%	16.75%	21.59%	26.18%	30.44%	34.38%
51%	0.00%	0.58%	3.50%	7.97%	13.02%	18.10%	22.98%	27.53%	31.74%	35.61%
53%	0.00%	0.79%	4.20%	9.04%	14.29%	19.47%	24.36%	28.88%	33.03%	36.82%
55%	0.00%	1.05%	4.96%	10.15%	15.59%	20.84%	25.73%	30.22%	34.31%	38.03%
57%	0.00%	1.36%	5.78%	11.31%	16.91%	22.22%	27.11%	31.55%	35.58%	39.24%
59%	0.00%	1.72%	6.66%	12.49%	18.25%	23.60%	28.47%	32.88%	36.84%	40.43%
61%	0.00%	2.13%	7.59%	13.72%	19.60%	24.98%	29.84%	34.19%	38.09%	41.61%
63%	0.00%	2.60%	8.58%	14.97%	20.96%	26.36%	31.19%	35.49%	39.33%	42.77%
65%	0.01%	3.13%	9.61%	16.25%	22.33%	27.74%	32.54%	36.78%	40.56%	43.93%
67%	0.01%	3.72%	10.69%	17.55%	23.70%	29.12%	33.87%	38.06%	41.77%	45.08%
69%	0.02%	4.36%	11.81%	18.87%	25.08%	30.49%	35.20%	39.33%	42.98%	46.21%
71%	0.03%	5.05%	12.96%	20.20%	26.46%	31.85%	36.52%	40.59%	44.17%	47.34%
73%	0.05%	5.81%	14.15%	21.55%	27.84%	33.21%	37.83%	41.83%	45.35%	48.45%
75%	0.08%	6.61%	15.37%	22.91%	29.23%	34.56%	39.12%	43.06%	46.51%	49.55%
77%	0.11%	7.47%	16.62%	24.28%	30.60%	35.90%	40.40%	44.28%	47.66%	50.64%
79%	0.16%	8.38%	17.90%	25.65%	31.98%	37.23%	41.68%	45.49%	48.80%	51.71%
81%	0.21%	9.33%	19.19%	27.03%	33.35%	38.55%	42.93%	46.68%	49.93%	52.78%
83%	0.29%	10.33%	20.50%	28.41%	34.71%	39.86%	44.18%	47.86%	51.04%	53.83%
85%	0.38%	11.37%	21.83%	29.79%	36.06%	41.16%	45.41%	49.02%	52.14%	54.86%
87%	0.49%	12.45%	23.18%	31.17%	37.41%	42.45%	46.63%	50.17%	53.22%	55.89%
89%	0.62%	13.57%	24.53%	32.55%	38.74%	43.72%	47.83%	51.31%	54.30%	56.90%
91%	0.78%	14.72%	25.90%	33.93%	40.07%	44.98%	49.02%	52.43%	55.35%	57.89%
93%	0.97%	15.91%	27.27%	35.30%	41.38%	46.22%	50.20%	53.54%	56.40%	58.88%
95%	1.19%	17.12%	28.65%	36.66%	42.69%	47.46%	51.36%	54.63%	57.42%	59.85%
97%	1.44%	18.37%	30.03%	38.01%	43.98%	48.67%	52.50%	55.70%	58.44%	60.80%
99%	1.72%	19.63%	31.41%	39.36%	45.25%	49.87%	53.63%	56.77%	59.44%	61.75%
101%	2.04%	20.92%	32.79%	40.70%	46.52%	51.06%	54.74%	57.81%	60.42%	62.67%

Profitability Ratio (% in-the-money)

Volatility	0%	10%	20%	30%	40%	50%	60%	70%	80%	90%	100%
1%	13.93%	21.75%	28.27%	33.79%	38.52%	42.62%	46.21%	49.37%	52.18%	54.70%	56.96%
3%	13.93%	21.75%	28.27%	33.79%	38.52%	42.62%	46.21%	49.37%	52.18%	54.70%	56.96%
5%	14.06%	21.76%	28.27%	33.79%	38.52%	42.62%	46.21%	49.37%	52.18%	54.70%	56.96%
7%	14.51%	21.84%	28.28%	33.79%	38.52%	42.62%	46.21%	49.37%	52.18%	54.70%	56.96%
9%	15.22%	22.09%	28.35%	33.81%	38.52%	42.62%	46.21%	49.37%	52.18%	54.70%	56.96%
11%	16.10%	22.54%	28.54%	33.88%	38.55%	42.63%	46.21%	49.37%	52.18%	54.70%	56.96%
13%	17.08%	23.14%	28.86%	34.03%	38.62%	42.66%	46.22%	49.38%	52.19%	54.70%	56.96%
15%	18.13%	23.87%	29.32%	34.29%	38.76%	42.73%	46.26%	49.40%	52.19%	54.71%	56.97%
17%	19.22%	24.69%	29.88%	34.66%	38.99%	42.87%	46.34%	49.44%	52.22%	54.72%	56.98%
19%	20.35%	25.57%	30.53%	35.13%	39.31%	43.08%	46.48%	49.53%	52.28%	54.76%	57.00%
21%	21.50%	26.51%	31.26%	35.67%	39.71%	43.37%	46.68%	49.67%	52.38%	54.83%	57.05%
23%	22.67%	27.48%	32.05%	36.28%	40.18%	43.72%	46.95%	49.87%	52.52%	54.93%	57.12%
25%	23.84%	28.49%	32.88%	36.96%	40.71%	44.14%	47.27%	50.12%	52.72%	55.08%	57.24%
27%	25.02%	29.52%	33.75%	37.68%	41.30%	44.62%	47.66%	50.43%	52.96%	55.27%	57.39%
29%	26.21%	30.56%	34.65%	38.44%	41.94%	45.15%	48.09%	50.78%	53.25%	55.51%	57.58%
31%	27.40%	31.62%	35.57%	39.23%	42.61%	45.72%	48.57%	51.19%	53.59%	55.79%	57.82%
33%	28.59%	32.68%	36.51%	40.05%	43.32%	46.33%	49.09%	51.63%	53.97%	56.11%	58.09%
35%	29.78%	33.76%	37.46%	40.89%	44.06%	46.97%	49.65%	52.12%	54.38%	56.48%	58.41%
37%	30.96%	34.84%	38.43%	41.75%	44.82%	47.64%	50.24%	52.63%	54.84%	56.87%	58.75%
39%	32.15%	35.92%	39.41%	42.63%	45.60%	48.34%	50.85%	53.18%	55.32%	57.30%	59.13%
41%	33.33%	37.00%	40.39%	43.52%	46.40%	49.05%	51.49%	53.75%	55.83%	57.75%	59.54%
43%	34.50%	38.08%	41.38%	44.41%	47.21%	49.78%	52.15%	54.34%	56.36%	58.24%	59.97%
45%	35.67%	39.16%	42.37%	45.32%	48.03%	50.53%	52.83%	54.96%	56.92%	58.74%	60.43%
47%	36.83%	40.23%	43.36%	46.22%	48.86%	51.29%	53.52%	55.59%	57.50%	59.26%	60.90%
49%	37.99%	41.31%	44.35%	47.14%	49.70%	52.05%	54.23%	56.23%	58.09%	59.81%	61.40%
51%	39.14%	42.38%	45.34%	48.05%	50.54%	52.83%	54.94%	56.89%	58.69%	60.36%	61.92%
53%	40.28%	43.44%	46.33%	48.97%	51.39%	53.61%	55.66%	57.56%	59.31%	60.93%	62.44%
55%	41.42%	44.50%	47.31%	49.88%	52.24%	54.40%	56.39%	58.23%	59.94%	61.52%	62.99%
57%	42.55%	45.55%	48.29%	50.79%	53.08%	55.19%	57.13%	58.92%	60.57%	62.11%	63.54%
59%	43.66%	46.60%	49.27%	51.70%	53.93%	55.98%	57.87%	59.61%	61.22%	62.71%	64.10%
61%	44.77%	47.64%	50.24%	52.61%	54.78%	56.77%	58.61%	60.30%	61.86%	63.32%	64.67%
63%	45.87%	48.67%	51.21%	53.52%	55.63%	57.57%	59.35%	60.99%	62.52%	63.93%	65.25%
65%	46.96%	49.69%	52.17%	54.42%	56.47%	58.36%	60.09%	61.69%	63.17%	64.55%	65.83%
67%	48.04%	50.71%	53.12%	55.31%	57.31%	59.15%	60.84%	62.39%	63.83%	65.17%	66.41%
69%	49.11%	51.71%	54.06%	56.20%	58.15%	59.94%	61.58%	63.09%	64.49%	65.79%	67.00%
71%	50.17%	52.71%	55.00%	57.08%	58.98%	60.72%	62.32%	63.79%	65.15%	66.42%	67.60%
73%	51.22%	53.70%	55.93%	57.96%	59.81%	61.50%	63.06%	64.49%	65.82%	67.05%	68.19%
75%	52.25%	54.67%	56.85%	58.83%	60.63%	62.28%	63.79%	65.18%	66.47%	67.67%	68.79%
77%	53.28%	55.64%	57.77%	59.69%	61.45%	63.05%	64.52%	65.88%	67.13%	68.30%	69.38%
79%	54.29%	56.60%	58.67%	60.55%	62.25%	63.81%	65.25%	66.57%	67.79%	68.92%	69.97%
81%	55.30%	57.54%	59.57%	61.39%	63.06%	64.57%	65.97%	67.25%	68.44%	69.54%	70.57%
83%	56.29%	58.48%	60.45%	62.23%	63.85%	65.33%	66.68%	67.93%	69.09%	70.16%	71.16%
85%	57.27%	59.41%	61.33%	63.06%	64.64%	66.07%	67.39%	68.61%	69.73%	70.78%	71.75%
87%	58.23%	60.32%	62.19%	63.88%	65.41%	66.81%	68.10%	69.28%	70.37%	71.39%	72.33%
89%	59.19%	61.22%	63.05%	64.69%	66.18%	67.55%	68.80%	69.95%	71.01%	72.00%	72.91%
91%	60.13%	62.11%	63.89%	65.49%	66.95%	68.27%	69.49%	70.61%	71.64%	72.60%	73.49%
93%	61.06%	62.99%	64.72%	66.28%	67.70%	68.99%	70.17%	71.26%	72.27%	73.20%	74.06%
95%	61.97%	63.86%	65.55%	67.07%	68.44%	69.70%	70.85%	71.91%	72.88%	73.79%	74.63%
97%	62.88%	64.72%	66.36%	67.84%	69.18%	70.40%	71.52%	72.55%	73.50%	74.38%	75.20%
99%	63.77%	65.56%	67.16%	68.60%	69.90%	71.09%	72.18%	73.18%	74.10%	74.96%	75.76%
101%	64.65%	66.39%	67.95%	69.35%	70.62%	71.77%	72.83%	73.81%	74.70%	75.54%	76.31%

Real Options Analysis Values (5-year maturity at 5% risk-free rate)

Volatility	Profitability Ratio (% in-the-money)									
	-99%	-90%	-80%	-70%	-60%	-50%	-40%	-30%	-20%	-10%
1%	0.00%	0.00%	0.00%	0.00%	0.00%	0.00%	0.00%	0.00%	2.77%	13.47%
3%	0.00%	0.00%	0.00%	0.00%	0.00%	0.00%	0.00%	0.17%	4.17%	13.50%
5%	0.00%	0.00%	0.00%	0.00%	0.00%	0.00%	0.04%	1.07%	5.85%	13.95%
7%	0.00%	0.00%	0.00%	0.00%	0.00%	0.01%	0.35%	2.43%	7.57%	14.86%
9%	0.00%	0.00%	0.00%	0.00%	0.00%	0.12%	1.05%	3.99%	9.30%	16.05%
11%	0.00%	0.00%	0.00%	0.00%	0.04%	0.43%	2.07%	5.66%	11.04%	17.39%
13%	0.00%	0.00%	0.00%	0.01%	0.15%	1.00%	3.32%	7.38%	12.78%	18.81%
15%	0.00%	0.00%	0.00%	0.03%	0.41%	1.80%	4.74%	9.14%	14.51%	20.28%
17%	0.00%	0.00%	0.00%	0.12%	0.84%	2.82%	6.27%	10.91%	16.24%	21.78%
19%	0.00%	0.00%	0.02%	0.29%	1.46%	4.01%	7.88%	12.69%	17.96%	23.31%
21%	0.00%	0.00%	0.05%	0.58%	2.26%	5.34%	9.56%	14.47%	19.67%	24.84%
23%	0.00%	0.00%	0.13%	1.00%	3.22%	6.78%	11.27%	16.26%	21.38%	26.39%
25%	0.00%	0.00%	0.26%	1.57%	4.33%	8.30%	13.01%	18.04%	23.07%	27.93%
27%	0.00%	0.01%	0.48%	2.29%	5.57%	9.90%	14.77%	19.81%	24.76%	29.47%
29%	0.00%	0.04%	0.80%	3.15%	6.92%	11.55%	16.55%	21.58%	26.43%	31.01%
31%	0.00%	0.08%	1.23%	4.14%	8.35%	13.24%	18.33%	23.33%	28.10%	32.54%
33%	0.00%	0.16%	1.77%	5.24%	9.87%	14.96%	20.11%	25.08%	29.75%	34.07%
35%	0.00%	0.28%	2.43%	6.46%	11.44%	16.71%	21.90%	26.81%	31.38%	35.59%
37%	0.00%	0.46%	3.21%	7.77%	13.07%	18.48%	23.67%	28.53%	33.00%	37.09%
39%	0.00%	0.70%	4.11%	9.17%	14.74%	20.25%	25.45%	30.24%	34.61%	38.59%
41%	0.00%	1.03%	5.11%	10.64%	16.45%	22.03%	27.21%	31.93%	36.20%	40.07%
43%	0.00%	1.44%	6.22%	12.18%	18.18%	23.82%	28.96%	33.60%	37.78%	41.54%
45%	0.00%	1.94%	7.42%	13.77%	19.94%	25.60%	30.70%	35.26%	39.34%	42.99%
47%	0.00%	2.53%	8.71%	15.41%	21.71%	27.38%	32.42%	36.90%	40.88%	44.43%
49%	0.01%	3.23%	10.07%	17.09%	23.48%	29.15%	34.13%	38.52%	42.40%	45.86%
51%	0.01%	4.02%	11.51%	18.79%	25.27%	30.91%	35.82%	40.12%	43.91%	47.26%
53%	0.03%	4.90%	13.01%	20.53%	27.05%	32.66%	37.50%	41.71%	45.40%	48.65%
55%	0.05%	5.88%	14.57%	22.28%	28.83%	34.39%	39.15%	43.27%	46.86%	50.03%
57%	0.08%	6.95%	16.17%	24.05%	30.61%	36.11%	40.79%	44.81%	48.31%	51.38%
59%	0.12%	8.10%	17.82%	25.83%	32.38%	37.81%	42.40%	46.33%	49.74%	52.72%
61%	0.19%	9.33%	19.50%	27.61%	34.13%	39.50%	43.99%	47.83%	51.14%	54.04%
63%	0.28%	10.64%	21.21%	29.39%	35.88%	41.16%	45.56%	49.30%	52.52%	55.33%
65%	0.39%	12.02%	22.95%	31.17%	37.61%	42.80%	47.11%	50.76%	53.89%	56.61%
67%	0.55%	13.46%	24.70%	32.95%	39.32%	44.42%	48.64%	52.19%	55.23%	57.87%
69%	0.74%	14.96%	26.47%	34.72%	41.01%	46.02%	50.14%	53.59%	56.55%	59.11%
71%	0.99%	16.51%	28.25%	36.48%	42.69%	47.60%	51.61%	54.97%	57.84%	60.32%
73%	1.28%	18.11%	30.03%	38.22%	44.34%	49.15%	53.06%	56.33%	59.11%	61.52%
75%	1.63%	19.75%	31.81%	39.95%	45.97%	50.67%	54.49%	57.67%	60.36%	62.69%
77%	2.04%	21.42%	33.60%	41.66%	47.58%	52.17%	55.89%	58.97%	61.59%	63.85%
79%	2.52%	23.12%	35.37%	43.35%	49.16%	53.65%	57.26%	60.26%	62.79%	64.98%
81%	3.06%	24.85%	37.14%	45.03%	50.71%	55.10%	58.61%	61.52%	63.97%	66.09%
83%	3.68%	26.60%	38.90%	46.67%	52.25%	56.52%	59.93%	62.75%	65.13%	67.17%
85%	4.37%	28.36%	40.64%	48.30%	53.75%	57.91%	61.23%	63.96%	66.26%	68.24%
87%	5.13%	30.13%	42.37%	49.90%	55.23%	59.27%	62.50%	65.14%	67.37%	69.28%
89%	5.97%	31.92%	44.08%	51.48%	56.68%	60.61%	63.74%	66.30%	68.46%	70.30%
91%	6.88%	33.70%	45.77%	53.02%	58.10%	61.92%	64.95%	67.44%	69.52%	71.30%
93%	7.87%	35.48%	47.43%	54.55%	59.49%	63.20%	66.14%	68.54%	70.55%	72.27%
95%	8.93%	37.26%	49.08%	56.04%	60.85%	64.46%	67.30%	69.62%	71.57%	73.23%
97%	10.06%	39.03%	50.70%	57.50%	62.18%	65.68%	68.44%	70.68%	72.56%	74.16%
99%	11.26%	40.79%	52.29%	58.94%	63.49%	66.88%	69.54%	71.71%	73.52%	75.07%
101%	12.52%	42.54%	53.86%	60.34%	64.76%	68.05%	70.62%	72.72%	74.47%	75.95%

					Profitability Ratio (% in-the-money)						
Volatility	0%	10%	20%	30%	40%	50%	60%	70%	80%	90%	100%
1%	22.12%	29.20%	35.10%	40.09%	44.37%	48.08%	51.32%	54.19%	56.73%	59.01%	61.06%
3%	22.12%	29.20%	35.10%	40.09%	44.37%	48.08%	51.32%	54.19%	56.73%	59.01%	61.06%
5%	22.16%	29.20%	35.10%	40.09%	44.37%	48.08%	51.32%	54.19%	56.73%	59.01%	61.06%
7%	22.44%	29.26%	35.11%	40.09%	44.37%	48.08%	51.32%	54.19%	56.73%	59.01%	61.06%
9%	23.03%	29.50%	35.19%	40.12%	44.38%	48.08%	51.33%	54.19%	56.73%	59.01%	61.06%
11%	23.86%	29.95%	35.41%	40.22%	44.42%	48.10%	51.33%	54.19%	56.73%	59.01%	61.06%
13%	24.87%	30.60%	35.80%	40.44%	44.55%	48.17%	51.37%	54.21%	56.74%	59.02%	61.06%
15%	26.00%	31.40%	36.35%	40.80%	44.77%	48.31%	51.46%	54.26%	56.78%	59.04%	61.08%
17%	27.21%	32.33%	37.03%	41.29%	45.11%	48.55%	51.62%	54.37%	56.85%	59.09%	61.11%
19%	28.49%	33.35%	37.82%	41.89%	45.57%	48.88%	51.86%	54.56%	56.98%	59.18%	61.18%
21%	29.80%	34.43%	38.70%	42.59%	46.11%	49.31%	52.20%	54.81%	57.18%	59.34%	61.30%
23%	31.14%	35.57%	39.64%	43.36%	46.75%	49.82%	52.61%	55.14%	57.45%	59.55%	61.47%
25%	32.50%	36.75%	40.64%	44.21%	47.45%	50.41%	53.10%	55.55%	57.78%	59.83%	61.70%
27%	33.88%	37.95%	41.69%	45.10%	48.22%	51.06%	53.65%	56.02%	58.18%	60.16%	61.99%
29%	35.26%	39.18%	42.77%	46.05%	49.04%	51.77%	54.26%	56.55%	58.64%	60.56%	62.33%
31%	36.65%	40.42%	43.87%	47.02%	49.89%	52.52%	54.92%	57.13%	59.15%	61.01%	62.72%
33%	38.04%	41.68%	44.99%	48.02%	50.79%	53.31%	55.63%	57.75%	59.70%	61.50%	63.16%
35%	39.43%	42.94%	46.13%	49.05%	51.71%	54.14%	56.37%	58.41%	60.30%	62.03%	63.64%
37%	40.81%	44.20%	47.28%	50.09%	52.65%	54.99%	57.14%	59.11%	60.93%	62.60%	64.15%
39%	42.19%	45.46%	48.43%	51.14%	53.60%	55.86%	57.93%	59.83%	61.58%	63.20%	64.70%
41%	43.56%	46.72%	49.59%	52.20%	54.58%	56.75%	58.75%	60.58%	62.27%	63.83%	65.28%
43%	44.92%	47.98%	50.75%	53.26%	55.56%	57.65%	59.58%	61.34%	62.98%	64.48%	65.88%
45%	46.27%	49.23%	51.90%	54.33%	56.54%	58.57%	60.42%	62.13%	63.70%	65.15%	66.50%
47%	47.61%	50.47%	53.06%	55.40%	57.53%	59.48%	61.27%	62.92%	64.44%	65.84%	67.14%
49%	48.94%	51.71%	54.20%	56.47%	58.53%	60.41%	62.13%	63.72%	65.19%	66.54%	67.80%
51%	50.25%	52.93%	55.34%	57.53%	59.52%	61.33%	63.00%	64.53%	65.94%	67.25%	68.47%
53%	51.55%	54.14%	56.48%	58.59%	60.51%	62.26%	63.87%	65.34%	66.71%	67.97%	69.14%
55%	52.84%	55.34%	57.60%	59.64%	61.49%	63.18%	64.73%	66.16%	67.48%	68.70%	69.83%
57%	54.10%	56.53%	58.71%	60.68%	62.47%	64.11%	65.60%	66.98%	68.25%	69.42%	70.52%
59%	55.36%	57.71%	59.82%	61.72%	63.45%	65.02%	66.47%	67.79%	69.02%	70.15%	71.21%
61%	56.59%	58.87%	60.90%	62.74%	64.41%	65.93%	67.33%	68.61%	69.79%	70.89%	71.90%
63%	57.81%	60.01%	61.98%	63.76%	65.37%	66.84%	68.18%	69.42%	70.56%	71.62%	72.60%
65%	59.01%	61.14%	63.04%	64.76%	66.32%	67.73%	69.03%	70.22%	71.32%	72.34%	73.29%
67%	60.19%	62.25%	64.09%	65.75%	67.25%	68.62%	69.87%	71.02%	72.09%	73.07%	73.98%
69%	61.36%	63.35%	65.13%	66.73%	68.18%	69.50%	70.71%	71.82%	72.84%	73.79%	74.67%
71%	62.50%	64.43%	66.15%	67.69%	69.09%	70.37%	71.53%	72.60%	73.59%	74.50%	75.35%
73%	63.63%	65.49%	67.15%	68.64%	69.99%	71.22%	72.35%	73.38%	74.33%	75.21%	76.03%
75%	64.73%	66.53%	68.13%	69.58%	70.88%	72.07%	73.15%	74.15%	75.06%	75.91%	76.70%
77%	65.82%	67.56%	69.10%	70.50%	71.75%	72.90%	73.94%	74.90%	75.79%	76.61%	77.37%
79%	66.88%	68.56%	70.06%	71.40%	72.61%	73.72%	74.72%	75.65%	76.50%	77.29%	78.03%
81%	67.93%	69.55%	70.99%	72.29%	73.46%	74.52%	75.49%	76.39%	77.21%	77.97%	78.68%
83%	68.95%	70.52%	71.91%	73.16%	74.29%	75.31%	76.25%	77.11%	77.90%	78.64%	79.32%
85%	69.96%	71.47%	72.81%	74.02%	75.10%	76.09%	76.99%	77.82%	78.59%	79.29%	79.95%
87%	70.94%	72.40%	73.69%	74.86%	75.90%	76.86%	77.73%	78.52%	79.26%	79.94%	80.57%
89%	71.90%	73.31%	74.56%	75.68%	76.69%	77.61%	78.44%	79.21%	79.92%	80.57%	81.18%
91%	72.84%	74.20%	75.41%	76.48%	77.46%	78.34%	79.15%	79.89%	80.57%	81.20%	81.78%
93%	73.76%	75.07%	76.23%	77.27%	78.21%	79.06%	79.84%	80.55%	81.20%	81.81%	82.37%
95%	74.66%	75.93%	77.04%	78.05%	78.95%	79.77%	80.51%	81.20%	81.83%	82.41%	82.95%
97%	75.54%	76.76%	77.84%	78.80%	79.67%	80.46%	81.17%	81.83%	82.44%	83.00%	83.52%
99%	76.40%	77.57%	78.61%	79.54%	80.37%	81.13%	81.82%	82.45%	83.04%	83.58%	84.08%
101%	77.24%	78.37%	79.36%	80.26%	81.06%	81.79%	82.45%	83.06%	83.62%	84.14%	84.62%

Real Options Analysis Values (7-year maturity at 5% risk-free rate)

Volatility	Profitability Ratio (% in-the-money)									
	-99%	-90%	-80%	-70%	-60%	-50%	-40%	-30%	-20%	-10%
1%	0.00%	0.00%	0.00%	0.00%	0.00%	0.00%	0.00%	0.76%	11.91%	21.70%
3%	0.00%	0.00%	0.00%	0.00%	0.00%	0.00%	0.07%	2.85%	12.09%	21.70%
5%	0.00%	0.00%	0.00%	0.00%	0.00%	0.02%	0.78%	4.96%	13.03%	21.85%
7%	0.00%	0.00%	0.00%	0.00%	0.01%	0.27%	2.13%	7.07%	14.46%	22.41%
9%	0.00%	0.00%	0.00%	0.00%	0.09%	0.94%	3.83%	9.18%	16.10%	23.36%
11%	0.00%	0.00%	0.00%	0.02%	0.38%	2.01%	5.71%	11.28%	17.85%	24.56%
13%	0.00%	0.00%	0.00%	0.11%	0.94%	3.39%	7.70%	13.37%	19.65%	25.93%
15%	0.00%	0.00%	0.01%	0.34%	1.79%	4.99%	9.74%	15.45%	21.49%	27.41%
17%	0.00%	0.00%	0.06%	0.75%	2.91%	6.75%	11.82%	17.52%	23.34%	28.95%
19%	0.00%	0.00%	0.18%	1.38%	4.25%	8.63%	13.92%	19.58%	25.20%	30.54%
21%	0.00%	0.01%	0.41%	2.23%	5.78%	10.59%	16.03%	21.62%	27.06%	32.16%
23%	0.00%	0.03%	0.77%	3.29%	7.45%	12.61%	18.14%	23.65%	28.91%	33.80%
25%	0.00%	0.08%	1.30%	4.53%	9.24%	14.66%	20.25%	25.67%	30.76%	35.45%
27%	0.00%	0.17%	2.00%	5.94%	11.12%	16.75%	22.35%	27.66%	32.59%	37.10%
29%	0.00%	0.33%	2.87%	7.49%	13.07%	18.85%	24.43%	29.64%	34.42%	38.75%
31%	0.00%	0.59%	3.91%	9.17%	15.08%	20.96%	26.50%	31.60%	36.22%	40.40%
33%	0.00%	0.94%	5.11%	10.95%	17.13%	23.07%	28.56%	33.54%	38.02%	42.04%
35%	0.00%	1.43%	6.45%	12.81%	19.20%	25.18%	30.59%	35.45%	39.79%	43.67%
37%	0.00%	2.04%	7.93%	14.74%	21.30%	27.27%	32.61%	37.34%	41.54%	45.28%
39%	0.00%	2.79%	9.52%	16.73%	23.41%	29.36%	34.60%	39.21%	43.27%	46.88%
41%	0.01%	3.68%	11.22%	18.76%	25.52%	31.42%	36.56%	41.05%	44.98%	48.46%
43%	0.02%	4.70%	13.00%	20.82%	27.63%	33.47%	38.50%	42.86%	46.67%	50.02%
45%	0.04%	5.86%	14.87%	22.91%	29.73%	35.50%	40.42%	44.65%	48.33%	51.56%
47%	0.07%	7.14%	16.79%	25.01%	31.82%	37.50%	42.30%	46.41%	49.97%	53.08%
49%	0.12%	8.55%	18.77%	27.12%	33.89%	39.47%	44.16%	48.14%	51.58%	54.58%
51%	0.20%	10.06%	20.80%	29.23%	35.95%	41.42%	45.98%	49.84%	53.17%	56.06%
53%	0.32%	11.68%	22.85%	31.34%	37.98%	43.34%	47.77%	51.52%	54.72%	57.51%
55%	0.48%	13.38%	24.94%	33.43%	39.98%	45.22%	49.53%	53.16%	56.25%	58.94%
57%	0.70%	15.17%	27.03%	35.52%	41.96%	47.08%	51.26%	54.77%	57.75%	60.34%
59%	0.99%	17.03%	29.14%	37.58%	43.91%	48.90%	52.96%	56.34%	59.22%	61.71%
61%	1.34%	18.95%	31.25%	39.62%	45.83%	50.69%	54.62%	57.89%	60.67%	63.06%
63%	1.78%	20.92%	33.36%	41.64%	47.72%	52.44%	56.25%	59.40%	62.08%	64.38%
65%	2.31%	22.93%	35.46%	43.63%	49.57%	54.15%	57.84%	60.88%	63.46%	65.67%
67%	2.93%	24.98%	37.55%	45.59%	51.38%	55.83%	59.39%	62.33%	64.81%	66.93%
69%	3.65%	27.06%	39.62%	47.52%	53.16%	57.47%	60.91%	63.74%	66.13%	68.17%
71%	4.47%	29.15%	41.66%	49.42%	54.91%	59.08%	62.40%	65.12%	67.41%	69.37%
73%	5.40%	31.25%	43.69%	51.28%	56.61%	60.65%	63.85%	66.47%	68.67%	70.55%
75%	6.44%	33.36%	45.68%	53.10%	58.27%	62.17%	65.26%	67.78%	69.89%	71.70%
77%	7.58%	35.47%	47.65%	54.88%	59.90%	63.66%	66.63%	69.06%	71.09%	72.82%
79%	8.82%	37.58%	49.58%	56.62%	61.48%	65.12%	67.97%	70.30%	72.25%	73.91%
81%	10.16%	39.67%	51.47%	58.33%	63.03%	66.53%	69.28%	71.51%	73.38%	74.97%
83%	11.60%	41.74%	53.33%	59.99%	64.53%	67.90%	70.54%	72.69%	74.48%	76.00%
85%	13.13%	43.80%	55.15%	61.61%	65.99%	69.24%	71.77%	73.83%	75.54%	77.00%
87%	14.74%	45.83%	56.93%	63.19%	67.42%	70.54%	72.97%	74.94%	76.58%	77.97%
89%	16.43%	47.83%	58.67%	64.73%	68.80%	71.79%	74.13%	76.01%	77.58%	78.91%
91%	18.20%	49.80%	60.37%	66.22%	70.14%	73.02%	75.25%	77.06%	78.56%	79.83%
93%	20.03%	51.74%	62.02%	67.67%	71.44%	74.20%	76.34%	78.07%	79.50%	80.71%
95%	21.93%	53.64%	63.63%	69.08%	72.70%	75.34%	77.39%	79.05%	80.41%	81.57%
97%	23.87%	55.50%	65.19%	70.44%	73.92%	76.45%	78.41%	79.99%	81.30%	82.40%
99%	25.86%	57.32%	66.71%	71.77%	75.10%	77.52%	79.40%	80.90%	82.15%	83.20%
101%	27.88%	59.10%	68.19%	73.05%	76.24%	78.56%	80.35%	81.79%	82.98%	83.98%

	Profitability Ratio (% in-the-money)										
Volatility	0%	10%	20%	30%	40%	50%	60%	70%	80%	90%	100%
1%	29.53%	35.94%	41.28%	45.79%	49.67%	53.02%	55.96%	58.55%	60.85%	62.91%	64.77%
3%	29.53%	35.94%	41.28%	45.79%	49.67%	53.02%	55.96%	58.55%	60.85%	62.91%	64.77%
5%	29.55%	35.94%	41.28%	45.79%	49.67%	53.02%	55.96%	58.55%	60.85%	62.91%	64.77%
7%	29.71%	35.98%	41.28%	45.79%	49.67%	53.02%	55.96%	58.55%	60.85%	62.91%	64.77%
9%	30.16%	36.16%	41.36%	45.82%	49.67%	53.02%	55.96%	58.55%	60.85%	62.91%	64.77%
11%	30.88%	36.57%	41.57%	45.93%	49.73%	53.05%	55.97%	58.55%	60.85%	62.91%	64.77%
13%	31.84%	37.19%	41.96%	46.17%	49.87%	53.14%	56.02%	58.58%	60.87%	62.92%	64.77%
15%	32.95%	38.00%	42.53%	46.56%	50.14%	53.31%	56.14%	58.66%	60.92%	62.96%	64.80%
17%	34.18%	38.95%	43.24%	47.09%	50.53%	53.60%	56.35%	58.82%	61.04%	63.04%	64.86%
19%	35.49%	40.01%	44.08%	47.75%	51.04%	54.00%	56.66%	59.06%	61.22%	63.18%	64.97%
21%	36.87%	41.15%	45.02%	48.52%	51.67%	54.51%	57.07%	59.38%	61.49%	63.40%	65.14%
23%	38.28%	42.36%	46.04%	49.37%	52.38%	55.10%	57.56%	59.80%	61.83%	63.69%	65.38%
25%	39.73%	43.61%	47.13%	50.30%	53.18%	55.78%	58.14%	60.29%	62.25%	64.05%	65.69%
27%	41.20%	44.90%	48.26%	51.29%	54.03%	56.53%	58.79%	60.86%	62.75%	64.48%	66.06%
29%	42.68%	46.22%	49.42%	52.32%	54.94%	57.33%	59.50%	61.48%	63.30%	64.96%	66.50%
31%	44.16%	47.55%	50.62%	53.38%	55.90%	58.18%	60.26%	62.16%	63.91%	65.51%	66.99%
33%	45.65%	48.90%	51.83%	54.48%	56.88%	59.07%	61.06%	62.88%	64.56%	66.10%	67.52%
35%	47.14%	50.25%	53.06%	55.59%	57.89%	59.98%	61.90%	63.65%	65.25%	66.73%	68.10%
37%	48.61%	51.60%	54.29%	56.72%	58.92%	60.93%	62.76%	64.44%	65.98%	67.40%	68.71%
39%	50.08%	52.95%	55.53%	57.86%	59.97%	61.89%	63.64%	65.25%	66.73%	68.10%	69.36%
41%	51.54%	54.30%	56.77%	59.00%	61.02%	62.86%	64.55%	66.09%	67.51%	68.82%	70.03%
43%	52.99%	55.63%	58.01%	60.15%	62.08%	63.85%	65.46%	66.94%	68.30%	69.56%	70.72%
45%	54.42%	56.96%	59.24%	61.29%	63.15%	64.84%	66.38%	67.80%	69.11%	70.31%	71.43%
47%	55.83%	58.27%	60.46%	62.43%	64.21%	65.83%	67.31%	68.67%	69.92%	71.08%	72.15%
49%	57.22%	59.57%	61.67%	63.56%	65.27%	66.82%	68.24%	69.54%	70.74%	71.85%	72.88%
51%	58.60%	60.85%	62.87%	64.68%	66.32%	67.81%	69.17%	70.42%	71.57%	72.63%	73.62%
53%	59.95%	62.12%	64.05%	65.79%	67.36%	68.79%	70.09%	71.29%	72.39%	73.41%	74.36%
55%	61.29%	63.37%	65.22%	66.89%	68.39%	69.76%	71.01%	72.16%	73.22%	74.20%	75.10%
57%	62.60%	64.59%	66.37%	67.97%	69.42%	70.73%	71.93%	73.03%	74.04%	74.98%	75.85%
59%	63.88%	65.80%	67.51%	69.04%	70.43%	71.68%	72.83%	73.89%	74.86%	75.75%	76.59%
61%	65.14%	66.99%	68.62%	70.09%	71.42%	72.63%	73.73%	74.74%	75.67%	76.53%	77.32%
63%	66.38%	68.15%	69.72%	71.13%	72.40%	73.56%	74.61%	75.58%	76.47%	77.29%	78.05%
65%	67.59%	69.29%	70.80%	72.15%	73.37%	74.47%	75.48%	76.41%	77.26%	78.05%	78.78%
67%	68.78%	70.41%	71.85%	73.15%	74.31%	75.37%	76.34%	77.22%	78.04%	78.80%	79.50%
69%	69.94%	71.50%	72.88%	74.12%	75.24%	76.26%	77.18%	78.03%	78.81%	79.53%	80.20%
71%	71.07%	72.57%	73.90%	75.08%	76.15%	77.12%	78.01%	78.82%	79.57%	80.26%	80.90%
73%	72.18%	73.61%	74.88%	76.02%	77.04%	77.97%	78.82%	79.60%	80.31%	80.97%	81.58%
75%	73.26%	74.63%	75.85%	76.94%	77.92%	78.80%	79.61%	80.36%	81.04%	81.67%	82.26%
77%	74.31%	75.63%	76.79%	77.83%	78.77%	79.62%	80.39%	81.10%	81.75%	82.36%	82.92%
79%	75.34%	76.60%	77.71%	78.71%	79.60%	80.41%	81.15%	81.83%	82.45%	83.03%	83.57%
81%	76.34%	77.54%	78.61%	79.56%	80.41%	81.19%	81.89%	82.54%	83.14%	83.69%	84.20%
83%	77.31%	78.46%	79.48%	80.39%	81.20%	81.94%	82.62%	83.24%	83.81%	84.33%	84.82%
85%	78.25%	79.35%	80.33%	81.19%	81.97%	82.68%	83.32%	83.91%	84.46%	84.96%	85.42%
87%	79.17%	80.22%	81.15%	81.98%	82.72%	83.40%	84.01%	84.58%	85.09%	85.57%	86.01%
89%	80.06%	81.06%	81.95%	82.74%	83.45%	84.09%	84.68%	85.22%	85.71%	86.17%	86.59%
91%	80.92%	81.88%	82.73%	83.48%	84.16%	84.77%	85.33%	85.84%	86.31%	86.75%	87.15%
93%	81.76%	82.67%	83.48%	84.20%	84.84%	85.43%	85.96%	86.45%	86.90%	87.31%	87.70%
95%	82.57%	83.44%	84.21%	84.89%	85.51%	86.07%	86.57%	87.04%	87.47%	87.86%	88.23%
97%	83.35%	84.18%	84.92%	85.57%	86.15%	86.69%	87.17%	87.61%	88.02%	88.39%	88.74%
99%	84.11%	84.90%	85.60%	86.22%	86.78%	87.28%	87.74%	88.16%	88.55%	88.91%	89.24%
101%	84.84%	85.60%	86.26%	86.85%	87.38%	87.86%	88.30%	88.70%	89.07%	89.41%	89.72%

Real Options Analysis Values (10-year maturity at 5% risk-free rate)

				Profitability Ratio (% in-the-money)						
Volatility	-99%	-90%	-80%	-70%	-60%	-50%	-40%	-30%	-20%	-10%
1%	0.00%	0.00%	0.00%	0.00%	0.00%	0.00%	0.80%	13.35%	24.18%	32.61%
3%	0.00%	0.00%	0.00%	0.00%	0.00%	0.08%	3.28%	13.61%	24.19%	32.61%
5%	0.00%	0.00%	0.00%	0.00%	0.03%	0.93%	5.81%	14.81%	24.41%	32.63%
7%	0.00%	0.00%	0.00%	0.01%	0.32%	2.56%	8.33%	16.56%	25.15%	32.88%
9%	0.00%	0.00%	0.00%	0.09%	1.11%	4.62%	10.84%	18.54%	26.34%	33.48%
11%	0.00%	0.00%	0.01%	0.39%	2.39%	6.89%	13.35%	20.63%	27.82%	34.42%
13%	0.00%	0.00%	0.07%	1.02%	4.06%	9.29%	15.84%	22.77%	29.47%	35.60%
15%	0.00%	0.00%	0.26%	2.01%	6.01%	11.75%	18.31%	24.95%	31.23%	36.96%
17%	0.00%	0.01%	0.65%	3.33%	8.15%	14.25%	20.77%	27.13%	33.06%	38.44%
19%	0.00%	0.05%	1.28%	4.93%	10.43%	16.77%	23.20%	29.32%	34.94%	40.00%
21%	0.00%	0.16%	2.18%	6.76%	12.81%	19.29%	25.61%	31.50%	36.83%	41.62%
23%	0.00%	0.36%	3.34%	8.78%	15.25%	21.81%	28.00%	33.66%	38.74%	43.28%
25%	0.00%	0.71%	4.74%	10.95%	17.74%	24.31%	30.36%	35.81%	40.66%	44.96%
27%	0.00%	1.23%	6.37%	13.24%	20.25%	26.80%	32.69%	37.93%	42.56%	46.66%
29%	0.00%	1.94%	8.18%	15.61%	22.77%	29.26%	34.99%	40.03%	44.46%	48.36%
31%	0.00%	2.85%	10.16%	18.04%	25.30%	31.69%	37.26%	42.11%	46.34%	50.06%
33%	0.01%	3.97%	12.28%	20.52%	27.81%	34.09%	39.49%	44.15%	48.20%	51.74%
35%	0.02%	5.29%	14.51%	23.03%	30.30%	36.46%	41.69%	46.17%	50.04%	53.42%
37%	0.04%	6.79%	16.84%	25.54%	32.77%	38.79%	43.84%	48.15%	51.86%	55.08%
39%	0.09%	8.48%	19.23%	28.07%	35.21%	41.08%	45.96%	50.10%	53.64%	56.72%
41%	0.18%	10.32%	21.68%	30.58%	37.62%	43.32%	48.04%	52.01%	55.40%	58.33%
43%	0.31%	12.30%	24.16%	33.08%	40.00%	45.53%	50.07%	53.88%	57.12%	59.92%
45%	0.51%	14.41%	26.67%	35.56%	42.33%	47.69%	52.07%	55.71%	58.81%	61.48%
47%	0.79%	16.62%	29.20%	38.01%	44.62%	49.81%	54.01%	57.51%	60.47%	63.02%
49%	1.17%	18.92%	31.72%	40.43%	46.86%	51.87%	55.91%	59.26%	62.09%	64.52%
51%	1.67%	21.30%	34.23%	42.80%	49.06%	53.89%	57.77%	60.97%	63.67%	65.99%
53%	2.29%	23.73%	36.73%	45.14%	51.20%	55.86%	59.58%	62.64%	65.22%	67.42%
55%	3.05%	26.20%	39.20%	47.43%	53.30%	57.78%	61.34%	64.27%	66.72%	68.82%
57%	3.95%	28.70%	41.64%	49.67%	55.34%	59.64%	63.06%	65.85%	68.19%	70.19%
59%	5.01%	31.22%	44.04%	51.85%	57.33%	61.46%	64.72%	67.39%	69.62%	71.52%
61%	6.21%	33.74%	46.40%	53.99%	59.26%	63.22%	66.34%	68.88%	71.00%	72.81%
63%	7.57%	36.26%	48.72%	56.07%	61.14%	64.93%	67.91%	70.33%	72.35%	74.06%
65%	9.07%	38.76%	50.98%	58.09%	62.96%	66.59%	69.43%	71.73%	73.65%	75.28%
67%	10.72%	41.24%	53.19%	60.06%	64.73%	68.19%	70.90%	73.09%	74.91%	76.46%
69%	12.50%	43.70%	55.35%	61.97%	66.44%	69.75%	72.32%	74.41%	76.14%	77.61%
71%	14.41%	46.11%	57.45%	63.82%	68.10%	71.25%	73.70%	75.68%	77.32%	78.71%
73%	16.43%	48.49%	59.49%	65.60%	69.69%	72.70%	75.02%	76.90%	78.46%	79.78%
75%	18.56%	50.82%	61.47%	67.33%	71.24%	74.09%	76.30%	78.09%	79.56%	80.81%
77%	20.78%	53.10%	63.39%	69.00%	72.72%	75.44%	77.54%	79.22%	80.62%	81.80%
79%	23.08%	55.32%	65.25%	70.61%	74.16%	76.73%	78.72%	80.32%	81.64%	82.76%
81%	25.44%	57.49%	67.04%	72.16%	75.53%	77.98%	79.86%	81.37%	82.62%	83.68%
83%	27.86%	59.59%	68.77%	73.66%	76.86%	79.17%	80.96%	82.39%	83.56%	84.56%
85%	30.33%	61.64%	70.44%	75.09%	78.13%	80.32%	82.01%	83.36%	84.47%	85.41%
87%	32.82%	63.61%	72.04%	76.47%	79.35%	81.42%	83.01%	84.29%	85.34%	86.22%
89%	35.34%	65.53%	73.58%	77.79%	80.51%	82.47%	83.98%	85.18%	86.17%	87.00%
91%	37.86%	67.38%	75.06%	79.05%	81.63%	83.48%	84.90%	86.03%	86.96%	87.74%
93%	40.38%	69.16%	76.48%	80.26%	82.70%	84.44%	85.78%	86.84%	87.72%	88.46%
95%	42.89%	70.87%	77.84%	81.42%	83.72%	85.36%	86.62%	87.62%	88.45%	89.14%
97%	45.38%	72.52%	79.14%	82.52%	84.69%	86.24%	87.42%	88.36%	89.14%	89.79%
99%	47.84%	74.10%	80.38%	83.57%	85.62%	87.07%	88.19%	89.07%	89.80%	90.40%
101%	50.26%	75.61%	81.56%	84.58%	86.50%	87.87%	88.91%	89.74%	90.42%	90.99%

	Profitability Ratio (% in-the-money)										
Volatility	0%	10%	20%	30%	40%	50%	60%	70%	80%	90%	100%
1%	39.35%	44.86%	49.46%	53.34%	56.68%	59.56%	62.09%	64.32%	66.30%	68.08%	69.67%
3%	39.35%	44.86%	49.46%	53.34%	56.68%	59.56%	62.09%	64.32%	66.30%	68.08%	69.67%
5%	39.35%	44.86%	49.46%	53.34%	56.68%	59.56%	62.09%	64.32%	66.30%	68.08%	69.67%
7%	39.42%	44.88%	49.46%	53.34%	56.68%	59.56%	62.09%	64.32%	66.30%	68.08%	69.67%
9%	39.70%	45.00%	49.51%	53.37%	56.69%	59.57%	62.09%	64.32%	66.30%	68.08%	69.67%
11%	40.25%	45.32%	49.69%	53.46%	56.74%	59.60%	62.11%	64.33%	66.31%	68.08%	69.67%
13%	41.06%	45.85%	50.04%	53.69%	56.88%	59.69%	62.17%	64.37%	66.33%	68.10%	69.69%
15%	42.07%	46.59%	50.57%	54.07%	57.15%	59.88%	62.31%	64.47%	66.40%	68.15%	69.72%
17%	43.24%	47.50%	51.27%	54.60%	57.56%	60.20%	62.55%	64.65%	66.55%	68.26%	69.81%
19%	44.52%	48.54%	52.11%	55.28%	58.11%	60.63%	62.90%	64.93%	66.77%	68.44%	69.96%
21%	45.89%	49.68%	53.06%	56.07%	58.76%	61.18%	63.35%	65.31%	67.09%	68.71%	70.18%
23%	47.31%	50.90%	54.10%	56.96%	59.52%	61.83%	63.90%	65.79%	67.50%	69.05%	70.48%
25%	48.78%	52.18%	55.22%	57.93%	60.36%	62.56%	64.54%	66.34%	67.98%	69.48%	70.85%
27%	50.28%	53.51%	56.38%	58.96%	61.27%	63.36%	65.25%	66.97%	68.54%	69.98%	71.30%
29%	51.80%	54.86%	57.59%	60.04%	62.24%	64.22%	66.03%	67.67%	69.17%	70.54%	71.81%
31%	53.33%	56.24%	58.83%	61.15%	63.24%	65.13%	66.85%	68.41%	69.85%	71.16%	72.37%
33%	54.86%	57.62%	60.09%	62.29%	64.28%	66.08%	67.71%	69.20%	70.57%	71.82%	72.98%
35%	56.39%	59.01%	61.35%	63.45%	65.34%	67.05%	68.61%	70.03%	71.33%	72.52%	73.63%
37%	57.90%	60.40%	62.63%	64.62%	66.42%	68.04%	69.52%	70.88%	72.12%	73.26%	74.31%
39%	59.41%	61.79%	63.90%	65.80%	67.51%	69.05%	70.46%	71.75%	72.93%	74.02%	75.02%
41%	60.90%	63.16%	65.17%	66.98%	68.60%	70.07%	71.41%	72.63%	73.76%	74.79%	75.75%
43%	62.37%	64.52%	66.43%	68.15%	69.69%	71.09%	72.36%	73.53%	74.60%	75.58%	76.49%
45%	63.81%	65.86%	67.68%	69.31%	70.78%	72.11%	73.32%	74.43%	75.44%	76.38%	77.25%
47%	65.23%	67.18%	68.92%	70.46%	71.86%	73.12%	74.27%	75.33%	76.29%	77.18%	78.01%
49%	66.63%	68.48%	70.13%	71.60%	72.93%	74.13%	75.22%	76.22%	77.14%	77.99%	78.77%
51%	68.00%	69.76%	71.33%	72.73%	73.99%	75.13%	76.16%	77.11%	77.99%	78.79%	79.54%
53%	69.33%	71.01%	72.50%	73.83%	75.03%	76.11%	77.10%	78.00%	78.83%	79.59%	80.30%
55%	70.64%	72.24%	73.65%	74.91%	76.05%	77.08%	78.01%	78.87%	79.66%	80.38%	81.06%
57%	71.92%	73.43%	74.78%	75.97%	77.05%	78.03%	78.92%	79.73%	80.48%	81.17%	81.80%
59%	73.16%	74.60%	75.88%	77.01%	78.04%	78.96%	79.80%	80.57%	81.28%	81.94%	82.54%
61%	74.37%	75.74%	76.95%	78.03%	79.00%	79.87%	80.67%	81.40%	82.08%	82.70%	83.27%
63%	75.55%	76.84%	77.99%	79.01%	79.93%	80.77%	81.52%	82.22%	82.85%	83.44%	83.98%
65%	76.69%	77.92%	79.01%	79.98%	80.85%	81.64%	82.35%	83.01%	83.61%	84.17%	84.68%
67%	77.80%	78.96%	79.99%	80.91%	81.74%	82.48%	83.16%	83.78%	84.35%	84.88%	85.37%
69%	78.87%	79.98%	80.95%	81.82%	82.60%	83.31%	83.95%	84.54%	85.08%	85.57%	86.04%
71%	79.91%	80.95%	81.88%	82.70%	83.44%	84.11%	84.71%	85.27%	85.78%	86.25%	86.69%
73%	80.91%	81.90%	82.77%	83.55%	84.25%	84.88%	85.46%	85.98%	86.46%	86.91%	87.32%
75%	81.88%	82.82%	83.64%	84.38%	85.04%	85.63%	86.18%	86.67%	87.13%	87.55%	87.94%
77%	82.81%	83.70%	84.48%	85.17%	85.80%	86.36%	86.87%	87.34%	87.77%	88.17%	88.53%
79%	83.71%	84.55%	85.29%	85.94%	86.53%	87.06%	87.54%	87.98%	88.39%	88.76%	89.11%
81%	84.58%	85.37%	86.06%	86.68%	87.24%	87.74%	88.19%	88.61%	88.99%	89.34%	89.67%
83%	85.41%	86.16%	86.81%	87.39%	87.92%	88.39%	88.82%	89.21%	89.57%	89.90%	90.21%
85%	86.21%	86.91%	87.53%	88.08%	88.57%	89.01%	89.42%	89.79%	90.13%	90.44%	90.73%
87%	86.98%	87.64%	88.22%	88.74%	89.20%	89.62%	90.00%	90.34%	90.66%	90.96%	91.23%
89%	87.71%	88.33%	88.88%	89.37%	89.80%	90.19%	90.55%	90.88%	91.18%	91.45%	91.71%
91%	88.42%	89.00%	89.51%	89.97%	90.38%	90.75%	91.08%	91.39%	91.67%	91.93%	92.17%
93%	89.09%	89.64%	90.12%	90.55%	90.93%	91.28%	91.59%	91.88%	92.15%	92.39%	92.62%
95%	89.73%	90.25%	90.70%	91.10%	91.46%	91.79%	92.08%	92.35%	92.60%	92.83%	93.04%
97%	90.34%	90.83%	91.25%	91.63%	91.97%	92.27%	92.55%	92.80%	93.03%	93.25%	93.45%
99%	90.93%	91.38%	91.78%	92.13%	92.45%	92.73%	92.99%	93.23%	93.45%	93.65%	93.84%
101%	91.48%	91.91%	92.28%	92.61%	92.91%	93.18%	93.42%	93.64%	93.85%	94.03%	94.21%

Real Options Analysis Values (15-year maturity at 5% risk-free rate)

Volatility	-99%	-90%	-80%	-70%	-60%	-50%	-40%	-30%	-20%	-10%
				Profitability Ratio (% in-the-money)						
1%	0.00%	0.00%	0.00%	0.00%	0.00%	5.65%	21.27%	32.52%	40.95%	47.51%
3%	0.00%	0.00%	0.00%	0.00%	0.43%	7.80%	21.35%	32.52%	40.95%	47.51%
5%	0.00%	0.00%	0.00%	0.08%	2.27%	10.58%	22.17%	32.64%	40.97%	47.52%
7%	0.00%	0.00%	0.01%	0.66%	4.84%	13.48%	23.75%	33.24%	41.16%	47.57%
9%	0.00%	0.00%	0.12%	1.96%	7.70%	16.39%	25.76%	34.36%	41.71%	47.83%
11%	0.00%	0.00%	0.52%	3.87%	10.71%	19.31%	27.98%	35.84%	42.63%	48.38%
13%	0.00%	0.03%	1.36%	6.20%	13.77%	22.21%	30.31%	37.56%	43.84%	49.21%
15%	0.00%	0.14%	2.66%	8.83%	16.86%	25.09%	32.71%	39.44%	45.27%	50.27%
17%	0.00%	0.42%	4.39%	11.66%	19.95%	27.94%	35.13%	41.42%	46.84%	51.51%
19%	0.00%	0.95%	6.47%	14.61%	23.02%	30.76%	37.57%	43.45%	48.52%	52.88%
21%	0.00%	1.79%	8.85%	17.63%	26.06%	33.54%	39.99%	45.52%	50.27%	54.35%
23%	0.00%	2.96%	11.46%	20.71%	29.07%	36.27%	42.40%	47.61%	52.06%	55.89%
25%	0.00%	4.45%	14.24%	23.79%	32.04%	38.96%	44.78%	49.69%	53.87%	57.47%
27%	0.02%	6.25%	17.14%	26.88%	34.95%	41.61%	47.13%	51.76%	55.70%	59.07%
29%	0.05%	8.33%	20.14%	29.95%	37.82%	44.19%	49.44%	53.81%	57.52%	60.69%
31%	0.13%	10.65%	23.19%	32.98%	40.63%	46.73%	51.70%	55.84%	59.33%	62.31%
33%	0.27%	13.18%	26.27%	35.97%	43.37%	49.21%	53.93%	57.83%	61.12%	63.93%
35%	0.50%	15.88%	29.36%	38.91%	46.06%	51.62%	56.10%	59.79%	62.88%	65.52%
37%	0.87%	18.71%	32.44%	41.80%	48.67%	53.97%	58.22%	61.70%	64.62%	67.10%
39%	1.39%	21.64%	35.49%	44.62%	51.22%	56.26%	60.28%	63.57%	66.31%	68.65%
41%	2.11%	24.65%	38.51%	47.37%	53.69%	58.49%	62.29%	65.39%	67.97%	70.17%
43%	3.03%	27.71%	41.47%	50.05%	56.09%	60.64%	64.24%	67.16%	69.59%	71.66%
45%	4.17%	30.80%	44.38%	52.65%	58.41%	62.73%	66.12%	68.88%	71.17%	73.11%
47%	5.54%	33.89%	47.22%	55.18%	60.66%	64.75%	67.95%	70.54%	72.70%	74.52%
49%	7.15%	36.96%	49.99%	57.62%	62.83%	66.70%	69.72%	72.15%	74.18%	75.89%
51%	8.98%	40.01%	52.69%	59.98%	64.93%	68.58%	71.42%	73.71%	75.61%	77.21%
53%	11.03%	43.01%	55.30%	62.26%	66.94%	70.39%	73.06%	75.21%	76.99%	78.50%
55%	13.28%	45.96%	57.82%	64.45%	68.88%	72.12%	74.64%	76.65%	78.32%	79.73%
57%	15.70%	48.85%	60.26%	66.56%	70.74%	73.79%	76.15%	78.04%	79.60%	80.92%
59%	18.30%	51.67%	62.61%	68.58%	72.52%	75.39%	77.60%	79.37%	80.83%	82.06%
61%	21.03%	54.40%	64.87%	70.52%	74.23%	76.92%	78.99%	80.65%	82.01%	83.16%
63%	23.87%	57.05%	67.04%	72.37%	75.86%	78.38%	80.32%	81.86%	83.14%	84.21%
65%	26.81%	59.61%	69.11%	74.14%	77.41%	79.77%	81.58%	83.03%	84.22%	85.22%
67%	29.82%	62.08%	71.09%	75.82%	78.89%	81.10%	82.79%	84.14%	85.24%	86.17%
69%	32.88%	64.45%	72.99%	77.43%	80.30%	82.36%	83.94%	85.19%	86.22%	87.09%
71%	35.96%	66.73%	74.79%	78.95%	81.64%	83.56%	85.03%	86.19%	87.15%	87.95%
73%	39.05%	68.90%	76.50%	80.40%	82.91%	84.70%	86.06%	87.14%	88.03%	88.78%
75%	42.12%	70.98%	78.13%	81.77%	84.11%	85.77%	87.04%	88.04%	88.87%	89.56%
77%	45.17%	72.96%	79.67%	83.07%	85.24%	86.79%	87.96%	88.90%	89.66%	90.30%
79%	48.18%	74.84%	81.13%	84.30%	86.31%	87.75%	88.84%	89.70%	90.41%	91.00%
81%	51.13%	76.62%	82.50%	85.45%	87.32%	88.65%	89.66%	90.46%	91.11%	91.66%
83%	54.01%	78.31%	83.80%	86.54%	88.28%	89.50%	90.44%	91.17%	91.78%	92.28%
85%	56.81%	79.91%	85.02%	87.56%	89.17%	90.30%	91.16%	91.85%	92.40%	92.87%
87%	59.53%	81.42%	86.17%	88.52%	90.01%	91.06%	91.85%	92.48%	92.99%	93.42%
89%	62.15%	82.83%	87.25%	89.42%	90.79%	91.76%	92.49%	93.07%	93.54%	93.93%
91%	64.67%	84.16%	88.26%	90.27%	91.53%	92.42%	93.09%	93.62%	94.05%	94.41%
93%	67.09%	85.41%	89.20%	91.05%	92.21%	93.03%	93.65%	94.13%	94.53%	94.86%
95%	69.41%	86.58%	90.08%	91.79%	92.85%	93.60%	94.17%	94.62%	94.98%	95.28%
97%	71.61%	87.68%	90.90%	92.47%	93.45%	94.14%	94.66%	95.06%	95.40%	95.68%
99%	73.70%	88.70%	91.67%	93.11%	94.00%	94.63%	95.11%	95.48%	95.79%	96.04%
101%	75.69%	89.65%	92.38%	93.70%	94.52%	95.09%	95.53%	95.87%	96.15%	96.38%

				Profitability Ratio (% in-the-money)						
Volatility	0%	10%	20%	30%	40%	50%	60%	70%	80%	90%	100%
1%	52.76%	57.06%	60.64%	63.66%	66.26%	68.51%	70.48%	72.21%	73.76%	75.14%	76.38%
3%	52.76%	57.06%	60.64%	63.66%	66.26%	68.51%	70.48%	72.21%	73.76%	75.14%	76.38%
5%	52.76%	57.06%	60.64%	63.66%	66.26%	68.51%	70.48%	72.21%	73.76%	75.14%	76.38%
7%	52.78%	57.06%	60.64%	63.66%	66.26%	68.51%	70.48%	72.21%	73.76%	75.14%	76.38%
9%	52.90%	57.11%	60.66%	63.68%	66.26%	68.51%	70.48%	72.21%	73.76%	75.14%	76.38%
11%	53.22%	57.30%	60.77%	63.74%	66.30%	68.53%	70.49%	72.22%	73.76%	75.14%	76.38%
13%	53.78%	57.68%	61.02%	63.91%	66.42%	68.61%	70.54%	72.26%	73.79%	75.16%	76.40%
15%	54.56%	58.26%	61.45%	64.22%	66.65%	68.78%	70.67%	72.36%	73.86%	75.22%	76.44%
17%	55.53%	59.02%	62.04%	64.69%	67.02%	69.08%	70.91%	72.54%	74.01%	75.33%	76.53%
19%	56.65%	59.93%	62.79%	65.30%	67.52%	69.49%	71.25%	72.82%	74.25%	75.53%	76.70%
21%	57.89%	60.96%	63.66%	66.03%	68.14%	70.02%	71.70%	73.21%	74.58%	75.82%	76.95%
23%	59.20%	62.09%	64.63%	66.87%	68.87%	70.65%	72.25%	73.69%	75.00%	76.19%	77.27%
25%	60.58%	63.29%	65.68%	67.80%	69.68%	71.37%	72.88%	74.26%	75.50%	76.64%	77.68%
27%	61.99%	64.55%	66.79%	68.79%	70.56%	72.16%	73.59%	74.89%	76.08%	77.16%	78.15%
29%	63.44%	65.84%	67.95%	69.83%	71.50%	73.00%	74.36%	75.59%	76.72%	77.74%	78.68%
31%	64.89%	67.15%	69.14%	70.90%	72.48%	73.90%	75.18%	76.34%	77.40%	78.38%	79.27%
33%	66.35%	68.47%	70.34%	72.00%	73.49%	74.82%	76.03%	77.13%	78.13%	79.05%	79.90%
35%	67.81%	69.80%	71.56%	73.12%	74.52%	75.77%	76.91%	77.95%	78.89%	79.76%	80.56%
37%	69.25%	71.12%	72.77%	74.24%	75.55%	76.74%	77.81%	78.79%	79.68%	80.50%	81.25%
39%	70.67%	72.43%	73.98%	75.36%	76.60%	77.71%	78.72%	79.64%	80.48%	81.25%	81.96%
41%	72.07%	73.72%	75.18%	76.48%	77.64%	78.68%	79.63%	80.49%	81.28%	82.01%	82.68%
43%	73.44%	74.99%	76.36%	77.58%	78.67%	79.65%	80.54%	81.35%	82.09%	82.78%	83.41%
45%	74.78%	76.24%	77.52%	78.66%	79.69%	80.61%	81.44%	82.21%	82.90%	83.55%	84.14%
47%	76.09%	77.46%	78.66%	79.73%	80.69%	81.55%	82.34%	83.05%	83.71%	84.31%	84.87%
49%	77.36%	78.64%	79.77%	80.77%	81.67%	82.48%	83.22%	83.89%	84.50%	85.06%	85.59%
51%	78.59%	79.79%	80.85%	81.79%	82.63%	83.39%	84.08%	84.70%	85.28%	85.81%	86.30%
53%	79.79%	80.91%	81.90%	82.78%	83.56%	84.27%	84.92%	85.51%	86.04%	86.54%	87.00%
55%	80.94%	81.99%	82.92%	83.74%	84.47%	85.14%	85.74%	86.29%	86.79%	87.25%	87.68%
57%	82.05%	83.03%	83.90%	84.66%	85.35%	85.97%	86.53%	87.05%	87.52%	87.95%	88.35%
59%	83.12%	84.04%	84.84%	85.56%	86.20%	86.78%	87.31%	87.78%	88.22%	88.63%	89.00%
61%	84.15%	85.00%	85.75%	86.42%	87.02%	87.56%	88.05%	88.50%	88.91%	89.28%	89.63%
63%	85.13%	85.93%	86.63%	87.25%	87.81%	88.31%	88.77%	89.18%	89.57%	89.92%	90.24%
65%	86.07%	86.81%	87.47%	88.05%	88.57%	89.03%	89.46%	89.85%	90.20%	90.53%	90.83%
67%	86.97%	87.66%	88.27%	88.81%	89.29%	89.73%	90.12%	90.48%	90.81%	91.11%	91.40%
69%	87.83%	88.47%	89.03%	89.53%	89.98%	90.39%	90.75%	91.09%	91.39%	91.68%	91.94%
71%	88.64%	89.24%	89.76%	90.23%	90.64%	91.02%	91.36%	91.67%	91.95%	92.22%	92.46%
73%	89.42%	89.97%	90.46%	90.89%	91.27%	91.62%	91.94%	92.22%	92.49%	92.73%	92.96%
75%	90.15%	90.67%	91.12%	91.51%	91.87%	92.19%	92.49%	92.75%	93.00%	93.22%	93.43%
77%	90.85%	91.32%	91.74%	92.11%	92.44%	92.74%	93.01%	93.25%	93.48%	93.69%	93.88%
79%	91.51%	91.95%	92.33%	92.67%	92.98%	93.25%	93.50%	93.73%	93.94%	94.13%	94.31%
81%	92.13%	92.53%	92.89%	93.20%	93.49%	93.74%	93.97%	94.18%	94.37%	94.55%	94.71%
83%	92.71%	93.09%	93.42%	93.71%	93.97%	94.20%	94.41%	94.61%	94.78%	94.95%	95.10%
85%	93.26%	93.61%	93.91%	94.18%	94.42%	94.63%	94.83%	95.01%	95.17%	95.32%	95.46%
87%	93.78%	94.10%	94.38%	94.62%	94.84%	95.04%	95.22%	95.39%	95.54%	95.67%	95.80%
89%	94.27%	94.56%	94.81%	95.04%	95.24%	95.42%	95.59%	95.74%	95.88%	96.01%	96.12%
91%	94.72%	94.99%	95.22%	95.43%	95.62%	95.78%	95.94%	96.07%	96.20%	96.32%	96.43%
93%	95.15%	95.39%	95.61%	95.80%	95.97%	96.12%	96.26%	96.39%	96.50%	96.61%	96.71%
95%	95.54%	95.77%	95.97%	96.14%	96.30%	96.44%	96.56%	96.68%	96.79%	96.88%	96.97%
97%	95.91%	96.12%	96.30%	96.46%	96.60%	96.73%	96.85%	96.95%	97.05%	97.14%	97.22%
99%	96.26%	96.45%	96.61%	96.76%	96.89%	97.00%	97.11%	97.21%	97.29%	97.38%	97.45%
101%	96.58%	96.75%	96.90%	97.03%	97.15%	97.26%	97.35%	97.44%	97.52%	97.60%	97.67%

Real Options Analysis Values (30-year maturity at 5% risk-free rate)

Volatility				Profitability Ratio (% in-the-money)						
	-99%	-90%	-80%	-70%	-60%	-50%	-40%	-30%	-20%	-10%
1%	0.00%	0.00%	0.05%	25.62%	44.22%	55.37%	62.81%	68.12%	72.11%	75.21%
3%	0.00%	0.00%	2.62%	25.82%	44.22%	55.37%	62.81%	68.12%	72.11%	75.21%
5%	0.00%	0.02%	6.64%	27.30%	44.34%	55.38%	62.81%	68.12%	72.11%	75.21%
7%	0.00%	0.37%	10.94%	29.75%	45.00%	55.54%	62.85%	68.13%	72.11%	75.21%
9%	0.00%	1.57%	15.31%	32.67%	46.31%	56.06%	63.06%	68.22%	72.15%	75.22%
11%	0.00%	3.71%	19.66%	35.80%	48.08%	57.01%	63.56%	68.49%	72.30%	75.31%
13%	0.00%	6.63%	23.98%	39.03%	50.16%	58.30%	64.37%	69.00%	72.63%	75.53%
15%	0.01%	10.13%	28.22%	42.28%	52.43%	59.86%	65.45%	69.76%	73.16%	75.91%
17%	0.04%	14.03%	32.38%	45.51%	54.80%	61.59%	66.72%	70.71%	73.89%	76.47%
19%	0.18%	18.17%	36.44%	48.70%	57.23%	63.44%	68.15%	71.83%	74.77%	77.18%
21%	0.50%	22.46%	40.40%	51.83%	59.66%	65.36%	69.67%	73.06%	75.78%	78.01%
23%	1.13%	26.82%	44.23%	54.88%	62.08%	67.30%	71.26%	74.37%	76.87%	78.94%
25%	2.15%	31.19%	47.94%	57.84%	64.47%	69.25%	72.88%	75.73%	78.03%	79.94%
27%	3.64%	35.51%	51.51%	60.70%	66.79%	71.18%	74.50%	77.11%	79.23%	80.98%
29%	5.62%	39.75%	54.94%	63.46%	69.06%	73.07%	76.11%	78.51%	80.45%	82.05%
31%	8.09%	43.88%	58.22%	66.10%	71.24%	74.92%	77.70%	79.89%	81.66%	83.13%
33%	11.01%	47.89%	61.36%	68.63%	73.35%	76.71%	79.25%	81.25%	82.87%	84.21%
35%	14.34%	51.74%	64.35%	71.04%	75.36%	78.43%	80.75%	82.57%	84.05%	85.28%
37%	18.02%	55.44%	67.18%	73.34%	77.28%	80.08%	82.19%	83.85%	85.20%	86.32%
39%	21.96%	58.96%	69.87%	75.51%	79.11%	81.66%	83.58%	85.09%	86.31%	87.33%
41%	26.11%	62.31%	72.40%	77.56%	80.84%	83.15%	84.90%	86.27%	87.38%	88.31%
43%	30.39%	65.48%	74.78%	79.49%	82.47%	84.57%	86.15%	87.39%	88.40%	89.24%
45%	34.74%	68.47%	77.01%	81.30%	84.00%	85.90%	87.34%	88.46%	89.37%	90.13%
47%	39.11%	71.28%	79.09%	82.99%	85.44%	87.16%	88.45%	89.47%	90.29%	90.98%
49%	43.44%	73.90%	81.04%	84.57%	86.78%	88.33%	89.50%	90.41%	91.16%	91.77%
51%	47.69%	76.35%	82.84%	86.04%	88.03%	89.43%	90.48%	91.30%	91.97%	92.52%
53%	51.82%	78.63%	84.52%	87.40%	89.19%	90.44%	91.39%	92.12%	92.72%	93.22%
55%	55.80%	80.74%	86.06%	88.65%	90.26%	91.39%	92.23%	92.89%	93.43%	93.87%
57%	59.62%	82.68%	87.49%	89.81%	91.25%	92.26%	93.01%	93.60%	94.08%	94.48%
59%	63.24%	84.47%	88.79%	90.87%	92.16%	93.06%	93.73%	94.26%	94.68%	95.04%
61%	66.67%	86.12%	89.99%	91.85%	92.99%	93.79%	94.39%	94.86%	95.24%	95.55%
63%	69.88%	87.62%	91.08%	92.73%	93.75%	94.46%	95.00%	95.41%	95.75%	96.03%
65%	72.88%	88.99%	92.07%	93.54%	94.45%	95.08%	95.55%	95.91%	96.21%	96.46%
67%	75.67%	90.23%	92.98%	94.28%	95.08%	95.63%	96.05%	96.37%	96.64%	96.86%
69%	78.25%	91.36%	93.79%	94.94%	95.65%	96.14%	96.50%	96.79%	97.02%	97.21%
71%	80.61%	92.38%	94.53%	95.54%	96.16%	96.59%	96.91%	97.16%	97.37%	97.54%
73%	82.78%	93.29%	95.19%	96.08%	96.62%	97.00%	97.28%	97.50%	97.68%	97.83%
75%	84.76%	94.11%	95.78%	96.56%	97.04%	97.37%	97.61%	97.81%	97.96%	98.09%
77%	86.55%	94.85%	96.31%	96.99%	97.41%	97.70%	97.91%	98.08%	98.22%	98.33%
79%	88.17%	95.50%	96.78%	97.37%	97.74%	97.99%	98.18%	98.32%	98.44%	98.54%
81%	89.63%	96.09%	97.20%	97.72%	98.03%	98.25%	98.41%	98.54%	98.64%	98.73%
83%	90.93%	96.60%	97.57%	98.02%	98.29%	98.48%	98.62%	98.73%	98.82%	98.90%
85%	92.10%	97.06%	97.90%	98.28%	98.52%	98.68%	98.81%	98.90%	98.98%	99.04%
87%	93.14%	97.46%	98.18%	98.52%	98.72%	98.86%	98.97%	99.05%	99.12%	99.17%
89%	94.06%	97.81%	98.44%	98.73%	98.90%	99.02%	99.11%	99.18%	99.24%	99.29%
91%	94.87%	98.12%	98.66%	98.91%	99.06%	99.16%	99.24%	99.30%	99.35%	99.39%
93%	95.58%	98.39%	98.85%	99.06%	99.19%	99.28%	99.35%	99.40%	99.44%	99.48%
95%	96.21%	98.63%	99.02%	99.20%	99.31%	99.39%	99.44%	99.49%	99.52%	99.55%
97%	96.76%	98.83%	99.17%	99.32%	99.41%	99.48%	99.53%	99.56%	99.59%	99.62%
99%	97.23%	99.01%	99.29%	99.42%	99.50%	99.56%	99.60%	99.63%	99.65%	99.68%
101%	97.65%	99.16%	99.40%	99.51%	99.58%	99.62%	99.66%	99.69%	99.71%	99.72%

					Profitability Ratio (% in-the-money)						
Volatility	**0%**	**10%**	**20%**	**30%**	**40%**	**50%**	**60%**	**70%**	**80%**	**90%**	**100%**
1%	77.69%	79.72%	81.41%	82.84%	84.06%	85.12%	86.05%	86.87%	87.60%	88.26%	88.84%
3%	77.69%	79.72%	81.41%	82.84%	84.06%	85.12%	86.05%	86.87%	87.60%	88.26%	88.84%
5%	77.69%	79.72%	81.41%	82.84%	84.06%	85.12%	86.05%	86.87%	87.60%	88.26%	88.84%
7%	77.69%	79.72%	81.41%	82.84%	84.06%	85.12%	86.05%	86.87%	87.60%	88.26%	88.84%
9%	77.69%	79.72%	81.41%	82.84%	84.06%	85.12%	86.05%	86.87%	87.60%	88.26%	88.84%
11%	77.74%	79.75%	81.43%	82.85%	84.07%	85.13%	86.06%	86.88%	87.61%	88.26%	88.84%
13%	77.89%	79.85%	81.49%	82.90%	84.10%	85.15%	86.08%	86.89%	87.62%	88.26%	88.85%
15%	78.17%	80.06%	81.65%	83.02%	84.20%	85.23%	86.13%	86.94%	87.65%	88.29%	88.87%
17%	78.61%	80.40%	81.92%	83.24%	84.37%	85.37%	86.25%	87.03%	87.73%	88.36%	88.93%
19%	79.18%	80.87%	82.31%	83.56%	84.65%	85.60%	86.45%	87.20%	87.88%	88.49%	89.04%
21%	79.88%	81.46%	82.81%	83.99%	85.01%	85.92%	86.73%	87.45%	88.09%	88.68%	89.21%
23%	80.67%	82.14%	83.40%	84.50%	85.47%	86.32%	87.08%	87.77%	88.38%	88.94%	89.44%
25%	81.53%	82.90%	84.07%	85.10%	86.00%	86.80%	87.51%	88.15%	88.73%	89.26%	89.74%
27%	82.45%	83.71%	84.80%	85.75%	86.59%	87.33%	88.00%	88.60%	89.14%	89.63%	90.08%
29%	83.41%	84.57%	85.57%	86.45%	87.22%	87.91%	88.53%	89.09%	89.59%	90.05%	90.47%
31%	84.38%	85.44%	86.36%	87.17%	87.89%	88.53%	89.10%	89.61%	90.08%	90.51%	90.90%
33%	85.35%	86.33%	87.17%	87.92%	88.57%	89.16%	89.69%	90.16%	90.60%	90.99%	91.35%
35%	86.32%	87.21%	87.99%	88.67%	89.27%	89.81%	90.29%	90.73%	91.13%	91.49%	91.83%
37%	87.27%	88.08%	88.79%	89.41%	89.96%	90.46%	90.90%	91.30%	91.67%	92.00%	92.31%
39%	88.19%	88.94%	89.58%	90.15%	90.65%	91.10%	91.51%	91.87%	92.21%	92.52%	92.80%
41%	89.09%	89.76%	90.35%	90.87%	91.33%	91.74%	92.11%	92.44%	92.75%	93.02%	93.28%
43%	89.95%	90.56%	91.10%	91.56%	91.98%	92.35%	92.69%	92.99%	93.27%	93.53%	93.76%
45%	90.77%	91.33%	91.81%	92.23%	92.61%	92.95%	93.25%	93.53%	93.78%	94.01%	94.23%
47%	91.56%	92.06%	92.49%	92.88%	93.22%	93.52%	93.80%	94.05%	94.28%	94.49%	94.68%
49%	92.30%	92.75%	93.14%	93.48%	93.79%	94.07%	94.32%	94.54%	94.75%	94.94%	95.11%
51%	92.99%	93.40%	93.75%	94.06%	94.34%	94.59%	94.81%	95.01%	95.20%	95.37%	95.53%
53%	93.64%	94.01%	94.32%	94.60%	94.85%	95.08%	95.28%	95.46%	95.63%	95.78%	95.92%
55%	94.25%	94.58%	94.86%	95.11%	95.33%	95.53%	95.71%	95.88%	96.03%	96.17%	96.29%
57%	94.82%	95.11%	95.36%	95.59%	95.78%	95.96%	96.12%	96.27%	96.40%	96.53%	96.64%
59%	95.34%	95.60%	95.83%	96.02%	96.20%	96.36%	96.51%	96.64%	96.76%	96.87%	96.97%
61%	95.82%	96.05%	96.25%	96.43%	96.59%	96.73%	96.86%	96.98%	97.08%	97.18%	97.27%
63%	96.27%	96.47%	96.65%	96.81%	96.95%	97.07%	97.19%	97.29%	97.38%	97.47%	97.55%
65%	96.67%	96.85%	97.01%	97.15%	97.27%	97.38%	97.49%	97.58%	97.66%	97.74%	97.81%
67%	97.04%	97.20%	97.34%	97.46%	97.57%	97.67%	97.76%	97.84%	97.91%	97.98%	98.05%
69%	97.38%	97.52%	97.64%	97.75%	97.85%	97.93%	98.01%	98.08%	98.15%	98.21%	98.26%
71%	97.68%	97.81%	97.91%	98.01%	98.09%	98.17%	98.24%	98.30%	98.36%	98.41%	98.46%
73%	97.96%	98.07%	98.16%	98.24%	98.32%	98.38%	98.44%	98.50%	98.55%	98.60%	98.64%
75%	98.20%	98.30%	98.38%	98.45%	98.52%	98.58%	98.63%	98.68%	98.72%	98.76%	98.80%
77%	98.43%	98.51%	98.58%	98.64%	98.70%	98.75%	98.80%	98.84%	98.88%	98.91%	98.95%
79%	98.62%	98.70%	98.76%	98.81%	98.86%	98.91%	98.95%	98.98%	99.02%	99.05%	99.08%
81%	98.80%	98.86%	98.92%	98.97%	99.01%	99.05%	99.08%	99.11%	99.14%	99.17%	99.19%
83%	98.96%	99.01%	99.06%	99.10%	99.14%	99.17%	99.20%	99.23%	99.25%	99.28%	99.30%
85%	99.10%	99.14%	99.18%	99.22%	99.25%	99.28%	99.31%	99.33%	99.35%	99.37%	99.39%
87%	99.22%	99.26%	99.29%	99.33%	99.35%	99.38%	99.40%	99.42%	99.44%	99.46%	99.47%
89%	99.33%	99.36%	99.39%	99.42%	99.44%	99.46%	99.48%	99.50%	99.52%	99.53%	99.54%
91%	99.42%	99.45%	99.48%	99.50%	99.52%	99.54%	99.55%	99.57%	99.58%	99.60%	99.61%
93%	99.50%	99.53%	99.55%	99.57%	99.59%	99.60%	99.62%	99.63%	99.64%	99.65%	99.66%
95%	99.58%	99.60%	99.62%	99.63%	99.65%	99.66%	99.67%	99.68%	99.69%	99.70%	99.71%
97%	99.64%	99.66%	99.67%	99.69%	99.70%	99.71%	99.72%	99.73%	99.74%	99.75%	99.75%
99%	99.69%	99.71%	99.72%	99.73%	99.74%	99.75%	99.76%	99.77%	99.78%	99.78%	99.79%
101%	99.74%	99.75%	99.76%	99.77%	99.78%	99.79%	99.80%	99.81%	99.81%	99.82%	99.82%

Answers to End of Chapter Questions

CHAPTER 1   Moving Beyond Uncertainty

1. Risk is important in decision making as it provides an added element of insight into the project being evaluated. Projects with higher returns usually carry with them higher risks, and neglecting the element of risk means that the decision maker may unnecessarily select the riskiest projects.
2. Bang for the buck implies selecting the best project or combination of projects that yields the highest returns subject to the minimum amount of risk. That is, given some set of risk, what is the best project or combination of projects that provides the best returns? Conversely, it also answers what the minimum level of risk is, subject to some prespecified level of return. This concept is the Markowitz efficient frontier in portfolio optimization discussed later in the book.
3. Uncertainty implies an event's outcome in which no one knows for sure what may occur. Uncertainties can range from the fluctuation in the stock market to the occurrences of sunspots. In contrast, uncertainties that affect the outcome of a project or asset's value directly or indirectly are termed risks.

CHAPTER 2   From Risk to Riches

1. The efficient frontier was first introduced by Nobel laureate Harry Markowitz, and it captures the concept of bang for the buck, where projects or assets are first grouped into portfolios. Then, the combinations of projects or assets that provide the highest returns subject to the varying degrees of risk are calculated. The best and most efficient combinations of projects or assets are graphically represented and termed the *efficient frontier.*
2. Inferential statistics refers to the branch of statistics that performs statistical analysis on smaller-size samples to infer the true nature of the population. The steps undertaken include designing the experiment, collecting the data, analyzing the data, estimating or predicting alternative conditions, testing of the hypothesis, testing of goodness-of-fit, and making decisions based on the results.
3. Standard deviation measures the average deviation of each data point from the mean, which implies that both upside and downside deviations are captured in a standard deviation calculation. In contrast, only the downside deviations are captured in the semi-standard deviation measure. The semi-standard deviation when used as a measure of risk is more appropriate if only downside occurrences are deemed as risky.

4. Holding everything else constant, projects with negative skew are preferred as the higher probability of occurrences are weighted more on the higher returns.

5. The answer depends on the type of project. For instance, for financial assets such as stocks, clearly a lower kurtosis stock implies a lower probability of occurrence in the extreme areas, or that catastrophic losses are less likely to occur. However, the disadvantage is that the probability of an extreme upside is also lessened.

6. Value at Risk (VaR) measures the worst-case outcome for a particular holding period with respect to a given probability. For instance, the worst-case 5 percent probability VaR of a particular project is $1 million for a 10-year economic life with a 90 percent statistical confidence. Compare that to a simplistic worst-case scenario, which in most cases are single-point estimates, for example, the worst-case scenario for the project is a $10,000 loss. Worst-case scenarios can be added to probabilistic results as in the VaR approach but are usually single-point estimates (usually just a management assumption or guesstimate).

CHAPTER 3   A Guide to Model-Building Etiquette

For the answers to Chapter 3's Exercises, refer to the enclosed DVD. The files are located in the folder: *Answers to End of Chapter Questions.*

CHAPTER 4   On the Shores of Monaco

1. Parametric simulation is an approach that requires distributional parameters to be first assigned before it can begin. For instance, a Monte Carlo simulation of 1,000 trials using input assumptions in a normal distribution with an average of 10 and standard deviation of 2 is a parametric simulation. In contrast, non-parametric simulation uses historical or comparable data to run the simulation, where specific distributional assumptions (i.e., size and shape of the distribution, type of distribution and its related inputs such as average or standard deviation) are not required. Nonparametric simulation is used when the data is "left alone to tell the story."

2. The term "stochastic" means the opposite of "deterministic." Stochastic variables are characterized by their randomness, for example, a stock's price movement over time. A stochastic process is a mathematical relationship that captures this random characteristic over time. The most common stochastic process is the Brownian motion or random walk used to simulate stock prices.

3. The *RAND()* function in Excel creates a random number from the uniform distribution between 0 and 1. Hitting the F9 key repeatedly will generate additional random numbers from the same distribution.

4. The *NORMSINV()* function in Excel calculates the inverse of the standard cumulative normal distribution with a mean of zero and a standard deviation of one.

5. When used in conjunction, the function *NORMSINV(RAND())* simulates a standard normal distribution random variable.

CHAPTER 5 Test Driving Risk Simulator

1. Starting a new profile is like starting a new file in Excel, but a profile is part of the Excel file and holds all the information on the simulation parameters; that is, you can perform scenario analysis on simulation by creating multiple similar profiles and changing each profile's distributional assumptions and parameters and see what the resulting differences are.

2. Pearson's product moment correlation coefficient is a linear parametric correlation where the two variables being correlated are assumed to be linearly related and the underlying assumption is that the correlation's distribution is normal. Spearman's rank-based correlation is a nonparametric correlation that can account for nonlinearities between variables and is hence more robust and better suited for use in simulation where different distributions can be correlated to one another due to their nonparametric properties that do not rely on the normal assumption.

3. More simulation trials are required to obtain a lower error level, a higher precision level, and a narrower confidence interval.

4. Error and precision are related but at the same time, they are not the same thing. Error relates to how far off a particular value is, that is, its forecast interval. For example, the mean is 10 with an error of 1, which means that the forecast interval is between 9 and 11. However, precision indicates the level of confidence of this forecast interval. For example, this error has a 90 percent precision, which means that 90 percent of the time, the error will be between 9 and 11.

5. Yes. Even using rough rules of thumb such as ± 0.25 (low correlation), ± 0.50 (moderate correlation), and ± 0.75 (strong correlation) when in fact there are correlations among the variables, although their exact values are unknown, will provide better estimates than not applying these correlations.

CHAPTER 6 Pandora's Toolbox

1. Tornado and spider charts are used to obtain the static sensitivities of a variable to its precedents by perturbing each of the precedent variables one at a time at a prespecified range. They are typically applied before a simulation is run and no simulation assumptions are required in the analysis. In contrast, sensitivity analysis is applied after a simulation run and requires both assumptions and forecasts. The assumptions are applied in a dynamic environment (with the relevant correlations and truncations) and the sensitivities of the forecast to each of the assumptions are then computed.

2. Some of the distributions are fairly closely related to one another (for instance, the Poisson and binomial distributions become normally distributed when their rates and number of trials increase) and it will be no surprise that some other distribution may be a better fit. In addition, distributions like the beta are highly flexible and can assume multiple shapes and forms, and hence can be used to fit multiple distributions and data sets.

3. A hypothesis test is used to test if a certain value or parameter is similar to or different from another hypothesized value—for example, whether two means from two different distributions are statistically similar or different.
4. Bootstrap simulation is used to obtain a forecast statistic's confidence interval and hence can be used to determine a statistic's precision and error level.
5. The square of the nonlinear rank correlation coefficient is an approximation of the percent variation in a sensitivity analysis.

CHAPTER 8 Tomorrow's Forecast Today

1. Time-series forecasting can be used to incorporate linear trends and seasonality in the forecasts while nonlinear extrapolation can only incorporate a nonlinear trend in its forecast. The former cannot include a nonlinear trend while the latter cannot have a seasonality component in its forecasts.
2. All forecasting methods require data except for stochastic process forecasts, which do not require any historical or comparable data, albeit the existence of data can be exploited by using these data to compute the relevant growth rate, volatility, reversion rate, jump rates, and so forth, used in generating these stochastic processes.
3. A Delphi survey method can be applied and the results of the survey can be used to generate a custom distribution. Simulation can, hence, be applied on this custom distribution.
4. Go through and replicate the examples in the chapter.
5. This statement is true. Seasonality is, in most cases, easy to forecast, but cyclicality is more difficult if not impossible to forecast. Examples of seasonality effects include the sales levels of ski passes (peaks during winter and troughs during summer and, hence, are fairly easy to predict year after year) versus cyclicality effects like the business cycle or stock price cycles (extremely hard to predict as the timing, frequency, and magnitude of peaks and troughs are highly unpredictable).

CHAPTER 9 Using the Past to Predict the Future

1. a. Time-series analysis
      The application of forecasting methodology on data that depends on time.
   b. Ordinary least squares
      A type of regression analysis that minimizes the sum of the square of errors.
   c. Regression analysis
      The estimation of the best-fitting line through a series of historical data used to predict a statistical relationship or to forecast the future based on this relationship.
   d. Heteroskedasticity
      The variance of the errors of a regression analysis is unstable over time.
   e. Autocorrelation
      The historical data of a variable depends on or is correlated to itself over time.

   f. Multicollinearity

     The independent variables are highly correlated to each other or there exists an exact linear relationship between the independent variables.

   g. ARIMA

     Autoregressive Integrated Moving Average—a type of forecasting methodology.

2. The R-squared or coefficient of determination is used on bivariate regressions, whereas the adjusted R-squared is used on multivariate regressions. The latter penalizes the excessive use of independent variables through a degree of freedom correction, making it a more conservative measure useful in multivariate regressions.

3. a. Heteroskedasticity

     In the event of heteroskedasticity, the estimated R-squared is fairly low and the regression equation is both insufficient and incomplete, leading to potentially large estimation errors.

   b. Autocorrelation

     If autocorrelated dependent variable values exist, the estimates of the slope and intercept will be unbiased, but the estimates of their variances will not be reliable and hence the validity of certain statistical goodness-of-fit tests will be flawed.

   c. Multicollinearity

     In perfect multicollinearity, the regression equation cannot be estimated at all. In near-perfect collinearity, the estimated regression equation will be inefficient and inaccurate. The corresponding R-squared is inflated and the t-statistics are lower than actual.

4. Nonlinear independent variables can be transformed into linear variables by taking the logarithm, square (or higher powers), square root, or multiplicative combinations of the independent variables. A new regression is then run based on these newly transformed variables.

CHAPTER 10   The Search for the Optimal Decision

1. Deterministic optimization means that the input variables are single-point deterministic values, whereas optimization under uncertainty means that the input variables are uncertain and simulated while the optimization process is occurring.

2. a. Objective

     An objective is the forecast output value that is to be maximized or minimized in an optimization (e.g., profits).

   b. Constraint

     A constraint is a restriction that is observed in an optimization (e.g., budget constraint).

   c. Decision variable

     The variables that can be changed based on management decisions such that the objective is achieved. These variables are usually subject to the constraints in the model.

3. Some problems arising from a graphical linear programming approach include nonlinear constraints, unbounded solutions, no feasible solutions, multiple solutions, and too many constraints. These problems cannot be easily solved graphically.
4. The graphical approach is simple to implement but may sometimes be too tedious if too many constraints or nonlinear constraints exist. Optimization can also be solved mathematically by taking first and second derivatives but is more difficult to do. Excel's Solver add-in can be used to systematically search by brute force through a series of input combinations to find the optimal solution, but the results may be local minimums or local maximums, providing incorrect answers. Risk Simulator also can be used to solve an optimization problem under uncertainty when the input assumptions are unknown and simulated.

CHAPTER 11   Optimization Under Uncertainty

1. Discrete decision variables are typically integers such as 0, 1, 2, 3, and so forth, whereas continuous variables can vary between any two values (e.g., between 0 and 1, we can have an infinite number of values such as 0.113354, 0.00012546).

CHAPTER 12   What Is So Real About Real Options, and Why Are They Optional?

1. Real options analysis is an integrated risk analysis process that is used to hedge risks and to take advantage of upside uncertainties, and is used for strategic decision analysis.
2. Real options can be solved using closed-form models, simulation approaches, binomial and multinomial lattices, as well as other more advanced numerical approaches such as variance reduction and partial differential equations.
3. The method must be valid, accurate, replicable, tractable, robust, explainable, and, most importantly, flexible enough to handle various inputs and able to mirror real-life conditions.
4. A model must exist or can be built; there must exist uncertainties and risks in the decision; these uncertainties and risks must affect the outcomes and hence the decisions in the project; there must be strategic flexibility or options in the project; and the decision makers or senior management must be credible enough to execute the options when they become optimal to do so.
5. The risks and uncertainties are not hedged or taken advantage of; that is, simulation can be used to forecast, predict, and quantify risks, but only real options analysis can be applied to hedge these risks or to take advantage of the upside.

CHAPTER 15   The Warning Signs

1. "Negligent entrustment" simply means that management takes the results from some fancy analytics generated by an analyst as is, without any due diligence

performed on them. This situation usually occurs because management does not understand the approach used or know the relevant questions to ask.

2. Some general types of errors encountered when creating a model include model errors, assumption and input errors, analytical errors, user errors, and interpretation errors.

3. If truncation is not applied when it should be, then the resulting forecast distribution will be too wide and the errors of estimations too large. Therefore, truncation is important as it provides results that are more accurate with lower errors.

4. A critical success factor is an input variable that has significant impact on the output result. By itself, the input variable is also highly uncertain and should be simulated.

5. A skewness of 0 and a kurtosis of 3 or excess kurtosis of 0 are considered normal-looking statistics.

6. Structural breaks occur when the underlying variable undergoes certain economic, business, or financial shifts (e.g., merger or divestiture). Specification errors occur when the underlying variable follows some nonlinearities (e.g., growth curves, exponential, or cyclical curves) but the regression is estimated based on a strict linear model.

About the DVD-ROM

This appendix provides you with information on the contents of the DVD that accompanies this book. For the latest and greatest information, please refer to the ReadMe file located at the root of the DVD.

SYSTEM REQUIREMENTS

- IBM PC or compatible computer with Pentium IV or higher processor, dual core recommended
- 1 GB RAM required (2 GB RAM or more recommended) and 300 MB hard-disk space
- DVD-ROM drive, SVGA monitor with 256 Color
- Excel XP, 2003, 2007, 2010, or later
- Windows XP, Windows Vista, Windows 7, or later
- Microsoft .Net Framework 2.0, 3.0, 3.5, or later
- Administrative rights to install software (all personal computers have this right by default)

WHAT'S ON THE DVD

The following sections provide a summary of the software and other materials you'll find on the DVD.

Content

The enclosed DVD contains a 30-day license of Real Options Valuation, Inc.'s Risk Simulator software and Real Options SLS Super Lattice Solver software. Included in the software are sample readings, presentation slides, getting started videos, brochures, and example models (Excel models and SLS models which require these two software to be installed in order to run).

How to Install and License the Software

- To obtain your 30-day trial of the full version of Risk Simulator, first install the Risk Simulator software from the DVD's SOFTWARE folder. Please note that the trial license is for Risk Simulator version 2010 only. After installing the software, start Excel and click on *Risk Simulator | License | Install License* and browse to the DVD and look for the LICENSE folder and select the *RS2010 License* file. Please note that this license file will expire in 30 days after it is first installed and works only with version 2010 and not any other versions.

- To install your 30-day trial of the full version of Real Options SLS, first install the Real Options SLS software from the DVD's SOFTWARE folder, then click *Start | Programs | Real Options Valuation | Real Options SLS | Real Options SLS* and on the main screen, click on *1. License Real Options SLS | Activate* and browse to the DVD and look for the LICENSE folder and select the *SLS2010 License* file. Please note that this license file will expire in 30 days after it is first installed and works only with version 2010. Then, on the main screen, click on *2. License Functions and Options Valuator* and enter in the following name and license key:

  NAME = SLS2010   Trial KEY = 794C-9327-1046-1FEF

- When your 30 days are up, you can uninstall the software applications and then visit www.realoptionsvaluation.com/download.html and scroll down to the section for downloading Risk Simulator and Real Options SLS. Download and install the latest versions of these two software applications for another default 10-day trial. Version 2010 is the latest version at the time of this book's printing, but by the time you install the software, newer versions might be out and these are all available on the Web.

- Visit www.realoptionsvaluation.com/faq.html for troubleshooting tips and installation issues. Visit www.realoptionsvaluation.com/download .html for free getting started videos, modeling videos, case studies, examples, whitepapers, and application papers.

You can purchase these software applications by visiting www .realoptionsvaluation.com and clicking on the Purchase link. Once the purchase is confirmed, you will be provided with instructions to send us your Hardware ID (10 to 20 digits) and Hardware Fingerprint (8 digits) and we will generate permanent licenses for you.

CUSTOMER CARE

If you have trouble with the DVD-ROM, please call the Wiley Product Technical Support phone number at (800) 762-2974. Outside the United States, call 1(317) 572-3994. You can also contact Wiley Product Technical Support at http://support.wiley.com. John Wiley & Sons will provide technical support only for installation and other general quality control items. For technical support on the applications themselves, consult the program's vendor or author.

To place additional orders or to request information about other Wiley products, please call (877) 762-2974.

Index

For more information regarding the DVD-ROM, see the
About the DVD-ROM section on page 959.

WILEY

John Wiley & Sons, Inc.